CAREER CENTER
Loyola University Chicago
6525 N. Sheridan Road
Chicago, IL 60626

AMERICAN JOBS ABROAD

AMERICAN JOBS ABROAD

A New England Publishing Associates Book

Edited by

Victoria Harlow
&
Edward W. Knappman

Gale Research Inc. · DETROIT · WASHINGTON, D.C. · LONDON

Gale Research Inc. staff:
Christine Nasso, *Acquisitions Editor*
Rebecca Nelson and Leslie Joseph, *Developmental Editors*
Kelle S. Sisung, *Associate Developmental Editor*
Lawrence W. Baker, *Senior Developmental Editor*

Mark C. Howell, *Cover and Page Designer*
Cynthia Baldwin, *Art Director*
Barbara J. Yarrow, *Graphic Services Supervisor*
C. J. Jonik, *Desktop Publisher*
Willie F. Mathis, *Camera Operator*

Theresa Rocklin, *Supervisor of Systems and Programming*
Timothy Richardson, *Computer Programmer*

Mary Beth Trimper, *Production Director*
Evi Seoud, *Assistant Production Manager*

Benita L. Spight, *Data Entry Supervisor*
Gwendolyn S. Tucker, *Data Entry Group Leader*
Constance J. Wells, *Data Entry Associate*

While every effort has been made to ensure the reliability of the information presented in this publication, Gale Research Inc. does not guarantee the accuracy of the data contained herein. Gale accepts no payment for listing; and inclusion in the publication of any organization, agency, institution, publication, service, or individual does not imply endorsement of the editors or publisher. Errors brought to the attention of the publisher and verified to the satisfaction of the publisher will be corrected in future editions.

∞™ This book is printed on acid-free paper that meets the minimum requirements of American National Standard for Information Sciences Permanent Paper for Printed Library Materials. ANSI Z39.48-1984.

The trademark **ITP** is used under license.

C O N T E N T S

PREFACE *vii*

HOW TO USE THIS BOOK *xii*

GETTING THE JOB

• IDENTIFYING PROSPECTIVE PRIVATE EMPLOYERS: TIPS AND TECHNIQUES FOR APPLYING /
TAILORING YOUR RESUME AND COVER LETTER / OUTLOOK FOR PRIVATE EMPLOYERS /
HOT SPOTS FOR THE 1990S / POTENTIAL HOT INDUSTRIES FOR THE 1990S

• IDENTIFYING PROSPECTIVE FEDERAL EMPLOYERS: FOCUSING YOUR SEARCH / TAILORING A
FEDERAL APPLICATION FORM AND COVER LETTER / COPING WITH THE FEDERAL JOB
APPLICATION PROCESS / OUTLOOK FOR FEDERAL EMPLOYERS / HOT SPOTS FOR THE 1990S

• IDENTIFYING PROSPECTIVE INTERNATIONAL ORGANIZATIONS: HOT SPOTS FOR THE 1990S
• NEGOTIATING THE BEST DEAL

MAKING THE MOVE

GETTING A PASSPORT • GETTING A VISA • GETTING A WORK PERMIT • NECESSARY
SHOTS AND OTHER MEDICAL TREATMENTS • WHAT TO DO ABOUT YOUR HOUSE
• OTHER ASSETS YOU LEAVE BEHIND • HELPING YOUR FAMILY MAKE THE MOVE
• WHAT TO TAKE WITH YOU • U.S. TAXATION OF FOREIGN INCOME
• ABSENTEE VOTING BALLOTS

LIVING ABROAD 73

EMBASSY AND CONSULATE DIRECTORY • REGISTERING WITH THE U.S. EMBASSY • FOREIGN CUSTOMS INSPECTION • CHILDREN BORN ABROAD • DUAL NATIONALITY • GETTING ARRESTED ABROAD • MISSING PERSONS • DEATHS ABROAD • ADJUSTING TO A JOB ABROAD • GETTING ACCLIMATED • COUNTRIES WITH LARGE AMERICAN COMMUNITIES • COMING HOME: RE-ENTERING THE DOMESTIC JOB MARKET

COMPANY LISTINGS 107

DESCRIPTIONS OF AND SPECIFICS ON MORE THAN 800 U.S. CORPORATIONS THAT EMPLOY AMERICANS OVERSEAS—FROM A.L. LABORATORIES TO YOUNG & RUBICAM

ORGANIZATION LISTINGS 535

DETAILS ON ALMOST 100 GOVERNMENT AGENCIES AND OTHER NOT-FOR-PROFIT ORGANIZATIONS THAT EMPLOY AMERICANS OVERSEAS—FROM THE ACADEMY FOR EDUCATIONAL DEVELOPMENT TO THE WORLD WILDLIFE FUND

COUNTRY PROFILES 589

DESCRIPTIONS OF 110 COUNTRIES—FROM ALBANIA TO ZIMBABWE: LOCATION • POPULATION, MAJOR CITIES, AMERICAN COMMUNITIES • LANGUAGE(S) AND CURRENCY • WORK PERMITS, VISAS, ETC. • TAXATION • PRINCIPAL INTERNATIONAL SCHOOLS • HEALTH CARE • CRIME • PROS AND CONS OF WORKING AND LIVING THERE

JOB CATEGORY INDEX 839

LISTING OF MORE THAN 150 JOBS AVAILABLE ABROAD—FROM ATTORNEYS TO VETERINARIANS

American Jobs Abroad provides job hunters with the most accurate, detailed, and useful information available on overseas employment opportunities with U.S. companies, government agencies, and not-for-profit organizations.

Armed with *American Jobs Abroad,* you will have everything you need to begin a comprehensive and effective job search for overseas employment. You will be able to target the type of position you want, the countries you are interested in, and the companies or organizations whose needs most closely match your qualifications.

- **Selection Criteria**

In compiling this work, our goal has been to provide comprehensive coverage of genuine, ongoing, long-term job opportunities with reputable U.S. companies and organizations. These were important criteria for identifying and screening the companies to be included in this sourcebook:

GENUINE: At least two previously published directories list up to 3,000 U.S. companies that are said to offer employment opportunities abroad. In the course of our research we checked directly with almost every company listed in those directories and were told by the vast majority that they did not employ any Americans abroad. Indeed, many of the companies listed said they do not now and never have had foreign operations of any sort. Quite a few had been out of business for several years when these directories were published.

In contrast, all the information in the company listings in *American Jobs Abroad* has been provided by company sources within 18 months of publication, and every company or organization received a proof of its final profile to check for accuracy. While companies are in a state of constant flux and reorganization, we have made every effort to ensure that the companies and organizations listed in *American Jobs Abroad* were accurate up to the time this book was put into production.

ONGOING OR LONG-TERM: We have sought to include only those companies and organizations that offer American citizens jobs abroad on an ongoing or long-term basis. We have excluded those companies that send U.S.-based employees overseas for brief stays or only occasionally employ U.S. citizens on a contract basis. However, it should be noted that some companies (particularly in the construction and technical services industries) and many not-for-profit organizations are project-based operations. Therefore, the number of Americans employed abroad may vary greatly from year to year.

REPUTABLE: In the past few years, particularly during the recession, the news media have uncovered a number of scams in which fly-by-night employment agencies promise—but rarely deliver—high-paying overseas jobs. For example, *Time* magazine reported in its March 8, 1993, issue that such "overseas job scams rake in at least $100 million a year" in fees paid by job hunters.

While we can't vouch for the probity of every firm listed here, each is a reputable U.S. company; no employment agencies of any sort are included.

The other selection criterion is reflected in the book's title: Our coverage is limited to "American Jobs," by which we mean jobs with U.S. companies, U.S. government agencies, and not-for-profit organizations that are offered at wages and with working conditions comparable to those found in the domestic labor market. A small number of international agencies, particularly those affiliated with the United Nations, are included because they employ significant numbers of Americans at comparable wages and conditions to those in the United States. A few of the companies listed are subsidiaries of foreign-owned corporations, but are functioning in the United States in the same fashion as U.S.-owned corporations.

Understandably, a number of companies replied to our inquiries, saying they require or prefer that a candidate has work experience with the domestic company before s/he is considered for an overseas slot. We decided to include them if they offer job tracks that lead to overseas postings.

When we began compiling the data for *American Jobs Abroad*, we intended to include only those companies that acknowledged employing a sizeable number of U.S. citizens abroad. However, from our research and conversations with hundreds of human resources professionals, it became clear that most U.S. companies with overseas operations prefer to employ local nationals to fill all but a few senior managerial, professional, and technical positions. (Among the exceptions are the construction and petroleum industries, which still recruit and employ large numbers of U.S. citizens overseas.) We also discovered there are many small and growing U.S. companies with strong foreign operations. Thus, we chose *not* to impose a minimum number of U.S. citizens employed abroad as cutoff criterion. We have included those companies and organizations that have an ongoing presence overseas—no matter how small.

- **Gathering the Information**

    Our first task in compiling *American Jobs Abroad* was to draft lists of companies that were candidates for inclusion. We began with all the companies listed in the *Fortune* 500 and the *Business Week* 1,000, except for those that were clearly local in nature. We also compiled lists from sources such as Standard & Poors, Moody's Manuals, *Million Dollar Directory*, *Ward's Business Directory*, Value Line Investment Survey, *Hoover's Handbook of American Business*, the *Directory of American Firms Operating in Foreign Countries*, the *Encyclopedia of Associations*, *The Job Seeker's Guide*, the U.S. Chambers of Commerce in foreign countries, the *International Employment Gazette*, the International Employment Hotline, the "Job Opportunities Bulletin," and dozens of other directories and periodicals.

    We then mailed questionnaires to the directors of human resources at each of the approximately 3,500 companies, government agencies, and not-for-profit agencies identified as candidates for inclusion in *American Jobs Abroad*. Those who did not reply were mailed a follow-up questionnaire. Each company that failed to respond, or responded without fully completing the questionnaire, was then telephoned or faxed until an interview could be conducted with a corporate spokesperson who had access to the necessary information and was willing to disclose it.

    In a few cases, reluctance by the company spokesperson—probably for security and competitive reasons—to provide more than cursory information required us to consult secondary sources to provide general information about a company's history and products. (Also, human resources representatives likely want to reduce the number of unsolicited resumes they receive and therefore they attempt to discourage listings in directories.)

- **How This Book is Organized**

    American Jobs Abroad is divided into seven sections—Getting the Job, Making the Move, Living Abroad, Company Listings, Organization Listings, Country Profiles, and Job Category Index:

    GETTING THE JOB: Advice on beginning your hunt—whether it's in the private, government, or non-profit sector.

    MAKING THE MOVE: Important information for anyone who is about to move overseas: getting passports, visas, and work permits; what to do about U.S. taxes and voting; what to take with you; and more.

    LIVING ABROAD: Tells you what to do when you arrive at your destination, including registering with the U.S. Embassy, tips on adjusting to the new surroundings and the new job, and what to do in special cases (such as childbirth).

    COMPANY LISTINGS: The heart of *American Jobs Abroad*, this section lists and describes 814 U.S. companies that employ a significant number of Americans abroad.

    ORGANIZATION LISTINGS: This section provides information on 87 government agencies and not-for-profit organizations.

Company/organization listings include the following:

- o Company/organization name
- o Headquarters address
- o Recruiter's name and title
- o Recruiter's contact information, including address and telephone and fax numbers
- o Chief executive officer's name and title
- o Products/services offered
- o Profile: a brief description of the company's/organization's history and recent sales figures
- o Total (number of) Employees*
- o U.S. Employees Abroad*
- o Countries (where Americans are employed abroad)
- o Application Information*
- o Salaries* (usually an average salary or salary range for overseas positions)
- o Job Categories (for which Americans are employed abroad)
- o General Requirements* (includes information on relevant work experience and or degree requirements)
- o Average Overseas Assignment* (duration of assignment)
- o Language Requirement*
- o Training*
- o Benefits* (travel, health, housing, and education)
- o Comments* (miscellaneous information provided by the company/organization)

This information is provided whenever it was made available by the company/organization.

Note on organization listings: *Because the overseas projects of many government agencies and other not-for-profit organizations are on an as-needed basis (in other words, these organizations often set up temporary operations in countries), we list regions (Latin America, Middle East, North Africa, etc.) where operations have occurred or in which operations are likely to occur. For a listing of countries, the serious applicant should contact the organization s/he is interested in.*

COUNTRY PROFILES: This section includes brief profiles of 111 countries. At the end of each profile, there is a list of the companies and organizations that reported employing Americans there. This list enables anyone who is interested in working in a particular country to locate the U.S. companies/organizations that offer opportunities there.

If more than 3 companies or organizations reported employing Americans in a country, that country's profile covers: Capital; Locations; Population, Cities, and American Residents; Language and Currency; Climate; Economy and Resources; Cost of Living; Work Permits, Visas, etc.; Taxation; Principal International Schools; Health

Care; Crime; Pros and Cons of Living and Working there; Embassy and Consulate Contact Information; and Other Sources of Information (including some print sources).

If fewer than three employers reported having operations in a country, that country's profile includes only the basic information—Capital; Location; Language and Currency; Embassy and Consulate Contact Information; and Other Sources of Information (including some print sources).

For anyone who is seriously considering a long-term stay abroad, these country profiles will provide a starting point for research into the country of destination.

JOB CATEGORY INDEX: The final section of *American Jobs Abroad* is an index of job categories, allowing you to identify the companies that offer job opportunities in your field or profession.

Please note that these categories are, for the most part, listed according to how the companies and organizations reported the information. While some standardization and consolidation did occur, it was nor always possible. Therefore, the job seeker should check all possible variations of a job title or category.

• Future Editions

Much of the time-sensitive information found in this sourcebook is subject to change. We welcome information on or from companies or organizations that would like to be included in future editions, as well as additional information on the companies and organizations that are profiled in this edition.

SUGGESTIONS AND COMMENTS MAY BE SENT TO:
EDITOR
AMERICAN JOBS ABROAD
NEW ENGLAND PUBLISHING ASSOCIATES
P.O. BOX 5
CHESTER, CT 06412

• Acknowledgments

We are obliged to the staff of Gale Research/Visible Ink Press for their support during this project: Chris Nasso enthusiastically supported the initial concept for *American Jobs Abroad*, Leslie Joseph helped get it off the ground, and Becky Nelson talked us through to a safe landing. We also owe thanks to Stephen Christianson, who researched and wrote the articles on pages 1–106, and to Sue Brainard for her assistance with this project from beginning to end.

—Victoria Harlow & Edward W. Knappman
February 1994

HOW TO USE THIS BOOK

- **If you know the name of a company or organization you are interested in** and you are reasonably sure it has overseas operations, consult the Company Listings, beginning on page 107, or the Organization Listings, beginning on page 535. Both of these sections are arranged alphabetically, with the company listings containing more than 800 entries for American businesses that operate abroad and the organization listings containing almost 100 not-for-profit associations or government agencies. *Note:* The company names have been alphabetized word by word, so that, for example, A. L. Laboratories precedes ABB Lummus Crest, New York Times Company precedes Newmont Mining Corporation, Inter-American Foundation precedes International City Management, and so forth.

Once you have identified the company or organization listing you are interested in, you will find a brief description of its operations—both domestic and overseas, as well as a list of the kinds of jobs that might be available abroad and the countries where those jobs are located. (You could then refer to the Country Profiles, beginning on page 589, to read about the countries where that company/organization operates.)

In many entries you will also find important application information, general requirements, language skills requirements, salaries, training, average overseas assignment duration, benefits for overseas employees, and comments from the company.

In every entry, the recruiter's contact information appears next to the company/ organization name, to help you direct your inquiries to the right person and place.

SAMPLE LISTING:

① **BRISTOL-MEYERS SQUIBB COMPANY**

② 345 Park Ave., 3rd Floor
New York, NY 10154

③ RECRUITER: MICHAEL MCDONNELL
DIRECTOR, CONSUMER PRODUCTS
GROUP-INT'L.
④ 345 PARK AVE., 3RD FLOOR
NEW YORK, NY 10154-0037
TEL: (212) 546-3751
FAX: (212) 546-9707

⑤ Richard L. Gelb, Chairman. ⑥ Pharmaceutical, health-care, and consumer products. ⑦ Bristol-Meyers Squibb is a public company. Both Squibb and Bristol-Meyers originated in the 19th century. Squibb was founded by Edward Squibb in New York City in 1858. Bristol-Meyers was begun as Clinton Pharmaceutical of Clinton, New York, in 1887 by William Bristol and John Meyers. Bristol-Meyers bought Squibb in 1989 for $12.7 billion. It is now a major drug and consumer-products company and a global leader in anti-cancer drugs and treatments for high blood pressure. Worldwide revenues for 1992: $11.2 billion.

- ⑧ **Total Employees:** 50,000
- ⑨ **U.S. Employees Abroad:** 95
- ⑩ **Countries:** Australia, Belgium, Brazil, Canada, Ecuador, France, Germany, Greece, Hong Kong, Indonesia, Italy, Japan, Malaysia, Mexico, Netherlands, New

Zealand, Philippines, Portugal, Spain, Switzerland, Taiwan, Thailand, United Kingdom, and Venezuela.

- ⑪ **Application Information:** Most foreign positions are filled internally.
- ⑫ **Salaries:** $50,000-$250,000 per year.
- ⑬ **Job Categories:** Executive Management, Finance, Human Resources.
- ⑭ **General Requirements:** Degree in related field.
- ⑮ **Average Overseas Assignment:** 3-5 years.
- ⑯ **Language Requirement:** Knowledge of local language a plus but not essential.
- ⑰ **Training:** Cultural orientation training optional for entire family; language courses optional for entire family.
- ⑱ **Benefits:** TRAVEL: Annual home leave provided with air fare for employee and family. Air fare for dependent children to visit parents is provided twice each year. HEALTH: Provides continuing U.S. benefits, where possible. If coverage under local benefit program is compulsory, appropriate offsets are made. HOUSING: If employee's housing expense exceeds the cost of comparable U.S. housing (based on U.S. national average) company provides a subsidy. EDUCATION: Covered for grades K-12; cost for language training provided if curriculum at local school is not conducted in a language in which child is proficient.
- ⑲ **Comments:** Other allowances/subsidies may be available for appropriate employees on international assignments for less than five years.

KEY:

① Company/organization name

② Headquarters address

③ Recruiter's name and title

④ Recruiter's contact information, including address and telephone and fax numbers

⑤ Chief executive officer's name and title

⑥ Products/services offered

⑦ Profile: a brief description of the company's/organization's history and recent sales figures

⑧ Total (number of) Employees*

⑨ U.S. Employees Abroad*

⑩ Countries (where Americans are employed abroad)

⑪ Application Information*

⑫ Salaries* (usually an average salary or salary range for overseas positions)

⑬ Job Categories* (for which Americans are employed abroad)

⑭ General Requirements* (includes information on relevant work experience and or degree requirements)

⑮ Average Overseas Assignment* (duration of assignment)

⑯ Language Requirement*

⑰ Training*

⑱ Benefits* (travel, health, housing, and education)

⑲ Comments* (miscellaneous information provided by the company/organization)

*This information is provided whenever it was made available by the company/organization.

- **If you know the country or countries you would like to live in** and would like to know which American companies do business there, refer to the Country Profiles, beginning on page 589. Here you will find descriptions of 111 countries of the world including nations of Europe, Latin America, Africa, the Middle East, and Asia.

From Albania to Zimbabwe, you can get a fix on a country's location, population, major cities, and the American community there; find out what language(s) are spoken and what the currency and exchange rate are; determine what work permits, visas, or other papers are required; learn how your income will be taxed by that country's government; see what international schools might be available (if you have children who would move abroad with you); know what to expect from the health care systems; become aware of the kinds of crime that occur and where; and finally, get an assessment of the pros and cons of both working and living in that country. *Note:* If fewer than three employers reported having operations in a country, that country's profile includes only the basic information—Capital; Location; Language and Currency; Embassy and Consulate Contact Information; and Other Sources of Information (including some print sources).

Each country profile is followed by an alphabetical list of the American companies and organizations that have operations there, each with the page number where you will find the listing for the company/organization.

The country profiles allow you to investigate the country or countries you are interested in and find out which U.S. employers might provide working opportunities there.

If you want to find out which American companies and organizations offer overseas employment opportunities in your field, consult the Job Category Index, beginning on page 839, for a listing of the companies and organizations that have reported employing in any of nearly 200 areas, including attorneys, computer programmers, engineers, gardeners, journalists, nurses, sales representatives, teachers, translators, and veterinarians.

Each job title or category is followed by the company/organization names and page references, so that you may target your search by investigating only those firms that employ within your area of expertise.

SOURCES OF FURTHER INFORMATION

- **Travel Advisories for U.S. Citizens Going Abroad**

  DEPARTMENT OF STATE'S CITIZENS EMERGENCY CENTER
  WASHINGTON, DC
  INFORMATION: 202-647-5225
  Call from a touch-tone telephone.

- **Information Concerning Travel Abroad**

  SUPERINTENDENT OF GOVERNMENT DOCUMENTS
  U.S. GOVERNMENT PRINTING OFFICE
  WASHINGTON, DC 20402
  TEL: 202-783-3238
  Ask for information regarding a specific country where you will travel.

- **Medical or Personal Emergencies**

  SOS ASSISTANCE
  PO BOX 11568
  PHILADELPHIA PA 19116
  TEL: 215-244-1500
  FAX: 244-9617

- **Medical Questions or Assistance**

  INTERNATIONAL ASSOCIATION FOR MEDICAL ASSISTANCE TO TRAVELERS (IAMAT)
  417 CENTER ST.
  LEWISTON NY 14092
  TEL: 716-754-4883

  CENTERS FOR DISEASE CONTROL (ATLANTA, GEORGIA)
  INTERNATIONAL TRAVELER'S HOTLINE: 404-332-4559
  Call from a touch-tone telephone.

- **Education Abroad**

  OFFICE OF OVERSEAS SCHOOLS (A/OS)
  U.S. DEPARTMENT OF STATE
  ROOM 245, SA-29
  WASHINGTON, DC 20522-2902
  TEL: 703-875-7800

  EUROPEAN COUNCIL OF INTERNATIONAL SCHOOLS
  21B LAVANT ST.
  PETERSFIELD, HAMPSHIRE
  GU32 3EL ENGLAND
  TEL: 44 (0) 730 68244/6
  FAX: 44 (0) 730 67914

- **Legal Assistance**

  INTERNATIONAL LEGAL DEFENSE COUNCIL
  111 SOUTH 15TH ST.
  PHILADELPHIA PA 19102
  TEL: 215-977-9982

Working abroad can be financially and culturally rewarding. Many American jobs abroad, in both the public and private sectors, offer high salaries and generous benefits to attract qualified employees willing to pull up their roots and commit to a move overseas.

Armed with the information provided in *American Jobs Abroad,* you will have everything you need to begin a comprehensive and effective job search for overseas employment. You will be able to target the type of position you want, the countries you are interested in, and the companies/organizations whose needs most closely match your qualifications.

IDENTIFYING PROSPECTIVE PRIVATE EMPLOYERS

The Company Listings (beginning on page 107) describe companies that hire Americans to fill overseas postings. Each of the more than 800 entries lists the types of jobs that are available abroad, the countries where the company operates, and whenever possible, the job qualifications. Carefully review these profiles and match your experience with the companies and the countries that interest you. Employers look for prospective employees whose experience indicates the closest match with the required job qualifications.

If your experience and qualifications aren't a precise fit with the job requirements, or aren't even close, the best fall back is to emphasize the aspects of your experience that are most applicable to the position. For example, assume there is a job opening in a company's management division and your job experience is as a senior technician. Look at the situation creatively: if you are experienced in supervising junior technicians, that supervision is a type of management skill, and therefore potentially a strength you can stress in your job application.

In many companies, most overseas postings are filled internally. If you're truly interested in working abroad, don't automatically dismiss those companies. Serving a year or two in a domestic job for such companies may be an essential stepping-stone to a better job overseas than may be available from companies that offer immediate foreign postings.

- **Job Opportunities in the Private Sector** In a survey of human resources personnel in more than twenty U.S. companies that hire Americans for jobs abroad, the respondents unanimously stated that there is no generic category of jobs or job qualifications for working abroad. Because of the diverse needs of the many American companies operating abroad, however, there is a broad spectrum of job opportunities.

For persons looking for executive, managerial or professional positions abroad, American companies routinely hire

   o Seasoned senior managers, especially those with experience in starting up new offices or branches
   o Accountants
   o Lawyers
   o Doctors
   o Engineers
   o Geologists
   o Economists

American companies routinely hire the following for technical or service positions abroad:

   o Translators
   o Computer operators and programmers
   o Administrative assistants
   o Electricians
   o Specialty equipment operators and technicians
   o Secretaries and word processing specialists

For persons looking for support positions abroad, American companies routinely hire skilled workers for these jobs:

   o Pipefitters and welders
   o Heavy equipment operators
   o Laborers
   o Drivers
   o Custodians and maintenance technicians
   o Clerks
   o Mechanics, carpenters, painters and plumbers

The foregoing categories are not all-inclusive and should not be read as excluding any particular occupation.

- **Tips and Techniques for Applying to Private Employers** In addition to any standard application form and other materials that an employer might require, you will probably have to submit a resume detailing your work experience, job qualifications, education, and other background information. You should also submit a cover letter with your resume and application materials, regardless of whether it is required. A cover letter is often the most effective means of selling yourself and presenting yourself in the best light possible in a concise, effective form.

- **Tailoring Your Resume and Cover Letter to the Job Opening** The basic rules of good resume writing are the same for jobs abroad as they are for jobs in the United States, with just a few wrinkles. The most important rules are as follows and sources of further information about preparing resumes and cover letters are given on page 4.

  - Be specific and concise about your work experience. Long-winded job descriptions bore the reader and smack of resume padding. Use generalizations only if your work experience wasn't good, or the position you are applying for is a bit of a stretch given your qualifications.
  - Don't go over two 8-½-X-11 pages unless absolutely necessary.
  - Use power words in describing your experience and qualifications, such as accomplished, achieved, brought, completed, controlled, decided, delegated, developed, directed, established, formulated, guided, improved, initiated, led, managed, organized, planned, promoted, solved, and supervised.
  - Note any foreign language you speak or read. If you are proficient in a language few Americans can speak, such as Russian, Japanese, Arabic, or Chinese, mention it, even if it's not directly relevant to the position. The company may keep your resume on file and contact you if another position opens up where that language is useful.
  - Be sure that the resume is up-to-date and written clearly for a reader who does not know you personally.
  - Be sure there are no typos or grammatical errors.
  - Be sure there are no unexplained gaps in your work or education history. If you are or have been unemployed, put the best face on it. If there is any plausible way, you can describe yourself as "self-employed" or "sole proprietor."
  - If possible, tailor each resume to the individual job opening, add or stress significant items, and delete the irrelevant. Consider investing in a personal computer (PC) for this purpose and putting your resume on disk.
  - Don't mix different resume styles. The most conventional and accepted method is to proceed in reverse chronological order.

o Use a high-quality, bond paper, preferably white or ivory. You don't have to spend a lot of money getting it professionally printed, but you should use a good, letter-quality printer.

o Update your resume periodically, especially in case of significant promotions, awards, or other noteworthy changes.

SAMPLE RESUME FORMAT: Following is a sample resume for fictional John Doe, who is seeking a management position abroad. Look at it as a guide to style and format: the fictional educational history and work experience are irrelevant. (*See* sample, p. 5.)

SAMPLE COVER LETTER FORMAT: A good cover letter is just as important as a good resume. It is the means by which you introduce yourself to the reader. The basic rules for writing a good cover letter are

o Always use a "re" line (*see* sample cover letter format on page 6). If the person who reads your job application is busy, s/he may only glance at the mail each day to decide whether it is worth reading in full. The re line announces the purpose of your letter up front, and catches the reader's eye.

o Be direct and concise about your objective, namely, that you want a job.

o If you have a particularly strong credential, or personal connection with the reader, say so in the letter even if it is covered in your resume. You don't want to be redundant, but you do want the reader to be interested enough to look at your resume.

o Refer to your enclosed resume.

A sample cover letter format is shown on page 6.

SOURCES OF FURTHER INFORMATION

Bostwick, Burdette E. *Resume Writing: A Comprehensive How-To-Do-It Guide.* New York: Wiley, 1990.

Cohen, Hiyaguha. *The No-Pain Resume Workbook: A Complete Guide to Job-Winning Resumes.* Homewood, Ill.: Business One Irwin, 1992.

Fournier, Myra. *Encyclopedia of Job-Winning Resumes.* Ridgefield, Conn.: Round Lake Publications, 1991.

Jackson, Acy L. *How to Prepare Your Curriculum Vitae.* Lincolnwood, Ill.: VGM Career Horizons, 1992.

Krannich, Ronald L. *Job Search Letters That Get Results.* Manassas Park, Va.: Impact Publications, 1992.

Marino, Kim. *The Resume Guide for Women of the '90s.* Berkeley, Calif.: Ten Speed Press, 1992.

Montag, William E. *Best Resumes for $75,000 Executive Jobs.* New York: Wiley, 1992.

Reed, Jean. *Resumes That Get Jobs.* New York: Prentice-Hall, 1992.

John Doe
101 Maple Street
Anywhere, USA
(000) 000-0000

Employment Experience
1985--Present, Senior Administrative Officer for the XYZ Corporation.
    Supervise over 20 employees.
    Implemented a comprehensive restructuring program that reduced corporate overhead costs by 30 percent.

1980--1985, Associate Administrator for the ABC Corporation.
    Developed and oversaw implementation of new and more effective hiring procedures for the Sales Department.
    Named Employee of the Year in 1984.

1976--1980, Assistant Sales Executive for the LMN Corporation.
    Achieved 70 percent increase in sales for product lines under my supervision, twice the corporate average.

Education
State College, Collegetown, USA
Major: Business
B.A. Awarded: May 1976
GPA: 3.6
Class Rank: 67 out of 1540
Activities: Debate Team regional competitions, Student Council Vice-President 1975, Fencing Team

Languages
Fluent in Spanish. Conversational ability in Russian.

Professional Organizations
American Association of Sales Professionals, 1977--present
Anywhere Jaycees, 1983--present
State College Alumni Association, Treasurer 1986--1989

Personal
Personal interests: fencing, baseball
Born: August 1, 1954
Married

Availability
Available for employment on four weeks' notice.

Awards and Honors
Anywhere Civic Association Man of the Year, 1990
Alpha Alpha Alpha Honor Society, State College, 1976

SAMPLE RESUME.

John Doe
101 Maple Street
Anywhere, USA
(000) 000-0000

Today's date, 199_

Ms. Jane Smith
PDQ Corporation
500 Industrial Lane
Somewhere, USA 54321

Re: Senior Management Executive Job Opening in Madrid, Spain

Dear Ms. Smith:

I noticed your company's advertisement for the above-referenced position in the *Anywhere Gazette,* and I want to be considered for the job.

As described in my enclosed resume, I am currently the senior administrative officer for the XYZ Corporation, and I am confident that I have the necessary qualifications for the position. Furthermore, I am fluent in Spanish.

I have always wanted to work abroad, especially in Europe, and I am willing to leave my current employer in order to pursue this opportunity.

I look forward to hearing from you in the near future. Please do not hesitate to contact me at (000) 000-0000 any time.

Yours truly,

John Doe

SAMPLE COVER LETTER.

Smith, Michael Holley. *The Resume Writer's Handbook*. New York: Barnes & Noble, 1987.

The Editors. *The Guide to Basic Resume Writing*. Lincolnwood, Ill.: VGM Career Horizons, 1991.

Wilson, Robert F. *Better Resumes for Executives and Professionals*. New York: Barron's Educational Series, 1991.

• **Outlook for Private Employers** Four factors determine whether a particular country presents good opportunities for your job search abroad: (1) the size of the economy, (2) the economic growth rate, (3) the size of the population, and (4) the importance of international trade in the country's economy. If a country has a large economy, a high economic growth rate, a large population, and an active import-export trade, then there are bound to be American companies there and thus above-average prospects for landing a job.

Even if a country doesn't have all four factors in its favor, the presence of one or more positive factors may make it a logical candidate for your job search. For example, American companies are present in every country with a sizable economy, regardless of the other three factors, because of the market size of those countries. Therefore, you can expect to find an American corporate presence in the following two dozen countries, which boast the largest economies in the world after the United States, as determined by 1990 gross domestic product (GDP):

COUNTRY / GDP (000,000,000)

1. *JAPAN / $2,932
2. GERMANY / $1,493
3. FRANCE / $1,190
4. ITALY / $1,072
5. UNITED KINGDOM / $971
6. CANADA / $579
7. SPAIN / $492
8. BRAZIL / $355
9. AUSTRALIA / $295
10. THE NETHERLANDS / $276
11. MEXICO / $238
12. INDIA / $231
13. SOUTH KOREA / $228
14. SWEDEN / $228
15. SWITZERLAND / $228
16. BELGIUM / $198
17. TAIWAN / $157

18. DENMARK / $128

19. TURKEY / $109

20. INDONESIA / $104

21. SOUTH AFRICA / $101

22. SAUDI ARABIA / $95

23. THAILAND / $83

24. GREECE / $68

* This list does not include Russia, the other former republics of the Soviet Union, Eastern Europe, or China. Although Russia, China, and possibly the Ukraine would qualify as having among the world's largest economies, it is not yet possible to calculate these countries' economic size in free-market terms such as the dollar value of their GDP.

The second factor determining how good job opportunities are in a particular country, economic growth, also strongly influences the hiring practices of American companies abroad. American companies in countries with small economies but high economic growth rates may be expanding faster and hiring more people than American companies in countries with large economies but stagnant growth rates. Following is a list of the economic growth rates for members of the Organization for Economic Cooperation and Development (OECD), which includes the world's most developed economies, and other countries for which reliable statistics are available. The growth rates given are for the 1980s and thus portray long-term growth history and potential but not the impact of the current worldwide recession. Once again, this list does not include Russia, the other former republics of the Soviet Union, Eastern Europe, or China, because of their non–free market economies. The list is in descending order of annual growth rate.

COUNTRY / ANNUAL GROWTH RATE (%)

1. SOUTH KOREA / 9.0

2. HONG KONG / 7.6

3. TAIWAN / 7.5

4. SINGAPORE / 6.6

5. PAKISTAN / 6.3

6. INDIA / 5.7

7. THAILAND / 5.5

8. EGYPT / 5.4

9. TURKEY / 5.3

10. MALAYSIA / 5.1

11. SRI LANKA / 4.2

12. JAPAN / 4.1

13. INDONESIA / 4.0

14. MOROCCO / 3.6

15. CANADA / 3.5

16. AUSTRALIA / 3.4

17. COLOMBIA / 3.3

18. FINLAND / 3.2

19. BURMA / 3.2

20. LUXEMBOURG / 3.0

21. UNITED STATES / 3.0

22. ALGERIA / 2.9

23. GREAT BRITAIN / 2.8

24. NORWAY / 2.7

25. SPAIN / 2.6

26. ISRAEL / 2.6

27. BRAZIL / 2.4

28. ICELAND / 2.3

29. PORTUGAL / 2.2

30. ITALY / 2.2

31. CHILE / 2.1

32. FRANCE / 1.9

33. DENMARK / 1.9

34. SWITZERLAND / 1.9

35. AUSTRIA / 1.8

36. SWEDEN / 1.8

37. IRELAND / 1.7

38. NEW ZEALAND / 1.7

39. GERMANY / 1.7

40. SOUTH AFRICA / 1.5

41. BELGIUM / 1.5

42. GREECE / 1.4

43. THE NETHERLANDS / 1.4

44. PHILIPPINES / 1.3

45. MEXICO / 1.0

46. VENEZUELA / 0.9

47. PERU / 0.7

48. ARGENTINA / -0.9

49. BOLIVIA / -1.1

50. NIGERIA / -1.3

51. UNITED ARAB EMIRATES / -3.7

52. SAUDI ARABIA / -5.1

Population size, the third factor determining job opportunities, is important because American companies are attracted to countries with sizable potential markets. For companies such as Pepsi that market low-cost consumer products, sheer population size is as important as economic size and annual growth. Therefore, depending on the type of job you are seeking, you might want to consider countries such as Mexico, Nigeria, Argentina, and the Philippines. Despite their relatively small economies and unimpressive growth statistics, these countries are heavily populated and offer vast markets to American corporations.

The fourth factor determinant of job opportunities, the importance of international trade in the country's economy, may be extremely important in your job search. Hong Kong, the Netherlands, and Singapore, for example, are centers of international trade and their economies depend on the presence of multinational corporations, including American ones. Therefore, in addition to manufacturing, such places present job opportunities in the following trade-related fields:

o Insurance
o Banking and finance
o Transportation and travel
o Communications
o Consulting
o Data Processing and information technology
o Professional services such as law and accounting

- **Hot Spots for the 1990s**

THE PACIFIC RIM: Take another look at the list of worldwide economic growth rates. Notice anything significant? In case you didn't notice, the high-growth end of the list is dominated by Asian countries in the area commonly called the Pacific Rim. South Korea, Hong Kong, Taiwan, Singapore, Thailand, Malaysia, Japan, Indonesia, and even nearby countries such as India, Australia, and Burma experienced above-average growth rates. Given the large economies of countries such as Japan and others on the "top two dozen" list, the area's tremendous population, and its continuing importance in international trade, the Pacific Rim is likely to be one of the top growth areas for American jobs abroad in the 1990s.

SOUTH AMERICA: Despite the unimpressive growth rates of most South American countries during the 1980s, the region presents significant growth opportunities for American companies in the 1990s. Countries such as Argentina and Chile are now committed to free-market economics and privatization of state-owned industries, and South American stock markets have enjoyed considerable growth over the past few years. American companies are expanding their operations in South America, so you may find job opportunities with their new or expanding operations there. Remember that

South America is still largely a Third World region, so communication fluency with the nationals is a highly valuable skill. If you are fluent in Spanish or Portuguese (for Brazil), you should stress this point in your resumes and interviews.

UNIFIED EUROPE: The countries of western Europe are already well penetrated by American companies and present large job markets. If European unification proceeds apace, then there may be more job opportunities as cross-border trade increases.

THE NORTH AMERICAN FREE TRADE AGREEMENT COUNTRIES—MEXICO AND CANADA: If the recently completed North American Free Trade Agreement goes into full effect and the Mexican and Canadian economies become more intertwined with the U.S. economy, then you may be able to get a job with a company operating across North American borders. Already the Zenith Corporation is relocating its television picture tube manufacturing plants to Mexico, and other American corporations are considering similar moves to take advantage of lower labor costs.

- **Growth Areas** Eastern Europe, China, Russia, and the other republics of the former Soviet Union offer tremendous economic potential for the visionary and patient American corporations willing to invest in them. It will be some time, however, before Eastern Europe and the former members of the Soviet Union adjust to free-market economics. Job prospects in those countries are more likely to be in the areas of U.S. government agencies, international agencies, and nonprofit organizations that are assisting with the transition from communism. China, despite impressive economic growth in its coastal free trade regions, has yet to reject central planning for the bulk of the country or prepare for the inevitable political turmoil that will result when the octogenarians who control Peking die.

    You may also have noticed how oil-exporting countries dominate the lower echelon of the economic growth rate list (see pages 8–10). Although Saudi Arabia is still the world's twenty-second-largest economic power (excluding the United States), it has experienced an economic decline exceeding 5 percent a year because of falling oil prices and increased alternative production sources. Some other oil-dependent countries, such as the United Arab Emirates and Nigeria, have suffered a similar fate. Finally, still other countries (for example, Iran) did not invest their oil wealth wisely during the boom days of the 1970s and are now back on the United Nations' list of impoverished countries qualifying for international aid. There is still potential for landing a job, however. American oil companies maintain large operations in the Middle East, and they always need engineers and other technical personnel. Other job opportunities may depend on the fluctuations of local politics and regional conflicts, as shown by American companies' involvement in the reconstruction of Kuwait after Operation Desert Storm.

- **Potential Hot Industries for the 1990s**

AEROSPACE: One of the unexpected legacies of U.S. defense and space spending is an aerospace industry that is still the world's leader. America is the world's largest exporter of civilian and military aircraft, and the companies that manufacture and sell them maintain a presence abroad. For example, despite competition from Europe's Airbus Industries and other foreign manufacturers, Boeing continues to be the primary supplier of planes to airlines across the world. Companies that make military aircraft, such as General Dynamics and McDonnell Douglas, are planning to expand their overseas exports even further as the domestic defense budget shrinks. Both civilian and military aircraft companies need qualified sales and support personnel, managers, and technical personnel abroad.

ENTERTAINMENT: U.S. entertainment companies continue to be strong abroad, and American movie companies are world leaders. The entertainment industry offers Americans an increasing number of technical, managerial, and support job opportunities abroad.

FOOD AND DRINK: More than a few large American multinational corporations are active abroad in the food and drink industry. Coca-Cola and Pepsico maintain plants and sales offices in virtually every major country. McDonald's, Pizza Hut, and Burger King are actively expanding their franchises abroad. The Philip Morris conglomerate is expanding its presence in Europe by acquiring leading European food processing companies.

PETROLEUM: The large American oil companies have always been active abroad, and their worldwide search for new oil fields to develop probably will continue as U.S. domestic production declines steadily year after year. American companies are actively exploring and developing new oil fields, both on-shore and offshore, in China, Latin America, and the Middle East. Their hiring needs range from highly skilled geologists and engineers to pipefitters, welders, and mechanics.

TELECOMMUNICATIONS: Deregulation of the American telecommunications market and the breakup of AT&T has resulted in the emergence of several highly competitive American telecommunications companies abroad. The Baby Bells are active in joint ventures with European state telephone companies in both western and eastern Europe. In many eastern European countries, cellular phone networks set up by American companies are the primary means of communication, because the old Soviet-style telephone lines can't handle the increased volume of traffic. American companies also actively pursue new markets abroad in fiber optics and information processing.

IDENTIFYING PROSPECTIVE FEDERAL EMPLOYERS

The Organization Listings (beginning on page 535) provide information on federal employers (and other not-for-profit organizations) that offer job opportunities abroad, including positions in the following occupations:

o Economists

- o Statisticians
- o Translators
- o Agricultural specialists
- o Teachers
- o Journalists
- o Computer programmers
- o Engineers

- **Focusing Your Search** It is important that your job search campaign with federal employers be very focused. It is fine to say to yourself, "I want to work for the State Department" or "I want to use my engineering experience to build hospitals in the Third World," but you also have to look at (1) what agencies, and what divisions or bureaus within that agency, are hiring, (2) whether there are hiring freezes or budgetary restrictions that prevent particular agencies from conducting any hiring, and (3) whether you have all the credentials required by the frequently very detailed federal job announcements and vacancy postings.

  Following is a list of the federal agencies that hire Americans for jobs abroad. You can obtain descriptions of available openings by contacting them. As with private employers, look for the positions that most closely match your experience in the countries where you are interested in working. As in the private sector, federal hiring officials look for prospective employees whose experience indicates the closest match with the required job qualifications. There are so many agencies who hire Americans for jobs abroad, however, that you shouldn't be pessimistic about your chances of landing a position.

- **Federal Employers Who Hire Americans for Jobs Abroad**

FOREIGN SERVICE: The Foreign Service, part of the Department of State, is responsible for running America's diplomatic relations abroad. There are thousands of Foreign Service officers, and they work in every American embassy, consulate, and mission abroad.

To enter the Foreign Service, you must take the Foreign Service Examination, which is a written test given every December. You should contact the State Department for registration and test information materials four or five months beforehand. If you pass the written test, you will then be invited to take a much more rigorous oral exam. If you pass the oral exam, and there are positions available, you will be offered a Foreign Service officer (FSO) position. Although in time you will be able to obtain assignment to the country or region of your choice, a Foreign Service rule requires that all FSOs must be available for worldwide assignment. This means that when you enter the Foreign Service, your first tour of duty may be as the visa officer in Tanzania or deputy assistant vice-consul in Oran, Algeria. The Foreign Service is potentially very rewarding and stimulating, but you must approach it as a long-term career, one in which you may have to pay your dues before you get that choice assignment that you covet in London, Paris, or Saint Petersburg. However, you are not committed to spending the rest of your life abroad if you don't want to. FSOs get vacation time in the United States between tours of duty (a tour of duty is one to three years), and they are usually rotated back to the United States for a domestic tour of duty (primarily in Washington, D.C.) after two or three foreign tours of duty.

Foreign Service officers fill four types of posts: administrative, consular, economic/commercial, and political. Administrative officers manage the nuts-and-bolts financial, travel, housing, personnel, and other aspects of embassies, consulates, and, of course, the central State Department complex in Washington, D.C. Consular officers help Americans abroad in emergencies, such as accidents or imprisonment, and intervene with local authorities if Americans are being mistreated. Consular officers get a good deal of field work and contact with the local nationals. Economic/commercial officers gather economic data and statistics, help promote American exports, and cooperate with American corporations operating in the same country. Finally, political officers handle the actual political and diplomatic relations with the foreign governments. They do everything from help negotiate agreements to prepare reports for Washington on recent developments in their host country.

Sometimes the Foreign Service admits people with particular skills without requiring them to take the Foreign Service Examination, for example, language translators, lawyers, and technicians. These exceptions are very rare, however. For further information contact:

> **THE DEPARTMENT OF STATE**
> FOREIGN SERVICE RECRUITMENT DIVISION
> P.O. BOX 9317
> ROSSLYN, VA 22209
> (202) 647-4000

THE AGENCY FOR INTERNATIONAL DEVELOPMENT: The AID oversees the expenditure of that portion of U.S. foreign aid dedicated to promoting economic development abroad. AID employees are stationed in more than sixty countries, primarily in Third World areas such as Central America, South America, Asia, and Africa. The AID projects include agricultural assistance, developing rural infrastructure, and medical and science technology transfer. AID hires persons with a wide variety of skills, including agronomists, economists, and educators, depending on the needs of particular projects and the needs of AID offices in particular countries. For further information contact:

> **THE AGENCY FOR INTERNATIONAL DEVELOPMENT**
> RECRUITMENT DIVISION
> 320 21ST STREET NW
> WASHINGTON, DC 20523
> (202) 663-1451

THE UNITED STATES INFORMATION AGENCY: The USIA has over 200 offices in more than 100 countries. The USIA attempts to promote a positive image abroad for America, the American people, and the policies of the American government. The USIA operates the Voice of America broadcasting network, which broadcasts radio and television programs in nearly fifty languages. The USIA also publishes and distributes magazines and other literature on American life, and USIA staff members oversee cultural and educational exchange programs.

The USIA hires persons with skills relevant to its activities, such as journalists, translators, broadcasters, and radio and television technicians. Because the USIA is part of the Department of State, most USIA jobs require that you take and pass the Foreign Service Examination, which is given every December. For further information contact:

THE DEPARTMENT OF STATE
FOREIGN SERVICE RECRUITMENT DIVISION
P.O. BOX 9317
ROSSLYN, VA 22209
(202) 647-4000

For further information concerning the Voice of America in particular, contact:

VOICE OF AMERICA
OFFICE OF PERSONNEL
330 INDEPENDENCE AVE. SW, ROOM 1543
WASHINGTON, DC 20547
(202) 619-4700

DEFENSE AND INTELLIGENCE AGENCIES: The United States spends hundreds of billions of dollars a year to maintain its worldwide superpower status. In addition to military personnel, the Defense Department and the affiliated intelligence community employ tens of thousands of civilians, many of whom are stationed abroad. Despite the almost certain prospect of downsizing throughout the 1990s, the civilian element of the worldwide defense and intelligence apparatus will likely continue to be significant and present many employment opportunities abroad.

The types of jobs available are incredibly diverse. Persons with technical and scientific backgrounds are in high demand, including computer science experts, mathematicians, engineers, physicists, statisticians, chemists, and military technology experts. In addition, there is a demand for translators, particularly those fluent in exotic languages such as Arabic and Chinese, and other professionals such as economists and sociologists. However, there is no easy way to apply for these positions. The Defense Department and the intelligence community are divided into a multitude of agencies, each of which conducts its own hiring, has its own application procedures and forms, and each has to be contacted separately for further information. Four of the most active employers of Americans for jobs abroad are:

ARMS CONTROL AND DISARMAMENT AGENCY
320 21ST STREET NW
WASHINGTON, DC 20451
(202) 647-2034

G
E
T
T
I
N
G

T
H
E

J
O
B

A
M
E
R
I
C
A
N

J
O
B
S

A
B
R
O
A
D

CENTRAL INTELLIGENCE AGENCY
DIRECTOR OF PERSONNEL
MCLEAN, VA 22102
(703) 482-1100

DEFENSE INTELLIGENCE AGENCY
THE PENTAGON
ARLINGTON, VA 20301
(703) 284-1124

NATIONAL SECURITY AGENCY
EMPLOYMENT OFFICE
FORT MEADE, MD 20755
(410) 859-6444

OTHER FEDERAL EMPLOYERS: Finally, within the massive bureaucracy of the federal government are numerous agencies whose functions require hiring Americans for jobs abroad. Again, the agencies have to be contacted one by one. They hire persons with experience in banking, finance, economics, trade, agriculture, and other areas. Five of the most active of these employers are as follows:

(1) EXPORT-IMPORT BANK
OFFICE OF PERSONNEL
811 VERMONT AVENUE NW
WASHINGTON, DC 20571
(202) 566-8834

(2) FOREIGN AGRICULTURAL SERVICE
DIRECTOR, PERSONNEL DIVISION
U.S. DEPARTMENT OF AGRICULTURE
INDEPENDENCE AVENUE, 12TH & 14TH STREETS NW
WASHINGTON, DC 20250
(202) 720-8732

(3) FOREIGN COMMERCIAL SERVICE
INTERNATIONAL TRADE ADMINISTRATION
DEPARTMENT OF COMMERCE
14TH, E STREET AND CONSTITUTION AVENUE NW
WASHINGTON, DC 20230
(202) 377-2000

(4) INTERNATIONAL TRADE COMMISSION
PERSONNEL DIVISION
500 E STREET NW
WASHINGTON, DC 20436
(202) 205-2000

(5) OVERSEAS PRIVATE INVESTMENT CORPORATION
EMPLOYMENT OFFICE
1615 M STREET NW
WASHINGTON, DC 20527
(202) 457-7013

Both the Foreign Agricultural Service and the Foreign Commercial Service are run by primarily domestic executive branch departments, namely, the Department of Agriculture and the Department of Commerce. Many such domestic agencies have job openings abroad for Americans, including the Department of Health and Human Services, whose Public Health Service is active internationally; the Department of Justice, which runs the Foreign Claims Settlement Commission and the Drug Enforcement Administration; and the Federal Reserve System with its International Finance Division. Although most of these domestic executive branch departments do not hire Americans for jobs abroad in great numbers, their job openings are much easier to research collectively than those of nondomestic employers such as the Foreign Service, because domestic executive branch departments are required to conduct their hiring in accordance with standards set forth by the Office of Personnel Management. The OPM publishes all its job openings abroad in job information centers located in virtually every state. Following are the addresses of the OPM Job Information Centers. Their telephone numbers change constantly, and therefore are not included in this list, but Directory Assistance should be able to provide you with the number of the center nearest you.

ALABAMA: $\quad$ 3322 MEMORIAL PARKWAY SOUTH
BUILDING 600, SUITE 341
HUNTSVILLE, AL 35801

ALASKA: $\quad$ THE FEDERAL BUILDING
701 C STREET, BOX 22
ANCHORAGE, AK 99513

ARIZONA: $\quad$ U.S. POSTAL SERVICE BUILDING
522 N. CENTRAL AVENUE, ROOM 120
PHOENIX, AZ 85004

ARKANSAS: $\quad$ CONTACT THE OKLAHOMA JOB
INFORMATION CENTER

CALIFORNIA: $\quad$ LINDER BUILDING, THIRD FLOOR
845 S. FIGUEROA
LOS ANGELES, CA 90017

1029 J STREET, SECOND FLOOR
SACRAMENTO, CA 95814

THE FEDERAL BUILDING
ROOM 4-S-9
880 FRONT STREET
SAN DIEGO, CA 92188

211 MAIN STREET, SECOND FLOOR
SAN FRANCISCO, CA 94120

COLORADO: $\quad$ 12345 W. ALAMEDA PARKWAY
LAKEWOOD, CO 80225

A
M
E
R
I
C
A
N

J
O
B
S

A
B
R
O
A
D

CONNECTICUT: THE FEDERAL BUILDING, ROOM 613
450 MAIN STREET
HARTFORD, CT 06103

DELAWARE: CONTACT THE PHILADELPHIA JOB
INFORMATION CENTER

**DISTRICT OF
COLUMBIA:** 1900 E STREET NW, ROOM 1416
WASHINGTON, DC 20415

FLORIDA: COMMODORE BUILDING, SUITE 150
3444 MCCRORY PLACE
ORLANDO, FL 32803

GEORGIA: THE FEDERAL BUILDING, ROOM 960
75 SPRING STREET SW
ATLANTA, GA 30303

GUAM: PACIFIC DAILY NEWS BUILDING
ROOM 902
AGANA, GUAM 96910

HAWAII: THE FEDERAL BUILDING, ROOM 5316
300 ALA MOANA BLVD.
HONOLULU, HI 96850

IDAHO: CONTACT THE WASHINGTON JOB
INFORMATION CENTER

ILLINOIS: 175 W. JACKSON BLVD., ROOM 530
CHICAGO, IL 60604

INDIANA: THE FEDERAL BUILDING
575 N. PENNSYLVANIA STREET
INDIANAPOLIS, IN 46204

IOWA: CONTACT THE KANSAS CITY, MISSOURI JOB
INFORMATION CENTER

KANSAS: 120 BUILDING, ROOM 101
120 S. MARKET STREET
WICHITA, KS 67202

KENTUCKY: CONTACT THE OHIO JOB INFORMATION
CENTER

LOUISIANA: 1515 POYDRAS STREET, SUITE 608
NEW ORLEANS, LA 70112

MAINE: CONTACT THE NEW HAMPSHIRE JOB
INFORMATION CENTER

MARYLAND: THE FEDERAL BUILDING
                  101 W. LOMBARD STREET
                  BALTIMORE, MD 21201

MASSACHUSETTS:
                  THE FEDERAL BUILDING
                  10 CAUSEWAY STREET
                  BOSTON, MA 02222

MICHIGAN: 477 MICHIGAN AVENUE, ROOM 565
                  DETROIT, MI 48226

MINNESOTA: THE FEDERAL BUILDING
                  FORT SNELLING
                  TWIN CITIES, MN 55111

MISSISSIPPI: CONTACT THE ALABAMA JOB
                  INFORMATION CENTER

MISSOURI: THE FEDERAL BUILDING, ROOM 134
                  601 E. 12TH STREET
                  KANSAS CITY, MO 64106

                  OLD POST OFFICE BUILDING,
                  ROOM 400
                  815 OLIVE STREET
                  SAINT LOUIS, MO 63101

MONTANA: CONTACT THE COLORADO JOB
                  INFORMATION CENTER

NEBRASKA: CONTACT THE KANSAS JOB INFORMATION
                  CENTER

NEVADA: CONTACT THE SACRAMENTO, CALIFORNIA,
                  JOB INFORMATION CENTER

**NEW
HAMPSHIRE:**   THE FEDERAL BUILDING, ROOM 104
                  80 DANIEL STREET
                  PORTSMOUTH, NH 03801

NEW JERSEY: THE FEDERAL BUILDING
                  970 BROAD STREET
                  NEWARK, NJ 07102

NEW MEXICO: THE FEDERAL BUILDING
                  421 GOLD AVENUE SW
                  ALBUQUERQUE, NM 87102

NEW YORK: THE FEDERAL BUILDING
                  26 FEDERAL PLAZA
                  NEW YORK, NY 10278

A
M
E
R
I
C
A
N

J
O
B
S

A
B
R
O
A
D

THE FEDERAL BUILDING
100 S. CLINTON STREET
SYRACUSE, NY 13260

NORTH CAROLINA: 4565 FALLS OF NEUSE ROAD,
SUITE 4445
RALEIGH, NC 27609

NORTH DAKOTA: CONTACT THE MINNESOTA JOB
INFORMATION CENTER

OHIO: THE FEDERAL BUILDING, ROOM 506
200 W. 2ND STREET
DAYTON, OH 45402

OKLAHOMA: 200 NW FIFTH STREET, SECOND FLOOR
OKLAHOMA CITY, OK 73102

OREGON: THE FEDERAL BUILDING, ROOM 376
1220 SW THIRD AVENUE
PORTLAND, OR 97204

PENNSYLVANIA: THE FEDERAL BUILDING, ROOM 168
HARRISBURG, PA 17108

THE FEDERAL BUILDING
600 ARCH STREET, ROOM 1416
PHILADELPHIA, PA 19106

THE FEDERAL BUILDING
1000 LIBERTY AVENUE, ROOM 119
PITTSBURGH, PA 15222

PUERTO RICO: THE FEDERAL BUILDING
CARLOS E. CHARDON STREET
HATO REY, PR 00918

RHODE ISLAND: THE FEDERAL BUILDING, ROOM 310
KENNEDY PLAZA
PROVIDENCE, RI 02903

SOUTH CAROLINA: CONTACT THE NORTH CAROLINA
JOB INFORMATION CENTER

SOUTH DAKOTA: CONTACT THE MINNESOTA JOB
INFORMATION CENTER

TENNESSEE: 200 JEFFERSON AVENUE, SUITE 1312
MEMPHIS, TN 38103

TEXAS: 1100 COMMERCE STREET, ROOM 6B12
DALLAS, TX 75242
643 E. DURANGO BLVD.
SAN ANTONIO, TX 78206

UTAH: CONTACT THE COLORADO JOB INFORMATION
CENTER

VERMONT: CONTACT THE NEW HAMPSHIRE JOB
INFORMATION CENTER

VIRGINIA: THE FEDERAL BUILDING, ROOM 220
200 GRANBY STREET
NORFOLK, VA 23510

WASHINGTON: THE FEDERAL BUILDING
915 SECOND AVENUE
SEATTLE, WA 98174

WEST VIRGINIA: CONTACT THE OHIO JOB
INFORMATION CENTER

WISCONSIN: CONTACT THE MINNESOTA JOB
INFORMATION CENTER

WYOMING: CONTACT THE COLORADO JOB
INFORMATION CENTER

The federal job openings are updated on the first and fifteenth of every month.

- **Tailoring a Federal Application Form and Cover Letter to the Job Opening** Virtually every federal agency will require you to prepare and submit a Standard Form 171 Application for Federal Employment in connection with your job application. There may be additional required materials, but the SF-171 is the basic application form, and how you fill it out will determine whether you get the job. In the SF-171, you must describe your personal background, work availability, applicable veteran status, work history for the past ten years, education, skills, and accomplishments, references, and legal matters such as criminal violations, court-martials, and debt delinquencies. A well-prepared SF-171 is critical in getting a federal job abroad.

The most recent version of the SF-171, which went into effect on December 31, 1990, is shown on pages 22–27.

Question-by-question instructions for filling out the SF-171 follow. You should strive to present yourself in the most positive light. Regardless of the question, however, remember that if you don't tell the truth, there are significant criminal penalties for deliberate falsifications.

Question 1. Leave this blank until you are actually ready to submit your SF-171 for a specific federal job opening. Then, fill in the precise title of the job opening and the announcement number, if any. This way, you can use your basic SF-171 format many times, making copies as necessary and filling in Question 1 with the information specific

Standard Form 171   # Application for Federal Employment

Read The Following Instructions Carefully Before You Complete This Application

- DO NOT SUBMIT A RESUME INSTEAD OF THIS APPLICATION.
- TYPE OR PRINT CLEARLY IN DARK INK.
- IF YOU NEED MORE SPACE for an answer, use a sheet of paper the same size as this page. On each sheet write your name, Social Security Number, the announcement number or job title, and the item number. Attach all additional forms and sheets to this application at the top of page 3.
- If you do not answer **all** questions fully and correctly, you may delay the review of your application and lose job opportunities.
- Unless you are asked for additional material in the announcement or qualification information, **do not attach** any materials, such as: official position descriptions, performance evaluations, letters of recommendation, certificates of training, publications, etc. Any materials you attach which were not asked for may be removed from your application and will **not** be returned to you.
- We suggest that you keep a copy of this application for your use. If you plan to make copies of your application, we suggest you leave items 1, 48 and 49 blank. Complete these blank items each time you apply. YOU MUST SIGN AND DATE, IN INK, EACH COPY YOU SUBMIT.
- To apply for a specific Federal civil service examination (whether or not a written test is required) or a specific vacancy in an Federal agency:
  - Read the announcement and other materials provided.
  - Make sure that your work experience and/or education meet the qualification requirements described.
  - Make sure the announcement is open for the job and location you are interested in. Announcements may be closed to receipt of applications for some types of jobs, grades, or geographic locations.
  - Make sure that you are allowed to apply. Some jobs are limited to veterans, or to people who work for the Federal Government or have worked for the Federal Government in the past.
  - Follow any directions on "How to Apply". If a written test is required, bring any material you are instructed to bring to the test session. For example, you may be instructed to "Bring a completed SF 171 to the test." If a written test is not required, mail this application and all other forms required by the announcement to the address specified in the announcement.

Work Experience (*Item 24*)

- Carefully complete each experience block you need to describe your work experience. Unless you qualify based on education alone, your rating will depend on your description of previous jobs. Do not leave out any jobs you held during the last ten years.
- Under Description of Work, write a clear and brief, but complete description of your major duties and responsibilities for each job. Include any supervisory duties, special assignments, and your accomplishments in the job. We may verify your description with your former employers.
- If you had a major change of duties or responsibilities while you worked for the same employer, describe each major change as a separate job.

Veteran Preference in Hiring (*Item 22*)

- DO NOT LEAVE **Item 22 BLANK.** If you do **not** claim veteran preference, place an "X" in the box next to "NO PREFERENCE".
- You **cannot** receive veteran preference if you are retired or plan to retire at or above the rank of major or lieutenant commander, **unless** you are disabled or retired from the active military Reserve.
- To receive veteran preference your separation from active duty must have been under honorable conditions. This includes honorable and general discharges. A clemency discharge does not meet the requirements of the Veteran Preference Act.
- Active duty for training in the military Reserve and National Guard programs is not considered active duty for purposes of veteran preference.
- To qualify for preference you must meet ONE of the following conditions:
  1. Served on active duty anytime between December 7, 1941, and July 1, 1955; (If you were a Reservist called to active duty between February 1, 1955 and July 1, 1955, you must meet condition 2, below.)
     or
  2. Served on active duty any part of which was between July 2, 1955 and October 14, 1976 or a Reservist called to active duty between February 1, 1955 and October 14, 1976 and who served for more than 180 days;
     or
  3. Entered on active duty between October 15, 1976 and September 7, 1980 or a Reservist who entered on active duty between October 15, 1976 and October 13, 1982 and received a Campaign Badge or Expeditionary Medal or are a disabled veteran;
     or
  4. Enlisted in the Armed Forces after September 7, 1980 or entered active duty other than by enlistment on or after October 14, 1982 and:
     a. completed 24 months of continuous active duty or the full period called or ordered to active duty, or were discharged under 10 U.S.C. 1171 or for hardship under 10 U.S.C. 1173 and received or were entitled to receive a Campaign Badge or Expeditionary Medal; or
     b. are a disabled veteran.
- If you meet one of the four conditions above, you qualify for 5-point preference. If you want to claim 5-point preference and do not meet the requirements for 10-point preference, discussed below, place an "X" in the box next to "5-POINT PREFERENCE".
- If you think you qualify for 10-Point Preference, review the requirements described in the Standard Form (SF) 15, Application for 10-Point Veteran Preference. The SF 15 is available from any Federal Job Information Center. The 10-point preference groups are:
  - Non-Compensably Disabled or Purple Heart Recipient.
  - Compensably Disabled (less than 30%).
  - Compensably Disabled (30% or more).
  - Spouse, Widow(er) or Mother of a deceased or disabled veteran.
- If you claim 10-point preference, place an "X" in the box next to the group that applies to you. To receive 10-point preference you must attach a completed SF 15 to this application together with the proof requested in the SF 15.

Privacy Act and Public Burden Statements

THE STANDARD FORM 171 APPLICATION FOR FEDERAL EMPLOYMENT (SF-171). (The form is continued on pages 23-27.)

Application for Federal Employment—SF 171

Read the instructions before you complete this application. *Type or print clearly in dark ink.*

Form Approved
OMB No. 3206-0012

GENERAL INFORMATION

1 What kind of job are you applying for? *Give title and announcement no. (if any)*

2 Social Security Number

3 Sex
☐ Male ☐ Female

4 Birth date *(Month, Day, Year)*

5 Birthplace *(City and State or Country)*

6 Name *(Last, First, Middle)*

Mailing address *(include apartment number, if any)*

City　　　　State　　ZIP Code

7 Other names ever used *(e.g., maiden name, nickname, etc.)*

8 Home Phone
Area Code　Number

9 Work Phone
Area Code　Number　　Extension

10 Were you ever employed as a civilian by the Federal Government? If **"NO"**, go to Item 11. If **"YES"**, mark each type of job you held with an **"X"**.

☐ Temporary ☐ Career-Conditional ☐ Career ☐ Excepted
What is your **highest** grade, classification series, and job title?

Dates at **highest** grade: FROM　　TO

FOR USE OF EXAMINING OFFICE ONLY

Date entered register

Form reviewed:
Form approved:

Option	Grade	Earned Rating	Veteran Preference	Augmented Rating
			☐ No Preference Claimed	
			☐ 5 Points (Tentative)	
			☐ 10 Pts. (30% Or More Comp. Dis.)	
			☐ 10 Pts. (Less Than 30% Comp. Dis.)	
			☐ Other 10 Points	
			☐ Disallowed	☐ Being Investigated

Initials and Date

FOR USE OF APPOINTING OFFICE ONLY

Preference has been verified through proof that the separation was under honorable conditions, and other proof as required.

☐ 5-Point ☐ 10-Point - 30% or More Compensable Disability ☐ 10-Point - Less than 30% Compensable Disability ☐ 10-Point - Other

Signature and Title

Agency　　　　Date

AVAILABILITY

11 When can you start work? *(Month and Year)*

12 What is the **lowest** pay you will accept? *(You will not be considered for jobs which pay less than you indicate.)*
Pay $ _____ per _____ OR Grade _____

13 In what geographic area(s) are you willing to work?

14 Are you willing to work:

	YES	NO
A. 40 hours per week *(full-time)?*		
B. 25-32 hours per week *(part-time)?*		
C. 17-24 hours per week *(part-time)?*		
D. 16 or fewer hours per week *(part-time)?*		
E. An intermittent job *(on-call/seasonal)?*		
F. Weekends, shifts, or rotating shifts?		

15 Are you willing to take a temporary job lasting:

A. 5 to 12 months *(sometimes longer)?*
B. 1 to 4 months?
C. Less than 1 month?

16 Are you willing to travel away from home for:

A. 1 to 5 nights each month?
B. 6 to 10 nights each month?
C. 11 or more nights each month?

MILITARY SERVICE AND VETERAN PREFERENCE

17 Have you served in the United States Military Service? *If your only active duty was training in the Reserves or National Guard, answer "NO". If "NO", go to item 22.* .... YES NO

18 Did you or will you retire at or above the rank of major or lieutenant commander? ....

MILITARY SERVICE AND VETERAN PREFERENCE

19 Were you discharged from the military service under honorable conditions? *(If your discharge was changed to "honorable" or "general" by a Discharge Review Board, answer "YES". If you received a clemency discharge, answer "NO".)* If "NO", provide below the date and type of discharge you received. YES NO

Discharge Date *(Month, Day, Year)*	Type of Discharge

20 List the dates *(Month, Day, Year)*, and branch for all active duty military service.

From	To	Branch of Service

21 If all your active military duty was after October 14, 1976, list the full names and dates of all campaign badges or expeditionary medals you received or were entitled to receive.

22 Read the instructions that came with this form before completing this item. When you have determined your eligibility for veteran preference from the instructions, place an "X" in the box next to your veteran preference claim.

☐ NO PREFERENCE

☐ 5-POINT PREFERENCE -- You must show proof when you are hired.

10-POINT PREFERENCE -- If you claim 10-point preference, place an "X" in the box below next to the basis for your claim. To receive 10-point preference you must also complete a Standard Form 15, Application for 10-Point Veteran Preference, which is available from any Federal Job Information Center. ATTACH THE COMPLETED SF 15 AND REQUESTED PROOF TO THIS APPLICATION.

☐ Non-compensably disabled or Purple Heart recipient.

☐ Compensably disabled, less than 30 percent.

☐ Spouse, widow(er), or mother of a deceased or disabled veteran.

☐ Compensably disabled, 30 percent or more.

THE FEDERAL GOVERNMENT IS AN EQUAL OPPORTUNITY EMPLOYER
PREVIOUS EDITION USABLE UNTIL 12-31-90

NSN 7540-00-935-7150　　171-110

Standard Form 171 (Rev. 6-88)
U.S. Office of Personnel Management
FPM Chapter 295

Page 1

AMERICAN JOBS ABROAD

WORK EXPERIENCE *If you have no work experience, write "NONE" in A below and go to 25 on page 3.*

23 May we ask your present employer about your character, qualifications, and work record? *A "NO" will not affect our review of your qualifications. If you answer "NO" and we need to contact your present employer before we can offer you a job, we will contact you first. . . . .* | YES | NO |

24 READ WORK EXPERIENCE IN THE INSTRUCTIONS BEFORE YOU BEGIN.

- Describe your current or most recent job in Block A and work backwards, describing each job you held **during the past 10 years.** If you were **unemployed for longer than 3 months** within the past 10 years, list the dates and your address(es) in an experience block.
- You may sum up in one block work that you did **more than 10 years ago.** But if that work **is related** to the type of job you are applying for, describe each related job in a separate block.
- INCLUDE VOLUNTEER WORK *(non-paid work)*--**If the work** *(or a part of the work)* **is like the job** you are applying for, complete all parts of the experience block just as you would for a paying job. You may receive credit for work experience with religious, community, welfare, service, and other organizations.

- INCLUDE MILITARY SERVICE--You should complete all parts of the experience block just as you would for a non-military job, including all supervisory experience. Describe each major change of duties or responsibilities in a separate experience block.
- IF YOU NEED MORE SPACE TO DESCRIBE A JOB--Use sheets of paper the same size as this page (be sure to include all information we ask for in A and B below). On each sheet show your name, Social Security Number, and the announcement number or job title.
- IF YOU NEED MORE EXPERIENCE BLOCKS, use the SF 171-A or a sheet of paper.
- IF YOU NEED TO UPDATE (ADD MORE RECENT JOBS), use the SF 172 or a sheet of paper as described above.

A | Name and address of employer's organization *(include ZIP Code, if known)* | Dates employed *(give month, day and year)* | Average number of hours per week | Number of employees you supervise |
From:	To:
Salary or earnings	Your reason for wanting to leave
Starting $	per
Ending $	per

Your immediate supervisor
Name | Area Code | Telephone No. | Exact title of your job | If Federal employment *(civilian or military)* list series, grade or rank, and, if promoted in this job, the date of your last promotion

Description of work: Describe your specific duties, responsibilities and accomplishments in this job, including the job title(s) of any employees you supervise. *If you describe more than one type of work (for example, carpentry and painting, or personnel and budget), write the approximate percentage of time you spent doing each.*

For Agency Use (skill codes, etc.)

B | Name and address of employer's organization *(include ZIP Code, if known)* | Dates employed *(give month, day and year)* | Average number of hours per week | Number of employees you supervised |
From:	To:
Salary or earnings	Your reason for leaving
Starting $	per
Ending $	per

Your immediate supervisor
Name | Area Code | Telephone No. | Exact title of your job | If Federal employment *(civilian or military)* list series, grade or rank, and, if promoted in this job, the date of your last promotion

Description of work: Describe your specific duties, responsibilities and accomplishments in this job, including the job title(s) of any employees you supervised. *If you describe more than one type of work (for example, carpentry and painting, or personnel and budget), write the approximate percentage of time you spent doing each.*

For Agency Use (skill codes, etc.)

Page 2 IF YOU NEED MORE EXPERIENCE BLOCKS, USE SF 171-A *(SEE BACK OF INSTRUCTION PAGE).*

← ATTACH ANY ADDITIONAL FORMS AND SHEETS HERE

EDUCATION

25 Did you graduate from high school? *If you have a GED high school equivalency or will graduate within the next nine months, answer "YES".*

26 Write the name and location *(city and state)* of the last high school you attended or where you obtained your GED high school equivalency.

YES ____	If "YES", give month and year graduated or received GED equivalency: ....
NO ____	If "NO", give the highest grade you completed: ____

27 Have you ever attended college or graduate school?   YES ____   NO ____   If "YES", continue with 28. If "NO", go to 31.

28 NAME AND LOCATION *(city, state and ZIP Code)* OF COLLEGE OR UNIVERSITY. *If you expect to graduate within nine months, give the month and year you expect to receive your degree:*

	Name	City	State	ZIP Code	MONTH AND YEAR ATTENDED From	To	NUMBER OF CREDIT HOURS COMPLETED Semester	Quarter	TYPE OF DEGREE *(e.g. B.A., M.A.)*	MONTH AND YEAR OF DEGREE
1)										
2)										
3)										

29

CHIEF UNDERGRADUATE SUBJECTS *Show major on the first line*	NUMBER OF CREDIT HOURS COMPLETED Semester	Quarter
1)		
2)		
3)		

30

CHIEF GRADUATE SUBJECTS *Show major on the first line*	NUMBER OF CREDIT HOURS COMPLETED Semester	Quarter
1)		
2)		
3)		

31 If you have completed any **other courses or training** related to the kind of jobs you are applying for *(trade, vocational, Armed Forces, business)* give information below.

NAME AND LOCATION *(city, state and ZIP Code)* OF SCHOOL	MONTH AND YEAR ATTENDED From	To	CLASS-ROOM HOURS	SUBJECT(S)	TRAINING COMPLETED YES	NO
School Name 1) City ____ State ____ ZIP Code						
School Name 2) City ____ State ____ ZIP Code						

SPECIAL SKILLS, ACCOMPLISHMENTS AND AWARDS

32 Give the title and year of any honors, awards or fellowships you have received. List your special qualifications, skills or accomplishments that may help you get a job. *Some examples are: skills with computers or other machines; most important publications (do not submit copies); public speaking and writing experience; membership in professional or scientific societies; patents or inventions; etc.*

33 How many words per minute can you:
TYPE? ____ TAKE DICTATION? ____
Agencies may test your skills before hiring you.

34 List **job-related** licenses or certificates that you have, such as: *registered nurse; lawyer; radio operator; driver's; pilot's; etc.*

	LICENSE OR CERTIFICATE	DATE OF LATEST LICENSE OR CERTIFICATE	STATE OR OTHER LICENSING AGENCY
1)			
2)			

35 Do you speak or read a language other than English *(include sign language)? Applicants for jobs that require a language other than English may be given an interview conducted solely in that language.*   YES ____   NO ____   If "YES", list each language and place an "X" in each column that applies to you. If "NO", go to 36.

LANGUAGE(S)	CAN PREPARE AND GIVE LECTURES Fluently	With Difficulty	CAN SPEAK AND UNDERSTAND Fluently	Passably	CAN TRANSLATE ARTICLES Into English	From English	CAN READ ARTICLES FOR OWN USE Easily	With Difficulty
1)								
2)								

REFERENCES

36 List three people who are not related to you and are not supervisors you listed under 24 who know your qualifications and fitness for the kind of job for which you are applying. At least **one** should know you well on a personal basis.

FULL NAME OF REFERENCE	TELEPHONE NUMBER(S) *(Include Area Code)*	PRESENT BUSINESS OR HOME ADDRESS *(Number, street and city)*	STATE	ZIP CODE
1)				
2)				
3)				

Page 3

A
M
E
R
I
C
A
N

J
O
B
S

A
B
R
O
A
D

BACKGROUND INFORMATION-- *You must answer each question in this section before we can process your application*

37 Are you a citizen of the United States? *(In most cases you must be a U.S. citizen to be hired. You will be required to submit proof of identity and citizenship at the time you are hired.)* If **"NO"**, give the country or countries you are a citizen of: _____ | YES | NO |

NOTE: It is important that you give complete and truthful answers to questions 38 through 44. If you answer "YES" to any of them, provide your explanation(s) in **Item 45.** Include convictions resulting from a plea of nolo contendere *(no contest)*. **Omit:** 1) traffic fines of $100.00 or less; 2) any violation of law committed before your 16th birthday; 3) any violation of law committed before your 18th birthday, if finally decided in juvenile court or under a Youth Offender law; 4) any conviction set aside under the Federal Youth Corrections Act or similar State law; 5) any conviction whose record was expunged under Federal or State law. We will consider the date, facts, and circumstances of each event you list. In most cases you can still be considered for Federal jobs. However, **if you fail to tell the truth or fail to list all relevant** events or circumstances, this may be grounds for not hiring you, for firing you after you begin work, or for criminal prosecution (18 USC 1001).

	YES	NO
38 During the last **10 years**, were you **fired from any job** for any reason, did you **quit after being told that you would be fired**, or did you leave by mutual agreement because of specific problems?.		
39 Have you **ever** been convicted of, or forfeited collateral for **any felony violation?** *(Generally, a felony is defined as any violation of law punishable by imprisonment of longer than one year, except for violations called misdemeanors under State law which are punishable by imprisonment of two years or less.)*.		
40 Have you **ever** been convicted of, or forfeited collateral for **any firearms or explosives violation?**.		
41 Are you **now** under charges for **any** violation of law?.		
42 During the **last 10 years** have you forfeited collateral, been convicted, been imprisoned, been on probation, or been on parole? Do **not** include violations reported in 39, 40, or 41, above.		
43 Have you **ever** been convicted by a military **court-martial?** If no military service, answer "NO".		
44 Are you **delinquent** on any Federal debt? *(Include delinquencies arising from Federal taxes, loans, overpayment of benefits, and other debts to the U.S. Government **plus** defaults on Federally guaranteed or insured loans such as student and home mortgage loans.)*.		

45 If **"YES"** in: 38 - Explain for each job the problem(s) and your reason(s) for leaving. Give the employer's name and address.
39 through 43 - Explain each violation. Give place of occurrence and name/address of police or court involved.
44 - Explain the type, length and amount of the delinquency or default, and steps you are taking to correct errors or repay the debt. Give any identification number associated with the debt and the address of the Federal agency involved.
NOTE: If you need more space, use a sheet of paper, and include the item number.

Item No.	Date (Mo./Yr.)	Explanation	Mailing Address
			Name of Employer, Police, Court, or Federal Agency
			City State ZIP Code
			Name of Employer, Police, Court, or Federal Agency
			City State ZIP Code

	YES	NO
46 Do you receive, or have you ever applied for retirement pay, pension, or other pay based on military, Federal civilian, or District of Columbia Government service?.		

47 Do any of your relatives work for the United States Government or the United States Armed Forces? Include: *father; mother; husband; wife; son; daughter; brother; sister; uncle; aunt; first cousin; nephew; niece; father-in-law; mother-in-law; son-in-law; daughter-in-law; brother-in-law; sister-in-law; stepfather; stepmother; stepson; stepdaughter; stepbrother; stepsister; half brother; and half sister.*. . . . . If **"YES"**, provide details below. If you need more space, use a sheet of paper.

Name	Relationship	Department, Agency or Branch of Armed Forces

SIGNATURE, CERTIFICATION, AND RELEASE OF INFORMATION

YOU MUST SIGN THIS APPLICATION. Read the following carefully before you sign.

- A false statement on any part of your application may be grounds for not hiring you, or for firing you after you begin work. Also, you may be punished by fine or imprisonment (U.S. Code, title 18, section 1001).
- If you are a male born after December 31, 1959 you must be registered with the Selective Service System or have a valid exemption in order to be eligible for Federal employment. You will be required to certify as to your status at the time of appointment.
- **I understand** that any information I give may be investigated as allowed by law or Presidential order.
- **I consent** to the release of information about my ability and fitness for Federal employment **by** *employers, schools, law enforcement agencies and other individuals and organizations,* **to** *investigators, personnel staffing specialists, and other authorized employees of the Federal Government.*
- **I certify** that, to the best of my knowledge and belief, **all** of my statements are true, correct, complete, and made in good faith.

48 SIGNATURE *(Sign each application in dark ink)*	**49** DATE SIGNED *(Month, day, year)*

Page 4

*U.S. Government Printing Office: 1991 — 312-071/40218

Standard Form 171-A— *Continuation Sheet for SF 171*

● Attach all SF 171-A's to your application at the top of page 3.

Form Approved:
OMB No. 3206-0012

1. Name *(Last, First, Middle Initial)*	2. Social Security Number

3. Job Title or Announcement Number You Are Applying For	4. Date Completed

ADDITIONAL WORK EXPERIENCE BLOCKS

Name and address of employer's organization *(include ZIP Code, if known)*	Dates employed *(give month, day and year)* From: To:	Average number of hours per week	Number of employees you supervised
	Salary or earnings Starting $ per Ending $ per	Your reason for leaving	

Your immediate supervisor Name	Area Code	Telephone No.	Exact title of your job	If Federal employment *(civilian or military)* list series, grade or rank, and, if promoted in this job, the date of your last promotion

Description of work: Describe your specific duties, responsibilities and accomplishments in this job, including the job title(s) of any employees you supervised. *If you describe more than one type of work (for example, carpentry and painting, or personnel and budget), write the approximate percentage of time you spent doing each.*

For Agency Use *(skill codes, etc.)*

Name and address of employer's organization *(include ZIP Code, if known)*	Dates employed *(give month, day and year)* From: To:	Average number of hours per week	Number of employees you supervised
	Salary or earnings Starting $ per Ending $ per	Your reason for leaving	

Your immediate supervisor Name	Area Code	Telephone No.	Exact title of your job	If Federal employment *(civilian or military)* list series, grade or rank, and, if promoted in this job, the date of your last promotion

Description of work: Describe your specific duties, responsibilities and accomplishments in this job, including the job title(s) of any employees you supervised. *If you describe more than one type of work (for example, carpentry and painting, or personnel and budget), write the approximate percentage of time you spent doing each.*

For Agency Use *(skill codes, etc.)*

THE FEDERAL GOVERNMENT IS AN EQUAL OPPORTUNITY EMPLOYER
PREVIOUS EDITION USABLE

Standard Form 171-A (Rev. 6-88)
U.S. Office of Personnel Management
FPM Chapter 295

to each job opening. You should also leave item 48 (your signature line) and item 49 (the date of signature) blank, if you plan to submit photocopies of your original SF-171. Copies are perfectly acceptable, as long as you sign and date each copy you submit separately and individually in ink.

Questions 2 through 10. Complete these questions, on the upper left side of page one, but leave the upper right section blank. This is for the Examining Office and the Appointing Office only. Obvious as this may seem, many people nevertheless fill in these sections by mistake and are thus denied consideration for the job position.

Question 11. Answer truthfully, of course, but consider simply saying "immediately," which is an acceptable response. Even if in fact you will need several weeks or months to organize your affairs before you can start, remember that the government hiring process takes time. It is likely that the inevitable bureaucratic delays, processing requirements and/or security clearance and background checks will give you the time you need anyway.

Question 12. Consider your response carefully. Naturally, you want as much money as possible. But, as the question says, you will not be considered for jobs that pay less than you indicate. Consider leaving this question blank as well, until you submit an SF-171 or a copy for a specific job. That way, you can tailor your response to the salary figure named in the job announcement.

Question 13. An important question! Some federal jobs, such as the Foreign Service, require that you be available for worldwide assignment. Other federal jobs and federal agencies have similar requirements. If you fill in "worldwide," you won't have any problems. This may mean that you get a job offer for an assignment in a Third World country or some other location you don't like. Remember, however, that it is better to get a job offer that you will turn down than to get no job offer at all.

Question 14. Answer yes to subquestion A and no to subquestions B, C, and D. Unless you see something to the contrary in a job announcement, don't plan on getting a part-time job overseas. Subquestions E and F are up to you, but again, answering yes doesn't mean you have to actually accept any job offer you receive that contains unacceptable work hours.

Question 15. Answer no to subquestions B and C, since it simply wouldn't be worth the effort of moving abroad for a job lasting only a couple of months. Subquestion A, however, deserves some thought. A temporary job of five to twelve months may lead to a longer assignment or even a permanent position. Check this out beforehand, however, and remember that a temporary job may not include medical benefits, vacation leave, sick leave, or other perks.

Question 16. Obviously, the answers to subquestions A, B, and C must be yes.

Questions 17 through 22. Unless you have a military service history that qualifies you for a 5-point or 10-point preference under Question 22, these questions aren't very important. Note how Question 22 says that, to claim a 5-point preference, "you must show proof when you are hired." Proof may include any Campaign Badge or Expeditionary Medal that you have received and a copy of Form DD-214, Report of

Military Transfer or Discharge, which you should have received after your final discharge from the military.

Question 23. Unless you have a strong reason to the contrary, answer yes to this question. Don't kid yourself that "a 'no' will not affect our review of your qualifications." Good references are just as important in government hiring as in private-sector hiring.

Question 24. This is the most important question in the SF-171. Fill out every block, even if you have to answer "not applicable," in every subquestion, working your way backward for a full ten years from your most recent job. Attach copies of SF-171-A, the Continuation Sheet for SF-171, if you need additional space.

The "Description of Work" portion of each subquestion is key, because it is here that you list your qualifications and sell yourself as the best candidate for the job. Ten years is a long time, of course, and so in your response to some of the subquestions (particularly on your continuation sheets) you may be describing summer jobs during school, other temporary employment, or other old jobs not relevant to the position you are seeking. Don't waste too much time on those, unless there is something unique that may help you get the job, since the person reviewing your SF-171 is just going to skim over them anyway. A terse summary—one or two sentences—of your duties will suffice. Concentrate on your most recent jobs—subquestions A, B, and so forth—where you presumably gained the experience that qualifies you for certain positions. Remember, it is perfectly acceptable to respond "see attached resume" and then staple a copy of your resume or vita to the SF-171. The portion of this Introduction titled "Tips and Techniques for Applying to Private Employers" contains a sample resume and is fine to use as a model for your attachment, as long as you convey your work experience and qualifications in the most positive light. Attaching your resume to Form SF-171 also gives you the flexibility of tailoring the resume to the specific job you're applying for. If you have a PC and your resume is on a disk, you can adapt it for each individual job.

Regardless of whether you attach a copy of your resume or type your description of work in the space provided, however, be sure to highlight your credentials, skills, and qualifications most relevant to the position you are seeking. If you previously worked in the government and got favorable job evaluations, say so and attach copies of the evaluation reports if you have them. If the job you are applying for requires a security clearance and you already have one, mention that also. Some federal agencies will accept security clearances issued by other federal agencies, and you may get favorable consideration for the job opening, if only because the hiring officer is relieved at not having to deal with his or her agency's security procedures.

Questions 25 through 31. These questions concern your educational background. If you have completed classes or seminars in the subjects covered by questions 29, 30, or 31, and these are relevant to the position you want, consider not only mentioning this but also attaching a copy of your transcript or certificate of completion.

Question 32. Include anything relevant to this question. Also include anything impressive, even if not relevant, such as awards or public offices held. Attach copies of

A
M
E
R
I
C
A
N

J
O
B
S

A
B
R
O
A
D

relevant documents, but not too many, since you don't want your SF-171 to become overloaded with attachments.

Questions 33 and 34. Self-explanatory. Don't list anything but job-related licenses or certificates in your response to question 34.

Question 35. If you are fluent in languages other than English, this could be very helpful in getting a job abroad. You can attach an additional sheet if you are fluent in more than two foreign languages as long as it is clearly marked "Continuation Sheet for Question Number 35."

Question 36. Self-explanatory. Be sure to give their current telephone numbers, since the hiring officer will probably want to call them rather than write them, and he or she will be irritated if you list a wrong or out-of-date number. If a reference is employed in a federal agency, particularly if it is the same agency to which you are applying, name that agency in the business address portion of your response.

Question 37. Self-explanatory.

Questions 38 through 47. Again, these questions are relatively self-explanatory. They are not trivial, however, and you should take to heart the warning about potential criminal penalties for false responses. A background check, which involves consulting appropriate federal, state, and military records, may uncover any lie or misstatement and not only disqualify you for the job, but expose you to prosecution as well. Question 38, however, allows you a bit more latitude, since it calls for a conclusion as to why you left a job. It is more difficult to check, particularly for older jobs where the supervisor listed in your response to question 24 may no longer be there or you can't obtain an accurate current phone number.

Questions 48 and 49. As stated earlier in this section, you should keep these items blank if you plan to submit copies of your basic SF-171 format. Copies are perfectly acceptable, as long as you sign and date each one separately in ink. It is recommend that you sign copies in blue ink, so it is immediately apparent to the person reviewing your application that you personally signed the SF-171.

SAMPLE COVER LETTER FORMAT: You can easily adapt the sample cover letter for American companies (on page 6) for use in applying for federal jobs. The most important modification is in the "re" line. It should reference the job announcement or notice of vacancy number right up front, so your application and SF-171 go into the correct file. Also, be sure to mention that you have enclosed your SF-171.

- **Coping with the Unique Aspects of the Federal Job Application Process** The federal hiring process is marked by some unique requirements. Furthermore, although many federal agencies are efficient and timely in processing job applications, lost applications and hiring delays of months or even years are not uncommon. Be prepared to follow up on your application by periodically telephoning the agency to make sure it was received, it hasn't been lost, it is being processed, and so forth.

John Doe
101 Maple Street
Anywhere, USA
(000) 000-0000

Today's date, 199_

Ms. Jane Smith
U.S. Dept of Paperwork
500 Bureaucracy Avenue
Washington, D.C. 20000

Re: Job Announcement Number 92-11123, GS-13 Senior Management
Executive Job Opening in Madrid, Spain, Field Office

Dear Ms. Smith:

I noticed your agency's advertisement for the above-captioned
position in the Federal Job Center in Anywhere, USA, and I want to be
considered for the job.

As described in my enclosed form SF-171 and resume, I am
currently the senior administrative officer for the XYZ Corporation, and I am
confident that I have the necessary qualifications for the position.
Furthermore, I am fluent in Spanish. I have always wanted to work abroad,
especially in Europe, and I am willing to leave my current employer in order
to pursue this opportunity.

I look forward to hearing from you in the near future. Please do not
hesitate to contact me at (000) 000-0000 any time.

Yours truly,

John Doe

SAMPLE COVER LETTER FOR A FEDERAL EMPLOYER.

A
M
E
R
I
C
A
N

J
O
B
S

A
B
R
O
A
D

In addition to the basic SF-171, there may be particular application forms and procedures required by the individual agencies you contact. With respect to the forms, you will have to get them directly from the agencies. With respect to the procedures, some of the most common and significant requirements are as follows:

SECURITY CLEARANCES AND BACKGROUND CHECKS: Many federal jobs abroad require a security clearance so that you can be permitted access to sensitive documents and other material related to your duties. There are three major categories of sensitive material: *classified,* for material of low importance; *secret,* for material of some importance; and *top secret,* for material of such significant importance that disclosure is deemed to be seriously detrimental to American interests. You may be required to get a secret or top secret security clearance; classified doesn't mean much.

To get a security clearance, you will have to undergo a background investigation. Every agency has its own security division, which conducts these investigations. Understand that there is no generic form of security clearance. A security clearance issued by one federal agency won't necessarily be accepted by another federal agency, and so even if you have undergone a background investigation before you may have to go through one again. The investigation may involve

- o Checking with the FBI, state, and local authorities concerning your criminal record
- o For agencies that deal primarily in intelligence, such as the CIA, a lie-detector test
- o Contacting your present and former employers to validate your work experience
- o Contacting your spouse, friends, and neighbors concerning your personal habits
- o Medical and psychological evaluation, including drug testing
- o A language evaluation, if you claim proficiency in a particular language

"TOUR OF DUTY" REQUIREMENTS: Many federal agencies require that you commit to working abroad for a minimum period of time, called a tour of duty. The requirement can be one, two, or more years.

- **Outlook for Federal Employers** Despite budget problems and downsizing of major federal employers of Americans abroad, such as the Department of Defense, the government is going to continue to need experienced men and women serving it abroad. As long as the United States is a world power and an active member of the international community, there will continue to be federal employees abroad. Given fiscal concerns, however, it is likely that hiring freezes, salary caps, and cost-of-living adjustment limits will continue to plague federal agencies. Furthermore, since the number of federal jobs abroad is likely to experience no real growth for some time, the competition for good positions will probably increase.

- **Hot Spots for the 1990s** Eastern European countries and the former Soviet Republics are two of the potentially strong growth areas in federal employment abroad. While private employers go where the profit-making opportunities are, federal employers are influenced by diplomatic and political considerations, which in the 1990s are primarily related to the post-cold war world order.

EASTERN EUROPE: In varying degrees, the countries of eastern Europe have turned to the United States and the rest of the West for help in building democratic societies and capitalist economies. Nations such as the Czech Republic, Hungary, and Poland are particularly active. Although there was an initial surge in enthusiasm in the private sector concerning eastern European economic opportunities following the fall of communism in 1989, that has been somewhat dampened owing to sluggish growth and the worldwide recession. As a result, the presence of agencies such as the Agency for International Development and others that distribute American assistance is likely to continue to grow.

THE FORMER SOVIET REPUBLICS: Like Eastern Europe, the countries of the former Soviet Union need American assistance as they undergo the transition from socialist, centrally planned economies to ones based on free market principles. In particular, the Foreign Service and the State Department are hiring more people, because instead of one country there are now over a dozen, each of which requires setting up an American embassy and various consulates.

SOURCES OF FURTHER INFORMATION

Fed-West Publishing. *How to Get a Government Job: A Reference Guide to Government Employment.* Seattle, Wash.: Fed-West Publishing, 1988.

Government Reprint Services. *Government Jobs Guide.* St. Louis, Mo.: Government Reprint Services, 1984.

Krannich, Ronald L. *Almanac of American Government Jobs and Careers.* Woodbridge, Va.: Impact Publications, 1991.

Lauber, Daniel. *Government Job Finder.* River Forest, Ill: National Book Network, 1992.

National Information Center. *Government Employment Guide.* Elgin, Ill.: National Information Center, 1987.

Office of Personnel Management. *America's Federal Jobs: A Complete Directory of Federal Career Opportunities.* Indianapolis, Ind.: JIST Works, 1991.

Pickard, Steven. *Government Employment Guide, Containing Useful Information On Obtaining Employment With the Government.* Chandler, Ariz.: WesLyn, 1990.

Robison, William C. *The Federal Employment Handbook.* New York: J. Messner, 1981.

U.S. Information Bureau. *The Complete Government Job Seekers Directory.* U.S. Information Bureau, 1988.

Vogel, Stephen E. *Directory of Employment Opportunities in the Federal Government.* New York: Arco Publishing, 1985.

A
M
E
R
I
C
A
N

J
O
B
S

A
B
R
O
A
D

Worldwide Marketing. *State & Federal Employment Guide: Including a Directory of State and Federal Employment Opportunities in Both the U.S. and Abroad.* St. Louis, Mo.: Worldwide Marketing, 1985.

IDENTIFYING PROSPECTIVE INTERNATIONAL ORGANIZATIONS

In addition to private and federal employers, many international organizations hire Americans for positions abroad. Some of the largest ones are discussed here. (For a complete list of international organizations, *see* the Organization Listings, beginning on page 535 .)

THE WORLD BANK GROUP: The World Bank Group and the International Bank for Reconstruction and Development are interrelated bodies, and they include the International Development Association and the International Finance Corporation. All four entities are involved in providing development assistance to countries around the world and have a continuing need for qualified persons in the areas of banking, business, economic development, economics, finance, and statistics. For further information, contact:

> **WORLD BANK GROUP: INTERNATIONAL BANK FOR RECONSTRUCTION AND DEVELOPMENT**
> 1818 H ST. NW
> WASHINGTON, DC 20433
> (202) 477-1234

THE INTERNATIONAL MONETARY FUND: Like the World Bank, the IMF is involved in international finance, but it has much more clout because of its greater assets. For example, it was the IMF that lent the United Kingdom billions of dollars in the 1970s to avert a balance-of-payments crisis. The IMF needs people skilled in banking, business, economic development, economics, finance, and statistics. For further information, contact:

> **INTERNATIONAL MONETARY FUND**
> RECRUITING DIVISION
> 700 19TH ST. NW
> WASHINGTON, DC 20431
> (202) 623-7000

THE UNITED NATIONS: The UN and its affiliated organizations, such as UNESCO, UNICEF, and the World Health Organization, have a truly worldwide bureaucracy. Their hiring needs run the entire spectrum of occupations, from economists to zoologists. For further information, contact:

UNITED NATIONS
OFFICE OF PERSONNEL SERVICES
ONE U.N. PLAZA
NEW YORK, NY 10017
(212) 963-1234

OTHER ORGANIZATIONS: Several other international organizations, most of which are connected to the UN in some manner, hire Americans for jobs abroad. The UN can provide you with a list of them. For example, there are regional bodies such as the Inter-American Development Bank and the Organization of American States, both of which need persons with backgrounds in banking, economic development, economics, and Central and South American studies. For further information, contact:

INTER-AMERICAN DEVELOPMENT BANK
RECRUITING OFFICE
1300 NEW YORK AVE. NW
WASHINGTON, DC 20005
(202) 623-1000

ORGANIZATION OF AMERICAN STATES
ATTENTION: HIRING DEPARTMENT
CONSTITUTION AVENUE AND 17TH STREET NW
WASHINGTON, DC 20006
(202) 458-3000

- **Hot Spots for the 1990s** Although international organizations are active worldwide, in some areas their presence is expected to grow considerably throughout the 1990s and beyond. The major growth areas are described here. Of course, there is no guarantee that events will transpire as expected.

EASTERN EUROPE: As discussed previously, Eastern Europe is expected to be a growth area for American agencies involved in international assistance. The same is generally regarded to be true for international agencies as well.

THE FORMER SOVIET REPUBLICS: As with federal employment abroad, the breakup of the former Soviet Union means employment opportunities with international agencies active in helping the former Soviet republics shed the legacy of centrally planned economies. Look for the primary growth to be in the larger economies of Russia, Ukraine, and possibly Kazakhstan.

THE THIRD WORLD: Unfortunately, regional famines, the spread of AIDS, and continued economic deprivation in the Third World mean that international organizations involved in agricultural assistance, health care, and development assistance will continue to be active and growing. These may not be the most glamorous of jobs, however, given the hardships of living in the Third World.

A
M
E
R
I
C
A
N

J
O
B
S

A
B
R
O
A
D

SOURCES OF FURTHER INFORMATION

Clark, Teresa S. *Directory of International, Inter-American, U.S., and Canadian Organizations Concerned with Latin American Development.* Washington: United Nations Food and Agricultural Organization, 1974.

Gale Research. *Encyclopedia of Associations: International Organizations.* Detroit, Mich.: Gale Research, 1994.

Smith, Devon Cottrell and James LaVeck. *Great Careers: The Fourth of July Resource Guide for the Promotion of Careers in Public, Community, and International Service.* Garrett Park, Md.: Garrett Park Press, 1990.

NEGOTIATING THE BEST DEAL BEFORE YOU ACCEPT AN OFFER

- **Private Employers: Potential Perks and Benefits** Your prospective employer may offer certain perks and benefits as part of a standard benefits package or cost-of-living adjustment, or as part of its job offer for a specific position in a specific country. If there is no standard benefits package, you might have to negotiate with the company. Depending on the nature of the position, the number of applicants, the economy, and how much you want the job, consider inquiring about the following concerns:

FOREIGN TAX OBLIGATIONS PAID BY THE EMPLOYER: As discussed more thoroughly on page 60, some employers offer tax equalization plans that relieve you of the responsibility for paying taxes to the foreign government, and withhold what you would have paid in taxes on your income if you had been working in the United States. Because of the $70,000 exclusion, however, a tax equalization plan only benefits you if the foreign country's personal income tax rate is higher than that of the United States.

TRAVEL AND RELOCATION EXPENSES: Will the company pay your expenses for traveling to, and relocating in, your new country? Will it pay for your travel back to the United States during your vacations, or for your spouse and dependents in the United States who visit you? *(See sections 5, 9, and 15 of the sample employment agreement in the next section, which relate to travel and relocation matters.)*

HOUSING: Will the company give you a housing allowance, or provide you with company-owned housing? This is particularly important in high-cost cities such as London and Tokyo. *(See section 6 of the sample employment agreement.)*

AUTOMOBILE: Will the company provide you with an automobile, or give you a car allowance? Take into account the cost of gasoline abroad. In some European countries, it can be as high as $5 a gallon.

MEDICAL CARE: Does the company have a health insurance plan? In countries such as Russia or those of the Third World, where medical supplies are scarce and the quality of care is low, will the company give you free access to any in-house medical clinic it operates?

OTHER PERKS AND BENEFITS: Some other perks and benefits you might look for, and which companies are known to agree to, include (1) language instruction classes, such as Berlitz, (2) educational allowances, and (3) a property management allowance to hire a professional realty company to rent and manage your house while you are abroad. Finally, don't forget to ask about some of the benefits you would normally expect to find in a job in the United States, such as dental plans, profit sharing, and 401(k) or other retirement plans.

- **Understanding Employment Agreements** On pages 38–44 is a sample employment agreement form used for jobs abroad with American companies. After every clause, there is a brief annotation of the meaning of that clause and its importance to you. Some clauses are more important than others, and some involve benefits discussed previously or other matters subject to negotiation between you and the company. The clauses in any actual employment agreement that you encounter won't necessarily be in the same order or bear the same heading, but you should be able to recognize the counterparts to the clauses in this sample form.

  Finally, this sample employment agreement is only for corporate employers. Other employers, such as government agencies and international organizations operating abroad, may operate on the basis of (1) their own particular employment agreements, which are subject to little or no negotiation or modification, and/or (2) rules and regulations governing employee rights and responsibilities rather than employment agreement. In the latter situation, you need to get a copy of the appropriate rules and regulations to understand what you're getting into. Again, there may be little or no room for negotiation or modification of the agency's or organization's policies. However, there will probably be grievance procedures and rights to a hearing that aren't provided by private employers if you face termination, demotion, or other disciplinary action.

- **Federal Employers Federal Rank or GS Status** Every federal agency ranks it employees according to a grade system. The higher your grade is, the greater your salary, your responsibility, and your benefits are. Try to get the hiring officer to commit to a particular rank—the higher the better—before you accept an offer.

  There are several different federal rank systems. For most domestic and some foreign federal jobs, the GS (General Schedule) system is used. GS ranks begin at GS-1, and salary increases with each rise in rank. The GS system usually ends at GS-15 or GS-16, after which you have to be appointed to the Senior Executive Service or other senior bureaucratic rank. Depending on their experience and qualifications, clerks and support personnel usually are hired at between GS-3 and GS-7, technical and skilled service

EMPLOYMENT AGREEMENT

THIS AGREEMENT, entered into this ____ day of _____, 19___, is by and between _____ (the "Employee") and _____, Inc. (the "Employer"), a corporation existing under the laws of the state of _____.

[This is the standard preface to an employment agreement. It should state the exact date on which the agreement was signed, your full, legal name, and the full, legal name of the employer. It should also name the state in which the company was incorporated.]

WITNESSETH:

WHEREAS, the Employer wishes to employ the Employee and the Employee wishes to be employed by the Employer, and

WHEREAS, the parties have decided to set forth the terms upon which the Employer will employ the Employee in this Agreement,

NOW, THEREFORE, in consideration of the promises set forth herein and other good and valuable consideration, the receipt and sufficiency of which is hereby acknowledged by the Employer and the Employee, the parties hereto agree as follows:

[These are called the recitals. They usually don't involve anything substantive, but exist to satisfy an arcane legal doctrine called "consideration," which is the prerequisite to any legally enforceable contract.]

Section 1: Employment. Subject to the terms and conditions set forth herein, the Employer hereby employs the Employee and the Employee hereby accepts such employment. The Employee shall perform the following services:

_____
_____
_____

The Employee will work at the Employer's offices located in the country of _____, city of _____ (the "Place of Work"). The Employer will not relocate, reassign, or otherwise require the Employee to move from the Place of Work during the Term of Employment as defined in Section 2 below without the Employee's prior written consent, which shall not be unreasonably withheld.

[This section should describe in reasonable detail your work duties and, if relevant, your official title. It should name the country and city in which you'll be working. If possible, you should also get the company to agree not to reassign you without your consent. The company is entitled, however, to your reasonable consent. For example, if the company asked you to transfer from the Frankfurt, Germany, office to the Heidelberg, Germany, office only 50 miles away, barring unusual circumstances, it would not be reasonable for you to refuse. If the company asked you to transfer from Frankfurt to a hardship location such as Somalia, however, your refusal probably would be reasonable. Finally, if your job will require some travel while you are abroad, consider a compromise on the final sentence of this section, such as "The Employer will not relocate, reassign, or otherwise require the Employee to move or travel from the Place of Work for more than one week a month during the Term of Employment as defined in Section 2 below without the Employee's prior written consent, which shall not be unreasonably withheld."

A SAMPLE EMPLOYMENT AGREEMENT, WHICH AMERICAN COMPANIES MAY USE FOR JOBS ABROAD. (The agreement is continued on pages 39–44.)

Section 2: Term of Employment. The Employee will report to the Place of Work on _____, 19__. Unless otherwise terminated earlier pursuant to the provisions of this Agreement, the term of the Employee's employment shall be for ___ year/s commencing on the date that the Employee is required to report to work. This Agreement shall automatically renew from year to year thereafter unless terminated upon written notice by either Employer or Employee not less than (thirty) 30 calendar days prior to the expiration of this Agreement or prior to the expiration of any renewal period.

[This is a very important clause, because you cannot sue the Employer for wrongful termination unless the employment agreement specifically says that you were hired for a year, five years, or another specified term. The automatic renewal clause enables you to stay on the job if you want to and the company wants you to, without having to sign a whole new employment agreement. Of course, before you let the agreement renew, you should look at the salary terms and other benefits that you may want increased.]

Section 3: Salary. For services performed, the Employer shall pay the Employee a salary of $_____ a year (the ''Initial Salary''), to be paid in United States dollars. During any renewal period, the Employer shall pay the Employee the Initial Salary plus such other amounts in excess of the Initial Salary as the Employer and the Employee may agree upon. The Employee's compensation shall be paid in such manner as salaries are normally paid to other comparable employees of the Employer. The Employee shall be entitled to an annual compensation review, and shall be entitled to participate in any life, accident and health insurance, incentive and profit-sharing, pension, 401(k), retirement, or other plan or benefit provided by the Employer to its employees generally or to employees with duties comparable to the Employee's in particular.

[Obviously, your salary is one of the most important terms. The agreement should state specifically your beginning salary. Furthermore, depending on the country, you may want the agreement to specify payment in U.S. dollars. In countries with strong, convertible currencies like England, Germany, and Japan, this is not so much of a concern, although you should ask how the company calculates its conversion rate. For example, suppose you sign a two-year employment agreement to work in Germany for $50,000 a year and you are to be paid in German marks. In year one the exchange rate is 1.5-marks per dollar, but in year two it falls to 2 marks per dollar. In year two, do you get paid 75,000 marks (the 1.5 mark rate in effect when you signed the agreement) or 100,000 marks (the 2-mark rate now in effect)? The reverse is also possible. If the exchange rate becomes 1 mark per dollar in year two, do you now get paid only 50,000 marks? Not only should you find out what the payment procedure is concerning conversion rates and the local currency, but you should also consider the potential risks and rewards of being paid in U.S. dollars.

In countries with weak currencies and where there are restrictions on converting it into hard currency, such as in eastern Europe and most of the Third World, you will certainly want to be paid in U.S. dollars. Not only will dollars get you further in the local economy, but at the end of your overseas employment you will be able to bring back any accumulated savings to the

United States without having to worry about converting it into dollars. In addition, some countries, such as Hungary, tolerate black-market currency trading; so you may be able to get a better conversion rate for your dollars "on the street" than through the company.]

[Finally, if you are to be paid by the hour instead of a salary, the agreement should state (1) how much you are to be paid per hour, (2) how many hours a week you are to work, (3) how much you will be paid per hour of overtime, and (4) whether your regular pay and your overtime pay includes travel time. Remember that you may not be protected by overtime compensation laws while you are working overseas.]

Section 4: Taxes. The Employer shall pay, without cost to the Employee, (1) any and all income taxes, and (2) any other taxes arising out of Employee's employment at the Place of Work, that are imposed by the national, regional, and/or local authorities. The Employee understands that the Employee is potentially subject to U.S. income tax and other U.S. taxes, and that the Employer will make the necessary withholdings and deductions necessary to satisfy these U.S. obligations.

[As discussed more fully on pages 60-61, you may face both U.S. and foreign income tax on your salary. Large multinational companies may have some sort of tax equalization plan, under which the company takes care of the foreign taxes so that your net pay is equivalent to what you would be receiving if you were working for the company in the United States. This may or may not be to your benefit.]

Section 5: Relocation. The Employer shall pay for the following relocation costs of the Employee:

(i) Travel by commercial airline to the Place of Work by the Employee and the Employee's spouse and children.

(ii) Hotel accommodations, meals, passport photos, inoculations, physical and other medical examinations, transportation of the Employee's and the Employee's family's baggage and personal effects, and other expenses relating to the Employee's and the Employee's family's relocation, not to exceed a total of $_____. Employee shall submit such receipts and other reasonable documentation of expenses that the Employer may require.

[The company should pay for your travel costs and other reasonable expenses. Travel is usually by airplane, unless for some reason another mode of transportation, such as by ship, is required. You might also consider specifying first-class or business-class seats, but of course common sense applies: if you are traveling alone, the company may agree to pay for an upgraded seat, but not if you are bringing a wife and eight kids. Furthermore, the company should agree to help you with your relocation expenses. You are entitled to a fixed amount of expenses, but whether the company agrees to pay $1,000, $5,000, $10,000, or more in expenses depends on the size of the company, where and how far you are traveling, and how much it wants you for the job. If possible, get your expense money up front, so that you don't have to dip into your own resources while you wait for reimbursement.]

Section 6: Housing. The Employer will, during the term of this agreement, either (1) provide the Employee and the Employee's family with reasonable housing accommodations, within a reasonable distance of the Place of Work, at a cost to the Employee not to exceed $_____ a month, or (2) pay the Employee a housing allowance of $_____ a month over and above the Employee's other compensation. The Employer is not responsible for paying for household furnishings and other personal effects.

[Whether you can get the company to help you with your housing needs depends on two factors: (1) the company's size and willingness to share the burden of getting you on board, and (2) where you're going. Help with housing is much more of an issue in high-priced locations such as Tokyo or London, but not much of a concern in low-cost Mexico City. Be sure to get accurate information about housing costs in the country you are moving to, however, before you decide to ask for a housing assistance clause in your employment agreement. For example, despite a relatively low cost of living overall, housing in Budapest, Hungary, is nearly as expensive as in London.]

Section 7: Exclusivity and Confidentiality. The Employee agrees to devote his full-time best efforts and attention to his duties with the Employer and not to enter into any outside employment or engage in any other business activities.

The Employee shall not, directly or indirectly, whether during the term of this Agreement or at any time thereafter, disclose or cause to be disclosed any confidential information of the Employer's. Confidential information includes any information that might be used in a manner adverse to the Employer's interests, including but not limited to trade secrets, patents, marketing research, client lists, client information, business methods, assets, finances, contracts, product research, and technical data. Upon leaving the Employer's employment, the Employee shall return any and all written material, computer disks, and other items containing confidential information in tangible form. Confidential material does not include information (i) learned or acquired by the Employee independently of his employment with the Employer, (ii) disclosed to the Employee by a third party not affiliated with or employed by the Employer, or (iii) that becomes disclosed by means or by causes that do not violate the terms of this Agreement.

[You will probably be asked to pledge that you will not work for anyone else, or pursue independent business activities, during the term of your employment. This is a fairly standard clause. It is also fairly standard to require you to not disclose any confidential information. There is another clause, however, that is common in domestic employment agreements but that you should be wary of concerning foreign employment: the "stipulation to injunctive relief" clause, which says that you agree that the company shall have the right to get a court order preventing you from disclosing any confidential information. Such a stipulation may be fine within the United States, but since you probably have no idea about how foreign laws and foreign courts operate, be leery of consenting to their jurisdiction.]

Section 8: Rights to Intellectual Property. The Employer shall be deemed the owner of all right, title, and interest in and of any patentable process, invention, and improvements in methods or business operations discovered by the Employee in connection with his employment with the Employer during the term of this Agreement. The Employee shall execute such documents and perform such acts as may reasonably be required by the Employer to give effect to this Section.

[The company has the right to claim ownership to any new inventions and other discoveries that you make while on the job, since you are using their facilities and are working on their time. The scope of this clause should be limited to the term of the agreement, however. The company is not entitled to your ideas and inventions after you leave the job.]

Section 9: Vacations. The Employee is entitled to __ weeks of vacation per calendar year, at full pay, to be taken at such times as the Employee and the Employer shall mutually agree upon. For partial calendar years, the __ weeks of vacation shall be prorated accordingly. The Employee may not carry over more than __ week/weeks of unused vacation time from any previous calendar year or years into any succeeding calendar year. In addition to vacation time, the Employee shall be entitled to take __ holiday days off, at full pay, to be allocated between customary American holidays and customary local holidays as the Employee and the Employer shall mutually agree upon.

[Four weeks of paid vacation a year is reasonable and customary, although it depends on the nature of the job. Remember, however, that in some countries people may get more or less vacation time than Americans are used to. For example, in France, Germany, and most of western Europe, six weeks of paid vacation a year is the norm. In Japan, however, people take very little vacation time. Be prepared to adapt to local customs, for better or for worse.]

Section 10: Workers' Compensation. The Employer shall maintain workers' compensation insurance in accordance with the laws of the state of _____ during the term of this Agreement, which insurance shall cover any injuries received by the Employee in the course of Employee's employment at the Place of Work, to the extent permitted by _____ law and the laws of the country of _____.

[In the United States, state law requires companies to provide workers' compensation insurance so that your medical bills will be paid if you are injured and your lost wages will be reimbursed to you. This section is designed to maintain that protection while you are abroad, where there may not be any workers' compensation protection. Of course, if you are going to a country such as Sweden where the laws provide greater benefits than are available under U.S. law, you don't need to insist on this section.]

Section 11: Termination with Cause. The Employer may discharge the Employee at any time prior to the expiration of this Agreement for (1) fraud, gross negligence, wanton and willful misconduct and/or incompetency, (2) conviction of serious criminal offense under local law or of a felony under Unites States law, or (3) a material breach of the terms of this Agreement. If the Employee is terminated for cause, the Employee shall be entitled to receive one month's salary as severance pay.

[The company is entitled to fire you for certain types of flagrant misconduct, although "just cause" should be limited to serious and material violations of law.]

Section 12: Termination without Cause. The Employer may, at any time, and upon 30 days prior written notice, discharge the Employee without cause. If the Employee is discharged without cause, the Employee shall be entitled to receive the Employee's salary for the remainder of the term or any renewal term of this Agreement, to be paid in the same manner and at the same times as if the Employee had not been terminated. The Employee shall be entitled to continue to receive all of the benefits provided by this Agreement, and shall not be obligated to seek or assume other employment.

[Corporations typically reserve the right to fire you without cause, so that they can eliminate personality conflicts, institute organizational reforms, and so forth. In this situation, it is only fair that the company pay more than it would if it fired you for cause.]

Section 13: Termination by Employee. The Employee may, at any time, and upon 30 days prior written notice, terminate this Agreement for any reason. In the event of such termination by the Employee, the Employer shall have no further obligations to the Employee other than to pay any and all sums then currently due and owing to the Employee, including wages to the date of termination.

[You should reserve the right to quit for any reason, but you can expect to receive practically nothing in the way of severance benefits if you do so.]

Section 14: Sick Leave and Discharge for Medical Reasons. The Employee shall be entitled to __ weeks of sick leave per calendar year. For partial calendar years, the __ weeks of sick leave shall be prorated accordingly. The Employee may not carry over more than __ week/weeks of unused sick leave from any previous calendar year or years into any succeeding calendar year. If a doctor certifies that the Employee is unable to perform his duties under this Agreement by reason of illness or injury, then the Employer in its sole discretion may deem this Agreement terminated and the Employee shall be entitled to __ months' salary as severance pay.

[You should get two to three weeks of sick leave per year. In addition, if the company decides to fire you because an illness or injury prevents you from working, this section will give you some protection.]

Section 15: Travel Back to the United States. In the event of (1) the expiration of the term of this Agreement or any renewal term thereafter, (2) the Employee's discharge without cause pursuant to Section 12, or (3) the Employee's discharge for medical reasons pursuant to Section 14, then the Employer shall pay for the following travel costs of the Employee back to the United States:

(i) Travel by commercial airline back to the Employee's point of departure from the United States under Section 5 for the Employee and the Employee's spouse and children.

(ii) Hotel accommodations, meals, passport photos, inoculations, physical and other medical examinations, transportation of the Employee's and the Employee's family's baggage and personal effects, and other expenses relating to the Employee's and the Employee's family's return to the United States, not to exceed a total of $_____. Employee shall submit such receipts and other reasonable documentation of expenses that the Employer may require.

[This section is the "travel home" counterpart to Section 5. The same comments after Section 5 concerning what assistance you can expect from the employer apply to this section as well.]

Section 16: Invalidity. The invalidity or unenforceability of any particular provision of this Agreement shall not affect the other provisions hereof, and this Agreement shall be construed in all respects as if such invalid or unenforceable provision were omitted.

[This is standard legalese, so that any invalid or illegal clause doesn't throw out the whole agreement.]

Section 17: Modification and Waiver. No change, modification, or waiver of this Agreement shall be valid unless the same is in writing and signed by both Employer and Employee. The failure of any party at any time to insist upon strict performance of any term, covenant, condition, or promise set forth herein shall not be construed as a waiver of performance of the same term, covenant, condition, or promise at a future time.

[Standard legalese. This section makes sure that all changes to the agreement will be in writing and that you won't waive any of your rights inadvertently.]

Section 18: Complete Agreement. This Agreement sets forth and is intended to be an integration of all of the promises, agreements, conditions, understandings, covenants, warranties, and representations among the parties with respect to the subject matter hereof and there are no promises, agreements, conditions, understandings, covenants, warranties, or representations, oral or written, express or implied, among the parties with respect to the subject matter hereof other than as set forth herein.

[The purpose of this section is to state that this agreement constitutes the complete deal between you and the company, so nobody can claim otherwise at a later date.]

Section 19: Multiple Counterparts. This Agreement may be executed in multiple counterparts, each one of which shall be deemed to be an original, and all of which together shall constitute one and the same Agreement.

[Self-explanatory legalese.]

Section 20: Headings. The headings and captions herein are inserted solely for the purpose of convenience of reference and are not a part hereof and are not intended to govern, limit or aid in the construction of any term or provision hereof.

[Self-explanatory legalese.]

Section 21: Choice of Law. This Agreement shall be governed by, and construed in accordance with, the laws of the state of _____.

[This section is fairly important, since you want to be sure that the agreement will be subject to U.S. law if there is ever a legal dispute. As far as which state's law should govern, it can be either (1) the state where you live, (2) the company's state of incorporation, or (3) the state where the company's principal place of business is located.]

Executed and acknowledged by the parties hereto as of the date set forth above.

EMPLOYEE:

_____

EMPLOYER:

_____, Inc.
By:_____, Authorized Officer

personnel at between GS-7 and GS-11, and executive, managerial, and professional personnel at between GS-11 and GS-15.

- **Federal Employers: Potential Perks and Benefits** Unlike the private sector, in federal jobs there is not much room for negotiating better perks and benefits. You may be able to insist on a higher GS or other rank, if the hiring officer has the authority to grant it, but any perks and benefits depend on the agency's budget, regulations, and appropriations legislation. You may be faced with a take-it-or-leave it situation. Still, it is worth inquiring about whether you will be entitled to any of the following benefits:

  HARDSHIP PAY: If you will be working in a Third World country or other country with a severe lack of Western conveniences and a low standard of living, ask about whether you will qualify for hardship pay. Some federal positions abroad entitle you to extra pay as partial compensation for such conditions.

  HAZARDOUS DUTY PAY: Akin to the concept of hardship pay, hazardous duty pay may be available if you will be working in a country near or in a war zone, or a country undergoing dangerous political unrest.

  U.S. GOVERNMENT HOUSING: Depending on the agency and the country, you may be able to live in a government-owned house for free or at subsidized rates. As an alternative, you might be entitled to receive a housing allowance for yourself and your family.

  COMMISSARY PRIVILEGES: Many government jobs abroad, such as the Foreign Service, include the right to buy groceries and other items at U.S. government-operated commissaries. These commissaries are usually, but not necessarily, located at U.S. military bases abroad. Goods can be purchased for discount prices, and in some countries the commissary may be the only source of American products.

  MEDICAL CARE: The U.S. government maintains an extensive network of hospitals and health care facilities abroad for its civilian and military personnel. In some countries, they are the only source of sophisticated medical care for Americans abroad. Check to see if you will be entitled to treatment at any U.S. facilities in the country of your assignment.

- **Your Salary** A critical factor, whether you are working in the private sector or for the government abroad, is whether your salary is adequate in relationship to the local cost of living. A princely salary in Bangkok or Mexico City may be a pauper's salary in London or Tokyo. Perks and benefits, or cost-of-living adjustments, are a significant part of the equation in addition to your salary. If you have a high salary and a good benefits package in Bangkok or Mexico City, you will probably live well and return to the United States with a tidy nest egg of accumulated savings. If you don't have a good salary and your benefits are low in London or Tokyo, you may find yourself living rather modestly and returning to the United States with only your memories to show for the experience.

A WORD OF CAUTION

The growing interest in overseas employment has unfortunately attracted some con men and scam artists who set up bogus employment firms and run advertisements in the newspaper or on television promising spectacular overseas job opportunities. There's one catch: you have to pay a fee of several hundred dollars or more in advance. However, in most cases once you pay the fee you never hear from the agency again, and the odds of catching up with it through civil or criminal legal actions are slim.

Most employment agencies are honest. To avoid dishonest ones, the rules are simple. First, be reluctant to pay any fee in advance. It's safer if the firm collects its fee from the employer, or by taking a portion of your first year's salary if you get the job. If you have to pay in advance, try to go with a local firm. Then, you can visit the firm personally and research its reputation with your local business regulatory authorities. Second, exercise common sense. If an advertisement describes wonderful job opportunities that sound too good to be true, they probably are. Be skeptical if the employment agency pursues you aggressively. If the job involves a great salary and benefits, a legitimate employment firm wouldn't use aggressive sales hype to get your interest and your money, since job seekers would be coming to them.

Leaving the United States for a job abroad involves planning, especially if you have a family that is going with you. Although your new employer probably will be able to help you, it is in your best interest to plan some things for yourself. In addition, you should always be aware of where you can go for help if you run into trouble while abroad.

Although some of the more important matters must be resolved before you move abroad, remember that the best thing you can do is to keep an open mind to the experience. You have voluntarily embarked upon this adventure; now it is time to realize that not everything connected with it will be easy.

LEGAL MATTERS

- **Getting a Passport** As a U.S. citizen, you need a U.S. passport if you plan to work or travel abroad, no matter how long you plan to stay outside the United States. Although some tourist travel between the United States and Canada or Mexico, and some travel to a few Third World nations, requires only proof of identity, there is no substitute for a valid passport if you are serious about working abroad.

  If you don't have a passport, you will need to apply for one. Even if you have one now, there are two other situations in which you will need to apply for a new passport. First, as described in the following section on visas, some foreign countries won't give you a visa if your passport is due to expire in less than a year. Check the expiration date of your current passport: a U.S. passport expires ten years after the date it is issued. If your passport expires while you are abroad, you can expect delays by the immigration authorities and a $100 fine upon reentering the United States. Second, all members of your family are now required by the government to have their own passport. Therefore, if you have an older passport that includes your children, you will need to get (1) a new passport for yourself, and (2) new passports for your children if they are accompanying you abroad.

To get a passport, you must obtain and complete a U.S. Department of State Form DSP-11 or Form DSP-82, Application for Passport (*see* pages 49 and 50). You can obtain these forms at (1) one of the thirteen U.S. passport agencies, (2) an authorized U.S. post office, or (3) an authorized state or federal court clerk's office.

Following are the addresses and telephone numbers of the thirteen U.S. passport offices. Not only can they answer your questions concerning passports and passport applications, they can also direct you to the post office or courthouse nearest you that is authorized to hand out and process DSP-11s. Also included are the passport offices recorded information numbers, which are twenty-four-hour recordings containing general passport information.

(1) Boston Passport Agency
The Federal Building, Room 247
10 Causeway St.
Boston, MA 02222
(617) 565-6990
Recording: (617) 565-6998

(2) Chicago Passport Agency
The Federal Building, Suite 380
230 South Dearborn St.
Chicago, IL 60604
(312) 353-7155 or (312) 353-7163
Recording: (312) 353-5426

(3) Honolulu Passport Agency
New Federal Building, Room C-106
300 Ala Moana Blvd.
Honolulu, HI 96850
(808) 541-1918
Recording: (808) 541-1919

(4) Houston Passport Agency
Concord Towers
1919 Smith St., Suite 1100
Houston, TX 77002
(713) 653-3153
Recording: (713) 653-3159

UNITED STATES DEPARTMENT OF STATE

APPLICATION FOR PASSPORT REGISTRATION

SEE INSTRUCTIONS—TYPE OR PRINT IN INK IN WHITE AREAS

1. NAME   FIRST NAME   MIDDLE NAME

LAST NAME

2. MAILING ADDRESS

STREET

CITY, STATE,
ZIP CODE

COUNTRY   IN CARE OF

☐ 5 Yr. ☐ 10 Yr.   Issue
R   D   DP   Date _____
End.#   Exp. _____

3. SEX   4. PLACE OF BIRTH City, State or Province, Country   5. DATE OF BIRTH   6. SEE FEDERAL TAX LAW NOTICE ON REVERSE SIDE   SOCIAL SECURITY NUMBER

Male Female   Mo. Day Year

7. HEIGHT   8. COLOR OF HAIR   9. COLOR OF EYES   10. (Area Code) HOME PHONE   11. (Area Code) BUSINESS PHONE

Feet Inches   12. PERMANENT ADDRESS (Street, City, State, ZIP Code)   13. OCCUPATION

FOLD

14. FATHER'S NAME   BIRTHPLACE   BIRTH DATE   U.S. CITIZEN   16. TRAVEL PLANS (Not Mandatory)
                                                      YES NO   COUNTRIES   DEPARTURE DATE
15. MOTHER'S MAIDEN NAME   BIRTHPLACE   BIRTH DATE   U.S. CITIZEN   LENGTH OF STAY
                                                      YES NO

17. HAVE YOU EVER BEEN ISSUED A U.S. PASSPORT?   YES   NO   IF YES, SUBMIT PASSPORT IF AVAILABLE. ☐ Submitted
IF UNABLE TO SUBMIT MOST RECENT PASSPORT, STATE ITS DISPOSITION: COMPLETE NEXT LINE
NAME IN WHICH ISSUED   PASSPORT NUMBER   ISSUE DATE (Mo., Day, Yr.)   DISPOSITION

SUBMIT TWO RECENT
IDENTICAL PHOTOS

FROM 1" TO
1-3/8"

2" x 2"

18. HAVE YOU EVER BEEN MARRIED? ☐ YES   ☐ NO   DATE OF MOST RECENT MARRIAGE
                                                      Mo. Day Year

WIDOWED/DIVORCED?   ☐ YES   ☐ NO   IF YES, GIVE DATE
                                                      Mo. Day Year

SPOUSE'S FULL BIRTH NAME   SPOUSE'S BIRTHPLACE

19. IN CASE OF EMERGENCY, NOTIFY (Person Not Traveling With You)   RELATIONSHIP
(Not Mandatory)
FULL NAME

ADDRESS   (Area Code) PHONE NUMBER

FOLD

20. TO BE COMPLETED BY AN APPLICANT WHO BECAME A CITIZEN THROUGH NATURALIZATION
I IMMIGRATED TO THE U.S.   I RESIDED CONTINUOUSLY IN THE U.S.   DATE NATURALIZED (Mo., Day, Yr.)
(Month, Year)   From (Mo., Yr.) To (Mo., Yr.)
                                                      PLACE

21. DO NOT SIGN APPLICATION UNTIL REQUESTED TO DO SO BY PERSON ADMINISTERING OATH
I have not, since acquiring United States citizenship, performed any of the acts listed under "Acts or Conditions" on the reverse of this application form (unless explanatory statement is attached). I solemnly swear (or affirm) that the statements made on this application are true and the photograph attached is a true likeness of me.

Subscribed and sworn to (affirmed) before me   (SEAL)   X
Month Day Year
                                                      ☐ Clerk of Court or
                                                      ☐ PASSPORT Agent   (Sign in presence of person authorized to accept application)
                                                      ☐ Postal Employee
(Signature of person authorized to accept application)   ☐ (Vice) Consul USA At _____

22. APPLICANT'S IDENTIFYING DOCUMENTS ☐ PASSPORT ☐ DRIVER'S LICENSE ☐ OTHER (Specify)   No.
ISSUE DATE   EXPIRATION DATE   PLACE OF ISSUE   ISSUED IN THE NAME OF
Month Day Year   Month Day Year

23. FOR ISSUING OFFICE USE ONLY (Applicant's evidence of citizenship)
☐ Birth Cert.   SR CR City Filed/Issued: APPLICATION APPROVAL
☐ Passport   Bearer's Name:
☐ Report of Birth   Examiner Name
☐ Naturalization/Citizenship Cert.   No.:
☐ Other: Office, Date
☐ Seen & Returned
☐ Attached   24.
                  FEE _____ EXEC. _____ POST _____

FORM DSP-11 (12–87)   (SEE INSTRUCTIONS ON REVERSE)   Form Approved OMB No. 1405-0004 (Exp. 8/1/89)

APPLICATION FOR PASSPORT, DSP-11 (FOR APPLYING IN PERSON).

A
M
E
R
I
C
A
N

J
O
B
S

A
B
R
O
A
D

UNITED STATES DEPARTMENT OF STATE

APPLICATION FOR PASSPORT BY MAIL

TYPE OR PRINT IN INK IN WHITE AREAS ONLY   USE BLOCK LETTERS/NUMBERS

NAME	FIRST	MIDDLE

LAST

MAIL PASSPORT TO

STREET / RFD # OR P.O. BOX   APT. #

CITY   STATE   ZIP CODE

IN CARE OF (IF APPLICABLE)

R   D   O   DP   Issue Date _____

End.# _____   Exp. _____

SEX	PLACE OF BIRTH		DATE OF BIRTH
☐ Male ☐ Female	City & State or City & Country	Month Day Year	

SOCIAL SECURITY NUMBER (SEE FEDERAL TAX LAW NOTICE ON REVERSE SIDE)

HEIGHT Feet Inches	HAIR COLOR	EYE COLOR	HOME TELEPHONE ( )	BUSINESS TELEPHONE ( )

NOTE: Most recent passport MUST be enclosed!

PASSPORT NUMBER	ISSUE DATE Month Day Year	PLACE OF ISSUANCE	OCCUPATION (Not Mandatory)

DEPARTURE DATE	TRAVEL PLANS (Not Mandatory) COUNTRIES TO BE VISITED	LENGTH OF STAY (Not Mandatory)

PERMANENT ADDRESS (Do not list P.O.Box)

STREET / R.F.D. #   CITY   STATE   ZIP CODE

2" X 2"   FROM 1" TO 1-3/8"

SUBMIT TWO RECENT IDENTICAL PHOTOS WITH LIGHT, PLAIN BACKGROUND

NOT MANDATORY

IN CASE OF EMERGENCY WHEN TRAVELING ABROAD, NOTIFY (Person in U.S. Not Traveling With You)

NAME

STREET

CITY   STATE   ZIP CODE

TELEPHONE ( )   RELATIONSHIP

OATH AND SIGNATURE (If any of the below-mentioned acts or conditions have been performed by or apply to the applicant the portion which applies should be lined out, and a supplementary explanatory statement should be attached, signed, and made a part of this application.)

I have not, since acquiring United States citizenship, been naturalized as a citizen of a foreign state; taken an oath, or made an affirmation or other formal declaration of allegiance to a foreign state; entered or served in the armed forces of a foreign state; accepted or performed the duties of any office, post, or employment under the Government of a foreign state or political subdivision thereof; made a formal renunciation of nationality either in the United States or before a diplomatic or consular officer of the United States in a foreign state; or been convicted by a court or court martial of competent jurisdiction of committing any act of treason against, or attempting by force to overthrow, or bearing arms against the United States, or conspiring to overthrow, put down or destroy by force the Government of the United States.

WARNING: False statements made knowingly and willfully in passport applications or affidavits or other supporting documents are punishable by fine and/or imprisonment under the provisions of 18 USC 1001 and/or 18 USC 1542. The alteration or mutilation of a passport issued pursuant to this application is punishable by fine and/or imprisonment under 18 USC 1543. The use of a passport in violation of the restrictions therein is punishable by fine and/or imprisonment under 18 USC 1544.

DECLARATION: I declare that the statements made in this application are true and complete to the best of my knowledge and belief, that the attached photographs are a true likeness of me, and that I have not been issued or included in a passport issued subsequent to the one submitted herein.

➤ **NOTE: APPLICANT MUST SIGN & DATE**

SIGNATURE	DATE

DO NOT WRITE BELOW THIS SPACE   **– FOR PASSPORT SERVICES USE ONLY –**   DO NOT WRITE BELOW THIS SPACE

Application Approval	Evidence of Name Change	Fees
	☐ Marriage Cert. ☐ Court Order	
	Date _____	
	Place _____	
	From _____	
	To _____	

FORM DSP-82 (2-93)   OMB No. 1405-0020 (Exp. 7/31/93) Estimated Burden - 5 Minutes*

APPLICATION FOR PASSPORT, DSP-82 (FOR APPLYING BY MAIL).

(5) Los Angeles Passport Agency

11000 Wilshire Blvd., Room 13100

Los Angeles, CA 90024

(213) 209-7075

Recording: (213) 209-7070

(6) Miami Passport Agency

Federal Office Building, 16th Floor

51 Southwest First Ave.

Miami, FL 33130

(305) 536-4681

Recordings: (305) 536-5395 (English)

(305) 536-4448 (Spanish)

(7) New Orleans Passport Agency

Postal Services Building, Room T-12005

701 Loyola Ave.

New Orleans, LA 70113

(504) 589-6161

Recording: (504) 589-6728

(8) New York Passport Agency

Rockefeller Center, Room 270

630 Fifth Ave.

New York, NY 10111

(212) 541-7710

Recording: (212) 541-7700

(9) Philadelphia Passport Agency

Federal Office Building, Room 4426

600 Arch St.

Philadelphia, PA 19106

(215) 597-7480

Recording: (215) 597-7482

(10) San Francisco Passport Agency

525 Market St., Suite 200

San Francisco, CA 94105

(415) 974-9941

Recording: (415) 974-7972

(11) Seattle Passport Agency

Federal Office Building, Room 992

915 Second Ave.

Seattle, WA 98174

(206) 442-7945

Recording: (206) 442-7941

(12) Stamford Passport Agency

One Landmark Square
Broad and Atlantic Streets
Stamford, CT 06901
(203) 325-3538 or (203) 325-3530
Recording: (203) 325-4401

(13) Washington, D.C., Passport Agency

1425 K St. NW
Washington, DC 20524
(202) 647-0518
Recording: (202) 647-0518, during non-office hours (other than
8:00 A.M. to 4:45 P.M. EST Monday through Friday)

HOW TO APPLY: For your first passport, you must apply in person at the proper passport agency, post office, or courthouse. If you have children between the ages of 13 and 18, they must also apply in person to get passports. The DSP-11 is the form used for applying in person. Along with your completed but unsigned DSP-11, you will need the following items.

- *Proof of your U.S. citizenship.* You can use a certified copy of your birth certificate if you were born in the United States. The local courthouse, state bureau of vital statistics, or other appropriate repository of birth records in the locality of your birth should be able to help you. Notifications of birth registration, birth announcements, or birth certificates filed more than one year after the date of birth probably won't be accepted. If you can't get a birth certificate, take with you a notice from the state or local official stating that no birth certificate exists, together with the best alternative evidence possible, such as a baptismal certificate, hospital birth record, affidavits of persons having personal knowledge of the facts of your birth, an early census, school records, family Bible records, or newspaper files. Personal knowledge affidavits should be supported by at least one public record supporting the fact of your birth in the United States.

If you were not born in the United States, you can use a Certificate of Naturalization, Certificate of Citizenship, Form FS-240 Report of Birth Abroad of a Citizen of the United States of America, or a Form FS-545 or DS-1350, Certification of Birth.

- *Proof of your identity.* In addition to proving your U.S. citizenship, you must bring an acceptable ID containing your signature and your physical description or photograph. For example, you can use a valid driver's license, Certificate of Naturalization, Certificate of Citizenship, or government ID issued by your federal, state or local government employer. You cannot use your Social Security card, learner's or temporary driver's license, or credit card, nor can you use any temporary or expired ID or any ID that has been altered or changed.

If you can't produce an acceptable proof of identity, you must take with you someone who has known you for at least two years and who is a U.S. citizen or permanent resident alien of the United States. That person will have to execute an affidavit and also be able to establish his or her own identity.

o *Two copies of a recent photograph* of yourself, preferably within the last six months, no larger than 2" $\times$ 2". The photographs may be in black and white or in color, with only your head and shoulders featured, without hat, head covering, dark glasses, or other obscuring attire.

o *The application fee,* which is $65 for persons age 18 and over and $40 for persons under age 18.

You may use the Form DSP-82, Application for Passport by Mail, if you can meet four conditions. First, you must have had a passport before, issued within the past twelve years. Second, you must have your old passport in your possession, since you will have to send it in with your DSP-82. Third, your old passport must have been issued on or after your sixteenth birthday. Finally, you must be using the same name, unless it has been changed by marriage or court order.

If you can meet all four of these conditions, you can apply for your new passport by mail. Your old passport will act as your proof of U.S. citizenship and proof of identity. You will still need two photographs and the application fee will be $55.

OTHER PASSPORT INFORMATION: If you will be working abroad for a U.S. government agency, you may have to obtain a U.S. official or diplomatic passport. These are special passports only for government employees, which your agency can help you obtain.

If your job will require frequent travel while you are abroad to countries that require visas, consider getting a forty-eight-page passport when you submit your passport application. A regular passport has twenty-four pages, with seventeen pages for visa stamps. If you will be traveling to visa countries often, these seventeen pages may run out quickly, but a forty-eight-page passport gives you twenty-four extra visa pages. There is no extra charge for a forty-eight-page passport.

If you don't need a new passport, but your name has changed, you must get your passport amended. Obtain, fill out and file Form DSP-19, Passport Amendment/ Validation Application, available at a passport agency or an authorized post office or courthouse. You must submit a marriage certificate, divorce decree, certified court order, or other proof of your name change with the DSP-19.

If you lose your passport while abroad, or it is stolen from you, contact the U.S. embassy or consulate nearest you. It can help you get a new passport. It would help if you knew your passport number and date and place of issuance, or left this information with a friend or relative in the United States. If the loss or theft of your passport occurs in the United States, report it immediately to the State Department:

U.S. DEPARTMENT OF STATE, PASSPORT SERVICES
1425 K ST. NW
WASHINGTON, DC 20524
(202) 646-0518

- **Getting a Visa** A visa is a stamp or endorsement placed by an official representative of a foreign country in your passport that allows you to visit and stay in that country. Obviously, you must have a valid U.S. passport to get a visa. The passport agency, court clerk's office, or post office where you obtained your passport cannot give you a visa. You must contact the embassy in Washington that represents the foreign country in which you plan to work, or the consulate nearest you, to get the proper visa. Ordinarily you must get your visa before you leave the United States. Check the expiration date of your passport if you already have a passport: some countries won't give you a visa if your passport is scheduled to expire in less than six months or a year.

  The most common type of visa is a tourist visa, valid for three months or less. The United States, Canada, Japan, Great Britain, and most countries in western Europe belong to the Visa Waiver Program and don't even require a visa for short-term tourist travel by citizens from other program countries. To live and work in these and other countries, however, you will need either a business visa, permanent resident visa, work visa, or whatever other category of visa is appropriate. Describe your work plans and contemplated length of stay to the officials at the embassy or consulate in full, so that you get the proper visa. In addition to your passport, you may be required to produce additional photographs of yourself and complete an application. Therefore, you should allow several weeks at least for bureaucratic processing over and above that which would ordinarily be required for a tourist visa.

- **Visa Requirements for Major Countries** For Americans working abroad, visa requirements vary from country to country. The requirements examined here are for the same countries listed in the directory of embassies and consulates beginning on page 75. For further information and visa applications, call or write the relevant country's embassy in Washington or the consulate nearest you. In addition, for more information on visa and other entry requirements of all countries, including those that follow, you can order Department of State Publication M-264, Foreign Entry Requirements, for fifty cents by writing to:

  CONSUMER INFORMATION CENTER
  PUEBLO, CO 81009

  Although Publication M-264 and the following information are intended to give the most current foreign visa requirements, you should double-check with the country's embassy or consulate. Some countries, for example are beginning to impose mandatory AIDS testing for some categories of visa applicants, and they may or may not accept U.S. test results.

ALGERIA: Business visa or permanent resident visa required for persons staying longer than three months. Visa won't be given if your passport has an Israeli or South African visa in it.

ARGENTINA: Business visa or permanent resident visa required for persons staying longer than three months.

AUSTRALIA: Visa required. AIDS test may be required for persons over the age of 16.

AUSTRIA: Business visa or permanent resident visa required for persons staying longer than three months.

BELGIUM: Business visa or permanent resident visa required for persons staying longer than three months.

BOLIVIA: Business visa or permanent resident visa required for persons staying longer than thirty days.

BRAZIL: Business visa or permanent resident visa required for persons staying longer than three months.

BULGARIA: Visa required for persons staying longer than one month. AIDS test may be required.

CANADA: Business visa or permanent resident visa required for persons staying longer than three months.

CHILE: Business visa or permanent resident visa required for persons staying longer than three months.

CHINA: Visa required. Medical examination required for persons staying one year or longer.

COLOMBIA: Business visa or permanent resident visa required for persons staying longer than three months.

CZECH REPUBLIC: Business visa or permanent resident visa required for persons staying longer than thirty days.

DENMARK: Business visa or permanent resident visa required for persons staying longer than three months.

ECUADOR: Visa required for persons staying longer than three months.

EGYPT: Business visa or permanent resident visa required for persons staying longer than three months. Currency declaration and registration with local authorities required upon arrival. AIDS test may be required.

FINLAND: Business visa or permanent resident visa required for persons staying longer than three months.

FRANCE: Business visa or permanent resident visa required for persons staying longer than three months.

GERMANY: Business visa or permanent resident visa required for persons staying longer than three months. AIDS test required of applicants for Bavarian residence permits planning to stay longer than 180 days.

GREECE: Business visa or permanent resident visa required for persons staying longer than three months.

HONG KONG: Visa required for work or study.

HUNGARY: Business visa or permanent resident visa required for persons staying longer than ninety days.

INDIA: Visa required. AIDS test required of any person over age 18 staying longer than a year.

INDONESIA: Business visa or permanent resident visa required for persons staying longer than two months.

IRELAND: Business visa or permanent resident visa required for persons staying longer than ninety days.

ISRAEL: Business visa or permanent resident visa required for persons staying longer than three months.

ITALY: Business visa or permanent resident visa required for persons staying longer than three months.

JAPAN: Business visa or permanent resident visa required for persons staying longer than ninety days.

KAZAKHSTAN: Visa required.

KENYA: Visa required.

KUWAIT: Visa required.

LUXEMBOURG: Business visa or permanent resident visa required for persons staying longer than three months.

MALAYSIA: Business visa or permanent resident visa required for persons staying longer than three months.

MEXICO: Business visa or permanent resident visa required for persons staying longer than ninety days.

NETHERLANDS: Business visa or permanent resident visa required for persons staying longer than ninety days.

NEW ZEALAND: Business visa or permanent resident visa required for persons staying longer than three months.

NIGERIA: Visa required.

NORWAY: Business visa or permanent resident visa required for persons staying longer than three months.

PAKISTAN: Visa required. AIDS test may be required for persons staying longer than one year.

PERU: Business visa or permanent resident visa required for persons staying longer than ninety days.

PHILIPPINES: Business visa or permanent resident visa required for persons staying longer than twenty-one days. AIDS test required for persons seeking permanent residency.

POLAND: Business visa or permanent resident visa required for persons staying longer than ninety days. Persons must register with local authorities after arrival.

PORTUGAL: Business visa or permanent resident visa required for persons staying longer than sixty days.

ROMANIA: Business visa or permanent resident visa required for persons staying longer than sixty days.

RUSSIA: Visa required.

SAUDI ARABIA: Visa required. A medical report and an official invitation from the Saudi Foreign Ministry probably will be required.

SINGAPORE: Business visa or permanent resident visa required for persons staying longer than three months.

SOUTH AFRICA: Visa required.

SOUTH KOREA: Business visa or permanent resident visa required for persons staying longer than fifteen days.

SPAIN: Business visa or permanent resident visa required for persons staying longer than six months.

SWEDEN: Business visa or permanent resident visa required for persons staying longer than three months.

SWITZERLAND: Business visa or permanent resident visa required for persons staying longer than three months.

THAILAND: Business visa or permanent resident visa required for persons staying longer than fifteen days.

TURKEY: Business visa or permanent resident visa required for persons staying longer than three months.

UNITED ARAB EMIRATES: Visa required. AIDS test required upon arrival for persons planning to work in the country.

UNITED KINGDOM: Business visa or permanent resident visa required for persons staying longer than six months.

VENEZUELA: Business visa or permanent resident visa required for persons staying longer than sixty days.

- **Getting a Work Permit** In addition to getting a visa you will almost certainly have to get a work permit to work abroad. The vast majority of visas issued to Americans are for tourist travel, and while a country may have lax visa requirements or none at all, the work permit requirements may be detailed, strict, and time-consuming. It probably won't be you who has to prepare the work permit application. According to Elizabeth Wallace, who runs a company called Visa Advisors in Washington, which offers professional assistance in getting work permits and visas, most of the time the American company arranges for the work permit. The information required to arrange for the work permit, however, does involve you. For example, many countries have begun requiring AIDS tests, and some have other specific requirements such as medical X rays or police background checks.

  Work permit requirements vary by country and range from the relatively easy to the very onerous. Eastern Europe, except for Russia, is on the easy end of the spectrum. Most eastern European countries simply issue you a form of business visa upon your arrival that serves as your work permit. In the middle of the spectrum are countries such as Nigeria, which doesn't require a great deal of documentation but does impose a quota on work permits. At the hard end of the spectrum are countries such as Saudi Arabia, which requires, among other items, a letter from your employer confirming your job offer and bearing an official seal, verification of your professional qualifications, and verification of the authenticity of your graduate and/or postgraduate diplomas by the Saudi Ministry of Education.

- **Getting the Proper Shots and Other Necessary Medical Treatment** Pursuant to regulations issued by the World Health Organization, countries may require that you get an International Certificate of Vaccination attesting that you have had yellow fever or cholera vaccinations. If your doctor doesn't have any certificates, you can buy one from the Government Printing Office (*see* address on page 103). Although not required, you should also get a typhoid vaccination if you are planning to work in a country with non-Western sanitation and lower water quality standards. You should check with your doctor concerning your diphtheria, measles, mumps, polio, pertussis, rubella, and tetanus vaccination status. In addition, some countries require HIV testing for long-term visitors, and they don't always accept U.S. test results. Finally, if you are going to work in Africa, tropical Asia, the Caribbean, Central or South America, India, or the Middle East, check with your doctor concerning malaria risks and taking preventive treatment.

Before you leave the United States, consider your and your family's health insurance needs. Medicare does not pay for non-U.S. medical and hospital treatment. In some countries, such as Great Britain, there may be national health insurance programs that provide coverage to foreign residents as well. In other countries with large American communities, such as Mexico, there may be local private international health insurance companies that provide coverage to U.S. citizens and their families. Finally, your employer may provide or offer coverage. If none of these options is available, or the coverage isn't adequate for your needs, check with a U.S. health insurance company about getting coverage abroad.

- **What to Do about Your House: Selling vs. Other Options** If you own a house in the United States, you have three options concerning what to do with it while you are abroad. First, you can sell it if the economy and real estate market make that a realistic option. Second, you can put it up for rent. However, since you will be abroad, if your tenant abandons the premises or is late with the rent you could be in a difficult situation. Your third option is to contract with your local realtor for professional real estate management services. For a reasonable fee, such as half the first month's rent and 10 percent of each succeeding month's rent, a realtor will find you a credit-worthy tenant and make sure that the rent is paid on time and the premises are well maintained.

- **What to Do about Other Assets You Leave Behind** Deciding what to do with other assets you may own, such as real estate or business interests, is a complex matter, because so much depends on your individual circumstances. Generally speaking, however, the following options are known to work for Americans working abroad who have to leave real estate and business interests behind:
    - As discussed above, consider using a professional real estate management company for your personal and business-related real estate assets in the United States.
    - If you have business interests, consider using a trust company, bank, lawyer, or accountant to oversee them.
    - If you have reliable relatives or other family members, consider requiring the realtor or trust company managing your real estate or business interests to get their authorization before spending any money. This operates as a safeguard against any mismanagement.

- **Helping Your Family Make the Move** Although there is no easy way to solve the problems associated with moving abroad, you can make the adjustment easier on your spouse and children by getting them involved in the process from the very beginning. Take them with you when you get the passports, visas, and work permits, encourage them to learn the local language at Berlitz or elsewhere before you leave, and try to get them interested in the country's culture and history. Everyone in your family has to cope with the prospect of leaving old friends and neighbors for a foreign land. If you encourage them to treat it as an adventure and get them excited about the opportunity to experience new things, however, you can lessen the problems associated with adjustment to life abroad.

- **What to Take with You** What to take with you depends on where you are going. In Canada, western Europe, and Japan, American products and Western conveniences are readily available. In Third World countries, the items you might want to take with you are too numerous to list here. The following is a list of some of the most basic and important items you will want to take with you to any destination.

  o Money in the form of travelers checks. You will need money when you arrive and travelers checks are convenient and widely accepted. Also, you can get new ones if they are stolen.
  o Credit cards. As with travelers checks, credit cards enjoy almost universal acceptance and can be replaced easily. They also give a surprisingly good exchange rate between U.S. dollars and foreign currencies.
  o Electrical adapters. Many foreign countries use different electrical currents and different types of plug outlets. Your local Radio Shack or other electrical supply outlet can help you.
  o Bilingual dictionaries and phrase books in the local language.
  o Several different forms of identification, including your driver's license, credit cards, and perhaps a duplicate passport. If there is ever any trouble with the local authorities, you want to be sure that you can identify yourself as an American.

- **U.S. Taxation of Foreign Income**

  FOREIGN EARNED INCOME EXCLUSION AND THE TAX HOME, BONA FIDE RESIDENCE, AND PHYSICAL PRESENCE REQUIREMENTS: The U.S. income tax system is unique in that the United States is one of only a few countries that tax the worldwide income of its citizens. This places an extra burden on Americans working abroad that foreigners working in the United States don't face. For example, a European working in the United States must pay U.S. income tax, but generally not income tax to his or her home country. Americans working in Europe, however, face potential income tax liability to both the United States and the country in which they work. If you meet certain requirements, however, your foreign earned income up to $70,000 a year is tax-free as far as the United States is concerned. Furthermore, you may qualify for foreign housing cost deductions and a credit for any foreign taxes that you have to pay.

  Most of the large American multinational corporations operating abroad have some sort of equalization plan under which the company takes care of the foreign taxes so that your net pay is equivalent to what you would be receiving if you were working for the company in the United States. The company's accountants calculate your income, allowances, bonuses, benefits, and other items that may be taxable under U.S. and/or foreign law, then prepare and file your foreign income tax return and U.S. Form 1040. They withhold from your pay only the exact equivalent of what you would have paid under American tax law, and the company absorbs the cost of any additional tax burden out of its own pocket.

A tax equalization plan is good for you if the personal income tax rate in the country in which you will be working is higher than in the United States. You end up paying the lower U.S. rate, and the company has to pay the excess. Tax equalization plans are bad for you, however, if the foreign tax rate is lower than in the United States. You end up losing the benefit of the $70,000 exclusion, which effectively is benefiting only the company. Although many companies offer tax equalization plans as a benefit to their prospective employees in high-tax countries, you should do your homework and check the personal income tax rate of the country where you will be working. On pages 75–92 is a directory of foreign embassies and consulates in the United States that you can contact for further information

To qualify for the $70,000 exclusion and other tax benefits, you must be able to (1) meet the "bona fide residence test" or the "physical presence test," and (2) your "tax home" must be in a foreign country. The bona fide residence test means that you were a legitimate resident abroad for an uninterrupted period that includes at least one complete tax year. The physical presence test means that, during any consecutive twelve-month period, you were physically present abroad for at least 330 full days. If either the bona fide residence test or the physical presence test applies to you, you must then pass the tax home requirement. For most purposes, your tax home for each tax year is the country in which you were working, which in tax language is "your regular or principal place of business, employment, or post of duty, regardless of where you maintain your family residence."

The basic form for reporting foreign earned income is IRS Form 2555, which you attach to your Form 1040 personal tax return. A copy of the Form 2555 and the instructions for filling it out are shown on pages 62–68. You may also order IRS Publication 54, Tax Guide for U.S. Citizens and Resident Aliens Abroad, by writing to the IRS at the address listed in the Form 2555 instructions.

FOREIGN HOUSING DEDUCTIONS: In addition to the $70,000 exclusion, you can deduct some of your "reasonable" foreign housing costs, including these:

- Homeowner's insurance
- Household utilities (except telephone and cable TV bills)
- Ordinary household repairs
- Parking costs
- Rent

TAX CREDIT FOR FOREIGN TAXES PAID: You may qualify for a credit for any foreign taxes that you have to pay while you are abroad. IRS Publication 514, Foreign Tax Credit for Individuals, is available from the IRS at the address given in the Form 2555 instructions.

Form **2555**	**Foreign Earned Income**	OMB No. 1545-0067
Department of the Treasury Internal Revenue Service	▶ See separate instructions. ▶ Attach to front of Form 1040.	**1993** Attachment Sequence No. **34**

For Use by U.S. Citizens and Resident Aliens Only

Name shown on Form 1040	Your social security number

Part I   **General Information**

1   Your foreign address (including country) | 2   Your occupation

3   Employer's name ▶ ....
4a   Employer's U.S. address ▶ ....
  b   Employer's foreign address ▶ ....
5   Employer is (check   a ☐ A foreign entity   b ☐ A U.S. company   c ☐ Self
    any that apply):   d ☐ A foreign affiliate of a U.S. company   e ☐ Other (specify) ▶ ....
6a   If, after 1981, you filed Form 2555 to claim either of the exclusions or Form 2555-EZ to claim the foreign earned income
    exclusion, enter the last year you filed the form. ▶ ....
  b   If you did not file Form 2555 or 2555-EZ after 1981 to claim either of the exclusions, check here ▶ ☐ and go to line 7 now.
  c   Have you ever revoked either of the exclusions?   .   .   .   .   ☐ Yes ☐ No
  d   If you answered "Yes," enter the type of exclusion and the tax year for which the revocation was effective. ▶ ....
7   Of what country are you a citizen/national? ▶ ....
8a   Did you maintain a separate foreign residence for your family because of adverse living conditions at your
    tax home? See **Second foreign household** on page 3 of the instructions   .   .   .   .   ☐ Yes ☐ No
  b   If "Yes," enter city and country of the separate foreign residence. Also, enter the number of days during your tax year that
    you maintained a second household at that address. ▶ ....
9   List your tax home(s) during your tax year and date(s) established. ▶ ....

**Next, complete either Part II or Part III. If an item does not apply, write "NA." If you do not give
the information asked for, any exclusion or deduction you claim may be disallowed.**

Part II   **Taxpayers Qualifying Under Bona Fide Residence Test** (See page 2 of the instructions.)

10   Date bona fide residence began ▶ ...., and ended ▶ ....
11   Kind of living quarters in foreign country ▶ a ☐ Purchased house b ☐ Rented house or apartment c ☐ Rented room
             d ☐ Quarters furnished by employer
12a   Did any of your family live with you abroad during any part of the tax year?.   .   .   .   .   ☐ Yes ☐ No
  b   If "Yes," who and for what period? ▶ ....
13a   Have you submitted a statement to the authorities of the foreign country where you claim bona fide residence
    that you are not a resident of that country? (See instructions.)   .   .   .   .   ☐ Yes ☐ No
  b   Are you required to pay income tax to the country where you claim bona fide residence? (See instructions.)   ☐ Yes ☐ No
    **If you answered "Yes" to 13a and "No" to 13b, you do not qualify as a bona fide resident. Do not complete the rest of
    Part II.**
14   If you were present in the United States or its possessions during the tax year, complete columns (a)-(d) below. **Do not** include
    the income from column (d) in Part IV, but report it on Form 1040.

(a) Date arrived in U.S.	(b) Date left U.S.	(c) Number of days in U.S. on business	(d) Income earned in U.S. on business (attach computation)	(a) Date arrived in U.S.	(b) Date left U.S.	(c) Number of days in U.S. on business	(d) Income earned in U.S. on business (attach computation)

15a   List any contractual terms or other conditions relating to the length of your employment abroad. ▶ ....
    ....
  b   Enter the type of visa under which you entered the foreign country. ▶ ....
  c   Did your visa limit the length of your stay or employment in a foreign country? If "Yes," attach explanation   ☐ Yes ☐ No
  d   Did you maintain a home in the United States while living abroad?.   .   .   .   .   ☐ Yes ☐ No
  e   If "Yes," enter address of your home, whether it was rented, the names of the occupants, and their relationship
    to you. ▶ ....

For Paperwork Reduction Act Notice, see page 1 of separate instructions.   2555

IRS FORM 2555 IS USED FOR REPORTING FOREIGN EARNED INCOME TO THE U.S.
GOVERNMENT. (The form is continued on pages 63–68.)

Form 2555 (1993)   Page **2**

Part III   **Taxpayers Qualifying Under Physical Presence Test** (See page 2 of the instructions.)

16   The physical presence test is based on the 12-month period from ▶......................... through ▶ ....
17   Enter your principal country of employment during your tax year. ▶...
18   If you traveled abroad during the 12-month period entered on line 16, complete columns **(a)-(f)** below. Exclude travel between foreign countries that did not involve travel on or over international waters, or in or over the United States, for 24 hours or more. If you have no travel to report during the period, enter "Physically present in a foreign country or countries for the entire 12-month period." **Do not** include the income from column **(f)** below in Part IV, but report it on Form 1040.

(a) Name of country (including U.S.)	(b) Date arrived	(c) Date left	(d) Full days present in country	(e) Number of days in U.S. on business	(f) Income earned in U.S. on business (attach computation)	

Part IV   **All Taxpayers**

Note: *Enter on lines 19 through 23 all income, including noncash income, you earned and actually or constructively received during your 1993 tax year for services you performed in a foreign country. If any of the foreign earned income received this tax year was earned in a prior tax year, or will be earned in a later tax year (such as a bonus), see the instructions. **Do not** include income from line 14, column **(d)**, or line 18, column **(f)**. Report amounts in U.S. dollars, using the exchange rates in effect when you actually or constructively received the income.*

If you are a cash basis taxpayer, report on Form 1040 all income you received in 1993, no matter when you performed the service.

1993 Foreign Earned Income		Amount (in U.S. dollars)	
19 Total wages, salaries, bonuses, commissions, etc., ...	**19**		
20 Allowable share of income for personal services performed (see instructions):			
a In a business (including farming) or profession	**20a**		
b In a partnership. List partnership's name and address and type of income. ▶	**20b**		
21 Noncash income (market value of property or facilities furnished by employer—attach statement showing how it was determined):			
a Home (lodging)	**21a**		
b Meals	**21b**		
c Car	**21c**		
d Other property or facilities. List type and amount. ▶	**21d**		
22 Allowances, reimbursements, or expenses paid on your behalf for services you performed:			
a Cost of living and overseas differential	**22a**		
b Family	**22b**		
c Education	**22c**		
d Home leave	**22d**		
e Quarters	**22e**		
f For any other purpose. List type and amount. ▶	**22f**		
g Add lines 22a through 22f	**22g**		
23 Other foreign earned income. List type and amount. ▶	**23**		
24 Add lines 19 through 21d, line 22g, and line 23	**24**		
25 Total amount of meals and lodging included on line 24 that is excludable (see instructions) .	**25**		
26 Subtract line 25 from line 24. Enter the result here and on line 27 on page 3. This is your **foreign earned income** . . . . ▶	**26**		

Form 2555 (1993)   Page **3**

Part V	**All Taxpayers**		

27 Enter the amount from line 26 . . . . **27**

  • If you choose to claim the housing exclusion or are claiming the housing deduction, complete Part VI.
  • All others, go to Part VII.

Part VI	**For Taxpayers Claiming the Housing Exclusion AND/OR Deduction**		

28 Qualified housing expenses for the tax year (see instructions) **28**

29 Number of days in your qualifying period that fall within your 1993 tax year (see instructions) **29**

30 Multiply $23.94 by the number of days on line 29. Enter the result but do not enter more than $8,737.00   **30**

31 Subtract line 30 from line 28. If zero or less, do not complete the rest of Part VI or any of Part IX **31**

32 Enter employer-provided amounts (see instructions) **32**

33 Divide line 32 by line 27. Enter the result as a decimal (to two places), but do not enter more than "1.00". . . . .   **33**   × .

34 **Housing exclusion.** Multiply line 31 by line 33. Enter the result but do not enter more than the amount on line 32. Also, complete Part VIII ▶   **34**

  Note: *The housing deduction is figured in Part IX. If you choose to claim the foreign earned income exclusion, complete Parts VII and VIII before Part IX.*

Part VII	**For Taxpayers Claiming the Foreign Earned Income Exclusion**		

35 Maximum foreign earned income exclusion **35** $70,000 00

36 • If you completed Part VI, enter the number from line 29.
    • All others, enter the number of days in your qualifying period that fall within your 1993 tax year (see the instructions for line 29).   **36**

37 • If line 36 and the number of days in your 1993 tax year (usually 365) are the same, enter "1.00."
    • Otherwise, divide line 36 by the number of days in your 1993 tax year and enter the result as a decimal (to two places).   **37**   × .

38 Multiply line 35 by line 37 . . . .   **38**

39 Subtract line 34 from line 27 . . . .   **39**

40 **Foreign earned income exclusion.** Enter the **smaller** of line 38 or line 39. Also, complete Part VIII ▶   **40**

Part VIII	**For Taxpayers Claiming the Housing Exclusion, Foreign Earned Income Exclusion, or Both**		

41 Add lines 34 and 40 . . . .   **41**

42 Deductions allowed in figuring your adjusted gross income (Form 1040, line 31) that are allocable to the excluded income. See instructions and attach computation **42**

43 Subtract line 42 from line 41. Enter the result here and in parentheses on Form 1040, line 22. Next to the amount write "Form 2555." On Form 1040, subtract this amount from your income to arrive at total income on Form 1040, line 23 . . . . ▶   **43**

Part IX	**For Taxpayers Claiming the Housing Deduction**—Complete this part only if (a) line 31 is more than line 34 and (b) line 27 is more than line 41.		

44 Subtract line 34 from line 31 . . . .   **44**

45 Subtract line 41 from line 27 . . . .   **45**

46 Enter the **smaller** of line 44 or line 45 . . . .   **46**

  Note: *If line 45 is more than line 46 and you couldn't deduct all of your 1992 housing deduction because of the 1992 limit, use the worksheet on page 4 of the instructions to figure the amount to enter on line 47. Otherwise, go to line 48.*

47 Housing deduction carryover from 1992 (from worksheet on page 4 of the instructions) . . .   **47**

48 **Housing deduction.** Add lines 46 and 47. Enter the total here and on Form 1040 to the left of line 30. Next to the amount on Form 1040, write "Form 2555." Add it to the total adjustments reported on that line . . . . ▶   **48**

1993

 Department of the Treasury
Internal Revenue Service

Instructions for Form 2555

Foreign Earned Income

Section references are to the Internal Revenue Code.

Paperwork Reduction Act Notice

We ask for the information on this form to carry out the Internal Revenue laws of the United States. You are required to give us the information. We need it to ensure that you are complying with these laws and to allow us to figure and collect the right amount of tax.

The time needed to complete and file this form will vary depending on individual circumstances. The estimated average time is: **Recordkeeping,** 2 hr., 11 min.; **Learning about the law or the form,** 26 min.; **Preparing the form,** 1 hr., 40 min.; and **Copying, assembling, and sending the form to the IRS,** 49 min.

If you have comments concerning the accuracy of these time estimates or suggestions for making this form more simple, we would be happy to hear from you. You can write to both the IRS and the Office of Management and Budget at the addresses listed in the Instructions for Form 1040.

General Instructions

Items To Note

● You may be able to use **Form 2555-EZ,** Foreign Earned Income Exclusion, if none of your foreign earned income was from self-employment, your total foreign earned income did not exceed $70,000, you do not have any business or moving expenses, and you do not claim the housing exclusion. For more details, get Form 2555-EZ and its separate instructions.

● Do not include on Form 1040, line 54 (Federal income tax withheld), any taxes a foreign employer withheld from your pay and paid to the foreign country's tax authority instead of to the U.S. Treasury.

Purpose of Form

If you are a U.S. citizen or a U.S. resident alien living in a foreign country, you are subject to the same U.S. income tax laws that apply to citizens and resident aliens living in the United States. But if you qualify, use Form 2555 to exclude a limited amount of your foreign earned income. Also, use it to claim the housing exclusion or deduction. You may not exclude or deduct more than your foreign earned income for the tax year.

Note: *Specific rules apply to determine if you are a resident or nonresident alien of*

the United States. Get **Pub. 519,** U.S. Tax Guide for Aliens, for details.

Who Qualifies

You qualify for the tax benefits available to taxpayers who have foreign earned income if you meet the **tax home test** (defined later) **and** you are one of the following:

● A U.S. citizen who is a bona fide resident of a foreign country, or countries, for an uninterrupted period that includes a complete tax year **(bona fide residence test),** or

● A U.S. resident alien who is a citizen or national of a country with which the United States has an income tax treaty in effect and who is a bona fide resident of a foreign country, or countries, for an uninterrupted period that includes a complete tax year **(bona fide residence test),** or

● A U.S. citizen or a U.S. resident alien who is physically present in a foreign country, or countries, for at least 330 full days during any period of 12 months in a row **(physical presence test).**

Note: *If your only earned income from work abroad is pay you received from the U.S. Government as its employee, you do not qualify for either of the exclusions or the housing deduction. Do not file Form 2555.*

Tax home test.—Your **tax home** must be in a foreign country, or countries, throughout your period of bona fide residence or physical presence, whichever applies. For this purpose, your period of physical presence is the 330 full days during which you were present in a foreign country, not the 12 consecutive months during which those days occurred.

Your **tax home** is your regular or principal place of business, employment, or post of duty, regardless of where you maintain your family residence. If you do not have a regular or principal place of business because of the nature of your trade or business, your tax home is your regular place of abode (the place where you regularly live).

You are not considered to have a tax home in a foreign country for any period during which your abode is in the United States. However, if you are temporarily present in the United States, or you maintain a dwelling in the United States (whether or not that dwelling is used by your spouse and dependents), it does not necessarily mean that your abode is in the United States during that time.

Example. You are employed on an offshore oil rig in the territorial waters of a foreign country and work a 28-day on/28-day off schedule. You return to your family residence in the United States during your off periods. You are considered to have an abode in the United States and **do not** meet the tax home test. You **may not** claim either of the exclusions or the housing deduction.

Foreign country.—A foreign country is any territory (including the air space, territorial waters, seabed, and subsoil) under the sovereignty of a government other than the United States. It does not include U.S. possessions or territories.

Violation of Travel Restrictions

Generally, if you were in a foreign country in violation of U.S. travel restrictions, the following rules apply: **(1)** any time spent in that country may not be counted in determining if you qualify under the bona fide residence or physical presence test; **(2)** any income earned in that country is not considered foreign earned income; and **(3)** any housing expenses in that country (or housing expenses for your spouse or dependents in another country while you were in that country) are not considered qualified housing expenses. See page 4 for a list of countries to which U.S. travel restrictions apply.

Additional Information

Pub. 54, Tax Guide for U.S. Citizens and Resident Aliens Abroad, contains more information about the bona fide residence test, the physical presence test, the foreign earned income exclusion, and the housing exclusion and deduction. You can get this publication from most U.S. embassies and consulates or by writing to either: Eastern Area Distribution Center, P.O. Box 25866, Richmond, VA 23286-8107; or Western Area Distribution Center, Rancho Cordova, CA 95743-0001, whichever is closer.

Waiver of Time Requirements

If your tax home was in a foreign country and you were a bona fide resident of, or physically present in, a foreign country and had to leave because of war, civil unrest, or similar adverse conditions, the minimum time requirements specified under the bona fide residence and physical presence tests may be waived. You must be able to show that you reasonably could have expected to meet the minimum time requirements if you had not been required to leave. If you left one of the countries listed on page 4 during the period indicated, you can claim the tax benefits on Form 2555, but only for the number of days you were a bona fide resident of, or physically present in, the foreign country.

If you can claim either of the exclusions or the housing deduction because of the waiver of time requirements, attach a statement to your return explaining that you expected to meet the applicable time requirement, but the conditions in the foreign country prevented you from the normal conduct of business. Also, write

Form 2555.

"Claiming Waiver" in the top margin on page 1 of your 1993 Form 2555.

Where To Attach

Attach Form 2555 to the front of your Form 1040. **Do not** attach it in the order of the "Attachment Sequence No." shown in the upper right corner of the form.

Where To File

Send your return to the Internal Revenue Service Center, Philadelphia, PA 19255.

When To File

A 1993 calendar year Form 1040 is generally due April 15, 1994.

However, you are automatically granted a 2-month extension of time to file (to June 15, 1994, for a 1993 calendar year return) if, on the due date of your return, you live outside the United States and Puerto Rico, AND your tax home (defined earlier) is outside the United States and Puerto Rico. If you take this extension, you must attach a statement to your return explaining that you meet these two conditions.

The automatic 2-month extension also applies to paying the tax. However, interest is charged on the unpaid tax from the regular due date (April 15 for a calendar year return) until it is paid.

Special extension of time.—If you plan to take the foreign earned income exclusion and/or the housing exclusion or deduction, but do not expect to qualify until after the end of the automatic 2-month extension period described earlier, you may apply for an extension to a date after you expect to qualify.

To apply for this extension, complete and file **Form 2350,** Application for Extension of Time To File U.S. Income Tax Return, with the Internal Revenue Service Center, Philadelphia, PA 19255, before the due date of your return. Interest is charged on the tax not paid by the regular due date as explained above.

Choosing the Exclusion(s)

To choose either of the exclusions, complete the appropriate parts of Form 2555 and file it with your Form 1040 or **Form 1040X,** Amended U.S. Individual Income Tax Return. Your initial choice to claim the exclusion must usually be made on a timely filed return (including extensions) or on a return amending a timely filed return. However, there are exceptions. See Pub. 54 for details.

Once you choose to claim an exclusion, that choice remains in effect for that year and all future years unless it is revoked. To revoke your choice, you must attach a statement to your return for the first year you do not wish to claim the exclusion(s). If you revoke your choice, you may not claim the exclusion(s) for your next 5 tax years without the approval of the Internal Revenue Service. See Pub. 54 for more information.

Earned income credit.—If you claim either of the exclusions or the housing deduction, you cannot take the earned income credit.

Specific Instructions

Part II

Bona Fide Residence Test

This test applies only to U.S. citizens and U.S. resident aliens who are citizens or nationals of a country with which the United States has an income tax treaty in effect. Get **Pub. 901,** U.S. Tax Treaties, for a list of these countries.

To qualify under this test, you must be a bona fide resident of a foreign country, or countries, for an uninterrupted period that includes a **complete tax year** (January 1–December 31, if you file a calendar year return).

No specific rule determines if you are a bona fide resident of a foreign country because the determination involves your intention about the length and nature of your stay. Evidence of your intention may be your words and acts. If these conflict, your acts carry more weight than your words. Generally, if you go to a foreign country for a definite, temporary purpose and return to the United States after you accomplish it, you are not a bona fide resident of the foreign country. If accomplishing the purpose requires an extended, indefinite stay, and you make your home in the foreign country, you may be a bona fide resident. See Pub. 54 for more information and examples.

Lines 13a and 13b.—If you submitted a statement to the authorities of a foreign country in which you earned income that you are not a resident of that country, and the authorities will not require that you are not subject to their income tax laws as a resident, you are not considered a bona fide resident of that country.

If you submitted such a statement and the authorities have not made an adverse determination of your nonresident status, you are not considered a bona fide resident of that country.

Part III

Physical Presence Test

To qualify under this test, you must be a U.S. citizen or resident alien who is physically present in a foreign country, or countries, for at least 330 **full days** during any period of 12 months in a row. A **full day** means the 24-hour period that starts at midnight.

To figure the minimum of 330 full days' presence, add all separate periods you were present in a foreign country during the 12-month period shown on line 16. The 330 full days may be interrupted by periods when you are traveling over international waters or are otherwise not in a foreign country. See Pub. 54 for more information and examples.

Note: A nonresident alien who, with a U.S citizen or U.S. resident alien spouse,

chooses to be taxed as a resident of the United States may qualify under this test if the time requirements are met. See Pub. 54 for details on how to make this choice.

Part IV

Enter in this part the total foreign earned income you **earned and received** (including income constructively received) during the tax year. If you are a cash basis taxpayer, report on Form 1040 all income you received during the tax year regardless of when you earned it.

Income is earned in the tax year you perform the services for which you receive the pay. But if you are a cash basis taxpayer and, because of your employer's payroll periods, you received your last salary payment for 1992 in 1993, that income may be treated as earned in 1993. If you cannot treat that salary payment as income earned in 1993, the rules explained on page 3 under **Income earned in prior year** apply. See Pub. 54 for more details.

Foreign earned income for this purpose means wages, salaries, professional fees, and other compensation received for personal services you performed in a foreign country during the period for which you meet the tax home test and either the bona fide residence test or the physical presence test. It also includes noncash income (such as a home or car) and allowances or reimbursements.

Foreign earned income does not include amounts that are actually a distribution of corporate earnings or profits rather than a reasonable allowance as compensation for your personal services. It also does not include the following types of income:

● Pension and annuity income (including social security and railroad retirement benefits treated as social security).

● Interest, dividends, capital gains, alimony, etc.

● Portion of 1992 moving expense deduction allocable to 1993 that is included in your 1993 gross income. For details, see **Recapture of Moving Expense Deduction** in the Instructions for Form 3903-F or under **Moving Expenses** in Pub. 54.

● Amounts paid to you by the U.S. Government or any of its agencies if you were an employee of the U.S. Government or any of its agencies.

● Amounts received after the end of the tax year following the tax year in which you performed the services.

● Amounts you must include in gross income because of your employer's contributions to a nonexempt employees' trust or to a nonqualified annuity contract.

Note: If you received income in 1993 for services performed before 1963, you may be able to exclude the income if a right to receive it existed on March 12, 1962. For more information, write to:

Internal Revenue Service
Attn: IN:C:TPS
950 L'Enfant Plaza South, SW
Washington, DC 20024

Form 2555.

Income received in prior year.—Foreign earned income received in 1992 for services you performed in 1993 may be excluded from your 1992 gross income if, and to the extent, the income would have been excludable if you had received it in 1993. To claim the additional exclusion, you must amend your 1992 tax return. To do this, file Form 1040X.

Income earned in prior year.—Foreign earned income received in 1993 for services you performed in 1992 may be excluded from your 1993 gross income if, and to the extent, the income would have been excludable if you had received it in 1992. Do not include this income in Part IV.

If you are excluding income under this rule, attach a statement to Form 2555 showing how you figured the exclusion. Enter the amount that would have been excludable in 1992 on Form 2555 to the left of line 43. Next to the amount write "Exclusion of Income Earned in 1992." Include it in the total reported on line 43.

Note: *If you claimed any deduction, credit, or exclusion on your 1992 return that is definitely related to the 1992 foreign earned income you are excluding under this rule, you may have to amend your 1992 income tax return to adjust the amount you claimed. To do this, file Form 1040X.*

Line 20.—If you engaged in an unincorporated trade or business in which both personal services and capital were material income-producing factors, a reasonable amount of compensation for your personal services will be considered earned income. The amount treated as earned income, however, may not be more than 30% of your share of the net profits from the trade or business after subtracting the deduction for one-half of self-employment tax.

If capital is not an income-producing factor and personal services produced the business income, the 30% rule does not apply. Your entire gross income is earned income.

Line 25.—Enter the value of meals and/or lodging provided by, or on behalf of, your employer that is excludable from your income under section 119. To be excludable, the meals and lodging must have been provided for your employer's convenience and on your employer's business premises. In addition, you must have been required to accept the lodging as a condition of your employment. If you lived in a camp provided by, or on behalf of, your employer, the camp may be considered to be part of your employer's business premises. See Pub. 54 for details.

Part VI

Line 28.—Enter the total reasonable expenses paid or incurred during the tax year by you, or on your behalf, for your foreign housing and the housing of your spouse and dependents if they lived with you. You may also include the reasonable expenses of a **second foreign household** (defined later). Housing expenses are

considered reasonable to the extent they are not lavish or extravagant under the circumstances.

Housing expenses include rent, utilities (other than telephone charges), real and personal property insurance, nonrefundable fees paid to obtain a lease, rental of furniture and accessories, residential parking, and household repairs. You may also include the fair rental value of housing provided by, or on behalf of, your employer if you have not excluded it on line 25.

Do not include deductible interest and taxes, any amount deductible by a tenant-stockholder in connection with cooperative housing, the cost of buying or improving a house, principal payments on a mortgage, or depreciation on the house. Also, do not include the cost of domestic labor, pay television, or the cost of buying furniture or accessories.

Include expenses for housing only during periods for which:

● The value of your housing is not excluded from gross income under section 119 (unless you maintained a second foreign household), and

● You meet the tax home test and either the bona fide residence test or physical presence test.

Second foreign household.—If you maintained a separate foreign household for your spouse and dependents at a place other than your tax home because the living conditions at your tax home were dangerous, unhealthful, or otherwise adverse, you may include the expenses of the second household on line 28.

Married couples.—If both you and your spouse qualify for the tax benefits of Form 2555, you each may choose to exclude or deduct part of your foreign housing expenses.

If you and your spouse lived in the same foreign household and file a joint return, the total qualified expenses for the household may be claimed on either your Form 2555 or your spouse's Form 2555. However, if you and your spouse have different periods of residence or presence and the one with the shorter period claims the expenses on his or her Form 2555, only the qualified expenses paid or incurred during the shorter period may be claimed. If you file separate returns, the total qualified housing expense may either be claimed on your Form 2555 or your spouse's Form 2555, or you each may claim part of the expenses on your separate Forms 2555.

If you and your spouse lived in separate foreign households, you each may claim qualified expenses for your own household on your separate Forms 2555 only if **(1)** your tax homes **were not** within a reasonable commuting distance of each other, and **(2)** each spouse's household **was not** within a reasonable commuting distance of the other spouse's tax home. This is true even if you and your spouse file a joint return. If the requirements in **(1)** and **(2)** above are not met, only one of you may claim the housing exclusion or deduction. This is true even if you and your

spouse file separate returns. If your spouse qualifies for, but does not claim, a housing exclusion or deduction, you may include on your Form 2555 the qualified expenses of your spouse's household if the home qualifies as a **second foreign household**.

Line 29.—Enter the number of days in your qualifying period that fall within your 1993 tax year. Your qualifying period is the period during which you meet the tax home test and either the bona fide residence test or the physical presence test.

Example. You establish a tax home and bona fide residence in a foreign country on August 14, 1993. You maintain the tax home and residence until January 31, 1995. You are a calendar year taxpayer. The number of days in your qualifying period that fall within your 1993 tax year is 140 (August 14 through December 31, 1993).

Nontaxable U.S. Government allowances.—If you or your spouse received a nontaxable housing allowance as a military or civilian employee of the U.S. Government, see Pub. 54 for information on how that allowance may affect your housing exclusion or deduction.

Line 32.—Enter any amount your employer paid or incurred on your behalf that is foreign earned income included in your gross income for the tax year (without regard to section 911).

Examples of employer-provided amounts are:

● Wages and salaries received from your employer.

● The fair market value of compensation provided in kind (such as the fair rental value of lodging provided by your employer as long as it is not excluded on line 25).

● Rent paid by your employer directly to your landlord.

● Amounts paid by your employer to reimburse you for housing expenses, educational expenses of your dependents, or as part of a tax equalization plan.

Self-employed individuals.—If all of your foreign earned income (Part IV) is self-employment income, skip lines 32 and 33 and enter zero on line 34. If you qualify, be sure to complete Part IX.

Part VII

Married couples.—If both you and your spouse qualify for, and choose to claim, the foreign earned income exclusion, the amount of the exclusion is figured separately for each of you. You each must complete Part VII of your separate Forms 2555.

Community income.—The amount of the exclusion is not affected by the income-splitting provisions of community property laws. The sum of the amounts figured separately for each of you is the total amount excluded on a joint return.

Part VIII

If you claim either of the exclusions, you may not claim any deduction, exclusion,

Form 2555.

moving expenses), credit, or exclusion that is definitely related to the excluded income. If only part of your foreign earned income is excluded, you must prorate such items based on the ratio that your excludable earned income bears to your total foreign earned income. See Pub. 54 for details on how to figure the amount allocable to the excluded income.

The exclusion under section 119 and the housing deduction are **not** considered definitely related to the excluded income.

Line 42.—Report in full on Form 1040 and related forms and schedules all deductions allowed in figuring your adjusted gross income (Form 1040, line 31). Enter on line 42 the total amount of those deductions (such as the deduction for one-half of self-employment tax) that are not allowed because they are allocable to the excluded income. This applies only to deductions definitely related to the excluded earned income. See Pub. 54 for details on how to report your itemized deductions (such as unreimbursed employee business expenses) that are allocable to the excluded income.

IRA deduction.—The IRA deduction is not definitely related to the excluded income. However, special rules apply in figuring the amount of your IRA deduction. For details, get **Pub. 590**, Individual Retirement Arrangements (IRAs).

Foreign taxes.—You may not take a credit or deduction for foreign income taxes paid or accrued on income that is excluded under either of the exclusions.

If all of your foreign earned income is excluded, you may not claim a credit or deduction for the foreign taxes paid or accrued on that income.

If only part of your income is excluded, you may not claim a credit or deduction for the foreign taxes allocable to the excluded income. Get **Pub. 514**, Foreign Tax Credit for Individuals, for details on how to figure the amount allocable to the excluded income.

Part IX

If line 31 is more than line 34 and line 27 is more than line 41, complete this part to figure your housing deduction. Also, complete this part to figure your housing deduction carryover from 1992.

One-year carryover.—If the amount on line 44 is **more than** the amount on line 45, you may carry the difference over to your 1994 tax year. If you cannot deduct the excess in 1994 because of the 1994 limit, you may not carry it over to any future tax year.

Housing Deduction Carryover Worksheet—Line 47 (keep for your records)

1. Enter the amount from your 1992 Form 2555, line 40 . . . . **1** _____
2. Enter the amount from your 1992 Form 2555, line 44 . . . . **2** _____
3. Subtract line 2 from line 1. If the result is zero, stop here; enter -0- on line 47 of your 1993 Form 2555. You do not have any housing deduction carryover from 1992 . . . . **3** _____
4. Enter the amount from your 1993 Form 2555, line 45 . . . . . . **4** _____
5. Enter the amount from your 1993 Form 2555, line 46 . . . . . . **5** _____
6. Subtract line 5 from line 4 . . . . **6** _____
7. Enter the **smaller** of line 3 or line 6 here and on line 47 of your 1993 Form 2555. If line 3 is **more than** line 6, you **may** not carry the difference over to any future tax year . . . . ▶ **7** _____

List of Countries To Which U.S. Travel Restrictions Apply

Country	Time Periods Beginning	and	Ending
Cuba	January 1, 1987		Still in effect
Libya	January 1, 1987		Still in effect
Iraq	August 2, 1990		Still in effect

List of Qualifying Countries and Time Periods—Waiver of Time Requirements

Country	Time Periods Beginning	and	Ending
Afghanistan	April 23, 1979		Still in effect
Bahrain	January 17, 1991		April 9, 1991
Bosnia and Herzegovina	April 7, 1992		Still in effect
China	June 7, 1989		August 9, 1989
Colombia	August 29, 1989		November 22, 1989
Ethiopia	April 25, 1991		July 9, 1991
Haiti	October 29, 1991		April 6, 1992
Iran	September 1, 1978		Still in effect
Iraq	August 3, 1990		April 9, 1991
Jordan	December 26, 1990		April 1, 1991
Kuwait	August 3, 1990		April 9, 1991
Lebanon	August 31, 1979		Still in effect
Liberia	June 1, 1990		October 21, 1990
Libya	August 31, 1979		August 31, 1992
Mauritania	January 13, 1991		April 1, 1991
Morocco	January 11, 1991		March 22, 1991
Oman	January 17, 1991		April 9, 1991
Pakistan	January 15, 1991		April 11, 1991
Panama	May 12, 1989		November 6, 1989
Philippines	November 15, 1990		December 14, 1990
Qatar	January 17, 1991		April 9, 1991
Saudi Arabia	January 17, 1991		April 9, 1991
Somalia	December 21, 1990		July 5, 1991
Sudan	December 26, 1990		April 8, 1991
Tanzania	January 25, 1991		March 16, 1991
United Arab Emirates	January 17, 1991		April 9, 1991
Yemen	August 18, 1990		March 29, 1991
Yugoslavia	July 4, 1991 / September 19, 1991 / June 13, 1992		August 8, 1991 / December 25, 1991 / Still in effect
Zaire	September 24, 1991		Still in effect

Note: *The above list reflects the changes made up to and including August 31, 1992. When this list is updated, it will be published in the Internal Revenue Bulletin.*

 Printed on recycled paper

TRAVEL RESTRICTIONS: The U.S. government forbids its citizens to visit Cambodia, Cuba, Libya, North Korea, or Vietnam without special permission. In the unlikely event that you were ever to work in one of these countries, you would be ineligible for the $70,000 exclusion and other U.S. tax privileges.

TAX-FREE SALARIES: If you will be working for the United Nations, or one of its affiliated agencies, you will be happy to know that one of the principal benefits is a salary that is tax-free under U.S. law and the laws of virtually every foreign country.

- **Absentee Voting Ballots** While you are overseas, you will probably want to retain your right to vote in federal and state elections in the United States. Most Americans abroad eventually return to the United States, and maintain an interest in the politics of their native country and state.

FEDERAL ELECTIONS: Absentee voting in federal elections for president, senator, and representative is relatively easy. Under federal law, the states are required to permit any person "who resides outside the United States and (but for such residence) would be qualified to vote in the last place in which the person was domiciled before leaving the United States" to vote in federal elections. The states, as well as the District of Columbia, Puerto Rico, Guam, the Virgin Islands, and American Samoa, must provide you with all the necessary absentee voter ballots, registration forms, and so forth. Therefore, you should be able to get everything you need to vote in federal elections while you are overseas from your local voting commissioner or other appropriate state official.

STATE ELECTIONS: To vote in state and local elections for governor, the state legislature, and judicial posts and on matters such as state referendums, you must comply with state absentee voter laws. Every state's laws are different, and you may or may not be allowed to vote while you are working overseas. Following is a summary of state absentee voter laws indicating who is entitled to vote by absentee ballot. Some absentee voter categories are included even though they are not strictly related to a job abroad. For example, if your state would not normally permit you to vote solely because you are working abroad, it may permit you to vote because (1) you are disabled, (2) you are out of state temporarily, (3) you are connected with the military, or (4) you are pursuing academic studies abroad. In addition, the list indicates whether you can register to vote by mail in your state.

ALABAMA: Only military personnel stationed abroad. Your absentee ballot must be notarized.

ALASKA: All eligible voters. You are permitted to register to vote by mail with the appropriate state authorities. Your absentee ballot must be notarized.

AMERICAN SAMOA: Only military personnel stationed abroad. You are permitted to register to vote by mail with the appropriate authorities.

ARIZONA: Senior citizens and anyone out of state. You are permitted to register to vote by mail with the appropriate state authorities.

ARKANSAS: Anyone absent from the state on business, handicapped persons, students abroad, and persons temporarily out of state.

CALIFORNIA: All eligible voters. You are permitted to register to vote by mail with the appropriate state authorities.

COLORADO: Handicapped persons and persons temporarily out of state.

CONNECTICUT: All eligible voters. You are permitted to register to vote by mail with the appropriate state authorities. Your absentee ballot must be notarized.

DELAWARE: All eligible voters. You are permitted to register to vote by mail with the appropriate state authorities. Your absentee ballot must be notarized.

THE DISTRICT OF COLUMBIA: All eligible voters. You are permitted to register to vote by mail with the appropriate authorities.

FLORIDA: Anyone absent from the state on business, handicapped persons, anyone absent for religious reasons, students abroad, and persons temporarily out of state.

GEORGIA: Anyone out of state.

GUAM: All eligible voters. You are permitted to register to vote by mail with the appropriate authorities.

HAWAII: All eligible voters. You are permitted to register to vote by mail with the appropriate state authorities.

IDAHO: Persons temporarily out of state.

ILLINOIS: Only military personnel stationed abroad.

INDIANA: Anyone absent from the state on business, handicapped persons, students abroad, and persons temporarily out of state. You are permitted to register to vote by mail with the appropriate state authorities.

IOWA: All eligible voters. You are permitted to register to vote by mail with the appropriate state authorities.

KANSAS: All eligible voters. You are permitted to register to vote by mail with the appropriate state authorities.

KENTUCKY: All eligible voters. You are permitted to register to vote by mail with the appropriate state authorities.

LOUISIANA: Handicapped persons.

MAINE: All eligible voters. You are permitted to register to vote by mail with the appropriate state authorities.

MARYLAND: All eligible voters. You are permitted to register to vote by mail with the appropriate state authorities.

MASSACHUSETTS: Handicapped persons.

MICHIGAN: Handicapped persons and persons temporarily out of state. Your absentee ballot must be notarized.

MINNESOTA: All eligible voters. You are permitted to register to vote by mail with the appropriate state authorities.

MISSISSIPPI: Only military personnel stationed abroad, and their absentee ballots must be notarized. You are permitted to register to vote by mail with the appropriate state authorities.

MISSOURI: Anyone absent from the state on business, handicapped persons, anyone absent for religious reasons, students abroad, and persons temporarily out of state.

MONTANA: All eligible voters. You are permitted to register to vote by mail with the appropriate state authorities.

NEBRASKA: All eligible voters. You are permitted to register to vote by mail with the appropriate state authorities.

NEVADA: Only military personnel stationed abroad. You are permitted to register to vote by mail with the appropriate state authorities.

NEW HAMPSHIRE: Anyone absent from the state on business, handicapped persons, anyone absent for religious reasons, students abroad, and persons temporarily out of state.

NEW JERSEY: All eligible voters. You are permitted to register to vote by mail with the appropriate state authorities.

NEW MEXICO: Persons temporarily out of state.

NEW YORK: All eligible voters. You are permitted to register to vote by mail with the appropriate state authorities.

NORTH CAROLINA: Only military personnel stationed abroad.

NORTH DAKOTA: No one. There is no procedure for absentee voting.

OHIO: All eligible voters. You are permitted to register to vote by mail with the appropriate state authorities.

OKLAHOMA: Only military personnel stationed abroad.

OREGON: All eligible voters. You are permitted to register to vote by mail with the appropriate state authorities.

PENNSYLVANIA: All eligible voters. You are permitted to register to vote by mail with the appropriate state authorities.

PUERTO RICO: All eligible voters. You may not be able to register to vote by mail, however.

RHODE ISLAND: Handicapped persons. Your absentee ballot must be notarized.

SOUTH CAROLINA: All eligible voters. You are permitted to register to vote by mail with the appropriate state authorities.

SOUTH DAKOTA: Anyone absent from the state on business and handicapped persons.

TENNESSEE: All eligible voters. You are permitted to register to vote by mail with the appropriate state authorities.

TEXAS: All eligible voters. You are permitted to register to vote by mail with the appropriate state authorities.

U.S. VIRGIN ISLANDS: No one. There is no procedure for absentee voting.

UTAH: All eligible voters. You are permitted to register to vote by mail with the appropriate state authorities.

VERMONT: All eligible voters. You are permitted to register to vote by mail with the appropriate state authorities. Your absentee ballot must be notarized.

VIRGINIA: Persons temporarily out of state.

WASHINGTON: Only military personnel stationed abroad.

WEST VIRGINIA: All eligible voters. You are permitted to register to vote by mail with the appropriate state authorities.

WISCONSIN: All eligible voters. You are permitted to register to vote by mail with the appropriate state authorities.

WYOMING: Anyone absent from the state on business, handicapped persons, anyone absent for religious reasons, students abroad, and persons temporarily out of state.

Working abroad means an opportunity for personal growth and intellectual stimulation. You will be exposed to a new culture, probably a different language, different foods, new sights, new customs, and a new way of life.

Of course, there are drawbacks to living abroad, and they range from the trivial to the serious. Often the biggest downside stems from cultural differences and feeling like a stranger in a society that you don't fully understand. Many of the familiar aspects of home, such as American stores and television shows, will be absent even in western Europe, which has been significantly permeated by American culture. In eastern Europe, Latin America, and other places, things you take for granted in the United States, such as reliable telephone service and electrical power or drinkable tap water may be undependable. You may have to learn a new language in order to get around, and you will have to make a whole new set of friends and acquaintances if you are to have any regular social life.

Some of the most serious challenges to living abroad include religion, particularly if you will be working in the Middle East or elsewhere in the Arab world. Local religious sensibilities may require significant restrictions on your dress and public behavior, as well as on what is permissible in private life. You may be living in a country that isn't a Western-style democracy or doesn't have American-style judicial protection, and you will have to pay much more attention to staying out of trouble than you are accustomed to. Other challenges may include political unrest, war in areas like the Middle East or the Balkans, disease, pollution, anti-American sentiment, and the local climate.

You don't have to give up your dreams of working abroad because of the presence of some of these potential challenges, but you should look at them objectively and approach any job opportunity abroad knowledgeably and with willingness to adapt to new circumstances. If you do, you will increase the likelihood of having an enjoyable and rewarding experience.

WHERE TO GO FOR MORE INFORMATION ON YOUR NEW COUNTRY AND FOR HELP WHEN YOU GET THERE

The following directory lists the addresses and telephone numbers of major foreign country embassies in the United States, broken down by country. *Note: "Major" in this context means those countries most likely to offer employment opportunities for Americans looking for jobs abroad, rather than referring to size, population, or any other factor. For example, Switzerland is included in this directory, but Sudan is not, because despite its much greater size and population, Sudan is far less likely than Switzerland to present employment opportunities.*

The directory also includes the U.S. cities in which the country has consulates. Consulates are like regional branch offices of the foreign embassy in Washington. The embassy in Washington or Directory Assistance should be able to give you the address and phone number of the consulate closest to you, if you want to visit it to ask more questions and get further information.

- **Registering with the U.S. Embassy** Under each entry in the directory, the address and telephone number (prefaced by the international dialing code) of the American embassy in that country is included. Not only can you contact it for more information about your new country, but once you get there, the American embassy can help you should you get into trouble or otherwise need assistance. Once you arrive in your new country, call or visit the U.S. embassy or the consulate nearest you and register your whereabouts and passport data with them. In case of an emergency, registration means that the U.S. authorities can find you. Registration also makes it easier to replace a lost or stolen passport.

This directory also lists the cities containing regional consulates of American embassies abroad. The embassy should be able to direct you to the local consul for your area if you will be living outside the nation's capital. The consul can help you if you have difficulties with the local authorities and may be a source of assistance with your other needs.

Although most U.S. embassies and consulates abroad are open for business from Monday through Friday, in Algeria, Saudi Arabia, and the United Arab Emirates the workweek is Saturday through Wednesday, and in Egypt and Pakistan the workweek is Sunday through Thursday. This is because these countries and other Islamic nations observe different days of rest and prayer than Americans do.

ALGERIA: EMBASSY IN THE UNITED STATES:
2137 WYOMING AVE. NW
WASHINGTON, DC 20008
(202) 265-2800

CONSULATES: NONE

U.S. EMBASSY:
4 CHEMIN CHEIKH BACHIR EL-IBRAHIMI
ALGIERS, ALGERIA
(213) (2) 601-425/255/186

CONSULATE: ORAN

ARGENTINA: EMBASSY IN THE UNITED STATES:
1600 NEW HAMPSHIRE AVE. NW
WASHINGTON, DC 20009
(202) 939-6400

CONSULATES: LOS ANGELES AND SAN FRANCISCO, CALIFOR-
NIA; MIAMI, FLORIDA; ATLANTA, GEORGIA; AND CHICAGO, ILLI-
NOIS

U.S. EMBASSY:
4300 COLOMBIA, 1425
BUENOS ARIES, ARGENTINA
(54) (1) 774-7611/8811/9911

CONSULATES: NONE

AUSTRALIA: EMBASSY IN THE UNITED STATES:
1601 MASSACHUSETTS AVE. NW
WASHINGTON, DC 20036
(202) 797-3000

CONSULATES: PAGO PAGO, AMERICAN SAMOA; LOS ANGELES
AND SAN FRANCISCO, CALIFORNIA; HONOLULU, HAWAII; CHICA-
GO, ILLINOIS; NEW YORK, NEW YORK; AND HOUSTON, TEXAS

U.S. EMBASSY:
MOONAH PLACE
CANBERRA, AUSTRALIA
(61) (6) 270-5000

CONSULATES: BRISBANE, MELBOURNE, PERTH, AND SYDNEY

AUSTRIA: EMBASSY IN THE UNITED STATES:
3524 INTERNATIONAL COURT NW
WASHINGTON, DC 20008
(202) 895-6700

CONSULATES: LOS ANGELES, CALIFORNIA; CHICAGO, ILLINOIS;
AND NEW YORK, NEW YORK

A
M
E
R
I
C
A
N

J
O
B
S

A
B
R
O
A
D

U.S. EMBASSY:
BOLTZMANNGASSE 16, A-1091
VIENNA, AUSTRIA
(43) (1) 31-55-11

CONSULATE: SALZBURG

BAHRAIN   EMBASSY IN THE UNITED STATES:
3502 INTERNATIONAL DR. NW
WASHINGTON, DC 20008
(202) 342-0741

U.S. EMBASSY:
BUILDING #979, ROAD 3119, ZINJ DIST.
MANAMA, BAHRAIN
(973) 273-300

BELGIUM: EMBASSY IN THE UNITED STATES:
3330 GARFIELD ST. NW
WASHINGTON, DC 20008
(202) 333-6900

CONSULATES: LOS ANGELES, CALIFORNIA; ATLANTA, GEORGIA;
CHICAGO, ILLINOIS; AND NEW YORK, NEW YORK

U.S. EMBASSY:
27 BOULEVARD DU REGENT; B-1000
BRUSSELS, BELGIUM
(32) (2) 513-3830

CONSULATES: NONE

BOLIVIA: EMBASSY IN THE UNITED STATES:
3014 MASSACHUSETTS AVE. NW
WASHINGTON, DC 20008
(202) 483-4410

CONSULATES: LOS ANGELES AND SAN FRANCISCO, CALIFOR-
NIA; MIAMI, FLORIDA; AND NEW YORK, NEW YORK

U.S. EMBASSY:
BANCO POPULAR DEL PERU BUILDING
CALLES MERCADO Y COLON
LA PAZ, BOLIVIA
(591) (2) 350251

CONSULATES: NONE

BRAZIL: EMBASSY IN THE UNITED STATES:
3006 MASSACHUSETTS AVE. NW
WASHINGTON, DC 20008
(202) 745-2700

CONSULATES: LOS ANGELES AND SAN FRANCISCO, CALIFOR-
NIA; MIAMI, FLORIDA; CHICAGO, ILLINOIS; NEW ORLEANS, LOUI-
SIANA; NEW YORK, NEW YORK; DALLAS AND HOUSTON, TEXAS

U.S. EMBASSY:
AVENIDA DAS NACOES, LOTE 3
BRASÁLIA, BRAZIL
(55) (61) 321-7272

CONSULATES: RIO DE JANEIRO, SÁO PAULO

BULGARIA: EMBASSY IN THE UNITED STATES:
1621 22ND ST. NW
WASHINGTON, DC 20008
(202) 387-7969

CONSULATE: NEW YORK, NEW YORK

U.S. EMBASSY:
1 SABORNA ST.
SOFIA, BULGARIA
(359) (2) 88-48-01

CONSULATES: NONE

CANADA: EMBASSY IN THE UNITED STATES:
501 PENNSYLVANIA AVE. NW
WASHINGTON, DC 20001
(202) 682-1740

CONSULATES: LOS ANGELES, SAN DIEGO AND SAN FRANCIS-
CO, CALIFORNIA; DENVER, COLORADO; MIAMI, FLORIDA; ATLAN-
TA, GEORGIA; CHICAGO, ILLINOIS; BOSTON, MASSACHUSETTS;
DETROIT, MICHIGAN; MINNEAPOLIS, MINNESOTA; ST. LOUIS,
MISSOURI; PRINCETON, NEW JERSEY; BUFFALO AND NEW
YORK, NEW YORK; CINCINNATI AND CLEVELAND, OHIO; PHILA-
DELPHIA AND PITTSBURGH, PENNSYLVANIA; SAN JUAN, PUER-
TO RICO; DALLAS AND HOUSTON, TEXAS; AND SEATTLE,
WASHINGTON

U.S. EMBASSY:
100 WELLINGTON ST
OTTAWA, ONTARIO, CANADA K1P 5T1
(613) 238-5335

CONSULATES: CALGARY, ALBERTA; HALIFAX, NOVA SCOTIA;
MONTREAL, QUEBEC; QUEBEC, QUEBEC; AND TORONTO, ON-
TARIO; VANCOUVER, BRITISH COLUMBIA

CHILE: EMBASSY IN THE U.S.:
1732 MASSACHUSETTS AVE. NW
WASHINGTON, DC 20036
(202) 785-1746

CONSULATES: LOS ANGELES AND SAN FRANCISCO, CALIFOR-
NIA; MIAMI, FLORIDA; NEW YORK, NEW YORK; PHILADELPHIA,
PENNSYLVANIA; AND HOUSTON, TEXAS

U.S. EMBASSY:
CODINA BUILDING, 1343 AGUSTINAS
SANTIAGO, CHILE
(56) (2) 671-0133

CONSULATES: NONE

CHINA: EMBASSY IN THE UNITED STATES:
2300 CONNECTICUT AVE. NW
WASHINGTON, DC 20008
(202) 328-2500

CONSULATES: LOS ANGELES AND SAN FRANCISCO, CALIFOR-
NIA; CHICAGO, ILLINOIS; NEW YORK, NEW YORK; AND HOUS-
TON, TEXAS

U.S. EMBASSY:
XIU SHUI BEI JIE 3; 100600
BEIJING, CHINA
(86) (1) 532-3831

CONSULATES: CHENGDU, GUANGZHOU, SHANGHAI, AND SHE-
NYANG

COLOMBIA: EMBASSY IN THE UNITED STATES:
2118 LEROY PLACE NW
WASHINGTON, DC 20008
(202) 387-8338

CONSULATES: LOS ANGELES AND SAN FRANCISCO, CALIFOR-
NIA; MIAMI AND TAMPA, FLORIDA; ATLANTA, GEORGIA; CHICA-
GO, ILLINOIS; NEW ORLEANS, LOUISIANA; BOSTON, MASSACHU-
SETTS; DETROIT, MICHIGAN; MINNEAPOLIS, MINNESOTA; NEW
YORK, NEW YORK; SAN JUAN, PUERTO RICO; AND HOUSTON,
TEXAS

U.S. EMBASSY:
CALLE 38, NO. 8-61
BOGOTÁ, COLOMBIA
(57) (1) 320-1300

CONSULATE: BARRANQUILLA

**CZECH
REPUBLIC:** EMBASSY IN THE UNITED STATES:
3900 LINNEAN AVE. NW
WASHINGTON, DC 20008
(202) 363-6315

CONSULATES: NONE

U.S. EMBASSY:
TRZISTE 15
125 48 PRAGUE 1, CZECHOSLOVAKIA
(42) (2) 536-641

CONSULATES: NONE

DENMARK: EMBASSY IN THE UNITED STATES:
3200 WHITEHAVEN ST. NW
WASHINGTON, DC 20008
(202) 234-4300

CONSULATES: LOS ANGELES, CALIFORNIA; CHICAGO, ILLINOIS;
AND NEW YORK, NEW YORK

U.S. EMBASSY:
DAG HAMMARSKJOLDS ALLE 24
2100 COPENHAGEN O, DENMARK
(45) (31) 42-31-44

CONSULATES: NONE

ECUADOR: EMBASSY IN THE UNITED STATES:
2535 15 ST. NW
WASHINGTON D.C. 20009
(202) 234-7200

CONSULATES: NEW YORK, NEW YORK

U.S. EMBASSY:
AVENIDA 12 DE OCTUBRE Y
AVENIDA PATRIA
QUITO, ECUADOR
(593) (2) 562-890

CONSULATE: GUAYAQUIL

EGYPT: EMBASSY IN THE UNITED STATES:
2310 DECATUR PLACE NW
WASHINGTON, DC 20008
(202) 232-5400

CONSULATES: SAN FRANCISCO, CALIFORNIA; CHICAGO, ILLI-
NOIS; NEW YORK, NEW YORK; AND HOUSTON, TEXAS

U.S. EMBASSY:
(NORTH GATE) 8, KAMAL EL-DIN SALAH STREET
CAIRO, EGYPT
(20) (2) 355-7371

CONSULATE: ALEXANDRIA

A
M
E
R
I
C
A
N

J
O
B
S

A
B
R
O
A
D

FINLAND: EMBASSY IN THE UNITED STATES:
3216 NEW MEXICO AVE. NW
WASHINGTON, DC 20016
(202) 363-2430

CONSULATES: LOS ANGELES, CALIFORNIA; CHICAGO, ILLINOIS;
AND NEW YORK, NEW YORK

U.S. EMBASSY:
ITAINEN PUISTOTIE 14A, SF-00140
HELSINKI, FINLAND
(358) (0) 171931

CONSULATES: NONE

FRANCE: EMBASSY IN THE UNITED STATES:
4101 RESERVOIR ROAD NW
WASHINGTON, DC 20007
(202) 944-6000

CONSULATES: LOS ANGELES AND SAN FRANCISCO, CALIFOR-
NIA; MIAMI, FLORIDA; ATLANTA, GEORGIA; HONOLULU, HAWAII;
CHICAGO, ILLINOIS; NEW ORLEANS, LOUISIANA; BOSTON, MAS-
SACHUSETTS; NEW YORK, NEW YORK; SAN JUAN, PUERTO
RICO; AND HOUSTON, TEXAS

U.S. EMBASSY:
2 AVENUE GABRIEL
75382 PARIS CEDEX 08, FRANCE
(33) (1) 42-96-12-02

CONSULATES: BORDEAUX, MARSEILLE, AND STRASBOURG

GERMANY: EMBASSY IN THE UNITED STATES:
4645 RESERVOIR ROAD NW
WASHINGTON, DC 20007
(202) 298-4000

CONSULATES: LOS ANGELES AND SAN FRANCISCO, CALIFOR-
NIA; MIAMI, FLORIDA; ATLANTA, GEORGIA; CHICAGO, ILLINOIS;
BOSTON, MASSACHUSETTS; DETROIT, MICHIGAN; NEW YORK,
NEW YORK; HOUSTON, TEXAS; AND SEATTLE, WASHINGTON

U.S. EMBASSY:
DEICHMANNS AUE
5300 BONN 2, GERMANY
(49) (228) 3391

CONSULATES: BERLIN, FRANKFURT AM MAIN, HAMBURG, LEIP-
ZIG, MUNICH, AND STUTTGART

GREECE: EMBASSY IN THE UNITED STATES:
2221 MASSACHUSETTS AVE. NW
WASHINGTON, DC 20008
(202) 667-3168

CONSULATES: LOS ANGELES AND SAN FRANCISCO, CALIFOR-
NIA; ATLANTA, GEORGIA; CHICAGO, ILLINOIS; NEW ORLEANS,
LOUISIANA; BOSTON, MASSACHUSETTS; NEW YORK, NEW
YORK; AND HOUSTON, TEXAS

U.S. EMBASSY:
91 VASILISSIS SOPHIAS BOULEVARD
10160 ATHENS, GREECE
(30) (1) 721-2951

CONSULATE: THESSALONÍKI

HONG KONG: EMBASSY IN THE UNITED STATES:
EMBASSY OF GREAT BRITAIN
HONG KONG GOVERNMENT OFFICE
1233 20TH ST. NW, SUITE 504
WASHINGTON, DC 20038
(202) 331-8947

U.S. EMBASSY:
26 GARDEN RD.
HONG KONG
(852) 523-9011

HUNGARY: EMBASSY IN THE UNITED STATES:
3910 SHOEMAKER ST. NW
WASHINGTON, DC 20008
(202) 362-6730

CONSULATE: NEW YORK, NEW YORK

U.S. EMBASSY:
SZABADSAG TER 12
BUDAPEST, HUNGARY
(36) (1) 112-6450

CONSULATES: NONE

INDIA: EMBASSY IN THE UNITED STATES:
2107 MASSACHUSETTS AVE. NW
WASHINGTON, DC 20008
(202) 939-7000

CONSULATES: SAN FRANCISCO, CALIFORNIA; CHICAGO, ILLI-
NOIS; AND NEW YORK, NEW YORK

A
M
E
R
I
C
A
N

J
O
B
S

A
B
R
O
A
D

U.S. EMBASSY:
SHANTI PATH, CHANAKYAPURI 110021
NEW DELHI, INDIA
(91) (11) 600651

CONSULATES: BOMBAY, CALCUTTA AND MADRAS

INDONESIA: EMBASSY IN THE UNITED STATES:
2020 MASSACHUSETTS AVE. NW
WASHINGTON, DC 20008
(202) 775-5200

CONSULATES: LOS ANGELES AND SAN FRANCISCO, CALIFOR-
NIA; CHICAGO, ILLINOIS; NEW YORK, NEW YORK; AND HOUS-
TON, TEXAS

U.S. EMBASSY:
MEDAN MERDEKA SELATAN 5
JAKARTA, INDONESIA
(62) (21) 360-360

CONSULATES: MEDAN AND SURABAYA

IRELAND: EMBASSY IN THE UNITED STATES:
2234 MASSACHUSETTS AVE. NW
WASHINGTON, DC 20008
(202) 462-3939

CONSULATES: SAN FRANCISCO, CALIFORNIA; CHICAGO, ILLI-
NOIS; BOSTON, MASSACHUSETTS; AND NEW YORK, NEW YORK

U.S. EMBASSY:
42 ELGIN ROAD, BALLSBRIDGE
DUBLIN, IRELAND
(353) (1) 6689612

CONSULATES: NONE

ISRAEL: EMBASSY IN THE UNITED STATES:
3514 INTERNATIONAL DRIVE NW
WASHINGTON, DC 20008
(202) 364-5500

CONSULATES: LOS ANGELES AND SAN FRANCISCO, CALIFOR-
NIA; MIAMI, FLORIDA; ATLANTA, GEORGIA; CHICAGO, ILLINOIS;
BOSTON, MASSACHUSETTS; NEW YORK, NEW YORK; PHILADEL-
PHIA, PENNSYLVANIA; AND HOUSTON, TEXAS

U.S. EMBASSY:
71 HAYARKON ST.
TEL AVIV, ISRAEL
(972) (3) 517-4338

CONSULATES: NONE

ITALY:	EMBASSY IN THE UNITED STATES: 1601 FULLER ST. NW WASHINGTON, DC 20009 (202) 328-5500

CONSULATES: LOS ANGELES AND SAN FRANCISCO, CALIFOR-
NIA; CHICAGO, ILLINOIS; NEW ORLEANS, LOUISIANA; BOSTON,
MASSACHUSETTS; DETROIT, MICHIGAN; NEWARK, NEW JERSEY;
NEW YORK, NEW YORK; PHILADELPHIA, PENNSYLVANIA; AND
HOUSTON, TEXAS

U.S. EMBASSY:
VIA VENETO 119/A
00187-ROME, ITALY
(39) (6) 46741

CONSULATES: FLORENCE, GENOA, MILAN, NAPLES, AND PAL-
ERMO

JAPAN: EMBASSY IN THE UNITED STATES:
2520 MASSACHUSETTS AVE. NW
WASHINGTON, DC 20008
(202) 939-6700

CONSULATES: ANCHORAGE, ALASKA; LOS ANGELES AND SAN
FRANCISCO, CALIFORNIA; ATLANTA, GEORGIA; AGANA, GUAM;
HONOLULU, HAWAII; CHICAGO, ILLINOIS; NEW ORLEANS, LOUI-
SIANA; BOSTON, MASSACHUSETTS; KANSAS CITY, MISSOURI;
NEW YORK, NEW YORK; PORTLAND, OREGON; HOUSTON,
TEXAS; AND SEATTLE, WASHINGTON

U.S. EMBASSY:
10-5, AKASAKA 1-CHOME, MINATO-KU (107)
TOKYO, JAPAN
(81) (3) 3224-5000

CONSULATES: FUKUOKA, NAHA (OKINAWA), OSAKA-KOBE, AND
SAPPORO

KAZAKHSTAN   EMBASSY IN THE UNITED STATES:
3421 MASSACHUSETTS AVENUE NW
WASHINGTON, DC 20008
(202) 333-4504

U.S. EMBASSY
99/97 FURMANOVA ST.
ALMATY, KAZAKHSTAN 480012
(7) (3272) 63-17-70

KENYA: EMBASSY IN THE UNITED STATES:
2249 R ST. NW
WASHINGTON, DC 20008
(202) 387-6101

LIVING ABROAD

CONSULATE: NEW YORK, NEW YORK

U.S. EMBASSY:
MOI/HAILE SELASSIE AVE.
NAIROBI, KENYA
(254) (2) 334141

CONSULATE: MOMBASA

KUWAIT: EMBASSY IN THE UNITED STATES:
2940 TILDEN ST. NW
WASHINGTON, DC 20008
(202) 966-0702

CONSULATE: NEW YORK, NEW YORK

U.S. EMBASSY:
13001 SAFAT
KUWAIT, KUWAIT
(965) 242-4151

CONSULATES: NONE

LUXEMBOURG: EMBASSY IN THE UNITED STATES:
2200 MASSACHUSETTS AVE. NW
WASHINGTON, DC 20008
(202) 265-4171

CONSULATE: SAN FRANCISCO, CALIFORNIA

U.S. EMBASSY:
22 BOULEVARD EMMANUEL-SERVAIS
2535 LUXEMBOURG
(352) 460123

CONSULATES: NONE

MALAYSIA: EMBASSY IN THE UNITED STATES:
2401 MASSACHUSETTS AVE. NW
WASHINGTON, DC 20008
(202) 328-2700

CONSULATES: LOS ANGELES, CALIFORNIA; AND NEW YORK,
NEW YORK

U.S. EMBASSY:
376 JALAN TUN RAZAK
50400 KUALA LUMPUR, MALAYSIA
(60) (3) 248-9011

CONSULATES: NONE

MEXICO:　EMBASSY IN THE UNITED STATES:
1911 PENNSYLVANIA AVE. NW
WASHINGTON, DC 20007
(202) 728-1600

CONSULATES: NOGALES, PHOENIX, AND TUCSON, ARIZONA;
CALEXICO, FRESNO, LOS ANGELES, OXNARD, SACRAMENTO,
SAN BERNARDINO, SAN DIEGO, SAN FRANCISCO, SAN JOSE,
AND SANTA ANA, CALIFORNIA; DENVER, COLORADO; MIAMI,
FLORIDA; ATLANTA, GEORGIA; CHICAGO, ILLINOIS; NEW ORLE-
ANS, LOUISIANA; BOSTON, MASSACHUSETTS; DETROIT, MICHI-
GAN; ST. LOUIS, MISSOURI; ALBUQUERQUE, NEW MEXICO; NEW
YORK, NEW YORK; PHILADELPHIA, PENNSYLVANIA; SAN JUAN,
PUERTO RICO; AUSTIN, BROWNSVILLE, CORPUS CHRISTI, DAL-
LAS, DEL RIO, EAGLE PASS, EL PASO, HOUSTON, LAREDO,
MCALLEN, MIDLAND, AND SAN ANTONIO, TEXAS; SALT LAKE
CITY, UTAH; AND SEATTLE, WASHINGTON

U.S. EMBASSY:
PASEO DE LA REFORMA 305
COLONIA CUAUHTEMOC
06500 MEXICO CITY, D.F., MEXICO
(52) (5) 211-0042

CONSULATES: CIUDAD JUAREZ, GUADALAJARA, HERMOSILLO,
MATAMOROS, MAZATLÍN, MERIDA, MONTERREY, NUEVO LARE-
DO, AND TIJUANA

NETHERLANDS:　EMBASSY IN THE UNITED STATES:
4200 LINNEAN AVE. NW
WASHINGTON, DC 20008
(202) 244-5300

CONSULATES: LOS ANGELES, CALIFORNIA, CHICAGO, ILLINOIS;
NEW YORK, NEW YORK; AND HOUSTON, TEXAS

U.S. EMBASSY:
LANGE VOORHOUT 102
THE HAGUE, NETHERLANDS
(31) (70) 310-9209

CONSULATE: AMSTERDAM

NEW ZEALAND:　EMBASSY IN THE UNITED STATES:
37 OBSERVATORY CIRCLE NW
WASHINGTON, DC 20008
(202) 328-4800

CONSULATE: LOS ANGELES, CALIFORNIA

U.S. EMBASSY:
29 FITZHERBERT TERRACE, THORNDON
WELLINGTON, NEW ZEALAND
(64) (4) 472-2068

A
M
E
R
I
C
A
N

J
O
B
S

A
B
R
O
A
D

CONSULATE: AUCKLAND

NIGERIA: EMBASSY IN THE UNITED STATES:
2201 M ST. NW
WASHINGTON, DC 20037
(202) 822-1500

CONSULATE: NEW YORK, NEW YORK

U.S. EMBASSY:
2 ELEKE CRESCENT
LAGOS, NIGERIA
(234) (1) 2610050

CONSULATE: KADUNA

NORWAY: EMBASSY IN THE UNITED STATES:
2720 34TH ST. NW
WASHINGTON, DC 20008
(202) 333-6000

CONSULATES: LOS ANGELES AND SAN FRANCISCO, CALIFOR-
NIA; MIAMI, FLORIDA; MINNEAPOLIS, MINNESOTA; NEW YORK,
NEW YORK; AND HOUSTON, TEXAS

U.S. EMBASSY:
DRAMMENSVEIEN 18
0244 OSLO 2, NORWAY
(47) (2) 44-85-50

CONSULATES: NONE

PAKISTAN: EMBASSY IN THE UNITED STATES:
2315 MASSACHUSETTS AVE. NW
WASHINGTON, DC 20008
(202) 939-6200

CONSULATES: LOS ANGELES, CALIFORNIA; AND NEW YORK,
NEW YORK

U.S. EMBASSY:
DIPLOMATIC ENCLAVE, RAMNA 5
ISLAMABAD, PAKISTAN
(92) (51) 826161

CONSULATES: KARACHI, LAHORE AND PESHAWAR

PANAMA: EMBASSY IN THE UNITED STATES:
2862 MCGILL TERRACE NW
WASHINGTON, DC 20008
(202) 483-1407

CONSULATE: NEW YORK, NEW YORK

L
I
V
I
N
G

A
B
R
O
A
D

U.S. EMBASSY
APARTADO 6959
PANAMA CITY, PANAMA
(507) 27-1777

CONSULATES: NONE

PERU: EMBASSY IN THE UNITED STATES:
1700 MASSACHUSETTS AVE. NW
WASHINGTON, DC 20036
(202) 833-9860

CONSULATES: LOS ANGELES AND SAN FRANCISCO, CALIFOR-
NIA; MIAMI, FLORIDA; CHICAGO, ILLINOIS; PATERSON, NEW
JERSEY; NEW YORK, NEW YORK; AND HOUSTON, TEXAS

U.S. EMBASSY:
AVENIDAS INCA GARCILASO DE LA VEGA Y ESPAÑA
LIMA, PERU
(51) (14) 33-8000

CONSULATES: NONE

PHILIPPINES: EMBASSY IN THE UNITED STATES:
1617 MASSACHUSETTS AVE. NW
WASHINGTON, DC 20036
(202) 483-1414

CONSULATES: LOS ANGELES, SAN DIEGO, AND SAN FRANCIS-
CO, CALIFORNIA; AGANA, GUAM; HONOLULU, HAWAII; CHICAGO,
ILLINOIS; NEW YORK, NEW YORK; HOUSTON, TEXAS; AND
SEATTLE, WASHINGTON

U.S. EMBASSY:
1201 ROXAS BOULEVARD
MANILA, THE PHILIPPINES
(63) (2) 521-7116

CONSULATE: CEBU

POLAND: EMBASSY IN THE UNITED STATES:
2640 16TH ST. NW
WASHINGTON, DC 20009
(202) 234-3800

CONSULATES: LOS ANGELES, CALIFORNIA; CHICAGO, ILLINOIS;
AND NEW YORK, NEW YORK

U.S. EMBASSY:
ALEJE UJAZDOWSKIE 29/31
WARSAW, POLAND
(48) (2) 628-3041

CONSULATES: KRAKOW AND POZNAN

PORTUGAL:

EMBASSY IN THE UNITED STATES:
2125 KALORAMA ROAD NW
WASHINGTON, DC 20008
(202) 328-8610

CONSULATES: LOS ANGELES AND SAN FRANCISCO, CALIFOR-
NIA; BOSTON AND NEW BEDFORD, MASSACHUSETTS; NEWARK,
NEW JERSEY; NEW YORK, NEW YORK; AND PROVIDENCE,
RHODE ISLAND

U.S. EMBASSY:
AVENIDA DAS FORCAS ARMADAS
1600 LISBON, PORTUGAL
(351) (1) 726-6600

CONSULATE: PONTA DELGADA

ROMANIA:

EMBASSY IN THE UNITED STATES:
1607 23RD ST. NW
WASHINGTON, DC 20008
(202) 232-4747

CONSULATES: NONE

U.S. EMBASSY:
STRADA TUDOR ARGHEZI 7-9
BUCHAREST, ROMANIA
401-312-0149

CONSULATES: NONE

RUSSIA:

EMBASSY IN THE UNITED STATES:
1825 PHELPS PLACE NW
WASHINGTON, DC 20008
(202) 939-8908

CONSULATES: SAN FRANCISCO, CALIFORNIA, AND NEW YORK,
NEW YORK

U.S. EMBASSY:
NOVINSKY BUL'VAR 19/23
MOSCOW, RUSSIA
(7) (095) 252-2450

CONSULATES: SAINT PETERSBURG, VLADIVOSTOK

Note: For a period after the breakup of the Soviet Union, the Russian Embassy was the conduit for the diplomatic affairs of several of the other newly independent states. The U.S. and the largest of these newly independent states have now established embassies in each other's capitols, which can also be contacted for information about consulates that have been or will soon be established.

SAUDI ARABIA: EMBASSY IN THE UNITED STATES:
601 NEW HAMPSHIRE AVE. NW
WASHINGTON, DC 20037
(202) 342-3800

CONSULATES: LOS ANGELES, CALIFORNIA; NEW YORK, NEW
YORK; AND HOUSTON, TEXAS

U.S. EMBASSY:
COLLECTOR ROAD M, RIYADH DIPLOMATIC QUARTER
RIYADH, SAUDI ARABIA
(966) (1) 488-3800

CONSULATES: DHAHRAN AND JEDDAH

SINGAPORE: EMBASSY IN THE UNITED STATES:
1824 R ST. NW
WASHINGTON, DC 20009
(202) 667-7555

CONSULATES: NONE

U.S. EMBASSY:
30 HILL STREET
SINGAPORE 0617
(65) 338-0251

CONSULATES: NONE

SOUTH AFRICA: EMBASSY IN THE UNITED STATES:
3051 MASSACHUSETTS AVE. NW
WASHINGTON, DC 20008
(202) 232-4400

CONSULATES: BEVERLY HILLS, CALIFORNIA; CHICAGO, ILLINOIS;
NEW YORK, NEW YORK; AND HOUSTON, TEXAS

U.S. EMBASSY:
877 PRETORIUS ST., ARCADIA 0083
PRETORIA, SOUTH AFRICA
(27) (12) 342-1048

CONSULATES: CAPE TOWN, DURBAN, AND JOHANNESBURG

SOUTH KOREA: EMBASSY IN THE UNITED STATES:
2600 VIRGINIA AVE. NW
WASHINGTON, DC 20037
(202) 939-5660

CONSULATES: ANCHORAGE, ALASKA; LOS ANGELES AND SAN
FRANCISCO, CALIFORNIA; MIAMI, FLORIDA; ATLANTA, GEORGIA;
AGANA, GUAM; HONOLULU, HAWAII; CHICAGO, ILLINOIS; BOS-
TON, MASSACHUSETTS; NEW YORK, NEW YORK; HOUSTON,
TEXAS; AND SEATTLE, WASHINGTON

A
M
E
R
I
C
A
N

J
O
B
S

A
B
R
O
A
D

U.S. EMBASSY:
82 SEJONG-RO; CHONGRO-KU
SEOUL, KOREA
(82) (2) 397-4000

CONSULATE: PUSAN

SPAIN: EMBASSY IN THE UNITED STATES:
2700 15TH ST. NW
WASHINGTON, DC 20009
(202) 265-0190

CONSULATES: LOS ANGELES AND SAN FRANCISCO, CALIFOR-
NIA; MIAMI, FLORIDA; CHICAGO, ILLINOIS; NEW ORLEANS, LOUI-
SIANA; BOSTON, MASSACHUSETTS; NEW YORK, NEW YORK;
SAN JUAN, PUERTO RICO; AND HOUSTON, TEXAS

U.S. EMBASSY:
SERRANO 75
28006 MADRID, SPAIN
(34) (1) 577-4000

CONSULATES: BARCELONA AND BILBAO

SWEDEN: EMBASSY IN THE UNITED STATES:
600 NEW HAMPSHIRE AVE. NW
WASHINGTON, DC 20037
(202) 944-5600

CONSULATES: LOS ANGELES, CALIFORNIA; CHICAGO, ILLINOIS;
AND NEW YORK, NEW YORK

U.S. EMBASSY:
STRANDVAGEN 101, S-115
89 STOCKHOLM, SWEDEN
(46) (8) 783-5300

CONSULATES: NONE

SWITZERLAND: EMBASSY IN THE UNITED STATES:
2900 CATHEDRAL AVE. NW
WASHINGTON, DC 20008
(202) 745-7900

CONSULATES: LOS ANGELES AND SAN FRANCISCO, CALIFOR-
NIA; ATLANTA, GEORGIA; CHICAGO, ILLINOIS; AND HOUSTON,
TEXAS

U.S. EMBASSY:
JUBILAEUMSTRASSE 93
3005 BERN, SWITZERLAND
(41) (31) 437-011

CONSULATES: GENEVA AND ZURICH

THAILAND:
EMBASSY IN THE UNITED STATES:
2300 KALORAMA ROAD NW
WASHINGTON, DC 20008
(202) 483-7200

CONSULATES: LOS ANGELES, CALIFORNIA; CHICAGO, ILLINOIS;
AND NEW YORK, NEW YORK

U.S. EMBASSY:
95 WIRELESS ROAD
BANGKOK, THAILAND
(66) (2) 252-5040

CONSULATES: CHIANG MAI, SONGKHLA, AND UDORN

TURKEY:
EMBASSY IN THE UNITED STATES:
1714 MASSACHUSETTS AVE. NW
WASHINGTON, DC 20008
(202) 659-8200

CONSULATES: LOS ANGELES, CALIFORNIA; CHICAGO, ILLINOIS;
NEW YORK, NEW YORK; AND HOUSTON, TEXAS

U.S. EMBASSY:
110 ATATURK BOULEVARD
ANKARA, TURKEY
(90) (4) 426-54-70

CONSULATES: ADANA, ISTANBUL, AND IZMIR

UKRAINE
EMBASSY IN THE UNITED STATES:
1828 L STREET NW, #711
WASHINGTON, DC 20036
(202) 333-0606

U.S. EMBASSY:
10 YURIA KOTSYUBINSKOVO
252053 KIEV 53 UKRAINE
(7) (044) 244-7349

**UNITED ARAB
EMIRATES:**
EMBASSY IN THE UNITED STATES:
600 NEW HAMPSHIRE AVE. NW
WASHINGTON, DC 20037
(202) 338-6500

CONSULATES: NONE

U.S. EMBASSY:
AL-SUDAN STREET
ABU DHABI, UNITED ARAB EMIRATES
(971) (2) 336691

CONSULATE: DUBAI

LIVING ABROAD

A
M
E
R
I
C
A
N

J
O
B
S

A
B
R
O
A
D

UNITED KINGDOM:

EMBASSY IN THE UNITED STATES:
3100 MASSACHUSETTS AVE. NW
WASHINGTON, DC 20008
(202) 462-1340

CONSULATES: LOS ANGELES AND SAN FRANCISCO, CALIFOR-
NIA; MIAMI, FLORIDA; ATLANTA, GEORGIA; CHICAGO, ILLINOIS;
BOSTON, MASSACHUSETTS; NEW YORK, NEW YORK; CLEVE-
LAND, OHIO; DALLAS AND HOUSTON, TEXAS; AND SEATTLE,
WASHINGTON

U.S. EMBASSY:
24/31 GROSVENOR SQUARE, W.1A 1AE
LONDON, ENGLAND
(44) (71) 499-9000

CONSULATES: BELFAST, NORTHERN IRELAND, AND EDINBURGH,
SCOTLAND

VENEZUELA:

EMBASSY IN THE UNITED STATES:
1099 30TH ST. NW
WASHINGTON, DC 20007
(202) 342-2214

CONSULATES: SAN FRANCISCO, CALIFORNIA; MIAMI, FLORIDA;
CHICAGO, ILLINOIS; NEW ORLEANS, LOUISIANA; BALTIMORE,
MARYLAND; BOSTON, MASSACHUSETTS; NEW YORK, NEW
YORK; PHILADELPHIA, PENNSYLVANIA; SAN JUAN, PUERTO
RICO; AND HOUSTON, TEXAS

U.S. EMBASSY:
AVENIDA FRANCISCO DE MIRANDA AND AVENIDA PRINCIPAL DE
LA FLORESTA CARACAS, VENEZUELA
(58) (2) 285-2222

CONSULATE: MARACAIBO

SOURCES OF FURTHER INFORMATION

U.S. Government. *Key Officers of Foreign Service Posts.* Washington, D.C.: Government
Printing Office, 1992. Stock number 744-006-00000-7, $1.75.

OTHER MATTERS

- **Foreign Customs Inspection** Learn about the country in which you will be living
  and what you can and cannot take with you. Use the directory of foreign embassies and
  consulates in the United States (*see* pages 75–92) to obtain further information. Items
  most commonly subject to customs restrictions are foreign currency, firearms,

pornography, alcoholic beverages, electronic equipment, and perishable food items. Islamic countries and the few remaining Communist countries have particularly strict customs inspection and potentially severe penalties for violations.

• **Children Born Abroad** Assuming that you and your spouse are U.S. citizens, if you have children abroad, they will automatically become U.S. citizens. However, as soon as possible after the birth of your child, you should contact the U.S. embassy or the consulate nearest you and obtain a form called Report of Birth Abroad of a U.S. Citizen. The report is legal proof of your child's U.S. citizenship.

• **Dual Nationality** Before you leave the United States, you should check with the embassy or consulate nearest you representing the foreign country in which you will be working if any of the following situations apply:

   o You were born in that country.
   o One or both of your parents were born in or were citizens of that country.
   o You are a naturalized U.S. citizen and are still potentially a citizen of that country.
   o You are married to a citizen of that country.

If any of these situations applies to you, you might have dual citizenship in the United States and that country. Find out for certain whether that country will treat you as one of its citizens. Such dual nationality could involve military service requirements and other legal obligations that you didn't expect and don't want. You might also be rendered ineligible for protection under international law if you are arrested there or face other legal trouble.

You can get further information about dual nationality from the State Department:

U.S. DEPARTMENT OF STATE
OFFICE OF CITIZENS CONSULAR SERVICES
BUREAU OF CONSULAR AFFAIRS
ROOM 4817
WASHINGTON, DC 20520
(202) 647-4000

• **Getting Arrested Abroad** For as long as you are overseas, you are subject to your host country's laws. These include criminal laws and penalties. Under international law, you are entitled to speak with and meet an American consul if you are arrested. American consuls can help you, but only to a limited degree. They can help you get a local lawyer, but they can't help you with your legal fees and expenses, nor can they do much about prison conditions except forward clothing, food, and money from your family or friends. The U.S. embassy can issue diplomatic protests and exercise other forms of pressure, but it will usually do so only in particularly egregious cases, such as those involving torture, extortion, or arrest for alleged political crimes.

Drug arrests are especially serious. Many countries have penalties for drug possession or trafficking that are much harsher than in the United States, ranging from years of imprisonment at hard labor to the death penalty. Also, most countries don't have the legal protection for individual rights that we take for granted. You may not get a jury trial, pretrial bail, a sanitary cell, or adequate food.

- **Missing Persons** If family, friends, or relatives lose contact with you abroad, the American consul is the primary conduit for information requests about your health and whereabouts. If you have registered with the embassy or consulate, a consul will make contact and relay any urgent messages, and ask for permission to reveal your whereabouts to the inquiring parties. If you haven't registered with U.S. authorities, or have registered but disappeared, the consul will contact the local authorities. At that point, the chances for locating you will depend on the efficiency of the local police force or other body.

- **Deaths Abroad** If a U.S. citizen dies abroad, any surviving family abroad should contact the U.S. embassy or the nearest consulate and also report the death to the next of kin and the executor named in the deceased's will. In addition to a local death certificate, relatives should also obtain a Form OF-180, Report of Death of an American Citizen Abroad, from the consul to assist with estate and probate matters back in the United States. (One would hope that the employer would handle these matters if the person lives alone overseas.) Finally, the family will have to pay for the cost of transporting the body back to the United States if burial is not to be abroad.

SOURCES OF FURTHER INFORMATION

There are many good sources of information on foreign countries. Government publications can be ordered from the Government Printing Office in Washington for very reasonable prices. A copy of the form you must use to order GPO publications is included at the end of these sources. The GPO will accept a photocopy of the form. Note that the form requires you to supply the GPO stock number and GPO price per unit. This information is provided below for every GPO publication, and is given everywhere else in this Introduction where a GPO publication is cited as a source of further information.

Gale Research. *Countries of the World.* Detroit: Gale Research, 1994.

U.S. Government. *Health Information for International Travel.* Washington, D.C.: Government Printing Office, 1992. Stock number 017-023-00189-2, $5.

U.S. Government. *International Certificate of Vaccination.* Washington, D.C.: Government Printing Office, 1992. Stock number 017-001-00440-5, $2.

U.S. Government. *Tips for Americans Residing Abroad.* Washington, D.C.: Government Printing Office, 1992. Stock number 044-000-02281-8, $1.

U.S. Government. *Your Trip Abroad.* Washington, D.C.: Government Printing Office, 1992. Stock number 044-000-02335-1, $1.25.

BEFORE USING THIS FORM, READ IMPORTANT INFORMATION ON REVERSE SIDE
PLEASE PRINT OR TYPE ALL INFORMATION

S284

Customer's Telephone No.'s

Area Code　Home　Area Code　Office

MasterCard　VISA

ORDER FORM

MAIL TO:

Superintendent of Documents
U. S. Government Printing Office
Washington, D. C. 20402

Date.............................. Your Order Number.......................

Credit Card No.

Customer's Name and Address

Expiration Date Month/Year

ZIP

FOR OFFICE USE ONLY	
QUANTITY	CHARGES
_____ Publications	_____
_____ Subscriptions	_____
Special shipping charges	_____
International handling ..	_____
Special charges	_____
OPNR.................	_____
_____ UPNS	
_____ Balance Due	
_____ Discount	
_____ Refund	

Deposit Account Number

Charge orders may be telephoned to the GPO order
desk at (202)783-3238 from 8:00 a.m. to 4:00 p.m.
eastern time, Monday-Friday (except holidays).

Stock No.	Quantity	Unit of Issue	List ID	☐ Publication　　　Title of　　☐ Subscription	Unit Price	Total
					TOTAL ENCLOSED $	

SHIP TO: (if different from above)

ZIP

Unit of Issue	Explanation
EA	Each - single copy
KT	Kit of multiple items in a special container
PD	Pad containing multiple sheets
PK	Package containing multiple copies
SE	Set of multiple items
SU	Subscription

THE GOVERNMENT PRINTING OFFICE (GPO) ORDER FORM. (CONTINUED ON PAGE 96.)

INFORMATION CONCERNING YOUR ORDER

Payment is required in advance of shipment of publications. You may order using check or money order drawn on a bank located in Canada, the United States, or United States possessions, in U.S. dollars. (NOTE: In accordance with U.S. Department of the Treasury regulations, we cannot accept checks drawn on Canadian banks or Candian money orders for amounts of less than four U.S. dollars ($4.00). If your order totals less than $4.00, we suggest that you use your MasterCard or VISA account.) Make checks/money orders payable to the Superintendent of Documents. Checks returned by the bank as uncollectible are subject to a penalty of up to 10 percent of the amount of the check, with a minimum charge of five dollars ($5.00). You may also order by using your VISA, MasterCard, or Superintendent of Documents Prepaid Deposit Account. Do not send currency (bills or coins) or postage stamps.

Shipping is by non-priority mail or United Parcel Service (UPS). First class and airmail services are available for an additional charge if requested. Please contact us in advance for rates if you desire this service (202-783-3238) and indicate on your order if you desire special postage.

DISCOUNTS:

With the exception of certain publications and subscriptions, a discount of 25% from the domestic price is allowed on orders of 100 or more units of issue mailed to a single address. A discount of 25% from the domestic price is also applicable on orders from bookdealers, for orders of any quantity, mailed to the dealer's business address. (The maximum discount allowable is 25%).

INTERNATIONAL CUSTOMERS:

Mailing regulations require special handling for orders mailed to addresses outside the United States or its possessions for which we charge an additional 25% of the domestic price. Payment is required in advance by one of the methods stated above. You may also remit by UNESCO coupons or by International Postal Money Order, made payable to the Superintendent of Documents. Foreign currency and foreign checks will not be accepted. All orders must be in English. International customers are allowed the same discounts stated above.

Orders are sent via surface mail unless otherwise requested. Should you desire airmail service, please contact us in advance by letter, telephone (202-783-3238), or Telex (#710-822-9413;ANSWERBACK USGPO WSH) for the total cost of your order.

To Order, Use Form On Reverse Side

1. A separate order form must be used for ordering publications and subscriptions.

2. Type or print your complete name and address, home and office telephone numbers, date, order number (if any), Deposit Account Number (if applicable), VISA or MasterCard number and expiration date (if applicable), in proper places at the top of the form. If order is to be shipped to another location, enter address at bottom of form. All prices include postage and handling.

3. When ordering publications, type or print the stock number, unit of issue (see front), quantity, title, price, and total payment enclosed. Allow 4 weeks for delivery (longer for International Orders).

4. When ordering a subscription service, type or print the quantity, title, price, List ID (when available), and total payment enclosed. Allow 2-6 weeks, plus mailing time, for processing. All subscriptions are for one year, unless otherwise noted. Subscribers will be notified by mail in ample time to renew.

5. Mail your order form to Superintendent of Documents, U.S. Government Printing Office, Washington, D.C. 20402.

6. Orders and inquiries can be placed with our order/information desk (202-783-3238) from 8:00 a.m. to 4:00 p.m., Eastern Time.

7. This form may be reproduced.

ADJUSTING TO A JOB ABROAD

Once you are abroad, it is important that you adjust effectively to your new job and your new country. This will not always be an easy process. The following pointers should help.

- **Interacting with Local Nationals** If you want to get along with your new neighbors, the foremost thing you have to do is understand that American customs and manners may be very much out of place. Some dos and don'ts:

  o Address people by their formal official titles, or as "Mr." or "Mrs.," until they indicate that a more casual address is acceptable. Many countries are much more formal than the United States regarding personal interaction. The sort of friendly familiarity Americans usually exude could generate alienation and hostility unless it is tempered with some formality.

  o Avoid flashy or extravagant clothing and jewelry, but don't be excessively casual. In most countries, you are judged almost immediately by what you are wearing. You don't want to be treated as the vulgar rich American, but you also don't want to be considered as a lower-class bumpkin because you go out in public wearing jeans with holes in them. Women in skimpy shorts or revealing dresses may invite unwelcome attention.

  o Learn some local phrases and greetings. English may be the world's language of business, but people will appreciate your effort to learn their language.

- **Getting Acclimated** Getting used to the local culture will require a certain amount of involvement. These ideas are worth considering:

  o Send your children to local schools if they are safe and of sufficient quality, rather than one of the many schools for expatriate children abroad. They will learn the local language and culture much quicker and more easily.

  o Do your own shopping at local stores and shops rather than relying on servants or the U.S. commissary. You'll learn local customs much faster.

  o Resist the temptation to socialize exclusively with other Americans in the expatriate community. Make an effort to make local friends and acquaintances. Understand that in many foreign countries, home entertainment is restricted to family and relatives. People outside that circle are usually invited to restaurants or clubs for dinner or for other occasions. An invitation to one's home is to be regarded as a special honor not to be taken lightly.

- **Countries with Large American Communities** The following summaries of eight selected countries with sizeable expatriate populations highlight economic conditions in each country to help you gauge your potential job opportunities there. Obviously, there is more to life in any foreign country than can be detailed here. Therefore, you are encouraged to contact the country's embassy or consulate for further information. In addition, refer to the list of sources of further information about living abroad, on page 94.

The eight countries examined here are Canada, France, Germany, Great Britain, Italy, Japan, Mexico, and Saudi Arabia.

The information in these summaries is intended to be as accurate as possible as of the date of publication, but of course conditions are bound to change over time, particularly if and when the current worldwide economic recession ends. You should also refer to the descriptions of these nations in the Country Profiles section, beginning on page 589. Beyond the following eight summaries and the nearly one hundred Country Profiles, excellent and concise sources of information about current conditions in other countries are the Department of State's country *Background Notes,* which are updated annually and cover every country in the world. If your local public library doesn't have the *Background Notes,* or the most current updates, in its reference section, see if the library has *Countries of the World,* a reference book published annually by Gale Research. *Countries of the World* contains reprints of all the most recent background notes. You can purchase *Background Notes* by mail from the Government Printing Office for the nominal cost of $1 per country. You can order as many or as few countries as you want, and the procedure for ordering GPO publications is described on page 94.

CANADA: Canada has the world's seventh-largest economy and is the largest recipient of American investment abroad. Virtually every large American multinational corporation and a growing number of medium-size and small companies have a Canadian subsidiary. Perhaps because we are accustomed to taking our northern neighbor for granted, most Americans don't realize that Canada, not Japan, is America's largest trading partner. In addition, Canada is the world's second-largest country and has vast natural resources.

American culture dominates Canada, so most Americans experience little difficulty in adjusting to life there. Although Canada is officially a bilingual country, because of the French-Canadian population of Quebec province, English is spoken everywhere. Most American products are available in Canada, and the unit of currency is the Canadian dollar, which currently is worth about 20 percent less than the U.S. dollar. Some minor cultural differences stem from Canada's continued close ties to Great Britain and the British Commonwealth. For example, public holidays include the Queen's Birthday in May. The imperial gallon, not the slightly smaller U.S. gallon, is the common form of liquid measurement.

The already large number of American companies in Canada will probably get even larger if Canada ratifies the North American Free Trade Agreement (NAFTA). If your background is in the automotive, finance, forest products, manufacturing, mineral extraction or petroleum industries, you should strongly consider Canada. American automakers, mining companies, paper and pulp producers, and other basic industries have a strong presence in Canada because of the abundance of mineral deposits, forests, and other natural resources.

FRANCE: France has the fourth-largest economy in the world and has benefitted from strong investment and export growth in recent years. The healthy French economy continues to attract American companies seeking to expand abroad. However, France has a long history of economic protectionism, particularly in agriculture, and the franc is notoriously unstable against other European currencies such as the German mark.

If you are fortunate enough to land a job in France, you will certainly enjoy France's well-deserved reputation for fine culture and excellent cuisine. However, the French have been accused of a certain "cultural superiority" complex. Although English is widely spoken, you may find it difficult to gain acceptance and fit easily into French life unless you learn how to speak French. Consider taking a Berlitz course or other French-language class before you leave the United States if you are not fluent in French.

The United States and France enjoy a strong trade partnership, valued at more than $25 billion annually. America's strengths in this trade relationship are computers, electronics and electronic equipment, medical equipment, and telecommunications. If you have a background in one of these areas, consider including France in your job search program.

GERMANY: Since the end of World War II, the German "economic miracle" has produced steady economic growth and has given Germany the largest economy in Europe and the third largest economy in the world (as of 1990). Germany enjoys a reputation for producing high-quality manufactured goods, and the German mark is the strongman in the European currency system. Germany does have its economic problems, however. Its economy is heavily export-oriented, and so Germany has been hurt by the current global economic slowdown. Furthermore, the integration of the former East Germany into a unified state adhering to Western economic principles has caused high interest rates and other economic dislocations.

Germany's high interest rates have driven the dollar to historic lows against the mark, so Americans find that the cost of living is high in Germany. The quality of life is high as well, however. The German custom is to take six weeks of vacation leave a year, social services are excellent, and German cities are clean and have low crime rates. Germany still has significant eastern-western and other regional differences. The north and the east are mostly Protestant, with liberal laws regarding social issues such as abortion. The south and the west are mostly Catholic and conservative.

Ironically for a country that produces Mercedes and BMWs, American automobile companies are particularly strong in Germany. Other American industries with a strong presence in Germany are aircraft, chemical, electrical equipment, machinery, and petroleum industries. If movement toward a unified Europe and the economic integration of the old East Germany proceed apace, the number of Americans working in Germany should continue to increase as American corporate subsidiaries benefit from German growth.

GREAT BRITAIN: Great Britain has the sixth-largest economy in the world. With the oldest cultural ties to the United States of any nation, it is the second-largest target of American investment abroad. The British government has embarked on a program of privatization, aimed at reducing the large state involvement in the private sector. Great Britain suffers from a chronic trade imbalance, however, and the pound has to be propped up repeatedly by the Bank of England.

Life in Great Britain, for most Americans, means life in London. London is by far the largest city, containing roughly 10 percent of the entire British population. It is the economic hub of the country. London has an excellent public transportation system and an abundance of cultural and historic diversions, but some public utilities, such as the telephone system, are disappointing by American standards. London is expensive, particularly for housing. A modest one- or two-bedroom London "flat" could easily eat up the bulk of your salary. See whether your prospective employer provides housing or housing subsidies before you take a job in London.

As with the American presence in Canada, there are quite a few American companies with U.K. subsidiaries, and they cover a broad spectrum of American industry. The service sector, however, is where some of the most notable growth is occurring. London's financial district, known as The City, is Europe's financial capital and was recently opened up to foreign competition. Therefore, American brokerage houses, commercial banks, and other financial services companies have been expanding in London and hiring American employees.

ITALY: One of the most recent, and largely unrecognized, economic success stories in the world is Italy. Now boasting the world's fifth-largest economy, Italy has transformed itself from an agrarian country into an industrial powerhouse, overtaking Great Britain in gross domestic product. The country suffers from political instability, however, resulting in continual reshuffling of the government. The lira has been steadily devalued since the early 1970s, particularly against the mark, and the country has imposed currency controls on persons entering and leaving the country.

Significant economic and cultural disparities exist between northern and southern Italy. Most of the country's economic activity and growth is north of Rome, and living standards there are comparable to the rest of western Europe. South of Rome, the economy is still heavily agrarian and backward, the unemployment rate is more than triple that of the north, and the government is engaged in a continual battle against the influence of the Mafia. If for some reason you should wind up in the south, be prepared for a dramatic reduction in the quality of public services, transportation, health care, and crime prevention.

The Italian economy is dominated by small and medium-size firms that compete by producing high-quality, low-cost processed consumer goods, frequently for foreign partners seeking to avoid high labor costs at home. Therefore, in addition to the usual large American multinational corporate presence, look for smaller textile, apparel, leather goods, and other consumer-oriented companies in your search for a job in Italy.

JAPAN: Japan has the second-largest economy in the world, roughly half that of the United States, and is the United States' second-largest trading partner. Japan has a strong export economy and a massive annual trade surplus with the United States and the rest of the world. The Japanese are not only the world's top manufacturers but also are increasingly dominant in the financial sector as well: nine of the world's ten largest banks are Japanese. However, the Japanese economy has been hurt by the worldwide recession, and the Japanese stock market has lost more than 50 percent of its value. The Japanese government is rife with corruption and top-level political scandals.

Life in Japan can be difficult for Americans, but with patience and an open mind many find it rewarding. Japan is a homogeneous society, with none of America's ethnic diversity, and the Japanese believe that their lack of racial division has helped their economic success. Therefore, despite Japan's infatuation with Western culture, it takes time for Americans to gain acceptance and make Japanese friends. Japan also is expensive, thanks to the plummeting value of the dollar against the yen. Find out whether your prospective employer provides housing or housing subsidies before you take a job in Japan.

Many American companies have offices in Japan, and they range from high-technology companies to financial services institutions to agricultural exporters. Look for job opportunities in other areas as well, particularly among American companies seeking to break into the vast Japanese market. For example, Toys R Us recently established a Japanese subsidiary, seeking to export American-style mass-discount retailing into a country still dominated by small mom-and-pop stores.

MEXICO: Although many still consider it a Third World country, Mexico has been undergoing an economic boom, thanks in large part to a surge in American and other foreign investment. Many American manufacturers have relocated their factories from the United States to Mexico to take advantage of Mexico's skilled but low-cost work force. The average Mexican worker may earn one-tenth the wage of an American worker, but he or she earns an average of ten times the working wage in truly Third World countries such as India. Still, the country is far from achieving a Western standard of living. Organized crime and the drug trade are rampant, and the government's campaign against corruption has yet to succeed.

With certain adjustments, life for an American in Mexico can be very pleasant. The cost of living is low, thanks to an exchange rate of approximately three new pesos (three thousand old pesos) to the dollar, and "yanquis" can expect first-class treatment everywhere. Although you can get by on English, you must learn Spanish if you are serious about staying in Mexico for any length of time. You must also be prepared to accept Mexico for what it is, namely, a country whose first priority has been economic development. Pollution is a serious health hazard in Mexico City, because of practically nonexistent environmental standards, and shantytowns populated by rural immigrants ring every major city.

Cheap labor and the North American Free Trade Agreement ensure that American companies will continue to expand their presence in Mexico. Look for companies that would benefit from "outsourcing" basic manufacturing or assembly operations to expand in Mexico, such as Zenith, which recently relocated a major picture tube plant. These companies still need Americans in technical and managerial positions.

SAUDI ARABIA: Saudi Arabia is a desert country, large in size but with a small population. Oil wealth has made it the world's twenty-third-largest economy, which in itself wouldn't be that important except for the very large foreign presence there. When the oil money began to flow into Saudi Arabia in the 1970s and the Saudis wanted to build roads, hospitals, factories, and other amenities, they allowed a flood of Western workers, engineers, technicians, and managers to settle in the country. Roughly 3.5 million non-Saudis live there. Although Saudi Arabia is the richest country in the Middle East it still needs Westerners. Because the Saudi economy depends on the price of oil, however, it has been severely hurt by price drops and new production sources not aligned with the Organization of Petroleum Exporting Countries (OPEC).

Saudi Arabia is the most difficult of the eight countries discussed here for Americans to adjust to. It is an Islamic country, so alcohol is strictly forbidden and women must wear very conservative clothing in public. Women are even forbidden to drive. Moreover, the country is not a democracy but a kingdom, ruled by the Saud family clan. The local princes wield great power, and there are harsh penalties for violating Islamic law. Although many Americans enjoy their stay in Saudi Arabia, it is definitely not a country for persons who don't like changes in their life-style.

Most of the American jobs in Saudi Arabia are in construction, defense, petroleum, or related industries and services. Salaries are frequently very generous to attract qualified personnel.

SOURCES OF FURTHER INFORMATION

Fodor's Publications. *The Wall Street Journal Guides to Business Travel: Europe.* New York: Fodor's Travel Publications, 1992.

Fodor's Publications. *The Wall Street Journal Guides to Business Travel: Pacific Rim.* New York: Fodor's Travel Publications, 1992.

Gale Research. *Countries of the World.* Detroit, Mich.: Gale Research, 1994.

U.S. Government. *Destination Japan: A Business Guide.* Washington, D.C.: Government Printing Office, 1992. Stock number 003-009-00602-3, $4.

U.S. Government. *Safe Trip Abroad.* Washington, D.C.: Government Printing Office, 1992. Stock number 044-000-02292-3, $1.

U.S. Government. *Tips for Americans Residing Abroad.* Washington, D.C.: Government Printing Office, 1992. Stock number 044-000-02281-8, $1.

U.S. Government. *Tips for Travelers to the Caribbean.* Washington, D.C.: Government Printing Office, 1992. Stock number 044-000-02329-6, $1.

U.S. Government. *Tips for Travelers to Central and South America.* Washington, D.C.: Government Printing Office, 1992. Stock number 044-000-02252-4, $1.

U.S. Government. *Tips for Travelers to Eastern Europe.* Washington, D.C.: Government Printing Office, 1992. Stock number 044-000-02307-5, $1.

U.S. Government. *Tips for Travelers to Mexico.* Washington, D.C.: Government Printing Office, 1992. Stock number 044-000-02269-9, $1.

U.S. Government. *Tips for Travelers to the Middle East and North Africa.* Washington, D.C.: Government Printing Office, 1992. Stock number 044-000-02201-0, $1.

U.S. Government. *Tips for Travelers to the People's Republic of China.* Washington, D.C.: Government Printing Office, 1992. Stock number 044-000-02245-1, $1.

U.S. Government. *Tips for Travelers to South Asia.* Washington, D.C.: Government Printing Office, 1992. Stock number 044-000-02205-2, $1.

U.S. Government. *Tips for Travelers to the USSR.* Washington, D.C.: Government Printing Office, 1992. Stock number 044-000-02288-5, $1.

U.S. Government. *Travel Tips for Older Americans.* Washington, D.C.: Government Printing Office, 1992. Stock number 044-000-02270-2, $1.

U.S. Government. *Your Trip Abroad.* Washington, D.C.: Government Printing Office, 1992. Stock number 044-000-02335-1, $1.25.

You can purchase State Department *Background Notes* by mail from the Government Printing Office for the nominal cost of $1 per country. The stock numbers for each country's *Background Notes* are listed in GPO subject bibliographies, which list not only all the *Background Notes* for a particular region of the world but also other government publications with valuable information as well. The subject bibliographies are free. All you have to do is fill out a copy of the Subject Bibliography Order Form shown on page 105 and mail it to:

SUPERINTENDENT OF DOCUMENTS
U.S. GOVERNMENT PRINTING OFFICE
WASHINGTON, DC 20402

Once you receive your subject bibliography or bibliographies and decide which *Background Notes* and other materials you want to purchase, you can, of course, use a photocopy of the standard GPO order form *(see* pages 94–96).

SUBJECT BIBLIOGRAPHY / SB NO.

AFRICA / 284

ASIA AND OCEANIA / 288

CANADA / 278

CHINA / 299

EUROPE (INCLUDING THE U.K.) / 289

LATIN AMERICA AND THE CARIBBEAN / 287

MIDDLE EAST / 286

(THE FORMER) SOVIET UNION / 279

COMING HOME: RE-ENTERING THE DOMESTIC JOB MARKET

Most Americans who work abroad return to the United States. If you want to come back to the United States with a reasonable prospect of obtaining a job, you should think well ahead before your job period expires. Of course, if you can transfer back to a U.S. office of the company you worked for abroad, that solves the problem.

- **Maintaining Job Contacts While You Are Abroad** Most job placement experts agree that making personal contacts, known as networking, is the most effective means of getting a job. Here are some suggestions for creative networking while you are abroad:
  - o Keep in touch with your contacts periodically by writing letters and sending cards on holidays.
  - o Make personal visits and telephone calls when you are in the United States on vacation or home leave.
  - o Maintain subscriptions to professional journals while you are abroad. The classified section may contain job opportunities in the United States, and you will be able to keep abreast of industry trends and hiring practices.

A FINAL WORD

Anyone looking into working abroad should do so with her/his eyes wide open and with an understanding of both the positive and negative aspects of overseas employment. Naturally, much depends on where you want to work and the particular conditions in that country. Many Americans enjoy their new home abroad so much that they stay longer than they originally intended, and some never return to the United States at all.

For anyone who has dreamed of working and living overseas, the pages that follow will provide the information you need to crack the overseas job market.

SUPERINTENDENT OF DOCUMENTS
UNITED STATES GOVERNMENT PRINTING OFFICE
WASHINGTON, DC 20402
Telephone 202-783-3238

Subject Bibliography Order Form

To order, indicate the quantity desired beside each SB number, complete the mailing label, and return to the address above.

SB No.	SB No.	SB No.	SB No.	SB No.	SB No.	SB No.
2	44	106	154	207	257	307
3	46	107	156	209	258	308
4	48	108	157	210	259	310
6	49	109	158	211	261	311
8	50	110	160	213	263	312
9	51	111	161	215	270	314
10	53	114	162	216	273	
12	57	115	163	217	276	
13	64	116	165	218	277	
14	66	117	166	221	278	
16	67	118	167	222	279	
17	69	119	168	223	280	
18	72	121	169	225	281	
19	73	122	171	226	284	
21	75	123	173	227	285	
22	76	125	176	228	286	
23	77	126	177	229	287	
24	80	127	181	231	288	
25	82	128	182	234	289	
27	83	129	183	236	290	
29	85	130	185	237	291	
30	86	131	187	238	294	
31	87	137	191	239	295	
32	88	140	192	241	296	
34	90	141	195	243	297	
35	91	142	196	244	298	
36	93	144	197	245	299	
37	95	146	198	246	300	
39	97	149	200	247	302	
40	98	150	201	249	303	
41	99	151	202	250	304	
42	100	152	204	252	305	
43	102	153	205	256	306	

Missing numbers are obsolete or superseded by newer lists.

Please send me............... additional copies of the Subject Bibliography Index.
Please send me............... copies of Price List 36.

U.S. GOVERNMENT PRINTING OFFICE
SUPERINTENDENT OF DOCUMENTS
WASHINGTON, DC 20402

OFFICIAL BUSINESS

PENALTY FOR PRIVATE USE, $300

Name...

Street address...

City and State .... ZIP Code ....

THE SUBJECT BIBLIOGRAPHY ORDER FORM CAN BE USED TO ORDER BACKGROUND
NOTES FROM THE GOVERNMENT PRINTING OFFICE.

COMPANY | LISTINGS

A. L. LABORATORIES INC.

1 Executive Dr.
Fort Lee, NJ 07024 USA

RECRUITER: LORRAINE CATRACIL
PERSONNEL MANAGER
1 EXECUTIVE DR.
FORT LEE, NJ 07024
TEL: (201) 947-7774
FAX: (201) 947-5541

I. Roy Cohen, President. Pharmaceuticals. A. L. Laboratories is a public company founded in 1975 as a subsidiary of a Norwegian health care company. It was then reincorporated under Delaware law in 1983 and its stock was first offered to the public in February 1984. Today, the firm operates on a global basis in the manufacture and sale of specialized pharmaceuticals, animal health micronutrients, and other human nutrition items. Worldwide revenues for 1992: $289 million.

- **Total Employees:** 1,700

- **U.S. Employees Abroad:** Not available.

- **Countries:** Denmark, Indonesia.

- **Job Categories:** Administrative, Marketing—Pharmaceuticals, Research & Development, Sales—Pharmaceuticals.

ABB LUMMUS CREST

PO Box 79570
Houston, TX 77279 USA

RECRUITER: KATHLEEN RYAN
MANAGER, EMPLOYEE RELATIONS
PO BOX 79570
HOUSTON, TX 77279
TEL: (713) 531-4000
FAX: (713) 589-3514

Steven Solomon, Chairperson. Engineering and construction services. ABB Lummus Crest was founded in 1988 and is a division of Asea Brown Boveri of Stamford, Connecticut. It is a diversified company primarily involved in the engineering and construction fields. Worldwide revenues for 1992: $615 million.

- **Total Employees:** 2,000
- **U.S. Employees Abroad:** 75
- **Countries:** Worldwide including Brazil, Canada, People's Republic of China, Germany, Netherlands, Saudi Arabia, Venezuela.
- **Application Information:** Do not call.
- **Job Categories:** Accountants, Design, Engineers.
- **Average Overseas Assignment:** 2-3 years.
- **Language Requirement:** Knowledge of local language a plus but not essential.
- **Training:** No special training provided.
- **Benefits:** All benefits are individually determined.

ABB VETCO GRAY, INC.

PO Box 2291
Houston, TX 77001 USA

RECRUITER: ODESSA COLE
INTERNATIONAL PERSONNEL
ADMINISTRATOR
PO BOX 2291
HOUSTON, TX 77001
TEL: (713) 683-2480
FAX: (713) 683-2659

Donald Grierson, President. Well-head and sub-sea equipment. ABB Vetco Gray is a private company founded in 1906. It manufactures and sells machinery for oil and gas fields and drilling water wells. Worldwide revenues for 1991: $330 million.

- **Total Employees:** 7,000
- **U.S. Employees Abroad:** 88
- **Countries:** Angola, Brazil, Congo, Indonesia, Kuwait, Malaysia, Nigeria, Singapore, Republic of South Africa, United Arab Emirates, United Kingdom, Venezuela.
- **Application Information:** Hiring for most foreign positions is done at the specific country location.
- **Job Categories:** Management, Marketing—Scientific, Sales—Scientific.
- **Average Overseas Assignment:** 2 years.

- **Language Requirement:** Varies with each posting.

- **Training:** No special training provided.

- **Benefits:** All benefits are individually determined.

ABBOTT LABORATORIES

D6PB AP30
One Abbott Park Rd.
Abbott Park, IL 60064 USA

RECRUITER: HUMAN RESOURCES
DIRECTOR (SPECIFIC AREA)
D6PP AP30, ONE ABBOTT PARK RD.
ABBOTT PARK, IL 60064
TEL: (708) 938-8302
FAX: (708) 938-8325

Duane Burnham, Chairman. Pharmaceuticals. Wallace Abbott founded the Abbott Alkaloidal Company in Chicago in 1888. Abbott Laboratories is now a major, worldwide pharmaceutical company, with over half its revenues attained from nutritional and diagnostic equipment markets. The company also supplies hospitals and bloodbanks worldwide with intravenous fluids, pumps, screening tests, and critical care equipment. Worldwide revenues for 1992: $7.9 billion.

- **Total Employees:** 45,000

- **U.S. Employees Abroad:** 60

- **Countries:** Twenty-five including Canada, Hong Kong, India, Italy, Japan, Mexico, United Kingdom.

- **Application Information:** Recruitment areas include: Africa, Asia, Europe, Latin America, and the Pacific.

- **Job Categories:** Executive Management, Sales—Pharmaceuticals.

- **General Requirements:** Usually must be a current employee of the company in order to qualify for overseas assignment.

- **Average Overseas Assignment:** 2-3 years.

- **Language Requirement:** Depends on location; decided on a case-by-case basis.

- **Training:** No special training provided.

- **Benefits:** TRAVEL: Annual home leave provided. HEALTH: Same coverage as U.S. employees. HOUSING: Employee must pay U.S. assumed housing cost. EDUCATION: Company pays education costs, if local schools are unsuitable.

- **Comments:** Abbott generally recruits from within for overseas positions. The company does not send entry-level employees overseas. A typical expatriate employee is at the senior management level.

A
M
E
R
I
C
A
N

J
O
B
S

A
B
R
O
A
D

ABEX INC./FISHER SCIENTIFIC INTERNATIONAL, INC.

Liberty Lane
Hampton, NH 03842 USA

RECRUITER: SHERRY LOUDON
PERSONNEL DIRECTOR
LIBERTY LANE
HAMPTON, NH 03842
TEL: (603) 926-5911
FAX: (603) 929-1940

Michael D. Dingman, Chairman. Aerospace systems and components; laboratory and medical products. Abex Inc./Fisher Scientific International, Inc. is a public company founded in 1959. It is a technology-based business and acts as a manufacturer and distributor of various products in the aerospace industry and the laboratory and medical areas. The Fisher Scientific Division supplies more than 100,000 items and services to various industrial and medical laboratories on a global basis. Worldwide revenues for 1991: $704 million.

- **Total Employees:** 11,400
- **U.S. Employees Abroad:** 25
- **Countries:** Canada, Germany, India, Mexico.
- **Application Information:** Hiring for most foreign positions is done at the specific country location.
- **Job Categories:** Engineers, Marketing—Health & Medical Supplies, Marketing—Scientific, Research & Development, Sales—Health & Medical Supplies, Sales—Scientific.
- **Language Requirement:** Varies with each posting.

ACCO WORLD CORPORATION

770 South Acco Plaza
Wheeling, IL 60090 USA

RECRUITER: JOAN CORN
DIRECTOR, HUMAN RESOURCES
770 SOUTH ACCO PLAZA
WHEELING, IL 60090
TEL: (708) 541-9500
FAX: (708) 541-0614

Norman H. Wesley, President. Office and computer-related supplies. ACCO World Corporation was founded in 1960 and is a subsidiary of American Brands Inc. of Old Greenwich, Connecticut. It is a leading manufacturer and marketer of office and computer-related items, accessories, and furniture. Worldwide revenues for 1992: $1 billion.

- **Total Employees:** 1,500
- **U.S. Employees Abroad:** 25
- **Countries:** France, Germany, Italy, Japan, Netherlands, United Kingdom, Venezuela.
- **Job Categories:** Management, Marketing, Sales.
- **Language Requirement:** None.

ACUSHNET COMPANY

333 Bridge St.
PO Box 965
Fairhaven, MA 02719-0965 USA

RECRUITER: JACKIE CAHILL
MANAGER, STAFFING
333 BRIDGE ST.
PO BOX 965
FAIRHAVEN, MA 02719-0965
TEL: (508) 979-3122
FAX: (508) 979-3900

John T. Ludes, President and Chairman. Specialty businesses including sporting goods, housewares, and rubber goods. Acushnet Company was founded in 1910 and is a subsidiary of American Brands, Inc. of Old Greenwich, Connecticut. Businesses include: the Titleist and Foot-Joy golf and leisure group; Dollond & Aitchison, an optical goods and services company in the United Kingdom and Europe; Gallaher's distribution businesses (tobacco retailing, candy chains and vending companies throughout the UKI); a rubber division, which makes precision-molded and synthetic rubber products; and Prestige, a leading manufacturer of housewares in the UKI. Worldwide revenues for 1992: $2.2 billion.

- **Total Employees:** 1,760
- **U.S. Employees Abroad:** 40
- **Countries:** Germany, United Kingdom.
- **Application Information:** Most foreign positions are filled internally.
- **Job Categories:** Management, Marketing—Consumer Goods, Sales—Consumer Goods.
- **Language Requirement:** Varies with each posting.

ADVANCE MACHINE COMPANY

14600 21st Ave.
Plymouth, MN 55447 USA

RECRUITER: KENNETH FRIDERES
DIRECTOR, HUMAN RESOURCES
14600 21ST AVE.
PLYMOUTH, MN 55447
TEL: (612) 473-2235
FAX: (612) 475-9718

Edward T. Michalek, Chief Executive Officer. Miscellaneous machinery and equipment for service industries, including floor maintenance equipment. Advance Machine is a private company founded in 1912. Worldwide revenues for 1992: $100 million.

- **Total Employees:** 850
- **U.S. Employees Abroad:** 3
- **Countries:** Singapore, United Kingdom.
- **Application Information:** Hiring for most foreign positions is done at the specific country location.
- **Job Categories:** Manufacturing, Marketing—Industrial, Sales—Industrial.

- **Average Overseas Assignment:** 3-5 years.

- **Language Requirement:** None.

- **Training:** No special training provided.

- **Benefits:** TRAVEL: No defined policy; usually an employee is allowed 2-3 trips home per year; family, if applicable, one per year. HEALTH: UK employees are covered under National Health Program. Singapore employees are carried under standard indemnity plan (payment converted to U.S. dollars). HOUSING: Individually determined. EDUCATION: None offered.

ADVANCED MICRO DEVICES, INC.

901 Thompson Place
Box #3453
Sunnyvale, CA 94088 USA

RECRUITER: FRANK BURNS
PERSONNEL MANAGER
901 THOMPSON PLACE, BOX #3453
SUNNYVALE, CA 94088
TEL: (408) 749-2094
FAX: (408) 749-3009

W. J. Sanders III, Chairman. Integrated circuits. Advanced Micro Devices is a public company founded in 1969. It is the fifth largest manufacturer and marketer of integrated circuits in the United States. Its products include: APX86 microprocessors, programmable logic devices, EPROMS erasable, and programmable read-only memories. Sales offices are located worldwide with manufacturing plants in the United States, Japan, Malaysia, Singapore, Thailand, and the UK. Worldwide revenues for 1992: $1.5 billion.

- **Total Employees:** 1,000

- **U.S. Employees Abroad:** 60

- **Countries:** Eighteen including Japan, Malaysia, Singapore, Thailand, United Kingdom.

- **Application Information:** Most foreign positions are filled internally. Americans are sent abroad for developmental positions only.

- **Job Categories:** Engineers, Manufacturing, Marketing—Electronics, Sales—Electronics.

- **Language Requirement:** None.

- **Training:** No special training provided.

AIRBORNE EXPRESS

3101 Western Ave.
Seattle, WA 98111 USA

RECRUITER: DARBY LANGDON
INTERNATIONAL RECRUITMENT
3101 WESTERN AVE.
SEATTLE, WA 98111
TEL: (206) 285-4600
FAX: (206) 282-2104

Bob Brazier, President. Air transportation service. Airborne Express is a private company founded in 1947. Until 1979 the company was an air-freight forwarder. It was then changed to an air-express business. Airborne is involved with overseas express-shipment companies including Purolator Courier Ltd. of Canada and Overseas Express Couriers. It also has a combined venture with two Japanese firms: Misui & Company and Tonami Transportation. Worldwide revenues for 1992: $1.3 billion.

- **Total Employees:** 11,800

- **U.S. Employees Abroad:** Not available.

- **Countries:** Australia, Hong Kong, Japan, New Zealand, Singapore, Taiwan, United Kingdom.

- **Job Categories:** Management, Marketing, Technicians.

AKZO AMERICA, INC.
300 South Riverside Plaza
Chicago, IL 60606 USA

RECRUITER: FERN A. SOHN
STAFFING/RECRUITMENT
300 SOUTH RIVERSIDE PLAZA
CHICAGO, IL 60606
TEL: (312) 906-7500
FAX: (312) 906-7680

Eugene F. Wilcauskas, President. Chemicals, salt, manmade fibers, coatings, health-care products. AKZO America, Inc. is a major international corporation headquartered in the Netherlands. Its main focus is on providing solutions that enhance the efficiency of processes or the properties of intermediate or finished products. It manufactures and markets basic and specialty chemicals, salt, manmade fibers, coatings, and health-care products. For 1992, AKZO's reasearch and development investment totaled $528 million, or 5.5 percent of worldwide revenues.

- **Total Employees:** 61,800

- **U.S. Employees Abroad:** 18

- **Countries:** Brazil, Canada, Germany, Japan, Netherlands, United Kingdom.

- **Application Information:** Most foreign positions are filled internally or from the parent company.

- **Job Categories:** Management, Marketing—Chemicals, Marketing—Health & Medical Supplies, Product Development, Sales—Chemicals, Sales—Health & Medical Supplies.

- **Language Requirement:** None.

- **Benefits:** All benefits are individually determined.

- **Comments:** The number of Americans reported working abroad varies greatly from quarter to quarter, fluctuating with the number and scope of projects under contract at the time.

ALARM DEVICE MANUFACTURING COMPANY

125 Eileen Way
Syosset, NY 11791 USA

RECRUITER: ALAN WACHTEL
VP, INTERNATIONAL OPERATIONS
125 EILEEN WAY
SYOSSET, NY 11791
TEL: (516) 921-6704

Leo A. Guthart, Chief Executive Officer. Security/alarm devices. Alarm Device Manufacturing Company was founded in 1929 and is a division of the Pittway Corporation of Northbrook, Illinois. It produces communications equipment including security alarms, traffic signals, and sirens.

- **Total Employees:** 1,400
- **U.S. Employees Abroad:** 25
- **Countries:** Australia, Canada, Germany, Greece, Hong Kong, Italy, Singapore, United Kingdom.
- **Job Categories:** Administrative, Marketing—Electronics, Sales—Electronics.

ALBANY INTERNATIONAL CORPORATION

PO Box 1907
Albany, NY 12201 USA

RECRUITER: FRANCIS MCKONE
DIRECTOR, HUMAN RESOURCES
INTERNATIONAL
PO BOX 1907
ALBANY, NY 12201
TEL: (518) 447-6506
FAX: (518) 445-2265

Francis L. McKone, President. Engineered textiles used in the manufacture of paper. Albany International was incorporated in New York in 1895 and was reincorporated in Delaware in August 1983. It is the largest maker of paper machine clothing, the fabric upon which wood pulp is formed. The fabric is then, pressed and dried to produce paper and paperboard. The company operates on a worldwide basis. Worldwide revenues for 1992: $561 million.

- **Total Employees:** 5,700
- **U.S. Employees Abroad:** Not available.
- **Countries:** Australia, Brazil, Canada, Finland, France, Germany, Mexico, Netherlands, Norway, Sweden, United Kingdom.
- **Application Information:** Most foreign positions are filled internally.
- **Job Categories:** Executive Management.
- **Average Overseas Assignment:** 3-5 years.
- **Language Requirement:** Knowledge of local language a plus but not essential.
- **Training:** No special training provided.
- **Benefits:** TRAVEL: Corporate policy covers relocation and travel allowances.

HEALTH: Corporate policy. HOUSING: Corporate policy covers housing subsidies. EDUCATION: Corporate policy covers educational subsidies.

ALBERTO-CULVER COMPANY

2525 Armitage Ave.
Melrose Park, IL 60160 USA

RECRUITER: M. R. LLOYD
ALBERTO-CULVER INTERNATIONAL,
    INC.
2525 ARMITAGE AVE.
MELROSE PARK, IL 60160
TEL: (708) 450-3000
FAX: (708) 450-3300

Leonard H. Lavin, Chairman. Toiletries, professional hair-care products, and food items. Alberto-Culver is a public company founded in 1961. Today, the business is divided into five manufacturing and marketing sections: Domestic Toiletries, Household/Grocery, Professional, and International Divisions, and the Sally Beauty Company. Popular brand names include Alberto VO5 haircare products and Mrs. Dash spice mix. Worldwide revenues for 1992: $1.1 billion.

- **Total Employees:** 5,600
- **U.S. Employees Abroad:** Not available.
- **Countries:** Australia, Belgium, Canada, France, Germany, Hong Kong, Italy, Guatemala, Mexico, Netherlands, Spain, Sweden, United Kingdom, Venezuela.
- **Job Categories:** Administrative, Manufacturing, Marketing—Consumer Goods, Marketing—Food/Food Services.

ALDUS CORPORATION

411 1st Ave., South
Seattle, WA 98104 USA

RECRUITER: MARILYN BECKER
HUMAN RESOURCES
    REPRESENTATIVE
411 1ST AVE., SOUTH
SEATTLE, WA 98104
TEL: (206) 622-5500

Paul Brainerd, Chairman. Microcomputer software. Aldus Corporation is a public company engaged in the design, production, and sale of microcomputer software in the United States and abroad. Worldwide revenues for 1992: $174 million.

- **Total Employees:** 570
- **U.S. Employees Abroad:** Not available.
- **Countries:** Australia, France, Germany, Sweden, United Kingdom.
- **Job Categories:** Executive Management, Design, Engineers, Marketing—Electronics, Sales—Electronics.
- **Language Requirement:** None.
- **Training:** No special training provided.

ALEXANDER & ALEXANDER SERVICES, INC.

1211 Avenue of the Americas
New York, NY 10036 USA

RECRUITER: HARRY LOESHELLE
PERSONNEL DEPARTMENT
1211 AVENUE OF THE AMERICAS
NEW YORK, NY 10036
TEL: (212) 973-4200
FAX: (212) 973-4081

Tinsley H. Irwin, President. Insurance services. Alexander & Alexander Services is a public company founded in 1898. It acts as an independent insurance agency specializing in risk management consulting. Worldwide revenues for 1992: $1.2 billion.

- **Total Employees:** 14,700

- **U.S. Employees Abroad:** 90

- **Countries:** Australia, Bermuda, Brazil, Guatemala, Italy, Japan, Saudi Arabia, United Kingdom.

- **Job Categories:** Agents—Insurance, Brokers—Insurance, Management, Marketing—Financial Services.

ALLEN-BRADLEY COMPANY, INC.

PO Box 2086
Milwaukee, WI 53201 USA

RECRUITER: WILLIAM FLETCHER
SENIOR VP, INTERNATIONAL
PO BOX 2086
MILWAUKEE, WI 53201
TEL: (414) 382-2000
FAX: (414) 382-4444

Don Davis, President. Electrical control products. Allen-Bradley was founded in 1903 and is a subsidiary of the Rockwell International Corporation of El Segundo, California. It is a manufacturer of relays, motor starters, and controllers. It also produces other industrial controls and accessories as well as various electronic components. Worldwide revenues for 1992: $1.4 billion.

- **Total Employees:** 11,200

- **U.S. Employees Abroad:** 35

- **Countries:** Australia, Brazil, Canada, France, Germany, India, Italy, Japan, Mexico, United Kingdom.

- **Job Categories:** Administrative, Marketing—Electronics, Sales—Electronics.

- **Training:** No special training provided.

ALLERGAN, INC.

2525 DuPont Dr.
PO Box 19354
Irvine, CA 92713-9354 USA

RECRUITER: DRINA WILSON
HUMAN RESOURCES
    REPRESENTATIVE
2525 DUPONT DR.
PO BOX 19354
IRVINE, CA 92713-9354
TEL: (714) 752-4500
FAX: (714) 752-4223
FREE: (800) 347-4500

Gavin S. Herbert, Chairman. Pharmaceuticals and skin-care products. Allergan is a public company founded in 1948. It produces and markets prescription and non-prescription eye products including contact lenses and related items. It is also a manufacturer of opthalmic surgical products and pharmaceuticals. Worldwide revenues for 1992: $898 million.

- **Total Employees:** 6,800

- **U.S. Employees Abroad:** 25

- **Countries:** Argentina, Australia, Brazil, Canada, Colombia.

- **Job Categories:** Marketing—Pharmaceuticals, Product Development, Sales—Pharmaceuticals.

- **Language Requirement:** None.

ALLIED-SIGNAL, INC.

101 Columbia Rd.
Morristown, NJ 07962 USA

RECRUITER: ALBERT GESLER
PERSONNEL OFFICER
101 COLUMBIA RD.
MORRISTOWN, NJ 07962
TEL: (201) 455-3587
FAX: (201) 455-2608

Lawrence A. Bossidy, Chairman. Aerospace, automotive, and engineered materials. Allied-Signal is a public company begun in 1920 by *Washington Post* publisher Eugene Meyer and scientist William Nichols. They organized the Allied Chemical & Dye Corporation from five existing companies. It became the Allied Chemical Company in 1958, and in 1985 Allied merged with the Signal Companies to form Allied-Signal. Today, its products are sold in more than 100 countries worldwide. Forty-two percent of the company's aerospace revenue is attributed to the U.S. government. Worldwide revenues for 1992: $12 billion.

- **Total Employees:** 98,000

- **U.S. Employees Abroad:** 75

- **Countries:** Worldwide including Belgium, France, Germany, Japan, Republic of Korea, Spain.

- **Application Information:** Employees are hired in various locations throughout the United States. Hiring locations include California, Michigan, and New Jersey.
- **Job Categories:** Management, Marketing—Automotive, Marketing—Scientific, Sales—Automotive, Sales—Scientific.
- **Language Requirement:** Competency in local language is required.
- **Training:** No special training provided.
- **Benefits:** TRAVEL: Offered. HEALTH: Same coverage as U.S. employees. HOUSING: Offered. EDUCATION: Offered.

ALLIS MINERAL SYSTEMS/ SVEDALA INDUSTRIES, INC.

20965 Crossroads Circle
Waukesha, WI 53186 USA

RECRUITER: WILLIAM G. LENHART
MANAGER, CORPORATE HUMAN
RESOURCES
PO BOX 1655
WAUKESHA, WI 53187-1655
TEL: 414-798-6266
FAX: 414-798-6211

W. A. Guernsy, Vice President. Construction and mining equipment. Allis Mineral Systems is a subsidiary of Switzerland-based Svedala Industries, Inc. Worldwide revenues for 1991: $15 million.

- **Total Employees:** 250
- **U.S. Employees Abroad:** Not available.
- **Countries:** Switzerland, United Kingdom.
- **Job Categories:** Management, Manufacturing, Marketing—Industrial, Sales—Industrial.

ALUMINUM COMPANY OF AMERICA

1501 Alcoa Building
Pittsburgh, PA 15219 USA

RECRUITER: R. W. PORTER
DIRECTOR, PROFESSIONAL
EMPLOYMENT
1501 ALCOA BUILDING
PITTSBURGH, PA 15219
TEL: (412) 553-4545
FAX: (412) 553-4929

Paul H. O'Neil, Chairman. Aluminum chemical/products, metals, chemicals, areospace and industrial products, packaging systems, and electrical products. The Aluminum Company of America (ALCOA), is a public company founded in 1888. It is the largest aluminum company in the world with a production system encompassing operations at every step of the aluminum making process. It supplies aluminum to manufacturers, including producers of soda cans and the new aluminum-intensive automobile. ALCOA manufactures and markets its products in 100 countries. Worldwide revenues for 1992: $9.5 billion.

- **Total Employees:** 60,000
- **U.S. Employees Abroad:** 100
- **Countries:** Australia, Brazil, Jamaica, Japan, Mexico, Norway, Spain, Suriname.
- **Application Information:** Unsolicited resumes accepted in person or by mail.
- **Job Categories:** Management, Marketing—Chemicals, Marketing—Electronics, Marketing—Industrial, Marketing—Scientific, Product Development, Sales—Chemicals, Sales—Electronics, Sales—Industrial, Sales—Scientific.

AM INTERNATIONAL, INC.
333 West Wacker Dr.
Chicago, IL 60606-1265 USA

RECRUITER: BRYAN VALENTINE
VICE PRESIDENT, HUMAN
    RESOURCES
333 WEST WACKER DR., SUITE #900
CHICAGO, IL 60606-1265
TEL: (312) 558-1966
FAX: (312) 558-7965

Merle H. Banta, Chairman. Information-handling equipment and systems. AM International is a public company founded in 1924. Today it produces, sells, and services a variety of graphics equipment and supplies on a worldwide basis. Through its three operating divisions, AM International supplies more than 1,000,000 customers. Worldwide revenues for 1992: $619 million.

- **Total Employees:** 5,022
- **U.S. Employees Abroad:** Not available.
- **Countries:** Australia, Belgium, Canada, Finland, France, Germany, Japan, Mexico, Netherlands, New Zealand, Republic of South Africa, Sweden, Switzerland, United Kingdom.
- **Job Categories:** Marketing—Electronics, Sales—Electronics.

AMAX, INC.
200 Park Ave.
New York, NY 10166 USA

RECRUITER: VIC TAMANINI
HUMAN RESOURCES DEPARTMENT
200 PARK AVE.
NEW YORK, NY 10166
TEL: (212) 856-5963
FAX: (212) 856-6042

Allen Born, President and Chairman. Aluminum and aluminum products. AMAX is a public company founded in 1887. German immigrant Berthold Hochschild arrived in New York in 1884 hoping to trade metals for a German banking firm. By 1887 his successful operation became American Metal, abbreviated AMCO. A merger with Climax Molybdenum founded AMAX in 1957, its official name accepted in 1974. Today, AMAX is the 6th largest U.S. metals company. It oversees affiliated companies, developing a wide scope of natural resources. Subsidiaries include: AMAX Oil & Gas,

Inc.; AMAX Gold, Inc.; Alumax, Inc.; and Climax Metals Company. Worldwide revenues for 1992: $3.7 billion.

- **Total Employees:** 20,200
- **U.S. Employees Abroad:** Not available.
- **Countries:** Australia, Canada, Mexico, New Zealand.
- **Job Categories:** Management, Marketing.

AMDAHL CORPORATION

1250 East Arques Ave.
Sunnyvale, CA 94088 USA

RECRUITER: JANICE NAKAMURA
HUMAN RESOURCES DEPARTMENT
1250 EAST ARQUES AVE.
SUNNYVALE, CA 94088
TEL: (408) 746-6000

John C. Lewis, Chairman. Designs, produces, and services large-scale, high-performance data processing systems; also educational and consulting services. A fairly new company, Amdahl began in 1970 when Gene Amdahl, principal architect of IBM's mainframe computer systems, left to start his own company. Amdahl is now a $2.2-billion manufacturer of IBM-compatible mainframe computers and peripherals. Amdahl was the first company to successfully compete in design and manufacture with IBM computers. This international firm does business in 18 countries. Worldwide revenues for 1992: $2.5 billion.

- **Total Employees:** 9,400
- **U.S. Employees Abroad:** 17
- **Countries:** Eighteen including Australia, Canada, France, Italy, Japan, United Kingdom.
- **Application Information:** Hiring for most foreign positions is done at the specific country location. Direct inquiries to the recruiter's address.
- **Job Categories:** Engineers, Finance, Marketing—Electronics, Sales—Electronics.
- **General Requirements:** Job skills may be required that are not available in the local business unit.
- **Average Overseas Assignment:** 2-3 years.
- **Language Requirement:** Knowledge of local language a plus but not essential.
- **Training:** Language training provided.
- **Benefits:** TRAVEL: The employee, spouse, and children are provided round-trip economy air tickets for the purpose of visiting their original location each anniversary year. HEALTH: While on assignment the employee continues, to the extent possible, on the home country's benefits. HOUSING: The company provides foreign furnished housing and utilities (excluding phone and cable). Comparable U.S. costs are deducted from assignee's salary. EDUCATION: Educational assistance is provided for grades K-12. Costs include tuition and books.
- **Comments:** It is not Amdahl's practice to send entry-level employees abroad.

AMERACE CORPORATION (ELASTIMOLD)

Esna Park
Hackettstown, NJ 07840 USA

RECRUITER: SID ELLIS
HUMAN RESOURCES DIRECTOR
ESNA PARK
HACKETTSTOWN, NJ 07840
TEL: (908) 852-1122
FAX: (908) 852-6168

William K. Hall, President. Chemicals, rubber products, and plastics. Amerace Corporation (Elastimold) is a subsidiary company of Eagle Industries, Incorporated, presently operating in four foreign countries. Worldwide revenues for 1992: $238 million.

- **Total Employees:** 1,836
- **U.S. Employees Abroad:** 30
- **Countries:** Canada, France, Japan, Luxembourg.
- **Job Categories:** Manufacturing, Management, Marketing—Chemicals, Sales—Chemicals.
- **Language Requirement:** None.
- **Training:** No special training provided.
- **Benefits:** All benefits are individually determined.

AMERADA HESS CORPORATION

1185 Avenue of the Americas
New York, NY 10036 USA

RECRUITER: LARRY FOX
MANAGER, EMPLOYEE RELATIONS
1185 AVENUE OF THE AMERICAS
NEW YORK, NY 10036
TEL: (212) 997-8500

Leon Hess, Chairman. Crude oil, natural gas. Amerada Hess is a public company founded in 1920, whose business is the production of oil and natural gas and oil refining. One of its major products is Hess gasoline. Worldwide revenues for 1992: $5.9 billion.

- **Total Employees:** 8,700
- **U.S. Employees Abroad:** 10
- **Countries:** United Kingdom.
- **Job Categories:** Executive Management.

AMERICAN APPRAISAL ASSOCIATES, INC.

100 East Wisconsin Ave.
Milwaukee, WI 53202 USA

RECRUITER: PAULA BARNETT
PERSONNEL ADMINISTRATOR
100 EAST WISCONSIN AVE.
MILWAUKEE, WI 53202
TEL: (414) 271-7240
FAX: (414) 271-1041

Richard Giesen, President. Valuation consulting services. American Appraisal Associates was founded in 1984 and is a subsidiary of R. L. M. Investments, Inc. of Wisconsin. It provides clients with professional appraisal services in the United States and in 12 foreign countries. Worldwide revenues for 1991: $85 million.

- **Total Employees:** 800

- **U.S. Employees Abroad:** Not available.

- **Countries:** Canada, Hong Kong, Italy, Mexico, Philippines, Spain, Thailand, United Kingdom.

- **Job Categories:** Appraisers.

- **Language Requirement:** Varies with each posting.

- **Training:** No special training provided.

- **Benefits:** All benefits are individually determined.

AMERICAN BANKERS INSURANCE GROUP, INC.

11222 Quail Roost Dr.
Miami, FL 33157 USA

RECRUITER: MS. ELLEN RIFKIN
EMPLOYEE STAFFING COORDINATOR
11222 QUAIL ROOST DR.
MIAMI, FL 33157
TEL: (305) 253-2244
FAX: (305) 252-6987

R. Kirk Landon, Chairman. Insurance services. American Bankers Insurance Group was founded in 1947. It is engaged in the underwriting of fire, marine, and casualty insurance. Total worldwide assets 1992: $1.4 billion

- **Total Employees:** 1,761

- **U.S. Employees Abroad:** Not available.

- **Countries:** Canada, United Kingdom.

- **Application Information:** Direct inquiries to Human Resources, 1st floor.

- **Job Categories:** Agents—Insurance, Marketing—Financial Services, Management, Sales—Financial Services.

- **Average Overseas Assignment:** 2-3 years.

- **Language Requirement:** Knowledge of local language a plus but not essential.

- **Training:** No special training provided.

- **Benefits:** TRAVEL: Offered. HEALTH: Offered. HOUSING: Offered. EDUCATION: Offered.

AMERICAN BUILDING MAINTENANCE INDUSTRIES, INC.

50 Freemont St., 26th Floor
San Francisco, CA 94105 USA

RECRUITER: GAYLE HUTT
PERSONNEL ASSISTANT
50 FREEMONT ST., 26TH FLOOR
SAN FRANCISCO, CA 94105
TEL: (415) 597-4500
FAX: (415) 597-7160

Sydney J. Rosenberg, Chairman. Maintenance services (janitorial, elevator, etc.). American Building Maintenance Industries is a public company founded in 1909. Today it provides a variety of building maintenance services in the United States and foreign countries. In 1990, major stockholders Theodore and Sydney Rosenberg opposed taking the company private, causing the stock to take a downward spin. The company remains public. Worldwide revenues for 1992: $761 million.

- **Total Employees:** 35,000
- **U.S. Employees Abroad:** 50
- **Countries:** Canada, Mexico.
- **Application Information:** Hiring for most foreign positions is done at the specific country location.
- **Job Categories:** Administrative, Maintenance.
- **Language Requirement:** None.
- **Training:** No special training provided.
- **Benefits:** All benefits are individually determined.

AMERICAN CANADIAN CARIBBEAN LINE

PO Box 368
Warren, RI 02885 USA

RECRUITER: LARRY WEINER
PERSONNEL DIRECTOR
PO BOX 368
WARREN, RI 02885
TEL: (401) 247-0955
FAX: (401) 245-8303
FREE: (800)556-7450

Luther Blount, President. Small cruise-ship line. American Canadian Caribbean Line is a private company offering cruise ship travel to passengers around the world. Its vessel has a capacity for 90. It travels to various ports-of-call throughout the Caribbean and Central America.

- **Total Employees:** 15
- **U.S. Employees Abroad:** 15
- **Countries:** Antigua-Barbuda, Aruba, Bahamas, Belize, Grenada, Netherlands Antilles, Virgin Islands of the United States.
- **Job Categories:** Captains, Mates, Chefs, Deck Hands, Stewards.

A
M
E
R
I
C
A
N

J
O
B
S

A
B
R
O
A
D

- **General Requirements:** Deck hands should have mechanical knowledge (for engine repair work).
- **Language Requirement:** None.
- **Training:** No special training offered.
- **Benefits:** HEALTH: Employee remains on U.S. coverage

AMERICAN CYANAMID COMPANY

One Cyanamid Plaza
Wayne, NJ 07470 USA

RECRUITER: RON HADLEY
PERSONNEL MANAGER
ONE CYANAMID PLAZA
WAYNE, NJ 07470
TEL: (201) 831-2000
FAX: (201) 831-3151

George J. Sella, Chairman. Biologicals (vaccines), surgical products, chemicals, and consumer products. American Cyanamid is a public company begun in 1907 by civil engineer Frank Washburn. He began producing calcium cyanamide, the world's first synthetic fertilizer, in Maine. Today the company is a global leader and supplier of biologicals and surgical supplies. The company's focus is on research-driven agricultural, medical, and chemical businesses. It now markets its products in 135 countries. Worldwide revenues for 1992: $5.2 billion.

- **Total Employees:** 33,000
- **U.S. Employees Abroad:** 100
- **Countries:** Australia, Austria, Brazil, Canada, Denmark, France, Germany, Japan, Kenya, Philippines, Portugal, Spain, Taiwan, Thailand, United Kingdom.
- **Job Categories:** Management, Marketing—Health & Medical Supplies, Marketing—Pharmaceuticals, Sales—Health & Medical Supplies, Sales—Pharmaceuticals.
- **Language Requirement:** Competency in local language required.
- **Training:** No special training provided.
- **Benefits:** All benefits are individually determined.

AMERICAN EXPRESS BANK, LTD.

American Express Tower
World Financial Center
New York, NY 10285 USA

RECRUITER: CRAIG DINSELL
DIRECTOR, HUMAN RESOURCES
AMERICAN EXPRESS TOWER, WORLD FINANCIAL CENTER
NEW YORK, NY 10285
TEL: (212) 298-3924
FAX: (212) 619-7352

Steven D. Goldstein, President. International banking services. American Express Bank, Ltd. is a subsidiary of the American Express Company of New York City. It provides banking services to clients in 83 locations in 40 countries. Worldwide total assets for 1991: $14.4 billion.

- **Total Employees:** 4,000
- **U.S. Employees Abroad:** 75
- **Countries:** Worldwide including Hong Kong, Japan, Mexico, United Kingdom.
- **Job Categories:** Executive Management, Finance, Marketing—Financial Services, Sales—Financial Services.
- **General Requirements:** Usually must be a current employee of the company in order to qualify for overseas assignment.
- **Language Requirement:** Varies with each posting.

AMERICAN EXPRESS COMPANY—TRAVEL RELATED SERVICES

TRS Services
American Express Tower
World Financial Center
New York, NY 10285 USA

RECRUITER: BARBARA KURZ
DIRECTOR, MANAGEMENT
RESOURCES
AMERICAN EXPRESS TOWER
WORLD FINANCIAL CENTER
NEW YORK, NY 10285
TEL: (212) 640-5548
FAX: (212) 619-9769

Jonathan S. Linen, President, American Express TRS. Diversified travel-related and financial services. American Express is a public company that was started in 1850 by Henry Wells and two others. (When company directors refused to move the operation to California in 1852, Wells and VP William Fargo formed Wells Fargo in California.) While traveling in Europe, Fargo experienced a great deal of trouble cashing letters of credit. As a result, Travelers Cheques were introduced in 1891 and services for Americans traveling abroad soon followed. In 1959, the American Express card was introduced. Today, this worldwide company is the largest U.S. diversified financial services organization. It operates throughout the United States and has offices in more than 160 countries. Worldwide revenues for 1992: $27 billion.

- **Total Employees:** 106,000
- **U.S. Employees Abroad:** 125
- **Countries:** Worldwide including Australia, Brazil, Canada, Chile, France, Germany, Hong Kong, India, Japan, Netherlands, United Kingdom, Venezuela.
- **Job Categories:** Executive Management, Finance, Marketing—Financial Services, Marketing—Travel, Sales—Financial Services, Sales—Travel.
- **Language Requirement:** Varies with each posting.
- **Comments:** Travel Related Services (TRS) is a division of American Express.

AMERICAN GREETINGS CORPORATION

10500 American Rd.
Cleveland, OH 44144 USA

RECRUITER: RON NOVACK
EMPLOYMENT MANAGER
10500 AMERICAN RD.
CLEVELAND, OH 44144
TEL: (216) 252-7300
FAX: (216) 252-6519

Morry Weiss, President. Greeting cards and related products. American Greetings Corporation is a public company founded in 1906. Today its products are sold in 97,000 outlets in more than 50 countries. These items include cards, gift wrap, hair-care products, stationery, and candles. Worldwide revenues for 1992: $1.7 billion. Foreign revenues for 1992: $291.8 million

- **Total Employees:** 21,400

- **U.S. Employees Abroad:** 25

- **Countries:** Fifty including Canada, France, Mexico, United Kingdom.

- **Job Categories:** Management, Marketing—Consumer Goods, Sales—Consumer Goods.

- **Comments:** American Greetings also has licensees located in more than 50 countries.

AMERICAN HOME PRODUCTS CORPORATION

685 3rd Ave.
New York, NY 10017 USA

RECRUITER: CRAIG PORTER
HUMAN RESOURCES ADMINISTRATOR
685 3RD AVE.
NEW YORK, NY 10017
TEL: (212) 878-5379
FAX: (212) 878-5012

John R. Stafford, Chairman. Over-the-counter medicines and prescription drugs, medical supplies, and food products. American Home Products Corporation is a public company founded in 1926. It produces and sells health-care and consumer products, hospital and medical supplies, and food items. Brand names include Dimetapp, a cold/allergy liquid, and Chef Boyardee food products. It operates on a worldwide basis. Worldwide revenues for 1992: $7.9 billion.

- **Total Employees:** 50,816

- **U.S. Employees Abroad:** 110

- **Countries:** Argentina, Australia, Canada, Chile, France, Germany, India, Italy, Japan, Kenya, Switzerland, Venezuela, United Kingdom.

- **Job Categories:** Chemical Engineers, Marketing—Food/Food Services, Marketing—Health & Medical Supplies, Marketing—Pharmaceuticals, Public Health Administrators, Sales—Food/Food Services, Sales—Health & Medical Supplies, Sales—Pharmaceuticals.

AMERICAN INTERNATIONAL GROUP

70 Pine St.
New York, NY 10270 USA

RECRUITER: DIRECTOR OF
PERSONNEL
INTERNATIONAL RECRUITMENT
70 PINE ST.
NEW YORK, NY 10270
TEL: (212) 770-7000
FAX: (212) 770-3576

Maurice R. Greenberg, President. Insurance services. American International Group (AIG), is a public company, which was originally started in Shanghai in 1919. Cornelius Starr founded the C.V. Starr and Company and moved its operations to the United States in 1941, prior to WWII. In 1954, multinational companies were added and an international benefits pool was established to provide coverage to employees as they moved from country to country. Today, AIG is the largest international insurer in the United States, and the only one founded abroad. This international company has 424 offices in the United States and abroad. Worldwide revenues for 1992: $18.4 billion.

- **Total Employees:** 33,000

- **U.S. Employees Abroad:** 45

- **Countries:** People's Republic of China, Hong Kong, Hungary, Japan, Malaysia, Saudi Arabia, Singapore.

- **Job Categories:** Accountants, Insurance, Brokers—Insurance, Management.

AMERICAN MANAGEMENT SYSTEMS, INC.

1777 North Kent St.
Arlington, VA 22209 USA

RECRUITER: ELIZABETH GROELLER
STAFFING/RECRUITMENT
1777 NORTH KENT ST.
ARLINGTON, VA 22209
TEL: (703) 841-6000
FAX: (703) 841-6146

Charles Rossotti, Chairman. Information technology and systems, engineering services, design and service of computer systems. American Management Systems is a public company founded in 1970. Its mission is to help clients make productive use of computer technology. Targeted markets include financial service institutions, insurance companies, state and local governments, colleges and universities, and other large institutions and companies. Worldwide operating revenues for 1992: $296 million.

- **Total Employees:** 3,200

- **U.S. Employees Abroad:** 25

- **Countries:** Belgium, Canada, Germany, United Kingdom.

- **Job Categories:** Marketing—Electronics, Management, Sales—Electronics.

AMERICAN PRESIDENT COMPANIES, LTD.

1800 Harrison St.
Oakland, CA 94612 USA

RECRUITER: MIKE MAHR
PERSONNEL DIRECTOR
1800 HARRISON ST.
OAKLAND, CA 94612
TEL: (415) 272-8000
FAX: (510) 272-8679

W. Bruce Seaton, Chairman. Transportation and distribution of intermodal containers by sea, rail, and truck worldwide. Also sells real estate. American President Companies, Ltd. was begun in 1848. William Aspinwall founded the Pacific Mail Steamship Company, planning to launch the first mail shipping line between California and Panama. Various changes occurred over the years, and in 1926 the firm was acquired by the Dollar Steamship Company. In 1938, the Maritime Commission forced the Dollar family to transfer control of the company to the government, and it was reorganized as American President Lines. It now offers a worldwide, integrated transportation system. Its fleet of 23 containerships and a network of feeder vessels serves more than 3,500 delivery points on five continents. Worldwide revenues for 1992: $2.5 billion.

- **Total Employees:** 4,994
- **U.S. Employees Abroad:** Not available.
- **Countries:** Canada, Guam, Hong Kong, Japan, Republic of Korea, Pakistan, Philippines, Singapore, Taiwan, Thailand.
- **Job Categories:** Management, Marketing, Sales.

AMERICAN STANDARD, INC.

1114 Avenue of the Americas
New York, NY 10036 USA

RECRUITER: STEVE WILSON
PERSONNEL DEPARTMENT
1114 AVENUE OF THE AMERICAS
NEW YORK, NY 10036
TEL: (212) 703-5100
FAX: (212) 703-5352

Emmanuel A. Kampouris, President. Suppliers of air conditioning, heating, and plumbing products; producer of braking devices and control systems for large trucks and buses. American Standard was founded in 1929 and is now a subsidiary of ASI Holding Corporation of New York. The company is a major supplier of plumbing products including vitreous china fixtures and bathroom accessories. Operations are in the United States, Canada, and 32 European countries. Worldwide revenues for 1992: $3.5 billion.

- **Total Employees:** 32,900
- **U.S. Employees Abroad:** Not available.
- **Countries:** Austria, Belgium, Brazil, Canada, Costa Rica, Dominican Republic, France, Germany, Guatemala, Israel, Italy, Mexico, Netherlands, Philippines, Thailand, United Kingdom.
- **Job Categories:** Executive Management, Finance, Marketing, Sales.

AMERICAN TOOL COMPANIES, INC.

301 South 13th St.
Lincoln, NE 68508 USA

RECRUITER: SHERRY SAVENER
HUMAN RESOURCES DEPARTMENT
301 SOUTH 13TH ST.
LINCOLN, NE 68508
TEL: (402) 435-3300
FAX: (402) 435-3619

A. D. Petersen, Chief Executive Officer. Hand tools. American Tool is a private company founded in 1929. The business concentrates on the production of hand and edge tools. Worldwide revenues for 1992: $65 million.

- **Total Employees:** 818
- **U.S. Employees Abroad:** Not available.
- **Countries:** Australia, Belgium, Canada, France, Germany, Netherlands, Taiwan.
- **Job Categories:** Accountants, Management, Marketing—Consumer Goods.
- **Training:** No special training provided.

AMERICAN UNIFORM COMPANY

PO Box 2130
Cleveland, TN 37320 USA

RECRUITER: DOUG SMITH
PERSONNEL OFFICER
PO BOX 2130
CLEVELAND, TN 37320
TEL: (615) 476-6561
FAX: (615) 479-6241

Gary K. Smith, Chief Executive Officer. Washable work clothing. American Uniform was founded in 1932 and is a subsidiary of the Steiner Corporation. Worldwide revenues for 1992: $95 million.

- **Total Employees:** 1,500
- **U.S. Employees Abroad:** 4
- **Countries:** Canada, Italy, United Kingdom.
- **Job Categories:** Management.
- **Average Overseas Assignment:** 5 years or more.
- **Language Requirement:** Competency in local language required.
- **Training:** Basic orientation (1-30 days) provided.
- **Benefits:** TRAVEL: Negotiable. HEALTH: Comprehensive health coverage offered. HOUSING: None offered. EDUCATION: None offered.
- **Comments:** The number of Americans reported working abroad varies from quarter to quarter, fluctuating with the number and scope of projects under contract at the time.

AMERIWOOD, INC.

PO Box 470
Dowagiac, MI 49047 USA

RECRUITER: RICHARD COMPTON
STAFFING/RECRUITMENT
4301 CANAL SW
GRANVILLE, MI 49418
TEL: (616) 530-6300
FAX: (616) 530-3044

Joseph J. Miglore, President. Wood furniture and related products. Ameriwood, Inc. is a public company founded in 1915. It was formerly known as the Rospatch Corporation. It is enagaged as a manufacturer of converted paper products and household furniture made of wood. Worldwide revenues for 1992: $87.7 million.

- **Total Employees:** 650
- **U.S. Employees Abroad:** 18
- **Countries:** Canada, Japan, Mexico.
- **Job Categories:** Management, Marketing, Sales.
- **Language Requirement:** None.
- **Training:** No special training provided.

AMETEK, INC.

Station Square
Paoli, PA 19301 USA

RECRUITER: JAMES WALSH
PERSONNEL DIRECTOR
STATION SQUARE
PAOLI, PA 19301
TEL: (215) 647-2121
FAX: (215) 296-3412

Walter Blankley, President. Instruments, motors, and engineered materials. Ametek was first incorporated in Delaware in 1930 as American Machines & Metals, Incorporated. Its present name was adopted in 1961. The company develops, designs, and manufactures a diverse line of products including electro-mechanical and precision instruments and industrial materials. It has plants in 14 states and four foreign countries. Worldwide revenues for 1991: $715.1 million.

- **Total Employees:** 6,100
- **U.S. Employees Abroad:** 100
- **Countries:** Canada, Denmark, Italy, Mexico, United Kingdom.
- **Job Categories:** Management, Manufacturing, Marketing—Industrial, Sales—Industrial.
- **Average Overseas Assignment:** 2-3 years.
- **Language Requirement:** None.
- **Training:** No special training provided.
- **Benefits:** Vary with each assignment.

AMGEN, INC.

1840 DeHavilland Dr.
Thousand Oaks, CA 91320-1789
USA

RECRUITER: SALLY FOX
VP, HUMAN RESOURCES
1840 DEHAVILLAND DR.
THOUSAND OAKS, CA 91320-1789
TEL: (805) 499-5725
FAX: (805) 498-8131

Gordon M. Binder, Chairman. Biotechnology products. Amgen is a public company founded in 1980. It began as Applied Molecular Genetics. Today it is the largest independent biotechnology venture in the United States. Two recent products developed are Epogen, a red blood cell stimulator, and Neupogen, an infection-fighting white blood cell stimulant. Neupogen is used in chemotherapy treatment. Amgen has offices in the United States and abroad. Worldwide revenues for 1992: $1.1 billion.

- **Total Employees:** 1,179

- **U.S. Employees Abroad:** 20

- **Countries:** Belgium, Canada, France, Germany, Italy, Netherlands, Spain, Switzerland, United Kingdom.

- **Job Categories:** Marketing—Scientific, Product Development, Sales—Scientific.

AMOCO CORPORATION

200 East Randolph Dr.
Chicago, IL 60601 USA

RECRUITER: CINDY REDDING
SENIOR HUMAN RESOURCES
REPRESENTATIVE
200 EAST RANDOLPH DR.
CHICAGO, IL 60601
TEL: (312) 856-3200
FAX: (312) 616-0395

H. Laurance Fuller, President. Petroleum and chemicals. Amoco Corporation was begun in 1882 when John D. Rockefeller organized the Standard Oil Trust. In 1889 Standard Oil organized Standard Oil of Indiana in Chicago. A strong retail marketing organization was instrumental in building the company. Standard changed its name to Amoco in 1985, and today it operates in more than 40 countries. It is the 2nd largest U.S. natural gas producer, the 7th largest U.S. crude oil producer and ranks as the 9th largest petroleum company in the western world. Worldwide revenues for 1992: $25.3 billion.

- **Total Employees:** 54,000

- **U.S. Employees Abroad:** 400

- **Countries:** Worldwide including Argentina, Australia, Austria, Azerbaijan, Belgium, Brazil, Canada, People's Republic of China, Congo, Denmark, Egypt, Gabon, Germany, Hong Kong, Indonesia, Italy, Japan, Republic of Korea, Malta, Mauritania, Myanmar, Netherlands, Norway, Oman, Pakistan, Singapore, Switzerland, Taiwan, Thailand, Trinidad and Tobago, Tunisia, United Kingdom, Yugoslavia.

- **Application Information:** Hiring for most foreign positions is done at the specific country location.

- **Job Categories:** Management, Marketing—Chemicals, Marketing—Petroleum/Natural Gas, Sales—Chemicals, Sales—Petroleum/Natural Gas.

- **Average Overseas Assignment:** 3-5 years.

- **Language Requirement:** Knowledge of local language a plus but not essential.

- **Training:** Basic orientation (1-30 days) provided; this includes cross-cultural orientation.

- **Benefits:** TRAVEL: Annual home leave is provided for employees. HEALTH: Same coverage as U.S. employees. HOUSING: Individually determined. EDUCATION: Tuition is offered for children in grades K-12; college is not included.

AMP, INC.

441 Friendship Rd.
Harrisburg, PA 17111 USA

RECRUITER: DONALD PROWELL
DIRECTOR, EMPLOYMENT/EMPLOYEE
RELATIONS
441 FRIENDSHIP RD.
HARRISBURG, PA 17111
TEL: (717) 564-0100
FAX: (717) 780-7019

Harold Mcinnes, Chairman. Electrical connectors and components. AMP was started in 1941, when U.A. Whitaker founded Aircraft-Marine Products in Elizabeth, New Jersey, just two months prior to the attack on Pearl Harbor. The company flourished as a supplier of parts for aircraft, etc., but experienced a rapid decline after the war ended. International expansion was started in the 1950s, and AMP now operates in 24 countries. It is the world's largest supplier of electrical and electronic components. Over 50 percent of sales and earnings come from international operations. Worldwide revenues for 1992: $3.3 billion.

- **Total Employees:** 24,000

- **U.S. Employees Abroad:** 100

- **Countries:** Argentina, Australia, Austria, Brazil, Denmark, Finland, France, Germany, Hong Kong, Ireland, Italy, Japan, Republic of Korea, Mexico, Netherlands, New Zealand, Norway, Portugal, Singapore, Spain, Sweden, Switzerland, Taiwan, United Kingdom.

- **Job Categories:** Engineers, Manufacturing, Marketing—Electronics.

- **Average Overseas Assignment:** 2-3 years.

- **Language Requirement:** None.

- **Training:** No special training provided.

- **Benefits:** All benefits are individually determined.

AMPEX CORPORATION

401 Broadway
Redwood City, CA 94063 USA

RECRUITER: MARILYN METZ
INTERNATIONAL RECRUITMENT
401 BROADWAY
REDWOOD CITY, CA 94063
TEL: (415) 367-4623
FAX: (415) 367-2905

Thomas J. Wheeler, President. Audio and video equipment for use in recording audio, video, or other signals. Ampex has been a privately held company since 1987. It was founded in San Francisco in 1944 by Alexander Poniatoff, an electrical engineer born in Russia. Its first products included radar motors and generators for the U.S. Navy. In 1956 the firm introduced the world's first commercial videotape recorder. Today, Ampex is the world's leading professional television equipment company. It derives half of its revenues from outside the United States and operates businesses in 115 countries. Worldwide revenues for 1992: $430 million.

- **Total Employees:** 2,700
- **U.S. Employees Abroad:** 70
- **Countries:** Argentina, Australia, Brazil, Canada, Israel, Italy, Japan, Mexico, Taiwan.
- **Job Categories:** Finance, Manufacturing, Marketing—Electronics, Sales—Electronics.
- **Average Overseas Assignment:** Less than two years.
- **Language Requirement:** None.
- **Training:** No special training provided.

AMR/AMERICAN AIRLINES

4333 Amon Carter
MO 5115
Fort Worth, TX 76155 USA

RECRUITER: LINDA K. SAPITSKY
MANAGING DIRECTOR, INT'L
PERSONNEL
4333 AMON CARTER MO 5115
FORT WORTH, TX 76155
TEL: (817) 967-1424
FAX: (817) 967-4380

Robert L. Crandall, President and Chairman. Airline, computer programming, travel information services, and airport ground handling contractors. This company had its beginning in 1929 when Sherman Fairchild's Fairchild Aviation Corporation started a New York City holding company called the Aviation Corporation. Within a year they owned 85 small airline companies. In 1934, postal regulations forced the company to split off its transportation divisions, and American Airlines was a result of this split. American now flies to 187 cities in the United States and abroad. Worldwide revenues for 1992: $14.4 billion.

- **Total Employees:** 130,000
- **U.S. Employees Abroad:** 130

- **Countries:** France, Germany, Hong Kong, Japan, United Kingdom.
- **Application Information:** Due to current industry status, external hiring is limited.
- **Salaries:** $20,000-$75,000.
- **Job Categories:** Airport Management, Airline Workers, Computer Programmers.
- **General Requirements:** Most foreign positions are filled internally as they require familiarity with the company's structure, policies, and procedures.
- **Average Overseas Assignment:** 3-5 years.
- **Language Requirement:** None.
- **Training:** Basic orientation (1-30 days) provided.
- **Benefits:** TRAVEL: Two home leave trips per year, cost of living, relocation assistance, miscellaneous allowance, home or rental support. HEALTH: Same coverage as U.S. employees. HOUSING: Housing contribution; call recruitment officer for details. EDUCATION: K-12 school tuition at American schools abroad paid in full by company.

ANACOMP, INC.

PO Box 40888
Indianapolis, IN 46240 USA

RECRUITER: PAT WILKINS
PERSONNEL REPRESENTATIVE
PO BOX 40888
INDIANAPOLIS, IN 46240
TEL: (317) 844-9666
FAX: (317) 848-1360

Louis P. Ferrero, President and Chairman. Information management services. Anacomp is a public company founded in 1968. Its clients include governments, industries, banks, financial institutions, and other large businesses around the world. Major products include Sunflex magnetics products and the XFP 2000 COM recorder. Worldwide revenues for 1992: $629 million.

- **Total Employees:** 7,500
- **U.S. Employees Abroad:** Not available.
- **Countries:** Japan.
- **Job Categories:** Administrative, Marketing, Sales.

ANDREW CORPORATION

10500 West 153rd St.
Orland Park, IL 60462 USA

RECRUITER: ROD MOSS
EMPLOYMENT MANAGER
10500 WEST 153RD ST.
ORLAND PARK, IL 60462
TEL: (708) 349-3300
FAX: (708) 349-5943

Floyd L. English, President. Electronic communication products and systems. Andrew Corporation is a public company founded in 1937. It supplies electronic communication products and systems to clients around the world. These include commercial, government, and military markets. Products include radar and communications reconnaissance systems and weather navigational radar antennas. Worldwide revenues for 1991: $416.2 million.

- **Total Employees:** 2,700
- **U.S. Employees Abroad:** Not available.
- **Countries:** Australia, Brazil, Canada, France, Italy, Japan, Mexico, Switzerland, United Kingdom.
- **Application Information:** Most foreign positions are filled internally.
- **Job Categories:** Administrative, Marketing—Electronics, Sales—Electronics.

ANSELL INTERNATIONAL

2500 Corporate Exchange Dr.,
Suite #200
Columbus, OH 43231 USA

RECRUITER: LYNN PHILLIPS
SENIOR VP, HR/ADMINISTRATION
2500 CORPORATE EXCHANGE DR.,
    SUITE #200
COLUMBUS, OH 43231
TEL: (614) 891-0033
FAX: (614) 891-2816

Rubber and plastic products. Ansell International was founded in 1981 and is a subsidiary of Pacific Dunlop, Ltd., of Australia. It manufactures rubber and related products. Worldwide revenues for 1992: $150 million.

- **Total Employees:** 1,000
- **U.S. Employees Abroad:** 20
- **Countries:** Australia, France, Germany, Hong Kong, Sri Lanka, United Kingdom.
- **Job Categories:** Management, Marketing, Sales.
- **Language Requirement:** None.

ANTHONY INDUSTRIES

4900 S. Eastern Ave.
Los Angeles, CA 90040 USA

RECRUITER: PERSONNEL OFFICER
PERSONNEL DEPARTMENT,
    INTERNATIONAL DIV.
4900 SOUTH EASTERN AVE.
LOS ANGELES, CA 90040
TEL: (213) 724-2800
FAX: (213) 724-0470

B. I. Forester, Chairman. Sporting goods and supplies. Anthony Industries is a public company founded in 1949. It is a worldwide manufacturer and distributor of sporting goods with name brands including Olin skis and Shakespeare fishing tackle. Worldwide revenues for 1992: $402 million.

- **Total Employees:** 3,500
- **U.S. Employees Abroad:** 10

- **Countries:** Australia, Belgium, Canada, Germany, Hong Kong, Japan, Netherlands, Norway, United Kingdom.

- **Application Information:** Hiring for most foreign positions is done at the specific country location.

- **Job Categories:** Administrative, Manufacturing.

- **Language Requirement:** None.

- **Training:** No special training provided.

- **Benefits:** All benefits are individually determined.

AON CORPORATION

123 North Wacker Dr.
Chicago, IL 60606 USA

RECRUITER: CAROL WOLF
HUMAN RESOURCES
REPRESENTATIVE
123 NORTH WACKER DR.
CHICAGO, IL 60606
TEL: (312) 701-3000

Patrick G. Ryan, President. Insurance and financial services. Aon Corporation is a public company founded in 1922. It offers clients services in the insurance or financial markets. It provides brokerage and consulting services on an international basis. Worldwide revenues for 1992: $3.3 billion.

- **Total Employees:** 11,000

- **U.S. Employees Abroad:** Not available.

- **Countries:** Australia, Canada, Germany, Japan, United Kingdom.

- **Job Categories:** Agents—Insurance, Brokers—Securities & Financial, Office Management, Marketing—Financial Services.

- **Training:** No special training provided.

APPLE COMPUTER, INC.

20525 Mariani Ave., MS 38-A
Cupertino, CA 95014 USA

RECRUITER: DIRECTOR
PROFESSIONAL STAFFING
20525 MARIANI AVE., MS 39-A
CUPERTINO, CA 95014
TEL: (408) 996-1010
FAX: (408) 974-6944

John Sculley, Chairman. Personal computers, peripherals, and software. Apple Computer is a public company founded in 1976. After dropping out of college, Steven Jobs and Stephen Wozniak began the Apple business in the Santa Clara Valley, originally to sell circuit boards. However, plans changed rapidly when Job's first sales call resulted in an order for 50 fully assembled microcomputers. The Apple I was produced in Job's garage, and they sold it without a monitor, keyboard, or casing. By 1990, Apple had become the 2nd largest producer of personal computers in the world.

Today, the company has manufacturing facilities in California, Singapore, and the United Kingdom. Business is transacted in more than 120 countries. Worldwide revenues for 1992: $7.2 billion.

- **Total Employees:** 14,500
- **U.S. Employees Abroad:** 60
- **Countries:** Australia, Belgium, Canada, France, Germany, Hong Kong, Italy, Japan, Mexico, Netherlands, Singapore, Spain, Sweden, United Kingdom.
- **Job Categories:** Management, Manufacturing, Marketing—Electronics, Sales—Electronics.

APPLIED BIOSCIENCE INTERNATIONAL, INC.

210 Carnegie Center
Princeton, NJ 08540 USA

RECRUITER: DIRECTOR
INTERNATIONAL HUMAN RESOURCES
210 CARNEGIE CENTER
PRINCETON, NJ 08540
TEL: (609) 452-9000
FAX: (609) 452-0284

K. H. Harper, President. Physical and biological research and development for commercial markets. Applied Bioscience International Inc. (ABI) is a public company founded in 1987. It was formed as a holding company for two wholly-owned toxicology laboratory subsidiaries: Bio/dynamics, Inc. of New Jersey and Life Science Research Limited in Suffolk, United Kingdom. Worldwide revenues for 1992: $181 million.

- **Total Employees:** 2,200
- **U.S. Employees Abroad:** Not available.
- **Countries:** Australia, Germany, United Kingdom.
- **Job Categories:** Chemists, Engineers, Management, Marketing—Scientific.

APPLIED MATERIALS, INC.

3050 Bowers Ave.
Santa Clara, CA 95054 USA

RECRUITER: AL GITSON
HUMAN RESOURCES
3050 BOWERS AVE.
SANTA CLARA, CA 95054
TEL: (408) 727-5555
FAX: (408) 235-4586

James W. Bagley, President. Systems for water fabrication, dry plasma etching, and other related systems. Applied Materials, Inc. is a public company founded in 1967. It is a global manufacturer of various systems including water fabrication, chemical vapor deposition, physical vapor deposition, and epitaxial deposition. Major products include Precision 5000 CVD and Endura 5500 PVD. Worldwide revenues for 1992: $800 million.

- **Total Employees:** 2,651

- **U.S. Employees Abroad:** Not available.
- **Countries:** People's Republic of China, Japan, United Kingdom.
- **Job Categories:** Manufacturing, Marketing—Scientific, Research & Development, Sales—Scientific.
- **Training:** No special training provided.

ARBY'S, INC.
6917 Collins Ave.
Miami, FL 33141 USA

RECRUITER: JOSEPH LANGTEAU
PERSONNEL DIRECTOR
6917 COLLINS AVE.
MIAMI, FL 33141
TEL: (305) 866-1904
FAX: (305) 866-0252

Frank J. Belatti, President. Operates fast-food restaurants. Arby's is a private company founded in 1964. It operates fast-food franchises and currently has 2,250 locations in the United States and 110 in foreign countries. Worldwide revenues for 1991: $90.3 million.

- **Total Employees:** 8,500
- **U.S. Employees Abroad:** 30
- **Countries:** Worldwide including Canada, France, Germany, Japan.
- **Job Categories:** Administrative, Management, Management Training, Marketing—Food/Food Services, Sales—Food/Food Services.
- **Language Requirement:** Varies with each posting.

ARCHER-DANIELS-MIDLAND COMPANY
PO Box 1470
Decatur, IL 62525 USA

RECRUITER: HOWARD BUFFETT
VP, EMPLOYEE RELATIONS
PO BOX 1470
DECATUR, IL 62525
TEL: (217) 424-5235
FAX: (217) 424-5307

Dwayne O. Andreas, Chairman. Agricultural products, oilseeds, corn, wheat, barley, rice, sugarcane, and milo. A-D-M is a public company founded in 1902. The business is involved in procuring, transporting, storing, processing, and merchandising agricultural products. It operates 121 processing plants in the United States and has an ownership interest in 25 foreign plants. The grain operations are scattered throughout the contiguous 48 U.S. states, Canada, and seven European countries. Worldwide net revenues for 1992: $9.6 billion.

- **Total Employees:** 13,500
- **U.S. Employees Abroad:** Not available.
- **Countries:** Canada, Netherlands, United Kingdom.

- **Application Information:** Hiring for most foreign positions is done at the specific country location.
- **Job Categories:** Administrative, Manufacturing, Marketing—Agricultural, Office Management, Plant Managers.
- **Language Requirement:** Competency in local language required.
- **Training:** Basic orientation (1-30 days) provided.
- **Benefits:** All benefits are individually determined.

ARCO COAL COMPANY

555 17th St.
Denver, CO 80202 USA

RECRUITER: EFFIE MACGOWAN
VP, EMPLOYEE RELATIONS
DEPARTMENT
555 17TH ST.
DENVER, CO 80202
TEL: (303) 293-4900
FAX: (303) 293-4186

Anthony G. Fernandez, President. Mining. ARCO Coal is a subsidiary of the Atlantic Richfield Company. ARCO is involved in the development of bituminous coal or lignite surface mines and the production of bituminous coal or lignite at those mines.

- **Total Employees:** 1,300
- **U.S. Employees Abroad:** 25
- **Countries:** Australia, Canada, Mexico, United Kingdom.
- **Job Categories:** Administrative, Management.
- **Average Overseas Assignment:** 2-3 years.
- **Language Requirement:** Knowledge of local language a plus but not essential.
- **Training:** No special training provided.
- **Benefits:** Individually determined.

ARCO INTERNATIONAL OIL AND GAS COMPANY

PO Box 260888
Plano, TX 75026-0888 USA

RECRUITER: KENNETH HAIGLER
HUMAN RESOURCES DEPARTMENT
PO BOX 260888
PLANO, TX 75026-0888
TEL: (214) 754-4011
FAX: (214) 754-4057

James A. Middleton, President. Petroleum refining; gasoline sales. ARCO International Oil and Gas Company was founded in 1870 and is a division of the Atlantic Richfield Company based in Los Angeles, California. ARCO Oil and Gas operates oil and gas field properties.

- **Total Employees:** 5,200
- **U.S. Employees Abroad:** Not available.

- **Countries:** Australia, Canada, Mexico, United Kingdom.

- **Job Categories:** Engineers, Management, Marketing—Petroleum/Natural Gas.

- **Language Requirement:** None.

- **Training:** No special training provided.

- **Benefits:** All benefits are individually determined.

ARETHUSA OFFSHORE

PO Box 2085
Houston, TX 77252 USA

RECRUITER: JIM TRABOR
STAFFING/RECRUITMENT
PO BOX 2085
HOUSTON, TX 77252
TEL: (713) 226-6141
FAX: (713) 226-6005

Offshore drilling and petroleum exploration. Arethusa Offshore is a subsidiary of Zapata Corporation of Houston, Texas. It is engaged in offshore drilling and petroleum exploration on a global basis.

- **Total Employees:** 5,000

- **U.S. Employees Abroad:** 40

- **Countries:** Canada, Costa Rica, Mexico, Nigeria, United Kingdom.

- **Job Categories:** Engineers, Management, Marketing—Petroleum/Natural Gas.

- **Language Requirement:** Varies with each posting.

ARMCO, INC.

300 Interpace Pkwy.
Parsippany, NJ 07054 USA

RECRUITER: JOHN BILICH
HUMAN RESOURCES
REPRESENTATIVE
300 INTERPACE PKWY.
PARSIPPANY, NJ 07054
TEL: (201) 316-5200
FAX: (201) 316-5203

Robert E. Boni, Chairman. Steel and related products. Armco is a public company founded in 1899. It manufactures and sells stainless, electrical, and carbon steel products, including drilling and production equipment process pumps, and process control equipment. It operates on a worldwide basis. Worldwide revenues for 1992: $2.1 billion.

- **Total Employees:** 230,000

- **U.S. Employees Abroad:** 325

- **Countries:** Belgium, Brazil, Canada, Chile, Italy, Peru, Philippines, United Kingdom.

- **Job Categories:** Engineers, Management, Marketing, Sales.

ARMOUR SWIFT ECKRICH, INC.

2001 Butterfield Rd.
Downers Grove, IL 60515 USA

RECRUITER: VAUGHN LARRISON
MANAGER, SWIFT INTERNATIONAL
2001 BUTTERFIELD RD.
DOWNERS GROVE, IL 60515
TEL: (708) 512-1000
FAX: (708) 512-1746

Leroy D. Lochman, President and Chief Operating Officer. Meat, poultry, and food products. Armour Swift-Eckrich, Inc. was founded in 1920 and is now a subsidiary of Beatrice Company of Chicago, Illinois. It is engaged as a manufacturer of various meat products including hot dogs, cold cuts, and sausage. Worldwide revenues for 1991: $1.1 billion.

- **Total Employees:** 4,000
- **U.S. Employees Abroad:** 30
- **Countries:** Belgium, France, Italy, Netherlands, Panama, United Kingdom.
- **Job Categories:** Management, Marketing—Food/Food Services, Sales—Food/Food Services.
- **Language Requirement:** None.

ARMSTRONG WORLD INDUSTRIES, INC.

PO Box 3001
Lancaster, PA 17604 USA

RECRUITER: B. G. SPITLER
MANAGER, COLLEGE RELATIONS
PO BOX 3001
LANCASTER, PA 17604
TEL: (717) 396-2541
FAX: (717) 396-2126

William W. Adams, President. Resilient flooring, ceramic tile, acoustical ceilings, insulation materials, adhesives, gaskets, and furniture. Armstrong World Industries, Inc. was begun in 1860 when Thomas Armstrong and John Glass began the Armstrong Brothers Cork Cutting Shop in Pittsburgh. A decreasing cork market forced the company to change to another product, linoleum. In 1980, the name was changed to Armstrong World Industries and the company began a period of rapid expansion. Today, Armstrong is the largest domestic manufacturer of resilient flooring and ceramic tile. It is also a leading manufacturer of interior furnishings. Armstrong has 66 manufacturing plants in the United States and 17 plants in eight other countries. Worldwide revenues for 1992: $2.6 billion.

- **Total Employees:** 23,000
- **U.S. Employees Abroad:** Not available.
- **Countries:** Australia, Canada, People's Republic of China, France, Germany, Hong Kong, India, Italy, Netherlands, Spain, United Kingdom.
- **Application Information:** Most foreign positions are filled internally; transfers usually occur after some years with Armstrong.

- **Job Categories:** Management, Marketing, Sales.

- **General Requirements:** B.S. or B.A. degree.

- **Average Overseas Assignment:** 3-5 years.

- **Language Requirement:** Knowledge of local language a plus but not essential.

- **Training:** Varies with each posting.

- **Benefits:** TRAVEL: Annual home leave provided. HEALTH: Same as offered in the United States unless better coverage is offered in the host country. HOUSING: Company pays the difference for comparable U.S. housing. EDUCATION: Tuition provided for grades K-12.

ASARCO, INC.

180 Maiden Lane
New York, NY 10038 USA

RECRUITER: JOHN CORBETT
VICE PRESIDENT, PERSONNEL
180 MAIDEN LANE
NEW YORK, NY 10038
TEL: (212) 510-2000
FAX: (212) 510-2271

Richard O. Osborne, President and Chairman. Nonferrous metals, specialty chemicals, and minerals. Asarco, Inc. is a public company and was founded in 1899 when Henry Rogers and others formed the American Smelting and Refining Company. It was renamed Asarco in 1975. It mines, smelts, and refines metals and produces chemicals for finishing and processing metals. It is also engaged in the production of crushed stone, ready-mix concrete, and asphalt. It has principal mining operations in the United States and abroad. Worldwide revenues for 1992: $1.9 billion.

- **Total Employees:** 9,055

- **U.S. Employees Abroad:** 40

- **Countries:** Australia, Canada, Mexico, Peru.

- **Job Categories:** Administrative, Engineers, Marketing—Chemicals, Marketing, Sales—Chemicals, Sales.

- **Language Requirement:** Varies with each posting.

- **Training:** Varies with each posting.

ASEA BROWN BOVERI

900 Long Ridge Rd.
PO Box 9308
Stamford, CT 06904 USA

RECRUITER: DOROTHY ARNETTE
DIRECTOR OF STAFFING
900 LONG RIDGE RD.
PO BOX 9308
STAMFORD, CT 06904
TEL: (203) 329-8771
FAX: (203) 328-2263

C. E. Hugel, President. Technical products. Asea Brown Boveri was founded in 1910 and is a subsidiary of Asea Brown Boveri Incorporated of Stamford, Connecticut. It was formerly Combustion Engineering Incorporated. Today the firm manufactures fabricated plate work, motors, generators, and various measuring or controlling devices. Worldwide revenues for 1992: $5.5 billion.

- **Total Employees:** 30,000

- **U.S. Employees Abroad:** 45

- **Countries:** Argentina, France, Germany, Italy, Japan, Mexico, New Zealand, Philippines, Venezuela, United Kingdom.

- **Job Categories:** Management, Marketing, Research & Development, Sales.

- **Language Requirement:** None.

ASHLAND OIL, INC.

PO Box 391
Ashland, KY 41114 USA

RECRUITER: EARLENE BALESTRINO
EMPLOYMENT SUPERVISOR
PO BOX 391
ASHLAND, KY 41114
TEL: (606) 329-3333
FAX: (606) 329-3693

John R. Hall, Chief Executive Officer. Diversified energy products. Ashland Oil is a public company founded in 1924. Based in Ashland, Kentucky, this energy corporation has operations which include refining, supplying petroleum products, transportation and marketing, retail gasoline marketing, construction, oil and gas exploration and production. A major product is Valvoline motor oil. Ashland Oil operates on a worldwide basis. Worldwide revenues for 1992: $10.2 billion.

- **Total Employees:** 33,000

- **U.S. Employees Abroad:** 13

- **Countries:** Australia, Canada, Italy, Japan, Mexico, Nigeria, Saudi Arabia, Singapore, United Kingdom.

- **Job Categories:** Engineers, Management, Marketing—Petroleum/Natural Gas, Sales—Petroleum/Natural Gas.

- **General Requirements:** Usually must be a current employee of the company in order to qualify for overseas assignment.

- **Average Overseas Assignment:** 2-3 years.

- **Language Requirement:** Knowledge of local language a plus but not essential.

- **Training:** No special training provided.

- **Benefits:** TRAVEL: Individually determined. HOUSING: Individually determined. EDUCATION: Up to authorized limit.

ASSOCIATED PRESS

50 Rockefeller Plaza
New York, NY 10020-1666 USA

RECRUITER: JACK STOKES
DIRECTOR, HUMAN RESOURCES
50 ROCKEFELLER PLAZA
NEW YORK, NY 10020-1666
TEL: (212) 621-1500
FAX: (212) 621-5447

Louis D. Boccardi, President. News service. Associated Press is a private company founded in 1848. The company acts as an operator of news syndicates in the United States and abroad. Worldwide operating revenues for 1992: $311 million.

- **Total Employees:** 3,125
- **U.S. Employees Abroad:** 25
- **Countries:** Australia, Belgium, Brazil, Egypt, United Kingdom, Germany, Italy, Japan, Kenya, Lebanon, Malaysia, Mexico, Norway, Peru, Portugal, Switzerland, Turkey, Uruguay, Venezuela.
- **Job Categories:** Reporters.
- **Training:** No special training provided.

AST RESEARCH, INC.

16215 Alton Pkwy.
Irvine, CA 92713-9658 USA

RECRUITER: RICHARD OTTAVIANO
PERSONNEL DIRECTOR
16215 ALTON PKWY.
PO BOX 19658
IRVINE, CA 92713-9658
TEL: (714) 727-4141
FAX: (714) 727-9355

Safi U. Qureshey, President and Co-Chairman. Personal computers. AST Research, Inc. is a public company incorporated in 1980 by Albert Wong, Safi Qureshey, and Tom Yuen. In 1981, IBM introduced its personal computer and within months of that, AST produced a memory enhancer. In 1983, sales reached $12 million. The company introduced its first PC in 1986 and today, it is a leader of notebook computers and PCs based on Intel's 486 microprocessor. Rapid expansion is taking place in Europe and Asia. Currently, AST has plants in the United States and abroad and sales offices in 17 countries. Worldwide revenues for 1992: $944 million.

- **Total Employees:** 2,960
- **U.S. Employees Abroad:** 20
- **Countries:** Australia, Canada, France, Germany, Hong Kong, Japan, Taiwan.
- **Job Categories:** Engineers, Management, Marketing—Electronics, Sales—Electronics.
- **Language Requirement:** Varies with each posting.

ASTRONAUTICS CORPORATION OF AMERICA

PO Box 523
Milwaukee, WI 53201 USA

RECRUITER: DIANE BROADHEAD
PERSONNEL DEPARTMENT,
EMPLOYEE RELATIONS
PO BOX 523
MILWAUKEE, WI 53201
TEL: (414) 447-8200
FAX: (414) 447-8231
FREE: (800) 733-7375

Nathaniel K. Delazo, Chief Executive Officer. Airborne displays, avionic instrumentation, fire control systems, secure computers, and thermal magnetic devices. Astronautics Corporation of America is a private company founded in 1959 for the purpose of designing and manufacturing state-of-the art electronic equipment and systems. Today, the company is a world leader in its field. Worldwide revenues for 1992: $400 million.

- **Total Employees:** 5,200
- **U.S. Employees Abroad:** 25
- **Countries:** Germany, Israel.
- **Job Categories:** Computer Programmers, Engineers, Manufacturing, Management, Marketing, Technical Field Support, Technicians.
- **Language Requirement:** None.
- **Training:** In-depth orientation (30 days) provided.

AT&T INTERNATIONAL

32 Avenue of the Americas
New York, NY 10013 USA

RECRUITER: KENNETH MAGNANI
MANAGER, PERSONNEL
ADMINISTRATION
PO BOX 1955
MORRISTOWN, NJ 07960-1955
TEL: (201) 898-8000
FAX: (201) 898-8712

Robert E. Allen, Chairman. Telecommunications services and network systems; communications and computers; financial services and leasing. AT&T began with Alexander Graham Bell and his supporters—the fathers of deaf students Bell was tutoring. They organized Bell Telephone in 1877 and New United Kingdom Telephone in 1878. The company was incorporated in New York in 1885. It the largest U.S. telecommunications company, providing domestic and international services. The company's worldwide intelligent network carries voice, data, image, and facsimile around the world. Worldwide revenues for 1992: $69.9 billion.

- **Total Employees:** 274,000
- **U.S. Employees Abroad:** 310
- **Countries:** Australia, Canada, Egypt, Greece, Hong Kong, Ireland, Italy, Japan,

Republic of Korea, Mexico, Singapore, Spain, Sweden, Taiwan, Thailand, United Kingdom.

- **Job Categories:** Finance, Marketing—Financial Services, Marketing—Telecommunications, Sales—Financial Services, Sales—Telecommunications.

ATARI CORPORATION

1196 Borregas Ave.
Sunnyvale, CA 94086 USA

RECRUITER: DIRECTOR
DIRECTOR, HUMAN RESOURCES
1196 BORREGAS AVE.
SUNNYVALE, CA 94086
TEL: (408) 745-2000
FAX: (408) 745-2088

Sam Tramiel, President. Video games, accessories and personal computer hardware, software and peripherals. Atari is a public company founded in 1972 by Nolan Bushnell. He sold Atari to Warner Communications in 1976. In 1984, Warner sold Atari to Jack Tramiel (former CEO of Commodore), and Atari experienced a turnaround after major losses during the early 1980s. Today, this company is a major producer and distributor of personal computers and related items. Worldwide revenues for 1992: $260 million.

- **Total Employees:** 1,270
- **U.S. Employees Abroad:** 22
- **Countries:** Japan, Taiwan, United Kingdom.
- **Job Categories:** Finance, Marketing—Electronics, Office Management, Sales—Electronics.
- **Language Requirement:** None.

AUGAT, INC.

89 Forbes Blvd.
Mansfield, MA 02048 USA

RECRUITER: BARBARA PELLERIN
PERSONNEL DIRECTOR
89 FORBES BLVD.
MANSFIELD, MA 02048
TEL: (508) 543-4300

Marcel P. Joseph, President and Chairman. Interconnection products. Augat is a public company founded in 1946. The firm designs and produces electrical mechanical components, sockets and connectors for telecommunications and automotive industries. Worldwide revenues for 1992: $362 million.

- **Total Employees:** 1,880
- **U.S. Employees Abroad:** Not available.
- **Countries:** Australia, Canada, France, Germany, Italy, Japan, Singapore, Sweden, Switzerland, United Kingdom.
- **Job Categories:** Management, Marketing—Electronics, Sales—Electronics.

AUTOMATIC SWITCH COMPANY

50 Hanover Rd.
Florham Park, NJ 07932 USA

RECRUITER: RICHARD ROONEY
VICE PRESIDENT, ADMINISTRATION
50 HANOVER RD.
FLORHAM PARK, NJ 07932
TEL: (201) 966-2189
FAX: (201) 966-2628

J. Hans Kluge, President. Valves and pressure temperature switches. Automatic Switch Company is a manufacturing subsidiary of the Emerson Electric Company. It currently has operations in eight foreign countries. Worldwide revenues for 1992: $316 million.

- **Total Employees:** 2,000
- **U.S. Employees Abroad:** 50
- **Countries:** Australia, Brazil, Canada, Germany, Japan, Mexico, Netherlands, United Kingdom.
- **Application Information:** Hiring for most foreign positions is done at the specific country location.
- **Job Categories:** Marketing—Industrial, Sales—Industrial.
- **Average Overseas Assignment:** 2-3 years.
- **Language Requirement:** Knowledge of local language a plus but not essential.
- **Training:** Basic orientation (1-30 days) provided.
- **Benefits:** All benefits are individually determined.

AVERY DENNISON CORPORATION

150 North Orange Grove Blvd.
Pasadena, CA 91109 USA

RECRUITER: TERESA MCCASLIN
DIRECTOR, HUMAN RESOURCES
150 NORTH ORANGE GROVE BLVD.
PASADENA, CA 91109
TEL: (818) 304-2000
FAX: (818) 577-5338

Charles D. Miller, Chairman. Office supplies and related products. Avery Dennison is a public company founded in 1990 as the result of a merger of Dennison Manufacturing Company and Avery International. Its products include self-adhesive base materials, tapes, and stationery. Some of its popular brand names are Dennison stationery and Click Hi-Lighter, a retractable highlighting marker. Worldwide revenues for 1992: $2.6 billion.

- **Total Employees:** 15,000
- **U.S. Employees Abroad:** Not available.
- **Countries:** Worldwide including Australia, Brazil, Denmark, France, Germany, Mexico, Republic of South Africa, United Kingdom.
- **Job Categories:** Administrative, Finance, Management, Marketing—Consumer Goods, Sales—Consumer Goods.

AVIS, INC.
900 Old Country Rd.
Garden City, NY 11530 USA

RECRUITER: CAROL RILEY
DIRECTOR, EQUAL OPPORTUNITY
900 OLD COUNTRY RD.
GARDEN CITY, NY 11530
TEL: (516) 222-3000
FAX: (516) 222-4351

Joseph V. Vittoria, Chairman. Car rentals. Avis is a private company begun in the mid-1940s by car dealer Warren Avis. Realizing that there were no car rental agencies at airport locations, he was the first to open them at Detroit's Willow Run Airport and Miami International Airport. In 1948, his business expanded to inter-city locations serving hotels and office buildings. Avis's international operations involve joint ventures in 68 countries. It operates through 4,900 locations in 138 countries. Worldwide revenues for 1991: $1.2 billion.

- **Total Employees:** 13,500
- **U.S. Employees Abroad:** 5
- **Countries:** Australia, New Zealand.
- **Job Categories:** Management, Management Training.
- **General Requirements:** Usually must be a current employee of the company in order to qualify for overseas assignment.
- **Average Overseas Assignment:** 2-3 years.
- **Language Requirement:** None.
- **Training:** No special training required.
- **Benefits:** Vary with each posting.
- **Comments:** The number of Americans reported working abroad varies greatly from quarter to quarter, fluctuating with the number and scope of projects under contract at the time.

AVNET, INC.
80 Cutter Mill Rd.
Great Neck, NY 11021 USA

RECRUITER: ROBERT ZIERK
DIRECTOR, HUMAN RESOURCES
10950 WEST WASHINGTOM BLVD.
CULVER CITY, CA 90230
TEL: (310) 558-2000
FAX: (310) 838-7419

Leon Machiz, Chairman. Distributor of components, video communication equipment, and computer products. Avnet, Inc. is a public company founded in 1955. Major products include Brownell electric motors, Channel Master television antennas and rotators. Avnet operates on an international basis. Worldwide revenues for 1992: $2 billion.

- **Total Employees:** 6,800

- **U.S. Employees Abroad:** 50
- **Countries:** Canada, Denmark, France, Malaysia, Mexico, Sweden, Taiwan, United Kingdom.
- **Application Information:** Hiring for most foreign positions is done at the specific country location.
- **Job Categories:** Management, Marketing—Electronics, Sales—Electronics.
- **General Requirements:** Avnet prefers that applicants have 10 years experience in sales and marketing.
- **Average Overseas Assignment:** Less than two years.
- **Language Requirement:** Competency in local language is required.
- **Training:** No special training provided.
- **Benefits:** All benefits are individually determined.

AVON PRODUCTS, INC.

9 West 57th St.
New York, NY 10019 USA

RECRUITER: HAROLD RUSH
DIRECTOR, INTERNATIONAL HUMAN
    RESOURCES
9 WEST 57TH ST.
NEW YORK, NY 10019
TEL: (212) 546-6015
FAX: (212) 546-6704

James E. Preston, President and Chairman. Cosmetics, fragrances, and toiletries. Avon Products is a public company originally established in 1886. It was incorporated under New York laws in 1916 as the California Perfume Company. Various name changes occurred over the years. It became Avon Products, Inc. on December 3, 1950. Avon is a diversified business specializing in beauty products and direct selling. As of 1992, sales continue to increase, especially in Latin America. Worldwide revenues for 1992: $2.5 billion.

- **Total Employees:** 19,600
- **U.S. Employees Abroad:** 75
- **Countries:** Austria, Belgium, Brazil, Canada, Chile, People's Republic of China, Dominican Republic, El Salvador, France, Guatemala, Hong Kong, Italy, Japan, Mexico, Peru, Portugal, Russia, Venezuela.
- **Application Information:** Hiring for most foreign positions is done at the specific country location.
- **Job Categories:** Finance, Sales—Consumer Goods.
- **General Requirements:** Expertise necessary in certain areas. Contact company for more information.
- **Average Overseas Assignment:** 3-5 years.
- **Language Requirement:** Competence in local language required.

- **Training:** Training available in specific work skills.
- **Benefits:** All benefits are individually determined.

AVX CORPORATION

750 Lexington Ave.
New York, NY 10022-1208 USA

RECRUITER: RICHARD AIOSA
VP, HUMAN RESOURCES MANAGER
PO BOX 867
MYRTLE BEACH, SC 29578
TEL: (803) 448-9411
FAX: (803) 448-7139

Benedict Rosen, Chairman. Multilayer ceramic capacitors. AVX is a manufacturing subsidiary of the Kyosera Corporation in Japan. Worldwide revenues for 1991: $568 million.

- **Total Employees:** 5,000
- **U.S. Employees Abroad:** 25
- **Countries:** El Salvador, France, Israel, Japan, Mexico, United Kingdom.
- **Job Categories:** Manufacturing, Marketing.
- **Average Overseas Assignment:** 2-3 years.
- **Language Requirement:** None.
- **Training:** No special training provided.
- **Benefits:** All benefits are individually determined.

BACKER SPIELVOGEL & BATES WORLDWIDE, INC.

405 Lexington Ave.
New York, NY 10174 USA

RECRUITER: JOHN DEBRECINI
MANAGER, EXECUTIVE TRAINING &
DEVELOPMENT
405 LEXINGTON AVE.
NEW YORK, NY 10174
TEL: (212) 297-7000
FAX: (212) 297-7761

Carl Spielvogel, Chairman. Advertising agency. Backer, Spielvogel & Bates Worldwide, Inc. was founded in 1940 and is a subsidiary of Backer, Spielvogel & Bates A/S of Oslo, Norway. It operates advertising agencies throughout the United States and abroad. Worldwide gross billings for 1991: $4.2 billion.

- **Total Employees:** 8,041
- **U.S. Employees Abroad:** 60
- **Countries:** Worldwide including Argentina, Australia, Brazil, Canada, Colombia, France, Germany, Hong Kong, India, Indonesia, Japan, Mexico, Netherlands, Philippines, Singapore, Spain, Thailand, United Kingdom, Venezuela.
- **Job Categories:** Executive Management, Finance, Marketing, Sales—Advertising.

- **Training:** No special training provided.

BADGER COMPANY, INC.

One Broadway
Cambridge, MA 02142 USA

RECRUITER: ROBERT HALE
SENIOR VP, HUMAN RESOURCES
ONE BROADWAY
CAMBRIDGE, MA 02142
TEL: (617) 494-7257
FAX: (617) 494-7258

Lazzaro G. Modigliani, President. Engineering and contruction services for clients in the process industry fields. The Badger Company was founded in 1968 and is a subsidiary of the Raytheon Company of Lexington, Massachusettes. Its services include professional engineering and construction of chemical plants and refineries, food-packing plants, and pharmaceutical plants. Worldwide revenues for 1991: $480 million.

- **Total Employees:** 2,000
- **U.S. Employees Abroad:** 20
- **Countries:** Italy, Netherlands, United Kingdom.
- **Job Categories:** Administrative, Engineers, Finance.
- **Training:** No special training provided.

BAILEY CONTROLS COMPANY

29801 Euclid Ave.
Wickliffe, OH 44092 USA

RECRUITER: JIM JACKMAN
MANAGER, STAFFING
29801 EUCLID AVE.
WICKLIFFE, NJ 44092
TEL: (216) 585-8500
FAX: (216) 585-5101

Gene Yon, Chief Operating Officer. Analog and digital instruments, controls, and control systems. Bailey Controls is a subsidiary of Elsag Bailey Incorporated of New York City. It manufactures instruments that measure, display, transmit or control process variables in industry. Worldwide revenues for 1991: $320 million.

- **Total Employees:** 6,500
- **U.S. Employees Abroad:** 75
- **Countries:** Australia, Brazil, Canada, People's Republic of China, Italy, Japan, Jordan, Mexico, Norway, United Kingdom.
- **Job Categories:** Marketing—Electronics, Sales—Electronics.
- **Average Overseas Assignment:** 2-3 years.
- **Language Requirement:** Competency in local language required.
- **Training:** Basic orientation (1-30 days) provided.

BAKER HUGHES, INC.

3900 Essex Lane
PO Box 4740
Houston, TX 77210-4740 USA

RECRUITER: SHANNON NINI
INTERNATIONAL RECRUITMENT
PO BOX 4740
HOUSTON, TX 77210-4740
TEL: (713) 439-8417
FAX: (713) 439-8782

James D. Woods, President and Chairman. Products and services for the petroleum and mining industries. Baker Hughes is a public company founded in 1913. Originally, Howard R. Hughes and a partner, Robert Sharp, opened a plant to manufacture rock drill bits in 1909. When Sharp died in 1912, Hughes purchased his half of the business and incorporated it as Hughes Tool. When Hughes died in 1924, the firm was passed on to H. R. Hughes, Jr. In 1928, Carl Baker founded Baker Oil Tools, and the company prospered for many years. By the late 1980s, both Baker and Hughes began to experience declining revenues, and in 1987, the two companies merged. Due to the 1990 acquisition of ChemLink, it is now the largest U.S. oilfield chemical company. It has more than 115 plants located in the United States and abroad. Worldwide revenues for 1992: $2.5 billion. Foreign revenues for 1991: $1.4 billion.

- **Total Employees:** 19,600
- **U.S. Employees Abroad:** Not available.
- **Countries:** Argentina, Australia, Canada, Egypt, France, Germany, Indonesia, Italy, Nigeria, Singapore, Republic of South Africa, United Kingdom.
- **Application Information:** Hiring for most foreign postings is done at the specific country location of the 24 Baker Hughes companies.
- **Job Categories:** Executive Management.
- **General Requirements:** A history with the firm is preferred; international experience is important.
- **Average Overseas Assignment:** 2-3 years.
- **Language Requirement:** Knowledge of local language a plus but not essential.
- **Training:** Basic orientation (1-30 days) provided.
- **Benefits:** TRAVEL: One trip home per year is provided. HEALTH: Same coverage as U.S. employees. HOUSING: Individually determined. EDUCATION: Individually determined; some Baker Hughes companies subsidize elementary-high school education in private schools.

BANCTEC, INC.

4435 Spring Valley Rd.
Dallas, TX 75244 USA

RECRUITER: CINDY MACFARLANE
MANAGER, HUMAN RESOURCES
4435 SPRING VALLEY RD.
DALLAS, TX 75244
TEL: (214) 450-7700
FAX: (214) 450-7867

Grahame N. Clark, Jr., Chairman. Computerized systems for financial transaction document processing. BancTec, Inc. is a public company founded in 1979. It provides computerized systems for processing checks, remittance advices, and sales drafts. It designs, processes, and sells products that use state-of-the-art document processing and image processing technologies to read, digitize, encode, sort, and process financial documents. Major products include Image FIRST 5500 second generation high-speed multi-application system, and CheckMender brand or trade name. Worldwide revenues for 1992: $191 million.

- **Total Employees:** 1,743
- **U.S. Employees Abroad:** 22
- **Countries:** Australia, Canada, Germany, United Kingdom.
- **Job Categories:** Finance, Management, Marketing—Electronics, Sales—Electronics.
- **Language Requirement:** None.
- **Training:** No special training offered.

BANDAG, INC.

Bandag Center
Muscatine, IA 52761-5886 USA

RECRUITER: MEL HERSHEY
PERSONNEL DEPARTMENT
BANDAG CENTER
MUSCATINE, IA 52761-5886
TEL: (319) 262-1400
FAX: (319) 262-1344

Martin G. Carver, President and Chairman. Rubber and related equipment and supplies. Bandag, Inc. is a public company founded in 1957. It produces rubber and other supplies used for retreading tires. The company is also involved in the sale of tires. Worldwide revenues for 1992: $591 million.

- **Total Employees:** 2,400
- **U.S. Employees Abroad:** Not available.
- **Countries:** Japan, Philippines, Taiwan, Thailand, United Kingdom.
- **Job Categories:** Marketing, Sales.

BANK OF BOSTON CORPORATION

100 Federal St.
Boston, MA 02110 USA

RECRUITER: JANE MURRAY
DIRECTOR, HUMAN RECOURCES,
GLOBAL
100 FEDERAL ST., MS-01-11-11
BOSTON, MA 02110
TEL: (617) 434-2200
FAX: (617) 434-5854

Ira Stepanian, Chairman. Banking services. Bank of Boston is a public company founded in 1784. This multi-bank holding company has three divisions: New United Kingdom

Banking Group, National Banking Group, and the Global Banking Group. It has operations in the United States and in more than 20 foreign countries. Worldwide average assets for 1992: $32.3 billion.

- **Total Employees:** 17,400
- **U.S. Employees Abroad:** 25
- **Countries:** Argentina, Australia, Brazil, Costa Rica, France, Germany, Republic of South Africa.
- **Job Categories:** Accountants, Finance, Management, Marketing—Financial Services.
- **Language Requirement:** Varies with each posting.

THE BANK OF NEW YORK COMPANY, INC.

One Wall St., 13th Floor
New York, NY 10028 USA

RECRUITER: DOUGLAS TANTILLO
VICE PRESIDENT, HUMAN RESOURCES
ONE WALL ST., 13TH FLOOR
NEW YORK, NY 10028
TEL: (212) 635-7735
FAX: (212) 635-7910

J. Carter Bacot, Chairman. Commercial banking. The Bank of New York is a public company founded in 1784 by Alexander Hamilton and a group of influential New York merchants and lawyers. In 1922 it merged with the New York Insurance & Trust Company. It now conducts a general banking and trust business with 145 offices in New York and 45 in other states. It also has additional offices in several overseas locations. The Bank of New York is the 15th largest bank holding company in the United States. Worldwide assets for 1992: $40.9 billion.

- **Total Employees:** 12,000
- **U.S. Employees Abroad:** 19
- **Countries:** Argentina, Australia, Brazil, Egypt, France, Germany, Hong Kong, Italy, Japan, Republic of Korea, Spain, Taiwan, Thailand, Turkey, United Kingdom.
- **Job Categories:** Accountants, Brokers—Securities & Financial, Office Management.
- **General Requirements:** When a foreign assignment becomes available, bank employees submit their names to the head of the foreign sector for consideration.
- **Average Overseas Assignment:** 2-3 years.
- **Language Requirement:** Knowledge of language skills a plus but not essential.
- **Training:** No special training required.
- **Benefits:** TRAVEL: If employees are expatriates, they are entitled to annual home leave. HEALTH: SOS worldwide medical assistance available. HOUSING: Housing allowances are available for expatriate employees and are determined by income level and family size. EDUCATION: Children of expatriates are reimbursed for elementary and secondary education; college costs are paid by employees.

BANKAMERICA CORPORATION

Bank of America Building
Box #37000
San Francisco, CA 94137 USA

RECRUITER: ROBERT N. BECK
EXECUTIVE VP, HUMAN RESOURCES
BOX #37000
SAN FRANCISCO, CA 94137
TEL: (415) 622-3456
FAX: (415) 622-4508

Richard M. Rosenberg, Chairman. Financial services. BankAmerica Corporation is a public company founded in 1906. Today, this diversified corporation offers financial products and services to clients including businesses, government agencies, and individuals on an international scale. Worldwide assets for 1992: $200 billion.

- **Total Employees:** 80,000
- **U.S. Employees Abroad:** 250
- **Countries:** Worldwide including Australia, Bahamas, Brazil, Canada, Cayman Islands, People's Republic of China, France, Hong Kong, Indonesia, Netherlands, Switzerland, United Kingdom.
- **Application Information:** Hiring for most foreign positions is done at the specific country location.
- **Job Categories:** Administrative, Executive Management.
- **General Requirements:** Specialized, high-level, financial services skills.
- **Average Overseas Assignment:** 2-5 years.
- **Language Requirement:** Varies with each posting.
- **Training:** No special training offered.
- **Benefits:** TRAVEL: Varies with each posting. HOUSING: Varies with each posting. EDUCATION: None offered.
- **Comments:** Only senior-level executives are hired for foreign postings.

BANKERS TRUST NEW YORK CORPORATION

280 Park Ave.
New York, NY 10017 USA

RECRUITER: ROLAND SEIDEL
PERSONNEL OFFICER,
   INTERNATIONAL
280 PARK AVE.
NEW YORK, NY 10017
TEL: (212) 775-2500
FAX: (212) 454-1151

Charles Sanford, Chairman. Banking services. This corporation owns Bankers Trust, one the largest U.S. banks. It was founded in 1903 by 35-year-old New York banker, Henry Davison. He and his banker friends handled trust business referred by commercial banks. In 1908, the business expanded to include foreign departments. Today, it provides corporate finance, money and securities market trading, and trust services. The corporation conducts business on an international basis. Worldwide assets for 1992: $72.2 billion.

- **Total Employees:** 12,000

- **U.S. Employees Abroad:** 180

- **Countries:** Argentina, Australia, Austria, Bahrain, Belgium, Brazil, Canada, Chile, Colombia, Denmark, France, Germany, Greece, Hong Kong, India, Indonesia, Italy, Cote d'Ivoire, Japan, Republic of Korea, Mexico, Netherlands, Nigeria, Panama, Philippines, Portugal, Singapore, Switzerland, Taiwan, Thailand, Tunisia, United Kingdom, Venezuela, Yugoslavia.

- **Application Information:** Hiring for most foreign positions is done at the specific country location.

- **Job Categories:** Brokers—Securities & Financial, Executive Management, Finance, Training Specialists.

- **Average Overseas Assignment:** 2-3 years.

- **Language Requirement:** Knowledge of local language skills a plus but not essential.

- **Training:** No special training provided.

- **Benefits:** TRAVEL: Basic firm policy provides home leave for employee and family. HEALTH: Same coverage as U.S. employees. HOUSING: Offered. EDUCATION: Education subsidy is offered if child is living with employee at overseas posting site.

BANYAN SYSTEMS, INC.

115 Flanders Rd.
Westborough, MA 01581 USA

RECRUITER: TONY ABRAHAM
STAFFING/RECRUITMENT
115 FLANDERS RD.
WESTBOROUGH, MA 01581
TEL: (508) 898-1660

David C. Mahoney, Chairman. Corporate-wide PC networking systems. Banyan Systems, Inc. is a private company founded in 1983. It offers PC networking systems that link personal computers to minicomputers and mainframes. It has operations in the United States and throughout Europe. Worldwide revenues for 1992: $113 million.

- **Total Employees:** 635

- **U.S. Employees Abroad:** 30

- **Countries:** France, Germany, United Kingdom.

- **Job Categories:** Customer Services, Engineers, Marketing—Electronics, Sales— Electronics.

- **General Requirements:** Applicants should have three or more years experience, and senior-level applicants should have 10 or more years job experience.

- **Language Requirement:** None.

- **Training:** No special training offered.

- **Benefits:** All benefits are individually determined.

C. R. BARD, INC.

730 Central Ave.
Murray Hill, NJ 07974 USA

RECRUITER: EUGENE B. SCHULTZ
VP, PERSONNEL
730 CENTRAL AVE.
MURRAY HILL, NJ 07974
TEL: (908) 277-8000
FAX: (908) 277-8098

George T. Maloney, President. Health-care products. C. R. Bard, Inc. is a public company founded in 1923. It produces and markets various health care products and focuses on cardiovascular, urological, and surgical items. It sells products to hospitals and health-care facilities throughout the United States and abroad. Worldwide revenues for 1992: $990 million.

- **Total Employees:** 8,850
- **U.S. Employees Abroad:** 25
- **Countries:** Australia, Brazil, Canada, Japan, United Kingdom.
- **Job Categories:** Management, Marketing—Health & Medical Supplies, Product Development, Sales—Health & Medical Supplies.
- **General Requirements:** Usually must be a current employee of the company in order to qualify for overseas assignment.
- **Language Requirement:** None.

THE BARDEN CORPORATION

200 Park Ave.
PO Box 2449
Danbury, CT 06813 USA

RECRUITER: PHILLIP BROCKELMAN
DIRECTOR, HUMAN RESOURCES
200 PARK AVE.
PO BOX 2449
DANBURY, CT 06813-2449
TEL: (203) 744-2211
FAX: (203) 797-0651

Robert H. Buch, President. Precision ball bearings. The Barden Corporation is a division of the FAG Bearings Corporation, established in Connecticut on June 4, 1942. Barden is a world leader in the manufacture of precision ball bearing components and sub-assemblies for aircraft missiles, spacecraft guidance, flight control, and other precision instruments. Worldwide revenues for 1991: $86 million.

- **Total Employees:** 1,500
- **U.S. Employees Abroad:** 50
- **Countries:** Australia, Brazil, Canada, France, Germany, Israel, Japan, Switzerland, United Kingdom.
- **Job Categories:** Engineers, Management, Sales.
- **Language Requirement:** None.
- **Training:** No special training provided.

- **Benefits:** All benefits are individually determined.

BAROID CORPORATION

PO Box 60087
Houston, TX 77205 USA

RECRUITER: MARY SPOLYAR
DIRECTOR, COMPENSATION &
BENEFITS
PO BOX 60087
HOUSTON, TX 77205
TEL: (713) 987-5900
FAX: (713) 987-5565

J. Landis Martin, Chairman. Petroleum services and equipment. Baroid was founded in 1926 and is a subsidiary of Valhi, Inc. of Dallas, Texas. It is a global supplier of petroleum services and equipment. Prior to 1988, its parent company was NL Industries. Worldwide revenues for 1992: $648.1 million.

- **Total Employees:** 3,700

- **U.S. Employees Abroad:** Not available.

- **Countries:** Greece, Indonesia, Italy, Nigeria, Singapore.

- **Job Categories:** Administrative, Engineers, Marketing—Petroleum/Natural Gas. Technicians, Sales—Petroleum/Natural Gas.

BASF CORPORATION

8 Campus Dr.
Parsippany, NJ 07054 USA

RECRUITER: ELLEN NASH
STAFFING/RECRUITMENT
8 CAMPUS DR.
PARSIPPANY, NJ 07054
TEL: (201) 397-2740
FAX: (201) 292-1227

J. Dieter Stein, Chief Executive Officer. Chemicals, coatings, and optical recording equipment. BASF Corporation is a subsidiary of BASF AG of Germany. Major products include Optiset ink, Silky Touch polyester, Ferro Maxima audio cassetts, and T120 videocassettes. Worldwide revenues for 1991: $5.4 billion.

- **Total Employees:** 22,000

- **U.S. Employees Abroad:** 20

- **Countries:** Germany.

- **Job Categories:** Management, Marketing—Chemicals, Marketing—Scientific, Sales—Chemicals, Sales—Scientific.

- **Language Requirement:** None.

BATTELLE MEMORIAL INSTITUTE

505 King Ave.
Columbus, OH 43201 USA

RECRUITER: FELIX TROJER
INTERNATIONAL MARKETING/
PERSONNEL
505 KING AVE.
COLUMBUS, OH 43201
TEL: (614) 424-6424
FAX: (614) 424-5263

Dr. Douglas E. Olesen, President. Research and development. Battelle Memorial Institute is a private company founded in 1929. It conducts high-level research in lasers, robotics, fiber optics, marine engineering, computer science, and materials handling. It is also a security consultant for government-run, lotteries. Worldwide operating revenues for 1991: $222.2 million.

- **Total Employees:** 8,200
- **U.S. Employees Abroad:** 10
- **Countries:** Brazil, France, Germany, Japan, Republic of Korea, Saudi Arabia, Switzerland.
- **Application Information:** Hiring for most foreign positions is done at the specific country location.
- **Job Categories:** Executive Management, Finance, Research & Development, Sales— Scientific.
- **General Requirements:** College degree in related fields.
- **Language Requirement:** Competency in local language required.
- **Training:** No special training provided.
- **Benefits:** All benefits are individually determined by specific Hiring Technical Center.
- **Comments:** The number of Americans reported working abroad varies greatly from quarter to quarter, fluctuating with the number and scope of projects under contract at the time.

BAUSCH & LOMB, INC.

42 East Ave.
Rochester, NY 14673 USA

RECRUITER: JAMES GREENAWALT
CORPORATE VICE PRESIDENT,
HUMAN RESOURCES
1 LINCOLN 1ST SQUARE
ROCHESTER, NY 14604
TEL: (716) 338-6873
FAX: (716) 338-6000

Daniel Gill, Chief Executive Officer. Optical and health-care equipment and pharmaceuticals. Bausch & Lomb is a public company incorporated on March 20, 1908, in New York as the Bausch & Lomb Optical Company. Its present name was adopted on July 1, 1960. The business is divided into two industry segments: health care and optics. Today, Bausch & Lomb operates on a worldwide basis with facilities in

25 countries and distribution operations in over 70 nations. Wordwide revenues for 1992: $1.7 billion.

- **Total Employees:** 5,500
- **U.S. Employees Abroad:** 50
- **Countries:** Australia, Austria, Bermuda, Brazil, Canada, Denmark, France, Germany, Hong Kong, Japan, Republic of Korea, Netherlands, Spain, Switzerland, Taiwan, United Kingdom.
- **Job Categories:** Finance, Management, Marketing—Health & Medical Supplies, Marketing—Pharmaceuticals, Sales—Health & Medical Supplies, Sales—Pharmaceuticals.
- **Average Overseas Assignment:** 2-3 years.
- **Language Requirement:** None.
- **Training:** Language training if necessary.
- **Benefits:** All benefits are individually determined.
- **Comments:** The corporate structure is currently being reorganized and no international hiring is planned until this is completed in late 1993.

BAXTER HEALTHCARE CORPORATION

One Baxter Pkwy.
Deerfield, IL 60015-4625 USA

RECRUITER: ANNE VEXTER
INTERNATIONAL RECRUITMENT
ONE BAXTER PKWY.
DEERFIELD, IL 60015-4625
TEL: (708) 948-4198
FAX: (708) 948-4353

Vernon Loucks, Chief Executive Officer. Health-care products. Baxter Healthcare Corporation was founded as The Don Baxter Intravenous Products Corporation in 1931. It is now the largest producer and marketer of health-care products, systems, and services in the world. The company offers more than 120,000 products and an electronic order-entry system (ASAP) that connects customers with over 1,500 vendors. It strives for efficiency, offering services and savings to hospitals worldwide. Baxter Healthcare attempts to reduce costs while improving the quality of patient care. Worldwide revenues for 1992: $8.4 billion.

- **Total Employees:** 60,000
- **U.S. Employees Abroad:** 80
- **Countries:** One hundred countries including Australia, Canada, France, Germany, Italy, Japan, Mexico, Spain, Venezuela, United Kingdom.
- **Application Information:** Most foreign positions are filled internally.
- **Job Categories:** Finance, Management, Marketing—Health & Medical Supplies.
- **General Requirements:** Must meet full list of criteria including flexibility, multicultural interests, family willing to relocate, proven management skills.

- **Average Overseas Assignment:** 2-3 years.
- **Language Requirement:** Competency in local language is required.
- **Training:** Basic orientation (1-30 days) and language training provided.
- **Benefits:** Vary with each posting.
- **Comments:** Usually expatriates are sent on international assignment for developmental purposes when difficulty arises in staffing with local people.

JIM BEAM BRANDS COMPANY

510 Lake Cook Rd.
Deerfield, IL 60015 USA

RECRUITER: MARK CHAFITZ
MANAGER, HUMAN RESOURCES
510 LAKE COOK RD.
DEERFIELD, IL 60015
TEL: (708) 948-8888
FAX: (708) 948-0416

Barry M. Berish, President. Distilled spirits. Jim Beam Brands was founded in 1795 and is a subsidiary of American Brands, Inc. of Old Greenwich, Connecticut. The business includes the Whyte & Mackay Group PLC in the United Kingdom. Major brands include Kessler, an American blended whiskey, Ronrico rum, and Vladivar vodka. Worldwide revenues for 1992: $1.3 billion.

- **Total Employees:** 1,300
- **U.S. Employees Abroad:** 30
- **Countries:** Australia, Germany, Japan, United Kingdom.
- **Job Categories:** Management, Marketing—Food/Food Services, Sales—Food/Food Services.
- **Language Requirement:** None.

BEAR STEARNS COMPANIES, INC.

245 Park Ave.
New York, NY 10167 USA

RECRUITER: ANNE CORWIN
VP, EMPLOYMENT
245 PARK AVE.
NEW YORK, NY 10167
TEL: (212) 272-2000
FAX: (212) 952-2040

A. C. Greenberg, Chief Executive Officer. Investment banking; trading. Bear Stearns is a public company founded in 1923. It is engaged in investment banking and provides security and brokerage services. The firm operates on an international basis. Worldwide revenues for 1992: $2.6 billion

- **Total Employees:** 6,100
- **U.S. Employees Abroad:** 75
- **Countries:** France, Hong Kong, Netherlands, Switzerland, United Kingdom.
- **Job Categories:** Executive Management, Finance, Marketing—Financial Services.

BECHTEL GROUP, INC.

PO Box 193965
San Francisco, CA 94119-3965
USA

RECRUITER: BRYON SANDERSON
STAFFING/RECRUITMENT
MS-14-014
PO BOX 193965
SAN FRANCISCO, CA 94119-3965
FAX: (415) 768-3247

Riley J. Bechtel, President. Global design, engineering, and construction. Bechtel Group, one of the world's largest privately held companies, was begun by Warren Bechtel in 1898. After its incorporation in 1925, Bechtel became the West's largest construction company. It is now one of the world's largest engineering and construction firms. The firm's 15,000 projects are in more than 135 countries on all seven continents. These projects include electric-power generation, environmental cleanups, oil and gas pipelines, chemical plants, transportation systems, mining, telecommunications, and buildings. Worldwide revenues for 1991: $7.5 billion.

- **Total Employees:** 30,900
- **U.S. Employees Abroad:** Not available.
- **Countries:** Algeria, Chile, Indonesia, Republic of Korea, Kuwait, Nigeria, Saudi Arabia, Taiwan, United Arab Emirates, Venezuela.
- **Application Information:** Mail resumes or inquiries to recruiter's address. No phone calls.
- **Salaries:** Varies depending on seniority, length of assignment, and degree of hardship on specific assignment.
- **Job Categories:** Construction Workers, Design Engineers, Engineers, Management.
- **General Requirements:** Engineering degree with 10 years experience in the engineering and construction industry.
- **Average Overseas Assignment:** Less than two years.
- **Language Requirement:** Knowledge of local language a plus but not essential.
- **Training:** Basic orientation (1-30 days) provided.
- **Benefits:** TRAVEL: Varies with each assignment; both R & R and home leave are offered on most projects. HEALTH: Same coverage as U.S. employees. HOUSING: Varies; in many cases housing is provided at no charge. Often, a subsidy is available to defray housing costs. EDUCATION: Varies; usually, if local schools are not adequate, a subsidy is offered to defray costs.

BECKMAN INSTRUMENTS, INC.

2500 Harbour Blvd.
Box #3100
Fullerton, CA 92634 USA

RECRUITER: THOMAS MONTGOMERY
DIRECTOR, INTERNATIONAL HUMAN
RESOURCES
2500 HARBOUR BLVD., BOX #3100
FULLERTON, CA 92634
TEL: (714) 871-4848
FAX: (714) 773-8220

Lewis T. Rosso, President and Chairman. Research and chemical laboratory instruments, systems, and software. Beckman Instruments is a public company founded in 1935. The company designs, manufactures, markets, distributes, and services a wide range of products that address the needs of bioanalytical laboratories in the life sciences market. The company has 37 facilities worldwide. Worldwide revenues for 1992: $908 million.

- **Total Employees:** 6,880
- **U.S. Employees Abroad:** 50
- **Countries:** Australia, Austria, Canada, France, Germany, Hong Kong, Italy, Japan, Mexico, Netherlands, Singapore, Republic of South Africa, Spain, Sweden, Switzerland, Taiwan, United Kingdom.
- **Application Information:** Hiring for most foreign positions is done at the specific country location.
- **Job Categories:** Management, Marketing—Electronics, Marketing—Scientific, Sales—Electronics, Sales—Scientific, Technicians.
- **Language Requirement:** Competency in local language required.
- **Training:** No special training provided.
- **Benefits:** All benefits are individually determined.

BELL HELICOPTER TEXTRON, INC.

PO Box 482
Fort Worth, TX 76101 USA

RECRUITER: DICK DAVIES
VICE PRESIDENT, HUMAN RESOURCES
PO BOX 482
FORT WORTH, TX 76101
TEL: (817) 280-2011
FAX: (817) 280-2321

Webb F. Joiner, President. Helicopters and helicopter parts. Bell Helicopter Textron was founded in 1935 and is a subsidiary of Textron, Inc. of Providence, Rhode Island. It manufactures and repairs aircraft. This also includes research and development of aircraft. Worldwide revenues for 1991: $1.1 billion.

- **Total Employees:** 6,000
- **U.S. Employees Abroad:** 50
- **Countries:** Worldwide including Canada, Singapore, United Kingdom.
- **Job Categories:** Customer Services, Marketing, Sales.
- **General Requirements:** Service technicians must be helicopter and helicopter-maintenance rated.
- **Language Requirement:** Knowledge of local language a plus but not essential.
- **Training:** Basic orientation (1-30 days) provided.
- **Benefits:** All benefits are individually determined.

BELL & HOWELL COMPANY

5215 Old Orchard Rd.
Skokie, IL 60077 USA

RECRUITER: MARIA RUBLY
VICE PRESIDENT, HUMAN
RESOURCES
5215 OLD ORCHARD RD.
SKOKIE, IL 60077
TEL: (708) 470-7612
FAX: (708) 470-9425

William J. White, President and Chairman. Information management; mail-handling equipment. Bell & Howell is a private company founded in 1907. It is involved in mail handling, publishing, and document management. Its principal businesses are the Phillipsburg Company, University Microfilms Inc., Document Management Products Company, and the Publications Systems Company. In May 1988, the Robert M. Bass Group acquired this firm. Today, Bell & Howell operates on an international basis. Worldwide revenues for 1992: $642 million.

- **Total Employees:** 6,000
- **U.S. Employees Abroad:** 1,200
- **Countries:** Canada, United Kingdom, France, Germany, Japan, Netherlands.
- **Job Categories:** Finance, Manufacturing, Marketing—Electronics, Marketing—Publishing, Sales—Electronics, Sales—Publishing.
- **Language Requirement:** Competency in local language required.
- **Training:** No special training provided.
- **Benefits:** All benefits are individually determined.

BEMIS COMPANY, INC.

222 South 9th St., Suite #2300
Minneapolis, MN 55402 USA

RECRUITER: MARILYN PEARSON
HUMAN RESOURCES
REPRESENTATIVE
222 SOUTH 9TH ST., SUITE #2300
MINNEAPOLIS, MN 55402
TEL: (612) 376-3000
FAX: (612) 376-3180

John H. Roe, President. Flexible packaging products. Bemis is a public company founded in 1858. The company produces polyethelene packaging, pressure-sensitive materials, paper packaging, specialty containers mainly used in food industries. Worldwide revenues for 1992: $1.2 billion.

- **Total Employees:** 7,700
- **U.S. Employees Abroad:** 50
- **Countries:** Belgium, Canada, Germany, Italy, Mexico.
- **Job Categories:** Management, Marketing, Sales.
- **General Requirements:** Usually must be a current employee of the company in order to qualify for overseas assignment.

- **Language Requirement:** Knowledge of local language a plus but not essential.

- **Training:** No special training provided.

- **Benefits:** All benefits are individually determined.

BENDIX FIELD ENGINEERING CORPORATION

1 Bendix Rd.
Columbia, MD 21045-1897 USA

RECRUITER: RALPH SCHIFLETT
MANAGER, EMPLOYMENT
1 BENDIX RD.
COLUMBIA, MD 21045-1897
TEL: (301) 964-7515
FAX: (301) 964-7498

Joseph Engle, President. Aerospace engineering services. Bendix Field Engineering was founded in 1950 and is a subsidiary of Allied-Signal Aerospace Company. It provides engineering services to aerospace industries in the United States and abroad. Worldwide operating revenues for 1991: $500 million.

- **Total Employees:** 7,000

- **U.S. Employees Abroad:** 15

- **Countries:** Saudi Arabia.

- **Job Categories:** Design Engineers, Field Engineers, Management.

- **Language Requirement:** None.

LOUIS BERGER INTERNATIONAL INC.

100 Halsted St.
East Orange, NJ 07019 USA

RECRUITER: RICHARD BERGAILO
PERSONNEL DIRECTOR
100 HALSTED ST.
EAST ORANGE, NJ 07019
TEL: (201) 678-1960
FAX: (201) 672-4284

Derish M. Wolff, President. Research. Louis Berger International is a private company founded in 1952. It is funded by endowments, contributions, and grants, enabling the firm to offer engineering and architectural services, economists and researchers to clients on a global basis.

- **Total Employees:** 500

- **U.S. Employees Abroad:** Not available.

- **Countries:** Bolivia, People's Republic of China, France, India, Cote d'Ivoire, Pakistan, Philippines, United Republic of Tanzania, Zaire, United Kingdom.

- **Job Categories:** Engineers, Finance, Management.

BETZ LABORATORIES

4636 Somerton Rd.
Trevose, PA 19053 USA

RECRUITER: RONNIE JACOBS
HUMAN RESOURCES
REPRESENTATIVE
4636 SOMERTON RD.
TREVOSE, PA 19053
TEL: (215) 355-3300
FAX: (215) 355-2869

John F. McCaughan, Chairman. Chemical treatment of water, wastewater, and process systems. Also, manufactures specialty chemicals. Betz Laboratories is a public company founded in 1925. Its business concentrates on the chemical treatment of water, wastewater, and process systems for industrial and commercial markets. Operations include 15 plants in the United States and in seven foreign countries. Worldwide revenues for 1992: $707 million.

- **Total Employees:** 3,400
- **U.S. Employees Abroad:** 35
- **Countries:** Australia, Belgium, Canada, France, Italy, Singapore, United Kingdom.
- **Job Categories:** Chemists, Engineers, Management, Marketing—Chemicals, Product Development.

BIO-RAD LABORATORIES

1000 Alfred Nobel Dr.
Hercules, CA 94547 USA

RECRUITER: JOE HARDY
MANAGER, HUMAN RESOURCES
SERVICES
1000 ALFRED NOBEL DR.
HERCULES, CA 94547
TEL: (415) 724-7000
FAX: (415) 724-0423

Tony Brown, Chief Operating Officer. Diagnostic and analytical instruments. Bio-Rad Laboratories is a public company founded in 1957. It manufactures life sciences research products, clinical diagnostics, and analytical instruments in the biological research field. Worldwide revenues for 1992: $330 million.

- **Total Employees:** 2,500
- **U.S. Employees Abroad:** 15
- **Countries:** Australia, Austria, Belgium, France, Hong Kong, Italy, Japan, Netherlands, Switzerland, United Kingdom.
- **Application Information:** Most foreign positions are filled internally.
- **Job Categories:** Finance, Management, Marketing—Health & Medical Supplies, Marketing—Scientific, Sales—Scientific.
- **Average Overseas Assignment:** Less than two years.
- **Language Requirement:** None.
- **Training:** No special training provided.

• **Benefits:** All benefits are individually determined.

BISSELL, INC.

2345 Walker Rd.
Grand Rapids, MI 49504 USA

RECRUITER: GARY BLYMSA
VP, CORPORATE HUMAN RESOURCES
2345 WALKER RD.
GRAND RAPIDS, MI 49504
TEL: (616) 791-1562
FAX: (616) 784-5880

J. M. Bissell, President. Home-cleaning products. Bissell was founded in 1876 by Melville Bissell. Bissell is a manufacturer of a diverse line of products, including carpet sweepers, vacuum cleaners, floor scrubbers, and chemical specialty products. It is a market leader in the deep cleaning, carpet machine category. Worldwide revenues for 1991: $310 million.

• **Total Employees:** 2,500

• **U.S. Employees Abroad:** 20

• **Countries:** France, United Kingdom.

• **Job Categories:** Management, Marketing—Consumer Goods.

• **Average Overseas Assignment:** Less than two years.

• **Language Requirement:** None.

• **Training:** No special training provided.

• **Benefits:** All benefits are individually determined.

BLACK & DECKER CORPORATION

701 East Joppa Rd.
Towson, MD 21286 USA

RECRUITER: PARTICIA ROGERS
HUMAN RESOURCES TW270
701 EAST JOPPA RD.
TOWSON, MD 21286
TEL: (410) 716-3900
FAX: (410) 583-3967

Nolan Archibald, President and Chairman. Tools and other products for home and commercial applications. Black & Decker is a public company founded in 1910, when S. Duncan Black and Alonzo G. Decker opened the Black & Decker Manufacturing Company in Baltimore. It manufactures and markets power tools. Major reconstruction began in 1985, when CEO Nolan Archibald joined the firm. It now operates 63 manufacturing facilities, 30 of which are in 11 foreign countries. Black & Decker is the 7th strongest brand name in the United States and 19th in Europe. Wordwide revenues for 1992: $4.8 billion.

• **Total Employees:** 38,000

• **U.S. Employees Abroad:** 40

- **Countries:** Argentina, Australia, Belgium, Brazil, Colombia, Germany, Japan, Mexico, New Zealand, Singapore, United Arab Emirates, United Kingdom.

- **Salaries:** $50,000-$100,000 per year.

- **Job Categories:** Management.

- **Average Overseas Assignment:** 3-5 years.

- **Language Requirement:** Knowledge of local language skills a plus but not essential.

- **Training:** Language training provided.

- **Benefits:** TRAVEL: Foreign service premium, cost-of-living and hardship allowances; relocation allowance of one month's base salary and annual home leave. HEALTH: U.S. high option medical plan plus local plans if applicable. HOUSING: A housing differential is offered. The amount reflects the difference betweeen host country housing and home country housing norms. EDUCATION: Educational assistance provided when host country public schools are inadequate. 100 percent of incremental education expense is paid by firm.

BLACK & VEATCH

8400 Ward Pkwy.
Kansas City, MO 64114 USA

RECRUITER: DEAN SHARP
PERSONNEL MANAGER, POWER
   DIVISION
8400 WARD PKWY.
KANSAS CITY, MO 64114
TEL: (913) 339-8700
FAX: (913) 339-7481

Jack Robinson, Chairman. Engineering and architectural design services. Black & Veatch is a private company founded in 1915. The firm provides professional engineering as well as architectural services on a worldwide scale. Worldwide revenues for 1991: $502 million.

- **Total Employees:** 4,500

- **U.S. Employees Abroad:** 80

- **Countries:** Australia, Egypt, Indonesia, Japan, Thailand, Turkey, United Kingdom.

- **Job Categories:** Architects, Engineers, Management.

- **Language Requirement:** Competency in local language required.

- **Training:** Basic orientation (1-30 days) provided.

- **Benefits:** All benefits are individually determined.

BLOCK DRUG COMPANY, INC.

257 Cornelison Ave.
Jersey City, NJ 07302-9988 USA

RECRUITER: THOMAS MCNAMARA
VP, HUMAN RESOURCES
257 CORNELISON AVE.
JERSEY CITY, NJ 07302-9988
TEL: (201) 434-3000
FAX: (201) 451-8424

Thomas R. Block, President. Pharmaceuticals. Block Drug is a public company founded in 1907. It produces and sells various items in three categories: dental products, consumer products, and ethical pharmaceuticals. Brand names include Polident denture cleanser and 2,000 Flushes toilet bowl cleaner. It has operations in more than 20 countries. Worldwide revenues for 1992: $585.3 million.

- **Total Employees:** 3,300
- **U.S. Employees Abroad:** 40
- **Countries:** Argentina, Belgium, Brazil, Germany, Italy, Japan, Mexico, Philippines, Spain, Taiwan, United Kingdom.
- **Application Information:** Hiring for most foreign positions is done at the specific country location.
- **Job Categories:** Administrative, Marketing—Pharmaceuticals, Research & Development, Sales—Pharmaceuticals.
- **Language Requirement:** Varies with each posting.

BLOUNT, INC. (BLOUNT CONSTRUCTION DIVISION)

PO Box 949
Montgomery, AL 36101 USA

RECRUITER: RICHARD GOBER
VICE PRESIDENT, HUMAN
   RESOURCES
PO BOX 949
MONTGOMERY, AL 36101-0949
TEL: (205) 244-4370
FAX: (205) 271-8130

John Panettiere, President. General contractor and manufacturer of industrial and power equipment. Blount Construction is a division of Blount, Inc., which was founded in 1946 by Winton M. Blount. It is a public company involved in various construction fields. Blount Construction employs general contractors in the construction of industrial warehouses and buildings. The company is also engaged in the construction of non-residential and non-industrial buildings. Worldwide revenues for 1992: $637.3 million.

- **Total Employees:** 6,500
- **U.S. Employees Abroad:** 50
- **Countries:** Australia, Belgium, Brazil, Canada, Germany, Kuwait, Japan, Sweden, United Kingdom.
- **Job Categories:** Administrative, Construction Workers, Management.
- **Average Overseas Assignment:** Less than two years.

- **Language Requirement:** Competency in local language required.
- **Training:** No special training provided.
- **Benefits:** All benefits are individually determined.

BOEING COMPANY

7755 East Marginal Way South
Seattle, WA 98108 USA

RECRUITER: WILLIAM CRACKER
HUMAN RESOURCES MANAGER
PO BOX 3707
MAIL STOP 31-11
SEATTLE, WA 98124
TEL: (206) 655-2121
FAX: (206) 393-6370

F. A. Shrontz, Chairman. Commercial and military aircraft. Boeing is a public company founded in 1916 when Bill Boeing constructed his first airplane. His Seattle factory was called Pacific Aero Products Company and in 1917 the name was changed to Boeing Airplane Company. World War I created a need for the production of training planes. After the war, international passenger service was started. Today, this diversified company designs and builds commercial and military aircraft, missiles, and helicopters. It operates on an international basis and leads all U.S. companies in export sales, which account for more than 50 percent of Boeing's revenues. Worldwide revenues for 1992: $30.2 billion.

- **Total Employees:** 155,000
- **U.S. Employees Abroad:** Not available.
- **Countries:** Canada, France, Germany, Italy, Saudi Arabia.
- **Job Categories:** Design Engineers, Engineers, Management, Marketing, Sales—Defense Industry, Sales.

BORDEN, INC.

277 Park Ave.
New York, NY 10172 USA

RECRUITER: PHILIP E. PERRY
CORP. DIRECTOR, STAFFING/
DEVELOPMENT
180 EAST BROAD ST.
COLUMBUS, OH 43215
TEL: (614) 225-4505
FAX: (614) 225-7263

Anthony S. D'Amato, Chairman. Foods and other diversified products. Borden, Inc. is a public company founded in 1857 by Gail Borden, Jr. Today, Borden is a worldwide producer of foods, non-food consumer products, and packaging and industrial items. It is the largest producer of dairy products in the United States. Other items include: frozen deserts, pasta, wallcoverings, and vinyl foodwrap films. It has over 100 plants in the United States and in 47 foreign countries. Worldwide revenues for 1992: $7.1 billion.

- **Total Employees:** 41,900

- **U.S. Employees Abroad:** 40

- **Countries:** Australia, Brazil, Canada, Costa Rica, Colombia, Italy, Japan, Malaysia, Netherlands, Panama, Philippines, Singapore, United Kingdom.

- **Salaries:** $50,000-$110,000 per year.

- **Job Categories:** Finance, Management.

- **General Requirements:** Prior overseas experience is preferred.

- **Average Overseas Assignment:** 5 years or more.

- **Language Requirement:** Knowledge of local language a plus but not essential.

- **Training:** Basic orientation (1-30 days) provided.

- **Benefits:** TRAVEL: Offered; home leave, economy airfare, and rental car included, annually. HEALTH: Same coverage as U.S. employees HOUSING: Offered. EDUCATION: Offered for children in grades K-12.

BORG-WARNER CORPORATION

200 South Michigan Ave.
Chicago, IL 60604 USA

RECRUITER: ANGELA J. D'AVERSA
DIRECTOR, HUMAN RESOURCES
200 SOUTH MICHIGAN AVE.
CHICAGO, IL 60604
TEL: (312) 322-8648
FAX: (312) 322-8599

Donald C. Trauscht, President. Automotive parts; protective and securities services. Borg-Warner is a private company begun in 1928 when four major auto parts companies (Borg & Beck, Warner Gear, Mechanics Universal Joint, and Marvel Carburetor) merged in Chicago. It now manufactures automotive parts and is a leading provider of protective and security services. The automotive segment operates 17 facilities in the United States, Canada, Germany, Italy, Japan, Korea, and the United Kingdom. The protective services group operates in North and South America. Worldwide revenues for 1991: $2.3 billion. Foreign revenues for 1991: $283 million.

- **Total Employees:** 83,000

- **U.S. Employees Abroad:** 100

- **Countries:** Brazil, Germany, Italy, Japan, Republic of Korea, United Kingdom, Canada.

- **Job Categories:** Accountants, Engineers, Manufacturing.

- **Language Requirement:** Competency in local language required.

BORLAND INTERNATIONAL, INC

1800 Green Hills Rd.
Scotts Valley, CA 95066 USA

RECRUITER: JILL STANGER
STAFFING/RECRUITMENT
1800 GREEN HILLS RD.
SCOTTS VALLEY, CA 95067-0001
TEL: (408) 438-8400
FAX: (408) 439-9327

Phillippe R. Kahn, President and Chairman. Prepackaged software. Borland International, Inc. is a private company founded in 1983. Today, it is the third largest manufacturer of PC sofware in the world. It is engaged as a developer and marketer of software as well as providing installation and instructions on the usage of its products. Worldwide net revenues 1992: $483 million.

- **Total Employees:** 1,893
- **U.S. Employees Abroad:** 23
- **Countries:** Australia, Canada, Denmark, France, Germany, Italy, Japan, New Zealand, Spain, Sweden, United Kingdom.
- **Application Information:** Job Hotline number 408/439-1598
- **Job Categories:** Accountants, Administrative, Engineers, Management, Public Relations, Technical Writers.
- **Language Requirement:** Varies with each posting.

BOSE CORPORATION

100 The Mountain Rd.
Framingham, MA 01701 USA

RECRUITER: DIRECTOR
PERSONNEL DEPARTMENT
100 THE MOUNTAIN RD.
FRAMINGHAM, MA 01701
TEL: (508) 879-7330

Shewin Greenblat, President. Electronic equipment. Bose is a private company founded in 1964. It manufactures electronic audio and video equipment for home and auto and public address systems or music distribution apparatus. Bose also produces radio and television broadcasting or communications equipment. Worldwide revenues for 1991: $470 million.

- **Total Employees:** 1,200
- **U.S. Employees Abroad:** 25
- **Countries:** Australia, Belgium, Canada, Denmark, France, Germany, Greece, Italy, Japan, Spain, Switzerland, United Kingdom.
- **Job Categories:** Manufacturing, Marketing—Electronics, Sales—Electronics.
- **Language Requirement:** None.
- **Training:** No special training provided.
- **Benefits:** All benefits are individually determined.

BP AMERICA, INC.

200 Public Square
Cleveland, OH 44114-2375 USA

RECRUITER: VP, HUMAN RESOURCES
HUMAN RESOURCES
REPRESENTATIVE
200 PUBLIC SQUARE
CLEVELAND, OH 44114-2375
TEL: (216) 586-4141
FAX: (216) 586-4050

James Ross, President. Crude oil production, chemicals, and natural gas. BP America, Inc. was founded in 1987 and is a wholly owned subsidiary of British Petroleum Company of London, UK. BP America's main businesses include oil, natural gas, and chemicals. It is also a refiner and marketer of petroleum products. Worldwide revenues for 1991: $16.2 billion.

- **Total Employees:** 39,000

- **U.S. Employees Abroad:** 100

- **Countries:** Worldwide including France, Germany, Japan, United Kingdom.

- **Application Information:** Most foreign positions are filled internally.

- **Job Categories:** Administrative, Engineers, Marketing—Chemicals, Marketing—Petroleum/Natural Gas, Sales—Chemicals, Sales—Petroleum/Natural Gas.

- **General Requirements:** Applicant must have a degree related to area of employment.

W. H. BRADY COMPANY

PO Box 571
Milwaukee, WI 53201 USA

RECRUITER: JOSEPH DAVIA
INTERNATIONAL COMPENSATION
MANAGER
PO BOX 571
MILWAUKEE, WI 53201
TEL: (414) 332-8100
FAX: (414) 332-0861

Paul G. Gengler, President. Industrial identification and coated film products. W. H. Brady is a public company founded in 1914. Major products include Letterizer Portable Lettering System and Permasleeve wire markers. Business is conducted in the United States and abroad. Worldwide revenues for 1991: $211.1 million.

- **Total Employees:** 1,765

- **U.S. Employees Abroad:** 40

- **Countries:** Australia, Belgium, Canada, France, Germany, Hong Kong, Italy, Sweden, United Kingdom.

- **Job Categories:** Management, Marketing—Industrial, Sales—Industrial.

BRIDGESTONE-FIRESTONE, INC.

50 Century Blvd.
Nashville, TN 37214 USA

RECRUITER: DONALD E. OKEY
MANAGER, INTERNATIONAL HUMAN
RESOURCES
50 CENTURY BLVD.
NASHVILLE, TN 37214
TEL: (615) 872-1442
FAX: (615) 872-1575

Yoichiro Kaizaki, Chairman. Auto and aircraft tires, automotive components, and industrial rubber products. Bridgestone-Firestone was founded in 1900 and is a manufacturing subsidiary of Bridgestone Corporation of Tokyo, Japan. Worldwide revenues for 1991: $8 billion.

- **Total Employees:** 41,000
- **U.S. Employees Abroad:** 60
- **Countries:** Argentina, Australia, Belgium, Brazil, Canada, Denmark, France, Germany, Indonesia, Italy, Japan, Malaysia, Mexico, Netherlands, New Zealand, Portugal, Singapore, Spain, Sweden, Switzerland, Taiwan, Thailand, Turkey, United Kingdom.
- **Job Categories:** Accountants, Factory Management, Finance, Management, Plant Engineers, Plant Managers, Sales—Automotive, Technicians.
- **Average Overseas Assignment:** 3-5 years.
- **Language Requirement:** Knowledge of local language skills a plus but not essential.
- **Training:** Basic orientation (1-30 days) provided.
- **Benefits:** TRAVEL: Annual or bi-annual plans are offered; round-trip air transportation (only) to employee and dependents to home base. HEALTH: Same coverage as U.S. employees. HOUSING: Offered; cost-of-living, foreign service premium, hardship premium for designated areas, and housing allowances. EDUCATION: Offered; allowances for grades 1-12 when local free schooling is unavailable or inadequate.

BRISTOL BABCOCK, INC.

1100 Buckingham St.
Watertown, CT 06795 USA

RECRUITER: DAN DIDRIO
HUMAN RESOURCES SUPERVISOR
1100 BUCKINGHAM ST.
WATERTOWN, CT 06795
TEL: (203) 575-3000
FAX: (203) 575-3170

Gregory Altman, President. Process controls; gas and power; and waste water treatment. Bristol Babcock was founded in 1889 and is a subsidiary of FKI Babcock, Inc. of Fairfield, Connecticut. It produces instruments for industries that measure, display, or control process variables. Worldwide revenues for 1991: $63 million.

- **Total Employees:** 1,600
- **U.S. Employees Abroad:** 25
- **Countries:** Australia, Mexico.

- **Application Information:** Hiring for most foreign positions is done at the specific country location.
- **Job Categories:** Engineers, Management, Marketing—Industrial, Sales—Industrial.
- **Average Overseas Assignment:** Less than two years.
- **Language Requirement:** None.
- **Training:** No special training provided.
- **Benefits:** All benefits are individually determined.

BRISTOL-MEYERS SQUIBB COMPANY

345 Park Ave., 3rd Floor
New York, NY 10154 USA

RECRUITER: MICHAEL MCDONNELL
DIRECTOR, CONSUMER PRODUCTS
GROUP- INTERNATIONAL
345 PARK AVE., 3RD FLOOR
NEW YORK, NY 10154-0037
TEL: (212) 546-3751
FAX: (212) 546-9707

Richard L. Gelb, Chairman. Pharmaceutical, health-care, and consumer products. Bristol-Meyers Squibb is a public company. Both Squibb and Bristol-Meyers originated in the 19th century. Squibb was founded by Edward Squibb in New York City in 1858. Bristol-Meyers was begun as Clinton Pharmaceutical of Clinton, New York, in 1887 by William Bristol and John Meyers. Bristol-Meyers bought Squibb in 1989 for $12.7 billion. It is now a major drug and consumer-products company and a global leader in anti-cancer drugs and treatments for high blood pressure.   Worldwide revenues for 1992: $11.2 billion.

- **Total Employees:** 50,000
- **U.S. Employees Abroad:** 95
- **Countries:** Australia, Belgium, Brazil, Canada, Chile, People's Republic of China, Dominican Republic, Ecuador, Egypt, France, Germany, Greece, Hong Kong, Indonesia, Italy, Jamaica, Japan, Republic of Korea, Malaysia, Mexico, Netherlands, New Zealand, Philippines, Portugal, Puerto Rico, Spain, Switzerland, Taiwan, Thailand, United Kingdom, Venezuela.
- **Application Information:** Most foreign positions are filled internally.
- **Salaries:** $50,000–$250,000 per year.
- **Job Categories:** Human Resources, Finance, Executive Management.
- **Average Overseas Assignment:** 3-5 years.
- **Language Requirement:** Knowledge of local language a plus but not essential.
- **Training:** Cultural orientation training optional for entire family; language courses optional for entire family.
- **Benefits:** TRAVEL: Annual home leave provided with air fare for employee and family. Air fare for dependent children to visit parents is provided twice each year. HEALTH: Provides continuing U.S. benefits, where possible. If coverage under local benefit

program is compulsory; appropriate offsets are made. HOUSING: If employee's housing expense exceeds the cost of comparable U.S. housing (based on U.S. national average) company provides a subsidy. EDUCATION: Covered for grades K-12; cost for language training provided if curriculum at local school is not conducted in a language in which child is proficient.

- **Comments:** Other allowances/subsidies may be available for appropriate employees on international assignments for less than five years.

BROWN GROUP, INC.

8400 Maryland Ave.
St. Louis, MO 63105 USA

RECRUITER: ART CROCI
PERSONNEL DEPARTMENT
8400 MARYLAND AVE.
ST. LOUIS, MO 63105
TEL: (314) 854-4000
FAX: (314) 854-4274

B. A. Bridgewater, Jr., President and Chairman. Footwear and specialty retailing. Brown Group is a public company founded in 1878. Today, the firm is a major marketer of footwear. Popular brand names include Naturalizer and Life Stride women's shoes. The company operates on an international scale. Worldwide revenues for 1992: $1.8 billion. Foreign Sales for 1992: $383 million.

- **Total Employees:** 23,000
- **U.S. Employees Abroad:** 70
- **Countries:** Brazil, People's Republic of China, Hong Kong, Indonesia, Italy, Taiwan.
- **Application Information:** Most foreign positions are filled internally.
- **Job Categories:** Finance, Management, Quality Assurance.
- **Language Requirement:** Knowledge of local language a plus but not essential.
- **Training:** Basic orientation (1-30 days) provided.

BROWN & SHARPE MANUFACTURING COMPANY

Precision Park
North Kingstown, RI 02852 USA

RECRUITER: RALPH W. CHASE, JR.
MANAGER, DEVELOPMENT &
RECRUITMENT
PRECISION PARK
NORTH KINGSTON, RI 02852
TEL: (401) 886-2000
FAX: (401) 886-2762

Dr. Fred Stuber, President. Metrology products: hand-operated measuring tools, precision tools coordinate measuring machines. Brown & Sharpe is a public company founded in 1833. Today, it designs, manufactures, and markets a diversified line of metrology products and a line of metal-cutting machine tools on an international scale. Worldwide revenues for 1991: $175.8 million.

- **Total Employees:** 2,000

- **U.S. Employees Abroad:** 5
- **Countries:** Germany, Switzerland, United Kingdom.
- **Job Categories:** Management, Marketing—Scientific, Sales—Scientific.
- **Language Requirement:** Fluency in local language required.
- **Training:** No special training provided.
- **Benefits:** Vary with each posting.
- **Comments:** The number of Americans reported working abroad varies greatly from quarter to quarter, fluctuating with the number and scope of projects under contract at the time.

BROWN & WILLIAMSON TOBACCO CORPORATION

PO Box 35090
Louisville, KY 40232 USA

RECRUITER: JERRY W. HUMPHREY
MANAGER, INT'L. RECRUITMENT &
   TRAINING
PO BOX 35090
LOUISVILLE, KY 40232
TEL: (502) 568-7892
FAX: (502) 568-7120

R. J. Pritchard, Chairman. Tobacco products. Brown & Williamson was founded in 1929 and it is a subsidiary of London-based BAT Industries. It manufactures, distributes, and sells tobacco products. Worldwide revenues for 1991: $2.6 billion.

- **Total Employees:** 216
- **U.S. Employees Abroad:** 8
- **Countries:** Worldwide including Costa Rica, Turkey.
- **Job Categories:** Administrative, Marketing—Consumer Goods, Sales—Consumer Goods.
- **Average Overseas Assignment:** 2-3 years.
- **Language Requirement:** Knowledge of local language a plus but not essential.
- **Training:** No special training provided.
- **Comments:** The number of Americans reported working abroad varies greatly from quarter to quarter, fluctuating with the number and scope of projects under contract at the time.

BROWNING-FERRIS INDUSTRIES

PO Box 3151
Houston, TX 77253 USA

RECRUITER: STEVE FLEWELLING
HUMAN RESOURCES
PO BOX 3151
HOUSTON, TX 77253
TEL: (713) 870-8100
FAX: (713) 589-3131

William D. Ruckelhaus, Chairman. Waste services. Browning-Ferris Industries is a public company founded in 1967 by Tom Fatjo and Louis Waters. The business began with one garbage truck to collect refuse and today the company operates on a worldwide basis. It collects, treats, and disposes of commercial, municipal, and residential solid waste. It has over 450 locations in the United States and abroad. Worldwide revenues for 1992: $3.3 billion.

- **Total Employees:** 25,200
- **U.S. Employees Abroad:** Not available.
- **Countries:** Australia, Canada, Hong Kong, Italy, Netherlands, New Zealand, Spain, United Kingdom, Venezuela.
- **Job Categories:** Management, Marketing, Sales.
- **Language Requirement:** None.
- **Training:** No special training provided.

BRUSH WELLMAN, INC.

1200 Hanna Building
Cleveland, OH 44115 USA

RECRUITER: DANIEL SKOCH
DIRECTOR, HUMAN RESOURCES
1200 HANNA BUILDING
CLEVELAND, OH 44115
TEL: (216) 486-4200
FAX: (216) 486-4091

Henry G. Piper, President. International supplier of engineered materials. Brush Wellman is a public company founded in 1931. It is a totally integrated source of beryllium, beryllium alloys, and beryllia ceramic, as well as a supplier of precious metal products. Worldwide revenues for 1992: $265 million.

- **Total Employees:** 1,830
- **U.S. Employees Abroad:** Not available.
- **Countries:** Germany, Japan, United Kingdom.
- **Job Categories:** Finance, Management, Marketing, Sales.

BUCK CONSULTANTS, INC.

500 Plaza Dr.
Secaucus, NJ 07096-1533 USA

RECRUITER: LAURIE J. ZAYAT
RECRUITING SPECIALIST
500 PLAZA DR.
SEACAUCUS, NJ 07096-1533
TEL: (201) 902-2300
FAX: (201) 902-2450

William E. Geigerich, President. Consulting services. Buck Consultants is a private company servicing clients on a worldwide scale. The firm acts as acturial and compensation consultants and concentrates on pension and retirement planning. Worldwide revenues for 1991: $150 million.

- **Total Employees:** 1,400
- **U.S. Employees Abroad:** 25
- **Countries:** Australia, Belgium, Canada, Hong Kong, Mexico, United Kingdom.
- **Job Categories:** Consultants—Financial, Finance, Marketing.
- **Language Requirement:** None.

BURLINGTON AIR EXPRESS

18200 Von Karman Ave.
Irvine, CA 92715 USA

RECRUITER: CHRISTINE HOERSCH
MANAGER OF EMPLOYMENT
18200 VON KARMAN AVE.
IRVINE, CA 92715
TEL: (714) 752-4000
FAX: (714) 851-3917

David C. Marshall, Chairman. Domestic and international air freight. Burlington Air Express was founded in 1972. It is a subsidiary of the Pittston Company of Greenwich, Connecticut. It is a provider of air courier services for letters and packages. Worldwide revenues for 1991: $975 million.

- **Total Employees:** 5,000
- **U.S. Employees Abroad:** 60
- **Countries:** Australia, Belgium, Canada, France, Germany, Hong Kong, Japan, Malawi, Malaysia, Netherlands, New Zealand, Singapore, Republic of South Africa, Taiwan, United Kingdom, Zambia.
- **Application Information:** Hiring for most foreign positions is done at the specific country location.
- **Job Categories:** Customer Services, Management, Marketing, Sales.
- **Language Requirement:** Knowledge of local language a plus but not essential.
- **Training:** No special training provided.
- **Benefits:** All benefits are individually determined.

BURNS INTERNATIONAL SECURITY SERVICES

2 Campus Dr.
Parsippany, NJ 07054 USA

RECRUITER: BARRY KINGMAN
TRAINING & DEVELOPMENT
2 CAMPUS DR.
PARSIPPANY, NJ 07054
TEL: (201) 397-2000
FAX: (201) 397-2493

Rodger Comstock, President. Physical security, investment services. Burns International Security Services is a subsidiary of Borg-Warner Corporation of Chicago, Illinois. This firm provides security guard services, investment and counseling services for industrial and institutional clients. Worldwide revenues for 1991: $920 million.

- **Total Employees:** 40,000

- **U.S. Employees Abroad:** 75
- **Countries:** Canada, Colombia, United Kingdom.
- **Job Categories:** Security Officers.
- **Language Requirement:** Knowledge of local language a plus but not essential.
- **Training:** Basic orientation (1-30 days) provided.
- **Benefits:** All benefits are individually determined.

BURNS & ROE, INC.

550 Kinderkamack Rd.
Oradell, NJ 07649 USA

RECRUITER: JAMES ROWAN
DIRECTOR, EMPLOYEE RELATIONS
550 KINDERKAMACK RD.
ORADELL, NJ 07649
TEL: (201) 265-2000
FAX: (201) 265-2997

K. Keith Roe, President. Heavy construction and related services. Burns & Roe, Inc. is a private company founded in 1932. It offers architectural, engineering, and heavy construction services on a global basis. Projects include nuclear power plants. Worldwide operating revenues for 1991: $130 million.

- **Total Employees:** 1,600
- **U.S. Employees Abroad:** 40
- **Countries:** Australia, Dominican Republic, Hong Kong.
- **Job Categories:** Architects, Engineers, Technical Field Support.
- **Language Requirement:** None.
- **Training:** No special training provided.

BURSON-MARSTELLER

230 Park Ave.
New York, NY 10003-1566 USA

RECRUITER: GREG WALDRON
HUMAN RESOURCES
REPRESENTATIVE
230 PARK AVE.
NEW YORK, NY 10003-1566
TEL: (212) 614-4000
FAX: (212) 614-4489

William Noonan, President. Consulting services, public relations/public affairs. Burson-Marsteller was founded in 1979 and is a subsidiary of Young & Rubicam Inc. of New York City. Business is conducted in the United States and abroad.

- **Total Employees:** 2,100
- **U.S. Employees Abroad:** 35
- **Countries:** Australia, Belgium, Canada, Germany, Hong Kong, Italy, Japan, Netherlands, Singapore, Switzerland, United Kingdom.

- **Job Categories:** Consultants—Financial, Public Relations.

- **Training:** No special training provided.

CABOT CORPORATION

75 State St.
Boston, MA 02116 USA

RECRUITER: SARAH CUTHILL
MANAGER, INTERNATIONAL
    ASSIGNMENTS
75 STATE ST.
BOSTON, MA 02116
TEL: (617) 345-0100
FAX: (617) 342-6103

Samuel W. Bodman, Chairman. Specialty chemicals; importer of liquid natural gas. Cabot Corporation is a public company founded in 1882 by Godfrey L. Cabot. It was incorporated in Delaware in 1960 as a successor to G. L. Cabot and three of its domestic subsidiaries. The business is involved in specialty chemicals and materials and energy. The energy group searches for and produces oil and natural gas. It also distributes coal products. Cabot is the only global manufacturer of carbon black. Currently, it has 26 plants in 17 countries. Worldwide revenues for 1992: $1.6 billion.

- **Total Employees:** 5,500

- **U.S. Employees Abroad:** 40

- **Countries:** Argentina, Australia, Belgium, Brazil, Canada, People's Republic of China, France, Germany, Indonesia, Italy, Japan, Malaysia, Mexico, Netherlands, Spain, United Kingdom, Venezuela.

- **Job Categories:** Chemical Engineers, Marketing—Chemicals, Marketing—Petroleum/Natural Gas, Plant Managers.

- **General Requirements:** Usually must be a current employee of the company in order to qualify for overseas assignment.

- **Average Overseas Assignment:** 3-5 years.

- **Language Requirement:** Knowledge of local language a plus but not essential.

- **Training:** A cross-cultural orientation (2-3 days) and language training are provided.

- **Benefits:** All benefits are individually determined.

- **Comments:** Depending on the requirements of the job, the company provides expatriate employees with some cost-of-living allowances. A technical degree is required for plant manager positions.

CALGON CORPORATION

PO Box 1346
Pittsburgh, PA 15230 USA

RECRUITER: MICHAEL KNOLL
MANAGER, EMPLOYMENT AND
STAFFING
PO BOX 1346
PITTSBURGH, PA 15230
TEL: (412) 777-8000
FAX: (412) 777-8104

A. Fred Kerst, President. Industrial inorganic chemicals and preparations; personal care items. Calgon was founded in 1918 and is a subsidiary of Merck and Company of Rahway, New Jersey. Worldwide revenues for 1992: $200 million.

- **Total Employees:** 1,100

- **U.S. Employees Abroad:** Not available.

- **Countries:** Belgium, Canada, Japan, Mexico, Saudi Arabia, Republic of South Africa, Venezuela, United Kingdom.

- **Application Information:** Most foreign positions are filled internally.

- **Job Categories:** Management, Manufacturing, Marketing—Chemicals, Marketing—Consumer Goods, Sales—Chemicals, Sales—Consumer Goods.

CALIFORNIA PELLET MILL COMPANY

150 Burke St.
Nashua, NH 03061 USA

RECRUITER: JOHN CLANCY
VP, EMPLOYEE RELATIONS
150 BURKE ST.
NASHUA, NH 03061
TEL: (603) 882-2711
FAX: (603) 883-7238

Larry Pitsch, President. Machinery for pelletizing machines. California Pellet Mill was founded in 1974 and is a subsidiary of Ingersoll-Rand Company of Woodcliff Lake, New Jersey.

- **Total Employees:** 450

- **U.S. Employees Abroad:** Not available.

- **Countries:** Ireland, Netherlands, Singapore, United Kingdom.

- **Job Categories:** Administrative, Sales—Industrial.

- **Language Requirement:** Knowledge of local language a plus but not essential.

- **Training:** No special training provided.

CAMP DRESSER & MCKEE INTERNATIONAL, INC.

1 Cambridge Center
Cambridge, MA 02142 USA

RECRUITER: PHILIP STEFANINI
MANAGER, HUMAN RESOURCES
1 CAMBRIDGE CENTER
CAMBRIDGE, MA 02142
TEL: (617) 252-8000
FAX: (617) 577-7504

Joseph E. Henry, President. Contract engineers. Camp Dresser & McKee is a private company founded in 1947. It offers professional engineering services to clients in the United States and abroad. Worldwide operating revenues for 1991: $268 million.

- **Total Employees:** 2,000
- **U.S. Employees Abroad:** Not available.
- **Countries:** Australia, Egypt, Jamaica, Philippines, Singapore, Sri Lanka, Uruguay.
- **Job Categories:** Administrative, Engineers.
- **Language Requirement:** Varies with each posting.
- **Comments:** The number of Americans reported working abroad varies greatly from quarter to quarter, fluctuating with the number and scope of projects under contract at the time.

CAMPBELL SOUP COMPANY

Campbell Place
Camden, NJ 08103 USA

RECRUITER: TOM ALGEO
RECRUITMENT STAFF-INTERNATIONAL
CAMPBELL PLACE
CAMDEN, NJ 08103
TEL: (609) 342-4800
FAX: (609) 338-0501

David W. Johnson, President. Food products. Campbell Soup is a public company founded in 1869. It produces and sells food products including soups, canned and microwaveable food items, snack foods, and vegetable juices. Worldwide revenues for 1992: $6.5 billion.

- **Total Employees:** 45,000
- **U.S. Employees Abroad:** 25
- **Countries:** Belgium, Canada, France, Hong Kong, Mexico, United Kingdom.
- **Job Categories:** Finance, Management, Product Development, Sales—Food/Food Services.
- **General Requirements:** Usually must be a current employee of the company in order to qualify for overseas assignment.
- **Average Overseas Assignment:** 3-5 years.
- **Language Requirement:** Varies with each posting.
- **Training:** No special training provided.
- **Benefits:** All benefits are individually determined.

CAPITOL CITIES/ABC, INC.

77 West 66th St.
New York, NY 10023-6298 USA

RECRUITER: ELIZABETH HINDS
DIRECTOR, EMPLOYEE RELATIONS
77 WEST 66TH ST.
NEW YORK, NY 10023-6298
TEL: (212) 456-7777
FAX: (212) 456-7112

Thomas S. Murphy, Chairman. Communications: television, radio, and print. Capitol Cities/ABC is a public company founded in 1934. Operating from New York City, this company is a spin-off from RCA's Blue Network. In 1986, Capitol Cities Communications purchased ABC for $3.5 billion. Today, ABC broadcasts through 227 television affiliates and eight owned television stations. Capitol Cities publishes newspapers, magazines, and trade publications. Worldwide revenues for 1992: $5.3 billion.

- **Total Employees:** 20,000
- **U.S. Employees Abroad:** 150
- **Countries:** France, Germany, Japan, Venezuela.
- **Job Categories:** Administrative, Finance, Marketing, Marketing—Publishing, Public Relations, Sales, Sales—Publishing.
- **Training:** No special training provided.

CARGILL INCORPORATED

PO Box 9300
Minneapolis, MN 55440 USA

RECRUITER: CHRISTIE L. NEWMAN
HUMAN RESOURCES DEPARTMENT
PO BOX 9300
MINNEAPOLIS, MN 55440
TEL: (612) 475-7833
FAX: (612) 475-6208

Whitney Macmillan, Chairman. Food products; grains and seeds; animal products; and financial and agricultural consulting services. Cargill is a private company founded in 1865 by William Cargill when he became the owner of the first grain flat house in Conover, Iowa, soon after the Civil War. During the Depression, Cargill expanded, building river barges necessary to transport its products. Currently, Cargill is the largest privately held company in the United States. Cargill's diversified enterprises include 300 active companies with more than 60,000 employees in 58 countries. Largest operations are in Canada, Brazil, Argentina, and Europe. Worldwide revenues for 1991: $42.0 billion.

- **Total Employees:** 60,000
- **U.S. Employees Abroad:** 150
- **Countries:** Worldwide including Argentina, Australia, Bahamas, Brazil, Canada, France, Hong Kong, Indonesia, Japan, Singapore, United Kingdom.

- **Job Categories:** Consultants—Financial, Management, Marketing—Agricultural, Marketing—Food/Food Services, Sales—Agricultural, Sales—Food/Food Services.
- **Average Overseas Assignment:** 2-3 years.

CARLSON TRAVEL NETWORK

PO Box 59159
Minneapolis, MN 55459 USA

RECRUITER: TOM DYBSKY
VP, HUMAN RESOURCES
PO BOX 59159
MINNEAPOLIS, MN 55459-8206
TEL: (612) 540-8941
FAX: (612) 449-2311

Charles Schmid, President. Travel services. Carlson Companies, Inc. was founded in 1938 when Curtis Carlson, son of Swedish immigrants, formed the Gold Bond Stamp Company. He and his wife, Arlene, were so successful that by 1960, they were able to invest in other enterprises, including the purchase of travel agencies. Today, this worldwide business is a travel/hotel/marketing company. The Travel Group has 2,100 offices in the United States, Canada, and the United Kingdom. Worldwide revenues for 1992: $6 billion.

- **Total Employees:** 14,000
- **U.S. Employees Abroad:** 20
- **Countries:** Nineteen including Canada, France, Germany, Netherlands, United Kingdom.
- **Application Information:** Accepts unsolicited resumes; may be filled out on site or mailed to recruiter's address.
- **Job Categories:** Management, Marketing—Travel, Sales—Travel.
- **Language Requirement:** Local language skills a plus but not essential.
- **Training:** Basic orientation (1-30 days) provided.
- **Benefits:** All benefits are individually determined.

CARNIVAL CRUISE LINES

Carnival Place
3655 NW 87th Ave.
Miami, FL 33178 USA

RECRUITER: STEVE SMITH AND
GLENN FUSFIELD
STAFFING/RECRUITMENT
CARNIVAL PLACE
3655 NW 87TH AVE.
MIAMI, FL 33178
TEL: (305) 599-2600
FAX: (305) 471-4807
FREE: (800) 327-7373

Micky Arison, President. Hotel and passenger cruise line. Carnival Cruise Lines, Inc. is a public company founded in 1974. It offers cruises on a variety of ships, including Carnivale, Holland America, Premier, and Windstar. It earns most of its revenues from passenger tickets and the goods and services sold aboard ship. It is a leading wholesale tour operator (Westours) and it also operates the largest hotel chain in Alaska and western Canada (Westmark). Worldwide revenues for 1991: $1.4 billion.

- **Total Employees:** 16,000
- **U.S. Employees Abroad:** 75
- **Countries:** Bahamas, Canada, Mexico.
- **Job Categories:** Entertainers, Hotel Management, Pursers.
- **Language Requirement:** None.
- **Training:** No special training provided.
- **Benefits:** HOUSING: Housing is provided on board ship.
- **Comments:** Staffing/Recruitment has two divisions: Steve Smith (Entertainment) and Glenn Fusfield (Hotel Management and Pursers).

CARRIER CORPORATION

PO Box 4806
Syracuse, NY 13221 USA

RECRUITER: PERSONNEL DEPARTMENT
DIRECTOR, HUMAN RESOURCES
PO BOX 4806
SYRACUSE, NY 13221
TEL: (315) 432-6000
FAX: (315) 432-7709

William A. Wilson, President. Air-conditioning and refrigeration products. Carrier is a subsidiary of United Technologies Corporation of Hartford, Connecticut. It was established in 1915. It produces refrigeration equipment and systems as well as air-conditioning units and warm-air furnace systems. Worldwide revenues for 1992: $3.8 billion.

- **Total Employees:** 28,000
- **U.S. Employees Abroad:** 45
- **Countries:** Argentina, Australia, Bahamas, France, Italy, Japan, Mexico, Saudi Arabia, Singapore, Switzerland, United Kingdom.
- **Application Information:** Three offices abroad handle hiring for international assignments.
- **Job Categories:** Management, Marketing, Sales, Technicians.
- **General Requirements:** Usually must be a current employee of the company in order to qualify for overseas assignment.
- **Average Overseas Assignment:** 3-5 years.
- **Language Requirement:** Competency in local language required.
- **Training:** Basic orientation and specific work skills training provided.
- **Benefits:** TRAVEL: Included in employee benefits. HEALTH: Included in employee benefits. HOUSING: Offered. EDUCATION: Offered.

CARTER-WALLACE, INC.

1345 Avenue of the Americas
New York, NY 10105-0021 USA

RECRUITER: MIGUEL FERNANDEZ
PRESIDENT, INTERNATIONAL
2 RESEARCH WAY
PRINCETON, NJ 08450-6628
TEL: (609) 520-3100
FAX: (609) 520-3114

Henry H. Hoyt, Jr., Chairman. Consumer and health-products. Carter-Wallace, Inc. is a public company founded in 1937 as Carter Products. Well-known brands included Rise (shaving cream) and Nair (depilitory). It entered the drug industry in the 1950s and purchased Lambert-Kay, a pet drug and nutritional products business in 1968. Today, this company produces a variety of of prescription drugs, as well as items promoting safe sex (condoms) and early pregnancy detection products. Worldwide revenues for 1993: $635 million.

- **Total Employees:** 4,270

- **U.S. Employees Abroad:** 40

- **Countries:** Australia, Canada, Italy, Mexico, United Kingdom.

- **Job Categories:** Marketing—Consumer Goods, Marketing—Pharmaceuticals, Research & Development, Sales—Consumer Goods, Sales—Pharmaceuticals.

- **Language Requirement:** Varies with each posting.

J. I. CASE COMPANY

700 State St.
Racine, WI 53404 USA

RECRUITER: MARC CASTOR
SENIOR VP, EMPLOYEE RELATIONS
700 STATE ST.
RACINE, WI 53404
TEL: (414) 636-6011
FAX: (414) 636-7188

James K. Ashford, President. Industrial equipment for commercial markets. J. I. Case is a subsidiary of Tenneco Inc. of Houston, Texas. It manufactures and markets agricultural, construction, mining, and forestry equipment. Worldwide revenues for 1991: $4.4 billion.

- **Total Employees:** 29,300

- **U.S. Employees Abroad:** 125

- **Countries:** Australia, France, Germany, Singapore, United Kingdom.

- **Job Categories:** Management, Marketing—Industrial, Sales—Industrial.

CENTOCOR, INC.
244 Great Valley Pkwy.
Malvern, PA 19355 USA

RECRUITER: PAULA SANTRY
STAFFING/RECRUITMENT
244 GREAT VALLEY PKWY.
MALVERN, PA 19355
TEL: (215) 296-4488
FAX: (215) 651-6330

Hubert J. P. Schoemaker, Chairman. Biopharmaceuticals. Centocor, Inc. is a public company founded in 1979. It focuses on the development of monoclonal antibody products and diagnostic substances. Products are concentrated in four main disease areas: cardiovascular, infectious and autoimmune disease, and cancer. It has facilities in the United States and abroad. Worldwide revenues for 1992: $58.4 million.

- **Total Employees:** 1,400
- **U.S. Employees Abroad:** 15
- **Countries:** Japan, Netherlands.
- **Job Categories:** Management, Marketing—Pharmaceuticals, Research & Development, Sales—Pharmaceuticals.
- **Language Requirement:** None.

CENTRAL SOYA COMPANY
PO Box 1400
Fort Wayne, IN 46801 USA

RECRUITER: THOMAS A. THEARD
PERSONNEL MANAGER
PO BOX 1400
FORT WAYNE, IN 46801
TEL: (219) 425-5100

David H. Swanson, President. Livestock processing, poultry feed, soybeans. Central Soya is a private company founded in 1934. It produces soybeans and uses the meal as a protein ingredient for animal feeds. The business is divided into six major segments: canola processing; feed manufacturing; refined vegetable oils and shortening; research; soy proteins and lecithins; and soybean processing. Worldwide revenues for 1992: $1.9 billion.

- **Total Employees:** 3,500
- **U.S. Employees Abroad:** Not available.
- **Countries:** Canada, Italy, France.
- **Job Categories:** Marketing—Agricultural, Plant Managers, Sales—Agricultural.
- **Language Requirement:** None.

CHADBOURNE & PARKE

30 Rockefeller Plaza
New York, NY 10112 USA

RECRUITER: SUSANNE MANDEL
DIRECTOR, HUMAN RESOURCES-
INTERNATIONAL
30 ROCKEFELLER PLAZA
NEW YORK, NY 10112
TEL: (212) 408-5100

Legal services. Chadbourne & Parke is a private law firm founded in 1902. It offers legal advice and services to clients in the United States and abroad. Worldwide operating revenues for 1991: $100 million.

- **Total Employees:** 270
- **U.S. Employees Abroad:** 12
- **Countries:** United Arab Emirates, Russia.
- **Job Categories:** Attorneys, Legal Personnel.

CHAMPION INTERNATIONAL CORPORATION

One Champion Plaza
Stamford, CT 06921 USA

RECRUITER: KATHY PIERSA, NON-
EXEMPT STAFFING
JOHN LEWIS, PROFESSIONAL
STAFFING
ONE CHAMPION PLAZA
STAMFORD, CT 06921
TEL: (203) 358-7000
FAX: (203) 358-2776

Andrew S. Sigler, Chairman. Printing and writing papers; kraft, pulp and forest products. Champion is a public company founded in 1967 as a result of a merger of U.S. Plywood and Champion Paper & Fibre. Today this international firm is the 8th largest forest products company in the United States. It is a leading producer of paper for businesses and newspapers. Plant facilities are located in Brazil, Canada, and the United States. Worldwide revenues for 1992: $4.9 billion.

- **Total Employees:** 27,260
- **U.S. Employees Abroad:** 125
- **Countries:** Brazil, Canada.
- **Job Categories:** Administrative, Clerical Assistants, Management, Marketing, Sales.
- **Language Requirement:** None.
- **Training:** No special training provided.
- **Benefits:** All benefits are individually determined.

CHARTER MEDICAL CORPORATION

PO Box 209
Macon, GA 31298 USA

RECRUITER: RICHARD GODSCHALK
VICE PRESIDENT, INTERNATIONAL
PO BOX 209
MACON, GA 31298
TEL: (912) 742-1161
FAX: (912) 751-2909
FREE: (800) 841-9403

E. MacCrawford, Chief Executive Officer. Contract management of hospitals. Charter Medical Corporation began as a public company in 1969. It became private in 1988 in a leveraged buyout and went public again in 1992. Worldwide revenues for 1992: $1.2 billion.

- **Total Employees:** 12,000
- **U.S. Employees Abroad:** 20
- **Countries:** Switzerland, Saudi Arabia, United Kingdom.
- **Job Categories:** Hospital Administration, Medical Technicians, Nurses, Physicians, Psychiatrists.
- **Average Overseas Assignment:** Less than two years.
- **Language Requirement:** Knowledge of local language a plus but not essential.
- **Training:** No special training provided.
- **Benefits:** Competitive benefits package offered.

CHASE MANHATTAN CORPORATION

1 Chase Manhattan Plaza
New York, NY 10081 USA

RECRUITER: AMY SUDAL
DIRECTOR, HUMAN RESOURCES
1 CHASE MANHATTAN PLAZA
EMPLOYMENT, 22ND FLOOR
NEW YORK, NY 10081
TEL: (212) 552-2222
FAX: (212) 552-3875

Willard C. Butcher, Chairman. Commercial banking. Chase Manhattan is a public company founded in 1799 when the New York legislature created the Manhattan Company. It was created to bring pure water into the city. But, Alexander Hamilton lobbied to utilize any extra funds for other purposes. It proved successful and after the water company was sold to the city in 1808, the Bank of Manhattan managed to survive. In 1877, John Thompson began the Chase National Bank. Various changes and mergers occurred through the years and in 1955 Chase merged with the Bank of Manhattan. As of 1990, Chase Manhattan was the 3rd largest banking establishment in the United States. It operates in more than 50 foreign countries. Worldwide average assets for 1992: $95.9 billion.

- **Total Employees:** 41,100
- **U.S. Employees Abroad:** Not available.

- **Countries:** Worldwide including Australia, Bahamas, Brazil, Canada, Chile, Ecuador, Hong Kong, India, Philippines, Saudi Arabia, Sweden, Switzerland, Venezuela, United Kingdom.
- **Job Categories:** Administrative, Financial Advisors, Management, Marketing—Financial Services.
- **Training:** No special training provided.

BERNARD CHAUS, INC.

1410 Broadway
New York, NY 10018 USA

RECRUITER: ROBIN SANTELIA
HUMAN RESOURCES
REPRESENTATIVE
800 SEACAUCUS RD.
SEACAUCUS, NJ 07094
TEL: (201) 863-4646
FAX: (201) 863-1171

Josephine Chaus, Chairwoman. Women's apparel. Bernard Chaus, Inc. is a public company founded in 1975. It designs and markets women's clothing and related accessories. Brand names include Chaus and Josephine labels. Worldwide revenues for 1992: $254 million.

- **Total Employees:** 882
- **U.S. Employees Abroad:** 15
- **Countries:** Hong Kong, Republic of Korea, Philippines.
- **Job Categories:** Administrative, Design, Marketing—Consumer Goods, Sales—Consumer Goods.
- **Language Requirement:** None.

CHEMICAL BANKING CORPORATION

Grand Central Tower
New York, NY 10017 USA

RECRUITER: DAVID BROOKS
STAFFING/RECRUITMENT
55 WATER ST., ROOM #201
NEW YORK, NY 10014
TEL: (212) 310-6161
FAX: (212) 363-2986

Walter V. Shipley, Chairman. Commercial banking. Chemical Bank is a public company founded in 1956. In January 1993 it merged with Hanover's Corporation. It offers clients financial services throughout the world. Worldwide assets for 1992: $139.7 billion.

- **Total Employees:** 32,000
- **U.S. Employees Abroad:** Not available.
- **Countries:** Argentina, Bahamas, Canada, Hong Kong, Japan, Switzerland, United Kingdom, Venezuela.

● **Job Categories:** Executive Management, Finance, Marketing—Financial Services.

CHEMICAL FABRICS CORPORATION

701 Daniel Webster Hwy.
PO Box 1137
Merrimack, NH 03054 USA

RECRUITER: LINDA SHORT
HUMAN RESOURCES ADMINISTRATOR
701 DANIEL WEBSTER HWY.
PO BOX 1137
MERRIMACK, NH 03054
TEL: (603) 424-9000
FAX: (603) 424-9028

Duane C. Montopoli, President. Flexible composite products. Chemical Fabrics Corporation is a public company founded in 1968. It operates on an international basis as an advanced performance materials company. It produces and markets flexible composite products used in extreme environments. Products are sold to aerospace, architecture, chemical processing, military, protective clothing, and other industrial markets. Worldwide revenues for 1991: $51.1 million.

● **Total Employees:** 400

● **U.S. Employees Abroad:** 18

● **Countries:** Worldwide including Japan, United Kingdom.

● **Job Categories:** Marketing—Industrial, Product Development, Sales—Industrial.

● **Language Requirement:** None.

CHEVRON CHEMICAL COMPANY

PO Box 5047
San Ramon, CA 94583 USA

RECRUITER: KAREN MCGARY
HUMAN RESOURCES
PO BOX 5047
SAN RAMON, CA 94583-5047
TEL: (510) 842-5424
FAX: (510) 842-4505

John E. Peppercorn, President. Chemical production. Chevron Chemical was founded in 1928 and is a subsidiary of Chevron Corporation of San Francisco, California. It manufactures various industrial organic chemicals, agricultural chemicals, and pesticides. Worldwide revenues for 1991: $3.3 billion.

● **Total Employees:** 4,500

● **U.S. Employees Abroad:** 25

● **Countries:** Thirteen including Brazil, Canada, India, Mexico, Switzerland.

● **Job Categories:** Administrative, Chemists, Marketing—Chemicals, Sales—Chemicals.

● **General Requirements:** Usually must be a current employee of the company in order to qualify for overseas assignment.

● **Average Overseas Assignment:** 2-3 years.

● **Language Requirement:** Knowledge of local language skills a plus but not essential.

- **Training:** Language training provided.

- **Benefits:** All benefits are individually determined.

CHEVRON CORPORATION

PO Box 7318
San Francisco, CA 94120-7318
USA

RECRUITER: CHRIS LARDGE
PROFESSIONAL RECRUITING STAFF
PO BOX 7318
SAN FRANCISCO, CA 94120-7318
TEL: (415) 984-5104
FAX: (415) 894-0593

Kenneth T. Derr, Chairman. Crude oil exploration and production; refining and marketing; fuel transportation. Other products include chemicals, natural gas, and coal. Chevron is a public company founded in 1879. Wildcatter Frederick Taylor and other oil marketers formed the Pacific Oil Coast Company in California. John D. Rockefeller's Standard Oil Company purchased Pacific Coast Oil in 1900. After a number of mergers, the company was renamed Chevron in 1984, the same year it purchased Gulf Oil for a price of $13.3 billion. Today, Chevron is the 10th largest industrial company in the United States and conducts business in more than 100 countries. Worldwide revenues for 1992: $37.5 billion.

- **Total Employees:** 50,000

- **U.S. Employees Abroad:** 800

- **Countries:** Angola, Australia, Bolivia, Brazil, Canada, Chile, People's Republic of China, Congo, France, Indonesia, Ireland, Japan, Mexico, Netherlands, Guinea, Nigeria, Singapore, United Kingdom, Zaire.

- **Salaries:** $40,000 per year.

- **Job Categories:** Engineers, Geologists, Management.

- **General Requirements:** Usually a current employee. Overseas positions require specific skills and Chevron experience.

- **Average Overseas Assignment:** 3-5 years.

- **Language Requirement:** None.

- **Training:** Basic orientation (1-30 days) provided.

- **Benefits:** TRAVEL: A comprehensive assistance package for home visits and relocation is provided. HEALTH: Expatriates have the same medical plan that is provided to U.S. based employees. However, overseas employees do not have the option to enroll in HMOs. HOUSING: Housing equalization or rental reimbursement with home country deduction is provided. EDUCATION: Actual cost of local schools is reimbursed; average U.S. boarding school cost is reimbursed when local schools are not available.

- **Comments:** Chevron does not usually solicit applications for overseas positions from applicants outside of the company.

CHEVRON OVERSEAS PETROLEUM, INC.

6001 Bollinger Canyon Rd.
San Ramon, CA 94583 USA

RECRUITER: CAROL BRESLIN
HUMAN RESOURCES-RELOCATION &
DEVELOPMENT
6001 BOLLINGER CANYON RD.
SAN RAMON, CA 94583
TEL: (510) 842-1814

Richard Matzke, President. Petroleum explorer. Chevron Overseas Petroleum is a subsidiary of Chevron Corporation of San Francisco, California.

- **Total Employees:** 1,500
- **U.S. Employees Abroad:** 75
- **Countries:** Worldwide including Angola, People's Republic of China, Congo, Guinea, Nigeria, United Kingdom.
- **Job Categories:** Engineers, Finance, Management, Marketing—Petroleum/Natural Gas, Sales—Petroleum/Natural Gas.
- **General Requirements:** Usually must be a current employee of the company in order to qualify for overseas assignment.
- **Average Overseas Assignment:** 2-3 years.
- **Language Requirement:** Knowledge of local language skills a plus but not essential.
- **Training:** No special training provided.
- **Benefits:** All benefits are individually determined.

CHIRON CORPORATION

4560 Horton St.
Emeryville, CA 94608 USA

RECRUITER: CECILIA VITUG
DIRECTOR, HUMAN RESOURCES
4560 HORTON ST.
EMERYVILLE, CA 94608
TEL: (510) 655-8730
FAX: (510) 601-2541

Dr. Edward E. Penhoet, Vice Chairman. Global biotechnology/research. Chiron Corporation is a public company founded in 1981. It manufactures diagnostics, biopharmaceuticals, opthalmics, and vaccines. Much of the company's revenues are derived from research and development. It also has a 50 percent-owned venture with CIBA-GEIGY, Ltd., whose primary focus is vaccine development. Worldwide revenues for 1992: $174 million.

- **Total Employees:** 1,510
- **U.S. Employees Abroad:** 25
- **Countries:** Australia, Germany, Italy, Netherlands.
- **Job Categories:** Chemists, Executive Management, Marketing—Health & Medical Supplies, Marketing—Pharmaceuticals.
- **Language Requirement:** None.

CHRYSLER CORPORATION

12000 Chrysler Dr.
Highland Park, MI 48203 USA

RECRUITER: RAYMOND WILHEMN
EXPATRIATE ADMIN. & SERVICE
MANAGER
12000 CHRYSLER DR.
HIGHLAND PARK, MI 48203
TEL: (313) 956-5741
FAX: (313) 956-3747

Robert Eaton, Chairman. Automobiles; financial services. In 1920, Walter Chrysler was hired to reorganize the Maxwell Motor Company. In 1923 he became president of the firm, and in 1924 he introduced his own car, the Chrysler. In 1978, Lee Iacocca, former Ford president, became the CEO of Chrysler and became a widely known public spokesman. This worldwide company develops, produces and markets cars, minivans and light trucks. Chrysler Financial Corporation (CFC), a subsidiary, is the 4th largest non-bank finance company in North America. It provides financing for its dealers and customers through Chrysler Credit Corporation. Worldwide revenues for 1992: $36.9 billion.

- **Total Employees:** 124,000
- **U.S. Employees Abroad:** 75
- **Countries:** Canada, Mexico.
- **Application Information:** Most overseas positions are filled internally.
- **Job Categories:** Management, Manufacturing, Marketing—Automotive, Sales—Automotive.

CH2M HILL INTERNATIONAL, LTD.

PO Box 24548
Denver, CO 80222 USA

RECRUITER: STAFFING MANAGER 119
PO BOX 24548
DENVER, CO 80222
TEL: (303) 771-0900
FAX: (303) 796-8710

Lyle G. Hassebroek, President. Engineering consulting. CH2M Hill International, Ltd. is a private company founded in 1946. It operates as an engineering consulting firm, principally in the areas of environmental issues and services. Worldwide revenues for 1991: $400 million.

- **Total Employees:** 4,000
- **U.S. Employees Abroad:** 40
- **Countries:** Australia, Egypt, France, Hungary, Taiwan, United Kingdom.
- **Job Categories:** Consultants—Engineering.
- **General Requirements:** Master's Degree; professional registration; prefer 10 years experience for engineers and environmental scientists; prior overseas experience a plus.
- **Language Requirement:** Knowledge of local language a plus but not essential.

- **Training:** Varies with each posting.
- **Benefits:** Vary with each posting.

THE CHUBB & SON CORPORATION

15 Mountain View Rd.
Warren, NJ 07059 USA

RECRUITER: MARSHA DURKIN
MANAGER, COMPENSATION &
RELOCATION SERVICES
15 MOUNTAIN VIEW RD.
WARREN, NJ 07059
TEL: (908) 580-2000
FAX: (908) 580-3145

Dean R. O'Hare, Chairman. Holding company for subsidiaries in the insurance industry. Chubb & Son Corporation is a public company created in 1967. It was founded in 1882 as Chubb & Son, by Thomas Caldecot Chubb and his son Percy. They acted as underwriters for cargo and ship insurance in New York. Today, property and casualty premiums account for two-thirds of the parent company's revenues. Worldwide assets for 1992: $15 billion.

- **Total Employees:** 10,000
- **U.S. Employees Abroad:** 40
- **Countries:** Australia, Brazil, Canada, Colombia, Ecuador, Thailand.
- **Job Categories:** Finance, Management, Marketing.
- **Language Requirement:** Varies with each posting.

CHURCH & DWIGHT COMPANY, INC.

469 North Harrison
Princeton, NJ 08543 USA

RECRUITER: JIM BLAUVELT
MANAGER, HUMAN RESOURCES &
DEVELOPMENT
469 NORTH HARRISON
PRINCETON, NJ 08543
TEL: (609) 683-5900
FAX: (609) 497-7269

Dwight C. Minton, Chairman. Consumer products and specialty chemicals. Church & Dwight is a public company founded in 1946. It manufactures sodium bicarbonate and related products. One of its well-known products is Arm & Hammer baking soda. Worldwide revenues for 1991: $484.5 million.

- **Total Employees:** 1,070
- **U.S. Employees Abroad:** 20
- **Countries:** Canada, Venezuela.
- **Job Categories:** Management, Marketing—Chemicals, Marketing—Consumer Goods, Sales—Chemicals, Sales—Consumer Goods.
- **Language Requirement:** Varies with each posting.

- **Training:** No special training provided.

CIGNA CORPORATION

1 Liberty Place
1650 Market St.
Philadelphia, PA 19192-1550
USA

RECRUITER: SUSAN WOOD
DIRECTOR, HUMAN RESOURCES
2 LIBERTY PLACE
1601 CHESTNUT ST.
PHILADELPHIA, PA 19192
TEL: (215) 761-4829
FAX: (215) 761-5482

Wilson H. Taylor, Chairman. Insurance and financial services. CIGNA is a public company founded in 1982 when Connecticut General and INA merged to form the Cigna Corporation. Based on 1990 assets, it is estimated to be the 4th largest U.S. insurance company. It provides services in four areas: employee life and health; employee retirement and savings; property and casualty; and individual financial services. It has operations in 160 offices in 67 countries. Worldwide assets for 1992: $69.9 billion. Foreign Assets for 1991: $5.6 billion.

- **Total Employees:** 50,000
- **U.S. Employees Abroad:** 90
- **Countries:** Worldwide including Argentina, Australia, Bahamas, Canada, France, Germany, Indonesia, Japan, Netherlands, New Zealand, Panama, Singapore, Switzerland, Venezuela, United Kingdom.
- **Application Information:** Most overseas positions are filled internally.
- **Job Categories:** Underwriters.
- **General Requirements:** Product experience is required for overseas assignment.
- **Average Overseas Assignment:** 3-5 years
- **Language Requirement:** Competency in local language is required.
- **Training:** No special training provided.
- **Benefits:** All benefits are individually determined.

CINCOM SYSTEMS, INC.

2300 Montana Ave.
Cincinnati, OH 45211 USA

RECRUITER: RON CHILCOTT
MANAGER, COMPENSATION &
    BENEFITS
2300 MONTANA AVE.
CINCINNATI, OH 45211
TEL: (513) 662-2300
FAX: (513) 481-8332

Thomas M. Niles, President. Computer software. Cincom Systems was founded in 1968. It produces and distributes computer software and related products in the United States and abroad. Worldwide revenues for 1991: $158 million.

198 CINCOM SYSTEMS, INC.

sidebarA
M
E
R
I
C
A
N

J
O
B
S

A
B
R
O
A
D

- **Total Employees:** 1,380
- **U.S. Employees Abroad:** Not available.
- **Countries:** Australia, France, Germany, Japan, United Kingdom.
- **Job Categories:** Marketing—Electronics, Sales—Electronics.
- **Language Requirement:** None.

CITICORP

575 Lexington Ave., 12th Floor,
Zone 3
New York, NY 10043 USA

RECRUITER: HOYLE JONES
DIRECTOR, GLOBAL MA PROGRAMS
575 LEXINGTON AVE., 12TH FLOOR,
ZONE 3
NEW YORK, NY 10043
TEL: (212) 559-1664
FAX: (212) 793-6434
FREE: (800) 285-3000

John S. Reed, Chairman. Banking services. Citicorp is a public company founded in 1967. It operates through its primary concern, Citibank, the largest bank in the United States. It operates in 93 countries. Worldwide assets for 1992: $213.7 billion.

- **Total Employees:** 85,000
- **U.S. Employees Abroad:** 400
- **Countries:** Ninety-three including Argentina, Australia, Bahamas, Brazil, France, Germany, Hong Kong, Italy, Kenya, Mexico, Panama, Peru, Saudi Arabia, Sweden, Switzerland, Thailand, United Kingdom, Venezuela.
- **Application Information:** Citibank recruits candidates from major universities throughout the United States.
- **Job Categories:** Executive Management.
- **General Requirements:** College graduate with a degree in business/finance.
- **Average Overseas Assignment:** 3-5 years.
- **Language Requirement:** Knowledge of local language a plus but not essential.
- **Training:** Basic orientation (1-30 days) and language training provided.
- **Comments:** In development programs, the goal is to promote entry-level employees into professional bankers.

CLARCOR, INC.

2323 6th St.
PO Box 7007
Rockford, IL 61125 USA

RECRUITER: DAVID LINDSAY
VP, GROUP SERVICES
2323 6TH ST.
PO BOX 7007
ROCKFORD, IL 61125
TEL: (815) 962-8867
FAX: (815) 962-8874

Lawrence E. Gloyd, President and Chairman. Quality engineered products. CLARCOR, Inc. is a public company founded in 1904. It provides various engineered products and services to clients on a global scale. Sectors include environmental, and consumer and precision products markets. It is divided into two groups: Consumer Products Group and Filtration Products Group. Worldwide revenues for 1992: $189 million.

- **Total Employees:** 1,550
- **U.S. Employees Abroad:** 100
- **Countries:** Belgium, United Kingdom.
- **Job Categories:** Engineers, Management, Marketing.
- **Language Requirement:** Varies with each posting.
- **Benefits:** All benefits are individually determined.

CLIPPER CRUISE LINES

7711 Bonhomme Ave.
St. Louis, MO 63105-1908 USA

RECRUITER: LOUANN AYER
DIRECTOR, EMPLOYMENT
7711 BONHOMME AVE.
ST. LOUIS, MO 63105
TEL: (314) 727-2929
FAX: (314) 727-6576

Paul Duynhduweor, Chief Executive Officer. Cruise ship service. Clipper Cruise Line is a private company founded in 1982. It offers transportation through vacation cruise ships, which travel both the East and West coasts of the United States and various locations throughout the world, including Antarctica and Russia. Worldwide operating revenues for 1991: $20 million.

- **Total Employees:** 35
- **U.S. Employees Abroad:** 25
- **Countries:** Brazil, Costa Rica, Russia.
- **Job Categories:** Mates, Chefs, Deck Hands, Public Relations, Stewards.
- **Language Requirement:** None.
- **Training:** No special training provided.
- **Benefits:** HOUSING: Housing is provided on board.

CLOROX COMPANY

1221 Broadway
Oakland, CA 94612 USA

RECRUITER: BEN LAWRENCE
DIRECTOR, HUMAN RESOURCES-
   INTERNATIONAL
1221 BROADWAY
OAKLAND, CA 94612
TEL: (510) 271-4900
FAX: (510) 271-7883

G. Craig Sullivan, Chief Executive Officer. Household products. Clorox is a public company founded in 1913 by five Oakland, California, investors. Their intention was to produce bleach, using water from salt ponds in the bay area around San Francisco. The company was registered the following year and it was called Clorox. Its name was derived from the two main ingredients of the product—chlorine and sodium hydroxide. Today the company produces a wide variety of items including household cleaners (PineSol), charcoal (Kingsford), and salad dressing (Hidden Valley). Worldwide revenues for 1992: $1.8 billion.

- **Total Employees:** 5,500
- **U.S. Employees Abroad:** 10
- **Countries:** Hong Kong, Republic of Korea, Saudi Arabia, United Kingdom.
- **Application Information:** Job Hotline: 510-271-7625
- **Salaries:** $70,000-$90,000 per year.
- **Job Categories:** Manufacturing, Marketing—Consumer Goods, Sales—Consumer Goods.
- **Average Overseas Assignment:** 2-3 years.
- **Language Requirement:** None.
- **Training:** Basic orientation (1-30 days) provided.
- **Benefits:** TRAVEL: Relocation allowances, goods and services allowances, and annual home leave offered. HEALTH: Offered. HOUSING: Varies with each posting. There may be a goods and service allowance, automobile allowance, education, or appliance allowance. EDUCATION: Offered for dependents through the 12th grade.

CLUB CORPORATION INTERNATIONAL

PO Box 819012
Dallas, TX 75381-8190 USA

RECRUITER: PATRICIA MORRIS
STAFFING/RECRUITMENT
PO BOX 819012
DALLAS, TX 75381-8190
TEL: (214) 243-6191
FAX: (214) 288-7558

Robert H. Dedman, Jr., Chairman. Holding company of private sports/recreation clubs and resorts. Club Corporation International is a private company founded in 1957. Worldwide revenues for 1991: $450 million.

- **Total Employees:** 18,000
- **U.S. Employees Abroad:** 25
- **Countries:** Japan, United Kingdom.
- **Job Categories:** Finance, Management, Marketing.
- **Language Requirement:** None.
- **Training:** No special training provided.

CLUB MED, INC.

40 West 57th St.
New York, NY 10019 USA

RECRUITER: PERSONNEL DIRECTOR
2600 DOUGLAS RD., SUITE #500
CORAL GABLES, FL 33134
TEL: (305) 461-4033
FAX: (305) 461-4041

Jean-Luc Ozion-Chapon, Chief Executive Officer. Hotel and motel management. Club Med is a public company established in the U.S. in 1968. It offers management services and operates hotels, motels, and resorts around the globe. Worldwide operating revenues for 1991: $518.7 million.

- **Total Employees:** 6,445
- **U.S. Employees Abroad:** 45
- **Countries:** Bahamas, Guadeloupe, Martinique, Mexico.
- **Job Categories:** Finance, Management, Marketing—Travel.
- **Language Requirement:** Knowledge of local language a plus but not essential.
- **Training:** No special training offered.

THE COASTAL GROUP

Coastal Tower
Nine Greenway Plaza
Houston, TX 77046 USA

RECRUITER: KATHY PEEPLES
PERSONNEL DEPARTMENT
COASTAL TOWER, NINE GREENWAY
  PLAZA
HOUSTON, TX 77046
TEL: (713) 877-1400
FAX: (713) 877-1400

James R. Paul, President. Diversified energy services including refining, marketing, exploration and production of oil, coal, and natural gas. The Coastal Group is a public company founded in 1955 by Oscar Wyatt. He first began a small natural gas-gathering business in 1951 in Corpus Christi, Texas. It became the Coastal States Gas Producing Company in 1955. Today, Coastal is the 12th largest energy business in the United States. Its subsidiaries operate in the United States, Canada, Europe, and Aruba. These operations include tankers and barges, six refineries, and over 800 C-Mart convenience/gas stores. Worldwide revenues for 1992: $10.1 billion.

- **Total Employees:** 16,960
- **U.S. Employees Abroad:** 60
- **Countries:** Argentina, Aruba, Canada, Singapore, United Kingdom.
- **Job Categories:** Administrative, Management, Marketing—Petroleum/Natural Gas.
- **Average Overseas Assignment:** 2-3 years.
- **Language Requirement:** Knowledge of local language a plus but not essential.
- **Training:** No special training provided.
- **Benefits:** All benefits are individually determined.

THE COCA-COLA COMPANY

One Coca-Cola Plaza
Atlanta, GA 30301 USA

RECRUITER: LINDA BULLARD
HUMAN RESOURCES DEPARTMENT
PO DRAWER 1734
ATLANTA, GA 30301
TEL: (404) 676-3478
FAX: (404) 515-2560

Roberto Goizueta, Chairman. Soft drinks, beverages, and food products. Coca-Cola is a public company founded in 1886 when Atlanta pharmacist, John S. Pemberton first invented Coke. It was a combination of two ingredients, kola nuts and cocoa leaves. Asa Candler, a druggist, purchased the company in 1891 and today, the company is the largest soft drink producer in the world. Beverages are sold in more than 160 countries, and syrups and concentrates are produced in 44 plants worldwide. More than half the company's sales are generated overseas. Worldwide revenues for 1992: $13.1 billion.

- **Total Employees:** 24,000
- **U.S. Employees Abroad:** Not available.
- **Countries:** Argentina, Austria, Bahamas, Belgium, Bermuda, Brazil, Cameroon, Chile, Costa Rica, Denmark, Ecuador, Finland, Greece, Guatemala, Hong Kong, India, Ireland, Japan, Kenya, Republic of Korea, Mexico, Morocco, Netherlands, New Zealand, Norway, Pakistan, Panama, Peru, Philippines, Spain, Sweden, Switzerland, Thailand, Turkey, Uruguay, Venezuela, Zimbabwe.
- **Job Categories:** Accountants, Management, Marketing—Food/Food Services, Sales—Food/Food Services.
- **Language Requirement:** Varies with each posting.

COHERENT, INC.

5100 Patrick Henry Dr.
Santa Clara, CA 95054 USA

RECRUITER: BERNIE KINNEY
DIRECTOR, HUMAN RESOURCES
5100 PATRICK HENRY DR.
SANTA CLARA, CA 95054
TEL: (408) 764-4000
FAX: (408) 764-4820

James L. Hobart, Chairman. Lasers. Coherent, Inc. is a public company founded in 1966. It develops and manufacturers lasers used in the industrial, medical, and scientific fields. It also produces electronic components and related items for the company's equipment. Major products include Duralite articulated arm design laser and Innova 300 ion laser. Worldwide revenues for 1992. $215 million.

- **Total Employees:** 1,345
- **U.S. Employees Abroad:** 25
- **Countries:** Germany, Japan, United Kingdom.
- **Job Categories:** Management, Marketing—Scientific, Research & Development, Sales—Scientific.

- **Language Requirement:** None.

COIN ACCEPTORS, INC.

300 Hunter Ave.
Saint Louis, MO 63124 USA

RECRUITER: JAMES DOUGLASS
PERSONNEL DIRECTOR
300 HUNTER AVE.
SAINT LOUIS, MO 63124
TEL: (314) 725-0100
FAX: (314) 725-7198

Jack E. Thomas, Jr., President. Coin-handling equipment for vending machines. Coin Acceptors is a public company with 1991 worldwide revenues of $50 million.

- **Total Employees:** 1,200
- **U.S. Employees Abroad:** 20
- **Countries:** Canada, Germany.
- **Job Categories:** Engineers, Manufacturing, Marketing, Sales.
- **Average Overseas Assignment:** 2-3 years.
- **Language Requirement:** Knowledge of local language a plus but not essential.
- **Training:** Basic orientation (1-30 days) provided.
- **Benefits:** All benefits are individually determined.

COLGATE-PALMOLIVE COMPANY

300 Park Ave.
New York, NY 10022 USA

RECRUITER: ALLISON GOOD
BENEFITS ADMINISTRATOR
300 PARK AVE.
NEW YORK, NY 10022
TEL: (212) 310-2000
FAX: (212) 310-3284

Reuben Mark, President and Chairman. Personal hygiene products, cosmetics, and consumer and pet items. Colgate-Palmolive is a public company founded in 1806 by William Colgate. He began Colgate Company by making candles, soap, and starch. After his death, his son Samuel took over and renamed the firm, Colgate and Company taking it public in 1908. In 1898, the B. J. Johnson Soap Company began by producing a soap, Palmolive, which became so popular, the company renamed the business the Palmolive Company in 1917. In 1927 they joined with soap makers, Peet Brothers, who then merged with Colgate in 1928, to form the Colgate-Palmolive Company. Today, the company derives 67 percent of its sales from outside of the United States. Popular brand names include: Ultra Brite toothpaste, Palmolive dishwashing liquid, and Hill's pet food. It has 75 plants in the United States and 120 located in more than 40 foreign countries. Worldwide revenues for 1992: $7 billion.

- **Total Employees:** 24,000
- **U.S. Employees Abroad:** 50

- **Countries:** Worldwide including Australia, Canada, Denmark, Germany, France, Japan, Norway, Portugal, Sweden.
- **Job Categories:** Administrative, Marketing—Consumer Goods, Product Development, Sales—Consumer Goods.
- **Average Overseas Assignment:** Less than two years.
- **Language Requirement:** None.
- **Training:** No special training provided.

COLTEC INDUSTRIES, INC.

430 Park Ave.
New York, NY 10022 USA

RECRUITER: PATRICIA BURNS
MANAGER, CORPORATE HUMAN
RESOURCES
430 PARK AVE.
NEW YORK, NY 10022
TEL: (212) 940-1400
FAX: (212) 940-0595

David Margolis, President. Aerospace, automotive, and industrial products. Coltec Industries was founded in 1911 and is a subsidiary of Coltec Holdings, Inc. of New York City. Major products include Menasco landing gear assemblies and Holley carburetors. Worldwide revenues for 1992: $1.4 billion.

- **Total Employees:** 13,300
- **U.S. Employees Abroad:** Not available.
- **Countries:** Canada, France, United Kingdom.
- **Job Categories:** Management, Marketing—Automotive, Marketing—Industrial, Marketing—Scientific, Product Development, Sales—Automotive, Sales—Industrial, Sales—Scientific.
- **Language Requirement:** None.

COLUMBIAN ROPE COMPANY

PO Box 270
Guntown, MS 38849 USA

RECRUITER: JOSEPH
WESTMORELAND
HUMAN RESOURCES
REPRESENTATIVE
PO BOX 270
GUNTOWN, MS 38849
TEL: (601) 348-2241
FAX: (601) 348-5749

Stephen G. Ludt, President. Rope, twine, industrial fiber, and paper filler for electric cables. Columbian Rope was incorporated in New York in 1903. Worldwide revenues for 1991: $10 million

- **Total Employees:** 300

- **U.S. Employees Abroad:** 12
- **Countries:** Canada, Philippines.
- **Job Categories:** Plant Managers, Marketing, Sales.
- **Language Requirement:** None.
- **Training:** Varies with each posting.

COMMERCE CLEARING HOUSE

2700 Lake Cook Rd.
Riverwoods, IL 60015 USA

RECRUITER: DARDE GAERTNER
VP, HUMAN RESOURCES
2700 LAKE COOK RD.
RIVERWOODS, IL 60015
TEL: (708) 940-4600
FAX: (708) 940-0113

Edward Massie, President. Publisher of tax and business law reports and processor of income tax returns by computer. Commerce Clearing House is a public company founded in 1927. CCH grew out of the Corporation Trust Company, which was formed in 1892 to provide state-required legal representation for large companies. In 1913, the company began publishing the Income Tax Reporter, which detailed federal income tax laws. Subscriptions increased and shortly before 1920, William Kixmiller began publishing import/export and income tax guides as Commerce Clearing House. In 1927, the two joined to form Commerce Clearing House in Chicago. Today, legal reports are published in the United States and in six foreign countries. Worldwide revenues for 1991: $704 million. Foreign revenues for 1991: $109 million.

- **Total Employees:** 7,780
- **U.S. Employees Abroad:** 25
- **Countries:** Australia, Canada, Mexico, New Zealand, Singapore, United Kingdom.
- **Job Categories:** Executive Management, Marketing.
- **Language Requirement:** None.

COMMERCIAL INTERTECH CORPORATION

1775 Logan Ave.
Youngstown, OH 44501 USA

RECRUITER: JACK SAVAGE
DIRECTOR, EMPLOYEE RELATIONS
1775 LOGAN AVE.
YOUNGSTOWN, OH 44501
TEL: (216) 746-8011
FAX: (216) 746-1148

Paul J. Powers, President and Chairman. Hydraulic components and fluid purification equipment. Commercial Intertech is a public company founded in 1920. It first began as Commercial Shearing & Stamping Company, a steel-stamping business. Today, this international firm develops and produces hydraulic components, fluid purification equipment, and metal products. Worldwide revenues for 1992: $451 million.

- **Total Employees:** 4,000
- **U.S. Employees Abroad:** 40
- **Countries:** Australia, Brazil, Canada, France, Italy, Japan, Luxembourg, Sweden, United Kingdom.
- **Job Categories:** Marketing—Industrial, Sales—Industrial.
- **Training:** No special training provided.

COMMODORE CRUISE LINES

800 Douglas Rd., Suite 600
Coral Gables, FL 33134 USA

RECRUITER: V. MENPZONI
DIRECTOR, EMPLOYMENT
800 DOUGLAS RD.
CORAL GABLES, FL 33134
TEL: (305) 529-3000
FAX: (305) 441-8536

Ove Nordquist, Chief Executive Officer. Cruise line operator. Commodore Cruise Line was founded in 1986 and offers water transportation services for clients who wish to travel to the Caribbean. Worldwide operating revenues for 1991: $350 million.

- **Total Employees:** 170
- **U.S. Employees Abroad:** 50
- **Countries:** British Virgin Islands.
- **Job Categories:** Captains, Chefs, Deck Hands, Mates, Pursers, Stewards.
- **Language Requirement:** None.
- **Training:** No special training offered.
- **Benefits:** HOUSING: Housing is provided on board ship.

COMMODORE INTERNATIONAL LTD.

1200 Wilson Dr.
West Chester, PA 19380 USA

RECRUITER: PATRICIA REIKARD
DIRECTOR, HUMAN RESOURCES
1200 WILSON DR.
WEST CHESTER, PA 19380
TEL: (215) 431-9100
FAX: (215) 431-9156

Irving Gould, Chairman. Personal computers. Commodore International Ltd. is a public company founded in 1954 by Jack Tramiel as Commodore Portable Typewriter. Today, Commodore International Ltd. is a leading manufacturer of personal computers. The Amiga series of computers was responsible for 55 percent of company sales in 1991. It is currently selling one million units on a yearly basis. Products are manufactured and sold in the United States and abroad. Worldwide revenues for 1991: $1 billion. Foreign revenues for 1991: $937 million.

- **Total Employees:** 2,890
- **U.S. Employees Abroad:** 40

- **Countries:** Australia, Bahamas, Belgium, Hong Kong, Italy, Netherlands, New Zealand, Norway, Sweden, Switzerland, United Kingdom.

- **Job Categories:** Design Engineers, Management, Marketing—Electronics, Technicians.

- **Language Requirement:** Knowledge of local language a plus but not essential.

COMPAQ COMPUTERS CORPORATION

PO Box 692000
Houston, TX 77269-2000 USA

RECRUITER: MIKE BERMAN
SENIOR VP, HUMAN RESOURCES
PO BOX 692000
HOUSTON, TX 77269-2000
TEL: (713) 370-0670
FAX: (713) 370-1740

Joseph R. Canion, President. Computers. Compaq Computers is a public company founded in 1982 by Joseph R. Canion and two other ex-Texas Instrument executives. They began the production and sale of IBM compatible computers and today the company is the number one producer of IBM compatibles. The company manufactures desktop, portable, and laptop computers in the United States and abroad. Business is conducted in over 60 countries. Worldwide sales for 1992: $4.1 billion.

- **Total Employees:** 9,800

- **U.S. Employees Abroad:** Not available.

- **Countries:** Sixty including Singapore, United Kingdom.

- **Job Categories:** Finance, Research & Development, Management, Marketing—Electronics, Sales—Electronics.

- **Language Requirement:** Varies with each posting.

COMPUTER ASSOCIATES INTERNATIONAL, INC.

1 Computer Associates Plaza
Islandia, NY 11788-7000 USA

RECRUITER: LISA MARS
SENIOR VP, PERSONNEL
1 COMPUTER ASSOCIATES PLAZA
ISLANDIA, NY 11788-7000
TEL: (516) DIAL-CAI
FAX: (516) DIAL-FAX

Charles B. Wang, Chairman. Design, development, and distribution of application computer software. Computer Associates is a public company founded in 1976 by Charles Wang, who with four employees began a U.S. subsidiary of Swiss-owned Computer Associates in Manhattan. The company produced a file organizer for IBM storage systems. Today this global marketer is still operated by Charles Wang. It operates in the United States and in more than 27 foreign countries. Worldwide revenues for 1993: $1.8 billion.

- **Total Employees:** 7,200

- **U.S. Employees Abroad:** 100

- **Countries:** Austria, Belgium, Brazil, Canada, Denmark, Finland, France, Germany, Hong Kong, Israel, Japan, Republic of Korea, Malaysia, New Zealand, Norway, Singapore, Spain, Sweden, Switzerland.

- **Job Categories:** Management, Marketing—Electronics, Product Development, Sales—Electronics.

- **Language Requirement:** Knowledge of local language a plus but not essential.

COMPUTERVISION CORPORATION

201 Burlington Rd.
Bedford, MA 01730 USA

RECRUITER: SHARON REILLY
HUMAN RESOURCES
REPRESENTATIVE
201 BURLINGTON RD.
BEDFORD, MA 10730
TEL: (617) 275-1800
FAX: (617) 271-0268

John J. Shields, President. Automation systems and semiconductors. Computervision Corporation is a public company founded in 1972. Worldwide revenues for 1991: $1.2 billion.

- **Total Employees:** 5,900

- **U.S. Employees Abroad:** 35

- **Countries:** Australia, Belgium, Brazil, France, Japan, Netherlands, United Kingdom.

- **Job Categories:** Management, Marketing—Electronics, Marketing—Scientific, Sales—Electronics, Sales—Scientific.

- **Language Requirement:** None.

- **Training:** None provided.

- **Benefits:** All benefits are individually determined.

CONAGRA, INC.

One ConAgra Dr.
Omaha, NE 68102 USA

RECRUITER: GERALD B. VERNON
VP, HUMAN RESOURCES
ONE CONAGRA DR.
OMAHA, NE 68102
TEL: (402) 595-4365
FAX: (402) 595-4707

Charles M. Harper, Chairman. Diversified foods. ConAgra is a public company founded in 1919 when four flour mills were combined to form Nebraska Consolidated Mills in Omaha, Nebraska. Expansion to other states occurred in the 1940s. By 1970, poultry processing plants were established and in 1971 the name was changed to ConAgra (meaning parternership with the land). Today, the company is the second largest in the

U.S. food industry. It operates in over 25 countries. Worldwide revenues for 1992: $21.7 billion.

- **Total Employees:** 74,000

- **U.S. Employees Abroad:** Not available.

- **Countries:** Belgium, Canada, France, Portugal, Spain.

- **Job Categories:** Administrative, Management, Marketing—Food/Food Services, Sales—Food/Food Services.

- **Comments:** The number of Americans reported working abroad varies greatly from quarter to quarter, fluctuating with the number and scope of projects under contract at the time.

CONOCO, INC.
600 North Dairy Ashford Rd.
Houston, TX 77079 USA

RECRUITER: TOM PAULDINE
INTERNATIONAL RECRUITMENT
600 NORTH DAIRY ASHFORD RD.
HOUSTON, TX 77079
TEL: (713) 293-1000
FAX: (713) 293-4476

Constantine Nicandros, President. Oil exploration, production, marketing, and refining. Conoco was founded on November 25, 1875, as the Continental Oil and Transportaion Company. It is a subsidiary of E. I. du Pont de Nemours & Company, Inc. Worldwide revenues for 1991: $15.9 billion.

- **Total Employees:** 14,000

- **U.S. Employees Abroad:** 550

- **Countries:** Angola, Australia, Bahrain, Canada, Congo, France, Gabon, Germany, Indonesia, Ireland, Italy, Japan, Netherlands, Nigeria, Norway, Poland, Russia, Singapore, Somalia, Spain, Sweden, Switzerland, United Kingdom.

- **Job Categories:** Accountants, Engineers, Environmental Specialists, Geologists, Geophysicists, Management, Manufacturing.

- **Average Overseas Assignment:** 2-3 years.

- **Language Requirement:** Knowledge of local language a plus but not essential.

- **Training:** No special training provided.

- **Comments:** Most employees sent overseas are hired internally. Only a small percentage of people are recruited from outside the firm to be sent abroad.

CONTINENTAL AIRLINES HOLDINGS, INC.

2929 Allen Pkwy.
Houston, TX 77019 USA

RECRUITER: WILLIAM CROUCH
STAFFING/RECRUITMENT
2929 ALLEN PKWY., SUITE #2010
HOUSTON, TX 77019
TEL: (713) 834-2950
FAX: (713) 834-5362

Robert R. Ferguson, III, President. Airline service and computerized reservations systems. Continental Airlines Holdings is a public company founded by Frank Lorenzo in 1980. Eastern Airlines was purchased in 1986 and in 1990 bankruptcy proceedings followed. Today, the company continues to operate and remain a major carrier with hubs at Houston and Newark. It also operates the Chelsea catering service and computerized reservations systems. It operates in the United States and in more than 50 foreign countries. Worldwide revenues for 1992: $5.6 billion.

- **Total Employees:** 37,000
- **U.S. Employees Abroad:** Not available.
- **Countries:** Worldwide including Germany, Japan, Mexico, Spain, Thailand, United Kingdom.
- **Job Categories:** Administrative, Finance, Marketing—Travel, Sales—Travel.
- **Language Requirement:** Varies with each posting.

CONTINENTAL BANK CORPORATION

231 South LaSalle St.
Chicago, IL 60697 USA

RECRUITER: SUSAN SCHORN
PERSONNEL DIRECTOR
231 SOUTH LASALLE ST., ROOM 250
CHICAGO, IL 60697
TEL: (312) 828-2345
FAX: (312) 828-7150

Thomas C. Theobald, Chairman. Commercial banking services. Continental Bank is a public company founded in 1928. It was formed from a group of Chicago bank mergers that became the Illinois Merchants' Trust in 1924 and then combined with Continental and Commercial Banks in 1928 to become Continental Illinois Bank and Trust. In 1988 "Illinois" was dropped from the name. Today, the corporation is recovering from its 1984 banking collapse, the largest one in U.S. history. It operates in the United States and in 11 foreign countries. Worldwide assets for 1992: $22.5 billion. Foreign Assets for 1991: $5.4 billion.

- **Total Employees:** 8,000
- **U.S. Employees Abroad:** Not available.
- **Countries:** Argentina, Brazil, Chile, France, Germany, Hong Kong, Italy, Mexico, Singapore, Venezuela, United Kingdom.
- **Job Categories:** Administrative, Finance, Management, Marketing—Financial Services, Sales—Financial Services.

- **Language Requirement:** Varies with each posting.
- **Training:** No special training provided.

CONTINENTAL GRAIN COMPANY

277 Park Ave.
New York, NY 10172 USA

RECRUITER: DWIGHT COFFIN
VP, HUMAN RESOURCES
277 PARK AVE.
NEW YORK, NY 10172
TEL: (212) 207-5100
FAX: (212) 207-5043

Donald L. Staheli, President. Grain and commodities, livestock operations, food processing, and financial services. Continental Grain is a private company founded in 1913. Simon Fribourg began a commodity trading business in Belgium. As more countries began to trade grain, the business prospered. In 1921 Jules and Rene Fribourg reorganized the company as Continental Grain and opened the first United States branch in Chicago. Today, this company controls the world's largest grain and related commodities empire with estimated sales of nearly $15 billion. It has operations in 58 countries. Worldwide revenues for 1991: $15 billion.

- **Total Employees:** 13,000
- **U.S. Employees Abroad:** 50
- **Countries:** People's Republic of China, Netherlands, United Kingdom.
- **Job Categories:** Administrative, Finance, Marketing—Agricultural, Sales—Agricultural.
- **Language Requirement:** None.

CONTINUUM COMPANY, INC.

9500 Arboretum Blvd.
Austin, TX 78759-6399 USA

RECRUITER: CRAIG PARKS
STAFFING/RECRUITMENT
9500 ARBORETUM BLVD.
AUSTIN, TX 78759-6399
TEL: (512) 345-5700
FAX: (512) 338-6675

Ronald Carroll, Chairman. Consulting and computer services. Continuum is a public company founded in 1968. It produces and sells computer softwear for the insurance and financial markets. It also offers consulting services in the United States and abroad. Continuum recently purchased Computations Holdings Ltd. of Sydney, Australia, in 1990. Worldwide revenues for 1991: $113 million.

- **Total Employees:** 680
- **U.S. Employees Abroad:** Not available.
- **Countries:** Australia, France, Netherlands, Japan, United Kingdom.
- **Job Categories:** Administrative, Finance, Management.

CONVERSE, INC.

1 Fordham Rd.
North Reading, MA 01864 USA

RECRUITER: HUMAN RESOURCES
DEPARTMENT
1 FORDHAM RD.
NORTH READING, MA 01864
TEL: (508) 664-1100
FAX: (508) 664-7472

Gib Ford, President. Athletic footwear. Converse, Inc. was founded in 1908 and became part of Interco in 1986. It remains a subsidiary of Interco whose headquarters are in St Louis, Missouri. It produces and sells a broad line of athletic footwear for men, women, and children. It provides basketball shoes to players and teams in the National Basketball Association, the National Collegiate Athletic Association, and high school teams. Worldwide revenues for 1992: $180 million.

- **Total Employees:** 2,500
- **U.S. Employees Abroad:** Not available.
- **Countries:** Australia, People's Republic of China, Indonesia, Japan, Mexico, United Kingdom.
- **Job Categories:** Marketing—Consumer Goods, Product Development, Quality Assurance, Sales—Consumer Goods.
- **General Requirements:** Vary with each posting; current employee with company experience preferred.
- **Language Requirement:** None.
- **Training:** No special training provided.
- **Comments:** The number of Americans reported working abroad varies greatly from quarter to quarter, fluctuating with the number and scope of projects under contract at the time.

COOPER ENERGY SERVICES, LTD.

North Sandusky St.
Mt. Vernon, OH 43050 USA

RECRUITER: GREG LOSH
EMPLOYMENT DIRECTOR
NORTH SANDUSKY ST.
MT. VERNON, OH 43050
TEL: (614) 393-8200
FAX: (614) 393-8373

Kenneth Stevenson, President. Gas turbines, engines, and compressors. Cooper Energy Services, founded in 1833, is now a division of Cooper Industries of Houston, Texas. The company produces air and gas compressors, motors and generators and also non-agricultural spraying and dusting equipment. Worldwide revenues for 1991: $650 million

- **Total Employees:** 3,000
- **U.S. Employees Abroad:** 50
- **Countries:** Mexico, United Kingdom.

- **Application Information:** Hiring for most foreign positions is done at the specific country location.

- **Job Categories:** Maintenance, Marketing—Industrial, Sales—Industrial.

- **Average Overseas Assignment:** 2-3 years.

- **Language Requirement:** Knowledge of local language a plus but not essential.

- **Training:** No special training provided.

- **Benefits:** All benefits are individually determined.

COOPER INDUSTRIES, INC.

PO Box 4446
Houston, TX 77210 USA

RECRUITER: CARL J. PLESNICHER, JR.
VP, EMPLOYEE RELATIONS
PO BOX 4446
HOUSTON, TX 77210
TEL: (614) 393-8200
FAX: (614) 393-8373

Robert Cizik, President and Chairman. Electrical products, power equipment, tools and hardware, automotive products, and industrial and petroleum equipment. Cooper Industries is a public company founded in 1833 by Charles Cooper when he opened a foundry with his brother Elias. It was named C & E Cooper and the business made plows, troughs, stoves, and wagon boxes. In 1868, Cooper built the first Corliss steam engine and during the 1920s became the top-seller of compression engines for oil and gas pipelines. Today, Cooper Industries is a global manufacturer comprising five business segments. One of its well-known brand names is Champion Spark Plug. The business operates in the United States and in more than 20 countries. Worldwide revenues for 1992: $6.2 billion.

- **Total Employees:** 58,000

- **U.S. Employees Abroad:** 150

- **Countries:** Twenty-four including Canada, Germany, Mexico, United Kingdom.

- **Job Categories:** Engineers, Executive Management, Finance, Marketing—Automotive, Marketing—Electronics, Marketing—Industrial, Product Development, Sales—Automotive, Sales—Electronics, Sales—Industrial.

COOPER POWER SYSTEMS

PO Box 2850
Pittsburgh, PA 15230 USA

RECRUITER: DONALD DUTOIT
VP, INTERNATIONAL SALES & MARKETING
PO BOX 2850
PITTSBURGH, PA 15230
TEL: (412) 269-6700
FAX: (412) 269-6761

William D. Brewer, President. Products for the transmission and distribution of electric power. Cooper Power Systems is a subsidiary of Cooper Industries of Houston, Texas. It is engaged as a manufacturer of power transformers, distribution equipment, and related items. Worldwide revenues for 1991: $650 million.

- **Total Employees:** 5,300
- **U.S. Employees Abroad:** 2
- **Countries:** Australia, Greece, Taiwan.
- **Job Categories:** Management, Marketing—Industrial, Product Development, Sales—Industrial.

COOPERS & LYBRAND

1251 Avenue of the Americas
New York, NY 10020 USA

RECRUITER: BRETT MARSCHKE
EMPLOYMENT ADMINISTRATOR
1251 AVENUE OF THE AMERICAS
NEW YORK, NY 10020
TEL: (212) 536-2000
FAX: (212) 536-2124

Eugene M. Freedman, Chairman. Business services including, accounting, auditing, and bookkeeping. Coopers & Lybrand is a private company founded in 1898. It began with four partners, William L. Lybrand, T. Edward Ross, Adam A. Ross, and Robert H. Montgomery. The firm grew steadily through the years and international divisions were established in Berlin (1924) and Paris (1926). Today this firm is the fifth largest of the "Big 6" accounting firms in the United States. It operates 95 offices in the United States and 600 branches in over 100 foreign countries. Worldwide revenues for 1991: $5 billion. Foreign revenues for 1991: $3.5 billion.

- **Total Employees:** 16,000
- **U.S. Employees Abroad:** 70
- **Countries:** Worldwide including Australia, France, Germany, Hong Kong, Italy, Japan, United Kingdom.
- **Job Categories:** Accountants, Executive Management, Marketing.
- **Training:** No special training provided.

CORE LABORATORIES

10205 Westheimer, 4th Floor
PO Box 1407
Houston, TX 77251 USA

RECRUITER: JAY G. MILNER
HUMAN RESOURCE MANAGER
10205 WESTHEIMER, 4TH FL.
PO BOX 1407
HOUSTON, TX 77251
TEL: (713) 972-6318
FAX: (713) 972-6322

Joe. G. Saltamachia, President. Environmental services; petroleum testing and analysis. Core Laboratories performs analytical services for energy industries throughout the world. It begins with basin and exploration phases and extends to refining, petrochemical testing, and environmental monitoring services.

- **Total Employees:** 1,100
- **U.S. Employees Abroad:** 50
- **Countries:** Colombia, Indonesia, Malaysia, Netherlands, Nigeria, Singapore, United Arab Emirates, United Kingdom, Venezuela.
- **Salaries:** $30,000-$50,000 per year, depending on position and level of responsibility.
- **Job Categories:** Chemists, Geochemists, Geologists, Petroleum Engineers.
- **General Requirements:** Degree or advanced degree plus 7-10 years directly related experience.
- **Average Overseas Assignment:** 3-5 years.
- **Language Requirement:** Knowledge of local language skills a plus but not essential.
- **Training:** No special training provided.
- **Benefits:** TRAVEL: 20 working days per year of foreign assignment after completion of 12 months of service. HEALTH: Health insurance program is the same as for domestic U.S. employees. HOUSING: Housing provided by locally established budget. EDUCATION: Education allowances established annually.

CORE STATES FINANCIAL CORPORATION

1600 Market St.
Philadelphia, PA 19101 USA

RECRUITER: KIM MINER
HUMAN RESOURCES
BOX 7558, FC 1314-23
PHILADELPHIA, PA 19101
TEL: (215) 973-4280
FAX: (215) 973-2402

Terrence A. Larsen, Chairman. Financial services. Core States Financial Corporation is a public company founded in 1971. It offers various financial services to its clients in the United States and abroad. Worldwide assets for 1992: $23.7 billion.

- **Total Employees:** 11,880
- **U.S. Employees Abroad:** Not available.
- **Countries:** Australia, Bahamas, Hong Kong, Singapore, United Kingdom.
- **Job Categories:** Finance, Management, Marketing—Financial Services.
- **Training:** No special training provided.

CORNING INCORPORATED

Houghton Park
HP CBI-8
Corning, NY 14831 USA

RECRUITER: MICHELLE COX
RECRUITMENT DEPARTMENT
HOUGHTON PARK, HP CBI-8
CORNING, NY 14831
TEL: (607) 974-9000
FAX: (607) 974-8711

James R. Houghton, Chairman. Consumer products, communications, specialty materials, laboratory services, and opto-electronics. Corning is a public company founded in 1851 by Amory Houghton when he formed the Houghton Glass Works Company in Massachusetts. He moved to Corning, New York, in 1868 and renamed his company the Corning Glass Works. Joint ventures have featured in the company's growth. Early ones included Pittsburgh Corning (Pittsburgh Plate Glass) in 1937 and Dow Corning (Dow Chemical) in 1943. The company is best known for Pyrex and Corning kitchenware. It operates 48 plants in the United States and abroad. Worldwide revenues for 1992: $3.7 billion.

- **Total Employees:** 28,800
- **U.S. Employees Abroad:** 125
- **Countries:** Argentina, Australia, Belgium, Brazil, Canada, People's Republic of China, France, Germany, Hong Kong, India, Italy, Japan, Republic of Korea, Malaysia, Mexico, Philippines, Singapore, Spain, Sweden, Switzerland, Taiwan, Thailand, United Kingdom.
- **Application Information:** Hiring for most foreign postings is done at the specific country location.
- **Job Categories:** Engineers, Manufacturing, Marketing—Consumer Goods, Marketing, Sales—Consumer Goods, Sales.
- **Average Overseas Assignment:** 3-5 years.
- **Language Requirement:** Knowledge of local language a plus but not essential.
- **Training:** No special training provided.
- **Benefits:** All benefits are individually determined.

WILLIS CORROON

26 Century Blvd.
Nashville, TN 37214 USA

RECRUITER: MAUREEN COHEALY
HUMAN RESOURCES
    REPRESENTATIVE
26 CENTURY BLVD.
NASHVILLE, TN 37214
TEL: (615) 872-3044
FAX: (615) 872-3200

Richard M. Miller, Chairman. Worldwide insurance broker. Willis Corroon is a public company founded in 1928. It was formerly Corroon & Black Corporation of New York. This company operates on a global basis providing services in general brokerage insurance, reinsurance, risk management, employee benefits, and compensation and actuarial consulting. Worldwide revenues for 1991: $450 million.

- **Total Employees:** 5,000
- **U.S. Employees Abroad:** 35
- **Countries:** Japan, Singapore, United Kingdom.
- **Job Categories:** Administrative, Agents—Insurance, Brokers—Insurance, Sales—Financial Services.

COUDERT BROTHERS LAW FIRM

200 Park Ave.
New York, NY 10166 USA

RECRUITER: JANE DEAN
ADMINISTRATIVE MANAGER
200 PARK AVE.
NEW YORK, NY 10166
TEL: (212) 880-4874
FAX: (212) 557-8137

Jane Dean, Director of Administration. Legal services. Coudert Brothers is a private law firm providing legal services in the United States and abroad. Worldwide operating revenues for 1991: $118 million.

- **Total Employees:** 421
- **U.S. Employees Abroad:** Not available.
- **Countries:** Bahrain, Belgium, Brazil, People's Republic of China, Hong Kong, Japan, Saudi Arabia, Singapore.
- **Application Information:** Most overseas positions are filled internally.
- **Job Categories:** Attorneys.
- **Comments:** The number of Americans reported working abroad varies greatly from quarter to quarter, fluctuating with the number and scope of projects under contract at the time.

CPC INTERNATIONAL, INC.

PO Box 8000
Englewood Cliffs, NJ 07632-9976
USA

RECRUITER: LAURA W. BRODY
DIV. MANAGER, RESOURCES &
    DEVELOPMENT
PO BOX 8000
ENGLEWOOD CLIFFS, NJ 07632-9976
TEL: (201) 894-4000
FAX: (201) 894-2186

James R. Eiszner, Chairman. Consumer products and food processing. CPC International is a public company founded in 1906 as the Corn Products Refining Company. Expansion and diversification through the years proved successful. It now owns 18 businesses and operates on an international basis. In 1969, the company name was changed to CPC International to emphasize foreign expansion. Popular name brands include: Arnold baked goods, Niagara starch, and Mazola corn oil. Worldwide revenues for 1992: $6.6 billion.

- **Total Employees:** 38,000
- **U.S. Employees Abroad:** 35
- **Countries:** Worldwide including Canada, France, Germany, Italy, Netherlands, United Kingdom.
- **Job Categories:** Management, Marketing—Consumer Goods, Marketing—Food/Food Services, Sales—Consumer Goods, Sales—Food/Food Services.
- **Language Requirement:** Varies with each posting.

JOHN CRANE, INC.

6400 Oakton St.
Morton Grove, IL 60053 USA

RECRUITER: DON BIESACK
EMPLOYEE RELATIONS
6400 OAKTON ST.
MORTON GROVE, IL 60053
TEL: (708) 967-3712
FAX: (708) 967-2857

R. McLaughlin, President. Industrial sealing systems and related products and services for rotating equipment. John Crane is a subsidiary of TI Group PLC of London, United Kingdom. It is a major international engineering group, headquartered in the United States. Key John Crane businesses include industrial sealing systems, engineered welded bellows, and engineered polymers. Worldwide revenues for 1991: $120 million.

- **Total Employees:** 2,600
- **U.S. Employees Abroad:** 25
- **Countries:** Worldwide including Australia, Canada, People's Republic of China, United Kingdom.
- **Job Categories:** Engineers, Finance, Marketing—Industrial, Sales—Industrial.

CROWN CORK & SEAL COMPANY, INC.

9300 Ashton Rd.
Philadelphia, PA 19136 USA

RECRUITER: CHARLENE M.
  HERNANDEZ
MANAGER, HUMAN RESOURCES
9300 ASHTON RD.
PHILADELPHIA, PA 19136
TEL: (215) 968-5100
FAX: (215) 676-7245

William J. Avery, Chairman. Containers, crowns, closures, and various machinery. Crown Cork & Seal is a public company founded in 1892. It manufactures and sells metal cans, packaging, and handling material. Major products include aerosol cans, plastic closures, and machinery for the beer and beverage industries. It has 66 plants in the United States and 70 locations in foreign countries. Worldwide revenues for 1992: $3.8 billion.

- **Total Employees:** 18,000
- **U.S. Employees Abroad:** 25
- **Countries:** Argentina, Brazil, Canada, Colombia, Costa Rica, France, Germany, Kenya, Mexico, Nigeria, Singapore, Republic of South Africa, Zimbabwe.
- **Application Information:** Do not call.
- **Job Categories:** Administrative, Finance, Marketing—Industrial, Sales—Industrial.
- **General Requirements:** Prefer experience in container manufacturing.
- **Average Overseas Assignment:** 3-5 years.
- **Language Requirement:** Knowledge of local language a plus but not essential.

- **Training:** No special training provided.

CRS SIRRINE, INC.
1177 West Loop, Suite 300
Houston, TX 77027 USA

RECRUITER: DIRECTOR
HUMAN RESOURCES
1177 WEST LOOP, SUITE 300
HOUSTON, TX 77027
TEL: (713) 552-2000
FAX: (713) 599-2602

Bruce W. Wilkinson, President. Construction and engineering; insurance underwriters. CRS Sirrine is a public company founded in 1946. It has four major divisions: CRS Services, Inc., a design and construction business; CRS Capital, Inc. power and generation operations; NaTec Resources Inc., acid rain and pollution control; and Global Capital Group, insurances specialty underwriters. Worldwide operating revenues for 1991: $484 million.

- **Total Employees:** 2,700
- **U.S. Employees Abroad:** Not available.
- **Countries:** Mexico, Saudi Arabia, United Kingdom.
- **Job Categories:** Administrative, Engineers, Marketing, Sales.

CS FIRST BOSTON, INC.
Park Ave. Plaza
New York, NY 10055 USA

RECRUITER: TIM DAY
HUMAN RESOURCES
PARK AVE. PLAZA
NEW YORK, NY 10055
TEL: (212) 909-2000
FAX: (212) 759-1280

John M. Hennesey, President. Investment banking. CS First Boston is a private company founded in 1976. It offers investment banking services to its clients in the United States and abroad. Worldwide operating revenues for 1991: $134.4 million.

- **Total Employees:** 6,200
- **U.S. Employees Abroad:** Not available.
- **Countries:** Japan, Switzerland.
- **Job Categories:** Executive Management, Financial Advisors, Marketing—Financial Services.
- **Language Requirement:** None.

CTS CORPORATION

905 West Blvd. North
Elkhart, IN 46514 USA

RECRUITER: JIM CUMMINS
DIRECTOR, HUMAN RESOURCES
905 WEST BLVD., NORTH
ELKHART, IN 46514
TEL: (219) 293-7511
FAX: (219) 293-6146

Joseph P. Walker, President and Chairman. Electronic components and subsystems. CTS is a public company founded in 1896 which designs, manufactures, and markets resistor networks, frequency control devices, microcircuits, modems, and loudspeakers. Worldwide revenues for 1991: $229.5 million.

- **Total Employees:** 5,900

- **U.S. Employees Abroad:** 30

- **Countries:** Canada, Hong Kong, Mexico, Singapore, Taiwan, United Kingdom.

- **Job Categories:** Management, Marketing—Electronics, Product Development, Sales—Electronics.

CUBIC CORPORATION

9333 Balboa Ave.
San Diego, CA 92123 USA

RECRUITER: PAUL WEST
PROFESSIONAL STAFFING
9333 BALBOA AVE.
SAN DIEGO, CA 92123
TEL: (619) 277-6780
FAX: (619) 277-1878

Walter J. Zable, President and Chairman. Automatic fare collection equipment, training systems, and elevator systems. Cubic Corporation is a public company founded in 1951. It is the parent company of Cubic Defense Systems, U.S. Elevator, and the Automatic Revenue Collection Group. The company operates on an international basis. Worldwide revenues for 1992: $344 million.

- **Total Employees:** 3,100

- **U.S. Employees Abroad:** 100

- **Countries:** Australia, Egypt, Germany, Hong Kong, Japan, Republic of Korea, Netherlands, United Kingdom.

- **Job Categories:** Engineers.

- **General Requirements:** U.S. citizen; must be in good health and pass a physical exam.

- **Average Overseas Assignment:** 2-3 years.

- **Language Requirement:** Knowledge of local language a plus but not essential.

- **Training:** Basic orientation (1-30 days) provided.

- **Benefits:** Benefits vary with each posting. EDUCATION: None offered.

CUC INTERNATIONAL, INC.

707 Summer St.
Stamford, CT 06901 USA

RECRUITER: FELICE JOAQUIM
BENEFITS MANAGER
707 SUMMER ST.
STAMFORD, CT 06901
TEL: (203) 324-9261
FAX: (203) 324-3468

Walter A. Forbes, President and Chairman. Membership-based services. CUC International, Inc. is a public company founded in 1973. It is a membership-based company offering personnel services and consumer services in the United States and in more than 10 foreign countries. Worldwide revenues for 1992: $714 million.

- **Total Employees:** 4,500

- **U.S. Employees Abroad:** Not available.

- **Countries:** Canada, France, United Kingdom.

- **Application Information:** Hiring for most foreign positions is done at the specific country location.

- **Job Categories:** Management, Marketing.

- **Training:** No special training provided.

CUMMINS ENGINE COMPANY, INC.

PO Box 3005
Columbus, IN 47202 USA

RECRUITER: RON BRINER
DIRECTOR, HUMAN RESOURCES
PO BOX 3005
COLUMBUS, OH 47202
TEL: (812) 377-5000
FAX: (812) 377-4064

Henry B. Schacht, Chairman. Diesel engines. Cummins Engine is a public company founded in 1919. It designs and manufactures in-line and v-type diesel engines, ranging from 40-2000 horsepower. It also produces and markets a broad range of engine-related components and power systems. Worldwide revenues for 1992: $3.8 billion.

- **Total Employees:** 25,100

- **U.S. Employees Abroad:** 50

- **Countries:** Australia, Belgium, Brazil, People's Republic of China, Colombia, France, Germany, India, Italy, Japan, Mexico, Singapore, United Kingdom, Zimbabwe.

- **Job Categories:** Engineers, Management, Marketing.

CUNA MUTUAL INSURANCE GROUP

5910 Mineral Point Rd.
Madison, WI 53705 USA

RECRUITER: ANN ROBERTS
STAFFING/RECRUITMENT
5910 MINERAL POINT RD.
PO BOX 391
MADISON, WI 53705
TEL: (608) 238-5851
FAX: (608) 238-0830

Richard M. Heins, President. Insurance services. CUNA Mutual provides insurance for credit unions and its members. Worldwide revenues for 1991: $1.4 billion.

- **Total Employees:** 3,700
- **U.S. Employees Abroad:** Not available.
- **Countries:** Australia, Jamaica, Trinidad and Tobago.
- **Job Categories:** Accountants, Administrative, Marketing—Financial Services, Sales—Financial Services.
- **Language Requirement:** None.

D-M-E COMPANY

29111 Stephenson Hwy.
Madison Heights, MI 48071 USA

RECRUITER: DWIGHT E. HARDING
DIRECTOR, HUMAN RESOURCES
29111 STEPHENSON HWY.
MADISON HEIGHTS, MI 48071
TEL: (313) 398-6000

J. Lirette, President. Tools for plastic molding and die coating. D-M-E was founded in 1943 and is a subsidiary of Fairchild Industries Inc. of Chantilly, Virginia. It produces tools and other fixtures used with machine tools, hammers, die-casting machines, and pressers.

- **Total Employees:** 1,300
- **U.S. Employees Abroad:** Not available.
- **Countries:** Australia, Canada, Japan, Philippines, United Kingdom.
- **Job Categories:** Management, Marketing—Industrial, Sales—Industrial.

DAKA INTERNATIONAL

1 Corporate Place
Danvers, MA 01923 USA

RECRUITER: DAVID PARKER
PERSONNEL SERVICES
1 CORPORATE PLACE
DANVERS, MA 01923
TEL: (508) 774-9115
FAX: (508) 774-1802

Allen Maxwell, President. Food services and eating establishments. Also conducts research. DAKA International is a public company founded in 1973. It operates restaurants and contract food services and also conducts market research and provides management services for clients on a global basis. Worldwide revenues for 1992: $155 million.

- **Total Employees:** 10,000
- **U.S. Employees Abroad:** 30
- **Countries:** Mexico, Germany.
- **Job Categories:** Management, Marketing—Food/Food Services, Sales—Food/Food Services.
- **Language Requirement:** None.

LEO A. DALY COMPANY

8600 Indian Hills Dr.
Omaha, NE 68114-4039 USA

RECRUITER: FRANK THOMPSON
STAFFING/RECRUITMENT
8600 INDIAN HILLS DR.
OMAHA, NE 68114-4039
TEL: (402) 391-8564
FAX: (402) 391-8111

Leo A. Daly, President. Architectural and design services. Leo A. Daly offers design services to clients around the world. These include architects, engineers, and planners for interior design. Worldwide revenues for 1992: $52.8 million.

- **Total Employees:** 800
- **U.S. Employees Abroad:** Not available.
- **Countries:** Hong Kong, Japan, Saudi Arabia, Singapore, Spain, Taiwan.
- **Job Categories:** Architects, Design, Marketing.

DAMES & MOORE

911 Wilshire Blvd.
Los Angeles, CA 90017 USA

RECRUITER: ED STAPLETON
DIRECTOR, HUMAN RESOURCES
911 WILSHIRE BLVD.
LOS ANGELES, CA 90017
TEL: (213) 683-1560

George D. Leal, Chief Executive Officer. Engineering consulting services. Dames & Moore is a private company founded in 1938. It is an engineering and environmental consulting business specializing in earthquake engineering analysis. In 1989 it worked with the federal government to develop a national earthquake insurance or reinsurance program. Worldwide operating revenues for 1993: $344 million.

- **Total Employees:** 3,300
- **U.S. Employees Abroad:** 35
- **Countries:** Australia, Canada, Chile, France, Germany, Hong Kong, Indonesia, Japan, Kuwait, Malaysia, Guinea, Philippines, Saudi Arabia, Singapore, Spain, Taiwan, United Arab Emirates, United Kingdom.
- **Job Categories:** Accountants, Engineers, Technicians, Office Management.

• **Language Requirement:** Varies with each posting.

DANA CORPORATION

4500 Dorr St.
PO Box 1000
Toledo, OH 43697 USA

RECRUITER: JIM THOMPSON
HUMAN RESOURCES DIRECTOR
4500 DORR ST.
PO BOX 1000
TOLEDO, OH 43697
TEL: (419) 535-4000

Southwood J. Morcott, President and Chairman. Automotive industry supplier. Dana Corporation is a public company founded in 1904. It began as a U.S. automotive industry provider. It now manufactures and markets components and provides services for original equipment markets (highway and industrial) as well as for distribution markets. In 1990, it purchased Columbus Auto Parts. Worldwide revenues for 1992: $5 billion.

• **Total Employees:** 37,500

• **U.S. Employees Abroad:** 60

• **Countries:** Brazil, India.

• **Application Information:** Most foreign positions are filled internally.

• **Job Categories:** Finance, Management, Marketing—Automotive, Sales—Automotive.

DANIEL, MANN, JOHNSON & MENDENHALL

3250 Wilshire Blvd.
Los Angeles, CA 90010 USA

RECRUITER: RONALD GARCIA
SENIOR RECRUITMENT OFFICER
3250 WILSHIRE BLVD.
LOS ANGELES, CA 90010
TEL: (213) 381-3663
FAX: (213) 385-8669

Albert A. Dorman, Chairman. Architectural and engineering services. Daniel, Mann, Johnson & Mendenhall was founded in 1946 and is a subsidiary of AECOM Technology of Los Angeles, California. The firm offers professional design and engineering services to clients in the United States and abroad. Worldwide revenues for 1992: $108 million.

• **Total Employees:** 1,500

• **U.S. Employees Abroad:** 60

• **Countries:** Brazil, Republic of Korea, Malaysia, Sudan.

• **Job Categories:** Accountants, Architects, Design, Engineers.

• **Language Requirement:** None.

D'ARCY MASIUS BENTON & BOWLES INC.

1675 Broadway
New York, NY 10019-5809 USA

RECRUITER: JIM CARLSON
STAFFING/RECRUITMENT
1675 BROADWAY
NEW YORK, NY 10019-5809
TEL: (212) 468-3622
FAX: (212) 468-4385

Roy J. Bostock, President. Advertising and communications. D'Arcy Masius Benton & Bowles is a private company founded in 1985 as the result of a merger of D'Arcy Masius MacManus with Benton and Bowles. Worldwide gross billings for 1991: $4.5 billion.

- **Total Employees:** 360

- **U.S. Employees Abroad:** 40

- **Countries:** Argentina, Australia, Canada, Greece, Hong Kong, India, Netherlands, Saudi Arabia, Singapore, Thailand, United Arab Emirates, United Kingdom.

- **Job Categories:** Management, Marketing, Sales—Advertising.

DATA GENERAL CORPORATION

4400 Corporation Dr.
Westborough, MA 01580 USA

RECRUITER: AUDREY KING
STAFFING
4400 CORPORATION DR.
WESTBOROUGH, MA 01580
TEL: (508) 870-7595

Ronald L. Skates, President. Computers and computer products. Data General Corporation is a public company founded in 1968. It is a manufacturer of computers and communications systems. It also provides routine maintenance and repair service for products. Worldwide revenues for 1992: $1.1 billion.

- **Total Employees:** 13,700

- **U.S. Employees Abroad:** 25

- **Countries:** Australia, Austria, Belgium, Brazil, Canada, Chile, Hong Kong, Italy, Japan, Mexico, Netherlands, Philippines, Singapore, Switzerland, Thailand, United Kingdom, Venezuela.

- **Job Categories:** Accountants, Comptrollers, Marketing—Electronics, Technical Field Support.

- **General Requirements:** Usually must be a current employee of the company in order to qualify for overseas assignment

- **Language Requirement:** Varies with each posting.

DAY & ZIMMERMAN

1818 Market St.
Philadelphia, PA 19103 USA

RECRUITER: ANTHONY NATALE
VP, HUMAN RESOURCES
280 KING PRUSSIA HWY.
RADNOR, PA 19807
TEL: (215) 975-6860
FAX: (215) 299-8030
FREE: (800) 253-0786

Harold L. Yoh, Jr., Chairman. Architectural, construction management, and engineering services. Day & Zimmerman is a private company founded in 1901 by Charles Day and Kern Dodge, both engineers. The firm offers services and personnel to businesses, governments, and industries in more than 70 countries. Worldwide operating revenues for 1992: $627 million.

- **Total Employees:** 12,800
- **U.S. Employees Abroad:** 45
- **Countries:** Worldwide including France, Germany, United Kingdom.
- **Job Categories:** Architects, Engineers, Marketing, Technical Field Support.
- **Language Requirement:** Varies with each posting.

DAYCO PRODUCTS, INC.

PO Box 1004
Dayton, OH 45401-1004 USA

RECRUITER: TIM ALBRECHT
DIRECTOR, HUMAN RESOURCES
PO BOX 1004
DAYTON, OH 45401-1004
TEL: (513) 226-7000
FAX: (513) 226-4689

Donald E. Bethune, President. Diversified auto products. Dayco Products is a division of Mark IV Industries and produces various rubber products including industrial belts, hydraulic and appliance hoses, and hose fittings. Worldwide revenues for 1992: $600 million.

- **Total Employees:** 4,600
- **U.S. Employees Abroad:** Not available.
- **Countries:** Australia, France, Germany, Italy, United Kingdom.
- **Application Information:** Hiring for most foreign positions is done at the specific country location.
- **Job Categories:** Management, Marketing—Automotive.
- **General Requirements:** Usually must be a current employee of the company in order to qualify for overseas assignment
- **Language Requirement:** Varies with each posting.

DDB NEEDHAM WORLDWIDE, INC.

437 Madison Ave.
New York, NY 10022 USA

RECRUITER: ED FLATHERS
PERSONNEL DEPARTMENT
437 MADISON AVE.
NEW YORK, NY 10022
TEL: (212) 415-2000
FAX: (212) 415-3562

Keith Reinhard, President. Advertising. Founded in 1925, DDB Needham is now a subsidiary of Omnicom Group, Inc. of New York. It operates as an advertising agency on a worldwide basis. Worldwide gross billings for 1992: $4 billion.

- **Total Employees:** 3,900

- **U.S. Employees Abroad:** 35

- **Countries:** Fifty-three including Australia, Austria, Belgium, Canada, France, Japan, Mexico, Singapore, Spain, Switzerland, Taiwan, Thailand, United Kingdom.

- **Job Categories:** Accountants, Clerical Assistants, Finance.

- **General Requirements:** Usually must be a current employee of the company in order to qualify for overseas assignment

- **Language Requirement:** Knowledge of local language a plus but not essential.

- **Training:** No special training provided.

- **Benefits:** All benefits are individually determined.

DE KALB GENETICS CORPORATION

3100 Sycamore St.
De Kalb, IL 60115 USA

RECRUITER: THERESA BROWN
PERSONNEL MANAGER
3100 SYCAMORE RD.
DEKALB, IL 60115
TEL: (815) 758-3461
FAX: (815) 758-6953

Bruce Bickner, Chairman. Agriculture products including hybrid seed corn, hybrid sorghum seed, and genetic research. De Kalb Genetics is a public company founded in 1988. It became independent when it was spun off from the De Kalb Genetics Corporation on August 3, 1988. It concentrates on the improvement of agricultural products for farmers. Research on hybrid corn began in 1934 and it entered the animal genetics field in 1944. Worldwide revenues for 1993: $291.5 million.

- **Total Employees:** 2,250

- **U.S. Employees Abroad:** 25

- **Countries:** Argentina, Australia, Canada, Italy, Mexico, Spain, Thailand.

- **Job Categories:** Management, Marketing—Agricultural, Sales—Agricultural.

DE LEUW, CATHER INTERNATIONAL

1133 15th St. NW
Washington, DC 20005 USA

RECRUITER: ZIGMUND KOBES
INTERNATIONAL PERSONNEL
1133 15TH ST. NW
WASHINGTON, DC 20005
TEL: (202) 775-3300
FAX: (202) 775-3422

David S. Gedney, President. Engineering and project management. De Leuw Cather was founded in 1944 and is a subsidiary of the Parsons Corporation of Pasadena, California. It operates on an international basis providing clients with engineering, planning, and project management services. Also provides expertise for rail systems, resorts, environmental projects, and defense systems. Worldwide operating revenues for 1991: $100 million.

- **Total Employees:** 1,175

- **U.S. Employees Abroad:** 50

- **Countries:** Bolivia, Indonesia, Pakistan, Singapore, Turkey, United Arab Emirates.

- **Job Categories:** Architects, Engineers, Design, Management.

DEAN WITTER, DISCOVER & COMPANY

2 World Trade Center, 44th Floor
New York, NY 10048 USA

RECRUITER: DANIEL DEBIASE
EMPLOYMENT MANAGER
2 WORLD TRADE CENTER, 44TH
    FLOOR
NEW YORK, NY 10048
TEL: (212) 392-2222
FAX: (212) 392-1268

Philip J. Purcell, Chairman. Security brokerage and investment banking. Dean Witter, Discover & Company was established in 1992 when parent company Sears, Roebuck & Company transferred all its stock from NOVUS Credit Services Inc. to the company. In December 1992, the name was officially adopted (it was formerly Dean Witter Reynolds, Inc. and was founded in 1924). Today, it offers brokerage and investment services to clients around the world. Worldwide revenues for 1992: $5.1 billion.

- **Total Employees:** 25,600

- **U.S. Employees Abroad:** 10

- **Countries:** Switzerland, United Kingdom.

- **Job Categories:** Accountants, Brokers—Securities & Financial, Financial Advisors.

- **Comments:** The number of Americans reported working abroad varies greatly from quarter to quarter, fluctuating with the number and scope of projects under contract at the time.

DEBEVOISE & PLIMPTON

875 Third Ave.
New York, NY 10022 USA

RECRUITER: ETHEL LEICHTI &
RACHEL KAGAN
LEGAL STAFF & ADMINISTRATION
STAFF
875 THIRD AVE.
NEW YORK, NY 10022
TEL: (212) 909-6000
FAX: (212) 909-6836

Barry R. Bryan, Presiding Partner. Legal services. Debevoise & Plimpton was founded in 1931 and is a major international law firm. It now has over 370 lawyers and provides services in the fields of corporate, international, litigation, real estate, tax and trusts, and estates law. Debevoise & Plimpton has offices in New York, Washington, DC, Los Angeles, Paris, London, and Budapest. Worldwide operating revenues for 1991: $165 million.

- **Total Employees:** 1041
- **U.S. Employees Abroad:** 60
- **Countries:** France, Hungary, United Kingdom.
- **Job Categories:** Accountants, Attorneys, Legal Personnel.
- **Language Requirement:** Knowledge of local language skills a plus but not essential.
- **Training:** Basic orientation, training in specific work skills, and language training offered.
- **Benefits:** HEALTH: A variety of coverage options are available.
- **Comments:** Recruitment is handled by Rachel Kagan (Accounting Staff) and Ethel Leichti (Legal Staff).

DEERE & COMPANY

John Deere Rd.
Moline, IL 61265 USA

RECRUITER: RONALD H. LIKE
MANAGER, HUMAN RESOURCES
400 19TH ST.
MOLINE, IL 61265
TEL: (309) 765-3114
FAX: (309) 765-3130

H. W. Becherer, Chairman. Agricultural, lawn and garden, and construction equipment. Deere & Company is public and was founded in 1868. It is the world's leading producer of agricultural equipment and is a major supplier of construction and forestry equipment. It produces a wide variety of outdoor power equipment for home and commercial use. Worldwide revenues for 1992: $6.9 billion.

- **Total Employees:** 34,000
- **U.S. Employees Abroad:** Not available.
- **Countries:** Worldwide including Argentina, Australia, France, Germany, Mexico, United Kingdom.

- **Application Information:** Direct inquiries to John Deere Intercontinental GMBH Region at recruiter's address.

- **Job Categories:** Technical Field Support, Sales—Agricultural.

- **General Requirements:** Language skills required; graduate degrees preferred.

- **Average Overseas Assignment:** Usually 3-5 years

- **Language Requirement:** Fluency in local language required.

- **Training:** Training in specific work skills provided.

- **Benefits:** TRAVEL: Relocation expenses paid with cost-of-living considerations. HEALTH: Non-contributory for employee and dependents. HOUSING: Based on comparable U.S. cost-of-living. EDUCATION: Offered.

DEL MONTE CORPORATION

1 Market Plaza
PO Box 193575
San Francisco, CA 94119-3547
USA

RECRUITER: RICHARD MUTO
VICE PRESIDENT, EMPLOYEE
RELATIONS
1 MARKET PLAZA
PO BOX 193575
SAN FRANCISCO, CA 94119-3575
TEL: (415) 247-3000
FAX: (415) 247-3565

A. Ewan Macdonald, President. Canned goods, fruits, and vegetables. Del Monte is a private company founded in 1916. Worldwide revenues for 1992: $1.4 billion.

- **Total Employees:** 28,000

- **U.S. Employees Abroad:** 35

- **Countries:** Mexico, Philippines.

- **Application Information:** Hiring for most foreign positions is done at the specific country location.

- **Job Categories:** Management, Manufacturing, Marketing—Food/Food Services, Sales—Food/Food Services.

- **General Requirements:** A degree or related experience is preferred in the specific area of employment.

- **Average Overseas Assignment:** 2-3 years

- **Language Requirement:** Competency in local language required.

- **Training:** No special training provided.

- **Benefits:** All benefits are individually determined.

DELL COMPUTER CORPORATION

9505 Arboretum Blvd.
Austin, TX 78759 USA

RECRUITER: BILL MCBRIDE
DIRECTOR, INTERNATIONAL
    RECRUITMENT
9505 ARBORETUM BLVD.
AUSTIN, TX 78759
TEL: (512) 338-4400
FAX: (512) 339-5324

Michael S. Dell, Chairman. Designs, manufactures, and markets personal computer systems. Dell Computer is a public company founded in 1984 by Michael Dell. He began by selling RAM chips and disk drives for IBM personal computers. He then began to make and sell his own IBM-compatible computers under the brand name PCs Limited. Today, Dell is one of the fastest growing companies in its field. It operates on a worldwide basis with manufacturing plants in the United States and the United Kingdom. Worldwide revenues for 1992: $890 million.

- **Total Employees:** 2,400

- **U.S. Employees Abroad:** 30

- **Countries:** Canada, France, Germany, Italy, Japan, Sweden, United Kingdom.

- **Job Categories:** Management, Marketing—Electronics, Product Development, Sales—Electronics.

DELOITTE & TOUCHE

PO Box 820
Wilton, CT 06897-0820 USA

RECRUITER: LYNDA SPIELMAN
DIRECTOR, INTERNATIONAL
    MANAGEMENT
PO BOX 820
WILTON, CT 06897-0820
TEL: (203) 761-3000
FAX: (203) 761-3139

J. Michael Cook, Chairman. Professional accounting and auditing services. Deloitte & Touche is a private company founded in 1947. It provides accounting, auditing, and bookkeeping services for clients on a global basis. Worldwide operating revenues for 1992: $1.9 billion.

- **Total Employees:** 16,500

- **U.S. Employees Abroad:** 25

- **Countries:** France, United Kingdom.

- **Job Categories:** Accountants, Management, Marketing.

- **Language Requirement:** Varies with each posting.

- **Benefits:** TRAVEL: No special training provided.

DELTA AIR LINES, INC.

Hartsfield Atlanta International
Airport
Atlanta, GA 30320 USA

RECRUITER: H. M. JOHNSON
ASSISTANT VICE PRESIDENT,
EMPLOYMENT
HARTSFIELD ATLANTA
INTERNATIONAL AIRPORT
ATLANTA, GA 30320
TEL: (404) 715-2501
FAX: (404) 715-2100

Ronald W. Allen, Chairman. International air service for passengers, freight, and mail. Delta Air Lines is a public company founded in 1924. It began as the world's first crop dusting service, named Huff-Daland Dusters. In 1925, the company was purchased by field manager C. E. Woolman and two partners and renamed Delta Air Service. Expansion through the years has allowed Delta to become one of the world's largest airlines. Today, it serves 187 cities in the United States and abroad. Worldwide revenues for 1992: $11.6 billion.

- **Total Employees:** 75,000
- **U.S. Employees Abroad:** 3,500
- **Countries:** Canada, Denmark, Germany, Japan, Hong Kong, Singapore, Switzerland, United Kingdom.
- **Job Categories:** Accountants, Airport Management, Finance, Marketing—Travel, Sales—Travel.

DETROIT DIESEL CORPORATION

13400 West Outer Dr.
Detroit, MI 48239-4001 USA

RECRUITER: PAT LOWES
SALARIED PERSONNEL
ADMINISTRATOR
13400 WEST OUTER DR.
DETROIT, MI 48239-4001
TEL: (313) 592-5000
FAX: (313) 592-7089

Ludvik F. Koci, President. Diesel or internal combustion engines for various industries. Detroit Diesel was founded in 1938 and is a subsidiary of the Penske Corporation of New York. It is a joint venture with Detroit Diesel of Canada, Limited. Worldwide revenues for 1991: $520 million.

- **Total Employees:** 3,300
- **U.S. Employees Abroad:** 25
- **Countries:** Canada, Switzerland.
- **Job Categories:** Management, Marketing—Industrial, Sales—Industrial.
- **General Requirements:** Usually must be a current employee of the company in order to qualify for overseas assignment.
- **Language Requirement:** None.

- **Training:** No special training provided.

THE DEXTER CORPORATION

1 Elm St.
Windsor Locks, CT 06096 USA

RECRUITER: KEVIN LAKE
CORPORATE DIRECTOR, HUMAN
    RESOURCES
1 ELM ST.
WINDSOR LOCKS, CT 06096
TEL: (203) 292-7678
FAX: (203) 627-9713

K. Grahame Walker, President. Specialty materials and support services for various industries. The Dexter Corporation is a public company founded in 1767. It is the oldest known firm on the New York Stock Exchange. Dexter focuses its business in six major areas: aerospace, automotive, electronics, food packaging, industrial assembly, and medical. Major products include adhesives, structural materials, and specialty coatings for the aerospace industry; and medical fabrics and biotechnology products for the medical/health-care markets. Worldwide revenues for 1992: $951.4 million.

- **Total Employees:** 5,000
- **U.S. Employees Abroad:** 20
- **Countries:** Belgium, France, Germany, Italy, Mexico, New Zealand, Singapore, Switzerland, United Kingdom, Venezuela.
- **Job Categories:** Finance, Marketing—Industrial, Office Management, Sales—Industrial.

DH TECHNOLOGY, INC.

15070 Ave. of Science
San Diego, CA 92128 USA

RECRUITER: DAVID T. LEDWELL
VP, OPERATIONS
15070 AVE. OF SCIENCE
SAN DIEGO, CA 92128
TEL: (619) 451-3485
FAX: (619) 451-3573

William H. Gibbs, President and Chairman. Supplier of printers and related products. DH Technology, Inc. is a public company founded in 1983. It is engaged as a designer, builder, and marketer of advanced high-performance printheads, printer mechanisms, and specialty printers. It has operations and/or sales offices in the United States and in 10 foreign countries. Worldwide revenues for 1991: $46.5 million.

- **Total Employees:** 560
- **U.S. Employees Abroad:** 22
- **Countries:** Brazil, Canada, France, Germany, India, Japan, Republic of Korea, Netherlands, Taiwan, United Kingdom.
- **Job Categories:** Engineers, Marketing—Industrial, Product Development, Sales—Industrial.

- **Language Requirement:** Varies with each posting.

DIAMOND M-ODECO DRILLING, INC.

PO Box 4558
Houston, TX 77210 USA

RECRUITER: VIRGINIA BUTTERFRAS
ASSISTANT PERSONNEL MANAGER
PO BOX 4558
HOUSTON, TX 77210
TEL: (713) 492-5300

Robert E. Rose, President. Exploration services and mining. Diamond M-ODECO Drilling, Inc. is a subsidiary of the Loews Corporation of New York City. It provides mining and exploration services in the oil and gas fields to clients on a global basis. Worldwide revenues for 1991: $64.6 million.

- **Total Employees:** 900

- **U.S. Employees Abroad:** 25

- **Countries:** Singapore, United Kingdom.

- **Job Categories:** Engineers, Marketing—Petroleum/Natural Gas, Sales—Petroleum/Natural Gas.

- **Language Requirement:** None.

DIAMOND SHAMROCK R & M, INC.

PO Box 696000
San Antonio, TX 78230 USA

RECRUITER: ALEX PENA
HUMAN RESOURCES GROUP
MANAGER
PO BOX 696000
SAN ANTONIO, TX 78230
TEL: (512) 641-6800
FAX: (512) 641-8670

Roger R. Hemminghaus, Chairman. Organic and inorganic chemicals and specialties. Also, a petroleum products refiner. Diamond Shamrock R & M is a public company founded in 1986. It originated from the previous Diamond Shamrock Corporation (currently known as Maxus Energy). It markets gasoline through its Diamond Shamrock divisions in the United States and abroad. Worldwide revenues for 1992: $2.6 billion.

- **Total Employees:** 5,000

- **U.S. Employees Abroad:** 45

- **Countries:** Argentina, Brazil, Mexico, Venezuela.

- **Job Categories:** Accountants, Chemists, Engineers, Management Training, Marketing—Chemicals, Truck Drivers.

DIEBOLD INCORPORATED

PO Box 8230
Canton, OH 44711 USA

RECRUITER: JOHN R. GOTCH
STAFFING/RECRUITMENT
818 MULBERRY RD. SE
CANTON, OH 44707
TEL: (216) 497-4623
FAX: (216) 497-4549

Robert W. Mahoney, Chairman. Security systems and teller machines. Diebold Incorporated is a public company founded in 1859. It produces, sells, and repairs self-service transaction systems, automated teller machines, security systems, and computer software. It has facilities in the United States and abroad. Worldwide revenues for 1992: $543.9 million.

- **Total Employees:** 3,975

- **U.S. Employees Abroad:** 20

- **Countries:** Germany, Hong Kong, Mexico, United Kingdom.

- **Job Categories:** Management, Marketing—Electronics, Sales—Electronics.

- **Language Requirement:** None.

DIGICON, INC.

3701 Kirby Dr., Suite 112
Houston, TX 77098 USA

RECRUITER: LISA SEEKERS
PERSONNEL DIRECTOR
3701 KIRBY DR., SUITE 112
HOUSTON, TX 77098
TEL: (713) 526-5611
FAX: (713) 630-4460

Edward R. Prince, Jr., Chairman. Geophysical services. Digicon, Inc. is a public company founded in 1965. It provides various and extensive geophysical services for clients on a worldwide basis. It is primarily involved in the acquisition and compiliation of seismic data for use by petroleum industries in search of new oil and gas reserves. Worldwide revenues for 1991: $94.2 million.

- **Total Employees:** 1,015

- **U.S. Employees Abroad:** 25

- **Countries:** Canada, Indonesia, Malaysia, Netherlands, Nigeria, Singapore, United Kingdom, Venezuela.

- **Job Categories:** Engineers, Executive Management, Management.

- **General Requirements:** Usually must be a current employee of the company in order to qualify for overseas assignment.

- **Language Requirement:** Varies with each posting.

DIGITAL EQUIPMENT CORPORATION

146 Main St.
Maynard, MA 01754-2571 USA

RECRUITER: R. JOHNSON
CORPORATE EMPLOYMENT
146 MAIN ST.
MAYNARD, MA 01754-2571
TEL: (508) 493-5111
FAX: (508) 493-9490

Kenneth H. Olsen, President. Supplier of network computer systems, software, and services. Digital Equipment is a public company founded in 1957 by two MIT engineers, Kenneth Olsen and Harlan Anderson. Today, this company is the second largest information systems provider in the world. Digital is also a leader in networking and systems integration. Business is conducted in more than 80 countries. Worldwide revenues for 1992: $14.2 billion.

- **Total Employees:** 124,000

- **U.S. Employees Abroad:** 125

- **Countries:** Eighty countries including Australia, Austria, Brazil, People's Republic of China, France, Germany, Japan, Israel, Mexico, Netherlands, Norway, Panama, Taiwan, United Kingdom.

- **Job Categories:** Management, Marketing—Electronics, Research & Development, Technicians, Sales—Electronics.

- **General Requirements:** Usually must be a current employee of the company in order to qualify for overseas assignment.

DIXON TICONDEROGA COMPANY

2600 Maitland Center Pkwy.
Maitland, FL 32751 USA

RECRUITER: KENNETH BAER
STAFFING
2600 MAITLAND CENTER PKWY.
MAITLAND, FL 32751
TEL: (407) 875-5000
FAX: (407) 875-2574

Gino N. Pala, Chief Executive Officer. Writing tools and art supplies. Dixon Ticonderoga was founded in 1795. It manufactures mechanical pencils, writing tools for drawing, natural bulk graphite, and graphite oil and greases. It is also a developer of condominiums in Florida. Worldwide revenues for 1991: $70.6 million.

- **Total Employees:** 1,000

- **U.S. Employees Abroad:** 20

- **Countries:** Canada, Mexico, United Kingdom.

- **Job Categories:** Management, Marketing—Consumer Goods, Sales—Consumer Goods.

- **Language Requirement:** None.

DOMINO'S PIZZA, INC.

30 Frank Lloyd Wright Dr.
PO Box 997
Ann Arbor, MI 48106-0997 USA

RECRUITER: DAN FOLEY
VP, HUMAN RESOURCES
30 FRANK LLOYD DR.
PO BOX 997
ANN ARBOR, MI 48106-0997
TEL: (313) 930-3030
FAX: (313) 668-4614

Thomas S. Monaghan, President. Pizza delivery. Domino's Pizza, Inc. is a private company founded in 1960 by Thomas Monaghan. The company grew rapidly during the 1980s and international operations were begun in 1983. Today, it has 5,500 locations worldwide, with more than 5,000 in the United States. It operates in more than 25 countries. Worldwide revenues for 1991: $2.4 billion.

- **Total Employees:** 115,000

- **U.S. Employees Abroad:** 50

- **Countries:** Worldwide including Australia, Bahamas, Canada, Colombia, France, Germany, Hong Kong, Japan, Republic of Korea, Mexico, Singapore, United Kingdom, Venezuela.

- **Job Categories:** Management, Marketing—Food/Food Services, Sales—Food/Food Services.

- **General Requirements:** Usually must be a current employee of the company in order to qualify for overseas assignment.

- **Language Requirement:** Varies with each posting.

DONALDSON COMPANY, INC.

PO Box 1299
Minneapolis, MN 55440 USA

RECRUITER: JOHN THANER
DIRECTOR, HUMAN RESOURCES
PO BOX 1299
MINNEAPOLIS, MN 55440
TEL: (612) 887-3131

William A. Hodder, Chairman. Filtration systems and related products. Donaldson is a public company founded in 1915. It produces commercial and industrial fans, blowers, and air-purification products for heating, air conditioning, and ventilation systems. Worldwide revenues for 1993: $533 million.

- **Total Employees:** 3,800

- **U.S. Employees Abroad:** Not available.

- **Countries:** Australia, Belgium, Brazil, France, Germany, Hong Kong, Mexico, Netherlands, United Kingdom.

- **Job Categories:** Finance, Management, Product Development, Technical Field Support, Sales—Industrial.

DONALDSON LUFKIN & JENRETTE, INC.

140 Broadway
New York, NY 10005 USA

RECRUITER: PAMELA HAYNES
AVP
MOORGATE HALL, 155 MOORGATE
LONDON EC2M 6XB, ENGLAND
TEL: (071) 638-5822
FAX: (071) 588-0120

John S. Chalsty, Chairman. Brokerage services. Donaldson Lufkin & Jenrette was founded in 1959 and is a subsidiary of the Equitable Life Assurance Society of the United States. It is a securities broker for institutions. Worldwide operating revenues for 1992: $334 million.

- **Total Employees:** 3,240
- **U.S. Employees Abroad:** 5
- **Countries:** Japan, France, Switzerland, United Kingdom.
- **Job Categories:** Agents—Insurance, Brokers—Securities & Financial, Finance.
- **Language Requirement:** Fluency in local language required.
- **Training:** No special training provided.
- **Benefits:** TRAVEL: None offered. HEALTH: Same coverage as U.S. employees; additional benefits accomodate labor laws in specific country. HOUSING: None offered. EDUCATION: None offered.
- **Comments:** The number of Americans working abroad varies greatly from quarter to quarter, fluctuating with the number and scope of projects under contract at the time.

R. R. DONNELLEY & SONS COMPANY

2223 South Martin Luther King Dr.
Chicago, IL 60616-1471 USA

RECRUITER: JEFF ANDERSON
PERSONNEL DEPARTMENT
2223 SOUTH MARTIN LUTHER KING
    DR.
CHICAGO, IL 60616-1471
TEL: (312) 326-8030
FAX: (312) 326-8543

John R. Walter, President and Chairman. Information for direct-mail and in-store merchandisers and financial instutions. Also engaged in publishing. R. R. Donnelley & Sons is a public company founded in 1864. It comprises a group of companies operating a worldwide network in communications, through mail and book publishing. A major product is cross-referenced directories. Worldwide revenues for 1992: $4.2 billion.

- **Total Employees:** 25,000
- **U.S. Employees Abroad:** Not available.
- **Countries:** Japan, Mexico, United Kingdom.
- **Job Categories:** Office Management, Marketing, Sales.

REUBEN H. DONNELLY

287 Bowman Ave.
Purchase, NY 10577 USA

RECRUITER: ALLEN ROSS
VP, HUMAN RESOURCES
287 BOWMAN AVE.
PURCHASE, NY 10577
TEL: (914) 933-6800
FAX: (914) 933-6483

Kenneth O. Johnson, President. Publishing. Reuben H. Donnelly was founded in 1886 and was formerly called The Donnelly Directory. It is a subsidiary of Dun & Bradstreet Corporation of New York, New York, and publishes telephone directories and other printed sourcebooks.

- **Total Employees:** 4,000

- **U.S. Employees Abroad:** Not available.

- **Countries:** United Kingdom.

- **Job Categories:** Management, Marketing—Publishing, Sales—Publishing.

DOVER CORPORATION

280 Park Ave.
New York, NY 10172 USA

RECRUITER: GARY L. ROUBOS
PRESIDENT
280 PARK AVE.
NEW YORK, NY 10172
TEL: (212) 922-1640

Gary L. Roubos, President. Machinery and equipment for aerospace, construction, electronics, and petroleum industries. Dover Corporation is a public company founded in 1947. It is engaged as a manufacturer of machinery and equipment. Major products include machinery and pumps for service stations, elevators, and moving stairs. Worldwide net revenues for 1992: $2.2 billion.

- **Total Employees:** 18,827

- **U.S. Employees Abroad:** 35

- **Countries:** Canada, Germany, United Kingdom.

- **Job Categories:** Management, Marketing—Industrial, Sales—Industrial.

- **General Requirements:** Usually must be a current employee of the company in order to qualify for overseas assignment

- **Language Requirement:** None.

DOW CHEMICAL COMPANY

2030 Willard H. Dow Center
Midland, MI 48674 USA

RECRUITER: JAMES E. TOWNSEND
MANAGER, UNIVERSITY RELATIONS
2030 WILLARD H. DOW CENTER
MIDLAND, MI 48674
TEL: (517) 636-1463
FAX: (517) 636-0922
FREE: (800) 258-9002

Frank P. Popoff, President. Goods and services including chemicals and performance products. Dow Chemical is a public company founded in 1897. It manufactures and sells more than 2,000 products around the world. Major products include chlorinated solvents, calcium chloride, Styrofoam plastic products, and Ziploc plastic bags. It has 118 manufacturing plants in 32 countries. Worldwide revenues for 1992: $19 billion.

- **Total Employees:** 62,080

- **U.S. Employees Abroad:** 90

- **Countries:** Argentina, Australia, Brazil, Chile, Germany, India, Japan, Netherlands, Singapore, Thailand, Trinidad and Tobago, United Kingdom.

- **Job Categories:** Accountants, Finance, Marketing—Chemicals, Marketing—Consumer Goods, Research & Development, Sales—Chemicals, Sales—Consumer Goods.

DOW CORNING CORPORATION

PO Box 994
Midland, MI 48686 USA

RECRUITER: BURNETT KELLEY
DIRECTOR, HUMAN RESOURCES
PO BOX 994
MIDLAND, MI 48686
TEL: (517) 496-4748
FAX: (517) 496-6113

Lawrence Reed, President. Silicones, silicon chemicals, and related products. Dow Corning is a public company founded in 1943. It produces hyper-pure polycrystalline silicon, silicones, and other related products. Worldwide revenues for 1992: $2 billion.

- **Total Employees:** 8,600

- **U.S. Employees Abroad:** 25

- **Countries:** Argentina, Australia, Greece, Hong Kong, Israel, Italy, Mexico, Singapore, Taiwan, United Kingdom.

- **Job Categories:** Accountants, Marketing—Chemicals, Product Development, Sales—Chemicals.

DOW JONES & COMPANY, INC.

200 Liberty St.
New York, NY 10281 USA

RECRUITER: JOHN SAX
EMPLOYEE RELATIONS MANAGER
200 LIBERTY ST.
NEW YORK, NY 10281
TEL: (212) 416-3530
FAX: (212) 416-4348

Peter R. Kann, Chairman. Business and financial news publishing. Dow Jones is a public company founded in 1882 by three financial reporters. Charles Dow, Edward Jones, and Charles Bergstresser began by selling hand-written bulletins with stock and bond information to financial districts in New York. Today, the firm is best known for its publication of the *Wall Street Journal*, with a daily, worldwide circulation of over two million. Worldwide revenues for 1992: $1.8 billion.

- **Total Employees:** 10,000
- **U.S. Employees Abroad:** 115
- **Countries:** Australia, Austria, Belgium, Brazil, France, Germany, Hong Kong, Indonesia, Japan, Republic of Korea, Malaysia, Mexico, Netherlands, Russia, Singapore, Sweden, Switzerland, Thailand, United Kingdom.
- **Job Categories:** Editors, Reporters, Sales—Publishing.
- **General Requirements:** College degree, experience, and ability to speak a foreign language.
- **Average Overseas Assignment:** 3-5 years.
- **Language Requirement:** Competency in local language required.
- **Training:** No special training provided.
- **Benefits:** TRAVEL: Home leave is provided after eighteen months of service. Economy airfare is provided for spouse and dependent children. HEALTH: Same coverage as U.S. employees; including hospital coverage, surgical and medical benefits, prescriptions, vision and dental care. HOUSING: Offers a foreign exchange protection allowance and a housing subsidy, which is paid monthly. EDUCATION: Assists with the education of children from kindergarten through high school.

DRESSER INDUSTRIES, INC.

1600 Pacific Building
Dallas, TX 75221 USA

RECRUITER: DANNY SANCHEZ
PERSONNEL MANAGER
1600 PACIFIC BUILDING
DALLAS, TX 75221
TEL: (214) 740-6000
FAX: (214) 740-6715

John J. Murphy, President and Chairman. Diversified supplier of services and equipment to energy services and natural resource industries. Dresser Industries is a public company founded in 1880 by Solomon Dresser. In 1878 he began working in the oil fields and in 1880 invented the cap packer (a tool that prevents crude oil from mixing with other fluids) and was given a patent for it. He then invented the Dresser Coupling, a device that prevented leaks in pipeline connections. After his death in 1911, the family sold the company to W. A. Harriman & Company, which took Dresser public in 1928. Today, it is a major industrial equipment manufacturer that focuses on equipment for the petroleum markets. Dresser operates in the United States and in more than 60 foreign countries. Worldwide revenues for 1992: $3.8 billion.

- **Total Employees:** 31,400

- **U.S. Employees Abroad:** 110

- **Countries:** Algeria, Argentina, Australia, Belgium, Brazil, Canada, Chile, People's Republic of China, Germany, Greece, Hong Kong, Indonesia, Italy, Japan, Kuwait, Luxembourg, Mexico, Netherlands, Nigeria, Norway, Peru, Russia, Saudi Arabia, Singapore, Saudi Arabia, Spain, Sweden, Switzerland, Thailand, Tunisia, United Arab Emirates, United Kingdom, Venezuela.

- **Job Categories:** Management, Marketing—Scientific, Sales—Scientific.

DRUMMOND COMPANY, INC.

530 Beacon Pkwy. West
PO Box 10246
Birmingham, AL 35202 USA

RECRUITER: JOSEPH B. BILICH
VP, HUMAN RESOURCES
530 BEACON PKWY. WEST
PO BOX 10246
BIRMINGHAM, AL 35202
TEL: (205) 945-6500
FAX: (205) 945-6440

Gary N. Drummond, President. Coal. Drummond is a private company founded in 1935. It is a major, independent and privately owned coal company and one of the largest exporters of coal in the United States. It operates on a global basis. Worldwide revenues for 1991: $540 million.

- **Total Employees:** 3,300

- **U.S. Employees Abroad:** 16

- **Countries:** Italy, Japan, Netherlands, United Kingdom.

- **Job Categories:** Accountants, Marketing, Sales.

- **Language Requirement:** None.

- **Comments:** The number of Americans reported working abroad varies greatly from quarter to quarter, fluctuating with the number and scope of projects under contract at the time.

DUN & BRADSTREET CORPORATION

299 Park Ave.
New York, NY 10171 USA

RECRUITER: PETER ROSS
SR. VP, INTERNATIONAL HUMAN
RESOURCES
1 WORLD TRADE CENTER
NEW YORK, NY 10171
TEL: (212) 524-8200
FAX: (212) 593-4143

Charles W. Moritz, Chairman. Business information services. Dun & Bradstreet is a public company founded in 1841 by Lewis Tappan. He formed the Mercantile Agency in New York City, one of the first commercial credit reporting agencies created. Today, it is a marketing and business information services company. Included are A. C. Nielsen, which measures television audiences and does marketing research; and R. H. Donnelley, which produces the Yellow Pages telephone directories. It sells services in over 60 countries. Worldwide revenues for 1992: $4.7 billion.

- **Total Employees:** 71,000

- **U.S. Employees Abroad:** 70

- **Countries:** Worldwide including Australia, Canada, France, Germany, Italy, Japan, United Kingdom.

- **Job Categories:** Accountants, Management, Marketing, Marketing—Publishing, Sales, Sales—Publishing.

- **Language Requirement:** None.

DUPONT MERCK PHARMACEUTICAL COMPANY

1000 Stewart Ave.
Garden City, NY 11530 USA

RECRUITER: RICHARD F. MINEOS
MANAGER, HUMAN RESOURCES
1000 STEWART AVE.
GARDEN CITY, NY 11530
TEL: (516) 832-2213
FAX: (516) 832-2275

Robert Matthews, Director. Pharmaceuticals. Dupont Merck Pharmaceutical was founded in 1990 as an equally-owned joint venture between Dupont and Merck & Company. It is engaged in pharmaceutical research and marketing.

- **Total Employees:** 1,030

- **U.S. Employees Abroad:** 20

- **Countries:** Australia, Colombia, Mexico, Philippines.

- **Job Categories:** Management, Marketing—Pharmaceuticals, Research & Development, Sales—Pharmaceuticals.

DURACELL, INC.

Berkshire Industrial Park
Bethel, CT 06801 USA

RECRUITER: MICHELLE PORCH
HUMAN RESOURCES SUPERVISOR
BERKSHIRE INDUSTRIAL PARK
BETHEL, CT 06801
TEL: (203) 796-4000
FAX: (203) 730-8958

C. Robert Kidder, President. Duracell Alkaline and Durobeam products for consumer and commercial markets. Duracell is a private company founded in 1946. It manufactures lithium, zinc/air, mercuricoxide, and silver oxide batteries for such items as cameras, hearing aids, and watches. Worldwide revenues for 1992: $1.7 billion.

- **Total Employees:** 9,500

- **U.S. Employees Abroad:** 20

- **Countries:** Argentina, Australia, Brazil, Chile, Hong Kong, Japan, Mexico, United Kingdom.

- **Job Categories:** Management, Marketing, Sales.

DURIRON COMPANY, INC.

Research Blvd.
PO Box 8820
Dayton, OH 45401-8820 USA

RECRUITER: JULIA TREY
MANAGER, HUMAN RESOURCES
RESEARCH BLVD.
PO BOX 8820
DAYTON, OH 45401-8820
TEL: (513) 476-6100
FAX: (513) 476-6231

John S. Haddick, President. Fluid movement and control equipment, including pumps and valves. Duriron is a public company founded in 1912. It produces fluid movement and control equipment, which it markets to industries that have difficulty handling corrosive liquids and gases used in the manufacturing process. Duririon also produces and markets filters and filtration systems. Worldwide revenues for 1992: $300 billion.

- **Total Employees:** 2,500

- **U.S. Employees Abroad:** 20

- **Countries:** Australia, Canada, Belgium, France, Germany, United Kingdom.

- **Job Categories:** Engineers, Executive Management, Finance, Marketing—Industrial.

- **Language Requirement:** Varies with each posting.

- **Training:** No special training provided.

DURO-TEST INTERNATIONAL CORPORATION

9 Law Dr.
Fairfield, NJ 07004 USA

RECRUITER: MIKE R. DIAZ
VP, INTERNATIONAL OPERATIONS
9 LAW DR.
FAIRFIELD, NJ 07004
TEL: (201) 808-0906
FAX: (201) 808-2666

Dan E. Picini, Chief Executive Officer. Incandescent and flourescent lamps. Duro-Test International Corporation is a private company founded in 1929. It manufactures and sells electric bulbs, tubes, and similar products. It markets these items to commercial and industrial customers. Worldwide revenues for 1991: $92 million.

- **Total Employees:** 2,000
- **U.S. Employees Abroad:** 20
- **Countries:** Canada, Japan, Mexico.
- **Job Categories:** Management Training, Marketing—Electronics, Sales—Electronics.
- **Language Requirement:** Fluency in local language required.

DYNCORP

2000 Edmund Halley Dr.
Reston, VA 22091 USA

RECRUITER: RON GEIGER
VP, HUMAN RESOURCES
2000 EDMUND HALLEY DR.
RESTON, VA 22091
TEL: (703) 264-0330
FAX: (703) 264-8600

Dan Bannister, President. Technical services. Dyncorp is a private company founded in 1946. It provides general and specific trade contractors for work on heavy-equipment projects. This includes the operation and maintenance of airports as well as servicing and repairing aircraft. In the communications sector, it handles radar station operation and missile tracking. Worldwide operating revenues for 1991: $750 million.

- **Total Employees:** 18,000
- **U.S. Employees Abroad:** Not available.
- **Countries:** Germany, Republic of Korea.
- **Job Categories:** Contractors, Maintenance, Management, Marketing.

E-SYSTEMS, INC.

PO Box 660248
Dallas, TX 75266-0248 USA

RECRUITER: JERRY SHAVER
STAFFING/RECRUITMENT
PO BOX 660248
DALLAS, TX 75266-0248
TEL: (214) 661-1000
FAX: (214) 661-8508

A
M
E
R
I
C
A
N

J
O
B
S

A
B
R
O
A
D

E. Gene Keiffer, Chairman. High-tech defense and electronic systems and related products. E-Systems is a public company founded in 1964. It designs and manufactures electronic systems and military items for intelligence, surveillance, guidance and navigation, communications, electronic warfare, aircraft maintenance, and reconnaissance. Worldwide revenues for 1992: $2.1 billion.

- **Total Employees:** 17,920

- **U.S. Employees Abroad:** 300

- **Countries:** Germany, Japan, Taiwan.

- **Application Information:** Most foreign positions are filled internally.

- **Job Categories:** Electrical Engineers, Marketing—Electronics, Product Development, Sales—Defense Industry, Sales—Electronics.

- **Language Requirement:** None.

EAGLE-PICHER INDUSTRIES, INC.

580 Walnut St.
Cincinnati, OH 45202 USA

RECRUITER: ERNEST HIRSH
DIRECTOR, HUMAN RESOURCES
580 WALNUT ST.
CINCINNATI, OH 45202
TEL: (513) 721-7010
FAX: (513) 721-2341

Thomas E. Petry, Chairman. Hi-tech maintenance and research. Eagle-Picher Industries, Inc. is a public company founded in 1843. It manufactures various products ranging from minerals and plastics to other items in the defense, industrial machine, and automotive industries. Customers include the Ford Motor Company and NASA. Worldwide revenues for 1992: $611 million.

- **Total Employees:** 6,200

- **U.S. Employees Abroad:** 20

- **Countries:** Germany, Japan, Spain, United Kingdom.

- **Application Information:** Hiring for most foreign positions is done at the specific country location.

- **Job Categories:** Accountants, Marketing—Scientific, Sales, Sales—Scientific.

- **Language Requirement:** None.

EASTMAN KODAK COMPANY

343 State St.
Rochester, NY 14650 USA

RECRUITER: DIRECTOR,
RECRUITMENT/STAFFING
343 STATE ST.
ROCHESTER, NY 14650
TEL: (716) 724-4000
FAX: (716) 724-0633

Kay R. Whitmore, President and Chairman. Photo and chemical products; household and health products; Also, information systems. Eastman Kodak is a public company founded in 1880. Best known as a leader in the photography business, the Kodak brand name is used around the world. Through the years, this company has diversified and streamlined operations, entering the fields of electronic publishing and information systems. With the purchase of Sterling Drug in 1988, Bayer aspirin is now a part of Eastman Kodak Company. It has offices throughout the world. Worldwide revenues for 1992: $20.2 billion.

- **Total Employees:** 135,000

- **U.S. Employees Abroad:** 250

- **Countries:** Worldwide including Argentina, Australia, Brazil, Chile, France, Germany, Greece, Hong Kong, Japan, Kenya, Mexico, Portugal, Singapore, United Arab Emirates, United Kingdom.

- **Job Categories:** Accountants, Executive Management, Finance, Marketing—Chemicals, Marketing, Product Development, Sales—Chemicals, Sales.

EATON CORPORATION/CUTLER HAMMER

Eaton Center
Cleveland, OH 44114-2584 USA

RECRUITER: BOB CHAPPLE
DIRECTOR, HUMAN RESOURCES
4201 NORTH 27TH ST.
MILWAUKEE, WI 53216
TEL: (414) 449-6000
FAX: (414) 449-6221

James R. Stover, Chairman. Advanced technology products for transportation industry. Eaton Corporation/Cutler Hammer is a public company founded in 1911 when Joseph Eaton and Viggo Torbensen began as manufacturers of truck axles. Renovation and expansion occurred through the years and in 1991, Eaton regrouped into six smaller operating sectors in response to market conditions. Today, it is a leading manufacturer of automobile and truck components. Eaton's largest customer is Ford, with 20 percent of 1990 net sales generated by that company. Eaton has 130 factories in more than 20 countries. Worldwide revenues for 1992: $3.8 billion.

- **Total Employees:** 43,000

- **U.S. Employees Abroad:** 110

- **Countries:** Argentina, Australia, Brazil, Colombia, France, Greece, Israel, Italy, Malaysia, Mexico, United Kingdom.

- **Job Categories:** Accountants, Finance, Marketing—Automotive, Marketing, Sales—Automotive, Sales.

EBASCO OVERSEAS CORPORATION

2 World Trade Center
New York, NY 10048 USA

RECRUITER: WILLIAM BOSAKOWSKI
RECRUITMENT DIVISION
2 WORLD TRADE CENTER
NEW YORK, NY 10048
TEL: (212) 839-2658
FAX: (212) 849-4574

B. R. Mazo, President. Engineering, design and contruction of power generation plants and major infrastructure projects; environmental engineering and quality assurance services. Ebasco was founded in 1905 as a subsidiary of Enserch Corporation of Dallas, Texas. Ebasco operates as as professional engineering firm and provides services on an international basis. Worldwide revenues for 1991: $1.2 billion.

- **Total Employees:** 6,000
- **U.S. Employees Abroad:** 60
- **Countries:** People's Republic of China, Egypt, Germany, Italy, Republic of Korea, Netherlands, Pakistan, Philippines, Singapore, Taiwan, United Kingdom.
- **Salaries:** Industry average plus overseas allowance.
- **Job Categories:** Construction Workers, Contract Administration, Management, Engineers.
- **General Requirements:** Previous overseas experience is preferred.
- **Average Overseas Assignment:** Contract dependent; generally 2-3 years.
- **Language Requirement:** Knowledge of local language a plus but not essential.
- **Training:** Basic orientation provided.
- **Benefits:** General benefits package.

ECOLOGY AND ENVIRONMENT, INC.

368 Pleasantview Dr.
Lancaster, NY 14086 USA

RECRUITER: JANET A. STEINBRUCKNER
PERSONNEL DIRECTOR
368 PLEASANTVIEW DR.
LANCASTER, NY 14086
TEL: (716) 684-8060
FAX: (716) 684-0844

Gerhard Neumaier, President. Environmental consulting. Ecology and Environment, Inc. is a public company founded in 1970. As an environmental consulting firm, it offers services in the fields of toxic, hazardous, nuclear, and solid waste disposal management on a global basis. Worldwide operating revenues for 1991: $87.4 million.

- **Total Employees:** 1,000
- **U.S. Employees Abroad:** 10
- **Countries:** Austria, Bahrain, Bolivia, Brazil, Chile, Costa Rica, Egypt, Germany,

Cayman Islands, Indonesia, Cote d'Ivoire, Kuwait, Malaysia, Mexico, Nigeria, Oman, Panama, Peru, Qatar, Saudi Arabia, United Arab Emirates, United Kingdom, Venezuela.

- **Job Categories:** Environmental Specialists.
- **General Requirements:** Employee willing to relocate to specific area for a minimum of one year.
- **Language Requirement:** Varies with each posting; competency in local language required.
- **Training:** Varies with each posting; language training may be offered.
- **Benefits:** All benefits are individually determined.

EG & G, INC.

45 William St.
Wellesley, MA 02181 USA

RECRUITER: PETER MURPHY
CORP. DIRECTOR, TRAINING &
DEVELOPMENT
45 WILLIAM ST.
WELLESLEY, MA 02181
TEL: (617) 237-5000
FAX: (617) 431-4114

John M. Kucharski, Chairman. Technical services and advanced scientific products. EG & G is a public company founded in 1947. It is a diversified company divided into six business segments: technical services, aerospace, instruments, components, defense and department of energy support. It has many divisions in the United States and abroad, and is involved in several joint ventures with foreign affiliates. Worldwide revenues for 1992: $2.8 billion.

- **Total Employees:** 30,000
- **U.S. Employees Abroad:** Not available.
- **Countries:** Australia, Belgium, Egypt, India, Italy, Japan, Kuwait, Netherlands, Taiwan, United Kingdom.
- **Application Information:** Hiring for most foreign positions is done at the specific country location.
- **Job Categories:** Accountants, Engineers, Finance, Marketing—Scientific, Product Development.

ELECTRONIC DATA SYSTEMS CORPORATION

5400 Legacy Dr.
Plano, TX 75024 USA

RECRUITER: AMY MADDEN
STAFFING/RECRUITMENT
5400 LEGACY DR.
PLANO, TX 75024
TEL: (214) 605-2700
FAX: (214) 605-2643

Les Alberthal, President. Information technology services. Electronic Data Systems Corporation was founded in 1962 and is a subsidiary of General Motors Corporation of

Detroit, Michigan. It provides services and applications in the field of information technology in the United States and 27 foreign countries. Worldwide revenues for 1992: $8.2 billion.

- **Total Employees:** 71,000

- **U.S. Employees Abroad:** Not available.

- **Countries:** France, Germany, Hong Kong, Italy, Japan, United Kingdom.

- **Job Categories:** Accountants, Communications, Finance, Marketing.

- **General Requirements:** College degree required. Qualifying majors include accounting, business, CIS, communications, computer science, finance, marketing, and MIS.

ELI LILLY AND COMPANY

Lilly Corporate Center
Indianapolis, IN 46285 USA

RECRUITER: RON ANGLEA
MANAGER, CORPORATE
RECRUITMENT
LILLY CORPORATE CENTER
INDIANAPOLIS, IN 46285
TEL: (317) 276-1050
FAX: (317) 276-1876

Vaughn D. Bryson, President and Chairman. *Pharmaceuticals, medical instruments, and diagnostics; animal health products.* Eli Lilly is a public company founded in 1876 by Colonel Eli Lilly, a pharmacist and Union officer from the Civil War. This company is well-known for its life-saving product, insulin, which was introduced in 1923. It is a leading supplier of numerous, significant antibiotics. Other primary items include the anti-depressant, Prozac, and Humulin insulin. Products are marketed in over 100 countries. Worldwide revenues for 1992: $6.2 billion.

- **Total Employees:** 30,000

- **U.S. Employees Abroad:** 100

- **Countries:** Worldwide including Argentina, France, Germany, Italy, Japan, Malaysia, Singapore, Switzerland, Thailand, United Kingdom, Venezuela.

- **Job Categories:** Finance, Marketing—Health & Medical Supplies, Marketing—Pharmaceuticals.

- **General Requirements:** Usually a current employee with Eli Lilly company experience.

- **Average Overseas Assignment:** 2-3 years.

- **Language Requirement:** Knowledge of local language a plus but not essential.

- **Training:** Basic orientation (1-30 days) and language training provided.

- **Benefits:** TRAVEL: Offered. HEALTH: Offered; same as U.S. coverage. HOUSING: Offered. EDUCATION: Offered.

ELIZABETH ARDEN COMPANY

1345 Avenue of the Americas
New York, NY 10105 USA

RECRUITER: CHARLENE MULLEN
HUMAN RESOURCES
1345 AVENUE OF THE AMERICAS
NEW YORK, NY 10105
TEL: (212) 261-1000
FAX: (212) 261-1303

Robert M. Phillips, President. Cosmetics. Elizabeth Arden was founded in 1910 and is now a subsidiary of Unilever United States, Inc. of New York City. It was purchased along with Faberge, Inc. in 1989 for $1.55 billion. Elizabeth Arden produces cosmetics, including fragrances and toiletries. Worldwide revenues for 1991: $2.2 billion.

- **Total Employees:** 7,000

- **U.S. Employees Abroad:** 35

- **Countries:** Australia, Canada, Denmark, Italy, Japan, Mexico, New Zealand, Singapore, United Kingdom.

- **Job Categories:** Accountants, Marketing—Consumer Goods, Product Development, Sales—Consumer Goods.

EMERSON ELECTRIC COMPANY

PO Box 4100
St. Louis, MO 63136 USA

RECRUITER: EARL WEAVER
VP, HUMAN RESOURCES
PO BOX 4100
ST. LOUIS, MO 63136
TEL: (314) 553-2000
FAX: (314) 553-1213

C. F. Knight, Chairman. Electrical and electronic products. Emerson Electric is a public company founded in 1890. It manufactures various electric and electronic products and markets them to residential and commercial customers, including industrial groups and the U.S. government. Products include HP motors, variable speed drills, and airborne radar systems. Worldwide revenues for 1992: $7.9 billion.

- **Total Employees:** 72,600

- **U.S. Employees Abroad:** 60

- **Countries:** Belgium, Japan, Saudi Arabia.

- **Job Categories:** Electrical Engineers, Finance, Management, Marketing—Electronics, Sales—Electronics.

- **Language Requirement:** None.

- **Training:** No special training provided.

EMERY WORLDWIDE

3350 West Bayshore
Palo Alto, CA 94303 USA

RECRUITER: THOMAS RINK
DIRECTOR, EMPLOYEE RELATIONS
3350 WEST BAYSHORE
PALO ALTO, CA 94303
TEL: (415) 855-9100
FAX: (415) 857-0745

Donald G. Berger, President. Air cargo transportation. Emery Worldwide is a subsidiary of Consolidated Freightways of Palo Alto, California. It is engaged in air cargo transportation on a global basis. Worldwide revenues for 1991: $1.3 billion.

- **Total Employees:** 17,900

- **U.S. Employees Abroad:** 25

- **Countries:** Germany, Hong Kong, Japan, Netherlands, Switzerland, United Kingdom.

- **Job Categories:** Management, Marketing, Technical Field Support.

- **Language Requirement:** Varies with each posting.

ENCORE COMPUTER CORPORATION

6901 West Sunrise Blvd.
Plantation, FL 33313 USA

RECRUITER: HOPE LYNCH
PERSONNEL REPRESENTATIVE
6901 WEST SUNRISE BLVD.
PLANTATION, FL 33313
TEL: (305) 797-5471
FREE: (800) 933-6267

Kenneth G. Fisher, President and Chairman. Computer systems. Encore Computer Corporation is a private company founded in 1983. It designs, manufactures, and sells real-time computer systems and parallel/multiprocessing systems for commercial, technical, and government clients. Worldwide revenues for 1991 $153.3 million.

- **Total Employees:** 1,254

- **U.S. Employees Abroad:** 25

- **Countries:** Argentina, Australia, Brazil, Finland, Germany, Hong Kong, Italy, Japan, Mexico, Spain, Sweden.

- **Job Categories:** Engineers, Management, Marketing—Electronics, Sales—Electronics.

- **Language Requirement:** Varies with each posting.

- **Training:** Varies with each posting.

ENCYCLOPEDIA BRITANNICA, INC.

310 South Michigan Ave.
Chicago, IL 60604 USA

RECRUITER: SUSAN MARYNOWSKI
DIRECTOR, INTERNATIONAL
    MARKETING
310 SOUTH MICHIGAN AVE.
CHICAGO, IL 60604
TEL: (312) 347-7000
FAX: (312) 347-7135

Peter Norton, President. Reference publishing, video, and other educational products. Encyclopedia Britannica is a private company founded in 1768. Worldwide revenues for 1991: $627 million.

- **Total Employees:** 2,000
- **U.S. Employees Abroad:** 15
- **Countries:** Australia, Belgium, Canada, France, Germany, Israel, Italy, Japan, Switzerland, United Kingdom.
- **Application Information:** Hiring for most foreign positions is done at the specific country location.
- **Job Categories:** Executive Management, Marketing—Publishing, Sales—Publishing.
- **Training:** No special training provided.

ENGELHARD CORPORATION

101 Wood Ave.
Iselin, NJ 08830 USA

RECRUITER: SANDY STERNER
HUMAN RESOURCES
101 WOOD AVE.
ISELIN, NJ 08830
TEL: (908) 205-5000
FAX: (908) 205-6767

Orin R. Smith, President. Petroleum, chemical and environmental catalysts, and pigments. Engelhard Corporation is a public company founded in 1981. It originally dates back to 1902 when Charle Engelhard, Sr. began the business in Newark, New Jersey. It went through a restructuring period in 1990 when the gold and silver operations were sold. Worldwide revenues for 1992: $2.4 billion.

- **Total Employees:** 8,100
- **U.S. Employees Abroad:** 25
- **Countries:** Canada, France, Italy, Netherlands, United Kingdom.
- **Job Categories:** Management, Marketing—Chemicals, Marketing—Petroleum/Natural Gas, Sales—Chemicals, Sales—Petroleum/Natural Gas.
- **Language Requirement:** None.

ENRON CORPORATION

1400 Smith St.
PO Box 1188
Houston, TX 77251 USA

RECRUITER: MARY ANN LONG
HUMAN RESOURCES
1400 SMITH ST.
PO BOX 1188
HOUSTON, TX 77251
TEL: (713) 853-6161
FAX: (713) 853-3129

Kenneth L. Lay, Chairman. Natural gas. Enron Corporation is a public company founded in 1930. Through its divisions, it has a 38,000-mile pipeline system, the largest in the nation. It also owns 84 percent of Enron Oil & Gas Company and is a global leader in the marketing of natural gas liquids. Worldwide revenues for 1992: $6.3 billion.

- **Total Employees:** 6,900

- **U.S. Employees Abroad:** Not available.

- **Countries:** Canada, United Kingdom.

- **Application Information:** Most foreign positions are filled internally.

- **Job Categories:** Executive Management, Finance, Marketing—Petroleum/Natural Gas.

- **Language Requirement:** None.

ENSERCH INTERNATIONAL DEVELOPMENT, INC.

Enserch Center
301 South Harwood
Dallas, TX 75201 USA

RECRUITER: CHRIS BELL
HUMAN RESOURCES
ENSERCH CENTER
301 SOUTH HARWOOD
DALLAS, TX 75201
TEL: (214) 651-8700
FAX: (214) 670-2520

William C. McCord, President and Chairman. Diversified energy services. Enserch Corporation is a public company founded in 1909. It operates oil and gas field properties and also markets and distributes natural gas. Worldwide revenues for 1992: $2.8 billion.

- **Total Employees:** 10,400

- **U.S. Employees Abroad:** 25

- **Countries:** Switzerland, United Kingdom.

- **Job Categories:** Field Technicians, Management, Marketing—Petroleum/Natural Gas, Sales—Petroleum/Natural Gas.

ERNST & YOUNG

787 7th Ave.
20th Floor
New York, NY 10019 USA

RECRUITER: DAVID NUGENT
INTERNATIONAL RECRUITMENT
787 7TH AVE., 20TH FLOOR
NEW YORK, NY 10019
TEL: (212) 773-3000
FAX: (212) 977-8163

Ray J. Groves & William L. Gladstone, CEOs. Accounting services. Ernst & Young is a private company formed by a merger of two accounting firms, Ernst & Whinney and Arthur Young in 1989. Today it ranks 2nd in U.S. accounting firm revenues, and 2nd in the world, after KPMG. Representative clients include: American Airlines, British Petroleum, and Mobil. Worldwide revenues for 1991: $5.4 billion. Foreign revenues for 1991: $3.2 billion.

- **Total Employees:** 25,000
- **U.S. Employees Abroad:** 65
- **Countries:** Australia, Belgium, Brazil, Canada, Chile, France, Germany, Hungary, Indonesia, Italy, Japan, Republic of Korea, Mexico, Netherlands, Russia, Singapore, Spain, Switzerland, United Kingdom, Venezuela.
- **Job Categories:** Accountants, Financial Advisors, Marketing.
- **Language Requirement:** Varies with each posting.
- **Training:** No special training provided.
- **Benefits:** All benefits are individually determined.

ESCO CORPORATION

PO Box 10123
Portland, OR 97210 USA

RECRUITER: CAROLYN WILSON
MANAGER, PERSONNEL DEPARTMENT
PO BOX 10123
PORTLAND, OR 97210
TEL: (503) 228-2141
FAX: (503) 778-6360

Nick P. Collins, President. Steel for heavy construction; mining; and forest products. Esco Corporation is a diversified private company founded in 1913. Worldwide revenues for 1991: $290 million.

- **Total Employees:** 2,000
- **U.S. Employees Abroad:** 50
- **Countries:** Brazil, Canada, France, Singapore.
- **Job Categories:** Management, Marketing, Sales.
- **Language Requirement:** Varies with each posting. Usually, knowledge of local language a plus but not essential.
- **Training:** No special training provided.
- **Benefits:** All benefits are individually determined.

ETHICON, INC.

Route #22
Somerville, NJ 08876 USA

RECRUITER: W. A. PENCE
DIRECTOR, HUMAN RESOURCES
ROUTE #22
SOMERVILLE, NJ 08876
TEL: (908) 218-3293
FAX: (908) 218-3503

F. G. Fitzpatrick, President. Surgical products. Ethicon, Inc. is a subsidiary of Johnson & Johnson of New Brunswick, New Jersey. It produces surgical products and related items. Worldwide revenues for 1991: $540 million.

- **Total Employees:** 4,000

- **U.S. Employees Abroad:** Not available.

- **Countries:** Germany.

- **Job Categories:** Management, Marketing—Health & Medical Supplies.

- **Language Requirement:** None.

- **Training:** Varies with each posting.

ETHYL CORPORATION

330 South 4th St.
Richmond, VA 23217 USA

RECRUITER: WILLIAM KOENIG
PERSONNEL MANAGER
330 SOUTH 4TH ST.
RICHMOND, VA 23217
TEL: (804) 788-5000
FAX: (804) 788-6405

Floyd D. Gottwald, Jr., Chairman. Chemicals and plastics. Ethyl Corporation is a public company founded in 1887. It manufactures and markets chemicals for the petroleum and plastics industries. It also produces chemical intermediates for detergents, electronics, agricultural chemicals, and pharmaceuticals. This company is well-known as the only U.S. producer of ibuprofen, an active ingredient found in pain relievers. Worldwide revenues for 1992: $3 billion.

- **Total Employees:** 5,500

- **U.S. Employees Abroad:** 40

- **Countries:** Belgium, Canada, Greece, France.

- **Job Categories:** Management, Marketing—Chemicals, Sales—Chemicals.

- **Language Requirement:** None.

- **Training:** No special training provided.

EXPEDITORS INTERNATIONAL OF WASHINGTON, INC.

19119 16th Ave. South
Seattle, WA 98118 USA

RECRUITER: KEVIN M. WALSH
PRESIDENT & CEO
19119 16TH AVE. SOUTH
SEATTLE, WA 98118
TEL: (206) 246-3711

Peter J. Rose, Chairman. Importers/exporters. Expeditors International of Washington, Inc. is a public company founded in 1979. It is a major full-service import and export business as well as as ocean and air forwarder. It is also a U.S. custom house broker. Worldwide operating revenues for 1992: $333.1 million.

- **Total Employees:** 1,250

- **U.S. Employees Abroad:** Not available.

- **Countries:** Worldwide including Germany, Japan, United Kingdom.

- **Application Information:** Hiring for most foreign positions is done at the specific country location.

- **Job Categories:** Management, Marketing.

- **Comments:** The number of Americans reported working abroad varies greatly from quarter to quarter, fluctuating with the number and scope of projects under contract at the time.

EXXON CHEMICAL COMPANY

580 Westlake Blvd.
Houston, TX 77079-2638 USA

RECRUITER: M. ASIF BEG
MANAGER, HUMAN RESOURCES
580 WESTLAKE BLVD.
HOUSTON, TX 77079-2638
TEL: (713) 584-7600
FAX: (713) 584-7926

H. Eugene McBrayer, President. Petrochemicals. Exxon Chemical was founded in 1963 and is a subsidiary of Exxon Corporation of Irving, Texas. It produces and markets synthetic resins, plastic materials, and industrial organic chemicals. Also, it manufactures agricultural chemicals, including pesticides.

- **Total Employees:** 18,000

- **U.S. Employees Abroad:** Not available.

- **Countries:** Argentina, Brazil, Germany, Guatemala, Pakistan, Saudi Arabia, Sweden.

- **Job Categories:** Chemists, Executive Management, Marketing—Agricultural, Marketing—Chemicals, Product Development, Sales—Agricultural, Sales—Chemicals.

- **General Requirements:** Usually must be a current employee of the company in order to qualify for overseas assignment.

EXXON COMPANY, INTERNATIONAL

200 Park Ave.
Florham Park, NJ 07932 USA

RECRUITER: V. S. EDMONDS
RECRUITMENT
200 PARK AVE.
FLORHAM PARK, NJ 07932
TEL: (201) 765-5409
FAX: (201) 765-4209

Renee Dahan, President. Oil and gas production, refining, and marketing. Exxon Company, International is a subsidiary of the Exxon Corporation of Irving, Texas. It is responsible for oil and gas operations outside of the United States and Canada.

- **Total Employees:** 35,000
- **U.S. Employees Abroad:** 400
- **Countries:** Worldwide including Argentina, Australia, Bahamas, Belgium, Brazil, Colombia, France, Indonesia, Italy, Jamaica, Japan, Malaysia, Norway, Singapore, Thailand, United Kingdom.
- **Job Categories:** Management, Marketing—Petroleum/Natural Gas, Technical Field Support, Sales—Petroleum/Natural Gas.
- **General Requirements:** Usually must be a current employee of the company in order to qualify for overseas assignment.
- **Language Requirement:** Varies with each posting.
- **Benefits:** All benefits are individually determined.

EXXON CORPORATION

225 East John Carpenter Freeway
Irving, TX 75062-2298 USA

RECRUITER: M. E. GILLIS
VP, HUMAN RESOURCES
225 EAST JOHN CARPENTER
FREEWAY
IRVING, TX 75062-2298
TEL: (214) 444-1000
FAX: (214) 444-1348

Lawrence G. Rawl, Chairman. Worldwide operation of oil and gas properties. Also chemicals and mining. Exxon Corporation is a public company founded in 1882 when John D. Rockefeller and his associates formed the Standard Oil Trust in New Jersey. In 1934 the Supreme Court divided the Trust into 34 separate companies, the largest one was Jersey Standard. Changes occurred through the years and the company name was changed to Exxon in 1972. Today, it is the world's 3rd-largest industrial company. It operates in the United States and 75 foreign countries. Worldwide revenues for 1992: $103 billion.

- **Total Employees:** 96,000
- **U.S. Employees Abroad:** 300
- **Countries:** Worldwide including Argentina, Austria, Bahamas, Costa Rica, Germany, Hong Kong, Japan, Mexico, Panama, Saudi Arabia, Venezuela, United Kingdom.

- **Job Categories:** Executive Management, Field Engineers, Finance, Management, Marketing—Chemicals, Marketing—Petroleum/Natural Gas, Sales—Chemicals, Sales—Petroleum/Natural Gas.
- **General Requirements:** Usually must be a current employee of the company in order to qualify for overseas assignment.
- **Language Requirement:** Knowledge of local language a plus but not essential.

FAIRCHILD PUBLICATIONS, INC.

7 West 34th St.
New York, NY 10001 USA

RECRUITER: SHARON THORN
DIRECTOR, HUMAN RESOURCES
7 WEST 34TH ST.
NEW YORK, NY 10001
TEL: (212) 630-4000
FAX: (212) 630-4295

John B. Fairchild, Chairman. Publishing. Fairchild Publications is a subsidiary of Capital Cities/ABC, Inc. It is a major fashion and merchandising publisher headquartered in New York with European offices in London, Milan, and Paris.

- **Total Employees:** 1,200
- **U.S. Employees Abroad:** 25
- **Countries:** France, Italy, United Kingdom.
- **Job Categories:** Executive Management, Finance, Marketing—Publishing.
- **Language Requirement:** None.
- **Training:** No special training provided.

FALK CORPORATION

PO Box 492
Milwaukee, WI 53201 USA

RECRUITER: CHARLES KENDALL
HUMAN RESOURCES
PO BOX 492
MILWAUKEE, WI 53201
TEL: (414) 342-3131
FAX: (414) 937-4359

John M. Blank, President. Gears, devices, and couplings. Falk Corporation was founded in 1892 and is a subsidiary of Sundstrand Corporation of Rockford, Illinois. It produces steel castings, speed changers, industrial high-speed drives and gears. It also manufactures mechanical power transmission equipment and related items for industrial machinery. Worldwide revenues for 1991: $120 million.

- **Total Employees:** 1,475
- **U.S. Employees Abroad:** Not available.
- **Countries:** Brazil, Canada, Japan, Mexico.
- **Job Categories:** Marketing—Industrial, Plant Managers, Sales—Industrial.
- **Language Requirement:** None.

- **Training:** No special training provided.

FEDERAL EXPRESS CORPORATION

PO Box 727
Memphis, TN 38132 USA

RECRUITER: ARNETTA GREEN
HUMAN RESOURCES
PO BOX 727
MEMPHIS, TN 38132
TEL: (901) 395-3460
FAX: (901) 795-1027

Frederick W. Smith, President and Chairman. Transportation and distribution of goods. Federal Express Corporation is a public company founded in 1973 by Fred Smith. His idea was to create a business that would provide a reliable, overnight delivery service for its customers. His concept has made this company the world's largest expedited delivery service, with operations in 125 countries. Worldwide revenues for 1993: $7.8 billion.

- **Total Employees:** 75,000
- **U.S. Employees Abroad:** 160
- **Countries:** Belgium, France, Germany, Hong Kong, Italy, Japan, Netherlands, Singapore, Switzerland, United Kingdom.
- **Job Categories:** Accountants, Executive Management, Marketing, Sales.
- **Language Requirement:** Knowledge of local language a plus but not essential.

FEDERAL-MOGUL CORPORATION

PO Box 1966
Detroit, MI 48235 USA

RECRUITER: LARRY KARENKO
EMPLOYEE RELATIONS MANAGER
PO BOX 1966
DETROIT, MI 48235
TEL: (313) 354-7700
FAX: (313) 354-9807

Dennis J. Gormley, President. Precision parts. Federal-Mogul Corporation is a public company founded in 1899. Its major products are vehicular and industrial components. This company has more than 20 domestic operations and 15 facilities in foreign countries. It has more than 70 distribution centers around the globe. Worldwide revenues for 1992: $1.2 billion.

- **Total Employees:** 14,300
- **U.S. Employees Abroad:** 50
- **Countries:** Argentina, Australia, Belgium, Chile, France, Germany, Italy, Mexico, Spain, Venezuela.
- **Application Information:** Hiring for most foreign positions is done at the specific country location.
- **Job Categories:** Executive Management, Management, Marketing—Industrial, Sales—Industrial.

- **General Requirements:** Usually must be a current employee of the company in order to qualify for overseas assignment.
- **Language Requirement:** Varies with each posting.
- **Training:** No special training provided.

FERRO CORPORATION

1000 Lakeside
Cleveland, OH 44114 USA

RECRUITER: ROBERT PRICE
VP, INTERNATIONAL
1000 LAKESIDE
CLEVELAND, OH 44114
TEL: (216) 641-8580
FAX: (216) 696-5784

Albert C. Bersticker, President. Specialty chemicals, coatings, colors, ceramics, and plastics. Ferro Corporation is a public company founded in 1919. It produces specialty chemicals for industrial use. Worldwide revenues for 1992: $1.1 billion.

- **Total Employees:** 8,000
- **U.S. Employees Abroad:** 12
- **Countries:** Brazil, France, Indonesia, Mexico, Netherlands, Taiwan, Thailand.
- **Job Categories:** Technical Field Support.
- **Average Overseas Assignment:** 3-5 years.
- **Language Requirement:** Knowledge of local language a plus but not essential.
- **Training:** Language training offered.
- **Benefits:** TRAVEL: Four weeks annually. HEALTH: Participates in host country's plan. HOUSING: Employee pays for first 15 percent of base salary. EDUCATION: Tuition offered for grades K-12.
- **Comments:** The number of Americans working abroad varies greatly from quarter to quarter, fluctuating with the number and scope of projects under contract at the time.

FIBRONICS INTERNATIONAL, INC.

Communications Way
Independence Park
Hyannis, MA 02601-1892 USA

RECRUITER: JULIE SILVERMAN
CORP. DIRECTOR, HUMAN
RESOURCES
COMMUNICATIONS WAY,
INDEPENDENCE PARK
HYANNIS, MA 02601-1892
TEL: (617) 826-0099
FAX: (617) 826-7745

John C. Hale, President. Fiberoptic and various information transfer and distribution systems. Fibronics International is a public company founded in 1977. It is involved in the full-scale production of products. Designs, manufactures, sells, and services fiberoptic and high bandwidth information transfer and distribution systems. These units connect communications and peripheral equipment. Worldwide revenues for 1992: $54 million.

- **Total Employees:** 470
- **U.S. Employees Abroad:** 20
- **Countries:** Israel, Germany, United Kingdom.
- **Job Categories:** Engineers, Finance, Office Management, Sales—Scientific.
- **Language Requirement:** None.
- **Training:** No special training provided.

FIGGIE INTERNATIONAL, INC.

4420 Sherwin Rd.
Willoughby, OH 44094 USA

RECRUITER: WILLIAM SICKMAN
MANAGER, MANPOWER/
EMPLOYMENT
4420 SHERWIN RD.
WILLOUGHBY, OH 44094
TEL: (216) 946-9000
FAX: (216) 951-1724

Harry E. Figgie, Jr., Chairman. Security, fire protection, consumer products, and services. Figgie International is a public company founded in 1910. It is divided into seven major sectors: Technical; Fire Protection and Safety; Machinery and Allied Products; Consumers' Service; Automation; and Safety Supply America. Products and services range from fire extinguishers and sprinkler systems to sports equipment and insurance. Worldwide revenues for 1992: $1.2 billion.

- **Total Employees:** 17,000
- **U.S. Employees Abroad:** 75
- **Countries:** Australia, Bermuda, Brazil, Canada, Costa Rica, France, Italy, Japan, Mexico, Netherlands, United Kingdom.
- **Job Categories:** Accountants, Brokers—Securities & Financial, Finance, Marketing, Sales.

FIRST CHICAGO CORPORATION

1 First National Plaza
Chicago, IL 60670 USA

RECRUITER: SUSAN SCHLOMAS
INTERNATIONAL COMPENSATION &
BENEFITS
1 FIRST NATIONAL PLAZA
CHICAGO, IL 60670
TEL: (312) 732-4000
FAX: (312) 732-7288

Richard Thomas, President. Banking services. First Chicago Corporation is a public company founded in 1863. Acquisitions through the years proved to be successful and in 1969 reorganization occurred. It created First Chicago as the bank's holding corporation. Today, it is divided into two banking groups: The Global Corporate Bank, which provides commercial and investment services; and the Superregional Bank, which offers services to individuals. Worldwide assets for 1992: $49 billion.

- **Total Employees:** 17,500
- **U.S. Employees Abroad:** 60
- **Countries:** Australia, Canada, Hong Kong, Japan, Republic of Korea, Mexico, Philippines, Singapore, Spain, Switzerland, United Kingdom.
- **Job Categories:** Accountants, Executive Management.
- **General Requirements:** Business degree preferred.
- **Language Requirement:** Varies with each posting.
- **Training:** No special training provided.

FISCHER & PORTER COMPANY

125 East County Line Rd.
Warminster, PA 18974 USA

RECRUITER: LARRY WYATT
MANAGER OF PERSONNEL
ADMINISTRATION
125 EAST COUNTY LINE RD.
WARMINSTER, PA 18974
TEL: (215) 674-6000
FAX: (215) 441-5280

Jay H. Tolson, President and Chairman. Measurement control technologies. Fischer & Porter is a public company founded in 1937. The business produces measurement and control devices used in the processing of gases and liquids. Major products include flowmeters, transmitters, and analytical instruments. It conducts business in the United States and 49 foreign countries. Worldwide revenues for 1992: $231.3 million.

- **Total Employees:** 2,207
- **U.S. Employees Abroad:** 25
- **Countries:** Belgium, Canada, Netherlands, France, Italy, Mexico, Spain, Sweden, United Kingdom.
- **Job Categories:** Accountants, Management, Marketing—Scientific, Sales—Scientific.

FISHER CONTROLS INTERNATIONAL, INC.

8000 Maryland Ave., Suite 500
Saint Louis, MO 63105-3718
USA

RECRUITER: EDWARD FLOWERS
DIRECTOR, HUMAN RESOURCES
8000 MARYLAND AVE., SUITE 500
SAINT LOUIS, MO 63105-3718
TEL: (314) 746-9923
FAX: (314) 746-9974

Larry W. Solley, Chairman. Industrial process control equipment. Fisher Controls International was founded in 1880 and is a subsidiary of Emerson Electric of St. Louis,

Missouri. It produces hydraulic and pneumatic valves, hoses, and tube fittings and hose assemblies for fluid power systems. Worldwide revenues for 1992: $905 million.

- **Total Employees:** 6,200
- **U.S. Employees Abroad:** 75
- **Countries:** Australia, Austria, Belgium, Canada, Germany, Mexico, Netherlands, Spain, Sweden, United Kingdom.
- **Job Categories:** Accountants, Finance, Plant Managers, Marketing—Industrial, Sales—Industrial.
- **Training:** No special training provided.

FLEMING COMPANIES, INC.

6301 Waterford Blvd.
Oklahoma City, OK 73126 USA

RECRUITER: JUDY STRANCZEK
MANAGER, HUMAN RESOURCES
6301 WATERFORD BLVD.
OKLAHOMA CITY, OK 73126
TEL: (405) 840-7200
FAX: (405) 841-8149

E. Dean Werries, Chairman. Wholesale food distribution. Fleming Companies, Inc. is a public company founded in 1915 by O. A. Fleming, Gene Wilson, and Sam Lux. The present name was adopted in 1972. Today Fleming is the largest wholesale food distributor in the United States, servicing nearly one out of 10 supermarkets. Its distribution centers handle 4,800 stores throughout the United States and abroad. Worldwide revenues for 1992: $12.9 billion.

- **Total Employees:** 22,800
- **U.S. Employees Abroad:** 25
- **Countries:** Japan, Mexico, Brazil.
- **Job Categories:** Management, Marketing—Food/Food Services, Sales—Food/Food Services.
- **Language Requirement:** Varies with each posting.

FLORSHEIM SHOE COMPANY

130 South Canal St.
Chicago, IL 60606 USA

RECRUITER: JOHN DIEBOLD
DIRECTOR, HUMAN RESOURCES
130 SOUTH CANAL ST.
CHICAGO, IL 60606
TEL: (313) 559-2500
FAX: (312) 559-7408

R. J. Mueller, President. Men's quality footwear. Florsheim was founded in 1892 and joined Interco in 1952. It remains a subsidiary of Interco, whose headquarters are in St. Louis, Missouri. It produces and sells men's footwear throughout the United States and internationally through 5,000 independent dealer locations and 360 company-owned retail stores. Worldwide revenues for 1992: $1.2 billion.

- **Total Employees:** 2,950
- **U.S. Employees Abroad:** 25
- **Countries:** Worldwide including Canada, Australia.
- **Job Categories:** Marketing—Consumer Goods, Product Development, Sales—Consumer Goods.
- **Language Requirement:** None.

FLOW INTERNATIONAL CORPORATION

21440 68th Ave. South
Kent, WA 98032 USA

RECRUITER: ERIC BROWNING-LARSON
DIRECTOR, HUMAN RESOURCES
21440 68TH AVE. SOUTH
KENT, WA 98032
TEL: (206) 938-3569

Y. H. Pao, President. Ultra-high pressure waterjet cutting systems for automated factory cutting of miscellaneous nonmetallic and metallic materials. Flow International is a public company founded in 1974. It is engaged in all phases of production for ultra-high pressure water systems. Markets include aerospace, automotive, disposable product, food processing, glass, metal cutting, and paper industries. It operates in the United States and in 45 foreign countries. Worldwide revenues for 1992: $48 million.

- **Total Employees:** 344
- **U.S. Employees Abroad:** 35
- **Countries:** Worldwide including Germany, Japan, Taiwan.
- **Job Categories:** Accountants, Engineers, Manufacturing, Marketing—Industrial, Researchers, Customer Services, Sales—Industrial.
- **Language Requirement:** Varies with each posting.
- **Training:** No special training provided.

JOHN FLUKE MANUFACTURING COMPANY

PO Box 9090
Everett, WA 98206-9090 USA

RECRUITER: CAROL KOWALSKI
EMPLOYMENT MANAGER
PO BOX 9090
EVERETT, WA 98206-9090
TEL: (206) 347-6100
FAX: (206) 356-5998

George M. Winn, President. Electrical test and measurement instruments. John Fluke Manufacturing is a public company founded in 1948. It is a supplier of electronic instrumentation devices and services that improve productivity for technical clients in the research, service, design management, and calibration fields. Products are marketed and sold internationally. Worldwide revenues for 1991: $239.7 million.

- **Total Employees:** 2,400
- **U.S. Employees Abroad:** 35
- **Countries:** Canada, Japan.
- **Job Categories:** Plant Managers, Marketing—Electronics, Sales—Electronics.
- **Language Requirement:** Varies with each posting.
- **Training:** No special training provided.

FLUOR CORPORATION

3333 Michelson Dr.
Irvine, CA 92730 USA

RECRUITER: MARK LANDRY
MANAGER, INTERNATIONAL
  ADMINISTRATION
3333 MICHELSON DR.
IRVINE, CA 92730
TEL: (714) 975-2000
FAX: (714) 975-5271

Leslie G. McGraw, Chairman. Construction, engineering, and maintenance services. Fluor Corporation is a public company founded in 1912. Fluor Daniel is the company's main operating unit. It offers services in five business areas: industrial, process, power, hydrocarbon, and government. It operates in the United States and in 16 foreign countries. Worldwide revenues for 1992: $6.6 billion.

- **Total Employees:** 20,000
- **U.S. Employees Abroad:** 45
- **Countries:** Australia, Canada, Germany, Netherlands, Saudi Arabia, United Kingdom.
- **Job Categories:** Engineers, Finance, Management, Marketing, Sales.
- **General Requirements:** Usually must be a current employee of the company in order to qualify for overseas assignment.
- **Language Requirement:** Varies with each posting.

FMC CORPORATION

200 East Randolph St.
Chicago, IL 60601 USA

RECRUITER: NANCY GRIFFIN
HUMAN RESOURCES
200 EAST RANDOLPH ST.
CHICAGO, IL 60601
TEL: (312) 861-6000
FAX: (312) 861-5902

Robert H. Malott, Chairman. Manufacturing and mining for agriculture, government, and industry. FMC Corporation is a public company founded in 1928. It is divided into five operating units and numerous other groups and divisions. Major products include natural soda ash, sulfuric acid, and food additives. Services are offered to clients in automatic service equipment, food preparation, and processing eqiuipment fields. FMC has 89 facilities in the United States and operates in 14 foreign countries. Worldwide revenues for 1992: $4 billion.

- **Total Employees:** 24,000

- **U.S. Employees Abroad:** 75

- **Countries:** Argentina, Austria, Bangladesh, Canada, Colombia, Costa Rica, France, Germany, Greece, Netherlands, Saudi Arabia, Saudi Arabia, United Arab Emirates, United Kingdom.

- **Job Categories:** Accountants, Engineers, Finance, Marketing, Plant Managers, Sales.

- **Language Requirement:** Varies with each posting.

- **Training:** No special training provided.

FORD MOTOR COMPANY

The American Rd.
Dearborn, MI 48121 USA

RECRUITER: J. CRAIG HAUSMAN
EMPLOYEE RELATIONS
CENTRAL PLACEMENT, WORLD
    HEADQUARTERS, 12TH FLOOR
DEARBORN, MI 48121
TEL: (313) 322-3000
FAX: (313) 322-7896

Harold A. Poling, Chairman. Manufactures automobiles and trucks. Also, financial services. Ford is a public company founded in 1903 by Henry Ford in Dearborn, Michigan. He produced the Model T in 1908 and in 1919, Ford purchased all outstanding shares for $100 million. It wasn't until 1956 that outside ownership occurred. Today the family still owns 40 percent of the voting stock. This company ranks second in the United States and world auto sales and manufactures models under nameplates including Ford, Lincoln, Mercury, and Jaguar. It provides service to customers in over 200 countries and territories. Worldwide revenues for 1992: $100 billion.

- **Total Employees:** 367,000

- **U.S. Employees Abroad:** 125

- **Countries:** Twenty-five countries including Argentina, Australia, Brazil, Canada, Japan, Italy, Netherlands, Spain, Taiwan, United Kingdom, Venezuela.

- **Job Categories:** Accountants, Executive Management, Finance, Marketing—Automotive, Marketing—Financial Services, Sales—Automotive, Sales—Financial Services.

- **General Requirements:** Usually must be a current employee of the company in order to qualify for overseas assignment.

- **Language Requirement:** Varies with each posting.

FOSTER WHEELER CORPORATION

Perryville Corporate Park
Clinton, NJ 08809-4000 USA

RECRUITER: J. SCHESSLER
STAFFING/RECRUITMENT
PERRYVILLE CORPORATE PARK
CLINTON, NJ 08809-4000
TEL: (908) 730-5294
FAX: (908) 730-5300

Louis E. Azzato, President and Chairman. Design, engineering, environmental, construction, management, manufacturing, and real estate services. Foster Wheeler is a public company founded in 1990. This international firm provides a broad range of services to clients in the United States and abroad. Worldwide operating revenues for 1992: $2.5 billion.

- **Total Employees:** 2,000
- **U.S. Employees Abroad:** 400
- **Countries:** Kuwait, Saudi Arabia, Venezuela.
- **Salaries:** $4000-$8000 per month.
- **Job Categories:** Construction Workers, Engineers, Management.
- **General Requirements:** Experience in refinery engineering and construction.
- **Average Overseas Assignment:** Less than two years.
- **Language Requirement:** None.
- **Training:** Basic orientation (1-30 days) provided.
- **Benefits:** Vary with each posting.

FREEPORT-MCMORAN, INC.

1615 Poydras St.
New Orleans, LA 70151 USA

RECRUITER: JOHN BROUILETTE
MANAGER, EXPATRIATE
EMPLOYMENT
PO BOX 51777
NEW ORLEANS, LA 70151
TEL: (504) 582-4000
FAX: (504) 582-1639

James R. Moffett, Chairman. Mining. Freeport-McMoran is a public company founded in 1981. It is engaged in the exploration of mines, and the development, production, processing, and marketing of natural resources. Major products include phosphate rock, sulphur, oil, natural gas, and copper. Worldwide revenues for 1992: $1.7 billion.

- **Total Employees:** 7,300
- **U.S. Employees Abroad:** 50
- **Countries:** Australia, Indonesia, Tunisia.
- **Job Categories:** Accountants, Engineers, Management, Marketing, Marketing—Petroleum/Natural Gas.

COMPANY LISTINGS

FRITZ COMPANIES

735 Market St.
San Francisco, CA 94103 USA

RECRUITER: ROBERT DAVIDSON
DIRECTOR, HUMAN RESOURCES
735 MARKET ST.
SAN FRANCISCO, CA 94103
TEL: (415) 904-8227
FAX: (415) 904-8326

Lynn C. Fritz, President. Customs broker service. Fritz Companies is a private business founded in 1933. It offers total product documentation and transportation services to importers and exporters. Operations are in the United States and abroad. Worldwide revenues for 1991: $2.1 billion.

- **Total Employees:** 1,800
- **U.S. Employees Abroad:** 23
- **Countries:** Argentina, Bolivia, Brazil, Germany, Panama, United Kingdom, Venezuela.
- **Job Categories:** Management, Marketing—Financial Services, Sales—Financial Services.
- **General Requirements:** Usually must be a current employee of the company in order to qualify for overseas assignment.

FUGRO-MCCLELLAND USA, INC.

PO Box 740010
Houston, TX 77274 USA

RECRUITER: ALBERTA ROGERS
PERSONNEL DIRECTOR
PO BOX 740010
HOUSTON, TX 77274
TEL: (713) 772-3700

John Focht, Jr., Chairman. Soil engineering. Fugro-McClelland USA, Inc. was founded in 1987. It is engaged in all phases of soil engineering in the United States and abroad. Worldwide revenues for 1991: $50 million.

- **Total Employees:** 385
- **U.S. Employees Abroad:** 25
- **Countries:** Singapore, United Arab Emirates.
- **Job Categories:** Engineers, Management, Marketing.
- **Language Requirement:** None.

FULLER COMPANY

2040 Ave. C
Bethlehem, PA 18017-2188 USA

RECRUITER: JOSEPH MANGAN
MANAGER, EMPLOYEE DEVELOPMENT
2040 AVE. C
BETHLEHEM, PA 18017-2188
TEL: (215) 264-6011
FAX: (215) 264-6170

Elmer D. Gates, President. Industrial processing equipment. Fuller is a private company founded in 1924. It engineers and manufactures cement and mineral processing equipment. Worldwide revenues for 1991: $260 million.

- **Total Employees:** 1,300

- **U.S. Employees Abroad:** 5

- **Countries:** Australia, Canada, France, Germany, India, Mexico, Spain, United Kingdom.

- **Job Categories:** Engineers, Management, Service Engineers.

- **General Requirements:** Ability to travel, communications skills, cultural knowledge, and language skills.

- **Average Overseas Assignment:** Less than two years.

- **Training:** Training in specific work skills provided.

- **Benefits:** TRAVEL: Varies with each posting. HEALTH: Same coverage as U.S. employees. HOUSING: Offered, extended stays in foreign posting may lead to salary adjustments. EDUCATION: None offered.

- **Comments:** Only Project Site Managers are required to relocate to a foreign country. This may be for days, weeks, or months.

GAF CORPORATION

1361 Alps Rd.
Wayne, NJ 07470 USA

RECRUITER: GARY SCHNEID
HUMAN RESOURCES
1361 ALPS RD.
WAYNE, NJ 07470
TEL: (201) 628-3000

Samuel J. Heyman, Chairman. Building materials and chemicals. GAF Corporation is a private company founded in 1929. It produces chemicals for hair-styling and skin-care products and dentures. Major products in the building materials sector include GAF asphalt roofing shingles and Weather Coat roofing emulsion. Worldwide revenues for 1992: $1 billion.

- **Total Employees:** 4,500

- **U.S. Employees Abroad:** Not available.

- **Countries:** Australia, Canada, France, Germany, Italy, Japan, Mexico, Netherlands, Singapore, Saudi Arabia, United Kingdom.

- **Application Information:** Usually overseas applications are forwarded to Neal Ralley, Human Resources International in England.

- **Job Categories:** Chemists, Management, Marketing—Chemicals, Marketing, Product Development, Sales, Sales—Chemicals.

- **Training:** Varies with each posting.

GAFNEY, CLINE & ASSOCIATES, INC.

16775 Addison Rd., Suite 400
Dallas, TX 75248 USA

RECRUITER: GAYLE BRANDT
STAFFING/RECRUITMENT
PO BOX 796309
DALLAS, TX 75379
TEL: (214) 733-1183
FAX: (214) 380-0180

W. B. Cline, President. Energy advisors. Gafney, Cline & Associates was founded in 1962 and is a subsidiary of GCA International Limited. It is a consultant to the energy and mineral industries. Worldwide revenues for 1991: $3.1 million.

- **Total Employees:** 125

- **U.S. Employees Abroad:** 20

- **Countries:** Australia, Singapore, United Kingdom.

- **Job Categories:** Engineers, Marketing, Technical Field Support.

- **General Requirements:** Usually must be a current employee of the company in order to qualify for overseas assignment.

- **Language Requirement:** None.

GALEN HEALTH CARE

201 West Main St.
PO Box 1438
Louisville, KY 40201-1438 USA

RECRUITER: RUSSELL COX
STAFFING/RECRUITMENT
201 WEST MAIN ST.
PO BOX 1438
LOUISVILLE, KY 40201-1438
TEL: (502) 572-2000
FAX: (502) 572-2163

Carl F. Pollard, Chairman. Health-care services. Galen Health Care is a public company founded in February 1993. It was formed due to a company split of Humana, Inc. of Louisville, Kentucky. It operates health-care systems and acute-care hospitals in the United States and abroad.

- **Total Employees:** 51,700

- **U.S. Employees Abroad:** 25

- **Countries:** Switzerland, United Kingdom.

- **Job Categories:** Health Professionals.

- **Language Requirement:** None.

GANNETT COMPANY, INC.

1100 Wilson Blvd.
Arlington, VA 22209 USA

RECRUITER: THOMAS BATES
PERSONNEL DIVISION,
INTERNATIONAL
535 MADISON AVE., 27TH FLOOR
NEW YORK, NY 10022
TEL: (212) 715-5427
FAX: (212) 207-8982

John J. Corley, President and Chairman. News and information services. Gannett was founded in 1906 as a private company. It was incorporated in 1923 and became public in 1967. This diversified business publishes newspapers, operates broadcasting stations and outdoor advertising concerns. A well-known venture of Gannett is *USA Today*, a national daily newspaper. Worldwide revenues for 1992: $3.5 billion.

- **Total Employees:** 36,000
- **U.S. Employees Abroad:** 40
- **Countries:** Canada, Guam, France, Hong Kong, Singapore, Switzerland, United Kingdom.
- **Job Categories:** Accountants, Clerical Assistants, Mail Clerks, Researchers.
- **Language Requirement:** Varies with each posting.
- **Training:** Varies with each posting.

GANNETT FLEMING, INC.

PO Box 67100
Harrisburg, PA 17105-7100 USA

RECRUITER: JOHN G. PETERSON
DIRECTOR, INTERNATIONAL
PROJECTS
PO BOX 67100
HARRISBURG, PA 17106-7100
TEL: (717) 763-7211
FAX: (717) 763-8150

Maurice A. Wadsworth, President. Contract services in the transport sector area; also civil engineering. Gannett Fleming is a private company founded in 1915. It offers engineering services involved with engineering studies, construction supervision, and management. These include water and sewer mains and power lines as well as transportation areas. Worldwide operating revenues for 1991: $86 million.

- **Total Employees:** 1,241
- **U.S. Employees Abroad:** Not available.
- **Countries:** Republic of South Africa.
- **Salaries:** $3,500-$5,000 per month depending on financing institution/qualifications.
- **Job Categories:** Construction Workers, Maintenance Engineers, Economists, Technical Field Support.
- **General Requirements:** At least five years of experience in specific field.

- **Average Overseas Assignment:** 2-3 years or under six months; varies with each posting.
- **Language Requirement:** Fluency in local language required.
- **Training:** No special training provided.
- **Benefits:** TRAVEL: Usually project specific. HEALTH: Additional: medical evacuation coverage. HOUSING: Usually project specific. EDUCATION: Strictly on USAID-FCED project.
- **Comments:** Gannett Fleming, Inc. hires specialized consultants with international experience.

THE GATES RUBBER COMPANY	**RECRUITER:** A. L. STECKLEIN
PO Box 5887	EMPLOYMENT SERVICES
Denver, CO 80217 USA	PO BOX 5887
	DENVER, CO 80217
	TEL: (303) 744-1911
	FAX: (303) 744-4000

Donald E. Miller, President. Rubber products for automobile industry and other industries. Gates Rubber Company was founded in 1911 and is a subsidiary of the Gates Corporation of Denver, Colorado. It produces and sells rubber products including belts, hoses, and molded products for agriculture, construction, and transportation industries. It has operations in the United States and 20 plants in foreign countries. Worldwide revenues for 1991: $1 billion.

- **Total Employees:** 13,000
- **U.S. Employees Abroad:** 35
- **Countries:** Australia, Belgium, Brazil, Canada, Germany, Japan, Mexico, Spain, United Kingdom.
- **Job Categories:** Management, Manufacturing, Marketing, Sales.
- **Language Requirement:** Varies with each posting.
- **Training:** No special training provided.

GATX CORPORATION	**RECRUITER:** LARRY ROSS
120 South Riverside Dr.	HUMAN RESOURCES
Chicago, IL 60606 USA	120 SOUTH RIVERSIDE DR.
	CHICAGO, IL 60606
	TEL: (312) 621-6200
	FAX: (312) 977-3295

James J. Glasser, President and Chairman. Railcar leasing, bulk liquid storage, financial services, and other related services. GATX Corporation is a public company founded in 1916. It operates through its divisions and five major business segments on a worldwide basis. Major General Management Transportation Corporation, GATX Capital Corporation, GATX Terminals Corporation, American Steamship Company, and Associated Unit Companies, Incorporated. Worldwide operating revenues for 1992: $1 billion.

- **Total Employees:** 5,000

- **U.S. Employees Abroad:** 25

- **Countries:** Australia, Belgium, Canada, Japan, Malaysia, Mexico, Spain, United Kingdom.

- **Job Categories:** Accountants, Finance, Management, Marketing.

- **Language Requirement:** Varies with each posting.

- **Training:** No special training provided.

GENERAL DYNAMICS CORPORATION

3190 Fairview Park Dr.
Falls Church, VA 22042-4523
USA

RECRUITER: ROBERT KELLER
CORPORATE PERSONNEL
PO BOX 760
TROY, MI 48099-0760
TEL: (313) 244-7000
FAX: (313) 244-7001

William A. Anders, Chairman. Major U.S. defense contractor. General Dynamics Corporation is a public company founded in 1952. It originally began in 1899 as the Electric Boat Company in New Jersey by John Holland. The business diversified in 1947 with the purchase of Canadian aircraft builder, Canadair. In 1952, from the merger of Electric Boat and Canadair, General Dynamics was formed. Today, this company is the 2nd-largest defense contractor in the United States, providing major weapons and systems for all sectors of the armed forces. Worldwide revenues for 1992: $3.5 billion

- **Total Employees:** 32,000

- **U.S. Employees Abroad:** 500

- **Countries:** Egypt, Germany, Japan, Turkey.

- **Application Information:** Do not call.

- **Job Categories:** Executive Management, Engineers, Marketing, Sales—Defense Industry.

- **General Requirements:** Usually must be a current employee of the company in order to qualify for overseas assignment

- **Language Requirement:** Varies with each posting.

- **Comments:** At the time of publication, a hiring freeze was in effect.

GENERAL DYNAMICS SERVICES COMPANY

3190 Fairview Park Dr.
Falls Church, VA 22042 USA

RECRUITER: ROBERT KELLER
CORPORATE PERSONNEL
PO BOX 760
TROY, MI 48099-0760
TEL: (313) 244-7000
FAX: (313) 244-7001

A. W. Carion, Vice President. Service, training, and logistics support of land system vehicles (military tanks). General Dynamics Services Company is a division of General Dynamics Corporation of Falls Church, Virginia. General Dynamics Corporation is a major defense contractor in the United States. General Dynamics Corporation worldwide revenues for 1991: $8.8 billion.

- **Total Employees:** 400
- **U.S. Employees Abroad:** 100
- **Countries:** Egypt, Saudi Arabia, Taiwan.
- **Application Information:** Do not call.
- **Job Categories:** Engineers, Management, Marketing.

GENERAL ELECTRIC COMPANY (GE)

3135 Easton Turnpike
Fairfield, CT 06431 USA

RECRUITER: THOMAS DEXTER
INTERNATIONAL RECRUITMENT
3135 EASTON TURNPIKE
FAIRFIELD, CT 06431
TEL: (203) 373-2211
FAX: (203) 373-3131

John F. Welch, Jr., Chairman. Diversified manufacturer in technical and service areas; electrical products and financial services; broadcasting (NBC). General Electric is a public company founded in 1892 as a result of a merger between Thomson-Houston Company and Edison General Electric. Thomas Edison was one of its first directors, leaving the firm in 1894. GE's early success was due to its concentration in the research field. Today, its sales have made GE the 6th largest U.S. company and 10th largest worldwide. A major acquisition in 1986 was the purchase of RCA, which included the National Broadcasting Company (NBC) for 6.4 billion. Worldwide revenues for 1992: $57 billion.

- **Total Employees:** 298,000
- **U.S. Employees Abroad:** 2,000
- **Countries:** Worldwide including Brazil, Canada, Egypt, France, Germany, Hong Kong, Hungary, Italy, Mexico, Netherlands, Philippines, Saudi Arabia, United Kingdom.
- **Job Categories:** Accountants, Clerical Assistants, Executive Management, Marketing—Electronics, Marketing—Financial Services, Marketing, Sales—Electronics, Sales—Financial Services, Sales.
- **Language Requirement:** Varies with each posting.

- **Training:** No special training provided.

GENERAL FOODS USA

250 North St.
White Plains, NY 10625 USA

RECRUITER: JOSEPH TAGLIA
DIRECTOR, HUMAN RESOURCES
250 NORTH ST.
WHITE PLAINS, NY 10625
TEL: (914) 335-2500
FAX: (914) 335-9965

Miles S. Marsh, President. Food processing and distribution. General Foods USA is a subsidiary of Philip Morris Companies, Inc. of New York City. Food production and distribution includes such items as breakfast foods, cheeses, coffee, and specialty items. Worldwide revenues for 1991: $5.1 billion.

- **Total Employees:** 30,000

- **U.S. Employees Abroad:** 40

- **Countries:** Canada, Colombia, France, Hong Kong, Italy, Mexico, Philippines, Spain, Sweden, United Kingdom.

- **Job Categories:** Finance, Management, Marketing—Food/Food Services, Sales—Food/Food Services.

- **Language Requirement:** None.

- **Training:** No special training provided.

GENERAL INSTRUMENT CORPORATION

181 West Madison Ave.
49th Floor
Chicago, IL 60602 USA

RECRUITER: LEE KEENAN
DIRECTOR, HUMAN RESOURCES
181 WEST MADISON AVE., 49TH
   FLOOR
CHICAGO, IL 60602
TEL: (312) 541-5000
FAX: (313) 541-5049

F. G. Hickey, Chairman. Electronic components and related systems. General Instrument Corporation is a public company founded in 1923. It manufactures cable television equipment, with facilities in the United States and abroad. Worldwide revenues for 1992: $1.1 billion.

- **Total Employees:** 14,000

- **U.S. Employees Abroad:** 40

- **Countries:** Belgium, Canada, France, Malaysia, Mexico, Portugal, Taiwan, United Kingdom.

- **Job Categories:** Accountants, Marketing—Electronics, Sales—Electronics.

- **Language Requirement:** Varies with each posting.

GENERAL MILLS, INC.

1 General Mills Blvd.
PO Box 1113
Minneapolis, MN 55440 USA

RECRUITER: WILLIAM A. DITTMORE
DIRECTOR OF RECRUITMENT
1 GENERAL MILLS BLVD.
PO BOX 1113
MINNEAPOLIS, MN 55440
TEL: (612) 540-7504
FAX: (612) 540-2445

H. Brewster Atwater, Jr., Chairman. Consumer foods and restaurants. General Mills, Inc. is a public company founded in 1866 by Cadwallader Washburn. Gold Medal Flour was introduced in the 1880s. Today, General Mills is the 2nd largest breakfast cereal producer, with 12 brand names. Other brand name items include Hamburger Helper (a ready-to-make meal) and Pop Secret (microwave popcorn). It has more than 880 locations throughout the United States and abroad. It is also the operator of Red Lobster restaurant chains. Worldwide revenues for 1992: $8.1 billion.

- **Total Employees:** 108,000

- **U.S. Employees Abroad:** 110

- **Countries:** Canada, France, Japan, Netherlands.

- **Job Categories:** Executive Management, Marketing—Food/Food Services, Sales—Food/Food Services.

- **General Requirements:** Usually must be a current employee of the company in order to qualify for overseas assignment.

- **Language Requirement:** None.

GENERAL MOTORS CORPORATION (GM)

3044 West Grand Blvd.
Detroit, MI 48202 USA

RECRUITER: RICHARD J. RACHNER
DIRECTOR, INTERNATIONAL
PERSONNEL
3044 WEST GRAND BLVD.
DETROIT, MI 48202
TEL: (313) 556-7637
FAX: (313) 556-5108

Jack Smith, Chairman. Automobiles, trucks, related parts, and accessories; also financial services. General Motors Corporation is a public company founded in 1908 by William Durant. He began the General Motors Company in Flint, Michigan. The GM Acceptance Corporation for auto financing was created in 1978. Today, GM is the world's largest automobile manufacturer. Some well-known autos include Buick, Cadillac, and Geo. The newest nameplate is Saturn, which was introduced in 1990. GM has plants in the United States and in 36 foreign countries. Worldwide revenues for 1992: $132.4 billion.

- **Total Employees:** 700,000

- **U.S. Employees Abroad:** 150

- **Countries:** Worldwide including Australia, Belgium, Canada, Chile, Denmark, Germany, Italy, Japan, Kenya, Philippines, Singapore, Yugoslavia, United Kingdom.

- **Job Categories:** Executive Management, Design Engineers, Marketing—Automotive, Marketing—Financial Services, Product Development, Sales—Automotive, Sales—Financial Services.

- **General Requirements:** Usually must be a current employee of the company in order to qualify for overseas assignment.

GENERAL RAILWAY SIGNAL COMPANY

PO Box 20600
Rochester, NY 14602-0600 USA

RECRUITER: PAT HOPKINS
INTERNATIONAL HUMAN RESOURCES
PO BOX 20600
ROCHESTER, NY 14602-0600
TEL: (716) 783-2000
FAX: (716) 783-2000

Stuart Brown, President. Transportation control products and systems. General Railway Signal is a subsidiary of SASIB, a business group located in Italy. It designs and produces railway, rapid transit, and vehicle control systems in the United States and abroad. Worldwide revenues for 1991: $72 million.

- **Total Employees:** 700
- **U.S. Employees Abroad:** 18
- **Countries:** People's Republic of China.
- **Job Categories:** Electrical Engineers, Finance, Management, Project Managers.
- **General Requirements:** No entry-level positions available. Prefer experience in technical fields, and/or electrical engineering degree.
- **Average Overseas Assignment:** 2-3 years.
- **Language Requirement:** Competency in local language required.
- **Training:** No special training provided.

GENERAL SIGNAL CORPORATION

PO Box 10010
Stamford, CT 06904 USA

RECRUITER: LARRY RIST
DIRECTOR, RECRUITMENT
PO BOX 10110
STAMFORD, CT 06904
TEL: (203) 357-8800
FAX: (203) 329-4223

Edmund M. Carpenter, Chairman. Equipment and systems for electrical, process control, and semiconductor industries. General Signal Corporation is a public company founded in 1904 as General Railway Signal Company. It was first established to manufacture railway safety equipment. In 1960, it purchased Regina (vacuum cleaners), and within two years a major diversification occurred. Its present name was adopted in

1983. Today, it operates in the United States and in 12 foreign countries. Worldwide revenues for 1992: $1.6 billion.

- **Total Employees:** 19,300
- **U.S. Employees Abroad:** 35
- **Countries:** Germany, Japan, Singapore, Switzerland.
- **Application Information:** Hiring for most foreign positions is done at the specific country locations.
- **Job Categories:** Management, Marketing—Electronics, Sales—Electronics.
- **Language Requirement:** Varies with each posting.
- **Training:** No special training provided.

GENERAL TIRE, INC.
1 General St.
Akron, OH 44329 USA

RECRUITER: DAVID MALLORY
DIRECTOR, STAFFING &
    DEVELOPMENT
1 GENERAL ST.
AKRON, OH 44329
TEL: (216) 798-3000

Alan Ockene, President. Tires. General Tire was founded in 1915 and is a subsidiary of Continental Gummi-Werke AG located in Germany. It manufactures solid and cushion tires, inner tubes, and pneumatic casings. Worldwide revenues for 1991: $1.5 billion.

- **Total Employees:** 9,500
- **U.S. Employees Abroad:** 40
- **Countries:** Angola, Argentina, India, Mexico, Pakistan, Portugal.
- **Job Categories:** Accountants, Management, Marketing—Automotive.
- **Language Requirement:** Varies with each posting.
- **Training:** No special training provided.
- **Benefits:** Vary with each posting.
- **Comments:** Due to a technical agreement with foreign subsidiaries, expatriates are hired on a local basis in the specific country location.

GERAGHTY & MILLER, INC.
1099 18th St.
Denver, CO 80202 USA

RECRUITER: BOB ZIEGLER
VP, INTERNATIONAL OPERATIONS
901 HILDEBRAND LANE NE, SUITE
    203
BAINBRIDGE ISLAND, WA 98110
TEL: (206) 780-1707
FAX: (206) 780-2302

David W. Miller, President. Environmental services. Geraghty and Miller, Inc. is a public company founded in 1957. It offers consulting, engineering, hydrocarbon, and remediation services in the United States and in more than 30 foreign countries. It focuses on the development, management, and protection of ground water but other specialty fields include air quality assessment and risk evaluation. Worldwide operating revenues for 1992: $134 million.

- **Total Employees:** 1,104

- **U.S. Employees Abroad:** 30

- **Countries:** Worldwide including France, Italy.

- **Job Categories:** Engineers, Marketing, Technical Field Support.

- **General Requirements:** Usually must be a current employee of the company in order to qualify for overseas assignment.

- **Language Requirement:** Varies with each posting.

GERBER PRODUCTS COMPANY

445 State St.
Fremont, MI 49413 USA

RECRUITER: MELISSA REDINGER
INTERNATIONAL OPERATIONS
445 STATE ST.
FREMONT, MI 49413
TEL: (616) 928-2000
FAX: (616) 928-2819

Alfred A. Piergallini, President and Chairman. Baby foods and related items. Gerber Products is a public company founded in 1901 by Frank Gerber, the president of the Fremont Canning Company of Fremont, Michigan. In 1941, the name was changed to Gerber Products Company. Today, products are sold in more than 58 countries. Worldwide revenues for 1992: $1.3 billion.

- **Total Employees:** 12,400

- **U.S. Employees Abroad:** 25

- **Countries:** Costa Rica, Hong Kong, Mexico.

- **Job Categories:** Marketing—Food/Food Services, Product Development, Sales—Food/Food Services.

GERHARD'S BICYCLE ODYSSEYS

PO Box 757
Portland, OR 97207 USA

RECRUITER: GERHARD MENG
DIRECTOR
PO BOX 757
PORTLAND, OR 97207
TEL: (503) 223-2402
FAX: (503) 223-5901

Gerhard Meng, Director. European cycling tours. Gerhard's Bicycle Odysseys operates cycling tours throughout Europe and offers an opportunity for employment abroad as a tour leader.

- **Total Employees:** Not available.
- **U.S. Employees Abroad:** Not available.
- **Countries:** Austria, France, Germany, Italy, Norway, Switzerland.
- **Salaries:** $2,500 per month (minimum).
- **Job Categories:** Tour Leaders.
- **General Requirements:** College (4-year) degree.
- **Average Overseas Assignment:** Less than two years.
- **Language Requirement:** Fluency in local language required.
- **Training:** No special training provided.
- **Benefits:** None are offered.

GETZ BROTHERS COMPANY, INC.

150 Post Rd.
Suite 500
San Francisco, CA 94108 USA

RECRUITER: TRACY MOORE
MANAGER, HUMAN RESOURCES
150 POST RD., SUITE 500
SAN FRANCISCO, CA 94108
TEL: (415) 772-5500
FAX: (415) 772-5659

Robert E. Brindley, Chairman. Marketing and distribution service. Getz Borthers is a private company founded in 1981. It services clients in the United States and abroad. Worldwide revenues for 1991: $550 million.

- **Total Employees:** 2,500
- **U.S. Employees Abroad:** 24
- **Countries:** Australia, Hong Kong, Philippines, Singapore, United Kingdom.
- **Application Information:** Phone calls concerning foreign positions are not accepted.
- **Job Categories:** Executive Management, Management, Marketing.
- **General Requirements:** Some experience living abroad.
- **Average Overseas Assignment:** Five years or more.
- **Language Requirement:** Knowledge of local language a plus but not essential.
- **Training:** No special training provided.
- **Benefits:** HEALTH: Offered.

GIDDINGS & LEWIS, INC.

142 Doty St.
Fond du Lac, WI 54936 USA

RECRUITER: MICHELLE SCHLOSSER
HUMAN RESOURCES
142 DOTY ST.
FOND DU LAC, WI 54936
TEL: (414) 921-9400
FAX: (414) 929-4522

William J. Fife, Jr., President. Machinery, tools, and industrial automation. Giddings & Lewis is a public company founded in 1900; until 1989, it was privately owned. Today, it is the largest supplier and integrator of industrial automation and machine tools in North America, and one of the largest in the world. Its products are utilized in more than 50 countries and in 250 different industries. Worldwide revenues for 1992: $623 million.

- **Total Employees:** 3,942
- **U.S. Employees Abroad:** 20
- **Countries:** Germany, United Kingdom.
- **Job Categories:** Accountants, Design, Product Development, Marketing—Industrial, Sales—Industrial.
- **Language Requirement:** Fluency in local language required.
- **Training:** No special training provided.

GILBERT/COMMONWEALTH INTERNATIONAL, INC.

PO Box 1498
Reading, PA 19603 USA

RECRUITER: GREGORY W. JOHNSON
VP, HUMAN RESOURCES
PO BOX 1498
READING, PA 19603
TEL: (215) 775-2600
FAX: (215) 775-2670

Alexander F. Smith, Chairman. Professional engineering services. Gilbert/Commonwealth International, Inc. was founded in 1942 and is a subsidiary of Gilbert Associates, Inc. of Reading, Pennsylvania. It is principally engaged in designing and engineering power plants.

- **Total Employees:** 2,000
- **U.S. Employees Abroad:** 12
- **Countries:** Egypt, Indonesia, United Kingdom.
- **Job Categories:** Design, Engineers.
- **General Requirements:** Prefer experience in the engineering field; primarily power engineering.
- **Language Requirement:** None.
- **Training:** No special training provided.
- **Benefits:** All benefits are individually determined.

- **Comments:** The number of Americans working abroad varies greatly from quarter to quarter, fluctuating with the number and scope of projects under contract at the time.

THE GILLETTE COMPANY

Prudential Tower Building
Boston, MA 02199 USA

RECRUITER: FRANK O'CONNELL
HUMAN RESOURCES, INTERNATIONAL
PRUDENTIAL TOWER BUILDING
BOSTON, MA 02199
TEL: (617) 421-7000
FAX: (617) 421-7123

Colman M. Mockler, Jr., Chairman. Personal care items, stationery, and small appliances. Gillette is a public company founded in 1901. King C. Gillette invented the disposable razor in 1895. In 1901, MIT machinist William Nickerson combined efforts with Gillette to perfect the safety razor. They founded the American Razor Company in Boston. Today, Gillette also produces writing instruments, toiletries, and small appliances. Manufacturing plants are located in 26 foreign locations with products sold in more than 200 countries. Worldwide revenues for 1992: $5.1 billion.

- **Total Employees:** 30,400
- **U.S. Employees Abroad:** 110
- **Countries:** Argentina, Australia, Brazil, Canada, Mexico, Panama, Saudi Arabia, Switzerland, Venezuela, United Kingdom.
- **Job Categories:** Accountants, Marketing—Consumer Goods, Product Development, Sales—Consumer Goods.
- **Language Requirement:** Varies with each posting.
- **Training:** No special training provided.

GOLDMAN SACHS & COMPANY

85 Broad St.
New York, NY 10004 USA

RECRUITER: JIM MORRISON
VP, PERSONNEL
85 BROAD ST.
NEW YORK, NY 10004
TEL: (212) 902-7300
FAX: (212) 902-4079

Stephen Friedman, Chairman. Investment banking and brokerage services. Goldman Sachs is a private company founded in 1869 by Philadelphia retailer Marcus Goldman. In the 1970s the firm began expansion of its international market and today it has 18 offices located in foreign countries. Worldwide assets for 1991: $83.2 billion.

- **Total Employees:** 7,263
- **U.S. Employees Abroad:** 292
- **Countries:** Canada, People's Republic of China, Cayman Islands, France, Hong Kong, Italy, Republic of Korea, Russia, Spain, Taiwan.

- **Job Categories:** Brokers—Securities & Financial, Finance, Management, Marketing—Financial Services.

- **Language Requirement:** Varies with each posting.

GOODYEAR TIRE & RUBBER COMPANY

1144 East Market St.
Akron, OH 44316 USA

RECRUITER: D. C. JONES
MANAGER, CORPORATE COLLEGE
RELATIONS
1144 EAST MARKET ST., DEPT. #806
AKRON, OH 44316
TEL: (216) 796-7990
FAX: (216) 796-4099

Stanley C. Gault, Chairman. Rubber products including tires for passenger cars; also truck and off-the-road tires. Goodyear is a public company founded in 1898 in Akron, Ohio, by Frank and Charles Seiberling. The company was titled Goodyear after Charles Goodyear, who invented the vulcanization process in 1839. By 1916, Goodyear had become the largest tire manufacturer in the world. Today, it is the largest rubber producer in the world, operating 43 U.S. plants in 21 states and 43 plants in 25 foreign countries. Worldwide revenues for 1992: $11.8 billion.

- **Total Employees:** 97,000

- **U.S. Employees Abroad:** 217

- **Countries:** Worldwide including Brazil, Colombia, France, Germany, Guatemala, Indonesia, India, Spain, United Kingdom, Venezuela.

- **Application Information:** Hiring for most foreign positions is done at the specific country location.

- **Job Categories:** Executive Management, Marketing—Automotive.

- **General Requirements:** Knowledge of culture and characteristics of specific country a plus.

- **Average Overseas Assignment:** 3-5 years; most expatriates go into international work as a career.

- **Language Requirement:** Competency in local language required.

- **Training:** Basic orientation (1-30 days) provided; some basic language training at local site is offered.

- **Benefits:** TRAVEL: One month home leave per year for expatriate family. HEALTH: Same coverage as U.S. employees. HOUSING: Foreign service premiums are paid in foreign locations, plus goods & services allowances; it differs from location to location. EDUCATION: All children of expatriates are educated in American schools.

GOULD PUMPS, INC.

240 Fall St.
Seneca Falls, NY 13148 USA

RECRUITER: KANDIE DAVIS
HUMAN RESOURCES
240 FALL ST.
SENECA FALLS, NY 13148
TEL: (315) 568-2811
FAX: (315) 568-7125

Stephen V. Ardia, President. Water pumps and systems. Gould Pumps is a public company founded in 1848. Clients include industrial, agricultural, commercial, and consumer markets. Worldwide revenues for 1991: $566.6 million.

- **Total Employees:** 4,200
- **U.S. Employees Abroad:** 25
- **Countries:** Canada, Italy, Mexico, Philippines.
- **Job Categories:** Management, Marketing, Design, Sales.
- **Language Requirement:** None.
- **Training:** No special training provided.

W. R. GRACE & COMPANY

1 Town Center Rd.
Boca Raton, FL 33486 USA

RECRUITER: CHRIS HILKER
DIRECTOR, EMPLOYEE RELATIONS
1 TOWN CENTER RD.
BOCA RATON, FL 33486
TEL: (407) 362-2000
FAX: (407) 362-2306

J. P. Bolduc, President. Specialty chemicals, water treatment, packaging health care, and catalysts. W. R. Grace is a public company founded in 1854 by William R. Grace. By 1866, he relocated his business to New York. Diversification through the years has proven successful. Today, Grace is the world's largest specialty chemicals company with a leadership position in health care. Currently, it has operations in 49 countries. Worldwide revenues for 1992: $5.5 billion. billion.

- **Total Employees:** 44,000
- **U.S. Employees Abroad:** 16,000
- **Countries:** Worldwide including Argentina, Australia, Brazil, Canada, Finland, France, Germany, Hong Kong, Japan, Mexico, Philippines, Singapore, Sweden, Switzerland, United Kingdom.
- **Job Categories:** Chemical Engineers, Management, Marketing—Chemicals, Marketing, Product Development, Sales—Chemicals, Sales.
- **General Requirements:** Usually must be a current employee of the company in order to qualify for overseas assignment.
- **Language Requirement:** Varies with each posting.

GRACO, INC.

PO Box 1441
Minneapolis, MN 55440-1441
USA

RECRUITER: NANCY MOSIER
SENIOR COMPENSATIONS ANALYST
PO BOX 1441
MINNEAPOLIS, MN 55440-1441
TEL: (612) 623-6000
FAX: (612) 623-6640

David A. Koch, Chairman. Fluid handling equipment and systems. Graco is a public company founded in 1926. It was originally called The Gray Company and was privately held until 1969. Today, it manufactures and services systems that move, measure, control, dispense, or apply fluid materials. Worldwide revenues for 1992: $320 million.

- **Total Employees:** 2,010

- **U.S. Employees Abroad:** 35

- **Countries:** Canada, France, Germany, Hong Kong, Italy, Japan, Republic of Korea, Taiwan, United Kingdom.

- **Job Categories:** Manufacturing, Marketing—Industrial, Sales—Industrial.

- **Language Requirement:** Varies with each posting.

- **Training:** No special training provided.

GRANT THORNTON INTERNATIONAL

1 Prudential Plaza
Suite 800
Chicago, IL 60601 USA

RECRUITER: SANDRA KNIPP
DIRECTOR, HUMAN RESOURCES
1 PRUDENTIAL PLAZA, SUITE 800
CHICAGO, IL 60601
TEL: (312) 856-0001
FAX: (312) 861-1340

Pat Zorsch, Director of Systems. Accounting services. Grant Thornton International is a private company founded in 1924. It offers professional accounting, bookkeeping, and related auditing services on an international basis.

- **Total Employees:** 2,800

- **U.S. Employees Abroad:** 30

- **Countries:** Belgium, Canada, Germany, Italy, Mexico, Netherlands, Saudi Arabia, Spain, United Kingdom.

- **Job Categories:** Accountants, Management, Marketing.

- **General Requirements:** Usually must be a current employee of the company in order to qualify for overseas assignment.

- **Language Requirement:** Varies with each posting.

GREAT LAKES CARBON INTERNATIONAL CORPORATION

320 Old Briarcliff Rd.
Briarcliff Manor, NY 10510 USA

RECRUITER: MARY NILAND
DIRECTOR, HUMAN RESOURCES
320 OLD BRIARCLIFF RD.
BRIARCLIFF MANOR, NY 10510
TEL: (914) 941-7800
FAX: (914) 941-1098

Harry L. Walters, President. Carbon prouducts. Great Lakes Carbon International Corporation was founded in 1919 and is a subsidiary of Horsehead Industries of New York City. It produces various items made from carbon, graphite, or metal-graphite, including brushes and electrodes. Worldwide revenues for 1991: $300 million.

- **Total Employees:** 1,125
- **U.S. Employees Abroad:** 20
- **Countries:** Belgium, Canada, United Kingdom.
- **Job Categories:** Accountants, Finance, Marketing, Sales.

GREAT LAKES CHEMICAL CORPORATION

PO Box 2200
West Lafayette, IN 47906 USA

RECRUITER: GREG GRIFFITH
HUMAN RESOURCES
PO BOX 2200
WEST LAFAYETTE, IN 47906
TEL: (317) 494-6100
FAX: (317) 497-6234

Emerson Kampen, President and Chairman. Bromine and bromine derivatives. Great Lakes Chemical Corporation is a public company founded in 1933. It produces bromine, related specialty chemicals, and furfural derivatives. Worldwide revenues for 1992: $1.5 billion.

- **Total Employees:** 1,700
- **U.S. Employees Abroad:** Not available.
- **Countries:** Japan, United Kingdom.
- **Job Categories:** Management, Marketing—Chemicals, Product Development, Sales—Chemicals.
- **Language Requirement:** None.

A. P. GREEN INDUSTRIES, INC.

Green Blvd.
Mexico, MO 65265 USA

RECRUITER: DAVID ADAMS
MANAGER, HUMAN RESOURCES/
DEVELOPMENT
GREEN BLVD.
MEXICO, MO 65265
TEL: (314) 473-3454
FAX: (314) 473-3508

Paul F. Hummer, Chairman. Refractory products. A. P. Green Industries is a public company founded in 1910. In addition to refractory products, A. P. Green also produces industrial lime products used in the manufacture of steel, aluminum, and paper and other applications. It operates 15 plants in the United States and abroad. Worldwide revenues for 1992: $170.2 million.

- **Total Employees:** 1,698
- **U.S. Employees Abroad:** 128
- **Countries:** Canada, Mexico, Singapore, United Kingdom.
- **Job Categories:** Executive Management, Marketing, Sales.
- **Language Requirement:** Knowledge of local language a plus but not essential.
- **Training:** No special training provided.

GREY ADVERTISING, INC.

777 Third Ave.
25th Floor
New York, NY 10017 USA

RECRUITER: FRANK CLARKE
EXECUTIVE VP, AREA DIRECTOR
777 THIRD AVE., 25TH FLOOR
NEW YORK, NY 10017
TEL: (212) 546-2000
FAX: (212) 546-1495

Edward H. Meyer, President and Chairman. Advertising services. Grey Advertising is a public company founded in 1917. It operates advertising agencies in the United States and abroad. Worldwide gross billings for 1992: $4.5 billion.

- **Total Employees:** 6,000
- **U.S. Employees Abroad:** 35
- **Countries:** Sixty countries including Argentina, Australia, Canada, France, Hong Kong, Italy, Japan, Netherlands, Sweden, United Kingdom.
- **Job Categories:** Management, Marketing, Sales—Advertising.
- **Language Requirement:** Varies with each posting.

GTE CORPORATION

1 Stamford Forum
Stamford, CT 06904 USA

RECRUITER: BRUCE I. TAYLOR
DIRECTOR, FOREIGN SERVICE
1 STAMFORD FORUM
STAMFORD, CT 06901
TEL: (203) 965-2000
FAX: (203) 965-2277

James L. Johnson, Chairman. Telecommunications systems and electrical products. GTE is a public company founded in 1935 by Sigurd Odegard and John O'Connell. They began the Associated Telephone Utilities in 1926. The Great Depression affected the company as lenders took control and, in 1932, moved headquarters from Chicago to New York. Unable to survive, it went bankrupt and emerged as General Telephone in

1935. In 1959, Sylvania bought General Telephone and changed its product line and name. It became General Telephone and Electronics. Today, this multinational concern operates throughout the United States and in 41 foreign countries. Worldwide revenues for 1992: $20 billion.

- **Total Employees:** 155,000
- **U.S. Employees Abroad:** Not available.
- **Countries:** Worldwide including Argentina, Canada, India, Netherlands, Nigeria, Thailand.
- **Job Categories:** Executive Management, Technical Field Support.
- **General Requirements:** Usually must be a current employee of the company in order to qualify for overseas assignment.
- **Language Requirement:** None.

GTE DIRECTORIES CORPORATION

PO Box 619810
Dallas Fort Worth Airport
Dallas, TX 75261-9810 USA

RECRUITER: KATHY O'DAY
DIRECTOR OF BENEFITS &
    COMPENSATION
PO BOX 619810
DALLAS FORT WORTH AIRPORT
DALLAS, TX 75261-9810
TEL: (214) 453-7000

Thomas F. Lysaught, President. Directories publishing. GTE Directories was founded in 1934 and is a subsidiary of GTE Telephone Operations, Inc. of Irving, Texas. It publishes various printed materials including telephone directories. Worldwide revenues for 1991: $360 million.

- **Total Employees:** 4,500
- **U.S. Employees Abroad:** 25
- **Countries:** Canada, Costa Rica, Hong Kong, Singapore, Venezuela.
- **Job Categories:** Management, Marketing—Publishing, Sales—Publishing.
- **Language Requirement:** None.

GTECH CORPORATION

2006 Nooseneck Hill Rd.
Coventry, RI 02816 USA

RECRUITER: JOANNE ARBIGE
INTERNATIONAL HUMAN RESOURCES
2006 NOOSENECK HILL RD.
COVENTRY, RI 02816
TEL: (401) 392-1100
FAX: (401) 392-0251

Guy B. Snowden, Chairman. Computerized lottery systems. GTECH Corporation is a private company founded in 1980 by Guy B. Snowden, Victor Markowicz, and Robert

A
M
E
R
I
C
A
N

J
O
B
S

A
B
R
O
A
D

K. Stern. It began with the idea of controlling lottery systems with one main computer. Worldwide revenues for 1992: $275 million.

- **Total Employees:** 1,400
- **U.S. Employees Abroad:** 25
- **Countries:** Canada, Malaysia, Spain, Sweden.
- **Job Categories:** Accountants, Marketing—Electronics, Sales—Electronics.
- **Language Requirement:** None.
- **Training:** No special training provided.

GUARDIAN INDUSTRIES CORPORATION

43043 West Nine Mile Rd.
Northville, MI 48167 USA

RECRUITER: ROBERT MERRICK
PERSONNEL DIRECTOR
43043 WEST NINE MILE RD.
NORTHVILLE, MI 48167
TEL: (313) 347-9102
FAX: (313) 347-9108

William Davidson, President. Insulation materials and glass products. Guardian Industries Corporation is a private company founded in 1932. Today, it is the 5th largest glass maker in the world. Products include flat and fabricated glass for home and office use. It is also engaged in photographic development. Worldwide revenues for 1991: $520 million.

- **Total Employees:** 6,000
- **U.S. Employees Abroad:** 20
- **Countries:** Australia, Hungary, Indonesia.
- **Job Categories:** Engineers, Design, Management, Marketing, Sales.
- **General Requirements:** Usually must be a current employee of the company in order to qualify for overseas assignment.
- **Language Requirement:** None.

H. J. HEINZ COMPANY

PO Box 57
Pittsburgh, PA 15230-0057 USA

RECRUITER: WILLIAM FERA
PERSONNEL ADMINISTRATOR
1060 PROGRESS ST.
PITTSBURGH, PA 15212
TEL: (412) 456-5700
FAX: (412) 456-6128

Anthony J. F. O'Reilly, President and Chairman. Processed food products and nutritional services. H. J. Heinz is a public company founded in 1869 by Henry J. Heinz and partner, L. C. Noble. They combined talents to produce bottled horseradish sauce. Though bankruptcy soon followed, the company emerged again to form F. & J. Heinz. Major products were ketchup and pickles. The name was changed in 1888 to H. J.

Heinz Company. Today, Heinz produces over 3,000 varieties of foods with operations in 17 foreign countries. Worldwide revenues for 1992: $7 billion.

- **Total Employees:** 37,300

- **U.S. Employees Abroad:** 60

- **Countries:** Australia, Belgium, Botswana, Canada, People's Republic of China, France, Germany, Ghana, Italy, Japan, Mexico, Netherlands, Portugal, Thailand, United Kingdom, Venezuela.

- **Job Categories:** Executive Management, Manufacturing, Marketing—Food/Food Services, Product Development, Sales—Food/Food Services.

- **Language Requirement:** None.

H & R BLOCK

4410 Main St.
Kansas City, MO 64111 USA

RECRUITER: JIM BYERS
REGIONAL SATELLITE FRANCHISE
DIRECTOR
PO BOX 908
BLUE SPRINGS, MO 64014
TEL: (816) 228-6170
FAX: (816) 228-3552

Thomas M. Bloch, President. Tax services. Two brothers, Henry and Richard Block, first opened the United Business Company in Kansas City in 1946. They provided many services to local businesses, including bookkeeping, management, and income tax filing. In 1955, they focused on tax preparation and became H & R Block. It is now the largest U.S. tax preparer, filling out nearly 1 of every 9 returns that the IRS sees. It operates 8,955 offices worldwide. Worldwide revenues for 1991: $1.1 billion.

- **Total Employees:** 70,000

- **U.S. Employees Abroad:** 100

- **Countries:** Australia, Canada, Germany, Japan, New Zealand.

- **Job Categories:** Clerical Assistants, Management, Office Management, Tax Preparers.

- **General Requirements:** Usually must be a current employee of the company in order to qualify for overseas assignment.

- **Average Overseas Assignment:** 3-5 years.

- **Language Requirement:** Knowledge of local language a plus but not essential.

- **Training:** Basic orientation (1-30 days) provided.

- **Benefits:** EDUCATION: Offered.

HACH COMPANY

5600 Lindbergh Dr.
PO Box 389
Loveland, CO 80539 USA

RECRUITER: PAUL GOLTZ
INTERNATIONAL MARKETING
5600 LINDBERG DR.
PO BOX 389
LOVELAND, CO 80539
TEL: (303) 669-3050
FAX: (303) 669-2932

Kathryn Hach, Chairperson. Process analyzers and test kits. Hach is a public company founded in 1947 by Clifford C. Hach. Products manufactured are used to analyze chemical content in foods, drinking water, waste water, and soil. It operates in the United States and major cities throughout the world. Worldwide revenues for 1992: $84.7 million.

- **Total Employees:** 745
- **U.S. Employees Abroad:** 20
- **Countries:** Canada, Belgium.
- **Job Categories:** Marketing, Product Development, Sales.
- **Language Requirement:** None.
- **Training:** No special training provided.

HALLIBURTON COMPANY

3600 Lincoln Plaza
Dallas, TX 75201 USA

RECRUITER: KAREN S. STUART
HUMAN RESOURCES, VP-
ADMINISTRATION
3600 LINCOLN PLAZA
DALLAS, TX 75201
TEL: (214) 978-2600
FAX: (214) 978-2611

Thomas H. Kruikshank, Chairman. Oil field services; engineering and construction services. Halliburton is a public company founded in 1919 by Erle Halliburton. He started the Better Method Oil Well Cementing Company in Burkburnett, Texas. In 1924, the business was incorporated as Halliburton Oilwell Cementing Company. Acquisitons through the years have helped to make this business successful. Today, Halliburton is one of the world's largest oil field engineering and construction services companies. It operates in more than 115 foreign countries. Worldwide revenues for 1992: $6.6 billion.

- **Total Employees:** 77,000
- **U.S. Employees Abroad:** 60
- **Countries:** Brazil, Canada, Hong Kong, Mexico, Singapore, United Arab Emirates, United Kingdom.
- **Job Categories:** Accountants, Engineers, Field Engineers, Finance, Marketing.

HALLIBURTON COMPANY/ HALLIBURTON SERVICES DIVISION

PO Drawer 1431
Duncan, OK 73534 USA

RECRUITER: CHUCK JOHNSTON
PERSONNEL MANAGER,
    INTERNATIONAL
PO DRAWER 1431
DUNCAN, OK 73534
TEL: (405) 251-4773
FAX: (405) 251-4773

Ken LeSuer, President. Services wells. Halliburton Services is a division of the Halliburton Company of Dallas, Texas. It manufactures machinery and equipment for oil and gas fields and for drilling wells. Worldwide revenues for 1991: $1.6 billion.

- **Total Employees:** 11,000

- **U.S. Employees Abroad:** 35

- **Countries:** Hong Kong, Japan, Mexico, United Kingdom.

- **Job Categories:** Accountants, Engineers, Marketing.

- **General Requirements:** Usually must be a current employee of the company in order to qualify for overseas assignment. Applicant should have experience in well-services area.

- **Language Requirement:** Varies with each posting.

HALLIBURTON-NUS CORPORATION

910 Clopper Rd.
Gaithersburg, MD 20878 USA

RECRUITER: SUSAN YOUNG
EMPLOYMENT ADMINISTRATOR
910 CLOPPER RD.
GAITHERSBURG, MD 20878
TEL: (301) 258-6000
FAX: (301) 258-2571

Charles F. Jones, President. Contract services. Halliburton-NUS Corporation is a subsidiary of Halliburton Company of Dallas, Texas. It provides technical consultants and managers to the engineering and environmental fields. Worldwide revenues for 1991: $204 million.

- **Total Employees:** 1,500

- **U.S. Employees Abroad:** 25

- **Countries:** Germany, Japan, Saudi Arabia.

- **Job Categories:** Accountants, Technical Field Support.

- **Language Requirement:** None.

HALLMARK CARDS, INC.

PO Box 419580
Kansas City, MO 64141-9580
USA

RECRUITER: GREGORY FURSTNER
INTERNATIONAL PERSONNEL
PO BOX 419580
KANSAS CITY, MO 64141-9580
TEL: (816) 274-5111
FAX: (816) 545-6286

Irvine O. Hockaday, Jr., President. Greeting cards and related products. Hallmark Cards is a private company founded by Joyce C. Hall in 1910. He began by selling postcards and when his brother joined him in 1911, they added greeting cards. The first retail store was opened in 1950 and today Hallmark is the number-1 producer of greetings cards in the world. Other products include ribbon and gift wrap. Worldwide revenues for 1991: $2.9 billion.

- **Total Employees:** 20,500
- **U.S. Employees Abroad:** 35
- **Countries:** Australia, Canada, France, Germany, Mexico, New Zealand, United Kingdom.
- **Job Categories:** Accountants, Marketing—Consumer Goods, Product Development, Sales—Consumer Goods.
- **General Requirements:** Usually must be a current employee of the company in order to qualify for overseas assignment.
- **Language Requirement:** Fluency in local language required.
- **Training:** No special training provided.

HAMLIN, INC.

612 East Lake St.
Lake Mills, WI 53551 USA

RECRUITER: BRAD ANDERSON
PERSONNEL MANAGER
612 EAST LAKE ST.
LAKE MILLS, WI 53551
TEL: (414) 648-3000
FAX: (414) 648-3001

M. J. Fitzpatrick, President. Industrial controls and devices. Hamlin, Inc. is a private company founded in 1949. As an industrial manufacturer, products include motor starters, relays, and switches. Worldwide revenues for 1991: $40 million.

- **Total Employees:** 1,050
- **U.S. Employees Abroad:** 10
- **Countries:** France, Germany, Hong Kong, United Kingdom.
- **Job Categories:** Management, Manufacturing, Marketing—Industrial.
- **Language Requirement:** None.
- **Training:** No special training provided.

- **Comments:** The number of Americans working abroad varies greatly from quarter to quarter, fluctuating with the number and scope of projects under contract at the time.

M. A. HANNA COMPANY

1301 East 9th St.
Suite 3600
Cleveland, OH 44114-1860 USA

RECRUITER: GARTH W. HENRY
VP, OPERATIONS
1301 EAST 9TH ST., SUITE 3600
CLEVELAND, OH 44114-1860
TEL: (216) 589-4038
FAX: (216) 589-4329

Martin D. Walker, Chairman. Specialty chemicals. M. A. Hanna is a public company founded in 1885. Major products include plastic and rubber compounds, and the distribution of plastic resins and shapes, and printing blankets. Worldwide revenues for 1992: $1.3 billion.

- **Total Employees:** 6,275
- **U.S. Employees Abroad:** 25
- **Countries:** Belgium, Canada, France, Germany, Sweden.
- **Application Information:** Hiring for most foreign positions is done at the specific country location.
- **Job Categories:** Management, Marketing—Chemicals, Sales—Chemicals.
- **Language Requirement:** None.
- **Training:** Individually determined.
- **Benefits:** All benefits are individually determined.

HANSON INDUSTRIES

410 Park Ave.
New York, NY 10022 USA

RECRUITER: DOROTHY SANDERS
DIRECTOR, COMPENSATION &
　　BENEFITS
99 WOOD AVE. SOUTH
ISELIN, NJ 08830
TEL: (908) 603-6600
FAX: (908) 603-6878

H. Clarke, President. Industrial management and manufacturing. Hanson Industries was founded in 1973 and is a subsidiary of Hanson PLC of London, England. Subsidiaries and divisions of Hanson Industries are in the building products, consumer, and industrial industries. Products manufactured and/or sold include cement, chemicals, cookware, office furniture, and toys. Worldwide revenues for 1991: $27 billion.

- **Total Employees:** 52,000
- **U.S. Employees Abroad:** 60
- **Countries:** Brazil, Canada, Costa Rica, France, Germany, Guatemala, Panama, Singapore, Switzerland, United Kingdom.

- **Job Categories:** Executive Management, Finance, Marketing—Industrial, Sales—Industrial.

HARRIS CORPORATION

1025 West Nasa Blvd.
Melbourne, FL 32919 USA

RECRUITER: PETE PETERSON
PERSONNEL DEPARTMENT
1025 WEST NASA BLVD.
MELBOURNE, FL 32901
TEL: (407) 727-9100
FAX: (407) 724-3131

John T. Hartley, President. Communications and information-handling equipment. Harris Corporation is a public company founded in 1894. It manufactures computers and radio and television broadcasting equipment. It is also engaged in the production of semiconductors and related products. Worldwide revenues for 1992: $3.1 billion.

- **Total Employees:** 36,000

- **U.S. Employees Abroad:** 125

- **Countries:** Canada, Mexico, Panama, United Kingdom.

- **Job Categories:** Accountants, Marketing—Electronics, Product Development, Sales—Electronics.

- **Language Requirement:** None.

- **Training:** No special training provided.

HARTFORD STEAM BOILER INSPECTION/INSURANCE COMPANY

1 State St.
Hartford, CT 06102 USA

RECRUITER: ROSE MIHALY
DIRECTOR, HUMAN RESOURCES
1 STATE ST.
HARTFORD, CT 06102
TEL: (203) 722-1866

Wilson Wilde, President. Engineering services and specialty insurance products. Hartford Steam Boiler Inspection/Insurance is a public company founded in 1866. It provides services to clients on a global basis. Worldwide assets for 1992: $682.1 million.

- **Total Employees:** 4,000

- **U.S. Employees Abroad:** 25

- **Countries:** Canada, Singapore.

- **Job Categories:** Engineers, Marketing, Scientists, Technicians.

- **Language Requirement:** None.

C
O
M
P
A
N
Y

L
I
S
T
I
N
G
S

HASBRO, INC.

1027 Newport Ave.
Pawtucket, RI 02861 USA

RECRUITER: JAMES KERSHNER
PERSONNEL MANAGER
1027 NEWPORT AVE.
PAWTUCKET, RI 02861
TEL: (401) 726-4100

Alan G. Hassenfeld, Chairman. Toys and games. Hasbro, Inc. is public company founded in 1926. Divisions include Playskool, Inc. of Pawtucket, Rhode Island, and Milton Bradley of Longmeadow, Massachusetts. Well-known brand names are Cabbage Patch Kids and the Scrabble board game. Worldwide revenues for 1992: $2.5 billion.

- **Total Employees:** 10,500

- **U.S. Employees Abroad:** 25

- **Countries:** Canada, France, Switzerland.

- **Job Categories:** Accountants, Marketing—Consumer Goods, Product Development, Sales—Consumer Goods.

- **General Requirements:** Usually must be a current employee of the company in order to qualify for overseas assignment.

- **Language Requirement:** None.

- **Training:** Varies with each posting.

HAZLETON WASHINGTON CORPORATION

13873 Park Center Rd.
Herndon, VA 22071 USA

RECRUITER: MICHAEL J. MACKERT
VP, HUMAN RESOURCES
13873 PARK CENTER RD.
HERNDON, VA 22071
TEL: (703) 478-9450
FAX: (703) 478-9457

Donald P. Nielsen, President. Laboratory instruments; research and development. Hazleton Washington was founded in 1946 and is a subsidiary of Corning, Inc. of Corning, New York. It manufactures laboratory instruments for chemical or physical analysis. It also offers research and development services to commercial markets. Worldwide revenues for 1991: $94 million.

- **Total Employees:** 2,000

- **U.S. Employees Abroad:** 18

- **Countries:** France, Germany, Japan, United Kingdom.

- **Job Categories:** Accountants, Chemists, Marketing—Scientific, Sales—Scientific.

- **Language Requirement:** None.

HDR INCORPORATED

8404 Indian Hills Dr.
Omaha, NE 68114-4049 USA

RECRUITER: ROB JOHNSON
NATIONAL RECRUITMENT DIRECTOR
8404 INDIAN HILLS DR.
OMAHA, NE 68114-4049
TEL: (402) 399-1205
FREE: (800) 366-2701

Jean Tietz, Chairman. Architecture, engineering, and facilities management. HDR was founded in 1983 and is a subsidiary of Centerra Corporation of Omaha, Nebraska. Worldwide operating revenues for 1991: $130.0 million.

- **Total Employees:** 1,080
- **U.S. Employees Abroad:** Not available.
- **Countries:** Saudi Arabia, Spain.
- **Job Categories:** Architects, Engineers, Marketing.

HELENE CURTIS INDUSTRIES, INC.

325 North Wells St.
Chicago, IL 60610 USA

RECRUITER: MAILE MULLIGAN
HUMAN RESOURCES
325 NORTH WELLS ST.
CHICAGO, IL 60601
TEL: (312) 661-0222
FAX: (312) 222-1589

Ronald J. Gidwitz, President. Personal care items including cosmetics. Helene Curtis Industries is a public company founded in 1927. Its products include cosmetics, toiletries, and hair preparations. Worldwide revenues for 1992: $1 billion.

- **Total Employees:** 3,000
- **U.S. Employees Abroad:** 20
- **Countries:** Argentina, Belgium, Canada, India, Japan, New Zealand.
- **Job Categories:** Accountants, Finance, Marketing—Consumer Goods, Research & Development, Sales—Consumer Goods.
- **Language Requirement:** None.

HELLMUTH, OBATA & KASSABAUM, INC.

1831 Chestnut St.
St. Louis, MO 63103 USA

RECRUITER: JOE ESSER
MANAGER, HUMAN RESOURCES
1831 CHESTNUT ST.
ST. LOUIS, MO 63103
TEL: (314) 421-2000

G. Obata, Chairman. Diversified design. Hellmuth, Obata & Kassabaum, Inc. is a private company founded in 1955. Operating on a worldwide basis, it offers various services to architects, engineers, planners for interior design, graphic designers and computer specialists. Worldwide operating revenues for 1991: $140 million.

- **Total Employees:** 1,000
- **U.S. Employees Abroad:** 35
- **Countries:** Saudi Arabia, Japan, United Kingdom.
- **Job Categories:** Accountants, Architects, Computer Programmers, Draftsmen, Attorneys, Management.
- **Language Requirement:** None.

HERCULES, INC.

Hercules Plaza
1313 North Market St.
22nd Floor
Wilmington, DE 19894 USA

RECRUITER: THOMAS J. MCCARTHY
VP, HUMAN RESOURCES
HERCULES PLAZA
1313 NORTH MARKET ST., 22ND
    FLOOR
WILMINGTON, DE 19894
TEL: (302) 594-5000
FAX: (302) 594-7097

David S. Hollingsworth, Chairman. Specialty chemicals and engineered polymers. Also markets food ingredients and fragrances. Hercules, Inc. is a public company founded in 1913, after a federal court decision forced DuPont to spin off half of its U.S. explosive productions business. It was divided into two companies; Hercules Powder and Atlas Powder. Through the years, the business expanded and changed its focus from powders to chemicals. Today, the chemical specialties sector is the company's sales leader with 52 percent of annual sales. It has over 90 production facilities throughout the world. Worldwide revenues for 1992: $2.9 billion.

- **Total Employees:** 23,000
- **U.S. Employees Abroad:** 75
- **Countries:** Brazil, Canada, Mexico, Germany, Netherlands, New Zealand, Singapore, Taiwan, United Kingdom.
- **Job Categories:** Chemists, Management, Marketing—Chemicals, Marketing, Product Development, Sales—Chemicals, Sales.
- **Training:** Varies with each posting.

HERSHEY FOODS CORPORATION

Crystal A Dr.
Hershey, PA 17033 USA

RECRUITER: JACK BISHOP
INTERNATIONAL HUMAN RESOURCES
CRYSTAL A DR.
HERSHEY, PA 17033
TEL: (717) 543-4200
FAX: (717) 534-7915

Richard A. Zimmerman, Chairman. Chocolate, confectionary, and pasta products. Hershey Foods is a public company founded in 1900 by Milton Hershey. He began the Lancaster Caramel Company in 1887 and sold the business in 1900 to start a chocolate factory. Today, Hershey Foods is number 1 in confectionary products in North America. Worldwide revenues for 1992: $3.2 billion.

- **Total Employees:** 13,700
- **U.S. Employees Abroad:** 18
- **Countries:** Brazil, Canada, Germany, Japan, Mexico.
- **Job Categories:** Marketing—Food/Food Services, Sales—Food/Food Services.
- **Language Requirement:** None.

HERTZ CORPORATION

225 Brae Blvd.
Park Ridge, NJ 07656-0713 USA

RECRUITER: JOANNE PETRAGLIA
EMPLOYEE RELATIONS MANAGER
225 BRAE BLVD.
PARK RIDGE, NJ 07656-0713
TEL: (201) 307-2000
FAX: (201) 307-2644

Frank A. Olson, Chairman. Automobile rental service. Hertz was founded in 1918 and is a subsidiary of the Park Ridge Corporation of New Jersey. The business was started by John Jacobs when he opened a car rental service in Chicago. John Hertz purchased the business in 1923 when its annual revenue totaled $1 million. Today, Hertz has 5,100 locations in the United States and abroad. Worldwide revenues for 1991: $2.4 billion. Foreign revenues for 1991: $990 million.

- **Total Employees:** 18,000
- **U.S. Employees Abroad:** 25
- **Countries:** Australia, Belgium, Denmark, Germany, Israel, Italy, Japan, Netherlands, Panama, Portugal, Spain, Switzerland, United Kingdom.
- **Application Information:** Hiring for most foreign positions is done at the specific country location.
- **Job Categories:** Finance, Management Training, Marketing—Automotive, Sales—Automotive.
- **Training:** No special training provided.

HEWLETT-PACKARD COMPANY

3000 Hanover St.
Palo Alto, CA 94304 USA

RECRUITER: TOM ALDRICH
STAFFING MANAGER
3495 DEER CREEK RD.
PALO ALTO, CA 94304
TEL: (415) 857-1501
FAX: (415) 852-8467

John A. Young, President. Electronic measurement and testing equipment. Also produces computer workstations. Hewlett-Packard is a public company founded in 1938. Two Stanford engineers started the business in a garage and the first product was an audio oscillator. Walt Disney was one of HP's first customers to purchase the oscillators, which he needed for the film production of *Fantasia*. Today, Hewlett-Packard has over 12,000 products, which are sold throughout the world. Worldwide revenues for 1992: $17.1 billion.

- **Total Employees:** 95,000

- **U.S. Employees Abroad:** 45

- **Countries:** Worldwide including Argentina, Australia, Brazil, Canada, Hong Kong, Malaysia, Mexico, Singapore, Switzerland, United Kingdom.

- **Job Categories:** Finance, Marketing—Electronics, Product Development, Sales—Electronics.

- **General Requirements:** Usually must be a current employee of the company in order to qualify for overseas assignment.

- **Training:** No special training provided.

HILL & KNOWLTON, INC.

420 Lexington Ave.
New York, NY 10017 USA

RECRUITER: JULIA BLOOM
DIRECTOR, HUMAN RESOURCES
420 LEXINGTON AVE.
NEW YORK, NY 10017
TEL: (212) 697-5600
FAX: (212) 210-8715

R. L. Dilenschneider, Chief Executive Officer. Public relations services. Hill & Knowlton is a subsidiary of OWL GP, Inc. and was founded in 1927. It is involved in public relations and lobbying and operates in the United States and in over 15 foreign countries. Worldwide operating revenues for 1991: $173.5 million.

- **Total Employees:** 2,000

- **U.S. Employees Abroad:** 60

- **Countries:** Australia, Bahrain, Belgium, Brazil, Canada, People's Republic of China, France, Germany, Hong Kong, Ireland, Italy, Japan, Malaysia, New Zealand, Singapore, Switzerland, United Kingdom.

- **Application Information:** Hiring for most foreign positions is done at the specific country location.

- **Job Categories:** Management, Marketing.

- **Language Requirement:** None.

HOECHST CELANESE, INC.

Route 202-206 North
PO Box 2500
Somerville, NJ 08876 USA

RECRUITER: CORA DREWRY
SENIOR HR REPRESENTATIVE
ROUTE 202-206 NORTH
PO BOX 2500
SOMERVILLE, NJ 08876
TEL: (908) 231-2000
FAX: (908) 231-3225

Ernest H. Drew, President. Polymers, fibers, chemicals, and cosmetics. Hoechst Celanese, Inc. was founded in 1953 and is a subsidiary of Hoechst AG of Germany. It develops and produces chemicals, cosmetics, dyestuffs, waxes, pharmaceuticals, polymers, and fibers. Worldwide revenues for 1992: $6.8 billion.

- **Total Employees:** 31,000

- **U.S. Employees Abroad:** 35

- **Countries:** Belgium, Canada, Germany, United Kingdom.

- **Job Categories:** Clerical Assistants, Finance, Marketing—Chemicals, Sales—Chemicals.

- **General Requirements:** Usually must be a current employee of the company in order to qualify for overseas assignment.

- **Language Requirement:** Varies with each posting.

HOLIDAY INNS WORLDWIDE

3 Ravinia Dr.
Atlanta, GA 30346 USA

RECRUITER: JOHN HAGER
STAFFING/RECRUITMENT
3 RAVINIA DR.
ATLANTA, GA 30346
TEL: (404) 604-5337
FAX: (404) 604-5548

Bryan D. Langton, Chairman. Hotel, casino, and restaurant management. Holiday Inns Worldwide is a subsidiary of Bass PLC. It operates on a worldwide basis as owner and/or operator of hotels and restaurants. It also supplies and/or operates amusement and gaming machines and casinos. Worldwide operating revenues for 1991: $1.5 billion.

- **Total Employees:** 100,000

- **U.S. Employees Abroad:** 125

- **Countries:** Bahamas, Barbados, Belgium, Brazil, Canada, France, Greece, India, Italy, Japan, Mexico, Switzerland, United Arab Emirates.

- **Job Categories:** Accountants, Finance, Marketing—Food/Food Services, Marketing—Travel, Sales—Food/Food Services, Sales—Travel.

- **Language Requirement:** Varies with each posting.

HOLMES & NARVER, INC.

999 Town and Country Rd.
Orange, CA 92668 USA

RECRUITER: DELLA GILLILAND
HUMAN RESOURCES
999 TOWN AND COUNTRY RD.
ORANGE, CA 92668
TEL: (714) 567-2400
FAX: (714) 567-2562

F. C. Six, President. Architectural and construction services. Holmes & Narver was founded in 1933 and is a subsidiary of AECOM Technology of Los Angeles, California. It provides clients with special trade contractors involved in miscellaneous heavy construction projects. It also provides professional architectural services as well as land, water, and aerial surveying services. Worldwide operating revenues for 1991: $170 million.

- **Total Employees:** 3,700
- **U.S. Employees Abroad:** 15
- **Countries:** Germany, Saudi Arabia.
- **Job Categories:** Design, Engineers, Management, Marketing.
- **Language Requirement:** None.

HONEYWELL, INC.

PO Box 524
Minneapolis, MN 55440 USA

RECRUITER: ERNIE VON HEIMBURG
CORPORATE MANAGER, UNIVERSITY
RELATIONS
PO BOX 524
MINNEAPOLIS, MN 55440
TEL: (612) 870-5200
FAX: (612) 870-5780

Dr. James R. Renier, Chairman. Control products, systems, and services for home, industry, and the space and aviation sectors. Honeywell is a public company founded in 1927 as the Minneapolis-Honeywell Regulator Company. Its present name was adopted in 1964. Today, Honeywell is a global leader in the production of industrial control systems and aviation systems. It also produces environmental controls (thermostats) as well as security and industrial automation systems. It conducts business in over 90 countries. Worldwide revenues for 1992: $6.2 billion.

- **Total Employees:** 57,000
- **U.S. Employees Abroad:** 150
- **Countries:** Worldwide including Australia, Belgium, Canada, France, Germany, Hong Kong, Italy, Netherlands, Singapore, Switzerland, Taiwan, United Kingdom.
- **Job Categories:** Executive Management, Marketing—Electronics, Marketing—Scientific, Sales—Electronics, Sales—Scientific.
- **General Requirements:** Usually a current employee with Honeywell experience. Must be familiar with local language.

- **Average Overseas Assignment:** 3-5 years

- **Language Requirement:** Competency in local language required.

- **Training:** Basic orientation (1-30 days) provided.

- **Benefits:** TRAVEL: Offered after 12 months in foreign posting. HEALTH: Same coverage as U.S. employees. HOUSING: Varies with each posting. EDUCATION: Varies with each posting.

HORMEL FOODS CORPORATION

PO Box 800
Austin, MN 55912 USA

RECRUITER: MICHAEL G. MACLEAN
MANAGER, PROF. STAFFING/
RECRUITMENT
PO BOX 800
AUSTIN, MN 55912
TEL: (507) 437-5881
FAX: (507) 437-5113

R. L. Knowlton, Chairman. Processed foods. Hormel Foods Corporation is a public company founded in 1891 when George Hormel opened his first slaughterhouse in Austin, Minnesota. He introduced the first brand name, Dairy Brand, in 1903 and the following year began opening distribution centers throughout the United States. Today, the company is known for its pork products, Spam luncheon meat and Black Label bacon. It has facilities throughout the United States and abroad. Worldwide revenues for 1992: $2.9 billion.

- **Total Employees:** 8,300

- **U.S. Employees Abroad:** 10

- **Countries:** Australia, Japan, Philippines, United Kingdom.

- **Job Categories:** Accountants, Marketing—Food/Food Services, Sales—Food/Food Services.

- **Language Requirement:** Fluency in local language required.

- **Training:** Varies with each posting.

- **Comments:** The number of Americans working abroad varies greatly from quarter to quarter, fluctuating with the number and scope of projects under contract at the time.

**HOSPITAL CORPORATION
INTERNATIONAL, LTD.**

2515 Park Plaza
Nashville, TN 37203 USA

RECRUITER: NEIL V. LAMBERT
SENIOR INTERNATIONAL
REPRESENTATIVE
2515 PARK PLAZA
NASHVILLE, TN 37203
TEL: (615) 320-2440
FAX: (615) 320-2501
FREE: (800) 251-2561

Ronald C. Marston, President. International hospital recruitment. Hospital Corporation International, Ltd. (HCI), formerly HCA International Company, a subsidiary of Hospital Corporation of America for 17 years, is a wholly owned subsidiary of HCI Group, PLC, a public company incorporated in the United Kingdom. Its primary function is the development, ownership, and operation of medical/surgical hospitals and health-care facilities around the world.

- **Total Employees:** 4,500

- **U.S. Employees Abroad:** 500

- **Countries:** Saudi Arabia.

- **Job Categories:** Lab Technicians, Nurses, Physicians, Scientists, Technical Field Support.

- **Average Overseas Assignment:** Two years.

- **Language Requirement:** None.

- **Training:** One-day basic orientation is provided.

- **Benefits:** TRAVEL: Thirty-day annual home leave with round trip ticket to point of origin. HEALTH: Offered. HOUSING: Offered; utilities included. EDUCATION: Offered.

HOUSEHOLD INTERNATIONAL, INC.

2700 Sanders Rd.
Prospect Heights, IL 60070 USA

RECRUITER: GRETA SATEK
MANAGER, HUMAN RESOURCES
2700 SANDERS RD.
PROSPECT HEIGHTS, IL 60070
TEL: (708) 564-5000

Donald C. Clark, Chairman. Financial services. Household International is a public company founded in 1981. It operates credit institutions that provide loans and financing to clients. It also acts as an underwriter of life insurance and offers various other service-related activities. Worldwide revenues for 1992: $4.1 billion.

- **Total Employees:** 12,000

- **U.S. Employees Abroad:** 25

- **Countries:** Australia, United Kingdom.

- **Job Categories:** Finance, Management, Marketing—Financial Services.

- **General Requirements:** Usually must be a current employee of the company in order to qualify for overseas assignment.

- **Training:** No special training provided.

HUBBELL, INC.

584 Derby-Milford Rd.
Orange, CT 06477-4024 USA

RECRUITER: GEORGE ZURMAN
DIRECTOR, HUMAN RESOURCES
584 DERBY-MILFORD RD.
ORANGE, CT 06477-4024
TEL: (203) 799-4100

G. J. Ratcliffe, President and Chairman. Electrical and electronic products. Hubbell is a public company founded in 1905. It markets and sells products to the telecommunications, commercial utility, and business industries. The business is divided into three areas: low voltage, high voltage, and other. Major products include Acadia lighting products and Chem-Marine sporting goods. Worldwide revenues for 1992: $786 million.

- **Total Employees:** 5,300

- **U.S. Employees Abroad:** 20

- **Countries:** Canada, United Kingdom.

- **Job Categories:** Management, Manufacturing, Marketing—Electronics, Sales—Electronics, Technicians.

- **Language Requirement:** None.

- **Training:** No special training provided.

J. M. HUBER CORPORATION

333 Thornall St.
Edison, NJ 08818 USA

RECRUITER: DOREEN ROMEO
HUMAN RESOURCES
333 THORNALL ST.
EDISON, NJ 08818
TEL: (908) 549-8600
FAX: (908) 549-2239

George Schenk, President. Inks, carbon black; also crude oil, timber, and minerals. J. M. Huber is a private company founded in 1887. Primarily, it is engaged as a maunfacturer of printing ink and carbon black. Worldwide revenues for 1991: $870 million.

- **Total Employees:** 4,000

- **U.S. Employees Abroad:** Not available.

- **Countries:** Finland, Peru, Venezuela.

- **Job Categories:** Management, Marketing—Chemicals, Sales—Chemicals.

- **Language Requirement:** None.

HUGHES AIRCRAFT COMPANY

PO Box 45006
Los Angeles, CA 90045-0066
USA

RECRUITER: MARILYN FISCHER
HUMAN RESOURCES
PO BOX 45006
LOS ANGELES, CA 90045-0066
TEL: (310) 568-6547
FAX: (310) 216-1254

Malcolm R. Currie, Chairman. Aircraft, aerospace systems, and equipment. Hughes Aircraft was founded in 1953 and is a subsidiary of GM Hughes Electronic Corporation of Detroit, Michigan. It is involved in the manufacture, research and development of guided missiles and space vehicles. It also produces search, detection, navigation, guidance, aeronautical, and nautical systems and instruments. Worldwide revenues for 1991: $7.8 billion.

- **Total Employees:** 66,000
- **U.S. Employees Abroad:** 90
- **Countries:** Belgium, France, Germany, Italy, Japan, Kenya, Republic of Korea, Saudi Arabia, Spain, Sweden, Switzerland, Thailand, United Kingdom.
- **Job Categories:** Accountants, Engineers, Management, Marketing—Scientific, Sales—Scientific, Technical Design.
- **Language Requirement:** None.

HUGHES CHRISTENSEN COMPANY

PO Box 2539
Houston, TX 77252-2539 USA

RECRUITER: CHUCK HOOSE
PERSONNEL MANAGER
PO BOX 2539
HOUSTON, TX 77252-2539
TEL: (713) 363-6000
FAX: (713) 363-6025

W. A. Kistler, President. Equipment and services to the oil and gas industries. Hughes Christensen is a subsidiary of Baker Hughes, Inc. of Houston, Texas. It services the oil and gas industries and is a manufacturer of oil and gas drilling bits.

- **Total Employees:** 2,000
- **U.S. Employees Abroad:** 40
- **Countries:** Brazil, Colombia, Gabon, Hong Kong, Indonesia, Mexico, Netherlands, Nigeria, Saudi Arabia, Thailand, United Arab Emirates, United Kingdom.
- **Job Categories:** Management, Plant Engineers, Sales—Petroleum/Natural Gas.
- **Average Overseas Assignment:** 2-3 years.
- **Language Requirement:** Knowledge of local language a plus but not essential.
- **Training:** Language training offered.
- **Benefits:** TRAVEL: Thirty days vacation annually. HEALTH: Same as U.S. coverage.

HYATT INTERNATIONAL CORPORATION

200 West Madison St.
Chicago, IL 60606 USA

RECRUITER: WENDY STRACHAN
INTERNATIONAL RECRUITMENT
200 WEST MADISON ST.
CHICAGO, IL 60606
TEL: (312) 750-1234
FAX: (312) 750-8550

Jay Pritzker, Chairman. Hotel management. Hyatt Corporation is a private company founded in 1957. Nicholas Pritzker came to Chicago from Kiev in 1881. During the 1930s, his son, A. N., left the family law practice to invest in a variety of businesses. In 1957, A. N.'s son, Jay, bought a hotel called the Hyatt House, near the Los Angeles airport. By 1961, he had added five more locations and recruited his brother Donald to manage the company. The Pritzker family organized Hyatt International in 1969 for the operation of hotels overseas. Worldwide revenues for 1991: $2.9 billion.

- **Total Employees:** 55,000
- **U.S. Employees Abroad:** 100
- **Countries:** Australia, Hong Kong, Hungary, India, Indonesia, Japan, Republic of Korea, Malaysia, Mexico, New Zealand, Philippines, Saudi Arabia, Singapore, Switzerland, United Arab Emirates, United Kingdom.
- **Application Information:** Hiring for most foreign positions is done at the specific country location.
- **Job Categories:** Accountants, Finance, Marketing—Travel.
- **General Requirements:** Usually must be a current employee of the company in order to qualify for overseas assignment.
- **Language Requirement:** Competency in local language required.
- **Training:** Basic orientation (1-30 days) provided.
- **Benefits:** All benefits are individually determined.

ICF KAISER ENGINEERS

1800 Harrison St.
Oakland, CA 94612 USA

RECRUITER: DOROTHY REIHL
RECRUITMENT/INTERNATIONAL
1800 HARRISON ST.
OAKLAND, CA 94612
TEL: (510) 419-5235
FAX: (510) 419-5355

Carl Aben, Corporate Officer. General and special trade contract services. ICF Kaiser Engineers was founded in 1914 and is a subsidiary of ICF Corporation International of Fairfax, Virginia. It offers clients professional architectural and engineering services in the United States and abroad. Worldwide operating revenues for 1991: $500 million.

- **Total Employees:** 3,600
- **U.S. Employees Abroad:** 25

- **Countries:** Australia, Hong Kong, Portugal, Taiwan, United Kingdom.
- **Job Categories:** Architects, Engineers, Finance.
- **General Requirements:** Usually must be a current employee of the company in order to qualify for overseas assignment.
- **Language Requirement:** None.

IDB COMMUNICATIONS, INC.

10525 West Washington Blvd.
Culver City, CA 90232 USA

RECRUITER: MICHAEL SAUER
VP, INTERNATIONAL CARRIER
SERVICES
IDB WORLDCOM, 67 BROAD ST.
NEW YORK, NY 10004
TEL: (212) 607-2000
FAX: (212) 607-2274

Jeffrey Sudikoff, Chairman. Audio and video transmission signals. IDB Communications, Inc. is a public company founded in 1983. It is a provider of private line services, satellite transmissions, and transmission services for television and radio broadcasting around the world.

- **Total Employees:** 422
- **U.S. Employees Abroad:** 25
- **Countries:** Argentina, Australia, Belgium, Brazil, France, Germany, Japan, Republic of Korea, Singapore, Taiwan, United Kingdom, Venezuela.
- **Job Categories:** Management, Marketing—Electronics, Sales—Electronics.
- **Language Requirement:** Varies with each posting.
- **Training:** Varies with each posting.

ILLINOIS TOOL WORKS, INC.

3600 West Lake Ave.
Glenview, IL 60025-5811 USA

RECRUITER: ILEANA PREZ
MANAGER, HUMAN RESOURCES
3600 WEST LAKE AVE.
GLENVIEW, IL 60025-5811
TEL: (708) 724-7500
FAX: (708) 657-4271

John D. Nichols, Chairman. Engineered components and industrial systems and consumables. Illinois Tool Works, Inc. (ITW), is a public company founded in 1912. Its product line is primarily nuts and bolts with items ranging from fasteners to plastic ring binders. Heavy concentration is placed on research and development with small facility management operations. It has plants throughout the United States and in over 30 foreign countries. Worldwide revenues for 1992: $2.8 billion.

- **Total Employees:** 15,700
- **U.S. Employees Abroad:** Not available.

- **Countries:** Australia, Canada, Italy, Japan, Mexico, Taiwan, United Kingdom, Venezuela.
- **Application Information:** Hiring for most foreign positions is done at the specific country location.
- **Job Categories:** Design, Engineers, Management, Marketing—Industrial, Sales—Industrial.
- **Language Requirement:** Varies with each posting.
- **Benefits:** All benefits are individually determined.
- **Comments:** Decentralized management is the goal at ITW; hiring is done on a case-by-case basis at the specific country location.

IMCERA GROUP, INC.

2315 Sanders Rd.
Northbrook, IL 60062 USA

RECRUITER: SANDRA DORAN
MANAGER, ADMINISTRATION
2315 SANDERS RD.
NORTHBROOK, IL 60062
TEL: (708) 564-8600
FAX: (708) 205-2206

George D. Kennedy, Chairman. Business conglomerate with three business units including specialty chemicals, medical products, and cattle/poultry feed and health products. IMCERA Group, Inc. is a public company founded in 1909. It is divided into three business segments: Mallinckrodt Medical, Mallinckrodt Specialty Chemicals, and Pitman-Moore. The medical sector produces devices used in diagnostics. The specialty chemicals division produces cosmetics and drugs, and Pitman-Moore produces feed for cattle and poultry as well as vaccines and diagnostics for animals. Worldwide revenues for 1992: $1.8 billion.

- **Total Employees:** 10,000
- **U.S. Employees Abroad:** Not available.
- **Countries:** France, Germany, Japan, Mexico, New Zealand, Spain, United Kingdom.
- **Job Categories:** Management, Marketing—Chemicals, Marketing—Scientific, Product Development, Sales—Chemicals, Sales—Scientific.

IMO INDUSTRIES

3450 Princeton Pike
Lawrenceville, NJ 08648 USA

RECRUITER: DAVID CHRISTENSEN
DIRECTOR, HUMAN RESOURCES
3450 PRINCETON PIKE
PO BOX 6550
LAWRENCEVILLE, NJ 08648
TEL: (609) 896-7600
FAX: (609) 896-7688

William J. Holcombe, Chairman. Analytical and optical instruments, electronic and mechanical controls, and engineered power products. IMO Industries is a public company founded in 1901. It designs and produces analytical and optical instruments and electronic, mechanical, and engineered power products. It also provides parts/service for its power products. Worldwide revenues for 1992: $829.2 million.

- **Total Employees:** 8,880
- **U.S. Employees Abroad:** 35
- **Countries:** Australia, Germany, Japan, Netherlands, Singapore, Sweden, Switzerland, United Kingdom.
- **Application Information:** Hiring for most foreign positions is done at the specific country location.
- **Job Categories:** Management, Marketing—Electronics, Product Development, Sales—Electronics.

IMS AMERICA, LTD.

660 West Germantown Pike
Plymouth Meeting, PA 19462
USA

RECRUITER: BETTY BAILEY
DIRECTOR, STAFFING
660 WEST GERMANTOWN PIKE
PLYMOUTH MEETING, PA 19462
TEL: (215) 834-5000

Jeremy Allen, Chief Executive Officer. Market research information. IMS America, Ltd. was founded in 1972 and is a subsidiary of IMS International of New York City. It provides economic, business, market, opinion or related research for commercial markets. Worldwide operating revenues for 1991: $100 million.

- **Total Employees:** 1,500
- **U.S. Employees Abroad:** 15
- **Countries:** Australia, Germany, Italy, Japan, United Arab Emirates.
- **Job Categories:** Accountants, Marketing, Researchers.
- **Language Requirement:** None.

INDUCTOTHERM CORPORATION

10 Indel Ave.
Rancocas, NJ 08073 USA

RECRUITER: FRANCES BROWN
DIRECTOR, HUMAN RESOURCES
10 INDEL AVE.
RANCOCAS, NJ 08073
TEL: (609) 267-9000
FAX: (609) 267-3537

Henry M. Rowan, Jr., President. Induction melting furnaces. Inductotherm Corporation is a private company founded in 1954. It manufactures industrial process furnaces, ovens, heat equipment, and related devices. Worldwide revenues for 1991: $600 million.

- **Total Employees:** 3,000
- **U.S. Employees Abroad:** 25

- **Countries:** Australia, Belgium, Brazil, France, Germany, India, Japan, Taiwan, United Kingdom.
- **Job Categories:** Management, Marketing—Industrial, Technical Field Support.
- **Language Requirement:** Varies with each posting.
- **Training:** None provided.

INFORMATION BUILDERS, INC.

1250 Broadway
New York, NY 10001 USA

RECRUITER: DIANA KESSLER
RECRUITMENT
1250 BROADWAY
NEW YORK, NY 10001
TEL: (212) 736-4433
FAX: (212) 629-3612

Gerald D. Cohen, President. Computer software. Information Builders, Inc. develops, manufactures, and sells computer software and related products with facilities in the United States and abroad. Worldwide revenues for 1991: $191 million.

- **Total Employees:** 1,600
- **U.S. Employees Abroad:** 18
- **Countries:** Australia, Belgium, France, Germany, Netherlands, Spain, Switzerland, United Kingdom.
- **Application Information:** Hiring for most foreign positions is done at the specific country location.
- **Job Categories:** Management, Marketing—Electronics, Product Development, Sales—Electronics.
- **Language Requirement:** None.
- **Training:** Varies with each posting.

INGERSOLL ENGINEERS

1021 North Mulford Rd.
Rockford, IL 61107 USA

RECRUITER: MARY JO MURRAY
HUMAN RESOURCES ADMINISTRATOR
1021 NORTH MULFORD RD.
ROCKFORD, IL 61107
TEL: (815) 395-6440
FAX: (815) 395-6452

Robert L. Callahan, President. Management consultants to industry. Ingersoll Engineers is a private company founded in 1962. Worldwide revenues for 1991: $25 million.

- **Total Employees:** 60
- **U.S. Employees Abroad:** 35
- **Countries:** Australia, France, Germany, Italy, United Kingdom.
- **Job Categories:** Consultants—Management, Finance, Manufacturing.

- **Average Overseas Assignment:** Less than two years.
- **Language Requirement:** Knowledge of local language a plus but not essential.
- **Training:** No special training provided.
- **Benefits:** TRAVEL: Home leave varies according to length and nature of project. HEALTH: Same coverage as U.S. employees. HOUSING: None offered. EDUCATION: None offered.
- **Comments:** Ingersoll engineers work in most industalized countries, depending on project needs.

INGERSOLL INTERNATIONAL, INC.

707 Fulton Ave.
Rockford, IL 61103 USA

RECRUITER: BRIAN HOWARD
MANAGER, HUMAN RESOURCES
707 FULTON AVE.
ROCKFORD, IL 61103
TEL: (815) 987-6000
FAX: (815) 966-7688

Edson I. Gaylor, Chief Executive Officer. Machine cutting tools. Ingersoll International, Inc. is a private company founded in 1980. It manufactures and rebuilds machine-cutting tools and metal-forming machine tools.

- **Total Employees:** 4,500
- **U.S. Employees Abroad:** 35
- **Countries:** Germany, United Kingdom.
- **Job Categories:** Manufacturing, Marketing—Industrial, Sales—Industrial.
- **Language Requirement:** None.

INGERSOLL-RAND COMPANY

200 Chestnut Ridge Rd.
Woodcliff Lake, NJ 07675 USA

RECRUITER: DONNA VANDERMARK
MANAGER, INT'L SALARIED
ADMINISTRATION
200 CHESTNUT RIDGE RD.
WOODCLIFF LAKE, NJ 07675
TEL: (201) 573-3138
FAX: (201) 573-3168

Theodore H. Black, President and Chairman. Industrial machinery and equipment. Ingersoll-Rand is a public company founded in 1905, when Simon Ingersoll joined efforts with three Rand brothers, Albert, Jasper, and Addison. All had been involved with the invention and production of drills. Years later, the company began producing air compressors as well as rock drills. Today, it is an international manufacturer that owns 81 plants around the globe. Worldwide revenues for 1992: $3.8 billion.

- **Total Employees:** 36,000
- **U.S. Employees Abroad:** 50

- **Countries:** Belgium, Brazil, People's Republic of China, France, Germany, Indonesia, Italy, Japan, Singapore, United Kingdom, Venezuela.

- **Application Information:** Chief recruiter varies with each location. Contact company for more information.

- **Job Categories:** Engineers, Finance, Marketing—Industrial, Sales—Industrial.

- **Average Overseas Assignment:** 3-5 years.

- **Language Requirement:** Knowledge of local language a plus but not essential.

- **Training:** No special training provided.

- **Benefits:** TRAVEL: Four weeks every other year. HEALTH: Local insurance mandated by government. HOUSING: Housing differentials for U.S. employees. EDUCATION: Offered; paid tuition, uniforms, and transportation.

INTEL CORPORATION

3065 Bowers Ave.
Santa Clara, CA 95052 USA

RECRUITER: CARLENE M. ELLIS
DIRECTOR, HUMAN RESOURCES
3065 BOWERS AVE.
SANTA CLARA, CA 95052
TEL: (408) 765-8080
FAX: (408) 765-3979

Andrew S. Grove, President. Semiconductors; designs, develops, and produces microcomputer components and related items. Intel Corporation is a public company founded in 1968 by three PhD engineers from Fairchild Semiconductor. They began with 12 employees and concentrated on large-scale integration (LSI) technology for silicon-based chips. Today, the x86 chip designs provide the brains for over 75 percent of all existing desktop computers. Intel has manufacturing plants in the United States and in seven foreign countries with sales and distribution sites on a global scale. Worldwide revenues for 1992: $5.8 billion.

- **Total Employees:** 23,900

- **U.S. Employees Abroad:** 60

- **Countries:** Japan, Israel, Malaysia, Philippines, Singapore, United Kingdom.

- **Job Categories:** Accountants, Marketing—Electronics, Product Development, Sales—Electronics.

- **Language Requirement:** None.

INTERGRAPH CORPORATION

Mail Stop-IW-2000
Huntsville, AL 35894-0001 USA

RECRUITER: DAVE NAWROCKI
STAFFING/RECRUITMENT
MAIL STOP-IW-2000
HUNTSVILLE, AL 35894-0001
TEL: (205) 730-2164
FAX: (205) 730-7252

James M. Meadlock, Chairman. Computer hardware. Intergraph Corporation is a public company founded in 1969 when James Meadlock, his wife Nancy, Terry Schantzman, and other former IBM employees formed M & S Computing in Huntsville, Alabama. Concentration in the architectural, engineering, and construction markets followed in the 1970s and today the company ranks 1 in this area on a worldwide basis. Products are sold in more than 40 countries with operating units in the United States and abroad. Worldwide revenues for 1992: $1.2 billion.

- **Total Employees:** 10,300
- **U.S. Employees Abroad:** 45
- **Countries:** Canada, Hong Kong, Kuwait, Netherlands.
- **Job Categories:** Engineers, Design, Management, Marketing—Electronics, Sales—Electronics.
- **General Requirements:** College degree in related area preferred.
- **Language Requirement:** Varies with each posting.

INTERNATIONAL BUSINESS MACHINES (IBM)

44 South Broadway
White Plains, NY 10601-4495
USA

RECRUITER: CAROL MCCABE
MANAGER, INTERNATIONAL
ASSIGNMENTS
44 SOUTH BROADWAY
WHITE PLAINS, NY 10601-4495
TEL: (914) 642-3000

John F. Akers, Chairman. Information systems, products, and solutions. IBM is a public company founded in 1914 by Thomas J. Watson. He left the National Cash Register Company to save the Computing-Tabulating-Recording Company and manufactured punch card tabulator machines. He expanded the operations to other countries in 1924 and changed the company name to IBM. Soon after, IBM dominated the market for tabulators, time clocks, and electric typewriters. Today, it is the largest producer of computers throughout the world. Worldwide revenues for 1992: $64.5 billion.

- **Total Employees:** 350,000
- **U.S. Employees Abroad:** 700
- **Countries:** Worldwide including Argentina, Australia, Belgium, Bermuda, Bolivia, Canada, Chile, France, Germany, Hong Kong, Israel, Japan, Netherlands, Panama, Singapore, Turkey, United Kingdom.
- **Application Information:** Hiring for most foreign positions is done at the specific country location.
- **Job Categories:** Executive Management, Management, Technicians.
- **General Requirements:** Must be experienced in IBM practices and qualified to perform or train local staff to perform.
- **Average Overseas Assignment:** 2-3 years.
- **Language Requirement:** Knowledge of local language a plus but not essential.

- **Training:** None provided.

- **Benefits:** TRAVEL: Round-trip economy air fare offered annually to employee and dependents. HEALTH: Same coverage as U.S. employees. HOUSING: Offered; employee receives an allowance to cover housing costs comparable to U.S. coverage. EDUCATION: Offered.

INTERNATIONAL DAIRY QUEEN, INC.

5701 Green Valley Rd.
Minneapolis, MN 55437 USA

RECRUITER: MARK LOWDER
VP, INTERNATIONAL
5701 GREEN VALLEY RD.
MINNEAPOLIS, MN 55437
TEL: (612) 830-0200
FAX: (612) 830-0450

Michael P. Sullivan, President. Snack restaurants franchising. International Dairy Queen, Inc. is a public company founded in 1940 with the opening of the first Dairy Queen franchise in Joliet, Illinois. By 1960, the number of establishments reached 3,000 throughout the United States and abroad. Today, it operates 6,055 restaurants in more than 15 countries. Worldwide revenues for 1991: $287 million.

- **Total Employees:** 592

- **U.S. Employees Abroad:** Not available.

- **Countries:** Canada, Japan, United Kingdom.

- **Job Categories:** Accountants, Management, Marketing—Food/Food Services.

- **Language Requirement:** Varies with each posting.

INTERNATIONAL DATA GROUP, INC.

5 Speen St.
Framingham, MA 01701 USA

RECRUITER: MARY CORNETTA
HUMAN RESOURCES
5 SPEEN ST.
FRAMINGHAM, MA 01701
TEL: (508) 875-5000
FAX: (508) 935-4600

Patrick J. McGovern, Chief Executive Officer. Computer magazines publishing. International Data Group is a private company founded in 1954. It is divided into into four business sectors: publications, market research, trade expositions, and book publishing. Published titles include: *Computer World* and *Network World Newsweekly*. It operates in the United States and titles are sold in 40 countries. Worldwide revenues for 1991: $650 million.

- **Total Employees:** 3,800

- **U.S. Employees Abroad:** 45

- **Countries:** Republic of South Africa, Malaysia, Poland, Russia, Thailand, Turkey.

- **Job Categories:** Accountants, Journalists, Management, Marketing—Publishing, Sales—Publishing.
- **General Requirements:** Usually must be a current employee of the company in order to qualify for overseas assignment.
- **Language Requirement:** Knowledge of local language a plus but not essential.
- **Training:** No special training provided.
- **Benefits:** All benefits are individually determined.

INTERNATIONAL FLAVORS & FRAGRANCES, INC.

521 West 57th St.
New York, NY 10019 USA

RECRUITER: WILLIAM MEYERS, JR.
CORPORATE DIRECTOR, EMPLOYEE
RELATIONS
521 WEST 57TH ST.
NEW YORK, NY 10019
TEL: (212) 765-5500
FAX: (212) 708-7119

Eugene P. Grisanti, President and Chairman. Synthetic tastes and aromas. International Flavors & Fragrances is a public company founded in 1909 when Dutch immigrant and perfumer A. L. van Ameringen and William Haebler formed van Ameringen-Haebler in New York. In 1958, the company purchased a Dutch firm and the result was a combined new name of International Flavors & Fragrances. Today, it is a producer of perfumes, cosmetics, and household cleaners. It sells its products to various marketers including Proctor & Gamble and Estee Lauder. It has operations in over 20 countries. Worldwide revenues for 1992: $1.1 billion.

- **Total Employees:** 4,100
- **U.S. Employees Abroad:** 25
- **Countries:** Argentina, Australia, Brazil, Canada, Hong Kong, Indonesia, Italy, Japan, Mexico, Netherlands, Turkey, United Kingdom.
- **Job Categories:** Accountants, Management, Marketing, Product Development, Sales.
- **Language Requirement:** Knowledge of local language a plus but not essential.

INTERNATIONAL MARITIME RESOURCES

PO Box 120
Miami Beach, FL 33139 USA

RECRUITER: DIRECTOR
PERSONNEL DEPARTMENT
PO BOX 120
MIAMI BEACH, FL 33139
TEL: (305) 672-6453
FAX: (305) 531-1805

M. D. Burke, President. Ship chandler. International Maritime Resources is the exclusive ship chandler for Windjammer Barefoot Cruises.

- **Total Employees:** 300

- **U.S. Employees Abroad:** 15

- **Countries:** Grenada, Bahamas.

- **Application Information:** Letter of introduction, resume, and recent photo is required.

- **Salaries:** $150-$1,000 per month.

- **Job Categories:** Bartenders, Chefs, Engine Room Staff, Pursers, Seamen, Stewards.

- **General Requirements:** Hard-working and self-motivated; pursers must be nurses.

- **Language Requirement:** Must be fluent in English.

- **Training:** Onboard training.

- **Benefits:** TRAVEL: Individually determined. HEALTH: None offered. HOUSING: Room and board included. EDUCATION: Reimbursement up to $1,000 (U.S.).

INTERNATIONAL PAPER COMPANY

2 Manhattanville Rd.
Purchase, NY 10577 USA

RECRUITER: JANE RIDGLEY
MANAGER, SALARIED COMPENSATION PROGRAMS
INTERNATIONAL PLACE I, 6400 POPLAR AVE.
MEMPHIS, TN 38197
TEL: (901) 763-6000
FAX: (914) 397-1695

John A. Georges, Chairman. Paper and wood pulp. International Paper is a public company founded in 1898 when 18 pulp and paper companies comined to achieve lower operating costs. The result was 20 mills operating in various states. Today, the company is a world leader in the production of integrated paper. It ranks number 1 as a producer of bleached board, which is used in milk and food packaging. It has operations in over 20 countries and its products are sold around the globe. Worldwide revenues for 1992: $13.6 billion.

- **Total Employees:** 69,000

- **U.S. Employees Abroad:** 40

- **Countries:** Australia, Canada, Colombia, Hong Kong, Netherlands, Philippines, Sweden, Taiwan, Venezuela, United Kingdom.

- **Job Categories:** Executive Management, Marketing, Sales.

- **General Requirements:** Usually a current employee with International Paper Company experience.

- **Language Requirement:** None.

INTERNATIONAL RECTIFIER CORPORATION

233 Kansas St.
El Segundo, CA 90245 USA

RECRUITER: MOLLY DESSERT
MANAGER, EMPLOYMENT
233 KANSAS ST.
EL SEGUNDO, CA 90245
TEL: (310) 322-3331
FAX: (310) 607-8865

Eric Lidow, President. Semi-conductors. International Rectifier Corporation is a public company founded in 1947. It develops and manufactures power semi-conductors, with operations in the United States and abroad. Worldwide revenues for 1992: $281 million.

- **Total Employees:** 2,970
- **U.S. Employees Abroad:** 125
- **Countries:** Canada, Italy, Japan, Republic of Korea, Mexico, United Kingdom.
- **Job Categories:** Engineers, Management, Marketing—Scientific, Sales—Scientific.
- **Language Requirement:** Knowledge of local language a plus but not essential.
- **Training:** Basic orientation (1-30 days) provided.
- **Benefits:** All benefits are individually determined.

INTERNATIONAL TOTALIZATOR SYSTEMS, INC.

2131 Faraday Ave.
Carlsbad, CA 92008 USA

RECRUITER: RONALD DAVIDSON
DIRECTOR, PERSONNEL
ADMINISTRATION
2131 FARADAY AVE.
CARLSBAD, CA 92008
TEL: (619) 931-4000
FAX: (619) 931-1789

James T. Walters, President and Chairman. Customized ticketing systems. International Totalizer Systems, Inc. is a public company founded in 1978. It designs, produces, and markets ticketing systems for computerized wagering, lotteries, and the airline industry. It has operations in the United States and abroad. Worldwide revenues for 1991: $29.5 million.

- **Total Employees:** 225
- **U.S. Employees Abroad:** 20
- **Countries:** Australia, Norway, Singapore, United Kingdom.
- **Job Categories:** Marketing—Electronics, Sales—Electronics.
- **Language Requirement:** None.

INTERTRANS CORPORATION

125 East John Carpenter Freeway
Irving, TX 75063 USA

RECRUITER: STEVEN HANNAH
RECRUITMENT/EMPLOYEE RELATIONS
125 EAST JOHN CARPENTER
   FREEWAY
IRVING, TX 75063
TEL: (214) 830-8888
FAX: (214) 830-8869

M. Keith McKinney, Jr., President. Global transportation services. Intertrans Corporation is a public company engaged in worldwide transportation services, including ocean and air freight forwarding and customs brokerage. It also provides crating and packing services. It owns no planes or ships but arranges cost-effective shipping through commercial markets. Worldwide operating revenues for 1991: $161.1 million.

- **Total Employees:** 1,000
- **U.S. Employees Abroad:** 30
- **Countries:** Brazil, Hong Kong, Japan.
- **Job Categories:** Accountants, Clerical Assistants, Finance, Marketing.
- **Language Requirement:** None.

IOMEGA CORPORATION

1821 West Iomega Way
Roy, UT 84067 USA

RECRUITER: GALE HAMELWRIGHT
SENIOR VP, HUMAN RESOURCES
1821 WEST IOMEGA WAY
ROY, UT 84067
TEL: (801) 778-3225
FAX: (801) 778-4201

Fred Wenninger, President. Removable mass storage devices, disc drives, tape drives. Iomega Corporation is a public company incorporated in Delaware in 1980. It designs, produces, and sells market data storage devices in the United States and abroad. Worldwide revenues for 1991: $136.6 million.

- **Total Employees:** 1,150
- **U.S. Employees Abroad:** 5
- **Countries:** Germany, United Kingdom.
- **Job Categories:** Management, Marketing—Electronics, Sales—Electronics.
- **Average Overseas Assignment:** 2-3 years.
- **Language Requirement:** Competency in local language required.
- **Training:** Language training provided.
- **Benefits:** TRAVEL: One week per year paid home leave. HEALTH: Offered. HOUSING: Offered. EDUCATION: Individually determined.
- **Comments:** The number of Americans working abroad varies greatly from quarter to quarter, fluctuating with the number and scope of projects under contract at the time.

ITT CORPORATION

1330 Avenue of the Americas
New York, NY 10019 USA

RECRUITER: LYNDA SUSSMAN
DIRECTOR, INTERNATIONAL
PERSONNEL
1330 AVENUE OF THE AMERICAS
NEW YORK, NY 10019
TEL: (212) 258-1000
FAX: (212) 258-1297

Rand V. Araskog, President and Chairman. International telecommunications conglomerate. ITT Corporation is a public company founded in 1920 by Colonel Sosthenes Behn. This diversified company has interests that include communications services, defense projects, electronics, and insurance. Worldwide revenues for 1992: $21.7 billion.

- **Total Employees:** 119,000
- **U.S. Employees Abroad:** 125
- **Countries:** Worldwide including Australia, Brazil, Finland, France, Germany, Hong Kong, Japan, Mexico, Nigeria, Netherlands, Sweden, Taiwan, Turkey, United Kingdom, Zambia.
- **Job Categories:** Executive Management, Finance, Marketing—Telecommunications, Sales—Telecommunications.
- **General Requirements:** Usually must be a current employee of the company in order to qualify for overseas assignment.
- **Comments:** Company does not actively recruit for foreign job postings.

ITT HARTFORD INSURANCE GROUP

1 Hartford Plaza
Hartford, CT 06115 USA

RECRUITER: JERRY CLAIR
MANAGER, CORPORATE STAFFING
1 HARTFORD PLAZA
HARTFORD, CT 06115
TEL: (203) 547-5385
FAX: (203) 547-2680

Donald R. Frahm, Chairman. Insurance services. ITT Hartford Insurance Group is a subsidiary of ITT Corporation of New York City. It offers property, casualty, and life insurance, as well as reinsurance and insurance services to clients in the United States and abroad. Worldwide assets for 1992: $40 billion.

- **Total Employees:** 21,350
- **U.S. Employees Abroad:** Not available.
- **Countries:** Australia, Belgium, France, Germany, Hong Kong, Netherlands, Spain, Taiwan, United Kingdom.
- **Job Categories:** Accountants, Marketing—Financial Services.
- **General Requirements:** International insurance experience, with marketing or financial expertise.

- **Language Requirement:** Proficiency in English and a second major language required.
- **Training:** Varies with each posting.
- **Benefits:** Vary with each posting.

ITT SHERATON CORPORATION

60 State St.
Boston, MA 02108 USA

RECRUITER: JEFFREY CAVA
STAFFING, HUMAN RESOURCES
60 STATE ST.
BOSTON, MA 02108
TEL: (617) 367-5506
FAX: (617) 367-5676

John Kapioltas, President. Holding company; operator of hotels/motels. ITT Sheraton is a subsidiary of the ITT Corporation of New York City. It acts as a holding company, controlling the companies' activities. It operates hotels/motels around the globe. Worldwide operating revenues for 1991: $717 million.

- **Total Employees:** 125,000
- **U.S. Employees Abroad:** Not available.
- **Countries:** Worldwide including Argentina, Australia, Brazil, Canada, Chile, Hong Kong, India, Israel, Japan, Spain, Venezuela, United Kingdom.
- **Application Information:** Hiring for most foreign positions is done at the specific country location. Direct inquiries to recruiter's address for a copy of a worldwide directory.
- **Job Categories:** Finance, Management, Marketing—Travel.
- **Language Requirement:** Varies with each posting.
- **Training:** Varies with each posting.

ITW FINISHING SYSTEMS & PRODUCTS

3939 West 56th St.
Indianapolis, IN 46254 USA

RECRUITER: ILEANA PREZ
MANAGER, CORPORATE HUMAN
RESOURCES
3600 WEST LAKE AVE.
GLENVIEW, IL 60025-5811
TEL: (708) 724-7500
FAX: (708) 657-4271

Coating and engraving services. ITW Finishing Systems & Products, Inc. was founded in 1948 and is a subsidiary of Illinois Tool Works, Inc. of Glenview, Illinois. It was formerly known as the Ransburg Corporation. It is a provider of coating, engraving, and related services to the metal industry. This includes electrostatic coating systems. Worldwide assets for 1991: $188.8 million.

- **Total Employees:** 1,200

- **U.S. Employees Abroad:** Not available.
- **Countries:** Australia, Brazil, France, Germany, Italy, Japan, Netherlands, Spain, Switzerland, United Kingdom.
- **Application Information:** Hiring for most foreign positions is done at the specific country location.
- **Job Categories:** Management, Marketing, Sales.
- **Language Requirement:** Varies with each posting.
- **Training:** No special training provided.
- **Benefits:** All benefits are individually determined.
- **Comments:** Management is decentralized for ITW subsidiaries.

JAMES RIVER CORPORATION

120 Tredegar St.
Richmond, VA 23219 USA

RECRUITER: LARRY OLSZEWSKI
DIRECTOR, HUMAN RESOURCES
120 TREDEGAR ST.
RICHMOND, VA 23219
TEL: (804) 649-4430
FAX: (804) 649-4340

Robert C. Williams, President. Consumer products and packaging. James River Corporation was originally founded as a private company in 1969 by Ethyl executives, Brenton Halsey and Robert Williams. The company went public in 1973. Today, it manufactures and markets consumer products, food and consumer packaging, and consumer-related communications papers. Brand names include Dixie cups and Northern bath tissue. It has facilities throughout the United States and in more than 10 foreign countries. Worldwide revenues for 1992: $4.7 billion.

- **Total Employees:** 38,000
- **U.S. Employees Abroad:** 15
- **Countries:** Canada, France, Italy, Mexico, Turkey, United Kingdom.
- **Job Categories:** Management, Marketing—Consumer Goods, Marketing, Sales—Consumer Goods, Sales.
- **General Requirements:** Usually must be a current employee of the company in order to qualify for overseas assignment.
- **Language Requirement:** Knowledge of local language a plus but not essential.

JMK INTERNATIONAL/JAMACK FABRICATIONS, INC.

1401 North Bowie Rd.
Weatherford, TX 76086 USA

RECRUITER: JOHN DUSZA
HUMAN RESOURCES ADMINISTRATOR
1401 NORTH BOWIE RD.
WEATHERFORD, TX 76086
TEL: (815) 594-8771
FAX: (815) 594-8324

Alfred M. Micallef, President. Rubber gaskets and seals. JMK International/Jamack Fabrications is a private company organized in 1971 and incorporated on October 4, 1985. It manufactures silicone rubber, synthetic rubber, and fabricated rubber products, including gaskets and seals. Worldwide revenues for 1991: $42 million.

- **Total Employees:** 400
- **U.S. Employees Abroad:** 12
- **Countries:** Canada, United Kingdom.
- **Job Categories:** Management, Marketing, Sales.
- **Language Requirement:** None.
- **Training:** Varies with each posting.

JOHNSON CONTROLS, INC.

507 East Michigan St.
Milwaukee, WI 53202 USA

RECRUITER: BEVERLY EDWARDS
INTERNATIONAL HUMAN RESOURCES
507 EAST MICHIGAN ST.
MILWAUKEE, WI 53202
TEL: (414) 274-4625
FAX: (414) 228-4200

James H. Keyes, President. Control systems, automotive seating systems, batteries, and plastic beverage containers. Johnson Controls is a public company founded in 1885 as the Johnson Electric Service Company. The business diversified through the years and an international division was begun in 1960. The company was renamed Johnson Controls Inc. in 1974 and today, its products are manufactured and sold around the globe. Worldwide revenues for 1992: $5.5 billion.

- **Total Employees:** 43,000
- **U.S. Employees Abroad:** 70
- **Countries:** Belgium, Canada, Germany, Italy, Mexico, Netherlands, United Kingdom.
- **Job Categories:** Accountants, Engineers, Marketing—Electronics, Product Development, Sales—Electronics.

JOHNSON & HIGGINS

125 Broad St.
New York, NY 10004 USA

RECRUITER: MARGE HOWES
HUMAN RESOURCES
125 BROAD ST.
NEW YORK, NY 10004
TEL: (212) 574-7000
FAX: (212) 574-7039

Robert V. Hatcher, Jr., Chief Executive Officer. Insurance services. Johnson & Higgins is a private company founded in 1845. It operates as an independent insurance and brokerage firm, offering services to the insurance industry in the United States and abroad. Worldwide revenues for 1991: $690 million.

C
O
M
P
A
N
Y

L
I
S
T
I
N
G
S

- **Total Employees:** 7,600
- **U.S. Employees Abroad:** 40
- **Countries:** Argentina, Brazil, Hong Kong, Italy, Japan, Saudi Arabia, Taiwan, Venezuela.
- **Job Categories:** Agents—Insurance, Brokers—Securities & Financial, Management, Marketing—Financial Services.
- **Language Requirement:** Varies with each posting.
- **Training:** None provided.

JOHNSON & JOHNSON

1 Johnson & Johnson Plaza
New Brunswick, NJ 08901 USA

RECRUITER: MICHAEL LONGUA
DIRECTOR, INTERNATIONAL
  RECRUITMENT
1 JOHNSON & JOHNSON PLAZA
NEW BRUNSWICK, NJ 08901
TEL: (908) 524-3454
FAX: (908) 524-2587

Ralph S. Larsen, Chairman. Health care products; pharmaceuticals for consumer and hospital markets. Johnson & Johnson is a public company founded in 1885 by brothers James and Edward Johnson in New Brunswick, New Jersey. Today, this company is a leader in the consumer and pharmaceutical industries. Over half of its business concentrates on products other than drugs. These include diagnostic equipment, monitors, and other medical items. Well-known brand names include Tylenol and Johnson & Johnson baby products. It has over 190 facilities in the United States and abroad. Worldwide revenues for 1992: $3.8 billion.

- **Total Employees:** 83,000
- **U.S. Employees Abroad:** 90
- **Countries:** Worldwide including Argentina, Chile, Canada, Costa Rica, France, Hong Kong, Hungary, India, Indonesia, Italy, Poland, Taiwan, United Kingdom, Yugoslavia.
- **Job Categories:** Chemists, Management, Marketing—Health & Medical Supplies, Marketing—Pharmaceuticals, Product Development, Sales—Health & Medical Supplies, Sales—Pharmaceuticals.
- **Language Requirement:** Varies with each posting.

S. C. JOHNSON WAX

1525 Howe St.
Racine, WI 53403 USA

RECRUITER: AUDREY DITTER
INTERNATIONAL RECRUITMENT
1525 HOWE ST.
RACINE, WI 53403
TEL: (414) 631-2000
FAX: (414) 631-4951

Samuel C. Johnson, Chairman. Personal care products, laundry aids, and cleaners. S. C. Johnson Wax is a private company founded in 1886. It is one of the largest consumer-products companies in the United States today. Well-known brands include Agree shampoo, Edge shaving items, Glade air freshener, and Raid insect repellent. It has operations in 48 countries. Worldwide revenues for 1991: $3.4 billion.

- **Total Employees:** 13,000

- **U.S. Employees Abroad:** 30

- **Countries:** Belgium, Canada, Japan, Singapore.

- **Job Categories:** Executive Management, Marketing—Consumer Goods, Product Development, Sales—Consumer Goods.

- **Language Requirement:** Varies with each posting.

JONES, DAY, REAVIS & POGUE, INC.

901 Lakeside Dr.
Cleveland, OH 44114 USA

RECRUITER: MICHAEL H. CARPENTER
CHAIRMAN, RECRUITMENT
1900 HUNTINGTON CENTER
COLUMBUS, OH 43215
TEL: (216) 586-3939
FAX: (216) 579-0212

Richard W. Pogue, Managing Partner. Legal services. Jones, Day, Reavis & Pogue is a private firm founded in 1893. Currently, it has over 1,000 attorneys and offices in the United States and abroad. Categories include corporate, government, regulation, litigation, real estate consulting, and tax. Worldwide operating revenues for 1991: $390 million.

- **Total Employees:** 1,400

- **U.S. Employees Abroad:** 65

- **Countries:** Belgium, France, Hong Kong, Japan, Saudi Arabia, Switzerland, United Kingdom.

- **Job Categories:** Attorneys, Legal Personnel.

- **Language Requirement:** Competency in local language required.

- **Training:** None provided.

- **Benefits:** All benefits are individually determined.

JOURNAL OF COMMERCE

2 World Trade Center
New York, NY 10048 USA

RECRUITER: NANCY SCHLAKE
HUMAN RESOURCES DEPARTMENT
445 MARSHALL ST.
PHILLIPSBURG, NJ 08865
TEL: (908) 454-6293
FAX: (908) 454-6912

Don C. Becker, Publisher. Newspapers. Journal of Commerce is a private company founded in 1827. It is a subsidiary of Knight-Ridder, Inc. of Miami, Florida. It publishes and prints newspapers in the United States and abroad. Worldwide revenues for 1991: $35.1 million.

- **Total Employees:** 615

- **U.S. Employees Abroad:** Not available.

- **Countries:** Japan, United Kingdom.

- **Salaries:** $48,000-$70,000.

- **Job Categories:** Reporters.

- **Average Overseas Assignment:** Five years or more.

- **Language Requirement:** Competency in local language required.

- **Training:** No special training provided.

- **Benefits:** TRAVEL: Offered; cost of relocation and return trip to U.S. 1-2 times per year. HEALTH: Same coverage as U.S. employees (Indemnity Plan 10/80/20 coverage). HOUSING: None offered. EDUCATION: None offered.

- **Comments:** The number of Americans working abroad varies greatly from quarter to quarter, fluctuating with the number and scope of projects under contract at the time.

JOY TECHNOLOGIES, INC.

301 Grant St.
Pittsburgh, PA 15219 USA

RECRUITER: FRANK E. JOYCE
VP, HUMAN RESOURCES
301 GRANT ST.
PITTSBURGH, PA 15219
TEL: (412) 562-4500
FAX: (412) 562-4548

Marc Wray, President and Chairman. Mining machinery and equipment; other industrial products. Joy Technologies is a public company founded in 1919. It produces mining machinery, industrial and commercial fans, and air purification equipment for heating, cooling, or ventilation systems. Worldwide revenues for 1991: $608.6 million.

- **Total Employees:** 4,300

- **U.S. Employees Abroad:** 20

- **Countries:** Australia, Saudi Arabia, United Kingdom.

- **Job Categories:** Marketing—Industrial, Sales—Industrial.

- **Language Requirement:** None.

- **Training:** None provided.

JWP, INC.

6 International Dr.
Rye Brook, NY 10573-1058 USA

RECRUITER: SUSAN GARELLI
SENIOR VP, HUMAN RESOURCES
6 INTERNATIONAL DR.
RYE BROOK, NY 10573-1058
TEL: (914) 935-4000
FAX: (914) 935-4141

Andrew T. Dwyer, Chairman. Technical solutions, mechanical and electrical information services for the energy and environmental fields. JWP is a public company founded in 1950. It provides technical services to various industries including energy and environmental projects as well as water supply and distribution systems. It operates 120 offices on an international basis. Worldwide revenues for 1992: $4.2 billion.

- **Total Employees:** 22,000

- **U.S. Employees Abroad:** 75

- **Countries:** Worldwide including Canada, France, Germany, Japan, United Kingdom.

- **Job Categories:** Administrative, Finance, Management, Marketing—Electronics, Marketing—Scientific, Sales—Electronics, Sales—Scientific.

- **Language Requirement:** None.

- **Training:** Basic orientation (1-30 days) provided.

- **Benefits:** All benefits are individually determined.

KAMAN CORPORATION

PO Box 1
Bloomfield, CT 06002 USA

RECRUITER: DEBRA RUSSELL
CORPORATE PERSONNEL
PO BOX 1
BLOOMFIELD, CT 06002
TEL: (203) 243-8311
FAX: (203) 249-7922

Charles H. Kaman, President and Chairman. Aviation and aerospace products. Kaman Corporation is a public company founded in 1945. It designs and produces components for defense and commercial airline industries. It also provides aircraft maintenance service and distributes over 850,000 industrial products and 5,000 musical instruments and related products. Worldwide revenues for 1992: $783 million.

- **Total Employees:** 5,544

- **U.S. Employees Abroad:** Not available.

- **Countries:** Canada, France, United Kingdom.

- **Job Categories:** Management, Marketing, Product Development.

- **Language Requirement:** None.

KAYSER-ROTH CORPORATION

4905 Koger Blvd.
Greensboro, NC 27407 USA

RECRUITER: TOM O'SHEA
VICE PRESIDENT, HUMAN
   RESOURCES
4905 KOGER BLVD.
GREENSBORO, NC 27407
TEL: (919) 852-2030
FAX: (919) 547-4634

Bob Seelert, President. Cloth, clothing, legwear. Kayser-Roth Corporation was founded in 1911 and is a subsidiary of Collins & Aikman Group, Inc. of New York City. It manufactures broadwoven cotton cloth and operates knitting mills. It is also involved in producing shirts for boys and men.

- **Total Employees:** 8,000
- **U.S. Employees Abroad:** Not available.
- **Countries:** Germany.
- **Job Categories:** Management, Marketing—Consumer Goods, Sales—Consumer Goods.
- **Language Requirement:** None.

A. T. KEARNEY, INC.

222 South Riverside Plaza
Chicago, IL 60606 USA

RECRUITER: WILLIAM SEITHEL
VP, HUMAN RESOURCES
222 SOUTH RIVERSIDE DR.
CHICAGO, IL 60606
TEL: (312) 993-8935
FAX: (312) 648-1939

Fred G. Steingraber, President. Management consultants. A. T. Kearney is a private company founded in 1926. It offers clients management consulting services in the United States and abroad. Worldwide operating revenues for 1991: $178 million.

- **Total Employees:** 1,200
- **U.S. Employees Abroad:** 18
- **Countries:** Belgium, Canada, Germany, Italy, Japan, United Kingdom.
- **Job Categories:** Consultants—Management, Finance, Marketing.
- **Training:** No special training provided.

KEITHLEY INSTRUMENTS, INC.

28775 Aurora Rd.
Solon, OH 44139 USA

RECRUITER: BRUCE W. HARRIS
HUMAN RESOURCES MANAGER
28775 AURORA RD.
SOLON, OH 44139
TEL: (216) 248-0400
FAX: (216) 248-6168

Thomas G. Brick, President. Electronic measurements for researchers, universities, and manufacturers. Keithley Instruments is a public company founded in 1945. It designs and produces state-of-the-art instrumentation for researchers, universities, laboratories, and electronic manufacturers. These instruments accurately measure volts, amps, and currents at extremely low levels. Worldwide revenues for 1993: $91 million.

- **Total Employees:** 708
- **U.S. Employees Abroad:** 3
- **Countries:** Germany, Japan.
- **Salaries:** $40,000 (plus) per year.
- **Job Categories:** Finance, Marketing—Electronics, Sales—Electronics.
- **Average Overseas Assignment:** 2-3 years.
- **Language Requirement:** Fluency in local language preferred.
- **Training:** No special training; subsidized language training.
- **Benefits:** TRAVEL: Annual home leave after one year overseas. Paid air fare, along with incidental en-route expenses. HEALTH: Offered. HOUSING: Offered; this includes furniture, appliances, and utilities except phone. EDUCATION: Tuition is paid for at English-speaking school.

KELLOGG COMPANY

1 Kellogg Square
PO Box 3599
Battle Creek, MI 49016-3599
USA

RECRUITER: ROBERT L. CREVISTON
SENIOR VP, HUMAN RESOURCES
1 KELLOGG SQUARE
PO BOX 3599
BATTLE CREEK, MI 49016-3599
TEL: (616) 961-2000
FAX: (616) 961-2871

Arnold G. Langbo, Chairman. Food products. Kellogg is a public company founded in 1906 by William Keith Kellog. It was originally called the Battle Creek Toasted Corn Flake Company. Today, it is the world's leading producer of ready-to-eat cereal products. It also produces frozen pies and waffles, cereal bars, and other convenience foods. Currently, it has production facilities in 17 countries and distributes in more than 150 countries throughout the world. Worldwide revenues for 1992: $6.7 billion.

- **Total Employees:** 16,500
- **U.S. Employees Abroad:** 50
- **Countries:** Argentina, Australia, Brazil, Colombia, Denmark, Germany, Guatemala, Italy, Japan, Mexico, Saudi Arabia, Republic of Korea, Spain, United Kingdom, Venezuela.
- **Job Categories:** Administrative, Finance, Management, Product Development, Sales—Food/Food Services.
- **Language Requirement:** Varies with each posting.

M. W. KELLOGG COMPANY

3 Greenway Plaza
PO Box 4557
Houston, TX 77046 USA

RECRUITER: CHERYL FUTCH
HUMAN RESOURCES
3 GREENWAY PLAZA
PO BOX 4557
HOUSTON, TX 77046
TEL: (713) 960-2000
FAX: (713) 960-2032

Donald C. Vaughn, President. Design, engineering, and construction services for process and energy industries. M. W. Kellogg Company was founded in 1901 and is a subsidiary of Dresser Industries of Dallas, Texas. It acts as general and special trade contractors for heavy construction jobs. Worldwide operating revenues for 1991: $308 million.

- **Total Employees:** 2,400
- **U.S. Employees Abroad:** 25
- **Countries:** Argentina, Cayman Islands, People's Republic of China, Indonesia, Malaysia, Singapore, United Kingdom.
- **Job Categories:** Contractors, Engineers, Executive Management.
- **Language Requirement:** Varies with each posting.

KELLWOOD COMPANY

PO Box 14374
Saint Louis, MO 63178 USA

RECRUITER: JIM MAYS
EMPLOYMENT RELATIONS DIRECTOR
PO BOX 14374
SAINT LOUIS, MO 63178
TEL: (314) 576-3100
FAX: (314) 576-3462

William J. McKenna, President. Clothing, home fashions, and camping soft goods. Kellwood is a public company founded in 1961. It has operations in 10 states and eight foreign countries and produces such items as shirts and blouses, wool sweaters, bedspreads, and sleeping bags. Brand names include Robert Scott Ltd., and Tuftee labels. Worldwide revenues for 1992: $917 million.

- **Total Employees:** 15,750
- **U.S. Employees Abroad:** 20
- **Countries:** Hong Kong, United Kingdom.
- **Job Categories:** Management, Marketing—Consumer Goods, Sales—Consumer Goods.
- **Language Requirement:** None.

KELSEY-HAYES COMPANY

38481 Huron River Dr.
Romulus, MI 48174 USA

RECRUITER: BILL ZIUKEWICH
PERSONNEL DIRECTOR
38481 HURON RIVER DR.
ROMULUS, MI 48174
TEL: (313) 941-2000
FAX: (313) 941-2230

John F. DeVaney, President. Automobile parts. Kelsey-Hayes was founded in 1909 and is a subsidiary of the K-H Corporation of Romulus, Michigan. It produces motor vehicle parts and related accessories. Worldwide revenues for 1991: **$900 million.**

- **Total Employees:** 6,200
- **U.S. Employees Abroad:** 20
- **Countries:** Canada, Mexico, Venezuela.
- **Job Categories:** Management, Manufacturing, Marketing—Automotive, Sales—Automotive.
- **Language Requirement:** None.
- **Training:** No special training provided.

KENDALL INTERNATIONAL

15 Hampshire St.
Mansfield, MA 02048 USA

RECRUITER: LISA CHAYET
EMPLOYMENT MANAGER
15 HAMPSHIRE ST.
MANSFIELD, MA 02048
TEL: (508) 261-8125
FAX: (508) 261-8105

Ervin Shames, President. Medical products. Kendall International is a private company founded in 1904. It manufactures medical products and supplies for wound care, vascular therapy, urology, and specialty products markets, including hospitals and health care facilities. Worldwide revenues for 1991: **$730 million.**

- **Total Employees:** 9,150
- **U.S. Employees Abroad:** 12
- **Countries:** Malaysia, Mexico, Thailand, United Kingdom, Venezuela.
- **Application Information:** Do not call.
- **Job Categories:** Management, Manufacturing, Marketing—Health & Medical Supplies, Sales—Health & Medical Supplies.
- **Average Overseas Assignment:** 2-3 years.
- **Language Requirement:** Knowledge of local language a plus but not essential.
- **Training:** No special training provided.
- **Benefits:** TRAVEL: Competitive relocation packages offered. HEALTH: Competetive benefits offered. HOUSING: Competetive benefits offered. EDUCATION: Offered.

- **Comments:** The number of Americans working abroad varies greatly from quarter to quarter, fluctuating with the number and scope of projects under contract at the time.

KENNAMETAL, INC.

PO Box 231
Latrobe, PA 15650 USA

RECRUITER: JOHN JAMISON
HUMAN RESOURCES MANAGER
PO BOX 231
LATROBE, PA 15650
TEL: (412) 539-5000
FAX: (412) 539-5745

Robert L. McGeehan, President. Tools and supplies for the metalworking and construction industries. Kennemetal is a public company founded in 1938. It produces and distributes tools, tooling systems, and products for metalworking, coal mining, and construction industries. Worldwide revenues for 1992: $595 million.

- **Total Employees:** 5,000
- **U.S. Employees Abroad:** 25
- **Countries:** Germany, Japan, Republic of Korea, Thailand, United Kingdom.
- **Job Categories:** Management, Marketing—Industrial, Sales—Industrial.
- **General Requirements:** Usually must be a current employee of the company in order to qualify for overseas assignment.
- **Average Overseas Assignment:** 3-5 years.
- **Language Requirement:** Knowledge of local language a plus but not essential.
- **Training:** Basic orientation (1-30 days) provided.
- **Benefits:** TRAVEL: Individually determined. HEALTH: Same coverage as U.S. employees. HOUSING: Individually determined. EDUCATION: Individually determined.

KENNECOTT CORPORATION

10 East South Temple
Salt Lake City, UT 84133 USA

RECRUITER: SHERRY MCCLOUD
SENIOR ASSISTANT, HUMAN
    RESOURCES
10 EAST SOUTH TEMPLE
SALT LAKE CITY, UT 84133
TEL: (801) 322-7000
FAX: (801) 322-8160

G. F. Joklik, President. Mining. Kennecott Corporation was incorporated on March 8, 1989. It is engaged in copper mining and the preparation for and mining of other minerals and metals, including gold ore. Worldwide revenues for 1991: $930 million.

- **Total Employees:** 3,500
- **U.S. Employees Abroad:** 50
- **Countries:** Australia, Canada, United Kingdom.
- **Application Information:** Most foreign positions are filled internally.

- **Job Categories:** Engineers, Marketing, Sales.
- **Language Requirement:** None.
- **Training:** No special training provided.

KETCHUM INTERNATIONAL

1133 Avenue of the Americas
New York, NY 10036 USA

RECRUITER: SHARON M. RIBER
INTERNATIONAL OPERATIONS
1133 AVENUE OF THE AMERICAS
NEW YORK, NY 10036
TEL: (212) 536-8800
FAX: (212) 768-2152

David Drobis, President. Advertising and public relations. Ketchum International was founded in 1970 and is a subsidiary of Ketchum Communications, Inc. of Pennsylvania. Worldwide gross billings for 1991: $978.8 million.

- **Total Employees:** 150
- **U.S. Employees Abroad:** 20
- **Countries:** France, Germany, Hong Kong, Japan, United Kingdom.
- **Job Categories:** Administrative, Marketing, Sales—Advertising.
- **Language Requirement:** None.
- **Training:** No special training provided.

KEYSTONE INTERNATIONAL

96 West Gulf Bank
PO Box 40010
Houston, TX 77040 USA

RECRUITER: KATHY RUF
HUMAN RESOURCES
96 WEST GULF BANK
PO BOX 40010
HOUSTON, TX 77040
TEL: (713) 466-1176

Raymond A. LeBlanc, Chairman. Flow control products. Keystone International is a public company founded in 1947. It produces flow control devices, which regulate the flow of liquids, gases, and solid materials for various operations from food processing to power generation. Worldwide revenues for 1991: $520.5 million.

- **Total Employees:** 3,350
- **U.S. Employees Abroad:** 25
- **Countries:** Australia, Germany, Hong Kong, Mexico, Netherlands, Singapore, United Arab Emirates, United Kingdom.
- **Job Categories:** Management, Manufacturing, Marketing—Industrial, Sales—Industrial.
- **Language Requirement:** Varies with each posting.

KFC CORPORATION

PO Box 32070
Louisville, KY 40232 USA

RECRUITER: OLDEN LEE
SENIOR VP, HUMAN RESOURCES
PO BOX 32070
LOUISVILLE, KY 40232
TEL: (502) 456-8393
FAX: (502) 454-2195

John M. Cranor III, President and Chairman. Global operator of eating establishments. KFC (Kentucky Fried Chicken) was founded in 1939 and is a subsidiary of PepsiCo, Inc. of Somers, New York. It operates restaurants and owns or leases franchises, patents, and copyrights that are licensed to others. Worldwide revenues for 1991: $6.7 billion.

- **Total Employees:** 160,000
- **U.S. Employees Abroad:** 125
- **Countries:** Worldwide including Canada, People's Republic of China, France, Hong Kong, Hungary, Kuwait, Malaysia, Mexico, United Kingdom.
- **Application Information:** Hiring for most foreign positions is done at the specific country location.
- **Job Categories:** Finance, Management, Management Training, Marketing—Food/Food Services, Sales—Food/Food Services.
- **Language Requirement:** Varies with each posting.

KIDDER PEABODY GROUP & COMPANY, INC.

60 Broad St.
New York, NY 10004 USA

RECRUITER: JOSEPH M. LUCIANO
VP, PROFESSIONAL RECRUITING &
    PLACEMENT
60 BROAD ST.
NEW YORK, NY 10004
TEL: (212) 656-1509
FAX: (212) 656-1541

Michael L. Carpenter, Chairman. Brokerage and investment banking services. Kidder Peabody Group & Company was founded in 1865 and is a subsidiary of General Electric Capital Corporation of Stamford, Connecticut. Worldwide operating revenues for 1991: $3.3 billion.

- **Total Employees:** 5,000
- **U.S. Employees Abroad:** 40
- **Countries:** France, Hong Kong, Italy, Japan, Switzerland, United Kingdom.
- **Job Categories:** Executive Management.
- **Language Requirement:** None.
- **Training:** No special training provided.
- **Benefits:** All benefits are individually determined.

KIMBALL INTERNATIONAL, INC.

1600 Royal St.
Jasper, IN 47549 USA

RECRUITER: KATHY SUTTON
DIRECTOR, CORPORATE
RECRUITMENT
1600 ROYAL ST.
JASPER, IN 47549
TEL: (812) 482-1600
FAX: (812) 482-8803

Thomas L. Habig, Chairman. Office furniture and consumer goods. Kimball International is a public company founded in 1950. It manufactures consumer items and other goods for other manufacturing companies. Well-known brand names include Kimball pianos and National office furniture. Worldwide revenues for 1992: $624 million.

- **Total Employees:** 7,700
- **U.S. Employees Abroad:** 25
- **Countries:** Austria, Mexico, United Kingdom.
- **Job Categories:** Management, Marketing, Sales.
- **Language Requirement:** None.
- **Training:** No special training provided.

KIMBERLY-CLARK CORPORATION

PO Box 619100
Dallas, TX 75261-9100 USA

RECRUITER: GLENN GUTHRIE
INTERNATIONAL RECRUITMENT
PO BOX 2001
NEENAH, WI 54956
TEL: (414) 721-2000
FAX: (414) 721-4315

Darwin E. Smith, Chairman. Paper and fiber products for personal and industrial use. Kimberly-Clark is a public company founded in 1872 when John Kimberly, Charles Clark, Havilah Babcock, and Frank Shattuck established Kimberly Clark & Company in Neenah, Wisconsin, to produce newsprint from rags. Its present name was adopted in 1928. Its headquarters moved to Dallas, Texas, in 1985. Today, the product line includes barber toweling, business paper, disposable diapers, and newsprint. Worldwide revenues for 1992: $7.1 billion.

- **Total Employees:** 39,954
- **U.S. Employees Abroad:** 25
- **Countries:** Australia, Brazil, Canada, France, Germany, Indonesia, Mexico, Netherlands, Thailand, United Kingdom.
- **Job Categories:** Management, Marketing—Consumer Goods, Marketing, Product Development, Sales—Consumer Goods, Sales.
- **General Requirements:** Usually must be a current employee of the company in order to qualify for overseas assignment.

KINNEY SHOE CORPORATION

233 Broadway
New York, NY 10279 USA

RECRUITER: JOHN KOZLOWSKI
HUMAN RESOURCES DEPARTMENT
233 BROADWAY
NEW YORK, NY 10279
TEL: (212) 720-3700
FAX: (212) 720-4695

Harold C. Rowen, President. Footwear and related apparel. Kinney Shoe Corporation was founded in 1894 and is a subsidiary of F. W. Woolworth Company of New York City. It operates shoe stores in the United States and abroad. Worldwide revenues for 1991: $2.8 billion.

- **Total Employees:** 30,000
- **U.S. Employees Abroad:** Not available.
- **Countries:** Australia, Canada.
- **Job Categories:** Marketing—Consumer Goods, Sales—Consumer Goods.
- **Language Requirement:** None.
- **Training:** No special training provided.

KLYNVELD PEAT MARWICK GOERDELER (KPMG)

3 Chestnut Ridge Rd.
Montvale, NJ 07645 USA

RECRUITER: JUDY CROSSAN
DIRECTOR, PERSONNEL
ADMINISTRATION
3 CHESTNUT RIDGE RD.
MONTVALE, NJ 07645
TEL: (201) 307-7749
FAX: (201) 307-7086

Barry Baird, President. Accounting and consulting services. KPMG is a private company founded in 1987 when Peat, Marwick, Mitchell, and co-partners joined KMG, a global federation of accounting firms. Currently, KPMG is owned by 6,300 partners and is the biggest of the Big 6 accounting firms. It operates throughout the United States and has facilities in over 100 foreign countries. Worldwide revenues for 1991: $6.0 billion. Foreign revenues for 1991: $3.8 billion.

- **Total Employees:** 75,000
- **U.S. Employees Abroad:** 150
- **Countries:** Worldwide including Czech Republic, France, Germany, Hungary, Japan, Poland, Switzerland.
- **Job Categories:** Accountants, Consultants—Management, Financial Advisors.
- **General Requirements:** Usually must be a current employee of the company in order to qualify for overseas assignment
- **Language Requirement:** Varies with each job posting.
- **Training:** No special training required.

A
M
E
R
I
C
A
N

J
O
B
S

A
B
R
O
A
D

- **Benefits:** All benefits are individually determined.

KNIGHT-RIDDER, INC.

1 Herald Plaza
Miami, FL 33132 USA

RECRUITER: REBECCA BAYBROOK-
HECKENBACH
HUMAN RESOURCES ADMINISTRATOR
1 HERALD PLAZA
MIAMI, FL 33132
TEL: (305) 376-3800
FAX: (305) 995-8164

James K. Batten, Chairman. Newspaper publishing and information services. Knight-Ridder, Inc. was formed in 1974 from a merger of Knight Newspapers and Ridder Publications. Today, it publishes 29 daily newspapers including the *Journal of Commerce*, an international business newspaper. Information services includes DIALOG, the nucleus of its electronic publishing business. Other services offer on-line access to information including market data. Worldwide revenues for 1992: $2.3 billion.

- **Total Employees:** 21,000

- **U.S. Employees Abroad:** 35

- **Countries:** Australia, France, Germany, Hong Kong, Japan, United Kingdom.

- **Job Categories:** Finance, Management, Marketing—Publishing.

- **Language Requirement:** None.

- **Training:** No special training provided.

KNOLL INTERNATIONAL

655 Madison Ave.
New York, NY 10021 USA

RECRUITER: MARCIA THOMPSON
DIRECTOR, HUMAN RESOURCES
WATER ST.
EAST GREENVILLE, PA 18041
TEL: (215) 679-7991

Marshall S. Cogan, Chairman. Furniture and related products. Knoll International is a private company founded in 1974. It manufactures wooden office furniture and plastic foam products. Worldwide revenues for 1991: $673.3 million.

- **Total Employees:** 5,500

- **U.S. Employees Abroad:** Not available.

- **Countries:** Argentina, Belgium, Canada, Chile, France, Germany, Hong Kong, Italy, Japan, Netherlands, United Kingdom.

- **Job Categories:** Management, Marketing, Sales.

KOCH INDUSTRIES, INC.

PO Box 2256
Wichita, KS 67201 USA

RECRUITER: TAMARA JUST
COORDINATOR OF PROFESSIONAL
EMPLOYMENT
PO BOX 2256
WICHITA, KS 67201
TEL: (316) 832-5500
FAX: (316) 832-5913

Charles Koch, Chief Executive Officer. Chemical production and oil refining. Koch Industries is a private company founded in 1942. Its former name was Wood River Oil & Refining Company. Today, it is engaged in oil refining, coal mining, chemical manufacturing, and petroleum exploration. Worldwide revenues for 1991: $15 billion.

- **Total Employees:** 12,000
- **U.S. Employees Abroad:** Not available.
- **Countries:** France, Germany, Hong Kong, Italy, Japan, Republic of Korea, Singapore, Spain.
- **Application Information:** Hiring for most foreign positions is done at the specific country location.
- **Job Categories:** Management, Marketing—Chemicals, Marketing—Petroleum/Natural Gas, Sales—Chemicals, Sales—Petroleum/Natural Gas.
- **Language Requirement:** Varies with each posting.
- **Comments:** Koch Industries utilizes a decentralized hiring procedure.

KOHLER COMPANY

444 Highland Dr.
Kohler, WI 53044 USA

RECRUITER: RICHARD HOMISTON
PERSONNEL DIRECTOR
444 HIGHLAND DR.
KOHLER, WI 53044
TEL: (414) 457-4441
FAX: (414) 459-1583

Herbert V. Kohler, Jr., President and Chairman. Plumbing and specialty products, power systems, furniture, and hospitality services. Kohler is a private company founded in 1873 by Austrian immigrant, John Kohler. Today, it is one of the leading manufacturers of ceramic toilet bowls, sinks, and bathtubs. Worldwide revenues for 1991: $1 billion.

- **Total Employees:** 14,200
- **U.S. Employees Abroad:** 11
- **Countries:** Australia, France, Japan, United Kingdom.
- **Job Categories:** Engineers, Marketing.
- **Average Overseas Assignment:** 3-5 years.
- **Language Requirement:** Fluency in local language required.

- **Training:** Basic orientation (1-30 days) provided.
- **Benefits:** TRAVEL: Individually determined. HEALTH: Offered; coverage with specific country plan. HOUSING: Individually determined. EDUCATION: Individually determined.
- **Comments:** The number of Americans working abroad varies greatly from quarter to quarter, fluctuating with the number and scope of projects under contract at the time.

KOLMAR LABORATORIES, INC.

PO Box 1111
Port Jervis, NY 12771 USA

RECRUITER: NANCY PORTER
DIRECTOR, HUMAN RESOURCES
PO BOX 1111
PORT JERVIS, NY 12771
TEL: (914) 856-5311
FAX: (914) 856-3143

Richard Hossman, Chairman. Contract manufacturer of cosmetics, household items, and pharmaceuticals. Kolmar Laboratories Inc. is a subsidiary of Canadian-based CCL Industries. Worldwide revenues for 1991: $140 million.

- **Total Employees:** 1,500
- **U.S. Employees Abroad:** Not available.
- **Countries:** Australia, Canada, France, Germany, Japan, Mexico, Thailand.
- **Application Information:** Hiring for most foreign positions is done at the specific country location.
- **Job Categories:** Chemists, Marketing, Research & Development, Technical Field Support.
- **Language Requirement:** Knowledge of local language a plus but not essential.
- **Training:** Varies with each posting; language training offered in some cases.
- **Benefits:** All benefits are individually determined.

KORN/FERRY INTERNATIONAL

237 Park Ave.
New York, NY 10017 USA

RECRUITER: STEPHANIE ROSENFELT
HUMAN RESOURCES
237 PARK AVE.
NEW YORK, NY 10017
TEL: (212) 687-1834
FAX: (212) 661-0612

Richard M. Ferry, President and Chairman. Global executive search firm for large corporations. Korn/Ferry International is a private company founded in 1969. The firm covers all major industries for executive search. It operates throughout the United States and abroad.

- **Total Employees:** 500
- **U.S. Employees Abroad:** 50

- **Countries:** Austria, Argentina, Belgium, Brazil, Canada, Colombia, France, Germany, Hungary, Hong Kong, Italy, Japan, Malaysia, Mexico, Singapore, Spain, Switzerland, Thailand, United Kingdom, Venezuela.
- **Salaries:** Minimum of $100,000 per year.
- **Job Categories:** Executive Recruiters, Finance, Management.
- **Language Requirement:** Varies with each posting.
- **Training:** No special training provided.
- **Benefits:** All benefits are individually determined.

KRAFT GENERAL FOODS INTERNATIONAL

800 Westchester Ave.
Rye Brook, NY 10573 USA

RECRUITER: SUSAN HOLSNECK
MANAGER, EXPATRIATE PROGRAM
800 WESTCHESTER AVE.
RYE BROOK, NY 10573
TEL: (914) 335-1626
FAX: (914) 335-1468

John M. Keenan, President. Food products. Kraft General Foods International is a subsidiary of Philip Morris Companies, Inc. of New York City. Products that it manufactures and markets include coffee, cheese, and other food items. Popular brand names are Maxim freeze-dried and ground/roast coffee, Kraft tomato ketchup, and Yoplait yogurt. International Food accounted for 15 percent of operating revenues for 1992. $10.7 billion.

- **U.S. Employees Abroad:** Not available.
- **Countries:** Australia, Colombia, France, Germany, Greece, Hungary, Japan, Netherlands, Spain, Switzerland, Venezuela.
- **Job Categories:** Administrative, Marketing—Food/Food Services, Product Development, Sales—Food/Food Services.
- **Language Requirement:** Knowledge of local language a plus but not essential.

THE KULJIAN COMPANY

3700 Science Center
Philadelphia, PA 19104 USA

RECRUITER: ROBERT E. BALLARD
VICE PRESIDENT
3700 SCIENCE CENTER
PHILADELPHIA, PA 19104
TEL: (215) 243-1900
FAX: (215) 243-1909

Arthur H. Kuljian, President. Engineering, design, and consulting services for the power, desalination, and cement industries. Kuljian is a private company founded in 1930 and has been operating internationally for 40 years. It offers services throughout the United States and abroad.

- **Total Employees:** 200

- **U.S. Employees Abroad:** 20
- **Countries:** Egypt, Saudi Arabia.
- **Salaries:** $35,000-$70,000 per year.
- **Job Categories:** Architects, Construction Workers, Design, Engineers, Maintenance.
- **General Requirements:** Middle East experience is a plus.
- **Average Overseas Assignment:** 2-3 years.
- **Language Requirement:** Knowledge of local language a plus but not essential.
- **Training:** Basic training (1-30 days) provided.
- **Benefits:** TRAVEL: Offered; single status: 1-3 trips per year, duration 30 days total; married status: annual family trips, duration 30 days total. HEALTH: Blue Cross/Blue Shield for employee only; family is co-pay coverage. HOUSING: Offered or monthly substance is paid. EDUCATION: Not offered.
- **Comments:** Foreign postings include personnel with experience in power, desalination, or cement industries.

KYSOR INDUSTRIAL CORPORATION

1 Madison Ave.
Cadillac, MI 49601 USA

RECRUITER: TIMOTHY PETERSON
INTERNATIONAL OPERATIONS
1 MADISON AVE.
CADILLAC, MI 49601
TEL: (616) 775-3950
FAX: (616) 775-3950

George R. Kempton, Chairman. Industrial products and systems. Kysor Industrial Corporation is a public company founded in 1925. It produces heavy-duty vehicle and marine components, refrigerated display containers, and other building systems. Kysor has plant facilities in the United States and in two foreign countries. Sales offices are located throughout the world. Worldwide revenues for 1992: $262 million.

- **Total Employees:** 2,085
- **U.S. Employees Abroad:** 22
- **Countries:** Belgium, Germany.
- **Job Categories:** Marketing—Industrial, Office Management, Sales—Industrial.
- **Language Requirement:** None.
- **Training:** No special training provided.

L. A. GEAR, INC.

4221 Redwood Ave.
Los Angeles, CA 90066 USA

RECRUITER: CAROLYN HARPER
HUMAN RESOURCES
4221 REDWOOD AVE.
LOS ANGELES, CA 90066
TEL: (213) 822-1995
FAX: (213) 822-0843

Stanley P. Gold, Chairman. Leisure footwear and athletic-style clothing. L. A. Gear was founded as a private company in 1983 by Robert Greenberg. He began L. A. Gear, a women's clothing store in Los Angeles, and soon the company expanded. The company went public in 1986, and today it produces athletic shoes and sports-related clothing for both men and women. It is the 3rd largest U.S. producer of athletic shoes. It sells merchandise in over 100 countries. Worldwide revenues for 1992: $430.2 million.

- **Total Employees:** 750
- **U.S. Employees Abroad:** 25
- **Countries:** Republic of Korea, Taiwan, Venezuela.
- **Job Categories:** Finance, Marketing—Consumer Goods, Product Development, Sales—Consumer Goods.
- **Language Requirement:** None.
- **Training:** No special training provided.

LAMBDA ELECTRONICS, INC.

515 Broad Hollow Rd.
Melville, NY 11747 USA

RECRUITER: ARNOLD FRIEDLAND
PERSONNEL DIRECTOR
515 BROAD HOLLOW RD.
MELVILLE, NY 11747
TEL: (516) 694-4200
FAX: (516) 752-2666

Allen E. Bueching, President. Power supplies, semiconductors, and test equipment. Lambda Electronics was founded in 1946 and is a subsidiary of Veeco Instruments. It produces electric power converters and operates in the United States and abroad. Worldwide revenues for 1991: $3 million.

- **Total Employees:** 3,000
- **U.S. Employees Abroad:** 20
- **Countries:** Canada, France, Germany, Israel, Japan, Republic of Korea, Singapore, United Kingdom.
- **Job Categories:** Marketing—Electronics, Sales—Electronics.

LAW COMPANIES GROUP, INC.

1000 Abernathy Rd. NE
Atlanta, GA 30328 USA

RECRUITER: R. F. HEIGHTCHEW
CORPORATE RECRUITMENT
1000 ABERNATHY RD. NE
ATLANTA, GA 30328
TEL: (404) 396-8000
FAX: (404) 396-0291

R. K. Sehgal, Chairman. Professional architects and engineers. Law Companies Group is a private company that provides professional arcitectural and engineering services in the United States and abroad. Worldwide revenues for 1991: $400 million.

- **Total Employees:** 3,400
- **U.S. Employees Abroad:** 30
- **Countries:** Saudi Arabia, Spain, United Kingdom.
- **Application Information:** International headquarters is located in London.
- **Job Categories:** Architects, Engineers, Marketing.
- **Language Requirement:** None.

LAWTER INTERNATIONAL, INC.

909 Skokie Blvd.
Northbrook, IL 60062 USA

RECRUITER: SUE VOLLMER
DIRECTOR, EMPLOYMENT
909 SKOKIE BLVD.
NORTHBROOK, IL 60062
TEL: (708) 498-4700
FAX: (708) 498-0082

Daniel J. Terra, Chairman. Inorganic pigments and related products. Lawter International, Inc. is a public company founded in 1958. It manufactures inorganic pigments, synthetic resins, plastic materials, and printing ink. A major product is Top Gun 142, an acid-gum fountain solution. Worldwide revenues for 1992: $167.6 million.

- **Total Employees:** 485
- **U.S. Employees Abroad:** 16
- **Countries:** Australia, Belgium, Canada, People's Republic of China, Denmark, Germany, Italy, Republic of Korea, Netherlands Antilles, Singapore, United Kingdom.
- **Job Categories:** Management, Marketing—Chemicals, Sales—Chemicals.

LEVI STRAUSS ASSOCIATES, INC.

1115 Battery St.
San Francisco, CA 94111 USA

RECRUITER: KATHY BORNSTEIN
PERSONNEL MANAGER
1115 BATTERY ST.
SAN FRANCISCO, CA 94111
TEL: (415) 544-6000
FAX: (415) 544-1468

Robert D. Haas, Chairman. Apparel. Levi Strauss Associates is a private company founded in 1873 by Levi Strauss and Jacob Davis. They produced the first pair of Levi's Patent Riveted 501 Waist High Overalls. The 2-horse patch, on the back of each pair, was started in 1886. The company prospered through the years and went public in 1971. But, the family felt the tradition was declining and took the company private in 1985. Today, Levi Strauss is the world's largest apparel manufacturer and the 2nd largest U.S. jeans producer. It has 34 production facilities in the United States and 15 plants in foreign countries. Worldwide revenues for 1991: $4.9 billion. Foreign revenues for 1991: $1.9 billion.

- **Total Employees:** 32,000

- **U.S. Employees Abroad:** 75
- **Countries:** Australia, Belgium, Brazil, Canada, France, Germany, Hong Kong, Italy, Japan, Malaysia, Mexico, Philippines, Sweden, Switzerland.
- **Job Categories:** Administrative, Finance, Marketing—Consumer Goods, Product Development, Sales—Consumer Goods.
- **Language Requirement:** Varies with each posting.

LIANT SOFTWARE CORPORATION

959 Concord St.
Framingham, MA 01701-4613
USA

RECRUITER: ARNOLD SALVATORE
HUMAN RESOURCES
   REPRESENTATIVE
959 CONCORD ST.
FRAMINGHAM, MA 10701-4613
TEL: (508) 626-0006
FAX: (508) 626-2221

Roy A. Finney, Chief Executive Officer. Intergrated programming systems. Liant Software is a private company founded in 1980. It offers intergrated programming sytems in the construction of portable applications for clients throughout the world. Worldwide revenues for 1991: $20 million.

- **Total Employees:** 160
- **U.S. Employees Abroad:** 20
- **Countries:** Germany, Japan, United Kingdom.
- **Job Categories:** Management, Marketing—Electronics, Sales—Electronics.
- **Language Requirement:** None.
- **Training:** No special training provided.

THE LIMITED, INC.

2 Limited Pkwy.
PO Box 16000
Columbus, OH 43216 USA

RECRUITER: MARLA KRUPMAN
STAFFING/RECRUITMENT
100 OLD RIVER RD.
ANDOVER, MA 01810
TEL: (508) 794-0660

Leslie H. Wexner, President and Chairman. Women's fashions and related items. The Limited is a public company founded in 1963. It began as a single store in 1963 and has grown to 3,864 stores in the United States and Europe. It was privately held until 1969. Retail clothing divisions include Victoria's Secret, Lane Bryant, and Lerner. Worldwide revenues for 1992: $6.9 billion.

- **Total Employees:** 100,000
- **U.S. Employees Abroad:** Not available.
- **Countries:** Italy, United Kingdom.

- **Application Information:** Mast Industries is a division of The Limited that operates internationally.

- **Job Categories:** Marketing—Consumer Goods, Sales—Consumer Goods.

THE LINCOLN ELECTRIC COMPANY

22801 St. Clair Ave.
Cleveland, OH 44117 USA

RECRUITER: RICHARD SABO
DIRECTOR, HUMAN RESOURCES
22801 ST. CLAIR AVE.
CLEVELAND, OH 44117
TEL: (216) 481-8100
FAX: (216) 486-1751

George E. Willis, Chairman. Arc-welding products. Lincoln Electric is a private company founded in 1895. It was incorporated in 1906. In 1989 the company joined with GMF Robotics to enter the automated welding industry. Major products include electric motors, gas motors, and Welden Power welder/generators. Worldwide revenues for 1992: $862.3 million.

- **Total Employees:** 2,600

- **U.S. Employees Abroad:** Not available.

- **Countries:** Australia, Brazil, Canada, France, Japan, Mexico, United Kingdom.

- **Job Categories:** Management, Marketing—Industrial, Sales—Industrial.

- **General Requirements:** Usually must be a current employee of the company in order to qualify for overseas assignment.

LINTAS: WORLDWIDE

1 Dag Hammerskjold Plaza
New York, NY 10017 USA

RECRUITER: GARY BILLINGS
INTERNATIONAL RECRUITMENT
1 DAG HAMMERSKJOLD PLAZA
NEW YORK, NY 10017
TEL: (212) 605-8000
FAX: (212) 486-8099

William Weithas, President. Advertising agency. Lintas was founded in 1979 and is a subsidiary of Interpublic Group of Companies of New York City. Worldwide gross billings for 1991: $4.9 billion.

- **Total Employees:** 690

- **U.S. Employees Abroad:** 30

- **Countries:** Argentina, Belgium, Canada, France, Germany, Hong Kong, India, Saudi Arabia, Sweden, Switzerland, United Kingdom, Venezuela.

- **Job Categories:** Management, Marketing, Sales—Advertising.

- **Language Requirement:** Varies with each posting.

- **Training:** No special training provided.

LIQUID CARBONIC CORPORATION

135 South LaSalle St.
Chicago, IL 60603 USA

RECRUITER: JIM MORGAN
EMPLOYEE RELATIONS
135 SOUTH LASALLE ST.
CHICAGO, IL 60603
TEL: (312) 855-2500
FAX: (312) 855-2797

Robert J. Daniels, President. Compressed gases. Liquid Carbonic Corporation was founded in 1888 and is a subsidiary of CBI Industries of Oak Brook, Illinois. It is engaged as a manufacturer of industrial gases for sale in compressed, liquid, or solid forms. Worldwide revenues for 1991: $980 million.

- **Total Employees:** 5,300

- **U.S. Employees Abroad:** 24

- **Countries:** Argentina, Bolivia, Brazil, Colombia, Republic of Korea, Mexico, Peru, Venezuela.

- **Job Categories:** Office Management, Marketing—Industrial, Sales—Industrial.

- **Language Requirement:** Varies with each posting.

ARTHUR D. LITTLE, INC.

25 Acorn Park
Cambridge, MA 02140 USA

RECRUITER: DIANA FAHEY
DIRECTOR, HUMAN RESOURCES
25 ACORN PARK
CAMBRIDGE, MA 02140
TEL: (617) 864-5770

Charles R. LaMantia, President. Technology and management consulting. Arthur D. Little is a private company founded in 1885. It provides management consulting services to clients in the United States and abroad. Worldwide operating revenues for 1991: $318 million.

- **Total Employees:** 2,260

- **U.S. Employees Abroad:** 30

- **Countries:** Belgium, Brazil, Canada, France, Germany, Saudi Arabia, Spain, United Kingdom.

- **Job Categories:** Executive Management, Financial Advisors.

- **Language Requirement:** Varies with each posting.

- **Training:** No special training provided.

A
M
E
R
I
C
A
N

J
O
B
S

A
B
R
O
A
D

LITTON INDUSTRIES, INC.

360 North Crescent Dr.
Beverly Hills, CA 90210 USA

RECRUITER: KAREN R. SMITH
PERSONNEL DIRECTOR
360 NORTH CRESCENT DR.
BEVERLY HILLS, CA 90210
TEL: (310) 859-5940
FAX: (310) 859-5940

Orion L. Hoch, Chairman. Advanced electronics, industrial automation systems/products, marine engineering/production, and resource exploration services. Litton Industries is a public company founded by Charles "Tex" Thornton in 1953. He began Electro Dynamics to meet the demand for updated, technologically advanced, military products after the war years. He purchased Litton Industries and added eight smaller companies in the same year. It went public in 1954 and today, it has 50 locations throughout the world. Worldwide revenues for 1992: $5.6 billion.

- **Total Employees:** 50,000
- **U.S. Employees Abroad:** 10,000
- **Countries:** Algeria, Argentina, Australia, Belgium, Bolivia, Brazil, Canada, People's Republic of China, Egypt, France, Germany, Hong Kong, Italy, Japan, Republic of Korea, Mexico, Netherlands, Norway, Saudi Arabia, Singapore, Spain, Switzerland, Taiwan, United Kingdom, Venezuela.
- **Application Information:** Hiring for foreign positions is done at the specific country location; applicant should consult local unit.
- **Job Categories:** Engineers, Technicians.
- **Language Requirement:** Varies with each posting.
- **Training:** Varies with each posting.
- **Benefits:** Vary with each posting.
- **Comments:** Refer to local directory for Litton Divisions operating overseas. No hiring is done from the Corporate Office in Beverly Hills, California.

LIZ CLAIBORNE, INC.

1441 Broadway
New York, NY 10018 USA

RECRUITER: REMY NICHOLAS
INTERNATIONAL RECRUITMENT
1441 BROADWAY
NEW YORK, NY 10018
TEL: (212) 354-4900
FAX: (212) 626-5471

Jerome A. Chazen, Chairman. Clothing and accessories for women. Liz Claiborne began as a private company in 1976. Dress designer Liz Claiborne joined her husband Arthur Ortenberg, and two other partners, Jerome Chazen and Leonard Boxer, to start Liz Claiborne, Inc. It went public in 1981 and in 1986, after 10 years of growth, sales reached over $800 million. Today, it is the largest producer of clothing and related items for the working woman. Worldwide revenues for 1992: $2.2 billion.

- **Total Employees:** 6,000
- **U.S. Employees Abroad:** 35
- **Countries:** Brazil, Canada, People's Republic of China, Hong Kong, Philippines, Republic of Korea, Taiwan, United Kingdom.
- **Job Categories:** Design, Finance, Marketing—Consumer Goods, Product Development, Sales—Consumer Goods.
- **Language Requirement:** Knowledge of local language a plus but not essential.
- **Training:** No special training provided.

LOCKHEED CORPORATION

4500 Park Granada Blvd.
Calabasas, CA 91302 USA

RECRUITER: PATRICIA A. MURPHY
CORPORATE EMPLOYEE RELATIONS
4500 PARK GRANADA BLVD.
CALABASAS, CA 91302
TEL: (818) 712-2000
FAX: (818) 876-2416

Danial M. Tellep, Chairman. Aerospace. Lockheed is a public company that began in 1926 as Lockheed Aircraft. New owners Robert Gross, Carl Squier, and Lloyd Stearman, purchased the company in 1932. Today, Lockheed is the 6th largest defense contractor and the biggest defense R & D contractor in the United States. Worldwide revenues for 1992: $10 billion.

- **Total Employees:** 71,000
- **U.S. Employees Abroad:** 500
- **Countries:** Worldwide including Saudi Arabia.
- **Application Information:** Hiring for most foreign positions is done at the specific country location.
- **Salaries:** Individually determined.
- **Job Categories:** Management, Marketing—Scientific, Sales—Scientific.
- **Language Requirement:** None.
- **Training:** No special training provided.
- **Benefits:** All benefits are individually determined.

LOCTITE CORPORATION

Hartford Square North
10 Columbus Blvd.
Hartford, CT 06106 USA

RECRUITER: DON ATENCIO
VICE PRESIDENT, HUMAN
RESOURCES
705 NORTH MOUNTAIN RD.
NEWINGTOM, CT 06111
TEL: (203) 280-3552
FAX: (203) 280-3820

Kenneth W. Butterworth, Chairman. Adhesives and sealants. Loctite Corporation is a public company founded in 1956 by Vernon Krieble as the American Sealants Company. It became the Loctite Corporation in 1963. It produces industrial and household adhesives and sealants. A well-known product is Super Glue. Worldwide revenues for 1992: $608 million.

- **Total Employees:** 3,670
- **U.S. Employees Abroad:** 40
- **Countries:** Worldwide including Argentina, Australia, Austria, Brazil, Chile, Costa Rica, Germany, Hong Kong, Japan, Republic of Korea, Mexico, Netherlands, Thailand, United Kingdom, Venezuela.
- **Job Categories:** Marketing—Chemicals, Office Management, Sales—Chemicals.
- **Training:** Varies with each posting.

LORAL CORPORATION

600 Third Ave.
New York, NY 10016 USA

RECRUITER: SARAH HITCHEN
MANAGER, COMPENSATION &
BENEFITS
RIDGE HILL
YONKERS, NY 10710
TEL: (914) 968-2500
FAX: (914) 968-3598

Bernard L. Schwartz, Chairman. Defense electronics. Loral Corporation is a public company founded in 1948. Originally its business was the production of toys and defense equipment. When CEO Bernard Schwartz took office in 1972, the focus was given to defense products. Worldwide revenues for 1992: $3.1 billion.

- **Total Employees:** 9,700
- **U.S. Employees Abroad:** 50
- **Countries:** Belgium, France, Germany, United Kingdom.
- **Job Categories:** Administrative, Engineers, Marketing—Electronics, Sales—Electronics, Sales—Defense Industry.
- **Language Requirement:** None.
- **Training:** No special training provided.

LORD CORPORATION

2000 West Grandview Blvd.
Erie, PA 16514-0038 USA

RECRUITER: ANTHONY P. LOPRIORE
AND ROBERT H. FINE
HUMAN RESOURCES PERSONNEL
2000 WEST GRANDVIEW BLVD.
ERIE, PA 16514-0038
TEL: (814) 868-0924
FAX: (814) 864-3452

Donald M. Alstadt, Chairman. Adhesives, chemicals, sealants, and shock- and noise-control products. Lord Corporation is a private company founded in 1924. It manufacturers adhesives, coatings, sealants, and products that control noise, shock, and vibration. Products are sold to the aerospace and automotive industries as well as other commercial markets. Worldwide revenues for 1991: $246 million.

- **Total Employees:** 1,920
- **U.S. Employees Abroad:** 12
- **Countries:** Brazil, France, Germany, United Kingdom.
- **Application Information:** There are two Human Resources Managers: Anthony Lopriore (Mechanical Products Division) & Robert H. Fine (Chemical Products Division).
- **Job Categories:** Engineers, Marketing—Chemicals, Sales—Chemicals.
- **General Requirements:** Applicant should have some knowledge of the company's products.
- **Average Overseas Assignment:** 3-5 years.
- **Language Requirement:** Competency in local language required.
- **Training:** Basic orientation (1-30 days) offered.
- **Benefits:** All benefits are offered.

LOTUS DEVELOPMENT CORPORATION

55 Cambridge Pkwy.
Cambridge, MA 02142 USA

RECRUITER: RUSSELL J. CAMPANELLO
VP, HUMAN RESOURCES
55 CAMBRIDGE PKWY.
CAMBRIDGE, MA 02142
TEL: (617) 577-8500
FAX: (617) 613-1213

Jim P. Manzi, President and Chairman. Computer software. Lotus Development Corporation is a public company founded in 1980 by Mitch Kapor. He designed an electronic spreadsheet for the IBM-PC and named it Lotus 1-2-3. Within a year, sales reached $53 million. Today, Lotus concentrates on key application markets including spreadsheet, wordprocessing, graphics, and electronic mail software. The company has locations in 32 foreign countries. Worldwide revenues for 1992: $900 million.

- **Total Employees:** 3,500
- **U.S. Employees Abroad:** 40
- **Countries:** Australia, Brazil, Ireland, Japan, Singapore.
- **Job Categories:** Office Management, Marketing—Electronics, Product Development, Sales—Electronics.
- **Language Requirement:** None.

LOUISIANA LAND & EXPLORATION COMPANY

909 Poydras St.
PO Box 60350
New Orleans, LA 70160 USA

RECRUITER: DENNIS LEGENDRE
MANAGER, COMPENSATION &
  EMPLOYMENT
909 POYDRAS ST.
PO BOX 60350
NEW ORLEANS, LA 70160
TEL: (504) 566-6456
FAX: (504) 566-6565

H. Leighton Steward, Chairman. Petroleum and natural gas explorer. Louisiana Land & Exploration is a public company founded in 1926. It is engaged in the exploration and production of natural gas and petroleum. It also manufactures refined petroleum products. Worldwide revenues for 1992: $765.8 million.

- **Total Employees:** 709

- **U.S. Employees Abroad:** Not available.

- **Countries:** Australia, Canada, Colombia, Netherlands, United Kingdom.

- **Job Categories:** Engineers, Management, Technical Field Support.

- **Language Requirement:** None.

LTV STEEL CO.

PO Box 6778
Cleveland, OH 44115 USA

RECRUITER: CHUCK BUTTERS
DIRECTOR, HUMAN RESOURCES
PO BOX 6778
CLEVELAND, OH 44115
TEL: (216) 622-5000
FAX: (216) 622-1066

D. H. Hoag, President. Steel and related products. LTV Steel was founded in 1853 and is a subsidiary of LTV Corporation of Dallas, Texas. It manufactures cold-rolling steel sheets and strips, cold-drawing steel bars and steel shapes. It also produces cold-finished steel and welded-seamless or heavy-riveted steel pipes and tubes. Worldwide revenues for 1992: $3.8 billion.

- **Total Employees:** 17,000

- **U.S. Employees Abroad:** 25

- **Countries:** Brazil, Canada, Israel.

- **Job Categories:** Management, Marketing, Product Development, Sales.

- **Language Requirement:** None.

LTX CORPORATION

LTX Park
University Ave.
Westwood, MA 02090 USA

RECRUITER: RICHARD BOVE
DIRECTOR, HUMAN RESOURCES
LTX PARK AT UNIVERSITY AVE.
WESTWOOD, MA 02090
TEL: (617) 461-1000
FAX: (617) 461-0185

Graham C. C. Miller, President. Testing systems for linear, digital, and mixed-signal integrated circuits. LTX Corporation is a public company founded in 1976. It manufactures systems to measure electricity and systems used for the functional test and alignment of high-volume electronic assemblies. Worldwide revenues for 1992: $149 million.

- **Total Employees:** 946
- **U.S. Employees Abroad:** 20
- **Countries:** France, Germany, Israel, Italy, Malaysia, Netherlands.
- **Application Information:** Hiring for most foreign positions is done at the specific country location.
- **Job Categories:** Management, Marketing—Electronics, Product Development, Sales—Electronics.
- **Language Requirement:** Varies with each posting.

LUBRIZOL CORPORATION

29400 Lakeland Blvd.
Wickliffe, OH 44092 USA

RECRUITER: ELIZABETH MARTIN
SUPERVISOR, EMPLOYEE/COLLEGE
RELATIONS
29400 LAKELAND BLVD.
WICKLIFFE, OH 44092
TEL: (216) 943-4200
FAX: (216) 943-5337

L. E. Coleman, Chairman. Specialty chemicals. Lubrizol Corporation is a public company founded in 1928. This technology-based business creates high-performance chemicals and mechanical and biological products for various markets around the globe. Worldwide revenues for 1992: $1.6 billion.

- **Total Employees:** 5,000
- **U.S. Employees Abroad:** 50
- **Countries:** Austria, Australia, Belgium, Brazil, Canada, Chile, Germany, Hong Kong, Italy, Mexico, Singapore, Republic of South Africa, Spain, United Kingdom.
- **Application Information:** Hiring for most foreign positions is done at the specific country location.
- **Job Categories:** Accountants, Marketing—Chemicals, Sales—Chemicals.
- **Language Requirement:** Varies with each posting.

- **Training:** No special training provided.

- **Benefits:** All benefits are individually determined.

LYKES LINES

Lykes Center
300 Poydras St.
New Orleans, LA 70130 USA

RECRUITER: ARDLEY HANEMANN
HUMAN RESOURCES ADMINISTRATOR
LYKES CENTER, 300 POYDRAS ST.
NEW ORLEANS, LA 70130
TEL: (504) 523-6611
FAX: (504) 528-1769

W. J. Amos, Jr., Chairman. Ocean freight transportation. Lykes Lines is a private company founded in 1900. Today, it is one of the largest global cargo shipping firms in the United States. Operating revenues for 1991: $330 million.

- **Total Employees:** 1,200

- **U.S. Employees Abroad:** 25

- **Countries:** Worldwide including Mexico, Republic of South Africa, United Kingdom, Venezuela.

- **Job Categories:** Management, Marketing, Sales.

- **Language Requirement:** Varies with each posting.

MCCANN-ERICKSON WORLDWIDE

750 Third Ave.
New York, NY 10017 USA

RECRUITER: KATHLEEN YUILL
HUMAN RESOURCES
750 THIRD AVE.
NEW YORK, NY 10017
TEL: (212) 697-6000

Robert James, Chairman. Advertising services. McCann-Erickson Worldwide is a private company which operates advertising agencies in the United States and abroad. Worldwide gross billings for 1991: $5.4 billion.

- **Total Employees:** 8,000

- **U.S. Employees Abroad:** 70

- **Countries:** Worldwide including Argentina, Australia, Barbados, Belgium, Brazil, Chile, People's Republic of China, France, Japan, Kenya, Netherlands, United Kingdom.

- **Job Categories:** Administrative, Marketing, Sales—Advertising.

- **Language Requirement:** Varies with each posting.

- **Training:** No special training provided.

MCCORMICK & COMPANY, INC.

211 Schilling Rd.
Hunt Valley, MD 21031 USA

RECRUITER: ROBIN MORAN
INTERNATIONAL RECRUITMENT
211 SCHILLING RD.
HUNT VALLEY, MD 21031
TEL: (410) 527-8224
FAX: (410) 527-8195

Charles P. McCormick, Jr., Chairman. Seasonings, specialty foods, plastic tubing. McCormick & Company is a public company founded in 1889. It globally distributes seasonings, flavorings, and spices. It is also a manufacturer of plastic tubes for the health-care industry. Worldwide revenues for 1992: $1.5 billion.

- **Total Employees:** 7,500

- **U.S. Employees Abroad:** 40

- **Countries:** Australia, Brazil, Canada, People's Republic of China, Japan, Mexico, Singapore, Venezuela, United Kingdom.

- **Job Categories:** Administrative, Finance, Marketing—Food/Food Services, Sales—Food/Food Services.

- **Language Requirement:** Varies with each posting.

MACDERMID, INC.

245 Freight St.
Waterbury, CT 06720 USA

RECRUITER: JAN SCHWEICKER
INTERNATIONAL PERSONNEL
245 FREIGHT ST.
WATERBURY, CT 06720
TEL: (203) 575-5700
FAX: (203) 575-5630

Daniel H. Leever, Chief Executive Officer. High-technology specialty chemicals. MacDermid, Inc. is a public company founded in 1922. It is a leading producer of chemicals used in the manufacture of printed circuit boards and industrial finishing. Worldwide revenues for 1992: $145 million.

- **Total Employees:** 833

- **U.S. Employees Abroad:** 25

- **Countries:** France, Germany, United Kingdom.

- **Job Categories:** Management, Marketing—Chemicals, Sales—Chemicals.

- **General Requirements:** Usually must be a current employee of the company in order to qualify for overseas assignment.

- **Language Requirement:** Varies with each posting.

MCDERMOTT INTERNATIONAL, INC.

1010 Common St.
New Orleans, LA 70112 USA

RECRUITER: LOU SANNINO
DIRECTOR, HUMAN RESOURCES
1010 COMMON ST.
NEW ORLEANS, LA 70112
TEL: (504) 587-4411
FAX: (504) 587-6153

Robert E. Howson, Chairman. Energy services. McDermott International, Inc. is a public company founded in 1923 by R. Thomas McDermott. Today, it concentrates on marine construction services and power generation systems and equipment. It operates on a global basis. Worldwide revenues for 1992: $3.6 billion. Foreign revenues for 1991: $1.1 billion.

- **Total Employees:** 58,000
- **U.S. Employees Abroad:** 75
- **Countries:** Republic of South Africa, Australia, Germany, Indonesia, Kuwait, Saudi Arabia, United Arab Emirates, Venezuela.
- **Application Information:** Most overseas positions are filled internally.
- **Job Categories:** Administrative, Engineers.
- **Language Requirement:** Varies with each posting.

MCDONALD'S CORPORATION

1 McDonald's Plaza
Oak Brook, IL 60521 USA

RECRUITER: TIM GROSSCUP
DIRECTOR, INTERNATIONAL
PERSONNEL
1 MCDONALD'S PLAZA
OAK BROOK, IL 60521
TEL: (708) 575-3000
FAX: (708) 575-5211

Michael R. Quinlan, Chairman. Food service; restaurant franchising. McDonald's Corporation is a public company founded in 1948 by Dick and Mac McDonald. In 1954, they signed a franchise agreement with malt machine salesman, Ray Kroc. In 1958, the 100 millionth hamburger was sold, and today McDonald's is one of the most advertised brands in the world. Each day, 20 million people eat at these fast-serve restaurants. McDonald's has operations in over 50 countries. Worldwide revenues for 1992: $7.1 billion. Foreign sales for 1991: $3 billion.

- **Total Employees:** 175,000
- **U.S. Employees Abroad:** 125
- **Countries:** Worldwide including Australia, Canada, France, Germany, Japan, United Kingdom.
- **Job Categories:** Finance, Management, Management Training, Marketing—Food/Food Services.
- **Language Requirement:** Varies with each posting.

MCGRAW-HILL, INC.

1221 Avenue of the Americas
New York, NY 10020 USA

RECRUITER: FRANK DURANTE
MANAGER, CORPORATE STAFFING
1221 AVENUE OF THE AMERICAS
NEW YORK, NY 10020
TEL: (212) 512-2000

Joseph L. Dione, President and Chairman. Publishing. McGraw-Hill, Inc. is a public company founded in 1889. It publishes books, magazines, and newsletters. It offers access to information through on-line networks, videotapes, software, and compact discs. A major product is Standard & Poor's rating publication. Worldwide revenues for 1991: $2.1 billion.

- **Total Employees:** 14,000

- **U.S. Employees Abroad:** 25

- **Countries:** Australia, Belgium, Brazil, Canada, Germany, Hong Kong, Japan, Mexico, Switzerland, United Kingdom.

- **Job Categories:** Administrative, Editors, Finance, Marketing—Publishing.

- **Language Requirement:** Varies with each posting.

MCKINSEY & COMPANY, INC.

55 East 52nd St.
New York, NY 10022 USA

RECRUITER: KATHY FOCHT
MANAGER, INTERNATIONAL
RECRUITING
485 MADISON AVE.
NEW YORK, NY 10022
TEL: (212) 446-7000
FAX: (212) 832-0514
FREE: (800) 221-1026

Frederick W. Gluck, Managing Director. Management consulting services. McKinsey & Company, Inc. is a private company founded in 1929. It offers management consulting services throughout the United States and abroad. Worldwide operating revenues for 1991: $1 billion.

- **Total Employees:** 5,700

- **U.S. Employees Abroad:** 40

- **Countries:** Australia, Austria, Belgium, Brazil, Canada, Denmark, France, Germany, Finland, Hong Kong, India, Italy, Japan, Republic of Korea, Mexico, Netherlands, Norway, Portugal, Spain, Sweden, Switzerland, Taiwan, United Kingdom, Venezuela.

- **Job Categories:** Administrative, Consultants—Management, Researchers.

MACRO SYSTEMS, INC.

8630 Fenton St.
Suite 300
Silver Spring, MD 20910 USA

RECRUITER: TRACY WILLIAMS
DIRECTOR, HUMAN RESOURCES
8630 FENTON ST.,SUITE 300
SILVER SPRING, MD 20910
TEL: (301) 588-5484
FAX: (301) 588-4731

Martin Kotler, Chairman. Marketing research and management consulting. Macro Systems, Inc. is a private company founded in 1966. It offers management consulting and professional services to clients in the United States and abroad. Worldwide revenues for 1991: $35 million.

- **Total Employees:** 400

- **U.S. Employees Abroad:** 15

- **Countries:** Hungary.

- **Job Categories:** Administrative, Marketing.

- **Language Requirement:** Varies with each posting.

- **Training:** No special training provided.

MAGNETEK, INC.

11150 Santa Monica Blvd.
Los Angeles, CA 90025 USA

RECRUITER: MIKE HALE
HUMAN RESOURCES
11150 SANTA MONICA BLVD.
LOS ANGELES, CA 90025
TEL: (213) 473-6681

Frank Perna, Jr., President. Electrical equipment. MagneTek, Inc. is a public company founded in 1984. It rebuilds and manufactures transformers and generators. The Powers and Products division was established to meet the demands of utilities and other power generators. Worldwide revenues for 1992: $1.2 billion.

- **Total Employees:** 15,500

- **U.S. Employees Abroad:** Not available.

- **Countries:** France, Italy, Sweden, Switzerland.

- **Job Categories:** Management, Marketing—Electronics, Product Development, Sales—Electronics.

- **Language Requirement:** None.

- **Training:** No special training provided.

MALLINCKRODT, INC.

PO Box 5840
Saint Louis, MO 63134 USA

RECRUITER: JOSEPH BUTTICI
INTERNATIONAL HUMAN RESOURCES
PO BOX 5840
SAINT LOUIS, MO 63134
TEL: (314) 895-2964

Raymond Bentele, President. Medical and industrial chemicals and pharmaceuticals. Mallinckrodt, Inc. was founded in 1867 and is a subsidiary of IMCERA Group, Inc. of Northbrook, Illinois. It manufactures health-care products, medical equipment, and specialty chemicals. Worldwide revenues for 1991: $844 million.

- **Total Employees:** 4,700

- **U.S. Employees Abroad:** 40

- **Countries:** Australia, Austria, Brazil, Canada, France, Germany, Japan, Mexico, Spain, United Kingdom.

- **Job Categories:** Accountants, Chemists, Marketing—Chemicals, Marketing—Health & Medical Supplies, Marketing—Pharmaceuticals, Product Development.

- **Language Requirement:** Varies with each posting.

MARATHON PETROLEUM COMPANY

539 South Main St.
Findlay, OH 45840 USA

RECRUITER: GREG LARSON
INTERNATIONAL PERSONNEL
ADMINISTRATOR
539 SOUTH MAIN ST.
FINDLAY, OH 45840
TEL: (419) 422-2121
FAX: (404) 425-7040

Victor G. Beghini, President. Petroleum. Marathon Petroleum was founded in 1887 and is a subsidiary of USX Corporation of Pittsburgh, Pennsylvania. It is engaged in petroleum exploration on a global basis. It also distributes and markets crude oil, natural gas, and petroleum products.

- **Total Employees:** 20,700

- **U.S. Employees Abroad:** 40

- **Countries:** Egypt, Indonesia, Tunisia, United Kingdom.

- **Job Categories:** Administrative, Engineers, Marketing—Petroleum/Natural Gas, Office Management, Sales—Petroleum/Natural Gas.

- **Language Requirement:** None.

MARION MERRELL DOW, INC.

9300 Ward Pkwy.
PO Box 8480
Kansas City, MO 64114-8480
USA

RECRUITER: JOSEPH M. BOCCHINO
VP, HUMAN RESOURCES
9300 WARD PKWY.
PO BOX 8480
KANSAS CITY, MO 64114-8480
TEL: (816) 966-4000
FAX: (816) 966-3803

Joseph G. Temple, Jr., Chairman. Pharmaceutical products. Marion Merrell Dow, Inc. is a public company founded in 1989. It develops, produces, and sells pharmaceutical products and other items for hospital use, in the United States and abroad. Along with its subsidiaries, these products are marketed and sold in more than 100 countries. Worldwide revenues for 1992: $3.3 billion.

- **Total Employees:** 9,170
- **U.S. Employees Abroad:** 25
- **Countries:** Australia, Canada, France, Germany, Italy, Japan, United Kingdom.
- **Job Categories:** Management, Marketing—Pharmaceuticals, Product Development, Sales—Pharmaceuticals.

MARRIOTT CORPORATION

1 Marriott Dr.
Washington, DC 20058 USA

RECRUITER: JEFF LOO
REGIONAL DIRECTOR, INTERNATIONAL
MARRIOTT CORPORATION
LONDON WIR GAQ, ENGLAND
TEL: (447) 1734-2299
FAX: (447) 1734-5622

J. W. Marriott, Jr., President and Chairman. Lodging, hotels, and contract food and beverage services. Marriott Corporation is a public company founded in 1927 by John Marriott and his wife, Alice. Airline food service was established in 1937 with Eastern Airlines, and the first hotel was opened in Arlington, Virginia in 1957. Today, Marriott operates over 700 hotels worldwide, and is also the number one provider of food and services to management and business, health-care facilities, and education industries. Worldwide revenues for 1992: $8.7 billion.

- **Total Employees:** 230,000
- **U.S. Employees Abroad:** 125
- **Countries:** Worldwide including Chile, Greece, Kuwait, Peru, Saudi Arabia, United Kingdom.
- **Application Information:** U.S. contact is located in Washington, D.C. (301) 380-9000.
- **Job Categories:** Finance, Hotel Management, Marketing—Food/Food Services, Marketing—Travel, Sales—Food/Food Services, Sales—Travel.
- **Language Requirement:** Varies with each posting.

- **Training:** No special training provided.
- **Benefits:** All benefits are idividually determined.
- **Comments:** The number of Americans reported working abroad varies greatly from quarter to quarter, fluctuating with the number and scope of projects under contract at the time.

MASCO CORPORATION

21001 Van Born Rd.
Taylor, MI 48180 USA

RECRUITER: BILL WEST
DIRECTOR, GROUP EMPLOYMENT &
    RELATIONS
21001 VAN BORN RD.
TAYLOR, MI 48180
TEL: (313) 274-7400
FAX: (313) 374-6666

Richard A. Manoogian, Chairman. Plumbing supplies and home furnishings. Masco Corporation is a public company founded in 1929 by Alex Manoogian. He began the Masco Screw Products Company days before the stock market crash in 1929. The company survived and began to diversify through the years with automobile and defense products. In 1954, Masco produced a single-handle kitchen faucet under the Delta name which proved very successful. The company was renamed Masco Corporation in 1961, and currently it has over 300 manufacturing plants in the United States and 19 foreign countries. Worldwide revenues for 1992: $3.5 billion.

- **Total Employees:** 41,300
- **U.S. Employees Abroad:** Not available.
- **Countries:** Canada, People's Republic of China, Egypt, United Kingdom.
- **Job Categories:** Administrative, Marketing, Sales.
- **Language Requirement:** None.

MASONEILAN INDUSTRIES, INC.

275 Turnpike St.
Canton, MA 02021 USA

RECRUITER: BETTE CLARKIN
ADM. ASSISTANT, HUMAN
    RESOURCES
275 TURNPIKE ST.
CANTON, MA 02021
TEL: (617) 821-5100

L. W. Kinderman, President. Control and safety valves. Masoneilan Industries is a division of Dresser Industries of Dallas, Texas. It produces control, safety, and safety relief valves in the United States and abroad.

- **Total Employees:** 3,000
- **U.S. Employees Abroad:** 25
- **Countries:** Canada, Mexico, Netherlands, Singapore, United Kingdom.

- **Job Categories:** Manufacturing, Management, Sales—Industrial.
- **Language Requirement:** None.

MASONITE CORPORATION

1 South Wacker Dr.
Chicago, IL 60606 USA

RECRUITER: MARY KURYLO
HUMAN RESOURCES
REPRESENTATIVE
1 SOUTH WACKER DR.
CHICAGO, IL 60606
TEL: (312) 750-0900
FAX: (312) 750-9502

J. V. Faraci, President. Sawmills operator; wood products. Masonite is a subsidiary of International Paper Company of Purchase, New York. It operates sawmills, develops plans for mills, and manufactures various products made from wood, rattan, straw, veneer, and wicker. Worldwide revenues for 1991: $536 million.

- **Total Employees:** 5,000
- **U.S. Employees Abroad:** 25
- **Countries:** Canada, Netherlands, Republic of South Africa.
- **Job Categories:** Marketing, Plant Managers, Sales.
- **Language Requirement:** None.

MASTER LOCK COMPANY

2600 North 32nd St.
Milwaukee, WI 53210 USA

RECRUITER: PAULA KRAUS
VP, HUMAN RESOURCES
2600 NORTH 32ND ST.
MILWAUKEE, WI 53210
TEL: (414) 449-3171
FAX: (414) 449-3193

James Beardsley, Chairman. Padlocks and door hardware. Master Lock was founded in 1921 and is a subsidiary of Master Brands Industries of Deerfield, Illinois. It manufacturers metal hardware products including quality padlocks. It is the number one producer of padlocks with the strongest brand name in the industry. Worldwide revenues for 1992: $1 billion.

- **Total Employees:** 1,850
- **U.S. Employees Abroad:** Not available.
- **Countries:** France, United Kingdom.
- **Salaries:** $50,000-$75,000 per year.
- **Job Categories:** Marketing—Consumer Goods, Sales—Consumer Goods.
- **General Requirements:** Experience in overseas market and language skills are preferred.
- **Language Requirement:** Fluency in local language required.

- **Training:** No special training offered.

- **Benefits:** TRAVEL: French health insurance plan utilized for employees in Europe. HEALTH: None offered. HOUSING: None offered. EDUCATION: None offered.

MATTEL, INC.

333 Continental Blvd.

El Segundo, CA 90245 USA

RECRUITER: TRENT READY

HUMAN RESOURCES

333 CONTINENTAL BLVD.

EL SEGUNDO, CA 90245

TEL: (310) 524-2000

FAX: (310) 524-3537

John W. Amerman, Chairman. Games, hobbies, and toys. Mattel is a public company incorporated in 1948 and headquartered in El Segundo, California. Harold Matson and Elliot Handler composed the company name from initials of their first and last names. Today, Mattel is the 2nd largest toymaker in the United States. Popular brand names include the Barbie doll and Hot Wheels cars. It has been successful in foreign markets with operations in more than 20 countries. Products are sold in over 100 nations. Worldwide revenues for 1992: $1.8 billion.

- **Total Employees:** 12,000

- **U.S. Employees Abroad:** 45

- **Countries:** Australia, Canada, People's Republic of China, France, Germany, Hong Kong, Italy, Mexico, Philippines, Spain, Taiwan.

- **Application Information:** Hiring for most foreign positions is done at the specific country location.

- **Job Categories:** Marketing—Consumer Goods, Plant Managers, Product Development, Sales—Consumer Goods.

- **Language Requirement:** Varies with each posting.

- **Benefits:** All benefits are individually determined.

MAXUS ENERGY CORPORATION

717 North Harwood St.

Dallas, TX 75201 USA

RECRUITER: STEVE GINSBURGH

SENIOR HUMAN RESOURCES

REPRESENTATIVE

717 NORTH HARWOOD ST.

DALLAS, TX 75201

TEL: (214) 953-2000

Charles J. Blackburn, Chairman. Oil and gas exploration and production. Maxus Energy is a public company founded in 1910. Today, it is one of the largest independent companies engaged in oil and gas exploration in North America. Worldwide revenues for 1992: $718 million.

- **Total Employees:** 2,200

- **U.S. Employees Abroad:** 80
- **Countries:** Barbados, Ecuador, Indonesia.
- **Job Categories:** Administrative, Engineers, Geologists.
- **Language Requirement:** Knowledge of local language a plus but not essential.
- **Training:** No special training provided.
- **Benefits:** All benefits are offered.

GEORGE S. MAY INTERNATIONAL, INC.

303 South Northwest Hwy.
Park Ridge, IL 60068 USA

RECRUITER: JOY MCGURIL
PERSONNEL MANAGER
303 SOUTH NORTHWEST HWY.
PARK RIDGE, IL 60068
TEL: (708) 825-8806
FAX: (708) 825-7937

D. Fletcher, President. Computer consulting. George S. May International is a private company founded in 1925. It offers computer consulting and is a designer of customized computer systems with operations in the United States and abroad. Worldwide operating revenues for 1991: $53 million.

- **Total Employees:** 1,200
- **U.S. Employees Abroad:** 20
- **Countries:** Canada, Italy.
- **Job Categories:** Management, Marketing.
- **Language Requirement:** None.
- **Training:** No special training provided.

MAYTAG CORPORATION

403 West 4th St., North
Newton, IA 50208 USA

RECRUITER: ANNE WIGNALL
STAFFING MANAGER
1 DEPENDABILITY SQUARE
NEWTON, IA 50208
TEL: (515) 792-8000
FAX: (515) 791-8395

Daniel J. Krumm, Chairman. Home appliances and floor-care products. Maytag is a public company founded in 1893 by F. L. Maytag and three associates. Originally, they manufactured feeder attachments for grain threshing machines. The company name was changed to Maytag in 1903, and in 1906, the first washing machine was produced. Today, Maytag consists of nine companies and has facilities in seven foreign countries. Major brands include Jenn-Air and Maytag appliances. Worldwide revenues for 1992: $3 billion.

- **Total Employees:** 26,000
- **U.S. Employees Abroad:** 35

- **Countries:** Australia, France, Italy, Mexico, United Kingdom.
- **Job Categories:** Management, Marketing—Consumer Goods, Product Development, Sales—Consumer Goods.
- **Language Requirement:** None.
- **Training:** None provided.

MCI COMMUNICATIONS CORPORATION

1133 19th St. NW
Washington, DC 20036 USA

RECRUITER: ANGELA COLOLUCA
INTERNATIONAL RECRUITMENT
MCI INTERNATIONAL
2 INTERNATIONAL DR.
RYE BROOK, NY 10573
TEL: (914) 934-3444
FAX: (914) 934-6004

Bert C. Roberts Jr., Chairman. Telecommunications services. MCI Communications Corporation is a public company founded in 1968 by William McGowan. He acted as chairman of the firm until his death in 1992. By 1973, its network had reached more than 40 cities. Today, this company is the second largest long-distance telephone company in the United States. It provides services from the United States to more than 180 countries and has foreign offices in 50 countries. Worldwide revenues for 1992: $10.6 billion.

- **Total Employees:** 24,500
- **U.S. Employees Abroad:** 60
- **Countries:** Worldwide including Argentina, Belgium, France, Germany, Italy, Japan, Mexico, Netherlands.
- **Job Categories:** Accountants, Administrative, Marketing—Telecommunications, Sales—Telecommunications.
- **Language Requirement:** None.
- **Training:** No special training provided.

MEAD CORPORATION

Courthouse Plaza NE
Dayton, OH 45463 USA

RECRUITER: JANET WALSH
MEAD PACKAGING INTERNATIONAL
1040 WEST MARIETTA ST., NW
ATLANTA, GA 30302
TEL: (404) 875-2711
FAX: (404) 897-6386

Burnell R. Roberts, Chairman. Forest products including lumber, packaging, and paper; electronic publishing and color-imaging. Mead Corporation is a public company founded in 1882 by Daniel Mead. He started Mead Paper and, after his death in 1891, the company staggered until his grandson, George, took over in 1905. The company went public in 1906. Today, Mead is the ninth largest forest-products company in the United

States. It is also a leading electronic publisher with its Mead Data Central Division. Worldwide revenues for 1992: $4.7 billion.

- **Total Employees:** 21,800
- **U.S. Employees Abroad:** 30
- **Countries:** Canada, France, Germany, Italy, Netherlands, United Kingdom.
- **Application Information:** Other division contact is: Sharon Daily, Mead Coated Board, 950 Paces Ferry Road, Atlanta, GA 30326; (404) 262-7770, FAX: (404) 262-7150.
- **Job Categories:** Administrative, Clerical Assistants, Design, Engineers, Marketing, Sales.
- **Language Requirement:** Varies with each posting.
- **Training:** No special training provided.

MEASUREX CORPORATION

1 Results Way
Cupertino, CA 95014 USA

RECRUITER: PHIL PETERSON
HUMAN RESOURCES
REPRESENTATIVE
1 RESULTS WAY
CUPERTINO, CA 95014-5991
TEL: (408) 155-1500
FAX: (408) 996-2371

David A. Bossen, President. Computer systems and integrated manufacturing systems. Measurex is a public company founded in 1968. It designs and manufactures sensor-based computer systems that measure and control manufacturing processes used in various industries. It has over 40 offices in the United States and 23 foreign countries. Worldwide revenues for 1992: $253 million.

- **Total Employees:** 2,310
- **U.S. Employees Abroad:** 25
- **Countries:** Argentina, Australia, Brazil, Canada, France, Germany, Hong Kong, Italy, Japan, Mexico, Netherlands, Sweden, Switzerland, United Kingdom, Venezuela.
- **Job Categories:** Manufacturing, Marketing—Electronics, Product Development, Sales—Electronics.
- **Language Requirement:** Varies with each posting.

MEDTRONIC, INC.

7000 Central Ave. NE
Minneapolis, MN 55432-3576
USA

RECRUITER: PEGGY QUIRK
INTERNATIONAL HUMAN RESOURCES
7000 CENTRAL AVE., NE
MINNEAPOLIS, MN 55432-3576
TEL: (612) 574-4000
FAX: (612) 574-4720
FREE: (800) 328-2518

Winston R. Wallin, Chairman. Therapeutic medical devices. Medtronic, Inc. is a public company founded in 1949. It designs, manufactures, and sells therapeutic medical devices for cardiovascular and neurological health care. Customers include cardiologists and surgeons in the United States and in over 80 foreign countries. Worldwide revenues for 1993: $1.3 billion.

- **Total Employees:** 9,200
- **U.S. Employees Abroad:** Not available.
- **Countries:** Canada, France, Italy, Japan, Netherlands.
- **Job Categories:** Administrative, Marketing—Health & Medical Supplies, Sales—Health & Medical Supplies.
- **Language Requirement:** None.
- **Training:** No special training provided.
- **Benefits:** All benefits are individually determined.

MELROE COMPANY

112 University Dr.
Fargo, ND 58108 USA

RECRUITER: GREG SCHMALZ
DIRECTOR, HUMAN RESOURCES
112 UNIVERSITY DR.
PO BOX 6019
FARGO, ND 58108
TEL: (701) 241-8700
FAX: (701) 241-8704

Robert N. Spolum, President. Heavy equipment. Melroe Company was founded in 1974 and is a subsidiary of Clark Equipment Company of South Bend, Indiana. It manufactures farm equipment and forestry equipment and machinery. Worldwide revenues for 1991: $620 million.

- **Total Employees:** 1,500
- **U.S. Employees Abroad:** 20
- **Countries:** Belgium, Singapore.
- **Job Categories:** Marketing—Industrial, Sales—Industrial.
- **Language Requirement:** None.

MEMOREX TELEX CORPORATION

PO Box 1526
Tulsa, OK 74135 USA

RECRUITER: JOHN VENTURELLA
VP, HUMAN RESOURCES
PO BOX 1526
TULSA, OK 74135
TEL: (918) 717-1111
FAX: (918) 624-4581

Steve Jatras, President and Chairman. Computer equipment and related services. Memorex Telex is a private company based in Tulsa, Oklahoma, which began in 1983.

Telex joined with Memorex, a Dutch company, to form Memorex Telex Corporation. Today, it has operations in more than 25 countries and is a leading supplier of plug-compatible computer equipment and related items. This includes disk and tape storage devices, terminals, and printers. Worldwide revenues for 1991: $1 billion.

- **Total Employees:** 11,000

- **U.S. Employees Abroad:** 35

- **Countries:** Worldwide including France, Germany, Hong Kong, Japan, Netherlands, United Kingdom.

- **Job Categories:** Management, Marketing—Electronics, Product Development, Sales—Electronics.

- **Language Requirement:** None.

MERCK & COMPANY, INC.

PO Box 2000
Rahway, NJ 07065-0909 USA

RECRUITER: STEVEN DARIEN
VICE PRESIDENT, WORLDWIDE
    PERSONNEL
1 MERCK DR.
PO BOX 100
WHITEHOUSE STATION, NJ 08889-
    0100
TEL: (908) 423-1000
FAX: (908) 423-2958

P. Roy Vagelos, President and Chairman. Pharmaceuticals and specialty chemicals. Merck & Company is a public firm founded in 1887 by Theodore Weicker, a German chemist. George Merck joined the company in 1891 to form a partnership. Today, it is the third largest pharmaceutical concern in the world. In addition, the company also produces animal-health items, pesticides, and specialty chemicals. Worldwide revenues for 1992: $9.7 billion.

- **Total Employees:** 34,400

- **U.S. Employees Abroad:** 60

- **Countries:** Worldwide including Australia, Brazil, France, Germany, Hong Kong, Italy, Japan, Mexico, Republic of South Africa, Switzerland, United Kingdom.

- **Job Categories:** Marketing—Chemicals, Marketing—Pharmaceuticals, Research Technicians, Sales—Chemicals, Sales—Pharmaceuticals.

- **Language Requirement:** Knowledge of local language a plus but not essential.

MERISEL, INC.

200 Continental Dr.
El Segundo, CA 90245 USA

RECRUITER: CAROL BAKER
ASSOCIATE RELATIONS MANAGER
200 CONTINENTAL DR.
EL SEGUNDO, CA 90245
TEL: (310) 615-1383
FAX: (310) 615-6435

Michael Prickett, President. Microcomputer hardware and software. Merisel, Inc. is a public company founded in 1980. It acts as an independent wholesale distributor of microcomputer hardware and software products to retailers on a global basis. It has plant facilities and subsidiaries throughout the United States and abroad. Worldwide revenues for 1992: $2.2 billion.

- **Total Employees:** 1,300
- **U.S. Employees Abroad:** Not available.
- **Countries:** Australia, Canada, Germany, Switzerland, United Kingdom.
- **Application Information:** Hiring for most overseas positions is done at the specific country location.
- **Job Categories:** Marketing—Electronics, Management, Sales—Electronics.
- **Language Requirement:** Varies with each posting.
- **Training:** Varies with each posting.
- **Benefits:** All benefits vary with each posting.

MERRILL LYNCH & COMPANY, INC.

World Financial Center, North Tower
New York, NY 10281 USA

RECRUITER: JOHN W. RAE, JR.
RECRUITMENT
WORLD FINANCIAL CENTER, NORTH
TOWER, 31ST FLOOR
NEW YORK, NY 10281-1331
TEL: (212) 449-9836
FAX: (212) 449-3187

William A. Schreyer, Chairman. Diversified financial services. Merrill Lynch & Company, Inc. is a public company founded in 1914. Wall Street bond salesman Charles Merrill and soon-to-be partner, Edmund Lynch opened an underwriting firm in New York. Today, Merrill Lynch is organized into five business segments, each focusing on specific products to serve a particular group of clients. Institutional businesses include investment banking, debt markets, and equity markets for 6,000 corporate, institutional, and governmental clients on a worldwide basis. Investor businesses are private client and asset management, and they provide investment, banking, credit, money management, and insurance products and service to 6 million individuals and small businesses on a global basis. It currently operates in 29 countries. Worldwide revenues for 1992: $13.4 billion.

- **Total Employees:** 40,000

- **U.S. Employees Abroad:** Not available.

- **Countries:** Worldwide including Argentina, France, Germany, Hong Kong, Italy, Japan, Singapore, Switzerland, United Arab Emirates, United Kingdom.

- **Job Categories:** Brokers—Securities & Financial, Financial Advisors, Management, Marketing—Financial Services.

METALLURG CORPORATION

25 East 39th St.
New York, NY 10016 USA

RECRUITER: MARY HIGGINS
STAFFING/RECRUITMENT
    COORDINATOR
PO BOX 768
NEWFIELD, NJ 08346
TEL: (609) 692-4200
FAX: (609) 697-9025

Michael Standen, President. Primary metal products. Metallurg is a private company founded in 1914. It is a manufacturer of abrasive products, including grinding wheels, or abrasive-coated products. Worldwide revenues for 1991: $600 million.

- **Total Employees:** 4,500

- **U.S. Employees Abroad:** Not available.

- **Countries:** Brazil, Canada, Japan, Sweden, Switzerland, United Kingdom.

- **Job Categories:** Marketing—Industrial, Sales—Industrial.

- **Language Requirement:** Varies with each posting.

METCALF & EDDY INTERNATIONAL, INC.

30 Harvard Mill Square
Wakefield, MA 01880 USA

RECRUITER: EDWARD BURNS
STAFFING/RECRUITMENT
30 HARVARD MILL SQUARE
WAKEFIELD, MA 01880
TEL: (617) 246-5200
FAX: (617) 243-2143

George Bilcher, President. Contract engineering. Metcalf & Eddy International, Inc. is a private subsidiary of Air & Water Technologies (AWT) of Branchburg, New Jersey. It offers professional engineering services to clients in the United States and abroad. Worldwide total assets for 1991: $344.9 million.

- **Total Employees:** 2,600

- **U.S. Employees Abroad:** 45

- **Countries:** Egypt, Saudi Arabia.

- **Job Categories:** Engineers, Marketing.

- **Language Requirement:** None.

- **Training:** No special training provided.

METCO PERKIN-ELMER

1010 Prospect Ave.
Westbury, NY 11590-0201 USA

RECRUITER: EILEEN COLARASSI
STAFFING
1010 PROSPECT AVE.
WESTBURY, NY 11590-0201
TEL: (516) 334-1300
FAX: (516) 338-2296

Thomas R. Fisher, President. Spray-coating products. Metco Perkin-Elmer is a division of Perkin-Elmer of Norwalk, Connecticut. It manufactures and services thermal spray-coating equipment and supplies.

- **Total Employees:** 900
- **U.S. Employees Abroad:** 18
- **Countries:** Australia, Belgium, Brazil, Canada, France, Germany, Italy, Japan, Netherlands, Spain.
- **Job Categories:** Administrative Assistants, Marketing—Chemicals, Sales—Chemicals.
- **Language Requirement:** None.

METHODE ELECTRONICS, INC.

7444 West Wilson Ave.
Chicago, IL 60656 USA

RECRUITER: LOUISE MOIAMA
PERSONNEL MANAGER
7444 WEST WILSON AVE.
CHICAGO, IL 60656
TEL: (708) 867-9600
FAX: (708) 867-9130

William J. McGinley, President. Electronic controls and related devices. Methode Electronics is a public company founded in 1946. It manufactures electronic controls, including circuit board testing equipment.

- **Total Employees:** 1,925
- **U.S. Employees Abroad:** Not available.
- **Countries:** Singapore.
- **Application Information:** Hiring for most overseas positions is done at the specific country location.
- **Job Categories:** Marketing—Electronics, Sales—Electronics.

METROPOLITAN LIFE INSURANCE COMPANY

One Madison Ave.
New York, NY 10010 USA

RECRUITER: PATRICIA MISOVSKY
INTERNATIONAL STAFFING MANAGER
ONE MADISON AVE.
NEW YORK, NY 10010
TEL: (215) 578-2211
FAX: (212) 685-1224

Robert G. Schwartz, President and Chairman. Insurance services. Metropolitan Life Insurance Company is a mutual company founded in 1868 by Simeon Draper, a New York merchant. It began offering industrial insurance with workers' burial policies. Today, it is the largest North American life insurer. Other subsidiaries include real estate leasing, appraising, and finance and investment services. Worldwide assets for 1992: $118.2 billion.

- **Total Employees:** 57,000
- **U.S. Employees Abroad:** 50
- **Countries:** Canada, Republic of Korea, Spain, Taiwan, United Kingdom.
- **Job Categories:** Executive Management, Marketing—Financial Services, Underwriters.
- **Language Requirement:** None.

MGM INCORPORATED

10000 Washington Blvd.
Culver City, CA 90230 USA

RECRUITER: BENITA PALMER
STAFFING/RECRUITMENT
10000 WASHINGTON BLVD.
CULVER CITY, CA 90230
TEL: (310) 280-6000
FAX: (310) 836-1680

Giancarlo Parretti, Chairman. Motion pictures, home videos. MGM Incorporated is a multinational company that produces and distributes motion pictures and videocassettes. It also operates cinemas. It has production facilities in the United States and abroad. Worldwide operating revenues for 1991: $892 million.

- **Total Employees:** 2,300
- **U.S. Employees Abroad:** 40
- **Countries:** Denmark, Finland, France, Italy, Norway, Sweden, United Kingdom.
- **Job Categories:** Administrative, Marketing, Technicians.
- **Language Requirement:** Varies with each posting.

MILLER BREWING COMPANY

3939 West Highland Blvd.
Milwaukee, WI 53208 USA

RECRUITER: ANTHONY HUBBARD
MANAGER, CORPORATE
  RECRUITMENT
3939 WEST HIGHLAND BLVD.
MILWAUKEE, WI 53208
TEL: (414) 931-2000
FAX: (414) 931-2614

Warren H. Dunn, Chairman. Beer, ale, and nonalcoholic brew. Miller Brewing was founded in 1855 and is a subsidiary of Philip Morris Companies of New York City. It manufactures and markets beer and other brewed products. Popular brand names include Miller Genuine Draft, Lowenbrau, and Sharp's nonalcoholic brew. The beer division of Philip Morris Companies accounted for seven percent ($4.1 billion) of operating revenues for 1992.

- **Total Employees:** 10,229
- **U.S. Employees Abroad:** 35
- **Countries:** Canada, People's Republic of China, Mexico, United Kingdom.
- **Job Categories:** Management, Marketing—Food/Food Services, Sales—Food/Food Services.
- **Language Requirement:** None.

HERMAN MILLER, INC.

855 East Main Ave.
PO Box 302
Zeeland, MI 49464-0302 USA

RECRUITER: STEVEN CHAPPEL
MANAGER, CORPORATE
    COMMUNICATIONS
8500 BYRON RD.
ZEELAND, MI 49464
TEL: (616) 654-3000
FAX: (616) 654-3632

Richard R. Ruch, President. Furniture and related products. Herman Miller is a public company founded as the Star Furniture Company in 1905. Its current name was adopted in 1923. Today, this business manufacturers and markets furniture systems. Its customers include offices and health-care facilities in the United States and abroad. Worldwide revenues for 1992: $805 billion.

- **Total Employees:** 5,500
- **U.S. Employees Abroad:** 25
- **Countries:** Australia, Canada, France, Germany, Japan, Netherlands, United Kingdom.
- **Job Categories:** Management, Marketing, Product Development, Sales.
- **Language Requirement:** None.

MILLIKEN & COMPANY

920 Milliken Rd.
Spartanburg, SC 29303-9301
USA

RECRUITER: TOMMY HODGE
DIRECTOR, HUMAN RESOURCES
920 MILLIKEN RD.
SPARTANBURG, SC 29303-9301
TEL: (803) 573-2020
FAX: (803) 573-2100

Roger Milliken, Chairman. Textiles; fabrics. Milliken is a private company founded in 1865 by Seth Milliken and William Deering. It produces finished fabrics which are used in a variety of products, including the cloth used in Burger King and McDonald's uniforms. Other items are braided polyester cords used in Michelin tires, and stretch fabrics for sportswear and swimsuits. Currently, it has operations throughout the United

States and in more than 10 foreign countries. Worldwide revenues for 1992: $2.5 billion.

- **Total Employees:** 14,000
- **U.S. Employees Abroad:** 50
- **Countries:** Belgium, Canada, Denmark, France, Japan, United Kingdom.
- **Job Categories:** Management, Marketing, Sales, Technical Field Support.
- **Language Requirement:** Varies with each posting.

MILLIPORE CORPORATION

80 Ashby Rd.
Bedford, MA 01730 USA

RECRUITER: C. WILLIAM EHMANN
DIRECTOR, CORPORATE HUMAN
RESOURCES
80 ASHBY RD.
BEDFORD, MA 01730
TEL: (617) 275-9205
FAX: (617) 275-3236

John A. Gilmartin, President and Chairman. Separations technologies. Millipore Corporation is a public company founded in 1954. It is a multinational concern whose products are used for crucial applications in a wide variety of markets. These include the biotechnology, chemical, environmental, food and beverage, life science research, microelectronic, health care, and pharmaceutical industries. Worldwide revenues for 1992: $770 million.

- **Total Employees:** 5,800
- **U.S. Employees Abroad:** 10
- **Countries:** Australia, Brazil, France, Italy, Japan, Mexico, Netherlands, Sweden, Switzerland.
- **Job Categories:** Management, Marketing—Scientific, Sales—Scientific.
- **Language Requirement:** Varies with each posting.
- **Comments:** The number of Americans reported working abroad varies greatly from quarter to quarter, fluctuating with the number and scope of projects under contract at the time.

MMS INTERNATIONAL

1301 Shoreway Rd.
Belmont, CA 94002 USA

RECRUITER: KIMBERLY DELP
HUMAN RESOURCES COORDINATOR
1301 SHOREWAY RD.
BELMONT, CA 94002
TEL: (415) 637-4374
FAX: (415) 637-4303

Richard R. Green, Chairman. Investment services. MMS International was founded in 1974 and is a subsidiary of McGraw-Hill Inc. of New York City. It operates as an investment firm in the United States and abroad. Worldwide operating revenues for 1991: $38 million.

- **Total Employees:** 160
- **U.S. Employees Abroad:** 20
- **Countries:** Canada, United Kingdom.
- **Job Categories:** Investment Counselors, Management, Marketing—Financial Services.
- **Language Requirement:** None.
- **Training:** No special training provided.

MOBIL OIL CORPORATION

3225 Gallows Rd.
Fairfax, VA 22037 USA

RECRUITER: FRAN CODY
STAFFING/RECRUITMENT
3225 GALLOWS RD.
FAIRFAX, VA 22037
TEL: (703) 849-3000
FAX: (703) 846-4669

Allen E. Murray, President and Chairman. Oil and natural gas exploration and production; chemical production. Mobil Oil Corporation is a public company founded in 1882 as the Standard Oil Company of New York. It became Socony Mobil Oil in 1955, and the name was shortened to Mobil Oil in 1966. Today, it is the fourth largest petroleum company in the world with operations in 20 foreign countries. Worldwide revenues for 1992; $56.9 billion. Foreign sales for 1991: $36 billion.

- **Total Employees:** 67,900
- **U.S. Employees Abroad:** 110
- **Countries:** Worldwide including Angola, Australia, Belgium, Brazil, Canada, Chile, France, Germany, Hong Kong, Indonesia, Kenya, Mexico, Nigeria, Saudi Arabia, Turkey, United Kingdom.
- **Job Categories:** Chemical Engineers, Executive Management, Marketing—Chemicals, Marketing—Petroleum/Natural Gas, Researchers, Technical Field Support.
- **Language Requirement:** Varies with each posting.

MODINE MANUFACTURING COMPANY

1500 DeKoven Ave.
Racine, WI 53403 USA

RECRUITER: ABE BIXLER
RECRUITMENT COORDINATOR
1500 DEKOVEN AVE.
RACINE, WI 53403
TEL: (414) 636-1200
FAX: (414) 636-1424

Earl E. Richter, Chairman. Vehicular heat-transfer products. Modine Manufacturing is a public company founded in 1916. It produces and sells vehicular heat-transfer products. These include radiators, heating, ventilating, and evaporative cooling items. Customers include automotive aftermarket, nonresidential building materials, and original equipment manufacturers. Worldwide revenues for 1993: $570 million.

- **Total Employees:** 5,200
- **U.S. Employees Abroad:** Not available.
- **Countries:** Austria, Brazil, Japan, Mexico.
- **Job Categories:** Management, Marketing, Product Development, Sales.
- **Language Requirement:** None.
- **Training:** No special training provided.

MOLEX, INC.

2222 Wellington Court
Lisle, IL 60532 USA

RECRUITER: HERB GOSEWISCH
EMPLOYMENT MANAGER
2222 WELLINGTON COURT
LISLE, IL 60532
TEL: (708) 969-4550
FAX: (708) 908-1352

Frederick A. Krehbiel, Vice Chairman. Products for the electrical and electronics markets. Molex, Inc. is a public company founded in 1938. Its product line offers 30,000 items through direct sales, distribution and manufacturers' representatives. Currently, it has 50 operating facilities in 20 countries. Major products include electronic connectors and interconnection systems. Worldwide revenues for 1992: $818 million.

- **Total Employees:** 6,700
- **U.S. Employees Abroad:** 30
- **Countries:** Germany, Japan, Singapore.
- **Job Categories:** Management, Marketing—Electronics, Sales—Electronics.
- **Language Requirement:** Varies with each posting.
- **Training:** No special training provided.

MONROE AUTO EQUIPMENT COMPANY

1 International Dr.
Monroe, MI 48161 USA

RECRUITER: DENISE LENNARD
HUMAN RESOURCES
1 INTERNATIONAL DR.
MONROE, MI 48161
TEL: (313) 243-8000
FAX: (313) 243-8034

John P. Reilly, Chairman. Automobile equipment. Monroe Auto Equipment is a public company founded in 1916 and is a subsidiary of Tenneco Automotive, Inc. of Lincolnshire, Illinois. It is a manufacturer of motor vehicle parts and accessories. Worldwide revenues for 1991: $730 million.

- **Total Employees:** 7,000

- **U.S. Employees Abroad:** 40
- **Countries:** Argentina, Belgium, Brazil, Japan, Spain.
- **Job Categories:** Management, Marketing—Automotive, Sales—Automotive.
- **Language Requirement:** None.

MONSANTO COMPANY

1800 North Lindberg
St. Louis, MO 63137 USA

RECRUITER: ROBERT J. MASON
DIRECTOR, UNIVERSITY RELATIONS
1800 NORTH LINDBERG
ST. LOUIS, MO 63167
TEL: (314) 694-1000
FAX: (314) 394-7625

Richard G. Mahoney, Chairman. Chemicals, agricultural products, and pharmaceuticals. Monsanto is a public company founded in 1901 by John Queeney. Using his wife's maiden name, he began Monsanto Chemical Works to make saccharin. Other items soon followed and today, Monsanto is the third largest chemical company in the United States. It operates and sells its products on a global basis. Worldwide revenues for 1992: $7.8 billion.

- **Total Employees:** 42,000
- **U.S. Employees Abroad:** 70
- **Countries:** Argentina, Australia, Brazil, Canada, Costa Rica, France, Germany, Hong Kong, Norway, Republic of South Africa, Sweden, Switzerland, United Kingdom.
- **Job Categories:** Administrative, Marketing—Agricultural, Marketing—Chemicals, Marketing—Pharmaceuticals, Product Development, Sales—Agricultural, Sales—Chemicals, Sales—Pharmaceuticals.
- **General Requirements:** Usually must be a current employee of the company in order to qualify for overseas assignment.

MONTGOMERY WARD HOLDING COMPANY

One Montgomery Ward Plaza
Chicago, IL 60671 USA

RECRUITER: MICHELLE BENOIT
SENIOR VP, HUMAN RESOURCES
ONE MONTGOMERY WARD PLAZA,
    LOC-8-3
CHICAGO, IL 60671
TEL: (312) 467-2000
FAX: (312) 467-7158

Bernard F. Brennan, President and Chairman. Department store and mail order operations. Montgomery Ward Holding Corporation is a private company founded in 1874 by Aaron Montgomery Ward. It was the first general merchandise mail order/catalog business in the world. Today, it has changed the once traditional appearance and mail order business into a brand-conscious retailing concern. It has 353 retail outlets throughout the United States and abroad. Worldwide revenues for 1991: $5.7 billion.

- **Total Employees:** 65,000
- **U.S. Employees Abroad:** Not available.
- **Countries:** Italy, Japan, Singapore.
- **Application Information:** Hiring for most overseas positions is done at the specific country location.
- **Job Categories:** Finance, Marketing—Consumer Goods, Sales—Consumer Goods.
- **Language Requirement:** None.
- **Training:** Varies with each posting.
- **Benefits:** All benefits are individually determined.

MOORE PRODUCTS COMPANY

Sumneytown Pike
Spring House, PA 19477 USA

RECRUITER: MICHAEL MORAN
MANAGER, PERSONNEL DEPARTMENT
SUMNEYTOWN PIKE
SPRING HOUSE, PA 19477
TEL: (215) 646-7400

William B. Moore, President. Industrial components and systems. Moore Products is a public company founded in 1940 by Coleman Bassett Moore. It manufactures components for the agrichemical, automotive, food and beverage, mining, paper and pulp, steel, textile, tobacco, and waste treatment industries. It operates on a global basis. Worldwide revenues for 1992: $96 million.

- **Total Employees:** 1,030
- **U.S. Employees Abroad:** Not available.
- **Countries:** Canada, France, India, Mexico, Netherlands, United Kingdom.
- **Job Categories:** Marketing—Industrial, Sales—Industrial.
- **Language Requirement:** None.

J. P. MORGAN & COMPANY, INC.

60 Wall St.
New York, NY 10260 USA

RECRUITER: RICHARD MAHONEY
CORPORATE COMMUNICATIONS
60 WALL ST.
NEW YORK, NY 10260
TEL: (212) 483-2323
FAX: (212) 235-4945

Dennis Weatherstone, Chairman. Banking and financial services. J. P. Morgan is a public company founded in 1890. Its roots originate with Junius Spencer Morgan. He became a partner in a London-based banking house owned by George Peabody. When Peabody retired in the 1860s, Morgan took control and renamed the company J. S. Morgan and Company. His son started J. Pierpont Morgan and Company in New York in 1862. When Junius died in 1890, there was a reorganization. The two businesses became J. P. Morgan & Company. Today, this holding company is a major dealer in government securities, foreign currencies, and precious metals. Worldwide assets for 1992: $103 billion.

- **Total Employees:** 12,960
- **U.S. Employees Abroad:** Not available.
- **Countries:** Argentina, Australia, Bahamas, France, Hong Kong, Italy, Japan, Singapore, Republic of South Africa, Spain, United Kingdom.
- **Job Categories:** Accountants, Financial Consultants, Underwriters.
- **Language Requirement:** Varies with each posting.
- **Training:** No special training required.

MORGAN STANLEY GROUP, INC.

1251 Avenue of the Americas
New York, NY 10020 USA

RECRUITER: DIANA MANTZ
HUMAN RESOURCES
REPRESENTATIVE
1251 AVENUE OF THE AMERICAS
NEW YORK, NY 10020
TEL: (212) 703-4000
FAX: (212) 703-6503

Richard B. Fisher, Chairman. Securities. Morgan Stanley Group is a public company founded in 1935 by businessmen, Henry Morgan and Harold Stanley. It became a partnership in 1941. Today it serves institutional and individual clients on a global basis. Worldwide net revenues for 1992: $7.3 billion

- **Total Employees:** 7,200
- **U.S. Employees Abroad:** 35
- **Countries:** Australia, Canada, Hong Kong, Japan, Singapore, United Kingdom.
- **Application Information:** Applications are accepted for various levels of employment, from entry-level to upper-management.
- **Job Categories:** Financial Consultants, Investment Counselors.
- **Language Requirement:** Knowledge of local language a plus but not essential.
- **Training:** No special training provided.
- **Benefits:** TRAVEL: Individually determined. HEALTH: Individually determined. HOUSING: Individually determined. EDUCATION: Not offered.

MORRISON KNUDSEN CORPORATION

1 Morrison Knudsen Plaza
PO Box 73
Boise, ID 83707 USA

RECRUITER: BOOKER BROWN
DIRECTOR, HUMAN RESOURCES,
INTERNATIONAL
1 MORRISON KNUDSEN PLAZA
PO BOX 73
BOISE, ID 83707
TEL: (208) 386-5000
FAX: (208) 386-5631

William M. Agee, Chairman. Engineering and construction. Morrison and Knudsen Corporation is a public company founded in 1912. Its business concentrates in the areas of mining, environmental projects, rail systems, transportation, and water resources. Worldwide revenues for 1992: $2.3 billion.

- **Total Employees:** 12,560
- **U.S. Employees Abroad:** 30
- **Countries:** Brazil, Canada, United Kingdom.
- **Job Categories:** Construction Workers, Engineers, Management, Marketing.
- **Language Requirement:** Varies with each posting.

MORTON INTERNATIONAL

100 North Riverside Dr.
Chicago, IL 60606-1560 USA

RECRUITER: JOHN C. HADLEY
VP, HUMAN RESOURCES
100 NORTH RIVERSIDE DR.
CHICAGO, IL 60606-1560
TEL: (312) 807-2000
FAX: (312) 807-2241

Charles S. Locke, Chairman. Specialty chemicals, salt, and automotive products. Morton International is a public company founded in 1848 by Alonzo Richmond. He operated Richmond and Company in Chicago until Jay Morton became the controlling owner in 1886 and renamed the company Jay Morton and Company. In 1910 it became Morton Salt Company, well-known for its slogan "When it rains, it pours." Today, it has 75 plants in 24 countries with the specialty chemicals division accounting for 62 percent of its sales. Worldwide revenues for 1992: $2.1 billion.

- **Total Employees:** 9,700
- **U.S. Employees Abroad:** 25
- **Countries:** Bahamas, Canada, France, Germany, Hong Kong, Japan, Netherlands, Taiwan, United Kingdom.
- **Job Categories:** Accountants, Chemical Engineers, Marketing—Chemicals, Marketing, Sales—Chemicals, Sales.

MOTION PICTURE EXPORT ASSOCIATION OF AMERICA

1133 Avenue of the Americas
New York, NY 10036 USA

RECRUITER: DEBBIE FORTUNATO
STAFFING MANAGER
1113 AVENUE OF THE AMERICAS
NEW YORK, NY 10036
TEL: (212) 840-6160
FAX: (212) 391-3239

Jack J. Valenti, President. Motion pictures. Motion Picture Association of America was established in 1922 and is the principal producer and distributor of motion pictures in the United States. It strives to maintain a high morale and artistic standards in films by promoting the educational as well as entertainment value and usefullness of motion pictures.

- **Total Employees:** 125
- **U.S. Employees Abroad:** 15
- **Countries:** Brazil, India, Italy, Philippines, United Kingdom.
- **Application Information:** Hiring for most overseas positions is done at the specific country location.
- **Job Categories:** Management, Marketing.

MOTOROLA, INC.

1301 Algonquin Rd.
Schaumburg, IL 60196 USA

RECRUITER: JAMES DONNELLY
EXECUTIVE VP, PERSONNEL
    DEPARTMENT
1301 ALGONQUIN RD.
SCHAUMBURG, IL 60196
TEL: (708) 576-5000
FAX: (708) 576-8003

George M. C. Fisher, Chairman. Electronic systems and equipment supplier. Motorola is a public company founded in 1928 by Paul Galvin. Chicago-based Galvin Manufacturing Company produced car-radio receivers. Daniel Noble joined the company, and in 1947 it was renamed Motorola after the car radios it produced. Today, it is the fourth largest provider of semiconductors in the world. It has major facilities in the United States and abroad. Worldwide revenues for 1992: $13.3 billion.

- **Total Employees:** 104,000
- **U.S. Employees Abroad:** 70
- **Countries:** Australia, Belgium, Canada, Costa Rica, Republic of Korea, Malaysia, Mexico, Taiwan, Switzerland, United Kingdom.
- **Job Categories:** Administrative, Marketing—Electronics, Product Development, Sales—Electronics.

NABORS INDUSTRIES, INC.

515 West Greens Rd.
Houston, TX 77067 USA

RECRUITER: VERA BAKER
PERSONNEL ADMINISTRATION
515 WEST GREENS RD.
HOUSTON, TX 77067
TEL: (713) 874-0035
FAX: (713) 872-5205

Gene Isenberg, Chairman. Contract drilling. Nabors Industries, Inc. is a public company founded in 1978. It is engaged in mining and oil field drilling. Worldwide revenues for 1991: $240 million.

- **Total Employees:** 3,000

- **U.S. Employees Abroad:** 100
- **Countries:** Canada, United Kingdom.
- **Job Categories:** Administrative, Management, Field Technicians, Rigging Services.
- **Language Requirement:** Competency in local language required.
- **Training:** In-depth orientation (1-30 days) provided.
- **Benefits:** All benefits are offered.

NALCO CHEMICAL COMPANY

One Nalco Center
Naperville, IL 60563-1198 USA

RECRUITER: LOU HABERMAS
HUMAN RESOURCES COORDINATOR
ONE NALCO CENTER
NAPERVILLE, IL 60563-1198
TEL: (708) 305-1000
FAX: (708) 305-2920

W. H. Clark, Chairman. Chemicals. Nalco Chemical is a public company founded in 1928. It produces chemicals used in water and waste treatment, petroleum production and refining, and pollution control. Markets include automotive, electronics, food and beverage, and mining and mineral processing industries. Products are sold in more than 100 countries. Worldwide revenues for 1992: $1.4 billion.

- **Total Employees:** 6,714
- **U.S. Employees Abroad:** 30
- **Countries:** Argentina, Australia, Brazil, Canada, Chile, Colombia, France, Germany, Hong Kong, Italy, Japan, Mexico, Netherlands, Philippines, Singapore, Taiwan, United Kingdom.
- **Application Information:** Most overseas positions are filled internally.
- **Job Categories:** Marketing—Chemicals, Product Development, Sales—Chemicals.
- **Language Requirement:** Varies with each posting.

NATIONAL DATA CORPORATION

2 National Data Plaza
Atlanta, GA 30329 USA

RECRUITER: CAROL KING
HUMAN RESOURCES COORDINATOR
2 NATIONAL DATA PLAZA
ATLANTA, GA 30329
TEL: (404) 728-2000
FAX: (404) 728-3904

L. C. Whitney, Chairman. Data processing services. National Data Corporation is a public company founded in 1967. It supplies data processing services to financial institutions, health-care and communication sectors, and retail establishments. Worldwide operating revenues for 1992: $219 million.

- **Total Employees:** 2,000
- **U.S. Employees Abroad:** 30

- **Countries:** Canada, Italy, Germany, Japan, Spain, United Kingdom.
- **Job Categories:** Management, Marketing, Sales.
- **Language Requirement:** Varies with each posting.

NATIONAL SEMICONDUCTOR CORPORATION

2900 Semiconductor Dr.
Santa Clara, CA 95052 USA

RECRUITER: DAVID SCHOOF
DIRECTOR OF STAFFING & PLACEMENT
2900 SEMICONDUCTOR DR., MS-14-175
SANTA CLARA, CA 95052
TEL: (408) 721-5000
FAX: (408) 730-1520

Charles E. Sprock, President. Semiconductors and board-level connectivity products. National Semiconductor Corporation is a public company founded in 1959. It designs, produces, and sells semiconductors and board-level connectivity projects. Major products include Adversary home video game and Post-Script printer quality images software. Worldwide revenues for 1992: $1.9 billion.

- **Total Employees:** 30,000
- **U.S. Employees Abroad:** 35
- **Countries:** Australia, Brazil, Hong Kong, Indonesia, Israel, Italy, Japan, Singapore, Thailand.
- **Job Categories:** Administrative, Marketing—Electronics, Sales—Electronics, Technicians.

NAVISTAR INTERNATIONAL TRANSPORTATION CORPORATION

455 Cityfront Plaza Dr.
Chicago, IL 60611 USA

RECRUITER: CATHERINE HENLEY
MANAGER, ORGANIZATION DEVELOPMENT
455 CITYFRONT PLAZA CRIVE
CHICAGO, IL 60611
TEL: (312) 836-2029
FAX: (312) 836-2582

James C. Cotting, Chairman. Heavy-duty and medium-duty diesel trucks, diesel engines, and diesel school buses. Navistar International Transportation Corporation is a public company founded in 1902 as International Harvester, which at that time controlled 85 percent of the U.S. harvester production. The first overseas facility was begun in 1905 in Sweden. The company was renamed Navistar in 1986. Today, it is the leader in sales of medium and heavy-duty trucks in North America. Navistar Financing offers its services to customers throughout the world. Worldwide revenues for 1992: $4 billion.

- **Total Employees:** 14,000
- **U.S. Employees Abroad:** 14

- **Countries:** Canada, Dominican Republic, Mexico.

- **Job Categories:** Business Development, Marketing—Automotive, Sales—Automotive, Technical Service Managers.

- **General Requirements:** Bilingual-Spanish for Latin America. Also, must have knowledge in the field of international products and truck industry.

- **Average Overseas Assignment:** 3-5 years

- **Language Requirement:** Fluency in local language required; knowledge of local language in other regions a plus.

- **Training:** No special training offered.

- **Benefits:** TRAVEL: Offers home leave and relocation. HEALTH: Same coverage as U.S. employees. HOUSING: Offers special housing allowances. EDUCATION: Individually determined.

NCR CORPORATION

1700 South Patterson Blvd.
Dayton, OH 45479 USA

RECRUITER: GARY R. MOYER
HUMAN RESOURCES
REPRESENTATIVE
1700 SOUTH PATTERSON BLVD.
DAYTON, OH 45479
TEL: (515) 445-5000
FAX: (515) 445-1238

Charles E. Exley, Jr., Chairman. Business information processing systems. NCR is a public subsidiary of AT & T located in New York City. It was founded in 1844 by John Patterson. He began the National Cash Register Company in Dayton, Ohio. He introduced accounting machines in the 1920s and after World War II the company focused its attention on computing. Today, NCR is the 2nd largest manufacturer of ATMs in the United States. It develops, produces, sells, and services business information systems throughout the world. NCR became part of AT&T in 1991. Worldwide revenues for 1991: $6.3 billion.

- **Total Employees:** 55,000

- **U.S. Employees Abroad:** 75

- **Countries:** Worldwide including Republic of South Africa, Australia, Canada, Japan, Mexico.

- **Job Categories:** Accountants, Marketing—Electronics, Product Development, Sales—Electronics.

NELLCOR, INC.

25495 Whitesell St.
Hayward, CA 94545 USA

RECRUITER: PATRICIA BASHAW
STAFFING/RECRUITMENT
25495 WHITESELL ST.
HAYWARD, CA 94545
TEL: (510) 887-5858
FAX: (510) 293-4420

C. Raymond Larkin, Jr., President. Patient safety monitors; related sensors and accessories. Nellcor, Inc. is a public company which develops, produces, and sells electric monitors and related products. These include anesthesia safety monitors and pulse oximeters. Worldwide revenues for 1992: $81.1 million.

- **Total Employees:** 1,500
- **U.S. Employees Abroad:** Not available.
- **Countries:** Belgium, France, Germany, Hong Kong, Netherlands, United Kingdom.
- **Job Categories:** Engineers, Manufacturing, Marketing—Health & Medical Supplies, Sales—Health & Medical Supplies.
- **General Requirements:** Prior international experience is preferred.
- **Average Overseas Assignment:** 3-5 years.
- **Language Requirement:** Fluency in at least one major language required.
- **Training:** Varies with each posting.
- **Benefits:** All benefits are individually determined.

NEW YORK LIFE INSURANCE COMPANY

51 Madison Ave.
New York, NY 10010 USA

RECRUITER: WILLIAM MOWAT
DIRECTOR, HUMAN RESOURCES
51 MADISON AVE.
NEW YORK, NY 10010
TEL: (212) 576-1000
FAX: (212) 576-7619

Donald K. Ross, President and Chairman. Insurance. New York Life Insurance is a public company founded in 1841. It offers automobile, homeowners, and property insurance as well as fidelity and security services, deferred annuities, and multifunded annuities. It also offers group stop-loss insurance, single premium immediate annuities, and pensions. Worldwide total assets for 1992: $47 billion.

- **Total Employees:** 10,000
- **U.S. Employees Abroad:** 20
- **Countries:** Canada, Republic of Korea.
- **Job Categories:** Administrative, Agents—Insurance, Marketing—Financial Services, Sales—Financial Services.
- **Language Requirement:** None.

NEW YORK TIMES COMPANY

229 West 43rd St.
New York, NY 10036 USA

RECRUITER: BRENDA WATSON
DIRECTOR, STAFFING/RECRUITMENT
229 WEST 43RD ST.
NEW YORK, NY 10036
TEL: (212) 556-1234
FAX: (212) 556-4607

Authur Ochs Sulzberger, Chairman. Publishing and radio broadcasting. New York Times is a public company founded in 1851 by George Jones and Henry J. Raymond. It publishes and prints newspapers. It also operates radio broadcasting stations. *The New York Times* newspaper is sold in the United States and in 70 other countries. Worldwide revenues for 1992: $1.8 billion.

- **Total Employees:** 10,600
- **U.S. Employees Abroad:** 35
- **Countries:** Canada, United Kingdom.
- **Job Categories:** Editors, Marketing—Publishing, Reporters, Sales—Publishing.

NEWMONT MINING CORPORATION

1700 Lincoln St., Suite 270
Denver, CO 80203 USA

RECRUITER: SHARON HACKENBURG
EMPLOYEE RELATIONS
1700 LINCOLN ST., SUITE 2700
DENVER, CO 80203
TEL: (303) 837-6113
FAX: (303) 837-6131

G. R. Parker, Chairman. Gold mining. Newmont Mining Corporation is a public company founded in 1921. It is primarily engaged in gold exploration. It also has full control over its gold properties in the United States and mines gold on a worldwide basis through its division, Newmont Exploration Limited (NEL). Worldwide revenues for 1992: $613 million.

- **Total Employees:** 3,100
- **U.S. Employees Abroad:** 25
- **Countries:** Australia.
- **Application Information:** Most overseas positions are filled internally.
- **Job Categories:** Administrative, Marketing, Technical Field Support.
- **Language Requirement:** Varies with each posting.

NEWSWEEK INTERNATIONAL

444 Madison Ave.
New York, NY 10022 USA

RECRUITER: JEANNE SAKAS AND
CATHY FERNANDEZ
STAFFING/RECRUITMENT
444 MADISON AVE.
NEW YORK, NY 10022
TEL: (212) 350-4000

Joanne Hindman, Vice President. Publishing. Newsweek International was founded in 1933 and is a subsidiary of the Washington Post Company of Washington, D.C. It publishes and prints an international news magazine and has 26 news bureaus throughout the world. Total circulation of *Newsweek* is 960,000. Worldwide revenues for 1991: $340 million.

- **Total Employees:** 1,000
- **U.S. Employees Abroad:** 30
- **Countries:** France, Germany, Hong Kong, Japan, Netherlands, Poland, Singapore, Sweden, Switzerland, United Kingdom.
- **Application Information:** Hiring for most overseas positions is done at the specific country location.
- **Job Categories:** Editors, Finance, Reporters.

NICOLET INSTRUMENT CORPORATION

5225 Verona Rd.
Madison, WI 53711 USA

RECRUITER: CORY ERICKSON
HUMAN RESOURCES
5225 VERONA RD.
MADISON, WI 53711
TEL: (608) 271-3333
FAX: (608) 273-6880

Roland Pampel, Chief Executive Officer. Electronic instruments. Nicolet Instrument is a public company founded in 1965. It produces and sells electronic instruments, including medical dialog equipment. These products are used in various fields: chemical analysis and research, neurological diagnostics and monitoring, hearing health-care, and electronic test measurements. Worldwide revenues for 1992: $139 million.

- **Total Employees:** 1,200
- **U.S. Employees Abroad:** Not available.
- **Countries:** Belgium, Canada, France, Germany, Japan, United Kingdom.
- **Job Categories:** Management, Marketing—Electronics, Product Development, Sales—Electronics.
- **Language Requirement:** None.
- **Comments:** The number of Americans reported working abroad varies greatly from quarter to quarter, fluctuating with the number and scope of projects under contract at the time.

NIKE, INC.

One Bowerman Dr.
Beaverton, OR 97005 USA

RECRUITER: SUE SCHNEIDER
PERSONNEL DIRECTOR
ONE BOWERMAN DR.
BEAVERTON, OR 97005
TEL: (503) 671-6453
FAX: (503) 626-7252

Philip H. Knight, Chairman. Athletic and leisure footwear and related accessories. NIKE, Inc. is a public company founded in 1968 by Phil Knight and Bill Bowerman. Their idea was to create an acceptable American running shoe. The first attempt began in 1964 when they formed Blue Ribbon Sports and had a Japanese manufacturer produce them. Today, NIKE basketball, fitness, and running shoes and also other fitness and sportswear. A popular brand name is Air Jordan, a basketball shoe. Nearly all of its shoes and half of its apparel are produced overseas. Worldwide revenues for 1992: $3.8 billion.

- **Total Employees:** 4,500
- **U.S. Employees Abroad:** 40
- **Countries:** Canada, Japan, Netherlands, Republic of Korea, Taiwan.
- **Job Categories:** Management, Marketing—Consumer Goods, Product Development, Sales—Consumer Goods.
- **Language Requirement:** Varies with each posting.

NL INDUSTRIES, INC.

PO Box 60087
Houston, TX 77205 USA

RECRUITER: FRANK VAVRICA
MANAGER, COMPENSATION &
RECRUITMENT
PO BOX 60087
HOUSTON, TX 77205
TEL: (713) 987-4000
FAX: (713) 987-6326

J. Landis Martin, President. Petroleum services, metal products, and chemicals. NL Industries was founded in 1891 and is a subsidiary of Valhi, Inc. of Dallas, Texas. It is a global producer of titanium dioxide pigments, which add opacity and whiteness to paints, plastics, fibers, and ceramics. It is also a manufacturer of specialty chemicals. Worldwide revenues for 1992: $893 million.

- **Total Employees:** 3,600
- **U.S. Employees Abroad:** 25
- **Countries:** Brazil, Italy, Trinidad and Tobago, United Arab Emirates.
- **Job Categories:** Management, Product Development, Sales—Chemicals, Sales—Petroleum/Natural Gas.
- **Language Requirement:** None.

NORDSON CORPORATION

28601 Clemens Rd.
Westlake, OH 44145 USA

RECRUITER: BRUCE H. FIELDS
DIRECTOR, HUMAN RESOURCES
28601 CLEMENS RD.
WESTLAKE, OH 44145
TEL: (216) 892-1580
FAX: (216) 892-9507

William P. Madar, President. Industrial application equipment and packaging machinery. Nordson Corporation is a public company founded in 1935. It produces and sells equipment and systems used in the application of coatings, adhesives, and sealants during the manufacturing process. Major products include powder coating application systems and Select Coat systems for applying protective conformal coatings on printed circuit boards. Subsidiaries and affiliates are located in the United States and abroad. Worldwide revenues for 1992: $3.4 billion.

- **Total Employees:** 2,645
- **U.S. Employees Abroad:** 22
- **Countries:** Australia, Belgium, Brazil, Canada, Denmark, France, Germany, Hong Kong, Italy, Japan, Republic of Korea, Netherlands, Switzerland, United Kingdom.
- **Application Information:** Most overseas positions are filled internally (for developmental purposes).
- **Job Categories:** Management, Marketing—Industrial.
- **Average Overseas Assignment:** Less than three years.
- **Language Requirement:** Varies with each posting.

NORTH AMERICAN PHILIPS CORPORATION

100 East 42nd St.
New York, NY 10017 USA

RECRUITER: JUDY GORSKI
MANAGER, EXPATRIATE PROGRAM
100 EAST 42ND ST.
NEW YORK, NY 10017
TEL: (212) 850-5000
FAX: (212) 850-5362

Einar Kloster, President. Electronic equipment and components. North American Philips was founded in 1984 and is a wholly owned subsidiary of N.V. Philips of the Netherlands. It is one of the largest U.S. manufacturers and major exporters of electronic products, components, and lighting. Major products include Hot Stuff beverage containers and Norelco electric appliances. Worldwide revenues for 1991: $6.1 billion.

- **Total Employees:** 52,000
- **U.S. Employees Abroad:** 40
- **Countries:** Canada, Italy, Greece, Netherlands.
- **Job Categories:** Management, Marketing—Electronics, Sales—Electronics.

- **Language Requirement:** Varies with each posting.

NORTHWEST AIRLINES, INC.

5101 Northwest Dr., A2060
St. Paul, MN 55111 USA

RECRUITER: INTERNATIONAL OPERATIONS
DIRECTOR, INTERNATIONAL OPERATIONS
5101 NORTHWEST DR., A2060
ST. PAUL, MN 55111-3034
TEL: (612 727-4864
FAX: (612 726-6911

John Dasburg, President. Passenger and cargo air transportation. Northwest Airlines, Inc. (NWA) is a private company founded in 1926. It acted as a public company until 1989 when Wings Holdings (an investment group including KLM Royal Dutch Airlines), took NWA private through a $3.65 billion leveraged buy-out. Today, NWA is the fourth largest airline in the United States flying to 129 cities in 21 countries. Worldwide revenues for 1991: $7.5 billion. Foreign revenues for 1991: $3.2 billion.

- **Total Employees:** 44,000
- **U.S. Employees Abroad:** 150
- **Countries:** Canada, People's Republic of China, France, Cayman Islands, Guam, Hong Kong, Jamaica, Japan, Republic of Korea, Philippines, Singapore, Thailand, United Kingdom.
- **Salaries:** $35,000-$140,000 per year.
- **Job Categories:** Aircraft Maintenance, Customer Services, Finance, Management, Marketing—Travel, Sales—Travel.
- **General Requirements:** Functional expertise required.
- **Average Overseas Assignment:** 3-5 years.
- **Language Requirement:** Knowledge of local language a plus but not essential.
- **Training:** Language training provided.
- **Benefits:** TRAVEL: Annual home leave offered; car rental paid for one week per year. HEALTH: Same coverage as U.S. employees. HOUSING: Offered; housing contribution deducted from employee's salary. EDUCATION: Offered; tuition and transportation for dependents age 3 through 12, at an approved American or international school.

NORTON COMPANY

1 New Bond St.
PO Box 15008
Worcester, MA 01615-1500 USA

RECRUITER: DAVID V. THOMPSON SCRP
INTERNATIONAL RECRUITMENT SCRP
1 NEW BOND ST.
PO BOX 15008
WORCESTER, MA 01615-1500
TEL: (508) 795-5000

Michael L. Besson, President and Chairman. Abrasives, drill bits, and safety products. Norton is a public company founded in 1885. It is a developer and manufacturer of bonded abrasives, coated abrasives, super abrasives, performance plastics, and chemical process products. Major items include films and laminates, grinding wheels, and sandpaper. It has operations throughout the United States and abroad. Worldwide revenues for 1991: $1.4 billion.

- **Total Employees:** 16,600
- **U.S. Employees Abroad:** 45
- **Countries:** Argentina, Australia, Belgium, Brazil, Canada, India, Italy, Netherlands, Singapore, Spain, Sweden, United Kingdom, Venezuela.
- **Job Categories:** Administrative, Marketing—Industrial, Plant Managers, Sales—Industrial.
- **Language Requirement:** Varies with each posting.

NORWEST CORPORATION

Norwest Center
6th & Marquette
Minneapolis, MN 55479 USA

RECRUITER: PATRICK STONE
MANAGER, HUMAN RESOURCES
NORWEST BANK, NORWEST CENTER,
   6TH & MARQUETTE
MINNEAPOLIS, MN 55479
TEL: (612) 667-3557
FAX: (612) 667-0674

Richard Kovacevich, President. Banking services. Norwest Corporation is a public company formed in 1990 when Norwest Corporation merged its 17 Twin Cities area banks into Norwest Bank Minnesota. Today, it is a national, diversified, financial services company with 2,000 offices throughout the United States, Canada, and other international locations. Its current assets place Norwest as the fifteenth largest holding company in the United States. Worldwide revenues for 1992: $4.7 billion.

- **Total Employees:** 30,000
- **U.S. Employees Abroad:** 6
- **Countries:** Argentina, Brazil, Hong Kong, Singapore, Taiwan.
- **Salaries:** $60,000-$85,000 per year
- **Job Categories:** Management.
- **General Requirements:** Usually must be a current employee of the company in order to qualify for overseas assignment; banking experience.
- **Average Overseas Assignment:** 3-5 years
- **Language Requirement:** Competency in local language required.
- **Training:** No special training provided.
- **Benefits:** TRAVEL: One home trip annually for employee and family. HEALTH: Offered; comparable to U.S. coverage HOUSING: Offered; paid for by Norwest. EDUCATION: Offered.

- **Comments:** The number of Americans reported working abroad varies greatly from quarter to quarter, fluctuating with the number and scope of projects under contract at the time.

NOVELL, INC.

122 East 1700 St.
Provo, UT 84606 USA

RECRUITER: JACQUI CARLSON
STAFFING MANAGER, HUMAN
RESOURCES
122 EAST 1700 ST.
PROVO, UT 84606
TEL: (801) 429-3098
FAX: (801) 429-5775

Raymond J. Noorda, President and Chairman. Open, high-performance PC-based networking connectivity products. Novell, Inc. is a public company incorporated in 1983. It is an operating system software company and developer of network services and specialized and general purpose operating system software products. These include NetWare, UnixWare, and DR DOS. Novell's NetWare network computing products manage and control the sharing of services, data, and applications among computer workgroups, departmental networks, and across business-wide information systems. Worldwide revenues for 1992: $989 million.

- **Total Employees:** 3,600
- **U.S. Employees Abroad:** 25
- **Countries:** Australia, Brazil, France, Germany, Hong Kong, Italy, Japan, Mexico, Spain, United Kingdom.
- **Job Categories:** Marketing—Electronics, Technical Field Support.
- **General Requirements:** Usually must be a current employee of the company in order to qualify for overseas assignment.

NYNEX CORPORATION

335 Madison Ave.
New York, NY 10017 USA

RECRUITER: PAT PETRICH
INTERNATIONAL RECRUITMENT
335 MADISON AVE.
NEW YORK, NY 10017
TEL: (914) 644-3905
FAX: (914) 697-9520

William C. Fergusen, President. Information provider; telecommunications systems. Nynex Corporation is a public company incorporated in 1983. It began operations in 1984. In 1990, it was divided into two groups: Telecommunications and Worldwide Services. In 1991 it began to focus on its international operations. Today, it is the fourth largest of the "Baby Bell" companies with operations in over 60 countries. Worldwide revenues for 1992: $13.1 billion.

- **Total Employees:** 92,000

- **U.S. Employees Abroad:** 110
- **Countries:** Worldwide including Belgium, France, Hong Kong, Switzerland, United Kingdom.
- **Job Categories:** Administrative, Finance, Marketing—Telecommunications, Sales—Telecommunications.

OCCIDENTAL PETROLEUM CORPORATION

10889 Wilshire Blvd.
Los Angeles, CA 90024 USA

RECRUITER: PATRICK DAILEY
DIRECTOR, HUMAN RESOURCES
10889 WILSHIRE BLVD.
LOS ANGELES, CA 90024
TEL: (213) 208-8800
FAX: (213) 824-2372

Ray R. Irani, President and Chairman. Exploration, development, and sale of crude oil. Occidental Petroleum Corporation is a public company founded in 1920 by Dr. Armand Hammer. After his death in 1990, Ray R. Irani captured the CEO post, and currently the Occidental Chemical division is a leading producer of polyvinyl chloride (PVC) and chloralkali. Worldwide revenues for 1992: $8.5 billion.

- **Total Employees:** 55,000
- **U.S. Employees Abroad:** 100
- **Countries:** Belgium, Brazil, Canada, Colombia, Germany, Pakistan, Saudi Arabia, Spain, Switzerland, United Kingdom, Venezuela.
- **Job Categories:** Administrative, Engineers, Marketing—Petroleum/Natural Gas, Sales—Petroleum/Natural Gas.
- **Language Requirement:** Varies with each posting.

OCEANEERING INTERNATIONAL, INC.

PO Box 218130
Houston, TX 77218 USA

RECRUITER: JUANITA VERDIN
PERSONNEL OFFICER
PO BOX 218130
HOUSTON, TX 77218
TEL: (713) 578-8868

John Rossman Huff, President. Underwater services for energy industries. Oceaneering International, Inc. provides diving and other related services for offshore oil and gas industries. Worldwide revenues for 1993: $216 million.

- **Total Employees:** 1,200
- **U.S. Employees Abroad:** 20
- **Countries:** Australia, Nigeria, Norway, Singapore, United Arab Emirates, United Kingdom.
- **Application Information:** Hiring for most overseas positions is done at the specific country location.

- **Job Categories:** Administrative, Marketing—Petroleum/Natural Gas, Divers.

- **Language Requirement:** None.

OFFSHORE LOGISTICS

224 Rue deJohn
Lafayette, LA 70508 USA

RECRUITER: JIM WILLIAMS
OPERATIONS MANAGER
224 RUE DEJOHN
LAFAYETTE, LA 70508
TEL: (318) 233-1221

Kenneth M. Jones, President. Offshore oil services. Offshore Logistics, Inc. is a provider of services to offshore oil operations in the United States and abroad. These include helicopters and vessels. Worldwide operating revenues for 1991: $95.2 million.

- **Total Employees:** 1,500

- **U.S. Employees Abroad:** 25

- **Countries:** Singapore, United Arab Emirates.

- **Job Categories:** Administrative, Pilots, Vessel Operators.

- **Language Requirement:** None.

OFFSHORE PIPELINES, INC.

5718 Westheimer Rd.
Houston, TX 77057 USA

RECRUITER: DENNIS LUCE
HUMAN RESOURCES
REPRESENTATIVE
5718 WESTHEIMER RD.
HOUSTON, TX 77057
TEL: (713) 952-1000
FAX: (713) 267-7751

Frank C. Wade, Chairman. Offshore production of oil and gas; related oil-production services. Offshore Pipelines, Inc. is a public company founded in 1984. It began as a private company and remained so until 1990. It builds and installs fixed platforms and refurbishes or constructs marine pipelines. It engages divers to assist in offshore production and transportation of oil and gas. Worldwide revenues for 1992: $370 million.

- **Total Employees:** 1,965

- **U.S. Employees Abroad:** 25

- **Countries:** Bahrain, Singapore.

- **Job Categories:** Administrative, Construction Workers, Divers.

- **Language Requirement:** None.

OGDEN CORPORATION

Two Pennsylvania Ave.
New York, NY 10021 USA

RECRUITER: HANK MARTONE
CORPORATE DIRECTOR OF
    EMPLOYMENT
TWO PENNSYLVANIA AVE.
NEW YORK, NY 10021
TEL: (212) 868-6100
FAX: (212) 967-4929

R. Richard Ablon, President. Holding company. Ogden Corporation was founded in 1939. It was originally formed as a holding company for a failing public utilities firm. Today, the company is divided into two main parts; Ogden Services (100 percent owned) and Ogden Projects (85 percent owned). Ogden Services provides building, housekeeping, and management services. Ogden Projects, a public company, concentrates on recycling, waste-disposal, and waste-to-energy facilities. It operates throughout the United States and in 12 foreign countries. Worldwide operating revenues for 1992: $1.8 billion.

- **Total Employees:** 45,000

- **U.S. Employees Abroad:** Not available.

- **Countries:** Canada, Mexico, New Zealand, United Kingdom.

- **Application Information:** Most foreign positions are filled internally.

- **Job Categories:** Management, Technical Field Support, Sales.

- **Average Overseas Assignment:** Varies with each posting, usually under one year.

OGILVY & MATHER

309 West 49th St.
New York, NY 10019 USA

RECRUITER: PATTY ENRIGHT
HUMAN RESOURCES
309 WEST 49TH ST.
NEW YORK, NY 10019
TEL: (212) 237-4000
FAX: (212) 779-7717

Graham Phillips, Chairman. Advertising. Ogilvy & Mather was founded in 1964 and is a subsidiary of WPP Group USA of New York City. Worldwide gross billings for 1991: $5.5 billion.

- **Total Employees:** 10,000

- **U.S. Employees Abroad:** 45

- **Countries:** Argentina, Australia, Belgium, Canada, France, Germany, Hong Kong, Malaysia, Mexico, Netherlands, Republic of South Africa, United Kingdom.

- **Job Categories:** Management, Marketing.

- **Training:** No special training provided.

OLIN CORPORATION

120 Long Ridge Rd.
Stamford, CT 06904 USA

RECRUITER: MARK KILLIAN
DIRECTOR, HUMAN RESOURCES
120 LONG RIDGE RD.
STAMFORD, CT 06904
TEL: (203) 356-2000
FAX: (203) 356-3595

John W. Johnstone, Jr., President. Chemicals, metals, and applied physics. Olin Corporation is a public company founded in 1892. The business is divided into three operating segments: chemicals, metals and materials, and defense. Worldwide revenues for 1992: $2.4 billion.

- **Total Employees:** 2,200

- **U.S. Employees Abroad:** 20

- **Countries:** Australia, Belgium, France, Germany, Japan, Mexico, Taiwan, United Kingdom, Venezuela.

- **Job Categories:** Engineers, Management, Marketing—Chemicals, Marketing—Scientific.

- **Language Requirement:** Varies with each posting.

OMI INTERNATIONAL

21441 Hoover Rd.
Warren, MI 48089 USA

RECRUITER: STANLEY ZABROCKY
MANAGER, EMPLOYMENT SERVICES
PO BOX 1900
NEW HAVEN, CT 06508
TEL: (203) 934-8611
FAX: (203) 799-1513

F. Schneiders, Chief Executive Officer. Specialty chemical preparations and equipment for metal finishing. OMI International was founded in 1983 and is a subsidiary of Asarco, Inc. of New York City. It produces surface active preparations and related products as well as various chemical products.

- **Total Employees:** 1,200

- **U.S. Employees Abroad:** 20

- **Countries:** Netherlands, Spain.

- **Job Categories:** Administrative, Marketing—Chemicals, Sales—Chemicals.

- **Language Requirement:** None.

OMNICOM GROUP, INC.

437 Madison Ave.
New York, NY 10022 USA

RECRUITER: DONNA OSTRAU
PERSONNEL DEPARTMENT
437 MADISON AVE., 9TH FLOOR
NEW YORK, NY 10022
TEL: (212) 415-3600
FAX: (212) 414-3530

Bruce Crawford, President. Advertising, marketing, public relations. Omnicom Group, Inc. is a public company founded in 1986. It offers marketing consultation, consumer product research advice on merchandising, and sales promotion. It also provides services for direct mail advertising and public relations. Worldwide gross billings for 1991: $10.4 billion.

- **Total Employees:** 11,400

- **U.S. Employees Abroad:** 40

- **Countries:** Worldwide including Australia, France, Germany, Japan, Republic of South Africa, United Kingdom.

- **Job Categories:** Human Resources, Management, Marketing.

- **Language Requirement:** Varies with each posting.

- **Training:** No special training provided.

ONAN CORPORATION

1400 73rd Ave. NE
Minneapolis, MN 55432 USA

RECRUITER: SHANNON GREEN
DIRECTOR, HUMAN RESOURCES
1400 73RD AVE. NE
MINNEAPOLIS, MN 55432
TEL: (612) 574-5000
FAX: (612) 574-8087

Ronald Hoge, President. Electric generators and gasoline engines. Onan Corporation was founded in 1920 and is a subsidiary of Cummins Engine Company of Columbus, Indiana. It manufactures electric generators and gasoline engines. Worldwide revenues for 1992: $500 million.

- **Total Employees:** 3,800

- **U.S. Employees Abroad:** Not available.

- **Countries:** Canada, Japan, Republic of Korea, Singapore, United Kingdom.

- **Application Information:** Most overseas positions are filled internally.

- **Job Categories:** Engineers, Executive Management, Marketing.

- **Language Requirement:** Varies with each posting.

OPPENHEIMER GROUP

Oppenheimer Tower
World Financial Center
New York, NY 10281 USA

RECRUITER: LISA BELL
PERSONNEL DEPARTMENT
200 LIBERTY ST., 7TH FLOOR
NEW YORK, NY 10281
TEL: (212 667-7000
FAX: (212 667-6320

Stephen Robert, Chief Executive Officer. Investment services. Oppenheimer Group is a private company engaged in investment management services in the United States and abroad. Worldwide operating revenues for 1992: $773 million.

- **Total Employees:** 2,600
- **U.S. Employees Abroad:** 20
- **Countries:** United Kingdom.
- **Job Categories:** Analysts, Finance, Executive Management.

ORACLE SYSTEMS, INC.

500 Oracle Pkwy.
Redwood City, CA 94065 USA

RECRUITER: MICKEY SATTERWHITE
INTERNATIONAL HUMAN RESOURCES
500 ORACLE PKWY.
REDWOOD CITY, CA 94065
TEL: (415) 506-7000
FAX: (415) 506-7150

Lawrence J. Ellison, President and Chairman. Database management systems and software. Oracle Systems is a public company founded in 1977 by Lawrence Ellison, Robert Miner, and Edward Oates. Their primary intention was to create a relational database management system (DBMS). Today, it is a leader in this area and the third largest independent software developer. It has operations in over 40 U.S. cities and in over 90 foreign countries. Worldwide revenues for 1992: $1.3 billion.

- **Total Employees:** 6,800
- **U.S. Employees Abroad:** Not available.
- **Countries:** Worldwide including France, Japan, United Kingdom.
- **Job Categories:** Management, Marketing—Electronics, Product Development, Technical Field Support.
- **Training:** No special training provided.

ORYX ENERGY

13155 Noel Rd.
Dallas, TX 75240 USA

RECRUITER: PAULETTE MARCOULIDES
HUMAN RESOURCES
13155 NOEL RD.
PO BOX 2880
DALLAS, TX 75240
TEL: (214) 715-4000
FAX: (214) 715-8220

Robert P. Hauptfuhrer, Chairman. Gas and oilfield operations. Oryx Energy is a public company founded in 1982. It was formerly called the Sun Exploration & Production Company. It offers geological, geophysical, and other exploration services to oil and gas field operations. Worldwide revenues for 1992: $1.3 billion.

- **Total Employees:** 2,700
- **U.S. Employees Abroad:** 45
- **Countries:** Ecuador, Gabon, Indonesia, Mexico, United Kingdom.
- **Job Categories:** Field Engineers, Management, Marketing—Petroleum/Natural Gas.
- **Language Requirement:** None.
- **Training:** No special training provided.

OTIS ELEVATOR COMPANY: WORLD HEADQUARTERS

10 Farm Springs Rd.
Farmington, CT 06032 USA

RECRUITER: DEBORAH WILSON
HUMAN RESOURCES
REPRESENTATIVE
10 FARM SPRINGS RD.
FARMINGTON, CT 06032
TEL: (203) 674-4000

Karl J. Krapek, Chief Operating Officer. Elevators. Otis Elevator was founded in 1853 and is a subsidiary of United Technologies Corporation. It manufactures elevators and moving stairways. Worldwide revenues for 1992: $2.2 billion.

- **Total Employees:** 43,000
- **U.S. Employees Abroad:** 60
- **Countries:** Argentina, Australia, Brazil, Egypt, France, Germany, Hong Kong, Japan, Malaysia, Mexico, Taiwan, United Kingdom, Venezuela.
- **Job Categories:** Management, Manufacturing, Marketing, Sales.
- **Language Requirement:** None.

OUTBOARD MARINE CORPORATION

100 Seahorse Dr.
Waukegan, IL 60085 USA

RECRUITER: DENISE CHARTS
HUMAN RESOURCES
REPRESENTATIVE
100 SEAHORSE DR.
WAUKEGAN, IL 60085
TEL: (708) 689-6200
FAX: (708) 689-5555

Charles D. Strang, Chairman. Outboard engines. Outboard Marine Corporation is a public company founded in 1929 by Stephen Briggs and partner, Ole Evinrude. It was first named the Outboard Motors Corporation and introduced electric-starting outboard engines. Today, it is the world's largest producer of outboard motors. It has 21 plants in the United States and 10 facilities in foreign countries. Worldwide revenues for 1992: $1.1 billion.

- **Total Employees:** 14,000
- **U.S. Employees Abroad:** Not available.
- **Countries:** Australia, Belgium, Brazil, Canada, France, Hong Kong, Mexico, Sweden.
- **Job Categories:** Management, Marketing, Product Development, Sales.
- **Language Requirement:** None.

OVERSEAS SHIPHOLDING GROUP, INC.

1114 Avenue of the Americas
New York, NY 10036 USA

RECRUITER: RICHARD RASKIN
DIRECTOR, PERSONNEL DEPARTMENT
511-15 AVENUE OF THE AMERICAS
NEW YORK, NY 10017
TEL: (212) 578-1911
FAX: (212) 578-1960

Morton P. Hyman, President. Ocean transportation of bulk cargo. Overseas Shipholding Group, Inc. is a public company founded in 1969. Customers include governments, manufacturers, oil companies, and traders. Worldwide operating revenues for 1992: $370 million.

- **Total Employees:** 2,225
- **U.S. Employees Abroad:** 25
- **Countries:** Aruba, Japan, Panama, United Kingdom.
- **Job Categories:** Engineers, Marketing.
- **Language Requirement:** Varies with each posting.

OWENS-CORNING FIBERGLAS CORPORATION

Fiberglas Tower
Toledo, OH 43659 USA

RECRUITER: MARILYN KLINE
INTERNATIONAL HUMAN RESOURCES
FIBERGLAS TOWER
TOLEDO, OH 43659
TEL: (419) 248-8000
FAX: (419) 248-5337

Max O. Weber, Chairman. Insulation and glass fiber products. Owens-Corning Fiberglas Corporation is a public company founded in 1938. It is the largest fiberglass materials producer in the world. Other products include reinforcements, yarns, and resins to use in place of materials such as steel and wood. Customers include the aerospace, automotive, and construction industries. Worldwide revenues for 1992: $2.9 billion.

- **Total Employees:** 17,000
- **U.S. Employees Abroad:** 15
- **Countries:** Belgium, Brazil, France, Germany, Italy, Netherlands, Saudi Arabia, Sweden, United Kingdom.

- **Job Categories:** Executive Management.
- **General Requirements:** Usually must be a current employee of the company in order to qualify for overseas assignment.
- **Language Requirement:** Varies with each posting.
- **Training:** No special training provided.
- **Comments:** Most overseas positions are senior-level management.

OWENS-ILLINOIS, INC.

One SeaGate
Toledo, OH 43666 USA

RECRUITER: DELORES JONES
SALARIED PERSONNEL
ONE SEAGATE
TOLEDO, OH 43666
TEL: (419) 247-2671
FAX: (419) 247-2671

Joseph Lemieux, President. Glass, metal, and plastic packaging containers; U.S. healthcare facilities. Owens-Illinois, Inc. is a private company founded in 1903. The Owens Bottle Machine Corporation was incorporated in Toledo in 1907 as a successor to a New Jersey company with the same name. Through the years, the company acquired other small glass firms and, in 1929, it purchased the Illinois Glass Company. It was then renamed, Owens-Illinois Glass. Today, this company is said to be the producer of nearly half the glass containers manufactured in the world. It is also the sixth largest operator of investor-owned nursing and retirement homes in the United States. Manufacturing facilities are located in 13 foreign countries. Worldwide revenues for 1992: $3.7 billion.

- **Total Employees:** 50,000
- **U.S. Employees Abroad:** 50
- **Countries:** Australia, Brazil, Canada, Colombia, Germany, Italy, Japan, Singapore, Switzerland, Venezuela.
- **Job Categories:** Administrative, Management, Engineers, Manufacturing.
- **Average Overseas Assignment:** 3-5 years.
- **Language Requirement:** Knowledge of local language a plus but not essential.
- **Training:** Basic training (1-30 days) provided.
- **Benefits:** All benefits are offered.

PACCAR, INC.

777 106th Ave. NE
Bellevue, WA 98004 USA

RECRUITER: JULIE HORSMAN
HUMAN RESOURCES
777 106TH AVE. NE
BELLEVUE, WA 98004
TEL: (206) 455-7400
FAX: (206) 453-4900

Charles M. Pigot, Chairman. Heavy-duty vehicles and trucks. Paccar, Inc. is a public company founded in 1971. It produces heavy-duty on- and off-road Class 8 trucks and other vehicles. Nameplates include Foden, Kenworth, and Peterbilt. Other businesses include full-service truck leasing and financing services for truck sales and retail outlets that sell automotive parts and accessories. It has operations in the United States and abroad. Worldwide revenues for 1992: $2.7 billion.

- **Total Employees:** 13,700

- **U.S. Employees Abroad:** 25

- **Countries:** Australia, Canada, Mexico, United Kingdom.

- **Job Categories:** Executive Management, Finance, Marketing.

- **General Requirements:** Usually must be a current employee of the company in order to qualify for overseas assignment.

- **Benefits:** All benefits are individually determined.

PACIFIC ARCHITECTS & ENGINEERS, INC.

1601 North Kent St., Suite #900
Arlington, VA 22209 USA

RECRUITER: DAVID TERRAR
DIRECTOR, RECRUITMENT
1601 NORTH KENT ST., SUITE #900
ARLINGTON, VA 22209
TEL: (703) 243-6464
FAX: (703) 243-5607

Michael Gulino, Executive Vice President. Support services for U.S. embassies around the world. Pacific Architects & Engineers is a private company founded in 1955. It operates on a worldwide basis offering various support services to its clients. Worldwide operating revenues for 1991: $16 million.

- **Total Employees:** 150

- **U.S. Employees Abroad:** 100

- **Countries:** Russia.

- **Application Information:** Must meet general qualifications.

- **Job Categories:** Carpenters, Clerical Assistants, Drivers, Electricians, Gardeners, Maintenance, Painters, Plumbers, Translators.

- **General Requirements:** Must be a U.S. citizen; have a high school diploma equivalent; an international driver's license; diplomatic passport/visa required.

- **Average Overseas Assignment:** 2-3 years.

- **Language Requirement:** Competency in local language required.

- **Training:** Basic orientation (1-30 days); in some cases language training is provided.

- **Benefits:** TRAVEL: PAE provides or reimburses employee for air ticket and surface shipment to and from post; 1 round trip ticket to Rome or New York once each year. HEALTH: Pre-employment physical paid for by PAE (up to $400); medical insurance available. HOUSING: Offered. EDUCATION: None offered.

PACIFIC TELESIS INTERNATIONAL

130 Kearney St.
San Francisco, CA 94108 USA

RECRUITER: JAMES R. MOBERG
EXECUTIVE VP, HUMAN RESOURCES
130 KEARNEY ST., 37TH FLOOR
SAN FRANCISCO, CA 94108
TEL: (415) 394-3000
FAX: (415) 362-2913

Sam Ginn, President and Chairman. Telecommunications and information systems. Pacific Telesis International is a public company founded in 1983. It provides telecommunication systems and related services within the United States and abroad through its many subsidiaries. Customers include businesses, consumers, interexchange and exchange carriers. Subsidiaries include Pacific Bell and PacTel Business Systems. Worldwide revenues for 1992: $9.9 billion.

- **Total Employees:** 65,800

- **U.S. Employees Abroad:** 70

- **Countries:** France, Germany, Japan, Republic of Korea, Thailand, United Kingdom.

- **Job Categories:** Administrative, Marketing—Telecommunications, Sales—Telecommunications.

- **Language Requirement:** Knowledge of local language a plus but not essential.

PAINE WEBBER GROUP, INC.

1285 Avenue of the Americas
New York, NY 10019 USA

RECRUITER: JOSH NABOZNY
STAFFING/RECRUITMENT
PAINE WEBBER GROUP, 1200
 HARPER BLVD.
WEEHAWKEN, NJ 07087
TEL: (201) 902-3782

Donald B. Marron, Chairman. Brokerage and securities services. Paine Webber Group, Inc. is a public company founded in 1880 by William Paine and Wallace Webber when the firm opened its first brokerage house. It joined the New York Stock Exchange in 1890 and opened its first branch office in Houghton, Michigan in 1899. Today, it acts as a holding company for Paine Webber, Inc., the fourth largest brokerage firm in the United States. It has 275 offices throughout the United States and abroad. Worldwide revenues for 1992: $3.3 billion.

- **Total Employees:** 13,000

- **U.S. Employees Abroad:** 200

- **Countries:** France, Greece, Hong Kong, Japan, Switzerland, United Kingdom.

- **Job Categories:** Brokers—Securities & Financial, Financial Advisors, Investment Counselors, Management, Marketing—Financial Services, Sales—Financial Services.

- **Language Requirement:** Varies with each posting.

PALL CORPORATION

30 Sea Cliff Ave.
Glen Cove, NY 11542 USA

RECRUITER: GERI SCHWALB
CORPORATE EMPLOYMENT MANAGER
2200 NORTHERN BLVD.
EAST HILL, NY 11548
TEL: (516) 671-4000
FAX: (516) 621-5434

Maurice G. Hardy, President. Filters and fluid clarification equipment. Pall Corporation is a public company founded in 1946. It specializes in fluid clarification by using various applications to remove microscopic contaminants from liquids and gases. Brand names include Dire Alert and Ultipor blood filters. Worldwide revenues for 1992: $697 million.

- **Total Employees:** 5,500
- **U.S. Employees Abroad:** 25
- **Countries:** Canada, Japan, United Kingdom.
- **Job Categories:** Management, Marketing—Health & Medical Supplies, Sales—Health & Medical Supplies.
- **Language Requirement:** None.

PARAMOUNT COMMUNICATIONS, INC.

15 Columbus Circle
New York, NY 10023-7780 USA

RECRUITER: BETTY PANARELLA
DIRECTOR, HUMAN RESOURCES
15 COLUMBUS CIRCLE
NEW YORK, NY 10023-7780
TEL: (212) 373-8036
FAX: (212) 373-8558

Martin S. Davis, Chairman. Entertainment and publishing. Paramount Communications is a public company founded by Charles G. Bluhdorn, an Austrian who arrived in the United States in 1942. Various business ventures led to the start of Gulf & Western Industries in 1959. By 1965, it had 27 regional warehouses with sales reaching $182 million. It then purchased Paramount Pictures in 1966 and adopted its present name in 1989. Today, its business activities include motion pictures, video production and distribution, education and consumer publishing, and other interests. Worldwide revenues for 1992: $4.1 billion.

- **Total Employees:** 12,200
- **U.S. Employees Abroad:** 35
- **Countries:** Australia, Belgium, Dominican Republic, Mexico, Netherlands.
- **Job Categories:** Management, Marketing, Marketing—Publishing, Technical Field Support.
- **Language Requirement:** None.

PARKER DRILLING COMPANY

Parker Building
8 East 3rd St.
Tulsa, OK 74103 USA

RECRUITER: BRENT THOMPSON
DIRECTOR, HUMAN RESOURCES
PARKER BUILDING
8 EAST 3RD ST.
TULSA, OK 74103
TEL: (918) 585-8221
FAX: (918) 631-1368

Robert L. Parker, Sr., Chairman. Contract drilling services. Parker Drilling is a public company founded in 1954. It offers contract drilling services to oil companies and industrial clients on a global basis. Subsidiary companies design and manufacture drilling rigs and components and are engaged in electromagnetic accelerator research. Worldwide revenues for 1992: $123.3 million.

- **Total Employees:** 1,700
- **U.S. Employees Abroad:** 25
- **Countries:** Barbados, Ecuador, Kenya, Kuwait, Singapore.
- **Job Categories:** Drilling Operators, Marketing—Petroleum/Natural Gas, Research & Development.
- **Language Requirement:** Varies with each posting.

PARKER HANNIFIN CORPORATION

17325 Euclid Ave.
Cleveland, OH 44112 USA

RECRUITER: DUANE CROCKROM
HUMAN RESOURCES DEVELOPMENT
  MANAGER
17325 EUCLID AVE.
CLEVELAND, OH 44112
TEL: (216) 531-3000
FAX: (215) 486-9380

Paul G. Schloemer, President. Motion-control products. Parker Hannifin Corporation is a public company founded in 1924. It manufactures products that control motion. Specific lines are for electrical, hydraulic, and pneumatic applications for the aerospace and industrial markets. Major brand names include Parshield and Tastemate Plus. Worldwide revenues for 1992: $2.4 billion.

- **Total Employees:** 30,000
- **U.S. Employees Abroad:** 40
- **Countries:** Argentina, Australia, Brazil, Canada, Denmark, France, Germany, Italy, Japan, Republic of Korea, Mexico, Netherlands, Singapore, Sweden, United Kingdom.
- **Job Categories:** Engineers, Management, Marketing—Industrial, Sales—Industrial.
- **Language Requirement:** Varies with each posting.

PARSONS BRINKERHOFF

1 Penn Plaza
New York, NY 10019 USA

RECRUITER: PATRICK SCHAFFNER
MANAGER, HUMAN RESOURCES
455 SPRING PARK PLACE, SUITE
#100
HERNDON, VA 22070
TEL: (703) 709-1170
FAX: (703) 471-8684

James L. Lammie, President. Engineering consultants and related services. Parsons Brinkerhoff is a private company founded in 1885. It offers architectural, engineering, and design planning services to its clients in the United States and abroad. Worldwide operating revenues for 1992: $290 million.

- **Total Employees:** 3,000

- **U.S. Employees Abroad:** 50

- **Countries:** Australia, Egypt, Hong Kong, Japan, Singapore, Taiwan, Thailand, Turkey, United Kingdom.

- **Job Categories:** Architects, Engineers, Management, Marketing.

- **Language Requirement:** None.

PARSONS CORPORATION

100 West Walnut St.
Pasadena, CA 91124 USA

RECRUITER: JOANNE PARENT
PROFESSIONAL STAFFING
100 WEST WALNUT ST.
PASADENA, CA 91124
TEL: (818) 440-2000
FAX: (818) 440-2630

William E. Leonhard, Chairman. Engineering and construction services. Parsons Corporation is a private company founded in 1944. It is engaged in engineering, planning design, project management, and related services. Clients include corporations and government agencies in the United States and abroad. Worldwide operating revenues for 1992: $1.3 billion.

- **Total Employees:** 8,000

- **U.S. Employees Abroad:** Not available.

- **Countries:** Indonesia, Japan, Republic of Korea, Kuwait, Philippines, Sudan, Thailand, United Arab Emirates, United Kingdom.

- **Job Categories:** Administrative, Field Engineers, Finance, Marketing.

PARSONS MAIN, INC.

Southeast Tower
Prudential Center
Boston, MA 02199 USA

RECRUITER: ANDREW REGAN
EMPLOYMENT MANAGER
SOUTHEAST TOWER, PRUDENTIAL
   CENTER
BOSTON, MA 02199
TEL: (617) 262-3200
FAX: (617) 859-2575

James T. Callahan, President. Engineering consultants. Parsons Main, Inc., formerly CT Main International, was founded in 1893 and is a subsidiary of the Parsons Corporation of Pasadena, California. Worldwide operating revenues for 1991: $100 million.

- **Total Employees:** 500
- **U.S. Employees Abroad:** Not available.
- **Countries:** Australia, Liberia.
- **Job Categories:** Consultants—Engineering.
- **Language Requirement:** Varies with each posting.
- **Training:** No special training provided.

J. C. PENNEY COMPANY, INC.

6501 Legacy Dr.
Plano, TX 75024-3698 USA

RECRUITER: GALE DUFF-BLOOM
DIRECTOR, CORP. PERSONNEL/
   ADMINISTRATION
6501 LEGACY DR.
PLANO, TX 75204-3698
TEL: (214) 431-1000
FAX: (214) 431-1315

William R. Howell, Chairman. Department stores. J. C. Penney is a public company founded in 1902 by James Cash Penney. He and two others opened The Golden Rule, a dry goods store, in Kemmerer, Wyoming. Five years later, Penney bought out his partners and in 1913, the company was incorporated in Utah as the J. C. Penney Company. Headquarters moved to New York City in 1914. Today, it is the fourth largest retailer in the United States, with over 2,500 department stores. It also operates a catalog service which produced 17 percent of its sales for 1991. J. C. Penney is now located in Plano, Texas. Worldwide revenues for 1992: $19.1 billion.

- **Total Employees:** 188,000
- **U.S. Employees Abroad:** 50
- **Countries:** Hong Kong, India, Japan, Republic of Korea, Singapore, Taiwan, Thailand.
- **Job Categories:** Administrative, Finance, Marketing—Consumer Goods, Sales—Consumer Goods.
- **Language Requirement:** None.

PENNZOIL COMPANY

Pennzoil Place
PO Box 2967
Houston, TX 77252-2967 USA

RECRUITER: WILLIAM USNER
COMPENSATION & BENEFITS
ADMINISTRATOR
PENNZOIL PLACE
PO BOX 2967
HOUSTON, TX 77252-2967
TEL: (713) 546-4000
FAX: (713) 546-6664

James L. Pate, President. Natural gas, oil, and sulphur. Pennzoil is a public company founded after WW II by two brothers, J. Hugh and Bill Liedtke, and George Bush. They formed Zapata Petroleum, which produced more than 120 oil fields in West Texas. Today, it focuses on overseas exploration rather than domestic production. It is the 18th largest oil company in the United States and well-known for its top selling motor oil. Worldwide revenues for 1992: $2.2 billion.

- **Total Employees:** 11,690

- **U.S. Employees Abroad:** 40

- **Countries:** Indonesia, Canada, Netherlands, Russia.

- **Job Categories:** Management, Marketing—Chemicals, Marketing—Petroleum/Natural Gas, Sales—Chemicals, Sales—Petroleum/Natural Gas, Technical Field Support.

- **Language Requirement:** None.

PENROD DRILLING CORPORATION

2200 Thanksgiving Tower
Dallas, TX 75201 USA

RECRUITER: JAY HUNT
PERSONNEL MANAGER
1405 PINHOOK
LAYFAYETTE, LA 70503
TEL: (318) 232-7032
FAX: (318) 231-1745

Marshall Ballard, Chairman. Oil and gas drilling. Penrod Drilling is a private company founded in 1923. It is engaged in oil and gas exploration and drilling in the United States and abroad. Worldwide revenues for 1991: $113 million

- **Total Employees:** 2,000

- **U.S. Employees Abroad:** 20

- **Countries:** Brazil, Greece, United Arab Emirates.

- **Application Information:** Most foreign positions are filled internally.

- **Job Categories:** Management, Field Technicians, Marketing—Petroleum/Natural Gas.

- **Language Requirement:** None.

PENTAIR, INC.

1500 County Rd., B-2
Saint Paul, MN 55113 USA

RECRUITER: RON LINDBERG
CORP. DIRECTOR, HUMAN
    RESOURCES
1500 COUNTY RD., B-2
SAINT PAUL, MN 55113
TEL: (612) 636-7920
FAX: (612) 639-5209

D. Eugene Nugent, President and Chairman. Industrial products. Pentair, Inc. is a public company founded in 1966. It is a manufacturer of industrial products and paper. Markets include automotive, construction, publishing and printing, and recreation. Currently, it has 24 locations throughout the United States and abroad. Worldwide revenues for 1992: $1.24 billion.

- **Total Employees:** 8,400
- **U.S. Employees Abroad:** 625
- **Countries:** Canada, Germany, Mexico, Taiwan, United Kingdom.
- **Job Categories:** Executive Management, Marketing—Industrial, Sales—Industrial.
- **Language Requirement:** None.

PEPSICO FOODS INTERNATIONAL

7701 Legacy Dr.
Plano, TX 75024 USA

RECRUITER: MATTHEW J. DURFEE
DIRECTOR, HUMAN RESOURCES
7701 LEGACY DR.
PLANO, TX 75024
TEL: (214) 334-3733
FAX: (214) 334-3609

Roger Enrico, Chairman. Snack foods. PepsiCo Foods International is a subsidiary of PepsiCo, Inc. of Somers, New York. It is a manufacturer of snack foods including potato chips and corn chips. Worldwide revenues for 1992: $3.9 billion.

- **Total Employees:** 50,000
- **U.S. Employees Abroad:** 40
- **Countries:** Argentina, Australia, Brazil, Canada, Chile, France, Italy, Mexico, Singapore, Thailand, United Arab Emirates, United Kingdom, Venezuela.
- **Job Categories:** Finance, Human Resources, Marketing—Food/Food Services.
- **General Requirements:** Availablity for permanent foreign relocation and international work experience, preferably in brand products.
- **Language Requirement:** Fluency in local language required.
- **Training:** No special training offered.
- **Benefits:** TRAVEL: None offered. HEALTH: Varies with each posting. HOUSING: Varies with each posting. EDUCATION: None offered.

PEPSICO, INC.

One Pepsi Way
Somers, NY 10589-2201 USA

RECRUITER: J. ROGER KING
SENIOR VP, PERSONNEL
6-NORTH, 600
SOMERS, NY 10589-2201
TEL: (914) 767-6000
FAX: (914) 253-2070

D. Wayne Calloway, Chairman. Fast-food restaurants, snack foods, and soft drinks. PepsiCo, Inc. is a public company founded in 1898 by Caleb D. Bradham. He invented the drink Pepsi and registered the trademark in 1903. He soon started a system of bottling franchises and Pepsi-Cola was soon being bottled by 300 dealers. Today, PepsiCo's soft drink division controls 33 percent of the U.S. market and 16 percent of the international market. Its restaurant segment includes Kentucky Fried Chicken and Pizza Hut and has more units than any other restaurant system throughout the world. Popular snack food brands include Doritos and Ruffles potato chips. Worldwide revenues for 1992: $22 billion.

- **Total Employees:** 266,000
- **U.S. Employees Abroad:** 150
- **Countries:** Worldwide including Australia, Brazil, Canada, Italy, Kenya, Mexico, Thailand, United Kingdom, Venezuela.
- **Job Categories:** Clerical Assistants, Management, Marketing—Food/Food Services, Product Development, Sales—Food/Food Services, Technical Field Support.
- **Language Requirement:** Varies with each posting.

PERKIN-ELMER CORPORATION

761 Main St.
Norwalk, CT 06859 USA

RECRUITER: MICHAEL J.
MCPARTLAND
VP, HUMAN RESOURCES
761 MAIN ST.
NORWALK, CT 06859
TEL: (203) 761-2590
FAX: (203) 274-1268

Gaynor N. Kelley, Chairman. Analytical instruments, computers, and related equipment. Perkin-Elmer Corporation is a public company founded in 1937. It is engaged as a manufacturer and marketer of various products, including instruments for chemical or physical analysis, burgular and fire alarms, machinery for industrial use, and thermal spray systems. Worldwide revenues for 1992: $911.1 million.

- **Total Employees:** 6,442
- **U.S. Employees Abroad:** 25
- **Countries:** Australia, Brazil, Canada, Germany, Hong Kong, Israel, Italy, Japan, Spain, United Kingdom.
- **Application Information:** Most foreign positions are filled internally.

- **Job Categories:** Management, Marketing—Electronics, Sales—Electronics.
- **Benefits:** All benefits vary with each posting.

PETROLITE CORPORATION

369 Marshall Ave.
St. Louis, MO 63119 USA

RECRUITER: THOMAS ETTE
MANAGER, EMPLOYEE RELATIONS
369 MARSHALL AVE.
ST. LOUIS, MO 63119
TEL: (314) 961-3500
FAX: (314) 968-6165

Ellis L. Brown, Chairman. Industrial equipment, components, and chemical preparations. Petrolite Corporation is a public company founded in 1930. It manufactures synthetic resins, plastics, and nonvulcanizable elastomers. It also produces various chemical preparations. Worldwide revenues for 1991: $323.5 million.

- **Total Employees:** 2,400
- **U.S. Employees Abroad:** 22
- **Countries:** Ecuador, France, Germany, Japan, Malaysia, Mexico, Netherlands, Republic of South Africa, Singapore, United Kingdom.
- **Job Categories:** Management, Marketing—Chemicals, Marketing—Industrial, Sales—Chemicals, Sales—Industrial.
- **Language Requirement:** Knowledge of local language a plus but not essential.

PFAUDLER COMPANIES, INC.

1000 West Ave.
Rochester, NY 14692 USA

RECRUITER: RICHARD KINSLEY
VP, HUMAN RESOURCES
1000 WEST AVE.
PO BOX 1600
ROCHESTER, NY 14692
TEL: (716) 235-1000
FAX: (716) 235-6732

Anthony R. Vasile, Senior Vice President. Glassware and textile glass fibers. Pfaudler Companies, Inc. was founded in 1884 and is a subsidiary of Eagle Industries of Chicago, Illinois. It manufactures glass, glassware, and textile glass fibers, including glass-lined reactor vessels.

- **Total Employees:** 1,400
- **U.S. Employees Abroad:** 15
- **Countries:** Germany, Mexico, United Kingdom.
- **Job Categories:** Management, Product Development, Sales—Consumer Goods.
- **Language Requirement:** None.

PFIZER, INC.

235 East 42nd St.
New York, NY 10017 USA

RECRUITER: MARJORY BOT
PERSONNEL, INTERNATIONAL
OPERATIONS
235 EAST 42ND ST.
NEW YORK, NY 10017
TEL: (212) 573-2323
FAX: (212) 573-1240

Edmund T. Pratt, Jr., Chairman. Pharmaceuticals, medical products, and specialty chemicals. Pfizer is a public company founded in 1849 by Charles B. Pfizer and cousin, Charles Erhard. They began to manufacture chemicals in Brooklyn and the business was incorporated in 1900. Heavy concentration in research and development has kept company growth steady through the years. Well-known brand names include Visine and Ben-Gay. Two of the newest medical products are Norvask (for hypertension) and Procardia XL (for cardiovascular disease). This diversified company operates on a global basis. Worldwide revenues for 1992: $7.2 billion.

- **Total Employees:** 42,000
- **U.S. Employees Abroad:** 75
- **Countries:** Australia, Belgium, Canada, Chile, Colombia, Costa Rica, France, Germany, Italy, Japan, Mexico, Netherlands, Switzerland, Singapore, Taiwan, United Arab Emirates, United Kingdom.
- **Job Categories:** Administrative, Finance, Marketing—Health & Medical Supplies, Marketing—Pharmaceuticals, Product Development, Sales—Health & Medical Supplies, Sales—Pharmaceuticals.
- **Language Requirement:** Varies with each posting.

PHELPS DODGE CORPORATION

2600 North Central Ave.
Phoenix, AZ 85004-3014 USA

RECRUITER: CAROLYN DERRON
MANAGER, COMPENSATION &
BENEFITS
2600 NORTH CENTRAL AVE.
PHOENIX, AZ 85004-3014
TEL: (602) 234-8100
FAX: (602) 234-8337

Douglas C. Yearley, President and Chairman. Minerals, metals, and specialty engineered products. Phelps Dodge Corporation is a public company founded in 1834 when Anson Greene Phelps and his sons-in-law formed a partnership. During the 1830s, the company invested in coal, iron, and timber in Pennsylvania and soon manufactured metals in Connecticut. Today, the company is the world's 2nd largest copper producer, yielding 1 billion pounds of copper in 1991. It is also a world leader in the production of copper rod (used for electrical wire and cable). It has operations in more than 20 foreign countries. Worldwide revenues for 1992: $2.6 billion.

- **Total Employees:** 13,391

- **U.S. Employees Abroad:** 45
- **Countries:** Canada, Chile, Costa Rica, El Salvador, France, Germany, Guatemala, India, Italy, Japan, Mexico, Panama, Republic of South Africa, United Kingdom, Venezuela.
- **Job Categories:** Engineers, Management, Sales—Industrial.
- **Language Requirement:** Varies with each posting.

PHIBRO ENERGY, INC.

500 Nyala Farms
Westport, CT 06880 USA

RECRUITER: LIZ BRINGMAN
HUMAN RESOURCES
   REPRESENTATIVE
500 NYALA FARMS
WESTPORT, CT 06880
TEL: (203) 221-5800

Ernst Weil, Chairman. Petroleum refining. Phibro Energy, Inc. was founded in 1902 and is a subsidiary of Salomon, Inc. of New York City. It is engaged in petroleum refining and acts as a wholesale distributor of crude oil or petroleum products from bulk liquid storage facilities. Worldwide revenues for 1991: $256 million.

- **Total Employees:** 2,150
- **U.S. Employees Abroad:** 22
- **Countries:** Russia, United Kingdom.
- **Job Categories:** Management, Marketing—Petroleum/Natural Gas, Sales—Petroleum/Natural Gas, Technical Field Support.
- **Language Requirement:** None.

PHILIP MORRIS COMPANIES, INC.

120 Park Ave.
New York, NY 10017-5592 USA

RECRUITER: CAROL YOUNG
MANAGER, WORLDWIDE EXPATRIATE
   PROGRAM
800 WESTCHESTER AVE.
ROCHESTER, NY 10573-1301
TEL: (914) 335-5000
FAX: (914) 335-9122

Michael A. Miles, Chairman. Consumer packaged goods. Philip Morris is a public company founded in 1919. Its combined business sectors make Philip Morris the number one cigarette company in the world, the number two global beer company, and the number one U.S. food company. Divisions include General Foods, Kraft, and Miller Brewing. Well-known brand names include Breyer ice cream, Marlboro cigarettes, and Post cereals. Tobacco is the company's most successful concern, producing 72 percent of operating profits. Worldwide revenues for 1992: $50.1 billion.

- **Total Employees:** 166,000

- **U.S. Employees Abroad:** 400
- **Countries:** Worldwide including Argentina, Bulgaria, Dominican Republic, France, Germany, Japan, Netherlands, Poland, Romania, Russia, Switzerland, Turkey, Venezuela.
- **Job Categories:** Executive Management, Finance, Marketing—Consumer Goods, Marketing—Food/Food Services, Sales—Consumer Goods, Sales—Food/Food Services.
- **Language Requirement:** Knowledge of local language a plus but not essential.
- **Benefits:** All benefits are individually determined.

PHILIPP BROTHERS CHEMICALS, INC.

1 Parker Plaza
Fort Lee, NJ 07024 USA

RECRUITER: PEGGY HAGEL
PERSONNEL DEPARTMENT
1 PARKER PLAZA
FORT LEE, NJ 07024
TEL: (201) 944-6020

Charles Bendheim, Chairman. Agricultural and inorganic chemicals. Philipp Brothers Chemicals is a public company incorporated in 1946. It has two main divisions: Agtrol Chemicals and Fertilzer & Agricultural Chemicals. Worldwide revenues for 1991: $140.0 million.

- **Total Employees:** 800
- **U.S. Employees Abroad:** 18
- **Countries:** People's Republic of China, France, Japan, Switzerland, United Kingdom.
- **Job Categories:** Management, Marketing—Agricultural, Marketing—Chemicals, Sales—Agricultural, Sales—Chemicals.

PHILIPS TECHNOLOGIES

7 McKee Place
Cheshire, CT 06410 USA

RECRUITER: DOUGLAS E. STOEHR
DIRECTOR OF PERSONNEL
7 MCKEE PLACE
CHESHIRE, CT 06410
TEL: (203) 271-6000
FAX: (203) 271-6522

H. F. Rice, Jr., President. Stepper motors and digital linear acuators. Philips Technologies (formerly Airpax) was founded in 1945 and is a division of Consolidated Electronic Industries.

- **Total Employees:** 3,850
- **U.S. Employees Abroad:** Not available.
- **Countries:** Belgium, Malaysia, Mexico, Singapore.
- **Application Information:** Most foreign positions are filled internally.
- **Job Categories:** Management.

- **General Requirements:** Managerial skills required.
- **Average Overseas Assignment:** 2-3 years.
- **Language Requirement:** Competency in local language required.
- **Training:** No special training provided.
- **Benefits:** All benefits are offered. Contact company for more information.

PHILLIPS PETROLEUM COMPANY

Plaza Building
Bartlesville, OK 74004 USA

RECRUITER: E. L. BAUGHN
DIRECTOR, EMPLOYEE RELATIONS
PLAZA BUILDING
BARTLESVILLE, OK 74004
TEL: (918) 661-6600
FAX: (918) 661-7636

C. J. Silas, Chairman. Chemicals and petroleum. Phillips Petroleum is a public company founded in 1917 by brothers, L. E. and Frank Phillips. After success in their productive oil wells in Oklahoma, the business branched out to include refining and marketing. Today, Phillips is the ninth largest integrated petroleum company in the United States and the largest U.S. producer of natural gas liquids. It operates throughout the world. It recently (1990) began exploration of 700,000 acres of offshore Australia. Worldwide revenues for 1992: $12 billion.

- **Total Employees:** 22,680
- **U.S. Employees Abroad:** 70
- **Countries:** Australia, Colombia, Costa Rica, Denmark, France, Germany, Hong Kong, Indonesia, Guinea, Pakistan, Republic of South Africa, United Kingdom, Venezuela.
- **Job Categories:** Engineers, Marketing—Chemicals, Marketing—Petroleum/Natural Gas, Sales—Chemicals, Sales—Petroleum/Natural Gas, Technical Field Support.

PHILLIPS-VAN HEUSEN CORPORATION

1290 Avenue of the Americas
New York, NY 10104 USA

RECRUITER: PERSONNEL DIRECTOR
1290 AVENUE OF THE AMERICAS
NEW YORK, NY 10104
TEL: (212) 541-5200
FAX: (212) 468-7064

Lawrence C. Phillips, Chairman. Apparel. Phillips-Van Heusen Corporation is a public company founded in 1881. It is engaged as a manufacturer of men's and women's clothing and shoes. It also produces its own private label items. Worldwide revenues for 1991: $806.3 million.

- **Total Employees:** 9,000
- **U.S. Employees Abroad:** 24
- **Countries:** Brazil, Cayman Islands, Costa Rica, Guatemala, Honduras, Hong Kong, Mexico.

- **Job Categories:** Management, Marketing—Consumer Goods, Sales—Consumer Goods.

- **Language Requirement:** Knowledge of local language a plus but not essential.

PILLSBURY COMPANY

200 South 6th St.
Minneapolis, MN 55404-1464
USA

RECRUITER: MARY ADAIR
RECRUITMENT COORDINATOR
200 SOUTH 6TH ST.
MINNEAPOLIS, MN 55404-1464
TEL: (612) 330-4966
FAX: (612) 330-7355

Ian Martin, President. Food products. Pillsbury was founded in 1935 and is a subsidiary of Grand Metropolitan, Inc. of Montvale, New Jersey. Subsidiaries include the Burger King restaurants and the Haagen-Daz ice cream chain. Other products include cake mixes and frozen vegetables. Worldwide revenues for 1992: $4.1 billion.

- **Total Employees:** 103,000
- **U.S. Employees Abroad:** 110
- **Countries:** Worldwide including Canada, France, Germany, Guatemala, Mexico, United Kingdom, Venezuela.
- **Application Information:** Most foreign positions are filled internally.
- **Job Categories:** Executive Management, Finance, Marketing—Food/Food Services, Sales—Food/Food Services.
- **Language Requirement:** Varies with each posting.

PINKERTON'S, INC.

6727 Odessa Ave.
Van Nuys, CA 91406-5796 USA

RECRUITER: NANCY JOSEPH
DIRECTOR, MARKETING
6717 ODESSA AVE.
VAN NUYS, CA 94106
TEL: (818) 373-8800
FAX: (818) 373-6267

Thomas W. Walthen, Chairman. Security and investigation services. Pinkerton's, Inc. is a public company founded in 1850. It offers security services for clients in the United States and abroad. These include detective, guard, and armored car services. Worldwide revenues for 1992: $703 million.

- **Total Employees:** 43,000
- **U.S. Employees Abroad:** 30
- **Countries:** Canada, United Kingdom.
- **Job Categories:** Guards, Management.
- **Language Requirement:** None.

PIONEER HI-BRED INTERNATIONAL, INC.

700 Capitol Square
400 Locust St.
Des Moines, IA 50309 USA

RECRUITER: GARY WALLJASPER
HUMAN RESOURCES
6800 PIONEER PKWY.
PO BOX 202
JOHNSTON, IA 50131
TEL: (515) 245-3500
FAX: (515) 270-3106

Thomas N. Urban, President. Seed corn and related products. Pioneer Hi-Bred International, Inc. is a public company founded in 1926. It manufactures and distributes grain seeds for commercial farmers. It has research facilities in the United States and abroad. Major products include hybrid corn, soybean, and sunflower seed. Worldwide revenues for 1992: $1.2 billion.

- **Total Employees:** 4,500
- **U.S. Employees Abroad:** 35
- **Countries:** Argentina, Australia, Brazil, Chile, France, Germany, India, Italy, Japan, Mexico, Philippines, Spain, Thailand.
- **Job Categories:** Management, Marketing—Agricultural, Research & Development, Sales—Agricultural.
- **Language Requirement:** Varies with each posting.

PITNEY BOWES, INC.

World Headquarters
Stamford, CT 06926 USA

RECRUITER: GUS STEPP, JR.
EMPLOYMENT DIRECTOR
WORLD HEADQUARTERS
STAMFORD, CT 06926
TEL: (203) 356-5000
FAX: (203) 351-7681

George B. Harvey, President and Chairman. Business equipment. Pitney Bowes, Inc. is a public company founded in 1920 when Walter Bowes formed a partnership with Arthur Pitney. The business was called the Pitney-Bowes Postage Meter Company. In 1929, Pitney-Bowes began leasing its machines to customers, and started operations abroad. By 1932, revenues totaled $1.5 million. The present name was adopted in 1945. Today, it is a world leader in the mailing systems market, which accounts for 60 percent of its sales. Other businesses include copier systems, facsimile machines, and shipping and weighing systems. Products are sold in more than 115 countries. Worldwide revenues for 1992: $3.4 billion.

- **Total Employees:** 29,421
- **U.S. Employees Abroad:** 40
- **Countries:** Austria, Brazil, Canada, France, Germany, Switzerland, United Kingdom.
- **Job Categories:** Executive Management, Marketing—Consumer Goods, Sales—Consumer Goods.

- **Language Requirement:** None.

PITTSBURGH-DES MOINES CORPORATION

3400 Grand Ave.
Pittsburgh, PA 15225 USA

RECRUITER: CAROLYN PRICE
HUMAN RESOURCES ADMINISTRATOR
3400 GRAND AVE.
PITTSBURGH, PA 15225
TEL: (412) 331-3000
FAX: (412) 331-7403

W. W. McKee, President. Contractors and builders of industrial buildings. Pittsburgh-Des Moines Corporation is a public company founded in 1893. It constructs industrial warehouses and buildings and manufactures fabricated plate work, including boilers and tanks. Worldwide operating revenues for 1992: $383 million.

- **Total Employees:** 2,058
- **U.S. Employees Abroad:** 18
- **Countries:** Australia, Mexico, Saudi Arabia, United Kingdom.
- **Job Categories:** Contractors, Management.
- **Language Requirement:** None.

PITTWAY CORPORATION

200 South Wacker Dr.
Chicago, IL 60606 USA

RECRUITER: PEGGY ODEGAARD
OFFICE MANAGER, RECRUITMENT
200 SOUTH WACKER DR., SUITE #700
CHICAGO, IL 60606
TEL: (312) 831-1070
FAX: (312) 831-0828

King Harris, President. Security systems and publishing. Pittway Corporation is a public company whose former name was Standard Shares. It has two main operating divisions: The Ademco Security Group and Pittway System Technology Group, which manufacture and market burglar alarms and fire detectors, etc.; and Penton Publishing, Inc. which publishes trade and professional magazines. It has other smaller businesses, including Pittway Real Estate. Worldwide revenues for 1992: $568.3 million.

- **Total Employees:** 4,500
- **U.S. Employees Abroad:** Not available.
- **Countries:** Australia, Canada, Italy, Mexico, Spain, United Kingdom.
- **Job Categories:** Management, Marketing—Electronics, Marketing—Publishing, Sales—Electronics, Sales—Publishing.
- **Language Requirement:** Varies with each posting.

PIZZA HUT, INC.

PO Box 428
Wichita, KS 67207 USA

RECRUITER: ALVIN WHITE, JR.
VP, INTERNATIONAL HUMAN
   RESOURCES
PO BOX 428
WICHITA, KS 67207
TEL: (316) 681-9638
FAX: (316) 687-8483

Allan Huston, President. Food service management. Pizza Hut, Inc. was founded in 1958 and is a public subsidiary of PepsiCo, Inc. of Somers, New York. It operates pizza chains throughout the United States and has establishments in more than 70 foreign countries. Worldwide revenues for 1992: $3.5 billion.

- **Total Employees:** 132,000

- **U.S. Employees Abroad:** 50

- **Countries:** Worldwide including Australia, France, Germany, Japan, Spain, United Kingdom.

- **Job Categories:** Management, Marketing—Food/Food Services, Sales—Food/Food Services.

- **Average Overseas Assignment:** 2-3 years.

- **Language Requirement:** Varies with each posting; local language skills are usually required. flEDC

PLAYTEX APPAREL, INC.

Ridgley St.
PO Box 631
Dover, DE 19903-0631 USA

RECRUITER: RICHARD SMITH
VP, HUMAN RESOURCES
RIDGLEY ST.
PO BOX 631
DOVER, DE 19903-0631
TEL: (302) 674-6666
FAX: (302) 674-6938

Joel E. Smilow, President and Chairman. Intimate apparel and related products. Playtex Apparel, Inc. is a private company founded in 1932. It manufactures such items as brassieres, girdles, and corsets. It also produces sanitary paper and fabricated rubber products. Worldwide revenues for 1991: $390 million.

- **Total Employees:** 7,200

- **U.S. Employees Abroad:** 22

- **Countries:** Australia, Canada, France, Italy, Mexico, Spain, United Kingdom.

- **Job Categories:** Management, Marketing—Consumer Goods, Sales—Consumer Goods.

- **Language Requirement:** None.

PMI FOOD EQUIPMENT GROUP

World Headquarters Building
Troy, OH 45374 USA

RECRUITER: NEAL BAILEYS
VP, HUMAN RESOURCES
WORLD HEADQUARTERS BUILDING
TROY, OH 45374
TEL: (513) 332-2501
FAX: (513) 332-2722

Robert J. Fisher, President. Machinery for food equipment industry. PMI Food Equipment was founded in 1897 and is a subsidiary of Premark International, Inc. of Deerfield, Illinois. It manufactures machinery for the food products and beverage industries and is also a producer of packaging machinery. Worldwide revenues for 1991: $1 billion.

- **Total Employees:** 10,000

- **U.S. Employees Abroad:** 20

- **Countries:** Belgium, Germany, United Kingdom.

- **Job Categories:** Manufacturing, Marketing—Industrial, Sales—Industrial.

- **Language Requirement:** None.

POLAROID CORPORATION

549 Technology Square
Cambridge, MA 02139 USA

RECRUITER: JON HANCHUS
MANAGER, INTERNATIONAL HUMAN
    RESOURCES
549 TECHNOLOGY SQUARE
CAMBRIDGE, MA 02139
TEL: (617) 577-2000
FAX: (617) 577-5618

I. MacAllister Booth, President and Chairman. Instant cameras and film. Polaroid Corporation is a public company founded in 1932 by Edwin Land. He established a company to market his newly developed product–the world's first synthetic light-polarizing material named Polaroid. Various products were introduced through the years, although today its core business remains instant photography. It is also involved in the fast-growing total imagery market. Worldwide revenues for 1992: $2.2 billion.

- **Total Employees:** 12,000

- **U.S. Employees Abroad:** 30

- **Countries:** Mexico, Netherlands, United Kingdom.

- **Job Categories:** Management, Marketing—Electronics, Product Development, Sales—Electronics.

R. L. POLK & COMPANY

1155 Brewery Park Blvd.
Detroit, MI 48207 USA

RECRUITER: JOSLYN GARTH
EMPLOYMENT INTERVIEWER
1155 BREWERY PARK BLVD.
DETROIT, MI 48207
TEL: (313) 393-0880
FAX: (313) 393-2862

John O'Hara, President. Publishing. R. L. Polk is a private company founded in 1870. It is a publisher of various materials including directories and direct mail advertising. Worldwide revenues for 1991: $280 million.

- **Total Employees:** 6,235
- **U.S. Employees Abroad:** 20
- **Countries:** Australia, Belgium, Canada, United Kingdom.
- **Job Categories:** Management, Marketing—Publishing, Sales—Publishing.

PPG INDUSTRIES

One PPG Place
Pittsburgh, PA 15272 USA

RECRUITER: LAWRENCE R. CUMMINS
MANAGER, INTERNATIONAL
    COMPENSATION
ONE PPG PLACE
PITTSBURGH, PA 15272
TEL: (412) 434-3438
FAX: (412) 434-2011

Vincent A. Sarni, Chairman. Commodity products, including coatings, fiberglass, and biomedical products. PPG Industries is a public company founded in 1883 by John Ford when he started a plate glass factory in Creighton, Pennsylvania, called Pittsburgh Plate Glass. Business soon focused on the automobile and construction markets during the 1900s. During the 1980s, PPG concentrated on global expansion. Today, it is the largest supplier of automobile and industrial finishes in the world, and the second largest producer of fiberglass. It has 75 plants throughout the United States and abroad. Worldwide revenues for 1992: $5.8 billion.

- **Total Employees:** 32,300
- **U.S. Employees Abroad:** 100
- **Countries:** Australia, Canada, People's Republic of China, Denmark, France, Germany, Italy, Japan, Republic of Korea, Mexico, Netherlands, Taiwan, Thailand, United Kingdom, Venezuela.
- **Job Categories:** Engineers, Finance, Management, Marketing—Chemicals, Sales—Chemicals.
- **Average Overseas Assignment:** 3-5 years.
- **Language Requirement:** Competency in local language required.
- **Training:** Basic orientation (1-30 days) is provided.

- **Benefits:** TRAVEL: All transportation costs paid; 4 weeks annual home leave; hardship premium in some locations. HEALTH: Same coverage as U.S. employees. HOUSING: Company pays the difference between U.S. housing costs and host country housing costs. EDUCATION: Full tuition costs paid grades K-12.

PRC, INC.
1500 PRC Dr.
Mc Lean, VA 22102 USA

RECRUITER: HUMAN RESOURCES
DEPARTMENT
1500 PRC DR.
MCLEAN, VA 22102
TEL: (703) 556-1000
FAX: (703) 556-1381

Jim Leto, President. Information systems and service. PRC, Inc. was founded in 1954 and is a subsidiary of the Black & Decker Corporation of Towson, Maryland. It produces computer integrated systems and designs, offers services for computer facilities management, and provides technical services as environmental and engineering consultants. Worldwide operating revenues for 1991: $734 million.

- **Total Employees:** 7,300
- **U.S. Employees Abroad:** 100
- **Countries:** Australia, Canada, Finland, Germany, United Kingdom.
- **Job Categories:** Consultants—Management, Technicians, Management, Marketing.
- **Language Requirement:** None.

PRECISION VALVE CORPORATION
PO Box 309
Yonkers, NY 10702 USA

RECRUITER: KENNETH CORSU
DIRECTOR, INDUSTRIAL RELATIONS
PO BOX 309
YONKERS, NY 10702
TEL: (914) 969-6500
FAX: (914) 969-1985

Robert Abplanalp, President and Chairman. Aerosol valves. Precision Valve Corporation is a private company founded in 1949. It manufactures aerosol and industrial valves. Worldwide revenues for 1991: $200 million.

- **Total Employees:** 2,100
- **U.S. Employees Abroad:** 14
- **Countries:** Canada, France, Germany, India, Italy, Japan, Mexico, Singapore, Spain, United Kingdom, Venezuela.
- **Job Categories:** Management, Marketing—Industrial, Sales—Industrial.
- **Language Requirement:** None.

PREFORMED LINE PRODUCTS COMPANY

660 Beta Dr.
Mayfield Village, OH 44143 USA

RECRUITER: ROBERT L. WEBER
PERSONNEL DIRECTOR
660 BETA DR.
MAYFIELD VILLAGE, OH 44143
TEL: (216) 461-5200

Jon. R. Ruhlman, President. Plastic products and current-carrying wiring devices. Preformed Line Products is a private company engaged as a manufacturer of various products for telecommunications systems. These include current-carrying and noncurrent-carrying wiring devices. It also manufactures communication equipment such as burglar and fire alarms and traffic systems. Currently, it operates with 17 facilities in the United States and abroad. Worldwide revenues for 1991: $115.0 million.

- **Total Employees:** 1,400
- **U.S. Employees Abroad:** 18
- **Countries:** Australia, Brazil, Canada, India, Japan, Mexico, Republic of South Africa, Spain, United Kingdom.
- **Job Categories:** Management, Marketing, Sales.
- **Training:** No special training offered.

PREMARK INTERNATIONAL, INC.

1717 Deerfield Rd.
Deerfield, IL 60015 USA

RECRUITER: GEORGE SHAFER
HUMAN RESOURCES
1717 DEERFIELD RD.
DEERFIELD, IL 60015
TEL: (708) 405-6000
FAX: (708) 405-6311

Warren L. Batts, Chairman. Consumer products. Premark International, Inc. is a public company formed in 1986 as the result of a spinoff of the former Dart & Kraft. Originally, Justin Dart began with the Walgreen Company, then went on to Rexall Drug, moving the location from Boston to Los Angeles, California in 1945. He purchased the Tupper Corporation, and in 1980, the business merged with Kraft, the Chicago-based food company, and was spunoff in 1986. Today, it is a worldwide leader in plastic storage and serving containers (Tupperwear). It produces and sells its products in more than 100 countries. Worldwide revenues for 1992: $2.9 billion.

- **Total Employees:** 25,000
- **U.S. Employees Abroad:** 60
- **Countries:** Worldwide including Argentina, Australia, Brazil, Canada, France, Germany, Italy, Japan, Republic of Korea, Mexico, Netherlands, Thailand, United Kingdom, Venezuela.
- **Job Categories:** Management, Marketing—Consumer Goods, Product Development, Sales—Consumer Goods.

PRICE WATERHOUSE

1251 Avenue of the Americas
New York, NY 10036 USA

RECRUITER: RICHARD F. KEARNS
DIRECTOR, HUMAN RESOURCES
1251 AVENUE OF THE AMERICAS
NEW YORK, NY 10036
TEL: (212) 944-9750
FAX: (212) 790-6620

Shaun F. O'Malley, Chairman. Accounting. Price Waterhouse is an international association of partnerships. It was founded in 1860 by S. H. Price and Edwin Waterhouse in England. By the late 1890s, representation was established in the United States and in 1902, U.S. Steel chose Price Waterhouse as its auditors. Today, it is the sixth largest of the Big 6 in the United States and abroad. It currently has more than 110 offices throughout the world. Worldwide revenues for 1991: $3.6 billion. Foreign revenues for 1991: $2.3 billion.

- **Total Employees:** 12,630
- **U.S. Employees Abroad:** 125
- **Countries:** Worldwide including France, Germany, Hungary, Italy, Netherlands, Switzerland, United Kingdom.
- **Job Categories:** Accountants, Administrative, Marketing.
- **Language Requirement:** Knowledge of local language a plus but not essential.

PRIMERICA CORPORATION

65 East 55th St.
New York, NY 10022 USA

RECRUITER: BARRY L. MANNES
SENIOR VICE PRESIDENT, HUMAN
RESOURCES
1355 AVENUE OF THE AMERICAS
NEW YORK, NY 10022
TEL: (212) 891-8900
FAX: (212) 891-8910

Sanford I. Weill, Chairman. Financial services. Primerica Corporation is a joint effort of the former American Can Company and the Commercial Credit Company. American Can started in New Jersey in 1901 and Commercial Credit began in 1912. In 1981, American Can bought Associated Madison, a life insurance firm, and began to focus on financial services. In 1987, the name was changed to Primerica. In 1988, Commercial Credit bought Primerica. Today, it has operations throughout the United States and in 100 foreign countries. More than 100,000 agents are associated with Primerica. Worldwide revenues for 1992: $5.1 billion.

- **Total Employees:** 16,500
- **U.S. Employees Abroad:** 100
- **Countries:** Canada, France, Germany, Italy, Japan, Netherlands, United Kingdom.
- **Job Categories:** Administrative, Finance, Marketing—Financial Services, Sales—Financial Services.

- **Language Requirement:** None.

PRINTRONIX, INC.

17500 Cartwright Rd.
Irvine, CA 92713 USA

RECRUITER: SHARON FERGUSON
HUMAN RESOURCES
  REPRESENTATIVE
17500 CARTWRIGHT RD.
PO BOX 19559
IRVINE, CA 92713
TEL: (714) 863-1900
FAX: (714) 660-8682

Robert A. Kleist, President. Computer peripheral equipment. Printronix, Inc. is a public company founded in 1974. It manufactures computer peripheral equipment, including printers or graphic displays. Worldwide revenues for 1992: $88.5 million.

- **Total Employees:** 1,500
- **U.S. Employees Abroad:** 15
- **Countries:** France, Germany, Netherlands, Singapore, United Kingdom.
- **Job Categories:** Engineers, Management, Marketing—Electronics, Sales—Electronics.
- **Language Requirement:** None.

PROCTER & GAMBLE COMPANY

One Procter & Gamble Plaza
Cincinnati, OH 45202 USA

RECRUITER: WILLIAM REINA
MANAGER, INTERNATIONAL
  RECRUITMENT
TWO PROCTER & GAMBLE PLAZA
CINCINNATI, OH 45202
TEL: (513) 983-1100
FAX: (513) 983-6758

Edwin L. Artzt, Chairman. Products for the home, personal care items, and food and beverages. Procter & Gamble is a public company founded in 1837 by William Procter and James Gamble. By 1859 it had become one of the biggest companies in Cincinnati, with sales of $1 million. In 1879, it introduced Ivory Soap, with a great deal of success. Today, it sells its products throughout the world with brand names including Cheer laundry detergent, Crisco Oil, and Gleem toothpaste. Worldwide revenues for 1992: $30.4 billion.

- **Total Employees:** 73,000
- **U.S. Employees Abroad:** 90
- **Countries:** Worldwide including Austria, Canada, Germany, France, Japan, Mexico, Netherlands, Philippines, Taiwan, United Kingdom.
- **Job Categories:** Management, Marketing—Food/Food Services, Marketing—Con-

sumer Goods, Product Development, Sales—Food/Food Services, Sales—Consumer Goods.

- **Language Requirement:** Varies with each posting.
- **Training:** No special training provided.

PROCTER & GAMBLE COSMETICS AND FRAGRANCE PRODUCTS

11050 York Rd.
Hunt Valley, MD 21030 USA

RECRUITER: WILLIAM REINA
MANAGER, INTERNATIONAL STAFFING
TWO PROCTER & GAMBLE PLAZA
CINCINNATI, OH 45202
TEL: (513) 983-1100
FAX: (513) 983-6758

George L. Bunting, Jr., President. Cosmetics and fragrances. Procter and Gamble Cosmetics and Fragrance Products was founded in 1917. It was formerly called Noxell, and it merged with Procter and Gamble of Cincinnati, Ohio in 1989. Today, it is a manufacturer of cosmetics, fragrances, and household cleaning products. Popular brand names include All-Day cosmetics and Navy, a Cover Girl fragrance for women.

- **Total Employees:** 2,400
- **U.S. Employees Abroad:** 25
- **Countries:** People's Republic of China, France, Germany, United Kingdom.
- **Application Information:** Applications for foreign postings go through the parent company, Procter & Gamble of Cincinnati, Ohio.
- **Job Categories:** Administrative, Marketing—Consumer Goods, Research & Development, Sales—Consumer Goods.
- **Language Requirement:** None.

PROCTER & GAMBLE PHARMACEUTICALS, INC.

17 Eaton Ave.
Norwich, NY 13815 USA

RECRUITER: WILLIAM REINA
MANAGER, INTERNATIONAL RECRUITMENT
TWO PROCTER & GAMBLE PLAZA
CINCINNATI, OH 45202
TEL: (513) 983-1100
FAX: (513) 983-6758

H. Tecklenburg, President. Pharmaceuticals. Procter & Gamble Pharmeceuticals is a subsidiary of Procter & Gamble Company of Cincinnati, Ohio. Its former name was Norwich Eaton Pharmaceuticals, Inc. It produces chemicals, health products, and pharmaceuticals in the United States and abroad. Worldwide revenues for 1991: $400 million.

- **Total Employees:** 2,700
- **U.S. Employees Abroad:** Not available.

- **Countries:** Australia, Belgium, Greece, Netherlands, Philippines, Venezuela.
- **Job Categories:** Chemists, Marketing—Pharmaceuticals, Sales—Pharmaceuticals.
- **Language Requirement:** None.

PRUDENTIAL INSURANCE COMPANY OF AMERICA

751 Broad St.
Newark, NJ 07102 USA

RECRUITER: COLETTE ROAN
INDUSTRY COORDINATOR
751 BROAD ST.
NEWARK, NJ 07102
TEL: (201) 877-6000
FAX: (201) 802-3812

Robert C. Winters, Chairman. Insurance services. Prudential is a mutual company owned by its 12 million policyholders. It was founded in 1873 by John Fairfield Dryden. He began the Widows and Orphans Friendly Society of New Jersey. In 1875 he changed the name to Prudential Friendly Society for the Prudential Assurance Company of England after visiting them and gaining valuable insight in the insurance field. Today, it is the largest insurance company in the United States with operations in 10 foreign countries. Worldwide revenues for 1992: $45 billion.

- **Total Employees:** 63,000
- **U.S. Employees Abroad:** 75
- **Countries:** Australia, Guam, Hong Kong, Italy, Japan, Republic of Korea, Spain, Taiwan.
- **Job Categories:** Executive Management, Finance, Marketing—Financial Services, Underwriters.
- **Language Requirement:** Varies with each posting.

PUROLATOR PRODUCTS COMPANY

2 Warren Place
Tulsa, OK 74136 USA

RECRUITER: DEBBIE THOMPSON
MANAGER, CORPORATE HUMAN
    RESOURCES
2 WARREN PLACE
TULSA, OK 74136
TEL: (918) 481-2500
FAX: (918) 481-3911

Roman E. Boruto, President. Vehicle filters and related products. Purolator Products was founded in 1923 and is a subsidiary of Pennzoil Company of Houston, Texas. It produces various motor vehicle parts and accessories including fuel oil and filters. Worldwide revenues for 1991: $402.4 million.

- **Total Employees:** 3,800
- **U.S. Employees Abroad:** 25
- **Countries:** Argentina, Canada, India, Switzerland, Venezuela.

- **Job Categories:** Management, Marketing—Automotive, Sales—Automotive.
- **Language Requirement:** None.

QUAKER CHEMICAL CORPORATION

Elm & Lee St.s
Conshohocken, PA 19428 USA

RECRUITER: CLIFF MONTGOMERY
VP, HUMAN RESOURCES
ELM & LEE ST.S
CONSHOHOCKEN, PA 19428
TEL: (215) 832-4000
FAX: (215) 832-4494

S. W. W. Lubsen, President. Specialty chemical products. Quaker Chemical Corporation is a public company founded in 1918. It produces various chemical specialty products for the aerospace, automotive, construction, petroleum, pulp and paper, and steel industries. Products include metalworking compounds, coatings, and sealants. Worldwide revenues for 1992: $212 million.

- **Total Employees:** 982
- **U.S. Employees Abroad:** 25
- **Countries:** Australia, Canada, France, Italy, Japan, Mexico, Netherlands, Republic of South Africa, Spain, United Kingdom.
- **Job Categories:** Engineers, Management, Marketing—Chemicals, Sales—Chemicals.
- **Language Requirement:** None.

QUAKER OATS COMPANY

Quaker Tower
PO Box 9001
Chicago, IL 60604-9001 USA

RECRUITER: ANGELA HILL
HUMAN RESOURCES, INTERNATIONAL
QUAKER TOWER
PO BOX 9001
CHICAGO, IL 60604-9001
TEL: (312) 222-7111
FAX: (312) 222-8304

William D. Smithburg, President and Chairman. Food products and pet food. Quaker Oats is a public company founded in 1891 by Henry Crowell when he began the American Cereal Company of Chicago. The current name was adopted in 1901 along with the logo of the Quaker Oats Man, which is well-known throughout the world today. Popular brand names include Life and Quaker Oats cereals, and Gravy Train dog food. It is currently focusing its attention on cereals, pet foods, and microwave items. Worldwide revenues for 1992: $5.7 billion.

- **Total Employees:** 20,900
- **U.S. Employees Abroad:** 45
- **Countries:** Australia, Brazil, Canada, Colombia, Denmark, France, Italy, Malaysia, Mexico, Netherlands, Philippines, Taiwan, United Kingdom.

- **Job Categories:** Management, Marketing—Food/Food Services, Product Development, Sales—Food/Food Services.
- **Training:** Varies with each posting

QUME CORPORATION

500 Yosemite Dr.
Milpitas, CA 95035 USA

RECRUITER: ROSE MUNOZ
HUMAN RESOURCES
REPRESENTATIVE
500 YOSEMITE DR.
MILPITAS, CA 95035
TEL: (408) 942-4004
FAX: (408) 942-4052

David S. Lee, President and Chairman. Computer peripheral products. Qume Corporation is a public company founded in 1979 as Data Technology Corporation. It purchased Qume Corporation Taiwan, Qume Ltd., and Qume Peripherals, Inc. in 1988 from Alcatel, N.V. Currently, it produces and markets computer peripheral products with operations in the United States and abroad. Major products include storage controllers, chip sets, and video display items. Worldwide revenues for 1992: $97 million.

- **Total Employees:** 512
- **U.S. Employees Abroad:** 30
- **Countries:** France, Germany, Hong Kong, Taiwan, Singapore, United Kingdom.
- **Job Categories:** Administrative, Product Development, Engineers, Marketing—Electronics, Sales—Electronics.
- **Language Requirement:** None.
- **Training:** No special training provided.

R. J. REYNOLDS TOBACCO COMPANY

401 North Main St.
Winston-Salem, NC 27102 USA

RECRUITER: CHRISTIAN TRINE
DIRECTOR, INTERNATIONAL HUMAN
RESOURCES
401 NORTH MAIN ST.
WINSTON-SALEM, NC 27102
TEL: (919) 741-5000
FAX: (919) 741-2178

James W. Johnston, Chairman. Tobacco products. R. J. Reynolds Tobacco Company was founded in 1875 and is a subsidiary of RJR Nabisco of New York City. It is engaged as a tobacco producer with manufacturing and distribution operations in the United States and abroad. Worldwide revenues for 1991: $8.5 billion.

- **Total Employees:** 12,000
- **U.S. Employees Abroad:** 25

A
M
E
R
I
C
A
N

J
O
B
S

A
B
R
O
A
D

- **Countries:** Australia, Canada, Switzerland.

- **Job Categories:** Administrative, Finance, Marketing—Consumer Goods.

- **Language Requirement:** None.

RAIN BIRD SPRINKLER MANUFACTURING CORPORATION

145 North Grand
Glendora, CA 91740 USA

RECRUITER: TIM YOUNG
MANAGER, MARKETING AND SALES
145 NORTH GRAND
GLENDORA, CA 91740
TEL: (818) 963-9311
FAX: (818) 963-4287

Tony LaFerta, President. Plumbing fittings, farm machinery. Rainbird Sprinkler Manufacturing Corporation is a private company founded in 1934. It manufactures metal plumbing fixtures, fittings, and trim. It also produces farm machinery, including irrigation equipment and sprinklers. Worldwide revenues for 1991: $100 million.

- **Total Employees:** 850

- **U.S. Employees Abroad:** 18

- **Countries:** Australia, Canada, France.

- **Job Categories:** Management, Marketing—Agricultural, Sales—Agricultural.

- **Language Requirement:** None.

RALSTON PURINA COMPANY

Checkerboard Square
St. Louis, MO 63164-0001 USA

RECRUITER: RON YOUNG
DIRECTOR, HUMAN RESOURCES
CHECKERBOARD SQUARE
ST. LOUIS, MO 63164
TEL: (314) 982-1000
FAX: (314) 982-1211

William P. Stiritz, President and Chairman. Food products, pet food, and batteries. Ralston Purina is a public company founded in 1894 by William Danforth when he began the Robinson-Danforth Commission Company. It was a small St. Louis feed producer and Danforth introduced "Purina" in 1898, a whole wheat cereal product. Everett Ralston, an advocate of whole grain items, endorsed the cereal and Danforth renamed the company Ralston Purina in 1902, to capitalize on all the publicity the cereal had received. Today, Ralston Purina produces such brands as Eveready batteries, Hostess Twinkies snack food, Purina dog food, and Wonder bread. Worldwide revenues for 1992: $7.9 billion.

- **Total Employees:** 57,000

- **U.S. Employees Abroad:** 125

- **Countries:** Australia, Brazil, Canada, People's Republic of China, France, Germany,

Hungary, Italy, Mexico, Netherlands, Panama, Philippines, Singapore, Spain, Switzerland, United Kingdom.

- **Job Categories:** Administrative, Finance, Marketing—Food/Food Services, Marketing—Consumer Goods, Sales—Food/Food Services, Sales—Consumer Goods.
- **Benefits:** All benefits are individually determined.

RANCO, INC.
8161 US Route #42
Plain City, OH 43064 USA

RECRUITER: VINCE MEYER
VP, HUMAN RESOURCES
8161 US ROUTE #42
PLAIN CITY, OH 43064
TEL: (614) 873-9200
FAX: (614) 873-9290

William A. Chapman, President. Industrial products and controls. Ranco, Inc. was founded in 1913 and is an industrial manufacturer of various products including electronic controls and devices, environmental controls, motor vehicle parts and accessories, and semiconductors and related items. Worldwide assets for 1991: $134 million.

- **Total Employees:** 4,700
- **U.S. Employees Abroad:** 12
- **Countries:** Canada, France, Germany, Italy, Japan, Mexico, United Kingdom.
- **Job Categories:** Management, Marketing—Electronics, Marketing—Industrial, Sales—Electronics, Sales—Industrial.
- **General Requirements:** Usually must be a current employee of the company in order to qualify for overseas assignment.
- **Language Requirement:** None.

RAYOVAC CORPORATION
601 Rayovac Dr.
Madison, WI 53711 USA

RECRUITER: RUSSELL E. LEFEVRE
STAFFING/RECRUITMENT
601 RAYOVAC DR.
MADISON, WI 53711
TEL: (608) 275-3340
FAX: (608) 275-4577

Thomas F. Pyle, Jr., President and Chairman. Batteries and lighting products. Rayovac is a private company founded in 1906. It produces electric and non-electric lighting fixtures and related items, and storage batteries. Worldwide revenues for 1991: $402.2 million.

- **Total Employees:** 2,500
- **U.S. Employees Abroad:** Not available.
- **Countries:** Canada.

A M E R I C A N   J O B S   A B R O A D

- **Job Categories:** Accountants, Finance.
- **Average Overseas Assignment:** 3-5 years.
- **Language Requirement:** None.
- **Training:** Basic orientation (1-30 days) provided.
- **Benefits:** All benefits are individually determined.

RAYTHEON COMPANY

141 Spring St.
Lexington, MA 02173 USA

RECRUITER: FRANK UMANZIO
VICE PRESIDENT, HUMAN
  RESOURCES
141 SPRING ST.
LEXINGTON, MA 02173
TEL: (617) 862-6600
FAX: (617) 860-2172

Dennis J. Picard, Chairman. Aviation, electronics, appliances; engineering and construction services. Raytheon is a public company founded in 1922 as the American Appliance Company to market machinery, motors, and their components. It became successful in the fast-growing market for radios. Today, Raytheon is well-known for its production of the Patriot missile (Gulf War). The anti-Scud Patriot was credited with $1.2 billion in sales in 1992. Currently, Raytheon has operations in 38 states and 23 foreign countries. Worldwide revenues for 1992: $9.1 billion. Foreign revenues for 1992: $512 million.

- **Total Employees:** 63,900
- **U.S. Employees Abroad:** 2,500
- **Countries:** Canada, Germany, Japan, Kuwait, Netherlands, Spain, Saudi Arabia, United Kingdom.
- **Job Categories:** Engineers, Marketing—Electronics, Marketing—Scientific, Sales—Electronics, Sales—Scientific.

READER'S DIGEST ASSOCIATION, INC.

Reader's Digest Rd.
Pleasantville, NY 10570-7000
USA

RECRUITER: MARTHA STROHL
HUMAN RESOURCES
  REPRESENTATIVE
READER'S DIGEST RD.
PLEASANTVILLE, NY 10570-7000
TEL: (914) 241-5354
FAX: (914) 238-4559

George V. Grune, Chairman. Magazines and book publishing. Reader's Digest Association, Inc. is a public company founded in 1922 by DeWitt and Lila Wallace in New York City. In 1925 the company moved to Pleasantville, New York. International operations were started in 1940 with the opening of five offices abroad. Today, it publishes books, magazines, recorded music, and videocassettes. Currently, worldwide circulation of *Reader's Digest* is 28 million subscribers and it is published in 17 languages. Worldwide revenues for 1992: $2.8 billion.

- **Total Employees:** 7,400
- **U.S. Employees Abroad:** 30
- **Countries:** Australia, Belgium, Canada, Denmark, France, Germany, Hong Kong, Italy, Mexico, Netherlands, New Zealand, Singapore, Sweden, Switzerland, United Kingdom.
- **Job Categories:** Editors, Management, Marketing—Publishing, Sales—Publishing.
- **General Requirements:** Usually must be a current employee of the company in order to qualify for overseas assignment.

READING & BATES

PO Box 79627
Houston, TX 77279 USA

RECRUITER: ARCHIE MOORE
STAFFING/RECRUITMENT
PO BOX 79627
HOUSTON, TX 77279
TEL: (713) 496-5000
FAX: (713) 496-0153

D. K. McIntosh, Chairman. Offshore drilling contractor. Reading & Bates is a public company founded in 1955. It is a global exploratory and development drilling contractor that provides equipment, manpower, and expertise for offshore drilling projects. Worldwide revenues for 1991: $126.8 million.

- **Total Employees:** 1,300
- **U.S. Employees Abroad:** 25
- **Countries:** Argentina, People's Republic of China, India, Italy, Malaysia, Netherlands, Singapore, United Arab Emirates, United Kingdom.
- **Job Categories:** Administrative, Engineers, Management, Marketing—Petroleum/ Natural Gas.
- **Language Requirement:** Varies with each posting.

RECOGNITION EQUIPMENT, INC.

2701 East Grauwyler
Irving, TX 75061 USA

RECRUITER: HUMAN RESOURCES
DEPARTMENT
DIRECTOR, HUMAN RESOURCES
2701 EAST GRAUWYLER
IRVING, TX 75061
TEL: (214) 579-6000
FAX: (214) 579-6877

Thomas Hurley, Chief Executive Officer. Computer data and document processing systems and equipment. Recognition Equipment, Inc. is a public company founded in 1961. It sells and services data capture, document scanning, and image processing systems, which include art terminal-based keyboard items and fully integrated systems. Major brands include System 1000 and System 100 trade names. Worldwide revenues for 1992: $199.2 million.

- **Total Employees:** 1,700
- **U.S. Employees Abroad:** 22
- **Countries:** France, Germany, Japan, Netherlands, United Kingdom.
- **Application Information:** Hiring for most overseas positions is done at the specific country location. Please call company for correct contact information. Do not mail resumes to recruiter's address.
- **Job Categories:** Engineers, Product Development, Sales—Electronics.
- **Language Requirement:** Varies with each posting.
- **Training:** Varies with each posting.

REDKEN LABORATORIES, INC.

6625 Variel Ave.
Canoga Park, CA 91303 USA

RECRUITER: TREVA VOHNIG
MANAGER, HUMAN RESOURCES
6625 VARIEL AVE.
CANOGA PARK, CA 91303
TEL: (818) 992-2700

P. K. Meehan, Chief Executive Officer. Hair- and skin-care products. Redken Laboratories, Inc. is a private company founded in 1960. It is a manufacturer of cosmetics, hair-care and beauty products.

- **Total Employees:** 700
- **U.S. Employees Abroad:** 17
- **Countries:** Australia, Canada, Germany, Japan, New Zealand, United Kingdom.
- **Application Information:** Most overseas positions are filled internally.
- **Job Categories:** Marketing—Consumer Goods, Product Development, Sales—Consumer Goods.
- **Language Requirement:** None.

REED TOOL COMPANY

6501 Navigation Blvd.
Houston, TX 77011 USA

RECRUITER: TIM BRUEGGER
MANAGER, COMPENSATION &
EMPLOYMENT
6501 NAVIGATION BLVD.
HOUSTON, TX 77011
TEL: (713) 747-4000
FAX: (713) 747-5667

R. Caldwell, Chief Executive Officer. Services and machinery for oil and gas industries and well-drilling. Reed Tool is a subsidiary of Camco Products and Services of Houston, Texas. It provides services to businesses engaged in nonmetallic minerals, mines, or quarries. It also produces equipment for oil and gas fields and the drilling of water wells. Worldwide revenues for 1991: $90 million.

- **Total Employees:** 800
- **U.S. Employees Abroad:** 18
- **Countries:** France, Italy, Netherlands, Singapore, United Kingdom.
- **Job Categories:** Management, Marketing—Petroleum/Natural Gas, Technical Field Support.
- **Language Requirement:** None.

REEVES BROTHERS, INC.

Box #892
Spartanburg, SC 29304 USA

RECRUITER: PAT WALSH
VP, HUMAN RESOURCES
BOX #892
SPARTANBURG, SC 29304
TEL: (803) 576-1210
FAX: (803) 576-8544

James W. Hart, President and Chairman. Textiles. Reeves Brothers is a private company, incorporated in 1922. It manufactures woven cotton, synthetic fabrics, textile job finishing, filter cloth, and industrial fabric products. It operates broadwoven cotton fabric mills and is also a manufacturer of mechanical rubber goods. Worldwide revenues for 1991: $257 million.

- **Total Employees:** 2,700
- **U.S. Employees Abroad:** 20
- **Countries:** Italy, Portugal, United Kingdom.
- **Job Categories:** Marketing, Plant Managers, Sales.
- **Language Requirement:** None.

RELIANCE ELECTRIC COMPANY

6065 Parkland Blvd.
Cleveland, OH 44124 USA

RECRUITER: DAVE BURKE
MANAGER, HUMAN RESOURCES
6065 PARKLAND BLVD.
CLEVELAND, OH 44124
TEL: (216) 266-7000
FAX: (216) 266-7666

John C. Morley, President. Equipment for industrial automation. Reliance Electric is a public company founded in 1986. It is a global manufacturer of industrial motors, process drive systems, and industrial control products. Primany clients are in the industrial and utility markets. Worldwide revenues for 1992: $1.6 billion.

- **Total Employees:** 14,000
- **U.S. Employees Abroad:** 40

- **Countries:** Australia, Brazil, Canada, France, Germany, Italy, Japan, Mexico, New Zealand, Sweden, Switzerland, United Kingdom.

- **Job Categories:** Management, Marketing—Industrial, Product Development, Sales—Industrial.

RELIANCE INTERNATIONAL

78 Water St.
New York, NY 10055 USA

RECRUITER: DIANE VOTINELLI
INTERNATIONAL STAFFING/
RECRUITMENT
78 WATER ST.
NEW YORK, NY 10055
TEL: (212) 858-3600
FAX: (212) 858-5699

Saul P. Sterling, Chairman. Financial services. Reliance International is a subsidiary of Reliance Group, Inc. of New York City. It offers life insurance, and financial and management services to clients on a global basis. Worldwide assets for 1991: $8.9 billion.

- **Total Employees:** 9,000
- **U.S. Employees Abroad:** 35
- **Countries:** Japan, United Kingdom.
- **Job Categories:** Agents—Insurance, Financial Advisors, Management, Marketing—Financial Services.
- **Language Requirement:** None.

REMINGTON PRODUCTS, INC.

60 Main St.
Bridgeport, CT 06604 USA

RECRUITER: MICHAEL DUDA
PERSONNEL MANAGER
60 MAIN ST.
BRIDGEPORT, CT 06602
TEL: (203) 367-4400
FAX: (203) 366-6039

Victor K. Kiam II, President. Electric shaving and toiletry items. Remington Products, Inc. is a private company founded in 1979. It manufactures various products including electric shavers; nonaluminum, nonferrous die castings; and household electric appliances. Major brands include Triple Action electric shavers and Close aftershave lotion. Worldwide revenues for 1991: $400 million.

- **Total Employees:** 1,700
- **U.S. Employees Abroad:** 22
- **Countries:** Australia, Canada, Germany, Japan, United Kingdom.
- **Job Categories:** Management, Marketing—Consumer Goods, Sales—Consumer Goods.

- **Language Requirement:** None.

RESOURCES MANAGEMENT INTERNATIONAL

3100 Zinfandel Dr., Suite 600
Rancho Cordova, CA 95670 USA

RECRUITER: GHASSAN NAKAD
DIRECTOR, INTERNATIONAL DIVISION
3100 ZINFANDEL DR., SUITE 600
RANCHO CORDOVA, CA 95670
TEL: (916) 852-1300
FAX: (916) 852-1073

Lloyd H. Harvego, President. Engineering (energy, water, and environment) and management consulting services. Resources Management International (RMI) is a public company founded in 1980. It provides services to clients in the United States and abroad. Worldwide operating revenues for 1991: $13 million.

- **Total Employees:** 300
- **U.S. Employees Abroad:** Not available.
- **Countries:** Egypt, Jordan, Indonesia, Philippines, Uruguay.
- **Application Information:** Do not call.
- **Job Categories:** Engineers, Management.
- **Language Requirement:** Varies with each posting.
- **Training:** None provided.
- **Benefits:** HEALTH: Offered. HOUSING: Offered for long-term assignments. EDUCATION: Offered for long-term assignments.

REVLON, INC.

625 Madison Ave.
New York, NY 10022 USA

RECRUITER: CHARLES SCHIFFER
VP, HUMAN RESOURCES
625 MADISON AVE.
NEW YORK, NY 10021
TEL: (212) 527-4000
FAX: (212) 527-4547

R. O. Perelman, Chairman. Cosmetics, toiletries, and pharmaceuticals. Revlon is a subsidiary of Banner Industries, Inc. of Ohio and was established in 1935. Major products include cosmetics, perfumes, and drugs for pharmaceutical preparations. Popular brand names include Bill Blass fragrances and Pedi-Care footcare products. All testing of products and ingredients on animals recently ceased as a result of a boycott against the company by an animal rights organization.

- **Total Employees:** 24,000
- **U.S. Employees Abroad:** 35
- **Countries:** Argentina, Australia, Brazil, Canada, France, Germany, Italy, Japan, Kenya, Mexico, Spain, Switzerland, United Kingdom, Venezuela.

- **Job Categories:** Management, Marketing—Consumer Goods, Marketing—Pharmaceuticals, Sales—Consumer Goods, Sales—Pharmaceuticals.
- **Training:** No special training provided.

REYNOLDS METALS COMPANY

PO Box 27003
Richmond, VA 23261-7003 USA

RECRUITER: JOHN MCGILL
VP, HUMAN RESOURCES
PO BOX 27003
RICHMOND, VA 23261-7003
TEL: (804) 261-2000
FAX: (804) 261-4160

Richard G. Holder, President. Aluminum and related products; also plastics and mining. Reynolds Metals is a public company founded in 1928 when Richard Reynolds, already owner of U.S. Foil, bought Robertshaw Thermostat, Fulton Sylphon, and a part of Beechnut Foil to form the Reynolds Metal Company. Today, it is the second largest producer of aluminum foil in the United States. It has facilities in 20 countries. Worldwide revenues for 1992: $5.6 billion.

- **Total Employees:** 30,900
- **U.S. Employees Abroad:** 60
- **Countries:** Australia, Canada, Germany, Jamaica, Japan, Russia, Switzerland, United Kingdom.
- **Job Categories:** Executive Management, Marketing—Industrial, Sales—Industrial.
- **Language Requirement:** Varies with each posting.

RHONE-POULENC RORER

500 Arcola Dr.
PO Box 1200
Collegeville, PA 19426-0107 USA

RECRUITER: ROBBIE LAROCCA
UNIVERSITY RELATIONS
500 ARCOLA DR.
PO BOX 1200
ARCOLA, PA 19426-0107
TEL: (215) 454-5233
FAX: (215) 454-5200

Robert E. Cawthord, Chief Executive Officer. Pharmaceuticals. Rhone-Poulenc Rorer is a public company founded in 1920. It researches and produces human pharmaceuticals and agricultural chemicals in the United States and abroad. Worldwide revenues for 1992: $4 billion.

- **Total Employees:** 23,000
- **U.S. Employees Abroad:** 100
- **Countries:** Worldwide including France, United Kingdom.
- **Job Categories:** Management, Marketing—Pharmaceuticals, Product Development, Sales—Pharmaceuticals.

- **Language Requirement:** Knowledge of local language a plus but not essential.
- **Training:** No special training provided.
- **Benefits:** All benefits are individually determined.

RIVERWOOD INTERNATIONAL, INC.

3350 Cumberland Circle
Atlanta, GA 30339 USA

RECRUITER: TONY ORTA
STAFFING/RECRUITMENT
3350 CUMBERLAND CIRCLE
ATLANTA, GA 30339
TEL: (404) 916-7925
FAX: (404) 644-2927

Tom Johnson, President. Forest products and paper. Riverwood International was founded in 1989 and is a subsidiary of Riverwood Corporation of Atlanta, Georgia. Worldwide revenues for 1992: $1.1 billion.

- **Total Employees:** 8,500
- **U.S. Employees Abroad:** 22
- **Countries:** Brazil.
- **Job Categories:** Management, Marketing, Sales.
- **Language Requirement:** None.
- **Training:** No special training provided.

RJR NABISCO

345 Park Ave.
New York, NY 10019 USA

RECRUITER: MICHAEL HICKEY
VP, INTERNATIONAL HUMAN
RESOURCES
345 PARK AVE.
NEW YORK, NY 10019
TEL: (212) 572-3047
FAX: (212) 826-4220

Louis V. Gerstner, Jr., Chairman. Tobacco and food industry products. RJR Nabisco is a public company founded in 1875 as the R. J. Reynolds Tobacco Company in Winston, North Carolina. It operated as one of the largest tobacco businesses in the world. Diversification occured as anti-smoking sentiment prompted the company to create other products. Today, it is a world leader in both the tobacco and food industries. Major brands include Camel cigarettes, Oreo cookies, and Grey Poupon mustard. Worldwide revenues for 1992: $15.8 billion.

- **Total Employees:** 55,000
- **U.S. Employees Abroad:** 75
- **Countries:** Worldwide including Brazil, Canada, Mexico, United Kingdom.
- **Job Categories:** Administrative, Marketing—Consumer Goods, Marketing—Food/Food Services, Sales—Consumer Goods, Sales—Food/Food Services.

- **Language Requirement:** None.

ROBERT HALF INTERNATIONAL, INC.

2884 Sand Hill Rd.
Menlo Park, CA 94025 USA

RECRUITER: ANNETTE MOWINCKLE
PERSONNEL DEPARTMENT
2884 SAND HILL RD., SUITE #200
MENLO PARK, CA 94025
TEL: (415) 854-9700

Harold M. Messmer, Jr., Chairman. Personnel services company. Robert Half International, Inc. is a public company founded in 1948. It offers financial services and employee placement through its franchises in the United States and abroad.

- **Total Employees:** 1,000

- **U.S. Employees Abroad:** 35

- **Countries:** Belgium, Canada, Israel, United Kingdom.

- **Job Categories:** Data Processors, Finance, Human Resources, Office Management, Marketing.

- **Language Requirement:** Knowledge of local language a plus but not essential.

ROBERTSON CECO

222 Berkley St., 20th floor
Boston, MA 02116 USA

RECRUITER: KEITH HUDSON
DIRECTOR, COMPENSATION &
BENEFITS
222 BERKLEY ST.
BOSTON, MA 02116
TEL: (617) 424-5500
FAX: (617) 424-5555

Andrew G. C. Sage II, President. Building products and related services. Robertson Ceco was formed due to the merger of H. H. Robertson Company and Ceco Company. It is an exporter of nonresidential building products and provider of erection services. It is also a manufacturer of metal door frames and sheet metal roofing and siding. Worldwide revenues for 1992: $401 million.

- **Total Employees:** 3,500

- **U.S. Employees Abroad:** 35

- **Countries:** Australia, Canada, Denmark, Hong Kong, Netherlands, New Zealand, Republic of South Africa, Sweden, United Kingdom.

- **Job Categories:** Management, Marketing, Sales.

ROCKWELL GRAPHIC SYSTEMS

600 East Oakmont Lane
Westmont, IL 60559-5546 USA

RECRUITER: ANSON KRANMER
DIRECTOR, HUMAN RESOURCES
600 EAST OAKMONT LANE
WESTMOUNT, IL 60559-5546
TEL: (708) 850-5600
FAX: (708) 8505851

James Cavenaugh, President. Printing machinery. Rockwell Graphic Systems was founded in 1885 and is a subsidiary of Rockwell International Corporation of Seal Beach, California. It manufactures machinery for the printing and bookbinding trades. Worldwide revenues for 1991: $11 billion.

- **Total Employees:** 5,000

- **U.S. Employees Abroad:** 25

- **Countries:** France, Germany, Japan, United Kingdom.

- **Job Categories:** Marketing—Industrial, Sales—Industrial, Technical Field Support.

ROCKWELL INTERNATIONAL CORPORATION

2201 Seal Beach Blvd.
Seal Beach, CA 90740-8250 USA

RECRUITER: ROBERT H. MURPHY
SENIOR VP, HUMAN RESOURCES
2201 SEAL BEACH BLVD.
SEAL BEACH, CA 90740-8250
TEL: (310) 797-5066
FAX: (310) 797-5690

Donald R. Beall, Chairman. Aerospace; electronics and automotive parts. Rockwell International Corporation is a public company formed in 1967 when Rockwell Standard merged with North American Aviation creating North American Rockwell. Its current name was adopted in 1973. It is widely known for its contracts for the space shuttle, but Rockwell is also a leader in the field of avionics (aircraft and electronic systems). Other areas include the automotive and graphics industries. Worldwide revenues for 1992: $10.9 billion.

- **Total Employees:** 87,000

- **U.S. Employees Abroad:** 125

- **Countries:** Australia, Brazil, Canada, France, Germany, Hong Kong, Italy, Japan, Republic of Korea, Singapore, Taiwan, United Kingdom.

- **Job Categories:** Administrative, Finance, Marketing—Automotive, Marketing—Electronics, Marketing—Scientific, Product Development, Sales—Automotive, Sales—Electronics, Sales—Scientific.

- **Language Requirement:** Varies with each posting.

ROGERS CORPORATION

1 Technology Dr.
Rogers, CT 06263 USA

RECRUITER: DIANE BEECH
EMPLOYMENT MANAGER
1 TECHNOLOGY DR.
ROGERS, CT 06263
TEL: (203) 774-9605
FAX: (203) 774-5852

Norman L. Greenman, President. Plastic components and related items. Rogers Corporation is a public company founded in 1832. It is an industrial manufacturer of plastic components and flexible interconnection products for the automotive, electronics, and telecommunications industries. Worldwide revenues for 1992: $172.4 million.

- **Total Employees:** 3,150

- **U.S. Employees Abroad:** 22

- **Countries:** Belgium, France, Germany, Japan, United Kingdom.

- **Job Categories:** Administrative, Marketing, Sales.

- **Language Requirement:** None.

ROHM & HAAS COMPANY

Independence Mall West
Philadelphia, PA 19105 USA

RECRUITER: MAURICE MARIETTI
DIRECTOR, HUMAN RESOURCES
INDEPENDENCE MALL WEST
PHILADELPHIA, PA 19105
TEL: (215) 592-3000
FAX: (215) 592-2679

J. Lawrence Wilson, Chairman. Plastics and specialty chemicals. Rohm & Haas is a public company founded in 1909. It produces such items as laundry detergent, house paints, motor oils, and agricultural products in the United States and abroad. Worldwide revenues for 1992: $3.1 billion.

- **Total Employees:** 12,870

- **U.S. Employees Abroad:** 22

- **Countries:** Argentina, Australia, Bermuda, Brazil, Canada, Costa Rica, Germany, France, Hong Kong, India, Indonesia, Mexico, Netherlands, Philippines, Singapore, Taiwan.

- **Application Information:** Most overseas positions are filled internally.

- **Job Categories:** Management, Marketing—Chemicals, Sales—Chemicals.

- **Language Requirement:** Knowledge of local language a plus but not essential.

ROLLINS HUDIG HALL INTERNATIONAL

123 North Wacker Dr.
Chicago, IL 60606 USA

RECRUITER: FRED FELDMAN
DIRECTOR, HUMAN RESOURCES
123 NORTH WACKER DR.
CHICAGO, IL 60606
TEL: (312) 701-4541
FAX: (312) 701-4580

Insurance services. Rollins Hudig Hall International was formed in 1992 due to a merger of Frank B. Hall of New York and Rollins Burdick Hunter International of Illinois. It offers insurance services to clients in the United States and abroad.

- **Total Employees:** 7,000

- **U.S. Employees Abroad:** 25

- **Countries:** Argentina, Hong Kong.

- **Job Categories:** Agents—Insurance, Marketing—Financial Services, Sales—Financial Services.

- **General Requirements:** Usually must be a current employee of the company in order to qualify for overseas assignment.

ROSEMOUNT, INC.

12001 Technology Dr.
Eden Prairie, MN 55344 USA

RECRUITER: DOUGLAS WALTERS
MANAGER, INTERNATIONAL HUMAN
RESOURCES
12001 TECHNOLOGY DR.
EDEN PRAIRIE, MN 55344
TEL: (612) 941-5560
FAX: (612) 828-7795

Robert Bateman, Chief Executive Officer. Aerospace and industrial instrumentation. Rosemount, Inc. was founded in 1956 and is a subsidiary of Emerson Electric of St. Louis, Missouri. Its main business focuses on the process controls industry. Worldwide revenues for 1991: $456 million

- **Total Employees:** 5,880

- **U.S. Employees Abroad:** 40

- **Countries:** Australia, Austria, Belgium, Canada, People's Republic of China, Denmark, France, Germany, Hong Kong, India, Italy, Japan, Republic of Korea, Mexico, Netherlands, Sweden, United Kingdom.

- **Job Categories:** Management, Marketing—Industrial, Marketing—Scientific, Research & Development, Sales—Industrial, Sales—Scientific.

ROWAN COMPANIES, INC.

2800 Post Oak Blvd., Suite #5450
Houston, TX 77056 USA

RECRUITER: ROBERT J. TEDRETT
DIRECTOR, HUMAN RESOURCES
2800 POST OAK BLVD., SUITE #5450
HOUSTON, TX 77056
TEL: (713) 621-7800
FAX: (713) 960-7560

C. R. Palmer, President and Chairman. Global offshore drilling services. Rowan Companies, Inc. is a public company founded in 1923. It provides offshore drilling services and also operates charter aviation services in the United States and abroad. Worldwide revenues for 1991: $272.2 million.

- **Total Employees:** 2,330

- **U.S. Employees Abroad:** 25

- **Countries:** Canada, Indonesia, Netherlands, Singapore, United Kingdom, Venezuela.

- **Job Categories:** Administrative, Contractors, Marketing—Petroleum/Natural Gas, Pilots.

- **General Requirements:** Usually must be a current employee of the company in order to qualify for overseas assignment.

- **Language Requirement:** Varies with each posting.

RPM, INC.

Box 777
Medina, OH 44258 USA

RECRUITER: J. MORRIS
STAFFING/RECRUITMENT
BOX #777
MEDINA, OH 44258
TEL: (216) 225-3192
FAX: (216) 225-8743

Thomas C. Sullivan, Chairman. Protective coatings, paint, and related products. RPM, Inc. is a public company founded in 1947 by Frank C. Sullivan. Its former name was Republic Powdered Metals. It has four major divisions: Industrial Corrosion Control, Specialty Chemicals, Consumer Do-It-Yourself, and Consumer Hobby and Leisure. It operates on a global basis. Worldwide revenues for 1991: $500.3 million.

- **Total Employees:** 2,700

- **U.S. Employees Abroad:** 30

- **Countries:** Canada, Luxembourg, Belgium.

- **Job Categories:** Management, Marketing—Chemicals, Sales—Chemicals.

- **Language Requirement:** None.

- **Training:** No special training provided.

RUBBERMAID, INC.
1147 Akron Rd.
Wooster, OH 44691-6000 USA

RECRUITER: LARRY BLACKBURN
VP, INTERNATIONAL
1147 AKRON RD.
WOOSTER, OH 44691-6000
TEL: (216) 264-6464
FAX: (216) 287-2739

Walter W. Williams, Chairman. Rubber and plastic products. Rubbermaid, Inc. is a public company founded in 1920 when five businessmen from Wooster, Ohio formed the Wooster Rubber Company to manufacture toy balloons. James Caldwell joined the group in the 1930s, and they began producing Rubbermaid products, a group of houseware items. Today, items produced include casual dinnerware, outdoor resin furniture, and toolboxes. It has manufacturing plants and warehouses in 15 states and 10 foreign countries. Worldwide revenues for 1992: $1.8 billion.

- **Total Employees:** 9,754
- **U.S. Employees Abroad:** 40
- **Countries:** Austria, Canada, France, Hungary, Mexico, Netherlands, Switzerland.
- **Job Categories:** Finance, Management, Marketing—Chemicals, Marketing—Consumer Goods, Sales—Chemicals, Sales—Consumer Goods.
- **General Requirements:** Usually must be a current employee of the company in order to qualify for overseas assignment.

RUDER FINN, INC.
301 East 57th St.
New York, NY 10022 USA

RECRUITER: KATHY BLOOMGARDEN
PRESIDENT
301 EAST 57TH ST.
NEW YORK, NY 10022
TEL: (212) 593-6400
FAX: (212) 593-6397

David Finn, Chief Executive Officer. Public relations. Ruder Finn is a private company founded in 1948. It offers public relations services which include advertising, art and graphic design, and commercial art and design.

- **Total Employees:** 300
- **U.S. Employees Abroad:** 20
- **Countries:** Australia, France, Germany, Italy, Japan, Sweden, Switzerland, United Kingdom.
- **Application Information:** Most overseas positions are filled internally.
- **Job Categories:** Administrative, Public Relations, Marketing.
- **Language Requirement:** None.

RUSSELL CORPORATION

PO Box 272
Alexander City, AL 35010 USA

RECRUITER: BOB SCIRE
MANAGER, INTERNATIONAL
OPERATIONS
PO BOX 272
ALEXANDER CITY, AL 35010
TEL: (205) 329-4000
FAX: (205) 329-5045

Dwight L. Carlisle, Jr., President. Athletic and casual apparel. Russell Corporation is a public company founded in 1902. It designs, manufactures, and markets leisure apparel, athletic uniforms, and other lightweight, yarn-dyed woven fabrics. These items are sold to various markets including: department and specialty stores, golf pro shops, mail order houses, and sporting goods dealers. Worldwide revenues for 1992: $899 million.

- **Total Employees:** 13,000
- **U.S. Employees Abroad:** 12
- **Countries:** Belgium, United Kingdom.
- **Job Categories:** Management, Marketing—Consumer Goods, Sales—Consumer Goods.
- **Language Requirement:** None.

RUSSELL REYNOLDS ASSOCIATES, INC.

200 Park Ave.
New York, NY 10166 USA

RECRUITER: JAMES BAGLEY
DIRECTOR, HUMAN RESOURCES
200 PARK AVE.
NEW YORK, NY 10166
TEL: (212) 351-2000
FAX: (212) 370-0896

Hobson Brown, Jr., President. Executive recruiting services. Russell Reynolds Associates, Inc. is a private company that functions as an employment agency for executive placement and recruitment.

- **Total Employees:** 600
- **U.S. Employees Abroad:** 25
- **Countries:** Australia, France, Germany, Hong Kong, Japan, Singapore, Spain, United Kingdom.
- **Job Categories:** Executive Management, Marketing.
- **General Requirements:** Usually must be a current employee of the company in order to qualify for overseas assignment.
- **Language Requirement:** Varies with each posting.

RUST INTERNATIONAL, INC.

PO Box 101
Birmingham, AL 35201 USA

RECRUITER: DONALD HAYSLETT
MANAGER, RECRUITMENT
PO BOX 101
BIRMINGHAM, AL 35201
TEL: (205) 995-7878
FAX: (205) 995-7684

David S. Rosendale, President. General contractors. Rust International Corporation was founded in 1905 and is a subsidiary of Wheelabrator Technologies of Hampton, New Hampshire. It offers general contracting, architecture and engineering services. It also constructs industrial buildings and warehouses. Worldwide operating revenues for 1992: $1.4 billion.

- **Total Employees:** 13,900
- **U.S. Employees Abroad:** 25
- **Countries:** Saudi Arabia.
- **Job Categories:** Architects, Engineers, Management, Marketing.
- **Comments:** The number of Americans reported working abroad varies greatly from quarter to quarter, fluctuating with the number and scope of projects under contract at the time.

RYDER SYSTEMS, INC.

3600 NW 82nd Ave.
Miami, FL 33166 USA

RECRUITER: SAM HINES
MANAGER, STAFFING
3600 NW 82ND AVE.
MIAMI, FL 33166
TEL: (305) 593-4396
FAX: (305) 596-4657

M. Anthony Burns, President and Chairman. Highway transportation services. Ryder Systems, Inc. is a public company founded in 1933 by Jim Ryder. It began by offering truck rentals in four southern states. Today, it is the world's best known supplier of highway transportation services. It is the number one provider of commercial truck rentals and has locations throughout the United States and abroad. It also offers many commercial airlines jet engine maintenance service through its Aviall and Caledonian Airmotive divisions. Aviall is the number number one independent distributor of new aviation parts and related items. Currently, Ryder operates with a fleet of 155,459 vehicles and 31 commercial aircraft. Worldwide revenues for 1992: $5.2 billion.

- **Total Employees:** 40,195
- **U.S. Employees Abroad:** 35
- **Countries:** Canada, Germany, United Kingdom.
- **Job Categories:** Management, Marketing, Sales.
- **Language Requirement:** None.

SAATCHI & SAATCHI

375 Hudson St.
New York, NY 10014 USA

RECRUITER: JOSEPH SANSAVERINO
DIRECTOR, HUMAN RESOURCES
375 HUDSON ST.
NEW YORK, NY 10014
TEL: (212) 463-2000

Stuart Upson, Chairman. Advertising. Saatchi & Saatchi was founded in 1923 and is a subsidiary of Saatchi & Saatchi Company PLC of London, England. It operates as an advertising firm in the United States and abroad.

- **Total Employees:** 7,200

- **U.S. Employees Abroad:** 60

- **Countries:** Australia, France, Germany, Japan, Singapore.

- **Application Information:** Hiring for most overseas positions is done at the specific country location.

- **Job Categories:** Finance, Marketing, Sales—Advertising.

- **Language Requirement:** None.

- **Training:** No special training provided.

SAINT JUDE MEDICAL, INC.

One Lillehi Plaza
St. Paul, MN 55117 USA

RECRUITER: TERESA HOINE
HUMAN RESOURCES COORDINATOR
ONE LILLEHI PLAZA
ST. PAUL, MN 55117
TEL: (612) 483-2000
FAX: (612) 482-8318

William C. Hendrickson, Chairman. Mechanical heart valves and related items. St. Jude Medical, Inc. is a public company founded in 1976 by medical entrepreneur, Manuel Villafana. He invented the bileaflet heart valve in 1972. Today, the company produces other related products including annuloplasty rings, centrifugal blood pumps and vascular grafts. It has facilities in seven countries and products are sold on a global basis. Worldwide revenues for 1992: $240 million.

- **Total Employees:** 600

- **U.S. Employees Abroad:** 25

- **Countries:** Belgium, Canada, France, Germany, Spain, United Kingdom.

- **Job Categories:** Finance, Management, Marketing—Health & Medical Supplies, Product Development, Sales—Health & Medical Supplies.

- **Language Requirement:** Varies with each posting.

SALOMON, INC.

Seven World Trade Center
New York, NY 10048 USA

RECRUITER: COLEEN O'HORA
VP, CORPORATE EMPLOYMENT
SEVEN WORLD TRADE CNTER, 28TH
    FLOOR
NEW YORK, NY 10048
TEL: (212) 783-7000
FAX: (212) 783-2110

Robert E. Denham, Chairman. Investment banking and securities trading; crude oil refiner and trader. Salomon, Inc. is a public company founded in 1910 by Arthur, Herbert, and Percy Salomon when they began Salomon Brothers, a money brokerage firm. Expansion occurred through the years and in the 1960s, foreign offices were established in London and Tokyo. Today, it offers diversified trading and financial services on a global basis. Clients include banks, financial institutions, and governments. Worldwide revenues for 1992: $8.2 billion.

- **Total Employees:** 8,972
- **U.S. Employees Abroad:** 40
- **Countries:** Worldwide including France, Germany, Hong Kong, Japan, Singapore, United Kingdom.
- **Application Information:** Hiring for most overseas positions is done at the specific country location.
- **Job Categories:** Finance, Management, Marketing—Financial Services, Sales—Financial Services, Underwriters.
- **Language Requirement:** Varies with each posting.
- **Benefits:** All benefits are individually determined.

SARA LEE CORPORATION

Three First National Plaza
Chicago, IL 60602 USA

RECRUITER: LENA C. COLDRAS
STAFFING/RECRUITMENT
THREE FIRST NATIONAL PLAZA
CHICAGO, IL 60602
TEL: (312) 726-2600
FAX: (312) 726-3712

John H. Bryan, Chairman. Food and consumer goods. Sara Lee Corporation is a public company founded in 1939 by Nathan Cummings. He purchased the C. D. Kenny Company, a wholesaler of coffee, tea, and sugar. Other store purchases soon followed along with a name change to Consolidated Grocers in 1945. It was renamed Consolidated Foods Corporation in 1956 and that same year, it purchased the Kitchens of Sara Lee. Because the name became so well-known, the entire company's name was changed in 1985 to the Sara Lee Corporation. Worldwide revenues for 1992: $13.9 billion.

- **Total Employees:** 113,000

- **U.S. Employees Abroad:** 60
- **Countries:** Australia, Canada, France, Netherlands.
- **Job Categories:** Management, Marketing—Food/Food Services, Product Development, Sales—Food/Food Services.
- **Language Requirement:** Varies with each posting.

SB POWER TOOLS, INC. (SKIL CORP.)

4300 West Peterson Ave.
Chicago, IL 60646 USA

RECRUITER: ELLEN REESE
MANAGER, EMPLOYEE RELATIONS
4300 WEST PETERSON AVE.
CHICAGO, IL 60646
TEL: (312) 286-7330
FAX: (312) 794-7481

G. Thomas McKane, President. Power tools. SB Power Tools was founded in 1924 and is a subsidiary of Emerson Electric Company of St. Louis, Missouri. Its former name was Skil Corporation. It manufactures power tools, cutting tools, machinist's measuring tools and related accessories. Worldwide revenues for 1991: $160.0 million.

- **Total Employees:** 2,300
- **U.S. Employees Abroad:** 24
- **Countries:** Australia, Mexico, Netherlands, Republic of South Africa, Sweden, Switzerland.
- **Job Categories:** Management, Marketing—Consumer Goods, Sales—Consumer Goods.
- **Language Requirement:** None.

SCHERING-PLOUGH CORPORATION

One Giralda Farms
Madison, NJ 07940-1000 USA

RECRUITER: EILEEN MULANEY
INTERNATIONAL PERSONNEL
ADMINISTRATOR
2000 GALLOPING HILL RD.
KENNILWORTH, NJ 07033
TEL: (908) 298-4000
FAX: (908) 298-4376

Robert P. Luciano, Chairman. Pharmaceutical and health-care products. Schering-Plough is a public company established in 1928 in the United States. It began in Germany, in 1864, when Ernst Schering began selling chemicals to local apothecary shops in Berlin. In 1971, the company merged with Plough, Inc. and expanded its product line to include cosmetics and consumer items. Today, Schering-Plough is a major producer of prescription and over-the-counter drugs, veterinary medicines, and cosmetics. Brand names include Coppertone, sun-care items, and Dr. Scholl's foot-care products. Worldwide revenues for 1992: $4.1 billion

- **Total Employees:** 20,200

- **U.S. Employees Abroad:** 60
- **Countries:** Belgium, Czech Republic, Hungary, Poland.
- **Job Categories:** Management, Marketing—Health & Medical Supplies, Marketing—Pharmaceuticals, Research & Development, Sales—Health & Medical Supplies, Sales—Pharmaceuticals.
- **Language Requirement:** Knowledge of local language a plus but not essential.

SCHLEGEL CORPORATION
PO Box 23197
Rochester, NY 14692 USA

RECRUITER: JAMES FAULKNER
DIRECTOR, HUMAN RESOURCES
PO BOX 23197
ROCHESTER, NY 14692
TEL: (716) 427-7200

Richard L. Turner, President. Engineered perimeter sealing systems. Schlegel is a subsidiary of BTR, Inc. Its systems are used for residential and commercial construction. Worldwide revenues for 1991: $180 million.

- **Total Employees:** 1,500
- **U.S. Employees Abroad:** 18
- **Countries:** Australia, Belgium, France, Germany, Greece, Japan, Spain.
- **Job Categories:** Management, Marketing—Industrial, Sales—Industrial.

A. SCHULMAN, INC.
3550 West Market St.
Akron, OH 44313 USA

RECRUITER: TOY FRIEDBERG
DIRECTOR, HUMAN RESOURCES
3550 WEST MARKET ST.
AKRON, OH 44313
TEL: (216) 666-3751
FAX: (216) 668-7204

William C. Zekan, Chairman. Plastic compounds and resins. A. Schulman, Inc. is a public company founded in 1928. It manufactures and markets high performance plastic compounds and resins used by product manufacturers on a global basis. It currently has eight manufacturing facilities in the United States and abroad. Worldwide revenues for 1992: $732 million.

- **Total Employees:** 1,590
- **U.S. Employees Abroad:** 25
- **Countries:** Belgium, Canada, France, Germany, Switzerland, United Kingdom.
- **Job Categories:** Management, Marketing—Chemicals, Sales—Chemicals.
- **General Requirements:** Usually must be a current employee of the company in order to qualify for overseas assignment.
- **Language Requirement:** None.

SCI SYSTEMS

PO Box 1000
Huntsville, AL 35807 USA

RECRUITER: MR. FRANCIS HENRY
PERSONNEL DIRECTOR
PO BOX 1000
HUNTSVILLE, AL 35807
TEL: (205) 882-4800
FAX: (205) 882-4804

Olin B. King, Chairman. Electronics. SCI Systems is a public company founded in 1961. It manufactures computer peripheral equipment including printers and graphic displays. It also produces aeronautical and nautical systems and instruments which measure, display, control, or transmit process variables for industrial establishments. Worldwide revenues for 1992: $1.1 billion.

- **Total Employees:** 8,575

- **U.S. Employees Abroad:** 22

- **Countries:** Singapore, United Kingdom.

- **Job Categories:** Engineers, Marketing—Electronics, Product Development, Sales—Electronics.

- **Language Requirement:** None.

SCIENTIFIC ATLANTA, INC.

1 Technology Pkwy. South
Norcross, GA 30092 USA

RECRUITER: NANCY BURNS
HUMAN RESOURCES
REPRESENTATIVE
1 TECHNOLOGY PKWY. SOUTH
ATLANTA, GA 30092
TEL: (410) 903-7000
FAX: (404) 903-4751

William E. Johnson, Chairman. Telecommunications equipment and instruments. Scientific Atlanta, Inc. is a public company founded in 1951. It is a leader in cable television electronics and satellite-based communications networks. It is also a major supplier of electronic instrumentation for industrial telecommunication and government sectors. Worldwide revenues for 1992: $581 million.

- **Total Employees:** 3,200

- **U.S. Employees Abroad:** 20

- **Countries:** Canada, France, Germany, Italy, Netherlands, United Kingdom.

- **Job Categories:** Administrative, Engineers, Design, Marketing—Telecommunications.

- **Language Requirement:** None.

SCM CHEMICALS

7 St. Paul St., Suite #1010
Baltimore, MD 21202 USA

RECRUITER: RICHARD LAMOND
DIRECTOR, ORGANIZATION &
   DEVELOPMENT
7 ST. PAUL ST., SUITE #1010
BALTIMORE, MD 21202
TEL: (410) 783-1032
FAX: (410) 783-1089

Donald V. Borst, President. Inorganic pigments. SCM Chemicals is a subsidiary of Hanson Industries of New York City. It produces and sells inorganic pigments, chemicals, coatings, and resins.

- **Total Employees:** 2,400
- **U.S. Employees Abroad:** 22
- **Countries:** France, Panama, Singapore, United Kingdom.
- **Job Categories:** Management, Marketing—Chemicals, Sales—Chemicals.
- **Language Requirement:** None.

SCOTT PAPER COMPANY

Scott Plaza
Philadelphia, PA 19113 USA

RECRUITER: DAVID HENDRICKS
STAFFING/RECRUITMENT
SCOTT PLAZA
PHILADELPHIA, PA 19113
TEL: (215) 522-5881
FAX: (215) 522-5129

Philip E. Lippincott, Chairman. Paper, related products, and bleached pulp. Scott Paper is a public company founded in 1879 by two brothers, Irvin and Clarence Scott. It was the first business to sell rolls of tissue for use as toilet paper. Overseas expansion was started prior to WW II, its first venture was with Japan. Today, it is a world leader of tissue products which include such brand names as Cottenelle bath tissue and Viva paper towels. Worldwide revenues for 1992: $4.9 billion.

- **Total Employees:** 29,100
- **U.S. Employees Abroad:** 40
- **Countries:** Belgium, Brazil, Canada, Costa Rica, France, Germany, Hong Kong, Italy, Japan, Republic of Korea, Mexico, Singapore, Taiwan, Thailand, United Kingdom.
- **Salaries:** N/a
- **Job Categories:** Administrative, Finance, Marketing—Consumer Goods, Sales—Consumer Goods.
- **Language Requirement:** Varies with each posting.

SEA-LAND SERVICE, INC.

379 Thornall St.
Edison, NJ 08837 USA

RECRUITER: JOSEPH GRANT
DIRECTOR, COMPENSATION &
BENEFITS
379 THORNALL ST.
EDISON, NJ 08837
TEL: (908) 558-6000
FAX: (908) 603-2837

Alex J. Mandl, Chairman. Container transport. Sea-Land Service, Inc. was founded in 1956 and is a subsidiary of CSX Corporation of Richmond, Virginia. It is engaged in the transportation of freight between the United States and foreign ports. Worldwide operating revenues for 1991: $3.3 billion.

- **Total Employees:** 9,284

- **U.S. Employees Abroad:** 30

- **Countries:** Brazil, Canada, Germany, Honduras, Hong Kong, India, Italy, Japan, Mexico, Netherlands, Switzerland, United Arab Emirates, United Kingdom.

- **Job Categories:** Marketing, Sales, Technical Field Support.

- **Language Requirement:** Varies with each position.

SEAGATE TECHNOLOGY, INC.

920 Disc Dr.
Scotts Valley, CA 95066 USA

RECRUITER: ROBERT MORQUECHO
STAFFING/RECRUITMENT
920 DISC DR.
SCOTTS VALLEY, CA 95067-0360
TEL: (408) 438-6550
FAX: (408) 438-6172

Gary B. Fuller, Chairman. Rigid magnetic disk drives. Seagate Technology, Inc. is a public company founded in 1979 by Alan Shugart, Tom Mitchell, and Douglas Mahon. In 1980, its first product was a 5 1/4-inch hard disk, ST506. By 1984, sales had reached $344 million and the company began to transfer manufacturing facilities to Singapore and then Thailand. Today, it is the largest independent supplier of rigid magnetic disk drives in the world and currently, it has a 25 percent market share. Worldwide revenues for 1992: $3.1 billion.

- **Total Employees:** 43,000

- **U.S. Employees Abroad:** 55

- **Countries:** Malaysia, Singapore, Portugal, Thailand, United Kingdom.

- **Job Categories:** Engineers, Management, Marketing—Electronics, Sales—Electronics.

- **Language Requirement:** None.

SEALED AIR CORPORATION

Park 80 Plaza East
Saddle Brook, NJ 07662 USA

RECRUITER: HEIDE HUFFIELD
HUMAN RESOURCES
    REPRESENTATIVE
PARK 80 PLAZA EAST
SADDLE BROOK, NJ 07662
TEL: (201) 791-7600
FAX: (201) 703-4173

T. J. Dermot Dunphy, President. Protective packaging materials. Sealed Air Corporation is a public company founded by Alfred Fielding and Mark Chavannes. Items produced include Instapak foam-in-place packaging systems and PolyMask coated masking materials. Worldwide revenues for 1991: $435.1 million.

- **Total Employees:** 2,400

- **U.S. Employees Abroad:** 25

- **Countries:** Canada, France, Germany, Hong Kong, Italy, Japan, Malaysia, Netherlands, Sweden, Singapore, Taiwan, United Kingdom.

- **Job Categories:** Engineers, Management, Marketing, Sales.

- **Language Requirement:** Knowledge of local language a plus but not essential.

- **Training:** Varies with eash posting.

SEARLE COMPANY

5200 Old Orchard
Skokie, IL 60077 USA

RECRUITER: PERSONNEL DIRECTOR
5200 OLD ORCHARD
SKOKIE, IL 60077
TEL: (708) 922-7000
FAX: (708) 470-6258

Sheldon Gilmore, M.D., President and Chairman. Pharmaceuticals. Searle Company was founded in 1888 and is a subsidiary of Monsanto Company of St. Louis, Missouri. It produces and sells various pharmaceuticals, its focus on the cardiovascular system, central nervous system, and gastrointestinal tract. It also manufactures oral contraceptives, low calorie sweeteners, and other related items. Worldwide revenues for 1991: $1.5 billion.

- **Total Employees:** 10,000

- **U.S. Employees Abroad:** 35

- **Countries:** Australia, Belgium, Canada, France, Germany, India, Japan, Republic of Korea, Mexico, Pakistan, Republic of South Africa, United Kingdom, Venezuela.

- **Job Categories:** Administrative, Marketing—Pharmaceuticals, Research & Development, Sales—Pharmaceuticals.

- **Language Requirement:** Varies with each posting.

SEARS ROEBUCK AND COMPANY

Building E-C 201-A
3333 Beverly Rd.
Hoffman Estates, IL 60179 USA

RECRUITER: ROSILAND BAKER
MANAGER, HUMAN RECOURCES
BUILDING E-C 201-A
3333 BEVERLY RD.
HOFFMAN ESTATES, IL 60179
TEL: (708) 286-2500
FAX: (708) 286-1517

Edward A. Brennan, President and Chairman. Merchandising, insurance, financial, and real estate services. Sears Roebuck is a public company founded in 1886 by Richard W. Sears, a railway agent, in Minnesota. He started the R. W. Watch Company and within six months, moved the business to Chicago. Today, its merchandising group operates more than 860 department stores and 950 specialty shops in North America. It is also a leader in the insurance business (Allstate). Its financial services division, Dean Witter, was purchased in 1981. Worldwide revenues for 1992: $52.3 billion.

- **Total Employees:** 450,000
- **U.S. Employees Abroad:** 125
- **Countries:** Canada, Mexico, Japan, Germany.
- **Job Categories:** Management, Marketing—Financial Services, Marketing—Consumer Goods, Sales—Financial Services, Sales—Consumer Goods.
- **Language Requirement:** None.

SENCO PRODUCTS

8485 Broadhollow Rd.
Cincinnati, OH 45244 USA

RECRUITER: WADE NOBLE
MANAGER, COMPENSATION &
BENEFITS
8485 BROADHOLLOW RD.
CINCINNATI, OH 45244
TEL: (513) 388-2000
FAX: (513) 388-3130

William Hess, President. Power-driven hand tools and related items. Senco Products is a private company founded in 1951. It manufacturers and sells fasteners and fastening systems, buttons, industrial nailers, and various power-driven hand tools. Worldwide revenues for 1991: $180 million.

- **Total Employees:** 1,900
- **U.S. Employees Abroad:** 12
- **Countries:** Canada, Germany, Republic of Korea, Netherlands, United Kingdom.
- **Job Categories:** Management, Marketing—Consumer Goods, Sales—Consumer Goods.
- **Language Requirement:** None.

SENSORMATIC ELECTRONICS CORPORATION

500 NW 12th Ave.
Deerfield Beach, FL 33442 USA

RECRUITER: BILL BEACH
MANAGER, HUMAN RESOURCES
500 NW 12TH AVE.
DEERFIELD BEACH, FL 33442
TEL: (305) 427-9700
FAX: (305) 428-9523

Ronald G. Assaf, President and Chairman. Electronic products. Sensormatic Electronics Corporation is a public company founded in 1968. It produces and sells electronic products involving surveillance equipment and related items. Major products include barcode scanners, and CCTV closed circuit television. Worldwide revenues for 1992: $253 million.

- **Total Employees:** 2,890

- **U.S. Employees Abroad:** 25

- **Countries:** Australia, Austria, Belgium, France, Germany, Hong Kong, Italy, Netherlands, New Zealand, Switzerland, United Kingdom.

- **Job Categories:** Marketing—Electronics, Product Development, Sales—Electronics.

- **Language Requirement:** Varies with each posting.

SEQUA CORPORATION

200 Park Ave.
New York, NY 10016 USA

RECRUITER: JESSE BATTINO
DIRECTOR, ORGANIZATION PLANNING
& DEV.
THREE UNIVERSITY PLAZA
HACKENSACK, NJ 07601
TEL: (201) 343-1122
FAX: (201) 343-7942

Norman E. Alexander, Chairman. Industrial manufacturing and professional services. Sequa Corporation is a public company founded in 1929. Its operating divisions include: aerospace, machinery and metal coatings, specialty chemicals, transportation, and financial and professional services. Clients include both commercial and government markets. Worldwide revenues for 1992: $1.9 billion.

- **Total Employees:** 15,700

- **U.S. Employees Abroad:** 30

- **Countries:** Barbados, France, United Kingdom.

- **Job Categories:** Finance, Management, Marketing—Industrial, Sales—Industrial.

- **Language Requirement:** None.

SGS CONTROL SERVICES

Societe Generale DeSurveillance
1 Place des Alps B.P. 898
CH 1211 Geneva, Switzerland
USA

RECRUITER: STEVEN BLOOM
STAFFING/RECRUITMENT
42 BROADWAY
NEW YORK, NY 10004
TEL: (212) 482-8700
FAX: (212) 480-9168

Werner Plus, President. Technical services. SGS Control Services Inc. is a subsidiary of Societe Gereral DeSurveillance of Geneva, Switzerland. It offers a wide range of quality and quality control checks and related technical services to clients in the United States and abroad.

- **Total Employees:** 500

- **U.S. Employees Abroad:** 20

- **Countries:** Worldwide including Argentina, Australia, Brazil, Canada, Chile, France, Germany, Hong Kong, Italy, Japan, Philippines, Sweden, Switzerland, United Kingdom, Venezuela.

- **Application Information:** World headquarters is located in Geneva, Switzerland. Direct inquiries to the New York address.

- **Job Categories:** Management, Marketing, Sales.

- **Language Requirement:** Competency in local language required.

SGS-THOMSON MICROELECTRONICS

1310 Electronics Dr.
Carrollton, TX 75006 USA

RECRUITER: DEBORAH CERBONE
EXPATRIATE STAFFING
1310 ELECTRONICS DR., MS #776
CARROLLTON, TX 75006
TEL: (214) 466-6000
FAX: (214) 466-7196

Daniel Queyssac, President. Integrated circuits and semiconductors. SGS-Thomson Microelectronics was founded in 1969 and is a subsidiary of the Thomson Corporation of America located in Arlington, Virginia. It designs and manufactures semiconductors in the United States and abroad. Worldwide revenues for 1991: $330 million.

- **Total Employees:** 1,900

- **U.S. Employees Abroad:** 25

- **Countries:** Belgium, Germany, Japan, Sweden, United Kingdom.

- **Job Categories:** Management, Marketing—Electronics, Product Development.

- **Language Requirement:** None.

- **Training:** No special training provided.

SHAKLEE CORPORATION

444 Market St.
San Francisco, CA 94111 USA

RECRUITER: MARTY BURSTEIN
DIRECTOR, HUMAN RESOURCES
444 MARKET ST.
SAN FRANCISCO, CA 94111
TEL: (415) 954-3000
FAX: (415) 986-0808

D. M. Chamberlain, President. Personal-care items and household products. Shaklee Corporation is a public company founded in 1956 by Forrest C. Shaklee and his two sons-in-law. It is now a subsidiary of Yamanouchi Pharmaceutical Company of Japan. It provides various personal-care items, nutritional and household products through its direct marketing and sales divisions. Major products include food and vitamins. Worldwide revenues for 1991: $650 million.

- **Total Employees:** 7,500

- **U.S. Employees Abroad:** 30

- **Countries:** Australia, Canada, Japan, Malaysia, Singapore, Taiwan, United Kingdom.

- **Job Categories:** Management, Marketing—Consumer Goods, Sales—Consumer Goods.

- **Language Requirement:** None.

SHEAFFER PEN, INC.

1 Crown Mark Plaza
PO Box 262
Lincoln, RI 02865 USA

RECRUITER: BARBARA THOMAS
HUMAN RESOURCES SPECIALIST
301 AVE. H
FORT MADISON, IA 52627
TEL: (319) 376-3300
FAX: (319) 372-3130

Michael Johnstone, Chief Executive Officer. Writing instruments. Sheaffer Pen, Inc. is a private company founded in 1908. It is a manufacturer of various types of writing instruments including pens, pencils, and markers. Worldwide revenues for 1991: $89 million.

- **Total Employees:** 2,100

- **U.S. Employees Abroad:** 20

- **Countries:** Canada, France, Italy, Japan, Netherlands, United Kingdom.

- **Job Categories:** Management, Marketing—Consumer Goods, Sales—Consumer Goods.

- **Language Requirement:** Knowledge of local language a plus but not essential.

SHEARMAN & STERLING

599 Lexington Ave.
New York, NY 10022 USA

RECRUITER: CHARLES MURRAY
DIRECTOR, HUMAN RESOURCES
599 LEXINGTON AVE.
NEW YORK, NY 10022
TEL: (212) 848-4000
FAX: (212) 848-7179

Edward D. Lorenzo, Director of Systems. Legal services. Shearman & Sterling is a private law firm founded in 1873. It offers legal services to clients in the United States and abroad. Worldwide operating revenues for 1991: $270 million.

- **Total Employees:** 600
- **U.S. Employees Abroad:** 45
- **Countries:** Canada, France, Germany, Japan, Hungary, Taiwan, United Arab Emirates, United Kingdom.
- **Job Categories:** Attorneys.
- **General Requirements:** Usually must be a current employee of the company in order to qualify for overseas assignment.
- **Language Requirement:** Varies with each posting.
- **Training:** No special training provided.
- **Benefits:** All benefits are individually determined.

SHEARSON LEHMAN BROTHERS

388 Greenwich St., 7th floor
New York, NY 10013 USA

RECRUITER: BOB DIBBLE
FIRST VICE PRESIDENT, HUMAN
    RESOURCES
388 GREENWICH ST., 7TH FLOOR
NEW YORK, NY 10013
TEL: (212) 464-2484
FAX: (212) 464-2458

Howard L. Clark, Jr., President. Securities. Shearson Lehman Brothers was founded in 1888 and is a subsidiary of American Express Company of New York City. It offers services to governments, institutions, and private investors in the United States and abroad. Services include investment and merchant banking, asset management, and administration and personal banking. Worldwide revenues for 1991: $207 million.

- **Total Employees:** 34,000
- **U.S. Employees Abroad:** 75
- **Countries:** Australia, Belgium, Canada, France, Germany, Greece, Hong Kong, Netherlands, Singapore, Spain, Switzerland, United Kingdom.
- **Job Categories:** Brokers—Securities & Financial, Executive Management, Investment Counselors, Marketing—Financial Services.

- **General Requirements:** Usually must be a current employee of the company in order to qualify for overseas assignment.
- **Language Requirement:** Varies withe each posting.

SHERWIN-WILLIAMS COMPANY

101 Prospect Ave.
Cleveland, OH 44115 USA

RECRUITER: QUENTIN M. RHINEHART
DIRECTOR, INTERNATIONAL
    PERSONNEL
101 PROSPECT AVE.
CLEVELAND, OH 44115
TEL: (216) 566-2419
FAX: (216) 566-2638

John G. Breen, Chairman. Paint and coatings for architectural, automotive, consumer, and industrial markets. Sherwin-Williams is a public company founded in 1870 by Henry Sherwin, Edward Williams, and A. T. Osborn. Today, it is the largest paint manufacturer in the world with facilities in the United States and licensees in 39 countries. Brand names include Cuprinol and Dutch Boy. Worldwide revenues for 1992: $2.8 billion.

- **Total Employees:** 16,682
- **U.S. Employees Abroad:** 35
- **Countries:** Australia, Canada, Germany, Japan, United Kingdom.
- **Application Information:** Hiring for most overseas positions is done at the specific country location.
- **Job Categories:** Management, Marketing—Chemicals, Sales—Chemicals.

SHIPLEY COMPANY, INC.

455 Forest St.
Marlborough, MA 01752 USA

RECRUITER: ART SHARKEY
STAFFING/RECRUITMENT
500 NICKERSON RD.
MARLBOROUGH, MA 01752
TEL: (508) 481-7950

Charles Shipley, President. Chemical manufacturing for printed circuit boards. Shipley is a public company engaged as a manufacturer and marketer of specialty chemicals for electroless plating on plastics and printed circuits. Worldwide revenues for 1991: $212 million.

- **Total Employees:** 900
- **U.S. Employees Abroad:** 18
- **Countries:** France, Germany, Hong Kong, Italy, Japan, Netherlands, Sweden, Switzerland, United Kingdom.
- **Application Information:** Hiring for most overseas positions is done at the specific country location.

A
M
E
R
I
C
A
N

J
O
B
S

A
B
R
O
A
D

- **Job Categories:** Management, Marketing—Chemicals, Sales—Chemicals.
- **Language Requirement:** Competency in local language required.

SIGNODE PACKAGING SYSTEMS

3610 West Lake Ave.
Glenview, IL 60025 USA

RECRUITER: JANET MACKIN
DIRECTOR, INTERNATIONAL STAFFING
3610 WEST LAKE AVE.
GLENVIEW, IL 60025
TEL: (708) 724-6100
FAX: (708) 657-5060

John G. Powers, President. Packaging systems. Signode Packaging Systems was founded in 1913 and is a subsidiary of Illinois Tool Works of Glenview, Illinois. It is a manufacturer of packaging machinery with facilities in the United States and abroad. Worldwide revenues for 1991: $650 million.

- **Total Employees:** 5,000
- **U.S. Employees Abroad:** Not available.
- **Countries:** Belgium, Brazil, Canada, People's Republic of China, Germany, Hong Kong, Japan, Netherlands, Philippines, United Kingdom.
- **Job Categories:** Management, Marketing, Sales.
- **Language Requirement:** Varies with each posting.
- **Comments:** The number of Americans reported working abroad varies greatly from quarter to quarter, fluctuating with the number and scope of projects under contract at the time.

SILICONIX

2201 Laurelwood Rd.
Santa Clara, CA 95056-0591
USA

RECRUITER: DIANE BERG
HUMAN RESOURCES MANAGER
2201 LAURELWOOD RD.
SANTA CLARA, CA 95056-0591
TEL: (408) 988-8000
FAX: (408) 970-3950

Richard E. Lee, President and Chairman. Semiconductor components. Siliconix is a public company founded in 1962. It produces and sells discrete semiconductor components and integrated circuits for original equipment manufacturers. Major industry sectors include automotive, consumer, industrial, and military/aerospace markets. It has six major facilities in the United States and abroad. Worldwide revenues for 1992: $156 million.

- **Total Employees:** 2,200
- **U.S. Employees Abroad:** 25
- **Countries:** France, Germany, Hong Kong, Italy, Taiwan, United Kingdom.

- **Job Categories:** Engineers, Marketing—Electronics, Product Development, Sales—Electronics.

SIMON & SCHUSTER, INC.

1230 Avenue of the Americas
New York, NY 10020 USA

RECRUITER: BENJAMIN ROTER
SENIOR VP, HUMAN RESOURCES
1230 AVENUE OF THE AMERICAS
NEW YORK, NY 10020
TEL: (212) 698-7000
FAX: (212) 461-8275

Richard E. Snyder, President. Publishing, software, and motion picture/videotape production. Simon & Schuster was founded in 1927 and is a subsidiary of Paramount Communications, Inc. of New York City. It publishes and prints books and pamphlets; it also designs and produces pre-packaged software. Another business sector includes motion picture and videotape production. Worldwide revenues for 1991: $1.5 billion.

- **Total Employees:** 9,800
- **U.S. Employees Abroad:** 35
- **Countries:** Australia, Brazil, India, Japan, Mexico, Singapore, United Kingdom.
- **Job Categories:** Editors, Marketing—Publishing, Sales—Publishing.
- **Language Requirement:** Varies with each posting.
- **Training:** No special training offered.

SIMPLEX TIME RECORDER COMPANY

One Simplex Plaza
Gardner, MA 01441 USA

RECRUITER: ROBERT WOODS
MANAGER, INTERNATIONAL GROUP
ONE SIMPLEX PLAZA
GARDNER, MA 01441
TEL: (508) 632-2500
FAX: (508) 632-1454

Edward G. Watkins, President and Chairman. Alarm systems and time recorders. Simplex Time Recorder is a private company founded in 1888. It is engaged as a manufacturer of various products including communications equipment, fire and burglar alarms, and traffic signals and sirens. It also produces office machinery including time recorders. Worldwide revenues for 1991: $510 million.

- **Total Employees:** 3,250
- **U.S. Employees Abroad:** 20
- **Countries:** Australia, Belgium, Canada, People's Republic of China, France, Germany, Israel, United Kingdom.
- **Job Categories:** Management, Marketing—Electronics, Sales—Electronics.
- **Language Requirement:** Knowledge of local language a plus but not essential.

**SIMPLICITY PATTERN
COMPANY INC.**

200 Madison Ave.
New York, NY 10016 USA

RECRUITER: JOANNE BOWMAN,
MANAGER, HUMAN RESOURCES
200 MADISON AVE.
NEW YORK, NY 19916
TEL: (212) 576-0500
FAX: (212) 576-0628

Louis R. Morris, President & CEO. Clothing patterns. Simplicity Pattern Company was founded in 1927 and is a subsidiary of Simplicity Holdings Inc. of New York City. It publishes various printed materials including patterns for clothing and other hobby-oriented accessories. Worldwide Sales for 1991: $100 million.

- **Total Employees:** 1,055

- **U.S. Employees Abroad:** 15

- **Countries:** Australia, Canada, New Zealand, Republic of South Africa, United Kingdom.

- **Job Categories:** Management, Marketing—Consumer Goods, Sales—Consumer Goods.

- **Language Requirement:** Local language skills not required

SIZZLER INTERNATIONAL

12655 West Jefferson Blvd.
Los Angeles, CA 90006 USA

RECRUITER: LOUIS LEIDELMEYER
DIRECTOR, HUMAN RESOURCES
12655 WEST JEFFERSON BLVD.
LOS ANGELES, CA 90006
TEL: (310) 827-2300

Thomas l. Gregory, President. Restaurant operator. Sizzler International is a public company that currently operates 207 establishments and 427 franchised units throughout the world. Worldwide revenues for 1991: $543.2 million.

- **Total Employees:** 17,800

- **U.S. Employees Abroad:** 25

- **Countries:** Australia.

- **Application Information:** Job Hotline Number: (310) 827-2300, ext. 3634

- **Job Categories:** Clerical Assistants, Management, Marketing—Food/Food Services, Sales—Food/Food Services.

- **Language Requirement:** Varies with each posting.

SKADDEN, ARPS, SLATE, MEAGHER & FLOM

919 3rd Ave.
New York, NY 10022 USA

RECRUITER: PETER P. MULLEN
MANAGING PARTNER
919 3RD AVE.
NEW YORK, NY 10022
TEL: (212) 735-2081
FAX: (212) 735-3596

Peter P. Mullen, Chief Executive Officer. Law services. Skadden, Arps, Slate, Meagher & Flom is a private company founded in 1948. It operates on a global basis and offers legal services in various fields which including environmental compliance, mergers and acquisitions, real estate, and white collar criminal defense. Worldwide operating revenues for 1991: $503 million.

- **Total Employees:** 1,145
- **U.S. Employees Abroad:** Not available.
- **Countries:** Australia, Belgium, Canada, France, Germany, Hong Kong, Japan, United Kingdom.
- **Job Categories:** Attorneys, Administrative, Marketing.
- **General Requirements:** Usually must be a current employee of the company in order to qualify for overseas assignment.
- **Language Requirement:** Varies with each posting.

SKIDMORE, OWINGS & MERRILL

220 East 42nd St.
New York, NY 10017-5806 USA

RECRUITER: PERSONNEL MANAGER
224 SOUTH MICHIGAN, SUITE #1000
CHICAGO, IL 60604
TEL: (312) 554-9090
FAX: (312) 360-4545

David M. Childs, Partner. Architectural and engineering services. Skidmore, Owings & Merrill is a private company founded in 1929 by Louis Skidmore and Nathanial Owings in Chicago after the 1933-34 Century of Progress Exposition. In 1938, the New York office was officially opened. Today, it is the largest architectural/engineering firm in the world with past and present projects in more than 40 counrtries. It offers architectural, civil engineering, environmental analysis, and site and space planning services. Worldwide revenues for 1992: $92.4 million.

- **Total Employees:** 515
- **U.S. Employees Abroad:** 3
- **Countries:** Pakistan, Hong Kong.
- **Job Categories:** Architects, Design Planners, Engineers.
- **General Requirements:** Degreed professionals.
- **Language Requirement:** None.
- **Training:** No special training provided.

- **Comments:** The number of Americans reported working abroad varies greatly from quarter to quarter, fluctuating with the number and scope of projects under contract at the time.

SMITH BARNEY, HARRIS UPHAM & COMPANY, INC.

1345 Avenue of the Americas
New York, NY 10105 USA

RECRUITER: SHARON ASIP
HUMAN RESOURCES ADMINISTRATOR
1345 AVENUE OF THE AMERICAS
NEW YORK, NY 10105
TEL: (212) 399-6000
FAX: (212) 698-5639

Frank G. Zarb, Chief Executive Officer. Brokerage services. Smith Barney, Harris Upham & Company, Inc. was founded in 1873. It was purchased by Primerica in 1987. It offers brokerage services to clients on a worldwide basis. Worldwide operating revenues for 1991: $1.6 billion.

- **Total Employees:** 7,500
- **U.S. Employees Abroad:** 35
- **Countries:** France, Switzerland.
- **Application Information:** Hiring for most overseas positions is done at the specific country location.
- **Job Categories:** Brokers—Securities & Financial, Finance, Marketing—Financial Services.
- **Language Requirement:** Varies with each posting.
- **Benefits:** All benefits are individually determined.

SMITH CORONA CORPORATION

Box #2020
Cortland, NY 13045 USA

RECRUITER: AL SCALLON
VP, INTERNATIONAL RECRUITING
BOX #2020
CORTLAND, NY 13045
TEL: (607) 753-6011

G. Lee Thompson, President and Chairman. Electronic typewriters and word processors. Smith Corona Corporation is a public company that designs and produces portable and compact electronic typewriters and personal word processors for use at home, in the office, or at school. Major brands include PWP personal word processor series and laptop personal word processors. Worldwide revenues for 1992: $372 million.

- **Total Employees:** 3,600
- **U.S. Employees Abroad:** 20
- **Countries:** United Kingdom.
- **Job Categories:** Management, Marketing—Electronics, Sales—Electronics.

A. O. SMITH CORPORATION

PO Box 23972
Milwaukee, WI 53223 USA

RECRUITER: DONNA COOK
HUMAN RESOURCES DEPARTMENT
11270 WEST PARK PLACE
MILWAUKEE, WI 55324
TEL: (414) 359-4101
FAX: (414) 359-4064

Robert J. O'Toole, President. Structural components for the automotive industry. A. O. Smith Corporation is a public company founded in 1874. It manufactures fractional horsepower, hermetic and variable speed electric motors. It also produces commercial heating systems, water storage tanks, and provides agricultural financial services. It has 28 plants in the United States and abroad. Worldwide revenues for 1992: $1 billion.

- **Total Employees:** 9,900

- **U.S. Employees Abroad:** 30

- **Countries:** Canada, Japan, Mexico, Netherlands, United Kingdom.

- **Job Categories:** Management, Marketing—Automotive, Sales—Automotive.

- **Language Requirement:** None.

- **Training:** No special training provided.

SMITH INTERNATIONAL, INC.

PO Box 60068
Houston, TX 77205 USA

RECRUITER: JOSEPH SIZEMORE
VP, HUMAN RESOURCES
PO BOX 60068
HOUSTON, TX 77205
TEL: (713) 443-3370
FAX: (713) 233-5997

Doug Rock, President. Goods and services for oil and gas drilling and mining industries. Smith International, Inc. is a public company founded in 1937. It is a major producer of bits, motors, and major drillstring components. Worldwide revenues for 1992: $211 million.

- **Total Employees:** 1,800

- **U.S. Employees Abroad:** 30

- **Countries:** Italy, Mexico, Singapore, United Arab Emirates.

- **Job Categories:** Engineers, Management, Marketing—Petroleum/Natural Gas, Technical Assistants.

- **Language Requirement:** Knowledge of local language a plus but not essential.

J. M. SMUCKER COMPANY

Strawberry Lane
Orrville, OH 44667 USA

RECRUITER: JOHN NICHOLAS
STAFFING/RECRUIRTMENT
STRAWBERRY LANE
ORRVILLE, OH 44667
TEL: (216) 682-0015
FAX: (216) 684-3370

Paul H. Smucker, Chairman. Food products. J. M. Smucker is a public company founded in 1897, and incorporated in 1921. It is engaged as a manufacturer of jams, jellies, fruit juices, and industrial food products. Major brands include Dutch Girl and Vita Juice products. Worldwide revenues for 1993: $491 million.

- **Total Employees:** 1,900

- **U.S. Employees Abroad:** 18

- **Countries:** Australia, Canada, United Kingdom.

- **Job Categories:** Management, Marketing—Food/Food Services, Sales—Food/Food Services.

- **Language Requirement:** None.

SNAP-ON TOOLS CORPORATION

2801 80th St.
Kenosha, WI 53141-1140 USA

RECRUITER: RANDY VIOLA
MANAGER, CORPORATE HUMAN
RESOURCES
2801 80TH ST.
KENOSHA, WI 53141-1140
TEL: (414) 656-5200
FAX: (414) 656-4961

Robert A. Cornog, President and Chairman. Tools. Snap-On Tools Corporation is a public company founded in 1920 by Joe Johnson and William Seidemann. Today, Snap-On Tools produces and distributes approximately 14,000 tools and products to more than 5,000 independent dealers in the United States and abroad. Items include sockets, wrenches, drills, tool chests, automotive diagnostic equipment, and other related products. Tools are used for the automotive service, manufacturing, repair, and maintenance industries. Offices and/or plant locations are located in the United States and abroad. Worldwide revenues for 1992: $986 million.

- **Total Employees:** 6,800

- **U.S. Employees Abroad:** 25

- **Countries:** Canada, Singapore, United Kingdom.

- **Job Categories:** Administrative, Marketing—Consumer Goods, Sales—Consumer Goods.

- **Language Requirement:** None.

SOLECTRON CORPORATION

542 Gibraltar Dr.
Milpitas, CA 95035 USA

RECRUITER: BILL WEBB
HUMAN RESOURCES
542 GIBRALTAR DR.
MILPITAS, CA 95035
TEL: (408) 957-8500
FAX: (408) 262-3973

Dr. Winston H. Chen, President. Integrated manufacturing services. Solectron Corporation is a public company founded in 1977. It operates independently as a supplier of integrated manufacturing services to computer and electronic system-original equipment manufacturers. It operates on both a consignment and turn-key basis. Worldwide revenues for 1992: $407 million.

- **Total Employees:** 2,980

- **U.S. Employees Abroad:** Not available.

- **Countries:** Malaysia.

- **Job Categories:** Marketing—Electronics, Product Development, Sales—Electronics.

- **Language Requirement:** None.

SONAT, INC.

PO Box 2563
Birmingham, AL 35202 USA

RECRUITER: JANE CLEMENTS
STAFFING/RECRUITMENT
PO BOX 2563
BIRMINGHAM, AL 35202-2563
TEL: (205) 325-3800
FAX: (205) 326-2059

Ronald L. Kuehn, Jr., President and Chairman. Energy. Sonat, Inc., a public company founded in 1929, explores, produces, markets, and transmits natural gas. It is also involved in oil services. Worldwide revenues for 1992: $1.5 billion.

- **Total Employees:** 5,300

- **U.S. Employees Abroad:** 25

- **Countries:** Brazil, Indonesia, Malaysia, Norway, Singapore, United Arab Emirates, United Kingdom.

- **Job Categories:** Engineers, Marketing—Petroleum/Natural Gas, Sales—Petroleum/Natural Gas, Technical Field Support.

- **General Requirements:** Usually must be a current employee of the company in order to qualify for overseas assignment.

- **Language Requirement:** Varies with each posting.

SONAT OFFSHORE

4 Greenway Plaza
Houston, TX 77046 USA

RECRUITER: BOB LABBE
OFFSHORE PERSONNEL
4 GREENWAY PLAZA
HOUSTON, TX 77046
TEL: (713) 871-7500
FAX: (713) 850-3817

William C. O'Malley, Chief Executive Officer. Offshore drilling services. Sonat Offshore is a subsidiary of Sonat, Inc. of Alabama. It provides offshore oil-well drilling services to customers around the world.

- **Total Employees:** 1,500
- **U.S. Employees Abroad:** 22
- **Countries:** Brazil, Egypt, India, Malaysia, Norway, Singapore, United Arab Emirates, United Kingdom.
- **Job Categories:** Management, Marketing—Petroleum/Natural Gas, Technical Field Support.

SONESTA INTERNATIONAL HOTELS CORPORATION

200 Clarendon St.
Boston, MA 02116 USA

RECRUITER: JACKIE SONNABEND
VP, HUMAN RESOURCES
200 CLARENDON ST.
BOSTON, MA 02116
TEL: (617) 421-5400
FAX: (617) 421-5402

R. P. Sonnabend, Chairman. Hotel management. Sonesta International Hotels Corporation is a public company founded in 1923. It operates hotels and motels around the globe.

- **Total Employees:** 2,150
- **U.S. Employees Abroad:** 20
- **Countries:** Bermuda, Egypt, Netherlands Antilles.
- **Job Categories:** Management.
- **General Requirements:** Experience in hotel management preferred.
- **Language Requirement:** None.
- **Benefits:** HOUSING: Offered.

SONOCO PRODUCTS COMPANY

PO Box 160
Hartsville, SC 29550 USA

RECRUITER: DICK PUFFER
STAFFING/RECRUITMENT
PO BOX 160
HARTSVILLE, SC 29550
TEL: (803) 383-7000
FAX: (803) 383-7008

Charles W. Coker, President. Packaging products. Sonoco Products is a public company founded in 1899 by Major James L. Coker and W. F. Smith. It was called the Southern Novelty Company until its present name was adopted in 1923. It manufactures and markets packaging products for the consumer and industrial markets. Items include: fibre and plastic drums; wood, plywood, and metal reels; and shipping tubes. Worldwide revenues for 1992: $1.8 billion.

- **Total Employees:** 15,000
- **U.S. Employees Abroad:** 35
- **Countries:** Worldwide including Argentina, Canada, France, Germany, Japan, Mexico, Netherlands, Singapore, Spain, Taiwan, United Kingdom.
- **Job Categories:** Management, Marketing, Sales.
- **Language Requirement:** Varies with each posting.

SONY PICTURES ENTERTAINMENT

711 Fifth Ave.
New York, NY 10020 USA

RECRUITER: TED SHUGRUE
HUMAN RESOURCES
10202 WEST WASHINGTON BLVD.
CULVER CITY, CA 90232
TEL: (310) 280-3095
FAX: (310) 280-1875

F. T. Vincent, Jr., President. Motion pictures, entertainment. Sony Pictures Entertainment was founded in 1968 and is a subsidiary of Sony, USA Incorporated. It produces motion pictures and videotapes.

- **Total Employees:** 7,095
- **U.S. Employees Abroad:** Not available.
- **Countries:** Australia, Argentina, Colombia, France, Germany, Hong Kong, Italy, Japan, Singapore, Spain, Venezuela, United Kingdom.
- **Application Information:** Direct all applications and inquiries to the address of the chief recruiter.
- **Job Categories:** Management, Marketing, Product Development, Sales.

SOTHEBY'S HOLDINGS, INC.

1334 Avenue of the Americas
New York, NY 10021 USA

RECRUITER: SUSAN GARBRECHT
SENIOR VP, HUMAN RESOURCES
1334 AVENUE OF THE AMERICAS
NEW YORK, NY 10021
TEL: (212) 606-7000
FAX: (212) 606-7028

Michael L. Ainslie, President. Holding company engaged in auctions and the sale of luxury real estate. Sotheby's Holdings, Inc. is a public company founded in 1733. Its subsidiaries arrange for the sale of fine art and jewelry through auctions held worldwide.

It is also engaged in art-related financing and it markets and sells luxury real estate. It currently operates in more than 35 countries. Worldwide operating revenues for 1992: $225 million.

- **Total Employees:** 1,576
- **U.S. Employees Abroad:** 30
- **Countries:** Worldwide including France, Germany, Republic of Korea, United Kingdom.
- **Job Categories:** Finance, Management, Marketing, Sales.
- **Language Requirement:** Competency in local language required.

SOUTHLAND CORPORATION

2711 North Haskell Ave.
Dallas, TX 75204-7011 USA

RECRUITER: DAVID M. FINLEY
HUMAN RESOURCES
2711 NORTH HASKELL DR.
DALLAS, TX 75204-7011
TEL: (214) 828-7011
FAX: (214) 828-7848

Clark J. Matthews II, President. Convenience stores. Southland Corporation was founded in 1927 as an ice company. Today, it is the largest convenience stores operator in the world. It operates under the 7-Eleven trademark throughout the United States and in over 20 foreign countries. Worldwide revenues for 1992: $6.5 billion.

- **Total Employees:** 45,000
- **U.S. Employees Abroad:** Not available.
- **Countries:** Canada, Mexico, Japan, Sweden, United Kingdom.
- **Application Information:** Most overseas positions are filled internally.
- **Job Categories:** Finance, Management, Marketing—Consumer Goods, Marketing—Food/Food Services.

SOUTHWIRE COMPANY

PO Box 1000
Carrollton, GA 30119 USA

RECRUITER: GARY ROYAL
STAFFING/RECRUITMENT
PO BOX 1000
CARROLLTON, GA 30119
TEL: (404) 832-4242
FAX: (404) 832-5469

Roy Richards, Jr., President. Electric conduits. Southwire is a private company founded in 1950. It manufactures copper and aluminum electrical wiring. Worldwide revenues for 1991: $1.3 billion.

- **Total Employees:** 5,000
- **U.S. Employees Abroad:** 22
- **Countries:** Brazil, United Arab Emirates.

- **Job Categories:** Management, Marketing—Electronics, Sales—Electronics.

- **Language Requirement:** None.

SPERRY-SUN, INC.

PO Box 60087
Houston, TX 77205 USA

RECRUITER: MURRAY COLGIN
VP, HUMAN RESOURCES
PO BOX 60087
HOUSTON, TX 77205
TEL: (713) 987-4261
FAX: (713) 987-5046

Patrick J. Murray, President. Oilfield services. Sperry-Sun was founded in 1981 and is a subsidiary of the Baroid Corporation of Houston, Texas. It is a manufacturer of machinery and related equipment for oil and gas fields and for drilling water wells. Worldwide revenues for 1991: $182 million.

- **Total Employees:** 1,800

- **U.S. Employees Abroad:** 20

- **Countries:** Saudi Arabia, United Arab Emirates.

- **Job Categories:** Management, Marketing—Petroleum/Natural Gas, Sales—Petroleum/Natural Gas.

- **Language Requirement:** None.

SPRINGS INDUSTRIES, INC.

205 North White St.
Fort Mill, SC 29715 USA

RECRUITER: R. N. SCHARFENBERGER
DIRECTOR, DEVELOPMENT &
    ADMINISTRATION
205 NORTH WHITE ST.
PO BOX 70
FORT MILL, SC 29715
TEL: (803) 547-1500
FAX: (813) 547-1636

Walter Y. Elisha, President and Chairman. Finished fabrics and textiles. Springs Industries, Inc. is a public company founded in 1887 as Fort Mill Manufacturing Company. Its present name was adopted in 1982. Today, it is a major manufacturer of sheets and bedding, and is the second largest public textile company in the United States. It has three divisions: finished fabrics, home furnishings, and industrial fabrics. Brand names include Bill Blass and Wamsutta. Worldwide revenues for 1992: $2 billion.

- **Total Employees:** 21,000

- **U.S. Employees Abroad:** 25

- **Countries:** Belgium, United Kingdom, Japan.

- **Job Categories:** Administrative, Marketing—Consumer Goods, Product Development, Sales—Consumer Goods.
- **Language Requirement:** None.

SPRINT CORPORATION

2330 Shawnee Mission Pkwy.
Westwood, KS 66205 USA

RECRUITER: COLEEN COOMBS
STAFFING/RECRUITMENT
12490 SUNRISE VALLEY DR.
RESTON, VA 22096
TEL: (703) 689-5128
FAX: (703) 689-7263

William T. Esrey, Chairman. Global telecommunications. Sprint Corporation is a public company founded in 1899 by Jacob Brown and his son, Cleyson. They began a franchise in Abilene, Kansas, for one of the first non-Bell telephone companies in the West. Within four years, they had 1,400 subscribers. It was then known as United Telephone Company. Today, it is the second largest non-Bell telephone company, following GTE. It has 4 million lines scattered throughout 14 of the U.S. states, and its long distance business serves 6 million people. Worldwide revenues for 1992: $9.2 billion.

- **Total Employees:** 43,200
- **U.S. Employees Abroad:** 70
- **Countries:** Worldwide including Netherlands, Sweden.
- **Job Categories:** Executive Management, Marketing—Telecommunications, Sales—Telecommunications.
- **General Requirements:** Usually must be a current employee of the company in order to qualify for overseas assignment.
- **Language Requirement:** Varies with each posting.

SPS TECHNOLOGIES, INC.

900 Newtown-Yardley Rd.
PO Box 1000
Newtown, PA 18940 USA

RECRUITER: JOHN MCGRATH
VP, CORPORATE SERVICES
HIGHLAND AVE.
JENKINTOWN, PA 19046
TEL: (215) 860-3000
FAX: (215) 860-3034

John R. Selby, Chairman. Global engineering and industrial manufacturing. SPS Technologies, Inc. is a public company founded in 1903. It produces aerospace and industrial fasteners, magnetic materials, and precision components. It has manufacturing plants, divisions, and market subsidiaries in more than 15 countries.

- **Total Employees:** 6,000
- **U.S. Employees Abroad:** 35

- **Countries:** Australia, Brazil, Canada, Denmark, France, Germany, Italy, Japan, Republic of Korea, Mexico, Singapore, Spain, United Kingdom.
- **Application Information:** Hiring for most overseas positions is done at the specific country location.
- **Job Categories:** Engineers, Marketing—Industrial, Product Development, Sales—Industrial.
- **Language Requirement:** Varies with each posting.

SQUARE D COMPANY

1415 South Roselle Rd.
Palatine, IL 60067 USA

RECRUITER: MICHELLE
PRENDEGRAST
INTERNATIONAL RECRUITMENT
1415 SOUTH ROSELLE RD.
PALATINE, IL 60067
TEL: (708) 397-2600
FAX: (708) 397-8105

Didier Pineau-Valencienne, Chairman. Power distribution and electric/electronic industrial control equipment. Square D is a private company founded in 1902. Two main sectors are electrical distribution and industrial control. Major products for electrical distribution include connectors, power equipment, and transformers. The industrial control division produces automation and control products, engineered systems, and technical services. It currently has 33 plants in the United States and 18 facilities in foreign countries. Worldwide revenues for 1991: $1.7 billion.

- **Total Employees:** 18,500
- **U.S. Employees Abroad:** 30
- **Countries:** Australia, Canada, Germany, Italy, Mexico, Spain, United Kingdom.
- **Application Information:** Most overseas positions are filled internally.
- **Job Categories:** Management, Marketing—Electronics, Sales—Electronics.
- **Language Requirement:** Varies with each posting.

SRI INTERNATIONAL

333 Ravenswood Ave.
Menlo Park, CA 94025 USA

RECRUITER: ALLISON HIGHLANDER
HUMAN RESOURCES
REPRESENTATIVE
333 RAVENSWOOD AVE.
MENLO PARK, CA 94025
TEL: (415) 859-5211
FAX: (415) 859-2125

William F. Miller, President. Research and consulting. SRI International is a private company founded in 1946. It acts as a contract research and consulting firm for business and government on a global basis. Worldwide operating revenues for 1991: $300 million.

- **Total Employees:** 3,000
- **U.S. Employees Abroad:** 25
- **Countries:** Australia, France, Germany, Italy, Japan, Republic of Korea, Mexico, Saudi Arabia, Singapore, Sweden, Switzerland, United Kingdom.
- **Job Categories:** Consultants—Management, Management, Marketing.
- **Language Requirement:** Varies with each posting.

STANDARD COMMERCIAL CORPORATION

2201 Miller Rd.
PO Box 450
Wilson, NC 27893 USA

RECRUITER: KEITH H. MERRICK
TREASURER
2201 MILLER RD.
WILSON, NC 27893
TEL: (919) 291-5507
FAX: (919) 237-1109

J. Alec G. Murray, Vice Chairman. Leaf tobacco and wool. Standard Commercial Corporation is a public company founded in 1910. Its principal activity is purchasing and processing various types of tobacco. It sells to global manufacturers of cigarettes, cigars, and other tobacco-related products. Other business interests include processing and selling wool for use in carpets and other wool items. It is also involved in the landscape and building supply business. Worldwide revenues for 1992: $1.2 billion.

- **Total Employees:** 2,000
- **U.S. Employees Abroad:** 25
- **Countries:** Argentina, Australia, Brazil, Chile, People's Republic of China, France, Greece, Republic of Korea, Malawi, New Zealand, Paraguay, Republic of South Africa, Switzerland, Thailand, Turkey, Republic of South Africa, United Kingdom.
- **Job Categories:** Management, Marketing—Consumer Goods, Sales—Consumer Goods.
- **Language Requirement:** Varies with each posting.
- **Comments:** The number of Americans reported working abroad varies greatly from quarter to quarter, fluctuating with the number and scope of projects under contract at the time.

STANDARD & POOR'S CORPORATION

25 Broadway
New York, NY 10044 USA

RECRUITER: SUSAN ROSSI
STAFFING/RECRUITMENT
25 BROADWAY
NEW YORK, NY 10004
TEL: (212) 208-8000
FAX: (212) 412-0200

Harold W. McGraw III, President. Financial services. Standard & Poor's was founded in 1860 and is a subsidiary of McGraw-Hill, Inc. of New York City. It offers financial and investment services as well as economic and marketing information to clients on a global basis. Worldwide revenues for 1991: $340 million.

- **Total Employees:** 1,900
- **U.S. Employees Abroad:** 30
- **Countries:** Japan, Philippines.
- **Job Categories:** Brokers—Securities & Financial, Management.
- **Language Requirement:** None.

STANDEX INTERNATIONAL

6 Manor Pkwy.
Salem, NH 03079 USA

RECRUITER: ELLEN CROMPTON
PERSONNEL DIRECTOR
6 MANOR PKWY.
SALEM, NH 03079
TEL: (603) 893-9701
FAX: (603) 893-7324

T. L. King, Chairman. Manufacturing. Standex International Corporation is a public company founded in 1955. It is divided into three operating segments: graphics/mail order, industrial products, and institutional products. Plant facilities are located in 13 countries and items are sold on a worldwide basis. These include: food service equipment, industrial hardware, mail order gift packages, and pumps. Worldwide revenues for 1991: $481.7 million.

- **Total Employees:** 5,000
- **U.S. Employees Abroad:** 35
- **Countries:** France, Germany, United Kingdom.
- **Job Categories:** Management, Marketing, Sales.
- **Benefits:** All benefits are individually determined.

STANHOME, INC.

333 Western Ave.
Westfield, MA 01085 USA

RECRUITER: JOHN ROGERS
RECRUITMENT
333 WESTERN AVE.
WESTFIELD, MA 01085
TEL: (413) 562-3631
FAX: (413) 568-2820

Alejandro Diaz Vargas, President. Giftwear, collectibles, and household product design. Stanhome, Inc. is a public company founded in 1931. Its former name was Stanley Home Products. Through its various divisions, products are sold throughout the world. Items include EZ Waxer wax applicator, Provide hair-care items, and Precious Moments collectible porcelain figurines. Worldwide revenues for 1992: $744 million.

- **Total Employees:** 6,000
- **U.S. Employees Abroad:** 30

- **Countries:** Canada, France, United Kingdom.

- **Job Categories:** Management, Marketing—Consumer Goods, Sales—Consumer Goods.

- **Language Requirement:** Varies with each posting.

STANLEY WORKS

1000 Stanley Dr.
New Britain, CT 06050 USA

RECRUITER: BARBARA BENNETT
STAFFING/RECRUITMENT
1000 STANLEY DR.
NEW BRITAIN, CT 06050
TEL: (203) 225-5111

Richard H. Ayers, Chairman. Tools, related items, and services for home improvement and consumer use. Stanley Works is a public company founded in 1843 by Frederick T. Stanley. It is a producer and supplier of items for industrial and professional applications including hand tools, equipment-rental operations, and power-operated doors and gates. Currently, Stanley Works has operations in 13 countries, and it sells its products in more than 113 nations. Worldwide revenues for 1992: $2.2 billion.

- **Total Employees:** 18,460

- **U.S. Employees Abroad:** 35

- **Countries:** Australia, Belgium, Brazil.

- **Application Information:** Hiring for most overseas positions is done at the specific country location.

- **Job Categories:** Management, Marketing—Consumer Goods, Sales—Consumer Goods.

- **Language Requirement:** Varies with each posting.

- **Training:** Varies with each posting.

STATE STREET BOSTON CORPORATION

225 Franklin St.
Boston, MA 02110 USA

RECRUITER: PATRICK CUNNIFF
VP, EMPLOYMENT/STAFFING
225 FRANKLIN ST.
BOSTON, MA 02110
TEL: (617) 786-3000
FAX: (617) 985-8055

Peter E. Madden, President. Banking services. State Street Boston Corporation is a public company founded in 1792. It offers various financial services to clients on a worldwide basis. These include mutual funds and pension plans. Worldwide revenues for 1992: $1.4 billion.

- **Total Employees:** 7,700

- **U.S. Employees Abroad:** 30

- **Countries:** Australia, Belgium, Canada, Germany, Hong Kong, Japan, United Kingdom.
- **Job Categories:** Finance, Executive Management, Marketing—Financial Services.
- **General Requirements:** Usually must be a current employee of the company in order to qualify for overseas assignment.
- **Language Requirement:** Varies with each posting.

STEBBINS ENGINEERING & MANUFACTURING CORPORATION

363 Eastern Blvd.
Watertown, NY 13601 USA

RECRUITER: ROSE BATISTA
PERSONNEL DIRECTOR
363 EASTERN BLVD.
WATERTOWN, NY 13601
TEL: (315) 782-3000
FAX: (315) 782-0481

Ken Sturges, Chief Executive Officer. Engineering construction services. Stebbins Engineering & Manufacturing Corporation is a private company founded in 1903. It operates as a special trade contractor and is manufactures structural clay products, fabricated plate work, and boiler shops. Worldwide operating revenues for 1991: $70 million.

- **Total Employees:** 400
- **U.S. Employees Abroad:** 20
- **Countries:** Canada, United Kingdom.
- **Job Categories:** Contractors, Engineers, Marketing.
- **General Requirements:** Usually must be a current employee of the company in order to qualify for overseas assignment.
- **Language Requirement:** None.

STERLING WINTHROP, INC.

90 Park Ave.
New York, NY 10016 USA

RECRUITER: CASSANDRA
    PHILIPPEAUX
MANAGER, EMPLOYEE RELATIONS
90 PARK AVE.
NEW YORK, NY 10016
TEL: (212) 907-2000
FAX: (212) 907-2159

Louis P. Mattis, President and Chairman. Pharmaceuticals and cosmetics. Sterling Winthrop, Inc. was founded in 1901 and is a subsidiary of the Eastman Kodak Company of Rochester, New York. It produces pharmaceutical preparations and nonprescription medicines. Worldwide revenues for 1991: $2.2 billion.

- **Total Employees:** 13,300
- **U.S. Employees Abroad:** 35

- **Countries:** Brazil, Chile, Ecuador, Mexico, Peru.
- **Job Categories:** Management, Marketing—Pharmaceuticals, Product Development, Sales—Pharmaceuticals.
- **Language Requirement:** Fluency in local language required.

STONE CONTAINER CORPORATION

150 North Michigan Ave.
Chicago, IL 60601 USA

RECRUITER: LINDA GIARDINI
EMPLOYMENT MANAGER
150 NORTH MICHIGAN AVE.
CHICAGO, IL 60601
TEL: (312) 346-6600
FAX: (312) 580-3486

Roger W. Stone, President and Chairman. Paper and paper packaging. Stone Container Corporation is a public company incorporated in 1945. It went public in 1947 and today it is a multinational paper company. It produces and markets paperboard and paper packaging and is the largest maker of unbleached containerboard and kraft paper throughout the world. Other products include newsprint, folding cartons, and lumber. Worldwide revenues for 1992: $5.5 billion.

- **Total Employees:** 31,800
- **U.S. Employees Abroad:** 40
- **Countries:** Belgium, Canada, Costa Rica, France, Mexico, Netherlands, United Kingdom.
- **Job Categories:** Executive Management, Marketing, Sales.
- **Language Requirement:** Varies with each posting.

STONE & WEBSTER ENGINEERING CORPORATION

PO Box 3546
Houston, TX 77253 USA

RECRUITER: CAROL DILLON
MANAGER, INTERNATIONAL HUMAN
RESOURCES
PO BOX 3546
HOUSTON, TX 77253
TEL: (713) 492-4351
FAX: (713) 492-3924

Walter F. Sullivan, President. Engineering and construction firm. Stone and Webster Engineering is a subsidiary of Stone & Webster, Inc. of New York City. It offers engineering, construction, and consulting services to clients on a worldwide basis.

- **Total Employees:** 8,000
- **U.S. Employees Abroad:** 40
- **Countries:** Canada, Republic of Korea, Malaysia, Saudi Arabia, United Arab Emirates, United Kingdom.
- **Job Categories:** Consultants—Management, Engineers, Management, Marketing.

- **Language Requirement:** Varies with each posting.
- **Training:** No special training offered.

STORAGE TECHNOLOGY CORPORATION

2270 South 88th St.
Louisville, CO 80028 USA

RECRUITER: BARB PORTILLOS
EMPLOYMENT MANAGER
2270 SOUTH 88TH ST.
LOUISVILLE, CO 80028
TEL: (303) 673-5151
FAX: (303) 673-5019

Ryal R. Poppa, President and Chairman. Information storage and retrieval systems design, production, and marketing. Storage Technology Corporation is a public company founded in 1969 by former IBM engineer, Jesse Aweida and three other associates. Today, it is a global leader in data storage and retrieval systems for mainframe and midrange computers. Manufacturing and marketing is done on a global basis. Worldwide revenues for 1991: $1.6 billion. Foreign revenues for 1991: $548 million.

- **Total Employees:** 10,100
- **U.S. Employees Abroad:** 35
- **Countries:** Australia, Canada, France, Germany, Italy, Japan, Switzerland, United Kingdom.
- **Job Categories:** Management, Marketing—Electronics, Product Development, Sales—Electronics.
- **Language Requirement:** Varies with each posting.
- **Training:** No special training provided.

STRUCTURAL DYNAMICS RESEARCH CORPORATION

2000 Eastman Dr.
Milford, OH 45150 USA

RECRUITER: DEREK D. JACKSON
RECRUITING SPECIALIST
2000 EASTMAN DR.
MILFORD, OH 45150
TEL: (513) 576-2400
FAX: (513) 576-2922

Ronald J. Friedsam, President and Chairman. Software products and services; engineering services. Structural Dynamics Research Corporation is a public company founded in 1967. It provides software products and related services as well as engineering services to industrial companies on a global basis. It helps in the development of mechanical products. Worldwide revenues for 1992: $163.6 million.

- **Total Employees:** 1,187
- **U.S. Employees Abroad:** 200
- **Countries:** Canada, France, Germany, Japan, Republic of Korea, Netherlands, United Kingdom.

A
M
E
R
I
C
A
N

J
O
B
S

A
B
R
O
A
D

- **Job Categories:** Engineers, Management, Marketing—Electronics, Sales—Electronics.
- **Language Requirement:** None.

STV GROUP

11 Robinson Rd.
Pottstown, PA 19464 USA

RECRUITER: PATRICK AUSTIN
MANAGER, HUMAN RESOURCES
11 ROBINSON RD.
POTTSTOWN, PA 19464
TEL: (215) 326-4000
FAX: (215) 326-3833

Richard L. Holland, Chairman. Design engineering and consulting. STV Group is a public company founded in 1945. As design engineers, STV offers its services to clients on a global basis. Clients include the Department of Agriculture, the Federal Aviation Administration, and the United States Agency for International Development. Worldwide operating revenues for 1992: $76 million.

- **Total Employees:** 900
- **U.S. Employees Abroad:** 35
- **Countries:** Indonesia, Philippines.
- **Job Categories:** Engineers, Marketing.
- **General Requirements:** Appropriate Bachelor's degree and five or more years experience required.
- **Language Requirement:** Varies with each posting.
- **Training:** No special training offered.
- **Comments:** Engineering positions include civil, electrical, and mechanical.

SULLAIR CORPORATION

3700 E. Michigan Blvd.
Michigan City, IN 46360 USA

RECRUITER: JIM PRICE
DIRECTOR, HUMAN RESOURCES
3700 E. MICHIGAN BLVD.
MICHIGAN CITY, IN 46360
TEL: (219) 879-5451
FAX: (219) 874-1235

Joe Weisiger, President. Air compressors and related products. Sullair Corporation was founded in 1965 and is a subsidiary of Sundstrand Corporation of Rockford, Illinois. It manufactures and sells air and gas compressors and rotary screw air compressors. Worldwide revenues for 1991: $72.0 million.

- **Total Employees:** 600
- **U.S. Employees Abroad:** 4
- **Countries:** France, Singapore.
- **Job Categories:** Sales—Industrial.

- **Average Overseas Assignment:** Less than two years.
- **Language Requirement:** Competency in local language required.
- **Training:** Basic orientation (1-30 days) provided.
- **Benefits:** TRAVEL: Offered. HEALTH: Remains on U.S. coverage. HOUSING: Offered; varies with each posting. EDUCATION: None offered.
- **Comments:** The number of Americans reported working abroad varies greatly from quarter to quarter, fluctuating with the number and scope of projects under contract at the time.

SULLIVAN & CROMWELL

125 Broad St.
New York, NY 10004 USA

RECRUITER: JAMES HINCHEY
PERSONNEL DIRECTOR
125 BROAD ST.
NEW YORK, NY 10004
TEL: (212) 555-4000
FAX: (212) 558-3351

John Merrow, Partner. Legal services. Sullivan & Cromwell is a law firm offering services to clients on a global basis. Worldwide operating revenues for 1991: $240 million.

- **Total Employees:** 440
- **U.S. Employees Abroad:** 25
- **Countries:** France, United Kingdom.
- **Application Information:** Most overseas positions are filled internally.
- **Job Categories:** Attorneys.
- **Language Requirement:** Varies with each posting.

SUN COMPANY, INC.

1801 Market St.
Philadelphia, PA 19103-1699
USA

RECRUITER: LULA HARDY
EMPLOYMENT SPECIALIST
1801 MARKET ST.
PHILADELPHIA, PA 19103-1699

Robert H. Campbell, President. Energy supplier. Sun is a public company founded when Joseph Newton Pew began his career in a Pennsylvania natural gas partnership. Pew Organized Sun Oil Line in 1886 (consolidated in 1890 as Sun Oil) and many changes occurred throughout the years. Today, Sun is the tenth largest petroleum refiner in the United States. It is engaged in oil and natural gas drilling on a global basis and has operations in the United States and in 13 foreign countries. Worldwide revenues for 1992: $8.6 billion.

- **Total Employees:** 16,963
- **U.S. Employees Abroad:** 35

- **Countries:** Canada, Japan, United Kingdom.
- **Job Categories:** Engineers, Marketing—Petroleum/Natural Gas, Sales—Petroleum/Natural Gas, Technical Field Support.
- **General Requirements:** Usually must be a current employee of the company in order to qualify for overseas assignment.
- **Language Requirement:** Varies with each posting.

SUN ELECTRIC CORPORATION

1 Sun Pkwy.
Crystal Lake, IL 60014 USA

RECRUITER: BETTY ZAMBON
MANAGER, HUMAN RESOURCES
1 SUN PKWY.
CRYSTAL LAKE, IL 60014
TEL: (815) 459-7700
FAX: (815) 459-7852

Gerald A. Kien, Chairman. Test and service equipment for the motor vehicle industry. Sun Electric Corporation is a public company founded in 1931. It produces, sells, and services various diagnostic, test, and service equipment for the motor vehicle services industry and motor vehicle manufacturers on a global basis. Worldwide revenues for 1991: $220.4 million.

- **Total Employees:** 2,205
- **U.S. Employees Abroad:** 30
- **Countries:** Australia, Austria, Belgium, Brazil, Canada, Germany, Mexico, Netherlands, United Kingdom.
- **Job Categories:** Management, Marketing—Automotive, Product Development, Sales—Automotive.
- **Language Requirement:** Varies with each posting.

SUN MICROSYSTEMS, INC.

2550 Garcia Ave.
Mountain View, CA 94043 USA

RECRUITER: LISA MARIE SABLAN
STAFFING/RECRUITMENT
2550 GARCIA AVE., MS MPK-01-20
MOUNTAIN VIEW, CA 94043
TEL: (415) 960-1300
FAX: (415) 336-0423

Scott G. McNealy, President and Chairman. Microprocessor-based computers used in networks and related areas. Sun Microsystems, Inc. is a public company founded in 1982. It is a major producer of computer workstations. Systems include SPARC server 470 and SPARCstation 1PC (graphics system). Software includes OpenWindows and SunLink network computing products. Currently, it has 68 foreign sales and service offices. Worldwide revenues for 1992: $3.8 billion.

- **Total Employees:** 12,480

- **U.S. Employees Abroad:** 30
- **Countries:** United Kingdom.
- **Job Categories:** Engineers, Marketing—Electronics, Sales—Electronics.
- **Language Requirement:** None.

SUNDSTRAND CORPORATION

4945 Harrison Ave.
PO Box 7083
Rockford, IL 61125 USA

RECRUITER: GARY HEDGES
CORPORATE VP, PERSONNEL
4945 HARRISON AVE.
PO BOX 7083
ROCKFORD, IL 61125
TEL: (815) 226-6000
FAX: (815) 394-2239

Harry Stonecipher, Chairman. Products for aerospace and other industries. Sundstrand Corporation is a public company founded in 1910. It manufactures aircraft parts and electronic components for commercial and government aircraft. Worldwide revenues for 1992: $1.7 billion.

- **Total Employees:** 13,700
- **U.S. Employees Abroad:** 35
- **Countries:** Belgium, France, Japan, Singapore, Switzerland.
- **Job Categories:** Engineers, Marketing—Scientific, Sales—Scientific.
- **General Requirements:** Usually must be a current employee of the company in order to qualify for overseas assignment.
- **Language Requirement:** Varies with each posting.

SYMBOL TECHNOLOGIES, INC.

116 Wilbur Place
Bohemia, NY 11716 USA

RECRUITER: DIANE WOLF
HUMAN RESOURCES COORDINATOR
116 WILBUR PLACE
BOHEMIA, NY 11716
TEL: (516) 563-2400
FAX: (516) 244-4103

Jerome Swartz, Chairman. Bar code scanning equipment, portable data terminals, and radio communication equipment. Symbol Technologies, Inc. is a public company founded in 1973. It produces, sells, and services laser-based bar code scanning equipment, portable data terminals, and radio frequency communication equipment. Customers include the health-care industry, manufacturers, and the military. Worldwide revenues for 1992: $344.9 million.

- **Total Employees:** 2,200
- **U.S. Employees Abroad:** 25
- **Countries:** Belgium, France, Germany, Italy, United Kingdom.

- **Job Categories:** Engineers, Finance, Marketing—Electronics, Sales—Electronics.
- **Language Requirement:** None.

SYNTEX CORPORATION

3401 Hillview Ave.
Palo Alto, CA 94304 USA

RECRUITER: LEO L. CONTOIS
VP, HUMAN RESOURCES
3401 HILLVIEW AVE.
PALO ALTO, CA 94304
TEL: (415) 855-5050
FAX: (415) 855-5103

Paul Freiman, Chairman. Pharmaceuticals. Syntex Corporation is a public company founded in 1944 by Russell Marker and two European scientists. It began by mass-producing progesterone and other hormones. Today, it is well-known for its arthritis drugs, Naprosyn and Anaprox. It is currently concentrating on research and development in the following areas: cancer, cardiology, gastroenterology, and neurology. It has operations in 23 countries. Worldwide revenues for 1991: $1.8 billion.

- **Total Employees:** 10,900
- **U.S. Employees Abroad:** 25
- **Countries:** Japan, Mexico, Panama, United Kingdom.
- **Job Categories:** Management, Marketing—Pharmaceuticals, Product Development, Researchers, Sales—Pharmaceuticals.
- **Language Requirement:** None.

TAMBRANDS, INC.

777 Westchester Ave.
White Plains, NY 10604 USA

RECRUITER: KEVIN PARADISE
VP, INTERNATIONAL HUMAN
RESOURCES
777 WESTCHESTER AVE.
WHITE PLAINS, NY 10604
TEL: (914) 696-6000
FAX: (914) 696-6757

Martin Emmett, Chairman. Feminine hygiene products. Tambrands, Inc. is a public company founded in 1936. It manufactures and sells feminine protection products and other related items in the United States and abroad. Items produced include Tampax and disposable diapers. Worldwide revenues for 1992: $684 million.

- **Total Employees:** 3,300
- **U.S. Employees Abroad:** 15
- **Countries:** Australia, Canada, People's Republic of China, France, Greece, Mexico, Russia, Ukraine, United Kingdom.
- **Job Categories:** Finance, Human Resources, Manufacturing, Marketing—Consumer Goods, Sales—Consumer Goods.

- **Average Overseas Assignment:** 2-3 years.
- **Language Requirement:** Knowledge of local language a plus but not essential.
- **Training:** Basic orientation (30 days) provided.
- **Benefits:** TRAVEL: Relocation fee paid; also moving and storage expenses provided. HEALTH: Same coverage as U.S. emloyees. HOUSING: Offered; usually a "housing norm" is deducted based on tables provided by outside firm. EDUCATION: Offered.
- **Comments:** The number of Americans reported working abroad varies greatly from quarter to quarter, fluctuating with the number and scope of projects under contract at the time.

TANDEM COMPUTERS, INC.

10600 Ridegeview Court
Cupertino, CA 95014 USA

RECRUITER: MARSHA LUDWIG
STAFFING SPECIALIST
10600 RIDGEVIEW COURT
CUPERTINO, CA 95014
TEL: (408) 725-6000
FAX: (408) 285-0035

Thomas J. Perkins, Chairman. Fault-tolerant computers. Tandem Computers, Inc. is a public company founded in 1974 by James Treybig and 2 computer engineers. Treybig discovered a way to link computers to work in tandem so that if one did not function, the other would take over without interruption. The first fail-safe minicomputer, the NonStop16, was introduced in 1976. Today, these computers are used in various applications around the world. Currently, Tandem has operations in more than 180 locations in the United States and abroad. Worldwide revenues for 1992: $2.1 billion.

- **Total Employees:** 11,167
- **U.S. Employees Abroad:** 35
- **Countries:** Germany, Mexico.
- **Job Categories:** Engineers, Marketing—Electronics, Sales—Electronics.
- **General Requirements:** Usually must be a current employee of the company in order to qualify for overseas assignment.
- **Language Requirement:** None.

TANDY CORPORATION

1800 One Tandy Center
Fort Worth, TX 76102 USA

RECRUITER: GEORGE BERGER
VP, HUMAN RESOURCES
1800 ONE TANDY CENTER
FORT WORTH, TX 76102
TEL: (817) 390-3700
FAX: (817) 390-2774

John V. Roach, Chairman. Consumer electronics and personal computers. Tandy Corporation is a public company founded in 1919 as a small, family-owned leather business in Fort Worth, Texas. Charles Tandy then began expansion in the 1950s and the business emerged as a nationwide chain of leathercraft and hobby stores. Today, Tandy is the largest retailer of consumer electronics in the world and a leader in the field of electronic products. One division includes Radio Shack retail outlets. Products are manufactured and marketed on a global basis. Worldwide revenues for 1992: $4.8 billion.

- **Total Employees:** 40,000

- **U.S. Employees Abroad:** 55

- **Countries:** Australia, Belgium, Canada, France, Germany, Hong Kong, Japan, Republic of Korea, Mexico, Taiwan, United Kingdom.

- **Application Information:** Most overseas positions are filled internally.

- **Job Categories:** Management, Marketing—Electronics, Product Development, Sales—Electronics.

- **Language Requirement:** Varies with each posting.

TEKTRONIX, INC.
14150 SW Karl Braun
Beaverton, OR 97077 USA

RECRUITER: BOB PHILLIPS
WORKFORCE PLANNING DEPARTMENT
PO BOX 1000
MS 63-819
WILSONVILLE, OR 97070-1000
TEL: (503) 627-7111
FAX: (503) 685-4017

David P. Friedley, President. Test, measurement, and communication products. Tektronix, Inc. is a public company founded in 1946. It is engaged as a manufacturer of measurement and test equipment, visual systems, and communications equipment. Major products include oscilloscopes and logic analyzers. Worldwide revenues for 1992: $1.3 billion.

- **Total Employees:** 15,708

- **U.S. Employees Abroad:** 35

- **Countries:** Australia, Belgium, Canada, France, Germany, Hong Kong, Italy, Japan, Mexico, Netherlands, Taiwan, United Kingdom.

- **Application Information:** Hiring for most overseas positions is done at the specific country location.

- **Job Categories:** Management, Marketing—Electronics, Sales—Electronics.

- **Language Requirement:** Varies with each posting.

- **Training:** Varies with each posting.

TELEDYNE, INC.

1901 Ave. of the Stars
Los Angeles, CA 90067 USA

RECRUITER: LEE RASPA
MANAGER, EXECUTIVE PLACEMENT
1901 AVE. OF THE STARS
LOS ANGELES, CA 90067
TEL: (301) 277-3311
FAX: (301) 551-4365

Donald Rice, President. Aerospace-defense products, consumer and industrial products and services, and specialty metals. Teledyne, Inc. is a public company founded in 1927. Products are marketed to the aviation and electronics industries as well as various consumer sectors. Major products include Doppler radar systems and Shower Massage showerheads. Worldwide revenues for 1992: $2.9 billion.

- **Total Employees:** 23,000
- **U.S. Employees Abroad:** 19
- **Countries:** Australia, Belgium, Brazil, France, Germany, Hong Kong, Israel, Italy, Japan, Republic of Korea, Mexico, Poland, Saudi Arabia, Singapore, Spain, Taiwan, United Kingdom.
- **Application Information:** Offices overseas are principally sales offices.
- **Salaries:** $80,000-$100,000 per year.
- **Job Categories:** Business Development, Management, Sales—Defense Industry, Sales—Industrial.
- **Average Overseas Assignment:** Five years or more.
- **Language Requirement:** Fluency in local language required.
- **Training:** No special training provided.
- **Benefits:** All benefits are individually determined.
- **Comments:** The number of Americans reported working abroad varies greatly from quarter to quarter, fluctuating with the number and scope of projects under contract at the time.

TELLABS OPERATIONS, INC.

4951 Indiana Ave.
Lisle, IL 60532 USA

RECRUITER: JIM COPPENS
INTERNATIONAL HUMAN RESOURCES
4951 INDIANA AVE.
LISLE, IL 60532
TEL: (208) 955-3153
FAX: (208) 955-0424

Michael J. Birck, President. Telecommunications. Tellabs Operations, Inc. is a public company founded in 1975. It produces and services data and voice communication equipment which is used on a global basis by interexchange carriers, business, government, and telephone markets. Worldwide revenues for 1992: $213 million.

- **Total Employees:** 2,500

- **U.S. Employees Abroad:** 400
- **Countries:** Belgium, Canada, Finland, Hong Kong, Mexico, United Kingdom.
- **Job Categories:** Engineers, Sales—Telecommunications.
- **General Requirements:** Telecommunications knowledge is preferred.
- **Average Overseas Assignment:** 2-3 years.
- **Language Requirement:** Competence in local language required.
- **Training:** Basic orientation (1-30 days) provided.
- **Benefits:** All benefits are individually determined.

TELXON CORP.

3330 West Market St.
Akron, OH 44334 USA

RECRUITER: JUDI EICHENLAUB
RECRUITMENT/STAFFING
PO BOX 5582
AKRON, OH 44334
TEL: (216) 867-3700
FAX: (216) 869-2269

Raymond D. Meyo, President. Microcomputer systems. Telxon Corporation is a public company founded in 1983. It produces and sells portable, hand-held, interactive microcomputer systems in the United States and abroad. Worldwide revenues for 1991: $215.0 million.

- **Total Employees:** 1,458
- **U.S. Employees Abroad:** 12
- **Countries:** Belgium, Singapore.
- **Application Information:** Hiring for most overseas positions is done at the specific country location.
- **Job Categories:** Engineers, Marketing—Electronics, Sales—Electronics.
- **Language Requirement:** Varies with each posting.
- **Training:** No special training provided.
- **Comments:** The number of Americans reported working abroad varies greatly from quarter to quarter, fluctuating with the number and scope of projects under contract at the time.

TENNANT COMPANY

PO Box 1452
Minneapolis, MN 55440 USA

RECRUITER: KATHRYN DESBLES
EMPLOYMENT SPECIALIST
PO BOX 1452
MINNEAPOLIS, MN 55440
TEL: (612) 540-1200

Roger L. Hale, President. Machinery and equipment for the service industries. Tennant is a public company founded in 1870. It manufactures various equipment for industrial floor-care in the United States and abroad. These include industrial floor-care sweepers, scrubbers, and roofing machines. Worldwide revenues for 1992: $215 million.

- **Total Employees:** 1,780

- **U.S. Employees Abroad:** 20

- **Countries:** Australia, Canada, Germany, Japan, Netherlands.

- **Application Information:** Most overseas positions are filled internally.

- **Job Categories:** Management, Manufacturing, Marketing—Industrial.

- **Language Requirement:** Varies with each posting.

- **Training:** Varies with each posting.

TENNECO AUTOMOTIVE

100 Tri-State International
Lincolnshire, IL 60069 USA

RECRUITER: BARBARA G. POSNER
VP, HUMAN RESOURCES/CORPORATE
  RELATIONS
100 TRI-STATE INTERNATIONAL,
  SUITE #300
LINCOLNSHIRE, IL 60069
TEL: (708) 940-6009
FAX: (708) 940-6022

John P. Reilly, President. Automotive parts. Tenneco Automotive was founded in 1977 and is a subsidiary of Tenneco, Inc. of Houston, Texas. It manufactures motor vehicle parts and related accessories. Worldwide revenues for 1991: $1.7 billion.

- **Total Employees:** 14,000

- **U.S. Employees Abroad:** 11

- **Countries:** Belgium, Canada, Japan, Mexico, Netherlands.

- **Salaries:** $60,000 minimum per year.

- **Job Categories:** Engineers, Finance, Marketing—Automotive, Sales—Automotive.

- **Average Overseas Assignment:** 3-5 years.

- **Language Requirement:** Knowledge of local language a plus but not required.

- **Training:** Basic orientation (1-30 days) provided.

- **Benefits:** TRAVEL: Annual home leave offered; also full relocation package including one month's salary as a relocation bonus. HEALTH: Same coverage as U.S. employees. HOUSING: Offered. EDUCATION: Offered; tuition reimbursement for secondary school level.

TENNECO, INC.

Tenneco Building
PO Box 2511
Houston, TX 77252 USA

RECRUITER: STEPHEN J. SMITH
EXECUTIVE DIRECTOR, HUMAN
RESOURCES
TENNECO BUILDING
PO BOX 2511
HOUSTON, TX 77252
TEL: (713) 757-3548
FAX: (713) 757-4342

Michael H. Walsh, Chairman. Petroleum refining and natural gas distribution. Tenneco, Inc. is a public company founded in 1943 as the Tennessee Gas & Transmission Company, a division of the Chicago Corporation. Today, it has major business interests in natural gas transportation and marketing, farm and construction equipment, automotive parts, shipbuilding, packaging, and chemicals. Worldwide revenues for 1992: $13.1 billion.

- **Total Employees:** 89,000
- **U.S. Employees Abroad:** 125
- **Countries:** Brazil, Canada, France, Japan, Spain, United Kingdom.
- **Job Categories:** Management, Marketing—Petroleum/Natural Gas, Sales—Petroleum/Natural Gas, Technical Field Support.
- **General Requirements:** Usually must be a current employee of the company in order to qualify for overseas assignment.
- **Language Requirement:** Varies with each posting.

TENNESSEE ASSOCIATES INTERNATIONAL, INC.

337 East Broadway Ave.
Maryville, TN 37801 USA

RECRUITER: JOSEPHINE ROGERS
STAFFING/RECRUITMENT
337 EAST BROADWAY AVE.
MARYVILLE, TN 37801
TEL: (617) 482-2700
FAX: (617) 422-2910

Gerald D. Sentell, President. Management consulting. Tennessee Associates International, Inc. is a private company offering management consultant services on an international basis. Worldwide revenues for 1991: $93 million.

- **Total Employees:** 170
- **U.S. Employees Abroad:** 30
- **Countries:** Canada, France, United Kingdom.
- **Job Categories:** Consultants—Management, Management, Marketing.
- **General Requirements:** Usually must be a current employee of the company in order to qualify for overseas assignment.
- **Language Requirement:** Varies with each posting.

TERADYNE, INC.

321 Harrison Ave.
Boston, MA 02118 USA

RECRUITER: FREDERICK VANVEEN
VP, CORPORATE RELATIONS
321 HARRISON AVE.
BOSTON, MA 02118
TEL: (617) 482-2700
FAX: (617) 422-2910

Alexander V. d'Arbeloff, President and Chairman. Automatic test systems and black plane connections systems. Teradyne, Inc. was founded in 1960 as a private company until it became public in 1970. It is a provider of automatic test systems for the electronics industries. The systems are used to test semiconductors, circuit boards, and related products. Worldwide revenues for 1992: $529.6 million.

- **Total Employees:** 4,000
- **U.S. Employees Abroad:** 20
- **Countries:** France, Japan, United Kingdom.
- **Job Categories:** Engineers, Management, Sales—Scientific.
- **Language Requirement:** Varies with each posting.
- **Training:** Varies with each posting.

TEXACO OIL COMPANY

2000 Westlake Ave.
White Plains, NY 10604 USA

RECRUITER: BRIAN GLADE
INTERNATIONAL EMPLOYMENT
2000 WESTLAKE AVE.
WHITE PLAINS, NY 10604
TEL: (914) 253-7187
FAX: (914) 253-7040

Alfred C. DeCrane, Jr., Chairman. Petroleum and related products. Texaco is a public company founded in 1897 by "Buckskin Joe" Cullinan when he formed his own oil company in Texas. In 1901 the Spindletop gusher attracted over 200 oil companies to the scene, and he decided the most profitable business was to sell oil that others had discovered. Today, Texaco is the third largest integrated oil company in the United States. It has operations in more than 50 foreign countries. Worldwide revenues for 1992: $36.8 billion.

- **Total Employees:** 37,000
- **U.S. Employees Abroad:** 70
- **Countries:** Worldwide including Angola, Australia, Bahamas, Brazil, Costa Rica, Dominican Republic, Guatemala, Hong Kong, Indonesia, Japan, Netherlands, Saudi Arabia, Switzerland, United Kingdom.
- **Job Categories:** Engineers, Field Technicians, Marketing—Petroleum/Natural Gas, Sales—Petroleum/Natural Gas.
- **General Requirements:** Usually must be a current employee of the company in order to qualify for overseas assignment.

- **Language Requirement:** Varies with each posting.

TEXAS INTRUMENTS, INC.

13500 North Central Expressway
Dallas, TX 75265 USA

RECRUITER: STEPHANIE VANN
CORPORATE COLLEGE RELATIONS
13500 NORTH CENTRAL
EXPRESSWAY
DALLAS, TX 75265
TEL: (214) 995-2011
FAX: (214) 995-3340

Jerry R. Junkins, President and Chairman. Electronics and semiconductor manufacturing. Texas Instruments is a public company founded in 1930 by "Doc" Karcher and Eugene McDermott in Newark, New Jersey. It was called Geophysical Services, Inc. In 1934, the business moved to Dallas, Texas and its name was changed to Texas Instruments (TI) in 1951. Once focusing on defense and semiconductor products, it now has interests in the consumer markets. Items include calculators, digital watches, computers, and related items. Worldwide revenues for 1992: $7.4 billion.

- **Total Employees:** 62,939
- **U.S. Employees Abroad:** 75
- **Countries:** Argentina, Australia, Brazil, Japan, Malaysia, Mexico, Netherlands, Philippines, Portugal, Singapore, Taiwan, United Kingdom.
- **Job Categories:** Management, Marketing—Electronics, Product Development, Sales—Electronics.
- **Language Requirement:** Varies with each posting.
- **Training:** No special training offered.

TEXTRON, INC.

40 Westminster St.
Providence, RI 02903 USA

RECRUITER: DONNA BLANEY
VICE PRESIDENT, STAFFING
40 WESTMINSTER ST.
PROVIDENCE, RI 02903
TEL: (401) 421-2800
FAX: (401) 421-2878

James F. Hardymon, President. Multi-industry company with three business sectors: aerospace technology, commercial products, and financial services. Textron, Inc. is a public company founded in 1930 as the Franklin Rayon Corporation in Providence, Rhode Island. Its name changed to Atlantic Rayon in 1938, and finally to Textron Inc. in 1944. "Textron" was derived from textile products made from synthetics. Today, products include Bell helicopters and Cessna business jets, Homelite chain saws, and Speidel watch bands. Other interests include automotive products and financial and insurance services. Currently, it has 133 plants in the United States and in five foreign countries. Worldwide revenues for 1992: $8.3 billion.

- **Total Employees:** 54,000
- **U.S. Employees Abroad:** 40
- **Countries:** Australia, Belgium, Canada, New Zealand, Spain, United Kingdom.
- **Application Information:** Hiring for most overseas positions is done at the specific counrty location.
- **Job Categories:** Administrative, Finance, Marketing—Financial Services, Marketing, Sales—Financial Services, Sales.
- **Language Requirement:** None.
- **Comments:** The number of Americans reported working abroad varies greatly from quarter to quarter, fluctuating with the number and scope of projects under contract at the time.

THERMCO SYSTEMS, INC.

1465 N. Batavia St.
Orange, CA 92667 USA

RECRUITER: CHRISTINA ARMENTA
HUMAN RESOURCES
REPRESENTATIVE
1465 N. BATAVIA ST.
ORANGE, CA 92667
TEL: (714) 639-2340
FAX: (714) 639-3373

Richard C. Pinto, President. Furnace and vacuum/gas systems. Thermco Systems, Inc. is a subsidiary of Allegheny International. It is engaged as a manufacturer of microprocessor-controlled diffusion furnace systems and vacuum gas systems for semiconductor processing.

- **Total Employees:** 700
- **U.S. Employees Abroad:** 15
- **Countries:** France, Germany, Hong Kong, United Kingdom.
- **Job Categories:** Management, Marketing—Scientific.
- **Language Requirement:** Varies with each posting.

THOMAS & BETTS

1001 Frontier St.
Bridgewater, NJ 08807 USA

RECRUITER: SUSAN KELLY
HUMAN RESOURCES
REPRESENTATIVE
1001 FRONTIER ST.
BRIDGEWATER, NJ 08807
TEL: (908) 685-1600
FAX: (908) 707-2056

T. Kevin Dunnigan, President. Electrical and electronic connectors. Thomas & Betts is a public company founded in 1912. It is engaged as a manufacturer of electric and electronic components and systems which are marketed to various sectors in the United

States and abroad. These include the automotive, industrial construction, and telecommunications markets. Worldwide revenues for 1992: $1 billion.

- **Total Employees:** 7,600

- **U.S. Employees Abroad:** 30

- **Countries:** Australia, Canada, France, Germany, Italy, Japan, Mexico, Sweden, United Kingdom.

- **Job Categories:** Management, Marketing—Electronics, Sales—Electronics.

- **Language Requirement:** Varies with each posting.

- **Training:** Varies with each posting.

3M COMPANY

3M Center
St. Paul, MN 55144-1000 USA

RECRUITER: BRUCE HOEFFEL
INTERNATIONAL OPERATIONS
3M CENTER
ST.PAUL, MN 55144-1000
TEL: (612) 733-1110
FAX: (612) 736-2041

L. D. DeSimone, Chairman. Abrasives, adhesives, chemicals, industrial and consumer tapes/diskettes, health-care products, and electrical connectors. 3M Company is a global leader in a wide variety of markets (50,000 by one estimate). The business was founded in 1902 by five businessmen in Two Harbors, Minnesota. Research and development are key factors in 3M's success with products such as Scotch brand masking tape (1925) and the Thermo-Fax copying machine (1950). One third of 1990 sales came from products introduced in the previous five years. Plans call for increased activity in overseas markets, which accounted for 50 percent of 3M's sales in 1990. Products are sold worldwide and at the present time, plants are located in 41 countries. Worldwide revenues for 1992: $13.6 billion. Foreign revenues for 1991: $6.5 billion.

- **Total Employees:** 89,601

- **U.S. Employees Abroad:** Not available.

- **Countries:** Argentina, Australia, Canada, People's Republic of China, Dominican Republic, France, Germany, Hong Kong, Japan, Kenya, Mexico, New Zealand, Philippines, Singapore, Thailand, United Arab Emirates, United Kingdom, Venezuela.

- **Application Information:** Most overseas positions are filled internally.

- **Job Categories:** Management, Manufacturing, Marketing—Consumer Goods, Research & Development, Sales—Consumer Goods.

- **Benefits:** All benefits are individually determined.

3M PHARMACEUTICALS

3M Center
275-3W-01
St. Paul, MN 55144 USA

RECRUITER: BERNICE SHAW
HUMAN RESOURCES
    REPRESENTATIVE
3M CENTER, 275-3W-01
ST. PAUL, MN 55144
TEL: (612) 733-8045
FAX: (612) 733-3451

Chemicals and pharmaceuticals. 3M Pharmaceuticals is a division of the 3M Company of St. Paul, Minnesota. It produces specialty chemicals and pharmaceuticals in facilities throughout the United States and abroad. Worldwide revenues for 1991: $125.0 million.

- **Total Employees:** 2,500

- **U.S. Employees Abroad:** 20

- **Countries:** Australia, Canada, France, Germany, Italy, Japan, United Kingdom.

- **Job Categories:** Manufacturing, Management, Marketing—Chemicals, Marketing—Pharmaceuticals, Sales—Chemicals, Sales—Pharmaceuticals.

- **General Requirements:** Usually must be a current employee of the company in order to qualify for overseas assignment.

TIME, INC.

Time & Life Building
Rockefeller Center
New York, NY 10020 USA

RECRUITER: CAROL DUCAS
STAFFING/DEVELOPMENT
TIME & LIFE BUILDING, ROCKEFELLER
    CENTER
NEW YORK, NY 10020
TEL: (212) 586-1212
FAX: (212) 522-0902

Reginald K. Brack, Jr., President and Chairman. Publishing. Time, Inc. is a subsidiary of Time-Warner Inc. of New York City. It publishes magazines in the United States and abroad. Well-known titles include *Fortune, People Weekly,* and *Sports Illustrated.*

- **Total Employees:** 5,000

- **U.S. Employees Abroad:** 30

- **Countries:** France, Germany, Hong Kong, Netherlands.

- **Job Categories:** Management, Marketing—Publishing, Sales—Publishing.

- **Language Requirement:** None.

TIME-WARNER, INC.

1271 Avenue of the Americas
New York, NY 10020 USA

RECRUITER: SUSAN GEISENHEIMER
DIRECTOR, HUMAN RESOURCES
1271 AVENUE OF THE AMERICAS
NEW YORK, NY 10020
TEL: (212) 522-1212

N. J. Nicholas, Jr., President. Media and entertainment. Time-Warner was founded in 1990 when Time, Inc., joined with Warner Communications, Inc., to form an entertainment conglomerate. As publishers, titles include *Time* and *People Weekly* magazines. It is also a global leader in the music industry with such popular artists as Madonna and R.E.M. Subsidiaries include Columbia House Records and Home Box Office (HBO). Worldwide revenues for 1992: $13.1 billion.

- **Total Employees:** 41,000

- **U.S. Employees Abroad:** Not available.

- **Countries:** Australia, France, Germany, Hong Kong, Italy, Japan, Mexico, Netherlands, United Kingdom.

- **Job Categories:** Executive Management, Marketing, Marketing—Publishing, Sales, Sales—Publishing.

- **Language Requirement:** Varies with each posting.

TLC BEATRICE INTERNATIONAL HOLDINGS, INC.

9 West 57th St.
New York, NY 10019 USA

RECRUITER: AVONDA PRESCOD
DIRECTOR, HUMAN RESOURCES
9 WEST 57TH ST. (48TH FLOOR)
NEW YORK, NY 10019
TEL: (212) 756-8906
FAX: (212) 888-3093

Gene Fugett, Chairman. Food products. TLC Beatrice is a private company founded in 1983 by Reginald F. Lewis and was first called TLC Group. A purchase of the international holdings of Beatrice (International Companies) for $985 million prompted a name change to TLC Beatrice International Holdings, Inc. in 1987. Most of its foreign operations are concentrated in Western Europe. Worldwide revenues for 1991: $1.5 billion. Foreign revenues for 1991: $541 million.

- **Total Employees:** 5,000

- **U.S. Employees Abroad:** 35

- **Countries:** Australia, Belgium, Denmark, France, Italy, Netherlands, Spain, Switzerland, Thailand.

- **Job Categories:** Management, Marketing—Food/Food Services, Sales—Food/Food Services.

- **Language Requirement:** Varies with each posting.

TORRINGTON COMPANY

59 Field St.
Torrington, CT 06790 USA

RECRUITER: MARIANNE GATTINELLA
MANAGER, ORGANIZATIONAL
    RESOURCES
59 FIELD ST.
TORRINGTON, CT 06790
TEL: (203) 482-9511
FAX: (203) 496-3603

J. Frank Travis, President. Ball and roller bearings. Torrington Company was founded in 1866 and is a subsidiary of Ingersoll-Rand Company of Woodcliff Lake, New Jersey. It is a manufacturer of ball or roller bearings and related products. Worldwide revenues for 1991: $1.2 billion.

- **Total Employees:** 11,000

- **U.S. Employees Abroad:** 30

- **Countries:** Australia, Brazil, Colombia, France, Germany, Italy, Japan, Mexico, Taiwan, United Kingdom.

- **Job Categories:** Management, Manufacturing, Marketing, Sales.

- **Language Requirement:** Varies with each posting.

- **Training:** No special training provided.

TOWERS PERRIN, INC.

100 Summit Lake Dr.
Valhalla, NY 10595 USA

RECRUITER: GEORGE MCMORAN
DIRECTOR, HUMAN RESOURCES
100 SUMMITT LAKE DR.
VALHALLA, NY 10595
TEL: (914) 745-5000
FAX: (914) 745-4555

James E. Kielley, Chairman. Management consulting services. Towers Perrin, Inc. is a private company founded in 1934. It offers management consultant services in the United States and abroad. Worldwide operating revenues for 1991: 680 million.

- **Total Employees:** 5,000

- **U.S. Employees Abroad:** 40

- **Countries:** Australia, Belgium, Brazil, Canada, France, Germany, Hong Kong, Italy, Japan, Mexico, Netherlands, Singapore, United Kingdom, Venezuela.

- **Job Categories:** Management, Marketing.

- **General Requirements:** Usually must be a current employee of the company in order to qualify for overseas assignment.

- **Language Requirement:** Varies with each posting.

- **Training:** No special training provided.

TOYS "R" US, INC.

461 From Rd.
Paramus, NJ 07652 USA

RECRUITER: JIM GORENC
MANAGER, RECRUITMENT/
    PLACEMENT
461 FROM RD.
PARAMUS, NJ 07652
TEL: (201) 262-7800
FAX: (201) 262-8112

Charles Lazarus, Chairman. Toy and children's clothing stores operator. Toys "R" Us, Inc. is a public company founded in 1948 by Charles Lazarus in Washington, D. C. What began as a children's fun store has turned into a $6.1 billion chain of toy and children's clothing outlets operated throughout the world. It is still run by Chairman and CEO Charles Lazarus and currently has 623 stores in the United States and abroad. Worldwide revenues for 1992: $7.2 billion. Foreign sales for 1991: $970 million.

- **Total Employees:** 78,000

- **U.S. Employees Abroad:** 50

- **Countries:** Canada, France, Germany, Hong Kong, Japan, Malaysia, Spain, Singapore, Taiwan, United Kingdom.

- **Job Categories:** Management, Marketing—Consumer Goods, Sales—Consumer Goods.

- **Language Requirement:** Varies with each posting.

TRACOR, INC.

6500 Tracor Lane
Austin, TX 78725 USA

RECRUITER: ED MOORE
SENIOR TECHNICAL RECRUITER
6500 TRACOR LANE
AUSTIN, TX 78725
TEL: (512) 926-2800
FAX: (512) 929-2241

James Skaggs, Chief Executive Officer. Time and frequency products; engineering services. Tracor, Inc. was founded in 1955 and is a subsidiary of Tracor Holdings, Inc. of Austin, Texas. It manufactures various products including search, detection, navigation, guidance, aeronautical, and nautical systems and instruments. Worldwide revenues for 1992: $261 million.

- **Total Employees:** 3,400
- **U.S. Employees Abroad:** 22
- **Countries:** Belgium, France, Germany, Mexico, Netherlands, Switzerland.
- **Job Categories:** Engineers, Management, Marketing—Scientific, Sales—Scientific.
- **Language Requirement:** None.
- **Training:** No special training required.

TRANE COMPANY

3600 Pammel Creek Rd.
La Crosse, WI 54601 USA

RECRUITER: ROGER HAGE
MANAGER, SALES & OFFICE
ADMINISTRATION
3600 PAMMEL CREEK RD.
LA CROSS, WI 54601
TEL: (608) 787-2000
FAX: (608) 787-4990

H. T. Smith, President. A/C equipment, fans, blowers, and refrigeration equipment. Trane Company was founded in 1885 and is a subsidiary of American Standard, Inc. of New York City. It manufactures various A/C equipment, fans, blowers, and air purification equipment for heating, air conditioning, or ventilating systems. Worldwide revenues for 1991: $1.1 billion.

- **Total Employees:** 13,000
- **U.S. Employees Abroad:** 35
- **Countries:** Argentina, Australia, Belgium, Brazil, Canada, France, Germany, Hong Kong, Japan, Mexico, Singapore, Switzerland, United Arab Emirates, United Kingdom, Venezuela.
- **Job Categories:** Management, Marketing, Sales.
- **Language Requirement:** Varies with each posting.

TRANSAMERICA, CORPORATION

600 Montgomery St.
San Francisco, CA 94111 USA

RECRUITER: RONA I. KING
VP, HUMAN RESOURCES
600 MONTGOMERY ST.
SAN FRANCISCO, CA 94111
TEL: (415) 983-4000
FAX: (415) 983-4234

James R. Harvey, Chairman. Financial services, real estate, and leasing services. Transamerica Corporation is a public company founded in1928. It has two basic divisions: finance and insurance. Transamerica finance deals with consumer and commercial lending, leasing, and real estate services. The insurance sector places Tranamerica as the eighth largest life insurer in North America. The latest addition to the company is the asset management group, formed in 1989. It includes Criterion Investment and Transamerica Fund management, and manages more than $11.5 billion in assets for the United States and United Kingdom investors. Worldwide assets for 1992: $33 billion.

- **Total Employees:** 15,000
- **U.S. Employees Abroad:** Not available.
- **Countries:** United Kingdom.
- **Job Categories:** Agents—Insurance, Management, Marketing—Financial Services.

- **General Requirements:** Usually must be a current employee of the company in order to qualify for overseas assignment.

- **Language Requirement:** None.

TRINOVA CORPORATION

3000 Strayer
PO Box 50
Maumee, OH 43537-0050 USA

RECRUITER: CINDY GORDON
INTERNATIONAL HUMAN RESOURCES
3000 STRAYER
PO BOX 50
MAUMEE, OH 43537-0050
TEL: (419) 867-2200
FAX: (419) 867-2390

Darryl F. Allen, President. Engineered components and systems. Trinova Corporation is a public company founded in 1916. It is a global leader in the manufacturing and distribution of engineered components and systems for industry. It has two main sectors: power and motion control, and plastics. Worldwide revenues for 1992: $1.7 billion.

- **Total Employees:** 16,000

- **U.S. Employees Abroad:** 35

- **Countries:** Australia, Belgium, Brazil, Canada, France, Germany, Hong Kong, Italy, Republic of Korea, Japan, Mexico, Norway, Singapore, United Kingdom.

- **Job Categories:** Engineers, Management, Marketing—Industrial, Sales—Industrial.

- **General Requirements:** Usually must be a current employee of the company in order to qualify for overseas assignment.

- **Language Requirement:** Varies with each posting.

TRITON ENERGY CORPORATION

6688 North Central Expressway
Dallas, TX 75206 USA

RECRUITER: DAVID MORMON
HUMAN RESOURCES
6688 NORTH CENTRAL EXPRESSWAY,
      SUITE #1400
DALLAS, TX 75206
TEL: (214) 691-5200
FAX: (214) 987-0571

David E. Gore, President and Chairman. Operation of oil and gas field properties. Triton Energy is a public company founded in 1962. It is engaged in oil and gas exploration and production on a global basis. Worldwide revenues for 1992: $227.5 million.

- **Total Employees:** 300

- **U.S. Employees Abroad:** 20

- **Countries:** Argentina, Australia, Colombia, France, Indonesia, Netherlands, Netherlands Antilles, New Zealand, Thailand, United Kingdom.

- **Job Categories:** Management, Marketing—Petroleum/Natural Gas, Technical Field Support.
- **General Requirements:** Usually must be a current employee of the company in order to qualify for overseas assignment.
- **Language Requirement:** None.

TRW, INC.
1900 Richmond Rd.
Cleveland, OH 44124 USA

RECRUITER: ELIZABETH LANZ
DIRECTOR, HUMAN RESOURCES
1900 RICHMOND RD.
CLEVELAND, OH 44124
TEL: (216) 291-7000
FAX: (216) 291-7321

Joseph T. Gorman, Chairman. Products manufacturer and provider of services for aerospace, defense, and informations systems industries. TRW, Inc. is a public company founded in 1901 as Cleveland Cap and Screw Company. Diversification through the years prompted a name change to TRW, Inc. in 1965. Today, this high-technology company has made contributions in the development of microprocessors, computer-aided design and manufacturing, and satellites. The automotive products division manufactures such items as airbag systems, engine valves, and pistons. It has manufacturing facilities in 29 states and 17 foreign countries. Worldwide revenues for 1992: $8.3 billion.

- **Total Employees:** 71,262
- **U.S. Employees Abroad:** 75
- **Countries:** Australia, Austria, Brazil, Canada, France, Germany, Italy, Japan, Mexico, Singapore, Switzerland, Taiwan, United Kingdom.
- **Job Categories:** Engineers, Management, Marketing, Marketing—Scientific, Sales—Defense Industry, Sales—Scientific.
- **Language Requirement:** Varies with each posting.

TURNER BROADCASTING SYSTEM, INC.

One CNN Plaza
100 International Blvd.
Atlanta, GA 30303 USA

RECRUITER: ALLAN DENIRO
CORPORATE VP, HUMAN RESOURCES
ONE CNN PLAZA
100 INTERNATIONAL BLVD.
ATLANTA, GA 30303
TEL: (404) 827-1700
FAX: (404) 827-2437

R. E. "Ted" Turner, President and Chairman. Broadcasting services. Turner Broadcasting System, Inc. is a public company founded by Ted Turner in 1970 and was originally called Turner Communications Corporation. Today, it focuses on its four cable channels: Cable News Network (CNN), Headline News, TBS Super Station, and Turner

Network Television (TNT). Other interests include the Turner Entertainment Company (films) and ownership in sports teams. Worldwide revenues for 1992: $1.8 billion.

- **Total Employees:** 4,370
- **U.S. Employees Abroad:** 35
- **Countries:** United Kingdom.
- **Job Categories:** Executive Management, Marketing, Sales.
- **General Requirements:** Usually must be a current employee of the company in order to qualify for overseas assignment.
- **Language Requirement:** Varies with each posting.
- **Training:** No special training provided.

TURNER STEINER INTERNATIONAL, INC.

375 Hudson St.
New York, NY 10014 USA

RECRUITER: ROGER TURNIER
PERSONNEL MANAGER
375 HUDSON ST.
NEW YORK, NY 10014
TEL: (212) 229-6000
FAX: (212) 229-6390

Ralph Beck, President. Construction. Turner Steiner International, Inc. is a subsidiary of the Turner Corporation of New York City. It operates in the construction and construction management fields. Worldwide revenues for 1991: $1 million.

- **Total Employees:** 125
- **U.S. Employees Abroad:** 20
- **Countries:** Hong Kong, Singapore, United Arab Emirates.
- **Job Categories:** Engineers, Marketing, Technical Field Support.
- **Language Requirement:** None.

TW HOLDINGS, INC.

203 East Main St.
Spartanburg, SC 29319 USA

RECRUITER: BARBARA MCCLENNAN
DIRECTOR, COMPENSATION &
BENEFITS
203 EAST MAIN ST.
SPARTANBURG, SC 29319
TEL: (803) 597-8700
FAX: (803) 597-8766

Jerome J. Richardson, President. Food services. TW Holdings, Inc. is a public company consolidated as the Trans World Corporation in 1979 after Trans World Airlines began purchasing other businesses outside the airline industry. Today, it owns and operates various resturants including Denny's, Quincy's Family Steakhouses, and El Pollo Loco (fast-food broiled chicken eatery). Other interests include vending accounts and commercial food service to factories, hospitals, offices, and other facilities in the United States and abroad. Worldwide revenues for 1992: $3.7 billion.

- **Total Employees:** 112,000

- **U.S. Employees Abroad:** 50

- **Countries:** Canada, Guam, Japan.

- **Job Categories:** Management, Marketing—Food/Food Services, Sales—Food/Food Services.

- **General Requirements:** Usually must be a current employee of the company in order to qualify for overseas assignment.

- **Language Requirement:** Competency in local language required.

TYSON FOODS, INC.
PO Box 2020
Springdale, AR 72764 USA

RECRUITER: KAREN PERCIVAL
COMPENSATION/HRIS
PO BOX 2020
SPRINGDALE, AK 72764
TEL: (501) 756-4000
FAX: (501) 290-7903
FREE: (800) 643-3410

Leland E. Tollett, President. Poultry-based food products. Tyson Foods, Inc. began as a private company and was incorporated in 1947 as Tyson Feed & Hatchery. In 1963, the company went public and adopted its present name. It is the largest poultry-based food products company in the world today. It has operations in 13 states and products are marketed and sold on a worldwide basis. Worldwide revenues for 1992: $4.3 billion.

- **Total Employees:** 50,000

- **U.S. Employees Abroad:** 4

- **Countries:** Mexico, Hong Kong.

- **Job Categories:** Management, Marketing—Food/Food Services, Sales—Food/Food Services.

- **General Requirements:** Usually must be a current employee of the company in order to qualify for overseas assignment.

- **Language Requirement:** Varies with each posting.

- **Comments:** The number of Americans reported working abroad varies greatly from quarter to quarter, fluctuating with the number and scope of projects under contract at the time.

UAL CORPORATION

PO Box 66100
Chicago, IL 60666 USA

RECRUITER: DAN GRENIER
DIRECTOR, INTERNATIONAL HUMAN
    RESOURCES
PO BOX 66100
CHICAGO, IL 60666
TEL: (708) 952-4000
FAX: (708) 952-7345

Stephen M. Wolf, President and Chairman. Global air passenger service. UAL is a public company founded in 1929 as United Aircraft and Transport and renamed United Airlines in 1931. This company was one of the first to offer coast-to-coast service from New York to San Francisco. Today, it serves 162 airports throughout the world. Its international network continues to grow with 27 percent of 1991 sales due to its strength in the Pacific region. Worldwide revenues for 1992: $12.9 billion.

- **Total Employees:** 81,242

- **U.S. Employees Abroad:** 75

- **Countries:** Worldwide including Australia, Japan, Mexico, United Kingdom.

- **Job Categories:** Airline Workers, Airport Management, Computer Programmers, Marketing—Travel, Technicians.

- **General Requirements:** Usually must be a current employee of the company in order to qualify for overseas assignment.

- **Language Requirement:** None.

UNILEVER UNITED STATES, INC.

Lever House
390 Park Ave.
New York, NY 10022 USA

RECRUITER: JAMES A. CURRY
HUMAN RESOURCES
LEVER HOUSE, 390 PARK AVE.
NEW YORK, NY 10022
TEL: (212) 418-8828
FAX: (212) 318-3700

Richard A. Goldstein, Chief Executive Officer. Cosmetics and consumer products. Unilever United States is a subsidiary of London based firm, Unilever-U.V., Rotterdam & Unilever PLC London.

- **Total Employees:** 30,000

- **U.S. Employees Abroad:** 60

- **Countries:** Australia, Argentina, Brazil, Japan, Mexico, United Kingdom.

- **Job Categories:** Management, Marketing—Consumer Goods.

- **Language Requirement:** None.

UNION CAMP CORPORATION

1600 Valley Rd.
Wayne, NJ 07470 USA

RECRUITER: GARY SCOTT
PERSONNEL SUPERVISOR
1600 VALLEY RD.
WAYNE, NJ 07470
TEL: (201) 628-2000
FAX: (201) 628-2592

Raymond E. Cartledge, Chairman. Chemicals, paper; wood and land resources. Union Camp Corporation is a public company founded in 1956. It has five main divisions: paper and paperboard, packaging production, chemicals production, building products production, and wood and land resources. Major products include kraft paper, corrugated containers, high performance polyamide resins and resinates, aroma chemicals, and plywood. Worldwide revenues for 1992: $3.1 billion.

- **Total Employees:** 16,646
- **U.S. Employees Abroad:** 40
- **Countries:** Canada, France, Germany, Hong Kong, Jamaica, Japan, Philippines, Singapore, Republic of South Africa, United Kingdom.
- **Job Categories:** Management, Marketing—Chemicals, Marketing, Sales—Chemicals, Sales.
- **General Requirements:** Usually must be a current employee of the company in order to qualify for overseas assignment.
- **Language Requirement:** Varies with each posting.

UNION CARBIDE CORPORATION

39 Old Ridgebury Rd.
Danbury, CT 06817 USA

RECRUITER: MALCOLM A. KESSINGER
VP, HUMAN RESOURCES
39 OLD RIDGEBURY RD.
DANBURY, CT 06817
TEL: (203) 794-2000
FAX: (203) 794-4336

Robert D. Kennedy, Chairman. Chemicals. Union Carbide Corporation is a public company founded in 1886 as the National Carbon Company. Major changes have occurred in the past 10 years leading to a smaller, more focused organization. Today, its major product is chemicals and it is the world's leading producer of ethylene glycol (antifreeze). It is also the number one U.S. supplier of solvents to industrial customers. It currently operates 50 facilities and laboratories in 17 countries. Worldwide revenues for 1992:$ 4.9 billion.

- **Total Employees:** 16,705
- **U.S. Employees Abroad:** 40
- **Countries:** Argentina, Canada, France, Germany, Indonesia, Taiwan, United Kingdom.
- **Job Categories:** Management, Marketing—Chemicals, Sales—Chemicals.
- **Language Requirement:** None.

UNISYS CORPORATION

PO Box 500
Blue Bell, PA 19424 USA

RECRUITER: RICHARD LORANGER
VP, HUMAN RESOURCES
PO BOX 500
BLUE BELL, PA 19424
TEL: (215) 542-4011
FAX: (215) 986-6850

James A. Unruh, Chairman. Computers. Unisys Corporation is a public company founded in 1986. It is a major systems integrator and producer of on-line transaction-processing systems. Unisys markets mainframes, peripherals, and related products to transaction-intensive businesses. These include airlines, banks, and government agencies. Currently, it has 90 facilities in the United States and 53 in foreign countries. Worldwide revenues for 1992: $8.4 billion.

- **Total Employees:** 60,300

- **U.S. Employees Abroad:** 75

- **Countries:** Worldwide including Argentina, Australia, France, Germany, Hong Kong, Italy, Japan, Republic of Korea, Netherlands, Singapore, United Kingdom, Venezuela.

- **Job Categories:** Executive Management, Marketing—Electronics, Product Development, Sales—Electronics.

- **Language Requirement:** Varies with each posting.

UNITED ENGINEERS & CONSTRUCTORS INTERNATIONAL

30 South 17th St.
Philadelphia, PA 19101 USA

RECRUITER: BARRY MABRY
SENIOR PERSONNEL
    REPRESENTATIVE
30 SOUTH 17TH ST.
PHILADELPHIA, PA 19101
TEL: (215) 422-4156
FAX: (215) 422-4684

Charles Miller, President. General contractors. United Engineers and Constructors International is a public company founded in 1928. It offers a diversified number of services which include energy, construction, maintenance, power, nuclear process, biotech, pharmaceutical, mining, steel, government, remediation, environmental. It operates throughout the United States and abroad. Worldwide operating revenues for 1991: $610 million.

- **Total Employees:** 5,100

- **U.S. Employees Abroad:** 200

- **Countries:** Canada, Mexico, Saudi Arabia, United Kingdom.

- **Job Categories:** Administrative, Construction Workers, Estimators, Field Engineers, Maintenance, Management, Technical Field Support.

- **General Requirements:** Degree preferred for upper-management; must have experience in overseas, direct hire, firm price, process/nuclear maintenance, and subcontract areas.

- **Average Overseas Assignment:** Less than two years.
- **Language Requirement:** Fluency in local language preferred.
- **Training:** Basic orientation (1-30 days) and training in specific work skills provided.
- **Benefits:** TRAVEL: Varies with each posting; usually, policy allows for periodic home leave or R & R. HEALTH: Same coverage as U.S. employees. HOUSING: Offered; or allowance made. EDUCATION: Offered; varies with each posting.

UNITED PARCEL SERVICE OF AMERICA, INC.

400 Perimeter Center
Terraces North
Atlanta, GA 30346 USA

RECRUITER: ROSA GILBERT
CORPORATE EMPLOYMENT
400 PERIMETER CENTER
TERRACES NORTH
ATLANTA, GA 30346
TEL: (404) 913-7123
FAX: (404) 913-6593

Kent C. Nelson, President and Chairman. Global package delivery service. United Parcel Service of America, Inc. is a private company founded as the Merchants Parcel Delivery Service in 1913. Today, it is the world's largest package delivery service and a key competitor in the air express market. It also delivers perishables in refrigerated rail containers. Overseas expansion continues to be profitable including the recent acquisition of Prost Transports in France (1991), Beemsterboer in the Netherlands (1992), and Star Air Parcel in Austria (1992). Worldwide revenues for 1991: $15 billion.

- **Total Employees:** 256,000
- **U.S. Employees Abroad:** 125
- **Countries:** Worldwide including Austria, Canada, France, Germany, Netherlands, Singapore.
- **Job Categories:** Finance, Management, Marketing, Sales.
- **Language Requirement:** Knowledge of local language a plus but not essential.

UNITED PRESS INTERNATIONAL

1400 Eye St. NW
Washington, DC 20005 USA

RECRUITER: STEVE GEIMANN
EXECUTIVE EDITOR/EXECUTIVE VP
1400 EYE ST. NW
WASHINGTON, DC 20005
TEL: (202) 898-8000
FAX: (202) 842-3625

Robert D. Kennedy, Chief Executive Officer. International news agency offering text, audio, and photo services. United Press International was founded in 1907 and is a subsidiary of Middle Eastern Broadcasting Company (MBC).

- **Total Employees:** 450
- **U.S. Employees Abroad:** 29
- **Countries:** Argentina, Australia, Brazil, Canada, Mexico, United Kingdom.
- **Salaries:** $500 per month–$30,000 per year depending on job responsibilities.
- **Job Categories:** Editors, Photographers, Reporters.
- **Average Overseas Assignment:** 3-5 years.
- **Language Requirement:** Varies with each posting; competency in local language required.
- **Training:** No special training provided.
- **Benefits:** TRAVEL: Offered; one return trip to United States or preferred destination per year. HEALTH: Offered. HOUSING: Varies with each posting; usually not offered. EDUCATION: Not offered.

U.S. ELECTRICAL MOTORS (EMERSON ELECTRIC)

8100 Florissant
PO Box 3946
Saint Louis, MO 63136 USA

RECRUITER: LINDA WILCOX
STAFFING/RECRUITMENT
8100 FLORISSANT, BLDG. L
PO BOX 3946
SAINT LOUIS, MO 63136
TEL: (314) 553-1125
FAX: (314) 553-2135

David Wathen, President. Electric motors and components. U.S. Electrical Motors is a division of Emerson Electric Company of St. Louis, Missouri. It manufactures electrical motors, components, and related items in the United States and abroad.

- **Total Employees:** 1,100
- **U.S. Employees Abroad:** 20
- **Countries:** Canada, Japan, Mexico, Philippines, United Kingdom.
- **Job Categories:** Management, Marketing—Electronics, Sales—Electronics.
- **Language Requirement:** Varies with each posting.

UNITED STATES SHOE CORPORATION

1 Eastwood Dr.
Cincinnati, OH 45227-1197 USA

RECRUITER: JIM CUNNINGHAM
SENIOR PERSONNEL OFFICER
1 EASTWOOD DR.
CINCINNATI, OH 45227-1197
TEL: (513) 527-7000
FAX: (513) 527-4052

Philip G. Barach, Chairman. Women's apparel stores and footwear. United States Shoe Corporation is a public company incorporated in 1923 to join the businesses of five smaller shoe manufacturers. Today, shoes account for only 27 percent of sales for U.S. Shoe Corporation. Other operations are women's apparel and the optical group. Well-known brand names include Capezio shoes and LensCrafter eyewear. Worldwide revenues for 1992: $2.6 billion.

- **Total Employees:** 41,000
- **U.S. Employees Abroad:** 25
- **Countries:** Canada, United Kingdom.
- **Job Categories:** Management, Marketing—Consumer Goods, Sales—Consumer Goods.
- **General Requirements:** Usually must be a current employee of the company in order to qualify for overseas assignment.
- **Language Requirement:** None.
- **Training:** No special training provided.

UNITED STATES SURGICAL CORPORATION

150 Glover Ave.
Norwalk, CT 06856 USA

RECRUITER: BILL MACDOUGALL
RECRUITMENT
150 GLOVER AVE.
NORWALK, CT 06856
TEL: (203) 845-1000
FAX: (203) 845-4125

Leon C. Hirsch, President and Chairman. Surgical products. United States Surgical Corporation is a public company founded in 1960. It has developed endoscopy instrumentation and other advanced sutures and markets its products directly to hospitals throughout the United States and 11 foreign countries. Worldwide revenues for 1992: $1.2 billion.

- **Total Employees:** 3,300
- **U.S. Employees Abroad:** 35
- **Countries:** France, Japan, United Kingdom.
- **Job Categories:** Administrative, Marketing—Health & Medical Supplies, Sales—Health & Medical Supplies.
- **Language Requirement:** None.

U.S. WHEAT ASSOCIATES

1620 Eye St. NW, Suite #801
Washington, DC 20006 USA

RECRUITER: KEVIN MCGARY
PRESIDENT
1620 EYE ST., SUITE #801
WASHINGTON, DC 20006
TEL: (202) 463-0999
FAX: (202) 785-1052

Winston Wilson, President. Market development for wheat products. U.S. Wheat Associates was incorporated on January 22, 1980. It develops markets for wheat products in the United States and abroad.

- **Total Employees:** 500

- **U.S. Employees Abroad:** 15

- **Countries:** Chile, Guatemala, India, Japan, Republic of Korea, Netherlands, Philippines, Taiwan.

- **Application Information:** Most overseas positions are filled with candidates from the U.S Department of Agriculture.

- **Job Categories:** Management, Marketing—Agricultural.

- **General Requirements:** Must have a degree or specific background in the field of agriculture.

- **Language Requirement:** Varies with each posting.

UNITED TECHNOLOGIES CORPORATION

One Financial Plaza
Hartford, CT 06101 USA

RECRUITER: PRATT & WHITNEY,
PERSONNEL DEPARTMENT
400 MAIN ST.
EAST HARTFORD, CT 06108
TEL: (203) 565-4321
FAX: (203) 565-0645

George David, President. Aerospace. United Technologies Corporation (UT) is a public company formed into a conglomerate in 1975. It originally began in 1925 when Frederick Rentschler and George Mead founded Pratt & Whitney Aircraft in Hartford, Connecticut. Mergers and acquisitions throughout the years led to changes and, today, UT is the second largest aerospace company in the United States. Other business sectors include Otis Elevator Company and Carrier Corp. (see separate entries). Worldwide revenues for 1992: $22 billion.

- **Total Employees:** 185,100

- **U.S. Employees Abroad:** 125

- **Countries:** Worldwide including Argentina, France, Germany, Italy, Japan, Netherlands, Singapore, Switzerland, United Kingdom, Venezuela.

- **Application Information:** Do not call.

- **Job Categories:** Engineers, Management, Marketing, Sales.

- **General Requirements:** Usually must be a current employee of the company in order to qualify for overseas assignment.

- **Language Requirement:** Varies with each posting.

UNIVERSAL FOODS CORPORATION

PO Box 25099
Richmond, VA 23260 USA

RECRUITER: KATHY DEUBIG
CORPORATE PERSONNEL
PO BOX 25099
RICHMOND, VA 23260
TEL: (804) 359-9311
FAX: (804) 254-3584

Henry H. Harrell, Chairman. Tobacco, agricultural products, and lumber. Universal Foods Corporation is a public company founded in 1918 as the Universal Leaf Company. Today, it is the world's largest tobacco dealer which buys and processes leaf tobacco for its sale to other tobacco product companies. Additional operations include agricultural products and building materials. Currently, it has tobacco operations in 28 countries. Worldwide revenues for 1992: $3.1 billion.

- **Total Employees:** 25,000
- **U.S. Employees Abroad:** 40
- **Countries:** Brazil, Canada, Guatemala, Germany, Netherlands.
- **Job Categories:** Executive Management, Marketing—Agricultural, Marketing, Sales—Agricultural, Sales.
- **General Requirements:** Usually must be a current employee of the company in order to qualify for overseas assignment.
- **Language Requirement:** Varies with each posting.

UNOCAL CORPORATION

1201 West 5th St.
Los Angeles, CA 90017 USA

RECRUITER: ELAINE PATTERSON
MANAGER, INTERNATIONAL HUMAN
RESOURCES
1201 WEST 5TH ST.
LOS ANGELES, CA 90017
TEL: (213) 977-7600
FAX: (213) 977-5362

Richard J. Stegemeier, President and Chairman. Petroleum. Unocal Corporation is a public company founded in 1890 when Lyman Stewart and Wallace Hardison joined together three oil companies in Southern California. The company was named Union Oil of California. It produced the West's first petroleum laboratory by 1901. Today, Unocal is the 11th largest petroleum company in the United States and the world's largest producer of geothermal energy. Production facilities are located in the United States and six foreign countries. Worldwide revenues for 1992: $8.9 billion.

- **Total Employees:** 17,500
- **U.S. Employees Abroad:** Not available.
- **Countries:** Indonesia, Netherlands, Thailand, United Kingdom, Venezuela.
- **Application Information:** Most overseas positions are filled internally.

- **Job Categories:** Chemical Engineers, Management, Marketing—Petroleum/Natural Gas.

- **Language Requirement:** None.

UNUM CORPORATION

2211 Congress St.
Portland, ME 04122 USA

RECRUITER: PETER MCDONALD
MANAGER, EMPLOYMENT
2211 CONGRESS ST.
PORTLAND, ME 04122
TEL: (207) 770-2211
FAX: (207) 770-3266

James F. Orr, III, Chairman. Life insurance. UNUM Corporation is a public company providing life insurance to clients in the United States and abroad. It is a major disability insurer in the United States and United Kingdom. Worldwide assets for 1992: $11.2 billion.

- **Total Employees:** 4,000

- **U.S. Employees Abroad:** 25

- **Countries:** Canada, United Kingdom.

- **Job Categories:** Agents—Insurance, Brokers—Securities & Financial, Marketing—Financial Services.

- **Language Requirement:** None.

UOP, INC.

25 East Algonquin Rd.
Des Plaines, IL 60017 USA

RECRUITER: ROGER ELLIOT
EMPLOYMENT MANAGER
25 EAST ALGONQUIN RD.
DES PLAINES, IL 60017
TEL: (708) 391-2000
FAX: (708) 391-2921

Jack F. Pittas, President. Industrial and inorganic chemicals. UOP, Inc. is a joint venture founded in 1914. It is engaged as a manufacturer of miscellaneous industrial and inorganic chemicals and catalysts. It is also a provider of engineering services in the United States and abroad. Worldwide revenues for 1991: $890 million.

- **Total Employees:** 3,600

- **U.S. Employees Abroad:** 50

- **Countries:** Argentina, Australia, Canada, Colombia, France, Germany, Hong Kong, Japan, Sweden, United Kingdom.

- **Job Categories:** Management, Marketing—Chemicals, Sales—Chemicals.

- **Language Requirement:** Varies with each posting.

THE UPJOHN COMPANY

7000 Portage Rd.
Kalamazoo, MI 49001 USA

RECRUITER: RICHARD G. TOMLINSON
SENIOR VP, HUMAN RESOURCES
7000 PORTAGE RD.
KALAMAZOO, MI 49001
TEL: (616) 323-4000
FAX: (616) 323-7034

Theodore Cooper, Chairman. Pharmaceuticals, animal health products, and chemicals. Upjohn is a public company founded in 1886 by Dr. William Upjohn and his brothers in Kalamazoo, Michigan. It was first called the Upjohn Pill and Granule Company. Two important products introduced in the early 1900s were antimalarial quinine, and the phenolax wafer laxative. The company's present name was adopted in 1902. Today, its well-known products include Motrin (pain reliever) and Rogaine (treatment for baldness) and it has research facilities in more than 200 countries. Worldwide revenues for 1992: $3.7 billion.

- **Total Employees:** 19,193

- **U.S. Employees Abroad:** 50

- **Countries:** Worldwide including Argentina, Australia, Brazil, Canada, Chile, France, Germany, Japan, Netherlands, Panama, Philippines, Taiwan, United Kingdom.

- **Job Categories:** Management, Marketing—Chemicals, Marketing—Pharmaceuticals, Research & Development, Sales—Chemicals, Sales—Pharmaceuticals.

- **Language Requirement:** Varies with each posting.

US WEST, INC.

9785 Maroon Circle
Englewood, CO 80112 USA

RECRUITER: BETH MOISE
EXECUTIVE DIRECTOR, ORG.
    DEVELOPMENT
9785 MAROON CIRCLE, SUITE #210
ENGLEWOOD, CO 80112
TEL: (303) 649-4600
FAX: (303) 793-6654

Richard D. McCormick, President and Chairman. Telecommunication services. US West, Inc. is a public company incorporated in 1983 as one of seven regional operating companies when AT&T was split. It is the fourth largest provider of local telephone service in the United States and has various business interests in several foreign countries. It has joint ventures in cable TV franchises throughout Europe and has cellular systems in Hungary, Moscow, and St. Petersburg. It is also a partner in development for future mobile communications in the United Kingdom. Worldwide revenues for 1992: $10.3 billion.

- **Total Employees:** 65,825

- **U.S. Employees Abroad:** 70

- **Countries:** Czech Republic, France, Hungary, Japan, Norway, Russia, Sweden, United Kingdom.

- **Job Categories:** Management, Marketing—Telecommunications, Sales—Telecommunications.

- **General Requirements:** Telecommunications knowledge preferred.

USAIR GROUP, INC.

2345 Crystal Dr.
Arlington, VA 22227 USA

RECRUITER: KATHRYN BROWN
DIRECTOR, REGIONAL EMPLOYMENT
2345 CRYSTAL DR.
ARLINGTON, VA 22227
TEL: (703) 418-5305
FAX: (703) 418-5307

Seth E. Schofield, President and Chairman. Airline services. USAir Group, Inc. is a public company founded in 1937 by pilot, Richard duPont. It was first called All American Aviation and it provided airmail service for northeastern communities. Passenger service began in 1949 after Edwin Colodny became the chairman. He renamed the company USAir in 1979. Today, it is the world's eighth largest airline, according to revenue passenger miles. It currently operates in 168 cities throughout the United States and abroad. Worldwide revenues for 1992: $6.7 billion.

- **Total Employees:** 48,700
- **U.S. Employees Abroad:** 55
- **Countries:** Bahamas, Bermuda, France, Germany, United Kingdom.
- **Job Categories:** Airline Workers, Management, Sales—Travel.
- **Language Requirement:** Varies with each posting.

USX CORPORATION

600 Grant St.
Pittsburgh, PA 15219-4776 USA

RECRUITER: DIRECTOR, CORPORATE
EMPLOYMENT
600 GRANT ST.
PITTSBURGH, PA 15219-4776
TEL: (412) 391-8115
FAX: (412) 391-7519

Charles A. Corry, Chairman. Petroleum refiner and steelmaker. USX Corporation is a public company founded in 1901 by financier J. P. Morgan. It has two major divisions: USX-Marathon Group (petroleum refiner) and USX-U.S. Steel Group. Marathon Oil is the eighth largest petroleum refiner in the United States. It explores, produces, refines, and markets oil and natural gas on a global basis. USX-U.S. Steel has manufacturing operations and also joint ventures in steelmaking, some with foreign competitors. Worldwide revenues for 1992: $17.2 billion.

- **Total Employees:** 42,552

- **U.S. Employees Abroad:** 75
- **Countries:** Australia, Egypt, Indonesia, Norway, Tunisia, United Kingdom.
- **Application Information:** Most overseas positions are filled internally.
- **Job Categories:** Engineers, Marketing, Marketing—Petroleum/Natural Gas, Sales, Sales—Petroleum/Natural Gas, Technical Field Support.
- **Language Requirement:** Varies with each posting.

VF CORPORATION
PO Box 1022
Reading, PA 19603 USA

RECRUITER: FRANK URBAN
VP, FINANCE & ADMINISTRATION
PO BOX 1022
READING, PA 19603
TEL: (215) 378-5511
FAX: (215) 371-0749

Lawrence R. Pugh, Chairman. Apparel. VF Corporation is a public company founded in 1899. It is a producer of jeanswear, sports and activewear, intimate clothing, and occupational apparel. Brand names include Jantzen, Lee, Vanity Fair, and Wrangler. Worldwide revenues for 1992: $3.8 billion.

- **Total Employees:** 50,000
- **U.S. Employees Abroad:** 15
- **Countries:** Australia, Belgium, Costa Rica, Finland, France, Germany, Hong Kong, Hungary, Malaysia, Mexico, Netherlands, Philippines, Poland, Spain, United Kingdom.
- **Job Categories:** Management, Marketing—Consumer Goods, Sales—Consumer Goods.
- **Language Requirement:** Varies with each posting.
- **Comments:** The number of Americans reported working abroad varies greatly from quarter to quarter, fluctuating with the number and scope of projects under contract at the time.

VISA INTERNATIONAL
3155 Clearview Way
San Mateo, CA 94402 USA

RECRUITER: FRAN YATES
EMPLOYMENT DIRECTOR
3155 CLEARVIEW WAY
SAN MATEO, CA 94402
TEL: (415) 570-3200
FAX: (415) 570-3273

Charles Russell, Chief Executive Officer, International. Electronic payment and transaction company. VISA International is a private company founded in 1977. Major products and services include VISA Classic trade name, VISA ATM Network trade name, and VISA Traveler's Cheques trade name.

- **Total Employees:** 1,700

- **U.S. Employees Abroad:** 25
- **Countries:** Worldwide including France, Japan, United Kingdom.
- **Job Categories:** Finance, Management, Marketing—Financial Services.
- **General Requirements:** Usually must be a current employee of the company in order to qualify for overseas assignment.
- **Language Requirement:** Varies with each posting.

VISHAY INTERTECHNOLOGY

63 Lincoln Hwy.
Malvern, PA 19355-2120 USA

RECRUITER: WILLIAM J. SPIRES
VP, HUMAN RESOURCES
63 LINCOLN HWY.
MALVERN, PA 19355-2120
TEL: (215) 644-1300
FAX: (215) 296-0657

Dr. Felix Zandman, President and Chairman. Electronic components. Vishay Intertechnology is a public company founded in 1962 by Dr. Felix Zandman and Alfred P. Slaner. As an electronics components manufacturer, it is the largest individual supplier of fixed resistors in the United States and Western European markets. Products are sold to various industries. These include the automobile, consumer electronic goods, medical equipment, and telecommunications markets. Worldwide revenues for 1991: $442.3 million.

- **Total Employees:** 11,500
- **U.S. Employees Abroad:** 35
- **Countries:** Canada, France, Germany, Israel, Japan, Republic of Korea, United Kingdom.
- **Job Categories:** Management, Marketing—Electronics, Marketing, Sales—Electronics, Sales.
- **Language Requirement:** Varies with each posting.

VTN CORPORATION

500 South Main St., Suite #1123
Orange, CA 92668 USA

RECRUITER: HOWARD ELLIOT
STAFFING/RECRUITMENT
500 SOUTH MAIN ST., SUITE #1123
ORANGE, CA 92668
TEL: (714) 547-4100

John M. Leach, President. Engineering and architectural services. VTN is a private company of achitects, engineers, and environmental consultants providing services for clients on a global basis.

- **Total Employees:** 460
- **U.S. Employees Abroad:** Not available.
- **Countries:** Kuwait, Saudi Arabia.

- **Job Categories:** Architects, Engineers, Management.
- **Language Requirement:** None.

WALKER MANUFACTURING COMPANY

1201 Michigan Blvd.
Racine, WI 53402 USA

RECRUITER: KARA MCCLURE
VP, HUMAN RESOURCES
1201 MICHIGAN BLVD.
RACINE, WI 53402
TEL: (414) 632-8871
FAX: (414) 631-6355

Richard A. Snell, General Manager. Automotive parts manufacturing. Walker Manufacturing was founded in 1888 and is a subsidiary of Tenneco, Inc. of Houston, Texas. It is a manufacturer of automotive parts, exhaust systems, and service equipment. Worldwide revenues for 1991: $851.3 million.

- **Total Employees:** 6,063
- **U.S. Employees Abroad:** 25
- **Countries:** Canada, France, Germany, Netherlands, Sweden, United Kingdom.
- **Job Categories:** Management, Marketing—Automotive, Sales—Automotive.
- **Language Requirement:** None.

WANG LABORATORIES, INC.

1 Industrial Ave.
Lowell, MA 01851 USA

RECRUITER: EDWARD J. DEVIN
SENIOR VP, HUMAN RESOURCES.
1 INDUSTRIAL AVE.
LOWELL, MA 01851
TEL: (508) 967-2277
FAX: (508) 967-7020

Richard W. Miller, Chairman. Computer-based information processing systems. Wang Laboratories, Inc. is a public company founded in 1951. It services customers in over 125 foreign countries as well as the United States. Systems produced include: data, text, image, and voice-processing products and related services. Other areas included are telecommunications and networking projects. Worldwide revenues for 1992: $1.9 billion.

- **Total Employees:** 12,800
- **U.S. Employees Abroad:** 11
- **Countries:** Belgium, Germany, United Kingdom.
- **Application Information:** Hiring for most overseas positions is done at the specific country location.
- **Salaries:** Custom Engineers, $27,000-$41,000 per year; Management, $45,000-$100,000 per year.
- **Job Categories:** Custom Engineers, Management.

- **Average Overseas Assignment:** 2-3 years.
- **Language Requirement:** Knowledge of local language a plus but not essential.
- **Training:** Basic orientation (1-30 days) provided.
- **Benefits:** TRAVEL: Offered; one return trip home per year; bereavement leave available for immediate family members. HEALTH: Same coverage as U.S. employees. HOUSING: Offered; cost-of-living adjustment included. EDUCATION: Offered; if English-speaking schools are not available, private tuition (grades K-12) is paid for.
- **Comments:** The number of Americans reported working abroad varies greatly from quarter to quarter, fluctuating with the number and scope of projects under contract at the time.

WARD HOWELL INTERNATIONAL, INC.

99 Park Ave.
New York, NY 10016 USA

RECRUITER: MICHAEL TAPPAN
VICE CHAIRMAN, INTERNATIONAL
99 PARK AVE.
NEW YORK, NY 10016
TEL: (212) 697-3730
FAX: (212) 697-1398

John Callen, Chief Executive Officer. Executive recruitment. Ward Howell International, Inc. is a private company engaged in executive recruitment and placement on an international basis.

- **Total Employees:** 100
- **U.S. Employees Abroad:** 20
- **Countries:** Australia, Belgium, Germany, Japan, Netherlands.
- **Job Categories:** Management, Marketing.
- **General Requirements:** Usually must be a current employee of the company in order to qualify for overseas assignment.
- **Language Requirement:** Varies with each posting.
- **Training:** No special training offered.

WARNACO, INC.

90 Park Ave.
New York, NY 10018 USA

RECRUITER: DEBBIE MORENO
STAFFING/RECRUITMENT
90 PARK AVE.
NEW YORK, NY 10018
TEL: (212) 661-1300

L. J. Wachner, President. Clothing. Warnaco, Inc. is a private company founded in 1874. It is a manufacturer of boys' and men's shirts and women's brassieres, corsets, and girdles. Worldwide revenues for 1992: $625 million.

- **Total Employees:** 12,700
- **U.S. Employees Abroad:** 25

- **Countries:** Canada, Mexico, United Kingdom.
- **Job Categories:** Management, Marketing—Consumer Goods, Sales—Consumer Goods.
- **General Requirements:** Usually must be a current employee of the company in order to qualify for overseas assignment.
- **Language Requirement:** Varies with each posting.

WARNER BROTHERS INTERNATIONAL

4000 Warner Blvd.
Burbank, CA 91522-0001 USA

RECRUITER: IVAN CHEEAH
VP, INTERNATIONAL ADMINISTRATION
3903 WEST OLIVE
LOS ANGELES, CA 91522
TEL: (814) 954-6009
FAX: (814) 954-6435

Robert Daly, President. Motion pictures, television, and video production. Warner Brothers International is a subsidiary of Warner Brothers, Inc. of Burbank, California. It produces and distributes motion picture films, television, video, and music recordings. Worldwide operating revenues for Warner Brothers, Inc. for 1991: $3.5 billion.

- **Total Employees:** 500
- **U.S. Employees Abroad:** Not available.
- **Countries:** Argentina, France, Germany, Japan, Netherlands, Singapore, Spain, Taiwan, Thailand.
- **Job Categories:** Management, Marketing, Sales.
- **Language Requirement:** Varies with each posting.

WARNER ELECTRIC BRAKE & CLUTCH COMPANY

449 Gardner St.
South Beloit, IL 61080 USA

RECRUITER: TIM SCHIRA
DIRECTOR, HUMAN RESOURCES
449 GARDNER ST.
SOUTH BELOIT, IL 61080
TEL: (815) 389-6611
FAX: (815) 389-2582

Michael Carrigan, Chief Executive Officer. Automotive parts. Warner Electric Brake & Clutch Company is a division of Dana Corporation of Toledo, Ohio. It manufactures and markets automotive and industrial brakes and clutches in the United States and abroad.

- **Total Employees:** 1,900
- **U.S. Employees Abroad:** 25
- **Countries:** Australia, Belgium, France, Germany, Italy, Japan, Sweden, Switzerland.
- **Job Categories:** Management, Marketing—Automotive, Sales—Automotive.
- **Language Requirement:** Varies with each posting.

WARNER-LAMBERT COMPANY

201 Tabor Rd.
Morris Plains, NJ 07950 USA

RECRUITER: COLIN T. WATMOUGH
VICE PRESIDENT, HUMAN
RESOURCES
201 TABOR RD.
MORRIS PLAINS, NJ 07950
TEL: (201) 540-2000

Joseph D. Williams, Chairman. Health-care products, consumer products, pharmaceuticals. Warner-Lambert is a public company founded in 1856 by pharmacist William Warner. The company prospered through the years, and went public in 1950. In 1955, the company assumed its present name after the purchase of Lambert Pharmacal. Many acquisitions occurred through the years and today, Warner-Lambert is best known for over-the-counter health-care products such as Listerine and Rolaids. The company has 75 plants in more than 39 countries. Worldwide revenues for 1992: $5.6 billion.

- **Total Employees:** 33,000
- **U.S. Employees Abroad:** 25
- **Countries:** Australia, Brazil, Canada, People's Republic of China, France, Germany, Hong Kong, Mexico, Venezuela, United Kingdom.
- **Job Categories:** Chemists, Management, Marketing—Consumer Goods, Marketing—Health & Medical Supplies, Marketing—Pharmaceuticals, Product Development, Sales—Consumer Goods, Sales—Health & Medical Supplies, Sales—Pharmaceuticals.

WASHINGTON POST COMPANY

1150 15th St. NW
Washington, DC 20071 USA

RECRUITER: BEVERLY KEIL
VP, HUMAN RESOURCES
1150 15TH ST. NW
WASHINGTON, DC 20071
TEL: (202) 334-6620
FAX: (202) 334-1031

Katharine Graham, Chairman. Communications and media. The Washington Post is a public company founded in 1947. It has interests in international newpaper and magazine publishing, network and cable television stations, newsprint production, and newswire services. Worldwide revenues for 1992: $1.4 billion.

- **Total Employees:** 5,950
- **U.S. Employees Abroad:** 20
- **Countries:** Canada, France, Japan.
- **Application Information:** Hiring for most overseas positions is done at the specific country location.
- **Job Categories:** Management, Marketing—Publishing.
- **General Requirements:** Communications background is preferred.
- **Language Requirement:** Varies with each posting.

- **Training:** Varies with each posting.

WATERS CHROMATOGRAPHY (MILLIPORE)

34 Maple St.
Milford, MA 01757 USA

RECRUITER: STEPHEN MELLOR
STAFFING/RECRUITMENT
34 MAPLE ST.
MILFORD, MA 01757
TEL: (617) 275-9200
FAX: (508) 478-8451

Betsy Dear, Chief Executive Officer. Chromatographic equipment. Waters Chromatography is a division of Millipore Corporation of Bedford, Massachusettes. It is a manufacturer and distributor of liquid chromatographic instruments and related accessories.

- **Total Employees:** 1,700
- **U.S. Employees Abroad:** 25
- **Countries:** Australia, Belgium, Canada, France, Germany, Japan, Netherlands, Singapore, United Kingdom.
- **Job Categories:** Manufacturing, Marketing—Scientific, Sales—Scientific.
- **Language Requirement:** Varies with each posting.

JERVIS B. WEBB COMPANY

34375 West Twelve Mile Rd.
Farmington Hills, MI 48331 USA

RECRUITER: DON SANDUSKY
VP, INTERNATIONAL RECRUITMENT
34375 WEST TWELVE MILE RD.
FARMINGTON HILLS, MI 48331
TEL: (313) 553-1000
FAX: (313) 553-1237

Joseph M. Hammond, Chairman. Conveyers and conveying systems. Jervis B. Webb is a private company founded in 1919. It designs, manufactures, and installs material-handling systems and conveyer systems.

- **Total Employees:** 1,500
- **U.S. Employees Abroad:** Not available.
- **Countries:** France, Taiwan, Venezuela.
- **Job Categories:** Engineers, Fabricators, Management, Sales—Industrial.
- **Average Overseas Assignment:** Less than 2 years.
- **Language Requirement:** Competency in local language required.
- **Training:** Basic orientation (1-30 days) provided.
- **Benefits:** TRAVEL: Individually determined. HEALTH: Individually determined. HOUSING: Individually determined. EDUCATION: None offered.

**WEIGHT WATCHERS
INTERNATIONAL, INC.**

Jericho Atrium
500 N. Broadway
Jericho, NY 11753 USA

RECRUITER: PALMA QUINN
HUMAN RESOURCES
JERICHO ATRIUM
500 NORTH BROADWAY
JERICHO, NY 11753
TEL: (516) 939-0400
FAX: (516) 949-0781

Lelio G. Parducci, President. Weight-loss programs and related products, including foods. Weightwatchers International, Inc. was founded in 1963 and is a subsidiary of H. J. Heinz Company of Pennsylvania. It operates weight-loss programs and produces related items, including foods. Worldwide revenues for 1991: $1.6 billion.

- **Total Employees:** 7,500

- **U.S. Employees Abroad:** 30

- **Countries:** France, Japan, United Kingdom.

- **Job Categories:** Finance, Management, Marketing—Consumer Goods.

- **Language Requirement:** Varies with each posting.

**WENDY'S INTERNATIONAL,
INC.**

4288 West Dublin-Granville Rd.
Dublin, OH 43017-0256 USA

RECRUITER: JAMES STERLING, SR.
SENIOR HUMAN RESOURCES
REPRESENTATIVE
PO BOX 256
DUBLIN, OH 43017-0256
TEL: (614) 764-3100
FAX: (617) 766-3866

James W. Near, President. Operator of fast-serve restaurants. Wendy's International, Inc. is a public company founded in 1968. It operates fast-serve restaurants throughout the United States and in 22 foreign countries. Worldwide revenues for 1993: $1.2 billion.

- **Total Employees:** 115,000

- **U.S. Employees Abroad:** 125

- **Countries:** Worldwide including Hong Kong, Mexico, Japan, Philippines, United Kingdom.

- **Job Categories:** Administrative, Management Training, Marketing—Food/Food Services.

WEST COMPANY, INC.

1041 West Bridge St.
Phoenixville, PA 19460 USA

RECRUITER: ELIZABETH BLIGAN
CORPORATE MANAGER,
RECRUITMENT
1041 WEST BRIDGE ST.
PHOENIXVILLE, PA 19460
TEL: (215) 935-4500

Rene L. Guerster, President. Packaging systems and components. West is a public company founded in 1923. It produces and sells packaging systems and components made from elastomers, glass, metal, and plastic. Products are used for pharmaceuticals, medical devices, personal-care items, food and beverages. Major products include seals and vials, and plastic closures or containers. Worldwide revenues for 1992: $333 million.

- **Total Employees:** 4,977
- **U.S. Employees Abroad:** 30
- **Countries:** Argentina, Australia, Brazil, Colombia, Germany, Italy, Japan, Mexico, Singapore, United Kingdom.
- **Job Categories:** Management, Marketing, Sales.
- **Language Requirement:** Varies with each posting.

WESTINGHOUSE ELECTRIC CORPORATION

Gateway Center
Pittsburgh, PA 15222 USA

RECRUITER: JAN HILDEBRAND
MANAGER, COMPENSATION &
BENEFITS
GATEWAY CENTER
PITTSBURGH, PA 15222
TEL: (412) 642-2437
FAX: (412) 642-3939

Paul E. Lego, Chairman. Defense electronics, electrical products, and financial services. Westinghouse Electric Corporation is a public company founded in 1886 by George Westinghouse in Pittsburgh, Pennsylvania. It was first called Westinghouse Electric, and the first invention involved a method for transmitting electric current over long distances. Then other products were introduced icluding light bulbs and related items. Today, it operates many industries including broadcasting, electrical systems for industry and defense, nuclear power plants, and environmental services. Worldwide revenues for 1992: $8.4 billion.

- **Total Employees:** 113,664
- **U.S. Employees Abroad:** 75
- **Countries:** Worldwide including Argentina, Australia, Canada, Germany, France, Netherlands, Mexico, Singapore, United Kingdom.
- **Application Information:** Hiring for most overseas positions is done at the specific country location.

- **Job Categories:** Management, Marketing—Electronics, Product Development, Sales—Defense Industry, Sales—Electronics.
- **Language Requirement:** Varies with each posting.
- **Training:** Varies with each posting.
- **Benefits:** All benefits are individually determined.

WEYERHAEUSER COMPANY

33663 32nd Dr. South
Tacoma, WA 98477 USA

RECRUITER: EFFENUS HENDERSON
DIRECTOR, INTERNATIONAL
ADMINISTRATION
33663 32ND DR. SOUTH (CH 1M26)
TACOMA, WA 98477
TEL: (206) 924-2345

George H. Weyerhaeuser, Chairman. Forest products, building materials, and related products. Weyerhaeuser is a public company founded in 1900. It manufactures forest products, building materials, and paperboard and has interests in real estate development and financial services. Worldwide revenues for 1992: $9.2 billion.

- **Total Employees:** 45,000
- **U.S. Employees Abroad:** 35
- **Countries:** Australia, Belgium, Canada, Hong Kong, Japan, Switzerland.
- **Job Categories:** Management, Marketing, Sales.
- **Language Requirement:** Varies with each posting.

WHIRLPOOL CORPORATION

2000 M-63
Benton Harbor, MI 49022-2962
USA

RECRUITER: LINDA KRAGER
RECRUITMENT/INTERNATIONAL
2000 M-63
BENTON HARBOUR, MI 49022-2962
TEL: (616) 926-5000
FAX: (616) 926-3568

David R. Whitwam, President and Chairman. Appliances. Whirlpool Corporation is a public company founded in 1929 as the Nineteen Hundred Corporation. At that time it was the largest washing machine concern in the world. The company began to market the machines under the Whirlpool name in 1947 and its current name was adopted in 1950. Today it produces other appliances including air conditioning units, dryers, and refrigerators. It also provides financial services for its distributors, commercial dealers, and retail dealers. Worldwide revenues for 1992: $7.3 billion.

- **Total Employees:** 37,886
- **U.S. Employees Abroad:** 40
- **Countries:** Argentina, Brazil, Canada, India, Italy, Japan, Mexico, Netherlands.

- **Job Categories:** Management, Marketing—Consumer Goods, Sales—Consumer Goods.
- **Language Requirement:** Varies with each posting.

WHITMAN CORPORATION

3501 Algonquin Rd.
Rolling Meadows, IL 60008 USA

RECRUITER: MURIEL RAMSEY
HUMAN RESOURCES
3501 ALGONQUIN RD.
ROLLING MEADOWS, IL 60008
TEL: (708) 818-5000
FAX: (708) 818-5045

Bruce S. Chelberg, Chairman. Consumer goods and services. Whitman Corporation is a public company founded in 1851. It started as the Illinois Central Railroad in 1851. Diversification throughout the years prompted a name change to IC Industries in 1975. By then, various companies were purchased; Pepsi-Cola Bottlers (1970) and Midas auto mufflers (1972). Its current name was adopted in 1988 and was derived from one of its well-known chocolate brands. Today, its three main subsidiaries are Pepsi-Cola Bottlers, Midas, and Hussmann refrigeration equipment. Worldwide revenues for 1992: $2.4 billion.

- **Total Employees:** 14,448
- **U.S. Employees Abroad:** 3,997
- **Countries:** Worldwide including Mexico, United Kingdom.
- **Job Categories:** Management, Manufacturing, Marketing—Consumer Goods, Sales—Consumer Goods.
- **Language Requirement:** Varies with each posting.
- **Benefits:** HOUSING: None offered.

WMX TECHNOLOGIES/WASTE MANAGEMENT, INC.

3003 Butterfield Rd.
Oak Brook, IL 60521 USA

RECRUITER: JAMES FORD
DIRECTOR, HUMAN RESOURCES
3003 BUTTERFIELD RD.
OAK BROOK, IL 60521
TEL: (708) 218-1500
FAX: (708) 571-6655

Dean L. Buntrock, Chairman. Waste management company. WMX Technologies/Waste Management is a public company founded in 1971. Today, it is the largest waste collection, disposal, and recycling company in the world. It has four sectors: Waste Management of North America, Chemical Waste Management, Wheelabrator (environmental services), and Waste Management International. It currently operates in 17 countries as well as the United States. Worldwide revenues for 1991: $7.6 billion. Foreign revenues for 1992: $8.7 billion.

- **Total Employees:** 63,040

- **U.S. Employees Abroad:** 75
- **Countries:** Argentina, Australia, Germany, Italy, Netherlands, United Kingdom.
- **Job Categories:** Engineers, Management, Marketing, Sales.
- **General Requirements:** Usually must be a current employee of the company in order to qualify for overseas assignment.
- **Language Requirement:** Varies with each posting.

WOODWARD GOVERNOR COMPANY

5001 North 2nd St.
Rockford, IL 61125 USA

RECRUITER: TOM PARLETTE
CORPORATE DIRECTOR, MEMBER
RELATIONS
5001 NORTH 2ND ST.
ROCKFORD, IL 61125
TEL: (815) 877-7441
FAX: (815) 877-0001

Calvin C. Covert, Chairman. Relays and industrial controls. Woodward Governor is a public company founded in 1870. It manufactures various industrial control products including turbine engine controls and speed control governors.

- **Total Employees:** 3,317
- **U.S. Employees Abroad:** 22
- **Countries:** Australia, Brazil, Japan, Netherlands, United Kingdom.
- **Job Categories:** Management, Marketing—Industrial, Sales—Industrial.
- **Language Requirement:** Varies with each posting.

WOOLWORTH CORPORATION

233 Broadway
New York, NY 10279 USA

RECRUITER: RAMONA FRAZIER
DIRECTOR, HUMAN RESOURCES
233 BROADWAY
NEW YORK, NY 10279
TEL: (212) 553-2000
FAX: (212) 553-2042

Harold E. Sells, Chairman. Specialty retailing. Woolworth Corporation is a public company founded in Utica, New York in 1879 as The Great Five Cent Store. Though it failed, another attempt was made in New York City in 1886. Dime-store chains were purchased and soon foreign expansion occurred. Today, it is a worldwide leader in specialty retailing with stores selling merchandies including clothing, sporting goods, and accessories. It currently has 6,386 stores in 20 countries. Worldwide revenues for 1992: $9.9 billion.

- **Total Employees:** 144,000
- **U.S. Employees Abroad:** Not available.
- **Countries:** Australia, Canada, Belgium, Italy, Mexico, Netherlands.

- **Application Information:** Overseas postings are administratively autonomous; hiring is done at specific country location.

- **Job Categories:** Management, Marketing—Consumer Goods, Sales—Consumer Goods.

- **Language Requirement:** Varies with each posting.

- **Training:** Varies with each posting.

- **Benefits:** All benefits vary with each posting.

WORLD COURIER MANAGEMENT, INC.

46 Southfield Ave.
Stamford, CT 06902 USA

RECRUITER: MONIQUE JORGO
STAFFING/RECRUITMENT
46 SOUTHFIELD AVE.
STAMFORD, CT 06902
TEL: (203) 975-9333
FAX: (203) 975-9798

Air courier services. World Courier, Management, Inc. is a private company providing air courier and transportation services in the United States and abroad. It currently operates in more than 25 countries.

- **Total Employees:** 1,000

- **U.S. Employees Abroad:** 20

- **Countries:** Argentina, Brazil, France, Germany, Hong Kong, Italy, Japan, Mexico, Netherlands, Singapore, Switzerland, United Kingdom, Venezuela.

- **Application Information:** Hiring for most overseas positions is done at the specific country location.

- **Job Categories:** Management, Marketing.

- **Language Requirement:** Varies with each posting.

- **Training:** Varies with each posting.

WILLIAM WRIGLEY JR. COMPANY

410 North Michigan Ave.
Chicago, IL 60611 USA

RECRUITER: WARREN BARSHES
DIRECTOR, INTERNATIONAL
PERSONNEL
410 NORTH MICHIGAN AVE.
CHICAGO, IL 60611
TEL: (312) 644-2121
FAX: (312) 644-0353

William Wrigley, President. Chewing gum and gum base. William Wrigley Jr. Company was founded in 1898 by William Wrigley, Jr. when he joined with Zeno Manufacturing to form the William Wrigley, Jr. Company. By 1910, Spearmint Gum was a major U.S. brand name and foreign expansion began. Today, Wrigley continues to establish foreign operations and currently it has facilities in more than 25 countries. Worldwide revenues for 1992: $1.3 billion.

- **Total Employees:** 6,250
- **U.S. Employees Abroad:** 15
- **Countries:** Australia, Canada, France, Germany, Hong Kong, Netherlands, New Zealand, Philippines, Singapore, Sweden, Taiwan, United Kingdom.
- **Application Information:** Most overseas positions are filled internally.
- **Job Categories:** Executive Management, Marketing—Food/Food Services, Sales—Food/Food Services.
- **Language Requirement:** None.
- **Comments:** The number of Americans reported working abroad varies greatly from quarter to quarter, fluctuating with the number and scope of projects under contract at the time.

WYETH-AYERST LABORATORIES

PO Box 8299
Philadelphia, PA 19101 USA

RECRUITER: JOHN WOODRUFF
HUMAN RESOURCES ADMINISTRATOR
PO BOX 8299
PHILADELPHIA, PA 19101
TEL: (215) 688-4400
FAX: (215) 688-6228

Fred Hassan, President. Pharmaceutical and biological products. Wyeth-Ayerst Laboratories was founded in 1862 and is a subsidiary of the American Home Products Corporation of New York City. Today, the company focuses heavily on the manufacture and sale of female health-care products and infant nutritional items. It is presently concentrating its product development on contraception and AIDS Research.

- **Total Employees:** 10,000
- **U.S. Employees Abroad:** Not available.
- **Countries:** Argentina, Colombia, France, Italy, Japan, Mexico, Philippines, United Kingdom.
- **Job Categories:** Chemists, Finance, Management, Marketing—Pharmaceuticals, Sales—Pharmaceuticals.

WYNN'S INTERNATIONAL, INC.

500 North State College Blvd.
Orange, CA 92668 USA

RECRUITER: JUDY VESTER
EMPLOYEE BENEFITS/RISK
  MANAGEMENT
500 NORTH STATE COLLEGE BLVD.,
  SUITE #700
ORANGE, CA 92668
TEL: (714) 938-3700

James Carroll, President. Automotive parts and accessories, petrochemical specialty products, and builder's hardware supplies. Wynn's International, Inc. is a public company founded in 1939. It supplies the automotive industry with various products including air conditioners and replacement parts, O-rings and other static and dynamic seals. The Petrochemical Specialties Division produces and markets industrial coolants and specialty fluids. It has operations in the United States and abroad.

- **Total Employees:** 1,979

- **U.S. Employees Abroad:** 25

- **Countries:** Australia, Belgium, Canada, France, Republic of South Africa, United Kingdom.

- **Job Categories:** Management, Marketing—Automotive, Marketing—Chemicals, Marketing—Consumer Goods, Sales—Automotive, Sales—Chemicals, Sales—Consumer Goods.

- **Language Requirement:** None.

XEROX CORPORATION

800 Long Ridge Rd.
PO Box 1600
Stamford, CT 06904 USA

RECRUITER: MARIA GARCIA-KEMP
INTERNATIONAL HUMAN RESOURCES
800 LONG RIDGE RD.
PO BOX 1600
STAMFORD, CT 06094
TEL: (203) 968-3000
FAX: (203) 968-4559

Paul A. Allaire, Chairman. Document processing. Xerox Corporation is a public company founded in 1906. Its products and systems are involved in the development, manufacture, marketing, and servicing of a wide range of document-processing products which make offices more efficient and productive. Major products include copiers and electronic printers and typewriters. Worldwide revenues for 1992: $18.7 billion.

- **Total Employees:** 109,400

- **U.S. Employees Abroad:** 75

- **Countries:** Canada, India, Japan, United Kingdom.

- **Job Categories:** Marketing—Electronics, Sales—Electronics.

- **Language Requirement:** Varies with each posting.

- **Training:** Varies with each posting.

YELLOW FREIGHT SYSTEM, INC.

10900 Roe Ave.
Overland Park, KS 66207 USA

RECRUITER: RALPH NOWELL
DIVISION VICE PRESIDENT
10900 ROE AVE.
PO BOX 7563
OVERLAND PARK, KS 66207
TEL: (914) 345-1020
FAX: (913) 349-3679

George E. Powell, Chairman. Provider of longhaul freight transportation. Yellow Freight System, Inc. is a major division of Yellow Corporation of Overland Park, Kansas. It focuses on longhaul freight transportation and shipment weighing less than 10,000 pounds account for the majority of freight carried. Yellow Corporation was founded by A. J. Harrell in 1924 as the Yellow Transit Company. Today, this corporation has 634 freight terminals throughout the United States, Canada, and Mexico. Worldwide revenues for 1992: $2.3 billion.

- **Total Employees:** 28,700
- **U.S. Employees Abroad:** 35
- **Countries:** Canada, Mexico.
- **Job Categories:** Drivers, Management, Marketing.
- **Language Requirement:** Varies with each posting.
- **Training:** Varies with each posting.

YORK INTERNATIONAL, INC.

PO Box 1592
York, PA 17405-1592 USA

RECRUITER: JEFFREY COOK
VP, INTERNATIONAL
PO BOX 1592
YORK, PA 17405-1592
TEL: (717) 771-7890
FAX: (717) 771-6843

James T. Dresher, Chairman. Air conditioning, refrigeration, and heating equipment. York International, Inc. is a subsidiary of privately held York Holdings Corporation of Pennsylvania. It is engaged as a manufacturer of refrigeration equipment for industrial and commercial use, air conditioning, and warm air furnaces. Worldwide revenues for 1992: $1.9 billion.

- **Total Employees:** 9,000
- **U.S. Employees Abroad:** 30
- **Countries:** Canada, France, Germany, Hong Kong, Malaysia, Mexico, Netherlands, Singapore, Taiwan, United Kingdom.
- **Job Categories:** Management, Marketing, Sales.
- **Language Requirement:** Varies with each posting.

YOUNG & RUBICAM, INC.

285 Madison Ave.
New York, NY 10017 USA

RECRUITER: STEVE MESSANA
DIRECTOR, INTERNATIONAL
    RECRUITMENT
285 MADISON AVE., 19TH FLOOR
NEW YORK, NY 10017
TEL: (212) 210-3000
FAX: (212) 210-5270

Alexander S. Kroll, Chairman. Advertising agency. Young & Rubicam is a private company founded in 1923 by Raymond Rubicam and John Orr Young. Y & R's first large client was General Foods. Today, this international firm is the largest privately held advertising agency in the United States. Accounts include Chevron Oil, Monsanto, and Pepsico. Worldwide billings for 1992: $7.8 billion.

- **Total Employees:** 10,400
- **U.S. Employees Abroad:** 60
- **Countries:** Argentina, Australia, Brazil, Canada, France, Germany, Hong Kong, Italy, Japan, Mexico, Switzerland, United Kingdom.
- **Job Categories:** Management, Marketing, Sales—Advertising.
- **Language Requirement:** None.
- **Training:** No special training provided.

ACADEMY FOR EDUCATIONAL DEVELOPMENT

1255 23rd St. NW
Washington, DC 20037 USA

RECRUITER: SUSAN H. TILSON
EXECUTIVE RECRUITMENT MANAGER
1255 23RD ST. NW
WASHINGTON, DC 20037
TEL: (202) 862-1900
FAX: (202) 862-1947

Stephen F. Mosley, Executive Director. Serves human development needs through education, communication, and information. The Academy for Educational Development is an independent, nonprofit organization which, through contracts and grants, operates programs for government and international agencies, educational institutions, foundations, and corporations.

- **Total Employees:** 350
- **U.S. Employees Abroad:** 60
- **Countries:** Information not available.
- **Salaries:** $30,000-$80,000 per year.
- **Job Categories:** Communications, Human Resources, Marketing, Teachers.
- **General Requirements:** Advanced degrees required; overseas experience preferred.
- **Language Requirement:** Varies with each posting; fluency in local language is usually preferred.
- **Training:** No special training.
- **Benefits:** TRAVEL: Varies with each posting. HEALTH: Full coverage for long-term

employees; consultants provide their own coverage. HOUSING: Varies with each posting. EDUCATION: Varies with each posting.

- **Comments:** In addition to the 60 Americans employed abroad on a long-term basis, an additional 1,000 people are hired for short-term consultant positions.

AGENCY FOR INTERNATIONAL DEVELOPMENT

2401 E St. NW
Washington, DC 20523-0116 USA

RECRUITER: PAMELA WHITE
CHIEF RECRUITER, DIVISION OF A.I.D.
2401 E ST. NW, ROOM #1026 SA-1
WASHINGTON, DC 20523-0116
TEL: (202) 663-2400
FAX: (202) 663-1805

Brian Atwood, Administrator. Federal government international service agency. The Agency for International Development (A.I.D.) helps implement U.S. economic assistance programs in developing countries. Created by Congress in 1961, it is the major U.S. government agency that provides funding and guidance for many public and private sector development efforts in Third and Fourth World countries. It focuses on agriculture, environment, health and nutrition, population planning, and rural development. Its purpose is to help people acquire the knowledge and resources to build the economic, political, and social institutions needed to maintain national development.

- **Total Employees:** 8,120

- **U.S. Employees Abroad:** 1,000

- **Countries:** Operations are in countries in Africa, Asia, the Caribbean, Latin America, and the Near East.

- **Salaries:** $22,948-$52,042 per year.

- **Job Categories:** Administrative, Agricultural Specialists, Economists, Human Resources, Finance, Teachers, Urban Development.

- **General Requirements:** 2-3 years of experience of A.I.D.-relevant work; experience in developing countries; U.S. citizenship.

- **Average Overseas Assignment:** 3-5 years.

- **Language Requirement:** Knowledge of (any) foreign language a plus but not essential.

- **Training:** In-depth orientation (30 days), language training, and training in specific work skills provided.

- **Benefits:** TRAVEL: Offered. HEALTH: Offered. HOUSING: Offered; also cost-of-living allowance included. EDUCATION: Offered.

AMERICAN FRIENDS SERVICE COMMITTEE

1501 Cherry St.
Philadelphia, PA 19102 USA

RECRUITER: RICK BOARDMAN
OVERSEAS RECRUITMENT
1501 CHERRY ST.
PHILADELPHIA, PA 19102
TEL: (215) 241-7102
FAX: (215) 241-7247

Kara Newell, Executive Secretary. Educational, humanitarian, and social change programs. The American Friends Service Committee (AFSC) was founded in 1917, during WWI, to provide conscientious objectors with an opportunity to serve in programs of relief and reconstruction for civilian war victims. Numerous administrative committees oversee various programs and services in the United States and abroad. The AFSC has nine regional offices throughout the United States.

- **Total Employees:** 402
- **U.S. Employees Abroad:** 30
- **Countries:** Information not available.
- **Application Information:** More information concerning financial support may be obtained by contacting the Home Cost Administrator at the recruiter's address.
- **Salaries:** Unsalaried; maintenance and savings are provided instead of salary.
- **Job Categories:** Medical Personnel, Rural Development.
- **Language Requirement:** Knowledge of local language a plus but not (always) essential.
- **Training:** Varies with each posting.
- **Benefits:** TRAVEL: Offered. HEALTH: Offered. HOUSING: Offered; AFSC provides from $5,000-8,000 for ongoing home expenses. EDUCATION: Offered.
- **Comments:** A savings plan offers $250 per month, per appointee, and $50 additional for accompanying dependents.

AMERICAN INSTITUTE FOR FREE LABOR DEVELOPMENT

1015 20th St. NW
Washington, DC 20036 USA

RECRUITER: CHRISTINA KOROLEVICH
RECRUITMENT
1015 20TH ST. NW
WASHINGTON, DC 20036
TEL: (202) 659-6300
FAX: (202) 466-6076

William C. Doherty, Executive Director. Labor studies. American Institute for Free Labor Development is a private organization governed by a board of trustees composed of AFL-CIO officials and is supported by labor institutes and public sources. It holds training programs, supports worker education seminars, and offers material support and technical advice for social development projects initiated by democratic trade unions. Its goal is to strengthen a free society through development of free and democratic trade unions.

- **Total Employees:** 70
- **U.S. Employees Abroad:** Not available.
- **Countries:** Operations are in countries in the Caribbean and Latin America.
- **Job Categories:** Administrative, Technical Field Support.
- **Language Requirement:** Competency in local language required.

AMERICAN RED CROSS

431 18th St. NW
Washington, DC 20006 USA

RECRUITER: MEG RILEY
H. R. ASSOCIATE, INTERNATIONAL
431 18TH ST. NW
WASHINGTON, DC 20006
TEL: (202) 639-3380
FAX: (202) 639-3711

Elizabeth Dole, President. Worldwide relief services. The American Red Cross, founded in 1881, provides preparedness and relief services for people in emergengy and disaster situations. It maintains more than 50 regional blood banks and trains volunteers for community services. It provides services to members of the armed forces, and works with sister Red Cross societies around the world for training and disaster situations. It currently has 1 million volunteers.

- **Total Employees:** 25,394
- **U.S. Employees Abroad:** 250
- **Countries:** Operations are in countries in Africa, Asia, the Caribbean, Europe, Latin America, and the Near East.
- **Job Categories:** Management, Medical Personnel.
- **General Requirements:** Applicant should have a strong medical background for field service positions; 1-2 years experience required.
- **Average Overseas Assignment:** Less than one year.
- **Language Requirement:** Competency in second language required.
- **Benefits:** HEALTH: Offered.

AMIDEAST

1100 17th St. NW, Suite 300
Washington, DC 20036 USA

RECRUITER: DIRECTOR, RECRUITMENT
1100 17TH ST. NW, SUITE #300
WASHINGTON, DC 20036
TEL: (202) 785-0002
FAX: (202) 822-6563

Robert S. Dillon, President. Assists Middle Eastern and North African countries. AMIDEAST (America-Mideast Educational and Training Services, Inc.) is a private nonprofit organization whose goal is to help Middle Eastern and North African countries to understand and utilize American resources so they may achieve their educational and training goals. This is accomplished through educational, informational development, and technical assistant programs. Areas covered include education, health care, and small business development.

- **Total Employees:** 200
- **U.S. Employees Abroad:** 50
- **Countries:** Operations are in countries in the Middle East and North Africa.
- **Job Categories:** Counselors, Teachers.
- **General Requirements:** A college or graduate degree in education, counseling, vocational skills, or Third-World development are preferred. Also, fluency in local language is required.
- **Language Requirement:** Fluency in local language required.

AMNESTY INTERNATIONAL, USA

322 Eighth Ave.
New York, NY 10001 USA

RECRUITER: CONNIE HARSHMAN
PROFESSIONAL RECRUITMENT
322 EIGHTH AVE.
NEW YORK, NY 10001
TEL: (212) 807-8400
FAX: (212) 627-1451

John G. Healey, Executive Director. Human rights organization. Amnesty International works for the release of people who are detained against their will anywhere in the world because of their color, beliefs, ethnic origin, language, religion, or sex.

- **Total Employees:** 100
- **U.S. Employees Abroad:** Not available.
- **Countries:** Operations are in countries in Africa, Asia, the Caribbean, Europe, Latin America, and the Near East.
- **Job Categories:** Health Professionals, Legal Personnel, Teachers.
- **General Requirements:** Degree in related field.
- **Language Requirement:** Competency in local language required.

ASA FOUNDATION

465 California St.
San Francisco, CA 94104 USA

RECRUITER: STAFFING SPECIALIST
465 CALIFORNIA ST., 14TH FLOOR
SAN FRANCISCO, CA 94104
TEL: (415) 982-4640
FAX: (415) 392-8863

William P. Fuller, President. Promotes social and economic development. The ASA Foundation was founded in 1954 and offers assistance to various agencies, governments, organizations, and individuals who help encourage social and economic development in the the following areas: private and voluntary sectors, representative government, public administration and government service, legal systems and human rights, education, management, business, economics, media and communications, international relations, and regional cooperation. One recent project included "Population and Family Planning Services" (Bangladesh, UDAID, $2.3 million).

- **Total Employees:** 225
- **U.S. Employees Abroad:** Not available.
- **Countries:** Operations are in countries in Asia and the Pacific Islands.
- **Job Categories:** Administrative, Technical Field Support, Teachers.
- **General Requirements:** Degree in related field.
- **Language Requirement:** Competency in local language required.
- **Training:** No special training provided.

ASIAN DEVELOPMENT BANK

6 ADB Ave., Mandaluyong
Manila, Philippines USA

RECRUITER: MR. CHARLES F. COE
MANAGER, HUMAN RESOURCES
DIVISION
6 ADB AVE., MANDALUYONG
MANILA, PHILIPPINES
TEL: (63) 2632-4444
FAX: (63) 2632-6816

Kimimasa Tarumizu, President and Chairman. Promotes economic and social progress of developing member countries. The Asian Development Bank is an international development institution owned by its 53 member countries. Objectives of the Bank include many areas that contribute to the economic development of its developing member countries (DMC). Main functions are: (1) to make loans and equity investments for the economic and social development of its DMCs, (2) to provide technical assistance to prepare and execute development projects, programs, and advisory service, (3) to promote investment of public and private capital for development, and (4) to respond to requests for assistance by DMCs in coordinating development plans and policies.

- **Total Employees:** 1,776
- **U.S. Employees Abroad:** 72
- **Countries:** Operations are in countries in Asia and the Pacific Islands.
- **Salaries:** $53,000-$64,000 per year.
- **Job Categories:** Economists, Engineers, Financial Advisors.
- **General Requirements:** Advanced university degree or equivalent, and experience working in an Asian developing country.
- **Average Overseas Assignment:** 3 years.
- **Language Requirement:** Proficiency in the English language is essential; knowledge of local language a plus.
- **Training:** Basic orientation (1-30 days), training in specific work skills, and language training provided.

- **Benefits:** TRAVEL: Offered. HEALTH: Comprehensive health care offered; contact organization for more information. HOUSING: Offered; contact organization for more information. EDUCATION: Education grant offered; contact organization for more information.

BOY SCOUTS OF AMERICA

PO Box 152079
Irving, TX 75015-2079 USA

RECRUITER: LEX JARVIS
PROFESSIONAL RECRUITMENT
PO BOX 152079
IRVING, TX 75015-2079
TEL: (214) 580-2000

Ben H. Love, Chief Scout Executive. Educational programs. Boy Scouts of America was founded in 1910. It conducts educational programs aimed at character development, citizenship training, and mental and physical fitness of boys and young adults. It operates councils, sponsors competitions, and offers camping programs on a global basis.

- **Total Employees:** 3,850
- **U.S. Employees Abroad:** Not available.
- **Countries:** Operations are in countries in Africa, Asia, the Caribbean, Europe, Latin America, and the Near East.
- **Job Categories:** Management, Teachers.
- **Language Requirement:** Varies with each posting.

CARE

660 First Ave.
New York, NY 10016 USA

RECRUITER: PATRICK SHIELDS
MANAGER, RECRUITMENT
660 FIRST AVE.
NEW YORK, NY 10016
TEL: (212) 686-3110
FAX: (212) 686-2467
FREE: (800) ICARE85

Dr. Phil Johnston, President. Private international aid and development. CARE (Cooperative for American Relief Everywhere, Inc.) is a private voluntary organization providing emergency relief for disaster victims. It also sponsors programs to improve education, employment, health, and nutrition of the poor on a worldwide basis.

- **Total Employees:** 8,800
- **U.S. Employees Abroad:** Not available.
- **Countries:** Operations are in countries in Asia, the Caribbean, Latin America, and Africa, including Egypt.
- **Job Categories:** Administrative, Health Professionals, Medical Personnel, Technical Field Support.

- **General Requirements:** Bachelor's degree and international experience or master's degree in an international project area required.
- **Language Requirement:** Competency in local language (French or Spanish) required.

CATHOLIC RELIEF SERVICES

209 West Fayette St.
Baltimore, MD 21201 USA

RECRUITER: MARIE E. WHITE
RECRUITMENT MANAGER
209 WEST FAYETTE ST.
BALTIMORE, MD 21201
TEL: (410) 625-2220
FAX: (410) 685-1635

Lawrence A. Pezzullo, Executive Director. Relief and development. Catholic Relief Services (CRS) is the official overseas development agency of the United States Catholic Conference. It operates relief and self-help development programs in the areas of agriculture, community development, education, health care, housing, and social welfare. It provides food, clothing and other necessities to people in need of relief.

- **Total Employees:** 1,580
- **U.S. Employees Abroad:** Not available.
- **Countries:** Operations are in 68 countries in Africa, Asia, the Caribbean, Europe Latin America, and the Near East.
- **Job Categories:** Administrative, Manufacturing, Teachers.
- **General Requirements:** Degree in related field.
- **Language Requirement:** Competency in local language required.

CHILD REACH INTERNATIONAL

804 Quaker Lane
East Greenwich, RI 02818 USA

RECRUITER: BOB YOUNT
INTERNATIONAL RECRUITMENT
804 QUAKER LANE
EAST GREENWICH, RI 02818
TEL: (401) 826-2500
FAX: (401) 826-2680

Virginia Mason, President. Assists children and their families around the globe. Child Reach International (formerly Foster Parents Plan Inc.) is a private voluntary organization that helps children and their families through health, education, and economic assistance. Major funding is derived from a sponsorship program, USAID, private contributions, and grants.

- **Total Employees:** 5,802.
- **U.S. Employees Abroad:** Not available.
- **Countries:** Operations are in countries in Asia, the Caribbean, Latin America, and Africa, including Egypt.

- **Job Categories:** Administrative, Finance, Management.
- **General Requirements:** A college degree or graduate degree in social sciences is required; also experience in Third World countries is preferred.
- **Language Requirement:** Fluency in at least one foreign language is preferred.

CHRISTIAN BLIND MISSION INTERNATIONAL

450 East Park Ave.
PO Box 19000
Greenville, SC 29601 USA

RECRUITER: DIRECTOR, RECRUITMENT
450 EAST PARK AVE.
GREENVILLE, SC 29601
TEL: (803) 239-0069
FAX: (803) 239-0069

Art Brooker, National Director. Provides medical support to developing countries. Christian Blind Mission International is a private organization founded in 1908. It is a medical mission offering support staffing to medical facilities in developing countries. In projects to date, the Mission has supplied staff to more than 100 hospitals, clinics, and institutions worldwide.

- **Total Employees:** Not available.
- **U.S. Employees Abroad:** 18
- **Countries:** Australia, Austria, Canada, Switzerland.
- **Job Categories:** Administrative, Medical Personnel, Nurses, Ophthalmologists, Physicians, Technical Field Support.
- **General Requirements:** Degree in related field.
- **Language Requirement:** Competency in local language.

CHRISTIAN CHILDREN'S FUND, INC.

PO Box 26484
Richmond, VA 23261-6484 USA

RECRUITER: ELLEN LAMPKIN
MANAGER, HUMAN RESOURCES
PO BOX 26484
RICHMOND, VA 23261-6484
TEL: (804) 756-2700
FAX: (804) 756-2718

Dr. Paul McCleary, Executive Director. Provides technical assistance and monthly support for children in need throughout the world. Christian Children's Fund is a private voluntary organization founded in 1938 that provides support through individual sponsors on a monthly basis for needy children. It offers assistance to more than 500,000 children in 28 developing countries, with a strong focus on community development, disaster relief, family planning, health, and nutritional training. Major funding comes from sponsorships, private donations, and grants.

- **Total Employees:** 560
- **U.S. Employees Abroad:** Not available.

A
M
E
R
I
C
A
N

J
O
B
S

A
B
R
O
A
D

- **Countries:** Operations are in countries in Africa, Asia, the Caribbean, and Latin America.

- **Job Categories:** Administrative, Family Planning Specialists.

- **Language Requirement:** Fluency in at least one foreign language (French, German, or Spanish) is preferred.

- **Training:** Contact organization for more information.

CHURCH WORLD SERVICE & WITNESS

475 Riverside Dr.
New York, NY 10115 USA

RECRUITER: PAUL YOUNT
INTERNATIONAL RECRUITMENT
475 RIVERSIDE DR., ROOM #668
NEW YORK, NY 10015
TEL: (212) 870-2061
FAX: (212) 870-2055

Lani Havens, Executive Director. Provides disaster relief, education, and other assistance to communities throughout the world. Church World Service & Witness is a private voluntary organization founded in 1947. It provides aid in the form of disaster relief, rehabilitation, agriculture, health, education, family planning, housing, social welfare, and community development. Major funding is derived from USAID, CARE, United Nations agencies, private foundations, and contributions.

- **Total Employees:** 200

- **U.S. Employees Abroad:** 55

- **Countries:** Operations are in countries in Africa, Asia, and Latin America.

- **Salaries:** $25,000-$29,000 per year.

- **Job Categories:** Development Specialists, Teachers, Technical Field Support.

- **General Requirements:** Having a church relationship is a plus, and/or experience in teaching; experience in development technology and management are preferred.

- **Average Overseas Assignment:** 2-3 years.

- **Language Requirement:** Varies with each posting; usually competency in local language is required.

- **Training:** Basic training (1-30 days) provided; in some cases language training provided.

- **Benefits:** TRAVEL: After two years of service, eight weeks home leave is offered. HEALTH: Comprehensive medical coverage provided; staff pays for one-third of premium. Also, reimbursement for all other expenses included. HOUSING: Housing and utilities are provided. EDUCATION: Not offered.

CONSERVATION INTERNATIONAL

1015 18th St. NW
Washington, DC 20036 USA

RECRUITER: JEFFREY MOSSER
HUMAN RESOURCES ADMINISTRATOR
1015 18TH ST. NW, SUITE #1000
WASHINGTON, DC 20036
TEL: (202) 429-5660
FAX: (202) 887-5188

Peter Seligmann, Chairman. Environmental protection and conservation. Conservation International is a private organizaton dedicated to the protection of natural ecosystems and the species that rely on these habitats for survival.

- **Total Employees:** 175
- **U.S. Employees Abroad:** 100
- **Countries:** Bolivia, Brazil, Botswana, Ecuador, Ghana, Guatemala, Madagascar, Mexico, Peru, Philippines.
- **Job Categories:** Anthropologists, Biologists, Conservation Specialists.
- **Average Overseas Assignment:** 2-3 years.
- **Language Requirement:** Fluency in local language required.
- **Training:** No special training provided.
- **Benefits:** TRAVEL: Varies with each posting. HEALTH: Usually overseas employees are hired by contract and obtain their own insurance. HOUSING: Varies with each posting. EDUCATION: Varies with each posting.

DEPARTMENT OF DEFENSE DEPENDENTS SCHOOLS

4040 N. Fairfax Dr.
Arlington, VA 22203-1634 USA

RECRUITER: CHERYL VINCI
CHIEF OF SERVICES, RECRUITMENT
4040 NORTH FAIRFAX DR.
ARLINGTON, VA 22203-1634
TEL: (703) 696-3068

Secretary of Defense. Provides education to American military and civilian service members stationed at overseas locations. The Department of Defense Dependents Schools (DoDDS) is a division of the U.S. Department of Defense. It was established in 1974 under the supervision of the assistant secretary of defense. Its mission is to provide adequate education to children (in grades K-12) of military and civilian service members on a worldwide basis.

- **Total Employees:** Not available.
- **U.S. Employees Abroad:** Not available.
- **Countries:** Operations are in countries in Africa, Asia, the Caribbean, Europe, Latin America, the Middle East, and the Near East.
- **Job Categories:** Teachers.
- **Benefits:** All benefits are individually determined.

FOOD & AGRICULTURE ORGANIZATION OF THE UNITED NATIONS

1001 22nd St. NW
Washington, DC 20437 USA

RECRUITER: DENNIS BRYDGES
EXECUTIVE OFFICER
1001 22ND ST. NW
WASHINGTON, DC 20437
TEL: (202) 653-2398
FAX: (202) 653-5760

James T. Hill, Officer-in-Charge. Raises levels of nutrition and standards of living in rural populations. The Food and Agriculture Organization (FAO) is a specialized agency of the United Nations, promoting better nutrition and improved production and distribution of food and agricultural products for rural populations. Since its inception, it has tried to alleviate poverty and hunger by promoting agricultural development, improved nutrition, and the pursuit of food security. The organization offers direct development assistance, collects, analyzes and disseminates information, advises governments, and acts as an international forum for debate on food and agricultural issues.

- **Total Employees:** 4,000
- **U.S. Employees Abroad:** Not available.
- **Countries:** Operations are in countries in Africa, Asia, the Caribbean, Europe, Latin America, the Middle East, and the Near East.
- **Application Information:** Contact the Liaison Office for North America of the FAO of the United Nations at (202) 635-2400.
- **Job Categories:** Agricultural Specialists, Fisheries, Forestry, Teachers.
- **General Requirements:** Graduate degree in related field; international experience is preferred; must complete a personal history form.
- **Language Requirement:** Varies with each posting; usually proficiency in one, preferably two, of the five major languages.
- **Benefits:** All benefits vary with each posting.

FORD FOUNDATION

320 East 43rd St.
New York, NY 10017 USA

RECRUITER: MARGARET LOWE
DIRECTOR, HUMAN RESOURCES
320 EAST 43RD ST.
NEW YORK, NY 10017
TEL: (212) 573-5000
FAX: (617) 687-9509

Franklin Thomas, President. Provides educational, research, and development grants to worldwide organizations. The Ford Foundation is a nonprofit organization founded in 1936 by Henry Ford and his son Edsel. Today, it is the largest philanthropic foundation in the United States with more than $7 billion given to organizations throughout the world. Grants focus on creative and performing arts, education, human rights, international affairs, and alleviating urban and rural poverty. Developing countries receive approximately 35 percent of the budget. Funds are derived from an internal stock and bond portfolio, which in 1991 was $5.2 billion.

- **Total Employees:** 350
- **U.S. Employees Abroad:** 40
- **Countries:** Operations are in countries in Africa, Asia, Latin America, and the Middle East.
- **Job Categories:** Executive Management, Finance, Technical Field Support.
- **Language Requirement:** Knowledge of local language a plus but not essential.

INTER-AMERICAN DEVELOPMENT BANK

1300 New York Ave. NW
Washington, DC 20005 USA

RECRUITER: JAMES WYLDE
INTERNATIONAL RECRUITMENT
SPECIALIST
1300 NEW YORK AVE. NW
WASHINGTON, DC 20005
TEL: (202) 623-1000
FAX: (202) 623-3178

Enrique V. Iglesias, President. Promotes regional economic and social development. The Inter-American Development Bank is an international financial institution under the jurisdiction of the United Nations. It encourages regional economic and social development by offering financial assistance for developing projects in Latin America/Caribbean. In addition, it helps mobilize private capital from international financial markets. It currently has 27 member nations.

- **Total Employees:** Not available.
- **U.S. Employees Abroad:** Not available.
- **Countries:** Operations are in countries in the Caribbean and Latin America.
- **Job Categories:** Administrative, Finance.
- **General Requirements:** Degree in related field.
- **Language Requirement:** Fluency in local language required; Spanish preferred.
- **Training:** No special training provided.

INTER-AMERICAN FOUNDATION

901 North Stuart St.
Arlington, VA 22203 USA

RECRUITER: MARCIA SAVOIE
PERSONNEL DIRECTOR
901 NORTH STUART ST., 11TH FLOOR
ARLINGTON, VA 22203
TEL: (703) 841-3800
FAX: (703) 841-0276

Bill K. Perrin, Ambassador. Civil, economic, and social assistance. The Inter-American Foundation was created by Congress in 1969 and is an independent corporation of the U.S. government. Grants are awarded to private, regional organizations that assist local groups by providing them with credit, technical assistance, training, and marketing services. Appropriations are derived from Congress and the Social Progress Trust Fund of the Inter-American Development Bank.

- **Total Employees:** 76
- **U.S. Employees Abroad:** Not available.
- **Countries:** Operations are in countries in the Caribbean and Latin America.
- **Job Categories:** Administrative, Computer Programmers, Finance, Technical Field Support.
- **General Requirements:** Bachelor's degreee and experience in international affairs preferred.
- **Average Overseas Assignment:** Less than six months; employees are sent abroad for temporary assignments only.
- **Language Requirement:** Fluency in Spanish is required.
- **Training:** No special training provided.
- **Benefits:** HEALTH: Same coverage as U.S. employees.

INTERNATIONAL CITY MANAGEMENT ASSOCIATION

777 Capitol St. NE
Washington, DC 20002 USA

RECRUITER: STEVEN MCCOY-
THOMPSON
RECRUITMENT
777 CAPITOL AVE. NE, SUITE #500
WASHINGTON, DC 20002
TEL: (202) 289-4262
FAX: (202) 962-3500

William Hansell, Executive Director. Management training. The ICMA (International City Management Association) is a private nonprofit organization for administrations serving cities, counties, and regions. It holds training seminars on various facets of municipal administration, collects data on local governments, provides management information services, and offers training on collection of urban data.

- **Total Employees:** 100
- **U.S. Employees Abroad:** 5
- **Countries:** Honduras, Kazakhstan, Poland.
- **Salaries:** Varies with each posting.
- **Job Categories:** Management Training.
- **General Requirements:** Should be experienced as a practioner of local government and have an economics background.
- **Average Overseas Assignment:** Varies with each posting; usually less than two years.
- **Language Requirement:** Fluency in local language required.
- **Training:** Basic training (1-30 days) provided.

INTERNATIONAL FERTILIZER DEVELOPMENT CENTER

PO Box 2040
Muscle Shoals, AL 35662 USA

RECRUITER: C. DAVID EDWARDS
PERSONNEL OFFICER
PO BOX 2040
MUSCLE SHOALS, AL 35662
TEL: (205) 381-6600
FAX: (205) 381-7408

Amitava H. Roy, President. Research and assistance in the fertilizer field and related technology. The International Fertilizer Development Center (IFDC) provides assistance, advisory services, and training in response to global needs—with special reference to the tropics and subtropics—for the transfer and use of improved fertilizer and related technology. It also helps implement economic policies that promote open, competitive markets and market-led associated institutions for increased agricultural productivity and economic development. It strives to conserve the natural resource base and the environment and to enhance the efficient use of plant nutrients.

- **Total Employees:** 120
- **U.S. Employees Abroad:** 6
- **Countries:** Albania, Bangladesh.
- **Salaries:** $40,000-$80,000 per year.
- **Job Categories:** Agricultural Specialists, Chemical Engineers, Marketing.
- **General Requirements:** Applicant should have seven or more years job related experience and overseas experience.
- **Average Overseas Assignment:** 2-3 years.
- **Language Requirement:** Competency in local language a plus but not essential.
- **Training:** No special training provided.
- **Benefits:** TRAVEL: Relocation expenses provided; rest and recuperation leave on an annual basis. HEALTH: $200 single and $400 family deductible; $2,000 catastrophe clause; 80 percent out-of-pocket expenses for doctor, precriptions, etc. HOUSING: Offered. EDUCATION: Offered.

INTERNATIONAL FUND FOR AGRICULTURAL DEVELOPMENT (IFAD)

1889 F St. NW
Washington, DC 20006 USA

RECRUITER: ALAN PRIEN
CHIEF OF PERSONNEL
107 VIA DEL SERAFICO
00-142 ROME, ITALY
TEL: (396) 54591
FAX: (396) 5043463

Fawzi Al-Sultan, President. Promotes worldwide increased agricultural production. The International Fund for Agricultural Development (IFAD) is a specialized agency under the jurisdiction of the Secretariat of the United Nations. Its goal is to expand food production and reduce malnutrition in developing countries. This is accomplished by

A
M
E
R
I
C
A
N

J
O
B
S

A
B
R
O
A
D

offering low-cost loans and providing technical assistance in education, fisheries, forestry, and rural development.

- **Total Employees:** 239
- **U.S. Employees Abroad:** 30
- **Countries:** Operations are in countries in Africa, Asia, the Caribbean, Europe, Latin America, the Middle East, and the Near East.
- **Application Information:** Send resume to Washington, DC, address (to be forwarded) or directly to Rome, Italy.
- **Job Categories:** Administrative, Finance, Technical Field Support, Teachers.
- **General Requirements:** Degree in related field.
- **Language Requirement:** Fluency in local language required.
- **Training:** Offered.

INTERNATIONAL LABOR OFFICE

1828 L St. NW
Washington, DC 20036 USA

RECRUITER: KAREN WALL DOGAN
RECRUITMENT OFFICER
1828 L ST. NW
WASHINGTON, DC 20036
TEL: (202) 653-7652
FAX: (202) 653-7687

Stephen Schlossberg, Director. Promotes peace through improved labor conditions and living standards. The International Labor Office is a specialized agency of the United Nations. It formulates international policies and plans to improve labor conditions, create employment opportunities, and develop international labor standards. It also offers technical expertise as well as training and research.

- **Total Employees:** 3,000
- **U.S. Employees Abroad:** 300
- **Countries:** Operations are in countries in Africa, Asia, the Caribbean, Europe, and Latin America.
- **Salaries:** $3,000-$5,000 per month, plus daily allowance.
- **Job Categories:** Attorneys, Economists, Management, Rural Development, Safety Inspectors, Statisticians, Training Specialists.
- **General Requirements:** 8-10 years professional experience with 2-3 years experience in developing countries.
- **Average Overseas Assignment:** Less than two years.
- **Language Requirement:** Knowledge of local language a plus but not essential.
- **Training:** No special training provided.
- **Benefits:** TRAVEL: Offered; includes travel and shipment of personal belongings. HEALTH: Offered; includes comprehensive medical coverage. HOUSING: Offered;

assignment grant, rental subsidy, and post adjustment is included. EDUCATION: Generous education allowance and scholastic travel is offered.

INTERNATIONAL MANAGEMENT DEVELOPMENT INSTITUTE

3J03 Forbes Quadrangle
University of Pittsburgh
Pittsburgh, PA 15260 USA

RECRUITER: IRENE M. SEREWICZ
DIRECTOR
3J03 FORBES QUADRANGLE
UNIVERSITY OF PITTSBURGH, PA
15260
TEL: (412) 648-7639
FAX: (412) 648-2222

Dr. Riall W. Nolan, Executive Director. Management training programs. The International Management Development Institute (IMDI) is a part of the Graduate School of Public and International Affairs of the University of Pittsburgh. It is engaged in development training programs for officials of foreign countries. It provides short-term, intensive, international training in development management and administration, and related areas. This is done through consulting and technical assistance activities and through research, publication, and links with other institutions.

- **Total Employees:** 13
- **U.S. Employees Abroad:** Not available.
- **Countries:** Operations are in countries in Africa, Asia, and the Middle East.
- **Application Information:** Management consultants hired for work overseas are sent for short-term intensive assignment (under six months) with no need for permanent housing.
- **Job Categories:** Administrative, Consultants—Management, Management Training.
- **General Requirements:** Master's degree or Ph.D. in a relevant discipline and three years international experience.
- **Average Overseas Assignment:** Less than two years.
- **Language Requirement:** Fluency in Arabic, French, Indian, or Russian is required.
- **Training:** Basic orientation (1-30 days) provided.
- **Benefits:** HEALTH: Same coverage as U.S. employees.

INTERNATIONAL MEDICAL CORPS

12233 West Olympic Blvd.
Los Angeles, CA 90064-1052
USA

RECRUITER: PERSONNEL RECRUITING
DEPARTMENT
12333 WEST OLYMPIC BLVD.
LOS ANGELES, CA 90064-1052
TEL: (310) 826-7800
FAX: (310) 442-6622

Nancy Aossey, Executive Director. Provides emergency medical relief. A nonprofit humanitarian organization, the International Medical Corps provides personnel and technical assistance for emergency medical relief. It offers qualified medical personnel who perform various functions in the health-care field.

- **Total Employees:** Not available.

- **U.S. Employees Abroad:** Not available.

- **Countries:** Operations are in countries in Africa, Asia, the Caribbean, Europe, and Latin America.

- **Job Categories:** Medical Personnel, Nurses, Nutritionists, Pediatricians.

- **General Requirements:** Degree in related field; also international experience preferred.

- **Average Overseas Assignment:** Usually less than two years.

- **Language Requirement:** Competency in local language required.

- **Benefits:** TRAVEL: Relocation airfare provided. HEALTH: Health, dental, life, and disability insurance paid by employer. HOUSING: Housing provided.

INTERNATIONAL MONETARY FUND

700 19th St. NW
Washington, DC 20431 USA

RECRUITER: STAFFING SPECIALIST
700 19TH ST., NW
WASHINGTON, DC 20431
TEL: (202) 623-7000
FAX: (202) 623-4661

Michael Camdessus, Managing Director. Consulting and collaboration services for monetary issues. The International Monetary Fund (IMF) is a specialized agency of the United Nations, which encourages international monetary cooperation, balanced international trade, and economic stability. It accomplishes this by providing a permanent institution for consultation and collaboration concerning international monetary problems. It provides financial assistance to improve the balance-of-payments problems of member nations.

- **Total Employees:** Not available.

- **U.S. Employees Abroad:** 18

- **Countries:** France, Switzerland.

- **Application Information:** Most foreign positions are filled internally.

- **Job Categories:** Administrative, Finance.

- **General Requirements:** Degree in related field.

- **Language Requirement:** Competency in local language required.

- **Training:** No special training offered.

INTERNATIONAL ORGANIZATION FOR MIGRATION

1750 K St. NW, Suite #1110
Washington, DC 20006 USA

RECRUITER: CLARISSA AZKOL
DIRECTOR OF OPERATIONS
1750 K ST. NW, SUITE #1110
WASHINGTON, DC 20006
TEL: (202) 862-1826
FAX: (202) 862-1879

Frances E. Sullivan, Chief of Missions. Resettles refugees and assists in the orderly migration of peoples. The International Organization for Migration (IOM) formerly Intergovernmental Committee for Migration, is a regional organization of the United Nations and was established in 1951. IOM is engaged in the resettlement and integration of refugees and migrants in countries for employment and educational purposes. It provides processing, language, and vocational training services.

- **Total Employees:** 400
- **U.S. Employees Abroad:** Not available.
- **Countries:** Operations are in countries in Africa, Asia, the Caribbean, Europe, Latin America, and the Near East.
- **Job Categories:** Administrative, Teachers.
- **Average Overseas Assignment:** Varies with each posting; usually less than two years.
- **Language Requirement:** Must be fluent in local language; usually Spanish.

INTERNATIONAL PLANNED PARENTHOOD FEDERATION

902 Broadway
New York, NY 10010 USA

RECRUITER: ANN FREIDMAN
MANAGER, PERSONNEL & ADMINISTRATION
902 BROADWAY, 10TH FLOOR
NEW YORK, NY 10010
TEL: (212) 995-8800
FAX: (212) 995-8853

Faye Wattleton, President. Family planning. International Planned Parenthood Federation is a private voluntary organization offering family planning services. It provides information and training programs on effective means of contraception; also offers infertility services and sterilization.

- **Total Employees:** 75
- **U.S. Employees Abroad:** Not available.
- **Countries:** Operations are in countries in the Caribbean and Latin America.
- **Application Information:** Hiring for most foreign positions is done at the specific country location. Direct inquiries to recruiter's address.
- **Job Categories:** Administrative, Family Planning Specialists, Teachers.
- **General Requirements:** Degree in related area.

- **Language Requirement:** Competency in local language required (Spanish).
- **Benefits:** HEALTH: Offered.

INTERNATIONAL REPUBLICAN INSTITUTE

1212 New York Ave., Suite #900
Washington, DC 20005 USA

RECRUITER: BRUCE MCCOLM
PRESIDENT
1212 NEW YORK AVE., SUITE #900
WASHINGTON, DC 20005
TEL: (202) 408-9450
FAX: (202) 408-9462

Bruce McColm, President. Supports democratic institutions. The International Republican Institute encourages and supports democratic institutions, with a focus on political parties. It provides technical training, organizational management, poll watching, electoral law and constitutional reform, and election observation.

- **Total Employees:** 40
- **U.S. Employees Abroad:** 6
- **Countries:** Operations are in countries in Africa, Asia, the Caribbean, Europe, Latin America, and the Middle East.
- **Job Categories:** Political Scientists, Project Managers, Training Specialists.
- **General Requirements:** Experience working in political campaigns and intercultural communications preferred.
- **Average Overseas Assignment:** Less than two years.
- **Language Requirement:** Usually fluency in local language is required.
- **Training:** Basic orientation (1-30 days), and training in specific work skills provided.
- **Benefits:** TRAVEL: Varies with each posting. HEALTH: Varies with each posting. HOUSING: Offered; housing is paid for by U.S. office. EDUCATION: Varies with each posting.

INTERNATIONAL RESCUE COMMITTEE

386 Park Ave. South
New York, NY 10016 USA

RECRUITER: LILIANA KEITH
RECRUITMENT COORDINATOR
386 PARK AVE. SOUTH
NEW YORK, NY 10016
TEL: (212) 689-3459
FAX: (212) 679-0010

Bob DeVecchi, President. Assistance for refugees and displaced people throughout the world. The International Rescue Committee is a private voluntary organization offering assistance resettlement programs for refugees and displaced people on a worldwide basis. It focuses on the areas of public health and sanitation with emphasis on training refugee health workers.

- **Total Employees:** Not available.

- **U.S. Employees Abroad:** 140
- **Countries:** Operations are in countries in Africa, Asia, the Caribbean, Europe, and the Middle East.
- **Application Information:** Positions overseas are contingent on the specific experience of the applicant. A strong medical or administrative background is required.
- **Salaries:** Competitive with other non-profit organizations.
- **Job Categories:** Accountants, Administrative, Engineers, Medical Personnel, Nurses, Physicians, Teachers.
- **General Requirements:** Graduate degree in medicine, immunology, infectious diseases or nutrition, nursing, or public health; experience working in Third World countries.
- **Average Overseas Assignment:** Less than two years.
- **Language Requirement:** Knowledge of local language a plus but not essential.
- **Training:** Basic orientation is provided at home and in host country.
- **Benefits:** TRAVEL: After one year of service, home leave is provided. HEALTH: Offered. HOUSING: Offered. EDUCATION: None offered.
- **Comments:** Having prior work experience in a refugee setting is preferred.

INTERNATIONAL VOLUNTARY SERVICES, INC.

1424 16th St. NW, Suite #204
Washington, DC 20036 USA

RECRUITER: RECRUITMENT OFFICER
1424 16TH ST. NW, SUITE #204
WASHINGTON, DC 20036
TEL: (202) 387-5533
FAX: (202) 387-4234

Linda Worthington, Executive Director. Community development. International Voluntary Services, Inc. is a private voluntary organization providing human resources, skills, knowledge, and advisory services to support and guide local development initiatives. Staff workers assist in agriculture, cooperatives, health care, and micro-enterprise development.

- **Total Employees:** 50
- **U.S. Employees Abroad:** Not available.
- **Countries:** Bolivia, Ecuador, Bangladesh, Thailand, Zimbabwe.
- **Salaries:** Based on the cost-of-living in the host country.
- **Job Categories:** Agricultural Specialists, Cooperative Development, Environmental Specialists, Management, Medical Personnel, Training Specialists.
- **General Requirements:** College degree or equivalent work experience, two years experience in developing world, and a 2-3 year commitment to posting.
- **Average Overseas Assignment:** 2-3 years.
- **Language Requirement:** Fluency in local language required.
- **Training:** Basic training (1-30 days) provided.

- **Benefits:** TRAVEL: Moving allowance; home leave after two years of four-year service. HEALTH: Health coverage offered; $300 optical (two years); and $300 dental (two years). HOUSING: Offered. EDUCATION: None offered.

- **Comments:** The number of Americans working abroad varies greatly from quarter to quarter, fluctuating with the number and scope of projects under contract at the time.

INTERNATIONAL WILDLIFE COALITION

1900 L St. NW, 5th floor
Washington, DC 20036 USA

RECRUITER: MARION NEWMAN
DIRECTOR, RECRUITMENT
1900 L ST. NW, 5TH FLOOR
WASHINGTON, DC 20036
TEL: (202) 872-8840
FAX: (202) 466-9042

Daniel J. Morast, President. Wildlife conservation. International Wildlife Coalition is a nonprofit organization established in 1982. Its goal is to preserve and protect wildlife and wildlife habitats throughout the world.

- **Total Employees:** 60
- **U.S. Employees Abroad:** Not available.
- **Countries:** Operations are in countries in Africa, Asia, the Caribbean, Europe, Latin America, and the Near East.
- **Job Categories:** Administrative, Environmental Specialists.
- **General Requirements:** Degree in related field (business or environmental studies).
- **Language Requirement:** Knowledge of local language a plus but not essential.

NATIONAL AERONAUTICS AND SPACE ADMINISTARTION (NASA)

300 E St. SW
Washington, DC 20546 USA

RECRUITER: PETER SMITH
DIRECTOR, EXTERNAL RELATIONS
300 E ST. SW
WASHINGTON, DC 20546
TEL: (202) 358-1650
FAX: (202) 358-3029

Daniel Goldin, Administrator. Space research and programs. NASA (National Aeronautics and Space Administration) was established by the National Aeronautics and Space Act of 1958. It conducts research and operates programs relating to flight within and outside the earth's atmosphere. Includes the nation's major space programs and centers.

- **Total Employees:** Not available.
- **U.S. Employees Abroad:** Not available.
- **Countries:** Operations are in Asia, Europe, and the Near East.
- **Job Categories:** Administrative, Technical Field Support.
- **Language Requirement:** None.

NATIONAL DEMOCRATIC INSTITUTE

1717 Massachusettes Ave. NW
Washington, DC 20036 USA

RECRUITER: JENNY COHAN
PERSONNEL DIRECTOR
1717 MASSACHUSETTES AVE. NW
WASHINGTON, DC 20036
TEL: (202) 328-3136
FAX: (202) 939-3166

Kenneth Wollack, President. Promotes democratic institutions around the world. The National Democratic Institute is engaged in promoting and strengthening democratic establishments throughout the world. It helps to organize political parties through experienced trainers in participating programs.

- **Total Employees:** 74
- **U.S. Employees Abroad:** 14
- **Countries:** Kazakhstan, Romania, Russia, Republic of South Africa, Ukraine.
- **Salaries:** $19,000-$36,000 per year.
- **Job Categories:** Administrative, Political Scientists, Training Specialists.
- **General Requirements:** Political organizing experience and/or international experience and language capabilities.
- **Average Overseas Assignment:** Less than two years.
- **Language Requirement:** Varies with each posting.
- **Training:** No special training provided.
- **Benefits:** TRAVEL: Varies with each posting; dependent on the funding for the project. HEALTH: Full-time staff are covered by health insurance; part-time staff (consultants) are only covered by basic travel accident insurance. HOUSING: Varies with each posting. EDUCATION: None offered.

OFFICE OF INTERNATIONAL HEALTH

5600 Fishers Lane, Rooms #18-87
Rockville, MD 20854 USA

RECRUITER: LINDA VOGEL
DEPUTY DIRECTOR
5600 FISHERS LANE, ROOMS #18-87
ROCKVILLE, MD 20854
TEL: (301) 443-1774
FAX: (301) 443-6288

Dr. James E. Saen, Deputy Assistant Secretary. Health research and policy. The Office of International Health is part of the U.S. Department of Health and Human Services. It works in conjunction with other countries to advance scientific knowledge for the better health of the American people. Its international activities focus on conducting research and promoting international health policy.

- **Total Employees:** 20,000
- **U.S. Employees Abroad:** 30
- **Countries:** Operations are in countries of Africa as well as in Switzerland.

- **Salaries:** $30,000-$60,000 per year.

- **Job Categories:** Medical Personnel, Epidemiologists, Researchers.

- **General Requirements:** Must be qualified in the fields of medical epidemiology and maternal and child health/child survival.

- **Average Overseas Assignment:** 2-3 years.

- **Language Requirement:** Fluency in local language required.

- **Training:** No special training provided.

- **Benefits:** All benefits are offered.

ORGANIZATION OF AMERICAN STATES

Constitution Ave. & 17th St. NW
Washington, DC 20006 USA

RECRUITER: MAURICIO GRANILLO
BARRERA
DIRECTOR, HUMAN RESOURCES
CONSTITUTION AVE. & 17TH ST. NW
WASHINGTON, DC 20006
TEL: (202) 458-3285
FAX: (202) 458-6276

Joao Clemente, Director. Inter-American negotiations. The Organization of American States (OAS), a United Nations organization, is the oldest multinational organization in the world. It was established on April 14, 1890. It encourages and promotes inter-American cooperation in various countries on a global basis. Included are cultural, economic, educational, political, and social cooperation of member states. It also acts as a forum for resolving political disagreements and promotes trade, investment, and technology transfer. Its current membership includes 35 nations in the Western Hemisphere.

- **Total Employees:** 725

- **U.S. Employees Abroad:** 50

- **Countries:** Operations are in countries of Africa, Asia, the Caribbean, Europe, Latin America, and the Near East.

- **Job Categories:** Administrative, Attorneys, Economists, Scientists, Teachers, Technical Field Support.

- **General Requirements:** Degree in related field.

- **Language Requirement:** Knowledge of French, Portuguese, or Spanish preferred.

- **Training:** Varies with each posting; contact General Secretariat of the OAS.

- **Benefits:** TRAVEL: Offered. HEALTH: Offered. HOUSING: Offered in field assignments. EDUCATION: Offered.

ORGANIZATION FOR ECONOMIC COOPERATION & DEVELOPMENT

2 rue Andre-Pascal, 75775
16 Paris, France USA

RECRUITER: ISABEL WARTELLE
HEAD OF RECRUITMENT
HUMAN RESOURCE MANAGEMENT, 2
  RUE ANDRE-PASCAL
75775 PARIS, CEDEX 16, FRANCE
TEL: (45) 24-17-01
FAX: (45) 24-79-11

M. Jean-Claude Paye, Secretary-General. Promotes economic growth among member European countries. The Organization for Economic Cooperation and Development (OECD) is a United Nations organization established by convention on September 30, 1961. It promotes economic growth and employment and a rising standard of living in member countries while maintaining financial stability. It contributes to the sound economic expansion in member and non-member countries in the process of economic development and to the expansion of world trade on a multilateral, non-discriminatory basis in accordance with international obligations.

- **Total Employees:** 1,873
- **U.S. Employees Abroad:** 185
- **Countries:** France.
- **Salaries:** Approximately 262,512 FF-375,708 FF per year plus allowances of up to 26 percent of base salary.
- **Job Categories:** Economists, Data Processors, Finance, Environmental Specialists, Translators.
- **General Requirements:** Ability to work in a multicultural environment.
- **Average Overseas Assignment:** 2-3 years.
- **Language Requirement:** Fluency required in French; also competency in other languages desired.
- **Training:** Training in specific work skills and language training provided.
- **Benefits:** TRAVEL: Travel expenses reimbursable; moving expenses reimbursable. HEALTH: All staff members must subscribe to the French Social Security for medical coverage. HOUSING: Expatriate allowance is 16-20 percent of basic salary. EDUCATION: Up to 70 percent of education costs are reimbursable.
- **Comments:** Applicants should have experience in the fields of energy, science, economic policy, financial policy, or industrial policy.

ORT INTERNATIONAL COOPERATION

2025 Eye St. NW
Washington, DC 20006 USA

RECRUITER: CHRISTINA GRIFFIN
RECRUITMENT
2025 EYE ST. NW
WASHINGTON, DC 20006
TEL: (202) 293-2560
FAX: (202) 293-2577

Celeste S. Angus, Executive Director. Technical and vocational education. A private voluntary organization, OTR International Cooperation encourages vocational and technical education through a network of institutions in 35 countries. It focuses on agriculture and rural and urban development. Major funding is derived from a variety of sources including USAID, CIDA, the World Bank, and Swiss Development Corporation.

- **Total Employees:** 4,000
- **U.S. Employees Abroad:** Not available.
- **Countries:** Operations are in countries in Africa, Asia, the Caribbean, Latin America, and the Middle East.
- **Job Categories:** Counselors, Teachers, Technical Field Support.
- **General Requirements:** Degree in related field; international experience a plus.
- **Language Requirement:** Fluency in local language required.

PAN AMERICAN HEALTH ORGANIZATION

525 23rd St. NW
Washington, DC 20037 USA

RECRUITER: CHIEF, STAFF
RECRUITMENT UNIT
525 23RD ST. NW
WASHINGTON, DC 20037
TEL: (202) 861-3200
FAX: (202) 861-3379

Dr. Carlyle Guerra de Macedo, Director. Serves as a regional office for the World Health Organization. The Pan American Health Organization, a part of the World Health Organization (WHO), became a specialized agency of the United Nations on November 15, 1947. WHO promotes medical research and the exchange of scientific information, collaborates in the issuance of health regulations for international travel, carries out constant surveillance of communicable diseases, disseminates data on health matters, and provides global assistance in the setting of standards for the quality control of drugs, vaccines, and other substances affecting health.

- **Total Employees:** 1,084
- **U.S. Employees Abroad:** 100
- **Countries:** Operations are in countries in the Caribbean and Latin America.
- **Job Categories:** Administrative, Medical Personnel.
- **General Requirements:** Degree in related field.
- **Language Requirement:** Competency in local language required.

PARTNERS IN ECONOMIC REFORM, INC.

1730 Rhode Island Ave. NW
Washington, DC 20036 USA

RECRUITER: SAM SIMON
DIRECTOR, HUMAN RESOURCES
PO BOX 65782
WASHINGTON, DC 20035
TEL: (202) 466-3840
FAX: (202) 296-1608

William J. Meagher, Executive Director. Provides technical assistance and training. Partners in Economic Reform, Inc. (PIER) provides technical assistance training as well as health and safety training throughout the coal basins of Russia, Ukraine, and Kazakhstan. Training sessions are generally 3 to 4 weeks in length.

- **Total Employees:** 60
- **U.S. Employees Abroad:** 7
- **Countries:** Russia.
- **Salaries:** $40,000-$60,000 per year.
- **Job Categories:** Project Managers, Training Specialists.
- **General Requirements:** Mining experience (coal, preferably).
- **Average Overseas Assignment:** Less than two years.
- **Language Requirement:** Knowledge of local language a plus but not essential.
- **Training:** Basic orientation (1-30 days) provided.
- **Benefits:** TRAVEL: Two trips home per year; one in conjunction with staff meeting. Also, 25 percent of base pay added as differential. HEALTH: Offered; also additional required DBA insurance policy provided by PIER.

PATHFINDERS INTERNATIONAL
9 Galen St.
Watertown, MA 02172 USA

RECRUITER: CHRISTINE RYAN
DIRECTOR, RECRUITMENT
9 GALEN ST.
WATERTOWN, MA 02172
TEL: (617) 924-7200
FAX: (617) 924-3833

Daniel E. Pellegrom, President. Promotes population planning. Pathfinders International is a private voluntary organization established in 1957. It encourages population planning through various methods to make fertility services more feasible, less expensive, and readily accessible to people in developing nations. It currently has operations in 39 countries.

- **Total Employees:** 165
- **U.S. Employees Abroad:** 12
- **Countries:** Operation African, Asia, Latin America, and the Middle East.
- **Job Categories:** Administrative, Family Planning Specialists, Medical Personnel.
- **General Requirements:** Master's degree in public health or business with emphasis in health services area. Also, experience in developing countries.
- **Language Requirement:** Fluency in local language required.
- **Comments:** Only qualified candidates with required degree or experience will be considered.

POPULATION COUNCIL

One Dag Hammarskjold Plaza
New York, NY 10017 USA

RECRUITER: MARIA VINARDELL
DEPUTY FOR PERSONNEL SERVICES
ONE DAG HAMMARSKJOLD PLAZA
NEW YORK, NY 10017
TEL: (212) 339-0545
FAX: (212) 755-6052

Margaret Catley-Carlson, President. Applies science and technology to the solution of population problems in developing countries. The Population Council works in three areas: biomedical research in human reproduction; social science research into causes of population change, societal implications of those changes and appropriate policy response; and provision of technical assistance to family planning and population-related programs at local, regional, and national levels. A recent USAID-funded project included "Support Program in Family Planning Research and Services" (Worldwide: $37 million).

- **Total Employees:** 334
- **U.S. Employees Abroad:** 17
- **Countries:** Bangladesh, Brazil, Bolivia, Egypt, Honduras, India, Indonesia, Kenya, Mexico, Peru, Pakistan, Thailand, Zimbabwe.
- **Salaries:** $47,500-$85,000 per year.
- **Job Categories:** Administrative, Physicians.
- **General Requirements:** PhD, MD, or MPH; experience in developing countries.
- **Average Overseas Assignment:** 2-3 years.
- **Language Requirement:** Competency in local language required.
- **Training:** Varies with each posting; basic orientation (1-30 days) provided in some cases.
- **Benefits:** TRAVEL: Staff member, family and personal affects sent to post; resettlement allowance paid; annual home leave. HEALTH: Same coverage as U.S. employees. HOUSING: Housing is paid for by the Council. EDUCATION: Offered for dependents grades K-12; partial reimbursement for dependents attending accredited college or university.

PROJECT CONCERN INTERNATIONAL

PO Box 86322
San Diego, CA 92138 USA

RECRUITER: PATTY BROWN
RECRUITMENT
PO BOX 86322
SAN DIEGO, CA 92138
TEL: (619) 279-9690
FAX: (619) 694-0294

Thomas McKay, Executive Director. Independent primary health-care training and development. Project Concern International was founded in 1961. Its goal is to provide low-cost health care through health-training programs. It focuses on international health issues covering such areas as hygiene, nutrition, and sanitation. It also provides assistance to overseas clinics, health-care facilities, and hospitals.

- **Total Employees:** 400
- **U.S. Employees Abroad:** Not available.
- **Countries:** Operations are in countries in Africa, Asia, the Caribbean, Europe, Latin America, the Middle East, and the Near East.
- **Job Categories:** Dentists, Physicians, Health Professionals, Public Health Administrators.
- **General Requirements:** Degree in related field.
- **Language Requirement:** Competency in local language required.
- **Training:** Varies with each posting.

PROJECT HOPE

Health Sciences Education Center
Millwood, VA 22646 USA

RECRUITER: SUE ADAMS
INTERNATIONAL HUMAN RESOURCES
    RECRUITER
HEALTH SCIENCES EDUCATION
    CENTER
MILLWOOD, VA 22646
TEL: (703) 837-2100
FAX: (703) 837-1813
FREE: (800) 544-4673

William B. Walsh, Jr., Executive Director. Works to improve medical care to developing areas of the world. Project HOPE was established in 1958 to bring improved medical care to developing countries in the world. Since that time, more than 12,000 HOPE educators have trained thousands of health-care personnel around the world. Engaged in the areas of medicine, dentistry, nursing, and biomedical engineering. Teaching is done at a local level, rather than bringing people to the United States to be trained. The objective is to teach people to help themselves. On an inividualized basis, HOPE professionals teach skills that bring longer, healthier lives to others.

- **Total Employees:** 250
- **U.S. Employees Abroad:** 40
- **Countries:** People's Republic of China, Costa Rica, Ecuador, Egypt, Guatemala, Honduras, Hungary, Kazakhstan, Malawi, Nicaragua, Poland, Romania, Russia, Switzerland.
- **Salaries:** Competitive with similar U.S-based positions.
- **Job Categories:** Health Professionals, Teachers.
- **General Requirements:** Certified health professional, master's degree and international experience preferred, teaching and faculty development experience desired.
- **Average Overseas Assignment:** Less than two years.

- **Language Requirement:** Varies with each posting; in some cases, fluency in local language is required.

- **Training:** None provided.

- **Benefits:** All benefits are offered.

- **Comments:** Areas of operations include African, Asia, the Caribbean, European, Latin America, the Middle East, and the Near East.

SAVE THE CHILDREN FEDERATION, INC.

54 Wilton Rd.
Westport, CT 06880 USA

RECRUITER: VICTORIA BANKS
DIRECTOR, RECRUITMENT
54 WILTON RD.
WESTPORT, CT 06880
TEL: (203) 221-4000
FAX: (203) 221-4077

James J. Bausch, President. Supports development projects involving children and their communities. Save the Children Federation, Inc. was founded in 1932 to support development projects focusing on children and their communities. Projects include building schools and houses and creating small industry. Major funding is derived from sponsorship programs, USAID, private foundations, corporations, and individual donors.

- **Total Employees:** 3,045

- **U.S. Employees Abroad:** 45

- **Countries:** Operations are in countries in Africa, Asia, the Caribbean, Latin America, and the Middle East.

- **Job Categories:** Administrative, Field Service Positions.

- **General Requirements:** Candidate should have a strong background in developing countries, and bachelor's degree or advanced degree in specific area.

- **Language Requirement:** Must be fluent in Arabic, French, or Spanish.

SOUTH PACIFIC COMMISSION

SPC B.P. D5
Noumea Cedex, New Caledonia
USA

RECRUITER: ATI GEORGE SOKOMANU
SECRETARY-GENERAL
SPC B.P. D5
NOUMEA CEDEX, NEW CALEDONIA
TEL: (687) 26.20.00
FAX: (687) 26.38.18

Ati George Sokomanu, Secretary-General. Technical assistance and cultural, economic, and social advisory services. The South Pacific Commission was established in 1947 by an agreement known as the Canberra Agreement, signed in Australia by various governments. Its goal was to assure economic and social stability of the island countries of the region. The South Pacific Commission is a non-political technical assistance agency and, when requested, will aid member countries by offering technical advice, training, and advisory services to administrations and governments.

- **Total Employees:** 158
- **U.S. Employees Abroad:** 9
- **Countries:** Operations are in countries in the Pacific Islands.
- **Job Categories:** Administrative, Teachers.
- **General Requirements:** Degree in related field.
- **Language Requirement:** Competency in French and English required.

TECHNOSERVE, INC.

148 East Ave.
Norwalk, CT 06851 USA

RECRUITER: MIGUEL GIRON
PERSONNEL ADMINISTRATOR
148 EAST AVE.
NORWALK, CT 06851
TEL: (203) 852-0377
FAX: (203) 838-6717

Edward P. Bullard, President. Development aid. Technoserve, Inc. was established in 1968. It is a private organization whose goal is to assist low-income people initiate their own community-based enterprises. It focuses on primary agricultural production, crop processing, livestock development, and savings and credit programs. The major funding sources come from the USAID.

- **Total Employees:** 200
- **U.S. Employees Abroad:** Not available.
- **Countries:** Costa Rica, El Salvador, Guatemala, Kenya, Panama, Peru, Poland.
- **Job Categories:** Administrative, Engineers, Finance.
- **General Requirements:** Candidate should have a background in developing countries and a degree in business, agribusiness, or engineering.
- **Average Overseas Assignment:** Less than two years.
- **Language Requirement:** Competency in local language required.

UNITED NATIONS CHILDRENS' FUND

UNICEF House
Three UN Plaza
New York, NY 10017 USA

RECRUITER: FUAD KRONFOL
RECRUITMENT & STAFF
    DEVELOPMENT
UNICEF HOUSE
THREE UN PLAZA
NEW YORK, NY 10017
TEL: (212) 326-7000
FAX: (212) 326-7536

James Grant, Secretary-Director. Protects and provides for children in developing countries. The UN Childrens' Fund (UNICEF) is a special program of the United

Nations, established in 1946. It operates in both rural and urban settings for the protection and well-being of children in developing countries. It is engaged in child nutrition, maternal health, sanitation, and training programs. It provides assistance to health centers, schools, and day-care and community centers. Its focus is on child survival and emphasizes breast-feeding, growth-monitoring, immunization, and a simple oral rehydration method.

- **Total Employees:** Not available.
- **U.S. Employees Abroad:** Not available.
- **Countries:** Operations are in countries in Africa, Asia, the Caribbean, Europe, Latin America, the Middle East, the Near East.
- **Job Categories:** Administrative, Health Professionals, Field Service Positions.
- **General Requirements:** Degree in related field and experience in developing countries.
- **Language Requirement:** Competency in local language required.

UNITED NATIONS EMPLOYMENT INFORMATION & ASSISTANCE DIVISION

IO/S/EA, Room #4808
Dept. of State
Washington, DC 20520 USA

RECRUITER: LAWRENCE T. SPRINGER
CHIEF
IO/S/EA, ROOM #4808, STATE DEPARTMENT
WASHINGTON, DC 20520-6319
TEL: (202) 647-3396
FAX: (202) 737-7320

Lawrence T. Springer, Chief. Assists United Nations in recruitment of Americans for international organizations. The office of United Nations Employment Assistance promotes equitable representation of Americans in the UN and specialized agencies, including the Food and Agriculture Organization (FAO) and the UN High Commission for Refugees (UNHCR). The department seeks professionals with an international orientation for work in various fields.

- **Total Employees:** Not available.
- **U.S. Employees Abroad:** Not available.
- **Countries:** Operations are in countries in Africa, Asia, the Caribbean, Europe, Latin America, and the Near East.
- **Application Information:** Applicants may write or fax resumes to recruiter's address.
- **Job Categories:** Agricultural Specialists, Attorneys, Demographers, Statisticians, Development Specialists, Economists, Environmental Specialists, Finance, Human Resources, Public Administrators, Press Officers.
- **General Requirements:** Master's degree; 3-4 years experience is required for entry-level positions.
- **Language Requirement:** Fluency in English or French, and knowledge of a second UN language.

- **Training:** Basic training (1-30 days) provided.
- **Benefits:** All benefits are offered.
- **Comments:** For senior-level positions, a Ph.D. may be required; for some foreign postings, prior working experience in developing countries is required.

UNITED NATIONS ENVIRONMENT PROGRAM

Two UN Plaza, Room 803
New York, NY 10017 USA

RECRUITER: TERESA MUIGAI
DIRECTOR, RECUITMENT
PO BOX 30552
NAIROBI, KENYA
TEL: (2542) 2308-00
FAX: (2542) 2268-86

Dr. Noel Brown, Executive Director. Monitors environmental issues. The United Nations Environment Program (UNEP) is under the Secretariat and Special Programs Division of the United Nations. It is a small coordinating group that regulates environmental issues and initiatives for the United Nations.

- **Total Employees:** 250
- **U.S. Employees Abroad:** Not available.
- **Countries:** Operations are in countries in Africa, Asia, the Caribbean, Europe, Latin America, the Middle East, the Near East.
- **Job Categories:** Administrative, Environmental Specialists.
- **General Requirements:** Degree in related (environmental or business) field.
- **Language Requirement:** Fluency in local language required.
- **Training:** Offered.

UNITED NATIONS HIGH COMMISSIONER FOR REFUGEES

1718 Connecticut Ave. NW
Washington, DC 20009 USA

RECRUITER: SUE MUNCH
RECRUITMENT UNIT
UNHCR HEADQUARTERS, CP2500
CH-1211 GENEVA 2 DEPOT,
  SWITZERLAND
TEL: (41)-227318111
FAX: (41)-227319546

Rene Rooyen, Representative. Provides for the welfare of refugees. The UN High Commissioner for Refugees (UNHCR) was established in 1950 and is a special program of the United Nations. It provides clothing, food, and shelter for refugees and works with governments to create safe conditions so that refugees may return to their home country. When that is not possible, it seeks to ensure that refugees receive asylum.

- **Total Employees:** 1,200
- **U.S. Employees Abroad:** Not available.

A
M
E
R
I
C
A
N

J
O
B
S

A
B
R
O
A
D

- **Countries:** Operations are in countries in Africa, Asia, Europe, Latin America, the Middle East, and the Near East.
- **Job Categories:** Administrative, Health Professionals, Field Service Positions.
- **Language Requirement:** Competency in local language required.

UNITED NATIONS INDUSTRIAL DEVELOPMENT ORGANIZATION (UNIDO)

One UN Plaza, Room DC1-1110
New York, NY 10017 USA

RECRUITER: E. SOEPRAPTO
CHIEF RECRUITMENT SECTION
VIENNA INTERNATIONAL CENTER
PO BOX 300
A-1400 VIENNA, AUSTRIA
TEL: (022) 33-39-93
FAX: (4122) 9170039

Domingo L. Siazon, Jr., Director-General. Promotes industrialization of developing countries. The United Nations Industrial Development Organization (UNIDO) was established in Vienna in January 1967 as part of the United Nations Secretariat. It assists developing countries by implementing industrial projects and arranging consultations between countries in an effort to transfer technology to developing countries.

- **Total Employees:** 1,400
- **U.S. Employees Abroad:** 200
- **Countries:** Worldwide including Austria, France, Germany, Italy, Japan, Poland, Republic of Korea, Switzerland.
- **Application Information:** The U.N. Liason Office is located at One U.N. Plaza, New York, NY 10017 (212)963-6890. Direct inquiries to that address.
- **Salaries:** Varies with each posting.
- **Job Categories:** Administrative, Chemical Engineers, Chemists, Economists, Engineers, Management, Field Service Positions.
- **General Requirements:** Applicant must have an advanced university degree and two years relavent work experience in field of interest to UNIDO.
- **Language Requirement:** Fluency in local language required (French); also Arabic, Chinese, Russian, or Spanish desired.
- **Training:** No special training offered.
- **Benefits:** All benefits vary with each posting.

UNITED NATIONS SECRETARIAT

United Nations Secretariat, Room #2475
New York, NY 10017 USA

RECRUITER: RECRUITMENT SPECIALIST, UN SECRETARIAT
ROOM #2745
NEW YORK, NY 10017
TEL: (212) 963-1234

Boutros Boutros-Ghali, Secretary-General. Worldwide peacekeeping organization with specialized agencies. The United Nations was officially founded on October 24, 1945, when the charter was ratified by China, France, the Soviet Union, the United Kingdom, the United States, and a majority of other signatories. It has four basic functions: to maintain global peace and security; to develop friendly relations between nations; to cooperate in solving international problems of cultural, economic, social, or humanitarian character, with respect for human rights and fundamental freedoms; and be the center for coordination among countries for the success of these goals.

- **Total Employees:** Not available.
- **U.S. Employees Abroad:** Not available.
- **Countries:** Operations are in countries of Africa, Asia, the Caribbean, Europe, Latin America, the Middle East, and the Near East.
- **Job Categories:** Field Service Positions, Economists.
- **General Requirements:** Advanced university degree and professional and/or international experience.
- **Language Requirement:** Competency in local language required.
- **Comments:** Professional positions are usually filled through competitive examinations, organized on a rotational basis for nationals of member states.

UNITED SERVICE ORGANIZATIONS, INC.

601 Indiana Ave. NW
Washington, DC 20007 USA

RECRUITER: MARLY GORMAN
DIRECTOR, HUMAN RESOURCES
601 INDIANA AVE. NW
WASHINGTON, DC 20007
TEL: (202) 783-8121
FAX: (202) 638-0901

Chapman B. Cox, President. Supports the social and recreational needs of U.S. service persons abroad. The United Service Organizations, Inc. (USO) was established to serve the social welfare, spiritual, and recreation needs of U.S. service persons and their dependents. Programs include family assistance, community outreach, and informal counseling and education. USO also sponsors celebrity entertainment programs at bases overseas. The USO strives to boost the morale and improve the quality of life for American service personnel stationed overseas.

- **Total Employees:** Not available.
- **U.S. Employees Abroad:** Not available.
- **Countries:** 175 locations in countries of Africa, Asia, the Caribbean, Europe, Latin America, the Middle East, and the Near East.
- **Salaries:** $20,500-22,500 per year.
- **Job Categories:** Administrative.
- **Language Requirement:** Competency in local language preferred.

- **Benefits:** TRAVEL: Airfare is paid for employee and dependent. HEALTH: Available at low cost. HOUSING: Allowance for housing; some locations on military bases.

U.S. ARMY CORPS OF ENGINEERS

PO Box 2250
Winchester, VA 22604-1450 USA

RECRUITER: D. DAVIS
CHIEF OF RECRUITMENT
PO BOX 2250
WINCHESTER, VA 22604-1450
TEL: (703) 665-3731
FAX: (703) 665-4039

Engineering and management services in foreign countries. The U.S. Army Corps of Engineers is engaged in the design and construction of facilities for U.S. government agencies in selected foreign countries. It also provides related engineering and management services for these facilities.

- **Total Employees:** 700
- **U.S. Employees Abroad:** 350
- **Countries:** Operations are in countries of Africa and in Germany, Kuwait.
- **Application Information:** Opportunities are limited due to the highly specified qualifications of candidates.
- **Salaries:** $41,000-$53,700 per year.
- **Job Categories:** Engineers.
- **General Requirements:** Must be a current federal government employee with a college engineering degree.
- **Average Overseas Assignment:** 2-3 years.
- **Language Requirement:** Knowledge of local language a plus but not essential.
- **Training:** No special training provided.
- **Benefits:** TRAVEL: Relocation costs provided. HEALTH: Same coverage as U.S. employees. HOUSING: Offered. EDUCATION: Offered.

U.S. CENTRAL INTELLIGENCE AGENCY

PO Box 9065
Mc Lean, VA 22102 USA

RECRUITER: CHIEF OF
REQUIREMENTS AND
RECRUITMENT
CIA EMPLOYMENT CENTER
PO BOX 1255
PITTSBURGH, PA 15230
TEL: (703) 482-4119
FREE: (800) JOBS-CIA

James Woolsey, Director. Provides information on trends and current events abroad. The Central Intelligence Agency (CIA) coordinates the nation's intelligence activities by collecting, evaluating, and disseminating intelligence that directly affects our national security. It coordinates the efforts of many federal intelligence organizations and provides the President and other policymakers with the information needed to formulate policy.

- **Total Employees:** Not available.
- **U.S. Employees Abroad:** Not available.
- **Countries:** Operations are in countries in Africa, Asia, the Caribbean, Europe, Latin America, and the Near East.
- **Application Information:** Do not call. Direct inquiries to recruiter's address.
- **Salaries:** $24,000-$54,000 per year.
- **Job Categories:** Administrative, Clerical Assistants, Telecommunications Officers.
- **Average Overseas Assignment:** 2-3 years.
- **Language Requirement:** Competency in local language required.
- **Training:** Training in specific work skills and language training offered.
- **Benefits:** TRAVEL: Offered. HEALTH: Same coverage as U.S. employees. HOUSING: Offered. EDUCATION: Offered.

U.S. DEFENSE INTELLIGENCE AGENCY

The Pentagon
Washington, DC 20340-0001 USA

RECRUITER: DIRECTOR, RECRUITMENT
CIVILIAN STAFFING OPERATIONS DIVISION
3100 CLARENDON BLVD.
ARLINGTON, VA 22201-5322
TEL: (703) 545-6700

U.S. Secretary of Defense. National security of the United States. The Defense Intelligence Agency (DIA) was founded by the U.S. government in 1961 to manage and coordinate the protection of foreign military intelligence information within the Department of Defense. It is engaged in a number of activities that are directly or indirectly involved in the national security of the United States. It is a major source for foreign military intelligence information within the Department of Defense.

- **Total Employees:** Not available.
- **U.S. Employees Abroad:** Not available.
- **Countries:** Operations are in countries in Africa, Asia, the Caribbean, Europe, Latin America, the Middle East, and the Near East.
- **Application Information:** Applicants may send a resume or a completed SF-171 form to recruiter's address.
- **Salaries:** Starting salaries are usually at the GG-05 through GG-07 levels.
- **Job Categories:** Clerical Assistants, Research Technicians.
- **General Requirements:** Applicants must be able to type a minimum of 40 w.p.m. and also possess position-related knowledge and experience. (See comments below.)

- **Average Overseas Assignment:** 3-5 years.

- **Language Requirement:** Fluency in local language required.

- **Training:** A 7-week specialized course of instruction is offered to civilians who will work abroad.

- **Benefits:** TRAVEL: Offered; 13 workdays a year, in addition to 5, 10, or 15 days home leave per year depending on the country assignment. HEALTH: Low-cost health insurance plan is offered. HOUSING: Government housing is offered.

- **Comments:** Required for secretarial: administrative background and three years work experience. For bilingual research/research technicians: listening comprehension, reading comprehension, and foreign language skills. Also, knowledge of automated computer systems.

U.S. DEPARTMENT OF THE AIR FORCE

AFDW-DPC
1460 Air Force Pentagon
Washington, DC 20330-1460 USA

RECRUITER: DAVE MULGREW
CIVILIAN PERSONNEL OFFICER
AFDW-DPC
1460 AIR FORCE PENTAGON
WASHINGTON, DC 20330-1460
TEL: (703) 697-1703
FAX: (703) 693-5392

Donald B. Rice, Secretary of the Air Force. Supports other armed forces in preservation of peace and security of the United States. The Department of the Air Force is part of the U.S. Department of Defense and was established as part of the National Security Act on September 18, 1947. It is responsible for supporting other branches of the armed forces by providing capable air power in the protection and security of the United States.

- **U.S. Employees Abroad:** Not available.

- **Countries:** Worldwide.

- **Application Information:** Civilian personnel management in the Department of the Air Force is decentralized. Direct inquiries to recruiter's address.

- **Job Categories:** Administrative, Technical Field Support.

- **General Requirements:** Applicant must be a current career federal civil service employee with reinstatement eligibility. If not, contact the Office of Personnel Management, 1900 E Street, Washington, DC 20415; (202) 606-2424.

- **Language Requirement:** Varies with each posting.

U.S. DEPARTMENT OF DEFENSE

The Pentagon
Washington, DC 20340 USA

RECRUITER: NANCY HILL
DEFENSE CIVILIAN PERSONNEL
THE PENTAGON
WASHINGTON, DC 20301-1115
TEL: (202) 697-1703
FAX: (202) 694-6981

U.S. Secretary of Defense. Responsible for the international security of the United States. The function of the Department of Defense (DoD), an agency of the U.S. government, is the defense and security of the people of the United States at home and overseas. It educates the children of U.S. military personnel and is engaged in global information and high-level policy matters.

- **Total Employees:** Not available.
- **U.S. Employees Abroad:** Not available.
- **Countries:** Operations are in countries in Africa, Asia, the Caribbean, Europe, Latin America, the Middle East, and the Near East.
- **Application Information:** Civilian personnel management in DoD is decentralized.
- **Job Categories:** Administrative, Management, Teachers.
- **General Requirements:** Applicant must be a current career federal civil service employee with reinstatement eligibility. If not, see comments.
- **Language Requirement:** Varies with each posting.
- **Comments:** For more information on where current overseas operations are located, contact the Office of Personnel Management, 1900 E Street, Washington, DC 20415; (202) 606-2424.

U.S. DEPARTMENT OF ENERGY

1000 Independence Ave. SW
Washington, DC 20585 USA

RECRUITER: WILLIAM PORTER
CHIEF OF RECRUITMENT
1000 INDEPENDENCE AVE. SW
WASHINGTON, DC 20585
TEL: (202) 586-8253
FAX: (202) 586-6789

Hazel O'Leary, Executive Director. Worldwide energy programs affecting the United States at home and overseas. An agency of the U.S. government, the Department of Energy's goal is to provide the United States with the knowledge, technology, policy, and institutional leadership necessary to achieve efficiency and diversity in energy use, a more productive and competitive economy, improved environmental quality, and a secure national defense.

- **Total Employees:** 20,000
- **U.S. Employees Abroad:** 70
- **Countries:** Austria, France, Japan.
- **Salaries:** $20,000-$90,000 per year.
- **Job Categories:** Engineers, Management, Scientists.
- **Average Overseas Assignment:** 3-5 years.
- **Language Requirement:** Knowledge of local language a plus but not essential.
- **Training:** No special training offered.
- **Benefits:** All benefits vary with each posting.

U.S. DEPARTMENT OF JUSTICE

Constitution Ave. & 10th St. NW
Washington, DC 20530 USA

RECRUITER: PAUL KRUMSIEK
ACTING DIRECTOR, JUSTICE MGMNT.
  DIVISION
CONSTITUTION AVE. & 10TH ST. NW
WASHINGTON, DC 20530
TEL: (202) 514-6877
FAX: (202) 514-6123

Janet Reno, Attorney General of the United States. Enforces federal laws. The Department of Justice is an agency of the U.S. government that serves as counsel for its citizens by representing them through the enforcement of laws. It protects against criminals and subversion, safeguards consumers, and enforces drug, immigration, and naturalization laws.

- **Total Employees:** Not available.
- **U.S. Employees Abroad:** Not available.
- **Countries:** Operations are in countries in Africa, Asia, the Caribbean, Europe, Latin America, the Middle East, and the Near East.
- **Job Categories:** Administrative, Agents—Investigative, Attorneys.
- **General Requirements:** Applicant should have experience in the criminal justice field.
- **Language Requirement:** Varies with each position.

U.S. DEPARTMENT OF THE NAVY

800 North Quincy St.
Arlington, VA 22203 USA

RECRUITER: POLLI BRUNELLI
STAFFING SPECIALIST
800 NORTH QUINCY ST.
ARLINGTON, VA 22203
TEL: (703) 696-4921
FAX: (703) 696-6292

Sean O'Keefe, Acting Secretary of the Navy. Preserves the security of the United States by maintaining freedom of the seas. The Department of the Navy is part of the U.S. Department of Defense and is under the direction of the President and the Secretary of Defense. Along with its Marine Corps component and other military department forces, it strives to protect the United States and preserve peace.

- **Total Employees:** Not available.
- **U.S. Employees Abroad:** Not available.
- **Countries:** Operations are in countries in Africa, Asia, the Caribbean, Europe, Latin America, the Middle East, and the Near East.
- **Application Information:** Civilian personnel management in the Department of the Navy is decentralized.
- **Job Categories:** Administrative, Technical Field Support.

- **General Requirements:** Applicant must be a current career Federal civil service employee with reinstatement eligibility. If not, see comments below.
- **Language Requirement:** Varies with each position.
- **Comments:** For more information on where current overseas operations are located, contact the Office of Personnel Management, 1900 E Street, Washington, DC 20415; (202) 606-2424.

U.S. DEPARTMENT OF STATE

PO Box 9317
Arlington, VA 22219 USA

RECRUITER: RECRUITMENT DIVISION
RECRUITMENT OFFICER
PO BOX 9317
ARLINGTON, VA 22219
TEL: (703) 875-7490
FAX: (703) 812-2265

Warren Christopher, Secretary of State. Official international relations arm of the President of the United States. The Foreign Service of the Department of State advises the President on foreign policy matters and is responsible for implementing U.S. foreign policy. It is the oldest executive department of the federal government and operates through a network of embassies and consulates overseas. It participates in the United Nations and 50 other worldwide organizations. It consists of both Foreign Service and Civil Service employees and has international specialists throughout the world. The Department of State is an equal opportunity employer.

- **Total Employees:** 26,000
- **U.S. Employees Abroad:** 5,000
- **Countries:** Operations are in countries in Africa, Asia, the Caribbean, Europe, Latin America, the Middle East, and the Near East.
- **Application Information:** Applicants should write to recruiter's address and request registration materials for the yearly Foreign Service written examination.
- **Salaries:** $21,000-$86,000 per year.
- **Job Categories:** Administrative, Clerical Assistants, Economists, Engineers, Medical Personnel, Political Scientists.
- **General Requirements:** Applicants must be U.S. citizens between the ages of 20 and 59, and a high school graduate or equivalent (some positions require a higher degree), and available to work anywhere in the world.
- **Average Overseas Assignment:** 2-4 years.
- **Language Requirement:** Knowledge of a foreign language a plus but not essential; may influence initial salary.
- **Training:** Basic orientation, training in specific work skills, and language training are provided.
- **Benefits:** TRAVEL: Home leave is mandatory by law; other benefits include shipment of automobiles to posts, and travel and lodging payments while enroute for employee and

dependents. HEALTH: A variety of health benefit plans are available including Blue Cross-Blue Shield and a Foreign Service Benefit Plan. HOUSING: Allowances include government-provided housing, furniture, and payment of utility bills, and may include cost-of-living allotment. EDUCATION: Offered; also dependents attending high school or college in the United States are offered annual travel expenses to and from post.

- **Comments:** Applicant must take the yearly Foreign Service written examination as it is the first step in becoming a Foreign Service Officer. A booklet describing application procedures will be sent upon request.

U.S. DEPARTMENT OF TRANSPORTATION

400 Seventh St. SW
Washington, DC 20590 USA

RECRUITER: EDWARD TURNER
DIRECTOR, INTERNATIONAL AFFAIRS
400 SEVENTH ST. SW
WASHINGTON, DC 20590
TEL: (202) 366-9392
FAX: (202) 366-3733

Federico Pena, Secretary of Transportation. Agency of the U.S. government responsible for transportation interests and policy. The Department of Transportation (DOT) is responsible for federal transportation policies and programs involving highways, mass transit, aviation, waterways, and ports. International interests are focused on aviation, maritime, and trade issues.

- **Total Employees:** Not available.
- **U.S. Employees Abroad:** Not available.
- **Countries:** Operations are in countries in Africa, Asia, the Caribbean, Europe, Latin America, the Middle East, and the Near East.
- **Job Categories:** Administrative, Technical Field Support.
- **Language Requirement:** Varies with each posting.

U.S. DEPARTMENT OF TREASURY

1500 Pennsylvania Ave. NW
Washington, DC 20220 USA

RECRUITER: DANIEL O'BRIEN
OFFICE OF INTERNATIONAL AFFAIRS
1500 PENNSYLVANIA AVE. NW
WASHINGTON, DC 20220
TEL: (202) 622-0060
FAX: (202) 622-0081

Lloyd Bentsen, Secretary of the Treasury. Agency of the U.S. government, engaged in economic, financial, fiscal, and tax policies. The Department of Treasury has four basic functions: formulating and recommending economic, financial, and fiscal policies; serving as financial agent of the U.S. government; enforcing tax laws; and manufacturing coins and currency. Global interests are concentrated in the areas of international tax and banking, finance, investment, and monetary and trade issues.

- **Total Employees:** Not available.

- **U.S. Employees Abroad:** Not available.
- **Countries:** Operations are in countries in Africa, Asia, the Caribbean, Europe, Latin America, the Middle East, and the Near East.
- **Job Categories:** Administrative, Finance.
- **General Requirements:** Degree in related field (business administration, finance); international experience preferred.
- **Language Requirement:** Varies with each posting.

U.S. ENVIRONMENTAL PROTECTION AGENCY

401 M St. NW
Washington, DC 20460 USA

RECRUITER: DIRECTOR, RECRUITMENT
401 M ST., NW
WASHINGTON, DC 20460
TEL: (202) 382-4870

William K. Reilly, Administrator. Environmental issues. An independent agency of the U.S. government, the Environmental Protection Agency's goal is to protect and enhance the environment for today and future generations. It controls and abates pollution in the areas of air and water, pesticides, radiation, solid waste, and toxic substances. It has an increasing interest in international environmental issues.

- **Total Employees:** Not available.
- **U.S. Employees Abroad:** Not available.
- **Countries:** Operations are in countries in Africa, Asia, the Caribbean, Europe, Latin America, and the Near East.
- **Job Categories:** Administrative, Conservation Specialists, Technical Field Support.
- **General Requirements:** Applicant should have a strong background in environmental or conservation studies.
- **Language Requirement:** Varies with each posting.

U.S. FEDERAL AVIATION ADMINISTRATION

800 Independence Ave. SW
Washington, DC 20591 USA

RECRUITER: JOAN BAUERLEIN
DIRECTOR, INTERNATIONAL AVIATION OFFICE
800 INDEPENDENCE AVE. SW
WASHINGTON, DC 20591
TEL: (202) 267-3213
FAX: (202) 267-5306

Barry L. Harris, Deputy Administrator. Administers the rules and regulations of navigable airspace, including civil and military operations. The Federal Aviation Administration (FAA) is an agency of the U.S. Department of Transportation. It is engaged in regulating air commerce; controlling the use of navigable airspace in the interest of safety and efficiency; promoting and developing civil aeronautics; conducting research and development in air navigation; installing and operating air navigation facilities; creating a common system of air traffic control for civil and military aircraft; and developing and implementing programs and laws to control aircraft noise, and other environmental effects of civil aviation.

- **Total Employees:** Not available.

- **U.S. Employees Abroad:** 700

- **Countries:** Worldwide including countries in Latin America as well as in Belgium, Germany, United Kingdom.

- **Job Categories:** Administrative, Safety Inspectors, Security Officers.

- **General Requirements:** Key licenses required for aviation positions; may include an Airframe & Powerplant (A & P) license.

- **Language Requirement:** Varies with each posting.

- **Training:** No special training offered.

U.S. FEDERAL BUREAU OF INVESTIGATION

10th & Pennsylvania Ave.
Washington, DC 20535 USA

RECRUITER: GWEN HUBBARD
RECRUITMENT/STAFFING
10TH & PENNSYLVANIA AVE.
WASHINGTON, DC 20535
TEL: (202) 324-4991
FAX: (202) 324-8255

Judge William S. Sessions, Executive Director. Investigative services for the U.S. Department of Justice. The Federal Bureau of Investigation (FBI) investigates all violations of criminal laws except for those assigned to other agencies (such as alcohol, counterfitting, postal and tobacco tax violations). It is involved in fingerprinting, lab services, and police training on a global basis.

- **Total Employees:** Not available.

- **U.S. Employees Abroad:** Not available.

- **Countries:** Operations are in countries in Africa, Asia, the Caribbean, Europe, Latin America, the Middle East, and the Near East.

- **Application Information:** Most foreign positions are filled internally.

- **Job Categories:** Administrative, Agents—Investigative.

- **General Requirements:** Applicant should have experience in the criminal justice field.

- **Language Requirement:** Varies with each posting.

- **Training:** Contact organization for information.

U.S. FOREIGN AGRICULTURE SERVICE

14th & Independence Ave. SW
Washington, DC 20250 USA

RECRUITER: RECRUITMENT
    COORDINATOR
EMPLOYMENT & CLASSIFICATION
14TH & INDEPENDENCE AVE. SW
WASHINGTON, DC 20250
TEL: (202) 720-1587
FAX: (202) 720-2016

Richard Schroeter, Acting Administrator. Expands exports of U.S. agricultural products. The Foreign Agriculture Service (FAS) is part of the U.S. Department of Agriculture. It is one of the largest employers of international specialists with expertise in agricultural issues affecting U.S. agriculture and trade policies. It has specialists in more than 60 American embassies and consulates throughout the world.

- **Total Employees:** 800
- **U.S. Employees Abroad:** 200
- **Countries:** Operations are in countries in Africa, Asia, the Caribbean, Europe, Latin America, and the Middle East.
- **Application Information:** Most foreign positions are filled from the existing Civil Service Pool.
- **Job Categories:** Economists, Forestry, Marketing.
- **General Requirements:** Degree in related field.
- **Language Requirement:** Varies with each posting.
- **Comments:** At the time of publication a hiring freeze was in effect.

U.S. GENERAL ACCOUNTING OFFICE

441 G St. NW
Washington, DC 20548 USA

RECRUITER: OLIVER LEWIS
DIRECTOR OF OPERATIONS,
    RECRUITMENT
441 G ST. NW
WASHINGTON, DC 20548
TEL: (202) 512-6092
FAX: (202) 512-2539
FREE: (800) WORK-GAO

Charles Bowsher, Comptroller-General. Involved in all matters pertaining to the receipt and disbursement of public funds. The General Accounting Office (GAO) is the investigative branch of Congress and monitors and audits all executive agencies involved in national and international matters. It is engaged in accounting systems audits, congressional support, program evaluation, and public policy review.

- **Total Employees:** 5,000
- **U.S. Employees Abroad:** 60
- **Countries:** Germany.
- **Salaries:** $40,000-$85,000 per year.

- **Job Categories:** Auditors, Evaluators.
- **General Requirements:** Usually must be a current employee with GAO in order to qualify for an overseas position.
- **Average Overseas Assignment:** 2-3 years.
- **Language Requirement:** Knowledge of local language a plus but not essential.
- **Training:** Basic orientation (1-30 days) provided.
- **Benefits:** TRAVEL: Home leave and travel expenses are offered once per year; also moving expenses are paid. HEALTH: Same coverage as U.S. employees. HOUSING: Varies with each posting; a percentage increase in base salary is allowed.

U.S. GENERAL SERVICES ADMINISTRATION

7th & D Streets SW
Washington, DC 20407 USA

RECRUITER: LENORE REESE
ACTING REGIONAL PERSONNEL
OFFICER
7TH & D STREETS SW
WASHINGTON, DC 20407
TEL: (202) 708-5300
FAX: (202) 708-5352

Richard G. Austin, Administrator. Provides economical and efficient management for various agencies and federal activities. The General Services Administration (GSA) is an independent agency of the U.S. government, engaged in the establishment of policy and the management of government property and records, including the construction and operation of buildings; the procurement and distribution of supplies; utilization and disposal of property; transportation, traffic, and communications operations; and the management of the government-wide automatic data processing resources program.

- **Total Employees:** Not available.
- **U.S. Employees Abroad:** Not available.
- **Countries:** Operation African, Asia, the Caribbean, European, Latin America, the Middle East, and the Near East.
- **Job Categories:** Administrative, Technical Field Support.
- **Language Requirement:** Varies with each posting.

UNITED STATES INFORMATION AGENCY

301 Fourth St. NW, Room #518
Washington, DC 20547 USA

RECRUITER: TINA GRAHAM
PERSONNEL OFFICE
301 FOURTH ST. NW, ROOM #518
WASHINGTON, DC 20547
TEL: (202) 619-4663
FAX: (202) 205-0496

Dr. Joseph Duffey, Director. Independent foreign affairs agency of the federal government. The United States Information Agency (USIA) is known abroad as the

United States Information Service (USIS). USIA's primary work is carried out by foreign service officers who advocate American foreign policy objectives through various channels, including the Voice of America program. It is also engaged in many communications activities, including Radio and TV Marti, the WORLDNET satellite television system, the daily Wireless File newswire, the Fulbright scholarship program, the International Visitor program, the U.S. Speakers Abroad program, publications translated in 15 languages, three Foreign Press Centers in the United States, and a network of overseas libraries and cultural centers. It has 210 posts in more than 140 countries.

- **Total Employees:** 9,000
- **U.S. Employees Abroad:** 1,000
- **Countries:** Operations are in countries in Africa, Asia, the Caribbean, Europe, Latin America, the Middle East, and the Near East.
- **Application Information:** Applicants may call (202) 619-4659 for current openings or information on job applications.
- **Job Categories:** Administrative, Finance, Field Service Positions, Teachers.
- **General Requirements:** International experience is preferred.
- **Language Requirement:** Competency in local language required.

U.S. MARINE CORPS

Headquarters, MPC-2 Navy Annex
Washington, DC 20301-1155 USA

RECRUITER: A. E. LAWRENCE
HUMAN RESOURCES OFFICER
CAMP S. D. BUTLER
FPO SEATTLE, WA 98773-5000
TEL: 001816117544

General C. E. Mundy, Jr., Commandant of the Marine Corps. Provides fleet marine forces for the Department of the Navy in the preservation of peace and protection of the United States. The Marine Corps was established by a resolution of the Continental Congress on November 10, 1775. It operates within the Department of the Navy, a division of the Department of Defense. Its job is to organize, train, equip, and provide fleet marine forces for the preservation and protection of the United States on a global basis.

- **Total Employees:** 18,000
- **U.S. Employees Abroad:** 500
- **Countries:** Japan.
- **Application Information:** Civilian personnel management in the Department of the Marine Corps is decentralized.
- **Job Categories:** Administrative, Technical Field Support.
- **General Requirements:** Applicant must be a current career federal civil service employee with reinstatement eligibility.
- **Language Requirement:** Varies with each posting.

U.S. PEACE CORPS

1990 K St. NW
Washington, DC 20526 USA

RECRUITER: JANET HADDAD
ACTING DIRECTOR, HUMAN
    RESOURCE MGMT.
1990 K ST. NW
WASHINGTON, DC 20526
TEL: (202) 606-3950
FREE: (800) 424-8580

John P. Hogan, Acting Director. Promotes peace, friendship, and understanding in developing countries through volunteer programs. The Peace Corps is an independent agency involved in many volunteer programs in more than 70 developing countries throughout the world. Its primary focus is on international development activities in agriculture, education, environment, health, small business development, urban development, and youth services.

- **Total Employees:** 1,297

- **U.S. Employees Abroad:** 246

- **Countries:** Operations are in countries in Africa, Asia, the Caribbean, Europe, Latin America, the Middle East, and the Near East.

- **Application Information:** Call to request copies of vacancy announcements; Federal Application, Supplemental Statement, and Intelligence Background Information are required.

- **Salaries:** Associate PC Directors: $35,438-$79,261; Country Directors: $43,734-$86,589 per year.

- **Job Categories:** Administrative.

- **General Requirements:** All Peace Corps employees must be U.S. citizens and cannot have worked for the CIA or other intelligence-gathering organizations.

- **Average Overseas Assignment:** 2-3 years.

- **Language Requirement:** Knowledge of local language a plus but not essential.

- **Training:** Basic training (1-30 days) provided.

- **Benefits:** TRAVEL: All employees receive five days home leave per year and may use it after completion of 18 months of service. HEALTH: Same coverage as U.S. employees. HOUSING: Offered. EDUCATION: Offered.

U.S. TOTAL ARMY PERSONNEL COMMAND

TAPC-CPF-Jim Hiltz
2200 Stovall St.
Alexandria, VA 22332-0340 USA

RECRUITER: PETER HORN
DIRECTOR, CIVILIAN PERSONNEL
TAPC-CPF-JIM HILTZ
2200 STOVALL ST.
ALEXANDRIA, VA 22332-0340
TEL: (703) 697-2961
FAX: (703) 325-4465

Michael P. W. Stone, Secretary of the Army. Defends and preserves the peace and security of the United States. The Department of the Army is a part of the U.S. Department of Defense. It was established by Congress as the American Continental Army on June 14, 1775. Its mission is to organize equipment and recruit active duty and reserve forces for the preservation and security of the United States at home and overseas.

- **Total Employees:** Not available.
- **U.S. Employees Abroad:** Not available.
- **Countries:** Operations are in countries in Africa, Asia, the Caribbean, Europe, Latin America, the Middle East, and the Near East.
- **Application Information:** Civilian personnel management in the Department of the Army is decentralized.
- **Job Categories:** Administrative, Field Service Positions.
- **General Requirements:** Applicant must be a* current career Federal civil service employee with reinstatement eligibility. If not, see comments below.
- **Language Requirement:** Varies with each posting.
- **Comments:** For more information on where current overseas operations are located, contact the Office of Personnel Management, 1900 E Street, Washington, DC 20415; (202) 606-2424.

VOICE OF AMERICA: BUREAU OF BROADCASTING

301 Fourth St. NW
Washington, DC 20547 USA

RECRUITER: JANICE BRAMBILLA
PERSONNEL DIRECTOR
301 FOURTH ST. NW
WASHINGTON, DC 20547
TEL: (202) 619-3117
FAX: (202) 205-8427

Joseph Bruns, Acting Director. Federal government international broadcasting. Voice of America (VOA) is part of the United States Information Agency (USIA). It is a divison of the Bureau of Broadcasting (one of the major functional elements of the USIA). VOA is the Bureau's main function for global radio broadcasting. Operating under a charter from Congress, it serves as a reliable, authoritative, accurate, objective, and comprehensive news source. It produces and broadcasts radio programs in English and 44 languages for overseas audiences.

- **Total Employees:** Not available.
- **U.S. Employees Abroad:** Not available.
- **Countries:** Operations are in countries in Africa, Asia, the Caribbean, Europe, Latin America, the Middle East, and the Near East.
- **Application Information:** For current job information, direct inquiries to: VOA, B/PF-Room 1274, 330 Independence Ave. SW, Washington, DC 20547.
- **Job Categories:** Radio Engineers.

- **General Requirements:** Applicants must be available for worldwide service; radio engineers must have experience working with high-powered transmitters.
- **Language Requirement:** Fluency in local language required.
- **Training:** Varies with each posting.
- **Benefits:** All benefits are offered.

VOLUNTEERS IN TECHNICAL ASSISTANCE, INC

1600 Wilson Blvd., Suite #500
Arlington, VA 22209 USA

RECRUITER: REGINA A. WYNN
DIRECTOR, RECRUITMENT
1600 WILSON BLVD., SUITE #500
ARLINGTON, VA 22209
TEL: (703) 276-1800
FAX: (703) 276-1865

Henry R. Norman, Executive Director. Supplies technological information and support. Volunteers in Technical Assistance, Inc. (VITA) was established in 1960 and provides information and assistance on the current technology to aid small businesses, farmers, community workers, and government agencies. Its goal is to help people in developing countries improve the quality of their lives through communications training and management courses. It produces a variety of publications and broadcasts a weekly Voice of America program. It enables people, even in remote areas of the world, to join the mainstream of development.

- **Total Employees:** 29
- **U.S. Employees Abroad:** 9
- **Countries:** Chad, Kenya, Pakistan.
- **Job Categories:** Agricultural Specialists, Communications, Environmental Specialists, Finance.
- **General Requirements:** Prior overseas experience (prefer Africa), a minimum of five years; M.A. degree preferred.
- **Average Overseas Assignment:** 2-3 years.
- **Language Requirement:** Fluency in local language required.
- **Training:** Basic training (1-30 days) provided.
- **Benefits:** All benefits are offered.

WORLD BANK GROUP

1818 H St. NW
Washington, DC 20433 USA

RECRUITER: SOROYA MASSOUD
ADMNISTRATIVE ASSISTANT
1818 H ST., NW
WASHINGTON, DC 20433
TEL: (202) 473-0828
FAX: (202) 477-4549

Lewis T. Preston, President. International lending institution of the United Nations. The World Bank Group, also known as the International Bank for Reconstruction and Development, promotes economic development in developing countries of Asia, Africa, and Latin America. It provides direct loans and policy advice and administers technical assistance programs.

- **Total Employees:** 2,500

- **U.S. Employees Abroad:** 70

- **Countries:** Operations are in countries in Africa, Asia, and Latin America.

- **Job Categories:** Administrative, Economists, Finance.

- **General Requirements:** Degree in related field.

- **Language Requirement:** Varies with each posting.

WORLD CONCERN

19303 Fremont Ave. North
Seattle, WA 98133 USA

RECRUITER: DUANE BREDIN
INTERNATIONAL PERSONNEL
SERVICES
19303 FREMONT AVE. NORTH
SEATTLE, WA 98133
TEL: (206) 546-7488
FAX: (206) 546-7269

Fred Gregory, Executive Director. Relief, rehabilitation, and self-help development programs in Third World countries. World Concern is a division of CRISTA Ministries. It provides personnel, commodities, and funds to aid projects in the areas of agriculture, community and economic development, education, emergency relief, health, refugee aid, and water development.

- **Total Employees:** 135

- **U.S. Employees Abroad:** 100

- **Countries:** Operations are in countries in Africa, Asia, and Latin America.

- **Salaries:** Basic expenses are covered as well as benefits, and a guaranteed, modest monthly stipend.

- **Job Categories:** Agricultural Specialists, Construction Workers, Economists, Management, Medical Personnel, Teachers, Technical Field Support, Veterinarians.

- **Average Overseas Assignment:** 2-3 years.

- **Language Requirement:** Knowledge of local language a plus but not essential.

- **Training:** Basic orientation (1-30 days) provided.

- **Benefits:** All benefits are offered.

WORLD INTELLECTUAL PROPERTY ORGANIZATION

34, chemin des Colombettes
Geneva, Switzerland USA

RECRUITER: CLIVE WOODFORD
HEAD, PERSONNEL RECRUITMENT
    SECTION
34 CHEMIN DES COLUMBETTES
1211 GENEVA 20, SWITZERLAND
TEL: (41)-227309111
FAX: (41)-227335428

Dr. Arpad Bogsch, Director General. Encourages the protection of intellectual property on a global basis. The World Intellectual Property Organization (WIPO) is a specialized agency of the United Nations. It promotes the protection of intellectual property by encouraging member states to cooperate in matters that involve industrial property (patents, trademarks, industrial designs, etc.) and copyrights. It also publishes newsletters, reports, and books.

- **Total Employees:** 423
- **U.S. Employees Abroad:** 15
- **Countries:** Switzerland.
- **Application Information:** The WIPO Liason Office is located at One U.N. Plaza, New York, NY 10017; (212) 963-6813. Direct inquiries to that address.
- **Salaries:** Common pay scales of the United Nations.
- **Job Categories:** Attorneys.
- **General Requirements:** Lawyers with intellectual property background and considerable experience.
- **Average Overseas Assignment:** Two years; renewable.
- **Language Requirement:** Fluency in local language (French) required.
- **Training:** No special training provided.
- **Benefits:** TRAVEL: Offered; home leave granted every two years. HEALTH: Offered. HOUSING: Rental subsidy is offered. EDUCATION: An allowance of up to 75 percent of education costs is offered.

WORLD LEARNING CENTER

Kipling Rd.
PO Box 676
Brattleboro, VT 05301 USA

RECRUITER: SUE BARNUM
EMPLOYEE RELATIONS/OUTREACH
    ASSISTANT
1015 15TH ST. NW, SUITE #750
WASHINGTON, DC 20005
TEL: (802) 257-7757
FAX: (802) 258-3248
FREE: (800) 451-4465

Alan Carter, Acting President. Operates cross-cultural and international exchange programs. World Learning Center (formerly known as U.S. Experiment in International Living) enables participants to develop knowledge, abilities, and skills needed to contribute effectively to international understanding and global development. World Learning has four areas of expertise: Advancing Citizen Exchange, Educating for Global Issues, Building Language Competence, and Training for International Development.

- **Total Employees:** 551
- **U.S. Employees Abroad:** 80
- **Countries:** Operations are in countries in Africa, Asia, the Caribbean, Europe, Latin America, the Middle East, and the Near East.
- **Application Information:** Recruitment in Washington, D.C., office is for Projects in International Training (PIDT). Recruitment in Vermont office is for Academic Studies Abroad (ASA) and Group Leader positions for Summer Abroad program.
- **Job Categories:** Academic Directors.
- **General Requirements:** Applicant must have international experience working abroad; Group Leaders must be 24 years old; Academic Studies Abroad requires a master's degree.
- **Average Overseas Assignment:** Duration for overseas positions varies with each posting, PIDT, 2-3 years; ASA, less than 2 years; Group Leader for Summer Abroad, 6-8 weeks.
- **Language Requirement:** Competency in local language required.
- **Training:** Basic orientation (1-30 days) provided.
- **Benefits:** TRAVEL: Offered; varies with each posting. HEALTH: Offered; varies with each posting. HOUSING: Offered; varies with each posting. EDUCATION: Not offered.

WORLD RELIEF

PO Box #WRC
Wheaton, IL 60189 USA

RECRUITER: JIM WATTERS
DIRECTOR, HUMAN RESOURCES
PO BOX #WRC
WHEATON, IL 60189
TEL: (708) 665-0235
FAX: (708) 653-9023

Dr. Arthur Evans Gay, Jr., Executive Director. Relief and development. World Relief is a private voluntary organization of the National Association of Evangelicals, promoting agriculture, community and rural development, health, nutrition, refugee relief, resettlement programs, and vocational training on a global basis. It also supplies emergency aid to disaster-stricken countries.

- **Total Employees:** 265
- **U.S. Employees Abroad:** 15
- **Countries:** Operations are in countries in Africa, Asia, and Latin America.
- **Job Categories:** Administrative, Health Professionals, Teachers.
- **General Requirements:** Degree in related field.
- **Average Overseas Assignment:** Varies with each posting; usually two years.

- **Language Requirement:** Competency in local language required.
- **Training:** Basic training (1-30 days) provided.
- **Benefits:** All benefits vary with each posting.

WORLD VISION RELIEF AND DEVELOPMENT, INC.

919 Huntington Dr.
Monrovia, CA 91016 USA

RECRUITER: DIRECTOR,
RECRUITMENT
919 HUNTINGTON AVE.
MONROVIA, CA 91016
TEL: (818) 357-7979
FAX: (818) 358-7615

Dr. Robert Seiple, President. Provides assistance through relief services and training. World Vision is a private international organization established in 1954. It provides disaster relief, primary health care and child survival services, water development, natural resource management, and community leadership training. Assistance is offered to Third World countries as well as to nine European nations.

- **Total Employees:** 700
- **U.S. Employees Abroad:** Not available.
- **Countries:** Operations are in countries in Africa, Asia, Europe, the Far East, and the Middle East.
- **Job Categories:** Administrative, Health Professionals, Medical Personnel, Relief Workers, Field Service Positions.
- **General Requirements:** Degree (business or medical) in related field.
- **Language Requirement:** Competency in local language required.

WORLD WILDLIFE FUND

1250 24th St. NW
Washington, DC 20037 USA

RECRUITER: PROFESSIONAL
RECRUITMENT/STAFFING
1250 24TH ST. NW
WASHINGTON, DC 20037
TEL: (202) 293-4800
FAX: (202) 292-9211

Kathryn Fuller, President. Promotes the protection of endangered wildlife and wildlands. World Wildlife Fund is a private voluntary organization established in 1961. It encourages the protection of endangered wildlife and wildlands with a strong focus on the conservation of tropical forest. Major funding is derived from USAID, foundations, and corporations.

- **Total Employees:** 325
- **U.S. Employees Abroad:** Not available.
- **Countries:** Operations are in countries in Africa, Asia, and Latin America.
- **Job Categories:** Environmental Specialists, Field Service Positions.
- **General Requirements:** Applicant should have a strong background in environmental or conservation studies.

C O U N T R Y | P R O F I L E S

PRINT SOURCES

   If you want to learn more about any of the countries that are profiled in the following pages, most public libraries house depositories for government pamphlets on foreign countries, or you may write to:

   SUPERINTENDENT OF DOCUMENTS
   U.S. GOVERNMENT PRINTING OFFICE
   WASHINGTON, DC 20402
   202-783-3238

   Ask for information regarding a specific country where you will travel

INTERNATIONAL SCHOOLS

   For current information on the availability, curricula, and fees of the principal international schools in the countries profiled in the following pages, contact:

   OFFICE OF OVERSEAS SCHOOLS (A/OS)
   OFFICE OF OVERSEAS SCHOOLS (A/OS)
   U.S. DEPARTMENT OF STATE
   ROOM 245, SA-29
   WASHINGTON, DC 20522-2902
   TEL: 703-875-7800

   OR

   EUROPEAN COUNCIL OF INTERNATIONAL SCHOOLS (ECIS)
   21B LAVANT ST.
   PETERSFIELD, HAMPSHIRE
   GU32 3EL ENGLAND
   TEL: 44 (0) 730 68244/6
   FAX: 44 (0) 730 67914

A
M
E
R
I
C
A
N

J
O
B
S

A
B
R
O
A
D

Note: When a cost of living figure is given, it is based on a scale in which the comparable figure for Washington, D.C., is 100.

ALBANIA

- **Official Name:** Republic of Albania
- **Capital:** Tiranδ
- **Location:** Albania is located on the Balkan Peninsula in southeastern Europe. It is bounded by Yugoslavia to the north, Macedonia to the east, Greece to the south, and the Adriatic and Ionian Seas to the west. The total land area is 11,100 square miles, making Albania slightly larger than Maryland. Much of the country is mountainous, especially in the northern section. The central uplands extending to the west form the Adriatic coastal plain. Nearly half of the territory is covered by forests.
- **Language and Currency:** The official language is Albanian. Having a working knowledge of this language is important if you are going to live or work in this country. The monetary unit is the lek. The exchange rate is 110 leks = U.S.$1 (December 1993).
- **Print Sources of Information:** *The Area Handbook For Albania* (1971). Available from the Superintendent of Documents, U.S. Government Printing Office, Washington, D.C., 20402.

EMBASSY AND CONSULATE CONTACT INFORMATION:

ALBANIAN EMBASSY
1511 K ST. NW
WASHINGTON, DC 20005
TEL: 202-223-4942

COMPANIES/ORGANIZATIONS WITH OPERATIONS IN ALBANIA:

INTERNATIONAL FERTILIZER
DEVELOPMENT CENTER, 549

ALGERIA

- **Official Name:** Democratic and Popular Republic of Algeria
- **Capital:** Algiers
- **Location:** Algeria is the tenth-largest country in the world and is located on the northern coast of Africa. It is bounded by the Mediterranean Sea to the north, Morocco and Mauritania to the west, Mali and Niger to the south, and Tunisia and Libya to the east. With a total land area of 919,595 square miles, Algeria is approximately one-third the size of the United States. More than three-fourths of its territory is comprised of desert, wasteland, and mountains, with most of the people living in the northern coastal

region, the Tell. The Atlas Mountains and Haut Plateau separate the Tell from the great Sahara Desert, which lies in the central and southern regions of Algeria.

- **Language and Currency:** The official language of Algeria is Arabic, but French is widely used throughout business circles. English and German are not common languages, so having a working knowledge of French, or preferably Arabic, is recommended. The unit of currency is the dinar, written as DA (or AD) and is considered soft currency. Only tourists are allowed to exchange dinars back into hard currency. The exchange rate is 23.90 Algerian dinars = U.S.$1 (November 1993).

COMPANIES/ORGANIZATIONS WITH OPERATIONS IN ALGERIA:

BECHTEL GROUP, INC., 162
DRESSER INDUSTRIES, INC., 241
LITTON INDUSTRIES, INC., 348

ANGOLA

- **Official Name:** People's Republic of Angola
- **Capital:** Luanda
- **Location:** Angola is located on the southwest coast of Africa, bounded on the north and northeast by Zaire, on the east by Zambia, on the south by Namibia, and on the west by the southern Atlantic Ocean. Cabinda, part of Angola, lies to its northwest corner, though it is separated from the rest of Angola by the Congo River and a narrow strip of Zaire. Most of Angola is a vast inland plateau. The land rises from the interior to the west, and then drops dramatically to a thin plain along the Atlantic coast. Total land area is 481,354 square miles, making Angola nearly twice the size of Texas.
- **Population, Cities, and American Residents:** The population of Angola totals 10.6 million people (1992 est.), and is almost entirely Black African. Of the many tribal groups, the largest are the Ovimbundu, the Mbundu, the Kongo, and the Luanda-Chokwe.

  Most American residents are employed in Angola's two major cities: Luanda with a population of 3 million, and Cabinda with 100,000 people (1992 est.).
- **Language and Currency:** The official language of Angola is Portuguese, which most educated Africans and Europeans speak. Various Bantu dialects also are used throughout the country, but only 30 percent of the population can read or write in any language. A working knowledge of Portuguese is useful. The unit of currency is the Novo kwanza. The exchange rate is U.S.$1 = 4,000 Novo kwanzas (August 25, 1993).

- **Climate:** The climate of Angola is mild with a yearly average temperature of 65°F along the coast and somewhat higher temperatures inland. Rain averages 55 inches yearly in the northern and coastal regions, but the southern areas receive only two inches during the year.

- **Economy and Resources:** The backbone of the Angolan economy is agriculture. Three-quarters of the people live in rural areas and live off the land, though industrial development and mining are growing in importance. Angola has abundant mineral resources, including diamonds, iron ore, and petroleum, with most of the latter found in the northern district of Cabinda. Of the labor force, 85 percent work in agriculture and 15 percent in industry. Chief exports are oil, coffee, diamonds, sisal, fish, and fish oil. Major export markets are the United States and Russia. Civil war and economic mismanagement have damaged the economy of Angola, but government and economic reforms have begun to show promising results. Business development is being stimulated through training and teaching programs, and foreign investment is being encouraged. Government officials have recognized a need for austerity and increased productivity. Most of the Angolan economy is nationalized, but some private concerns still operate. Unless the long civil war is settled by a peace agreement, the prospects for a stable economy are doubtful.

- **Cost of Living:** There is insufficient local retail price data to develop meaningful cost of living comparisons.

- **Work Permits, Visas, etc.:** A valid passport and visa are required for travel in Angola. If you are entering Angola from the United States, no vaccinations are required, though The Centers for Disease Control (CDC) has recommended yellow fever vaccinations for travelers under nine months of age who go outside the urban areas of Angola. For official or other information, direct inquiries to the embassy or consulate at the addresses below.

- **Taxation:** Expatriates are responsible for local taxes, which are usually collected by foreign-based firms in Angola.

- **Principal International Schools:** Currently there are no international schools in Angola.

- **Health Care:** Medical care is available in Luanda and other major cities, but there is a drastic shortage of supplies. Only simple procedures can be handled, so if a serious medical problem arises, leave the country to seek better professional care. Water is unsafe to drink in most areas. Sanitation also is poor. Cook all meats and fish until they are well done, and precautions should be taken with all fruits and vegetables.

- **Crime:** The war between UNITA (National Union for the Total Independence of Angola) and the Angolan government is ongoing, despite repeated cease-fire agreements. Violent crime exists throughout the country, with armed robbery and guerrilla attacks occurring along highways and in some tourist areas. The Department of State has issued a warning to U.S. citizens advising against travel to Angola, because of unsettled conditions (December 1992). Travel in rural areas is unsafe due to the presence of armed troops, roadside bandits, and numerous unexploded land mines, which are still being removed from the roadways and footpaths. Luanda is the only city considered safe to travel by day.

- **Pros and Cons of Living and Working in Angola:** The country is very unstable due to nearly continuous war and civil strife since its independence from Portugal in 1975. There are severe shortages of food, water, utilities, lodging, and transportation in all areas, including Luanda. Most medicines are unavailable, and malaria is prevalent throughout the country. Currently, the United States does not recognize or maintain diplomatic relations with Angola. There is one U.S. liaison office located at the Casa Inglesa, first floor, Rua Major Kanyangunla, in the capital of Luanda. However, in November 1992, the staff was reduced, and no consular personnel are assigned to this office. Only emergency services are provided to American citizens. Facilities for tourism are virtually nonexistent.

EMBASSY AND CONSULATE CONTACT INFORMATION:

EMBASSY OF THE PEOPLE'S REPUBLIC OF ANGOLA
1899 L ST. NW, STE. 500
WASHINGTON, DC 20036
202-785-1156

ANGOLA MISSION TO THE U.N.
PEOPLE'S REPUBLIC OF ANGOLA
125 EAST 73RD ST.
NEW YORK, NY 10021
TEL: 212-861-5657

OTHER SOURCES OF INFORMATION:

U.S. STATE DEPT.
DESK OFFICER FOR SOUTHERN AFRICAN AFFAIRS, RM. 4238
2201 C ST. NW
WASHINGTON, DC 20520
TEL: 202-647-8434
FAX: 202-647-5007

COMPANIES/ORGANIZATIONS WITH OPERATIONS IN ANGOLA:

ABB VETCO GRAY, INC., 108
CHEVRON CORPORATION, 193
CHEVRON OVERSEAS PETROLEUM, INC., 194

CONOCO, INC., 209
GENERAL TIRE, INC., 279
MOBIL OIL CORPORATION, 375
TEXACO OIL COMPANY, 493

ANTIGUA AND BARBUDA

- **Official Name:** Antigua and Barbuda

- **Capital:** St. John's

- **Location:** The islands of Antigua and Barbuda comprise an independent state of the United Kingdom (independence was gained on November 1, 1981). It is located in the eastern Caribbean Sea about 300 miles southeast of Puerto Rico. It is bounded by the Atlantic Ocean to the north and east, and the Caribbean Sea to the south and west. Its total land area is 171 square miles making it nearly three times the size of Washington, D.C. Its terrain is comprised primarily of limestone that is built up in hills. The islands' outer edges have many coral reefs, and the coastline is indented with coves, natural harbors, and numerous sandy beaches.

- **Language and Currency:** The official language of Antigua and Barbuda is English, which is used throughout business and government. Various other dialects are spoken throughout the two islands. The monetary unit is the East Caribbean (EC) dollar divided into 100 cents. The current exchange rate is 2.65 EC = U.S.$1 (March 1994).

- **Print Source of Information:** Zellers, Margaret, editor. *Fielding's Caribbean.* New York: Fielding Travel Books, William Morrow & Co., 1992.

EMBASSY AND CONSULATE CONTACT INFORMATION:

EMBASSY OF ANTIGUA AND BARBUDA
INTELSAT BUILDING, STE. 4M
3400 INTERNATIONAL DR. NW
WASHINGTON, DC 20008
TEL: 202-362-5122

COMPANIES/ORGANIZATIONS WITH OPERATIONS IN ANTIGUA-BARBUDA:

AMERICAN CANADIAN CARIBBEAN LINE,
    123

ARGENTINA

- **Official Name:** Republic of Argentina

- **Capital:** Buenos Aires

- **Location:** Argentina is the second largest country in South America and the third largest country in the Southern Hemisphere. It is about twice the size of Alaska, encompassing an area of 1.1 million square miles. The country is bounded by the Atlantic and Antarctic Oceans and has four primary divisions: The Andes, which runs the entire length of the country along the western border, is low and very cold in the south, and high and dry in the north. The second area is the North and Mesopotamia, which includes the forested plains of the Chaco and the rolling lands of the Mesopotamia between the Parana and Uruguay rivers. The third area is the Pampas, the extreme flat lands extending from the Chaco in the north to the Colorado River in the south. It also extends from the Andes in the west to the Atlantic Ocean and Parana River to the east. The last area is Patagonia, a dry wind-swept area south of the Colorado River.

- **Population, Cities, and American Residents:** The population of Argentina totals 32.7 million (1991 est.), with Argentines of European extraction accounting for 85 percent. The remaining 15 percent includes mestizo, Indian, and other nonwhite groups.

    Most American residents are employed in Argentina's three largest cities: Buenos Aires with 10 million, Cordoba with 1.1 million, and Rosario with 1 million people (1985 est.).

- **Language and Currency:** The official language is Spanish, but English is the second language, used primarily in populated areas. French and Italian also are widely spoken. The monetary unit is the Peso. The exchange rate is 1 Argentine peso = U.S.$1.01

C
O
U
N
T
R
Y

P
R
O
F
I
L
E
S

(July 30, 1993). Five thousand four hundred fifty dollars and fifty cents would appear: $5.450,50. In South America, decimals are commas, and vice versa.

- **Climate:** Seasons are in the reverse of those in the Northern Hemisphere with Argentine summers beginning in December and running through February. It is usually very hot and humid, especially in the capital city of Buenos Aires. Temperatures range from 80°F to 95°F during the summer season, with extreme temperatures reaching 102°F-104°F. The relative humidity averages 70 percent, and the pollen count, in season, can be very high. Winter begins in June and lasts through August. The average temperature is 50°F and though it can drop to below freezing (32°F), it rarely snows in the capital city of Buenos Aires. Spring and fall are most pleasant. Buenos Aires is not subject to earthquakes, hurricanes, or typhoons, and precipitation is divided evenly throughout the year.

- **Economy and Resources:** Argentina is one of the richest countries in South America. It has a strong focus on agriculture, which supplies the major part of its export earnings. The temperate plains, known as the pampas, are the country's richest area in natural resources. Its farms produce wheat, corn, sorghum, soybeans, and sunflower seeds. The land also supplies year-round pasturage for the country's cattle industry with exports selling to various buyers including China and the United States. Other exports include canned, precooked, and frozen beef, as well as sugar and fruits. The natural resources and food produced enable manufacturing plants to play a key role in the Argentine economy. After World War II an uneven economic performance and political conflict prevented Argentina from realizing its full economic potential. Inflation is still high (198 percent in July 1989), and the country's foreign debt still stands at $60 billion (June 1990). When Carlos Saul Menem was elected president in 1989, the economy was in the midst of a severe crisis. While his government's policies of privatization and free markets have lowered inflation and interest rates, this has resulted in higher unemployment rates.

- **Cost of Living:** At 138, the cost of living is higher than in the United States.

- **Work Permits, Visas, etc.:** You'll need a valid passport to travel in Argentina, but a visa is required for a tourist stay of more than three months. No vaccinations are required to enter the country. For official or other information, direct inquiries to the embassy or consulate at the addresses below.

- **Taxation:** All income derived from Argentine sources is subject to income tax irrespective of the individual's domicile, citizenship, or residence. Foreigners residing in Argentina for up to six months in any year are subject to income tax at an effective rate of 25.2 percent, which must be withheld by the local payer. The major U.S. international accounting firms have affiliates in Argentina which publish comprehensive studies in English on local tax laws. Consult the U.S. offices of these firms for more information.

- **Principal International Schools:** There are many international schools with high standards in Buenos Aires, including American, German, French, Italian, Japanese, Armenian, and Jewish institutions. The maximum annual tuition averages $1,600 for a French school and $6,000 for an American one. There are fewer choices in other cities throughout the country.

A
M
E
R
I
C
A
N

J
O
B
S

A
B
R
O
A
D

- **Health Care:** Argentine doctors, dentists, and other medical personnel are competent and readily available in the major cities of the country. Fees for medical services are very reasonable. Argentina has more physicians per capita than the United States, but its ratio of nurses is less than one tenth of that of the United States. It is safe to drink tap water in the more populated areas, and local vegetables and fruits are also safe for consumption.

- **Crime:** As a general rule, it is safe to travel throughout the more populated areas of Argentina. Buenos Aires is secure, and the streets are well lit at night, and usually busy with pedestrian traffic. However, poor economic conditions in the country have led to an increase in common crime. Though it isn't suggested that a woman leave her jewelry at home, you should take the same precautions you would in any large city.

- **Pros and Cons of Living and Working in Argentina:** Argentina has an exciting, exotic charm with incredible scenery such as canyons, deserts, glaciers, and jungles. Many areas of this country offer a great variety of culture, art, and spectator sports. Concerts and theater are of high quality, with shops and restaurants in abundance. Housing is readily available and affordable, and transportation is very good, available by airplane, auto, bus, or train. On the negative side, summers can be quite warm and humid with pollen presenting a problem for some visitors. The economy is still troubled, and inflation remains high by American standards, so some goods are costly. Currently, there are several thousand Americans who live and work in the country. Many U.S. industrial firms and banks have subsidiaries in Argentina, with U.S. private investment totaling about $2.6 billion.

EMBASSY AND CONSULATE CONTACT INFORMATION:

ARGENTINE EMBASSY
1600 NEW HAMPSHIRE AVE. NW
WASHINGTON, DC 20009
TEL: 202-939-6400

ARGENTINE CONSULATE GENERAL
12 WEST 56 ST.
NEW YORK, NY 10019
TEL: 212-603-0400

OTHER SOURCES OF INFORMATION:
ARGENTINE-AMERICAN CHAMBER OF COMMERCE
50 WEST 34 ST.
NEW YORK, NY 10001
TEL: 212-564-3855

COMPANIES/ORGANIZATIONS WITH OPERATIONS IN ARGENTINA:

ALLERGAN, INC., 117
AMERICAN HOME PRODUCTS CORPORATION, 126
AMOCO CORPORATION, 131
AMP, INC., 132
AMPEX CORPORATION, 133
ASEA BROWN BOVERI, 142
BACKER SPIELVOGEL & BATES WORLDWIDE, INC., 150
BAKER HUGHES, INC., 152
BANK OF BOSTON CORPORATION, 153
THE BANK OF NEW YORK COMPANY, INC., 154

BANKERS TRUST NEW YORK CORPORATION, 155
BLACK & DECKER CORPORATION, 167
BLOCK DRUG COMPANY, INC., 169
BRIDGESTONE-FIRESTONE, INC., 174
CABOT CORPORATION, 181
CARGILL INCORPORATED, 184
CARRIER CORPORATION, 186
CHEMICAL BANKING CORPORATION, 191
CIGNA CORPORATION, 197
CITICORP, 198
THE COASTAL GROUP, 201
THE COCA-COLA COMPANY, 202

CONTINENTAL BANK CORPORATION, 210

CORNING INCORPORATED, 215

CROWN CORK & SEAL COMPANY, INC., 218

D'ARCY MASIUS BENTON & BOWLES INC., 225

DE KALB GENETICS CORPORATION, 227

DEERE & COMPANY, 229

DIAMOND SHAMROCK R & M, INC., 234

DOW CHEMICAL COMPANY, 240

DOW CORNING CORPORATION, 240

DRESSER INDUSTRIES, INC., 241

DURACELL, INC., 244

EASTMAN KODAK COMPANY, 246

EATON CORPORATION/CUTLER HAMMER, 247

ELI LILLY AND COMPANY, 250

ENCORE COMPUTER CORPORATION, 252

EXXON CHEMICAL COMPANY, 257

EXXON COMPANY, INTERNATIONAL, 258

EXXON CORPORATION, 258

FEDERAL-MOGUL CORPORATION, 260

FMC CORPORATION, 266

FORD MOTOR COMPANY, 267

FRITZ COMPANIES, 269

GENERAL TIRE, INC., 279

THE GILLETTE COMPANY, 283

W. R. GRACE & COMPANY, 285

GREY ADVERTISING, INC., 288

GTE CORPORATION, 288

HELENE CURTIS INDUSTRIES, INC., 298

HEWLETT-PACKARD COMPANY, 300

IDB COMMUNICATIONS, INC., 309

INTERNATIONAL BUSINESS MACHINES (IBM), 315

INTERNATIONAL FLAVORS & FRAGRANCES, INC., 317

ITT SHERATON CORPORATION, 322

JOHNSON & HIGGINS, 324

JOHNSON & JOHNSON, 325

KELLOGG COMPANY, 330

M. W. KELLOGG COMPANY, 331

KNOLL INTERNATIONAL, 338

KORN/FERRY INTERNATIONAL, 340

LINTAS: WORLDWIDE, 346

LIQUID CARBONIC CORPORATION, 347

LITTON INDUSTRIES, INC., 348

LOCTITE CORPORATION, 349

MCCANN-ERICKSON WORLDWIDE, 354

MCI COMMUNICATIONS CORPORATION, 365

MEASUREX CORPORATION, 366

MERRILL LYNCH & COMPANY, INC., 369

MONROE AUTO EQUIPMENT COMPANY, 376

MONSANTO COMPANY, 377

J. P. MORGAN & COMPANY, INC., 378

NALCO CHEMICAL COMPANY, 382

NORTON COMPANY, 390

NORWEST CORPORATION, 391

OGILVY & MATHER, 395

OTIS ELEVATOR COMPANY: WORLD HEADQUARTERS, 399

PARKER HANNIFIN CORPORATION, 405

PEPSICO FOODS INTERNATIONAL, 409

PHILIP MORRIS COMPANIES, INC., 413

PIONEER HI-BRED INTERNATIONAL, INC., 417

PREMARK INTERNATIONAL, INC., 423

PUROLATOR PRODUCTS COMPANY, 427

READING & BATES, 433

REVLON, INC., 437

ROHM & HAAS COMPANY, 442

ROLLINS HUDIG HALL INTERNATIONAL, 443

SGS CONTROL SERVICES, 458

SONOCO PRODUCTS COMPANY, 470

SONY PICTURES ENTERTAINMENT, 471

STANDARD COMMERCIAL CORPORATION, 476

TEXAS INTRUMENTS, INC., 494

3M COMPANY, 496

TRANE COMPANY, 501

TRITON ENERGY CORPORATION, 502

UNILEVER UNITED STATES, INC., 506

UNION CARBIDE CORPORATION, 507

UNISYS CORPORATION, 508

UNITED PRESS INTERNATIONAL, 509

UNITED TECHNOLOGIES CORPORATION, 512

UOP, INC., 514

THE UPJOHN COMPANY, 515

WARNER BROTHERS INTERNATIONAL, 521

WEST COMPANY, INC., 525

WESTINGHOUSE ELECTRIC CORPORATION, 525

WHIRLPOOL CORPORATION, 526

WMX TECHNOLOGIES/WASTE MANAGEMENT, INC., 527

WORLD COURIER MANAGEMENT, INC., 529

WYETH-AYERST LABORATORIES, 530
YOUNG & RUBICAM, INC., 533

━━━━

ARUBA

- **Official Name:** Aruba
- **Capital:** Oranjestad
- **Location:** Part of the Netherlands Antilles, Aruba is an island country located a few miles off the north coast of Venezuela in the Caribbean Sea. Aruba's neighbors are Curaçao and Bonaire to the southeast, Netherlands Antilles 42 miles to the east, and Venezuela 16 miles to the south. Aruba is a rocky island with low hilly areas and little vegetation.
- **Language and Currency:** The official language of Aruba is Dutch. Papiamento (a combination of Dutch-English and Spanish-Portuguese) and English are widely spoken. The monetary unit is the Arubin florin (written Af). The exchange rate is U.S.$1 = Af 1.77 (November 1993).
- **Print Sources of Information:** *Fielding's Caribbean* edited by Mrgaret Zellers. New York: Fielding Travel Books, William Morrow & Co., 1992.

EMBASSY AND CONSULATE CONTACT INFORMATION:

EMBASSY OF THE NETHERLANDS ANTILLES
4200 LINNEAN AVE. NW,
WASHINGTON, DC 20008
TEL: 202-244-5300

COMPANIES/ORGANIZATIONS WITH OPERATIONS IN ARUBA:

AMERICAN CANADIAN CARIBBEAN LINE, 123
THE COASTAL GROUP, 201

OVERSEAS SHIPHOLDING GROUP, INC., 400

━━━━

AUSTRALIA

- **Official Name:** Commonwealth of Australia
- **Capital:** Canberra
- **Location:** Australia is the smallest continent and one of the largest countries in the world. It is located in the Southeast Asian archipelago, between the Indian and Pacific oceans. With a total land area of 2,966,151 square miles, it is slightly smaller than the United States.
- **Population, Cities, and American Residents:** The population of Australia totals 17.3 million (1991 est.). Nearly 95 percent of the population is Caucasian, four percent Asian, and 1 percent aboriginal or other.

Most American residents are employed in Australia's three largest cities: Sydney, with 3.5 million, Melbourne with 3 million, and the capital city, Canberra, with 290,000 people. (all 1985 estimates).

- **Language and Currency:** English is the official language of Australia with more than 99 percent of the people speaking it. However, the local slang and colorful expressions may be a little difficult for Americans to comprehend at first. Also, it's important to remember that the aboriginal peoples have their own language and specific cultures. The Australian dollar (written as A$ or written $ within the country), is divided into 100 cents. Bills are 1, 2, 5, 19, 20, and 50 dollars. Coins are 1, 2, 5, 10, 20, 50 cents and 1 and 2 dollars. The exchange rate is 1 Australian dollar = U.S.$.68 (July 30, 1993).

- **Climate:** Australia has a wide range of climates. It varies from mild to tropical, and is one of the drier continents on earth as the interior is particularly dry and arid. Yet, 40 percent of the country lies north of the Tropic of Capricorn where rainfall can exceed 200 inches annually. It is temperate in the island state of Tasmania, and tropical in the far north of the states of Western Australia and Queensland. The southern area has a Mediterranean-like climate, and temperatures are similar for Sydney, Melbourne, and Perth. Melbourne is coolest in winter, and Perth is usually the warmest of the main cities year round. Remember that the seasons of Australia are in reverse of those in the Northern Hemisphere. Average temperatures for summer (January-March) 57°F-86°F; fall (April-May) 47°F-76°F; winter (June-August) 42°F-63°F; and spring (September-December) 49°F-81°F.

- **Economy and Resources:** Australia is a rich country and the economy is driven by commodities. Although there is a free-enterprise economic system, government regulations are extensive and there is a strict tax and wage structure. Federal controls oversee agriculture, banking, credit, energy, and minerals, though privatization of some state-run enterprises may occur in the near future. Farm and mineral products account, respectively, for 46 percent and 37 percent of all goods sold overseas. Australia is one of the largest producers of wool and meat. It ranks second in the export of sugar and diamonds, and third in the export of apples, dairy products, and wheat. A major industry is mining extensive deposits of uranium, minerals, metals, and iron ore.

- **Cost of Living:** At an average of 132, the cost of living is higher than in the United States.

- **Work Permits, Visas, etc.:** A valid passport, visa, and onward/return transportation are required to travel in Australia. Employment in Australia is not permitted for aliens until they are given temporary residence status. Apply through the Department of Immigration and Ethnic Affairs and include an explanation with the application. If you are entering Australia from the United States no vaccinations are required, but an AIDS test is mandatory for permanent resident visa applicants over age 16 (U.S. test acceptable).

- **Taxation:** Australia taxes its resident individuals on a global basis, and individuals coming to work in Australia may be considered residents even if their length of stay is only temporary (2-4 years). Foreign nationals are usually taxed on salary and allowances related to work performed in the country, but taxes vary on a case-by-case basis.

- **Principal International Schools:** Australian schools follow the British system of education and are considered good for all age levels. The two categories are government-supported and private schools. International schools are located in Sydney and Melbourne, and they include English, French, and Japanese institutions. English schools also are located in other large cities. Maximum tuition for an American school averages $9,000 per year.

- **Health Care:** There are no unusual health problems in Australia, and water is chlorinated and safe to drink. Medical care is considered good with qualified doctors, dentists, and specialists readily available in major cities. Hospital facilities and services are modern and efficient, though very crowded. Australians are covered under the local health-insurance plan, called Medicare. Nonprofit local agencies offer government-funded health plans with excellent benefits; more medical bills are reimbursed under these plans than under U.S. medical insurance plans. The U.S. State Department suggests that long-term personnel join one of the nonprofit plans, even if it means additional coverage to what they already have. Prescription and over-the-counter drugs are available, and because of the government-sponsored (subsidized) pharmaceutical program, drugs cost much less than in the United States. Due to the intensity of the sun, particularly in the summer months, Australia has a very high rate of skin cancer.

- **Crime:** Crime is not a major problem in Australia. Populated areas are usually safe, day or night, but normal precautions should always be taken, especially in the larger, more populated cities.

- **Pros and Cons of Living and Working in Australia:** Australia is a fascinating country, especially the cities of Melbourne and Sydney which are considered a walker's paradise. The architecture is renowned, with iron lacework from the 19th century wrought in graceful shapes on doors, balconies, and porticos. Australia is the most urbanized country in the world with nine tenths of the population living in urban areas. Telecommunications and transportation are very good throughout the country, but seeing the sights can be costly. Australia encompasses a large area and domestic airfares are very high. Australians drive on the left, which may take some getting used to. Housing can be expensive, with apartments ranging from U.S.$200-$400 per week for rentals. Domestic help is almost impossible to find,

EMBASSY AND CONSULATE CONTACT INFORMATION:

AUSTRALIAN EMBASSY
1601 MASSACHUSETTS AVE. NW
WASHINGTON DC 20036
TEL: 202-797-3000

CONSULATE GENERAL/TRADE COMMISSION
636 FIFTH AVE.
NEW YORK, NY 10020
TEL: 212-245-4000

OTHER SOURCES OF INFORMATION:

AUSTRALIAN TOURIST COMMISSION
489 FIFTH AVE., 31ST FL.
NEW YORK NY 10017
TEL: 212-687-6300
FAX: 212-661-3340

and full-time help usually costs about $1,000 per month. Also, Australia does not admit any pets (birds, cats, or dogs) into the country from the United States.

U.S. STATE DEPT.
DESK OFFICER FOR AUSTRALIA
WASHINGTON, DC 20520
TEL: 202-647-9690

COMPANIES/ORGANIZATIONS WITH OPERATIONS IN AUSTRALIA:

AIRBORNE EXPRESS, 112

ALARM DEVICE MANUFACTURING COMPANY, 114

ALBANY INTERNATIONAL CORPORATION, 114

ALBERTO-CULVER COMPANY, 115

ALDUS CORPORATION, 115

ALEXANDER & ALEXANDER SERVICES, INC., 116

ALLEN-BRADLEY COMPANY, INC., 116

ALLERGAN, INC., 117

ALUMINUM COMPANY OF AMERICA, 118

AM INTERNATIONAL, INC., 119

AMAX, INC., 119

AMDAHL CORPORATION, 120

AMERICAN CYANAMID COMPANY, 124

AMERICAN EXPRESS COMPANY—TRAVEL RELATED SERVICES, 125

AMERICAN HOME PRODUCTS CORPORATION, 126

AMERICAN TOOL COMPANIES, INC., 129

AMOCO CORPORATION, 131

AMP, INC., 132

AMPEX CORPORATION, 133

ANDREW CORPORATION, 134

ANSELL INTERNATIONAL, 135

ANTHONY INDUSTRIES, 135

AON CORPORATION, 136

APPLE COMPUTER, INC., 136

APPLIED BIOSCIENCE INTERNATIONAL, INC., 137

ARCO COAL COMPANY, 139

ARCO INTERNATIONAL OIL AND GAS COMPANY, 139

ARMSTRONG WORLD INDUSTRIES, INC., 141

ASARCO, INC., 142

ASHLAND OIL, INC., 143

ASSOCIATED PRESS, 144

AST RESEARCH, INC., 144

AT&T INTERNATIONAL, 145

AUGAT, INC., 146

AUTOMATIC SWITCH COMPANY, 147

AVERY DENNISON CORPORATION, 147

AVIS, INC., 148

BACKER SPIELVOGEL & BATES WORLDWIDE, INC., 150

BAILEY CONTROLS COMPANY, 151

BAKER HUGHES, INC., 152

BANCTEC, INC., 152

BANK OF BOSTON CORPORATION, 153

THE BANK OF NEW YORK COMPANY, INC., 154

BANKAMERICA CORPORATION, 155

BANKERS TRUST NEW YORK CORPORATION, 155

C. R. BARD, INC., 157

THE BARDEN CORPORATION, 157

BAUSCH & LOMB, INC., 159

BAXTER HEALTHCARE CORPORATION, 160

JIM BEAM BRANDS COMPANY, 161

BECKMAN INSTRUMENTS, INC., 162

BETZ LABORATORIES, 166

BIO-RAD LABORATORIES, 166

BLACK & DECKER CORPORATION, 167

BLACK & VEATCH, 168

BLOUNT, INC. (BLOUNT CONSTRUCTION DIVISION), 169

BORDEN, INC., 170

BORLAND INTERNATIONAL, INC, 172

BOSE CORPORATION, 172

W. H. BRADY COMPANY, 173

BRIDGESTONE-FIRESTONE, INC., 174

BRISTOL BABCOCK, INC., 174

BRISTOL-MEYERS SQUIBB COMPANY, 175

BROWNING-FERRIS INDUSTRIES, 177

BUCK CONSULTANTS, INC., 178

BURLINGTON AIR EXPRESS, 179

BURNS & ROE, INC., 180

BURSON-MARSTELLER, 180

CABOT CORPORATION, 181

CAMP DRESSER & MCKEE INTERNATIONAL, INC., 183

CARGILL INCORPORATED, 184

CARRIER CORPORATION, 186

CARTER-WALLACE, INC., 187

A
M
E
R
I
C
A
N

J
O
B
S

A
B
R
O
A
D

J. I. CASE COMPANY, 187
CHASE MANHATTAN CORPORATION, 190
CHEVRON CORPORATION, 193
CHIRON CORPORATION, 194
CHRISTIAN BLIND MISSION
    INTERNATIONAL, 543
CH2M HILL INTERNATIONAL, LTD., 195
THE CHUBB & SON CORPORATION, 196
CIGNA CORPORATION, 197
CINCOM SYSTEMS, INC., 197
CITICORP, 198
COLGATE-PALMOLIVE COMPANY, 203
COMMERCE CLEARING HOUSE, 205
COMMERCIAL INTERTECH CORPORATION,
    205
COMMODORE INTERNATIONAL LTD., 206
COMPUTERVISION CORPORATION, 208
CONOCO, INC., 209
CONTINUUM COMPANY, INC., 211
CONVERSE, INC., 212
COOPER POWER SYSTEMS, 213
COOPERS & LYBRAND, 214
CORE STATES FINANCIAL CORPORATION,
    215
CORNING INCORPORATED, 215
JOHN CRANE, INC., 218
CUBIC CORPORATION, 220
CUMMINS ENGINE COMPANY, INC., 221
CUNA MUTUAL INSURANCE GROUP, 222
D-M-E COMPANY, 222
DAMES & MOORE, 223
D'ARCY MASIUS BENTON & BOWLES INC.,
    225
DATA GENERAL CORPORATION, 225
DAYCO PRODUCTS, INC., 226
DDB NEEDHAM WORLDWIDE, INC., 227
DE KALB GENETICS CORPORATION, 227
DEERE & COMPANY, 229
DIGITAL EQUIPMENT CORPORATION, 236
DOMINO'S PIZZA, INC., 237
DONALDSON COMPANY, INC., 237
DOW CHEMICAL COMPANY, 240
DOW CORNING CORPORATION, 240
DOW JONES & COMPANY, INC., 241
DRESSER INDUSTRIES, INC., 241
DUN & BRADSTREET CORPORATION, 243
DUPONT MERCK PHARMACEUTICAL
    COMPANY, 243
DURACELL, INC., 244
DURIRON COMPANY, INC., 244

EASTMAN KODAK COMPANY, 246
EATON CORPORATION/CUTLER HAMMER,
    247
EG & G, INC., 249
ELIZABETH ARDEN COMPANY, 251
ENCORE COMPUTER CORPORATION, 252
ENCYCLOPEDIA BRITANNICA, INC., 253
ERNST & YOUNG, 255
EXXON COMPANY, INTERNATIONAL, 258
FEDERAL-MOGUL CORPORATION, 260
FIGGIE INTERNATIONAL, INC., 262
FIRST CHICAGO CORPORATION, 262
FISHER CONTROLS INTERNATIONAL, INC.,
    263
FLORSHEIM SHOE COMPANY, 264
FLUOR CORPORATION, 266
FORD MOTOR COMPANY, 267
FREEPORT-MCMORAN, INC., 268
FULLER COMPANY, 269
GAF CORPORATION, 270
GAFNEY, CLINE & ASSOCIATES, INC., 271
THE GATES RUBBER COMPANY, 273
GATX CORPORATION, 273
GENERAL MOTORS CORPORATION (GM),
    277
GETZ BROTHERS COMPANY, INC., 281
THE GILLETTE COMPANY, 283
W. R. GRACE & COMPANY, 285
GREY ADVERTISING, INC., 288
GUARDIAN INDUSTRIES CORPORATION,
    290
H. J. HEINZ COMPANY, 290
H & R BLOCK, 291
HALLMARK CARDS, INC., 294
HERTZ CORPORATION, 300
HEWLETT-PACKARD COMPANY, 300
HILL & KNOWLTON, INC., 301
HONEYWELL, INC., 303
HORMEL FOODS CORPORATION, 304
HOUSEHOLD INTERNATIONAL, INC., 305
HYATT INTERNATIONAL CORPORATION,
    308
ICF KAISER ENGINEERS, 308
IDB COMMUNICATIONS, INC., 309
ILLINOIS TOOL WORKS, INC., 309
IMO INDUSTRIES, 310
IMS AMERICA, LTD., 311
INDUCTOTHERM CORPORATION, 311
INFORMATION BUILDERS, INC., 312
INGERSOLL ENGINEERS, 312

INTERNATIONAL BUSINESS MACHINES (IBM), 315
INTERNATIONAL FLAVORS & FRAGRANCES, INC., 317
INTERNATIONAL PAPER COMPANY, 318
INTERNATIONAL TOTALIZATOR SYSTEMS, INC., 319
ITT CORPORATION, 321
ITT HARTFORD INSURANCE GROUP, 321
ITT SHERATON CORPORATION, 322
ITW FINISHING SYSTEMS & PRODUCTS, 322
JOY TECHNOLOGIES, INC., 327
KELLOGG COMPANY, 330
KENNECOTT CORPORATION, 333
KEYSTONE INTERNATIONAL, 334
KIMBERLY-CLARK CORPORATION, 336
KINNEY SHOE CORPORATION, 337
KNIGHT-RIDDER, INC., 338
KOHLER COMPANY, 339
KOLMAR LABORATORIES, INC., 340
KRAFT GENERAL FOODS INTERNATIONAL, 341
LAWTER INTERNATIONAL, INC., 344
LEVI STRAUSS ASSOCIATES, INC., 344
THE LINCOLN ELECTRIC COMPANY, 346
LITTON INDUSTRIES, INC., 348
LOCTITE CORPORATION, 349
LOTUS DEVELOPMENT CORPORATION, 351
LOUISIANA LAND & EXPLORATION COMPANY, 352
LUBRIZOL CORPORATION, 353
MALLINCKRODT, INC., 359
MARION MERRELL DOW, INC., 360
MATTEL, INC., 363
MAYTAG CORPORATION, 364
MCCANN-ERICKSON WORLDWIDE, 354
MCCORMICK & COMPANY, INC., 355
MCDERMOTT INTERNATIONAL, INC., 356
MCDONALD'S CORPORATION, 356
MCGRAW-HILL, INC., 357
MCKINSEY & COMPANY, INC., 357
MEASUREX CORPORATION, 366
MERCK & COMPANY, INC., 368
MERISEL, INC., 369
METCO PERKIN-ELMER, 371
HERMAN MILLER, INC., 373
MILLIPORE CORPORATION, 374
MOBIL OIL CORPORATION, 375
MONSANTO COMPANY, 377

J. P. MORGAN & COMPANY, INC., 378
MORGAN STANLEY GROUP, INC., 379
MOTOROLA, INC., 381
NALCO CHEMICAL COMPANY, 382
NATIONAL SEMICONDUCTOR CORPORATION, 383
NCR CORPORATION, 384
NEWMONT MINING CORPORATION, 386
NORDSON CORPORATION, 389
NORTON COMPANY, 390
NOVELL, INC., 392
OCEANEERING INTERNATIONAL, INC., 393
OGILVY & MATHER, 395
OLIN CORPORATION, 396
OMNICOM GROUP, INC., 397
OTIS ELEVATOR COMPANY: WORLD HEADQUARTERS, 399
OUTBOARD MARINE CORPORATION, 399
OWENS-ILLINOIS, INC., 401
PACCAR, INC., 401
PARAMOUNT COMMUNICATIONS, INC., 404
PARKER HANNIFIN CORPORATION, 405
PARSONS BRINKERHOFF, 406
PARSONS MAIN, INC., 407
PEPSICO FOODS INTERNATIONAL, 409
PEPSICO, INC., 410
PERKIN-ELMER CORPORATION, 410
PFIZER, INC., 412
PHILLIPS PETROLEUM COMPANY, 415
PIONEER HI-BRED INTERNATIONAL, INC., 417
PITTSBURGH-DES MOINES CORPORATION, 418
PITTWAY CORPORATION, 418
PIZZA HUT, INC., 419
PLAYTEX APPAREL, INC., 419
R. L. POLK & COMPANY, 421
PPG INDUSTRIES, 421
PRC, INC., 422
PREFORMED LINE PRODUCTS COMPANY, 423
PREMARK INTERNATIONAL, INC., 423
PROCTER & GAMBLE PHARMACEUTICALS, INC., 426
PRUDENTIAL INSURANCE COMPANY OF AMERICA, 427
QUAKER CHEMICAL CORPORATION, 428
QUAKER OATS COMPANY, 428
R. J. REYNOLDS TOBACCO COMPANY, 429

COUNTRY PROFILES

RAIN BIRD SPRINKLER MANUFACTURING CORPORATION, 430

RALSTON PURINA COMPANY, 430

READER'S DIGEST ASSOCIATION, INC., 432

REDKEN LABORATORIES, INC., 434

RELIANCE ELECTRIC COMPANY, 435

REMINGTON PRODUCTS, INC., 436

REVLON, INC., 437

REYNOLDS METALS COMPANY, 438

ROBERTSON CECO, 440

ROCKWELL INTERNATIONAL CORPORATION, 441

ROHM & HAAS COMPANY, 442

ROSEMOUNT, INC., 443

RUDER FINN, INC., 445

RUSSELL REYNOLDS ASSOCIATES, INC., 446

SAATCHI & SAATCHI, 448

SARA LEE CORPORATION, 449

SB POWER TOOLS, INC. (SKIL CORP.), 450

SCHLEGEL CORPORATION, 451

SEARLE COMPANY, 455

SENSORMATIC ELECTRONICS CORPORATION, 457

SGS CONTROL SERVICES, 458

SHAKLEE CORPORATION, 459

SHEARSON LEHMAN BROTHERS, 460

SHERWIN-WILLIAMS COMPANY, 461

SIMON & SCHUSTER, INC., 463

SIMPLEX TIME RECORDER COMPANY, 463

SIMPLICITY PATTERN COMPANY INC., 464

SIZZLER INTERNATIONAL, 464

SKADDEN, ARPS, SLATE, MEAGHER & FLOM, 465

J. M. SMUCKER COMPANY, 468

SONY PICTURES ENTERTAINMENT, 471

SPS TECHNOLOGIES, INC., 474

SQUARE D COMPANY, 475

SRI INTERNATIONAL, 475

STANDARD COMMERCIAL CORPORATION, 476

STANLEY WORKS, 478

STATE STREET BOSTON CORPORATION, 478

STORAGE TECHNOLOGY CORPORATION, 481

SUN ELECTRIC CORPORATION, 484

TAMBRANDS, INC., 486

TANDY CORPORATION, 487

TEKTRONIX, INC., 488

TELEDYNE, INC., 489

TENNANT COMPANY, 490

TEXACO OIL COMPANY, 493

TEXAS INTRUMENTS, INC., 494

TEXTRON, INC., 494

THOMAS & BETTS, 495

3M COMPANY, 496

3M PHARMACEUTICALS, 497

TIME-WARNER, INC., 498

TLC BEATRICE INTERNATIONAL HOLDINGS, INC., 498

TORRINGTON COMPANY, 499

TOWERS PERRIN, INC., 499

TRANE COMPANY, 501

TRINOVA CORPORATION, 502

TRITON ENERGY CORPORATION, 502

TRW, INC., 503

UAL CORPORATION, 506

UNILEVER UNITED STATES, INC., 506

UNISYS CORPORATION, 508

UNITED PRESS INTERNATIONAL, 509

UOP, INC., 514

THE UPJOHN COMPANY, 515

USX CORPORATION, 516

VF CORPORATION, 517

WARD HOWELL INTERNATIONAL, INC., 520

WARNER ELECTRIC BRAKE & CLUTCH COMPANY, 521

WARNER-LAMBERT COMPANY, 522

WATERS CHROMATOGRAPHY (MILLIPORE), 523

WEST COMPANY, INC., 525

WESTINGHOUSE ELECTRIC CORPORATION, 525

WEYERHAEUSER COMPANY, 526

WMX TECHNOLOGIES/WASTE MANAGEMENT, INC., 527

WOODWARD GOVERNOR COMPANY, 528

WOOLWORTH CORPORATION, 528

WILLIAM WRIGLEY JR. COMPANY, 529

WYNN'S INTERNATIONAL, INC., 530

YOUNG & RUBICAM, INC., 533

AUSTRIA

- **Official Name:** Federal Republic of Austria
- **Capital:** Vienna
- **Location:** Austria is a landlocked country located in south-central Europe. It is bounded by Germany, the Czech Republic, and Slovakia to the north, Hungary to the east, Yugoslavia and Italy to the south, and Switzerland and Liechtenstein to the west. Its total land area is 32,369 square miles, comparable in size to Maine. Two-thirds of the territory is mountainous, and only one fifth of the land is under cultivation.
- **Population, Cities, and American Residents:** Austria has 7.6 million people (1991 est.), with Germans comprising 99.4 percent of the population. The remaining groups are: 0.3 percent Croatian, 0.2 percent Slovene, and 0.1 percent other.

  Most American residents are employed in Austria's three largest cities: Vienna with 1.5 million, Graz with 243,000, and Linz with 210,000 people (1991 est.).
- **Language and Currency:** German is the official language of Austria with native German-speakers comprising 98 percent of the total population. English is widely spoken in business and government areas, but having some knowledge of German is important. The monetary unit is the schilling, abbreviated as ATS internationally, and AS (or OS) internally. There are 100 grochens to one schilling. Bills are in 5,000, 1,000, 500, 100, 50, and 20 schillings. Coins are in 20, 10, 5, and 1 schilling and 50,10, 5, and 2 grochens. The exchange rate is 1 ATS = U.S.$.08 (July 30, 1993).
- **Climate:** Austria has a continental climate with warm summers and cold winters. The mountains have a significant effect, with temperatures decreasing and precipitation increasing with altitude. Though rain is frequent from April to November, it is usually sunny, warm, and quite enjoyable from May through October. Winter arrives early, along with the snow, which usually melts away quickly in Vienna. The capital city has a climate comparable to that of Boston, Massachusetts, with temperatures ranging from 4°F in winter to about 85°F in the summer.
- **Economy and Resources:** Austria has a social market economy with the government playing a key role. There are many state-owned or government-controlled industries. After World War II, the country went through a period of rapid industrialization and dramatic economic growth. Nearly 70 percent of the economy is based on industry. Food processing, iron, steel, and machinery are among the major industries. Austria is very dependent on trade, which accounts for more than one-third of the total gross domestic product. The neighboring European Community countries take 66 percent of Austrian exports and supply 70 percent of Austria's imports. Chief crops include: forest products, potatoes, and sugar beets. Livestock includes chickens, pigs, and cattle, and natural resources include iron ore, crude oil, and timber.
- **Cost of Living:** At 157, the cost of living is higher than in the United States.
- **Work Permits, Visas, etc.:** A valid passport is required to travel in Austria. Visas are not needed of U.S. citizens for stays up to ninety days in the country. For stays up to one year, a business or tourist visa is necessary, and for visits longer than one year, you must receive approval by the Austrian Minister of the Interior in Vienna. All residents

must register with the local police. If you are entering Austria from the United States, no vaccinations are required. For official or other information, direct inquiries to the embassy or consulate at the addresses below.

- **Taxation:** All residents of Austria are subject to an income tax. Regardless of citizenship, a person is considered a resident if living in Austria for at least 183 days of the fiscal year. Currently, there is a progressive income tax ranging from 21 percent on an annual taxable income of approximately U.S.$3,800 to about 62 percent of income exceeding approximately $114,000. Austria has a double-taxation agreement with the United States.

- **Principal International Schools:** There are many international schools with high educational standards in Vienna. Yearly tuition for a French school is about $2,350, $6,000 for a German school, and $9,000 for an American school.

- **Health Care:** Austrian water is safe to drink, and extremely pure, as it is piped in from mountain springs. Doctors and dentists are readily available; their standards are high and so are their fees. The cost of an average visit to the dentist is approximately U.S.$100. Local pharmacies are well equipped and hospitals are adequate.

- **Crime:** Crime and theft rates are low in Austria, but precautions should still be taken, especially in large cities or in the evening hours. Valuables should not be left in vehicles.

- **Pros and Cons of Living and Working in Austria:** Austria is a country of splendid scenery and many historical cities. Culturally, there is a great deal to offer, and sports facilities are unsurpassed, with western Austria regarded as one of the best skiing regions in the world. Vienna has a variety of museums, and excellent restaurants. Telecommunications are good as is transportation, with buses the most reliable and least expensive. Traveling by rail can be costly, however. An international driver's license and registration papers are necessary to drive a vehicle in Austria, and gasoline can be expensive compared to American standards (U.S.$2.80 per gallon). Though accommodations may be easily found at reasonable prices, utilities run slightly higher than U.S. rates (electricity for a family of four might average U.S.$125 per month). As medical fees can be very expensive in Austria, it is advisable to have adequate health insurance.

EMBASSY AND CONSULATE CONTACT INFORMATION:

AUSTRIAN EMBASSY
2343 MASSACHUSETTS AVE. NW
WASHINGTON, DC 20008
TEL: 202-483-4474

AUSTRIAN CONSULATE GENERAL
31 EAST 69 ST.
NEW YORK, NY 10021
TEL: 212-737-6400

OTHER SOURCES OF INFORMATION:

AUSTRIAN NATIONAL TOURIST OFFICE
500 FIFTH AVE.
NEW YORK, NY 10010
TEL: 212-944-6880

U.S. STATE DEPT.
DESK OFFICER FOR AUSTRIA
WASHINGTON, DC 20025
TEL: 202-647-2005

COMPANIES/ORGANIZATIONS WITH OPERATIONS IN AUSTRIA:

AMERICAN CYANAMID COMPANY, 124
AMERICAN STANDARD, INC., 128

AMOCO CORPORATION, 131
AMP, INC., 132

AVON PRODUCTS, INC., 149

BANKERS TRUST NEW YORK
   CORPORATION, 155

BAUSCH & LOMB, INC., 159

BECKMAN INSTRUMENTS, INC., 162

BIO-RAD LABORATORIES, 166

CHRISTIAN BLIND MISSION
   INTERNATIONAL, 543

THE COCA-COLA COMPANY, 202

COMPUTER ASSOCIATES INTERNATIONAL,
   INC., 207

DATA GENERAL CORPORATION, 225

DDB NEEDHAM WORLDWIDE, INC., 227

DIGITAL EQUIPMENT CORPORATION, 236

DOW JONES & COMPANY, INC., 241

ECOLOGY AND ENVIRONMENT, INC., 248

EXXON CORPORATION, 258

FISHER CONTROLS INTERNATIONAL, INC.,
   263

FMC CORPORATION, 266

GERHARD'S BICYCLE ODYSSEYS, 280

KIMBALL INTERNATIONAL, INC., 336

KORN/FERRY INTERNATIONAL, 340

LOCTITE CORPORATION, 349

LUBRIZOL CORPORATION, 353

MALLINCKRODT, INC., 359

MCKINSEY & COMPANY, INC., 357

MODINE MANUFACTURING COMPANY, 375

PITNEY BOWES, INC., 417

PROCTER & GAMBLE COMPANY, 425

ROSEMOUNT, INC., 443

RUBBERMAID, INC., 445

SENSORMATIC ELECTRONICS
   CORPORATION, 457

SUN ELECTRIC CORPORATION, 484

TRW, INC., 503

UNITED NATIONS INDUSTRIAL
   DEVELOPMENT ORGANIZATION
   (UNIDO), 568

UNITED PARCEL SERVICE OF AMERICA,
   INC., 509

U.S. DEPARTMENT OF ENERGY, 573

COUNTRY PROFILES

AZERBAIJAN

- **Official Name:** Azerbaijani Republic

- **Capital:** Baku

- **Location:** Located on the border of Europe and Asia, Azerbaijan lies on the western shore of the Caspian Sea. It is bounded by Georgia to the northwest, the Russian Federation to the north, the Caspian Sea to the east, Iran to the south, and Armenia to the southwest. Though the Nakhichevan Autonomous Republic (ASSR) is within Armenian territory, it is part of Azerbaijan. The total land area is 33,428 square miles making Azerbaijan comparable in size to Maine. Most of the republic is comprised of lowlands near the River Kura and its tributary, the Araks. Agriculture predominates in this region. Toward the north and west are pastures and meadows where herders graze their livestock in the Caucasus Mountains.

- **Language and Currency:** The official language of Azerbaijan is Azeri. Other ethnic languages, including Russian, are also spoken throughout the country. Familiarity with the language is essential if you are going to live or work in this country. The monetary unit is the manat (since August 1992). The current exchange rate is not available.

EMBASSY AND CONSULATE CONTACT INFORMATION:

REPUBLIC OF AZERBAIJAN
1825 PHELPS AVE. NW
WASHINGTON, DC 20008
TEL: 202-939-8916

COMPANIES/ORGANIZATIONS WITH OPERATIONS IN AZERBAIJAN:

AMOCO CORPORATION, 131

BAHAMAS

- **Official Name:** The Commonwealth of the Bahamas

- **Capital:** Nassau

- **Location:** The Bahamas is a group of more than 700 islands (only 20 of them inhabited), in an archipelago that extends 590 miles from northwest to southeast between Florida and Haiti. The islands are scattered over 100,000 square miles, and are bounded on all sides by the Atlantic Ocean. Its total land area is 5,382 square miles, making the country slightly larger than Connecticut.

- **Population, Cities, and American Residents:** The population of Nassau totals 252,100 (1991 est.). Bahamians of African descent account for 85 percent of the population; the remaining 15 percent are Caucasian, most of British descent.

    Most American residents are employed in the capital city of Nassau with 192,000 residents (1990 est.).

- **Language and Currency:** The official language of the Bahamian people is English with some Creole used among Haitian immigrants. The currency is the Bahamian dollar (plural-dollars) and 1 Bahamian dollar (B$) = 100 cents. The exchange rate (fixed rate) is 1 Bahamian dollar (B$) = U.S.$1 (July 30,1993).

- **Climate:** The Bahamas has a tropical marine climate moderated by the warm waters of the Gulf Stream and a refreshing trade-wind flow generating the ever-present breezes. Temperatures are moderate year round with little variation. The most pleasant months are between December and May, with daytime temperatures ranging from 70°F-75°F. The remainder of the year is hot, between 80°F-85°F, with frequent tropical storms.

- **Economy and Resources:** The Bahamas is an independent member of the Commonwealth, and a great many of its traditions follow those of the United Kingdom. The Bahamian economy is primarily based on tourism and offshore banking. Tourism accounts for 50 percent of GDP and directly or indirectly employs about 40 percent of the local people. About 80 percent of the tourists are American, so the Bahamian economy is affected by economic changes in the United States. Finance is the second most important sector in the country's economy, and its status as a tax haven has made it an international banking center. The government has been trying to diversify the economy and attract new business into the region. Operating in the Bahamas provides industrial firms access to U.S. and Canadian markets. Principal products exported to the United States, Canada, and Europe include: pharmaceuticals, petroleum products, rum, crawfish, and salt.

- **Cost of Living:** At 132, the cost of living is higher than in the United States.

- **Work Permits, Visas, etc.:** Proof of U.S. citizenship, photo ID, and return ticket are required for stay of up to eight months in the Bahamas. A passport and residence/work permit are needed to live and work in the country. A permit also is required to import pets. If you are entering the Bahamas from the United States, no vaccinations are necessary. For official or other information, direct inquiries to the embassy or consulate at the addresses below.

- **Taxation:** Income tax is not imposed on individuals in the Bahamas.

- **Principal International Schools:** Bahamian education is under the jurisdiction of the Ministry of Education and Culture, which is responsible for all educational institutions in the country. There are local public and several private schools in the Bahamas. Private Primary Schools (ages 3-11) include Lyford Cay School, where tuition ranges from $1,035-$1,160 per term (depending on grade), with three terms; Xavier's Lower School, West Bay Street, Nassau where tuition costs are $1,290 plus book fees ($3). Private Primary-Secondary Schools (ages 4-18) include Jordan-Prince Williams School, Cowpen Road, Nassau, where tuition is $400 per term, with three terms; and Kingsway Academy, Bernard Road, Nassau where tuition is $695-$795 per term (depending on grade), with three terms. Other public and private schools are available.

- **Health Care:** Though no vaccinations are required, health requirements change, so check with authorities before an extended stay in the Bahamas. Food and water are safe when purchased from reputable stores. Tap water is potable but saline, so most people use bottled water. Doctors, dentists, and medical facilities are adequate in the larger cities (Nassau and Freeport), but the out islands are sparsely populated and not equipped for medical problems. If prescriptions are needed, it is wise to obtain them in the United States beforehand.

- **Crime:** Tourism is the mainstay of the Bahamas and populated areas are usually filled with people shopping and sightseeing, but crime is relatively infrequent on the islands. At night, streets are well lit and patrolled by local police, so it is quite safe to travel during the day and evening hours. Take precautions, and do not leave valuables unattended.

- **Pros and Cons of Living and Working in the Bahamas:** The islands of the Bahamas offer visitors a tranquil, relaxing haven located close to the southeast region of the United States. It is a major tourist destination for Americans who are generally welcomed throughout the islands.

  Telecommunications are highly developed, and international airports on Grand Bahama and New Providence offer effi-

EMBASSY AND CONSULATE CONTACT INFORMATION:

BAHAMIAN EMBASSY
600 NEW HAMPSHIRE AVE. NW
WASHINGTON, DC 20037
TEL: 202-319-2660
FAX: 202-338-3940

cient transportation to and from the United States. Prices for necessities are high, especially for food, drugs, etc. Summers can be very warm and humid, and bugs (mosquitoes, termites, sandflies) can be annoying. Poisonous insects include the black widow spider and the scorpion. The weather can also wreak havoc, as the environment is subject to hurricanes and tropical storms, which can cause extensive flood damage.

BAHAMIAN CONSULATE GENERAL
INGRAHAM BUILDING
25 SE 2ND AVE.
MIAMI, FL 33131
TEL: 305-373-6295

OTHER SOURCES OF INFORMATION:

GOVERNMENT TOURIST OFFICE OF THE
BAHAMAS
150 EAST 52ND ST.
NEW YORK, NY 10022
TEL: 212-758-2777

COMPANIES/ORGANIZATIONS WITH OPERATIONS IN BAHAMAS:

AMERICAN CANADIAN CARIBBEAN LINE, 123
BANKAMERICA CORPORATION, 155
CARGILL INCORPORATED, 184
CARNIVAL CRUISE LINES, 185
CARRIER CORPORATION, 186
CHASE MANHATTAN CORPORATION, 190
CHEMICAL BANKING CORPORATION, 191
CIGNA CORPORATION, 197
CITICORP, 198
CLUB MED, INC., 201
THE COCA-COLA COMPANY, 202
COMMODORE INTERNATIONAL LTD., 206

CORE STATES FINANCIAL CORPORATION, 215
DOMINO'S PIZZA, INC., 237
EXXON COMPANY, INTERNATIONAL, 258
EXXON CORPORATION, 258
HOLIDAY INNS WORLDWIDE, 302
INTERNATIONAL MARITIME RESOURCES, 317
J. P. MORGAN & COMPANY, INC., 378
MORTON INTERNATIONAL, 380
TEXACO OIL COMPANY, 493
USAIR GROUP, INC., 516

BAHRAIN

- **Official Name:** State of Bahrain
- **Capital:** Manama
- **Location:** Bahrain is a group of 33 islands located in the western Persian Gulf halfway between Saudi Arabia and the Qatar peninsula. Bahrain is about four times the size of Washington, D.C., with a total land area of 260 square miles. Only five of the islands are inhabited. The main island of Bahrain comprises 85 percent of the total land area and is connected to Saudi Arabia by a 15-mile causeway that was opened in 1986.
- **Population, Cities, and American Residents:** The population of Bahrain totals 537,000 people (1991 est.). Approximately two-thirds of the population is Bahraini, with Asians, Arabs, Indians, Europeans, and Pakistanis accounting for the remainder.

  Most Americans are employed in Bahrain's two largest cities: Manama with 150,000 people and Al Muharraq with 65,000 (1989 est.).
- **Language and Currency:** The official language of Bahrain is Arabic, but Persian is used as well. English is widely spoken and is the principal language of commerce. The

monetary unit is the Bahraini Dinar, written as BD. There are 1,000 fils in one dinar. The exchange rate is 3.75 Bahraini Dinars = U.S.$1 (November 1993).

- **Climate:** The summer season of June through September is hot and humid in Bahrain. Temperatures often reach 104°F, and the humidity can be oppressive. From November through April, the weather improves, with a temperature range of 50°F-68°F, and evening temperatures often dropping off to 40°F. Heavy, unpredictable rainstorms occur, and because of poor drainage, flooded streets are common.

- **Economy and Resources:** Bahrain has been on the trade route between India and Arabia since the second millennium B.C. Oil reserves were discovered in 1932, and this resource still accounts for nearly two-thirds of the gross domestic product (GDP). In the near future, these reserves will be exhausted, and Bahrain is seeking new avenues for diversification. The government is promoting foreign investment in the financial and business services sectors. Currently, Bahrain's major industries are petroleum processing and refining accounting for 80 percent of the exports. Major trading partners are the United States and Japan. Nearly 85 percent of the labor force works in industry and commerce, and 42 percent of the labor force is Bahraini. Other than oil, Bahrain has almost no natural resources and must import many items. There is a small amount of agriculture and fishing in the north, but the country only produces 15 percent of domestic requirements.

  Bahrain faces many challenges in the future. It is in the middle of an unstable region. The local banks have been hurt by the default of their Latin American borrowers, and unemployment is high (reaching almost 10 percent). Because of the Persian Gulf war, trade was oppressed and it has been difficult to attract foreign business to the region. Bahrain's major concern, of course, is the depletion of its oil resources, making the economy's future strength and stability questionable.

- **Cost of Living:** At 122, the cost of living is higher than in the United States.

- **Work Permits, Visas, etc.:** You'll need a valid passport to travel in Bahrain. To obtain a work or residence permit, obtain an N.O.C. (No Objection Certificate) from the Immigration Department through the sponsoring firm in Bahrain. If you're entering Bahrain from the United States, no vaccinations are required. For official or other information, direct inquiries to the embassy or consulate at the addresses below.

- **Taxation:** Bahrain has no personal, corporate, or sales taxes.

- **Health Care:** Bahrain has a national health service program which expatriates may join. Contact your U.S.-based company to see if the medical care and insurance are free of charge. Medical services are adequate, and a list of doctors and dentists is found in the yellow pages of the telephone directory. Sanitation conditions are poor in much of Bahrain. Insects and rodents (ants, mosquitoes, and rats) are a problem, and it's vital that refuse be disposed of promptly. Tap water is not contaminated but brackish in taste, so it's best to buy "sweet water" as it's sold from house to house.

- **Crime:** Crime is not a serious problem in Bahrain. Take the normal precautions for traveling through any major tourist areas.

- **Pros and Cons of Working and Living in Bahrain:** Though Bahrain is a relatively small group of islands, it does offer tourists some historical and cultural sites.

There are forts, museums, mosques, the Tree of Life, Sakhir Palace, and an industrial tour exhibiting oil fields and refineries. The Al Areen Wildlife Park and Reserve exhibits many rare and endangered species from Arabia and East Africa. Telecommunications services are good throughout the country, and transportation is adequate. Tourists on extended visits may want to bring their own cars because purchasing an auto in Bahrain can be expensive. Housing is adequate but limited, so it's best to plan ahead and use a real estate agent. Electricity is unreliable, due to frequent power failures. Though the importation of pets is allowed, it is not recommended. The Arab attitudes toward house pets, along with the humid climate, make it difficult for family pets to adjust.

EMBASSY AND CONSULATE CONTACT INFORMATION:

EMBASSY OF BAHRAIN
3502 INTERNATIONAL DR. NW,
WASHINGTON, DC 20008
TEL: 202-342-0741

BAHRAIN CONSULATE GENERAL
2 UNITED NATIONS PLAZA, 25TH FL.
NEW YORK, NY 10017
TEL: 212-223-6200

OTHER SOURCES OF INFORMATION:

ARAB INFORMATION CENTER
747 THIRD AVE.
NEW YORK, NY 10017
TEL: 212-838-8700

U.S. STATE DEPT.
DESK OFFICER FOR BAHRAIN
WASHINGTON, DC 20204
TEL: 202-647-1794

COMPANIES/ORGANIZATIONS WITH OPERATIONS IN BAHRAIN:

BANKERS TRUST NEW YORK
    CORPORATION, 155
CONOCO, INC., 209
COUDERT BROTHERS LAW FIRM, 217

ECOLOGY AND ENVIRONMENT, INC., 248
HILL & KNOWLTON, INC., 301
OFFSHORE PIPELINES, INC., 394

BANGLADESH

- **Official Name:** People's Republic of Bangladesh

- **Capital:** Dhaka

- **Location:** An independent nation in southern Asia, Bangladesh is almost totally enveloped by India on its north, east, and west borders, and it is bounded by Myanmar to the east. The Bay of Bengal forms the southern boundary. With a total land area of 143,998 square miles, Bangladesh is slightly smaller than Wisconsin. A flat river plain comprises most of its territory, and numerous streams and waterways flow across this plain.

- **Population, Cities, and American Residents:** The population of Bangladesh totals 122 million (1992 est.), with 98 percent of Bengali stock. The remainder is from another ethnic group, the Biharis.

    Most American residents are employed in Bangladesh's two largest cities: Dhaka with 5 million people and Chittigong with 1.8 million (1990 est.).

- **Language and Currency:** The official language of Bangladesh is Bangla (also known as Bengali). English is widely used in business and government. The monetary unit is the taka. The exchange rate is 39.8 takas = U.S.$1 (December 1993).

- **Climate:** Bangladesh has a semitropical climate with warm, humid, and rainy weather. The monsoon season is from mid-May through September. Winters are cool and dry. The average annual temperature is 84°F. Bangladesh has one of the highest annual rainfalls in the world, as much as 85 inches in the northern sector of the country. Because the land is so flat, and covered by so many rivers and streams, flooding is a common problem during the rainy season. Travel is difficult, and much of the time must be done by boat.

- **Economy and Resources:** Bangladesh is a very poor nation, with an economy based on a limited number of agricultural products. Jute is a chief crop and major source of export earnings. Tea, rice, and cotton are other cash crops. The lack of natural resources, and the damage caused by natural disasters (monsoons, tornadoes, floods) have hurt the economy. Poor infrastructure and an escalating population growth are other hindrances. Despite these setbacks, a strong agricultural performance in the early 1990s pushed the gross domestic product (GDP) from 3.5 to 5.5 percent. Poverty is the main concern, as the nation cannot grow or import enough food for its people. Bangladesh has to deal with many serious social, economic, and political challenges. It relies on aid from the United States and Japan, as well as many organizations, including the World Bank, and the UN Development Program.

- **Cost of Living:** At 81, the cost of living is lower than in the United States.

- **Work Permits, Visas, etc.:** A passport and proof of return ticket are required for stays up to 14 days in Bangladesh. For longer stays, a visa is required. A business visa is valid for six months; when applying, you must include a company letter explaining the purpose of the trip and the proposed length of stay. If you are entering Bangladesh from the United States no vaccinations are required. For official or other information direct inquiries to the embassy or consulate at the addresses below.

- **Taxation:** Contact the embassy or consulate of the Republic of Bangladesh for current tax information.

- **Principal International Schools:** American schools are available in Bangladesh for kindergarten through grade 12.

- **Health Care:** Sanitation and health standards are below those found in the United States. Medical facilities are not inadequate for anything but a routine illness. Pharmaceuticals and medicines are in short supply. Supplemental medical insurance for overseas travel is highly recommended. It is suggested by the Centers for Disease Control (CDC) that tetanus, typhoid, polio, and gamma globulin shots be given prior to travel in Bangladesh. If visiting areas outside Dhaka, malaria suppressants should also be administered. Take precautions with dairy products, meats, and raw vegetables and fruits. Boil water for all usage.

- **Crime:** As one of the poorest nations in the world, poverty in endemic throughout Bangladesh. Street crime is on the rise, and travelers must take precautions and be especially careful when going out in the evening. Political demonstrations and labor strikes are common occurrences in Bangladesh, and travelers should avoid any involvement.

- **Pros and Cons of Working and Living in Bangladesh:** Bangladesh is one of the most heavily populated nations in the world, with few resources and not enough food to feed its people. The Bangladeshis are friendly, hospitable people who sell their crafts at unique marketplaces throughout the cities. The country, however, has constant weather-related problems, and natural disasters such as cyclones, tidal waves, monsoons, and floods are an ever-present threat. Food supplies are easily depleted, and contaminated floodwaters spread disease. Sanitary standards are, for the most part, unacceptable. Travelers in Bangladesh should remember that it is an Islamic country with strict rules. Conservative dress is recommended. Remember also that Bangladesh officials treat drug offenders seriously. Mandatory jail sentences, stiff fines, and even the death penalty may result if you are involved in the possession or sale of narcotics in this country.

- **Print Sources of Information:** *Bangladesh: a Country Study* (1989), available from the Superintendent of Documents, U.S. Government Printing Office, Washington, D.C., 20402.

EMBASSY AND CONSULATE CONTACT INFORMATION:

EMBASSY OF BANGLADESH
2201 WISCONSIN AVE. NW
WASHINGTON, DC 20007
TEL: 202-342-8373

CONSULATE OFFICE OF BANGLADESH
211 E. 43RD ST., STE. 502
NEW YORK, NY 10017

COMPANIES/ORGANIZATIONS WITH OPERATIONS IN BANGLADESH:

FMC CORPORATION, 266
INTERNATIONAL FERTILIZER
　　DEVELOPMENT CENTER, 549

INTERNATIONAL VOLUNTARY SERVICES,
　　INC., 555
POPULATION COUNCIL, 562

BARBADOS

- **Official Name:** Barbados
- **Capital:** Bridgetown
- **Location:** Surrounded by the Atlantic Ocean, Barbados is located 250 miles north of Venezuela and 200 miles northeast of Trinidad. Only 21 miles long and 14 miles wide, it is the most easterly island of the West Indies. Barbados has a total land area of 166 square miles, making it almost three times the size of Washington, D.C. Its territory is comprised of essentially flat land that rises gently to a central highland region.
- **Population, Cities, and American Residents:** The total population of Barbados is 256,000 (1992 est.). Approximately 80 percent of the people are African, with 16 percent of mixed origin, and Europeans accounting for the remainder.

　　Most Americans are employed in the capital city of Bridgetown (including outer districts), with 95,000 people (1990 est.).

- **Language and Currency:** English is the official language of Barbados. The monetary unit is the Barbados dollar. The current exchange rate is U.S.$1 equals Bds$2 (February 1994).

- **Climate:** Barbados has a tropical climate with a rainy season lasting from June to September. The average temperature is 78°F with an annual rainfall of 34 inches. Rain is more prevalent in northern areas. Barbados lies within the hurricane belt and is subject to storms from June to October.

- **Economy and Resources:** Barbados is one of the most thickly populated islands in the world. The nation relies on tourism, manufacturing and processing, and agriculture to maintain its developing economy. Of the labor force, 37 percent of the people work in government and services, 22 percent in commerce, and 22 percent in manufacturing. Chief exports are sugar products, rum, and electrical components, traded primarily to other Caribbean countries and the United States. With a per capita income of $6,500, Barbados has one of the highest standards of living among the eastern Caribbean nations. Despite this, it is struggling with a high unemployment rate of 18 percent. The government is trying to create new jobs and increase foreign exchange earnings in manufacturing and agricultural sectors. This has been a difficult task due to its dependence on imports and its accessibility to external economic developments. Barbados needs tourism for the creation of more jobs and a solution to improve the standard of living for all Barbadians.

- **Cost of Living:** At 133, the cost of living is higher than in the United States.

- **Work Permits, Visas, etc.:** No passport or visa is required if traveling to Barbados from the United States for stays up to 90 days. For longer stays or business travel, a visa is required, which may require a work permit. If entering Barbados from the United States, no vaccinations are required. For official or other information, direct inquiries to the embassy or consulate at the addresses below.

- **Taxation:** Any individual who is considered a resident or lives in Barbados is subject to taxes collected from worldwide income. You are considered a resident if you spend more than 182 days in Barbados in an income (calendar) year. Various deductions or exemptions may apply.

- **Health Care:** Health care and sanitation standards are adequate in Barbados. Though the Queen Elizabeth Hospital in Georgetown is overcrowded and understaffed, it offers qualified physicians, many of whom have trained in the United States, England, or Canada. There are a number of health clinics throughout the island. Air ambulance is available to Florida for serious medical problems, but the flight to the United States is long.

- **Crime:** Crime is not a major problem in Barbados. Take the normal precautions for traveling through any major tourist area.

- **Pros and Cons of Living and Working in Barbados:** Barbados offers a warm, inviting climate and unique British customs to its visitors. A popular winter haven for thousands of tourists, Barbados has sandy beaches, bustling harbors, and a beautiful landscape. It is a fairly modern country with good public transportation and efficient telecommunications services. Health standards are good and housing is readily available.

Barbados is easily reached by plane as it is relatively close to the United States. For best accommodations, it's smart to inquire about housing in advance.

- **Print Source of Information:** Zellers, Margaret, editor. *Fielding's Caribbean.* New York: Fielding Travel Books, William Morrow & Co., 1992.

EMBASSY AND CONSULATE CONTACT INFORMATION:

EMBASSY OF BARBADOS
2144 WYOMING AVE. NW
WASHINGTON, DC 20008
TEL: 202-938-9200

COMPANIES/ORGANIZATIONS WITH OPERATIONS IN BARBADOS:

HOLIDAY INNS WORLDWIDE, 302

MAXUS ENERGY CORPORATION, 363

MCCANN-ERICKSON WORLDWIDE, 354

PARKER DRILLING COMPANY, 405

SEQUA CORPORATION, 457

BELGIUM

- **Official Name:** Kingdom of Belgium

- **Capital:** Brussels

- **Location:** Belgium is a small country in the northwestern corner of Europe covering an area of 30,519 square miles. It is bordered from the north by the Netherlands, Germany, and Luxembourg, with France along its southern side. It is comparable in size to Maryland.

- **Population, Cities, and American Residents:** The population of Belgium totals 9.92 million (1991 est.). The country is divided into the Flemish-Dutch speaking areas of the north and the French-speaking Walloons of the south provinces. Flemings account for 56 percent of Belgium's population, with Walloons accounting for 32 percent, German for 1 percent and the remaining 11 percent mixed or other.

  Most American residents are employed in Belgium's three largest cities: Brussels with 970,100, Antwerp with 473,100, and Ghent with 231,000 people (1988 est.).

- **Language and Currency:** The official languages are Dutch, spoken by 56 percent of the residents, and French, spoken by 32 percent of the residents. The remaining people speak German. Of the total population, 11 percent speak both Dutch and French. Most Belgians are familiar with English, which is spoken by many government officials and business executives. The monetary unit is the Belgium franc (BFr), divided into 100 centimes. Bills are BFr 5,000, 1,000, 500, and 100. Coins are BFr 50, 20, 5, and 1. The exchange rate is 1 Belgian Franc = U.S.$.027 (July 30, 1993).

- **Climate:** The climate of Belgium is generally cool, temperate, and rainy. From the coastal areas to Brussels, it can be compared to the northeastern United States, but the southern Ardennes region has colder winters and hotter summers. During winter, expect wind, fog, and snow or drizzle. The mean temperatures in Brussels are 65°F in July and

37°F in January. Most of the year it is quite damp, so warmer clothing and rain gear are essential.

- **Economy and Resources:** Belgium is a highly industrialized country with one of the most open economies in the world. It is among the world's most industrialized areas, as it is within 100 miles of London, Paris, and most of the Netherlands. Belgium is an export-intensive country and 75 percent of its trade is with its fellow European Community (EC) countries. Years of deteriorating economic performance prompted a shake-up during the early 1980s. An economic austerity program began to show results in 1983, and though conditions for the consumer have not changed dramatically, people have accepted that the program will eventually lead to better economic conditions. Major industries include engineering, metal products, and chemicals. Belgian industry is concentrated in Flanders, with its railways, efficient highway systems, and inland waterways. Flemish industry consists primarily of international concerns, including assembly plants for General Motors and Volvo. Natural resources include natural gas and coal.

- **Cost of Living:** At an average of 149, the cost of living is higher than in the United States.

- **Work Permits, Visas, etc.:** A valid passport is required to travel in Belgium. A visa is not required for business/tourist stays of up to three months. A temporary residence permit and a work permit are required for longer stays, and must be obtained from the Ministry of Economic Affairs in Brussels. If you are entering Belgium from the United States, no vaccinations are required. For official or other information, direct inquiries to the embassy or consulate at the addresses below.

- **Taxation:** Permanent foreign residents must pay personal income tax on all income earned in Belgium, but under five years in Belgium is considered temporary residence. Also, U.S. citizens are eligible for benefits under a convention for the avoidance of double taxation between Belgium and the United States.

- **Principal International Schools:** English, French, and German schools are available to the international community of Belgium. International institutions are registered with the European Council of International Schools (ECIS) and are located in Antwerp and Brussels. Tuition for an American school is approximately U.S.$13,000 per year.

- **Health Care:** Belgium has many qualified English-speaking doctors and dentists. but medical costs are usually higher than in the United States. Belgium has a very advanced medical plan covering almost all health costs. Corporations are encouraged to join the health program or individuals can join independently. Health standards are very high in the country and no precautions are necessary. The cool, damp, winter weather may cause respiratory ailments for some people. Tap water is safe to drink, and bottled water is readily available.

- **Crime:** Crime is not considered a major problem in Belgium. Normal precautions should be taken, especially against pickpockets in areas where there are many tourists.

- **Pros and Cons of Living and Working in Belgium:** Though Belgium is one of the smallest countries in Europe, it is centrally located, and offers a great deal. It has an extensive transportation system, has a major seaport, and is a magnet for foreign

A
M
E
R
I
C
A
N

J
O
B
S

A
B
R
O
A
D

investment and multinational corporations. Cultural opportunity abounds, with many museums and monuments. Health and safety factors rank very high, though medical assistance and drugs can be expensive. There is still some hostility between the Dutch-speaking Flanders region in the north and the French-speaking Wallonia sector of the south. The Belgian economy has stabilized, but whether it will continue at this pace is uncertain. Housing can be very expensive, and prices continue to rise. Currently, the cost for a three-room furnished apartment in Brussels averages U.S.$1625 per month. The weather can also be an unpleasant factor, with the winter season being cold and damp most of the time.

EMBASSY AND CONSULATE CONTACT INFORMATION:

EMBASSY OF BELGIUM
3330 GARFIELD ST. NW
WASHINGTON, DC 20008
TEL: 202-333-6900

BELGIAN CONSULATE GENERAL
50 ROCKEFELLER PLAZA
NEW YORK, NY 10020
TEL: 212-586-5110

OTHER SOURCES OF INFORMATION:

U.S. STATE DEPT.
DESK OFFICER FOR BELGIUM
WASHINGTON, DC 20025
TEL: 202-647-6644

COMPANIES/ORGANIZATIONS WITH OPERATIONS IN BELGIUM:

ALBERTO-CULVER COMPANY, 115
ALLIED-SIGNAL, INC., 117
AM INTERNATIONAL, INC., 119
AMERICAN MANAGEMENT SYSTEMS, INC., 127
AMERICAN STANDARD, INC., 128
AMERICAN TOOL COMPANIES, INC., 129
AMGEN, INC., 131
AMOCO CORPORATION, 131
ANTHONY INDUSTRIES, 135
APPLE COMPUTER, INC., 136
ARMCO, INC., 140
ARMOUR SWIFT ECKRICH, INC., 141
ASSOCIATED PRESS, 144
AVON PRODUCTS, INC., 149
BANKERS TRUST NEW YORK CORPORATION, 155
BEMIS COMPANY, INC., 164
BETZ LABORATORIES, 166
BIO-RAD LABORATORIES, 166
BLACK & DECKER CORPORATION, 167
BLOCK DRUG COMPANY, INC., 169
BLOUNT, INC. (BLOUNT CONSTRUCTION DIVISION), 169
BOSE CORPORATION, 172
W. H. BRADY COMPANY, 173
BRIDGESTONE-FIRESTONE, INC., 174
BRISTOL-MEYERS SQUIBB COMPANY, 175

BUCK CONSULTANTS, INC., 178
BURLINGTON AIR EXPRESS, 179
BURSON-MARSTELLER, 180
CABOT CORPORATION, 181
CALGON CORPORATION, 182
CAMPBELL SOUP COMPANY, 183
CLARCOR, INC., 198
THE COCA-COLA COMPANY, 202
COMMODORE INTERNATIONAL LTD., 206
COMPUTER ASSOCIATES INTERNATIONAL, INC., 207
COMPUTERVISION CORPORATION, 208
CONAGRA, INC., 208
CORNING INCORPORATED, 215
COUDERT BROTHERS LAW FIRM, 217
CUMMINS ENGINE COMPANY, INC., 221
DATA GENERAL CORPORATION, 225
DDB NEEDHAM WORLDWIDE, INC., 227
THE DEXTER CORPORATION, 233
DONALDSON COMPANY, INC., 237
DOW JONES & COMPANY, INC., 241
DRESSER INDUSTRIES, INC., 241
DURIRON COMPANY, INC., 244
EG & G, INC., 249
EMERSON ELECTRIC COMPANY, 251
ENCYCLOPEDIA BRITANNICA, INC., 253
ERNST & YOUNG, 255
ETHYL CORPORATION, 256

EXXON COMPANY, INTERNATIONAL, 258

FEDERAL EXPRESS CORPORATION, 260

FEDERAL-MOGUL CORPORATION, 260

FISCHER & PORTER COMPANY, 263

FISHER CONTROLS INTERNATIONAL, INC., 263

THE GATES RUBBER COMPANY, 273

GATX CORPORATION, 273

GENERAL INSTRUMENT CORPORATION, 276

GENERAL MOTORS CORPORATION (GM), 277

GRANT THORNTON INTERNATIONAL, 286

GREAT LAKES CARBON INTERNATIONAL CORPORATION, 287

H. J. HEINZ COMPANY, 290

HACH COMPANY, 292

M. A. HANNA COMPANY, 295

HELENE CURTIS INDUSTRIES, INC., 298

HERTZ CORPORATION, 300

HILL & KNOWLTON, INC., 301

HOECHST CELANESE, INC., 302

HOLIDAY INNS WORLDWIDE, 302

HONEYWELL, INC., 303

HUGHES AIRCRAFT COMPANY, 307

IDB COMMUNICATIONS, INC., 309

INDUCTOTHERM CORPORATION, 311

INFORMATION BUILDERS, INC., 312

INGERSOLL-RAND COMPANY, 313

INTERNATIONAL BUSINESS MACHINES (IBM), 315

ITT HARTFORD INSURANCE GROUP, 321

JOHNSON CONTROLS, INC., 324

S. C. JOHNSON WAX, 325

JONES, DAY, REAVIS & POGUE, INC., 326

A. T. KEARNEY, INC., 329

KNOLL INTERNATIONAL, 338

KORN/FERRY INTERNATIONAL, 340

KYSOR INDUSTRIAL CORPORATION, 342

LAWTER INTERNATIONAL, INC., 344

LEVI STRAUSS ASSOCIATES, INC., 344

LINTAS: WORLDWIDE, 346

ARTHUR D. LITTLE, INC., 347

LITTON INDUSTRIES, INC., 348

LORAL CORPORATION, 350

LUBRIZOL CORPORATION, 353

MCCANN-ERICKSON WORLDWIDE, 354

MCGRAW-HILL, INC., 357

MCI COMMUNICATIONS CORPORATION, 365

MCKINSEY & COMPANY, INC., 357

MELROE COMPANY, 367

METCO PERKIN-ELMER, 371

MILLIKEN & COMPANY, 373

MOBIL OIL CORPORATION, 375

MONROE AUTO EQUIPMENT COMPANY, 376

MOTOROLA, INC., 381

NELLCOR, INC., 385

NICOLET INSTRUMENT CORPORATION, 387

NORDSON CORPORATION, 389

NORTON COMPANY, 390

NYNEX CORPORATION, 392

OCCIDENTAL PETROLEUM CORPORATION, 393

OGILVY & MATHER, 395

OLIN CORPORATION, 396

OUTBOARD MARINE CORPORATION, 399

OWENS-CORNING FIBERGLAS CORPORATION, 400

PARAMOUNT COMMUNICATIONS, INC., 404

PFIZER, INC., 412

PHILIPS TECHNOLOGIES, 414

PMI FOOD EQUIPMENT GROUP, 420

R. L. POLK & COMPANY, 421

PROCTER & GAMBLE PHARMACEUTICALS, INC., 426

READER'S DIGEST ASSOCIATION, INC., 432

ROBERT HALF INTERNATIONAL, INC., 440

ROGERS CORPORATION, 442

ROSEMOUNT, INC., 443

RPM, INC., 444

RUSSELL CORPORATION, 446

SAINT JUDE MEDICAL, INC., 448

SCHERING-PLOUGH CORPORATION, 450

SCHLEGEL CORPORATION, 451

A. SCHULMAN, INC., 451

SCOTT PAPER COMPANY, 453

SEARLE COMPANY, 455

SENSORMATIC ELECTRONICS CORPORATION, 457

SGS-THOMSON MICROELECTRONICS, 458

SHEARSON LEHMAN BROTHERS, 460

SIGNODE PACKAGING SYSTEMS, 462

SIMPLEX TIME RECORDER COMPANY, 463

SKADDEN, ARPS, SLATE, MEAGHER & FLOM, 465

SPRINGS INDUSTRIES, INC., 473

STANLEY WORKS, 478

STATE STREET BOSTON CORPORATION, 478

STONE CONTAINER CORPORATION, 480

SUN ELECTRIC CORPORATION, 484

SUNDSTRAND CORPORATION, 485

SYMBOL TECHNOLOGIES, INC., 485

TANDY CORPORATION, 487

TEKTRONIX, INC., 488

TELEDYNE, INC., 489

TELLABS OPERATIONS, INC., 489

TELXON CORP., 490

TENNECO AUTOMOTIVE, 491

TEXTRON, INC., 494

TLC BEATRICE INTERNATIONAL HOLDINGS, INC., 498

TOWERS PERRIN, INC., 499

TRACOR, INC., 500

TRANE COMPANY, 501

TRINOVA CORPORATION, 502

U.S. FEDERAL AVIATION ADMINISTRATION, 577

VF CORPORATION, 517

WANG LABORATORIES, INC., 519

WARD HOWELL INTERNATIONAL, INC., 520

WARNER ELECTRIC BRAKE & CLUTCH COMPANY, 521

WATERS CHROMATOGRAPHY (MILLIPORE), 523

WEYERHAEUSER COMPANY, 526

WOOLWORTH CORPORATION, 528

WYNN'S INTERNATIONAL, INC., 530

BELIZE

- **Official Name:** Belize

- **Capital:** Belmopan

- **Location:** Belize is located on the northeast coast of Central America. It is bounded by Mexico to the north, the Caribbean Sea to the east, and Guatemala to the south and west. Its total land area is 8,867 square miles making it slightly larger than Massachusetts. The Belizean coastline is relatively flat and swampy. A few low mountains exist in the interior region. Nearly half of its territory is covered by forests.

- **Language and Currency:** The official language of Belize, used in business and in government, is English. Mayan and Spanish are also spoken throughout the country. The monetary unit is the Belize dollar, linked to the U.S. dollar at a fixed rate of Belize $2 = U.S.$1.

- **Print Sources of Information:** *Belize: The Uncut Gem* by Judith Eckert. Worldwide Images Publishers, 1989.

EMBASSY AND CONSULATE CONTACT INFORMATION:

EMBASSY OF BELIZE
3400 INTERNATIONAL DR. NW, #2J
WASHINGTON, DC 20008
TEL: 202-363-4505

COMPANIES/ORGANIZATIONS WITH OPERATIONS IN BELIZE:

AMERICAN CANADIAN CARIBBEAN LINE, 123

BERMUDA

- **Official Name:** Bermuda

- **Capital:** Hamilton

- **Location:** Bermuda forms an archipelago of nearly 300 islands and islets in the North Atlantic Ocean, located about 670 miles southeast of New York City. It is a British dependent territory. With a coastline stretching for 64 miles, the total land area encompasses 21 square miles. Only about 20 of the islands are inhabited, and Bermuda's territory is comprised of beaches, hills, ridges, and caves, abundant throughout the island.

- **Population, Cities, and American Residents:** The population of Bermuda is 58,000 (1992 est.), with approximately 61 percent black and the remainder 39 percent white and other.

  Most American residents are employed in the capital city of Hamilton with 3,000 people (1989 est.).

- **Language and Currency:** The official language of Bermuda is English. The monetary unit is the dollar. The exchange rate is Bermuda $1 = U.S.$1.

- **Climate:** The climate of Bermuda is mild, with an average yearly temperature of 70°F. Precipitation averages about 58 inches yearly. Rain is extremely important to Bermuda as it has few underground sources of water. Rain is collected from rooftops and stored in tanks below buildings. Roofs are whitewashed and maintained for cleanliness. Bermuda's location makes it subject to tropical storms and hurricanes, especially in the fall.

- **Economy and Resources:** Bermuda has enjoyed steady economic growth since the end of World War II. Tourism is the mainstay of the economy and approximately 75 percent of the travelers are from the United States. There are also more than 6,000 foreign companies located in Bermuda, many U.S.-owned. Other economic interests include agriculture and fishing. There is a low unemployment (under 3 percent) due to numerous job opportunities, especially in tourism. Natural resources include limestone, and of course the climate, which fosters tourism.

- **Cost of Living:** At 144, the cost of living is higher than in the United States.

- **Work Permits, Visas, etc.:** A valid passport or proof of U.S. citizenship is required for travel in Bermuda. For tourist stays of more than six months, you'll need a visa. If you are entering Bermuda from the United States, no vaccinations are necessary. For official or other information, direct inquiries to the embassy or consulate at the addresses below.

- **Taxation:** Income tax is not imposed on individuals in Bermuda.

- **Health Care:** Sanitation standards and health facilities are good in Bermuda. Food available on the island is safe to eat and water from most areas is safe to drink. No health hazards exist that pose a risk to travelers.

- **Crime:** Crime is not a major problem in Bermuda. It is a popular tourist area, however, so take precautions. Don't leave valuables unattended, or carry large sums of cash on a casual basis. Tourism is very important to the local people, and authorities monitor the personal safety of travelers on this island very carefully.

- **Pros and Cons of Living and Working in Bermuda:** Bermuda is a popular resort area, with scenic beaches, and a mild enjoyable climate. Its transportation and telecommunications services are good, and its proximity to the United States is a plus. Health care and sanitary conditions are adequate, and crime is not a major problem. It is subject to tropical storms and hurricanes, though they may be infrequent. Almost all manufactured products and foodstuffs must be imported, and prices reflect this.

- **Print Sources of Information:** *Who's Who in Bermuda*, Background Notes: United Kingdom. Available from the Superintendent of Documents, U.S. Government Printing Office, Washington, D.C., 20402.

EMBASSY AND CONSULATE CONTACT INFORMATION:

UNITED KINGDOM
EMBASSY OF BERMUDA
3100 MASSACHUSETTS AVE. NW
WASHINGTON, DC 20008
TEL: 202-462-1340

COMPANIES/ORGANIZATIONS WITH OPERATIONS IN BERMUDA:

ALEXANDER & ALEXANDER SERVICES, INC., 116
BAUSCH & LOMB, INC., 159
THE COCA-COLA COMPANY, 202
FIGGIE INTERNATIONAL, INC., 262

INTERNATIONAL BUSINESS MACHINES (IBM), 315
ROHM & HAAS COMPANY, 442
SONESTA INTERNATIONAL HOTELS CORPORATION, 470
USAIR GROUP, INC., 516

BOLIVIA

- **Official Name:** Republic of Bolivia

- **Capital:** La Paz

- **Location:** Bolivia is a landlocked country in central South America covering 1.1 million square miles. Its size is comparable to the combined land area of California and Texas. Its terrain is a combination of mountains, a high plateau, valleys, and tropical lowlands. It is bounded by Brazil to the north and east, Paraguay and Argentina to the south, and Peru and Chile to the west. It shares control of Lake Tititaca, the world's highest navigable lake, with Peru.

- **Population, Cities, and American Residents:** The population of Bolivia totals 7.2 million (1992 est.). Approximately 30 percent of the population is Quecha and 25 percent Aymara. Those of European descent account for 5 to 15 percent of the population with the remaining 25 to 30 percent mixed.

Most American residents are employed in Bolivia's three largest cities: La Paz (administrative capital) with 1 million, Santa Cruz de la Sierra with 615,100, and Sucre (legal capital and seat of judiciary) with 95,600 people (1988 est.).

- **Language and Currency:** The official language of Bolivia is Spanish, but because of the low literacy rate in rural areas, fewer than half of the residents speak Spanish as their first language. Other languages spoken are Aymara and Quecha. The monetary unit of Bolivia is the boliviano. The rate of exchange is 4.30 bolivianos = U.S.$1 (August 25, 1993).

- **Climate:** The climate of Bolivia varies in different areas. Crossing the country from northwest to the southeast, a plateau splits the Andes into two mountain chains, along the eastern and western sides. La Paz has the highest elevation of any capital city in the world. Average temperature is 70°F. The lowland plain region covers the Beni and Santa Cruz areas, the most highly developed agricultural region in Bolivia. The northeastern area is part of the Amazon River basin and contains tropical forests and dense vegetation with hot and humid weather conditions prevailing. The rainy season for Bolivia is from December to March.

- **Economy and Resources:** Bolivia has the lowest per capita gross national product in South America. Poor weather conditions in the early 1980s set the country back, but annual productions of sugar, potatoes, corn, and rice have returned to normal levels. However, the country still has to import wheat. Agriculture (including forestry and fishing), is a major contributor to Bolivia's economy, employs most of the labor force, and has potential for considerable growth. Minerals and hydrocarbons account for 47.5 percent of Bolivia's total exports, with tin as a leading earner. Major industries are mining and petroleum refining.

- **Cost of Living:** At 88, the cost of living is lower than in the United States.

- **Work Permits, Visas, etc.:** You'll need a valid passport to travel in Bolivia. A visa is not required for a tourist stay of up to 30 days. For over 30 days, a business visa (cost, $50) and company letter stating the purpose of the trip are needed (no photo or application necessary). If you are entering Bolivia from the United States, no vaccinations are required. For official or other information, direct inquiries to the embassy or consulate at the addresses below.

- **Taxation:** Bolivia taxes it citizens and residents on Bolivian-source income only. Authorities collect taxes from any person who resides in Bolivia for more than 180 days during the calendar year. Domicile and citizenship do not affect the tax base.

- **Principal International Schools:** There are international schools in Bolivia for children of American residents. One is The Santa Cruz Cooperative School, Casilla 753, Santa Cruz, Bolivia, telephone 591-3-33-2990.

- **Health Care:** Sanitation is poor in Bolivia, so don't eat undercooked meats and fish, and precautions should be taken with all fruits and vegetables. Tap water is not potable. The altitude can present problems; to adjust, rest for the first few days, eat lightly, and avoid cigarettes and alcohol for the first week. Drink sufficient liquids and remain in the

La Paz area, where humidity is low. Bolivian officials recommend yellow fever vaccinations.

- **Crime:** As with many large cities of the world, Bolivia's major tourist areas are subject to common crime, including robberies and thefts. Lock car doors, and keep valuables out of sight. When walking, avoid dark alleys, and be wary of strangers and beggars. Avoid travel at night, and try to travel in a group when visiting isolated areas. Also, it is important to remember that many South American countries have strict laws against the use, possession, or sale of narcotics. Consequences are very serious. There is usually no bail, and jail sentences of 2 to 4 years are not uncommon.

- **Pros and Cons of Living and Working in Bolivia:** Bolivia has one of the world's oldest civilizations. In many respects, life in Bolivia is primitive, simple, and slow. The country has great natural beauty, from the dense jungles of the east to the arid Andean plains in the west. The Indian customs and culture are some of the most unusual and well-preserved in the world.

Bolivia has experienced more political instability and unrest than any other country in the world. It has poor sanitation, and two-thirds of its people live in poverty. The United States currently has friendly diplomatic relations with Bolivia, but there in no guarantee that will remain true. Principal underlying issues concern the continuation of a democratic process and the narcotics problem. An increasing amount of coca cultivation has been diverted to the illegal market for the manufacture of cocaine. Narcotics trafficking has become both a domestic and international problem for Bolivia and for the U.S. market as well.

EMBASSY AND CONSULATE CONTACT INFORMATION:

BOLIVIAN EMBASSY
3014 MASSACHUSETTS AVE. NW
WASHINGTON, DC 20008
TEL: 202-483-4410

BOLIVIAN CONSULATE GENERAL
21 EAST 43RD ST., STE. 702
NEW YORK, NY 10017
TEL: 212-687-0530

OTHER SOURCES OF INFORMATION:

FOR UPDATES ON TRAVEL IN BOLIVIA, CONTACT:
U.S. STATE DEPT.
FOREIGN TRAVEL ADVISORIES
WASHINGTON, DC 20520
TEL: 202-647-5225

COMPANIES/ORGANIZATIONS WITH OPERATIONS IN BOLIVIA:

LOUIS BERGER INTERNATIONAL INC., 165
CHEVRON CORPORATION, 193
CONSERVATION INTERNATIONAL, 545
DE LEUW, CATHER INTERNATIONAL, 228
ECOLOGY AND ENVIRONMENT, INC., 248
FRITZ COMPANIES, 269

INTERNATIONAL BUSINESS MACHINES
  (IBM), 315
INTERNATIONAL VOLUNTARY SERVICES,
  INC., 555
LIQUID CARBONIC CORPORATION, 347
LITTON INDUSTRIES, INC., 348
POPULATION COUNCIL, 562

BOTSWANA

- **Official Name:** Republic of Botswana
- **Capital:** Gaborone
- **Location:** Botswana is a landlocked country in the center of southern Africa. It is bounded by Zambia to the north and west, Zimbabwe to the northeast, and to the south and southeast by South Africa. Its land area is 224,607 square miles, making it slightly smaller than Texas. Nearly three-fourths of its territory is covered by forests and gently rolling tableland.
- **Language and Currency:** The official language of Botswana is English. Setswana is also spoken. The monetary unit is the pula. The exchange rate is 2.5 pulas = U.S.$1 (December 1993).

EMBASSY AND CONSULATE CONTACT INFORMATION:

EMBASSY OF BOTSWANA
4301 CONNECTICUT AVE. NW, STE. 404
WASHINGTON, DC 20008
TEL: 202-244-4990

COMPANIES/ORGANIZATIONS WITH OPERATIONS IN BOTSWANA:

CONSERVATION INTERNATIONAL, 545
H. J. HEINZ COMPANY, 290

BRAZIL

- **Official Name:** Federative Republic of Brazil
- **Capital:** Brasilia
- **Location:** Brazil occupies the central and northeastern sections of South America. It is bounded by Colombia, Venezuela, Guyana, Suriname, and French Guiana to the north; the Atlantic Ocean to the east; Uruguay, Paraguay, and Argentina to the south; and Peru and Bolivia to the west. It is the largest country in South America, with a land area totaling 3,286,488 square miles, making it slightly smaller than the United States. Nearly 70 percent of the territory is forest and woodland with only 7 percent of arable land. Two dominant features of Brazil's geography are the Amazon River system and the Serra do Mar cliff that follows the eastern coast. Most of the people live on the eastern coast of Brazil.
- **Population, Cities, and American Residents:** The population of Brazil totals 156 million (1992 est.). Nearly 55 percent is white (from Portuguese, Italian, and German extraction), 38 percent mixed, 6 percent black, and 1 percent other groups.

    Most American residents are employed in Brazil's three major cities: Brasilia with 1.8 million, Sao Paulo with 12 million, and Rio de Janeiro with 8 million people (1989 est.).
- **Language and Currency:** The official language of Brazil is Portuguese. English,

French, and Spanish are also spoken, but Portuguese is the language of business and government. A working knowledge of the language is essential to cope with daily life in the country. If you do not speak Portuguese, then an interpreter or translator is necessary to conduct business. The monetary unit is the cruzeiro (Cz$). It has replaced the former currency, the cruzado (NCz$) in which one thousand cruzeiros equal one old cruzado. Remember that decimals are commas (and vice versa) in South America, so five thousand five hundred dollars and fifty cents would read: $5.500,50. The exchange rate on July 30, 1993 was 1 Brazilian cruzeiro = U.S.$.000015; 66,452 cruzeiros equal U.S.$1. However, rampant inflation erodes the dollar value of the currency very rapidly.

- **Climate:** In Brazil, the seasons are in the reverse of those in the Northern Hemisphere. Humidity is rather high throughout most of the country, slightly less in the higher elevations like Sao Paulo. Summers (from December to February), can be very warm. The mean yearly temperature in the north is 82°F and 68°F. in the south. Toward the north and closer to the equator, there is only a slight difference between summer and winter. The rainy season is from June through August.

- **Economy and Resources:** Brazil's economy has experienced both high and low periods in the past decade. It has had dynamic growth and slumped during the world recession. After the escalation of world oil prices halted growth in the 1970s, a recovery began when exports improved during the 1980s. High inflation rates still linger, but the country's vast natural resources should strengthen Brazil's economy. More than 40 percent of the people work in services, 31 percent are engaged in agriculture, and 27 percent are in industry. Natural resources include iron ore, manganese, and uranium. The largest industries are: textiles, consumer goods, and chemicals. Chief exports are coffee, metallurgical products, food stuffs, and iron ore. Major trading partners are the United States and the European Community.

- **Cost of Living:** At an average of 121, the cost of living is higher than in the United States.

- **Work Permits, Visas, etc.:** A valid passport and visa are required when visiting or working in Brazil. Visas are valid for three months and may be extended while in the country. Visa applications are accepted by mail at all Brazilian Consular Offices, with the exception of New York. Allow ample time for their issue and return. If you are entering Brazil from the United States, no vaccinations are necessary. However, if you are visiting the Amazon region, a malaria prophylaxis is recommended (shots available in Brazil). AIDS is prevalent in Brazil. For official or other information, direct inquiries to the embassy or consulate at the addresses below.

- **Taxation:** All individuals residing in Brazil or deriving income from Brazilian sources are required to pay income tax. Nonresidents usually pay a 25 percent fee on revenues earned in the country. Foreign individuals who transfer their residence from abroad do not have to pay income tax on returns from their overseas holdings for the first five years of residency. For more information, contact the U.S. Commerce Department or the Brazilian Government Trade Bureau.

- **Principal International Schools:** Several international schools are available in Sao

Paulo and Rio de Janeiro for children of American residents. For an American school, the tuition averages $3,500 to $5,500 per year.

- **Health Care:** Medical care is satisfactory in major cities of Brazil, and most doctors speak English and are well trained. In rural areas, contact the nearest embassy or U.S. consulate for the best advice. Sanitation throughout the country is continuing to improve, but rural areas are not as good as major tourist areas. Except for the major hotels, which serve safe drinking water, all tap water should be boiled. Otherwise, drink bottled fluids and use bottled or boiled water for ice, and brushing your teeth. Take precautions with all fruits and vegetables and be careful where you eat, too, as establishments may not have been inspected properly by officials.

- **Crime:** Petty crime and theft are common in major tourist areas in Brazil. Don't carry a lot of cash with you, and lock the doors to your apartment and to your car. Don't flash around expensive jewelry, cameras, etc., either. Women especially should not travel alone at night. Keep identification with you at all times in case you're stopped by police, and do not become involved in any drug-related matters while in Brazil. Being arrested for any drug-related offense is very serious and the consequences can be severe.

- **Pros and Cons of Living and Working in Brazil:** Brazil is one of the most diverse countries of the world offering many sightseeing opportunities. From the huge cities to the jungles of the Amazon, Brazil has something of interest for everyone. It has a very receptive climate for foreign businessmen who are treated in a courteous fashion. Medical facilities are good and so is transportation, but telecommunication services are poor. Calling home will not be a problem, but telephones are in short supply. Try to rent a home or apartment in which there is already one installed. Apartments are preferred over houses because of lower risks of burglary. Sanitary standards are not acceptable in many regions. To live and work in Brazil, familiarity with the Portuguese language and knowing Spanish is a help. The cost of living in Brazil is slightly higher than in the United States, so be prepared to pay more for daily necessities.

EMBASSY AND CONSULATE CONTACT INFORMATION:

EMBASSY OF BRAZIL
3006 MASSACHUSETTS AVE. NW
WASHINGTON, DC 20008
TEL: 202-745-2700

CONSULATE GENERAL OF BRAZIL
401 N. MICHIGAN AVE., STE. 3050
CHICAGO, IL 60611
TEL: 312-464-0244

OTHER SOURCES OF INFORMATION:

BRAZILIAN GOVERNMENT TRADE BUREAU
551 FIFTH AVE.
NEW YORK, NY 10020
212-916-3200

U.S. COMMERCE DEPT.
MARKETING MANAGER FOR BRAZIL
WASHINGTON, DC 20230
TEL: 202-377-3871

COMPANIES/ORGANIZATIONS WITH OPERATIONS IN BRAZIL:

ABB LUMMUS CREST, 108
ABB VETCO GRAY, INC., 108
AKZO AMERICA, INC., 113
ALBANY INTERNATIONAL CORPORATION, 114

ALEXANDER & ALEXANDER SERVICES, INC., 116
ALLEN-BRADLEY COMPANY, INC., 116
ALLERGAN, INC., 117
ALUMINUM COMPANY OF AMERICA, 118

A
M
E
R
I
C
A
N

J
O
B
S

A
B
R
O
A
D

AMERICAN CYANAMID COMPANY, 124
AMERICAN EXPRESS COMPANY—TRAVEL
    RELATED SERVICES, 125
AMERICAN STANDARD, INC., 128
AMOCO CORPORATION, 131
AMP, INC., 132
AMPEX CORPORATION, 133
ANDREW CORPORATION, 134
ARMCO, INC., 140
ASSOCIATED PRESS, 144
AUTOMATIC SWITCH COMPANY, 147
AVERY DENNISON CORPORATION, 147
AVON PRODUCTS, INC., 149
BACKER SPIELVOGEL & BATES
    WORLDWIDE, INC., 150
BAILEY CONTROLS COMPANY, 151
BANK OF BOSTON CORPORATION, 153
THE BANK OF NEW YORK COMPANY,
    INC., 154
BANKAMERICA CORPORATION, 155
BANKERS TRUST NEW YORK
    CORPORATION, 155
C. R. BARD, INC., 157
THE BARDEN CORPORATION, 157
BATTELLE MEMORIAL INSTITUTE, 159
BAUSCH & LOMB, INC., 159
BLACK & DECKER CORPORATION, 167
BLOCK DRUG COMPANY, INC., 169
BLOUNT, INC. (BLOUNT CONSTRUCTION
    DIVISION), 169
BORDEN, INC., 170
BORG-WARNER CORPORATION, 171
BRIDGESTONE-FIRESTONE, INC., 174
BRISTOL-MEYERS SQUIBB COMPANY, 175
BROWN GROUP, INC., 176
CABOT CORPORATION, 181
CARGILL INCORPORATED, 184
CHAMPION INTERNATIONAL
    CORPORATION, 189
CHASE MANHATTAN CORPORATION, 190
CHEVRON CHEMICAL COMPANY, 192
CHEVRON CORPORATION, 193
THE CHUBB & SON CORPORATION, 196
CITICORP, 198
CLIPPER CRUISE LINES, 199
THE COCA-COLA COMPANY, 202
COMMERCIAL INTERTECH CORPORATION,
    205
COMPUTER ASSOCIATES INTERNATIONAL,
    INC., 207

COMPUTERVISION CORPORATION, 208
CONSERVATION INTERNATIONAL, 545
CONTINENTAL BANK CORPORATION, 210
CORNING INCORPORATED, 215
COUDERT BROTHERS LAW FIRM, 217
CROWN CORK & SEAL COMPANY, INC.,
    218
CUMMINS ENGINE COMPANY, INC., 221
DANA CORPORATION, 224
DANIEL, MANN, JOHNSON &
    MENDENHALL, 224
DATA GENERAL CORPORATION, 225
DH TECHNOLOGY, INC., 233
DIAMOND SHAMROCK R & M, INC., 234
DIGITAL EQUIPMENT CORPORATION, 236
DONALDSON COMPANY, INC., 237
DOW CHEMICAL COMPANY, 240
DOW JONES & COMPANY, INC., 241
DRESSER INDUSTRIES, INC., 241
DURACELL, INC., 244
EASTMAN KODAK COMPANY, 246
EATON CORPORATION/CUTLER HAMMER,
    247
ECOLOGY AND ENVIRONMENT, INC., 248
ENCORE COMPUTER CORPORATION, 252
ERNST & YOUNG, 255
ESCO CORPORATION, 255
EXXON CHEMICAL COMPANY, 257
EXXON COMPANY, INTERNATIONAL, 258
FALK CORPORATION, 259
FERRO CORPORATION, 261
FIGGIE INTERNATIONAL, INC., 262
FLEMING COMPANIES, INC., 264
FORD MOTOR COMPANY, 267
FRITZ COMPANIES, 269
THE GATES RUBBER COMPANY, 273
GENERAL ELECTRIC COMPANY (GE), 275
THE GILLETTE COMPANY, 283
GOODYEAR TIRE & RUBBER COMPANY,
    284
W. R. GRACE & COMPANY, 285
HALLIBURTON COMPANY, 292
HANSON INDUSTRIES, 295
HERCULES, INC., 299
HERSHEY FOODS CORPORATION, 299
HEWLETT-PACKARD COMPANY, 300
HILL & KNOWLTON, INC., 301
HOLIDAY INNS WORLDWIDE, 302
HUGHES CHRISTENSEN COMPANY, 307
IDB COMMUNICATIONS, INC., 309

INDUCTOTHERM CORPORATION, 311

INGERSOLL-RAND COMPANY, 313

INTERNATIONAL FLAVORS & FRAGRANCES, INC., 317

INTERTRANS CORPORATION, 320

ITT CORPORATION, 321

ITT SHERATON CORPORATION, 322

ITW FINISHING SYSTEMS & PRODUCTS, 322

JOHNSON & HIGGINS, 324

KELLOGG COMPANY, 330

KIMBERLY-CLARK CORPORATION, 336

KORN/FERRY INTERNATIONAL, 340

LEVI STRAUSS ASSOCIATES, INC., 344

THE LINCOLN ELECTRIC COMPANY, 346

LIQUID CARBONIC CORPORATION, 347

ARTHUR D. LITTLE, INC., 347

LITTON INDUSTRIES, INC., 348

LIZ CLAIBORNE, INC., 348

LOCTITE CORPORATION, 349

LORD CORPORATION, 350

LOTUS DEVELOPMENT CORPORATION, 351

LTV STEEL CO., 352

LUBRIZOL CORPORATION, 353

MALLINCKRODT, INC., 359

MCCANN-ERICKSON WORLDWIDE, 354

MCCORMICK & COMPANY, INC., 355

MCGRAW-HILL, INC., 357

MCKINSEY & COMPANY, INC., 357

MEASUREX CORPORATION, 366

MERCK & COMPANY, INC., 368

METALLURG CORPORATION, 370

METCO PERKIN-ELMER, 371

MILLIPORE CORPORATION, 374

MOBIL OIL CORPORATION, 375

MODINE MANUFACTURING COMPANY, 375

MONROE AUTO EQUIPMENT COMPANY, 376

MONSANTO COMPANY, 377

MORRISON KNUDSEN CORPORATION, 379

MOTION PICTURE EXPORT ASSOCIATION OF AMERICA, 380

NALCO CHEMICAL COMPANY, 382

NATIONAL SEMICONDUCTOR CORPORATION, 383

NL INDUSTRIES, INC., 388

NORDSON CORPORATION, 389

NORTON COMPANY, 390

NORWEST CORPORATION, 391

NOVELL, INC., 392

OCCIDENTAL PETROLEUM CORPORATION, 393

OTIS ELEVATOR COMPANY: WORLD HEADQUARTERS, 399

OUTBOARD MARINE CORPORATION, 399

OWENS-CORNING FIBERGLAS CORPORATION, 400

OWENS-ILLINOIS, INC., 401

PARKER HANNIFIN CORPORATION, 405

PENROD DRILLING CORPORATION, 408

PEPSICO FOODS INTERNATIONAL, 409

PEPSICO, INC., 410

PERKIN-ELMER CORPORATION, 410

PHILLIPS-VAN HEUSEN CORPORATION, 415

PIONEER HI-BRED INTERNATIONAL, INC., 417

PITNEY BOWES, INC., 417

POPULATION COUNCIL, 562

PREFORMED LINE PRODUCTS COMPANY, 423

PREMARK INTERNATIONAL, INC., 423

QUAKER OATS COMPANY, 428

RALSTON PURINA COMPANY, 430

RELIANCE ELECTRIC COMPANY, 435

REVLON, INC., 437

RIVERWOOD INTERNATIONAL, INC., 439

RJR NABISCO, 439

ROCKWELL INTERNATIONAL CORPORATION, 441

ROHM & HAAS COMPANY, 442

SCOTT PAPER COMPANY, 453

SEA-LAND SERVICE, INC., 454

SGS CONTROL SERVICES, 458

SIGNODE PACKAGING SYSTEMS, 462

SIMON & SCHUSTER, INC., 463

SONAT, INC., 469

SONAT OFFSHORE, 470

SOUTHWIRE COMPANY, 472

SPS TECHNOLOGIES, INC., 474

STANDARD COMMERCIAL CORPORATION, 476

STANLEY WORKS, 478

STERLING WINTHROP, INC., 479

SUN ELECTRIC CORPORATION, 484

TELEDYNE, INC., 489

TENNECO, INC., 492

TEXACO OIL COMPANY, 493

TEXAS INTRUMENTS, INC., 494

TORRINGTON COMPANY, 499

TOWERS PERRIN, INC., 499
TRANE COMPANY, 501
TRINOVA CORPORATION, 502
TRW, INC., 503
UNILEVER UNITED STATES, INC., 506
UNITED PRESS INTERNATIONAL, 509
UNIVERSAL FOODS CORPORATION, 513
THE UPJOHN COMPANY, 515

WARNER-LAMBERT COMPANY, 522
WEST COMPANY, INC., 525
WHIRLPOOL CORPORATION, 526
WOODWARD GOVERNOR COMPANY, 528
WORLD COURIER MANAGEMENT, INC.,
   529
YOUNG & RUBICAM, INC., 533

BRITISH VIRGIN ISLANDS

- **Official Name:** British Virgin Islands
- **Capital:** Road Town
- **Location:** The British Virgin Islands are comprised of more than 50 mountainous islands and islets located in the northeastern Caribbean Sea. Puerto Rico lies about 100 miles to the west. The main islands are Tortola, which houses the capital (Road Town), Beef Island, and Virgin Gorda. Its total land area is 59 square miles, making the British Islands just smaller than Washington, D.C. The terrain is exceptionally hilly and the climate is very pleasant with an annual average daytime temperature of 80°F. The British Virgin Islands group is a dependent territory of the United Kingdom.
- **Language and Currency:** The official language of the British Virgin Islands is English. The monetary unit is the U.S. dollar.
- **Print Source of Information:** Zellers, Margaret, editor. *Fielding's Caribbean.* New York: Fielding Travel Books, William Morrow & Co., 1992.

EMBASSY AND CONSULATE CONTACT INFORMATION:
BRITISH EMBASSY
3100 MASSACHUSETTS AVE. NW
WASHINGTON, DC 20008
TEL: 202-462-1340

COMPANIES/ORGANIZATIONS WITH OPERATIONS IN BRITISH VIRGIN ISLANDS:
COMMODORE CRUISE LINES, 206

BULGARIA

- **Official Name:** People's Republic of Bulgaria
- **Capital:** Sofia
- **Location:** Bulgaria is a moderately developed European nation located on the Balkan Peninsula, extending from the Black Sea on the east to Yugoslavia on the west. The Danube River, to the north, forms most of the boundary with Romania. Greece and

Turkey lie to the south and southeast. Bulgaria is mostly mountainous, with the Balkan Mountains running through the center of the country, from east to west. The climate is similar to the U.S. Midwest. At 44,365 square miles, Bulgaria is roughly the size of Ohio.

- **Language and Currency:** The official language is Bulgarian. The monetary unit is the leva, with an exchange rate of .41 leva = U.S.$1 (April 1989).

EMBASSY AND CONSULATE CONTACT INFORMATION:

BULGARIAN EMBASSY
1621 22ND ST. NW
WASHINGTON, DC 20008
TEL: 202-387-7969

BULGARIAN CONSULATE
TEL: 202-483-5885

COMPANIES/ORGANIZATIONS WITH OPERATIONS IN BULGARIA:

PHILIP MORRIS COMPANIES, INC., 413

CAMEROON

- **Official Name:** Republic of Cameroon
- **Capital:** Yaounde
- **Location:** Cameroon is located on the western coast of central Africa. It is bounded by Nigeria to the northwest, Chad to the northeast, the Central African Republic to the east, Congo to the southeast, Gabon and Equatorial Guinea to the south, and the Gulf of Guinea to the west. With a land area of 183,569 square miles, it is slightly larger than California. It has four main geographic regions: the northern area around Lake Chad; the central Adamaoua Plateau; the heavily forested area of the Mandara and Gote Mountains on the western border; and the tropical rain forests in the southern and eastern sections. More than half of Cameroon's territory is covered by forests.
- **Language and Currency:** The official languages of Cameroon are English and French and both are used throughout government and business. Three-fourths of the people speak French, the primary language. Other African languages are spoken throughout the country. The monetary unit is the CFA franc issued by the African Financial Community. The exchange rate is 250 CFA francs = U.S.$1 (November 1993).

EMBASSY AND CONSULATE CONTACT INFORMATION:

EMBASSY OF THE REPUBLIC OF CAMEROON
2349 MASSACHUSETTS AVE. NW
WASHINGTON, DC 20008
TEL: 202-265-8790

MISSION TO THE REPUBLIC OF CAMEROON
TO THE UNITED NATIONS
22 EAST 73RD ST.
NEW YORK, NY 10021
TEL: 212-794-2295

OTHER SOURCES OF INFORMATION:

U.S. DEPT. OF STATE, DESK OFFICER FOR CAMEROON
WASHINGTON, DC 20025
TEL: 202-647-0996

COMPANIES/ORGANIZATIONS WITH OPERATIONS IN CAMEROON:

THE COCA-COLA COMPANY, 202

CANADA

- **Official Name:** Canada
- **Capital:** Ottawa
- **Location:** Located just to the north of the continental United States, Canada is the second largest country in the world with an area of 3,558,087 square miles of land and fresh water. The longest undefended border in the world, 5,526 miles, is between Canada and the United States. Canada is divided into ten provinces and two territories. There are seven main physiographic areas: The Canadian Shield, the Great Lakes/St. Lawrence Lowlands, Prairies and Mackenzie Lowlands, Hudson Bay and Arctic Archipelago Lowlands, Appalachians, Western Cordillera, and the Arctic Regions.
- **Population, Cities, and American Residents:** Canada's population is 26.9 million people (1992 est.) ranking 31st in size among the nations. Nine cities have populations of over 500,000.

  The four largest cities where Americans are employed are Toronto with 3.5 million, Montreal with 2.9 million, Vancouver with 1.4 million, and Ottawa with 833,000 people. Nearly 40 percent of the population originated from the British Isles; 27 percent are of French origin, 20 percent European, and the remaining 13 percent are of Asian, Caribbean, indigenous Indian, or other origins.
- **Language and Currency:** The principal and official languages of Canada are English and French. Sixty percent of the population speaks English, 25 percent speaks French, and 15 percent speak both languages. The unit of currency is the Canadian dollar (c$) divided into 100 cents. Coins are issued in denominations of 1, 2, 5, 10, 25, and 50 cents and one dollar. The exchange rate is 1 Canadian dollar = U.S.$.78 (July 30, 1993).
- **Climate:** Canada's climate is diversified. British Columbia, on the Pacific Coast, has a moderate climate with mild, damp winters and warm summers. The flat, fertile plains of the Prairie Provinces produce a climate of extremes: summers are short and hot; winters are long and cold; precipitation is light throughout the entire year. Ontario's climate is also varied. In the southern areas winters are less severe and the summers last longer. The mean maximum temperature in Toronto in January is 31°F; in July it's 81°F. In the northeast, Quebec's climate is more extreme than Ontario's. Snowfalls are heavier, and winters are long and cold. The summers are hot and humid. Quebec City's mean maximum temperature in January is 19°F; in July it's 77°F. The Maritime Provinces of the East Coast, such as Nova Scotia, have damp and relatively mild climates due to their proximity to the warm Gulf Stream flowing north through the Atlantic.
- **Economy and Resources:** Canada is a free market economy in which the private

sector predominates. It is rich in natural resources and ranks seventh in the world in gross domestic product. Industry drives the nation's economy, employing one-third of the country's work force. The breakdown of the labor force is: agriculture (4 percent); industry and commerce (52 percent); and services (28 percent). Canada's economic development has been sustained by its natural resources. The nation ranks first in the world in mineral exports and third in mineral production. These minerals include: nickel, copper, zinc, gold, and silver. Forest products, crude oil reserves, livestock, and fishing are also major contributors to the Canadian economy.

The free-trade agreement established with the United States in 1989 created both opportunities and challenges for Canadian companies to compete in a larger economic arena. Canadians are wary of foreign ownership of Canadian businesses, particularly media companies. Canadian law now requires that majority control be held by Canadian citizens when a new business is started or the ownership of an existing business changes hands.

- **Cost of Living:** The cost of living in Canada ranges from 118 to 123, based on figures compiled from five major areas.

- **Work Permits, Visas, etc.:** U.S. citizens visiting Canada may be required to show proof of citizenship. U.S. firms sending employees to work on a temporary or permanent basis in Canada are asked to apply for employment visas in advance by contacting the Immigration Section of the Canadian Consulate General nearest them. Foreign workers must apply for an immigrant visa before going to work in Canada. For official or further information, direct inquiries to the embassy or consulate at the addresses below.

- **Taxation:** The Federal Government of Canada collects taxes from separate provinces, providing that the provincial tax structure is uniform with the federal system. All residents (anyone who has spent 183 days or more of a taxation year in Canada) pay taxes on their worldwide income. Nonresidents pay on their Canadian income. There are tax treaties in effect between Canada and the United States to avoid double taxation. Exemptions on salaries may be allowed based on the type of firm or type of employment.

- **Principal International Schools:** There are public and private international schools throughout Canada. The average cost of tuition for an American school is $9,000 per year.

- **Health Care:** Public health in Canada is comparable to that of the United States. Provinces and territories share with the federal government the cost of a national health insurance plan. U.S. citizens are not covered by this plan and are advised to provide their own health insurance while working in Canada. Health services are available through Canada's 1,048 hospitals. The many remote areas of the country are provided with flying ambulance services. No health precautions are necessary; local food and water are safe for consumption. However, the Toronto area has one of the highest pollen counts in North America so those affected by hay fever, etc. should realize medication is a must.

- **Crime:** Crime is not a major problem in Canada, though robberies and other common crime occur, as in any tourist area or large city. Be careful with your belongings and do not leave valuables unattended.

• **Pros and Cons of Living and Working in Canada:** The advantages to working and living in Canada include its proximity to the United States and the comparable living conditions to those in the U.S. The quality of health care also is a plus. Opportunities for outdoor recreation are as great or greater than any other country in the world. Canada's scenic beauty and abundant wildlife are the country's greatest attractions, although it also has a rich cultural life and interesting history. The climate, however, is regarded as a drawback by many Americans, with winters being long and severe in certain areas. Given the country's size, there are many remote areas far from the population centers that are expensive or time consuming to reach.

EMBASSY AND CONSULATE CONTACT INFORMATION:

EMBASSY OF CANADA
501 PENNSYLVANIA AVE. NW
WASHINGTON, DC 20001-2114
TEL: 202-682-1740

CONSULATE GENERAL OF CANADA
1251 AVENUE OF THE AMERICAS
NEW YORK, NY 10020-1194
TEL: 212-768-2400

COMPANIES/ORGANIZATIONS WITH OPERATIONS IN CANADA:

ABB LUMMUS CREST, 108
ABBOTT LABORATORIES, 109
ABEX INC./FISHER SCIENTIFIC INTERNATIONAL, INC., 110
AKZO AMERICA, INC., 113
ALARM DEVICE MANUFACTURING COMPANY, 114
ALBANY INTERNATIONAL CORPORATION, 114
ALBERTO-CULVER COMPANY, 115
ALLEN-BRADLEY COMPANY, INC., 116
ALLERGAN, INC., 117
AM INTERNATIONAL, INC., 119
AMAX, INC., 119
AMDAHL CORPORATION, 120
AMERACE CORPORATION (ELASTIMOLD), 121
AMERICAN APPRAISAL ASSOCIATES, INC., 121
AMERICAN BANKERS INSURANCE GROUP, INC., 122
AMERICAN BUILDING MAINTENANCE INDUSTRIES, INC., 123
AMERICAN CYANAMID COMPANY, 124
AMERICAN EXPRESS COMPANY—TRAVEL RELATED SERVICES, 125
AMERICAN GREETINGS CORPORATION, 126
AMERICAN HOME PRODUCTS CORPORATION, 126
AMERICAN MANAGEMENT SYSTEMS, INC., 127

AMERICAN PRESIDENT COMPANIES, LTD., 128
AMERICAN STANDARD, INC., 128
AMERICAN TOOL COMPANIES, INC., 129
AMERICAN UNIFORM COMPANY, 129
AMERIWOOD, INC., 130
AMETEK, INC., 130
AMGEN, INC., 131
AMOCO CORPORATION, 131
AMPEX CORPORATION, 133
ANDREW CORPORATION, 134
ANTHONY INDUSTRIES, 135
AON CORPORATION, 136
APPLE COMPUTER, INC., 136
ARBY'S, INC., 138
ARCHER-DANIELS-MIDLAND COMPANY, 138
ARCO COAL COMPANY, 139
ARCO INTERNATIONAL OIL AND GAS COMPANY, 139
ARETHUSA OFFSHORE, 140
ARMCO, INC., 140
ARMSTRONG WORLD INDUSTRIES, INC., 141
ASARCO, INC., 142
ASHLAND OIL, INC., 143
AST RESEARCH, INC., 144
AT&T INTERNATIONAL, 145
AUGAT, INC., 146
AUTOMATIC SWITCH COMPANY, 147
AVNET, INC., 148

AVON PRODUCTS, INC., 149
BACKER SPIELVOGEL & BATES
    WORLDWIDE, INC., 150
BAILEY CONTROLS COMPANY, 151
BAKER HUGHES, INC., 152
BANCTEC, INC., 152
BANKAMERICA CORPORATION, 155
BANKERS TRUST NEW YORK
    CORPORATION, 155
C. R. BARD, INC., 157
THE BARDEN CORPORATION, 157
BAUSCH & LOMB, INC., 159
BAXTER HEALTHCARE CORPORATION, 160
BECKMAN INSTRUMENTS, INC., 162
BELL HELICOPTER TEXTRON, INC., 163
BELL & HOWELL COMPANY, 164
BEMIS COMPANY, INC., 164
BETZ LABORATORIES, 166
BLOUNT, INC. (BLOUNT CONSTRUCTION
    DIVISION), 169
BOEING COMPANY, 170
BORDEN, INC., 170
BORG-WARNER CORPORATION, 171
BORLAND INTERNATIONAL, INC, 172
BOSE CORPORATION, 172
W. H. BRADY COMPANY, 173
BRIDGESTONE-FIRESTONE, INC., 174
BRISTOL-MEYERS SQUIBB COMPANY, 175
BROWNING-FERRIS INDUSTRIES, 177
BUCK CONSULTANTS, INC., 178
BURLINGTON AIR EXPRESS, 179
BURNS INTERNATIONAL SECURITY
    SERVICES, 179
BURSON-MARSTELLER, 180
CABOT CORPORATION, 181
CALGON CORPORATION, 182
CAMPBELL SOUP COMPANY, 183
CARGILL INCORPORATED, 184
CARLSON TRAVEL NETWORK, 185
CARNIVAL CRUISE LINES, 185
CARTER-WALLACE, INC., 187
CENTRAL SOYA COMPANY, 188
CHAMPION INTERNATIONAL
    CORPORATION, 189
CHASE MANHATTAN CORPORATION, 190
CHEMICAL BANKING CORPORATION, 191
CHEVRON CHEMICAL COMPANY, 192
CHEVRON CORPORATION, 193
CHRISTIAN BLIND MISSION
    INTERNATIONAL, 543

CHRYSLER CORPORATION, 195
THE CHUBB & SON CORPORATION, 196
CHURCH & DWIGHT COMPANY, INC., 196
CIGNA CORPORATION, 197
THE COASTAL GROUP, 201
COIN ACCEPTORS, INC., 203
COLGATE-PALMOLIVE COMPANY, 203
COLTEC INDUSTRIES, INC., 204
COLUMBIAN ROPE COMPANY, 204
COMMERCE CLEARING HOUSE, 205
COMMERCIAL INTERTECH CORPORATION,
    205
COMPUTER ASSOCIATES INTERNATIONAL,
    INC., 207
CONAGRA, INC., 208
CONOCO, INC., 209
COOPER INDUSTRIES, INC., 213
CORNING INCORPORATED, 215
CPC INTERNATIONAL, INC., 217
JOHN CRANE, INC., 218
CROWN CORK & SEAL COMPANY, INC.,
    218
CTS CORPORATION, 220
CUC INTERNATIONAL, INC., 221
D-M-E COMPANY, 222
DAMES & MOORE, 223
D'ARCY MASIUS BENTON & BOWLES INC.,
    225
DATA GENERAL CORPORATION, 225
DDB NEEDHAM WORLDWIDE, INC., 227
DE KALB GENETICS CORPORATION, 227
DELL COMPUTER CORPORATION, 231
DELTA AIR LINES, INC., 232
DETROIT DIESEL CORPORATION, 232
DH TECHNOLOGY, INC., 233
DIGICON, INC., 235
DIXON TICONDEROGA COMPANY, 236
DOMINO'S PIZZA, INC., 237
DOVER CORPORATION, 239
DRESSER INDUSTRIES, INC., 241
DUN & BRADSTREET CORPORATION, 243
DURIRON COMPANY, INC., 244
DURO-TEST INTERNATIONAL
    CORPORATION, 245
ELIZABETH ARDEN COMPANY, 251
ENCYCLOPEDIA BRITANNICA, INC., 253
ENGELHARD CORPORATION, 253
ENRON CORPORATION, 254
ERNST & YOUNG, 255
ESCO CORPORATION, 255

A
M
E
R
I
C
A
N

J
O
B
S

A
B
R
O
A
D

ETHYL CORPORATION, 256
FALK CORPORATION, 259
FIGGIE INTERNATIONAL, INC., 262
FIRST CHICAGO CORPORATION, 262
FISCHER & PORTER COMPANY, 263
FISHER CONTROLS INTERNATIONAL, INC.,
    263
FLORSHEIM SHOE COMPANY, 264
JOHN FLUKE MANUFACTURING COMPANY,
    265
FLUOR CORPORATION, 266
FMC CORPORATION, 266
FORD MOTOR COMPANY, 267
FULLER COMPANY, 269
GAF CORPORATION, 270
GANNETT COMPANY, INC., 272
THE GATES RUBBER COMPANY, 273
GATX CORPORATION, 273
GENERAL ELECTRIC COMPANY (GE), 275
GENERAL FOODS USA, 276
GENERAL INSTRUMENT CORPORATION,
    276
GENERAL MILLS, INC., 277
GENERAL MOTORS CORPORATION (GM),
    277
THE GILLETTE COMPANY, 283
GOLDMAN SACHS & COMPANY, 283
GOULD PUMPS, INC., 285
W. R. GRACE & COMPANY, 285
GRACO, INC., 286
GRANT THORNTON INTERNATIONAL, 286
GREAT LAKES CARBON INTERNATIONAL
    CORPORATION, 287
A. P. GREEN INDUSTRIES, INC., 287
GREY ADVERTISING, INC., 288
GTE CORPORATION, 288
GTE DIRECTORIES CORPORATION, 289
GTECH CORPORATION, 289
H. J. HEINZ COMPANY, 290
H & R BLOCK, 291
HACH COMPANY, 292
HALLIBURTON COMPANY, 292
HALLMARK CARDS, INC., 294
M. A. HANNA COMPANY, 295
HANSON INDUSTRIES, 295
HARRIS CORPORATION, 296
HARTFORD STEAM BOILER INSPECTION/
    INSURANCE COMPANY, 296
HASBRO, INC., 297
HELENE CURTIS INDUSTRIES, INC., 298

HERCULES, INC., 299
HERSHEY FOODS CORPORATION, 299
HEWLETT-PACKARD COMPANY, 300
HILL & KNOWLTON, INC., 301
HOECHST CELANESE, INC., 302
HOLIDAY INNS WORLDWIDE, 302
HONEYWELL, INC., 303
HUBBELL, INC., 306
ILLINOIS TOOL WORKS, INC., 309
INTERGRAPH CORPORATION, 314
INTERNATIONAL BUSINESS MACHINES
    (IBM), 315
INTERNATIONAL DAIRY QUEEN, INC., 316
INTERNATIONAL FLAVORS &
    FRAGRANCES, INC., 317
INTERNATIONAL PAPER COMPANY, 318
INTERNATIONAL RECTIFIER CORPORATION,
    319
ITT SHERATON CORPORATION, 322
JAMES RIVER CORPORATION, 323
JMK INTERNATIONAL/JAMACK
    FABRICATIONS, INC., 323
JOHNSON CONTROLS, INC., 324
JOHNSON & JOHNSON, 325
S. C. JOHNSON WAX, 325
JWP, INC., 328
KAMAN CORPORATION, 328
A. T. KEARNEY, INC., 329
KELSEY-HAYES COMPANY, 332
KENNECOTT CORPORATION, 333
KFC CORPORATION, 335
KIMBERLY-CLARK CORPORATION, 336
KINNEY SHOE CORPORATION, 337
KNOLL INTERNATIONAL, 338
KOLMAR LABORATORIES, INC., 340
KORN/FERRY INTERNATIONAL, 340
LAMBDA ELECTRONICS, INC., 343
LAWTER INTERNATIONAL, INC., 344
LEVI STRAUSS ASSOCIATES, INC., 344
THE LINCOLN ELECTRIC COMPANY, 346
LINTAS: WORLDWIDE, 346
ARTHUR D. LITTLE, INC., 347
LITTON INDUSTRIES, INC., 348
LIZ CLAIBORNE, INC., 348
LOUISIANA LAND & EXPLORATION
    COMPANY, 352
LTV STEEL CO., 352
LUBRIZOL CORPORATION, 353
MALLINCKRODT, INC., 359
MARION MERRELL DOW, INC., 360

MASCO CORPORATION, 361
MASONEILAN INDUSTRIES, INC., 361
MASONITE CORPORATION, 362
MATTEL, INC., 363
GEORGE S. MAY INTERNATIONAL, INC.,
    364
MCCORMICK & COMPANY, INC., 355
MCDONALD'S CORPORATION, 356
MCGRAW-HILL, INC., 357
MCKINSEY & COMPANY, INC., 357
MEAD CORPORATION, 365
MEASUREX CORPORATION, 366
MEDTRONIC, INC., 366
MERISEL, INC., 369
METALLURG CORPORATION, 370
METCO PERKIN-ELMER, 371
METROPOLITAN LIFE INSURANCE
    COMPANY, 371
MILLER BREWING COMPANY, 372
HERMAN MILLER, INC., 373
MILLIKEN & COMPANY, 373
MMS INTERNATIONAL, 374
MOBIL OIL CORPORATION, 375
MONSANTO COMPANY, 377
MOORE PRODUCTS COMPANY, 378
MORGAN STANLEY GROUP, INC., 379
MORRISON KNUDSEN CORPORATION, 379
MORTON INTERNATIONAL, 380
MOTOROLA, INC., 381
NABORS INDUSTRIES, INC., 381
NALCO CHEMICAL COMPANY, 382
NATIONAL DATA CORPORATION, 382
NAVISTAR INTERNATIONAL
    TRANSPORTATION CORPORATION, 383
NCR CORPORATION, 384
NEW YORK LIFE INSURANCE COMPANY,
    385
NEW YORK TIMES COMPANY, 386
NICOLET INSTRUMENT CORPORATION, 387
NIKE, INC., 388
NORDSON CORPORATION, 389
NORTH AMERICAN PHILIPS CORPORATION,
    389
NORTHWEST AIRLINES, INC., 390
NORTON COMPANY, 390
OCCIDENTAL PETROLEUM CORPORATION,
    393
OGDEN CORPORATION, 395
OGILVY & MATHER, 395
ONAN CORPORATION, 397

OUTBOARD MARINE CORPORATION, 399
OWENS-ILLINOIS, INC., 401
PACCAR, INC., 401
PALL CORPORATION, 404
PARKER HANNIFIN CORPORATION, 405
PENNZOIL COMPANY, 408
PENTAIR, INC., 409
PEPSICO FOODS INTERNATIONAL, 409
PEPSICO, INC., 410
PERKIN-ELMER CORPORATION, 410
PFIZER, INC., 412
PHELPS DODGE CORPORATION, 412
PILLSBURY COMPANY, 416
PINKERTON'S, INC., 416
PITNEY BOWES, INC., 417
PITTWAY CORPORATION, 418
PLAYTEX APPAREL, INC., 419
R. L. POLK & COMPANY, 421
PPG INDUSTRIES, 421
PRC, INC., 422
PRECISION VALVE CORPORATION, 422
PREFORMED LINE PRODUCTS COMPANY,
    423
PREMARK INTERNATIONAL, INC., 423
PRIMERICA CORPORATION, 424
PROCTER & GAMBLE COMPANY, 425
PUROLATOR PRODUCTS COMPANY, 427
QUAKER CHEMICAL CORPORATION, 428
QUAKER OATS COMPANY, 428
R. J. REYNOLDS TOBACCO COMPANY,
    429
RAIN BIRD SPRINKLER MANUFACTURING
    CORPORATION, 430
RALSTON PURINA COMPANY, 430
RANCO, INC., 431
RAYOVAC CORPORATION, 431
RAYTHEON COMPANY, 432
READER'S DIGEST ASSOCIATION, INC.,
    432
REDKEN LABORATORIES, INC., 434
RELIANCE ELECTRIC COMPANY, 435
REMINGTON PRODUCTS, INC., 436
REVLON, INC., 437
REYNOLDS METALS COMPANY, 438
RJR NABISCO, 439
ROBERT HALF INTERNATIONAL, INC., 440
ROBERTSON CECO, 440
ROCKWELL INTERNATIONAL
    CORPORATION, 441
ROHM & HAAS COMPANY, 442

A
M
E
R
I
C
A
N

J
O
B
S

A
B
R
O
A
D

ROSEMOUNT, INC., 443

ROWAN COMPANIES, INC., 444

RPM, INC., 444

RUBBERMAID, INC., 445

RYDER SYSTEMS, INC., 447

SAINT JUDE MEDICAL, INC., 448

SARA LEE CORPORATION, 449

A. SCHULMAN, INC., 451

SCIENTIFIC ATLANTA, INC., 452

SCOTT PAPER COMPANY, 453

SEA-LAND SERVICE, INC., 454

SEALED AIR CORPORATION, 455

SEARLE COMPANY, 455

SEARS ROEBUCK AND COMPANY, 456

SENCO PRODUCTS, 456

SGS CONTROL SERVICES, 458

SHAKLEE CORPORATION, 459

SHEAFFER PEN, INC., 459

SHEARMAN & STERLING, 460

SHEARSON LEHMAN BROTHERS, 460

SHERWIN-WILLIAMS COMPANY, 461

SIGNODE PACKAGING SYSTEMS, 462

SIMPLEX TIME RECORDER COMPANY, 463

SIMPLICITY PATTERN COMPANY INC., 464

SKADDEN, ARPS, SLATE, MEAGHER &
    FLOM, 465

A. O. SMITH CORPORATION, 467

J. M. SMUCKER COMPANY, 468

SNAP-ON TOOLS CORPORATION, 468

SONOCO PRODUCTS COMPANY, 470

SOUTHLAND CORPORATION, 472

SPS TECHNOLOGIES, INC., 474

SQUARE D COMPANY, 475

STANHOME, INC., 477

STATE STREET BOSTON CORPORATION,
    478

STEBBINS ENGINEERING &
    MANUFACTURING CORPORATION, 479

STONE CONTAINER CORPORATION, 480

STONE & WEBSTER ENGINEERING
    CORPORATION, 480

STORAGE TECHNOLOGY CORPORATION,
    481

STRUCTURAL DYNAMICS RESEARCH
    CORPORATION, 481

SUN COMPANY, INC., 483

SUN ELECTRIC CORPORATION, 484

TAMBRANDS, INC., 486

TANDY CORPORATION, 487

TEKTRONIX, INC., 488

TELLABS OPERATIONS, INC., 489

TENNANT COMPANY, 490

TENNECO AUTOMOTIVE, 491

TENNECO, INC., 492

TENNESSEE ASSOCIATES INTERNATIONAL,
    INC., 492

TEXTRON, INC., 494

THOMAS & BETTS, 495

3M COMPANY, 496

3M PHARMACEUTICALS, 497

TOWERS PERRIN, INC., 499

TOYS ''R'' US, INC., 500

TRANE COMPANY, 501

TRINOVA CORPORATION, 502

TRW, INC., 503

TW HOLDINGS, INC., 504

UNION CAMP CORPORATION, 507

UNION CARBIDE CORPORATION, 507

UNITED ENGINEERS & CONSTRUCTORS
    INTERNATIONAL, 508

UNITED PARCEL SERVICE OF AMERICA,
    INC., 509

UNITED PRESS INTERNATIONAL, 509

U.S. ELECTRICAL MOTORS (EMERSON
    ELECTRIC), 510

UNITED STATES SHOE CORPORATION, 510

UNIVERSAL FOODS CORPORATION, 513

UNUM CORPORATION, 514

UOP, INC., 514

THE UPJOHN COMPANY, 515

VISHAY INTERTECHNOLOGY, 518

WALKER MANUFACTURING COMPANY, 519

WARNACO, INC., 520

WARNER-LAMBERT COMPANY, 522

WASHINGTON POST COMPANY, 522

WATERS CHROMATOGRAPHY (MILLIPORE),
    523

WESTINGHOUSE ELECTRIC CORPORATION,
    525

WEYERHAEUSER COMPANY, 526

WHIRLPOOL CORPORATION, 526

WOOLWORTH CORPORATION, 528

WILLIAM WRIGLEY JR. COMPANY, 529

WYNN'S INTERNATIONAL, INC., 530

XEROX CORPORATION, 531

YELLOW FREIGHT SYSTEM, INC., 532

YORK INTERNATIONAL, INC., 532

YOUNG & RUBICAM, INC., 533

CAYMAN ISLANDS

- **Official Name:** Cayman Islands
- **Capital:** George Town
- **Location:** The Cayman Islands consist of three large and numerous smaller islands in the western Caribbean Sea. Cuba lies to its north, and Jamaica 180 miles to its southeast. Limestone cliffs (the remains of shells and coral), dry land, and vast beaches characterize the topography. The islands are dotted with palm trees and a few Australian pines. Its land area is 100 square miles, making it about twice the size of Washington, D.C.
- **Population, Cities, and American Residents:** The population of the Cayman Islands is 28,000 (1991 cst.). Nearly 40 percent of the people are from mixed groups, 20 percent black, 20 percent white, and the remainder are expatriates.

     Most American residents are employed in the Cayman Island's largest city of George Town, with approximately 10,000 people (1987 est.).
- **Language and Currency:** The official language of the Cayman Islands is English. The monetary unit is the Caymanian dollar (written as CI$), and divided into 100 cents. The exchange rate is fixed with the U.S. dollar; 1 Caymanian dollar per U.S.$1.25 (fixed rate).
- **Climate:** The Cayman Islands have a tropical climate, with warm, rainy summers from May through October. Average temperatures are 75°F-80°F. Winters are cooler and relatively dry, with abundant sunshine.
- **Economy and Resources:** The Cayman Islands depend on tourism, which accounts for 70 percent of the gross domestic product (GDP) and 75 percent of export earnings. The key industry is offshore financial services (banking and insurance) catering to visitors from North America. Most of the food used commercially must be imported. The Caymanians enjoy a high standard of living, one of the best in the Caribbean.
- **Cost of Living:** Current information is not available.
- **Work Permits, Visas, etc.:** If you are a U.S. citizen, proof of citizenship and return ticket are required for travel in the Cayman Islands for stays up to three months. No vaccinations are required to travel in the Cayman Islands, but an AIDS test is required to live or work in the country.
- **Taxation:** Contact the British Embassy for current tax information.
- **Health Care:** Medical care is good throughout the Cayman Islands. Many of the doctors have been trained in the United States, Canada, or Britain. Facilities are modern and well equipped, and the air ambulance service reaches Miami in just over an hour.
- **Crime:** Serious crime is not a problem on the Cayman Islands. Tourism is important and the officials try to keep the islands safe for tourists. Take precautions in busy shopping areas (against pickpockets) as you would in any major city.
- **Pros and Cons of Working and Living in the Cayman Islands:** These islands are a popular tourist destination, especially for North Americans. The warm climate, beaches, magnificent scenery, and the hospitality of the people are the main reasons. Another plus is its proximity to the United States. Telecommunications are good on the

main islands, but limited on the smaller ones. Transportation services are good, with car rentals available. It's wise to arrange for housing accommodations ahead of time for the best selection. Though the climate is pleasant, the Cayman Islands are within the hurricane belt, and travelers should be prepared in the event of bad weather.

- **Print Sources of Information:** *Fielding's Caribbean.* New York: William Morrow & Co. 1992.

EMBASSY AND CONSULATE CONTACT INFORMATION:

THE BRITISH EMBASSY
3100 MASSACHUSETTS AVE. NW
WASHINGTON, DC 20008
TEL: 202-462-1340

COMPANIES/ORGANIZATIONS WITH OPERATIONS IN CAYMAN ISLANDS:

BANKAMERICA CORPORATION, 155
ECOLOGY AND ENVIRONMENT, INC., 248
GOLDMAN SACHS & COMPANY, 283
M. W. KELLOGG COMPANY, 331

NORTHWEST AIRLINES, INC., 390
PHILLIPS-VAN HEUSEN CORPORATION, 415

CHAD

- **Official Name:** Republic of Chad
- **Capital:** N'Djamena
- **Location:** Chad is a landlocked country in the heart of Africa. The largest country of former French Equatorial Africa, its total land area is 495,755 square miles, making it three times the size of California. Chad is bounded by Libya to the north, Sudan to the east, the Central African Republic to the south, Cameroon and Nigeria to the southeast, and Niger to the west. Desert and rocky plateaus comprise most of the northern region, and a small, fertile area and forests comprise the southern area. Between these two areas lies the savanna, or grassy plain; part of the region known as the Sahel.
- **Language and Currency:** French and Arabic are the official languages of Chad. If you are on a long-term assignment, having a working knowledge of French is useful. The monetary unit is the CFA franc. The exchange rate is 300 CFA francs = U.S.$1 (November 1993).
- **Print Sources of Information:** American University's *Area Handbook of Chad* is available from the Superintendent of Documents, U.S. Government Printing Office, Washington, D.C., 20402.

EMBASSY AND CONSULATE CONTACT INFORMATION:

EMBASSY OF THE REPUBLIC OF CHAD
2002 R ST. NW
WASHINGTON, DC 20009
TEL: 202-462-4009

COMPANIES/ORGANIZATIONS WITH OPERATIONS IN CHAD:

VOLUNTEERS IN TECHNICAL ASSISTANCE, INC, 584

CHILE

- **Official Name:** Republic of Chile

- **Capital:** Santiago

- **Location:** Chile is a narrow strip of land, approximately 110 miles in width, located on the South Pacific coast of South America. It is bounded by Peru and Bolivia to the north, Argentina to the east, and the Pacific Ocean to the west. Many high mountain peaks surround the country, and it sits in the midst of an unstable land mass prone to earthquakes. Most of the population and farms are found in the central valley, an uneven plain stretching for 600 miles. It runs between the Andes and the low mountains along the coast, extending itself from the Atacama Desert in the north to the Puerto Mont in the south.

- **Population, Cities, and American Residents:** The population of Chile is 13.6 million (1992 est.), with Chileans of European and European-Indian extraction accounting for 95 percent. The remaining 5 percent are Indian and other groups.

  Most American residents are employed in Brazil's three largest cities: Santiago with 4.4 million, Concepción with 306,500, and Vina del Mar with 281,000 people (1990 est.).

- **Language and Currency:** The official language of Chile is Spanish, and you should have some knowledge of it before attempting to do business in the country. If that is not possible, consider using a translator or interpreter. The unit of currency is the peso. Bills are P5000, 1000, and 500. Coins are P100, 50, 10, 5, and 1. The exchange rate is 1 Chilean peso = U.S.$.0025; 392 pesos equal U.S.$1 (July 30, 1993).

- **Climate:** The climate is greatly affected by the chilly Humboldt Current, which runs northward along the Chilean coast from the Antarctic. The northern section of Chile contains the Atacama Desert and is one of the driest regions in the world. The central area has a Mediterranean climate, with dry summers and mild, wet winters. Summer temperatures average around 54°F. The southern region has mountains and fjords, and is known for its heavy rains and high winds. It rains in this area most of the year with an average rainfall of more than 200 inches annually.

- **Economy and Resources:** After many years of a sagging economy, Chile has done well in the 1990s and has a bright outlook for the future. Austerity programs and the expansion of exports in the 1980s helped to stabilize the economy, and it should continue on an upward scale for the next few years. Its inflation rate remains lower than neighboring countries, and it has succeeded in lowering its large external debt. Nearly 40 percent of the work force is in services (including government), with 31 percent engaged in industry, and 16 percent in agriculture. Natural resources are: copper, timber, iron ore, and precious metals. Leading industries are: copper and other minerals, foodstuffs, and fish processing. Exports totaled $8.6 billion in 1990, of which copper accounted for 48 percent. Chile is very dependent on the price of copper as this commodity has accounted for more than half of Chile's foreign-exchange income in the past. Major markets for exports are the United States and the European Community.

- **Cost of Living:** At 104, the cost of living is slightly higher than in the United States.

- **Work Permits, Visas, etc.:** A valid passport is required to travel in Chile. If you plan to stay or work in Chile for more than three months, a temporary resident visa is necessary. To obtain this, proof of financial security must be provided by your employer. Contact the Chilean consular office nearest you. You may apply by mail, but allow ample time for your visa's return. If you are entering Chile from the United States, no vaccinations are necessary, but typhoid and gamma globulin shots are recommended.

- **Taxation:** Nonresidents pay taxes only on income earned from Chilean sources. A nonresident is defined as anyone who lives in Chile for less than six months of any given year. Foreign nationals who live in Chile for up to three years pay taxes only on income derived from Chilean sources; after that they must pay on income earned from all sources. Chile does not have a tax treaty with the United States to avoid double taxation.

- **Principal International Schools:** There are many international schools in Chile for children of American residents. Tuition of an American school is about $1,400 per year.

- **Health Care:** Medical assistance in Santiago is considered good, with modern facilities and doctors who speak English. Dentists, orthodontists, and most medical supplies are available, including prescriptions and over-the-counter medicines. However, special prescriptions, (including eyeglasses) should be brought, as well as the generic name for the drugs. Sanitation standards are good compared to surrounding South American countries. In Santiago, there are efficient sewage and garbage-disposal systems, and the water is safe to drink. Use bottled water (or boil yourself) in rural areas, though. Unless you're at a major hotel, avoid raw fruits and vegetables, as they may come from farms that irrigate crops with unhealthy river water, and may carry typhoid or tetanus. Check labels, but milk is generally be pasteurized and safe to drink.

- **Crime:** Chile is not a major problem in Chile, but be as cautious as you would in any major tourist area. Keep your eye out for pickpockets, and be careful if you are out at night, and traveling alone.

- **Pros and Cons of Living and Working in Chile:** Chile has a diverse climate and terrain, many interesting sights, and offers beaches, mountain forests, skiing, and Indian archaeological sites. Medical facilities and communications services are good. Try to rent an apartment or home that already has a telephone there, as there is a shortage and chances aren't good that you'll be able to get one installed. Housing is reasonable and available, but Americans are expected to pay their rent in dollars. A knowledge of

EMBASSY AND CONSULATE CONTACT INFORMATION:

EMBASSY OF CHILE
1732 MASSACHUSETTS AVE. NW
WASHINGTON, DC 20036
TEL: 202-785-1746

Spanish is important. Without it, daily life will not be easy. In some areas, the weather can be very chilly and houses are not heated properly, so bring warm clothing. Santiago has a problem with smog, and people with allergies should come prepared. Chile is in a region of unstable land that has seen some severe earthquakes.

CONSULATE GENERAL OF CHILE
866 U.N. PLAZA
NEW YORK, NY 10017
TEL: 212-980-3366

OTHER SOURCES OF INFORMATION:

U.S. STATE DEPT.
DESK OFFICER FOR CHILE
WASHINGTON, DC 20025
TEL: 202-647-2575

COMPANIES/ORGANIZATIONS WITH OPERATIONS IN CHILE:

AMERICAN EXPRESS COMPANY—TRAVEL
    RELATED SERVICES, 125
AMERICAN HOME PRODUCTS
    CORPORATION, 126
ARMCO, INC., 140
AVON PRODUCTS, INC., 149
BANKERS TRUST NEW YORK
    CORPORATION, 155
BECHTEL GROUP, INC., 162
BRISTOL-MEYERS SQUIBB COMPANY, 175
CHASE MANHATTAN CORPORATION, 190
CHEVRON CORPORATION, 193
THE COCA-COLA COMPANY, 202
CONTINENTAL BANK CORPORATION, 210
DAMES & MOORE, 223
DATA GENERAL CORPORATION, 225
DOW CHEMICAL COMPANY, 240
DRESSER INDUSTRIES, INC., 241
DURACELL, INC., 244
EASTMAN KODAK COMPANY, 246
ECOLOGY AND ENVIRONMENT, INC., 248
ERNST & YOUNG, 255
FEDERAL-MOGUL CORPORATION, 260

GENERAL MOTORS CORPORATION (GM),
    277
INTERNATIONAL BUSINESS MACHINES
    (IBM), 315
ITT SHERATON CORPORATION, 322
JOHNSON & JOHNSON, 325
KNOLL INTERNATIONAL, 338
LOCTITE CORPORATION, 349
LUBRIZOL CORPORATION, 353
MARRIOTT CORPORATION, 360
MCCANN-ERICKSON WORLDWIDE, 354
MOBIL OIL CORPORATION, 375
NALCO CHEMICAL COMPANY, 382
PEPSICO FOODS INTERNATIONAL, 409
PFIZER, INC., 412
PHELPS DODGE CORPORATION, 412
PIONEER HI-BRED INTERNATIONAL, INC.,
    417
SGS CONTROL SERVICES, 458
STANDARD COMMERCIAL CORPORATION,
    476
STERLING WINTHROP, INC., 479
U.S. WHEAT ASSOCIATES, 511
THE UPJOHN COMPANY, 515

CHINA

- **Official Name:** People's Republic of China
- **Capital:** Beijing
- **Location:** China is the third largest nation in the world, occupying most of eastern Asia. It is bordered by North Korea, the former Soviet Union, Mongolia, Pakistan, India, Nepal, Bhutan, Burma, Laos, and Vietnam. Only one tenth of the land is arable, and two-thirds of China is mountains and semi-desert. Its total land area is 3,692,244 square miles which makes it slightly larger than the United States.

- **Population, Cities, and American Residents:** The population of China totals 1,140,000,000 (1992 est.), more than 93 percent of which is Han Chinese. The remaining 6.7 percent are Zhuang, Uygur, Hui, Yi, Tibetan, Miao, Manchu, Mongol, Buyi, and Korean.

    Most American residents are employed in China's three largest cities: Shanghai with 17 million, Beijing (formerly Peking) with 9.5 million, and Canton with 5.4 million people (1989 est.). Shanghai is one of the three largest cities in the world.

- **Language and Currency:** The official language of China is Mandarin Chinese (dialects include Fukienese, Shanghai, and Cantonese), spoken throughout business and government, with interpreters available upon request. Long-term residents may ask for a full-time interpreter through the Diplomatic Service Bureau. The currency is called renminbi (known as RMB, "the people's money"), and the monetary unit is the yuan, more commonly known as kuai. The yuan is a decimal currency; 1 yuan has 10 jiao, 1 jiao has 10 fen, and there are 100 fen in 1 yuan. Bills are in 50, 20, and 10 fen notes; and in 100, 50, 10, 5, 2, and 1 yuan notes. Coins are 5, 2, or 1 yen. The most frequently circulated note is 10 yuan. The exchange rate is 1 Chinese yuan = U.S.$.17 (July 30, 1993).

- **Climate:** Because of its size, the climate of China varies markedly from one region to the next. Rain and humidity are common factors in summer throughout most of the country, with monsoons occurring south of the Yangtze River. Winters are usually very dry, more so in the north towards Beijing. Here, winters are very cold, with the mean temperature at 23°F in January. Summers are hot and humid in this area, with an average temperature in July of 80°F. Shanghai has a more temperate climate all year. Canton in the southern region, has intense humidity most of the year, with warm, moist summers and an average temperature of 85°F in July, and cool, damp winters with an average temperature of 56°F in January.

- **Economy and Resources:** China was once very dependent on its agriculture to sustain its growth. It is now focused on industry, with a current output more than three times the dollar value of its agricultural products. Its major industrial items are iron, steel, textiles and petroleum. Chief crops include rice, wheat, corn, and other grains. Nearly one-quarter of its exports are from textiles, clothing, and yarn, with machinery, metal, and manufacturing goods among the rest. Major markets for exports are Hong Kong, Japan, and the United States. More than three-quarters of the population (750 million people) are in the work force. Under former leader Deng Xiaoping, private enterprise was encouraged, along with other open-door policies, and the economic growth surged under his decade of leadership. But the Tiananmen Square massacre in 1989 soured China's relationships with many of its neighbors and trading partners. Restrictions and sanctions, along with ill feelings, took their toll on the economy. Austerity programs also have made it more complex for foreign companies to succeed in this country of strict and diverse laws and regulations.

- **Cost of Living:** At 105, the cost of living is slightly higher than in the United States.

- **Work Permits, Visas, etc.:** A valid passport and visa are required for all foreign nationals entering China. Business travel in China is by invitation and sponsorship only.

The invitation must be issued from the People's Republic of China Foreign Trade Corporation or other government agency. Allow ample time to apply for this invitation prior to the trip. If you are entering China from the United States, no vaccinations are required, but typhoid shots are advisable, and gamma globulin is highly recommended. It is also suggested that long-term residents receive hepatitis-B shots. For official or further information, direct inquiries to the embassy or consulate at the addresses below.

- **Taxation:** All foreigners staying in China for more than three months are subject to tax on income earned in China. A tax treaty between China and the United States allows for taxes paid in China to be credited against U.S. taxes. China's tax code may be subject to change, so it's best to check with the U.S. Commerce Department or Trade Ministry for the latest information.

- **Principal International Schools:** There are international schools for children of American residents. Average tuition for an American School is $7,000 per year.

- **Health Care:** Sanitary conditions, compared to Western standards, are poor. Tap water, even in large hotels, is not potable. Boil it for drinking, making ice, and brushing your teeth. Hotels supply water in Thermos containers and ice made from clean water. Wash all fruits and vegetables in a chlorine solution or peel before eating. Simple medical problems can be treated locally. But for any serious ailments, you should leave the country. Facilities just aren't modern enough and herbal remedies and acupuncture may be the only available treatment. Western medicine is practiced in Beijing at the Capital Hospital, which is adequate and has a friendly staff. China does not have, nor does it store, RH-negative blood.

- **Crime:** Crime is not a major problem in China; it is relatively safe throughout the country. Take normal precautions against pickpockets, and lock valuables out of sight when you leave your hotel.

- **Pros and Cons of Living and Working in China:** The history and culture of China make it an interesting nation in which to travel. The Great Wall and the Forbidden City are popular tourist sites and dining can be an adventure, but certain areas are restricted to foreigners. Telecommunications and transportation services are good. Driving on your own is not recommended, as the streets are heavily congested with cars, bikes, and people. China is a communist country with strict laws and a different way of life. To work in the country, you must be invited. Sufficient working and living space in China has been a persistent problem for some years now. Housing is arranged, after application, through the Chinese Diplomatic Service Bureau (DSB), and virtually all foreigners must live in Beijing. Americans should be careful about certain articles they want to bring into the country that may be

EMBASSY AND CONSULATE CONTACT INFORMATION:

EMBASSY OF THE PEOPLE'S REPUBLIC OF CHINA
2300 CONNECTICUT AVE. NW
WASHINGTON, DC 20008
TEL: 202-328-2517

CONSULAR OFFICE OF CHINA
520 FIFTH AVE.
NEW YORK, NY 10036
TEL: 212-330-7409

considered objectionable by the Chinese government. If you plan on an extended stay in China, check in with the American Embassy in Beijing or the American Consulate in Shanghai very soon after arrival.

OTHER SOURCES OF INFORMATION:
CHINA NATIONAL TOURIST OFFICE
60 EAST 42ND ST., STE. 3136
NEW YORK, NY 10165
TEL: 212-867-0271

COMPANIES/ORGANIZATIONS WITH OPERATIONS IN CHINA:

ABB LUMMUS CREST, 108
AMERICAN INTERNATIONAL GROUP, 127
AMOCO CORPORATION, 131
APPLIED MATERIALS, INC., 137
ARMSTRONG WORLD INDUSTRIES, INC., 141
AVON PRODUCTS, INC., 149
BAILEY CONTROLS COMPANY, 151
BANKAMERICA CORPORATION, 155
LOUIS BERGER INTERNATIONAL INC., 165
BRISTOL-MEYERS SQUIBB COMPANY, 175
BROWN GROUP, INC., 176
CABOT CORPORATION, 181
CHEVRON CORPORATION, 193
CHEVRON OVERSEAS PETROLEUM, INC., 194
CONTINENTAL GRAIN COMPANY, 211
CONVERSE, INC., 212
CORNING INCORPORATED, 215
COUDERT BROTHERS LAW FIRM, 217
JOHN CRANE, INC., 218
CUMMINS ENGINE COMPANY, INC., 221
DIGITAL EQUIPMENT CORPORATION, 236
DRESSER INDUSTRIES, INC., 241
EBASCO OVERSEAS CORPORATION, 248
GENERAL RAILWAY SIGNAL COMPANY, 278
GOLDMAN SACHS & COMPANY, 283
H. J. HEINZ COMPANY, 290

HILL & KNOWLTON, INC., 301
INGERSOLL-RAND COMPANY, 313
M. W. KELLOGG COMPANY, 331
KFC CORPORATION, 335
LAWTER INTERNATIONAL, INC., 344
LITTON INDUSTRIES, INC., 348
LIZ CLAIBORNE, INC., 348
MASCO CORPORATION, 361
MATTEL, INC., 363
MCCANN-ERICKSON WORLDWIDE, 354
MCCORMICK & COMPANY, INC., 355
MILLER BREWING COMPANY, 372
NORTHWEST AIRLINES, INC., 390
PHILIPP BROTHERS CHEMICALS, INC., 414
PPG INDUSTRIES, 421
PROCTER & GAMBLE COSMETICS AND FRAGRANCE PRODUCTS, 426
PROJECT HOPE, 563
RALSTON PURINA COMPANY, 430
READING & BATES, 433
ROSEMOUNT, INC., 443
SIGNODE PACKAGING SYSTEMS, 462
SIMPLEX TIME RECORDER COMPANY, 463
STANDARD COMMERCIAL CORPORATION, 476
TAMBRANDS, INC., 486
3M COMPANY, 496
WARNER-LAMBERT COMPANY, 522

COLOMBIA

- **Official Name:** Republic of Colombia
- **Capital:** Bogota
- **Location:** Colombia is the continent's fourth largest country, situated on the northwestern coast of South America. It is bounded to the north by the Caribbean Sea, to the east by Brazil and Venezuela, to the south by Ecuador, and to the west by Panama and the Pacific Ocean. The total land area is 440,831 square miles, comparable to the combined areas of Texas, New Mexico, and Arkansas. Nearly half the land is covered by

forest and woodlands. Colombia is divided into the central highlands region, the flat areas along the coast, mountains, and the eastern plains. More than half of Colombia, east of the Bogota region, is virtually uninhabited and very inconvenient to reach. Most people live in the central mountains region, which stretches along the northern and western coasts.

- **Population, Cities, and American Residents:** The population of Colombia totals 33 million (1992 est.). Mestizos (those of mixed ancestry), account for 58 percent of the people, 20 percent are white, 14 percent are mulatto, 4 percent are black, and 4 percent are other mixed groups.

   Most American residents are employed in Colombia's three largest cities: Bogota with 4.4 million, Medellin with 2.2 million, and Cali with 1.8 million people (1989 est.).

- **Language and Currency:** The official language of Colombia is Spanish, used throughout government and business. English is spoken in tourist areas. The monetary unit is the Colombian peso. The exchange rate is 1 Colombian peso = U.S.$.0014; 679 pesos equal U.S.$1 (July 30, 1993).

- **Climate:** The climate in Colombia varies considerably with the altitude of the region. The Caribbean coast offers a year-round temperature of about 80°F. The capital city of Bogota has a higher altitude, with cooler temperatures averaging from the mid-50s-70s throughout the year. The country has two rainy seasons; one during March and April, and the other during October and November. Most of the rain occurs on the west coast and in the mountains.

- **Economy and Resources:** During the 1970s, Colombia began to expand and diversify its exports, which produced a marked growth rate in the gross domestic product (GDP). But the low prices on exported goods and the global economic recession left Colombia with many problems to solve. Annual inflation rates escalated (25-30 percent in 1990), and a sharp decline in coffee earnings slowed the country down. Agriculture remains the main sector of the economy with coffee as the major export earner, at 30 percent in 1988. Colombia is the world's second largest coffee producer. Other major exports include bananas, petroleum, coal, and nickel. Major industries are textiles, food processing, and oil. Major markets for exports are the United States and the European Community. Export diversification and strict financial management are strengthening the country's economic condition. It is the only large country in Latin America that has not had to renegotiate its foreign debt during the 1980s. Over 53 percent of the people work in services, with 26 percent in agriculture, and 21 percent in industry.

- **Cost of Living:** At 75, the cost of living is lower than in the United States.

- **Work Permits, Visas, etc.:** A passport is required for a stay of up to 30 days in Colombia. After that, you will need a visa from the nearest Colombian Embassy or Consulate. If you are entering Colombia from the United States, no vaccinations are necessary, but it is recommended that you have a gamma globulin injection before arriving in Colombia as hepatitis is very common there. The U.S. Center for Disease Control (CDC) recommends that children under the age of 9 months have a yellow fever vaccination if traveling outside the urban areas of Colombia. For official or other information, direct inquiries to the embassy or consulate at the addresses below.

- **Taxation:** Colombia taxes foreign nationals who reside in Colombia on Colombian income. It has a treaty with the United States to avoid double taxation. Rates are similar to those under the U.S. tax system, and are levied at a progressive rate.

- **Principal International Schools:** Various international schools are available for children of American residents in Colombia. These follow an American curriculum and are located in Bogota, Cali, and Cartagena.

- **Health Care:** Medical facilities are satisfactory in the major cities of Colombia. Doctors are well trained and many speak English. Medicines and drugs are also available. Sanitary conditions are below average, especially in the rural areas. Boil tap water for all usage, and take appropriate precautions with all fruits and vegetables. Be cautious when using dairy products as some may not be pasteurized.

- **Crime:** Common crime is prevalent throughout Colombia, especially in the tourist areas. Beware of pickpockets and muggers, and lock doors when you leave your home or automobile. Burglary attempts on the homes of foreign nationals happen frequently so don't be careless. The U.S. State Department has issued a travel advisory for U.S. visitors going to Colombia, as the drug trafficking and guerrilla wars continue to plague the country and care must be taken. There are certain regions of Colombia (basically the interior) that are danger zones. Contact the (State Department) Citizens' Emergency Center, at 202-647-5225, prior to your trip for current information. You may also contact the American Citizens' Services Unit of the U.S. Embassy in Bogota at 1-285-1300, ext. 206 or 215.

- **Pros and Cons of Living and Working in Colombia:** Colombia is a tropical destination offering a wide variety of attractions, from the Sierra Nevada chain to the small ports located on two seas. It has sandy white beaches, national parks, and historic monuments. However, sanitation standards need improvement, and the unsettled atmosphere in Columbia due to the drug trade is distressing to Americans. The drug barons seem to have as much power as elected officials, and the eruptions of violence between the two has had a significant effect on the economy and tourism. Be very careful, and adhere to travel advisories at all times. Be cautious in main tourist areas, and especially careful if traveling at night. It is especially important that you carry identification on you at all times as the police stop people on the streets for drug searches. Security is a main issue when deciding on a temporary residency in Colombia. Executives (especially foreign nationals) must take extreme precautions at home and at work to guard against crime and possibly kidnapping.

EMBASSY AND CONSULATE CONTACT INFORMATION:

COLOMBIAN EMBASSY
2118 LEROY PLACE NW
WASHINGTON, DC 20008
TEL: 202-387-8388

COLOMBIAN CONSULATE
10 EAST 46TH ST.
NEW YORK, NY 10017
TEL: 212-949-9898

OTHER SOURCES OF INFORMATION:

COLOMBIAN GOVERNMENT TOURIST OFFICE
140 EAST 57TH ST.
NEW YORK, NY 10022
TEL: 212-688-0151

COMPANIES/ORGANIZATIONS WITH OPERATIONS IN COLOMBIA:

ALLERGAN, INC., 117

BACKER SPIELVOGEL & BATES
WORLDWIDE, INC., 150

BANKERS TRUST NEW YORK
CORPORATION, 155

BLACK & DECKER CORPORATION, 167

BORDEN, INC., 170

BURNS INTERNATIONAL SECURITY
SERVICES, 179

THE CHUBB & SON CORPORATION, 196

CORE LABORATORIES, 214

CROWN CORK & SEAL COMPANY, INC.,
218

CUMMINS ENGINE COMPANY, INC., 221

DOMINO'S PIZZA, INC., 237

DUPONT MERCK PHARMACEUTICAL
COMPANY, 243

EATON CORPORATION/CUTLER HAMMER,
247

EXXON COMPANY, INTERNATIONAL, 258

FMC CORPORATION, 266

GENERAL FOODS USA, 276

GOODYEAR TIRE & RUBBER COMPANY,
284

HUGHES CHRISTENSEN COMPANY, 307

INTERNATIONAL PAPER COMPANY, 318

KELLOGG COMPANY, 330

KORN/FERRY INTERNATIONAL, 340

KRAFT GENERAL FOODS INTERNATIONAL,
341

LIQUID CARBONIC CORPORATION, 347

LOUISIANA LAND & EXPLORATION
COMPANY, 352

NALCO CHEMICAL COMPANY, 382

OCCIDENTAL PETROLEUM CORPORATION,
393

OWENS-ILLINOIS, INC., 401

PFIZER, INC., 412

PHILLIPS PETROLEUM COMPANY, 415

QUAKER OATS COMPANY, 428

SONY PICTURES ENTERTAINMENT, 471

TORRINGTON COMPANY, 499

TRITON ENERGY CORPORATION, 502

UOP, INC., 514

WEST COMPANY, INC., 525

WYETH-AYERST LABORATORIES, 530

COUNTRY PROFILES

CONGO

- **Official Name:** Republic of the Congo

- **Capital:** Brazzaville

- **Location:** Lying directly on the equator, Congo is located on the western coast of the African continent. Its name originated from the majestic Congo River that flows along the eastern border of the country. It is bounded by Cameroon to the northwest, the Central African Republic to the northeast, Zaire to the east and south, the Angolan district of Cabinda to the south, the Gulf of Guinea to the southwest, and Gabon to the west. Its total land area is 132,047 square miles, making Congo a little bigger than New Mexico. Most of the territory is covered by forests; pastures and meadows comprise nearly one-third of Congo. Most of the north is covered by tropical rain forests, and much of the southern region by plains and farming regions.

- **Population, Cities, and American Residents:** The population of Congo is 2 million (1990 est.). Most of the Congolese are part of four main black African groups: Kongo account for 48 percent of the population, Sangha 20 percent, Teke 17 percent, and M'Bochi for the remaining 12 percent. A very small European population (mainly

French) numbers about 8,500. Most American residents are employed in Congo's three main cities: Brazzaville with 600,000 people, Point Noire with 300,000, and Pool with 219,000 (1987 est.).

- **Language and Currency:** The official language of Congo is French, but many African languages are used. If you are on long-term assignment in Congo, having a working knowledge of French is very useful in daily life. The monetary unit is the CFA franc. The exchange rate is 375 CFA francs = U.S.$1 (November 1993).

- **Climate:** Congo has a tropical climate, typically hot and humid throughout the year. Higher temperatures and substantial rainfall occur more toward the interior sections of Congo. The average annual temperature is 75°F, and the average annual rainfall varies from 45 to 80 inches, depending on the specific location. The dry season runs from May through September.

- **Economy and Resources:** Oil and forestry are the mainstays of the Congolese economy. Oil has provided two-thirds of the government revenues and exports. Other natural resources include lead and zinc, with chief exports including crude petroleum (72 percent), lumber, plywood, coffee, and cocoa. The United States is the major importer of Congolese products. Of the labor force, 62 percent are employed in mining, farming, and fishing. Banking and services employs 26 percent, and industry and services accounts for the remainder of the work force. Because of the high oil prices during the 1980s, Congo was able to finance various development projects and sustain a 5 percent growth rate, one of the highest rates in Africa. But a fall in oil prices forced the nation to begin austerity programs to handle declining receipts and escalating foreign debt. Since 1989, the government has encouraged private enterprise and the reduction of state-owned businesses. Congo has a very efficient transportation system due to the Congo-Ubangi river system and the Congo-Ocean railroad, which allows Congo to transport goods to other countries within Africa. With the improvement of the country's infrastructure and other long-term projects, the economy should stabilize. The United States has good diplomatic relations with Congo, and the American presence in the nation is expanding. Congo receives foreign aid from the United States through agricultural, health, and development programs. Its primary source of foreign aid, however, is France.

- **Cost of Living:** At 186, the cost of living is very high compared the United States.

- **Work Permits, Visas, etc.:** You'll need a passport and visa to travel in Congo. Visas are valid for stays of up to 90 days. For business visas, you must apply prior to the trip, and the application must include a company letter stating the reason for the trip and the proposed length of stay. Allow ample time for this process. All persons entering Congo must show proof of vaccination against yellow fever. Health requirements change periodically, so check with the U.S. State Department for current information prior to your trip. For official or other information, direct inquiries to the embassy or consulate at the addresses below.

- **Taxation:** For current information on taxes, contact the embassy or consulate at the Republic of Congo.

- **Health Care:** Medical facilities, including hospitals, are located only in the major

---

towns of Congo. Health care is basic, and supplies are limited. Malaria is prevalent throughout the country, so malaria suppressants are recommended. Tap water is not potable, and it's important to take necessary precautions with all meats, dairy products, and raw fruits and vegetables.

- **Crime:** Serious crime is not a major problem in Congo. Take the normal precautions for any crowded tourist areas to be relatively safe.

- **Pros and Cons of Working and Living in Congo:** The culture of the native people of Congo is interesting, and wildlife is abundant in the northern regions of rain forests and tropical woodland. Photographers will find many unique opportunities to film plant life, animals, and scenery. Photography is restricted in some places (government or public buildings, airports, etc.), and it's best to check with the authorities upon arrival in Congo. Health and sanitation standards do not compare with those found in North America. Telecommunications services are only fair. Housing is available, but limited, so it's wise to make arrangements in advance. The climate can be oppressive, with extreme heat and high humidity that may cause problems for people with respiratory ailments.

- **Print Sources of Information:** *Historical Dictionary of the People's Republic of Congo*, 2d ed. Metuchen, NJ: Scarecrow Press, 1984.

EMBASSY AND CONSULATE CONTACT INFORMATION:

EMBASSY OF THE REPUBLIC OF CONGO
4891 COLORADO AVE. NW
WASHINGTON, DC 20011
TEL: 202-726-5500

COMPANIES/ORGANIZATIONS WITH OPERATIONS IN CONGO:

ABB VETCO GRAY, INC., 108
AMOCO CORPORATION, 131
CHEVRON CORPORATION, 193

CHEVRON OVERSEAS PETROLEUM, INC., 194
CONOCO, INC., 209

COSTA RICA

- **Official Name:** Republic of Costa Rica

- **Capital:** San Jose

- **Location:** Costa Rica is the second smallest country in Central America, located between Panama and Nicaragua. Its land area totals 19,652 square miles, making it slightly smaller than West Virginia. The terrain is mountainous and hilly with rivers and streams flowing through its countryside. Much of Costa Rica is forest. There is a wide coastal plain in the east, which reflects a narrower plain along the Pacific coast. In Costa Rica's mountainous interior, the Central Valley has only 600 square miles of land, but houses two-thirds of the population and is a major center for agriculture, industry, and government. This region contains the capital, San Jose, and is one of the most populated spots in Central America.

- **Population, Cities, and American Residents:** The population of Costa Rica totals 3.1 million people (1992 est.). About 96 percent of the people in Costa Rica are of European origin (mostly from Spain). The population is 3 percent black, and 1 percent Indian.

  Most American residents are employed in Costa Rica's three largest cities: San Jose with 284,600, Alajuela with 151,000, and Cartago with 103,900 people (1989 est.).

- **Language and Currency:** The official language of Costa Rica is Spanish. Without a familiarity in Spanish, hiring a translator/interpreter might be necessary. The monetary unit is the colon, divided into 100 centimos. Bills are in 1,000,500, 100, 50, 10, and 5 colones. Coins are in 20, 10, 5, 2, and 1 colon(es); and 50, 25, and 10 centimos. The exchange rate is 137 colones = U.S.$1 (August 25, 1993).

- **Climate:** The climate is extremely dependent on the altitude in Costa Rica. The lowlands have a mean maximum temperature of 90°F or higher, while the more populated highlands have a mean maximum temperature of 75°F. San Jose's climate is more temperate with a dry season from December through April. The Caribbean plain is primarily tropical and rainy throughout the year.

- **Economy and Resources:** Agriculture is the mainstay of Costa Rica's economy, responsible for 18 percent of the gross domestic product (GDP). Nearly one-third of the people work the land or are dependent on agriculture. Over 60 percent of the total export earnings are from agriculture. Chief crops are bananas, coffee, and rice. Manufacturing accounts for 20 percent of the GDP. Textiles, chemicals, petroleum refining, and pulp-and-paper processing are main industries. Tourism is also a major foreign-exchange earner. Costa Rica suffered a set-back during the 1980s when oil and commodity prices fell. The country had to borrow from abroad and tighten spending to recover from this shock. Although it has done better than most of its neighboring countries, it is still in a recovery process.

- **Cost of Living:** At 87, the cost of living is lower than in the United States.

- **Work Permits, Visas, etc.:** A valid passport is required to travel in Costa Rica. If you're visiting Costa Rica from the United States, you may stay up to three months and if an extended stay is required, you must apply for an exit visa. A foreign employee of a company operating in Costa Rica needs temporary or permanent resident status. Apply to the Costa Rican Embassy or Consulate Office for application forms. If you are entering Costa Rica from the United States, no vaccinations are required. But, it is recommended that you consider getting polio, typhoid, and tetanus booster shots prior to the trip. For those visiting outer lowland areas, malaria prophylaxis is recommended. For those staying in Costa Rica for more than 60 days, you must be tested for AIDS. U.S. tests are not acceptable. For official or other information, direct inquiries to the embassy or consulate at the addresses below.

- **Taxation:** All individuals are subject to income tax in Costa Rica, regardless of their nationality or resident status. A person living in Costa Rica for six months of a calendar year must file a regular return. From three to six months, a special return is filed. For under three months no taxes are collected as this is considered tourism.

- **Principal International Schools:** There are several English-language schools in

Costa Rica that follow the U.S. curriculum and calendar year. Two are the Costa Rica Academy and the Country Day School.

- **Health Care:** Medical facilities and personnel are quite good throughout Costa Rica. The major hospitals have English-speaking doctors (many of whom have trained in the United States). The Costa Rican Social Security system provides for low-cost care, even for foreign residents. A routine checkup is about $20. Sanitation is good in Costa Rica, with a few exceptions. Water is safe to drink in San Jose, but outside the major cities it should be boiled for all purposes. All vegetables and fruits from rural areas should be peeled or washed accordingly before eating. Most dairy products are safe as they are pasteurized and sold locally. Check labels.

- **Crime:** Costa Rica is an exotic, tranquil, and safe place to visit. However, an increasing number of refugees from surrounding areas and unemployment in Costa Rica warrant taking precautions. Don't take foolish chances. As you would in any tourist area, lock valuables out of sight. Autos are targets for thieves, so lock doors when you park your vehicle and don't leave it overnight unless it is in a safe (fenced) area. You should always carry your passport, in case officials ask to see it. Failure to produce proof of your identity could mean an unnecessary trip to the police station. Although prostitution is legal in Costa Rica, some women rob their clients and others may have AIDS.

- **Pros and Cons of Working and Living in Costa Rica:** Costa Rica offers a great deal to the visitor. Nearly one-quarter of the country consists of parks, reserves, and wildlife refuges. The country has miles of white sand beaches and numerous museums. Health standards are good, and housing is available and affordable. Speaking Spanish is essential to efficiently function in the country. Costa Rica has one of the highest per capita traffic accident rates. Many roads may appear safe but often are not. It is a mountainous and rainy country in most regions and drivers must watch for potholes, an occasional landslide, and livestock on the roadways. Be especially careful when driving at night.

EMBASSY AND CONSULATE CONTACT INFORMATION:

COSTA RICAN EMBASSY/CONSULATE
1825 CONNECTICUT AVE. NW
WASHINGTON, DC 20009
TEL: 202-234-2945

COSTA RICAN CONSULATE GENERAL
80 WALL ST., STE. 718-719
NEW YORK, NY 10005
TEL: 212-425-2620

OTHER SOURCES OF INFORMATION:

COSTA RICAN NATIONAL TOURIST BUREAU
1101 BRICKELL AVE.
BIV TOWER, STE. 801
MIAMI FL
TEL: 1-800-327-7033
FAX: 305-358-7915

COMPANIES/ORGANIZATIONS WITH OPERATIONS IN COSTA RICA:

AMERICAN STANDARD, INC., 128
ARETHUSA OFFSHORE, 140
BANK OF BOSTON CORPORATION, 153
BORDEN, INC., 170
BROWN & WILLIAMSON TOBACCO
   CORPORATION, 177
CLIPPER CRUISE LINES, 199

THE COCA-COLA COMPANY, 202
CROWN CORK & SEAL COMPANY, INC.,
   218
ECOLOGY AND ENVIRONMENT, INC., 248
EXXON CORPORATION, 258
FIGGIE INTERNATIONAL, INC., 262
FMC CORPORATION, 266

GERBER PRODUCTS COMPANY, 280
GTE DIRECTORIES CORPORATION, 289
HANSON INDUSTRIES, 295
JOHNSON & JOHNSON, 325
LOCTITE CORPORATION, 349
MONSANTO COMPANY, 377
MOTOROLA, INC., 381
PFIZER, INC., 412
PHELPS DODGE CORPORATION, 412
PHILLIPS PETROLEUM COMPANY, 415

PHILLIPS-VAN HEUSEN CORPORATION, 415
PROJECT HOPE, 563
ROHM & HAAS COMPANY, 442
SCOTT PAPER COMPANY, 453
STONE CONTAINER CORPORATION, 480
TECHNOSERVE, INC., 565
TEXACO OIL COMPANY, 493
VF CORPORATION, 517

CÔTE D'IVOIRE

- **Official Name:** Republic of Côte d'Ivoire
- **Capital:** Yamoussoukro
- **Location:** Côte d'Ivoire, also known as the Ivory Coast, lies along the Gulf of Guinea on the western coast of Africa. It is bounded by Mali and Burkina to the north, Ghana to the east, the Gulf of Guinea to the south, and Liberia and Guinea to the west. Its total land area is 122,780 square miles, making Côte d'Ivoire slightly bigger than New Mexico. It has a varied landscape comprised of flat and sandy coastal areas, tropical forests inland, the northern savanna, and the Guinea Highlands.
- **Language and Currency:** The official language of Côte d'Ivoire is French and it is the principal language spoken throughout business and government. English may be spoken by some executives, but if you are living or working in this country, you should have a basic knowledge of French or consider using a translator. The monetary unit is the CFA (Communauté Financière Africane) franc issued by the African Financial Community through the Bank of Central Africa. The CFA franc floats with the French franc and is guaranteed convertible to French francs at the rate of FF1 = CFA Fr50. The current exchange rate is 600 CFA francs = U.S.$1 (March 1994).
- **Print Source of Information:** Crowther, Geoff. *Africa on a Shoestring*. Berkeley, Cal.: Lonely Planet, 1989.

EMBASSY AND CONSULATE CONTACT INFORMATION:

CÔTE D'IVOIRE EMBASSY (AND TOURISM OFFICE)
2424 MASSACHUSETTS AVE. NW
WASHINGTON, DC 20008
TEL: 202-797-0344

COMPANIES/ORGANIZATIONS WITH OPERATIONS IN COTE D'IVOIRE:

LOUIS BERGER INTERNATIONAL INC., 165
ECOLOGY AND ENVIRONMENT, INC., 248

CZECH REPUBLIC

- **Official Name:** Czech Republic
- **Capital:** Prague
- **Location:** The Czech Republic is a landlocked country in central Europe. Until January 1, 1993, it was part of Czechoslovakia, which also included the Slovak Republic, or Slovakia. A peaceful separation divided the republics. The Czech Republic has a total land area of 30,449 miles, making it slightly smaller in size than Maine. It is bounded by Poland to the north, the Slovak Republic to the east, Austria to the south, and Germany to the west. The Czech Republic is a land of mountains, forests, and dominant rivers, which connect this country to the Black, North, and Baltic Seas.
- **Language and Currency:** The official language of the Czech Republic is Czech. It is the language of business and government. English is occasionally spoken. If you are going to live or work in the republic, you should have a basic knowledge of Czech to make daily life easier. The monetary unit is the koruna or (kcs). The current exchange rate is 29 kcs = U.S.$1 (March 1994).

EMBASSY AND CONSULATE CONTACT INFORMATION:

EMBASSY OF THE CZECH REPUBLIC
3900 SPRING OF FREEDOM ST. NW
WASHINGTON, DC 20008
TEL: 202-363-6315

OTHER SOURCES OF INFORMATION:

THE U.S.-CZECH ECONOMIC COUNCIL
C/O THE U.S. CHAMBER OF COMMERCE
1615 H STREET
WASHINGTON, DC 20062
TEL: 202-463-5482

COMPANIES/ORGANIZATIONS WITH OPERATIONS IN CZECH REPUBLIC:

KLYNVELD PEAT MARWICK GOERDELER (KPMG), 337

SCHERING-PLOUGH CORPORATION, 450
US WEST, INC., 515

DENMARK

- **Official Name:** Kingdom of Denmark
- **Capital:** Copenhagen
- **Location:** Denmark is located in northern Europe, and is bounded by the Skagerrak Channel to the north, the Baltic Sea to the east, Germany to the south, and the North Sea to the west. It comprises the Jutland Peninsula on the European mainland, the Zealand and Fyn islands, and other smaller islands. Other territories are Greenland, and the Faroe Islands, which are north of Scotland. The country has a long, meandering coastline, which stretches for 4,500 miles. It is a land of wooded hills and lakes with no predominant mountains or rivers. Its total land area is 16,632 square miles, making it slightly smaller than New Hampshire.
- **Population, Cities, and American Residents:** The population of Denmark totals

5.1 million (1992 est.). Scandinavian people account for a major part of the population; others are Eskimo, Faeroese, and German.

Most American residents are employed in Denmark's three largest cities: Copenhagen with 1.3 million, Aarhus with 261,000, and Odense with 176,000 people (1990 est.). Copenhagen is the largest city in Denmark and a major world port.

- **Language and Currency:** The official language of Denmark is Danish and it is spoken throughout the country. English is the second language of the local people and used often in business circles. German is often spoken as a second language, primarily in southern Jutland. The monetary unit is the Danish krone, abbreviated as Dkr. Bills are in Dkr 1,000, 500, 100, 50 and 20. Coins are in: 25, 10, and 5 ore; and Dkr10, 5, and 1. The exchange rate is 1 Danish krone = U.S.$.15 (July 30, 1993).

- **Climate:** The climate along the coast is temperate with damp and windy weather. Summer is the most enjoyable season with sunny, breezy days and a mean temperature of about 63°F. Winter is accompanied by snow, which is heavy at times. The mean temperature averages 32°F.

- **Economy and Resources:** Until this century, agriculture was the mainstay in Denmark's successful economy. Now, services is the largest sector, and is growing. It currently accounts for 70 percent of the gross domestic product (GDP). Denmark is a global leader in the export of foodstuffs, in part due to the vast amount of surplus food it produces. Agriculture accounts for about one-third of the total merchandise exports. Denmark's economy has shifted from agriculture to industry since World War II and now manufacturing accounts for 20 percent of the GDP. More than half the people in Denmark work in services, 34 percent are in industry, and government and agriculture account for the rest. The government is implementing economic reforms to trim the expansive bureaucracy and reduce the government-generated share of the GDP during the 1990s.

- **Cost of Living:** At 166, the cost of living is higher than in the United States.

- **Work Permits, Visas, etc.:** A valid passport is required to travel in Denmark. For visitors staying longer than three months, a visa is also necessary. Applications to work in Denmark should be completed before going to the country. When you arrive, register with the police within 24 hours. If you are entering Denmark from the United States, no vaccinations are required. For official or other information, direct inquiries to the addresses below.

- **Taxation:** Foreigners who live in Denmark for more than six months are considered residents and liable to Danish national and local taxes. There is a treaty in effect, however, between the United States and Denmark to avoid double taxation.

- **Principal International Schools:** There are some very good international schools in Denmark. Fees vary, but an average American school tuition will cost about $9,000 per year.

- **Health Care:** Medical services throughout the country are very good, with most physicians speaking English. In case of severe injury or illness, foreign patients are not charged for treatment or hospitalization. Bring any prescription drugs with you, as only those from Scandinavian doctors can be filled in the country. Costs for check-ups are reasonable. Sanitary standards are excellent, water is safe to drink, and there are no serious health risks or diseases.

- **Crime:** Crime is not a major problem in Denmark, but it is wise to be cautious, especially in tourist areas or when going out during the late evening hours.

- **Pros and Cons of Living and Working in Denmark:** Denmark's cultural and intellectual heritage is rich, and Copenhagen is one of the most charming cities in Europe. Denmark has museums, castles, and excellent cuisine. Medical facilities and sanitary standards are excellent, and so are transportation and telecommunications services. Be careful driving, though, as stiff fines accompany any arrest due to speeding, drunken driving, or accidents. Housing is difficult to find, and a lawyer should review any lease before signing. The weather is unpleasant during the winter; bring warm clothes and rain gear. The cost of living is very high in Denmark. Some over-the-counter drugs may be available on a prescription-only basis.

EMBASSY AND CONSULATE CONTACT INFORMATION:

ROYAL DANISH EMBASSY
3200 WHITEHAVEN ST. NW
WASHINGTON, DC 20008
TEL: 202-234-4300

ROYAL DANISH CONSULATE GENERAL
825 THIRD AVE.
NEW YORK, NY 10022
TEL: 212-223-4545

OTHER SOURCES OF INFORMATION:

DANISH INFORMATION CENTER
280 PARK AVE.
NEW YORK, NY 10017
TEL: 212-697-5107

COMPANIES/ORGANIZATIONS WITH OPERATIONS IN DENMARK:

A. L. LABORATORIES INC., 107
AMERICAN CYANAMID COMPANY, 124
AMETEK, INC., 130
AMOCO CORPORATION, 131
AMP, INC., 132
AVERY DENNISON CORPORATION, 147
AVNET, INC., 148
BANKERS TRUST NEW YORK
    CORPORATION, 155
BAUSCH & LOMB, INC., 159
BORLAND INTERNATIONAL, INC, 172
BOSE CORPORATION, 172
BRIDGESTONE-FIRESTONE, INC., 174
THE COCA-COLA COMPANY, 202
COLGATE-PALMOLIVE COMPANY, 203
COMPUTER ASSOCIATES INTERNATIONAL,
    INC., 207
DELTA AIR LINES, INC., 232
ELIZABETH ARDEN COMPANY, 251

GENERAL MOTORS CORPORATION (GM),
    277
HERTZ CORPORATION, 300
KELLOGG COMPANY, 330
LAWTER INTERNATIONAL, INC., 344
MCKINSEY & COMPANY, INC., 357
MGM INCORPORATED, 372
MILLIKEN & COMPANY, 373
NORDSON CORPORATION, 389
PARKER HANNIFIN CORPORATION, 405
PHILLIPS PETROLEUM COMPANY, 415
PPG INDUSTRIES, 421
QUAKER OATS COMPANY, 428
READER'S DIGEST ASSOCIATION, INC.,
    432
ROBERTSON CECO, 440
ROSEMOUNT, INC., 443
SPS TECHNOLOGIES, INC., 474
TLC BEATRICE INTERNATIONAL HOLDINGS,
    INC., 498

DOMINICAN REPUBLIC

- **Official Name:** Dominican Republic
- **Capital:** Santo Domingo
- **Location:** The Dominican Republic, located in the Caribbean Sea, is the second largest country in the Caribbean. It occupies the eastern two-thirds of the island, Hispaniola. The Dominican Republic is bounded by the North Atlantic Ocean to the north, the Mona Passage (which separates it from Puerto Rico) to the east, the Caribbean Sea to the south, and Haiti to the west. The land area totals 18,680 square miles, making it twice the size of New Hampshire. Nearly 23 percent of the territory is arable, and 43 percent of the land is covered by meadows and pastures.
- **Population, Cities, and American Residents:** The population of the Dominican Republic totals 7.4 million (1992 est.). Mulattos of mixed races account for 75 percent of the people, Caucasians for 15 percent, and blacks for 10.

  Most American residents are employed in the Dominican Republic's three largest cities: Santo Domingo with 1.8 million, Santiago de los Caballeros with 278,000 and La Romana with 92,000 people (1990 est.)
- **Language and Currency:** The official language of Santo Domingo is Spanish, which is spoken by almost everyone. With the expansion of tourism, English is used more frequently than in the past years, but a working knowledge of Spanish is essential, especially in dealings with business and the government. Qualified translators and interpreters are available upon request. The monetary unit is the peso, locally written as RD$ or $. It is divided into 100 centavos. The exchange rate is RD$ 12.50 = U.S.$1 (August 17, 1993).
- **Climate:** The climate of the Dominican Republic is primarily tropical. Winter temperatures range from 64°F to 84°F, and summer temperatures average from 73°F to 95°F. Temperatures vary slightly with altitude, as it is cooler in the Cordillera region. Most of the rain falls from May through November, and the country is subject to tropical storms and hurricanes, particularly in the late summer and early fall.
- **Economy and Resources:** The Dominican Republic is one of the poorest countries in Latin America. However, it is rich in various natural resources, including gold, silver, ferronickel, and bauxite. Mining accounts for a major part of the nonagricultural output. The Republic is highly dependent on trade, with agricultural products as the principal export. Traditional cash crops include coffee, sugar, and tobacco. Another emerging industry is tourism, which has overtaken sugarcane as the major foreign exchange earner. Of the labor force, nearly half are employed in agriculture, 33 percent work in services, and 18 percent in industry. A rapidly growing population, and an excessive foreign debt of $3.5 billion contracted in the 1970s, are two main problems this country faces. Inflation and unemployment rates are both high, but massive public works programs and increased tourism may alleviate some of the economic problems.
- **Cost of Living:** At 93, the cost of living is lower than in the United States.
- **Work Permits, Visas, etc.:** If you are a U.S. citizen entering the Dominican

Republic and your stay is limited to three months, only proof of citizenship is required. A valid passport or an immigration visa may be necessary for longer stays. If you plan to work in the country, you must submit a working contract with the local company to be legally registered with the Secretary of State for Employment in Santa Domingo. If you are entering the Dominican Republic from the United States, no vaccinations are required. However, it is recommended that long-term residents receive typhoid, tetanus, diphtheria, polio, and gamma globulin shots, along with malaria suppressants. For official or other information, direct inquiries to the embassy or consulate at the addresses below.

- **Taxation:** Individuals working in the Dominican Republic are subject to local government income taxes. Rates vary, and certain deductions may apply.

- **Principal International Schools:** There are several English-language schools available in Santa Domingo. The annual tuition ranges from $1,650 to $1,990.

- **Health Care:** Medical facilities in the Dominican Republic are adequate for minor health problems, and offer clinics with English-speaking doctors. Prescription drugs are available in all the major cities, but for any serious health problems, you should be flown to Puerto Rico where quality hospital care is available. Sanitary conditions throughout the Dominican Republic are below U.S. standards. Tap water is not safe to drink, so it's best to use bottled fluids. Appropriate precautions should be taken with all fruits and vegetables. Be careful in choosing restaurants. Take precautions when out in the sun, as bad burns are possible even on cloudy days.

- **Crime:** Although crime is not particularly prevalent in the Dominican Republic, street crimes do occur, particularly in Santo Domingo and other major tourist areas. Dominican politics and labor relations may become confrontational, and it's smart to avoid areas where demonstrations are being held.

- **Pros and Cons of Living and Working in the Dominican Republic:** The Dominican Republic offers a variety of historic, cultural and artistic attractions. There are many recreational facilities available, and the night life can be exciting, with casinos and an array of first-class restaurants. Health conditions are not comparable to U.S. standards, so be careful of what you eat and drink. Mail service is very slow and unreliable. Its best to use the telecommunications services, which offer satellite communications with any country in the world. Transportation services are adequate but it's expensive to drive in the Republic. Auto imports are very restricted. Local drivers tend to ignore the laws of the road. Housing is available, but rental rates vary dramatically due to inflation. Check costs prior to your trip to the Dominican Republic.

EMBASSY AND CONSULATE CONTACT INFORMATION:

DOMINICAN REPUBLIC EMBASSY
1715 22ND AVE. NW
WASHINGTON, DC 20008
TEL: 202-332-6280

DOMINICAN REPUBLIC CONSULATE
1 TIMES SQUARE, 11TH FL.
NEW YORK, NY 10036
TEL: 212-826-0750

OTHER SOURCES OF INFORMATION:

DOMINICAN REPUBLIC MISSION TO THE U.N.
144 EAST 44TH ST.
NEW YORK, NY 10017
TEL: 212-867-0833

COMPANIES/ORGANIZATIONS WITH OPERATIONS IN DOMINICAN REPUBLIC:

AMERICAN STANDARD, INC., 128

AVON PRODUCTS, INC., 149

BRISTOL-MEYERS SQUIBB COMPANY, 175

BURNS & ROE, INC., 180

NAVISTAR INTERNATIONAL
   TRANSPORTATION CORPORATION, 383

PARAMOUNT COMMUNICATIONS, INC., 404

PHILIP MORRIS COMPANIES, INC., 413

TEXACO OIL COMPANY, 493

3M COMPANY, 496

ECUADOR

- **Official Name:** Republic of Ecuador
- **Capital:** Quito
- **Location:** Ecuador is located on the Pacific coast of northwestern South America. It is bounded by Colombia to the north, Peru to the east and south, and the Pacific Ocean to the west. Its total land area is 109,483 square miles, making it almost the same size as Colorado. There are three distinctive geographical regions: the Costa (or coastal lowlands); the Sierra, including the Western and Eastern Cordilleras of the Andes mountains; and the Oriente, the eastern slope of the Andes and nearby lowlands. This region is located within the large Amazon River system. The Galapagos Islands lie 600 miles to the west and are considered another region.
- **Population, Cities, and American Residents:** The population of Ecuador totals 11.4 million (1992 est.). Over half the people are mestizos (of mixed race). Indians account for an additional 25 percent. Caucasians and Africans account for the remaining 20 percent.

  Most American residents are employed in Ecuador's three largest cities: Guayaquil with 1.8 million, Quito with 1.3 million, and Cuenca with 227,000 people (1990 est.).
- **Language and Currency:** The official language of Ecuador is Spanish, used throughout business and government. Any foreigner working there should have a working knowledge of the language, or an interpreter or translator will be needed. The monetary unit is the sucre, abbreviated as S/. There are 100 centavos in 1 sucre. The exchange rate is 1 Ecuadorian sucre = U.S.$.0005; 1,889 equals U.S.$1 (July 30, 1993).
- **Climate:** The climate of Ecuador varies from moderate in the central region to hot and humid in the coastal plains or Amazon jungle region. In the coastal regions, the rainy season is from December to May with a temperature range of 65°F to 95°F. During the dry season, it cools off slightly. In the central region, morning temperatures are about 50°F and reach about 73°F in the afternoons. Rain is most frequent from November to May in this area. In the Oriente, it is usually hot, humid, and rainy throughout the year.
- **Economy and Resources:** Until after World War II, Ecuador was very dependent on agricultural commodities, but other products have begun to play a key economic role. The development of oil resources in the 1970s enabled the country to compete in the

world petroleum market. Though Ecuadorian production is less than 1 percent of the world's total, petroleum and its derivatives account for 40 percent of exports by value. Even so, Ecuador is trying to diversify its exports, so it will not be heavily dependent on petroleum. Ecuador remains one of the biggest exporters of bananas and cocoa in the world, and shrimp and coffee are other important foreign exchange earners. Over half of Ecuador's exports go to the United States. Of the labor force, 52 percent work in agriculture, 20 percent in services, and 13 percent in manufacturing. Major industries include food processing, textiles, and chemicals. Ecuador's economy is highly regulated, but major tariff reforms are being put into effect. Inflation is high, and the country has an enormous $11 billion foreign debt.

- **Cost of Living:** At 72, the cost of living is significantly lower than in the United States.

- **Work Permits, Visas, etc.:** A valid passport and tourist card are required for stays of up to three months in Ecuador. For longer stays, a visa is necessary, along with a residence or work permit. Visitors must register within thirty days of arrival in Ecuador with the Provincial Director of External Affairs. If you are entering Ecuador from the United States, no vaccinations are required. However, shots against typhoid, paratyphoid, typhus, tetanus, and hepatitis are recommended. For official or other information, direct inquiries to the embassy or consulate at the addresses below.

- **Taxation:** Citizens and foreigners are taxed on their Ecuadorian source income. Foreigners who occasionally work in the country are subject to a flat 25 percent income tax rate withheld at the source.

- **Principal International Schools:** International schools are available in Quito and Guayaquil. The annual tuition for an American school is about $600.

- **Health Care:** Health care in Ecuador is adequate for simple medical problems. In some cases, doctors tend to over-prescribe antibiotics even for minor infections. One hospital used by foreign residents is the Clinica Kennedy in Guayaquil. Another American-run facility is the Hospital Voz Andes in Quito. Sanitation throughout Ecuador is very poor, and typhoid, diphtheria, and other diseases are endemic. All tap water should be boiled for twenty minutes, including water used for ice and brushing teeth. Take precautions with all fruits and vegetables and avoid dairy products unless you are sure they are pasteurized. Rodents and insects are ubiquitous, especially at lower altitudes. Mosquito netting is recommended.

- **Crime:** Ecuador has a problem with common crime, although it is safer than many other countries in Latin America. Take precautions against pickpockets and purse snatchers. Lock parked vehicles, and don't leave valuables unattended.

- **Pros and Cons of Living and Working in Ecuador:** Ecuador's climate is warm and inviting, and it has beaches, mountain ranges, Sierra vistas, and the Amazon jungle. The Galapagos Islands have unusual flora and fauna that attract amateur and professional naturalists. Telecommunica-

EMBASSY AND CONSULATE CONTACT INFORMATION:

ECUADORIAN EMBASSY
2535 15 ST. NW
WASHINGTON, DC 20009
TEL: 202-234-7200

tions and transportation are adequate, but the mail is very unreliable and is often lost or stolen. Housing is available at a reasonable cost, though new apartments or houses usually lack any appliances or furniture. Check before you rent. Diseases are prevalent, and annoying insects and rodents are commonplace. Unless you speak Spanish, daily life will not be easy.

ECUADORIAN CONSULATE GENERAL
18 EAST 41 ST., 18TH FL.
NEW YORK, NY 10017
TEL: 212-683-7555

OTHER SOURCES OF INFORMATION:
ECUADORIAN GOVERNMENT TRADE OFFICE
551 FIFTH AVE., STE. 910
NEW YORK, NY 10176
TEL: 212-687-0848

COMPANIES/ORGANIZATIONS WITH OPERATIONS IN ECUADOR:

BRISTOL-MEYERS SQUIBB COMPANY, 175
CHASE MANHATTAN CORPORATION, 190
THE CHUBB & SON CORPORATION, 196
THE COCA-COLA COMPANY, 202
CONSERVATION INTERNATIONAL, 545
INTERNATIONAL VOLUNTARY SERVICES,
   INC., 555

MAXUS ENERGY CORPORATION, 363
ORYX ENERGY, 398
PARKER DRILLING COMPANY, 405
PETROLITE CORPORATION, 411
PROJECT HOPE, 563
STERLING WINTHROP, INC., 479

EGYPT

- **Official Name:** Arab Republic of Egypt
- **Capital:** Cairo
- **Location:** Egypt is located in the northeastern corner of Africa. With its land area totaling 386,000 square miles, it is approximately one and a half times the size of Texas. Egypt is bordered to the north by the Mediterranean Sea, to the east by the Red Sea and Israel, to the south by the Sudan, and to the west by Libya. Nearly 90 per cent of the country is unused land, including the immense Sahara desert. From the Red Sea to the valley of the Nile it is mountainous. The Nile waters a narrow but fertile strip of green from the Aswan Dam north to the delta at Alexandria. Nearly all the population of Egypt is found in the Nile valley and delta, with more than 14,000,000 living in or near Cairo.
- **Population, Cities, and American Residents:** The population of Egypt totals 56.5 million (1992 est.). Approximately 90 percent is Eastern Hamitic, with the remaining 10 percent comprised of Greek, Italian, and Syro-Lebanese people.

  Most American residents are employed in Egypt's three largest cities: Cairo with 6.1 million, Giza with 3.7 million, and Alexandria with 2.9 million people (1986 est.).
- **Language and Currency:** The official language of Egypt is Arabic, but English is widely spoken in business and government. French is also used frequently, especially around Alexandria. The monetary unit is the Egyptian pound, written E£, divided into 100 piasters, written as PT. Bills are E£100, 20, 10, 5, and 1. Coins are PT50, 25, 10, 5, and 1. The exchange of money is regulated with strict enforcement in Egypt. Visitors may convert their money into pounds at local banks, hotels, or their embassies. Egypt

lacks enough hard currency, so laws concerning exchange are firm. The exchange rate is 34.5 Egyptian pounds = U.S.$1 (August 25, 1993).

- **Climate:** Egypt has a warm dry climate most of the year. Summer can be oppressive with temperatures ranging from 95°F in Cairo to 110°F toward the southern region of Aswan, but nights can get quite cool. The spring season is accompanied by the hot, dusty wind called el Khamaseen. The most pleasant months are October through March.
- **Economy and Resources:** The signing of the Camp David Accords in 1979 ending the 30-year state of war with Israel was a new beginning for Egypt. Major economic reorganization began under President Anwar el-Sadat. After Sadat's assassination in 1981, President Hosni Mubarak continued to expand his predecessor's policies, but Egypt's economy is still in sad shape. Oil revenues have been decreasing, acts of terrorism and rioting have hurt tourism, and the drought in the Ethiopian highlands have compounded the existing problems. Of the total labor force (15 million), nearly half work in agriculture, and 36 percent work in government (local and national). The remainder are engaged in privately owned enterprises. Major exports include raw cotton, crude and refined petroleum, and textiles.
- **Cost of Living:** At 81, the cost of living is lower than in the United States.
- **Work Permits, Visas, etc.:** A valid passport is required to travel in Egypt. Tourist or business visas are valid for six months from date of issue. To apply for a business visa, a company letter, stating the purpose of the visit, must accompany the application. All visitors in Egypt must register at the nearest police station within 48 hours of arrival. If you are entering Egypt from the United States, no vaccinations are necessary, but the U.S. State Department recommends shots against tetanus, polio, paratyphoid, and hepatitis. For official or other information, direct inquiries to the embassy or consulate at the addresses below.
- **Taxation:** Egypt's tax system can be complicated and highly progressive. Negotiations are established between the U.S. company and the Egyptian government and exemptions are granted on a case-by-case basis. For further assistance, contact the Country Marketing Manager for Egypt in Washington, D.C. (202-377-4652).
- **Principal International Schools:** These are several international schools in Cairo and Alexandria. Tuition for an American school is $1,100 per year.
- **Health Care:** Medical facilities are below Western standards, but for simple medical problems, hospitals in the major cities are adequate. The Maadi Military Hospital (on Corniche, near Maadi) is excellent, but you must receive permission from the U.S. Embassy for admittance. Depending on where you are in Egypt, always get a second opinion for serious problems, even if it means leaving the country. Sanitation is poor outside the major tourist areas. Pollution and noise are prevalent. Never drink tap water or water from the Nile; use bottled water or boil it yourself. Only use pasteurized dairy products. Appropriate precautions should be taken with all fruits and vegetables.
- **Crime:** Be cautious when visiting Egypt, as purse-snatchers and pickpockets thrive in tourist zones; overnight trains are targeted areas. Only carry enough cash for daily spending, and don't wear expensive, flashy jewelry. Remember to lock car doors when leaving them unattended.

• **Pros and Cons of Living and Working in Egypt:** Egypt has the world's oldest civilization, offering unique cultural monuments. Temples, pyramids, and the Nile are among the main tourist attractions. The country has acted as a bridge from Asia to Africa, and Africa to Europe, and it is rich in history. It is also very overcrowded, and half of its people live in poverty. English is not widely spoken outside of the main cities and sanitation is very poor. The desert wind spreads its dust throughout the cities and towns and can be a real health hazard to anyone with allergies. Egyptians are very strict with their drug laws. Being convicted of smuggling or selling narcotics could result in the death penalty. Terrorism sponsored by Islamic fundamentalists has become a threat in recent years, and tourists have been singled out for attacks. This information should be taken seriously.

EMBASSY AND CONSULATE CONTACT INFORMATION:
EMBASSY OF ARAB REPUBLIC OF EGYPT
2310 DECATUR PLACE NW
WASHINGTON, DC 20008
TEL: 202-232-5400

NEW YORK CONSULATE
1110 SECOND AVE.
NEW YORK, NY 10022
TEL: 212-759-7120

OTHER SOURCES OF INFORMATION:
U.S. STATE DEPARTMENT
DESK OFFICER FOR EGYPT
WASHINGTON, DC 20025
TEL: 202-647-2365

COMPANIES/ORGANIZATIONS WITH OPERATIONS IN EGYPT:

AMOCO CORPORATION, 131
ASSOCIATED PRESS, 144
AT&T INTERNATIONAL, 145
BAKER HUGHES, INC., 152
THE BANK OF NEW YORK COMPANY, INC., 154
BLACK & VEATCH, 168
BRISTOL-MEYERS SQUIBB COMPANY, 175
CAMP DRESSER & MCKEE INTERNATIONAL, INC., 183
CARE, 541
CHILD REACH INTERNATIONAL, 542
CH2M HILL INTERNATIONAL, LTD., 195
CUBIC CORPORATION, 220
EBASCO OVERSEAS CORPORATION, 248
ECOLOGY AND ENVIRONMENT, INC., 248
EG & G, INC., 249
GENERAL DYNAMICS CORPORATION, 274
GENERAL DYNAMICS SERVICES COMPANY, 275

GENERAL ELECTRIC COMPANY (GE), 275
GILBERT/COMMONWEALTH INTERNATIONAL, INC., 282
THE KULJIAN COMPANY, 341
LITTON INDUSTRIES, INC., 348
MARATHON PETROLEUM COMPANY, 359
MASCO CORPORATION, 361
METCALF & EDDY INTERNATIONAL, INC., 370
OTIS ELEVATOR COMPANY: WORLD HEADQUARTERS, 399
PARSONS BRINKERHOFF, 406
POPULATION COUNCIL, 562
PROJECT HOPE, 563
RESOURCES MANAGEMENT INTERNATIONAL, 437
SONAT OFFSHORE, 470
SONESTA INTERNATIONAL HOTELS CORPORATION, 470
USX CORPORATION, 516

EL SALVADOR

- **Official Name:** Republic of El Salvador

- **Capital:** San Salvador

- **Location:** El Salvador is located on the Pacific coast of Central America. The smallest country in Central America, its total land area is 8,124 square miles, making it about the same size as Massachusetts. It is bounded by Honduras to the north and east, the Pacific Ocean to the south, and Guatemala to the west. Its territory is very mountainous. The country is separated into three regions: a narrow coastal belt toward the southern region that has a tropical climate; the central area of valleys and plateaus; and a mountainous region in the north. Nearly all the territory of El Salvador is of volcanic origin.

- **Population, Cities, and American Residents:** The population of El Salvador is 5.5 million (1992 est.). Nearly 90 percent of the people are Mestizo (of European and Indian origin), and the balance are Indians and white Europeans. Most American residents are employed in El Salvador's two major cities: San Salvador with 1.4 million people, and Santa Ana with 230,000 (1986 est.).

- **Language and Currency:** El Salvador's official language is Spanish. Pipal Indian (Nahua) is also spoken. If you are on a long-term assignment, having a working knowledge of Spanish is essential. The monetary unit is the Salvadoran colon. The exchange rate is 8.20 colons = U.S.$1 (November 1993).

- **Climate:** The climate of El Salvador is tropical with temperatures varying with the altitude. Coastal areas have an average temperature of 80°F, while interior sections see temperatures of 73°F. The rainy season occurs from May to October with about 85 inches of annual rainfall on the coast and 60 inches toward the northwest regions.

- **Economy and Resources:** Though El Salvador is relatively small in area, it is the most heavily populated mainland nation in the Western Hemisphere. The population growth rate continues to increase, while El Salvador's farmland is shrinking. Agriculture plays a key role in the economy, accounting for 25 percent of the gross domestic product (GDP) and 66 percent of total exports. Almost half of the labor force is employed in this sector. Manufacturing accounts for 18 percent of the GDP and employs 15 percent of the work force. Coffee is a major export, along with sugar and cotton. The United States and Germany are El Salvador's biggest trading partners.

  Political and social conflicts have plagued El Salvador for two decades. Land reform has been a major issue. Prior to 1980, most of the territory was in the hands of plantation owners and absentee landlords. The plan and goal of the land reform program is to redistribute property in order to develop a rural middle class. Another major problem is the threat from various guerrilla groups (now about 5,000) who have disrupted the democratic and economic development of El Salvador. Economic losses due to guerrilla sabotage have cost over $2 billion since 1979. Although a cease-fire has been in effect over the past few years, the financial burden of supporting the military continues to constrain needed social services. For a stable economy to exist the government must provide a secure environment for the people. The United States has good diplomatic relations with El Salvador; it supports the government and provides assistance.

- **Cost of Living:** At 86, the cost of living is lower than in the United States.

- **Work Permits, Visas, etc.:** You'll need a passport and visa to travel in El Salvador. A visa is valid for three months. If you are entering El Salvador from the United States no vaccinations are required. For official or other information, direct inquiries to the embassy or consulate at the addresses below.

- **Taxation:** For current tax information, contact the embassy or consulate at the Republic of El Salvador.

- **Principal International Schools:** American schools are available.

- **Health Care:** Sanitation and health standards are not comparable to those found in North America. Take precautions with meats, dairy products, and raw fruits and vegetables. Boil water for all usage.

- **Crime:** The U.S. State Department has issued a travel warning for all people going to El Salvador. Guerrilla warfare still exists in various regions, and extreme caution is urged. All visitors traveling in El Salvador should register with the U.S. embassy immediately upon arrival.

- **Pros and Cons of Working and Living in El Salvador:** Two separate cultural groups, the Ladinos and Indians, offer a unique cultural experience for travelers in El Salvador, including colorful festivals and sidewalk markets. Health and sanitation standards are far below North American standards, as are telecommunications and transportation services. Though the guerrilla warfare has decreased in recent years, there are still sporadic attacks on people living or visiting in El Salvador. Check with the U.S. State Department for current information on the situation in El Salvador before your departure to this country.

- **Print Sources of Information:** *Revolution in El Salvador: Origins and Evolution* by Tommie Sue Montgomery. Boulder, CO: Westview Press, 1982.

EMBASSY AND CONSULATE CONTACT INFORMATION:

EMBASSY OF THE REPUBLIC OF EL SALVADOR
2308 CALIFORNIA ST. NW
WASHINGTON, DC 20008
TEL: 202-265-3480

COMPANIES/ORGANIZATIONS WITH OPERATIONS IN EL SALVADOR:

AVON PRODUCTS, INC., 149
AVX CORPORATION, 150

PHELPS DODGE CORPORATION, 412
TECHNOSERVE, INC., 565

FINLAND

- **Official Name:** Republic of Finland

- **Capital:** Helsinki

- **Location:** Finland is the fifth largest country (in area) in Europe, occupying one of the northernmost sections of the continent. It is bounded by Norway to the north, Russia to the east, the Baltic Sea to the south, and the Gulf of Bothina and Sweden to the west. Its total land area comprises 338,000 square miles. About 76 percent of the country is covered by forest and woodland, 10 percent by lakes, and 8 percent is suited for agriculture.

- **Population, Cities, and American Residents:** Finland is home to 5 million people (1992 est.). Finns, Swedes, Lapps, and Gypsies compose the population, with the majority being Finnish. The original inhabitants migrated from the countries of Estonia and Russia over two thousand years ago. The Lapps, already in Finland, today number about 2,000 people.

    Most American residents are employed in Finland's three major cities: Helsinki with 492,000, Espoo with 173,000 and Vanta with 155,000 people (1990 est.).

- **Language and Currency:** The official languages of Finland are Finnish and Swedish. Approximately 93.5 percent of the people speak Finnish, and 6.3 percent speak Swedish. A very small section comprise the Lapp- and Russian-speaking minorities. English is the second language used often in business circles and by the younger generation of Finland. The monetary unit is the Markka or Finnmark (Fmk, or FIM). It is divided into 100 pennis (p). The exchange rate is 1 Finnish Markka = U.S.$.17 (July 30, 1993).

- **Climate:** Finland's climate is fairly temperate, mainly because of the Gulf Stream. It is a little cooler than New England with a mean temperature in the summer of 64°F, and in the winter about 20°F in the Helsinki region. In Lapland, it is even cooler, with means of 57°F during the summer and 11°F in February. The humidity is always low. Although summers are short, they are sunny and offer clean crisp air. Winters are severe, and arrive early in the north, with snow beginning in October and lasting through April. In the south, winter is shorter, with snow falling from December until April. Snow apparel is a necessity in Finland.

- **Economy and Resources:** Much of Finland's economy is based on private ownership with high levels of capital investment and technology. Manufacturing is vital to the country's success, as it accounting for 30 percent of the GDP. Wood and steel are the main industries; other goods produced include electronics and motor vehicles. Finland is self-sufficient for some foodstuffs (dairy products, meats), but must import other food items including fruits and vegetables. Chief exports are timber, paper and pulp, ships, and machinery. Trade is an important sector. Major trading partners are the European Community and Russia. Even though Finland's market economy is based on privately owned enterprises, state-owned companies account for 15 percent of the nation's industrial output and employ 12 percent of the industrial work force. Finland has a highly developed social-welfare system; its people enjoy a high standard of living.

- **Cost of Living:** At 170, the cost of living is much higher than in the United States.

- **Work Permits, Visas, etc.:** A valid passport is required to travel in Finland. If you are a citizen of the United States and the length of stay is less than three months, no visa is necessary. Longer stays require residence or work permits. If you are entering Finland from the United States, no vaccinations are needed. For official or other information, direct inquiries to the embassy or consulate at the addresses below.

- **Taxation:** The main taxes in Finland are national income tax, local income taxes, and a net wealth tax. They are collected from companies and individuals. Currently, the tax structure is being reformed, and it is recommended that you contact a government agency of Finland for up-to-date information concerning taxes.

- **Principal International Schools:** An international school in Helsinki offers instruction through grade 10. Tuition is $8,500.

- **Health Care:** Medical facilities in Finland are quite good, especially in Helsinki. Fees for service are extremely reasonable, about $10 for a visit to an outpatient clinic, though private hospitals tend to be more expensive. A hospital used by American residents is the Helsinki University Central Hospital, open 24 hours a day for treatment. Medicines are available, with some pharmacies open 24 hours a day. Sanitary conditions throughout the country are good, water is safe to drink, and there are no prevalent diseases that pose a risk to travelers.

- **Crime:** Crime is not a major problem in Finland, but be careful in major tourist areas.

- **Pros and Cons of Living and Working in Finland:** Finland is a beautiful country, full of forests and lakes, as well as sophisticated cities filled with modern architecture. It offers museums, cathedrals, parks, and sporting events. Saunas (some 14 million of them), are a favorite Finnish form of relaxation. They are found almost everywhere: in homes, hotels, public baths, even car ferries. Telecommunications and transportation services are both adequate throughout the country. Arrests for intoxication (while driving or walking) are punished by stiff fines in Finland. It is expensive to live in Finland compared to U.S. standards; daily necessities are costly (gasoline is about U.S.$3.40 a gallon). Bring warm clothing, as winter is long and harsh with a good deal of snow in most areas.

EMBASSY AND CONSULATE CONTACT INFORMATION:

EMBASSY OF FINLAND
3216 NEW MEXICO AVE. NW
WASHINGTON, DC 20016
TEL: 202-363-2430

CONSULATE GENERAL OF FINLAND
FINLAND HOUSE
540 MADISON AVE.
NEW YORK, NY 10022
TEL: 212-832-6550

OTHER SOURCES OF INFORMATION:

U.S. COMMERCE DEPT.
COUNTRY SPECIALIST FOR FINLAND
WASHINGTON, DC 20230
TEL: 202-377-3254

COMPANIES/ORGANIZATIONS WITH OPERATIONS IN FINLAND:

ALBANY INTERNATIONAL CORPORATION, 114

AM INTERNATIONAL, INC., 119

AMP, INC., 132

THE COCA-COLA COMPANY, 202

COMPUTER ASSOCIATES INTERNATIONAL, INC., 207

ENCORE COMPUTER CORPORATION, 252

W. R. GRACE & COMPANY, 285

J. M. HUBER CORPORATION, 306

ITT CORPORATION, 321

MCKINSEY & COMPANY, INC., 357

MGM INCORPORATED, 372

PRC, INC., 422

TELLABS OPERATIONS, INC., 489

VF CORPORATION, 517

FRANCE

- **Official Name:** French Republic
- **Capital:** Paris
- **Location:** France is the second largest nation in Western Europe with a land area totaling 212,783 square miles. It is bounded by Belgium and the English Channel to the north; Belgium, Luxembourg, Germany, Switzerland, and Italy to the east; the Mediterranean Sea and Spain to the south; and the Atlantic Ocean to the west. Its land area is a mixture of mountains, meadows and pastures, and forests and woodland. Mont Blanc, near the Italian and Swiss borders, is the highest point in Europe.
- **Population, Cities, and American Residents:** The population of France totals 56.6 million people (1992 est.). The French are of various origins, including Celtic, Latin, and Teutonic with Slavic, North African, Indochinese, and Basque minorities.

  Most American residents are employed in France's three largest cities: Paris with the metropolitan population of 9 million, Lyon with 1.2 million, and Marseille with 1 million people (1989 est.).
- **Language and Currency:** The official language of France is French. English is widely used in business circles, but the French appreciate foreigners who are familiar with their language. The unit of currency is the French franc which is made up of 100 centimes. The exchange rate is 1 French franc = U.S.$.17 (July 30, 1993).
- **Climate:** The climate of France varies with location. Along the Mediterranean coastal areas, summers tend to be hot and winters are mild with the average low temperature around 50°F. Most of the country sees colder winters and mild summers. In Paris, temperatures average 45°F-75°F with rain frequent in the fall and winter arriving early. It also tends to drizzle though much of the spring in Paris. The south of France offers the most pleasant year-round climate for tourists.
- **Economy and Resources:** France currently has the fourth-largest economy in the free world, and is the fourth largest trading nation. France's major trading partners are the other members of the European Community. It is the leader in food products and exports among the European nations, and worldwide it ranks second in food exports following the United States. It is a world leader in nuclear power, a European leader in aerospace technology, and a rival of the United States in commercial satellite-launching endeavors. Services account for 61.5 percent of the labor force, and 31.3 percent are in industry. Natural resources include coal, iron ore, and timber. Major industries are steel, machinery, and equipment. Chief exports are machinery and transport equipment, foodstuffs, chemicals, and iron and steel products. During the early 1980s, a conservative government was in power and the economy was expanded through programs of privatization, major financial market reforms, tax reduction, and budget controls. During this period, 65 government-controlled banks, insurance companies, and industrial firms were privatized. The United States continues to be a major foreign investor in France.
- **Cost of Living:** At 174, the cost of living is much higher than in the United States.
- **Work Permits, Visas, etc.:** A valid passport is required to travel in France. If you

are a U.S. citizen and the length of your stay is less than three months, no visa is necessary. If the stay is longer, you will need a permit, of which there are three types. A residence permit is required for stays longer than three months; a work permit is required for anyone intending to work in France; and a business permit may be substituted for either, depending on the circumstances. If you are entering France from the United States no vaccinations are required, but you should get a flu shot prior to an extended stay. For official or other information, direct inquiries to the embassy or consulate at the addresses below.

- **Taxation:** The tax code in France is basic and simple to understand. A foreigner living in France for more than 183 days is subject to French personal income tax on income derived from French sources. Rates are steep, and there is no withholding, but certain deductions may be made. It is recommended that anyone going to work in France contact a French tax lawyer for assistance.

- **Principal International Schools:** There are several private and international schools for children of American residents. The annual tuition for an American school is about $10,000.

- **Health Care:** Medical facilities throughout France are considered good, with some doctors speaking fluent English. This group may charge higher fees, however. In Paris, one facility used often by American residents is the American Hospital of Paris (63 blvd Victor Hugo, 92200 Neuilly-sur-Seine). It is well equipped and has American doctors on staff. Please note that a permit is necessary to import any drugs. Permits are issued by the Ministry of Health in Paris. Drugs are tightly regulated in the country, so you may not be able to get the same kinds in France that you do in the United States. Sanitation is adequate in most areas of the country. Water is safe to drink but contains many minerals, so most people opt for bottled water. Make sure dairy products are safe, including milk, which should be pasteurized. The damp weather causes some respiratory problems, especially for tourists.

- **Crime:** Crime presents some problems in France, especially in the larger cities. Purse snatching, robberies, and muggings occur, so keep your purse snugly at your side and watch out for pickpockets in major tourist areas. In the evening, avoid the Bastille area and the rue du Faubourg-Montmarte in Paris. Don't ride the Paris metro after 10 P.M., as it may be unsafe.

- **Pros and Cons of Living and Working in France:** France is a country whose people are proud of their heritage and their influential role in global affairs. The country has a great deal to offer, including various historic sights, cultural institutions, and gardens. Its provincial cities as well as the countryside are popular tourist destinations. France has good transportation services, and medical facilities and health standards rank high. Telecommunications services are also very good, but be certain your housing accommodations include an installed phone, as new installation takes an extraordinarily long time. It is very expensive to live in France compared to the

EMBASSY AND CONSULATE CONTACT INFORMATION:

FRENCH EMBASSY
4101 RESERVOIR RD. NW
WASHINGTON, DC 20007
TEL: 202-944-6000

United States. Daily necessities are costly, as are rental apartments and houses. They usually come unfurnished and most landlords ask that tenants give six months notice when breaking a lease or risk losing their original deposit. Read your lease carefully. The climate is rather damp, so people with respiratory or sinus ailments may have problems.

CONSULATE GENERAL OF FRANCE
934 FIFTH AVE.
NEW YORK, NY 10021
TEL: 212-606-3600

OTHER SOURCES OF INFORMATION:

FRENCH GOVERNMENT TOURIST OFFICES
610 FIFTH AVE.
NEW YORK, NY 10020
TEL: 212-757-1125

COMPANIES/ORGANIZATIONS WITH OPERATIONS IN FRANCE:

ACCO WORLD CORPORATION, 110
ALBANY INTERNATIONAL CORPORATION, 114
ALBERTO-CULVER COMPANY, 115
ALDUS CORPORATION, 115
ALLEN-BRADLEY COMPANY, INC., 116
ALLIED-SIGNAL, INC., 117
AM INTERNATIONAL, INC., 119
AMDAHL CORPORATION, 120
AMERACE CORPORATION (ELASTIMOLD), 121
AMERICAN CYANAMID COMPANY, 124
AMERICAN EXPRESS COMPANY—TRAVEL RELATED SERVICES, 125
AMERICAN GREETINGS CORPORATION, 126
AMERICAN HOME PRODUCTS CORPORATION, 126
AMERICAN STANDARD, INC., 128
AMERICAN TOOL COMPANIES, INC., 129
AMGEN, INC., 131
AMP, INC., 132
AMR/AMERICAN AIRLINES, 133
ANDREW CORPORATION, 134
ANSELL INTERNATIONAL, 135
APPLE COMPUTER, INC., 136
ARBY'S, INC., 138
ARMOUR SWIFT ECKRICH, INC., 141
ARMSTRONG WORLD INDUSTRIES, INC., 141
ASEA BROWN BOVERI, 142
AST RESEARCH, INC., 144
AUGAT, INC., 146
AVERY DENNISON CORPORATION, 147
AVNET, INC., 148
AVON PRODUCTS, INC., 149
AVX CORPORATION, 150

BACKER SPIELVOGEL & BATES WORLDWIDE, INC., 150
BAKER HUGHES, INC., 152
BANK OF BOSTON CORPORATION, 153
THE BANK OF NEW YORK COMPANY, INC., 154
BANKAMERICA CORPORATION, 155
BANKERS TRUST NEW YORK CORPORATION, 155
BANYAN SYSTEMS, INC., 156
THE BARDEN CORPORATION, 157
BATTELLE MEMORIAL INSTITUTE, 159
BAUSCH & LOMB, INC., 159
BAXTER HEALTHCARE CORPORATION, 160
BEAR STEARNS COMPANIES, INC., 161
BECKMAN INSTRUMENTS, INC., 162
BELL & HOWELL COMPANY, 164
LOUIS BERGER INTERNATIONAL INC., 165
BETZ LABORATORIES, 166
BIO-RAD LABORATORIES, 166
BISSELL, INC., 167
BOEING COMPANY, 170
BORLAND INTERNATIONAL, INC, 172
BOSE CORPORATION, 172
BP AMERICA, INC., 173
W. H. BRADY COMPANY, 173
BRIDGESTONE-FIRESTONE, INC., 174
BRISTOL-MEYERS SQUIBB COMPANY, 175
BURLINGTON AIR EXPRESS, 179
CABOT CORPORATION, 181
CAMPBELL SOUP COMPANY, 183
CAPITOL CITIES/ABC, INC., 184
CARGILL INCORPORATED, 184
CARLSON TRAVEL NETWORK, 185
CARRIER CORPORATION, 186
J. I. CASE COMPANY, 187
CENTRAL SOYA COMPANY, 188

A
M
E
R
I
C
A
N

J
O
B
S

A
B
R
O
A
D

CHEVRON CORPORATION, 193
CH2M HILL INTERNATIONAL, LTD., 195
CIGNA CORPORATION, 197
CINCOM SYSTEMS, INC., 197
CITICORP, 198
COLGATE-PALMOLIVE COMPANY, 203
COLTEC INDUSTRIES, INC., 204
COMMERCIAL INTERTECH CORPORATION, 205
COMPUTER ASSOCIATES INTERNATIONAL, INC., 207
COMPUTERVISION CORPORATION, 208
CONAGRA, INC., 208
CONOCO, INC., 209
CONTINENTAL BANK CORPORATION, 210
CONTINUUM COMPANY, INC., 211
COOPERS & LYBRAND, 214
CORNING INCORPORATED, 215
CPC INTERNATIONAL, INC., 217
CROWN CORK & SEAL COMPANY, INC., 218
CUC INTERNATIONAL, INC., 221
CUMMINS ENGINE COMPANY, INC., 221
DAMES & MOORE, 223
DAY & ZIMMERMAN, 226
DAYCO PRODUCTS, INC., 226
DDB NEEDHAM WORLDWIDE, INC., 227
DEBEVOISE & PLIMPTON, 229
DEERE & COMPANY, 229
DELL COMPUTER CORPORATION, 231
DELOITTE & TOUCHE, 231
THE DEXTER CORPORATION, 233
DH TECHNOLOGY, INC., 233
DIGITAL EQUIPMENT CORPORATION, 236
DOMINO'S PIZZA, INC., 237
DONALDSON COMPANY, INC., 237
DONALDSON LUFKIN & JENRETTE, INC., 238
DOW JONES & COMPANY, INC., 241
DUN & BRADSTREET CORPORATION, 243
DURIRON COMPANY, INC., 244
EASTMAN KODAK COMPANY, 246
EATON CORPORATION/CUTLER HAMMER, 247
ELECTRONIC DATA SYSTEMS CORPORATION, 249
ELI LILLY AND COMPANY, 250
ENCYCLOPEDIA BRITANNICA, INC., 253
ENGELHARD CORPORATION, 253
ERNST & YOUNG, 255

ESCO CORPORATION, 255
ETHYL CORPORATION, 256
EXXON COMPANY, INTERNATIONAL, 258
FAIRCHILD PUBLICATIONS, INC., 259
FEDERAL EXPRESS CORPORATION, 260
FEDERAL-MOGUL CORPORATION, 260
FERRO CORPORATION, 261
FIGGIE INTERNATIONAL, INC., 262
FISCHER & PORTER COMPANY, 263
FMC CORPORATION, 266
FULLER COMPANY, 269
GAF CORPORATION, 270
GANNETT COMPANY, INC., 272
GENERAL ELECTRIC COMPANY (GE), 275
GENERAL FOODS USA, 276
GENERAL INSTRUMENT CORPORATION, 276
GENERAL MILLS, INC., 277
GERAGHTY & MILLER, INC., 279
GERHARD'S BICYCLE ODYSSEYS, 280
GOLDMAN SACHS & COMPANY, 283
GOODYEAR TIRE & RUBBER COMPANY, 284
W. R. GRACE & COMPANY, 285
GRACO, INC., 286
GREY ADVERTISING, INC., 288
H. J. HEINZ COMPANY, 290
HALLMARK CARDS, INC., 294
HAMLIN, INC., 294
M. A. HANNA COMPANY, 295
HANSON INDUSTRIES, 295
HASBRO, INC., 297
HAZLETON WASHINGTON CORPORATION, 297
HILL & KNOWLTON, INC., 301
HOLIDAY INNS WORLDWIDE, 302
HONEYWELL, INC., 303
HUGHES AIRCRAFT COMPANY, 307
IDB COMMUNICATIONS, INC., 309
IMCERA GROUP, INC., 310
INDUCTOTHERM CORPORATION, 311
INFORMATION BUILDERS, INC., 312
INGERSOLL ENGINEERS, 312
INGERSOLL-RAND COMPANY, 313
INTERNATIONAL BUSINESS MACHINES (IBM), 315
INTERNATIONAL MONETARY FUND, 552
ITT CORPORATION, 321
ITT HARTFORD INSURANCE GROUP, 321

ITW FINISHING SYSTEMS & PRODUCTS, 322

JAMES RIVER CORPORATION, 323

JOHNSON & JOHNSON, 325

JONES, DAY, REAVIS & POGUE, INC., 326

JWP, INC., 328

KAMAN CORPORATION, 328

KETCHUM INTERNATIONAL, 334

KFC CORPORATION, 335

KIDDER PEABODY GROUP & COMPANY, INC., 335

KIMBERLY-CLARK CORPORATION, 336

KLYNVELD PEAT MARWICK GOERDELER (KPMG), 337

KNIGHT-RIDDER, INC., 338

KNOLL INTERNATIONAL, 338

KOCH INDUSTRIES, INC., 339

KOHLER COMPANY, 339

KOLMAR LABORATORIES, INC., 340

KORN/FERRY INTERNATIONAL, 340

KRAFT GENERAL FOODS INTERNATIONAL, 341

LAMBDA ELECTRONICS, INC., 343

LEVI STRAUSS ASSOCIATES, INC., 344

THE LINCOLN ELECTRIC COMPANY, 346

LINTAS: WORLDWIDE, 346

ARTHUR D. LITTLE, INC., 347

LITTON INDUSTRIES, INC., 348

LORAL CORPORATION, 350

LORD CORPORATION, 350

LTX CORPORATION, 353

MACDERMID, INC., 355

MAGNETEK, INC., 358

MALLINCKRODT, INC., 359

MARION MERRELL DOW, INC., 360

MASTER LOCK COMPANY, 362

MATTEL, INC., 363

MAYTAG CORPORATION, 364

MCCANN-ERICKSON WORLDWIDE, 354

MCDONALD'S CORPORATION, 356

MCI COMMUNICATIONS CORPORATION, 365

MCKINSEY & COMPANY, INC., 357

MEAD CORPORATION, 365

MEASUREX CORPORATION, 366

MEDTRONIC, INC., 366

MEMOREX TELEX CORPORATION, 367

MERCK & COMPANY, INC., 368

MERRILL LYNCH & COMPANY, INC., 369

METCO PERKIN-ELMER, 371

MGM INCORPORATED, 372

HERMAN MILLER, INC., 373

MILLIKEN & COMPANY, 373

MILLIPORE CORPORATION, 374

MOBIL OIL CORPORATION, 375

MONSANTO COMPANY, 377

MOORE PRODUCTS COMPANY, 378

J. P. MORGAN & COMPANY, INC., 378

MORTON INTERNATIONAL, 380

NALCO CHEMICAL COMPANY, 382

NELLCOR, INC., 385

NEWSWEEK INTERNATIONAL, 387

NICOLET INSTRUMENT CORPORATION, 387

NORDSON CORPORATION, 389

NORTHWEST AIRLINES, INC., 390

NOVELL, INC., 392

NYNEX CORPORATION, 392

OGILVY & MATHER, 395

OLIN CORPORATION, 396

OMNICOM GROUP, INC., 397

ORACLE SYSTEMS, INC., 398

ORGANIZATION FOR ECONOMIC COOPERATION & DEVELOPMENT, 559

OTIS ELEVATOR COMPANY: WORLD HEADQUARTERS, 399

OUTBOARD MARINE CORPORATION, 399

OWENS-CORNING FIBERGLAS CORPORATION, 400

PACIFIC TELESIS INTERNATIONAL, 403

PAINE WEBBER GROUP, INC., 403

PARKER HANNIFIN CORPORATION, 405

PEPSICO FOODS INTERNATIONAL, 409

PETROLITE CORPORATION, 411

PFIZER, INC., 412

PHELPS DODGE CORPORATION, 412

PHILIP MORRIS COMPANIES, INC., 413

PHILIPP BROTHERS CHEMICALS, INC., 414

PHILLIPS PETROLEUM COMPANY, 415

PILLSBURY COMPANY, 416

PIONEER HI-BRED INTERNATIONAL, INC., 417

PITNEY BOWES, INC., 417

PIZZA HUT, INC., 419

PLAYTEX APPAREL, INC., 419

PPG INDUSTRIES, 421

PRECISION VALVE CORPORATION, 422

PREMARK INTERNATIONAL, INC., 423

PRICE WATERHOUSE, 424

PRIMERICA CORPORATION, 424

PRINTRONIX, INC., 425

A
M
E
R
I
C
A
N

J
O
B
S

A
B
R
O
A
D

PROCTER & GAMBLE COMPANY, 425
PROCTER & GAMBLE COSMETICS AND
FRAGRANCE PRODUCTS, 426
QUAKER CHEMICAL CORPORATION, 428
QUAKER OATS COMPANY, 428
QUME CORPORATION, 429
RAIN BIRD SPRINKLER MANUFACTURING
CORPORATION, 430
RALSTON PURINA COMPANY, 430
RANCO, INC., 431
READER'S DIGEST ASSOCIATION, INC.,
432
RECOGNITION EQUIPMENT, INC., 433
REED TOOL COMPANY, 434
RELIANCE ELECTRIC COMPANY, 435
REVLON, INC., 437
RHONE-POULENC RORER, 438
ROCKWELL GRAPHIC SYSTEMS, 441
ROCKWELL INTERNATIONAL
CORPORATION, 441
ROGERS CORPORATION, 442
ROHM & HAAS COMPANY, 442
ROSEMOUNT, INC., 443
RUBBERMAID, INC., 445
RUDER FINN, INC., 445
RUSSELL REYNOLDS ASSOCIATES, INC.,
446
SAATCHI & SAATCHI, 448
SAINT JUDE MEDICAL, INC., 448
SALOMON, INC., 449
SARA LEE CORPORATION, 449
SCHLEGEL CORPORATION, 451
A. SCHULMAN, INC., 451
SCIENTIFIC ATLANTA, INC., 452
SCM CHEMICALS, 453
SCOTT PAPER COMPANY, 453
SEALED AIR CORPORATION, 455
SEARLE COMPANY, 455
SENSORMATIC ELECTRONICS
CORPORATION, 457
SEQUA CORPORATION, 457
SGS CONTROL SERVICES, 458
SHEAFFER PEN, INC., 459
SHEARMAN & STERLING, 460
SHEARSON LEHMAN BROTHERS, 460
SHIPLEY COMPANY, INC., 461
SILICONIX, 462
SIMPLEX TIME RECORDER COMPANY, 463
SKADDEN, ARPS, SLATE, MEAGHER &
FLOM, 465

SMITH BARNEY, HARRIS UPHAM &
COMPANY, INC., 466
SONOCO PRODUCTS COMPANY, 470
SONY PICTURES ENTERTAINMENT, 471
SOTHEBY'S HOLDINGS, INC., 471
SPS TECHNOLOGIES, INC., 474
SRI INTERNATIONAL, 475
STANDARD COMMERCIAL CORPORATION,
476
STANDEX INTERNATIONAL, 477
STANHOME, INC., 477
STONE CONTAINER CORPORATION, 480
STORAGE TECHNOLOGY CORPORATION,
481
STRUCTURAL DYNAMICS RESEARCH
CORPORATION, 481
SULLAIR CORPORATION, 482
SULLIVAN & CROMWELL, 483
SUNDSTRAND CORPORATION, 485
SYMBOL TECHNOLOGIES, INC., 485
TAMBRANDS, INC., 486
TANDY CORPORATION, 487
TEKTRONIX, INC., 488
TELEDYNE, INC., 489
TENNECO, INC., 492
TENNESSEE ASSOCIATES INTERNATIONAL,
INC., 492
TERADYNE, INC., 493
THERMCO SYSTEMS, INC., 495
THOMAS & BETTS, 495
3M COMPANY, 496
3M PHARMACEUTICALS, 497
TIME, INC., 497
TIME-WARNER, INC., 498
TLC BEATRICE INTERNATIONAL HOLDINGS,
INC., 498
TORRINGTON COMPANY, 499
TOWERS PERRIN, INC., 499
TOYS "R" US, INC., 500
TRACOR, INC., 500
TRANE COMPANY, 501
TRINOVA CORPORATION, 502
TRITON ENERGY CORPORATION, 502
TRW, INC., 503
UNION CAMP CORPORATION, 507
UNION CARBIDE CORPORATION, 507
UNISYS CORPORATION, 508
UNITED NATIONS INDUSTRIAL
DEVELOPMENT ORGANIZATION
(UNIDO), 568

UNITED PARCEL SERVICE OF AMERICA,
    INC., 509
U.S. DEPARTMENT OF ENERGY, 573
UNITED STATES SURGICAL CORPORATION,
    511
UNITED TECHNOLOGIES CORPORATION,
    512
UOP, INC., 514
THE UPJOHN COMPANY, 515
US WEST, INC., 515
USAIR GROUP, INC., 516
VF CORPORATION, 517
VISA INTERNATIONAL, 517
VISHAY INTERTECHNOLOGY, 518
WALKER MANUFACTURING COMPANY, 519
WARNER BROTHERS INTERNATIONAL, 521
WARNER ELECTRIC BRAKE & CLUTCH
    COMPANY, 521

WARNER-LAMBERT COMPANY, 522
WASHINGTON POST COMPANY, 522
WATERS CHROMATOGRAPHY (MILLIPORE),
    523
JERVIS B. WEBB COMPANY, 523
WEIGHT WATCHERS INTERNATIONAL, INC.,
    524
WESTINGHOUSE ELECTRIC CORPORATION,
    525
WORLD COURIER MANAGEMENT, INC.,
    529
WILLIAM WRIGLEY JR. COMPANY, 529
WYETH-AYERST LABORATORIES, 530
WYNN'S INTERNATIONAL, INC., 530
YORK INTERNATIONAL, INC., 532
YOUNG & RUBICAM, INC., 533

COUNTRY PROFILES

GABON

- **Official Name:** Gabonese Republic
- **Capital:** Libreville
- **Location:** Lying directly on the equator, Gabon is located on the western coast of Africa. It is bounded by Equatorial Guinea to the northwest, Cameroon to the north, Congo to the east and south, and the Atlantic Ocean to the west. The total land area is 103,346 square miles, making Gabon slightly smaller than Colorado. More than three-fourths of Gabon is covered by tropical rain forests and other woodlands. There are many deep river valleys cutting through the highlands. Along the coastline there are palm-fringed beaches, mangrove swamps, and lagoons.
- **Population, Cities, and American Residents:** Gabon has a population of 905,000 (1992 est.) with black African groups (primarily Bantu) comprising nearly the entire population. The four main tribal groups are: the Fang, the Eshira, the Bapounou, and the Bateke. There are also about 27,000 French citizens living in Gabon.

    Most American residents live in Gabon's two main cities: Libreville with 400,000 people and Port-Gentil with 200,000 (1989 est.).
- **Language and Currency:** French is the official language of Gabon. A working knowledge of the language is vital to do business in Gabon. The monetary unit is the CFA franc (CFA Fr), issued by the African Financial Community. The exchange rate is approximately 300 CFA francs = U.S.$1 (November 1993).
- **Climate:** The climate of Gabon is hot and humid, with the humidity averaging around 85 percent. Four distinct seasons include the dry season from May to September, a rainy period from October to mid-December, and a brief dry season from then through

January. Heaviest precipitation begins in the middle of January and lasts through the middle of May, with almost 100 inches of rain falling annually. The average year-round temperature is about 79°F.

- **Economy and Resources:** Because of its abundance of natural resources and a relatively small population, Gabon is considered one of the richest nations in Sub-Saharan Africa. Natural resources include crude oil, manganese, timber, gold, uranium, and iron ore. Major industries are sawmills, petroleum, and mining. Gabon is a member of OPEC and has some of the richest deposits of iron and manganese in the world. Petroleum accounts for 45 percent of the gross domestic product (GDP), 80 percent of foreign exchange earnings, and 65 percent of government revenues. Though agriculture contributes only 4 percent to the GDP, it employs 65 percent of the labor force. The remaining people work in industry and commerce. Major exports are crude oil and wood, which go primarily to France and the United States. After recovering from an economic slump in the mid-1980s, Gabon has once again achieved economic stability. The International Monetary Fund (IMF) austerity programs have prompted growth and renewed foreign interest in Gabon's petroleum sector.

- **Cost of Living:** At 200, the cost of living is twice as high as living in the United States.

- **Work Permits, Visas, etc.:** You'll need a valid passport, visa, and current international health certificate to travel in Gabon. Visas may be obtained in person or by mail from the Gabonese embassy. An application for a business visa must include a letter from the company or organization responsible for the trip stating the reason and proposed length of stay. Allow ample time for this if it is done through the mail. All visitors staying in Gabon for more than 15 days must have an International Certificate of Vaccination against yellow fever. It is recommended that antimalarial medication be taken. For official or other information, direct inquiries to the embassy or consulate at the addresses below.

- **Taxation:** There are various taxes levied on expatriates working in Gabon. A personal income tax, based on a progressive scale of 5-55 percent, is collected on personal income. Various credits may apply for U.S. citizens. There is no treaty for the avoidance of double taxation between the United States and Gabon.

- **Principal International Schools:** American schools are available in Gabon for children of expatriates. The average annual tuition is about $8,000.

- **Health Care:** Adequate medical assistance for routine problems is available in Gabon. French or French-trained physicians and dentists are qualified to treat patients and specialists (gynecologists, pediatricians, etc.) are available. French-made pharmaceuticals are used in Gabon, so before departing the United States, it's a good idea to have your physician provide prescriptions written in French. AIDS is a major problem in Gabon, as it is in other African nations. Extreme caution is urged. Sanitation standards in Gabon are lower than in the United States. It's best to avoid swimming in pools, slow-moving streams, or fresh bodies of water. The constant heat and humidity may present problems for people with respiratory ailments. Boil all tap water and avoid drinking fresh milk. Cook all meat and fish thoroughly and take precautions with raw fruits and vegetables.

- **Crime:** Street crime is not a major problem in Gabon. However, it is smart to take precautions against pickpockets or purse snatchers in crowded areas. Carry personal identification with you at all times in case you are stopped by the local police. It will avoid a hassle.

- **Pros and Cons of Working and Living in Gabon:** Gabon has some of the finest and most modern cities on the African continent. There are wildlife preserves, sports, beaches, and many palaces and museums that attract tourists. Telecommunications are quite good, but having your own (or rented) auto is important, especially if you're on long-term assignment. Auto insurance (especially third-party liability) is exorbitant, and can run into a few thousand dollars annually. Gasoline is over $5 a gallon. In most areas, expatriates will pay a high cost to live in Gabon compared to the United States. Libreville, the capital city, is one of the most expensive cities in the world in which to live. Accommodations are available, but are limited and costly. Because of the uncomfortable climate, it is recommended that pets be left at home.

EMBASSY AND CONSULATE CONTACT INFORMATION:

EMBASSY OF THE REPUBLIC OF GABON
2034 20 ST. NW
WASHINGTON, DC 20008
TEL: 202-797-1000

GABON MISSION TO THE UNITED NATIONS
820 SECOND AVE., RM. 902
NEW YORK, NY 10016
TEL: 212-696-9720

OTHER SOURCES OF INFORMATION:

GABON TOURIST INFORMATION OFFICE/AIR GABON
347 FIFTH AVE.
NEW YORK, NY 10016
TEL: 212-447-6700

COMPANIES/ORGANIZATIONS WITH OPERATIONS IN GABON:

AMOCO CORPORATION, 131
CONOCO, INC., 209

HUGHES CHRISTENSEN COMPANY, 307
ORYX ENERGY, 398

GERMANY

- **Official Name:** Federal Republic of Germany

- **Capital:** Berlin

- **Location:** Germany is located in the north central section of Europe. It is bounded by Denmark and the Baltic Sea to the north, Poland and the Czech Republic to the east, Austria and Switzerland to the south, and France, Luxembourg, Belgium, the Netherlands, and the North Sea to the west. Its total land area at 137,855 square miles is slightly smaller than Montana. The country has three basic regions: the North German Plain, the Central German Uplands, and the South German Alpine Foothills. Its land is mountainous and hilly with meadows and pastures in the central and eastern areas. The west is heavily forested. Arable land accounts for 34 percent of Germany's area.

- **Population, Cities, and American Residents:** The population of Germany totals 77 million people (1992 est.). They are predominantly German with some Slavic and Danish minorities. The Jewish population is about 28,000.

  Most American residents are employed in Germany's three major cities: Berlin with 3 million, Hamburg with 1.6 million, and Frankfurt am Main with 500,000 people (1989 est.). Frankfurt am Main has more than 500 American businesses represented in the area and is the most American-influenced city in Germany.

- **Language and Currency:** German is the official language of the country, but English is certainly the most common used second language, and many Germans speak it fluently. Courtesy and protocol dictate which language will prevail. If German is used, interpreters are available if necessary. Any foreigner working in Germany should have some knowledge of the native language, as it is expected and appreciated by the Germans. The monetary unit is the Deutsche Mark (DM and usually referred to as the "mark"). The exchange rate is 1 Deutsche Mark = U.S.$.57 (July 30, 1993).

- **Climate:** Germany's climate varies with each region, but it basically has temperate, marine weather with cool, wet winters and summers. The northwest has mild winters and warm summers. The average winter temperature is about 35°F, and in the summer temperatures average about 63°F. The south, where elevations are higher, tends to be colder in the winter season, about 27°F, and warmer during the summer, averaging over 68°F. Winters in most areas are cold and damp, so warm clothing is a necessity.

- **Economy and Resources:** The unification of East and West Germany in 1990 created an extraordinary challenge that is far from over. Germany has the largest and most productive economy in the European Community. Although now joined together, East and West Germany are very different. Productivity in East Germany is only 40 percent of that in the West. In East Germany, almost 40 percent of the people work in industry, 21 percent in services, and 10 percent in agriculture. Natural resources are brown coal, uranium, and copper. Major industries include metal fabrication, chemicals, and brown coal. Chief exports consist of machinery and transport equipment (47 percent), and consumer goods (16 percent). Major trading partners are Russia and the European Community. In the West, 41.6 percent of the labor force work in industry, 34.7 percent in services, and 18 percent in trade and transport. Major industries include iron, steel, coal, and cement (Germany is a global leader in these industries). Nearly 87 percent of exports are manufactured products (machines and machine tools, motor vehicles, and steel products). More than half of the exports go to the European Community. Economic restructuring will take several years, yet despite all that Germany has had to overcome, the economy remains relatively strong. The total elimination of barriers in commerce among the European Communities will strengthen a reunited nation.

- **Cost of Living:** At 143, the cost of living is higher than in the United States.

- **Work Permits, Visas, etc.:** A valid passport is required to travel in Germany. If you are a U.S. citizen and your stay is under three months, no visa is necessary. If you are planning to stay longer, apply for a residence and work permit well in advance of your trip, at a German Consulate office in the United States, in person or through the mail. If you are entering Germany from the United States, no vaccinations are required. For official or other information, direct inquiries to the embassy or consulate at the addresses below.

- **Taxation:** The tax system of Germany is rather intricate and difficult to understand, and its tax structure is very progressive. If you are a resident of Germany, you are responsible for taxes on all income from inside and outside of the country. A resident is anyone who lives in the Federal Republic for more than six months or for six consecutive months in a calendar year. Nonresidents are taxed on German income only. Deductions or exemptions may apply. There is a treaty in effect between Germany and the United States to avoid double taxation.

- **Principal International Schools:** There are several international schools in Germany where children of American residents may attend classes. Tuition for an American school averages $10,000-$12,000 per year.

- **Health Care:** In the West, medical standards are quite good and comparable to U.S. standards. Doctors and dentists are qualified and have modern offices and adequate staffing. Sanitary conditions are good, with water and dairy products safe to drink and eat. Government inspectors strictly enforce health codes. In the East, however, conditions are not as pleasant. The larger cities offer competent medical service, but the rural areas do not have as many qualified medical personnel as the West because many went to the West when unification occurred. Pollution is also a major problem, prevalent throughout the countryside.

- **Crime:** There has been a noticeable rise in personal crime, especially in Berlin's eastern section. Be careful not to carry large amounts of cash, and lock car doors when vehicles are not being used. In the evening hours, avoid poorly lit streets and stay in the busier areas.

- **Pros and Cons of Living and Working in Germany:** Germany has many cultural attractions, among them cathedrals, museums, and the castles on the Rhine. Its cities are modern yet elegant. Telecommunications and transportation are very good in the West, and only fair in the East, where roadwork is desperately needed, so be careful when driving. It is recommended that you do not import your vehicle while staying in Germany. Cars are inspected and may need modifications to conform with German laws. The world-famous Autobahn network in the West totals 5,100 miles and links all major cities with smaller ones. The top speed is 81 mph on the Autobahn, but vehicles often are driven at speeds up to 110 mph. The right lane is for slower drivers, and that's a safe place to be. Otherwise you might be bumper-to-bumper with a tail-gater in a real hurry. The cost of living in Germany is higher than in the United States. You will most likely pay more for daily items, especially restaurant

EMBASSY AND CONSULATE CONTACT INFORMATION:

EMBASSY OF THE FEDERAL REPUBLIC OF GERMANY
4645 RESERVOIR RD. NW
WASHINGTON, DC 20007
TEL: 202-298-4000

CONSULATE GENERAL OF THE FEDERAL REPUBLIC OF GERMANY
460 PARK AVE.
NEW YORK, NY 10022
TEL: 212-308-3422

A
M
E
R
I
C
A
N

J
O
B
S

A
B
R
O
A
D

meals. Housing can be very expensive as rentals in or close to major cities are costly. Read the lease closely and consider having an attorney look over the paperwork before signing.

OTHER SOURCES OF INFORMATION:

GERMAN NATIONAL TOURIST OFFICE
747 THIRD AVE.
NEW YORK, NY 10017
TEL: 212-308-3300

COMPANIES/ORGANIZATIONS WITH OPERATIONS IN GERMANY:

ABB LUMMUS CREST, 108

ABEX INC./FISHER SCIENTIFIC INTERNATIONAL, INC., 110

ACCO WORLD CORPORATION, 110

ACUSHNET COMPANY, 111

AKZO AMERICA, INC., 113

ALARM DEVICE MANUFACTURING COMPANY, 114

ALBANY INTERNATIONAL CORPORATION, 114

ALBERTO-CULVER COMPANY, 115

ALDUS CORPORATION, 115

ALLEN-BRADLEY COMPANY, INC., 116

ALLIED-SIGNAL, INC., 117

AM INTERNATIONAL, INC., 119

AMERICAN CYANAMID COMPANY, 124

AMERICAN EXPRESS COMPANY—TRAVEL RELATED SERVICES, 125

AMERICAN HOME PRODUCTS CORPORATION, 126

AMERICAN MANAGEMENT SYSTEMS, INC., 127

AMERICAN STANDARD, INC., 128

AMERICAN TOOL COMPANIES, INC., 129

AMGEN, INC., 131

AMOCO CORPORATION, 131

AMP, INC., 132

AMR/AMERICAN AIRLINES, 133

ANSELL INTERNATIONAL, 135

ANTHONY INDUSTRIES, 135

AON CORPORATION, 136

APPLE COMPUTER, INC., 136

APPLIED BIOSCIENCE INTERNATIONAL, INC., 137

ARBY'S, INC., 138

ARMSTRONG WORLD INDUSTRIES, INC., 141

ASEA BROWN BOVERI, 142

ASSOCIATED PRESS, 144

AST RESEARCH, INC., 144

ASTRONAUTICS CORPORATION OF AMERICA, 145

AUGAT, INC., 146

AUTOMATIC SWITCH COMPANY, 147

AVERY DENNISON CORPORATION, 147

BACKER SPIELVOGEL & BATES WORLDWIDE, INC., 150

BAKER HUGHES, INC., 152

BANCTEC, INC., 152

BANK OF BOSTON CORPORATION, 153

THE BANK OF NEW YORK COMPANY, INC., 154

BANKERS TRUST NEW YORK CORPORATION, 155

BANYAN SYSTEMS, INC., 156

THE BARDEN CORPORATION, 157

BASF CORPORATION, 158

BATTELLE MEMORIAL INSTITUTE, 159

BAUSCH & LOMB, INC., 159

BAXTER HEALTHCARE CORPORATION, 160

JIM BEAM BRANDS COMPANY, 161

BECKMAN INSTRUMENTS, INC., 162

BELL & HOWELL COMPANY, 164

BEMIS COMPANY, INC., 164

BLACK & DECKER CORPORATION, 167

BLOCK DRUG COMPANY, INC., 169

BLOUNT, INC. (BLOUNT CONSTRUCTION DIVISION), 169

BOEING COMPANY, 170

BORG-WARNER CORPORATION, 171

BORLAND INTERNATIONAL, INC, 172

BOSE CORPORATION, 172

BP AMERICA, INC., 173

W. H. BRADY COMPANY, 173

BRIDGESTONE-FIRESTONE, INC., 174

BRISTOL-MEYERS SQUIBB COMPANY, 175

BROWN & SHARPE MANUFACTURING COMPANY, 176

BRUSH WELLMAN, INC., 178

BURLINGTON AIR EXPRESS, 179

BURSON-MARSTELLER, 180

CABOT CORPORATION, 181

CAPITOL CITIES/ABC, INC., 184

CARLSON TRAVEL NETWORK, 185

J. I. CASE COMPANY, 187

CHIRON CORPORATION, 194

CIGNA CORPORATION, 197

CINCOM SYSTEMS, INC., 197

CITICORP, 198

COHERENT, INC., 202

COIN ACCEPTORS, INC., 203

COLGATE-PALMOLIVE COMPANY, 203

COMPUTER ASSOCIATES INTERNATIONAL, INC., 207

CONOCO, INC., 209

CONTINENTAL AIRLINES HOLDINGS, INC., 210

CONTINENTAL BANK CORPORATION, 210

COOPER INDUSTRIES, INC., 213

COOPERS & LYBRAND, 214

CORNING INCORPORATED, 215

CPC INTERNATIONAL, INC., 217

CROWN CORK & SEAL COMPANY, INC., 218

CUBIC CORPORATION, 220

CUMMINS ENGINE COMPANY, INC., 221

DAKA INTERNATIONAL, 222

DAMES & MOORE, 223

DAY & ZIMMERMAN, 226

DAYCO PRODUCTS, INC., 226

DEERE & COMPANY, 229

DELL COMPUTER CORPORATION, 231

DELTA AIR LINES, INC., 232

THE DEXTER CORPORATION, 233

DH TECHNOLOGY, INC., 233

DIEBOLD INCORPORATED, 235

DIGITAL EQUIPMENT CORPORATION, 236

DOMINO'S PIZZA, INC., 237

DONALDSON COMPANY, INC., 237

DOVER CORPORATION, 239

DOW CHEMICAL COMPANY, 240

DOW JONES & COMPANY, INC., 241

DRESSER INDUSTRIES, INC., 241

DUN & BRADSTREET CORPORATION, 243

DURIRON COMPANY, INC., 244

DYNCORP, 245

E-SYSTEMS, INC., 245

EAGLE-PICHER INDUSTRIES, INC., 246

EASTMAN KODAK COMPANY, 246

EBASCO OVERSEAS CORPORATION, 248

ECOLOGY AND ENVIRONMENT, INC., 248

ELECTRONIC DATA SYSTEMS CORPORATION, 249

ELI LILLY AND COMPANY, 250

EMERY WORLDWIDE, 252

ENCORE COMPUTER CORPORATION, 252

ENCYCLOPEDIA BRITANNICA, INC., 253

ERNST & YOUNG, 255

ETHICON, INC., 256

EXPEDITORS INTERNATIONAL OF WASHINGTON, INC., 257

EXXON CHEMICAL COMPANY, 257

EXXON CORPORATION, 258

FEDERAL EXPRESS CORPORATION, 260

FEDERAL-MOGUL CORPORATION, 260

FIBRONICS INTERNATIONAL, INC., 261

FISHER CONTROLS INTERNATIONAL, INC., 263

FLOW INTERNATIONAL CORPORATION, 265

FLUOR CORPORATION, 266

FMC CORPORATION, 266

FRITZ COMPANIES, 269

FULLER COMPANY, 269

GAF CORPORATION, 270

THE GATES RUBBER COMPANY, 273

GENERAL DYNAMICS CORPORATION, 274

GENERAL ELECTRIC COMPANY (GE), 275

GENERAL MOTORS CORPORATION (GM), 277

GENERAL SIGNAL CORPORATION, 278

GERHARD'S BICYCLE ODYSSEYS, 280

GIDDINGS & LEWIS, INC., 282

GOODYEAR TIRE & RUBBER COMPANY, 284

W. R. GRACE & COMPANY, 285

GRACO, INC., 286

GRANT THORNTON INTERNATIONAL, 286

H. J. HEINZ COMPANY, 290

H & R BLOCK, 291

HALLIBURTON-NUS CORPORATION, 293

HALLMARK CARDS, INC., 294

HAMLIN, INC., 294

M. A. HANNA COMPANY, 295

HANSON INDUSTRIES, 295

HAZLETON WASHINGTON CORPORATION, 297

HERCULES, INC., 299

HERSHEY FOODS CORPORATION, 299

HERTZ CORPORATION, 300

HILL & KNOWLTON, INC., 301

HOECHST CELANESE, INC., 302

HOLMES & NARVER, INC., 303

HONEYWELL, INC., 303

A
M
E
R
I
C
A
N

J
O
B
S

A
B
R
O
A
D

HUGHES AIRCRAFT COMPANY, 307
IDB COMMUNICATIONS, INC., 309
IMCERA GROUP, INC., 310
IMO INDUSTRIES, 310
IMS AMERICA, LTD., 311
INDUCTOTHERM CORPORATION, 311
INFORMATION BUILDERS, INC., 312
INGERSOLL ENGINEERS, 312
INGERSOLL INTERNATIONAL, INC., 313
INGERSOLL-RAND COMPANY, 313
INTERNATIONAL BUSINESS MACHINES
    (IBM), 315
IOMEGA CORPORATION, 320
ITT CORPORATION, 321
ITT HARTFORD INSURANCE GROUP, 321
ITW FINISHING SYSTEMS & PRODUCTS,
    322
JOHNSON CONTROLS, INC., 324
JWP, INC., 328
KAYSER-ROTH CORPORATION, 329
A. T. KEARNEY, INC., 329
KEITHLEY INSTRUMENTS, INC., 329
KELLOGG COMPANY, 330
KENNAMETAL, INC., 333
KETCHUM INTERNATIONAL, 334
KEYSTONE INTERNATIONAL, 334
KIMBERLY-CLARK CORPORATION, 336
KLYNVELD PEAT MARWICK GOERDELER
    (KPMG), 337
KNIGHT-RIDDER, INC., 338
KNOLL INTERNATIONAL, 338
KOCH INDUSTRIES, INC., 339
KOLMAR LABORATORIES, INC., 340
KORN/FERRY INTERNATIONAL, 340
KRAFT GENERAL FOODS INTERNATIONAL,
    341
KYSOR INDUSTRIAL CORPORATION, 342
LAMBDA ELECTRONICS, INC., 343
LAWTER INTERNATIONAL, INC., 344
LEVI STRAUSS ASSOCIATES, INC., 344
LIANT SOFTWARE CORPORATION, 345
LINTAS: WORLDWIDE, 346
ARTHUR D. LITTLE, INC., 347
LITTON INDUSTRIES, INC., 348
LOCTITE CORPORATION, 349
LORAL CORPORATION, 350
LORD CORPORATION, 350
LTX CORPORATION, 353
LUBRIZOL CORPORATION, 353
MACDERMID, INC., 355

MALLINCKRODT, INC., 359
MARION MERRELL DOW, INC., 360
MATTEL, INC., 363
MCDERMOTT INTERNATIONAL, INC., 356
MCDONALD'S CORPORATION, 356
MCGRAW-HILL, INC., 357
MCI COMMUNICATIONS CORPORATION,
    365
MCKINSEY & COMPANY, INC., 357
MEAD CORPORATION, 365
MEASUREX CORPORATION, 366
MEMOREX TELEX CORPORATION, 367
MERCK & COMPANY, INC., 368
MERISEL, INC., 369
MERRILL LYNCH & COMPANY, INC., 369
METCO PERKIN-ELMER, 371
HERMAN MILLER, INC., 373
MOBIL OIL CORPORATION, 375
MOLEX, INC., 376
MONSANTO COMPANY, 377
MORTON INTERNATIONAL, 380
NALCO CHEMICAL COMPANY, 382
NATIONAL DATA CORPORATION, 382
NELLCOR, INC., 385
NEWSWEEK INTERNATIONAL, 387
NICOLET INSTRUMENT CORPORATION, 387
NORDSON CORPORATION, 389
NOVELL, INC., 392
OCCIDENTAL PETROLEUM CORPORATION,
    393
OGILVY & MATHER, 395
OLIN CORPORATION, 396
OMNICOM GROUP, INC., 397
OTIS ELEVATOR COMPANY: WORLD
    HEADQUARTERS, 399
OWENS-CORNING FIBERGLAS
    CORPORATION, 400
OWENS-ILLINOIS, INC., 401
PACIFIC TELESIS INTERNATIONAL, 403
PARKER HANNIFIN CORPORATION, 405
PENTAIR, INC., 409
PERKIN-ELMER CORPORATION, 410
PETROLITE CORPORATION, 411
PFAUDLER COMPANIES, INC., 411
PFIZER, INC., 412
PHELPS DODGE CORPORATION, 412
PHILIP MORRIS COMPANIES, INC., 413
PHILLIPS PETROLEUM COMPANY, 415
PILLSBURY COMPANY, 416

PIONEER HI-BRED INTERNATIONAL, INC., 417

PITNEY BOWES, INC., 417

PIZZA HUT, INC., 419

PMI FOOD EQUIPMENT GROUP, 420

PPG INDUSTRIES, 421

PRC, INC., 422

PRECISION VALVE CORPORATION, 422

PREMARK INTERNATIONAL, INC., 423

PRICE WATERHOUSE, 424

PRIMERICA CORPORATION, 424

PRINTRONIX, INC., 425

PROCTER & GAMBLE COMPANY, 425

PROCTER & GAMBLE COSMETICS AND FRAGRANCE PRODUCTS, 426

QUME CORPORATION, 429

RALSTON PURINA COMPANY, 430

RANCO, INC., 431

RAYTHEON COMPANY, 432

READER'S DIGEST ASSOCIATION, INC., 432

RECOGNITION EQUIPMENT, INC., 433

REDKEN LABORATORIES, INC., 434

RELIANCE ELECTRIC COMPANY, 435

REMINGTON PRODUCTS, INC., 436

REVLON, INC., 437

REYNOLDS METALS COMPANY, 438

ROCKWELL GRAPHIC SYSTEMS, 441

ROCKWELL INTERNATIONAL CORPORATION, 441

ROGERS CORPORATION, 442

ROHM & HAAS COMPANY, 442

ROSEMOUNT, INC., 443

RUDER FINN, INC., 445

RUSSELL REYNOLDS ASSOCIATES, INC., 446

RYDER SYSTEMS, INC., 447

SAATCHI & SAATCHI, 448

SAINT JUDE MEDICAL, INC., 448

SALOMON, INC., 449

SCHLEGEL CORPORATION, 451

A. SCHULMAN, INC., 451

SCIENTIFIC ATLANTA, INC., 452

SCOTT PAPER COMPANY, 453

SEA-LAND SERVICE, INC., 454

SEALED AIR CORPORATION, 455

SEARLE COMPANY, 455

SEARS ROEBUCK AND COMPANY, 456

SENCO PRODUCTS, 456

SENSORMATIC ELECTRONICS CORPORATION, 457

SGS CONTROL SERVICES, 458

SGS-THOMSON MICROELECTRONICS, 458

SHEARMAN & STERLING, 460

SHEARSON LEHMAN BROTHERS, 460

SHERWIN-WILLIAMS COMPANY, 461

SHIPLEY COMPANY, INC., 461

SIGNODE PACKAGING SYSTEMS, 462

SILICONIX, 462

SIMPLEX TIME RECORDER COMPANY, 463

SKADDEN, ARPS, SLATE, MEAGHER & FLOM, 465

SONOCO PRODUCTS COMPANY, 470

SONY PICTURES ENTERTAINMENT, 471

SOTHEBY'S HOLDINGS, INC., 471

SPS TECHNOLOGIES, INC., 474

SQUARE D COMPANY, 475

SRI INTERNATIONAL, 475

STANDEX INTERNATIONAL, 477

STATE STREET BOSTON CORPORATION, 478

STORAGE TECHNOLOGY CORPORATION, 481

STRUCTURAL DYNAMICS RESEARCH CORPORATION, 481

SUN ELECTRIC CORPORATION, 484

SYMBOL TECHNOLOGIES, INC., 485

TANDEM COMPUTERS, INC., 487

TANDY CORPORATION, 487

TEKTRONIX, INC., 488

TELEDYNE, INC., 489

TENNANT COMPANY, 490

THERMCO SYSTEMS, INC., 495

THOMAS & BETTS, 495

3M COMPANY, 496

3M PHARMACEUTICALS, 497

TIME, INC., 497

TIME-WARNER, INC., 498

TORRINGTON COMPANY, 499

TOWERS PERRIN, INC., 499

TOYS "R" US, INC., 500

TRACOR, INC., 500

TRANE COMPANY, 501

TRINOVA CORPORATION, 502

TRW, INC., 503

UNION CAMP CORPORATION, 507

UNION CARBIDE CORPORATION, 507

UNISYS CORPORATION, 508

A
M
E
R
I
C
A
N

J
O
B
S

A
B
R
O
A
D

UNITED NATIONS INDUSTRIAL
DEVELOPMENT ORGANIZATION
(UNIDO), 568
UNITED PARCEL SERVICE OF AMERICA,
INC., 509
U.S. ARMY CORPS OF ENGINEERS, 570
U.S. FEDERAL AVIATION ADMINISTRATION,
577
U.S. GENERAL ACCOUNTING OFFICE, 579
UNITED TECHNOLOGIES CORPORATION,
512
UNIVERSAL FOODS CORPORATION, 513
UOP, INC., 514
THE UPJOHN COMPANY, 515
USAIR GROUP, INC., 516
VF CORPORATION, 517
VISHAY INTERTECHNOLOGY, 518
WALKER MANUFACTURING COMPANY, 519

WANG LABORATORIES, INC., 519
WARD HOWELL INTERNATIONAL, INC., 520
WARNER BROTHERS INTERNATIONAL, 521
WARNER ELECTRIC BRAKE & CLUTCH
COMPANY, 521
WARNER-LAMBERT COMPANY, 522
WATERS CHROMATOGRAPHY (MILLIPORE),
523
WEST COMPANY, INC., 525
WESTINGHOUSE ELECTRIC CORPORATION,
525
WMX TECHNOLOGIES/WASTE
MANAGEMENT, INC., 527
WORLD COURIER MANAGEMENT, INC.,
529
WILLIAM WRIGLEY JR. COMPANY, 529
YORK INTERNATIONAL, INC., 532
YOUNG & RUBICAM, INC., 533

GHANA

- **Official Name:** Republic of Ghana

- **Capital:** Accra

- **Location:** Ghana lies on the Gulf of Guinea in western Africa. It is bounded by Burkina Faso to the north, Togo to the east, the Gulf of Guinea to the south, and the Ivory Coast to the west. Less than half of the country lies 500 feet above sea level, with most of the territory comprised of low plains with plateaus in the south-central region.

- **Language and Currency:** The official language is English. It is used throughout business and government and is taught in all the schools. The monetary unit is the (new) cedi. The exchange rate is 750 cedis = U.S.$1 (December 1993).

- **Print Sources of Information:** American University's *Area Handbook for Ghana* (1983) is available from the Superintendent of Documents, U.S. Government Printing Office, Washington, D.C., 20402.

EMBASSY AND CONSULATE CONTACT INFORMATION:

EMBASSY OF GHANA
3512 INTERNATIONAL DR. NW
WASHINGTON, DC 20008
TEL: 202-686-4520

CONSULATE GENERAL OF GHANA
19 E. 47TH ST.
NEW YORK, NY 10017
TEL: 212-832-1300

COMPANIES/ORGANIZATIONS WITH OPERATIONS IN GHANA:

CONSERVATION INTERNATIONAL, 545
H. J. HEINZ COMPANY, 290

GREECE

- **Official Name:** The Hellenic Republic

- **Capital:** Athens

- **Location:** Greece is located in Southeastern Europe on the edge of the Balkan peninsula. It is bounded by Albania, Yugoslavia, and Bulgaria to the north; Turkey to the northeast; the Aegean Sea to the east; the Mediterranean Sea to the south; and Ionic Sea to the west. Hundreds of islands surround the mainland of Greece and account for 9,000 square miles of its total land area. The mainland totals 50,948 square miles, making it slightly larger than New York. Greece has an extremely mountainous terrain, with only 23 percent considered arable land. Meadows and pastures account for 40 percent of the territory and 20 percent is covered by forests and woodlands.

- **Population, Cities, and American Residents:** The population of Greece totals 10.1 million people (1992 est.). Nearly everyone is Greek, accounting for 97.7 percent of the population. The remainder are Turkish (1.3 percent), and other groups including Vlach, Slav, Albanian, and Pomach.

   Most American residents are employed in Greece's three largest cities: Athens with 3.5 million, Thessaloniki with 800,000, and Patras with 120,000 people (1989 est.).

- **Language and Currency:** Greek is the official language of the country, but English is widely used in business and government. Most younger Greeks speak English, and some speak French. Only in special cases, or when dealing with small businesses, will you need a translator. The monetary unit is the drachma; written as "D." The exchange rate is 1 Greek drachma = U.S.$.004. It takes 237 drachma to equal U.S.$1 (July 30, 1993).

- **Climate:** The climate in Greece varies depending on what section of the country you are in. The winters in the northern section near Thessaloniki can turn very cold, with the average temperature about 42°F. In the south, around Athens, the typical winter temperature is about 45°F. Summers tend to be hot and dry with seasonal breezes off the ocean. In most areas the average temperature is 81°F, with streams drying up from June through August. In the evenings, temperatures are cool enough to wear a sweater or jacket.

- **Economy and Resources:** The Greek economy is primarily based on agriculture, tourism, and shipping. Industry accounts for 20 percent of the gross domestic product (GDP) and half of the country's exports. Most business concerns are small, family-owned businesses engaged in textiles, clothing, food processing, metal manufacture, and cement. Agriculture accounts for 17 percent of the GDP and 20 percent of exports. Agricultural exports include: wheat, barley, maize, fruits, vegetables, oil seeds, tobacco, cotton, and sugar beets. Major exports include manufactured goods, 28.1 percent; food and beverages, 25.6 percent; textiles, 21.8 percent; and petroleum products, 11.3 percent. The major export market is the European Community. In the last decade, problems have plagued the Greek government, including a large debt burden, high inflation, and low levels of investment. These, coupled with the government scandals in the late 1980s, under socialist leader Andreas Papandreou, left Greece with a host of problems. With a new government and austerity and stabilization programs in pace, Greece hopes to continue its trade with the European Community and expand trade with the United States, which has been minimal in the past. Research has helped to determine exactly what products should be exported to U.S. markets; they include food, wine, marble, and jewelry.

- **Cost of Living:** At 126, the cost of living is higher than in the United States.

- **Work Permits, Visas, etc.:** A valid passport is required to travel in Greece, but if you stay longer than three months, you must file an application with the Alien's Bureau of the Ministry of Internal Affairs in Athens. In most cases, work permits are obtained by the employer well in advance of the trip. If you are entering Greece from the United States, no vaccinations are required. For official or other information, direct inquiries to the embassy or consulate at the addresses below.

- **Taxation:** Income taxes are collected from all individuals who earn more than $686 yearly in Greece. Citizenship and permanent residence do not affect taxation. The rates are from 18-50 percent on income earned. There is a tax treaty between Greece and the United States to avoid double taxation.

- **Principal International Schools:** International schools are available in Greece for children of American residents. Tuition for an American School ranges from $4,200-$4,500 per year.

- **Health Care:** Medical care is adequate in most sections of Greece, with most physicians having trained in English-speaking countries. Hospital charges for outpatients are reasonable, but there is no free medical care available for foreign visitors. Sanitation standards throughout most of Greece are good, with water safe to drink in urban areas. Avoid drinking well water anywhere in Greece as it is not safe. Most foods are acceptable, but to avoid problems, do not eat raw meat or fish. Pharmaceuticals are available, but prescription drugs should be brought from home. There are no prevalent diseases or health hazards that pose a special risk to travelers, other than the heavy air pollution in the Athens area.

- **Crime:** Greece has one of the lowest crime rates in Western Europe. However, there have been isolated terrorist attacks in the recent past. The government and local police have increased security at airports and major tourist areas. If something does happen, contact the English-speaking "Tourist Police" who wear special green uniforms.

- **Pros and Cons of Living and Working in Greece:** Greece has many interesting tourist sites, including well-preserved relics of ancient Greece. Museums, archaeological sites, and the Greek Islands are some of the major attractions. Telecommunications services are adequate, but there is an equipment shortage. When renting a home or apartment, make sure it already has a phone, as it takes two years to have a new one installed, and the cost is high at about $300. Insist on air conditioning as the air pollution and heat are not easy to live with,

EMBASSY AND CONSULATE CONTACT INFORMATION:

THE GREEK EMBASSY
2221 MASSACHUSETTS AVE. NW
WASHINGTON, DC 20008
TEL: 202-667-3168

but bear in mind that electricity is very costly. Greece has one of the highest car rental rates in the world (around $500 a week for a subcompact). Read all fine print carefully on the auto rental lease. Driving after drinking is strictly prohibited. The Athens area has severe air pollution, and people with respiratory problems should come prepared.

GREEK CONSULATE GENERAL
69 EAST 79 ST.
NEW YORK, NY 10021
TEL: 212-988-5500

OTHER SOURCES OF INFORMATION:

GREEK NATIONALIST TOURIST INFORMATION
645 FIFTH AVE.
NEW YORK, NY 10022
TEL: 212-421-5777

COMPANIES/ORGANIZATIONS WITH OPERATIONS IN GREECE:

ALARM DEVICE MANUFACTURING
COMPANY, 114
AT&T INTERNATIONAL, 145
BANKERS TRUST NEW YORK
CORPORATION, 155
BAROID CORPORATION, 158
BOSE CORPORATION, 172
BRISTOL-MEYERS SQUIBB COMPANY, 175
THE COCA-COLA COMPANY, 202
COOPER POWER SYSTEMS, 213
D'ARCY MASIUS BENTON & BOWLES INC.,
225
DOW CORNING CORPORATION, 240
DRESSER INDUSTRIES, INC., 241
EASTMAN KODAK COMPANY, 246
EATON CORPORATION/CUTLER HAMMER,
247

ETHYL CORPORATION, 256
FMC CORPORATION, 266
HOLIDAY INNS WORLDWIDE, 302
KRAFT GENERAL FOODS INTERNATIONAL,
341
MARRIOTT CORPORATION, 360
NORTH AMERICAN PHILIPS CORPORATION,
389
PAINE WEBBER GROUP, INC., 403
PENROD DRILLING CORPORATION, 408
PROCTER & GAMBLE PHARMACEUTICALS,
INC., 426
SCHLEGEL CORPORATION, 451
SHEARSON LEHMAN BROTHERS, 460
STANDARD COMMERCIAL CORPORATION,
476
TAMBRANDS, INC., 486

GRENADA

- **Official Name:** Grenada

- **Capital:** St. George's

- **Location:** Grenada is an island nation located in the southeastern Caribbean Sea, approximately 100 miles from the island of Trinidad. It is bounded by the Atlantic Ocean to the northeast, east, and southeast, and the Caribbean Sea to the southwest, west, and northwest. Its land area totals 133 square miles, making Grenada nearly twice the size of Washington, D.C. The island is of volcanic origin, with a mountain range in the central region. Meadows, woodlands, and sandy beaches predominate throughout Grenada, with only 15 percent of arable land.

- **Language and Currency:** The official language of Grenada is English and it is used throughout business and government. The monetary unit is the East Caribbean (EC) dollar. The current exchange rate is EC$2.67 = U.S.$1 (March 1994).

- **Print Source of Information:** Zellers, Margaret, editor. *Fielding's Caribbean.* New York: Fielding Travel Books, William Morrow & Co., 1992.

EMBASSY AND CONSULATE CONTACT INFORMATION:

EMBASSY OF GRENADA
1701 NEW HAMPSHIRE AVE. NW
WASHINGTON, DC 20009
TEL: 202-265-2561

COMPANIES/ORGANIZATIONS WITH OPERATIONS IN GRENADA:

AMERICAN CANADIAN CARIBBEAN LINE, 123

INTERNATIONAL MARITIME RESOURCES, 317

GUADELOUPE

- **Official Name:** Department of Guadeloupe
- **Capital:** Basse-Terre
- **Location:** Guadeloupe is a group of islands in the Lesser Antilles, located in the eastern Caribbean Sea. It is bounded by Antigua and Barbuda to the north and Dominica to the south. It is comprised of two main islands, a small island group named Iles des Saintes, and five smaller islands. It has a total land area of 687 square miles, making it about ten times the size of Washington, D.C. Its terrain is varied, with one-third of the island occupied by forest. The eastern half consists of limestone beds, while Basse-Terre (the western half of the island) becomes more mountainous with steep gorges and rushing waterfalls. The coastlines are sheltered by banks of coral, which protect the vast white sand beaches.
- **Language and Currency:** French and Creole patois are the main languages spoken in Guadeloupe. If you are planning to live or work in Guadeloupe, you should have a basic knowledge of French. The monetary unit is the French franc. The current exchange rate is: 5.85 French francs = U.S.$1 (March 1994).
- **Print Source of Information:** Zeller, Margaret, editor. *Fielding's Caribbean.* New York: Fielding Travel Books, William Morrow & Co., 1992.

EMBASSY AND CONSULATE CONTACT INFORMATION:

EMBASSY OF FRANCE
4101 RESERVOIR RD. NW
WASHINGTON, DC 20007
TEL: 202-944-6000

COMPANIES/ORGANIZATIONS WITH OPERATIONS IN GUADELOUPE:

CLUB MED, INC., 201

GUAM

- **Official Name:** Territory of Guam

- **Capital:** Agana

- **Location:** A U.S. territory, Guam is the largest of the Mariana Islands in the western North Pacific Ocean. (Because Guam is a U.S. possession, it has no embassies or consulates.) The Marianas are the northernmost islands of Micronesia. With the exception of Guam, all of the other Mariana Islands are a commonwealth of the United States. Guam is about 1,350 miles south of Tokyo, Japan, and 3,300 miles southwest of Hawaii. Total land area is 209 square miles, or about three times the size of Washington, D.C. Guam's territory is covered by a mixture of mountains, forest, and farmland. In the southern region there are volcanic mountains. The island is surrounded by coral reefs, and the terrain features steep coastal cliffs and narrow coastal plains. Earthquakes occur occasionally.

- **Population, Cities, and American Residents:** The population of Guam is 145,000 (1991 est.). Over half the people are Chamorro, 25 percent are Filipino, and 10 percent are Caucasian. There are also some Chinese, Japanese, and Korean residents. The town of Agana is on the west coast of the island.

- **Language and Currency:** The official languages of Guam are English and Chamorro, and most people are bilingual. Japanese is also spoken in various parts of Guam. The monetary unit is the U.S. dollar.

- **Climate:** Guam has a tropical marine climate, usually very warm and humid, cooled off by northeast trade winds. It is dry from January to June, with the rainy season beginning in July and lasting until December. There is little temperature variation throughout the year.

- **Economy and Resources:** Guam is an organized, unincorporated territory of the United States, established in 1950. Today, Guam serves as a significant U.S. air and naval base in the Pacific. The economy is based primarily on military spending and tourism. Over the last two decades, tourism has seen rapid expansion; new hotels have been built and older ones restored. There is a small manufacturing sector that includes textiles, clothing, and food and beverages. There is also some petroleum refining. Well over half of the labor force is employed in the private sector, with the remainder employed by the government.

- **Cost of Living:** The cost of living is comparable to that of the United States.

- **Work Permits, Visas, etc.:** Guam is a U.S. territory, no visas or special documents are required for U.S. citizens.

- **Taxation:** Residents of Guam are subject to U.S. federal taxes.

- **Principal International Schools:** American schools are available.

- **Health Care:** Guam has modern medical facilities, and health standards are comparable to those in the United States.

- **Crime:** Tourist areas are subject to common crime, so it's wise to take the same precautions that you would in any large city in the United States.

- **Pros and Cons of Working and living in Guam:** Guam is a fairly modern island. Sanitation and health standards are good, as are telecommunications and transportation services. Housing is available, but arrangements should be made in advance to obtain the best selection and price. The balmy climate is Guam's major attraction. However, frequent squalls occur during the rainy season, and typhoons strike the island during August. Guam is also subject to earthquakes.

COMPANIES/ORGANIZATIONS WITH OPERATIONS IN GUAM:

AMERICAN PRESIDENT COMPANIES, LTD., 128
GANNETT COMPANY, INC., 272
NORTHWEST AIRLINES, INC., 390

PRUDENTIAL INSURANCE COMPANY OF AMERICA, 427
TW HOLDINGS, INC., 504

GUATEMALA

- **Official Name:** Republic of Guatemala

- **Capital:** Guatemala City

- **Location:** Guatemala lies in the northernmost section of Central America and has a total land area of 42,000 square miles, comparable in size to Tennessee. Guatemala's neighbors are Mexico, Belize, Honduras, and El Salvador. Its Pacific coastline is two hundred miles long and the northeast area of the country is bordered by an irregular Caribbean coastline of only 50 miles. The most populated area is in the Central Highland region which contains one fifth of the country's land surface. The Pacific plain is a narrow section between the mountains and the ocean, and the Caribbean lowlands have lush river valleys. The remaining and least populated third of Guatemala is in the north.

- **Population, Cities, and American Residents:** The population of Guatemala totals 9.7 million (1992 est.). Ladinos (mestizo, or those of mixed Indian and European ancestry) account for 56 percent of the population; the remaining 44 percent are Indian.

   Most American residents are employed in Guatemala's two largest cities: Guatemala City with 1.1 million, and Quezaltenango with 93,000 people (1991 est.).

- **Language and Currency:** The official language of Guatemala is Spanish, but English is widely spoken in the business sector. There are 23 other Indian languages spoken including Quiche, Cakchiquel, and Kekchi. The monetary unit is the quetzal. The exchange rate is 5.7 quetzals = U.S.$1 (August 30, 1993).

- **Climate:** Guatemala has a tropical climate, hot and humid in the lowlands, and cooler in the highlands. The country has two seasons; wet (from May through October), and dry (from November to April). Rain is most prevalent in central Guatemala with annual rainfall from 70-200 inches. In the dry months, rainfall averages 2 inches.

Temperatures in Guatemala are moderate year round, averaging 80°F. The country is subject to tropical storms and hurricanes.

- **Economy and Resources:** Guatemala's economy is dominated by the private sector, which is supported by government policies conducive to the flow of trade and investment. Agriculture and commerce each account for 25 percent of the GDP. Approximately 60 percent of the exports are agricultural and 57 percent of the labor force works in agriculture. Almost 35 percent of foreign trade is with the United States. Major exports include coffee, sugar, bananas, and crude petroleum. Guatemala has recently become self-sufficient in electrical energy due to the development of hydroelectric resources. As a result of poor economic conditions and political strife, the tourism industry struggled for some time.

- **Cost of Living:** At 85, the cost of living is lower than in the United States.

- **Work Permits, Visas, etc.:** A valid passport and visa are required to travel in Guatemala. If you are entering Guatemala from the United States, no vaccinations are necessary. For official or other information, direct inquiries to the embassy or consulate at the addresses below.

- **Taxation:** New tax laws are in effect as of July 1, 1992. Guatemala taxes its citizens, resident, and nonresident individuals on their compensation attributable to services rendered in the country. Nonresident aliens are taxed on earnings for work done in Guatemala regardless of where payment is made.

- **Principal International Schools:** International schools are available in Guatemala City. One is the American School of Guatemala, c/o the American Embassy Guatemala, Unit 3325, APO AA 34024, telephone 502-2-69-07-91.

- **Health Care:** Medical facilities are adequate in the more populated areas of Guatemala, such as Guatemala City. Do not rely on the advice of local pharmacists for medical advice; consult a local physician. Fees are very reasonable. Water in Guatemala City is chemically treated, but in rural areas may not be, so it should be boiled or filtered. It is recommended that visitors take malaria-preventive pills, and consider getting a typhoid booster vaccination if they are staying more than a few weeks. Be careful to eat only well-cooked meats, and take appropriate precautions with all vegetables and fruits. Tree bearing fruits are safe; however, fruits and vegetables that grow on the ground may be contaminated.

- **Crime:** Travelers to Guatemala are generally greeted with a courteous and friendly attitude, but as with many large cities, major tourist areas are a target for common crime. The State Department issues current travel advisories for any terrorist activity or banditry in affected areas. Contact them prior to departure for a recent update on any threatening conditions. Always lock vehicles; do not leave valuables in plain sight or unattended. In outlying areas, travel in a group and avoid any alleys or poorly lit areas. The use, possession, or sale of narcotics is prohibited and offenders are severely punished by law.

- **Pros and Cons of Living and Working in Guatemala:** Guatemala offers a varied and interesting cultural experience. The Ladino and Indian people each have unique traditions and handicrafts, and relics of Mayan civilization remain in the majestic mountains, tropical plains, and the lowland jungles and swamps. Despite the great progress Guatemala has made toward modernization, much of the country's folk customs remain unchanged. Because of the varied climate, almost anything will grow in Guatemala. More than 100 species of orchids grow among the forests. In its tropical location, it is subject to hurricanes and other storms. There are also numerous volcanoes in the mountains and frequent, violent earthquakes. Precautions must always be taken when preparing or buying food, or drinking the water.

- **Print Sources of Information:** *Guatemala Guide* by Paul Glassman, Passport Press, 1991.

EMBASSY AND CONSULATE CONTACT INFORMATION:

EMBASSY OF GUATEMALA
2220 R ST. NW
WASHINGTON, DC 20008
TEL: 202-745-4952

CONSULATE GENERAL OF GUATEMALA
57 PARK AVE.
NEW YORK, NY
TEL: 212-686-3837

COMPANIES/ORGANIZATIONS WITH OPERATIONS IN GUATEMALA:

ALBERTO-CULVER COMPANY, 115
ALEXANDER & ALEXANDER SERVICES, INC., 116
AMERICAN STANDARD, INC., 128
AVON PRODUCTS, INC., 149
THE COCA-COLA COMPANY, 202
CONSERVATION INTERNATIONAL, 545
EXXON CHEMICAL COMPANY, 257
GOODYEAR TIRE & RUBBER COMPANY, 284
HANSON INDUSTRIES, 295

KELLOGG COMPANY, 330
PHELPS DODGE CORPORATION, 412
PHILLIPS-VAN HEUSEN CORPORATION, 415
PILLSBURY COMPANY, 416
PROJECT HOPE, 563
TECHNOSERVE, INC., 565
TEXACO OIL COMPANY, 493
U.S. WHEAT ASSOCIATES, 511
UNIVERSAL FOODS CORPORATION, 513

GUINEA

- **Official Name:** Republic of Guinea
- **Capital:** Conakry
- **Location:** Guinea is located in western Africa and is bounded by Guinea-Bissau to the northwest, Senegal to the north, Mali to the northeast, Côte d'Ivoire to the southeast, Liberia and Sierra Leone to the south, and the Atlantic Ocean to the west. Its land area totals 95,000 square miles, making Guinea slightly smaller than Oregon. Its terrain is varied, ranging from flat lands along the coast to mountainous territory toward the interior section.
- **Language and Currency:** The official language of Guinea is French, which is spoken throughout business and govern-

EMBASSY AND CONSULATE CONTACT INFORMATION:

EMBASSY OF THE REPUBLIC OF GUINEA
2112 LEROY PLACE NW
WASHINGTON, DC 20008
TEL: 202-483-9420

ment. Other tribal languages are also spoken. If you plan to live or work in Guinea, you should have a basic knowledge of French. The monetary unit is the Guinean franc. The current exchange rate is: 1,000 Guinean francs = U.S.$1 (March 1994).

OTHER SOURCES OF INFORMATION:

FOR INFORMATION ON CURRENT ECONOMIC TRENDS, OR COMMERCIAL DEVELOPMENT CONTACT:

INTERNATIONAL TRADE ADMINISTRATION

U.S. DEPARTMENT OF COMMERCE

WASHINGTON, DC 20230

COMPANIES/ORGANIZATIONS WITH OPERATIONS IN GUINEA:

CHEVRON CORPORATION, 193

CHEVRON OVERSEAS PETROLEUM, INC., 194

DAMES & MOORE, 223

PHILLIPS PETROLEUM COMPANY, 415

HONDURAS

- **Official Name:** Republic of Honduras
- **Capital:** Tegucigalpa
- **Location:** Honduras is located on the land bridge of Central America. It is bounded by the Caribbean Sea to the north, Nicaragua to the south, and Guatemala and El Salvador to the west. With a total land area of 43,277 square miles, Honduras is slightly larger than Tennessee. It has four main regions: the northern coast has a rich fertile area, along with grasslands, swamps and forests; the southern coast is similar to the northern coast, but it receives less rain; the mountainous interior covers two-thirds of Honduras; and the northeastern plain, referred to as "the Mosquito Coast," is the least developed region in the country. Rain forests cover most of this sparsely populated section.
- **Population, Cities, and American Residents:** The population of Honduras totals 5.4 million (1992 est.), with Mestizos accounting for 90 percent, Indians 7 percent, blacks 2 percent, and white 1 percent.

   Most American residents are employed in Honduras's two largest cities: Tegucigalpa with 608,000 people and San Pedro Sula with 310,000.
- **Language and Currency:** The official language of Honduras is Spanish. English is widely spoken in northern areas, but familiarity with Spanish is helpful on long-term assignment in Honduras. The monetary unit is the lempira. The exchange rate is 7 lempiras = U.S.$1 (December 1993).
- **Climate:** Honduras has a tropical climate with an average year-round temperature of 88°F along the coast. The highlands tend to be a bit cooler. The rainy season lasts from May to December in the south-central regions; May to February in the north. Rain falls throughout the year in the northeast.
- **Economy and Resources:** The Hondurans have low average incomes. Agriculture dominates, accounting for 30 percent of the gross domestic product (GDP), and

employing two-thirds of the labor force. Agriculture also supplies two-thirds of the nation's major exports. The services sector accounts for nearly half of the GDP and employs another 20 percent of the work force. Chief exports are bananas, shrimp, lobster, and coffee, primarily to the United States and European nations.

Political unrest and civil disorders have plagued this struggling nation for some time. Many structural problems still face Honduras, including a rapidly growing population, a high unemployment rate of 15 percent, an underemployment rate as high as 40 percent of the work force, an inefficient public sector, and the lack of basic services. Its exports (mainly coffee and bananas) are subject to fluctuating market prices, which have led to economic setbacks in past years. Honduras is beginning to show signs of economic growth, due partly to direct foreign investments and economic assistance from the United States.

- **Cost of Living:** At 82, the cost of living is lower than in the United States.

- **Work Permits, Visas, etc.:** A passport is required for travel in Honduras. A business visa is required to work in Honduras, and may be applied for by mail. Allow ample time for this. Officials require a company letter stating the purpose of the trip and the proposed length of stay. If you are entering Honduras from the United States no vaccinations are required. For official or other information direct inquiries to the embassy or consulate at the addresses below.

- **Taxation:** Contact the embassy or consulate of Honduras for current tax information.

- **Principal International Schools:** American schools are available.

- **Health Care:** Medical facilities are limited to the major cities in Honduras. Having supplemental medical insurance for overseas coverage is highly recommended, because U.S. coverage is not always accepted. Sanitation standards are below those found in the United States. Water is not potable, and precautions should be taken with meats, dairy products, and raw fruits and vegetables. Several diseases are prevalent, including cholera, malaria, typhoid, and hepatitis.

- **Crime:** Border conflicts continue to erupt between Honduras and neighboring countries (primarily El Salvador and Nicaragua). Bandit groups and robbers are prevalent, especially in remote areas. Stay on the main roads. If you do cross the border your vehicle is likely to be thoroughly searched by officials. Street crime is also on the rise in Honduras, with robberies, muggings, and purse snatching occurring in major tourist areas. Leave all valuables at home or locked away. When traveling in your car it's safer to keep windows rolled up and doors locked.

- **Pros and Cons of Working and Living in Honduras:** Honduras offers tourists unique scenery, with beaches, volcanoes, and the Mayan ruins at Copan. However, it is a poor country with many problems and internal conflicts. Telecommunications and transportation services are adequate in tourist areas. Housing is available, but accommodations are limited so it's best to plan ahead. The climate is tropical but cooler during the winter. The rainy season is from May to December, and precipitation falls daily; rain gear is a must. Concerning currency, no personal checks are cashed for U.S.

citizens in this country. It is also very difficult to transfer funds from abroad to Honduras. Bring a sufficient amount of travelers checks, cash, or credit cards.

Crime is a main drawback. Currently, the travel warning from the U.S. State Department has been lifted, but precautions are still warranted. Border skirmishes are frequent, and there are mine fields in these areas, particularly on the Honduran/ Nicaraguan border. It is vital that travelers use only main roads, and avoid remote sections of the country. Check with the Department of State's Citizen Emergency Center (202-647-5225) for a current update on travel in Honduras.

- **Print Sources of Information:** American University's *Area Handbook for Honduras* (1984) is available from the Superintendent of Documents, U.S. Government Printing Office, Washington, D.C., 20402.

EMBASSY AND CONSULATE CONTACT INFORMATION:

EMBASSY OF THE REPUBLIC OF HONDURAS
3007 TILDEN ST. NW
WASHINGTON, DC 20008
TEL: 202-966-7702

COMPANIES/ORGANIZATIONS WITH OPERATIONS IN HONDURAS:

INTERNATIONAL CITY MANAGEMENT ASSOCIATION, 548

PHILLIPS-VAN HEUSEN CORPORATION, 415

POPULATION COUNCIL, 562

PROJECT HOPE, 563

SEA-LAND SERVICE, INC., 454

HONG KONG

- **Official Name:** British Dependent Territory of Hong Kong

- **Capital:** Victoria

- **Location:** Hong Kong is a colony of the United Kingdom located on the southeastern coast of China. It has two main islands, Hong Kong and Lantau, 235 smaller islands, and the mainland New Territories. The whole area totals 414 square miles, and is about five times the size of Washington, D.C. The two major urban areas are Victoria and Kowloon, which account for 10 percent of the colony's land. The remaining regions are hills, mountainous terrain, and lush valleys.

- **Population, Cities, and American Residents:** The population of Hong Kong totals 5.9 million people (1991 est.). Chinese account for 98 percent, with the remaining 2 percent Europeans and other ethnic origins.

  Most American residents are employed in Hong Kong's two major cities: Victoria with 1 million, and Kowloon with 2 million people (1990 est.).

- **Language and Currency:** The official languages are Chinese (Cantonese, a dialect of Chinese), and English. English is the accepted language of business and government. Throughout the colony, English is widely spoken, especially in daily life (taxis, storekeepers). The police who speak fluent English wear a red patch below their shoulder number. Comparative to the U.S. dollar, the monetary unit is the Hong Kong dollar (HK$) and it is divided into 100 cents. Bills are HK$1,000, 500, 100, 50, 20, and 10. Coins are HK$5, HK$2, HK$1, and 50, 20, and 10 cents. The exchange rate is 1 Hong Kong dollar = U.S.$.13 (July 30,1993).

- **Climate:** The climate of Hong Kong is subtropical, and subject to monsoons. Summers are usually hot and rainy with the winters cool and dry. Average temperatures range from 59°F in February to 90°F in July. September through December are the most enjoyable months.

- **Economy and Resources:** Hong Kong has a thriving economy with a major import-export market and it is one of the world's top financial centers, relying on trade and its skilled work force for its prosperity. Trade, manufacturing, finance, and tourism are all important sectors to the success of Hong Kong's economy. Manufacturing accounts for 36 percent of the work force, and overseas companies are responsible for 10 percent of the industrial employment. Key products include electronics, building materials, textiles, and chemicals. Major exports include clothing, textiles, and electrical goods. The colony operates as a very free economy with little government control over manufacturers. There are no import tariffs, and corporate and income taxes were decreased in 1987. Though it is now a British colony, Hong Kong is scheduled to revert back to China in 1997. The stability and success of the economy may be at risk when the change occurs, although the Chinese are sure to be reluctant to interfere too much with Hong Kong's booming economy.

- **Cost of Living:** At 135, the cost of living is higher than in the United States.

- **Work Permits, Visas, etc.:** A valid passport is necessary to travel in China, and visas are required of anyone coming to reside, study, or work in Hong Kong for more than one month. Submit the proper application two months before the planned trip, as it is sent to Hong Kong for approval. If you are entering Hong Kong from the United States, no vaccinations are needed. However, the U.S. State Department recommends shots against cholera and yellow fever, gamma globulin for hepatitis, and typhoid, tetanus, and polio shots for young children. For official or other information, direct inquiries to the embassy or consulate at the addresses below.

- **Taxation:** In 1989, Hong Kong decreased its tax rates to a maximum of 15 percent on personal income with several exemptions allowed. For a current update on tax laws, contact the Hong Kong Trade Development Council and ask for the pamphlet, Synopsis of Taxation in Hong Kong. Also, many international tax firms have offices in Hong Kong and publish concise studies on local tax regulations.

- **Principal International Schools:** Private international schools are available in Hong Kong. The average tuition for an American school is $7,500.

- **Health Care:** Both medical and dental facilities are excellent in Hong Kong with fees varying from clinic to clinic. The colony has been free from epidemics for some years now, but infectious hepatitis is an ever-present hazard. Because of the depletion of minerals in the soil through the years, taking vitamins is strongly recommended. Sanitary conditions are very good, and dairy products are safe for consumption. Cook all meats and fish thoroughly and take appropriate precautions with all fruits and vegetables. The government has approved the drinking of water from main systems. To be on the safe side, however, either boil tap water or use bottled water, but don't drink from wells and pumps; and be mindful of where your ice comes from.

- **Crime:** Hong Kong has a low crime rate. Walking the streets during the day or evening hours is safe, and people are friendly. Beware of pickpockets, however, as tourist areas are major targets for petty thieves.

- **Pros and Cons of Living and Working in Hong Kong:** Hong Kong is a vibrant and interesting colony. There is an exciting mixture of attractions from ultramodern skyscrapers and crowded harbors, to the local peasants who till the soil with plows drawn by water buffaloes. Transportation, telecommunications and the safety of tourist areas are all a plus. Medical care is excellent, and the sightseeing and sophisticated restaurants and night life offer something for everyone. However, the urban areas are very crowded, pollution is a problem, and it takes some time to get used to the contrast between air-conditioned offices and the blistering heat of the streets. As Hong Kong is a British colony, drive on the left. Also, as a visitor, keep your driver's license (or an ID with a photo) with you at all times. It is required by law.

EMBASSY AND CONSULATE CONTACT INFORMATION:

EMBASSY OF GREAT BRITAIN
HONG KONG GOVERNMENT OFFICE
1233 20TH ST. NW, STE. 504
WASHINGTON, DC 20038
TEL: 202-331-8947

HONG KONG ECONOMIC AFFAIRS OFFICE
126 EAST 56TH ST.
NEW YORK, NY 10022

OTHER SOURCES OF INFORMATION:

HONG KONG TRADE DEVELOPMENT COUNCIL
673 FIFTH AVE.
NEW YORK, NY 10022
TEL: 212-838-8688

COMPANIES/ORGANIZATIONS WITH OPERATIONS IN HONG KONG:

ABBOTT LABORATORIES, 109
AIRBORNE EXPRESS, 112
ALARM DEVICE MANUFACTURING COMPANY, 114
ALBERTO-CULVER COMPANY, 115
AMERICAN APPRAISAL ASSOCIATES, INC., 121
AMERICAN EXPRESS BANK, LTD., 124
AMERICAN EXPRESS COMPANY—TRAVEL RELATED SERVICES, 125
AMERICAN INTERNATIONAL GROUP, 127
AMERICAN PRESIDENT COMPANIES, LTD., 128
AMOCO CORPORATION, 131
AMP, INC., 132
AMR/AMERICAN AIRLINES, 133
ANSELL INTERNATIONAL, 135
ANTHONY INDUSTRIES, 135
APPLE COMPUTER, INC., 136

ARMSTRONG WORLD INDUSTRIES, INC., 141
AST RESEARCH, INC., 144
AT&T INTERNATIONAL, 145
AVON PRODUCTS, INC., 149
BACKER SPIELVOGEL & BATES WORLDWIDE, INC., 150
THE BANK OF NEW YORK COMPANY, INC., 154
BANKAMERICA CORPORATION, 155
BANKERS TRUST NEW YORK CORPORATION, 155
BAUSCH & LOMB, INC., 159
BEAR STEARNS COMPANIES, INC., 161
BECKMAN INSTRUMENTS, INC., 162
BIO-RAD LABORATORIES, 166
W. H. BRADY COMPANY, 173
BRISTOL-MEYERS SQUIBB COMPANY, 175
BROWN GROUP, INC., 176
BROWNING-FERRIS INDUSTRIES, 177

A
M
E
R
I
C
A
N

J
O
B
S

A
B
R
O
A
D

BUCK CONSULTANTS, INC., 178
BURLINGTON AIR EXPRESS, 179
BURNS & ROE, INC., 180
BURSON-MARSTELLER, 180
CAMPBELL SOUP COMPANY, 183
CARGILL INCORPORATED, 184
CHASE MANHATTAN CORPORATION, 190
BERNARD CHAUS, INC., 191
CHEMICAL BANKING CORPORATION, 191
CITICORP, 198
CLOROX COMPANY, 199
THE COCA-COLA COMPANY, 202
COMMODORE INTERNATIONAL LTD., 206
COMPUTER ASSOCIATES INTERNATIONAL,
    INC., 207
CONTINENTAL BANK CORPORATION, 210
COOPERS & LYBRAND, 214
CORE STATES FINANCIAL CORPORATION,
    215
CORNING INCORPORATED, 215
COUDERT BROTHERS LAW FIRM, 217
CTS CORPORATION, 220
CUBIC CORPORATION, 220
LEO A. DALY COMPANY, 223
DAMES & MOORE, 223
D'ARCY MASIUS BENTON & BOWLES INC.,
    225
DATA GENERAL CORPORATION, 225
DELTA AIR LINES, INC., 232
DIEBOLD INCORPORATED, 235
DOMINO'S PIZZA, INC., 237
DONALDSON COMPANY, INC., 237
DOW CORNING CORPORATION, 240
DOW JONES & COMPANY, INC., 241
DRESSER INDUSTRIES, INC., 241
DURACELL, INC., 244
EASTMAN KODAK COMPANY, 246
ELECTRONIC DATA SYSTEMS
    CORPORATION, 249
EMERY WORLDWIDE, 252
ENCORE COMPUTER CORPORATION, 252
EXXON CORPORATION, 258
FEDERAL EXPRESS CORPORATION, 260
FIRST CHICAGO CORPORATION, 262
GANNETT COMPANY, INC., 272
GENERAL ELECTRIC COMPANY (GE), 275
GENERAL FOODS USA, 276
GERBER PRODUCTS COMPANY, 280
GETZ BROTHERS COMPANY, INC., 281
GOLDMAN SACHS & COMPANY, 283

W. R. GRACE & COMPANY, 285
GRACO, INC., 286
GREY ADVERTISING, INC., 288
GTE DIRECTORIES CORPORATION, 289
HALLIBURTON COMPANY, 292
HALLIBURTON COMPANY/HALLIBURTON
    SERVICES DIVISION, 293
HAMLIN, INC., 294
HEWLETT-PACKARD COMPANY, 300
HILL & KNOWLTON, INC., 301
HONEYWELL, INC., 303
HUGHES CHRISTENSEN COMPANY, 307
HYATT INTERNATIONAL CORPORATION,
    308
ICF KAISER ENGINEERS, 308
INTERGRAPH CORPORATION, 314
INTERNATIONAL BUSINESS MACHINES
    (IBM), 315
INTERNATIONAL FLAVORS &
    FRAGRANCES, INC., 317
INTERNATIONAL PAPER COMPANY, 318
INTERTRANS CORPORATION, 320
ITT CORPORATION, 321
ITT HARTFORD INSURANCE GROUP, 321
ITT SHERATON CORPORATION, 322
JOHNSON & HIGGINS, 324
JOHNSON & JOHNSON, 325
JONES, DAY, REAVIS & POGUE, INC., 326
KELLWOOD COMPANY, 331
KETCHUM INTERNATIONAL, 334
KEYSTONE INTERNATIONAL, 334
KFC CORPORATION, 335
KIDDER PEABODY GROUP & COMPANY,
    INC., 335
KNIGHT-RIDDER, INC., 338
KNOLL INTERNATIONAL, 338
KOCH INDUSTRIES, INC., 339
KORN/FERRY INTERNATIONAL, 340
LEVI STRAUSS ASSOCIATES, INC., 344
LINTAS: WORLDWIDE, 346
LITTON INDUSTRIES, INC., 348
LIZ CLAIBORNE, INC., 348
LOCTITE CORPORATION, 349
LUBRIZOL CORPORATION, 353
MATTEL, INC., 363
MCGRAW-HILL, INC., 357
MCKINSEY & COMPANY, INC., 357
MEASUREX CORPORATION, 366
MEMOREX TELEX CORPORATION, 367
MERCK & COMPANY, INC., 368

MERRILL LYNCH & COMPANY, INC., 369
MOBIL OIL CORPORATION, 375
MONSANTO COMPANY, 377
J. P. MORGAN & COMPANY, INC., 378
MORGAN STANLEY GROUP, INC., 379
MORTON INTERNATIONAL, 380
NALCO CHEMICAL COMPANY, 382
NATIONAL SEMICONDUCTOR
    CORPORATION, 383
NELLCOR, INC., 385
NEWSWEEK INTERNATIONAL, 387
NORDSON CORPORATION, 389
NORTHWEST AIRLINES, INC., 390
NORWEST CORPORATION, 391
NOVELL, INC., 392
NYNEX CORPORATION, 392
OGILVY & MATHER, 395
OTIS ELEVATOR COMPANY: WORLD
    HEADQUARTERS, 399
OUTBOARD MARINE CORPORATION, 399
PAINE WEBBER GROUP, INC., 403
PARSONS BRINKERHOFF, 406
J. C. PENNEY COMPANY, INC., 407
PERKIN-ELMER CORPORATION, 410
PHILLIPS PETROLEUM COMPANY, 415
PHILLIPS-VAN HEUSEN CORPORATION,
    415
PRUDENTIAL INSURANCE COMPANY OF
    AMERICA, 427
QUME CORPORATION, 429
READER'S DIGEST ASSOCIATION, INC.,
    432
ROBERTSON CECO, 440
ROCKWELL INTERNATIONAL
    CORPORATION, 441
ROHM & HAAS COMPANY, 442
ROLLINS HUDIG HALL INTERNATIONAL,
    443
ROSEMOUNT, INC., 443
RUSSELL REYNOLDS ASSOCIATES, INC.,
    446
SALOMON, INC., 449
SCOTT PAPER COMPANY, 453

SEA-LAND SERVICE, INC., 454
SEALED AIR CORPORATION, 455
SENSORMATIC ELECTRONICS
    CORPORATION, 457
SGS CONTROL SERVICES, 458
SHEARSON LEHMAN BROTHERS, 460
SHIPLEY COMPANY, INC., 461
SIGNODE PACKAGING SYSTEMS, 462
SILICONIX, 462
SKADDEN, ARPS, SLATE, MEAGHER &
    FLOM, 465
SKIDMORE, OWINGS & MERRILL, 465
SONY PICTURES ENTERTAINMENT, 471
STATE STREET BOSTON CORPORATION,
    478
TANDY CORPORATION, 487
TEKTRONIX, INC., 488
TELEDYNE, INC., 489
TELLABS OPERATIONS, INC., 489
TEXACO OIL COMPANY, 493
THERMCO SYSTEMS, INC., 495
3M COMPANY, 496
TIME, INC., 497
TIME-WARNER, INC., 498
TOWERS PERRIN, INC., 499
TOYS "R" US, INC., 500
TRANE COMPANY, 501
TRINOVA CORPORATION, 502
TURNER STEINER INTERNATIONAL, INC.,
    504
TYSON FOODS, INC., 505
UNION CAMP CORPORATION, 507
UNISYS CORPORATION, 508
UOP, INC., 514
VF CORPORATION, 517
WARNER-LAMBERT COMPANY, 522
WENDY'S INTERNATIONAL, INC., 524
WEYERHAEUSER COMPANY, 526
WORLD COURIER MANAGEMENT, INC.,
    529
WILLIAM WRIGLEY JR. COMPANY, 529
YORK INTERNATIONAL, INC., 532
YOUNG & RUBICAM, INC., 533

C
O
U
N
T
R
Y

P
R
O
F
I
L
E
S

HUNGARY

- **Official Name:** Hungarian Republic
- **Location:** Hungary is a landlocked country located in Central Europe. It is bounded by Slovakia to the north, the Ukraine to the northeast, Romania to the east, Yugoslavia to

the south and Austria to the west. Its total land area is 93,030 square miles, making it slightly smaller than Indiana. Hungary's four main land regions are the Great Plain, Transdanubia, the Little Plain, and the Northern Highlands. Low-lying plains comprise two-thirds of the territory, the land rising no higher than 650 feet above sea level. The highest elevation in Hungary is in the Matra Hills area. Mount Kekes rises to 3,000 feet above sea level.

- **Population, Cities, and American Residents:** The population of Hungary totals 10.5 million people (1992 est.). Hungarians account for 96 percent, Germans for 1.6 percent, Slovaks for 1.1 percent, Southern Slavs for 0.3 percent, and Romanians for 0.2 percent.

  Most American residents are employed in Hungary's three largest cities: Budapest with 2 million people, Debrecen with 212,000, and Miskole with 196,000 people (1990 est.).

- **Language and Currency:** The official language is Hungarian, but German and English are widely used in business circles throughout the country. The monetary unit is the forint, written as Ft. The exchange rate is 1 Hungarian Ft = U.S.$.011; 94 forints = U.S.$1 (July 30, 1993).

- **Climate:** Hungary has a continental climate with cold winters and hot summers with little variation throughout the country. The annual mean temperature is 50°F. The coldest month is January, when temperatures range from 25°F to 32°F. July is the warmest month of the year with an average temperature of 68°F. Rain occurs most often in May.

- **Economy and Resources:** The mainstay of the Hungarian economy is manufacturing, which accounts for 36 percent of Gross Domestic Product (GDP), and along with construction, employs nearly 40 percent of the labor force. Main industries are metallurgy, machinery and equipment, chemicals, food processing, textiles, and engineering. Agriculture employs 17 percent of the labor force, with principal products including cereals, oil seeds, vegetables, sugar beets, grapes, potatoes, and livestock. A large percentage of foreign trade is controlled by a state monopoly. Major export customers are Russia and the European Community.

  In 1989, a parliamentary democracy was established, after four decades of rule by the Communist Party. Sweeping government reforms established a free market economy, a welcome change from the economic stagnation Hungary had struggled with for years. Its factories still need to be updated and modernized, central planning must be dismantled, and the foreign debt must be reduced, but he private sector is expanding, and joint ventures with foreign investors are increasing. Compared to other East European nations, Hungary has some advantages. It offers a favorable climate for foreign business, and has more experience in private enterprise systems. The financial services area is expected to be an economic growth sector. With austerity programs in effect, the Hungarian people are learning to cope with the social impact of this reconstruction period.

- **Cost of Living:** At 96, the cost of living is comparable to that of the United States.

- **Work Permits, Visas, etc.:** A valid passport is required to travel in Hungary, and depending on the length of stay, single and multiple-entry visas are available after arrival. When entering Hungary from the United States, no vaccinations are necessary. For official or other information, direct inquiries to the embassy or consulate at the addresses below.

- **Taxation:** Hungary's personal income tax is assessed on both foreign and domestic income for residents of Hungary. To qualify as a resident, one must live in Hungary for 183 days during a calendar year or own a home in Hungary. Various exemptions or deductions may apply to foreign residents.

- **Principal International Schools:** International schools are available in Budapest. Tuition for an American school is about $6,000 per year.

- **Health Care:** Medical services in Hungary are very good, with modern hospitals and clinics. First-aid and hospital transport services are free to foreign visitors, but fees are charged for examinations and treatment. Pharmacies are located throughout the country, but many medicines (especially painkillers) require a prescription. Sanitary standards are very high throughout Hungary. Water is safe to drink, and there are no special health hazards or diseases that pose a threat to tourists.

- **Crime:** Hungary is a relatively safe country to visit. The rate of common crime is very low, and it's rare to see a policeman patrolling the streets. No special precautions are necessary.

- **Pros and Cons of Living and Working in Hungary:** Hungary is a modern country with considerable old world charm. It has museums, opera houses, theaters, and an abundance of parks and gardens. A major attraction will be the 1995 World's Fair to be jointly held in Vienna and Budapest. Transportation services as well as health and sanitation standards are good. Telecommunications services are reliable but expensive. Housing is available and is usually obtainable through a rental agent, with one month's rent is usually required as a deposit. Try to find a furnished unit as local merchandise is of medium to low quality.

EMBASSY AND CONSULATE CONTACT INFORMATION:

HUNGARIAN EMBASSY
3910 SHOEMAKER ST. NW
WASHINGTON, DC 20008
TEL: 202-362-6737

CONSULATE GENERAL
8 EAST 75TH ST.
NEW YORK, NY 10021
TEL: 212-879-4126

OTHER SOURCES OF INFORMATION:

THE U.S.-HUNGARIAN BUSINESS COUNCIL
c/o U.S. CHAMBER OF COMMERCE
1615 H ST. NW
WASHINGTON, DC 20062
TEL: 202-463-5482

COMPANIES/ORGANIZATIONS WITH OPERATIONS IN HUNGARY:

AMERICAN INTERNATIONAL GROUP, 127
CH2M HILL INTERNATIONAL, LTD., 195
DEBEVOISE & PLIMPTON, 229
ERNST & YOUNG, 255
GENERAL ELECTRIC COMPANY (GE), 275

GUARDIAN INDUSTRIES CORPORATION, 290
HYATT INTERNATIONAL CORPORATION, 308
JOHNSON & JOHNSON, 325

KFC CORPORATION, 335
KLYNVELD PEAT MARWICK GOERDELER
    (KPMG), 337
KORN/FERRY INTERNATIONAL, 340
KRAFT GENERAL FOODS INTERNATIONAL,
    341
MACRO SYSTEMS, INC., 358
PRICE WATERHOUSE, 424

PROJECT HOPE, 563
RALSTON PURINA COMPANY, 430
RUBBERMAID, INC., 445
SCHERING-PLOUGH CORPORATION, 450
SHEARMAN & STERLING, 460
US WEST, INC., 515
VF CORPORATION, 517

INDIA

- **Official Name:** Republic of India

- **Capital:** New Delhi

- **Location:** India is regarded as a subcontinent because of its vast area; it dominates South Asia geographically. It is bordered on the east by the Bay of Bengal and on the west and south by the Arabian Sea, part of the Indian Ocean. Sri Lanka, formerly Ceylon, lies off the southeastern point of the peninsula. The total land area is 1,269,219 square miles and it is slightly larger than one-third of the size of the United States. It has three main geographic areas: the Himalayas, which run along the whole northern border; the densely populated Gangetic Plains in the North, whose water source is the Ganges River; and the peninsula, which includes the Deccan plateau.

- **Population, Cities, and American Residents:** The population of India totals 889 million (1992 est.). Indo-Aryan people account for 72 percent, and Dravidian 25 percent. The remaining 3 percent are Mongoloid and other ethnic groups.

    Most American residents are employed in India's three largest cities: Calcutta, with 9.2 million, Bombay with 8.2 million, and New Delhi with 7.2 million people (1991 est.). Calcutta is a major manufacturing, commercial, and shipping center.

- **Language and Currency:** The official language in India is Hindi. However, the language of business in English, and fourteen other languages are considered official and recognized for public use throughout India. Forty-five percent of the people speak Hindi or a related dialect. The monetary unit is the rupee (R, Rs). It is divided into 100 paise. Bills: Rs 500, 100, 20, 10, 5, 2, and 1. Coins: R1, and 50, 25, 20, 10, 5, 3, 2, and 1 paise. It is a good idea to always have a small amount of change on hand, as there is usually a shortage, especially with taxis or vendors. The exchange rate is 1 Indian rupee = U.S.$.032 (July 30, 1993).

- **Climate:** The climate of India varies due to the vast area, but most of the country is tropical or subtropical and subject to monsoon winds, which arrive with torrential rains during the summer season. New Delhi's temperatures range from 45°F in January to 117°F in July. Bombay has an annual average temperature of 80°F, with the rainy season from June through September (70-80 inches expected). Calcutta is damp a good part of the year, with humidity exceeding 90 percent from May through October. The more pleasant months are from mid-December through February when the temperatures are cooler, about 77°F during the day and 50°F at night.

- **Economy and Resources:** India has a per capita income of $300, and is one of the poorest countries in the world. Agriculture is the major economic sector, with 70 percent of the people earning a living from the land. Agriculture is responsible for one-third of the country's gross domestic product (GDP) and such major exports include cotton and jute textiles, tea, rice, and other cereals. There is an abundance of natural mineral resources, which have only been partially exploited. Coal is a major export (India has the fourth largest reserves in the world), and other mineral exports are iron ore, bauxite, and manganese. With so many natural resources, India has the potential for a prosperous, economic future, but intractable problems exist. Excessive government control, frequent power shortages, outdated physical plants, and overpopulation make economic progress very difficult.

- **Cost of Living:** At 75, the cost of living is lower than in the United States.

- **Work Permits, Visas, etc.:** A valid passport and visa are required to travel in India. A tourist visa is valid for up to a four month stay and must be obtained in advance. A business visa requires two application forms, two photos, and business letter stating the purpose of the trip. If you are entering India from the United States, no vaccinations are required, but anti-malaria tablets and typhoid and polio shots are recommended. An AIDS test is required for all students and anyone over eighteen years of age staying for more than one year; a U.S. test is usually accepted. For official or other information, direct inquiries to the embassy or consulate at the addresses below.

- **Taxation:** There is a personal income tax for all residents of India. The rates apply on a progressive scale against taxable income and are very high. The United States has some provisions for tax credits (education of children, etc.) with India.

- **Principal International Schools:** Two accredited international schools are located in the Delhi area. The American Embassy School and the Hebron School offer classes from K-12. The former teaches the U.S. curriculum and the latter teaches the British system. Tuition for the American Embassy School is $8,300 per year. The Hebron School's annual tuition is $1,100.

- **Health Care:** India is one of the most disease-ridden countries in the world, with poor sanitation throughout the country. None of its cities has complete sewage treatment systems, and it has been estimated that more than 80 percent of all sickness in India is related to unsafe water. All drinking water should be boiled, including water used for brushing teeth. Dairy products are unsafe as are many meat products, especially pork. Take appropriate precautions with all fruits and vegetables. Gastrointestinal upsets are common, so be careful when choosing a public restaurant. Malaria is endemic in India; begin anti-malaria pills two weeks before arrival. If domestic help is used, a medical check-up is recommended as TB is widespread throughout India. Local hospitals are not comparable to U.S. standards, but facilities in Bombay and Calcutta are better than those in New Delhi. Laboratory facilities are limited and very poor in quality. If you have a routine health problem, it's best to leave the country for treatment. (Singapore is fairly close and has good medical facilities.)

- **Crime:** Most areas of India are generally safe for travel, but social disintegration is widespread throughout India, and beggars are everywhere. There have been outbreaks of terrorism in the Kashmir portion of the State of Jammu and the State of Assam in recent years, so it is advisable to check with the Consular Section of the American Embassy of New Delhi for current information on the security situation in India.

- **Pros and Cons of Living and Working in India:** India is a very diverse nation of great natural beauty, with unique cultural heritage. The country has museums, historic sites, and galleries. Beaches are crowded, but adequate. Because of its size, India has a wide variety of cultures and peoples from tropical coasts along the Indian Ocean to the hill regions of Kashmir. With India's population growing at 2 percent a year, it will soon overtake China as the world's most populous country. It is chronically overcrowded, and sanitation is barely acceptable. Cows compete for road space with cars, and local transportation is slow, with the only subway available in Calcutta. There is a severe housing shortage especially in large urban areas, and it can take six months to establish permanent accommodations. Health standards are poor (TB and malaria are widespread, and there is a high incidence of typhoid). The climate in most areas is uncomfortably hot and muggy, and the seasonal monsoon winds and torrential rains that accompany them often wreak havoc during the summer season.

EMBASSY AND CONSULATE CONTACT INFORMATION:

EMBASSY OF INDIA
2107 MASSACHUSETTS AVE. NW
WASHINGTON, DC 20008
TEL: 202-939-7000
FAX: 202-939-7027

CONSULATE GENERAL OF INDIA
3 EAST 64TH ST.
NEW YORK, NY 10021
TEL: 212-879-7800

OTHER SOURCES OF INFORMATION:

GOVERNMENT OF INDIA TOURIST OFFICES
30 ROCKEFELLER PLAZA
15 NORTH MEZZANINE
NEW YORK, NY
FAX: 212-586-4901
TEL: 212-582-3274

COMPANIES/ORGANIZATIONS WITH OPERATIONS IN INDIA:

ABBOTT LABORATORIES, 109
ABEX INC./FISHER SCIENTIFIC
    INTERNATIONAL, INC., 110
ALLEN-BRADLEY COMPANY, INC., 116
AMERICAN EXPRESS COMPANY—TRAVEL
    RELATED SERVICES, 125
AMERICAN HOME PRODUCTS
    CORPORATION, 126
ARMSTRONG WORLD INDUSTRIES, INC.,
    141
BACKER SPIELVOGEL & BATES
    WORLDWIDE, INC., 150
BANKERS TRUST NEW YORK
    CORPORATION, 155
LOUIS BERGER INTERNATIONAL INC., 165

CHASE MANHATTAN CORPORATION, 190
CHEVRON CHEMICAL COMPANY, 192
CORNING INCORPORATED, 215
CUMMINS ENGINE COMPANY, INC., 221
DANA CORPORATION, 224
D'ARCY MASIUS BENTON & BOWLES INC.,
    225
DH TECHNOLOGY, INC., 233
DOW CHEMICAL COMPANY, 240
EG & G, INC., 249
FULLER COMPANY, 269
GENERAL TIRE, INC., 279
GOODYEAR TIRE & RUBBER COMPANY,
    284
GTE CORPORATION, 288

HELENE CURTIS INDUSTRIES, INC., 298
HOLIDAY INNS WORLDWIDE, 302
HYATT INTERNATIONAL CORPORATION, 308
INDUCTOTHERM CORPORATION, 311
ITT SHERATON CORPORATION, 322
JOHNSON & JOHNSON, 325
LINTAS: WORLDWIDE, 346
MCKINSEY & COMPANY, INC., 357
MOORE PRODUCTS COMPANY, 378
MOTION PICTURE EXPORT ASSOCIATION OF AMERICA, 380
NORTON COMPANY, 390
J. C. PENNEY COMPANY, INC., 407
PHELPS DODGE CORPORATION, 412
PIONEER HI-BRED INTERNATIONAL, INC., 417

POPULATION COUNCIL, 562
PRECISION VALVE CORPORATION, 422
PREFORMED LINE PRODUCTS COMPANY, 423
PUROLATOR PRODUCTS COMPANY, 427
READING & BATES, 433
ROHM & HAAS COMPANY, 442
ROSEMOUNT, INC., 443
SEA-LAND SERVICE, INC., 454
SEARLE COMPANY, 455
SIMON & SCHUSTER, INC., 463
SONAT OFFSHORE, 470
U.S. WHEAT ASSOCIATES, 511
WHIRLPOOL CORPORATION, 526
XEROX CORPORATION, 531

INDONESIA

- **Official Name:** Republic of Indonesia

- **Capital:** Jakarta

- **Location:** Indonesia is the largest archipelago in the world, forming a natural boundary between the Indian and Pacific oceans. There are five main islands and thirty smaller chains comprising more than 13,667 smaller (some uninhabited) islands. The five main islands are: Java, Sumatra, Sulawesi, two-thirds of Borneo (which it shares with Malaysia and calls Kalimantan), and the western half of New Guinea (which it shares with Papua New Guinea and calls Irian Jaya). The capital City of Jakarta is on the island of Java. The total land area is 2,000,000 square miles and the water area is five times as large as that. Stretching across 3,175 miles of equatorial waters, it is wider than the continental United States. Its comparative area is about three times the size of Texas. Indonesia's name was derived from the Greek words Indos, for east Indian, and nesos, for islands.

- **Population, Cities, and American Residents:** The population of Indonesia totals 186 million people (1992 est.), making it the fifth most populous nation. Forty-five percent of the population is of Malay stock, with the remainder comprised of 14 percent Sudanese, 7.5 percent Madurese, and 7.5 percent coastal Malays.

  Most American residents are employed in Indonesia's three main cities, Jakarta with 7.3 million, Bandung with 1.6 million, and Semarang with 1.2 million people (1983 est.).

- **Language and Currency:** The official language of the country is Bahasa Indonesia. English is used widely among the more educated Indonesians and throughout business circles. The ethnic Chinese speak a variation of Cantonese, and Dutch, the original language of the colonial rulers, is still used by some older residents. Less frequently used languages include Javanese and Balinese. The unit of currency is the rupiah (shortened to Rp.) Different colors distinguish denominations of Rp10,000, 5,000, 1,000, 500, and 100. Coins are various sizes in denominations of: Rp100, 50, 25, 10, and 5. The exchange rate is 1 rupiah = U.S.$.0005; 2,090 rupiah equal U.S.$1 (July 30, 1993).

- **Climate:** Basically, Indonesia has a tropical climate, with hot, humid weather and the typical monsoon rains from October through April. During the rainy season, humidity averages 83 percent. It is dry from May through October and daytime temperatures range from 85°F-95°F throughout the year.

- **Economy and Resources:** Indonesia is rich in natural resources, and is currently the tenth largest oil producer in the world. It ranks first as a major exporter of liquified natural gas, with Japan purchasing most of its supply. Its timber forests produce rubber and wood products. Other resources include gold and tin. Agriculture employs 64 percent of the people, accounting for 53 percent of production and 25 percent of the GDP. The main agricultural exports are tea and coffee.

   Unemployment is a problem; with such a dense population, jobs are scarce. The official unemployment rate is under ten percent but nearly half of the labor force (68,000,000) is jobless or currently under employed. The manufacturing sector is just emerging. Until recently, few Indonesians have had the necessary skills to make the country competitive with other cheap-labor economies like Thailand, or the Philippines.

- **Cost of Living:** At 95, the cost of living is lower than in the United States.

- **Work Permits, Visas, etc.:** A passport valid for six months from the date of application is required. A visa is not necessary for a stay of less than two months; after that you must apply to the Department of Immigration for a semi-permanent visa (called KIM-S). This is valid for one year, after which you must apply for a resident visa. Work permits must be obtained from the Ministry of Manpower, Transmigration, and Cooperatives for foreigners to work in Indonesia. If you are entering Indonesia from the United States, no vaccinations are required. For official or other information, direct inquiries to the embassy or consulate at the addresses below.

- **Taxation:** Anyone who resides in Indonesia for more than three months must pay personal income tax. A nonresident is taxed only on income earned in the country. Indonesia has agreements with the United States to avoid double taxation.

- **Principal International Schools:** Most of the major cities, including Jakarta, have a good selection of international schools. The average tuition for an American school is $6,000.

- **Health Care:** Medical care in Indonesia is far below U.S. standards. For serious health problems, including surgery, it is wise to go to Singapore. The tourist areas and large hotels have English-speaking doctors. The best available service is with the Medical Scheme in Kebayoran, Jakarta, which offers European and American-trained staff on call. There is a basic fee to join (currently $100 for enrollment, and $75 per year), which covers visits, prescriptions, etc. A frequently used facility by Americans in

Indonesia is the Metropolitan Medical Center, located on the first floor of the Wisata International Hotel in Jakarta. General dentistry is good especially in Jakarta, and a routine visit is about $30. Do not drink tap water anywhere in Indonesia. Boiled or bottled water is a must (even when brushing teeth). Appropriate precautions should be taken with all fruits and vegetables, and cook all meats and fish thoroughly. Be careful when using public toilets, as some may be unhealthy, and bring along tissue, as it is not supplied in public rest rooms.

- **Crime:** Crime is not a major concern in Indonesia. However, care should be taken with valuables (always lock them up and never leave anything out in plain sight). Beware of pickpockets and purse snatchers in the major cities. If you do have something lost or stolen, chances are it will not be recovered. The streets are generally safe to walk at night, but avoid alleys and poorly lit areas.

- **Pros and Cons of Living and Working in Indonesia:** Indonesia is a an exotic and fascinating nation. Its wild regions, jungles, volcanoes, and animal life appeal to most visitors. Interesting cabaret and theater productions also are popular. The business climate is favorable and housing is available but expensive, especially around Jakarta. A car is invaluable in Indonesia as traveling from one island to the next by boat or plane can be costly. The climate is unpleasant, especially the oppressive humidity that damages books, furniture, and fine fabrics. And then there's the monsoon season. Pack your rain gear; you'll need it.

EMBASSY AND CONSULATE CONTACT INFORMATION:

INDONESIAN EMBASSY
2020 MASSACHUSETTS AVE. NW
WASHINGTON, DC 20036
TEL: 202-775-5200

CONSULATES GENERAL
5 EAST 68TH ST.
NEW YORK, NY 10021
TEL: 212-879-0600

OTHER SOURCES OF INFORMATION:

AMERICAN INDONESIAN CHAMBER OF COMMERCE
711 THIRD AVE.
NEW YORK, NY 10017
TEL: 212-687-4505
FAX: 212-867-9882

COMPANIES/ORGANIZATIONS WITH OPERATIONS IN INDONESIA:

A. L. LABORATORIES INC., 107
ABB VETCO GRAY, INC., 108
BACKER SPIELVOGEL & BATES WORLDWIDE, INC., 150
BAKER HUGHES, INC., 152
BANKAMERICA CORPORATION, 155
BAROID CORPORATION, 158
BECHTEL GROUP, INC., 162
BLACK & VEATCH, 168
BRIDGESTONE-FIRESTONE, INC., 174
BRISTOL-MEYERS SQUIBB COMPANY, 175
BROWN GROUP, INC., 176
CABOT CORPORATION, 181
CARGILL INCORPORATED, 184

CHEVRON CORPORATION, 193
CIGNA CORPORATION, 197
CONOCO, INC., 209
CONVERSE, INC., 212
CORE LABORATORIES, 214
DAMES & MOORE, 223
DE LEUW, CATHER INTERNATIONAL, 228
DIGICON, INC., 235
DOW JONES & COMPANY, INC., 241
DRESSER INDUSTRIES, INC., 241
ECOLOGY AND ENVIRONMENT, INC., 248
ERNST & YOUNG, 255
EXXON COMPANY, INTERNATIONAL, 258
FERRO CORPORATION, 261

A
M
E
R
I
C
A
N

J
O
B
S

A
B
R
O
A
D

FREEPORT-MCMORAN, INC., 268

GILBERT/COMMONWEALTH
INTERNATIONAL, INC., 282

GOODYEAR TIRE & RUBBER COMPANY,
284

GUARDIAN INDUSTRIES CORPORATION,
290

HUGHES CHRISTENSEN COMPANY, 307

HYATT INTERNATIONAL CORPORATION,
308

INGERSOLL-RAND COMPANY, 313

INTERNATIONAL FLAVORS &
FRAGRANCES, INC., 317

JOHNSON & JOHNSON, 325

M. W. KELLOGG COMPANY, 331

KIMBERLY-CLARK CORPORATION, 336

MARATHON PETROLEUM COMPANY, 359

MAXUS ENERGY CORPORATION, 363

MCDERMOTT INTERNATIONAL, INC., 356

MOBIL OIL CORPORATION, 375

NATIONAL SEMICONDUCTOR
CORPORATION, 383

ORYX ENERGY, 398

PARSONS CORPORATION, 406

PENNZOIL COMPANY, 408

PHILLIPS PETROLEUM COMPANY, 415

POPULATION COUNCIL, 562

RESOURCES MANAGEMENT
INTERNATIONAL, 437

ROHM & HAAS COMPANY, 442

ROWAN COMPANIES, INC., 444

SONAT, INC., 469

STV GROUP, 482

TEXACO OIL COMPANY, 493

TRITON ENERGY CORPORATION, 502

UNION CARBIDE CORPORATION, 507

UNOCAL CORPORATION, 513

USX CORPORATION, 516

IRELAND

- **Official Name:** Ireland
- **Capital:** Dublin
- **Location:** Ireland is located in northwestern Europe, occupying five sixths of the island of Ireland. The remaining one fifth of the island is Northern Ireland and it is part of the United Kingdom of Great Britain and Northern Ireland. Ireland's total land area is 26,593 square miles, making it slightly larger than West Virginia. More than 70 percent of its territory is covered by meadows and pastures. Green countryside and farmland cover most of central Ireland, with mountains gently rising on the west coast. With a heavily indented coastline stretching for 900 miles, no part of Ireland is more than 70 miles from the sea.
- **Population, Cities, and American Residents:** The population of Ireland totals 3.8 million people (1992 est.). Most of the Irish population is of Celtic descent. There is a small English minority.

    Most American residents are employed in Ireland's two largest cities: Dublin with 930,000 people and Cork with 174,000 people.
- **Language and Currency:** The official languages of Ireland are English and Gaelic, but English predominates throughout the country in business and government circles. The monetary unit is the Irish pound or punt. To distinguish it from the British pound, the punt is always written as IRú. Pounds are divided into 100 pence, written as in Britain, as "p." The exchange rate is 1 IRú = U.S.$1.38 (July 30, 1993).
- **Climate:** The climate of Ireland is temperate with warm summers and mild winters.

Winter temperatures average about 40°F, and summer temperatures remain in the low 60s. Rainfall is considerable throughout the year, providing plenty of moisture for Ireland, which is sometimes referred to as the Emerald Isle because of its green landscape.

- **Economy and Resources:** The Irish Republic has a mixed economy. After hundreds of years of farming, Agriculture dominated the economy until a decline began in the 1920s. Now, Ireland's economy counts heavily on service industries and manufacturing, and industry accounts for 36 percent of the gross domestic product (GDP) and 65 percent of export earnings. Principal industries include food and beverages, textiles, paper, non-metallic minerals, and machinery. Recently American and European multinationals have introduced other skill-intensive industries such as chemicals and electronic engineering. Agriculture accounts for 12 percent of the GDP and 23 percent of export earnings, basically from livestock production. Major trading partners are the United Kingdom and fellow European Community members. Ireland is dependent on imports for 70 percent of its energy requirements, but it has the largest zinc and lead deposits in Europe, along with reserves of copper, pyrites, gypsum, coal, limestone, and marble. Of the labor force, 57 percent of the people work in banking and services, 27.4 percent in manufacturing and construction, and 15.6 percent in agriculture, fishing, and mining. Although Ireland has one of the youngest work forces in the world, unemployment remains high (12 percent in 1993). The cost of living also is high compared to the United States. Continued economic growth is expected, but many challenges remain. A reorganized tax structure should continue to increase revenues, and Ireland is in the midst of developing and repairing its infrastructure. The violence between Catholics and Protestants in Northern Ireland has declined somewhat in past few years, but terrorist acts still continue to plague the country.

- **Cost of Living:** At 154, the cost of living is higher than in the United States.

- **Work Permits, Visas, etc.:** A valid passport is required to travel in Ireland. Foreigners going to work there must obtain work permits from the Minister of Labor in Ireland, which can be done by mail prior to the trip. Bring the permit with you upon entering Ireland as the officer at the port of entry will ask to see it. Be aware that the importation of certain items is prohibited or restricted (animals, agricultural products, certain drugs, etc.). When entering Ireland from the United States, no vaccinations are required. For official or other information, contact the embassy or consulate at the addresses below.

- **Taxation:** All U.S. citizen residents not living permanently in Ireland must pay Irish income tax on all income from Irish and United Kingdom sources, and on payments to Ireland from foreign sources (other than the United Kingdom). Residence is established by owning a dwelling in Ireland or by living in the country for more than 183 days of the tax year.

- **Principal International Schools:** Free education is provided for grade school as well as high school levels. Private and international schools also are available in Dublin. Tuition for an American school ranges from $7,100 to $9,125 per year.

- **Health Care:** In Ireland, the Department of Health regulates health services through eight regional boards. Any foreign resident who earns more than $22,780 annually is required to pay social insurance tax to receive benefits. Health services are adequate throughout Ireland. Sanitary conditions are good, with drinking water, produce, and dairy products safe to eat and drink. Imported pharmaceuticals are readily available at reasonable prices.

- **Crime:** Ireland has its share of street crime. Pickpockets, purse snatchers, and car break-ins are common, and precautions should be taken. Lock valuables out of sight and don't carry large sums of cash.

- **Pros and Cons of Living and Working in Ireland:** Ireland is a modern country, with picturesque harbors, ports, and a lovely green countryside. The Irish people are hospitable, and their folk music and storytelling are famous throughout the world. Health and telecommunications standards are both good. Transportation is modern and affordable, but you should be careful if you travel near the border of Northern Ireland. The police and army patrol the area, and it's a good idea to have your passport or identification with you. Housing is available, and rentals are comparable in price to those in North America. Ireland has very strict regulations about importing animals, and most pets remain in quarantine for six months at the owner's expense. Rain gear is essential for any stay in Ireland, as precipitation is frequent throughout the year. Remember that the cost of living in Ireland is higher than in the United States, and daily necessities may cost more.

EMBASSY AND CONSULATE CONTACT INFORMATION:

IRISH EMBASSY
2234 MASSACHUSETTS AVE. NW
WASHINGTON, DC 20008
TEL: 202-462-3939

CONSULATE GENERAL OF IRELAND
515 MADISON AVE.
NEW YORK, NY 10022
TEL: 212-319-2555

OTHER SOURCES OF INFORMATION:

IRISH TOURIST BOARD
757 THIRD AVE.
NEW YORK, NY 10017
TEL: 212-418-0800

DEPARTMENT OF LABOUR
MINISTER OF LABOUR
MESPIL HOUSE
MESPIL RD.
DUBLIN 4, IRELAND

COMPANIES/ORGANIZATIONS WITH OPERATIONS IN IRELAND:

AMP, INC., 132
AT&T INTERNATIONAL, 145
CALIFORNIA PELLET MILL COMPANY, 182
CHEVRON CORPORATION, 193

CONOCO, INC., 209
HILL & KNOWLTON, INC., 301
LOTUS DEVELOPMENT CORPORATION, 351

ISRAEL

- **Official Name:** State of Israel
- **Capital:** Jerusalem

- **Location:** Israel is located on a narrow piece of land along the eastern shore of the Mediterranean Sea. It lies between Lebanon and Syria to the north, Jordan to the east, and Egypt to the south and west. Saudi Arabia is southeast of Israel across the Gulf of Aqaba. In size, Israel is comparable to New Jersey, covering an area of 8,473 square miles. The three main areas are the western coastal plain which includes Tel Aviv and Haifa; the mountain range with the Hills of Galilee, Samaria, Judea, and Jerusalem; and the Jordan and Arava river valleys, which link the Dead Sea and the Sea of Galilee with the River Jordan. The Dead Sea, at 1,286 feet below sea level, is the lowest point on earth. The most populous areas are the northern and central sections of Israel.

- **Population, Cities, and American Residents:** The population of Israel totals 4.7 million people (1992 est.). Jewish people account for 83 percent of the population with the remaining 17 percent mostly Arab.

   Most American residents are employed in Israel's three largest cities: Jerusalem with 457,000, Tel Aviv with 322,000, and Haifa with 224,000 people (1990 est.).

- **Language and Currency:** The official language of Israel is Hebrew, and English is the most widely used second language throughout the country. Arabic is a second official language for the Arab minority. The monetary unit is the New Shekel (NIS); the plural is Shekelim. There are 100 agorot to each Shekel. Bills are in 500, 50, 10, 5, and 1. Coins are in 50, 10, 5, and 1 agorot, and 1 Shekel. The exchange rate is 1 NIS = U.S.$.36 (July 30, 1993).

- **Climate:** Considering its small size, Israel has a very diverse climate. The coastal plain is warm and humid, while the hilly region near Jerusalem is cooler with little humidity. The southern deserts are hot and dry, year-round, and in the northern section near Galilee, winters can be quite cold. The temperatures in Tel Aviv average from 48°F-66°F in February, and 68°F-89°F in September. Toward the south in the area of Eilat, temperatures can often reach more than 100°F during the month of August.

- **Economy and Resources:** Israel has a democratic socialist economy. The government owns or shares in all industries and services, with the exception of agriculture, though efforts toward privatization are currently underway with a goal of creating a more efficient economy. The national labor union (the Histadrut) plays a key role in the economy. Manufacturing and mining account for one-quarter of gross domestic product (GDP). Other industries are leather goods, foods, and diamond cutting. Science-based industries such as bio-technology and chemicals are increasingly important and have the greatest growth potential. Israel has no sources of oil and must rely on others (Egypt and Mexico) to meet its needs. Israel trades largely with the United States and Europe. Its major exports are citrus and other fruits, textiles, fertilizer and chemical products. It is still not known what the Gulf War cost Israel, particularly in lost tourist revenues.

- **Cost of Living:** At 141, the cost of living is higher than in the United States.

- **Work Permits, Visas, etc.:** A valid passport is necessary to travel in Israel. A visa is not required of Canadian, British, or U.S. citizens if their passport is valid for nine months after arrival, they have a return ticket, and have sufficient funds for their stay in Israel. Upon arrival in Israel, passports are stamped with a valid renewable three-month visa, and extensions may be obtained from the Ministry of the Interior once you are in the country. Several categories are currently issued. If you are entering Israel from the United States, no vaccinations are required. For official or other information, direct inquiries to the embassy or consulate at the addresses below.

- **Taxation:** Israel has one of the highest tax rates in the world. Foreign residents noted as "approved specialists" may have to pay a flat 25 percent fee on earnings in Israel. Currently, there is no agreement between the U.S. and Israel for the avoidance of double taxation, but one is under discussion. For current information, contact the Income Tax Bureau, Ministry of Finance, Hakirya, Jerusalem.

- **Principal International Schools:** Education is very important in Israel. Although Hebrew is the official language for instruction, English is offered in most schools. American schools are located in Tel Aviv. The maximum tuition is $8,000.

- **Health Care:** Sanitation throughout Israel is generally good. Israel's food standards are high, and the water is safe to drink in most areas. Health care standards are comparable to those of United States, most doctors speak English, and medical costs are reasonable. The Mediterranean beaches are subject to urban and industrial pollution, and at times, the water and beaches may be unhealthy.

- **Crime:** Common crime is rarely seen in Israel, but terrorist acts sometimes occur. Avoid bus or train stations in large cities, especially at night, and always choose well-lit streets and ask local officials about unsafe areas.

- **Pros and Cons of Living and Working in Israel:** Israel is a modern, diversified nation, with a favorable business climate and trade agreements with both the United States and the European Community. Telecommunications and transportation services are good with telephone hook-ups readily available, and buses, trains, and taxis reasonably priced. Jerusalem has many tourist attractions and the Mediterranean shoreline and the Sea of Galilee have many facilities for water sports. The cuisine reflects Israel's mixture of various peoples. Among the offerings: Hungarian goulash, Middle Eastern humus and falafel, and Turkish coffee. From dusk on Friday to Sunday morning, no Jew is allowed to handle money, which is an inconvenience to visitors. Avoid traveling during the Sabbath as banks, stores, and gas stations are closed. Housing costs are reasonable, but accommodations are extremely difficult to find. Understand every part of a lease agreement in advance before signing. Domestic help is almost non-existent. Being virtually surrounded by enemies, Israel is in a constant state of alert. Skirmishes with Arab terrorists may occur and visitors should keep an eye on local political conditions before embarking going to or while staying in Israel.

EMBASSY AND CONSULATE CONTACT INFORMATION:

EMBASSY OF ISRAEL
3514 INTERNATIONAL DR. NW
WASHINGTON, DC 20008
TEL: 202-364-5500

CONSULATE GENERAL OF ISRAEL
800 SECOND AVE.
NEW YORK, NY 10017
TEL: 212-351-5200

OTHER SOURCES OF INFORMATION:

ISRAEL INFORMATION CENTER
U.S. DEPT. OF COMMERCE, RM. H2039
INTERNATIONAL TRADE ADMINISTRATION
WASHINGTON, DC 20230
TEL: 202-377-4652
FAX: 202-377-5444

COMPANIES/ORGANIZATIONS WITH OPERATIONS IN ISRAEL:

AMERICAN STANDARD, INC., 128

AMPEX CORPORATION, 133

ASTRONAUTICS CORPORATION OF AMERICA, 145

AVX CORPORATION, 150

THE BARDEN CORPORATION, 157

COMPUTER ASSOCIATES INTERNATIONAL, INC., 207

DIGITAL EQUIPMENT CORPORATION, 236

DOW CORNING CORPORATION, 240

EATON CORPORATION/CUTLER HAMMER, 247

ENCYCLOPEDIA BRITANNICA, INC., 253

FIBRONICS INTERNATIONAL, INC., 261

HERTZ CORPORATION, 300

INTEL CORPORATION, 314

INTERNATIONAL BUSINESS MACHINES (IBM), 315

ITT SHERATON CORPORATION, 322

LAMBDA ELECTRONICS, INC., 343

LTV STEEL CO., 352

LTX CORPORATION, 353

NATIONAL SEMICONDUCTOR CORPORATION, 383

PERKIN-ELMER CORPORATION, 410

ROBERT HALF INTERNATIONAL, INC., 440

SIMPLEX TIME RECORDER COMPANY, 463

TELEDYNE, INC., 489

VISHAY INTERTECHNOLOGY, 518

ITALY

- **Official Name:** Italian Republic
- **Capital:** Rome
- **Location:** Italy is located in southern Europe. Its peninsula is formed in the shape of a boot, and stretches for 708 miles from the Alps to the Mediterranean Sea. In addition to the mainland are two large islands, Sicily and Sardinia, and various smaller islands. France, Switzerland, Austria, and Yugoslavia share land borders with Italy. For the most part, Italy is a mountainous country, with scattered rivers and fertile plains throughout its territory. Its strategic location has enabled Italy to play a key role politically and economically throughout history.
- **Population, Cities, and American Residents:** The population of Italy totals 57.4 million (1992 est.). Most of the people are of Italian descent, and other small groups include German-, French-, and Slovene-Italians in the north, and Albanian-Italians and Greeks in the south.

  Most American residents are employed in Italy's three largest cities: Rome with 2.8 million, Milan with 1.4 million, and Naples with 1.2 million people.
- **Language and Currency:** Italian is the official language of Italy, and though many well-educated Italians speak English, their native language is the one used in business, government, and in trade literature, catalogs, etc. Having a working knowledge of the native tongue is essential. The monetary unit is the lira (plural is lire). The exchange rate is 1 Italian lira = U.S.$.0006. It takes 1,595 lire to equal U.S.$1 (July 30, 1993).
- **Climate:** Italy has a temperate climate in the north and a Mediterranean climate in the southern sections. However, local conditions are greatly affected by the sea and the mountains. The Alps in the north have very cold winters, while the Neapolitan coastlines

have relatively warm winters. Sicily's climate is much like that of southern California. The average temperature range for Rome is: 49°F-82°F; for Naples, 50°F-82°F; and Milan, 36°F-75°F.

- **Economy and Resources:** Italy has the fifth largest economy in the world, and much of its success can be attributed to its industrial sector. Major industries are machinery and transport equipment, steel, and chemicals. Chief exports are textiles, clothing, metals, and transport equipment. The major trading partners are other members of the European community.

  The north and the south of the country have very different economies, strengths, and weaknesses. Unemployment is three times worse in the south, which is primarily engaged in agriculture and produces only 24 percent of the gross domestic product (GDP). Southern crops include olive oil, wine, fruits, and vegetables. Much has been tried to boost industry in the south but with little success, and foreign investment has been minimized, mainly because of the presence of organized crime in the region. The north is engaged in heavy industry and is home to well known names, including Fiat and Pirelli. It also has a fertile farmland, producing meat, dairy, and cereal products. Tourism is also important to Italy's economy and accounts for 5 percent of GDP. Of the labor force, over half work in services, 37.9 in industry and 5.4 percent in agriculture.

- **Cost of Living:** Ranging from 153 to 168 (data was taken from four major cities), the cost of living in Italy is much higher than in the United States.

- **Work Permits, Visas, etc.:** A valid passport is required to travel in Italy. For stays up to three months, no visa is necessary. Any foreigner applying for work in Italy must request a work permit through the Italian Ministry of Foreign Affairs. If you are entering Italy from the United States, no vaccinations are required. For official or other information, direct inquiries to the embassy or consulate at the addresses below.

- **Taxation:** There are two income taxes in Italy; a personal income tax and a local income tax. Residents are taxed on worldwide income while nonresidents are taxed on income from Italian sources only. You qualify as a resident if your principal office or interests are in Italy, or if you live in Italy for more than six months of the year. Italy has a treaty in effect with the United States to avoid double taxation.

- **Principal International Schools:** International schools are available in all the major cities of Italy. The tuition for an American school costs $11,500 per year.

- **Health Care:** There are numerous hospitals, physicians, and clinics in the major cities of Italy, but the public hospitals are understaffed and do not have all the modern equipment that Americans may be accustomed to. Private hospitals also tend to cost more. In Rome, there is one hospital (Salvator Mundi Hospital) that is used often by Americans as it has U.S. trained staff and is sufficiently equipped. Sanitary conditions in most of Italy are good. Water is safe in the cities, but do not drink any well water in rural areas. There are no prevalent diseases or health hazards that pose a risk to travelers, other than the air pollution and smog in the larger cities.

- **Crime:** Common crime is a problem in Italy, especially in tourist areas. Watch out for purse snatchers, pickpockets, and petty thieves. Don't carry large amounts of cash or leave valuables in plain sight, or unattended. Women should be especially careful if going out alone during the evening hours.

- **Pros and Cons of Living and Working in Italy:** Italy has a rich cultural heritage, fascinating scenery, and many tourist areas, including Vatican City, the Colosseum, and the many museums. The Italian Riviera is elegant and features fishing villages, castles, and the sparkling sea. Transportation services throughout the country are good, but telecommunications services are not. Long-distance calls may take longer than usual and service can be erratic. Mail service is also quite bad. Housing is available and affordable, but read the lease carefully before you sign it. Many rental houses or apartments are poorly heated, so bringing an electric blanket is a good idea. Medical facilities and health standards are also good, but be prepared for smog and air pollution, especially in the larger cities.

EMBASSY AND CONSULATE CONTACT INFORMATION:

EMBASSY OF ITALY
1601 FULLER ST. NW
WASHINGTON, DC 20009
TEL: 202-328-5500

CONSULATE GENERAL OF ITALY
690 PARK AVE.
NEW YORK, NY 10021
TEL: 212-737-9100

OTHER SOURCES OF INFORMATION:

ITALIAN TRADE COMMISSION
499 PARK AVE.
NEW YORK, NY 10022
TEL: 212-980-1500

COMPANIES/ORGANIZATIONS WITH OPERATIONS IN ITALY:

ABBOTT LABORATORIES, 109
ACCO WORLD CORPORATION, 110
ALARM DEVICE MANUFACTURING COMPANY, 114
ALBERTO-CULVER COMPANY, 115
ALEXANDER & ALEXANDER SERVICES, INC., 116
ALLEN-BRADLEY COMPANY, INC., 116
AMDAHL CORPORATION, 120
AMERICAN APPRAISAL ASSOCIATES, INC., 121
AMERICAN HOME PRODUCTS CORPORATION, 126
AMERICAN STANDARD, INC., 128
AMERICAN UNIFORM COMPANY, 129
AMETEK, INC., 130
AMGEN, INC., 131
AMP, INC., 132
AMPEX CORPORATION, 133
ANDREW CORPORATION, 134
APPLE COMPUTER, INC., 136
ARMCO, INC., 140

ARMOUR SWIFT ECKRICH, INC., 141
ARMSTRONG WORLD INDUSTRIES, INC., 141
ASEA BROWN BOVERI, 142
ASHLAND OIL, INC., 143
ASSOCIATED PRESS, 144
AT&T INTERNATIONAL, 145
AUGAT, INC., 146
AVON PRODUCTS, INC., 149
BADGER COMPANY, INC., 151
BAILEY CONTROLS COMPANY, 151
BAKER HUGHES, INC., 152
THE BANK OF NEW YORK COMPANY, INC., 154
BAROID CORPORATION, 158
BAXTER HEALTHCARE CORPORATION, 160
BECKMAN INSTRUMENTS, INC., 162
BEMIS COMPANY, INC., 164
BETZ LABORATORIES, 166
BIO-RAD LABORATORIES, 166
BLOCK DRUG COMPANY, INC., 169
BOEING COMPANY, 170

A
M
E
R
I
C
A
N

J
O
B
S

A
B
R
O
A
D

BORDEN, INC., 170
BORG-WARNER CORPORATION, 171
BORLAND INTERNATIONAL, INC, 172
BOSE CORPORATION, 172
W. H. BRADY COMPANY, 173
BRIDGESTONE-FIRESTONE, INC., 174
BRISTOL-MEYERS SQUIBB COMPANY, 175
BROWN GROUP, INC., 176
BROWNING-FERRIS INDUSTRIES, 177
BURSON-MARSTELLER, 180
CABOT CORPORATION, 181
CARRIER CORPORATION, 186
CARTER-WALLACE, INC., 187
CENTRAL SOYA COMPANY, 188
CHIRON CORPORATION, 194
CITICORP, 198
COMMERCIAL INTERTECH CORPORATION, 205
COMMODORE INTERNATIONAL LTD., 206
CONOCO, INC., 209
CONTINENTAL BANK CORPORATION, 210
COOPERS & LYBRAND, 214
CORNING INCORPORATED, 215
CPC INTERNATIONAL, INC., 217
CUMMINS ENGINE COMPANY, INC., 221
DATA GENERAL CORPORATION, 225
DAYCO PRODUCTS, INC., 226
DE KALB GENETICS CORPORATION, 227
DELL COMPUTER CORPORATION, 231
THE DEXTER CORPORATION, 233
DOW CORNING CORPORATION, 240
DRESSER INDUSTRIES, INC., 241
DRUMMOND COMPANY, INC., 242
DUN & BRADSTREET CORPORATION, 243
EATON CORPORATION/CUTLER HAMMER, 247
EBASCO OVERSEAS CORPORATION, 248
EG & G, INC., 249
ELECTRONIC DATA SYSTEMS CORPORATION, 249
ELI LILLY AND COMPANY, 250
ELIZABETH ARDEN COMPANY, 251
ENCORE COMPUTER CORPORATION, 252
ENCYCLOPEDIA BRITANNICA, INC., 253
ENGELHARD CORPORATION, 253
ERNST & YOUNG, 255
EXXON COMPANY, INTERNATIONAL, 258
FAIRCHILD PUBLICATIONS, INC., 259
FEDERAL EXPRESS CORPORATION, 260
FEDERAL-MOGUL CORPORATION, 260

FIGGIE INTERNATIONAL, INC., 262
FISCHER & PORTER COMPANY, 263
FORD MOTOR COMPANY, 267
GAF CORPORATION, 270
GENERAL ELECTRIC COMPANY (GE), 275
GENERAL FOODS USA, 276
GENERAL MOTORS CORPORATION (GM), 277
GERAGHTY & MILLER, INC., 279
GERHARD'S BICYCLE ODYSSEYS, 280
GOLDMAN SACHS & COMPANY, 283
GOULD PUMPS, INC., 285
GRACO, INC., 286
GRANT THORNTON INTERNATIONAL, 286
GREY ADVERTISING, INC., 288
H. J. HEINZ COMPANY, 290
HERTZ CORPORATION, 300
HILL & KNOWLTON, INC., 301
HOLIDAY INNS WORLDWIDE, 302
HONEYWELL, INC., 303
HUGHES AIRCRAFT COMPANY, 307
ILLINOIS TOOL WORKS, INC., 309
IMS AMERICA, LTD., 311
INGERSOLL ENGINEERS, 312
INGERSOLL-RAND COMPANY, 313
INTERNATIONAL FLAVORS & FRAGRANCES, INC., 317
INTERNATIONAL RECTIFIER CORPORATION, 319
ITW FINISHING SYSTEMS & PRODUCTS, 322
JAMES RIVER CORPORATION, 323
JOHNSON CONTROLS, INC., 324
JOHNSON & HIGGINS, 324
JOHNSON & JOHNSON, 325
A. T. KEARNEY, INC., 329
KELLOGG COMPANY, 330
KIDDER PEABODY GROUP & COMPANY, INC., 335
KNOLL INTERNATIONAL, 338
KOCH INDUSTRIES, INC., 339
KORN/FERRY INTERNATIONAL, 340
LAWTER INTERNATIONAL, INC., 344
LEVI STRAUSS ASSOCIATES, INC., 344
THE LIMITED, INC., 345
LITTON INDUSTRIES, INC., 348
LTX CORPORATION, 353
LUBRIZOL CORPORATION, 353
MAGNETEK, INC., 358
MARION MERRELL DOW, INC., 360

MATTEL, INC., 363

GEORGE S. MAY INTERNATIONAL, INC., 364

MAYTAG CORPORATION, 364

MCI COMMUNICATIONS CORPORATION, 365

MCKINSEY & COMPANY, INC., 357

MEAD CORPORATION, 365

MEASUREX CORPORATION, 366

MEDTRONIC, INC., 366

MERCK & COMPANY, INC., 368

MERRILL LYNCH & COMPANY, INC., 369

METCO PERKIN-ELMER, 371

MGM INCORPORATED, 372

MILLIPORE CORPORATION, 374

MONTGOMERY WARD HOLDING COMPANY, 377

J. P. MORGAN & COMPANY, INC., 378

MOTION PICTURE EXPORT ASSOCIATION OF AMERICA, 380

NALCO CHEMICAL COMPANY, 382

NATIONAL DATA CORPORATION, 382

NATIONAL SEMICONDUCTOR CORPORATION, 383

NL INDUSTRIES, INC., 388

NORDSON CORPORATION, 389

NORTH AMERICAN PHILIPS CORPORATION, 389

NORTON COMPANY, 390

NOVELL, INC., 392

OWENS-CORNING FIBERGLAS CORPORATION, 400

OWENS-ILLINOIS, INC., 401

PARKER HANNIFIN CORPORATION, 405

PEPSICO FOODS INTERNATIONAL, 409

PEPSICO, INC., 410

PERKIN-ELMER CORPORATION, 410

PFIZER, INC., 412

PHELPS DODGE CORPORATION, 412

PIONEER HI-BRED INTERNATIONAL, INC., 417

PITTWAY CORPORATION, 418

PLAYTEX APPAREL, INC., 419

PPG INDUSTRIES, 421

PRECISION VALVE CORPORATION, 422

PREMARK INTERNATIONAL, INC., 423

PRICE WATERHOUSE, 424

PRIMERICA CORPORATION, 424

PRUDENTIAL INSURANCE COMPANY OF AMERICA, 427

QUAKER CHEMICAL CORPORATION, 428

QUAKER OATS COMPANY, 428

RALSTON PURINA COMPANY, 430

RANCO, INC., 431

READER'S DIGEST ASSOCIATION, INC., 432

READING & BATES, 433

REED TOOL COMPANY, 434

REEVES BROTHERS, INC., 435

RELIANCE ELECTRIC COMPANY, 435

REVLON, INC., 437

ROCKWELL INTERNATIONAL CORPORATION, 441

ROSEMOUNT, INC., 443

RUDER FINN, INC., 445

SCIENTIFIC ATLANTA, INC., 452

SCOTT PAPER COMPANY, 453

SEA-LAND SERVICE, INC., 454

SEALED AIR CORPORATION, 455

SENSORMATIC ELECTRONICS CORPORATION, 457

SGS CONTROL SERVICES, 458

SHEAFFER PEN, INC., 459

SHIPLEY COMPANY, INC., 461

SILICONIX, 462

SMITH INTERNATIONAL, INC., 467

SONY PICTURES ENTERTAINMENT, 471

SPS TECHNOLOGIES, INC., 474

SQUARE D COMPANY, 475

SRI INTERNATIONAL, 475

STORAGE TECHNOLOGY CORPORATION, 481

SYMBOL TECHNOLOGIES, INC., 485

TEKTRONIX, INC., 488

TELEDYNE, INC., 489

THOMAS & BETTS, 495

3M PHARMACEUTICALS, 497

TIME-WARNER, INC., 498

TLC BEATRICE INTERNATIONAL HOLDINGS, INC., 498

TORRINGTON COMPANY, 499

TOWERS PERRIN, INC., 499

TRINOVA CORPORATION, 502

TRW, INC., 503

UNISYS CORPORATION, 508

UNITED NATIONS INDUSTRIAL DEVELOPMENT ORGANIZATION (UNIDO), 568

UNITED TECHNOLOGIES CORPORATION, 512

COUNTRY PROFILES

WARNER ELECTRIC BRAKE & CLUTCH
    COMPANY, 521
WEST COMPANY, INC., 525
WHIRLPOOL CORPORATION, 526
WMX TECHNOLOGIES/WASTE
    MANAGEMENT, INC., 527

WOOLWORTH CORPORATION, 528
WORLD COURIER MANAGEMENT, INC.,
    529
WYETH-AYERST LABORATORIES, 530
YOUNG & RUBICAM, INC., 533

JAMAICA

- **Official Name:** Jamaica
- **Capital:** Kingston
- **Location:** Jamaica, located 480 miles south of Florida, is the third largest island in the Caribbean Sea. Similar to other islands in the West Indies, it is an outcrop of a submerged mountain range. Its land area totals 4,411 square miles making it comparable in size to Connecticut. Jamaica has three distinct regions: the coastal lowlands and valleys, the limestone plateau, and the interior highlands. Most of the country is mountainous, but there are excellent beaches on the northern and western coasts. The capital city of Kingston, in the south, is around one of the largest and finest natural harbors in the world.
- **Population, Cities, and American Residents:** The population of Jamaica totals 2.6 million people (1992 est.). More than ninety percent are of black African ancestry. Today, 76.3 percent of the people are African, 15.1 percent Afro-European, 3.4 percent East Indian and Afro-East Indian, 3.2 percent white, and 2 percent other.

    Most American residents are employed in Jamaica's two largest cities: Kingston with 800,000, and Montego Bay with 70,000 people (1989 est.)
- **Language and Currency:** The official language of Jamaica is English, which is spoken throughout business and government. The monetary unit is the Jamaican dollar (J$), divided into 100 cents. The exchange rate is 35.4 J$ = U.S.$1 (July 30, 1993).
- **Climate:** The climate of Jamaica is tropical, moderated by cool ocean breezes and mountain altitude. There is little temperature variation during the year, averaging about 75°F during the winter and 80°F in the summer. Rainfall is heaviest from May to June and September to October. Jamaica is subject to hurricanes, tropical storms, and earthquakes, with the official hurricane season beginning in June and lasting through October.
- **Economy and Resources:** Tourism is a major economic activity in Jamaica. Others are agriculture, mining, and manufacturing. Although agriculture contributes little to the GDP, it employs 33 percent of the labor force. Chief exports include sugar, bananas, and citrus fruits. Jamaica is the world's third largest producer of bauxite; other natural resources include gypsum and limestone. Industry and commerce employ 28 percent of the labor force, and government 13 percent. Major trading partners include the United States, United Kingdom, and Canada. The weather plays a key role in the Jamaican economy as agriculture and tourism can be severely affected by hurricanes. The outlook

for Jamaica's future is good, if political and social stability can be maintained, but the drug trade threatens the country's image. Jamaica has to curtail the production of marijuana to encourage tourism. Though it is considered illegal, ganga (marijuana) remains a major product of the rural economy with much of it being exported off the island. Narcotics traffickers using Jamaica as a transshipment point smuggle drugs into legitimate exports, driving up shipping costs. Government efforts to stabilize the economy and expand trade and investment will be difficult unless the drug problem is controlled.

- **Cost of Living:** At 92, the cost of living is slightly less than in the United States.
- **Work Permits, Visas, etc.:** A valid passport or two documents showing proof of citizenship are required for U.S. citizens to travel to Jamaica. Those who intend to work or reside in Jamaica must apply for a work permit through the Ministry of National Security by contacting an embassy official in the United States. If you are entering Jamaica from the United States, no vaccinations are necessary. For official or other information, direct inquiries to the embassy or consulate at the addresses below.
- **Taxation:** Individuals staying in Jamaica for less than six months or who do not plan to reside in Jamaica permanently, are not subject to Jamaican income taxes. For longer stays, nonresidents are subject to Jamaican income taxes only on income earned from Jamaican sources. There is a tax treaty in effect between Jamaica and the United States to avoid double taxation.
- **Principal International Schools:** International schools in Kingston and Mandeville follow the U.S. and British curriculum. Tuition ranges from $500 to $1,100 per year.
- **Health Care:** Medical facilities are adequate for minor procedures and simple health problems. Serious illnesses or injuries are treated elsewhere, usually in Puerto Rico, which has the highest quality health care in the Caribbean. Sanitation is good in the major cities throughout Jamaica; water is safe to drink. In rural areas, it's better to drink bottled water or boil water before drinking. The sun is especially strong in this tropical location, so take care to avoid heat stroke and sunburn.
- **Crime:** Jamaica's crime rate is lower than those of most American cities; Americans are usually welcomed and treated respectfully. As in any major tourist area or large city, beware of pickpockets or purse snatchers, and don't carry large amounts of cash. Be cautious when traveling in the evening hours, especially if you're alone. Drug trafficking is a problem in Jamaica, and narcotics are peddled in tourist areas. Possession or sale of any hard drug is a criminal offense and may be punishable by a long prison term.
- **Pros and Cons of Living and Working in Jamaica:** Jamaica has magnificent scenery and a pleasant year-round climate. It has more than 3,000 species of tropical flowers and plants, hundreds of miles of sandy beaches, and sunshine throughout the year. Popular attractions include historic plantations, reggae music, and a vibrant night life. Telecommunications services, transportation, and housing are adequate. Bring furniture with you, as the selection for sale in Jamaica is limited and expensive. Be careful on the roads; cars travel on the left, Jamaicans tend to drive very fast, and

EMBASSY AND CONSULATE CONTACT INFORMATION:

JAMAICAN EMBASSY
1850 K ST. NW, STE. 355
WASHINGTON, DC 20006
TEL: 202-452-0660

roads are narrow, with many curves. Prescriptions for medications will only be filled if issued by a Jamaican doctor. If certain medications are needed, bring the original prescription form signed by your doctor with you. Illegal drug use is prevalent in Jamaica. In order to curb drug exports, airport security is tight.

JAMAICAN CONSULATE GENERAL
866 SECOND AVE., 8TH FL.
NEW YORK, NY 10017

OTHER SOURCES OF INFORMATION:

U.S. STATE DEPT.
DESK OFFICER FOR JAMAICA
WASHINGTON, DC 20025
TEL: 202-647-2620

COMPANIES/ORGANIZATIONS WITH OPERATIONS IN JAMAICA:

ALUMINUM COMPANY OF AMERICA, 118

CAMP DRESSER & MCKEE
INTERNATIONAL, INC., 183

CUNA MUTUAL INSURANCE GROUP, 222

EXXON COMPANY, INTERNATIONAL, 258

NORTHWEST AIRLINES, INC., 390

REYNOLDS METALS COMPANY, 438

UNION CAMP CORPORATION, 507

JAPAN

- **Official Name:** Japan

- **Capital:** Tokyo

- **Location:** Japan consists of four main islands and more than 3,000 smaller ones, forming an archipelago that stretches for 1,300 miles northeast to southwest between the Sea of Japan and the western Pacific Ocean. It has a very indented, 18,600 mile coastline. The total land area is 377,657 square miles, making it comparable in size to Montana. Japan accounts for 3 percent of the world's total population. Only 16 percent of Japan's land mass is used for cultivation. Another 16 percent is built up, and about 72 percent of the country is mountainous. The main islands are: Hokkaido, Honshu, Shikoku, and Kyushu. The capital city of Tokyo is on Honshu, the island upon which 80 percent of Japan's population lives.

- **Population, Cities, and American Residents:** The population of Japan totals 124.6 million people (1992 est.), accounting for three percent of the world's total population. Japanese account for 99.4 percent of the country's people. The remaining 0.6 percent are mostly Korean.

  Most American residents are employed on the island of Honshu in Japan's three largest cities: Tokyo with 12 million, Yokohama with 3.2 million, and Osaka with 2.6 million people (1990 est.).

- **Language and Currency:** The official language of the country is Japanese, which is used in business and government throughout the country. Language courses are available in most cities. The monetary unit is the yen. Bills are in denominations of 10,000, 5,000, 1,000, and 500. Coins are in 500, 100, 50, 10, 5, and 1. The exchange rate is 1 Japanese yen = U.S.$.009; 106 yen equal U.S.$1 (July 30,1993).

- **Climate:** The climate of Japan has four seasons, with Tokyo's climate very much like that of Washington, D.C. There is little ice on the roads during the winters, which are cold and bright with daily temperatures around 30°F. Spring begins in March with an average temperature of 55°F, and the rainy season is from May through July. The average summer temperature is 77°F and is quite humid. September can see heavy rains and strong winds, though generally not of typhoon force. Autumn is the most pleasant season, with clear sunny days averaging around 62°F.

- **Economy and Resources:** At the end of World War II, Japan's economy lay in devastation. Almost fifty years later, hard work, keen business management, and strategic planning has made Japan a global leader in many sectors including the auto industry, shipbuilding, electronics, and steel. The nation continues to move ahead in the fields of high-technology. Factories are generally more modern and automated than those in other industrialized countries. The Japanese economy is meeting domestic needs, although less than 20 percent of the land is arable. Nearly 54 percent of the labor force is engaged in trade and services and 33 percent work in manufacturing, mining, and construction. Major exports include machinery, motor vehicles, and consumer electronics. Major trading partners are the United States and Southeast Asia.

- **Cost of Living:** The cost of living in Japan is very high, ranging from 146 to 196 (figures were taken from a selection of major areas).

- **Work Permits, Visas, etc.:** A valid passport is required to travel in Japan. If you are from the United States and plan on staying in Japan for ninety days or less, no visa is necessary. For longer stays, you'll need a long-term commercial visa, for which you can apply for after you arrive in Japan. If you are entering Japan from the United States, no vaccinations are required. For official or other information, direct inquiries to the embassy or consulate at the addresses below.

- **Taxation:** Japan has one of the highest rates of taxation in the world. There are withholding taxes on salaries, wages, bonuses, etc., and foreign residents are taxed only on income from sources earned in Japan. The United States and Japan have a treaty to avoid double taxation, and some credits are given.

- **Principal International Schools:** International schools, offering quality education at all levels, are widely available throughout Japan. Tuition for a typical American School in Tokyo or Osaka is $10,000 per year.

- **Health Care:** Medical care in Japan is excellent. Doctors and dentists are well trained, and many of them speak English. Western medicine is available, and Chinese medicine (kampo yaku) also is practiced. This includes acupuncture and acupressure massage. Doctor's fees are reasonable, but dental costs average about $150 for a routine visit. Sanitation is very good throughout Japan, with water safe to drink in all major areas. In the country, however, water should be boiled. Dairy products are safe to consume, and domestic drugs are reasonably priced.

- **Crime:** Crime is not a major problem in Japan. Streets are safe day or night, and the Japanese people are known for their helpful and friendly attitudes toward Westerners. It is best, however, to avoid dock areas and certain night-life districts during the evening hours.

● **Pros and Cons of Living and Working in Japan:** It's difficult to describe what
Japan has to offer the traveler in a few
words. Its culture is radically different
from ours. It is a modern, thriving country,
with excellent transportation and telecommunications services. Sanitation and
health care standards are well above
average and the people are very accommo-
dating to Westerners. However, roads are
poor, and traffic is heavily congested, even
in rural areas. Parking spaces are almost
non-existent, and cars travel in the left
lane. Also, road taxes and insurance rates
are very high, compared to U.S. standards.
Japan's cost of living is almost twice that
of the United States. Prices on some of the
essentials of daily life (food, clothing,
entertaining, etc.) can be staggering.

**EMBASSY AND CONSULATE CONTACT
INFORMATION:**

EMBASSY OF JAPAN
2520 MASSACHUSETTS AVE. NW
WASHINGTON, DC 20008
TEL: 202-939-6700

CONSULATE-GENERAL OF JAPAN
299 PARK AVE.
NEW YORK, NY 10017
TEL: 212-371-8222
FAX: 212-751-8344

OTHER SOURCES OF INFORMATION:

JAPANESE CHAMBER OF COMMERCE OF
NEW YORK
145 WEST 57TH ST.
NEW YORK, NY 10019
TEL: 212-246-9774

COMPANIES/ORGANIZATIONS WITH OPERATIONS IN JAPAN:

ABBOTT LABORATORIES, 109

ACCO WORLD CORPORATION, 110

ADVANCED MICRO DEVICES, INC., 112

AIRBORNE EXPRESS, 112

AKZO AMERICA, INC., 113

ALEXANDER & ALEXANDER SERVICES,
    INC., 116

ALLEN-BRADLEY COMPANY, INC., 116

ALLIED-SIGNAL, INC., 117

ALUMINUM COMPANY OF AMERICA, 118

AM INTERNATIONAL, INC., 119

AMDAHL CORPORATION, 120

AMERACE CORPORATION (ELASTIMOLD),
    121

AMERICAN CYANAMID COMPANY, 124

AMERICAN EXPRESS BANK, LTD., 124

AMERICAN EXPRESS COMPANY—TRAVEL
    RELATED SERVICES, 125

AMERICAN HOME PRODUCTS
    CORPORATION, 126

AMERICAN INTERNATIONAL GROUP, 127

AMERICAN PRESIDENT COMPANIES, LTD.,
    128

AMERIWOOD, INC., 130

AMP, INC., 132

AMPEX CORPORATION, 133

AMR/AMERICAN AIRLINES, 133

ANACOMP, INC., 134

ANDREW CORPORATION, 134

ANTHONY INDUSTRIES, 135

AON CORPORATION, 136

APPLE COMPUTER, INC., 136

APPLIED MATERIALS, INC., 137

ARBY'S, INC., 138

ASEA BROWN BOVERI, 142

ASHLAND OIL, INC., 143

ASSOCIATED PRESS, 144

AST RESEARCH, INC., 144

AT&T INTERNATIONAL, 145

ATARI CORPORATION, 146

AUGAT, INC., 146

AUTOMATIC SWITCH COMPANY, 147

AVON PRODUCTS, INC., 149

AVX CORPORATION, 150

BACKER SPIELVOGEL & BATES
    WORLDWIDE, INC., 150

BAILEY CONTROLS COMPANY, 151

BANDAG, INC., 153

THE BANK OF NEW YORK COMPANY,
    INC., 154

C. R. BARD, INC., 157

THE BARDEN CORPORATION, 157

BATTELLE MEMORIAL INSTITUTE, 159

BAUSCH & LOMB, INC., 159

BAXTER HEALTHCARE CORPORATION, 160
JIM BEAM BRANDS COMPANY, 161
BECKMAN INSTRUMENTS, INC., 162
BELL & HOWELL COMPANY, 164
BIO-RAD LABORATORIES, 166
BLACK & DECKER CORPORATION, 167
BLACK & VEATCH, 168
BLOCK DRUG COMPANY, INC., 169
BLOUNT, INC. (BLOUNT CONSTRUCTION
    DIVISION), 169
BORDEN, INC., 170
BORG-WARNER CORPORATION, 171
BORLAND INTERNATIONAL, INC, 172
BOSE CORPORATION, 172
BP AMERICA, INC., 173
BRIDGESTONE-FIRESTONE, INC., 174
BRUSH WELLMAN, INC., 178
BURLINGTON AIR EXPRESS, 179
BURSON-MARSTELLER, 180
CABOT CORPORATION, 181
CALGON CORPORATION, 182
CAPITOL CITIES/ABC, INC., 184
CARGILL INCORPORATED, 184
CARRIER CORPORATION, 186
CENTOCOR, INC., 188
CHEMICAL BANKING CORPORATION, 191
CHEMICAL FABRICS CORPORATION, 192
CHEVRON CORPORATION, 193
CIGNA CORPORATION, 197
CINCOM SYSTEMS, INC., 197
CLUB CORPORATION INTERNATIONAL, 200
COHERENT, INC., 202
COLGATE-PALMOLIVE COMPANY, 203
COMMERCIAL INTERTECH CORPORATION,
    205
COMPUTER ASSOCIATES INTERNATIONAL,
    INC., 207
COMPUTERVISION CORPORATION, 208
CONOCO, INC., 209
CONTINENTAL AIRLINES HOLDINGS, INC.,
    210
CONTINUUM COMPANY, INC., 211
CONVERSE, INC., 212
COOPERS & LYBRAND, 214
CORNING INCORPORATED, 215
WILLIS CORROON, 216
COUDERT BROTHERS LAW FIRM, 217
CS FIRST BOSTON, INC., 219
CUBIC CORPORATION, 220
CUMMINS ENGINE COMPANY, INC., 221

D-M-E COMPANY, 222
LEO A. DALY COMPANY, 223
DAMES & MOORE, 223
DATA GENERAL CORPORATION, 225
DDB NEEDHAM WORLDWIDE, INC., 227
DELL COMPUTER CORPORATION, 231
DELTA AIR LINES, INC., 232
DH TECHNOLOGY, INC., 233
DIGITAL EQUIPMENT CORPORATION, 236
DOMINO'S PIZZA, INC., 237
DONALDSON LUFKIN & JENRETTE, INC.,
    238
R. R. DONNELLEY & SONS COMPANY,
    238
DOW CHEMICAL COMPANY, 240
DOW JONES & COMPANY, INC., 241
DRESSER INDUSTRIES, INC., 241
DRUMMOND COMPANY, INC., 242
DUN & BRADSTREET CORPORATION, 243
DURACELL, INC., 244
DURO-TEST INTERNATIONAL
    CORPORATION, 245
E-SYSTEMS, INC., 245
EAGLE-PICHER INDUSTRIES, INC., 246
EASTMAN KODAK COMPANY, 246
EG & G, INC., 249
ELECTRONIC DATA SYSTEMS
    CORPORATION, 249
ELI LILLY AND COMPANY, 250
ELIZABETH ARDEN COMPANY, 251
EMERSON ELECTRIC COMPANY, 251
EMERY WORLDWIDE, 252
ENCORE COMPUTER CORPORATION, 252
ENCYCLOPEDIA BRITANNICA, INC., 253
ERNST & YOUNG, 255
EXPEDITORS INTERNATIONAL OF
    WASHINGTON, INC., 257
EXXON COMPANY, INTERNATIONAL, 258
EXXON CORPORATION, 258
FALK CORPORATION, 259
FEDERAL EXPRESS CORPORATION, 260
FIGGIE INTERNATIONAL, INC., 262
FIRST CHICAGO CORPORATION, 262
FLEMING COMPANIES, INC., 264
FLOW INTERNATIONAL CORPORATION, 265
JOHN FLUKE MANUFACTURING COMPANY,
    265
FORD MOTOR COMPANY, 267
GAF CORPORATION, 270
THE GATES RUBBER COMPANY, 273

COUNTRY

PROFILES

AMERICAN JOBS ABROAD

GATX CORPORATION, 273
GENERAL DYNAMICS CORPORATION, 274
GENERAL MILLS, INC., 277
GENERAL MOTORS CORPORATION (GM), 277
GENERAL SIGNAL CORPORATION, 278
W. R. GRACE & COMPANY, 285
GRACO, INC., 286
GREAT LAKES CHEMICAL CORPORATION, 287
GREY ADVERTISING, INC., 288
H. J. HEINZ COMPANY, 290
H & R BLOCK, 291
HALLIBURTON COMPANY/HALLIBURTON SERVICES DIVISION, 293
HALLIBURTON-NUS CORPORATION, 293
HAZLETON WASHINGTON CORPORATION, 297
HELENE CURTIS INDUSTRIES, INC., 298
HELLMUTH, OBATA & KASSABAUM, INC., 298
HERSHEY FOODS CORPORATION, 299
HERTZ CORPORATION, 300
HILL & KNOWLTON, INC., 301
HOLIDAY INNS WORLDWIDE, 302
HORMEL FOODS CORPORATION, 304
HUGHES AIRCRAFT COMPANY, 307
HYATT INTERNATIONAL CORPORATION, 308
IDB COMMUNICATIONS, INC., 309
ILLINOIS TOOL WORKS, INC., 309
IMCERA GROUP, INC., 310
IMO INDUSTRIES, 310
IMS AMERICA, LTD., 311
INDUCTOTHERM CORPORATION, 311
INGERSOLL-RAND COMPANY, 313
INTEL CORPORATION, 314
INTERNATIONAL BUSINESS MACHINES (IBM), 315
INTERNATIONAL DAIRY QUEEN, INC., 316
INTERNATIONAL FLAVORS & FRAGRANCES, INC., 317
INTERNATIONAL RECTIFIER CORPORATION, 319
INTERTRANS CORPORATION, 320
ITT CORPORATION, 321
ITT SHERATON CORPORATION, 322
ITW FINISHING SYSTEMS & PRODUCTS, 322
JOHNSON & HIGGINS, 324

S. C. JOHNSON WAX, 325
JONES, DAY, REAVIS & POGUE, INC., 326
JOURNAL OF COMMERCE, 326
JWP, INC., 328
A. T. KEARNEY, INC., 329
KEITHLEY INSTRUMENTS, INC., 329
KELLOGG COMPANY, 330
KENNAMETAL, INC., 333
KETCHUM INTERNATIONAL, 334
KIDDER PEABODY GROUP & COMPANY, INC., 335
KLYNVELD PEAT MARWICK GOERDELER (KPMG), 337
KNIGHT-RIDDER, INC., 338
KNOLL INTERNATIONAL, 338
KOCH INDUSTRIES, INC., 339
KOHLER COMPANY, 339
KOLMAR LABORATORIES, INC., 340
KORN/FERRY INTERNATIONAL, 340
KRAFT GENERAL FOODS INTERNATIONAL, 341
LAMBDA ELECTRONICS, INC., 343
LEVI STRAUSS ASSOCIATES, INC., 344
LIANT SOFTWARE CORPORATION, 345
THE LINCOLN ELECTRIC COMPANY, 346
LITTON INDUSTRIES, INC., 348
LOCTITE CORPORATION, 349
LOTUS DEVELOPMENT CORPORATION, 351
MALLINCKRODT, INC., 359
MARION MERRELL DOW, INC., 360
MCCANN-ERICKSON WORLDWIDE, 354
MCCORMICK & COMPANY, INC., 355
MCDONALD'S CORPORATION, 356
MCGRAW-HILL, INC., 357
MCI COMMUNICATIONS CORPORATION, 365
MCKINSEY & COMPANY, INC., 357
MEASUREX CORPORATION, 366
MEDTRONIC, INC., 366
MEMOREX TELEX CORPORATION, 367
MERCK & COMPANY, INC., 368
MERRILL LYNCH & COMPANY, INC., 369
METALLURG CORPORATION, 370
METCO PERKIN-ELMER, 371
HERMAN MILLER, INC., 373
MILLIKEN & COMPANY, 373
MILLIPORE CORPORATION, 374
MODINE MANUFACTURING COMPANY, 375
MOLEX, INC., 376

MONROE AUTO EQUIPMENT COMPANY, 376
MONTGOMERY WARD HOLDING COMPANY, 377
J. P. MORGAN & COMPANY, INC., 378
MORGAN STANLEY GROUP, INC., 379
MORTON INTERNATIONAL, 380
NALCO CHEMICAL COMPANY, 382
NATIONAL DATA CORPORATION, 382
NATIONAL SEMICONDUCTOR CORPORATION, 383
NCR CORPORATION, 384
NEWSWEEK INTERNATIONAL, 387
NICOLET INSTRUMENT CORPORATION, 387
NIKE, INC., 388
NORDSON CORPORATION, 389
NORTHWEST AIRLINES, INC., 390
NOVELL, INC., 392
OLIN CORPORATION, 396
OMNICOM GROUP, INC., 397
ONAN CORPORATION, 397
ORACLE SYSTEMS, INC., 398
OTIS ELEVATOR COMPANY: WORLD HEADQUARTERS, 399
OVERSEAS SHIPHOLDING GROUP, INC., 400
OWENS-ILLINOIS, INC., 401
PACIFIC TELESIS INTERNATIONAL, 403
PAINE WEBBER GROUP, INC., 403
PALL CORPORATION, 404
PARKER HANNIFIN CORPORATION, 405
PARSONS BRINKERHOFF, 406
PARSONS CORPORATION, 406
J. C. PENNEY COMPANY, INC., 407
PERKIN-ELMER CORPORATION, 410
PETROLITE CORPORATION, 411
PFIZER, INC., 412
PHELPS DODGE CORPORATION, 412
PHILIP MORRIS COMPANIES, INC., 413
PHILIPP BROTHERS CHEMICALS, INC., 414
PIONEER HI-BRED INTERNATIONAL, INC., 417
PIZZA HUT, INC., 419
PPG INDUSTRIES, 421
PRECISION VALVE CORPORATION, 422
PREFORMED LINE PRODUCTS COMPANY, 423
PREMARK INTERNATIONAL, INC., 423
PRIMERICA CORPORATION, 424
PROCTER & GAMBLE COMPANY, 425

PRUDENTIAL INSURANCE COMPANY OF AMERICA, 427
QUAKER CHEMICAL CORPORATION, 428
RANCO, INC., 431
RAYTHEON COMPANY, 432
RECOGNITION EQUIPMENT, INC., 433
REDKEN LABORATORIES, INC., 434
RELIANCE ELECTRIC COMPANY, 435
RELIANCE INTERNATIONAL, 436
REMINGTON PRODUCTS, INC., 436
REVLON, INC., 437
REYNOLDS METALS COMPANY, 438
ROCKWELL GRAPHIC SYSTEMS, 441
ROCKWELL INTERNATIONAL CORPORATION, 441
ROGERS CORPORATION, 442
ROSEMOUNT, INC., 443
RUDER FINN, INC., 445
RUSSELL REYNOLDS ASSOCIATES, INC., 446
SAATCHI & SAATCHI, 448
SALOMON, INC., 449
SCHLEGEL CORPORATION, 451
SCOTT PAPER COMPANY, 453
SEA-LAND SERVICE, INC., 454
SEALED AIR CORPORATION, 455
SEARLE COMPANY, 455
SEARS ROEBUCK AND COMPANY, 456
SGS CONTROL SERVICES, 458
SGS-THOMSON MICROELECTRONICS, 458
SHAKLEE CORPORATION, 459
SHEAFFER PEN, INC., 459
SHEARMAN & STERLING, 460
SHERWIN-WILLIAMS COMPANY, 461
SHIPLEY COMPANY, INC., 461
SIGNODE PACKAGING SYSTEMS, 462
SIMON & SCHUSTER, INC., 463
SKADDEN, ARPS, SLATE, MEAGHER & FLOM, 465
A. O. SMITH CORPORATION, 467
SONOCO PRODUCTS COMPANY, 470
SONY PICTURES ENTERTAINMENT, 471
SOUTHLAND CORPORATION, 472
SPRINGS INDUSTRIES, INC., 473
SPS TECHNOLOGIES, INC., 474
SRI INTERNATIONAL, 475
STANDARD & POOR'S CORPORATION, 476
STATE STREET BOSTON CORPORATION, 478

A
M
E
R
I
C
A
N

J
O
B
S

A
B
R
O
A
D

STORAGE TECHNOLOGY CORPORATION, 481
STRUCTURAL DYNAMICS RESEARCH CORPORATION, 481
SUN COMPANY, INC., 483
SUNDSTRAND CORPORATION, 485
SYNTEX CORPORATION, 486
TANDY CORPORATION, 487
TEKTRONIX, INC., 488
TELEDYNE, INC., 489
TENNANT COMPANY, 490
TENNECO AUTOMOTIVE, 491
TENNECO, INC., 492
TERADYNE, INC., 493
TEXACO OIL COMPANY, 493
TEXAS INTRUMENTS, INC., 494
THOMAS & BETTS, 495
3M COMPANY, 496
3M PHARMACEUTICALS, 497
TIME-WARNER, INC., 498
TORRINGTON COMPANY, 499
TOWERS PERRIN, INC., 499
TOYS ''R'' US, INC., 500
TRANE COMPANY, 501
TRINOVA CORPORATION, 502
TRW, INC., 503
TW HOLDINGS, INC., 504
UAL CORPORATION, 506
UNILEVER UNITED STATES, INC., 506
UNION CAMP CORPORATION, 507
UNISYS CORPORATION, 508
UNITED NATIONS INDUSTRIAL DEVELOPMENT ORGANIZATION (UNIDO), 568

U.S. DEPARTMENT OF ENERGY, 573
U.S. ELECTRICAL MOTORS (EMERSON ELECTRIC), 510
U.S. MARINE CORPS, 581
UNITED STATES SURGICAL CORPORATION, 511
U.S. WHEAT ASSOCIATES, 511
UNITED TECHNOLOGIES CORPORATION, 512
UOP, INC., 514
THE UPJOHN COMPANY, 515
US WEST, INC., 515
VISA INTERNATIONAL, 517
VISHAY INTERTECHNOLOGY, 518
WARD HOWELL INTERNATIONAL, INC., 520
WARNER BROTHERS INTERNATIONAL, 521
WARNER ELECTRIC BRAKE & CLUTCH COMPANY, 521
WASHINGTON POST COMPANY, 522
WATERS CHROMATOGRAPHY (MILLIPORE), 523
WEIGHT WATCHERS INTERNATIONAL, INC., 524
WENDY'S INTERNATIONAL, INC., 524
WEST COMPANY, INC., 525
WEYERHAEUSER COMPANY, 526
WHIRLPOOL CORPORATION, 526
WOODWARD GOVERNOR COMPANY, 528
WORLD COURIER MANAGEMENT, INC., 529
WYETH-AYERST LABORATORIES, 530
XEROX CORPORATION, 531
YOUNG & RUBICAM, INC., 533

JORDAN

- **Official Name:** Hashemite Kingdom of Jordan
- **Capital:** Amman
- **Location:** Jordan is an Arab kingdom in the Middle East. It is bounded by Syria to the north, Iraq to the northeast, Saudi Arabia to the southeast, and Israel to the west. Jordan is landlocked, except for a small stretch of land in the southern sector on the Gulf of 'Aqaba. Its total land area is 37,738 square miles, making Jordan a bit smaller than

Indiana. Nearly 90 percent of the territory is desert, with mountains and rolling plains comprising the rest. A major topographic feature is the great north-south Jordan Rift Valley that forms the depression of the Jordan River Valley, Lake Tiberias, and the Dead Sea, which is 1,300 feet below sea level.

- **Language and Currency:** The official language of Jordan is Arabic. English is widely used in business and government and among upper and middle classes. The monetary unit is Jordanian dinar. The exchange rate is 1.46 Jordanian dinar = U.S.$1 (July 1993).

EMBASSY AND CONSULATE CONTACT INFORMATION:

EMBASSY OF THE HASHEMITE KINGDOM OF JORDAN
3504 INTERNATIONAL DR. NW
WASHINGTON, DC 20008
TEL: 202-966-2664

OTHER SOURCES OF INFORMATION:

FOR INFORMATION ON ECONOMIC TRENDS, COMMERCIAL DEVELOPMENT, AND TRADE CONTACT:
INTERNATIONAL TRADE ADMINISTRATION
U.S. DEPARTMENT OF COMMERCE
WASHINGTON, DC 20230

COMPANIES/ORGANIZATIONS WITH OPERATIONS IN JORDAN:

BAILEY CONTROLS COMPANY, 151
RESOURCES MANAGEMENT
    INTERNATIONAL, 437

KAZAKHSTAN

- **Official Name:** Republic of Kazakhstan
- **Capital:** Almaty
- **Location:** Kazakhstan is an independent country in central Asia. It joined the Commonwealth of Independent States, formed when the Soviet Union was dissolved in 1991. Kazakhstan is bounded by the Russia to the north and northeast; China to the southeast; Kyrgystan, Uzbekistan, and Turkmenistan to the south; and the Caspian Sea to the west. The total land area is 1,049,155 square miles, making Kazakhstan nearly twice the size of Alaska. Most of its territory is covered by a wilderness of wide, sandy deserts, and grassy plateaus.
- **Language and Currency:** The official language is Kazakh. Russian and other languages are also spoken. Having a working knowledge of Kazakh is important if you live or work in the country. The monetary unit is the ruble. The current exchange rate is not available (December 1993).

EMBASSY AND CONSULATE CONTACT INFORMATION:

EMBASSY OF THE REPUBLIC OF KAZAKHSTAN
3421 MASSACHUSETTS AVE. NW
WASHINGTON, DC 20007
TEL: 202-333-4507

COMPANIES/ORGANIZATIONS WITH OPERATIONS IN KAZAKHSTAN:

INTERNATIONAL CITY MANAGEMENT
ASSOCIATION, 548

NATIONAL DEMOCRATIC INSTITUTE, 557
PROJECT HOPE, 563

KENYA

- **Official Name:** Republic of Kenya

- **Capital:** Nairobi

- **Location:** Kenya, an independent republic within the British Commonwealth, is located on the Indian Ocean coast of East Africa with the equator dividing it into almost equal halves. "East Africa" includes Kenya, Tanzania, and Uganda and contains the second largest freshwater lake in the world, Lake Victoria. The lake lies in all three countries and is the main source of the Nile. Kenya is slightly smaller than Texas with an area of 224,960 square miles.

- **Population, Cities, and American Residents:** The population of Kenya totals 27.2 million people (1992 est.), 98 percent of whom are African. The remaining 2 percent are comprised of Arab, Asian, and European people. Thirty ethnic groups comprise the African population; over 60 percent are Bantu, and the remaining groups are the Nilotic, the Hamitic, and the Nilo-Hamitic people. About 6,000 American citizens reside in Kenya.

  Most American residents are employed in Kenya's two largest cities: Nairobi with 1.1 million, and Mombasa with 400,000 people (1989 est.).

- **Language and Currency:** Kiswahili is the national language of Kenya, but English is the official language used and spoken throughout business and government sectors. The unit of currency is the Kenyan Shilling (KSh), divided into 100 cents. Coins include 5 and 10 cent copper pieces; 50 cent, 1 Shilling, and 5 Shilling silver pieces. Notes are in denominations of 5 Shillings, 10 Shillings, 20 Shillings, 50 Shillings, 100 Shillings, and 200 Shillings. There are no pound notes, but at times prices are quoted in pounds. One pound is equivalent to 20 Shillings. The exchange rate is 65 KSh = U.S.$1 (August 31, 1993).

- **Climate:** Altitude is a major factor in this country's climate. Although the equator runs through the center of Kenya, half of the country is more than 1500 meters above sea level, resulting in a relatively temperate climate. The terrain varies from lush rain forests to desert conditions. Temperatures are normally the same all year: 75°F in the daytime, falling to 52°F in the evening. Coastal areas have a tropical climate with an average of 27-51 inches of rainfall per year. Many inland areas are dry with semi-arid conditions.

- **Economy and Resources:** Kenya has a moderately free economy with a large and active private sector. It has shown steady growth in industry and agriculture, but tourism remains the main foreign exchange earner. Some 700,000 visitors come to Kenya each year bringing U.S.$350 million into the country's coffers (1988). Mineral production includes gold, limestone, and magnesite; other resources include timber, livestock, and fish. Agricultural production is a mainstay of the economy; chief crops are coffee, tea, and cotton. Population growth is a threat to economic gains, however. At 4.1 percent yearly, Kenya's population growth rate is now the highest in the world. Less than 20 percent of the land is arable, and it will be difficult for food production to keep pace with population growth.

- **Cost of Living:** At 82, the cost of living is lower than in the United States.

- **Work Permits, Visas, etc.:** A valid passport and visa are required for U.S. citizens who wish to study or work in Kenya. Work permits, of which there are several different classes, are essential. Visas must be obtained in advance, and a multiple-entry visa for up to one year is available. If you are entering Kenya from the United States, no vaccinations are required, but shots against cholera, yellow fever, and typhoid are highly recommended. For official or other information, direct inquiries to the embassy or consulate at the addresses below.

- **Taxation:** Residents are subject to Kenyan income tax on worldwide earned income. Nonresidents are subject to tax on income from Kenyan sources. The country's tax system follows the British unitary structure. All income is totaled and subject to a progressive tax rate. For more information, contact the Commissioner of Income Tax, ESC Building, Ngong Road, PO Box #30742, Nairobi (telephone-727430).

- **Principal International Schools:** A selection of schools in Nairobi offer a comparable American curriculum for children of American residents.

- **Health Care:** Kenyan doctors and dentists are well trained and speak fluent English. Hospitals are well equipped, but imported pharmaceuticals are costly. The Nairobi Hospital serves American citizens adequately for most medical problems, and the facility in Mombasa is fine for routine or emergency treatment. General dentistry is available in Nairobi. Water is safe to drink in tourist areas and in the capital city of Nairobi, but outside the capital, avoid tap water (or boil if necessary). Appropriate precautions should be taken with all fruits and vegetables. Remember that the high altitude in Kenya may produce fatigue for visitors when they first arrive.

- **Crime:** The U.S. State Department advises citizens to be careful when visiting Kenya. Specific areas, including Nairobi and Mombasa, have high rates of theft and robbery, and the danger becomes greater in the late evening. Foreign visitors, as well as wealthy Kenyans, are often targets for criminals. In the evening hours, visitors are advised to use taxis, and to avoid wearing expensive jewelry and clothing or displaying high-priced photographic equipment. Americans should also be careful not to leave valuables unattended at their home. U.S. visitors are encouraged to register with their embassy in Nairobi. Both the consulate in Mombasa and the U.S. embassy offer specific information on the present crime situation in Kenya.

- **Pros and Cons of Living and Working in Kenya:** Kenya offers an exotic cultural and living experience for Americans. The development of the tourist industry has modernized many of the cities, but the nation's vast natural preserves are still beautiful, with abundant wildlife. Transportation is quite good; airports are served by many international airlines, and there is good passenger train service as well as an efficient intercity bus system. Despite the government's efforts to preserve the environment, problems continue to worsen, and in many areas, poaching poses a serious threat to some species. The U.S. State Department has advised its citizens to travel in groups (accompanied by a game ranger) while visiting game preserves as thieves have been known to attack foreign visitors there. Overpopulation is a major problem that affects everyone in Kenya, and urban poverty and crime must be controlled if the country is to keep attracting foreign visitors.

EMBASSY AND CONSULATE CONTACT INFORMATION:

KENYA EMBASSY
2249 R ST. NW
WASHINGTON, DC 20008
TEL: 202-387-6101

KENYA CONSULATE GENERAL
424 MADISON AVE., 6TH FL.
NEW YORK, NY 10017
TEL: 212-486-1300

OTHER SOURCES OF INFORMATION:

KENYA TOURIST OFFICE
424 MADISON AVE., 6TH FL.
NEW YORK, NY 10017
TEL: 212-486-1300

COMPANIES/ORGANIZATIONS WITH OPERATIONS IN KENYA:

AMERICAN CYANAMID COMPANY, 124
AMERICAN HOME PRODUCTS
　　CORPORATION, 126
ASSOCIATED PRESS, 144
CITICORP, 198
CROWN CORK & SEAL COMPANY, INC.,
　　218
EASTMAN KODAK COMPANY, 246
GENERAL MOTORS CORPORATION (GM),
　　277
HUGHES AIRCRAFT COMPANY, 307

MCCANN-ERICKSON WORLDWIDE, 354
MOBIL OIL CORPORATION, 375
PARKER DRILLING COMPANY, 405
PEPSICO, INC., 410
POPULATION COUNCIL, 562
REVLON, INC., 437
TECHNOSERVE, INC., 565
3M COMPANY, 496
VOLUNTEERS IN TECHNICAL ASSISTANCE,
　　INC, 584

KUWAIT

- **Official Name:** State of Kuwait

- **Capital:** Kuwait City

- **Location:** Kuwait is located in the northwest corner of the Arabian-Persian Gulf. It is bounded by Iraq to the north, Saudi Arabia to the south, and the Persian Gulf to the east. The total land area, including several islands, is 6,880 square miles, comparable in size to New Jersey. Kuwait's territory is primarily an arid desert and has only 2 percent arable land. The only fertile regions lie along the coast and on the islands.

- **Population, Cities, and American Residents:** The population of Kuwait prior to the Gulf War was over 2 million people, of which nearly 40 percent was Kuwaiti. Two-thirds of the people fled the country because of the Gulf War but most have returned home. Other Arabs accounted for 39 percent, South Asians for 9 percent, Iranians for 9 percent, and others for 9 percent.

Most American residents are employed in Kuwait's two largest cities: Kuwait City with 1 million people (Prewar est.) and Ahmadi with 305,000 (Prewar est.).

- **Language and Currency:** The official language of Kuwait is Arabic. English is a second language and spoken widely in business circles. The monetary unit is the dinar. The exchange rate is 1 Kuwaiti dinar = U.S.$3.3 (July 30, 1993).

- **Climate:** In Kuwait, the humidity is usually high most of the year. In the summer months it is very hot with the mean daytime temperature about 112°F, though it may often exceed 120°F. The spring and autumn months offer a temperate climate, and winter may see temperatures drop to between 55°-60°F. Most of the rain falls in December and January, but dust storms occur throughout the year.

- **Economy and Resources:** The Gulf War had a devastating effect on Kuwait. Much of the country was destroyed, and fires that ignited more than 700 oil wells caused one of the worst environmental disasters in history. Kuwait was, and still is, very dependent on oil; reserves are said to be the third largest in the world. Only 5 percent of the total were lost in the war. Kuwait has foreign investment holdings estimated at $70 billion, which include European refineries and drilling exploration companies. Other interests include banks and financial institutions, which were not affected by the Gulf War. Kuwait continues to invite foreign investment in certain areas, especially when managerial and technical skills can be taught or transferred. Prior to the war, Japan was Kuwait's biggest trading partner, but it appears that the United States will play a major role now and in the future.

- **Cost of Living:** At 115, the cost of living is higher than in the United States.

- **Work Permits, Visas, etc.:** A valid passport is required, as is a visa, which may be obtained through a Kuwaiti embassy or consulate. No one with an Israeli stamp, visa, or endorsement in a passport is permitted to enter Kuwait. Work and residence permits are issued by the Ministry of the Interior and must be obtained prior to entering the country. If you are entering Kuwait from the United States, no vaccinations are required. For official or other information, direct inquiries to the embassy or consulate at the addresses below.

- **Taxation:** There are no personal income taxes collected for citizens or foreigners of Kuwait.

- **Principal International Schools:** English-speaking schools are available in Kuwait City.

- **Health Care:** Medical facilities in Kuwait are adequate with many European doctors on the staffs. There are also numerous Western-trained and Arab doctors. Prescription drugs are available.

- **Crime:** The Sharia or Islamic law, with its severe strictures prevails in Kuwait. Common crime is not a problem in Kuwait as punishments are very harsh.

A
M
E
R
I
C
A
N

J
O
B
S

A
B
R
O
A
D

- **Pros and Cons of Living and Working in Kuwait:** The Gulf War left its mark on this small country, and it will be rebuilding for some time. Kuwait was, prior to the war, one of the richest countries in the world, and very dependent on oil exports. There are abundant opportunities for Americans to work in Kuwait, in various phases of reconstruction. Public transportation and telecommunications are adequate as are the medical facilities, but sanitation is still poor. Remember that Kuwait observes Moslem customs quite rigorously, alcohol is strictly forbidden there. Do not get off the plane intoxicated, or consume alcohol at any time while visiting the country. Offenders will be fined. Have some familiarity with Islamic laws and customs before arriving in Kuwait.

EMBASSY AND CONSULATE CONTACT INFORMATION:

EMBASSY OF KUWAIT
2940 TILDEN ST NW
WASHINGTON, DC 20008
TEL: 202-966-0702

KUWAIT CONSULATE GENERAL,
801 SECOND AVE.
NEW YORK, NY 10017
TEL: 212-973-4318

OTHER SOURCES OF INFORMATION:

U.S. STATE DEPT.
DESK OFFICER FOR THE ARABIAN
PENINSULA
WASHINGTON, DC 20025
TEL: 202-647-6572

COMPANIES/ORGANIZATIONS WITH OPERATIONS IN KUWAIT:

ABB VETCO GRAY, INC., 108
BECHTEL GROUP, INC., 162
BLOUNT, INC. (BLOUNT CONSTRUCTION
    DIVISION), 169
DAMES & MOORE, 223
DRESSER INDUSTRIES, INC., 241
ECOLOGY AND ENVIRONMENT, INC., 248
EG & G, INC., 249
FOSTER WHEELER CORPORATION, 268

INTERGRAPH CORPORATION, 314
KFC CORPORATION, 335
MARRIOTT CORPORATION, 360
MCDERMOTT INTERNATIONAL, INC., 356
PARKER DRILLING COMPANY, 405
PARSONS CORPORATION, 406
RAYTHEON COMPANY, 432
U.S. ARMY CORPS OF ENGINEERS, 570
VTN CORPORATION, 518

LEBANON

- **Official Name:** Republic of Lebanon
- **Capital:** Beirut
- **Location:** Lebanon is located on the eastern edge of the Mediterranean Sea in western Asia. It is bounded by Syria to the north and east, Israel to the south, and the Mediterranean Sea to the west. Its total land area is 4,036 square miles, making Lebanon about half the size of New Jersey. The country has a rugged terrain, with a narrow coastal plain giving way to the steep Lebanon Mountains, which provide a protective barrier. The Bekaa Valley divides Lebanon and the Anti-Lebanon Mountains.
- **Language and Currency:** The official

EMBASSY AND CONSULATE CONTACT INFORMATION:

EMBASSY OF LEBANON
2560 28TH ST. NW
WASHINGTON, DC 20008
TEL: 202-939-6300

languages of Lebanon are Arabic and French. English and Armenian are also spoken, but having a knowledge of Arabic or French is helpful in daily life. The monetary unit is the Lebanese pound. The current exchange rate is 1,700 Lebanese pounds = U.S.$1 (March 1994).

OTHER SOURCES OF INFORMATION:

FOR INFORMATION ON CURRENT ECONOMIC TRENDS, OR COMMERCIAL DEVELOPMENT CONTACT:
INTERNATIONAL TRADE ADMINISTRATION
U.S. DEPARTMENT OF COMMERCE
WASHINGTON, DC 20230

COMPANIES/ORGANIZATIONS WITH OPERATIONS IN LEBANON:

ASSOCIATED PRESS, 144

LIBERIA

- **Official Name:** Republic of Liberia
- **Capital:** Monrovia
- **Location:** Liberia, Africa's first independent republic (1848), is located on the western coast of the continent. It is bounded by Sierra Leone and Guinea to the north, Côte d'Ivoire to the east, and the Atlantic Ocean to the south and west. With a total land area of 37,743 square miles, Liberia is almost half the size of Nebraska. Its territory is comprised of flat coastal plains, rolling plateaus, and low mountains in the northeast section of the country.
- **Language and Currency:** The official language of Liberia is English and it is used throughout business and government. More than 20 languages of the Niger-Congo group are also spoken. The monetary unit is the U.S. dollar. The Liberian dollar is also used.

EMBASSY AND CONSULATE CONTACT INFORMATION:

EMBASSY OF THE REPUBLIC OF LIBERIA
5201 16TH ST. NW
WASHINGTON, DC 20011
TEL: 202-723-0437

OTHER SOURCES OF INFORMATION:

FOR INFORMATION ON CURRENT ECONOMIC TRENDS, OR COMMERCIAL DEVELOPMENT CONTACT:
INTERNATIONAL TRADE ADMINISTRATION
U.S. DEPARTMENT OF COMMERCE
WASHINGTON, DC 20230

COMPANIES/ORGANIZATIONS WITH OPERATIONS IN LIBERIA:

PARSONS MAIN, INC., 407

LUXEMBOURG

- **Official Name:** Grand Duchy of Luxembourg
- **Capital:** Luxembourg

- **Location:** Luxembourg is a landlocked country in northwestern Europe. It is bounded by Belgium to the north, Germany to the east, and France to the south. Covering only 998 square miles, it is slightly smaller than Rhode Island. It has a landscape of hills, steep cliffs, and rolling farmland, with nearly 60 percent of its territory covered by meadows and pastures.
- **Language and Currency:** Letzeburgish is the official language of Luxembourg, but French and German are widely spoken throughout the country. French is the accepted language of business and government, and those on long-term assignments should have a working knowledge of French. The monetary unit is the Luxembourg franc (LFr), which is equal in value to the Belgian franc. The exchange rate is 35 Luxembourg francs = U.S.$1 (November 1993).

EMBASSY AND CONSULATE CONTACT INFORMATION:

LUXEMBOURG EMBASSY
2200 MASSACHUSETTS AVE. NW
WASHINGTON, DC 20008
TEL: 202-265-4171

LUXEMBOURG CONSULATE/NATIONAL
TOURIST OFFICE
801 SECOND AVE.
NEW YORK, NY 10017
TEL: 212-370-9850

OTHER SOURCES OF INFORMATION:

DEPARTMENT OF COMMERCE
BELGIUM/LUXEMBOURG DESK OFFICER
WASHINGTON, DC 20230
TEL: 202-377-5401

COMPANIES/ORGANIZATIONS WITH OPERATIONS IN LUXEMBOURG:

AMERACE CORPORATION (ELASTIMOLD),
121
COMMERCIAL INTERTECH CORPORATION,
205
RPM, INC., 444

MADAGASCAR

- **Official Name:** Republic of Madagascar
- **Capital:** Antananarivo
- **Location:** Madagascar lies in the western Indian Ocean off the southeast coast of Africa. Comprising one large island (Madagascar) and other smaller island dependencies, its land area totals 224,532 square miles, making Madagascar nearly twice the size of Arizona. More than half of the territory is covered by meadows and pastures, with the heart of the country a high plateau containing many hilly areas. Mountains in the center divide northern Madagascar from the south, which is mainly desert. In the west there are fertile plains, while the eastern coast is a narrow plain subject to storms. It is also a dangerous region for ships due to the abundance of offshore reefs.

- **Language and Currency:** The official languages of Madagascar are Malagasy and French. Having a working knowledge of French is important for a long-term assignment in Madagascar. The monetary unit is the Malagasy franc. The exchange rate is 1,900 francs = U.S.$1 (December 1993).

EMBASSY AND CONSULATE CONTACT INFORMATION:

EMBASSY OF THE REPUBLIC OF MADAGASCAR
2374 MASSACHUSETTS AVE. NW
WASHINGTON, DC 20008
TEL: 202-265-5525

COMPANIES/ORGANIZATIONS WITH OPERATIONS IN MADAGASCAR:

CONSERVATION INTERNATIONAL, 545

MALAWI

- **Official Name:** Republic of Malawi
- **Capital:** Lilongwe
- **Location:** Malawi is a small landlocked country in south-central Africa. It is bounded by Tanzania to the north, Mozambique to the east, south, and southwest, and Zambia to the west. Lake Malawi forms the largest portion of the eastern boundary. Its total land area is 45,747 square miles, making it slightly larger than Pennsylvania. Its territory is comprised of grasslands and savannas, hardwood forests, and narrow plateaus that stretch into an area of hills and low mountains.
- **Language and Currency:** The official languages are English and Chichewa. Tombuka is also spoken by some of its people. The monetary unit is the Malawi kwacha. The current exchange rate is unavailable.

EMBASSY AND CONSULATE CONTACT INFORMATION:

THE EMBASSY OF MALAWI
2408 MASSACHUSETTS AVE. NW
WASHINGTON, DC 20008
TEL: 202/797-1007

OTHER SOURCES OF INFORMATION:

FOR INFORMATION ON CURRENT ECONOMIC TRENDS, OR COMMERCIAL DEVELOPMENT CONTACT:
INTERNATIONAL TRADE ADMINISTRATION
U.S. DEPARTMENT OF COMMERCE
WASHINGTON, DC 20230

COMPANIES/ORGANIZATIONS WITH OPERATIONS IN MALAWI:

BURLINGTON AIR EXPRESS, 179
PROJECT HOPE, 563

STANDARD COMMERCIAL CORPORATION, 476

MALAYSIA

- **Official Name:** Malaysia
- **Capital:** Kuala Lumpur

- **Location:** Malaysia, located on the southeastern tip of Asia, is separated into two sections by 400 miles of ocean. West Malaysia (also called Peninsular Malaysia) has 11 of the country's 13 states and is located between the Strait of Malacca to the west and the South China Sea to the East. It is bounded by Thailand to the north, the South China Sea to the east, Singapore to the south, and Sumatra to the west. Across the South China Sea are the 2 states of East Malaysia, Sabah, and Sarawak. They share North Borneo with Indonesia and Brunei. Most of the country's territory is composed of coastal plains and jungle-covered mountains. A mountain range stretches down the length of the peninsula, where 80 percent of the Malaysian population lives. The area around the administrative capital of Kuala Lumpur is also the economic center of the country. It lies on the Malacca coast of the southern peninsula. The country's total land area is 127,317 square miles, making Malaysia slightly smaller than Japan.

- **Population, Cities, and American Residents:** Malaysia has 18 million people (1992 est.). Malays account for 59 percent of the population, Chinese for 32 percent, and Indians for 9 percent.

  Most American residents are employed in Malaysia's three largest cities: Kuala Lumpur with 1 million, Georgetown with 1 million, and Johore Bahru with 250,000 people (1990 est.).

- **Language and Currency:** The official language of Malaysia is Bahasa (Malay), but English is widely used in business and government throughout the country, and is taught as a second language. The unit of currency is the Malaysian dollar (ringgit), which has 100 sen (cents). Bills are M$1,000, 100, 50, 10, 5, and 1. Coins are 50, 20, 10, 5, and 1 sen; and M$1. The exchange rate is 1 Malaysian ringgit = U.S.$.39 (July 30, 1993).

- **Climate:** Although it lies extremely close to the equator, Malaysia has a moderate climate. The days are quite hot and humid, usually between 85-90 percent humidity, but the nights are cooler. In most areas, temperatures range from 73°F at night to 90°F during the day, although the highlands are a bit cooler. The rainy season lasts from September through December on the west coast and from October through February on the east coast, with the average rainfall of 80 to 104 inches. The heaviest precipitation is in the northeast monsoon area.

- **Economy and Resources:** Since gaining independence from Great Britain in 1957, Malaysia has had one of the fastest growing economies in the world. Although it suffered from a recession in the mid 1980s, the country has since regained economic momentum, fueled by an abundance of natural resources and investment in high technology. Over 1,200 international firms are located in Malaysia, in part for its desirable location on the crossroads of world travel; most are engaged in manufacturing operations. Malaysia is a global producer and exporter of tin, palm oil, tropical hardwoods, and pepper. Major crops include natural rubber, palm oil, and rice. Natural resources include tin, crude oil, and timber. The largest industries are processing and manufacturing, agricultural processing, and petroleum production and refining. Nearly 35 percent of the work force is employed in agriculture, 15.6 percent in manufacturing, and 14.9 percent in government. Major trading partners are Japan, Singapore, and the United States. Malaysia offers a very favorable climate for foreign investment.

- **Cost of Living:** At 107, the cost of living is slightly higher than in the United States.

- **Work Permits, Visas, etc.:** A valid passport is required to travel in Malaysia. If you are staying for up to three months as a tourist, or one month on business, no visa is necessary. "Visit Passes" are issued to foreigners for stays of up to one year and should be applied for through the Malaysian Embassy or Consulate before you leave the U.S. If business stays exceed one year, a Business Visa-Residence Permit is required, and are usually handled through your U.S. company or organization. If you are entering Malaysia from the United States, no vaccinations are necessary, but shots against malaria and cholera are recommended. For official or other information direct inquiries to the embassy or consulate at the addresses below.

- **Taxation:** Currently, foreign residents are taxed on all income from Malaysian sources, though deductions and personal allowances may apply in certain cases. The personal income tax rate begins at 5 percent. Currently, there is no agreement between the United States and Malaysia to avoid double-taxation. Current tax regulations are explained in a booklet available from the Malaysian Industrial Development Authority.

- **Principal International Schools:** An English-language international school in Kuala Lumpur follows U.S. curriculum guidelines, with tuition averaging $7,000-$13,000 per year.

- **Health Care:** Medical care in the larger cities is modern, with many English-speaking doctors. Medical costs are reasonable; routine check-ups are about $125 and dental check-ups are $25. Health standards in the larger cities are considered good. Although the government says the water is safe, use bottled water, especially in rural areas. Appropriate precautions should be taken with all fruits and vegetables. Insect repellent and anti-malarial tablets are necessary if you spend time in outlying rural areas.

- **Crime:** Common crime is not frequent in Malaysia. However, take normal precautions when traveling, especially in tourist areas. Safeguard valuables and lock car doors in public areas.

- **Pros and Cons of Living and Working in Malaysia:** Malaysia is located on one of the most important sea passages in the world. It is a modern, safe, and civilized country with beaches, gardens, temples, and mosques. Health standards are adequate, the costs for daily necessities are reasonable, and communications and housing accommodations are good. However, the tropical heat and intense humidity present problems. Don't bring fine furniture as it is likely be ruined by dampness or insects. Malaysia also is waging an aggressive war against drugs. There is a mandatory death

EMBASSY AND CONSULATE CONTACT INFORMATION:

EMBASSY OF MALAYSIA
2401 MASSACHUSETTS AVE. NW
WASHINGTON, DC 20008
TEL: 202-328-2700

PERMANENT MISSION TO THE U.N. AND
CONSULATE GENERAL OF MALAYSIA
140 EAST 45TH ST.
NEW YORK, NY 10017
TEL: 212-986-6310

penalty for possession of more than 15 grams of heroin. Protests from a number of nations and groups have done nothing to stop Malaysian officials from imposing the death penalty on foreigners for possession of narcotics.

OTHER SOURCES OF INFORMATION:

MALAYSIAN INDUSTRIAL DEVELOPMENT AUTHORITY (MIDA)
630 THIRD AVE.
NEW YORK, NY 10016
TEL: 212-687-2491

COMPANIES/ORGANIZATIONS WITH OPERATIONS IN MALAYSIA:

ABB VETCO GRAY, INC., 108
ADVANCED MICRO DEVICES, INC., 112
AMERICAN INTERNATIONAL GROUP, 127
ASSOCIATED PRESS, 144
AVNET, INC., 148
BORDEN, INC., 170
BRIDGESTONE-FIRESTONE, INC., 174
BURLINGTON AIR EXPRESS, 179
CABOT CORPORATION, 181
COMPUTER ASSOCIATES INTERNATIONAL, INC., 207
CORE LABORATORIES, 214
CORNING INCORPORATED, 215
DAMES & MOORE, 223
DANIEL, MANN, JOHNSON & MENDENHALL, 224
DIGICON, INC., 235
DOW JONES & COMPANY, INC., 241
EATON CORPORATION/CUTLER HAMMER, 247
ECOLOGY AND ENVIRONMENT, INC., 248
ELI LILLY AND COMPANY, 250
EXXON COMPANY, INTERNATIONAL, 258
GATX CORPORATION, 273
GENERAL INSTRUMENT CORPORATION, 276
GTECH CORPORATION, 289
HEWLETT-PACKARD COMPANY, 300
HILL & KNOWLTON, INC., 301

HYATT INTERNATIONAL CORPORATION, 308
INTEL CORPORATION, 314
INTERNATIONAL DATA GROUP, INC., 316
M. W. KELLOGG COMPANY, 331
KENDALL INTERNATIONAL, 332
KFC CORPORATION, 335
KORN/FERRY INTERNATIONAL, 340
LEVI STRAUSS ASSOCIATES, INC., 344
LTX CORPORATION, 353
MOTOROLA, INC., 381
OGILVY & MATHER, 395
OTIS ELEVATOR COMPANY: WORLD HEADQUARTERS, 399
PETROLITE CORPORATION, 411
PHILIPS TECHNOLOGIES, 414
QUAKER OATS COMPANY, 428
READING & BATES, 433
SEAGATE TECHNOLOGY, INC., 454
SEALED AIR CORPORATION, 455
SHAKLEE CORPORATION, 459
SOLECTRON CORPORATION, 469
SONAT, INC., 469
SONAT OFFSHORE, 470
STONE & WEBSTER ENGINEERING CORPORATION, 480
TEXAS INTRUMENTS, INC., 494
TOYS "R" US, INC., 500
VF CORPORATION, 517
YORK INTERNATIONAL, INC., 532

MARTINIQUE

- **Official Name:** Department of Martinique
- **Capital:** Fort-de-France
- **Location:** The French island of Martinique is part of the Lesser Antilles and is located in the eastern Caribbean Sea. It lies 25 miles south of the Dominican Republic and 20

miles north of the island of St. Lucia. Its total land area is 425 square miles, making it about six times the size of Washington, D.C. A popular tourist destination, this island has a varied and quite beautiful landscape. It is basically hilly, with rugged coastal areas and numerous sandy beaches.

- **Language and Currency:** Two languages spoken in Martinique are French and Creole patois. If you plan to live or work in Martinique, you should have some basic knowledge of the French language. The monetary unit is the French franc. The current exchange rate is 5.85 French francs = U.S.$1 (March 1994).
- **Print Source of Information:** Zeller, Margaret, editor. *Fielding's Caribbean.* New York: Fielding Travel Books, William Morrow & Co., 1992.

EMBASSY AND CONSULATE CONTACT INFORMATION:

EMBASSY OF FRANCE
4101 RESERVOIR RD. NW
WASHINGTON, DC 20007
TEL: 202-944-6000

COMPANIES/ORGANIZATIONS WITH OPERATIONS IN MARTINIQUE:

CLUB MED, INC., 201

MEXICO

- **Official Name:** United Mexican States
- **Capital:** Mexico City
- **Location:** Mexico is the southernmost country in North America. It is bordered by the United States to the north, the Gulf of Mexico to the east, Belize and Guatemala to the south, and the Pacific Ocean to the west. Its land area totals 756,066 square miles, making it slightly larger than Alaska. Its massive land area contains everything from tropical jungles to frigid mountain ranges. The northern plateau area accounts for 60 percent of the national territory, although only 19 percent of the people live there as the land is not suitable for cultivation. South of Mexico City, the land rises dramatically, exposing a volcanic range of mountains, and extraordinary peaks for which Mexico is famous. The mountains of the west are higher, and further north on the west coast there is a desert-like climate. The Pacific coast is less populous than the Caribbean side, which is fertile and heavily cultivated. Popular resort islands are located off the northeastern tip of the Yucatan Peninsula.
- **Population, Cities, and American Residents:** The population of Mexico totals 88.1 million (1992 est.). Approximately 60 million are mestizo (a mixture of Spanish and Indian), 30 percent Amerindian, 9 percent white, and 1 percent other.

    Most American residents are employed in Mexico City, which with 20 million people is the largest city in the world, Guadalajara with 2.8 million, and Monterrey with 2.3 million people (1990 est.). More than 15,000 Americans live in Guadalajara.
- **Language and Currency:** The official language of Mexico is Spanish, spoken in government and business circles. Many top executives and officials have studied in the

United States and speak fluent English, but mid- or lower-level employees do not. Anyone working in Mexico should speak Spanish as it is essential in business and daily life. The monetary unit in Mexico is the peso, written "P" outside the country, but within the country, it is written like the U.S. dollar ($). Bills are in 20,000, 10,000, 5,000, 2,000, 1,000, and 500 pesos. Coins are in 100, 50, 20, 10, and 5 pesos. The exchange rate is 1 Mexican peso = U.S.$.32 (July 30, 1993).

- **Climate:** The climate of Mexico varies with the altitude. Any region below 3,000 feet is the *tierra caliente,* and is usually very hot. Up to 6,000 feet is termed the *tierra templada,* a most temperate climate, and any area above that will see the *tierra fria,* an exceptionally cool and drier region. The inland highlands have the most enjoyable climate because of the altitude, but day and evening temperatures vary greatly (from around 78°F to 55°F). It is also dry in the highlands for most of the year. The country as a whole is exceptionally dry, but in the foothills behind the Caribbean coast it rains regularly throughout the year.

- **Economy and Resources:** Although some people consider Mexico a "poor" country, it has the thirteenth largest economy in the world and is a major global producer of oil. Mexico's interest in petroleum began in the late 1800s and its economy flourished for many years because of its huge deposits of oil. In 1981, it suffered the worst economic crisis in the history of the country due to a decrease of oil prices and other commodities. Austerity programs, an end to costly government subsidies, and foreign investment regulations finally enabled Mexico to recover. Today, expatriate residents have vast opportunities for business development. Natural resources include oil, silver, and gold. Major exports are food and beverages, tobacco, and chemicals. Most of the people are employed in services (31.4 percent) and agriculture (26 percent).

- **Cost of Living:** At 103, the cost of living is slightly higher than in the United States.

- **Work Permits, Visas, etc.:** No passports or visas are required when entering Mexico from the United States for a stay up to three months. For longer stays, a tourist card is required. Cards must be obtained in advance from the Tourism Office. If you are entering Mexico from the United States, no vaccinations are required. For official or other information, direct inquiries to the embassy or consulate at the addresses below.

- **Taxation:** If you live in Mexico for more than 183 days of the fiscal year, you are subject to personal income tax and to the limited foreign tax credit on foreign sources income. If you do not live there permanently, you are taxed only on what is earned in Mexico (currently at a standard rate of 21 percent).

- **Principal International Schools:** There is a good selection of international schools throughout Mexico. In Mexico City, the average tuition for an American school is approximately $1,000 per year.

- **Health Care:** Officials are working toward improving health conditions and sanitation in Mexico. Major health facilities in the larger cities are adequate and the civic hospitals are reasonably priced and open to all residents. A hospital used regularly by American residents is the American British Cowdray (ABC) Hospital in Mexico City. Unless you are in a major tourist area, boil all water (or use bottled), as the water may be contaminated from its source or tanks in which it is stored. Milk is unpasteurized and appropriate precautions should be taken with all fruits and vegetables. Stomach upset is quite common, especially during the first week or two in the country. Taking Doxycycline before the trip is a good preventive treatment. Respiratory problems may be caused by the air pollution, which is quite severe in Mexico City and other major cities. The worst time for pollution is between November and March.

- **Crime:** Be very careful in densely populated tourist areas (museums, airports, eateries) as pickpockets are frequent in such sites. Also, the police may solicit bribes, especially in drug-related arrests. Avoid such situations. Always lock car doors and don't leave valuables unattended or in plain sight. Unescorted women should wear shorts only in the beach areas and avoid local bars. Visit only the hotel bars and cocktail lounges where tourists gather.

- **Pros and Cons of Living and Working in Mexico:** Mexico is a popular tourist spot, with an interesting history, cultural sites, and a wide range of sightseeing opportunities, usually at reasonable prices. The country thrives on tourism, so restaurants are good, and transportation and telecommunications services are modern. Mexico is, of course, very convenient to the United States. Weather is also a plus, with warm temperatures. However, the health standards are low, and air pollution is a serious problem. Bringing the family pet is discouraged, as rabies is prevalent throughout the country. Do not let children play with stray pets of any kind.

EMBASSY AND CONSULATE CONTACT INFORMATION:

EMBASSY OF MEXICO
1911 PENNSYLVANIA AVE. NW
WASHINGTON, DC 20007
TEL: 202-728-1600

CONSULATE GENERAL OF MEXICO
8 EAST 41ST ST.
NEW YORK, NY 10017
TEL: 212-689-0456

OTHER SOURCES OF INFORMATION:

MEXICAN NATIONAL TOURIST OFFICE
405 PARK AVE.
NEW YORK, NY 10022
TEL: 212-755-7261

COMPANIES/ORGANIZATIONS WITH OPERATIONS IN MEXICO:

ABBOTT LABORATORIES, 109
ABEX INC./FISHER SCIENTIFIC INTERNATIONAL, INC., 110
ALBANY INTERNATIONAL CORPORATION, 114
ALBERTO-CULVER COMPANY, 115
ALLEN-BRADLEY COMPANY, INC., 116
ALUMINUM COMPANY OF AMERICA, 118
AM INTERNATIONAL, INC., 119
AMAX, INC., 119
AMERICAN APPRAISAL ASSOCIATES, INC., 121
AMERICAN BUILDING MAINTENANCE INDUSTRIES, INC., 123
AMERICAN EXPRESS BANK, LTD., 124
AMERICAN GREETINGS CORPORATION, 126
AMERICAN STANDARD, INC., 128

AMERIWOOD, INC., 130
AMETEK, INC., 130
AMP, INC., 132
AMPEX CORPORATION, 133
ANDREW CORPORATION, 134
APPLE COMPUTER, INC., 136
ARCO COAL COMPANY, 139
ARCO INTERNATIONAL OIL AND GAS COMPANY, 139
ARETHUSA OFFSHORE, 140
ASARCO, INC., 142
ASEA BROWN BOVERI, 142
ASHLAND OIL, INC., 143
ASSOCIATED PRESS, 144
AT&T INTERNATIONAL, 145
AUTOMATIC SWITCH COMPANY, 147
AVERY DENNISON CORPORATION, 147
AVNET, INC., 148

A
M
E
R
I
C
A
N

J
O
B
S

A
B
R
O
A
D

AVON PRODUCTS, INC., 149
AVX CORPORATION, 150
BACKER SPIELVOGEL & BATES
    WORLDWIDE, INC., 150
BAILEY CONTROLS COMPANY, 151
BAXTER HEALTHCARE CORPORATION, 160
BECKMAN INSTRUMENTS, INC., 162
BEMIS COMPANY, INC., 164
BLACK & DECKER CORPORATION, 167
BLOCK DRUG COMPANY, INC., 169
BRIDGESTONE-FIRESTONE, INC., 174
BRISTOL BABCOCK, INC., 174
BUCK CONSULTANTS, INC., 178
CABOT CORPORATION, 181
CALGON CORPORATION, 182
CAMPBELL SOUP COMPANY, 183
CARNIVAL CRUISE LINES, 185
CARRIER CORPORATION, 186
CARTER-WALLACE, INC., 187
CHEVRON CHEMICAL COMPANY, 192
CHEVRON CORPORATION, 193
CHRYSLER CORPORATION, 195
CITICORP, 198
CLUB MED, INC., 201
COMMERCE CLEARING HOUSE, 205
CONSERVATION INTERNATIONAL, 545
CONTINENTAL AIRLINES HOLDINGS, INC.,
    210
CONTINENTAL BANK CORPORATION, 210
CONVERSE, INC., 212
COOPER ENERGY SERVICES, LTD., 212
COOPER INDUSTRIES, INC., 213
CORNING INCORPORATED, 215
CROWN CORK & SEAL COMPANY, INC.,
    218
CRS SIRRINE, INC., 219
CTS CORPORATION, 220
CUMMINS ENGINE COMPANY, INC., 221
DAKA INTERNATIONAL, 222
DATA GENERAL CORPORATION, 225
DDB NEEDHAM WORLDWIDE, INC., 227
DE KALB GENETICS CORPORATION, 227
DEERE & COMPANY, 229
DEL MONTE CORPORATION, 230
THE DEXTER CORPORATION, 233
DIAMOND SHAMROCK R & M, INC., 234
DIEBOLD INCORPORATED, 235
DIGITAL EQUIPMENT CORPORATION, 236
DIXON TICONDEROGA COMPANY, 236
DOMINO'S PIZZA, INC., 237

DONALDSON COMPANY, INC., 237
R. R. DONNELLEY & SONS COMPANY,
    238
DOW CORNING CORPORATION, 240
DOW JONES & COMPANY, INC., 241
DUPONT MERCK PHARMACEUTICAL
    COMPANY, 243
DURACELL, INC., 244
DURO-TEST INTERNATIONAL
    CORPORATION, 245
EASTMAN KODAK COMPANY, 246
EATON CORPORATION/CUTLER HAMMER,
    247
ECOLOGY AND ENVIRONMENT, INC., 248
ELIZABETH ARDEN COMPANY, 251
ENCORE COMPUTER CORPORATION, 252
ERNST & YOUNG, 255
EXXON CORPORATION, 258
FALK CORPORATION, 259
FEDERAL-MOGUL CORPORATION, 260
FERRO CORPORATION, 261
FIGGIE INTERNATIONAL, INC., 262
FIRST CHICAGO CORPORATION, 262
FISCHER & PORTER COMPANY, 263
FISHER CONTROLS INTERNATIONAL, INC.,
    263
FLEMING COMPANIES, INC., 264
FULLER COMPANY, 269
GAF CORPORATION, 270
THE GATES RUBBER COMPANY, 273
GATX CORPORATION, 273
GENERAL ELECTRIC COMPANY (GE), 275
GENERAL FOODS USA, 276
GENERAL INSTRUMENT CORPORATION,
    276
GENERAL TIRE, INC., 279
GERBER PRODUCTS COMPANY, 280
THE GILLETTE COMPANY, 283
GOULD PUMPS, INC., 285
W. R. GRACE & COMPANY, 285
GRANT THORNTON INTERNATIONAL, 286
A. P. GREEN INDUSTRIES, INC., 287
H. J. HEINZ COMPANY, 290
HALLIBURTON COMPANY, 292
HALLIBURTON COMPANY/HALLIBURTON
    SERVICES DIVISION, 293
HALLMARK CARDS, INC., 294
HARRIS CORPORATION, 296
HERCULES, INC., 299
HERSHEY FOODS CORPORATION, 299

HEWLETT-PACKARD COMPANY, 300
HOLIDAY INNS WORLDWIDE, 302
HUGHES CHRISTENSEN COMPANY, 307
HYATT INTERNATIONAL CORPORATION,
    308
ILLINOIS TOOL WORKS, INC., 309
IMCERA GROUP, INC., 310
INTERNATIONAL FLAVORS &
    FRAGRANCES, INC., 317
INTERNATIONAL RECTIFIER CORPORATION,
    319
ITT CORPORATION, 321
JAMES RIVER CORPORATION, 323
JOHNSON CONTROLS, INC., 324
KELLOGG COMPANY, 330
KELSEY-HAYES COMPANY, 332
KENDALL INTERNATIONAL, 332
KEYSTONE INTERNATIONAL, 334
KFC CORPORATION, 335
KIMBALL INTERNATIONAL, INC., 336
KIMBERLY-CLARK CORPORATION, 336
KOLMAR LABORATORIES, INC., 340
KORN/FERRY INTERNATIONAL, 340
LEVI STRAUSS ASSOCIATES, INC., 344
THE LINCOLN ELECTRIC COMPANY, 346
LIQUID CARBONIC CORPORATION, 347
LOCTITE CORPORATION, 349
LUBRIZOL CORPORATION, 353
LYKES LINES, 354
MALLINCKRODT, INC., 359
MASONEILAN INDUSTRIES, INC., 361
MATTEL, INC., 363
MAYTAG CORPORATION, 364
MCCORMICK & COMPANY, INC., 355
MCGRAW-HILL, INC., 357
MCI COMMUNICATIONS CORPORATION,
    365
MCKINSEY & COMPANY, INC., 357
MEASUREX CORPORATION, 366
MERCK & COMPANY, INC., 368
MILLER BREWING COMPANY, 372
MILLIPORE CORPORATION, 374
MOBIL OIL CORPORATION, 375
MODINE MANUFACTURING COMPANY, 375
MOORE PRODUCTS COMPANY, 378
MOTOROLA, INC., 381
NALCO CHEMICAL COMPANY, 382
NAVISTAR INTERNATIONAL
    TRANSPORTATION CORPORATION, 383
NCR CORPORATION, 384

NOVELL, INC., 392
OGDEN CORPORATION, 395
OGILVY & MATHER, 395
OLIN CORPORATION, 396
ORYX ENERGY, 398
OTIS ELEVATOR COMPANY: WORLD
    HEADQUARTERS, 399
OUTBOARD MARINE CORPORATION, 399
PACCAR, INC., 401
PARAMOUNT COMMUNICATIONS, INC., 404
PARKER HANNIFIN CORPORATION, 405
PENTAIR, INC., 409
PEPSICO FOODS INTERNATIONAL, 409
PEPSICO, INC., 410
PETROLITE CORPORATION, 411
PFAUDLER COMPANIES, INC., 411
PFIZER, INC., 412
PHELPS DODGE CORPORATION, 412
PHILIPS TECHNOLOGIES, 414
PHILLIPS-VAN HEUSEN CORPORATION,
    415
PILLSBURY COMPANY, 416
PIONEER HI-BRED INTERNATIONAL, INC.,
    417
PITTSBURGH-DES MOINES CORPORATION,
    418
PITTWAY CORPORATION, 418
PLAYTEX APPAREL, INC., 419
POLAROID CORPORATION, 420
POPULATION COUNCIL, 562
PPG INDUSTRIES, 421
PRECISION VALVE CORPORATION, 422
PREFORMED LINE PRODUCTS COMPANY,
    423
PREMARK INTERNATIONAL, INC., 423
PROCTER & GAMBLE COMPANY, 425
QUAKER CHEMICAL CORPORATION, 428
QUAKER OATS COMPANY, 428
RALSTON PURINA COMPANY, 430
RANCO, INC., 431
READER'S DIGEST ASSOCIATION, INC.,
    432
RELIANCE ELECTRIC COMPANY, 435
REVLON, INC., 437
RJR NABISCO, 439
ROHM & HAAS COMPANY, 442
ROSEMOUNT, INC., 443
RUBBERMAID, INC., 445
SB POWER TOOLS, INC. (SKIL CORP.),
    450

A
M
E
R
I
C
A
N

J
O
B
S

A
B
R
O
A
D

SCOTT PAPER COMPANY, 453
SEA-LAND SERVICE, INC., 454
SEARLE COMPANY, 455
SEARS ROEBUCK AND COMPANY, 456
SIMON & SCHUSTER, INC., 463
A. O. SMITH CORPORATION, 467
SMITH INTERNATIONAL, INC., 467
SONOCO PRODUCTS COMPANY, 470
SOUTHLAND CORPORATION, 472
SPS TECHNOLOGIES, INC., 474
SQUARE D COMPANY, 475
SRI INTERNATIONAL, 475
STERLING WINTHROP, INC., 479
STONE CONTAINER CORPORATION, 480
SUN ELECTRIC CORPORATION, 484
SYNTEX CORPORATION, 486
TAMBRANDS, INC., 486
TANDEM COMPUTERS, INC., 487
TANDY CORPORATION, 487
TEKTRONIX, INC., 488
TELEDYNE, INC., 489
TELLABS OPERATIONS, INC., 489
TENNECO AUTOMOTIVE, 491
TEXAS INTRUMENTS, INC., 494
THOMAS & BETTS, 495
3M COMPANY, 496
TIME-WARNER, INC., 498
TORRINGTON COMPANY, 499
TOWERS PERRIN, INC., 499

TRACOR, INC., 500
TRANE COMPANY, 501
TRINOVA CORPORATION, 502
TRW, INC., 503
TYSON FOODS, INC., 505
UAL CORPORATION, 506
UNILEVER UNITED STATES, INC., 506
UNITED ENGINEERS & CONSTRUCTORS INTERNATIONAL, 508
UNITED PRESS INTERNATIONAL, 509
U.S. ELECTRICAL MOTORS (EMERSON ELECTRIC), 510
VF CORPORATION, 517
WARNACO, INC., 520
WARNER-LAMBERT COMPANY, 522
WENDY'S INTERNATIONAL, INC., 524
WEST COMPANY, INC., 525
WESTINGHOUSE ELECTRIC CORPORATION, 525
WHIRLPOOL CORPORATION, 526
WHITMAN CORPORATION, 527
WOOLWORTH CORPORATION, 528
WORLD COURIER MANAGEMENT, INC., 529
WYETH-AYERST LABORATORIES, 530
YELLOW FREIGHT SYSTEM, INC., 532
YORK INTERNATIONAL, INC., 532
YOUNG & RUBICAM, INC., 533

NETHERLANDS

- **Official Name:** Kingdom of the Netherlands
- **Capital:** Amsterdam
- **Location:** The Netherlands is located in western Europe at the mouths of three important rivers; the Rhine, the Scheldt, and the Meuse. It is bounded by the North Sea to the north and west, Germany to the east, and Belgium to the south. The total land area covers 13,103 square miles, making it slightly larger than Maryland. One-third of the country's land area is below sea level, and, for the most part, its territory is low and flat. The only region that has some elevation is in the southeast section of the country. The Netherlands is comprised of fourteen provinces, the major one being Holland, which is now divided into north and south sectors.
- **Population, Cities, and American Residents:** The population of the Netherlands totals 14.9 million people (1992 est.). The Dutch account for 99 percent of the population; the remaining 1 percent are Indonesian or other.

Most American residents are employed in the three largest cities: Amsterdam with 695,000 people, Rotterdam with 579,000, and Hague with 442,000 (1990 est.).

- **Language and Currency:** The official language of the Netherlands is Dutch. English is the second language and widely used in government and business. The monetary unit is the guilder (f) and is divided into 100 cents. The exchange rate is 1 Dutch guilder = U.S.$.51 (July 30, 1993).

- **Climate:** The climate of the Netherlands is much like North America's Pacific northwest region: temperate, with cool summers and mild winters. It is very damp and chilly during the long winter season, though the temperature rarely drops below 40°F. Summer temperatures usually range between 65°F-70°F.

- **Economy and Resources:** Known as the "gateway to Europe," the Netherlands has a prime geographical location which has enabled foreign trade to play a key role in its economy. With limited natural resources, much of the raw materials used in industry must be imported, but in the last twenty years, numerous natural gas deposits have been discovered in the North Sea, and have proved to be a valuable, as well as exploitable, resource. Exports account for 60 percent of the gross domestic product (GDP). These include natural gas, chemicals, agricultural products, and processed foods and tobacco. More than 70 percent of exports go to fellow members of the European Community. Of the labor force, 50.1 percent work in services, 28.2 percent in manufacturing and construction, and 15.9 percent in government.

  The Netherlands remains one of the most inviting nations for foreign capital and investments. The world's oldest stock exchange is in Amsterdam, which is one of the major financial centers in Europe. Heavy reliance on revenues from the natural gas industry, however, has subjected the Netherlands to the destabilizing fluctuations of the world market. A drop in natural gas prices has prompted the start of austerity programs in recent years. Pollution has also been a problem, and efforts have begun to clean up the environment, at a cost that will total billions of dollars over next several years.

- **Cost of Living:** At 131, the cost of living is slightly higher than in the United States.

- **Work Permits, Visas, etc.:** A valid passport is required, but for stays longer than three consecutive months, you'll need a residence permit. This is usually done after arrival. Working in the country requires a labor permit, which should be obtained prior to your trip. If you are entering the country from the United States, no vaccinations are required. For official or other information, direct inquiries to the embassy or consulate at the addresses below.

- **Taxation:** Residents of the Netherlands (including foreign nationals) are subject to personal income taxes on worldwide income. Nonresidents are responsible for taxes only on income from Dutch sources. Residence is determined by several factors: length of stay, type of work, employer's place of residence, and if an employee is accompanied by his/her family.

- **Principal International Schools:** The international schools in the Netherlands are considered excellent. The tuition for an American school is about $7,500 per year.

- **Health Care:** The Netherlands has the most extensive—and costly—health care plan in the world. The social welfare system provides quality health care and entitles a pension to all permanent residents who reach 65 years of age. Health standards remain very high, with water safe to drink and food establishments inspected regularly for cleanliness. Medical facilities are excellent, with many English-speaking doctors available. No diseases or health hazards pose a threat to travelers. However, the climate is damp, and respiratory problems may affect some people. Bringing antihistamines along might be a good idea.

- **Crime:** Crime is not a major problem in the Netherlands. However, Dutch society is more tolerant of behavior that would be regarded as vice in the United States. Drug use is widely accepted in the Netherlands, and prostitution is legal. Amsterdam is known throughout Europe as a center for pornography, and AIDS is a major problem. Although the crime rate is low, take precautions when going out at night, especially if you're traveling alone. Certain urban areas might be unsafe for tourists.

- **Pros and Cons of Living and Working in the Netherlands:** The people of the Netherlands are hard-working and very hospitable. The country is known for its beautiful flowers, postcard towns, and cultural and tourist attractions. Amsterdam has retained much of its past through its vast museums and its quaint and distinctive architecture. Its diamond cutting establishments are well worth a visit. Rotterdam is very modern and one of Europe's greatest ports. Health standards are very good, as are telecommunications services and transportation. There are numerous mopeds and bicycles on the Dutch roads and bicycles have the right of way, so drive alertly. Housing is available and affordable. Oral agreements can be legally binding, so make sure accommodations are exactly what you want. If not, you may have to forfeit your original deposit. The weather can be exceptionally damp, especially during the winter months, affecting those with respiratory problems. Drug use, pornography, and prostitution are tolerated and surprisingly out in the open in the Netherlands.

EMBASSY AND CONSULATE CONTACT INFORMATION:

EMBASSY OF THE NETHERLANDS
4200 LINNEAN AVE. NW
WASHINGTON, DC 20008
TEL: 202-244-5300

CONSULATE GENERAL OF THE NETHERLANDS
1 ROCKEFELLER PLAZA
NEW YORK, NY 10020
TEL: 212-246-1429

OTHER SOURCES OF INFORMATION:

NETHERLANDS BOARD OF TOURISM
355 LEXINGTON AVE.
NEW YORK, NY 10017
TEL: 212-370-7367

COMPANIES/ORGANIZATIONS WITH OPERATIONS IN NETHERLANDS:

ABB LUMMUS CREST, 108
ACCO WORLD CORPORATION, 110
AKZO AMERICA, INC., 113
ALBANY INTERNATIONAL CORPORATION, 114
ALBERTO-CULVER COMPANY, 115
AM INTERNATIONAL, INC., 119

AMERICAN EXPRESS COMPANY—TRAVEL RELATED SERVICES, 125
AMERICAN STANDARD, INC., 128
AMERICAN TOOL COMPANIES, INC., 129
AMGEN, INC., 131
AMP, INC., 132
ANTHONY INDUSTRIES, 135
APPLE COMPUTER, INC., 136

ARCHER-DANIELS-MIDLAND COMPANY, 138

ARMOUR SWIFT ECKRICH, INC., 141

ARMSTRONG WORLD INDUSTRIES, INC., 141

AUTOMATIC SWITCH COMPANY, 147

BACKER SPIELVOGEL & BATES WORLDWIDE, INC., 150

BADGER COMPANY, INC., 151

BANKAMERICA CORPORATION, 155

BAUSCH & LOMB, INC., 159

BEAR STEARNS COMPANIES, INC., 161

BECKMAN INSTRUMENTS, INC., 162

BELL & HOWELL COMPANY, 164

BIO-RAD LABORATORIES, 166

BORDEN, INC., 170

BRIDGESTONE-FIRESTONE, INC., 174

BROWNING-FERRIS INDUSTRIES, 177

BURLINGTON AIR EXPRESS, 179

BURSON-MARSTELLER, 180

CABOT CORPORATION, 181

CALIFORNIA PELLET MILL COMPANY, 182

CARLSON TRAVEL NETWORK, 185

CENTOCOR, INC., 188

CHEVRON CORPORATION, 193

CHIRON CORPORATION, 194

CIGNA CORPORATION, 197

COMMODORE INTERNATIONAL LTD., 206

COMPUTERVISION CORPORATION, 208

CONOCO, INC., 209

CONTINENTAL GRAIN COMPANY, 211

CONTINUUM COMPANY, INC., 211

CORE LABORATORIES, 214

CPC INTERNATIONAL, INC., 217

CUBIC CORPORATION, 220

D'ARCY MASIUS BENTON & BOWLES INC., 225

DATA GENERAL CORPORATION, 225

DH TECHNOLOGY, INC., 233

DIGICON, INC., 235

DIGITAL EQUIPMENT CORPORATION, 236

DONALDSON COMPANY, INC., 237

DOW CHEMICAL COMPANY, 240

DOW JONES & COMPANY, INC., 241

DRUMMOND COMPANY, INC., 242

EBASCO OVERSEAS CORPORATION, 248

EG & G, INC., 249

EMERY WORLDWIDE, 252

ENGELHARD CORPORATION, 253

ERNST & YOUNG, 255

FEDERAL EXPRESS CORPORATION, 260

FERRO CORPORATION, 261

FIGGIE INTERNATIONAL, INC., 262

FISCHER & PORTER COMPANY, 263

FISHER CONTROLS INTERNATIONAL, INC., 263

FLUOR CORPORATION, 266

FMC CORPORATION, 266

FORD MOTOR COMPANY, 267

GAF CORPORATION, 270

GENERAL ELECTRIC COMPANY (GE), 275

GENERAL MILLS, INC., 277

GRANT THORNTON INTERNATIONAL, 286

GREY ADVERTISING, INC., 288

GTE CORPORATION, 288

H. J. HEINZ COMPANY, 290

HERCULES, INC., 299

HERTZ CORPORATION, 300

HONEYWELL, INC., 303

HUGHES CHRISTENSEN COMPANY, 307

IMO INDUSTRIES, 310

INFORMATION BUILDERS, INC., 312

INTERGRAPH CORPORATION, 314

INTERNATIONAL BUSINESS MACHINES (IBM), 315

INTERNATIONAL FLAVORS & FRAGRANCES, INC., 317

INTERNATIONAL PAPER COMPANY, 318

ITT CORPORATION, 321

ITT HARTFORD INSURANCE GROUP, 321

ITW FINISHING SYSTEMS & PRODUCTS, 322

JOHNSON CONTROLS, INC., 324

KEYSTONE INTERNATIONAL, 334

KIMBERLY-CLARK CORPORATION, 336

KNOLL INTERNATIONAL, 338

KRAFT GENERAL FOODS INTERNATIONAL, 341

LOCTITE CORPORATION, 349

LOUISIANA LAND & EXPLORATION COMPANY, 352

LTX CORPORATION, 353

MASONEILAN INDUSTRIES, INC., 361

MASONITE CORPORATION, 362

MCCANN-ERICKSON WORLDWIDE, 354

MCI COMMUNICATIONS CORPORATION, 365

MEAD CORPORATION, 365

MEASUREX CORPORATION, 366

MEDTRONIC, INC., 366

A
M
E
R
I
C
A
N

J
O
B
S

A
B
R
O
A
D

MEMOREX TELEX CORPORATION, 367
METCO PERKIN-ELMER, 371
HERMAN MILLER, INC., 373
MILLIPORE CORPORATION, 374
MOORE PRODUCTS COMPANY, 378
MORTON INTERNATIONAL, 380
NALCO CHEMICAL COMPANY, 382
NELLCOR, INC., 385
NEWSWEEK INTERNATIONAL, 387
NIKE, INC., 388
NORDSON CORPORATION, 389
NORTH AMERICAN PHILIPS CORPORATION,
    389
NORTON COMPANY, 390
OGILVY & MATHER, 395
OMI INTERNATIONAL, 396
OWENS-CORNING FIBERGLAS
    CORPORATION, 400
PARAMOUNT COMMUNICATIONS, INC., 404
PARKER HANNIFIN CORPORATION, 405
PENNZOIL COMPANY, 408
PETROLITE CORPORATION, 411
PFIZER, INC., 412
PHILIP MORRIS COMPANIES, INC., 413
POLAROID CORPORATION, 420
PPG INDUSTRIES, 421
PREMARK INTERNATIONAL, INC., 423
PRICE WATERHOUSE, 424
PRIMERICA CORPORATION, 424
PRINTRONIX, INC., 425
PROCTER & GAMBLE COMPANY, 425
PROCTER & GAMBLE PHARMACEUTICALS,
    INC., 426
QUAKER CHEMICAL CORPORATION, 428
QUAKER OATS COMPANY, 428
RALSTON PURINA COMPANY, 430
RAYTHEON COMPANY, 432
READER'S DIGEST ASSOCIATION, INC.,
    432
READING & BATES, 433
RECOGNITION EQUIPMENT, INC., 433
REED TOOL COMPANY, 434
ROBERTSON CECO, 440
ROHM & HAAS COMPANY, 442
ROSEMOUNT, INC., 443
ROWAN COMPANIES, INC., 444
RUBBERMAID, INC., 445
SARA LEE CORPORATION, 449
SB POWER TOOLS, INC. (SKIL CORP.),
    450

SCIENTIFIC ATLANTA, INC., 452
SEA-LAND SERVICE, INC., 454
SEALED AIR CORPORATION, 455
SENCO PRODUCTS, 456
SENSORMATIC ELECTRONICS
    CORPORATION, 457
SHEAFFER PEN, INC., 459
SHEARSON LEHMAN BROTHERS, 460
SHIPLEY COMPANY, INC., 461
SIGNODE PACKAGING SYSTEMS, 462
A. O. SMITH CORPORATION, 467
SONOCO PRODUCTS COMPANY, 470
SPRINT CORPORATION, 474
STONE CONTAINER CORPORATION, 480
STRUCTURAL DYNAMICS RESEARCH
    CORPORATION, 481
SUN ELECTRIC CORPORATION, 484
TEKTRONIX, INC., 488
TENNANT COMPANY, 490
TENNECO AUTOMOTIVE, 491
TEXACO OIL COMPANY, 493
TEXAS INTRUMENTS, INC., 494
TIME, INC., 497
TIME-WARNER, INC., 498
TLC BEATRICE INTERNATIONAL HOLDINGS,
    INC., 498
TOWERS PERRIN, INC., 499
TRACOR, INC., 500
TRITON ENERGY CORPORATION, 502
UNISYS CORPORATION, 508
UNITED PARCEL SERVICE OF AMERICA,
    INC., 509
U.S. WHEAT ASSOCIATES, 511
UNITED TECHNOLOGIES CORPORATION,
    512
UNIVERSAL FOODS CORPORATION, 513
UNOCAL CORPORATION, 513
THE UPJOHN COMPANY, 515
VF CORPORATION, 517
WALKER MANUFACTURING COMPANY, 519
WARD HOWELL INTERNATIONAL, INC., 520
WARNER BROTHERS INTERNATIONAL, 521
WATERS CHROMATOGRAPHY (MILLIPORE),
    523
WESTINGHOUSE ELECTRIC CORPORATION,
    525
WHIRLPOOL CORPORATION, 526
WMX TECHNOLOGIES/WASTE
    MANAGEMENT, INC., 527
WOODWARD GOVERNOR COMPANY, 528

WOOLWORTH CORPORATION, 528   WILLIAM WRIGLEY JR. COMPANY, 529
WORLD COURIER MANAGEMENT, INC.,   YORK INTERNATIONAL, INC., 532
  529

NETHERLANDS ANTILLES

- **Official Name:** Netherlands Antilles

- **Capital:** Willemstad

- **Location:** The Netherlands Antilles is comprised of two island groups in the Caribbean Sea. The first group lies about 50 miles off the northwestern coast of Venezuela and is often called the "Leeward Islands." It consists of Bonaire and Curaçao. Saba and St. Eustatius Islands, and St. Maarten (which occupies the southern section of St. Martin), comprise the northern, or "Windward" group. This island chain is approximately 500 miles northeast of Bonaire and Curaçao. Aruba belonged to the Netherlands Antilles until 1986 when it became a separate part of the Netherlands. Though it is now self-governing, Aruba still relies on the Netherlands for military and foreign affairs support.

  The total land area is 309 square miles, making it nearly five times the size of Washington, D.C. The terrain varies on each island. Curaçao, the largest island (178 square miles), is low and hilly, with a good deal of cacti and aloes scattered throughout its territory. St. Maarten is the most tropical of the group, and less rocky and mountainous than other islands of the Antilles.

- **Population, Cities, and American Residents:** The population of the Netherlands Antilles is 188,000 (1991 est.). Black Africans of mixed origin account for 85 percent of the population with Carib Indian, European, Latin, and Asian accounting for the remainder.

  Most American residents are employed in the Netherlands Antilles' three largest islands: Curaçao with 150,000, St. Maarten with 25,000, and Bonaire with 10,000 people (1989 est.).

- **Language and Currency:** The official language of the Netherlands Antilles is Dutch. Other languages spoken are Papiamento (Spanish-Portuguese-Dutch-English dialect) and Spanish. English is widely used throughout business and government. The monetary unit is the Netherlands Antillean florin (fl) or guilder. The exchange rate is 2 fl (often called guldens) = U.S.$1 (February 1994).

- **Climate:** The climate is mildly tropical throughout the islands with rainfall varying in different locations. Bonaire and Curaçao have an average temperature of 82°F and annual rainfall of 22 inches. Constant trade winds prevail on these islands, which lie outside the hurricane belt. St. Maarten is a lush, tropical island with an average temperature of 80°F. It has about 45 inches of rainfall each year.

- **Economy and Resources:** The Netherlands Antilles depends on oil refining and tourism to maintain its stable economy. Venezuela exports oil to Curaçao for refining, and 98 percent of the Netherlands Antilles' exports are petroleum products. Phosphates (from Curaçao) account for the remaining 2 percent. The United States is a major trading partner.

Tourism continues to remain the backbone of the economy. Because of the pleasant year-round climate and an abundance of beaches, these islands draw thousands of visitors annually. Of the labor force, 65 percent of the people work in government, 28 percent in industry and commerce, and 7 percent are unemployed.

The Netherlands Antilles are an autonomous division of Kingdom of the Netherlands, with the islands being self-governing. A governor is appointed by the Dutch monarch. Each island-territory has its own council directed by a lieutenant governor.

- **Cost of Living:** At 109, the cost of living is comparable to the United States.

- **Work Permits, Visas, etc.:** A passport or proof of U.S. citizenship is required to travel in the Netherlands Antilles. Visas are not required for stays up to 90 days. If you are entering the Netherlands Antilles from the United States, no vaccinations are required. For official or other information, direct inquiries to the embassy or consulate at the addresses below.

- **Taxation:** Individual circumstances and residency status in the Netherlands Antilles determine taxes, which are collected on worldwide income. Exemptions are allowed for expatriates living/working in the Netherlands Antilles. For current information, contact the embassy or consulate of the Netherlands Antilles.

- **Principal International Schools:** American schools are available.

- **Health Care:** Health care is adequate throughout the islands of the Netherlands Antilles. Water is safe to drink (as its distilled from the sea) in all major tourist areas. Much of the food is imported and under strict health control supervision, so it's safe to eat in most areas on the islands. Overexposure to the sun can be a problem, so take precautions.

- **Crime:** The Netherlands Antilles thrives on tourism and crime is not a serious problem. Take the normal precautions for traveling through any major tourist areas.

- **Pros and Cons of Living and Working in the Netherlands Antilles:** The warm, pleasant climate and many sandy beaches lure many Americans here annually. Each of the islands has something special to offer visitors, from scuba diving in St. Maarten to the architecture of Curaçao. People are friendly and the island is relatively easy to reach from the United States. Health care and sanitary conditions are adequate. Telecommunications and transportation services are good. Most roads are paved and car rentals are readily available. For best selection, it's smart to arrange for accommodations in advance.

- **Print Source of Information:** Zellers, Margaret, editor. *Fielding's Caribbean.* New York: Fielding Travel Books, William Morrow & Co., 1992.

EMBASSY AND CONSULATE CONTACT INFORMATION:

EMBASSY OF THE NETHERLANDS
4200 LINNEAN AVE. NW
WASHINGTON, DC 20008
TEL: 202-244-5300

COMPANIES/ORGANIZATIONS WITH OPERATIONS IN NETHERLANDS ANTILLES:

AMERICAN CANADIAN CARIBBEAN LINE, 123

LAWTER INTERNATIONAL, INC., 344

SONESTA INTERNATIONAL HOTELS CORPORATION, 470

TRITON ENERGY CORPORATION, 502

NEW ZEALAND

- **Official Name:** New Zealand
- **Capital:** Wellington
- **Location:** New Zealand comprises three large islands and several smaller ones stretching across 992 miles of the South Pacific Ocean. Its land area totals 103,886 square miles, making it comparable to Colorado. With only 2 percent arable land, 53 percent of New Zealand is covered by meadows and pastures, and 38 percent by forest and woodland. The natural scenery is breathtaking, from tropical rain forests to rugged mountains and glaciers. The two largest islands are the North Island, whose volcanic system produces hot springs and geysers; and the South Island, which is very mountainous, and lacks any volcanic activity. The Southern Alps, stretching along almost all of the western edge of South Island, have high peaks (9,800 feet or higher) and glaciers. The third island is Stewart Island, which lies below South Island and has many lakes and picturesque mountain scenery. The most populated area is North Island where more than three-quarters of the people of New Zealand live.
- **Population, Cities, and American Residents:** The population of New Zealand totals 3.3 million people (1991 est.). Various groups of European extraction (English, Scottish, Dutch, and Welsh) account for 88 percent of the population. The remaining 12 percent are the indigenous people of New Zealand (Maoris, Pacific Islanders, and others).

  Most American residents are employed in New Zealand's three largest cities: Wellington with 326,000, Auckland with 865,000 people, and Christchurch with 300,000 people (1990 est.). The first two are on North Island and the latter on South Island.
- **Language and Currency:** The official language of New Zealand is English. New Zealand uses a decimal currency. The monetary unit is the New Zealand dollar (NZ$) and it is divided into 100 cents. The exchange rate is 1 New Zealand dollar = U.S.$.51 (July 30, 1993).
- **Climate:** New Zealand has a varied climate, similar to that of the Pacific Northeast region of United States, with the surrounding ocean influencing the weather. In the North Island area, it is subtropical, and South Island has a temperate climate. New Zealand is southeast of Australia, and is usually a bit cooler. The country does not reach extreme temperatures in any season, but the higher mountains in the Southern Alps are covered with snow for most of the year. The seasons are the reverse of those in the Northern Hemisphere. The North Island has average summer temperatures of 73°F and winter temperatures averaging about 60°F. The South Island has an average summer

temperature of 68°F and an average winter temperatures are about 55°F. Precipitation is more likely during the winter season, with North Island receiving more rainfall.

- **Economy and Resources:** New Zealand was once dependent on pastoral farming, but the country is developing resource-based industries. Forest industries, in particular, are expanding, and foreign exchange earners are pulp, logs, and paper products. Other natural resources include natural gas, iron ore, and coal. Primary products still account for 66 percent of export earnings. Major industries include food processing, wood and paper products, and textiles. Principal exports are dairy products, meat, wool, and timber. Of the labor force, nearly 70 percent work in services, and 19.8 percent in manufacturing. When the Labour Party came into office in 1984, there were many problems to resolve. Inflation was running over 10 percent annually, and public and private borrowing was pushing up the national debt. Government officials began reform programs, some of which were considered quite drastic measures. Inflation came down, but many problems remain to be resolved if the country is to sustain an open free market economy that can compete in the world market.

- **Cost of Living:** At 105, the cost of living is comparable to the United States.

- **Work Permits, Visas, etc.:** A valid passport is required to travel in New Zealand, and for stays of up to three months, no visa is necessary. However, if you plan to stay more than three months or work in New Zealand, you'll need a tourist or business visa. Those staying longer than one year must go through immigration formalities, which can take longer than three months to complete. There are no health requirements to enter New Zealand. For official or other information, direct inquiries to the embassy or consulate at the addresses below.

- **Taxation:** Individuals who are considered residents (anyone who has lived in New Zealand for 365 or more consecutive days) pay income taxes on their worldwide income. Nonresidents are taxed only on income earned from New Zealand sources.

- **Principal International Schools:** Schools in New Zealand are similar to those in the United Kingdom. There are several English-language private schools in Wellington and Auckland, and tuition averages about $3,000 per year.

- **Health Care:** Medical facilities in New Zealand are quite good. Costs are reasonable, but visitors are obligated to pay for any medical treatment received while in the country. You should have health insurance coverage prior to your trip. Sanitary standards are also very good. Water and most foods are safe to eat, and there are no communicable diseases or health hazards posing a threat to travelers.

- **Crime:** Crime is not a major problem in New Zealand. If you are in a busy tourist area, take the same precautions as you would at home.

- **Pros and Cons of Living and Working in New Zealand:** New Zealand is a country of great natural beauty. Though it is not large in area, it has beaches, volcanoes, mountains, and countless lakes. There are theater companies, art festivals, museums, and an array of sports activities. Health standards are excellent, and telecommunications and transportation are also very good. Housing is a little scarce, but a

EMBASSY AND CONSULATE CONTACT INFORMATION:

NEW ZEALAND EMBASSY
37 OBSERVATORY CIRCLE NW
WASHINGTON, DC 20008
TEL: 202-328-4800

rental agent should be able to provide suitable accommodations. Rentals might be sparsely furnished and lacking in appliances or furniture, and buying these items in New Zealand will be more expensive than in the United States. There are also strict rules concerning pets. No cats, dogs, or other animals are allowed in from North America. New Zealand also has tight restrictions on the importation of plants and fruits.

CONSULATE GENERAL OF NEW ZEALAND
630 FIFTH AVE.
NEW YORK, NY 10111
TEL: 212-698-4670

OTHER SOURCES OF INFORMATION:

NEW ZEALAND TOURIST AND PUBLICITY OFFICE
CITICORP CENTER, STE. 810
SANSOME ST.
SAN FRANCISCO, CA 94104
TEL: 415-788-7404

COMPANIES/ORGANIZATIONS WITH OPERATIONS IN NEW ZEALAND:

AIRBORNE EXPRESS, 112
AM INTERNATIONAL, INC., 119
AMAX, INC., 119
ASEA BROWN BOVERI, 142
AVIS, INC., 148
BLACK & DECKER CORPORATION, 167
BORLAND INTERNATIONAL, INC, 172
BRIDGESTONE-FIRESTONE, INC., 174
BROWNING-FERRIS INDUSTRIES, 177
BURLINGTON AIR EXPRESS, 179
CIGNA CORPORATION, 197
COMMERCE CLEARING HOUSE, 205
COMMODORE INTERNATIONAL LTD., 206
COMPUTER ASSOCIATES INTERNATIONAL, INC., 207
THE DEXTER CORPORATION, 233
ELIZABETH ARDEN COMPANY, 251
H & R BLOCK, 291
HALLMARK CARDS, INC., 294
HELENE CURTIS INDUSTRIES, INC., 298

HERCULES, INC., 299
HILL & KNOWLTON, INC., 301
HYATT INTERNATIONAL CORPORATION, 308
IMCERA GROUP, INC., 310
OGDEN CORPORATION, 395
READER'S DIGEST ASSOCIATION, INC., 432
REDKEN LABORATORIES, INC., 434
RELIANCE ELECTRIC COMPANY, 435
ROBERTSON CECO, 440
SENSORMATIC ELECTRONICS CORPORATION, 457
SIMPLICITY PATTERN COMPANY INC., 464
STANDARD COMMERCIAL CORPORATION, 476
TEXTRON, INC., 494
3M COMPANY, 496
TRITON ENERGY CORPORATION, 502
WILLIAM WRIGLEY JR. COMPANY, 529

NICARAGUA

- **Official Name:** Republic of Nicaragua

- **Capital:** Managua

- **Location:** Extending from the Pacific Ocean to the Caribbean Sea, Nicaragua is located on the land bridge in Central America. It is the largest of all the Central American countries with a total land area of 50,200 square miles, making Nicaragua slightly bigger than New York. It is bounded by Honduras to the north, the Caribbean Sea to the east, Costa Rica to the south, and the Pacific Ocean to the west. The terrain is varied. The Pacific region lies along the western coast, with Lake Managua in the center. Lake Nicaragua occupies most of the southern Pacific region. Volcanoes and steep mountains form the rim of the Pacific coast. The mountainous central highlands are covered with forests and volcanoes making it the coolest region. Another region extends along the Caribbean coast and is primarily a long, flat plain. Grasslands and some fertile land along the river banks are found here, but most of the section is covered by rain forests.

- **Language and Currency:** The official language of Nicaragua is Spanish. English and other Indian languages are also spoken, mainly throughout the Atlantic coastal region. Having a working knowledge of Spanish is helpful on a long-term assignment in Nicaragua. The monetary unit is the cordoba. The exchange rate is 6.30 cordobas = U.S.$1 (December 1993).

- **Print Sources of Information:** American University's *Area Handbook for Nicaragua* (1982) is available from the Superintendent of Documents, U.S. Government Printing Office, Washington, D.C., 20402.

EMBASSY AND CONSULATE CONTACT INFORMATION:

EMBASSY OF NICARAGUA
1627 NEW HAMPSHIRE AVE. NW
WASHINGTON, DC 20009
TEL: 202-387-4371

COMPANIES/ORGANIZATIONS WITH OPERATIONS IN NICARAGUA:
PROJECT HOPE, 563

NIGERIA

- **Official Name:** Federal Republic of Nigeria

- **Capital:** Abuja

- **Location:** Nigeria is located on the western coast of Africa. It is bounded by Niger and Chad to the north, Cameroon to the east, the Gulf of Guinea to the south, and Benin to the west. Its land area totals 351,649 square miles, making it almost one and a half times the size of Texas. Rivers, waterways, and lagoons are abundant throughout Nigeria; they play an important role in agriculture and as a transportation system.

- **Population, Cities, and American Residents:** The population of Nigeria is approximately 90 million (1992 est.), comprised of some 250 tribal groups. Approximately 65 percent of the people are members of the Hausa, Fulani, Yoruba, and Ibos tribes, which are based throughout Nigeria. Only about 27,000 of the Nigerian population are non-Africans.

  Most American residents are employed in Nigeria's three largest cities: Lagos with 5.5 million people, Ibadan with 4.5 million, and Kano with 1 million (1989 est.).

- **Language and Currency:** The official language of Nigeria is English. It is used widely in business and government circles. The monetary unit is the naira, written N. N1 = 100 kobo. The exchange rate is N30.31 = U.S.$1.

- **Climate:** The climate of Nigeria is tropical with some variation from one part of the country to another. The northern areas tend to be dry and hot, and the humidity gets worse toward the south. The coastal belt has an average rainfall of 85 inches and an average temperature of 82°F. The extreme north is very dry, with desert-like conditions. During the "dry" season in Nigeria, no rain falls. In the northern region, the dry season lasts from October through April, while in the south it lasts from November through March. When the rainy season starts, it rains every day.

- **Economy and Resources:** Nigeria's economy is dependent on oil. Crude oil accounts for 95 percent of the country's foreign exchange earnings, but this resource has been a mixed blessing. When oil prices fluctuated in the 1980s, Nigeria's prosperity temporarily ended, and it became burdened with debt, runaway inflation, and high unemployment. Agriculture contributes 25 percent to the gross domestic product (GDP) and 5 percent to exports, and also employs half of Nigeria's labor force. Cash crops include cocoa, coffee, rubber, and palm kernels. Nearly 20 percent of the people in Nigeria work in industry, services, and commerce. The major resource-based industries are mining, crude oil, natural gas, coal, and tin; manufacturing industries are textiles, cement, and food products. In the late 1980s, austerity programs were started to help Nigeria recover from the drop in oil prices, and the country continues to search for other avenues of economic development. Natural gas and agriculture are two areas targeted for development. Another Nigerian goal is to become more self-sufficient in food products, and the government recently banned imports of wheat, barley, and corn to encourage farmers to grow local grains. Nigeria is the most populous nation in Africa, and the eighth most populous in the world. Austerity programs include a campaign to lower the birth rates and monitor excessive population growth.

- **Cost of Living:** At 76, the cost of living is lower than in the United States.

- **Work Permits, Visas, etc.:** A valid passport and visa are required to travel in Nigeria. Visas may be obtained through an embassy or consulate in the United States, but long-term visas (over three months) are difficult to get. For short or long-term travel you must have a valid international health certificate stating that you are vaccinated against cholera. Antimalarial medication, yellow fever vaccinations, and tetanus/typhoid boosters are also recommended. For official or other information, direct inquiries to the embassy or consulate at the addresses below.

- **Taxation:** Foreign employees are responsible for Nigerian personal income taxes if they reside in Nigeria for more than 183 days. Various exemptions or deductions may apply. There is no treaty in effect between Nigeria and the United States to avoid double taxation.

- **Principal International Schools:** International schools are available in the urban areas of Nigeria. The tuition for an American school is $5,900 per year.

- **Health Care:** Public and private health facilities are available throughout Nigeria, but they are not up to Western standards. Some clinics and hospitals are better than others, and some foreign companies based in Nigeria will make arrangements for their employees to get adequate medical care. Over-the-counter drugs are available, but prescriptions may not be. Make sure to bring an extra pair of eyeglasses with you. Sanitation is poor in Nigeria, and tap water is not safe to drink. Appropriate precautions should be taken with all fruits and vegetables. Cook all meats and fish thoroughly to avoid gastrointestinal problems.

- **Crime:** Crime, especially armed robberies, has become a serious problem in Nigeria. Be very careful when traveling in major tourist areas. In the evening, try to go out with a group of people, rather than alone. Lock all doors and windows to your apartment, and never leave valuables in plain sight. Many people on long-term assignments in Nigeria hire security guards along with household help.

- **Pros and Cons of Living and Working in Nigeria:** Nigeria is a nation known for its art, culture, and varied landscape. Although tourists can visit mosques, palaces, and museums in the major cities and the country's Atlantic beaches, Nigeria does not have an abundance of tourist attractions. It is overpopulated, and health standards are poor. Lagos, the former capital, was voted the world's worst city in which to live in a 1990 survey. There is intolerable traffic congestion, pollution, and poor sanitation. Telecommunications are inadequate, and the mail system is no better. Housing is scarce and good accommodations are very expensive. Crime is becoming a major problem in Nigeria, and all valuables or expensive items should not be brought along. For your personal safety, it is strongly suggested that you do not travel outside urban areas in the evening hours.

EMBASSY AND CONSULATE CONTACT INFORMATION:

NIGERIAN EMBASSY
2201 M ST. NW
WASHINGTON, DC 20037
TEL: 202-822-1500

NIGERIAN CONSULATE GENERAL
575 LEXINGTON AVE.
NEW YORK, NY 10022
TEL: 212-715-7200

OTHER SOURCES OF INFORMATION:

U.S. STATE DEPT.
DESK OFFICER FOR NIGERIA
WASHINGTON, DC 20025
TEL: 202-647-3406

COMPANIES/ORGANIZATIONS WITH OPERATIONS IN NIGERIA:

ABB VETCO GRAY, INC., 108
ARETHUSA OFFSHORE, 140
ASHLAND OIL, INC., 143
BAKER HUGHES, INC., 152
BAROID CORPORATION, 158
BECHTEL GROUP, INC., 162
CHEVRON OVERSEAS PETROLEUM, INC., 194
CONOCO, INC., 209
CORE LABORATORIES, 214

CROWN CORK & SEAL COMPANY, INC., 218
DIGICON, INC., 235
ECOLOGY AND ENVIRONMENT, INC., 248
GTE CORPORATION, 288
HUGHES CHRISTENSEN COMPANY, 307
ITT CORPORATION, 321
MOBIL OIL CORPORATION, 375
OCEANEERING INTERNATIONAL, INC., 393

NORWAY

- **Official Name:** Kingdom of Norway
- **Capital:** Oslo
- **Location:** Located in northern Europe, Norway shares the Scandinavian peninsula with Sweden. The fifth largest country in Europe, its land area totals 125,181 square miles, making it slightly larger than New Mexico. In the north it shares land borders with Finland and the former U.S.S.R. Other Norwegian territories include the Arctic island groups of Spitzbergen and Jan Mayen. Norway has a heavily indented coastline, inland plateaus, and an abundance of clearwater lakes, though nearly three-quarters of the territory is mountains and wasteland with only 4 percent arable land. More than half of the Norwegian people live in the southeastern section of the country near the capital of Oslo.
- **Population, Cities, and American Residents:** The population of Norway totals 4.2 million (1992 est.). The country is ethnically homogeneous with a mixture of Germanic, Nordic, and Baltic peoples. There is also a relatively small minority group of 20,000 Lapps.

  Most American residents are employed in Norway's three largest cities: Oslo with 458,000 people, Bergen with 212,000, and Trondheim with 137,000 people (1990 est.).
- **Language and Currency:** The official language is Norwegian, broken down into two official versions: bokmaal, the traditional vernacular, which is similar to Danish; and nynorsk, or the new Norwegian. Bokmaal dates to the common Scandinavian tongue of early times and is the preferred language for everyday use. English is taught in school systems and is the leading foreign language, used frequently throughout business and government. The monetary unit is the Norwegian krone and divided into 100 ore. Bills are: Kr 1,000, 500, 100 and 50. Coins are: 50 and 10 ore; and Kr10, 5, and 1. The exchange rate is 1 Norwegian krone = U.S.$.13 (July 30, 1993).
- **Climate:** Because the Gulf stream passes along the Norwegian coast, the climate is mild. It is temperate along the coast, and much colder inland. It rains year-round in coastal sections, very heavily in the Bergen area.
- **Economy and Resources:** Norway is one of the richest countries in the world, mainly due to the recent discoveries of hydrocarbon reserves off its coasts. Previously, Norway was dependent on the sea and agriculture for its economic existence, but now agriculture accounts for only 1.6 percent of the gross domestic product (GDP). Major exports are petroleum products, natural gas, and fish. Major trading partners are the United Kingdom, and the European Free Trade Association (EFTA), which includes Austria, Finland, Iceland, Sweden, Switzerland,and Liechtenstein. Thanks to commercial development in the 1970s, Norway is now Europe's second-largest producer of crude oil following the United Kingdom, and gas reserves will last 100 years. Because Norway has more than enough domestic power (through hydroelectric sources), nearly all of its oil and gas is sold abroad. Being rich in oil reserves has presented some problems for Norway. Market stability and fluctuating prices in the 1980s led to unexpected

reductions in revenues, and many officials fear that oil and gas earnings are being relied on too much and are being wasted on current budget spending. To compensate, funds are now being invested for the future to produce income abroad when Norway's natural resources are eventually depleted. Natural resources besides oil and gas are copper, pyrites, and nickel. Of the labor force, 33 percent of the people are employed in services, 17.4 in commerce, and 17.2 percent in mining and manufacturing.

- **Cost of Living:** At 194, the cost of living is very high compared to the United States.

- **Work Permits, Visas, etc.:** For stays of up to three months, all that is required of U.S. citizens entering Norway is a valid passport. For longer stays, visas may be obtained from the consular offices in Norway. Work and residence permits are only issued to specialists in their field, and to key company personnel considered vital to the operation of the company. This reflects a ban on immigration which went into effect in 1975. If you are entering Norway from the United States, no vaccinations are necessary. For official or other information, direct inquiries to the embassy or consulate at the addresses below.

- **Taxation:** Foreigners working in Norway are subject to the same taxation as the citizens of Norway. Special tax provisions are made for the offshore oil industry. There is a treaty in effect between Norway and the United States to avoid double taxation.

- **Principal International Schools:** International schools available in the major cities of Norway. Tuition for an American school is about $6,500 per year.

- **Health Care:** Medical standards are high in Norway, with modern facilities in the major urban areas. The National Health Insurance plan provides coverage for all residents, regardless of citizenship. Facilities are extensive and costs are reasonable, but bring an adequate supply of any prescriptions or important medications, as they may not be available in the country. Sanitary conditions also are good, and the water is safe to drink. There are no prevalent diseases or health hazards that pose a threat to travelers.

- **Crime:** Crime is not a major problem in Norway, but in large cities or major tourist areas, lock vehicles when not in use and don't carry huge sums of cash.

- **Pros and Cons of Living and Working in Norway:** Norway is a fascinating country with much to offer visitors, especially those who love outdoor recreation. Norway's natural beauty may be seen by auto, cruise ship, or on foot. Sailing, mountain climbing, and fishing in the many lakes are popular activities, and Bergen, a seaport hidden among the mountains on the west coast, is a popular tourist spot. Communications are excellent and so is transportation. Highway laws are strictly enforced and fines are steep in Norway. Do not drink and drive; jail sentences for this infraction are mandatory. Housing is available but tends to be expensive compared to U.S. standards. Daily necessities cost more than in the United States. Bring any expensive pharmaceuticals or medications

EMBASSY AND CONSULATE CONTACT INFORMATION:

NORWEGIAN EMBASSY
2720 34 ST. NW
WASHINGTON, DC 20008
TEL: 202-333-6000

CONSULATE GENERAL OF NORWAY
825 THIRD AVE.
NEW YORK, NY 10022
TEL: 212-421-7333

with you. Because of the damp climate, and the shortage of sun, colds and respiratory problems are common, so be prepared if your stay in Norway is an extended one.

OTHER SOURCES OF INFORMATION:

SCANDINAVIAN TOURIST BOARD
655 THIRD AVE.
NEW YORK, NY 10017
TEL: 212-949-2333

COMPANIES/ORGANIZATIONS WITH OPERATIONS IN NORWAY:

ALBANY INTERNATIONAL CORPORATION, 114
ALUMINUM COMPANY OF AMERICA, 118
ANTHONY INDUSTRIES, 135
ASSOCIATED PRESS, 144
BAILEY CONTROLS COMPANY, 151
COLGATE-PALMOLIVE COMPANY, 203
COMMODORE INTERNATIONAL LTD., 206
COMPUTER ASSOCIATES INTERNATIONAL, INC., 207
CONOCO, INC., 209
DIGITAL EQUIPMENT CORPORATION, 236

EXXON COMPANY, INTERNATIONAL, 258
GERHARD'S BICYCLE ODYSSEYS, 280
INTERNATIONAL TOTALIZATOR SYSTEMS, INC., 319
MGM INCORPORATED, 372
MONSANTO COMPANY, 377
OCEANEERING INTERNATIONAL, INC., 393
SONAT, INC., 469
SONAT OFFSHORE, 470
TRINOVA CORPORATION, 502
US WEST, INC., 515
USX CORPORATION, 516

PAKISTAN

- **Official Name:** Islamic Republic of Pakistan

- **Capital:** Islamabad

- **Location:** Pakistan is located in southern Asia, at the beginning of the Arabian Sea. It is bounded by Afghanistan to the north, China to the far northeast, India to the east, the Arabian Sea to the south, and Iran to the west. Its land area totals 803,943 square miles, making it approximately twice the size of California. The climate and geography of Pakistan vary greatly from one location to another. There are four major provinces: Sind in the southeast, Baluchistan in the south and west, Punjab in the east-central region, and the Northwest Frontier. Pakistan's territory consists largely of rugged mountains, high valleys, scattered plains, plateaus, and deserts. Flowing southwest to the Arabian Sea, the Indus River and its four major tributaries provide a valuable transportation network for Pakistan.

- **Population, Cities, and American Residents:** The population of Pakistan totals 129.8 million people (1992 est.). Nearly all are from Indic and Indo-Iranian origin. About 66 percent of that group are Punjabi, 13 percent Sindhi, 8.5 percent Iranian, 7.6 percent Urdu, and 2.5 percent are Baluchi.

   Most American residents are employed in Pakistan's three major cities: Karachi with 8 million people, Lahore with 4 million, and the capital city of Islamabad with 400,000 (1990 est.).

- **Language and Currency:** The official language of Pakistan is English and it is used widely in business and government. Other local languages include Urdu, Punjabi, Pushto, and Sindhi. The monetary unit is the Pakistan rupee divided into 100 paisa (P). The exchange rate is 1 Pakistani rupee = U.S.$.034; 29.7 rupees equal U.S.$1 (July 30, 1993).

- **Climate:** Pakistan's climate is primarily subtropical in the south and temperate toward the northern mountain regions. Warmest temperatures occur from May through mid-July when daytime highs can reach more than 120°F in the Indus Valley. In winter, the northern sector may see some snow with temperatures as low as 32°F. Precipitation is light except when the monsoon season arrives in July. Most of the heavy rains predominate in the northern area.

- **Economy and Resources:** Pakistan is one of the poorest countries in the world. The economy is largely dependent on agriculture but most crops are used to feed its population of nearly 130 million people. The country's main resource is the Indus River, which irrigates its arable land and provides hydroelectric power. Agriculture employs more than half of the labor force and is responsible for one-quarter of the gross domestic product (GDP). Pakistan is a net food-exporter and is almost self-sufficient in food-grains. Major exports include rice, cotton, and textiles. Pakistan is engaged in natural-gas extraction, and its industrial sector produces engineering products, including power plants, dams, and irrigation equipment. The government is continuing to leave most industry in private hands and to channel public funds for infrastructure projects involving energy, water, health, and education. Services (finance, transport, and commerce) now account for 46 percent of the GDP. Private investment in Pakistan continues to be low, however. The government is trying to increase foreign investment by eliminating much of the red tape involved for foreigners to engage in business in the country.

- **Cost of Living:** At 81, the cost of living is lower than the United States.

- **Work Permits, Visas, etc.:** A valid passport and visa are required to travel in Pakistan. Business visas are good for a stay of up to one year and may be obtained through an embassy or consulate office. If your stay in Pakistan is longer than thirty days, you must register with the local police soon after arrival. If you are entering Pakistan from the United States, no vaccinations are required. However, vaccinations against typhoid, malaria, tetanus, diphtheria, and hepatitis are recommended before arriving in Pakistan. For official or other information, direct inquiries to the embassy or consulate at the addresses below.

- **Taxation:** Pakistan has a complicated tax system including corporate, personal, wealth, dividend, and local sales taxes. There is an agreement between Pakistan and the United States to avoid double taxation.

- **Principal International Schools:** English-language and international schools are available in the major cities of Pakistan. Tuition for an American school ranges from $1,000-$6,000 per year.

- **Health Care:** Medical care is good in most urban areas of Pakistan, and hospitals in the larger cities have American doctors on staff, but medical fees may be expensive. There are a few foreign-trained dentists available in major cities, but their fees will be higher than local professionals. Prescription drugs, eyeglasses, or special medications should be brought from home, as they may not be available in Pakistan. Sanitary conditions are poor throughout most of the country. Only the major hotels offer safe drinking water; boil or treat water from all other sources before using. Avoid dairy products unless you are sure they have been pasteurized, and take appropriate precautions with all fruits and vegetables before eating. There is a good deal of dust and smoke from trash heaps, which may affect people with respiratory ailments.

- **Crime:** Crime is an increasing problem in Pakistan. Robberies, kidnappings, and political murders affect the local population more than foreign visitors, but tourist areas attract pickpockets and purse snatchers, and bandits have been known to stop and rob vehicles, particularly near the Afghan border. Be especially cautious at night.

- **Pros and Cons of Living and Working in Pakistan:** Pakistan's tourist attractions include mosques, tombs, sculptures, and forts that remain from the ancient culture of the Indus Valley. That civilization was one of the world's first four civilizations, and many relics and ruins are still relatively well preserved. There are also bazaars, beaches, and beautiful mountain regions. Advantages to working in Pakistan include the widespread use of English, and the low cost of living. However, Pakistan is a poor and over-crowded nation, with poor sanitation throughout the country. Most entertaining is done at home, in part because strict Islamic cultural customs inhibit night life. Discos and nightclubs are rare in the country. Liquor is served only to foreigners, and may not be consumed in public. Crime is a major concern in Pakistan, and precautions must be taken while staying in the country. Leave expensive items or valuables at home. The tropical heat and oppressive humidity may cause some health problems and discomfort.

EMBASSY AND CONSULATE CONTACT INFORMATION:

EMBASSY OF PAKISTAN
2315 MASSACHUSETTS AVE. NW
WASHINGTON, DC 20008
TEL: 202-939-6200

CONSULATE GENERAL OF PAKISTAN
8 EAST 65TH ST.
NEW YORK, NY 10021
TEL: 212-879-8600

OTHER SOURCES OF INFORMATION:

PAKISTAN TOURIST DEVELOPMENT CORP.
747 3RD AVE., 16TH FL.
NEW YORK, NY 10026
TEL: 212-879-5800

COMPANIES/ORGANIZATIONS WITH OPERATIONS IN PAKISTAN:

AMERICAN PRESIDENT COMPANIES, LTD., 128
LOUIS BERGER INTERNATIONAL INC., 165
DE LEUW, CATHER INTERNATIONAL, 228
EBASCO OVERSEAS CORPORATION, 248
EXXON CHEMICAL COMPANY, 257
GENERAL TIRE, INC., 279

OCCIDENTAL PETROLEUM CORPORATION, 393
PHILLIPS PETROLEUM COMPANY, 415
POPULATION COUNCIL, 562
SEARLE COMPANY, 455
SKIDMORE, OWINGS & MERRILL, 465
VOLUNTEERS IN TECHNICAL ASSISTANCE, INC, 584

PANAMA

- **Official Name:** Republic of Panama
- **Capital:** Panama City
- **Location:** Panama is located on the southeastern end of the isthmus that creates the land bridge between North and South America. The Gulf of Mexico lies on its northern coast and the Pacific Ocean on the southern coast. Its total land area totals 29,762 square miles, making it comparable in size to South Carolina. Most of the territory is mountainous and hilly with the land to the east densely filled with tropical woodland. Nearly 54 percent of Panama is covered by forest or woodlands, with only 6 percent of the land arable.
- **Population, Cities, and American Residents:** The population of Panama totals 2.5 million (1992 est.). Most of the people are mestizo, accounting for 70 percent of the population. The remainder are 14 percent Indian, 10 percent white, and 6 percent Indian.

  Most Americans are employed in Panama's three largest cities: Panama City with 1.2 million people, Colon with 119,000, and David with 88,000 (1989 est.).
- **Language and Currency:** The official language of Panama is Spanish, though about 14 percent of the people speak English as a first language. Various other Indian languages are spoken throughout the country. The monetary unit is labeled the Balboa, but the official currency is the American dollar and U.S. and Panamanian coinage circulate interchangeably.
- **Climate:** The climate of Panama is tropical with high humidity, ranging from 78 to 98 percent on a year-round basis. The rainy season is from May through December, with the heaviest rain falling in September. It is fairly dry from December through April when temperatures average 85°F, except in the highlands region where it tends to be cooler. The Pacific side of Panama is the drier region.
- **Economy and Resources:** Because of the demand for goods and services related to its operation and defense, the Panama Canal has played a key role in the economy of Panama. For some time, the country has focused heavily on services for transit trade, international commerce, and finance. Political unrest during the late 1980s caused many banks to relocate, and massive capital flight occurred. Until then, the international banking community was the country's third largest employer (after the Panama and U.S. governments). The Banking Commission restricts depositors' access to some accounts. After the 1987 assault on the U.S. Embassy in Panama, the United States sanctions imposed on the country nearly crippled its economy. In 1989, the United States invaded Panama to arrest military dictator General Manuel Noriega, who had already removed one president from office and declared another presidential election invalid. He finally surrendered to U.S. officials in January of 1990. The economy is slowly improving, but it will not be fully stabilized until all political conflicts are resolved. Government and services employ 27.9 percent of the labor force, and agriculture 26.2 percent. Major industries are manufacturing and petroleum refining. Principal exports include bananas

C
O
U
N
T
R
Y

P
R
O
F
I
L
E
S

(40 percent), shrimp, coffee, and petroleum products. The major trading partner is the United States which accounts for 90 percent of Panama's exports.

- **Cost of Living:** At 96, the cost of living is comparable to the United States.

- **Work Permits, Visas, etc.:** A valid passport is required to travel in Panama, and for stays longer than one month you'll need a visa. Contact the embassy or consulate nearest your home for proper instructions. When entering Panama from the United States, no vaccinations are required, but the Centers for Disease Control (CDC) recommends yellow fever shots for travelers under nine months of age visiting rural sections outside of major tourist areas. For official or other information direct inquiries to the embassy or consulate at the addresses below.

- **Taxation:** Nonresidents are taxed on income earned from Panamanian sources. Taxes on any type of income received by nonresidents must be withheld by the payer. Contact the Panamanian consulate or embassy for more information.

- **Health Care:** Medical facilities in Panama City are generally good. Hospitals are well equipped and staffed with English-speaking doctors. The rural areas have limited facilities, and while sanitation in the main cities is satisfactory, in rural areas it is not. Outside the major urban areas, tap water must be boiled.

- **Crime:** Crime is not a major problem in Panama, but tourist areas are prone to common crime. Beware of pickpockets and do not leave valuables unattended.

- **Pros and Cons of Living and Working in Panama:** Panama's attractions include folklore and culture, native Indian art, lively music, sandy beaches, dormant volcanoes, and lush mountain ranges. The climate is exceptionally humid, and it rains much of the time between May and December. Continuing political unrest must be resolved if the economy is to improve.

- **Print Sources of Information:** *Panama: A Country Study* (1989), edited Sandra Meditz. Superintendent of Documents, U.S. Government Printing Office, Washington, D.C., 20402.

EMBASSY AND CONSULATE CONTACT INFORMATION:

PANAMANIAN EMBASSY
2862 MCGILL TERRACE NW
WASHINGTON, DC 20008
TEL: 202-483-1407

PANAMANIAN CONSULATE
1212 AVENUE OF THE AMERICAS, 10TH FL.
NEW YORK, NY 10036
TEL: 212-840-2450

COMPANIES/ORGANIZATIONS WITH OPERATIONS IN PANAMA:

ARMOUR SWIFT ECKRICH, INC., 141
BORDEN, INC., 170
CIGNA CORPORATION, 197
CITICORP, 198
DIGITAL EQUIPMENT CORPORATION, 236
EXXON CORPORATION, 258
FRITZ COMPANIES, 269
THE GILLETTE COMPANY, 283
HANSON INDUSTRIES, 295
HARRIS CORPORATION, 296
HERTZ CORPORATION, 300

INTERNATIONAL BUSINESS MACHINES
(IBM), 315
OVERSEAS SHIPHOLDING GROUP, INC.,
400
PHELPS DODGE CORPORATION, 412
RALSTON PURINA COMPANY, 430
SCM CHEMICALS, 453
SYNTEX CORPORATION, 486
TECHNOSERVE, INC., 565
THE UPJOHN COMPANY, 515

PARAGUAY

- **Official Name:** Republic of Paraguay
- **Capital:** Asuncion
- **Location:** Paraguay is a landlocked country located in central South America. It is bounded by Bolivia to the north, Brazil to the east, and Argentina to the south and west. Its total land area is 157,048 square miles, making it about the size of California. Nearly half the territory is meadows and pastures; forests comprise an additional 35 percent.
- **Language and Currency:** The official language of Paraguay is Spanish. If you plan to live or work in Paraguay, you should have a basic knowledge of Spanish in dealing with daily life. The monetary unit is the guarini. The current exchange rate is 1,600 guarini = U.S.$1 (March 1994).

EMBASSY AND CONSULATE CONTACT INFORMATION:

EMBASSY OF PARAGUAY
2400 MASSACHUSETTS AVE. NW
WASHINGTON, DC 20008
TEL: 202-483-6960

OTHER SOURCES OF INFORMATION:

FOR INFORMATION ON CURRENT ECONOMIC TRENDS, OR COMMERCIAL DEVELOPMENT CONTACT:
INTERNATIONAL TRADE ADMINISTRATION
U.S. DEPARTMENT OF COMMERCE
WASHINGTON, DC 20230

COMPANIES/ORGANIZATIONS WITH OPERATIONS IN PARAGUAY:

STANDARD COMMERCIAL CORPORATION,
476

PERU

- **Official Name:** Republic of Peru
- **Capital:** Lima
- **Location:** Peru, located on the western coast of South America, has a total land area of 496,222 square miles, and is slightly smaller than Alaska. Bounded to the north by Ecuador and Colombia, to the east by Bolivia, to the south by Chile, and to the west by the Pacific Ocean, Peru is the third largest country in South America. Over half the territory is covered by forest and woodland, and only 3 percent is arable land. It has three different geographic regions: the western coast is a dry stretch of desert land; the middle of Peru is a broad region of high mountains and deep canyons; and the eastern part of the country is a thick, tropical rain forest which encompasses more than half of Peru's territory. The Costa (coastal area) is the economic center of Peru, and is inhabited by 44 percent of the total population.
- **Population, Cities, and American Residents:** Peru is home to 23.4 million

people (1992 est.) The population is 45 percent Indian, 37 mestizo, and 15 percent white. The remaining 3 percent are black, Japanese, Chinese, and other mixed groups.

Most American residents are employed in Peru's three major cities: Lima with 6.7 million people, Arequipa with 1 million, and Callao with 500,000 (1991 est.).

- **Language and Currency:** The official language of Peru is Spanish and it is used throughout government and business. Without some working knowledge of Spanish, be prepared to use translators or interpreters. The unit of currency is the new sol. The rate of exchange is 1 new sol = U.S.$.51 (July 30, 1993).

- **Climate:** Situated south of the equator, the seasons are in reverse of those in the Northern Hemisphere. The climate in the Costa is unusual in that it is a desert with little or no rain, yet the humidity is high. Days are warm, evenings are cool, and an average temperature in February is 72°F. The winter season from May to November has a chilly, damp climate with foggy days and little sun. Temperatures average around 55°F. East of the Costa, the dry, warm, desert-like climate prevails year round. The Amazon and jungle regions are hot and rainy all year with high humidity and temperatures averaging between 80°F-100°F.

- **Economy and Resources:** Government changes and policies have had an effect on Peru's economy over the past several years. Global prices on the country's major exports have experienced repeated changes, and the weather has not been favorable for crops or fishing. It is a country rich in resources, but poor management by past leaders has not helped the country to achieve what it deserves. A deep recession, and inflation (which escalated prices by more than 6,000 percent in 1990), are two problems president Alberto Fujimori must handle. The major part of the work force is composed of 44 percent government and services, 37 percent agriculture, and 19 percent industry. Natural resources include copper, silver, gold, petroleum, and timber. Major industries are mining of metals, petroleum, and fishing. Chief exports include fish meal, cotton, sugar, coffee, and copper. Major trading partners for exports are the European Community and the United States.

- **Cost of Living:** At 105, the cost of living is comparable to living in the United States.

- **Work Permits, Visas, etc.:** A valid passport is needed. No visa is required if stay is limited to three months, but after that, you must apply for a work or residence permit. Usually the permit is applied for by the employer and is sent to the Minister of Labor and then to the Director General of Immigration in Peru for approval. If entering Peru from the United States, no vaccinations are required, but a yellow fever shot and malaria pills are recommended if you are traveling to the rural areas of the Amazon region. For official or other information, direct inquiries to the embassy or consulate at the addresses below.

- **Taxation:** Peru's tax system is now undergoing changes. Currently, residents are required to pay taxes on income earned globally, and nonresidents are responsible for income earned only from Peruvian sources. For tax reasons, a person is considered a resident if he or she has lived in Peru for two complete calendar years. Check with the U.S. State Department for a current update on the tax system of Peru.

- **Principal International Schools:** International schools are available in Lima for children of American residents. Tuition for an American school is about $6,000 per year.

- **Health Care:** There are medical facilities available in Lima that are acceptable by U.S. standards. Two used most often by foreigners are the Anglo-American Hospital and the Hospital de Ninas. Sanitary conditions are not very favorable; use bottled water or boil tap water yourself (from all areas). Be careful with produce; all raw vegetables and fruits should be peeled or washed accordingly before eating. Cook meat thoroughly and avoid shellfish and unpasteurized milk. Altitude can cause problems and may induce a syndrome called soroche. Symptoms include nausea, dizziness, and lethargy. Consult a physician if symptoms persist. Do not use local glazed pottery for food usage as it may contain lead.

- **Crime:** The U.S. State Department has issued a travelers' advisory for Peru. Terrorist groups have been known to use violent methods to uproot their government and Americans should avoid any confrontations. Drug trafficking is prevalent in certain Peruvian sectors and these are danger zones for travel. Stay with a group of people rather than traveling alone. This is especially important if you're going to any rural or remote areas of the country. Common crime and isolated acts of terrorism are serious throughout Peru. Street crime is prevalent, especially in major tourist areas, so watch out for pickpockets and purse snatchers. As demonstrations or labor strikes may occur, it's wise to avoid these unsettled areas. Check with the (State Department) Citizens' Emergency Center at 202-647-4225 for a current update on the travel situation in Peru.

- **Pros and Cons of Living and Working in Peru:** Peru is a fascinating country abundant in historic and natural attractions. From the lost city of the Inca to the white sand beaches, there are mountain climbing excursions, jungle expeditions, and much more. But crime is a serious matter on all levels throughout Peru and a deciding factor on whether or not to reside there. Common crime is a frequent occurrences in tourist areas, and the U.S. State Department has issued travel warnings. Travel outside of the capital region is difficult because of poor roads, and there is a chance you may be robbed on the highway. Travel by public bus is not recommended. Sanitation is not good in most areas, and there are widespread occurrences of cholera, so don't drink the water and be careful preparing foods.

EMBASSY AND CONSULATE CONTACT INFORMATION:

PERUVIAN EMBASSY
1700 MASSACHUSETTS AVE. NW
WASHINGTON, DC 20036
TEL: 202-833-9860

CONSULATE GENERAL
215 LEXINGTON AVE., 21ST FL.
NEW YORK, NY 10022
TEL: 212-481-7410

OTHER SOURCES OF INFORMATION:

PERUVIAN TOURIST OFFICE
1000 BRICKELL AVE., STE. 600
MIAMI, FL 33131
TEL: 305-374-0023

COMPANIES/ORGANIZATIONS WITH OPERATIONS IN PERU:

ARMCO, INC., 140
ASARCO, INC., 142
ASSOCIATED PRESS, 144
AVON PRODUCTS, INC., 149
CITICORP, 198
CONSERVATION INTERNATIONAL, 545

J. M. HUBER CORPORATION, 306
LIQUID CARBONIC CORPORATION, 347
MARRIOTT CORPORATION, 360
POPULATION COUNCIL, 562
STERLING WINTHROP, INC., 479
TECHNOSERVE, INC., 565

PHILIPPINES

- **Official Name:** Republic of the Philippines
- **Capital:** Manila
- **Location:** The Philippines form an archipelago of more than 7,000 islands that extend for 1,152 square miles across the South China Sea. Located 500 miles off southeastern Asia, the total land area is 116,000 square miles, making it slightly larger than Arizona. Eleven of the largest islands comprise 95 percent of the territory, most of which is covered by dense tropical rain forests. The Philippines have many bays, harbors, large lakes, and hundreds of rivers. Most rivers flow only during the rainy season, which occurs from June through February. The country is divided into three main regions: Luzon in the north, the Visayas in the center section, and Mindanao in the south. The Visayas comprises 96 percent of the total land area and include 8 of the 11 main islands.
- **Population, Cities, and American Residents:** The population of the Philippines totals 65 million Filipinos (1992 est.), of which 91.5 are Christian Malays, 4 percent Muslim Malays, 1.5 percent Chinese, and 3 percent other groups.

    Most American residents are employed in the Philippines' three largest cities: Manila with 9 million people (metropolitan population), Quezon City with 1.7 million, and Davao City with 850,000 (1990 est.).
- **Language and Currency:** The official languages of the Philippines are Pilipino and English. (Pilipino is based on Tagalog.) English is widely used in business circles. The monetary unit is the Philippine peso (P), divided into 100 centavos. The exchange rate is 1 Philippine peso = U.S.$.036 (July 30, 1993).
- **Climate:** The Philippines is exceptionally hot and humid throughout the year. Summer runs from November through May, with little or no precipitation. The wet winter months occur from June through October during when as much as 120 inches of rain may fall. The mean annual temperature averages about 80°F with highland areas slightly cooler. The Philippine Islands are located in the circum-Pacific belt, where frequent earthquakes occur. Volcanoes also lie along this belt, and Mount Pinatubo, near Manila has erupted many times.
- **Economy and Resources:** The Philippine economy has expanded rapidly since World War II. Industry accounts for 36 percent of the gross domestic product (GDP) and agriculture for 25 percent. Principal industries include cement, chemicals, cigars,

clothing, food and beverages, refined metals and petroleum, sugar, textiles, and wood products. The major crops are rice, maize, bananas, and coconut. The country also is rich in natural resources, which include copper, nickel, gold, timber, and crude oil. Of the labor force, 47 percent work in agriculture, 20 percent in industry and commerce, 13.5 in services, and 10 percent in government. Major trading partners are the United States and the European Community. The worldwide recession during the 1980s had a lasting effect on the Philippine economy; large-scale capital flight over many years siphoned billions of dollars of investments, profits, and foreign aid out of the national economy and into private accounts in foreign banks. Government reforms began in the late 1980s and included liberalization of trade and regulatory policies. Currently the focus is on land reform and economic redistribution to encourage agricultural development and the establishment of rural, labor-intensive industries. Massive poverty and high unemployment are major problems for President Fidel V. Ramos, who replaced Corazon Aquino. Despite several attempted military coups and years of unstable conditions and a corrupt system, the major export industries remain under Philippine control. The demand for industrial chemicals, plastics, and computer equipment remains strong, and Filipinos have begun to invest in their country once again.

- **Cost of Living:** At 82, the cost of living is lower than in the United States.
- **Work Permits, Visas, etc.:** A valid passport and an international health certificate are required for stays of up to three weeks. For pleasure trips longer than three weeks, a visa must be obtained from a diplomatic or consular office in the Philippines after arrival. To work in the Philippines, you must apply for a visa through an embassy or consulate in the United States. Applications must be notarized and include a letter from the employer, stating the nature of the trip and the financial responsibility for the employee. When entering the Philippines from the United States, no vaccinations are required. However, antimalarial precautions and vaccinations against typhoid and tetanus are recommended.
- **Taxation:** Individual foreign residents are subject to taxes at graduated rates ranging from 1 percent to 35 percent of gross income derived from all sources both within and outside the Philippines. Americans living in the Philippines may take taxes either as a deduction or as a credit when filing U.S. tax returns at home.
- **Principal International Schools:** International schools offering a U.S. curriculum are available in the major Philippine cities. Tuition for an American school is $4,500 per year.
- **Health Care:** Medical facilities are adequate in the major cities of the Philippines, but facilities are few and far between, and unacceptable in rural areas. Sanitation is better than in most other Asian countries, but is not up to American standards, and rodents, insects, and house pests are endemic in some areas. Check sources of all tap water before drinking. Take necessary precautions with all fruits and vegetables, and cook all meat and fish thoroughly.
- **Crime:** Common crime is a problem in the Philippines, attributable in part to the widespread poverty throughout the country. Pickpocketing and jewelry thefts are frequent. Police patrol the streets throughout the day and evening hours and are helpful to foreign visitors.

- **Pros and Cons of Living and Working in The Philippines:** The Philippines' national culture combines local European, and American traditions. Popular tourist attractions include churches, historic sites, museums, art galleries, and botanical gardens. Local festivals, beaches, and the many fishing villages also are appealing. Because English is spoken almost everywhere, you'll have few problems communicating with local residents, who are friendly and hospitable to tourists, especially Americans. Transportation throughout the cities is good, and taxis are inexpensive. However, telecommunications and sanitary conditions are poor. Only the larger cities offer adequate utilities, garbage collection, and sewage systems. Medical facilities are acceptable only in the more populous areas. Because of the high poverty level, crime is common. It's best to leave valuables, particularly expensive jewelry, at home. Furnished apartments and other housing are available in Manila, usually with a one-year security deposit required. Because of mildew caused by the humid climate, it's best to leave fine books, clothing, and furniture at home.
- **Print Sources of Information:** Karnow, Stanley. *In Our Image: America's Empire in the Philippines.* New York: Random House, 1989.

EMBASSY AND CONSULATE CONTACT INFORMATION:

EMBASSY OF THE PHILIPPINES
1617 MASSACHUSETTS AVE. NW
WASHINGTON, DC 20036
TEL: 202-483-1414

PHILIPPINE CONSULATE GENERAL
556 FIFTH AVE.
NEW YORK, NY 10036
TEL: 212-764-1330

COMPANIES/ORGANIZATIONS WITH OPERATIONS IN PHILIPPINES:

AMERICAN APPRAISAL ASSOCIATES, INC., 121
AMERICAN CYANAMID COMPANY, 124
AMERICAN PRESIDENT COMPANIES, LTD., 128
AMERICAN STANDARD, INC., 128
ARMCO, INC., 140
ASEA BROWN BOVERI, 142
BACKER SPIELVOGEL & BATES WORLDWIDE, INC., 150
BANDAG, INC., 153
LOUIS BERGER INTERNATIONAL INC., 165
BLOCK DRUG COMPANY, INC., 169
BORDEN, INC., 170
CAMP DRESSER & MCKEE INTERNATIONAL, INC., 183
CHASE MANHATTAN CORPORATION, 190
BERNARD CHAUS, INC., 191
COLUMBIAN ROPE COMPANY, 204
CONSERVATION INTERNATIONAL, 545
D-M-E COMPANY, 222
DAMES & MOORE, 223
DATA GENERAL CORPORATION, 225
DEL MONTE CORPORATION, 230
DUPONT MERCK PHARMACEUTICAL COMPANY, 243
EBASCO OVERSEAS CORPORATION, 248
FIRST CHICAGO CORPORATION, 262
GENERAL ELECTRIC COMPANY (GE), 275
GENERAL FOODS USA, 276
GENERAL MOTORS CORPORATION (GM), 277
GETZ BROTHERS COMPANY, INC., 281
GOULD PUMPS, INC., 285
W. R. GRACE & COMPANY, 285
HORMEL FOODS CORPORATION, 304
HYATT INTERNATIONAL CORPORATION, 308
INTEL CORPORATION, 314
INTERNATIONAL PAPER COMPANY, 318
LEVI STRAUSS ASSOCIATES, INC., 344
LIZ CLAIBORNE, INC., 348
MATTEL, INC., 363
MOTION PICTURE EXPORT ASSOCIATION OF AMERICA, 380
NALCO CHEMICAL COMPANY, 382

NORTHWEST AIRLINES, INC., 390
PARSONS CORPORATION, 406
PIONEER HI-BRED INTERNATIONAL, INC.,
   417
PROCTER & GAMBLE COMPANY, 425
PROCTER & GAMBLE PHARMACEUTICALS,
   INC., 426
QUAKER OATS COMPANY, 428
RALSTON PURINA COMPANY, 430
RESOURCES MANAGEMENT
   INTERNATIONAL, 437
ROHM & HAAS COMPANY, 442
SGS CONTROL SERVICES, 458
SIGNODE PACKAGING SYSTEMS, 462

STANDARD & POOR'S CORPORATION, 476
STV GROUP, 482
TEXAS INTRUMENTS, INC., 494
3M COMPANY, 496
UNION CAMP CORPORATION, 507
U.S. ELECTRICAL MOTORS (EMERSON
   ELECTRIC), 510
U.S. WHEAT ASSOCIATES, 511
THE UPJOHN COMPANY, 515
VF CORPORATION, 517
WENDY'S INTERNATIONAL, INC., 524
WILLIAM WRIGLEY JR. COMPANY, 529
WYETH-AYERST LABORATORIES, 530

POLAND

- **Official Name:** Republic of Poland

- **Capital:** Warsaw

- **Location:** Poland is located on a large plain in eastern Europe with a total land area of 120,700 square miles. It is bounded by the Baltic Sea to the north, the Ukraine to the east, Slovakia to the south, the Czech Republic to the southwest, and Germany to the west. Most of the territory is part of the Great European Plain, a vast flat countryside, running across Europe from France to the Ural Mountains. Beyond the plain, toward the southern area, are deep river gorges and dense forest woodlands. Poland has seven regions: the Coastal Lowlands, the Baltic Lakes Region, the Central Plains, the Polish Uplands, the Carpathian Forelands, the Sudetes Mountains, and the Western Carpathian Mountains.

- **Population, Cities, and American Residents:** The population of Poland is approximately 38.8 million (1992 est.). Most people (98.7 percent) are of Polish stock. The remainder are Ukrainian at 0.6 percent, and Byelorussian at 0.5 percent.

   Most American residents are employed in Poland's three largest cities: Warsaw with 1.7 million people, Lodz with 852,000, and Krakow with 784,000 (1989 est.).

- **Language and Currency:** The official language of Poland is Polish, which is a difficult language for foreigners to learn, but a working knowledge of Polish is essential in business or just to cope with daily life. Interpreters or translators are available, if necessary. English is spoken by some of the educated elite. The monetary unit is the zloty. The exchange rate is 1 Polish zloty = U.S.$.00006; 17,364 zlotys equal U.S.$1 (July 30, 1993).

- **Climate:** Summers in Poland are short, and winters are long and cold with a good deal of snow. The average winter temperature is 26°F. Summer temperatures average about

66°F. The climate is comparable to that of northern New England. The most pleasant months in Poland are from May through October.

- **Economy and Resources:** From 1947-1989, Poland was ruled by the Communist Party, under which industrial development was given high priority. Today, industry accounts for half of the gross domestic product (GDP) and 70 percent of exports. Major industries are steel, electricity, cement, and shipbuilding. Mineral resources include coal, lignite, and zinc. Coal and timber are important natural resources in Poland's economy. Of the labor force, 37 percent of the people work in industry and construction, 29 percent in agriculture, and 15 percent in trade, transport, and communications. Major trading partners are Russia and Germany. In 1989, the Polish government reached an agreement with the Solidarity labor union, which eventually legalized the union and completely changed the structure of government. Major reforms were initiated, with the goal of transforming the failed Communist system into a market economy as soon as possible. Subsidies and controls were removed, and many inefficient factories were closed. This eventually led to increased unemployment and escalating inflation rates, so drastic economic reforms, including an austerity plan, were put into effect. Within a year, positive signs began to emerge, but recovery has been slow. Poland continues to encourage foreign investment by placing few restrictions on the types of business located in the country. Joint ventures are taxed more favorably than Polish-owned enterprises. There is a good deal of development and change currently going on in Poland, and it's difficult to predict what the future will bring. The Polish people will have to continue to make sacrifices to achieve a stable, growing economy. Pollution is a major problem, as in other European countries. Heavy industry was a major polluter, and billions of dollars must be spent to clean the polluted air, land, and water resulting from years of neglect.

- **Cost of Living:** At 91, the cost of living is slightly less than in the United States.

- **Work Permits, Visas, etc.:** A valid passport is required to travel in Poland. If you plan to work in the country, you'll need a business visa, obtainable only after receiving an invitation from a government office or business in Poland. It is issued for a six-month period and is subject to renewal upon request. Allow ample time for processing. When entering Poland from the United States, no vaccinations are required. For official or other information, direct inquiries to the embassy or consulate at the addresses below.

- **Taxation:** Americans working in Poland are subject to personal income taxes, which, in some cases, may be taken care of by the employer. If not, the taxes are deductible from U.S. taxes up to the IRS limits.

- **Principal International Schools:** An international school in Warsaw offers education to children through the ninth grade. Tuition for the American school is about $6,000 per year.

- **Health Care:** Poland has a socialized medicine system, for which Americans do not qualify. Fees are very reasonable, however, and most facilities are acceptable for medical problems. Sanitary standards are lower than those in the United States, and tap water is unsafe. Appropriate precautions should be taken with all fruits and vegetables, and be careful to purchase only pasteurized milk.

- **Crime:** Street crime is common in Poland and pickpockets frequent bus and train stations. Take precautions when going out at night, especially if traveling alone.

- **Pros and Cons of Living and Working in Poland:** Poland has gone through many dramatic changes since the 1940s. Much of the country was destroyed during World War II, but the nation has rebuilt many historic and cultural sites. Warsaw's "Old Town" has museums, cobblestone paths, and marketplaces. The cost of living in Poland is slightly lower than in the United States, so daily needs can be met at a reasonable price, although there may be a smaller selection or shortage of some goods. Transportation is adequate, as roads are in good shape, but traffic laws are strictly enforced. Penalties include stiff fines for speeding or drunk driving, and watch out for pedestrians and horse carts, which are frequent along in rural roadways. Telecommunications are very unreliable with some overseas calls taking up to two hours. Suitable housing is scarce and cramped, particularly for families. Bring a good selection of clothing when staying for any length of time, as the selection and supply in Poland is limited and may not be suited to American tastes. Winters can be snowy and cold, so pack an electric blanket and extra sweaters. Without a working knowledge of the Polish language living in the country for any extended time period will be difficult.

EMBASSY AND CONSULATE CONTACT INFORMATION:

POLISH EMBASSY
2640 16TH ST. NW
WASHINGTON, DC 20009
TEL: 202-234-3800

POLISH CONSULATE GENERAL
233 MADISON AVE.
NEW YORK, NY 10016
TEL: 212-889-8360

OTHER SOURCES OF INFORMATION:

POLISH COMMERCIAL COUNSELOR
1 DAG HAMMARSKJÖLD PLAZA
NEW YORK, NY 10016
TEL: 212-486-3150

COMPANIES/ORGANIZATIONS WITH OPERATIONS IN POLAND:

INTERNATIONAL CITY MANAGEMENT
ASSOCIATION, 548
INTERNATIONAL DATA GROUP, INC., 316
JOHNSON & JOHNSON, 325
KLYNVELD PEAT MARWICK GOERDELER
(KPMG), 337
NEWSWEEK INTERNATIONAL, 387
PHILIP MORRIS COMPANIES, INC., 413

PROJECT HOPE, 563
SCHERING-PLOUGH CORPORATION, 450
TECHNOSERVE, INC., 565
TELEDYNE, INC., 489
UNITED NATIONS INDUSTRIAL
DEVELOPMENT ORGANIZATION
(UNIDO), 568
VF CORPORATION, 517

PORTUGAL

- **Official Name:** Republic of Portugal

- **Capital:** Lisbon

- **Location:** Portugal is located on the Atlantic side of the Iberian Peninsula in southwestern Europe. Rectangular in shape, its land area totals 36,390 square miles, comparable in size to Indiana. Portugal also comprises two archipelagos, the Azores and the Madeira Islands, located in the Atlantic Ocean. The country has an extremely indented coastline, with several deep harbors. Much of the land consists of flat coastal plains that climb slowly to mountainous terrain toward the center of the country. The Serra da Estrela mountain range has peaks reaching to nearly 6,600 feet. The southern coast of Portugal is a popular tourist spot, offering a mild climate, bright sunshine, and sandy beaches.

- **Population, Cities, and American Residents:** The population of Portugal totals 10.3 million people (1992 est.). The Portuguese are a mixture of many origins, with the majority of Mediterranean stock, many of whom migrated to Portugal after the prehistoric era. The Portuguese people are descendants of Celts, Phoenicians, Carthaginians, Romans, Jews, Germanic tribes, Arabs, and Berbers. There are also citizens of Black African descent who immigrated to Portugal during the decolonization period.

   Most American residents are employed in Portugal's two largest cities: Lisbon with 2 million people and Oporto with 1.5 million (1990 est.).

- **Language and Currency:** The official language of Portugal is Portuguese. However, English and French are spoken as second languages throughout the country and in the majority of large companies. Translators are available if needed. The monetary unit of Portugal is the escudo, divided into 100 centavos. It is written as $, and placed between the escudo and centavo units—40$20 = 40 escudos and 20 centavos. The exchange rate is 1 Portuguese escudo = U.S.$.006; 174 escudos equal U.S.$1 (July 30, 1993).

- **Climate:** Portugal has a moderate climate with an average yearly temperature of 61°F. The coastal regions are a bit cooler and have more precipitation throughout the year. The average temperature range in Lisbon is 46°F-57°F in January; and 63°F-81°F in July.

- **Economy and Resources:** Portugal is one of the oldest independent nations in Europe. It joined the European Community in 1986, but remains one of the poorer countries in the group, with a per capita gross domestic product (GDP) of less than $3,500. Portugal is highly dependent upon trade and light manufacturing (textiles and shoes), and tourism, agriculture, and fishing are the mainstays of the economy. Industry contributes 30 percent of the GDP, but much of what is produced is dependent on imported energy and raw materials. Agriculture accounts for 10 percent of the GDP, with wheat, maize, potatoes, grapes (and wine), and tomatoes as principal products. Nearly three-quarters of exports go to the European Community. Of the labor force, 44 percent of the people work in services, and 34 percent are engaged in agriculture. Portugal has an abundance of undeveloped mining resources, but relies heavily on imported fuel, especially oil. Conservation plans include a switch from oil to coal and hydroelectric power to meet energy needs. Today, hydroelectric sources account for half of the electricity generated in Portugal. During the 1970s, a new democratically elected government began restructuring the economy by promoting foreign investment, privatization, and deregulation. Inflation remains high and the social inequalities have been accentuated, rather than minimized, by economic growth.

Under the social democratic government of Prime Minister Cavco Silva, a stable business environment has developed, promoting economic growth. However, keeping the economy growing and curbing the escalating inflation rate remain difficult challenges.

- **Cost of Living:** At 120, the cost of living is higher than in the United States.

- **Work Permits, Visas, etc.:** A valid passport is required for visits up to sixty days. For longer stays, a visa must be obtained from a Portuguese embassy or consulate, and may be extended at the Foreign Registration Service in Lisbon after arriving in the country. If you are entering Portugal from the United States, no vaccinations are required. For official or other information, direct inquiries to the addresses below.

- **Taxation:** Residents of Portugal are required to pay income taxes on wages earned there. People are considered residents if they spend more than 183 days in Portugal during the year, or if they own homes there. According to the foreign investment code, earnings of foreign nationals in Portugal must be remitted abroad, net of taxes and living expenses, for up to three years without restrictions. There is no tax treaty between Portugal and the United States to avoid double taxation.

- **Principal International Schools:** Several international schools that offer quality education are available in Portugal. Tuition for an American school is $7,200-$8,000 per year.

- **Health Care:** Medical care in Portugal is not comparable to U.S. standards, mainly due to overcrowded and under-equipped facilities. Private hospitals are slightly better for simple medical procedures and minor surgery (including normal obstetrical care). Most pharmaceuticals are available from local drugstores. Sanitation standards in the country are fair. Tap water in the Lisbon area is only safe to drink during the rainy seasons (spring and autumn). In other seasons—and at other locations in the country—it's safer to drink bottled water. Appropriate precautions should be taken with all fruits and vegetables, and make sure that milk is pasteurized, as untreated milk is unsafe to drink. Do not eat raw fish of any kind; doing so may lead to stomach ailments.

- **Crime:** Common crime is quite frequent in Portugal, particularly theft from parked automobiles. It's important to lock all car doors, and to remove anything of value. Purse snatchers and pickpockets frequent tourist areas. Women should be especially careful if going out at night and should not visit bars or nightclubs unescorted.

- **Pros and Cons of Living and Working in Portugal:** Portugal is a pleasant country, with a relatively low cost of living, an excellent climate, and many tourist attractions. Each region specializes in its own cuisine, resulting in a variety of food on restaurant menus. There are museums, cathedrals, quaint fishing villages, and other cultural attractions. Transportation is good, but if you're driving, watch out for

EMBASSY AND CONSULATE CONTACT INFORMATION:

EMBASSY OF PORTUGAL
2125 KALORAMA RD. NW
WASHINGTON, DC 20008
TEL: 202-328-8610

pedestrians on the roadway and for drivers who have had too much to drink or ignore the posted speed limits. The country has one of the world's worst accident rates in Europe. Wearing seatbelts is mandatory in Portugal. Suitable housing is becoming expensive and difficult to find. Central heating is rare. Although the climate is temperate, bring electric blankets and sweaters if you plan to winter in Portugal.

PORTUGUESE CONSULATE OF
MASSACHUSETTS
899 BOYLSTON ST., 2ND FL.
BOSTON, MA 02115
TEL: 617-536-8740

OTHER SOURCES OF INFORMATION:

PORTUGUESE TRADE COMMISSION
590 FIFTH AVE.
NEW YORK, NY 10036
TEL: 212-354-4610

COMPANIES/ORGANIZATIONS WITH OPERATIONS IN PORTUGAL:

AMERICAN CYANAMID COMPANY, 124
ASSOCIATED PRESS, 144
COLGATE-PALMOLIVE COMPANY, 203
CONAGRA, INC., 208
EASTMAN KODAK COMPANY, 246
GENERAL INSTRUMENT CORPORATION, 276

GENERAL TIRE, INC., 279
H. J. HEINZ COMPANY, 290
HERTZ CORPORATION, 300
ICF KAISER ENGINEERS, 308
REEVES BROTHERS, INC., 435
SEAGATE TECHNOLOGY, INC., 454
TEXAS INTRUMENTS, INC., 494

ROMANIA

- **Official Name:** Romania
- **Capital:** Bucharest
- **Location:** Romania is the 12th-largest nation in Europe and is located in the southeastern area of the continent. It is bounded to the north by Ukraine, to the east by Moldova, to the west by Hungary and Yugoslavia, and to the south by Bulgaria. Its total land area is 91,700 square miles, making Romania twice the size of Pennsylvania. It is a mountainous country with the Carpathian Mountains stretching along the northern section, and the Sub-Carpathians extending from west to east through the middle. Quaint villages and farmlands surround these mountains and many beaches lie along the southeastern coast of the Black Sea.
- **Population, Cities, and American Residents:** The population of Romania totals 23.5 million. Nearly 90 percent of the people are Romanian. Eight percent are Hungarian. Germans, Ukrainians, Serbs, Croats, Russians, Turks, and Gypsies account for the remainder.

  Most American residents are employed in Romania's three major cities: Bucharest with 2 million, Brasov with 350,000, and Constanta with 333,000 people (1990 est.).
- **Language and Currency:** The official language of Romania is Romanian. German and Hungarian are also widely spoken. English is not frequently used in daily life. If you are going to live or work in the country, it is essential that you have a basic knowledge of Romanian. The monetary unit is the leu (plural, lei). The leu consists of 100 bani. The exchange rate is 1,450 lei = U.S.$1 (February 1994).

- **Economy and Resources:** Romania has gone through major changes in the past several years. A communist-led government began in March 1945 and continued until December 1989 when the transition to democracy began. Nicolae Ceausescu, general secretary and head of the Communist Party since 1965, controlled the government and politics of this nation. He and his family dynasty, with the help of the secret police, dominated the lives of Romanian citizens. At that time the Communist Party had nearly 3.5 million members, one-third of the active population. Economic hardships, civil issues, and controversial government programs led to the overthrow of the Communist regime in December 1989. Violent demonstrations followed, and though Ceausescu and his family tried to escape, they were captured, tried, and executed on Christmas Day 1989. The Communist Party was outlawed on January 12, 1990. However, no strong opposition movement followed, and former Communist Party member Ion Iliescu was elected president in the May 20, 1990, elections. Civil unrest continued for many months, as citizens were frustrated with their form of government. When elections were held in 1992, strong democratic gains were finally attained. A 14-party anti-Communist coalition was established, and it marked a realistic beginning for Romania in becoming a democratic nation.

  Today, Romania remains one of Europe's least-developed nations. The newly established government is loosening up the economy, which was so strictly enforced by former leader Ceausescu. Emerging from this transition are moderate land reforms, and privatization of enterprises as well as state firms. Industry accounts for one-third of the labor force and half of the GNP. Major sectors are mining, timber, and construction materials. Agriculture employs another 28 percent of the work force. Chief exports include machinery and equipment, and agricultural materials and forestry products. Primarily, these products go to various republics of the former Soviet Union and to Eastern Europe. For a more efficient economy, the government is concentrating on its agricultural sector rather than heavy industry. Farmers need to utilize modern technology, thereby allowing for increased production and the expansion of Romania's economic strengths.

- **Cost of Living:** Meaningful data is not currently available.

- **Work Permits, Visas, etc.:** A visa and passport are required to travel in Romania. If you are entering Romania from the United States, no vaccinations are required. For official or other information, direct inquiries to the embassy or consulate at the addresses below.

- **Taxation:** No taxes are collected on profits for the first two years of operation in Romania. For complete information, contact the Ministry of Finance in Romania.

- **Principal International Schools:** The American School of Bucharest opened in 1962. Yearly tuition is about $6,500.

- **Health Care:** Health care and sanitary conditions are below those found in the United States. Medical supplies are limited and you should bring any needed medications or pharmaceuticals with you. All tap water should be boiled as the plumbing systems are ancient and unhealthy. Although it is not required, a typhoid inoculation is highly recommended before traveling in Romania.

- **Crime:** Common crime is on the rise in Romania, especially in the black-market money exchange sector. Purse-snatchers and pickpockets are seen primarily in bus or train stations. Take the normal precautions you would when traveling in any major city.

- **Pros and Cons of Living and Working in Romania:** A country rich in history, Romania offers picturesque villages, ski resorts, and numerous hiking trails for tourists. The architecture of Bucharest and the region of Transylvania (home of the legendary Count Dracula's castle) are also attractions. However, Romania is going through profound economic and political changes in its attempt to become a democratic republic. Health and sanitation standards are both inadequate, and telecommunications services are erratic and unreliable. Public transportation is overcrowded and driving is adventurous, to say the least. Roadways are often in poor condition and used by pedestrians, bicyclists, agricultural vehicles, and animals. Housing is available but limited. Most appliances (microwaves, toasters) are unavailable and it's wise to bring your own with you. Because of the recent government transition, it's advisable to check with the State Department for current updates on travel in Romania before departure.

EMBASSY AND CONSULATE CONTACT INFORMATION:

EMBASSY OF ROMANIA
1607 23RD AVE. NW
WASHINGTON, DC 20008
TEL: 202-232-4747

OTHER SOURCES OF INFORMATION:

UNITED STATES DEPARTMENT OF
COMMERCE
ROMANIA DESK OFFICE
EAST EUROPEAN DIVISION, RM. 3413
WASHINGTON, DC 20230
TEL: 202-377-4915

COMPANIES/ORGANIZATIONS WITH OPERATIONS IN ROMANIA:

NATIONAL DEMOCRATIC INSTITUTE, 557
PHILIP MORRIS COMPANIES, INC., 413
PROJECT HOPE, 563

RUSSIA

- **Official Name:** Russian Federation

- **Capital:** Moscow

- **Location:** Russia is the largest and most dominant of the new nations created out of the former Union of Soviet Socialist Republics. Located in northeastern Europe and northern Asia, it is bounded to the north by the Baltic Sea, Barents Sea, Kara Sea, and East Siberian Sea; to the east by the Bering Sea, Sea of Okhotsk, and the Sea of Japan; to the south by China, North Korea, Mongolia, Kazakhstan, the Caspian Sea, Azerbaijan, Georgia, and the Black Sea; to the west by the Ukraine and Belarus; and the northwest by Latvia, Lithuania, Estonia, Finland, and Norway. Its coastline stretches for 26,582 miles, and with a total land area of 6,592,819 square miles, it is nearly twice the size of the United States. Most of this vast area is a plain, and a few low mountain ranges are sparsely scattered throughout the land.

- **Population, Cities, and American Residents:** The population of Russia totals 149 million people (1992 est.) Approximately 82.6 percent are Russian, 3.6 percent are Tartar, 2.7 percent Ukrainian, and the rest are Chuvash, Belarussian, Bashkir, and Jewish.

  Most American residents are employed in Russia's two largest cities: Moscow with 9 million people, and St. Petersburg with 5 million (1989 est.).

- **Language and Currency:** The official language of Russia is Russian. However, English is spoken by many business and government officials and interpreters are available when needed. The monetary unit in Russia is the ruble, made up of 100 kopeks. Bills are in 100, 50, 25, 10, 5, 3, and 1 ruble(s); coins are in 50, 20, 15,10, 5, 3, 2, and 1 kopek(s), and 1 ruble. Due to rapid inflation, the exchange rate with the dollar is currently meaningless.

- **Climate:** Considering its size, the climate in Russia is not as diverse might be expected. Snow covers much of the land in winter, with the average temperature below 32°F. Russians have adapted well to the severe winter weather, and snow does not hamper their daily lives. Rain is most frequent in spring and summer. The highs and lows in Moscow are 12°F in January and 65°F in July.

- **Economy and Resources:** Because of Russia's transformation from a Communist state, economic conditions remain very uncertain. Major changes are taking place including new governmental structures, economic systems, and trade alliances. Agriculture was once the mainstay of Russia, but now it is largely dependent on industry. Major industries include the extraction and processing of raw materials, as well as woven fabrics and steel pipes. Natural resources include coal, petroleum, natural gas, gold, manganese, molybdenum, and iron. Major agricultural exports are potatoes, sugar beets, and vegetables. (No export figures are available at the current time.) Economic reforms are being implemented, with a goal of replacing the previous Soviet command-administration with a market economy.

- **Cost of Living:** At 156, the cost of living is higher than in the United States.

- **Work Permits, Visas, etc.:** A valid passport and visa are required to travel in Russia. If you are entering Russia from the United States, no vaccinations are required, but those planning to stay for more than three months must show proof of an internationally accepted health certificate attesting that they do not have the AIDS virus. Those who do not have proof will be tested at the point of entry. For current official or other information, direct inquiries to the embassy or consulate at the addresses below.

- **Taxation:** At present, there is no tax on income earned by foreigners while in Russia. For a current update, direct inquiries to the U.S. Commerce Department, Dept. of East European and Soviet Affairs, Washington, DC 20230, 202-277-4655.

- **Principal International Schools:** There are no English-speaking schools in Russia that teach beyond the 9th grade. At the grammar-school level, tuition for an American school is $12,000 per year.

- **Health Care:** Medical care in Russia is adequate and approaching Western standards, but some anesthetics and antibiotics are scarce. Also, there are no disposable hypodermic needles, so avoid shots. Sanitary conditions in Russia are not equal to Western standards. Though water may be labeled safe to drink in Moscow, in most places use bottled water. Public establishments are quite often shabby and overcrowded, especially in rural areas. Be careful where you eat out or socialize. Local milk is unsafe to drink and remember that appropriate precautions should be taken with all fruits and vegetables.

- **Crime:** U.S. visitors in Russia should take precautions against street crime. Muggings, robberies, and burglaries are on the rise, and the U.S. State Department has recently issued various travel advisories. You should register at the U.S. Embassy or the Consulate General and may do this prior to your trip or when you arrive in the country. Registration information is helpful if you encounter any difficulties requiring government intervention or protection of your legal rights while in Russia.

- **Pros and Cons of Living and Working in Russia:** Transition and reconstruction is apparent everywhere throughout this region. The Russian people are very hospitable to Westerners, and are now able to express their feelings of freedom and openness—something they never would have done in the past. The country also offers museums, theaters, and concert halls. However, it also is facing numerous obstacles as it is preoccupied with many domestic problems. Housing is difficult to find and is expensive compared to Western standards. Sanitation is poor and the larger cities do not have the amenities Westerners are accustomed to. Western business practices are unfamiliar to most Russians, so patience is a key factor, as there is a good deal of red tape and bureaucracy associated with most business transactions.

EMBASSY AND CONSULATE CONTACT INFORMATION:

THE RUSSIAN EMBASSY/CONSULAR DIVISION
1825 PHELPS PLACE NW
WASHINGTON, DC 20008
TEL: 202-939-8916

THE U.S. EMBASSY IN RUSSIA
ULITSA CHAYKOVSKOGO, 19/21/23
MOSCOW, RUSSIA

AMERICAN EMBASSY, MOSCOW
A.P.O. NEW YORK 09862

OTHER SOURCES OF INFORMATION:

TRADE REPRESENTATION OF RUSSIA IN THE U.S.A.
2001 CONNECTICUT AVE. NW
WASHINGTON, DC 20008
TEL: 202-232-5988

COMPANIES/ORGANIZATIONS WITH OPERATIONS IN RUSSIA:

CHADBOURNE & PARKE, 189
CLIPPER CRUISE LINES, 199
DOW JONES & COMPANY, INC., 241
ERNST & YOUNG, 255
GOLDMAN SACHS & COMPANY, 283
INTERNATIONAL DATA GROUP, INC., 316
NATIONAL DEMOCRATIC INSTITUTE, 557
PACIFIC ARCHITECTS & ENGINEERS, INC., 402

PARTNERS IN ECONOMIC REFORM, INC., 560
PENNZOIL COMPANY, 408
PHIBRO ENERGY, INC., 413
PHILIP MORRIS COMPANIES, INC., 413
PROJECT HOPE, 563
REYNOLDS METALS COMPANY, 438
TAMBRANDS, INC., 486
US WEST, INC., 515

SAUDI ARABIA

- **Official Name:** Kingdom of Saudi Arabia

- **Capital:** Riyadh

- **Location:** Saudi Arabia occupies 80 percent of the Arabian peninsula, and is the largest country in the Middle East. Its land area totals 864,869 square miles, or about the size of Texas and Alaska combined. It is bounded by Jordan, Iraq, and Kuwait to the north; the Persian Gulf, Qatar, and United Arab Emirates to the east; Oman to the southeast; Yemen to the south; and the Red Sea to the west. Only 1 percent of the land is arable. It has six major regions: the Tihama, a barren plain stretching along the coast of the Red Sea; the Asir Mountains further east; the Asir region, a forested, well-populated area to the south; Rub'al Khali, an immense desert area to the east; the Nej'd, a dry plain with streams and grasslands, used by nomads and their flocks; and Al-Hasa, the Eastern Province, which is rich in oil and agriculture and is also densely populated.

- **Population, Cities, and American Residents:** The population of Saudi Arabia totals 15.2 million (1992 est.), with Arabs accounting for 90 percent of the people. The remaining 10 percent are Africans and Asians.

  Most American residents are employed in Saudi Arabia's three major cities: Riyadh with 1.5 million people, Jeddah with 1.4 million, and Dhahran proper (including the metropolitan district) with 1 million (1990 est.). Mecca and Medina are holy cities and anyone who is not a Moslem is not allowed to enter them.

- **Language and Currency:** The official language of Saudi Arabia is Arabic. However, many of the younger, well-educated Arabs employed in business have studied in English-speaking countries and are fluent in English. The English language is also taught in many secondary schools. The Arabs appreciate foreigners who are familiar with Arabic. The monetary unit is the riyal (SR-Saudi Riyals), and the currency exchange rate is fixed with the U.S. dollar and is easily converted. The exchange rate is 1 Saudi riyal = U.S.$.27 (July 30, 1993).

- **Economy and Resources:** Saudi Arabia's economy is primarily based on oil, which accounts for 88 percent of exports by value and 60 percent of government revenues. It is the world's leading exporter of oil with substantial reserves and active exploration programs to identify potential new fields. The Saudis are also investing in distribution and refining facilities in the United States and Europe, and the development of petrochemical industries. Foreign participation in the development of the country's economy is welcomed. The Saudi people have a high standard of living, with free medical and schooling expenses. There are no personal income taxes, and unemployment is nonexistent; almost 60 percent of the labor force consists of foreign workers. Nearly 34 percent of Saudi natives work in government, 28 percent in industry and oil, and 22 percent in services. Major trading partners are the United States and Japan. The Persian Gulf War threatened the stability and security of this country in 1990. While there were only skirmishes on Saudi Arabian soil, Iraq launched missile attacks against Riyadh, Dhahran, and other locations, and huge oil spills threatened the operation of important desalination facilities in the Persian Gulf. Since the war ended, Saudi Arabia has been a key diplomatic partner of the United States in trying to maintain peace and security in the Middle East.

- **Cost of Living:** At 103, the cost of living is slightly higher than in the United States.

- **Work Permits, Visas, etc.:** A valid passport and visa are required to travel in Saudi Arabia, and workers need a business visa. Write to the consulate and supply a letter from your company explaining the reason for the trip, the proposed length, and who bears financial responsibility for the traveler. Business visas are normally granted by invitation only. Visas are good for one month, but may be extended for longer stays. The Ministry of Foreign Affairs in Jeddah reviews and approves the applications. If you are entering Saudi Arabia from the United States, no vaccinations are necessary, but shots against meningitis and cholera are highly recommended. For official or other information, direct inquiries to the embassy or consulate at the addresses below.

- **Taxation:** There is no personal income tax collected in Saudi Arabia; in 1975, the government abolished income tax on foreigners working in the country.

- **Principal International Schools:** International schools are available in Riyadh for children of American residents. Tuition for an American school is about $4,400.

- **Health Care:** Health care standards in Saudi Arabia are below those in North America. A few doctors speak English, but some American firms opt to bring their own medical team with them for consultations and emergency treatment. Minor health problems can be handled locally; for serious ailments you should be flown to Europe or North America. In Riyadh, two facilities with 24 hour emergency services available are the Shumaisi Hospital, on Shumaisi Street, and Al Mubarak, on Wazir and Washm Streets. Over-the counter drugs are available but most prescription drugs are costly. If you bring a specific drug with you, bring a copy of the prescription signed by a doctor. Written permission should also be obtained; rules are very strict concerning narcotics or any drugs brought into the country. Sanitation is poor, and trachoma and tuberculosis are prevalent among the native population. Unless you are in a major hotel, boil water for all usage. Appropriate precautions should be taken with all fruits and vegetables, and cook meats thoroughly. Good sunglasses are essential, due to the intense sun and dusty conditions.

- **Crime:** The Islamic Sharia Law is imposed with diligence throughout the country, so common crime is almost nonexistent. Visitors to Saudi Arabia should familiarize themselves with the laws of the country. What is legal in the United States may not be in Saudi Arabia. For example, possession of alcohol is illegal; anyone arriving in Saudi Arabia who appears to be under the influence of alcohol will be refused entry and made to leave the country at his or her own expense. If you are arrested in the country, the consequences can be frightening and frustrating. You'd have to make a statement, recorded in Arabic, without the presence of an attorney, and may be held without trial while the authorities investigate the matter.

- **Pros and Cons of Living and Working in Saudi Arabia:** Saudi Arabia's culture is very different from what Americans are used to, and it takes a good deal of time to adjust to the lifestyle. Social activities focus on entertaining and meeting new people, and there are no movie theaters, discos, or sporting events. The influence of Islam is pervasive. Transportation and telecommunications services are good, but calls made to the United States from Saudi Arabia may be monitored. Sanitary and medical standards are also below those of the United States. The laws are very strict, and many items (pork products, alcohol, some reading material) are not allowed into the country. Recreation facilities are limited, and most entertaining is done at home. Housing and other items are costly and new phone installations take more than a year to complete. Women should always wear concealing clothing (long skirts, etc. in public), along with a scarf or hat to hide the face. No make-up should be worn in public.

EMBASSY AND CONSULATE CONTACT INFORMATION:

EMBASSY OF SAUDI ARABIA
601 NEW HAMPSHIRE AVE. NW
WASHINGTON, DC 20037
TEL: 202-342-3800

CONSULATE GENERAL OF SAUDI ARABIA
866 U.N. PLAZA, STE. 480
NEW YORK, NY 10017
TEL: 212-752-2740

OTHER SOURCES OF INFORMATION:

NATIONAL U.S.-ARAB CHAMBER OF
COMMERCE
1825 K ST. NW
WASHINGTON, DC 20006
TEL: 202-331-8010

COMPANIES/ORGANIZATIONS WITH OPERATIONS IN SAUDI ARABIA:

ABB LUMMUS CREST, 108
ALEXANDER & ALEXANDER SERVICES, INC., 116
AMERICAN INTERNATIONAL GROUP, 127
ASHLAND OIL, INC., 143
BATTELLE MEMORIAL INSTITUTE, 159
BECHTEL GROUP, INC., 162
BENDIX FIELD ENGINEERING CORPORATION, 165
BOEING COMPANY, 170
CALGON CORPORATION, 182
CARRIER CORPORATION, 186
CHARTER MEDICAL CORPORATION, 190
CHASE MANHATTAN CORPORATION, 190
CITICORP, 198
CLOROX COMPANY, 199
COUDERT BROTHERS LAW FIRM, 217
CRS SIRRINE, INC., 219
LEO A. DALY COMPANY, 223
DAMES & MOORE, 223
D'ARCY MASIUS BENTON & BOWLES INC., 225
EMERSON ELECTRIC COMPANY, 251

EXXON CHEMICAL COMPANY, 257
EXXON CORPORATION, 258
FLUOR CORPORATION, 266
FMC CORPORATION, 266
FOSTER WHEELER CORPORATION, 268
GAF CORPORATION, 270
GENERAL DYNAMICS SERVICES COMPANY, 275
GENERAL ELECTRIC COMPANY (GE), 275
THE GILLETTE COMPANY, 283
GRANT THORNTON INTERNATIONAL, 286
HALLIBURTON-NUS CORPORATION, 293
HDR INCORPORATED, 298
HELLMUTH, OBATA & KASSABAUM, INC., 298
HOLMES & NARVER, INC., 303
HOSPITAL CORPORATION INTERNATIONAL, LTD., 304
HUGHES AIRCRAFT COMPANY, 307
HUGHES CHRISTENSEN COMPANY, 307
HYATT INTERNATIONAL CORPORATION, 308
JOHNSON & HIGGINS, 324

JONES, DAY, REAVIS & POGUE, INC., 326
JOY TECHNOLOGIES, INC., 327
KELLOGG COMPANY, 330
THE KULJIAN COMPANY, 341
LAW COMPANIES GROUP, INC., 343
LINTAS: WORLDWIDE, 346
ARTHUR D. LITTLE, INC., 347
LOCKHEED CORPORATION, 349
MARRIOTT CORPORATION, 360
MCDERMOTT INTERNATIONAL, INC., 356
METCALF & EDDY INTERNATIONAL, INC., 370
MOBIL OIL CORPORATION, 375
OCCIDENTAL PETROLEUM CORPORATION, 393

OWENS-CORNING FIBERGLAS CORPORATION, 400
PITTSBURGH-DES MOINES CORPORATION, 418
RAYTHEON COMPANY, 432
RUST INTERNATIONAL, INC., 447
SPERRY-SUN, INC., 473
SRI INTERNATIONAL, 475
STONE & WEBSTER ENGINEERING CORPORATION, 480
TELEDYNE, INC., 489
TEXACO OIL COMPANY, 493
UNITED ENGINEERS & CONSTRUCTORS INTERNATIONAL, 508
VTN CORPORATION, 518

SINGAPORE

- **Official Name:** Republic of Singapore

- **Capital:** Singapore City

- **Location:** Singapore is an island off the southern Malay peninsula connected to the mainland by a causeway. In addition to the main island of Singapore there are 57 offshore islets. The main island is 27 miles wide and 14 miles long, comprising 240 square miles of land, making it smaller than the metropolitan area of New York. It is bounded by the Johor Strait to the north, the Pacific Ocean to the east, the Strait of Malacca to the southwest (which separates Singapore from the Indonesian Island of Sumatra), and the Indian Ocean to the west. Singapore is one of the most densely populated nations in the world.

- **Population, Cities, and American Residents:** The population of Singapore totals 2.8 million people (1992 est.), with Chinese accounting for 76.4 percent, Malays for 14.9 percent, Indians for 6.4 percent, and others for 2.3 percent.

  Most American residents are employed in Singapore's capital, Singapore City.

- **Language and Currency:** The language of business is English. Other languages spoken are Malay (the national language), Mandarin Chinese, and Tamil. The unit of currency is the Singapore dollar (S$) and it has 100 cents. The exchange rate is 1 Singapore dollar = U.S.$.62 (July 30, 1993).

- **Climate:** Singapore is hot and humid, with cooling sea breezes. Temperatures vary little. Although afternoons are sunny, rain usually occurs every day, occasionally as thunderstorms. The heaviest rains fall from October through March. The mean annual temperature is around 82°F.

- **Economy and Resources:** Singapore has one of the most successful economies in Southeast Asia. With a location vital to air and trade routes, it is the second busiest port in the world, and the busiest in Asia. Though it lacks natural resources, Singapore has become a major manufacturing and trading power in the last 25 years, with two-thirds of the gross domestic product (GDP) generated by trade. Exports and re-exports include crude rubber, computers and parts, consumer electronic items, telecommunications gear, electrical machinery, and clothing. Major trading partners are the United States, Japan, Malaysia, the European Community, and Taiwan. Other major sectors of the economy are tourism, finance and business services, transport and communications, construction and real estate, and utilities. Manufacturing employs nearly one-third of the work force and accounts for 24 percent of the GDP. Currently there are more than 500 international firms with plants or technical support facilities on the island. Manufacturing is the key to future economic success, and Singapore continues to encourage investment by foreign firms to broaden and increase its industrial base.

- **Cost of Living:** At 124, the cost of living is slightly higher than in the United States.

- **Work Permits, Visas, etc.:** A valid passport is required to for visits up to 14 days. For stays up to 90 days, report to the Immigration Office in Singapore for an extension. For stays longer than 90 days or if the trip involves employment or residence, you'll need a visa from the Singapore embassy or consulate nearest your home in the United States. Get it prior to the trip, and allow ample time for the application to be processed. If entering Singapore from the United States, no vaccinations are required, but typhoid, polio, tetanus, and hepatitis A shots are recommended. For official or other information, direct inquiries to the embassy or consulate at the addresses below.

- **Taxation:** Everyone present or employed in Singapore for at least 183 days of a calendar year is subject to personal income taxes. Income from outside Singapore is taxed only if it is received within Singapore. Personal income taxes are imposed at a progressive rate between 15 and 30 percent. Various deductions or exemptions may apply.

- **Principal International Schools:** Singapore has international schools offering quality education. Tuition for an American school is about $10,000 per year.

- **Health Care:** Medical and dental facilities are very good throughout Singapore, as many doctors and dentists have been trained in the United States or Europe. Most prescription drugs are available but bring prescriptions for generic drugs with you to insure availability. Sanitary standards are excellent; Singapore is the cleanest and one of the safest cities in Asia, and local officials plan to keep it that way, so fines are stiff for minor infractions (littering, spitting on the streets, jaywalking). Strict smoking laws prohibit smoking in taxis, elevators, theaters, or any public places.

- **Crime:** Common crime is rarely a problem in Singapore because of the country's draconian legal codes. Minor crimes are taken seriously and offenders are severely punished. Learn the laws of the country before planning an extended stay.

- **Pros and Cons of Living and Working in Singapore:** Singapore is a modern, exceptionally clean, and safe country to visit. The sightseeing, cultural, and entertainment attractions include a varied selection of gardens, museums, handicraft centers, and restaurants, which are exceptionally clean, and offer varied cuisines. Singapore has excellent transportation and telecommunications services, and English is spoken widely. Medical care and sanitary standards are high—the best in Asia. Suitable housing is getting harder to find, and it is expensive compared to U.S. standards. The cost of living is reasonable, though slightly higher than in the United States. If you plan on an extended stay in Singapore, remember that the tropical heat and humidity will take time to adjust to; guard against sunburn and heat exhaustion.

EMBASSY AND CONSULATE CONTACT INFORMATION:

EMBASSY OF SINGAPORE
1824 R ST. NW
WASHINGTON, DC 20009
TEL: 202-667-7555

SINGAPORE U.N. PERMANENT MISSION
2 U.N. PLAZA, 25TH FL.
NEW YORK, NY 10017
TEL: 212-826-0840

OTHER SOURCES OF INFORMATION:

SINGAPORE TOURIST PROMOTION BOARD
342 MADISON AVE.
NEW YORK, NY 10017
TEL: 212-302-4861

COMPANIES/ORGANIZATIONS WITH OPERATIONS IN SINGAPORE:

ABB VETCO GRAY, INC., 108
ADVANCE MACHINE COMPANY, 111
ADVANCED MICRO DEVICES, INC., 112
AIRBORNE EXPRESS, 112
ALARM DEVICE MANUFACTURING
    COMPANY, 114
AMERICAN INTERNATIONAL GROUP, 127
AMERICAN PRESIDENT COMPANIES, LTD.,
    128
APPLE COMPUTER, INC., 136
ASHLAND OIL, INC., 143
AT&T INTERNATIONAL, 145
AUGAT, INC., 146
BACKER SPIELVOGEL & BATES
    WORLDWIDE, INC., 150
BAKER HUGHES, INC., 152
BAROID CORPORATION, 158
BECKMAN INSTRUMENTS, INC., 162
BELL HELICOPTER TEXTRON, INC., 163
BETZ LABORATORIES, 166
BLACK & DECKER CORPORATION, 167
BORDEN, INC., 170
BURLINGTON AIR EXPRESS, 179
BURSON-MARSTELLER, 180
CALIFORNIA PELLET MILL COMPANY, 182
CAMP DRESSER & MCKEE
    INTERNATIONAL, INC., 183
CARGILL INCORPORATED, 184
CARRIER CORPORATION, 186

J. I. CASE COMPANY, 187
CIGNA CORPORATION, 197
THE COASTAL GROUP, 201
COMMERCE CLEARING HOUSE, 205
COMPAQ COMPUTERS CORPORATION, 207
CONTINENTAL BANK CORPORATION, 210
CORE LABORATORIES, 214
CORE STATES FINANCIAL CORPORATION,
    215
WILLIS CORROON, 216
COUDERT BROTHERS LAW FIRM, 217
CROWN CORK & SEAL COMPANY, INC.,
    218
CTS CORPORATION, 220
CUMMINS ENGINE COMPANY, INC., 221
LEO A. DALY COMPANY, 223
DAMES & MOORE, 223
D'ARCY MASIUS BENTON & BOWLES INC.,
    225
DATA GENERAL CORPORATION, 225
DDB NEEDHAM WORLDWIDE, INC., 227
DE LEUW, CATHER INTERNATIONAL, 228
DELTA AIR LINES, INC., 232
THE DEXTER CORPORATION, 233
DIAMOND M-ODECO DRILLING, INC., 234
DIGICON, INC., 235
DOMINO'S PIZZA, INC., 237
DOW CHEMICAL COMPANY, 240
DOW CORNING CORPORATION, 240

AMERICAN JOBS ABROAD

DOW JONES & COMPANY, INC., 241
EASTMAN KODAK COMPANY, 246
EBASCO OVERSEAS CORPORATION, 248
ELI LILLY AND COMPANY, 250
ELIZABETH ARDEN COMPANY, 251
ESCO CORPORATION, 255
EXXON COMPANY, INTERNATIONAL, 258
FEDERAL EXPRESS CORPORATION, 260
FIRST CHICAGO CORPORATION, 262
FUGRO-MCCLELLAND USA, INC., 269
GAF CORPORATION, 270
GAFNEY, CLINE & ASSOCIATES, INC., 271
GANNETT COMPANY, INC., 272
GENERAL MOTORS CORPORATION (GM), 277
GENERAL SIGNAL CORPORATION, 278
GETZ BROTHERS COMPANY, INC., 281
W. R. GRACE & COMPANY, 285
A. P. GREEN INDUSTRIES, INC., 287
GTE DIRECTORIES CORPORATION, 289
HALLIBURTON COMPANY, 292
HANSON INDUSTRIES, 295
HARTFORD STEAM BOILER INSPECTION/ INSURANCE COMPANY, 296
HERCULES, INC., 299
HEWLETT-PACKARD COMPANY, 300
HILL & KNOWLTON, INC., 301
HONEYWELL, INC., 303
HYATT INTERNATIONAL CORPORATION, 308
IDB COMMUNICATIONS, INC., 309
IMO INDUSTRIES, 310
INGERSOLL-RAND COMPANY, 313
INTEL CORPORATION, 314
INTERNATIONAL BUSINESS MACHINES (IBM), 315
INTERNATIONAL TOTALIZATOR SYSTEMS, INC., 319
S. C. JOHNSON WAX, 325
M. W. KELLOGG COMPANY, 331
KEYSTONE INTERNATIONAL, 334
KOCH INDUSTRIES, INC., 339
KORN/FERRY INTERNATIONAL, 340
LAMBDA ELECTRONICS, INC., 343
LAWTER INTERNATIONAL, INC., 344
LOTUS DEVELOPMENT CORPORATION, 351
LUBRIZOL CORPORATION, 353
MASONEILAN INDUSTRIES, INC., 361
MCCORMICK & COMPANY, INC., 355
MELROE COMPANY, 367
MERRILL LYNCH & COMPANY, INC., 369
METHODE ELECTRONICS, INC., 371
MOLEX, INC., 376
MONTGOMERY WARD HOLDING COMPANY, 377
J. P. MORGAN & COMPANY, INC., 378
MORGAN STANLEY GROUP, INC., 379
NALCO CHEMICAL COMPANY, 382
NATIONAL SEMICONDUCTOR CORPORATION, 383
NEWSWEEK INTERNATIONAL, 387
NORTHWEST AIRLINES, INC., 390
NORTON COMPANY, 390
NORWEST CORPORATION, 391
OCEANEERING INTERNATIONAL, INC., 393
OFFSHORE LOGISTICS, 394
OFFSHORE PIPELINES, INC., 394
ONAN CORPORATION, 397
OWENS-ILLINOIS, INC., 401
PARKER DRILLING COMPANY, 405
PARKER HANNIFIN CORPORATION, 405
PARSONS BRINKERHOFF, 406
J. C. PENNEY COMPANY, INC., 407
PEPSICO FOODS INTERNATIONAL, 409
PETROLITE CORPORATION, 411
PFIZER, INC., 412
PHILIPS TECHNOLOGIES, 414
PRECISION VALVE CORPORATION, 422
PRINTRONIX, INC., 425
QUME CORPORATION, 429
RALSTON PURINA COMPANY, 430
READER'S DIGEST ASSOCIATION, INC., 432
READING & BATES, 433
REED TOOL COMPANY, 434
ROCKWELL INTERNATIONAL CORPORATION, 441
ROHM & HAAS COMPANY, 442
ROWAN COMPANIES, INC., 444
RUSSELL REYNOLDS ASSOCIATES, INC., 446
SAATCHI & SAATCHI, 448
SALOMON, INC., 449
SCI SYSTEMS, 452
SCM CHEMICALS, 453
SCOTT PAPER COMPANY, 453
SEAGATE TECHNOLOGY, INC., 454
SEALED AIR CORPORATION, 455
SHAKLEE CORPORATION, 459
SHEARSON LEHMAN BROTHERS, 460

SIMON & SCHUSTER, INC., 463
SMITH INTERNATIONAL, INC., 467
SNAP-ON TOOLS CORPORATION, 468
SONAT, INC., 469
SONAT OFFSHORE, 470
SONOCO PRODUCTS COMPANY, 470
SONY PICTURES ENTERTAINMENT, 471
SPS TECHNOLOGIES, INC., 474
SRI INTERNATIONAL, 475
SULLAIR CORPORATION, 482
SUNDSTRAND CORPORATION, 485
TELEDYNE, INC., 489
TELXON CORP., 490
TEXAS INTRUMENTS, INC., 494
3M COMPANY, 496
TOWERS PERRIN, INC., 499
TOYS ''R'' US, INC., 500
TRANE COMPANY, 501
TRINOVA CORPORATION, 502

TRW, INC., 503
TURNER STEINER INTERNATIONAL, INC., 504
UNION CAMP CORPORATION, 507
UNISYS CORPORATION, 508
UNITED PARCEL SERVICE OF AMERICA, INC., 509
UNITED TECHNOLOGIES CORPORATION, 512
WARNER BROTHERS INTERNATIONAL, 521
WATERS CHROMATOGRAPHY (MILLIPORE), 523
WEST COMPANY, INC., 525
WESTINGHOUSE ELECTRIC CORPORATION, 525
WORLD COURIER MANAGEMENT, INC., 529
WILLIAM WRIGLEY JR. COMPANY, 529
YORK INTERNATIONAL, INC., 532

COUNTRY PROFILES

SOUTH AFRICA

- **Official Name:** Republic of South Africa
- **Capitals:** Cape Town, Pretoria, and Bloemfontein
- **Location:** South Africa is located in the southernmost region of the African continent, extending from the Limpopo River in the north to Cape Agulhas in the south. It is bounded by Namibia to the northwest; Botswana and Zimbabwe to the north; Mozambique to the northeast; Swaziland and the Indian Ocean to the east; and the Atlantic Ocean to the west. The independent kingdom of Lesotho is completely surrounded by South African territory and relies on stable relations with South Africa for its survival. South Africa has a diverse geography from rocky coastlines to mountains, plateaus, and desert regions. Its land area totals 471,455 square miles, making it nearly twice the size of Texas.
- **Population, Cities, and American Residents:** The total population of South Africa is 41.6 million (1992 est.). Nearly 70 percent is black, 17.8 percent white, 2.9 percent Indian, and 9.4 percent other.

    Most American residents are employed in Africa's three major cities: Cape Town with 1.5 million people, Johannesburg with 2.1 million, and Durban with 1.5 million (1989 est.). The three capital cities have different functions: Cape Town is the legislative capital, Pretoria is the administrative capital, and Bloemfontein is the judicial capital.
- **Language and Currency:** The official languages of South Africa are Afrikaans and English. Nearly 80 percent of South Africans are bilingual, and most foreign firms offer promotional literature in both languages. Most business people have a good working

knowledge of English and use it throughout the country. The monetary unit is the Rand, divided into 100 cents. The exchange rate is 1 African Rand = U.S.$.28 (July 30, 1993).

- **Climate:** South Africa has a temperate climate and is generally sunny and mild throughout the year. Because it is in the Southern Hemisphere, the seasons are in reverse of those in the North, with summers running from October to March, and temperatures often reaching 90°F before cooling off in the evening hours. Winter begins in June, with daily temperatures of approximately 75°F, dropping to 30°F at night. The heaviest rains fall during the spring and winter in the Durban and Cape Town areas, occasionally accompanied by high humidity and strong winds.

- **Economy and Resources:** Ever since its discovery during the 1880s, gold has been a major contributing factor in the South African economy. It is one of the world's chief mining nations and a major producer of gold, asbestos, chromite, coal, copper, diamonds, iron ore, limestone, manganese, platinum, phosphate, uranium, and vanadium. Mining accounts for 15 percent of the gross domestic product (GDP), and 75 percent of export earnings. Manufacturing and agriculture are also important sectors of the economy. Manufacturing accounts for 23.7 percent of the GDP, and the country is self-sufficient in manufactured goods, which include textiles, iron and steel products, chemicals, motor vehicles, and processed foods. Though agriculture only accounts for 6 percent of the GDP, South Africa is still a net food exporter. Major export markets are the United States and the European Community. The commercial white farmers produce nearly all the food South Africa needs for its people. Leading crops include corn, grapes (wine), oranges, pineapples, potatoes, tobacco, and wheat. South Africa is also engaged in livestock-raising, with wool being a major agricultural product. The black farmers do not use modern methods to work their land, resulting in poor crop production and barely enough food to sustain local populations. Of the work force, 34 percent are employed in services, 30 percent in agriculture, 29 percent in industry and commerce, and 7 percent in mining.

South Africans have witnessed dramatic changes in the economy and in their social and political systems. In the past, South Africa has attracted a great deal of foreign investors, drawn to the country by its vast natural resources and a large, cheap, black work force. However, government changes have caused dramatic differences in the past several years. Moving away from a policy of apartheid (legal separation of the races), toward a new policy of racial justice has stimulated mixed emotions. The apartheid laws were repealed in the early 1990s, but the government is still controlled by whites. Because of the confrontations and friction between the black majority and the white government, some U.S.-based firms have pulled out of the country. South Africa must deal with the pending transition to black majority rule if the nation is to effectively survive, much less prosper. Earnings for whites are five times greater than for Africans, and the unemployment rate for blacks is rising. With fluctuating gold prices in the world market, South Africa must develop other export products. The transition to majority rule could result in either new stability or even more unstable conditions that could scare off the financial community, discourage U.S. foreign trade, and prevent economic growth.

- **Cost of Living:** At 92, the cost of living is slightly lower than the United States.

- **Work Permits, Visas, etc.:** A valid passport and visa are required to travel in South Africa, and temporary residence permits are needed by all visitors who plan to work there. Apply for these at the embassy or consulate nearest to your home. Travelers with South African visas in their passports may be refused entry into other African countries. When entering South Africa from the United States, no vaccinations are required, but you must have a valid International Health Certificate. For official or other information, direct inquiries to the embassy or consulate at the addresses below.

- **Taxation:** Resident and nonresident individuals are taxed only on income earned from South African sources, based on a progressive scale of rates. For more information, the South African government publishes a booklet explaining the details of the South African tax system.

- **Principal International Schools:** Public and private schools are available throughout South Africa. Public schools are free, but most American residents send their children to private institutions, where the average yearly tuition runs about $3,900.

- **Health Care:** Health care in South Africa is very good, and many doctors have studied in the United States or the United Kingdom. Medical treatment must be completely paid for as there is no national medical program in South Africa. Prescription drugs are readily available, at reasonable costs. Sanitation is generally better in the white areas of the country. City water is potable, and fresh fruits and vegetables need only to be washed in plain water (not disinfected) before eating. Lakes and other fresh water bodies may be contaminated, so it's safer to swim in salt water or in chlorinated pools.

- **Crime:** Although there is racial unrest in the country, tourists are rarely affected by this. Common crime occurs, primarily as a result of drug problems, so take normal precautions as you would in any tourist area, especially when going out at night.

- **Pros and Cons of Living and Working in South Africa:** South Africa has magnificent landscapes, wildlife, and wilderness areas. Cape Town, founded in 1652, is the oldest European settlement in South Africa and has museums, gardens, castles, and sunny beaches. Transportation is good; rental cars are available and affordable. Telecommunications are also adequate. Housing is available and affordable, with properties usually rented through agents, who also collect the fees. Political and social unrest has not created the best environment for expatriates in the past several years. Remember that the police and military have the power to restrict travel, especially into black township areas, or to other African countries. Also, certain reading materials may be banned for their political or erotic content. Luggage is searched, and banned materials will not be allowed into the country. "Blue Laws" are

EMBASSY AND CONSULATE CONTACT INFORMATION:

EMBASSY OF SOUTH AFRICA
3051 MASSACHUSETTS AVE. NW
WASHINGTON, DC 20008
TEL: 202-232-4400

CONSULATE GENERAL OF NEW YORK
326 EAST 48TH ST.
NEW YORK, NY 10017
TEL: 212-371-7997

also observed in the country. It's wise to learn what they restrict. For up-to-date information, contact the U.S. State Department (202-377-5148) on current conditions in South Africa.

OTHER SOURCES OF INFORMATION:

U.S. STATE DEPT.
DESK OFFICER FOR SOUTH AFRICA
WASHINGTON, DC 20025
TEL: 202-647-3274

COMPANIES/ORGANIZATIONS WITH OPERATIONS IN REPUBLIC OF SOUTH AFRICA:

ABB VETCO GRAY, INC., 108
AM INTERNATIONAL, INC., 119
AVERY DENNISON CORPORATION, 147
BAKER HUGHES, INC., 152
BANK OF BOSTON CORPORATION, 153
BECKMAN INSTRUMENTS, INC., 162
BURLINGTON AIR EXPRESS, 179
CALGON CORPORATION, 182
CROWN CORK & SEAL COMPANY, INC., 218
GANNETT FLEMING, INC., 272
INTERNATIONAL DATA GROUP, INC., 316
LUBRIZOL CORPORATION, 353
LYKES LINES, 354
MASONITE CORPORATION, 362
MCDERMOTT INTERNATIONAL, INC., 356
MERCK & COMPANY, INC., 368
MONSANTO COMPANY, 377
J. P. MORGAN & COMPANY, INC., 378

NATIONAL DEMOCRATIC INSTITUTE, 557
NCR CORPORATION, 384
OGILVY & MATHER, 395
OMNICOM GROUP, INC., 397
PETROLITE CORPORATION, 411
PHELPS DODGE CORPORATION, 412
PHILLIPS PETROLEUM COMPANY, 415
PREFORMED LINE PRODUCTS COMPANY, 423
QUAKER CHEMICAL CORPORATION, 428
ROBERTSON CECO, 440
SB POWER TOOLS, INC. (SKIL CORP.), 450
SEARLE COMPANY, 455
SIMPLICITY PATTERN COMPANY INC., 464
STANDARD COMMERCIAL CORPORATION, 476
UNION CAMP CORPORATION, 507
WYNN'S INTERNATIONAL, INC., 530

SOUTH KOREA

- **Official Name:** Republic of Korea
- **Capital:** Seoul
- **Location:** South Korea (also called the Republic of Korea) is located in the lower half of the Korean peninsula in Eastern Asia. Its northern boundary is the demilitarized zone which separates it from North Korea. The Sea of Japan and the Korea Strait lie to the east and south, separating the peninsula from Japan. To the west, the Yellow Sea lies between Korea and the People's Republic of China. South Korea's land area totals 38,000 square miles making it comparable in size to Virginia. Much of South Korea is mountainous, leaving only one-third of the land arable.
- **Population, Cities, and American Residents:** The population of Korea totals 44.4 million (1992 est.), and the country is ethnically very homogeneous, with only a small Chinese minority (20,000).

    Most American residents are employed in Korea's three largest cities: Seoul with 10 million people, Pusan with 3.5 million, and Taegu with 2 million (1990 est.). One-fourth of the total population lives in Seoul, making it the fifth largest city in the world.

- **Language and Currency:** Korean is the official language of the country, and is part of the Ural-Altaic family, which includes Turkish and Mongolian. It is different from Japanese and Chinese, but the characters in the Korean alphabet (Hangul), are somewhat similar to some of the Chinese characters, and the grammar resembles that of the Japanese. Though English is used in commerce, Koreans find it hard to pronounce and use it only when necessary. The monetary unit is the Korean Won (W), and bills are in denominations of 10,000, 5,000, 1,000, and 500. Coins are 500, 100, 50, 10, 5, and 1. The exchange rate is 1 Korean won = U.S.$.0012; 808 won = U.S.$1 (July 30, 1993).

- **Climate:** Korea has a temperate continental climate, subject to monsoons in summer, and bitter cold snaps that bear down on the country from Siberia in winter. It has four distinct seasons, similar to those of the northeastern United States. Winters are cold and dry, with fair amounts of snow, and summer is hot (temperatures reaching 98°F), with high humidity. The best seasons are spring and fall, with warm days and cool, crisp nights.

- **Economy and Resources:** The Korean War had a devastating effect on the nation's economy, but rebuilding through focused development programs helped to make South Korea a stable, industrialized nation. Its economic future is still uncertain, however, as it must compete in export markets against Japan and other Asian rivals to remain strong. The country's natural resources include iron, lead, graphite, gold, silver, tungsten, and zinc. Agriculture, forestry, and fishing account for 15 percent of the gross domestic product (GDP). Major industries include textiles and food processing. About 52 percent of the work force is employed in services and commerce, while 21 percent of the people work in agriculture. South Korea's main trading partners are Japan and the United States, and major exports include textiles, clothing, electronic and electrical equipment, and steel.

- **Cost of Living:** At 117, the cost of living is higher than in the United States.

- **Work Permits, Visas, etc.:** For stays up to 14 days, a valid passport is required. Business visas are required for stays as short as one day. To apply for a business visa, you must contact the Seoul Immigration Office, 175-87, Anguk-dong, Chongno-ku, prior to the trip. Include a letter from the company or organization sponsoring the trip, the length of stay, and who bears the financial responsibility for the visit. Do this several weeks in advance of the trip. If entering South Korea from the United States, no vaccinations are required, but cholera shots are recommended, as is carrying a current international immunization card. For official or other information, direct inquiries to the embassy or consulate at the addresses below.

- **Taxation:** South Korea has numerous taxes and a highly complex tax system. Recent changes have occurred, so check with the American Chamber of Commerce in Seoul for the most current provisions. The United States has a treaty with South Korea to prevent double taxation of individuals and corporations.

- **Principal International Schools:** There are two good schools for children of American residents of South Korea: the Seoul Foreign School and the Seoul

International School. Both institutions offer quality education at a tuition averaging $8,500 per year.

- **Health Care:** Strict government controls oversee the licensing of medical personnel in South Korea. Standards remain high and are comparable to those found in the United States. Seoul hospitals used most often by Americans are Kangnam St. Mary's Hospital, the Catholic Medical Center, and the Severance Hospital Foreigners' Clinic at Seoul National University Hospital. Sanitation is good in Seoul, but outer areas have old water purification and sewage systems. Unless you are in a major tourist area, do not drink tap water or swim in any bodies of fresh water. Appropriate precautions should be taken with all fruits and vegetables, and cook all meat and fish thoroughly. Hepatitis is endemic throughout Asia, and shots of gamma globulin are recommended. Various diseases are also prevalent in the country, including typhoid, cholera, and leprosy.

- **Crime:** Korea is a safe country, especially in the urban areas, including Seoul. However, lock up valuables and don't carry large sums of cash. Police stations are numerous, and are identified by a yellow lighted sign on each street. If you have a communications problem, call the Korean National Tourism Corporation at: (02)735-0101.

- **Pros and Cons of Living and Working in South Korea:** Korea is a small country, with a fascinating culture and very friendly people. It is a mixture of the old and new, with museums, palaces, cultural art centers, and numerous shops and stores to purchase antiques and souvenirs. Transportation and telecommunications are both efficient and reasonably priced. Medical facilities are also good. Adequate housing is difficult (and expensive) to find, and driving in the main cities is horrendous, crowded by cars, carts, bicycles, and pedestrians, all ignoring traffic signals. The U.S Chamber of Commerce recommends against driving in South Korea, as it has one of the highest per capita motor vehicle accident and fatality rates in the world. If you do want to drive, a Korean license is required and costs $350 for three years. Insurance rates are also very high. Be prepared for soggy weather, especially during the summer months with the monsoon season. Typhoons are also common in South Korea.

EMBASSY AND CONSULATE CONTACT INFORMATION:

EMBASSY OF THE REPUBLIC OF KOREA
2320 MASSACHUSETTS AVE. NW
WASHINGTON, DC 20008
TEL: 202-939-5600
FAX: 202-797-0595

CONSULATE GENERAL OF THE REPUBLIC OF KOREA
460 PARK AVE.
NEW YORK, NY 10022
TEL: 212-752-1700

OTHER SOURCES OF INFORMATION:

KOREAN CHAMBER OF COMMERCE
981 SOUTH WESTERN AVE., RM. 201
LOS ANGELES, CA 90006
TEL: 213-733-4410

COMPANIES/ORGANIZATIONS WITH OPERATIONS IN REPUBLIC OF SOUTH KOREA:

ALLIED-SIGNAL, INC., 117
AMERICAN PRESIDENT COMPANIES, LTD., 128

AMP, INC., 132
AT&T INTERNATIONAL, 145

THE BANK OF NEW YORK COMPANY, INC., 154

BATTELLE MEMORIAL INSTITUTE, 159

BAUSCH & LOMB, INC., 159

BECHTEL GROUP, INC., 162

BORG-WARNER CORPORATION, 171

BERNARD CHAUS, INC., 191

CLOROX COMPANY, 199

COMPUTER ASSOCIATES INTERNATIONAL, INC., 207

CORNING INCORPORATED, 215

CUBIC CORPORATION, 220

DANIEL, MANN, JOHNSON & MENDENHALL, 224

DH TECHNOLOGY, INC., 233

DOMINO'S PIZZA, INC., 237

DOW JONES & COMPANY, INC., 241

DYNCORP, 245

EBASCO OVERSEAS CORPORATION, 248

ERNST & YOUNG, 255

FIRST CHICAGO CORPORATION, 262

GOLDMAN SACHS & COMPANY, 283

GRACO, INC., 286

HUGHES AIRCRAFT COMPANY, 307

HYATT INTERNATIONAL CORPORATION, 308

IDB COMMUNICATIONS, INC., 309

INTERNATIONAL RECTIFIER CORPORATION, 319

KELLOGG COMPANY, 330

KENNAMETAL, INC., 333

KOCH INDUSTRIES, INC., 339

L. A. GEAR, INC., 342

LAMBDA ELECTRONICS, INC., 343

LAWTER INTERNATIONAL, INC., 344

LIQUID CARBONIC CORPORATION, 347

LITTON INDUSTRIES, INC., 348

LIZ CLAIBORNE, INC., 348

LOCTITE CORPORATION, 349

MCKINSEY & COMPANY, INC., 357

METROPOLITAN LIFE INSURANCE COMPANY, 371

MOTOROLA, INC., 381

NEW YORK LIFE INSURANCE COMPANY, 385

NIKE, INC., 388

NORDSON CORPORATION, 389

NORTHWEST AIRLINES, INC., 390

ONAN CORPORATION, 397

PACIFIC TELESIS INTERNATIONAL, 403

PARKER HANNIFIN CORPORATION, 405

PARSONS CORPORATION, 406

J. C. PENNEY COMPANY, INC., 407

PPG INDUSTRIES, 421

PREMARK INTERNATIONAL, INC., 423

PRUDENTIAL INSURANCE COMPANY OF AMERICA, 427

ROCKWELL INTERNATIONAL CORPORATION, 441

ROSEMOUNT, INC., 443

SCOTT PAPER COMPANY, 453

SEARLE COMPANY, 455

SENCO PRODUCTS, 456

SOTHEBY'S HOLDINGS, INC., 471

SPS TECHNOLOGIES, INC., 474

SRI INTERNATIONAL, 475

STANDARD COMMERCIAL CORPORATION, 476

STONE & WEBSTER ENGINEERING CORPORATION, 480

STRUCTURAL DYNAMICS RESEARCH CORPORATION, 481

TANDY CORPORATION, 487

TELEDYNE, INC., 489

TRINOVA CORPORATION, 502

UNISYS CORPORATION, 508

UNITED NATIONS INDUSTRIAL DEVELOPMENT ORGANIZATION (UNIDO), 568

U.S. WHEAT ASSOCIATES, 511

VISHAY INTERTECHNOLOGY, 518

COUNTRY PROFILES

SPAIN

- **Official Name:** Kingdom of Spain
- **Capital:** Madrid

- **Location:** Spain is located in southwest Europe and occupies four fifths of the Iberian peninsula. It is bounded by the Bay of Biscay, France, and Andorra to the north; the Mediterranean Sea to the east; Morocco, across the Strait of Gibraltar, to the south; and Portugal and the Atlantic Ocean to the west. Its land area totals 194,897 square miles, making it twice the size of Oregon. The territory of Spain also includes the Canary Islands in the Atlantic off the coast of Morocco; the Balearic Islands in the Mediterranean off the coast of Spain; and Ceuta, Melilla, and other properties located in the north of Morocco. Spain has five main regions: the northern coastal belt; the central plateau; Andalucia in the south and southwest of Spain; the Levante; and Catalonia, where the city of Barcelona is located. The Canaries consist of 13 volcanic islands. The Balearic Islands are mountainous with fertile ranges and dense vegetation. Spain is basically rugged and mountainous, with lush valleys and forests scattered throughout its territory.

- **Population, Cities, and American Residents:** The population of Spain totals 39.4 million. The people are a mixture of Mediterranean and Nordic backgrounds. Latins predominate in the central and southern regions, and people of Celtic, Iberic, and Gothic extraction are concentrated in northern Spain.

   Most American residents are employed in Spain's three largest cities: Madrid with 3.1 million people, Barcelona with 1.7 million, and Valencia with 758,000 (1990 est.).

- **Language and Currency:** Spanish is the official language of Spain and used throughout in business and government. Except in Catalonia and the southern region, Castilian Spanish is spoken throughout the country. A working knowledge of Spanish makes daily life much easier and is appreciated by the Spaniards. The monetary unit is the Spanish peseta (pta). Bills are ptas 10,000, 5,000, 2,000, 1,000, 500, and 200; coins are ptas 500, 200, 100, 50, 25, 5, and 1. The exchange rate is 1 Spanish peseta = U.S.$.007; 140 pesetas equal U.S.$1 (July 30, 1993).

- **Climate:** Spain's climate varies widely with location. The north is generally cool and quite humid, with damp, cloudy winters. Temperatures average 50°F in January and 66°F in August. The central region, the Mesata, has slightly colder winters and warm summers. In Madrid, temperatures average 40°F in January and 73°F in July. The southern region and Mediterranean coastal belt are temperate, but on occasion summer temperatures may reach 104°F in the shade.

- **Economy and Resources:** On January 1, 1986, the country achieved its long-sought after goal and was admitted to the European Community on January 1, 1986. Spain is very dependent on industry which has replaced agriculture and mining as the engine of the economy. It has an abundance of natural resources, including coal, lignite, iron ore, uranium, and mercury. Major exports include foodstuffs, footwear, wood, machinery, and chemicals. Of the labor force, 44.8 percent are employed in services, and 30 percent are in industry. Spain's major export markets are its fellow members of the European Community. Since 1985, almost one million new jobs have been created but job growth has been outpaced by a substantial increase in the labor force, so unemployment is increasing. For the economy to remain stable, Spain must continue to increase public spending on infrastructure; building and maintaining highways and railroads is a priority. It must also increase public spending and continue to attract foreign investment to compete within the European Community.

- **Cost of Living:** At 147, the cost of living is higher than in the United States.

- **Work Permits, Visas, etc.:** A valid passport is required. To work in Spain for more than six months, a resident visa and/or work permit must be obtained in advance through the Ministry of Labor in Spain or through an embassy or consulate in the United States. When entering Spain from the United States, no vaccinations are necessary. However, hepatitis is increasing, and inoculations against this disease, as well as polio, typhoid, and tetanus, are recommended. For official or other information, direct inquiries to the embassy or consulate at the addresses below.

- **Taxation:** In Spain, taxes are collected at both local and national levels. Taxpayers are divided into two categories: residents of Spain who are taxed on worldwide income; and nonresidents who are taxed on income earned from Spanish sources only. You are considered a resident if you live in Spain for more than 183 days in a calendar year. Various credits or deductions may apply.

- **Principal International Schools:** Schools are available in all major cities throughout Spain. American schools are the most expensive, with yearly tuition averaging $10,000.

- **Health Care:** For the most part, medical facilities in Spain are modern and well-equipped. They are not equal to those in North America, but are adequate for the majority of medical problems. The best facility is the University Hospital on the outskirts of Madrid. English-speaking doctors are usually in demand, and may charge more for their services. Sanitary conditions are good in major cities, but it is best not to drink well water in rural areas. Water and most foods are safe in major tourist areas.

- **Crime:** Common crime is on the rise in Spain, and attributable to the high unemployment rate among young adults. Be careful of pickpockets and purse snatchers, and do not leave valuables unattended. Be especially cautious in the evening hours when going out alone.

- **Pros and Cons of Living and Working in Spain:** Spain has distinctive and well-preserved cultural traditions as well as sunny beaches, sporting events, mountain ranges, and great museums. Health and sanitary conditions are good, for the most part, and transportation is adequate. Remember that seat belts are mandatory and children are not allowed to ride in the front seat of any vehicle in Spain. Telecommunications are poor in most of Spain, and telephones are in short supply. When mailing anything, address envelopes correctly, and apply correct postage or it will travel by sea. It is relatively expensive to live in Spain, and the cost of housing, which is scarce,

EMBASSY AND CONSULATE CONTACT INFORMATION:

EMBASSY OF SPAIN
2700 15TH STREET NW
WASHINGTON, DC 20009
TEL: 202-265-0190

CONSULATE GENERAL OF SPAIN
150 EAST 58TH ST.
NEW YORK, NY 10022
TEL: 212-355-4080

typically equals 30 percent of a person's gross salary. Daily necessities cost more than in the United States. With street crime so prevalent, Leave any valuables or expensive items at home.

OTHER SOURCES OF INFORMATION:

NATIONAL TOURIST OFFICE OF SPAIN
665 FIFTH AVE.
NEW YORK, NY 10022
TEL: 212-759-8822

COMPANIES/ORGANIZATIONS WITH OPERATIONS IN SPAIN:

ALBERTO-CULVER COMPANY, 115
ALLIED-SIGNAL, INC., 117
ALUMINUM COMPANY OF AMERICA, 118
AMERICAN APPRAISAL ASSOCIATES, INC., 121
AMERICAN CYANAMID COMPANY, 124
AMGEN, INC., 131
APPLE COMPUTER, INC., 136
ARMSTRONG WORLD INDUSTRIES, INC., 141
AT&T INTERNATIONAL, 145
THE BANK OF NEW YORK COMPANY, INC., 154
BAUSCH & LOMB, INC., 159
BAXTER HEALTHCARE CORPORATION, 160
BECKMAN INSTRUMENTS, INC., 162
BLOCK DRUG COMPANY, INC., 169
BORLAND INTERNATIONAL, INC, 172
BOSE CORPORATION, 172
BROWNING-FERRIS INDUSTRIES, 177
CABOT CORPORATION, 181
CONAGRA, INC., 208
CONTINENTAL AIRLINES HOLDINGS, INC., 210
LEO A. DALY COMPANY, 223
DAMES & MOORE, 223
DDB NEEDHAM WORLDWIDE, INC., 227
DE KALB GENETICS CORPORATION, 227
EAGLE-PICHER INDUSTRIES, INC., 246
ENCORE COMPUTER CORPORATION, 252
FEDERAL-MOGUL CORPORATION, 260
FIRST CHICAGO CORPORATION, 262
FISCHER & PORTER COMPANY, 263
FISHER CONTROLS INTERNATIONAL, INC., 263
FORD MOTOR COMPANY, 267
FULLER COMPANY, 269
THE GATES RUBBER COMPANY, 273
GATX CORPORATION, 273
GENERAL FOODS USA, 276
GOLDMAN SACHS & COMPANY, 283

GOODYEAR TIRE & RUBBER COMPANY, 284
GRANT THORNTON INTERNATIONAL, 286
GTECH CORPORATION, 289
HDR INCORPORATED, 298
HERTZ CORPORATION, 300
HUGHES AIRCRAFT COMPANY, 307
IMCERA GROUP, INC., 310
INFORMATION BUILDERS, INC., 312
ITT HARTFORD INSURANCE GROUP, 321
ITT SHERATON CORPORATION, 322
ITW FINISHING SYSTEMS & PRODUCTS, 322
KELLOGG COMPANY, 330
KOCH INDUSTRIES, INC., 339
KRAFT GENERAL FOODS INTERNATIONAL, 341
LAW COMPANIES GROUP, INC., 343
ARTHUR D. LITTLE, INC., 347
LUBRIZOL CORPORATION, 353
MALLINCKRODT, INC., 359
MATTEL, INC., 363
METCO PERKIN-ELMER, 371
METROPOLITAN LIFE INSURANCE COMPANY, 371
MONROE AUTO EQUIPMENT COMPANY, 376
J. P. MORGAN & COMPANY, INC., 378
NATIONAL DATA CORPORATION, 382
NORTON COMPANY, 390
NOVELL, INC., 392
OCCIDENTAL PETROLEUM CORPORATION, 393
OMI INTERNATIONAL, 396
PERKIN-ELMER CORPORATION, 410
PIONEER HI-BRED INTERNATIONAL, INC., 417
PITTWAY CORPORATION, 418
PIZZA HUT, INC., 419
PLAYTEX APPAREL, INC., 419
PRECISION VALVE CORPORATION, 422

C
O
U
N
T
R
Y

P
R
O
F
I
L
E
S

PREFORMED LINE PRODUCTS COMPANY, 423

PRUDENTIAL INSURANCE COMPANY OF AMERICA, 427

QUAKER CHEMICAL CORPORATION, 428

RALSTON PURINA COMPANY, 430

RAYTHEON COMPANY, 432

REVLON, INC., 437

RUSSELL REYNOLDS ASSOCIATES, INC., 446

SAINT JUDE MEDICAL, INC., 448

SCHLEGEL CORPORATION, 451

SHEARSON LEHMAN BROTHERS, 460

SONOCO PRODUCTS COMPANY, 470

SONY PICTURES ENTERTAINMENT, 471

SPS TECHNOLOGIES, INC., 474

SQUARE D COMPANY, 475

TELEDYNE, INC., 489

TENNECO, INC., 492

TEXTRON, INC., 494

TLC BEATRICE INTERNATIONAL HOLDINGS, INC., 498

TOYS "R" US, INC., 500

VF CORPORATION, 517

WARNER BROTHERS INTERNATIONAL, 521

SRI LANKA

- **Official Name:** Democratic Socialist Republic of Sri Lanka

- **Capital:** Colombo

- **Location:** Sri Lanka is located in the Indian Ocean approximately 50 miles southeast of India. It is bounded by the Palk Strait to the north, Bay of Bengal to the east, Indian Ocean to the south and southwest, and the Gulf of Mannar to the northwest. Its total land area is 24,886 square miles, making Sri Lanka slightly larger than West Virginia. Its terrain is comprised of mainly low, flat rolling plains. There are mountains in the south-central interior sections.

- **Language and Currency:** The official language of Sri Lanka is Sinhala. Tamil is also a national language. English is used throughout business and government and spoken by 10 percent of the people. The monetary unit is the Sri Lankan rupee. The current exchange rate is 49 rupees = U.S.$1 (March 1994).

EMBASSY AND CONSULATE CONTACT INFORMATION:

EMBASSY OF THE DEMOCRATIC SOCIALIST REPUBLIC OF SRI LANKA
2148 WYOMING AVE. NW
WASHINGTON, DC 20008
TEL: 202-483-4025

OTHER SOURCES OF INFORMATION:

FOR INFORMATION ON CURRENT ECONOMIC TRENDS, OR COMMERCIAL DEVELOPMENT CONTACT:

INTERNATIONAL TRADE ADMINISTRATION
U.S. DEPARTMENT OF COMMERCE
WASHINGTON, DC 20230

COMPANIES/ORGANIZATIONS WITH OPERATIONS IN SRI LANKA:

ANSELL INTERNATIONAL, 135

CAMP DRESSER & MCKEE INTERNATIONAL, INC., 183

SUDAN

- **Official Name:** Republic of the Sudan
- **Capital:** Khartoum
- **Location:** Sudan is located in the northeastern section of Africa. It is bounded by Egypt to the north, the Red Sea and Ethiopia to the east, Kenya, Uganda, and Zaire to the south, and the Central African Republic, Chad, and Libya to the west. Its total land area is 967,500 square miles, making Sudan slightly larger than one-quarter the size of the United States. The terrain is basically comprised of flat plains with few distinguishable features. Mountains appear in the eastern and western sectors of the country.
- **Language and Currency:** The official language of Sudan is Arabic. Other Ethnic languages are also spoken, as well as English. A program of "Arabization" is currently under way. The monetary unit is the Sudanese pound. The current exchange rate is unavailable.

EMBASSY AND CONSULATE CONTACT INFORMATION:

EMBASSY OF THE REPUBLIC OF THE SUDAN
2210 MASSACHUSETTS AVE. NW
WASHINGTON, DC 20008
TEL: 202-338-8565

OTHER SOURCES OF INFORMATION:

FOR INFORMATION ON CURRENT ECONOMIC TRENDS, OR COMMERCIAL DEVELOPMENT CONTACT:
INTERNATIONAL TRADE ADMINISTRATION
U.S. DEPARTMENT OF COMMERCE
WASHINGTON, DC 20230

COMPANIES/ORGANIZATIONS WITH OPERATIONS IN SUDAN:

DANIEL, MANN, JOHNSON & MENDENHALL, 224
PARSONS CORPORATION, 406

SURINAME

- **Official Name:** Republic of Suriname
- **Capital:** Paramaribo
- **Location:** The smallest independent country in South America, Suriname is located on the northeastern coast of the continent. It is bounded by the north Atlantic Ocean to the north, French Guiana to the east, Brazil to the south, and Guyana to the west. Covering an area of 63,037 square miles, Suriname is slightly larger than Georgia. Nearly 97 percent of its territory is covered primarily by rain forests. Swampy flatland lies along the northern Atlantic coast, and inland a sandy plain rises to meet a high, grassy savanna that stretches along the southwest edge of the country.

- **Language and Currency:** The official language of Suriname is Dutch, with English as the accepted language of business and commerce. Sranan Tongo, also called Taki-Taki, is widely spoken by the Surinamese people. It is a mixture of Dutch, English, and several African languages. The monetary unit is the Suriname guilder. The exchange rate is 8 Suriname guilders = U.S.$1 (November 1993).

EMBASSY AND CONSULATE CONTACT INFORMATION:

THE EMBASSY OF THE REPUBLIC OF SURINAME
2600 VIRGINIA AVE. NW, STE. 201
WASHINGTON, DC 20037
TEL: 202-338-6980

OTHER SOURCES OF INFORMATION:

SURINAME TOURIST BOARD
ROCKEFELLER PLAZA
NEW YORK, NY 10020

COMPANIES/ORGANIZATIONS WITH OPERATIONS IN SURINAME:

ALUMINUM COMPANY OF AMERICA, 118

SWEDEN

- **Official Name:** Kingdom of Sweden
- **Capital:** Stockholm
- **Location:** Sweden is located in northwest Europe and shares the Scandinavian Peninsula with Norway, which lies on Sweden's northwest and western borders. It is bounded by Finland to the northeast, the Gulf of Bothina to the east, the Baltic Sea to the east and south, and the Skagerrak Channel to the southwest. Its land area totals 449,964 square miles, making it slightly larger than California. Only 7 percent of the land is arable, and 64 percent of the territory is covered by forest and woodland. The terrain is primarily flat, except for Noorland in the northern section, which contains Sweden's only mountainous area. Sweden has 96,000 lakes, which account for 10 percent of the country's land area. The south-central section of the Swedish coast is scattered with islands and is known as the Archipelago. It is a favorite area for vacation homes and sailing.
- **Population, Cities, and American Residents:** The population of Sweden totals 8.3 million people (1992 est.), consisting mainly of native Swedes, although there is a small Lappish minority, and about 12 percent of the population are foreign-born or first generation immigrants (Finns, Danes, Greeks, Norwegians, Turks, and Yugoslavs).

  Most American residents are employed in Sweden's three largest cities: Stockholm with 1.2 million people, Goteborg with 700,000, and Malmo with 467,000 (1989 est.).
- **Language and Currency:** The official language is Swedish, but English is a mandatory subject in all state schools, and is the major foreign language used in the country. Most Swedes know English and speak it fluently, especially in business circles. The monetary unit is the Swedish krona (Kr) and divided into 100 ore. The exchange rate is 1 Swedish krona = U.S.$.12.

- **Climate:** Because it is influenced by the Gulf Stream, Sweden's climate is not as cold as one might expect. Winter however, lasts six months, with an average temperature in Stockholm of 27°F. Generally, the snowfall is light. Days are sunny and brisk, although short, and nights are long. Summer is from May through August with an average temperature of 62°F. Average annual rainfall is about 22 inches, and usually is concentrated in early spring or the fall.

- **Economy and Resources:** Sweden has a productive and efficient industrial economy, and by remaining neutral in international conflicts, Sweden has avoided major wars, unlike some of its neighbors. Sweden is very dependent on trade, with 50 percent of industrial production and 30 percent of the gross domestic product (GDP) dependent upon exports. Services are the fastest growing sector of the economy and now employ two-thirds of the work force. Originally, Sweden's three vital natural resources were forests, iron ore, and hydroelectric power, and they helped the economy become what it is today. Currently, Sweden's chief exports are machinery, motor vehicles, paper products, pulp and wood, and iron and steel products, with more than half going to the European Community. During the last decade, Sweden's economy has showed signs of slowing down, and to avoid another slump, Sweden must secure its trade relations with the European community.

- **Cost of Living:** At 194, the cost of living is much higher than in the United States.

- **Work Permits, Visas, etc.:** A valid passport is required to travel in Sweden. If you are a citizen of the United States, and your stay is limited to three months, no visa is necessary, but for longer stays, you'll need a visa or residence permit. If you are entering Sweden from the United States, no vaccinations are required. For official or other information, direct inquiries to the embassy or consulate at the addresses below.

- **Taxation:** Sweden has one of the highest rates of taxation in the industrialized world. If you live in Sweden for less than six months, you are liable for only the income earned from Swedish sources. If you are in the country for six months or more, you are considered a resident (for tax purposes) and are responsible for assessment on income from all sources, whether or not located in Sweden. Exemptions or benefits may apply and the employer involved may be able to assist in the tax situation.

- **Principal International Schools:** Various international schools are available in Stockholm. Tuition is expensive compared to U.S. standards; expect to pay between $6,000 and $15,000 per year for an American school.

- **Health Care:** Medical and dental standards are comparable to those in the United States. Swedish doctors and dentists are qualified and work in modern facilities, and the U.S. embassy provides a list of physicians who take on new patients. Foreign residents must pay their own bills, unless there is a reciprocal arrangement with the patient's home health plan. Sanitation standards are very good throughout the country. Water and dairy products are safe, and there are no prevalent diseases that pose any threat to travelers.

- **Crime:** Crime is not a major problem in Sweden. Be careful though, especially in major tourist areas or large cities, and lock car doors.

- **Pros and Cons of Living and Working in Sweden:** The people of Sweden enjoy a very high standard of living, and the country offers many attractions, especially for those who enjoy outdoor activities. Stockholm is an ultramodern city with many museums, gardens, and elegant shopping. It is a safe country in which to live, with good medical facilities and high health standards. Transportation and telecommunications services are also comparable to those in the United States. The high tax rate and the high cost of living make residing in Sweden difficult for all but the highest paid expatriates. With a shortage in housing accommodations, housing arrangements must be made in advance. Alcohol abuse is taken very seriously in Sweden. Do not drink and drive, as alcohol tests are routinely given to drivers, and imprisonment is a typical punishment for driving under the influence.

EMBASSY AND CONSULATE CONTACT INFORMATION:

SWEDISH EMBASSY
600 NEW HAMPSHIRE AVE. NW
WASHINGTON, DC 20008
TEL: 202-944-5600

SWEDISH CONSULATE GENERAL AND
INFORMATION SERVICE
825 THIRD AVE.
NEW YORK, NY 10022
TEL: 212-751-5900

OTHER SOURCES OF INFORMATION:

U.S. COMMERCE DEPT.
COUNTRY SPECIALIST FOR SWEDEN
WASHINGTON, DC 20230
TEL: 202-377-4414

COMPANIES/ORGANIZATIONS WITH OPERATIONS IN SWEDEN:

ALBANY INTERNATIONAL CORPORATION, 114
ALBERTO-CULVER COMPANY, 115
ALDUS CORPORATION, 115
AM INTERNATIONAL, INC., 119
APPLE COMPUTER, INC., 136
AT&T INTERNATIONAL, 145
AUGAT, INC., 146
AVNET, INC., 148
BECKMAN INSTRUMENTS, INC., 162
BLOUNT, INC. (BLOUNT CONSTRUCTION DIVISION), 169
BORLAND INTERNATIONAL, INC, 172
W. H. BRADY COMPANY, 173
CHASE MANHATTAN CORPORATION, 190
CITICORP, 198
COLGATE-PALMOLIVE COMPANY, 203
COMMERCIAL INTERTECH CORPORATION, 205
COMMODORE INTERNATIONAL LTD., 206
DELL COMPUTER CORPORATION, 231
ENCORE COMPUTER CORPORATION, 252
EXXON CHEMICAL COMPANY, 257
FISCHER & PORTER COMPANY, 263
FISHER CONTROLS INTERNATIONAL, INC., 263
GENERAL FOODS USA, 276
W. R. GRACE & COMPANY, 285
GREY ADVERTISING, INC., 288

GTECH CORPORATION, 289
M. A. HANNA COMPANY, 295
HUGHES AIRCRAFT COMPANY, 307
IMO INDUSTRIES, 310
INTERNATIONAL PAPER COMPANY, 318
ITT CORPORATION, 321
LEVI STRAUSS ASSOCIATES, INC., 344
LINTAS: WORLDWIDE, 346
MAGNETEK, INC., 358
MEASUREX CORPORATION, 366
METALLURG CORPORATION, 370
MGM INCORPORATED, 372
MILLIPORE CORPORATION, 374
MONSANTO COMPANY, 377
NEWSWEEK INTERNATIONAL, 387
NORTON COMPANY, 390
OUTBOARD MARINE CORPORATION, 399
OWENS-CORNING FIBERGLAS CORPORATION, 400
PARKER HANNIFIN CORPORATION, 405
READER'S DIGEST ASSOCIATION, INC., 432
RELIANCE ELECTRIC COMPANY, 435
ROBERTSON CECO, 440
RUDER FINN, INC., 445
SB POWER TOOLS, INC. (SKIL CORP.), 450
SEALED AIR CORPORATION, 455
SGS CONTROL SERVICES, 458

SGS-THOMSON MICROELECTRONICS, 458

SHIPLEY COMPANY, INC., 461

SOUTHLAND CORPORATION, 472

SPRINT CORPORATION, 474

SRI INTERNATIONAL, 475

THOMAS & BETTS, 495

UOP, INC., 514

US WEST, INC., 515

WALKER MANUFACTURING COMPANY, 519

WARNER ELECTRIC BRAKE & CLUTCH
  COMPANY, 521

WILLIAM WRIGLEY JR. COMPANY, 529

SWITZERLAND

- **Official Name:** Swiss Confederation
- **Capital:** Bern
- **Location:** Switzerland is a landlocked country located in the Alpine highlands of Western Europe. It is bounded by Germany to the north, Austria to the east, Italy to the south, and France to the west. The total land area is 41,293 square miles, or about twice the size of New Jersey. The Alps occupy nearly 60 percent of the territory, running east to west in the southern section of Switzerland. Another group of mountains, the Juras, extend southwest to northeast in the western section of the country, and cover another 10 percent of Switzerland's land area. A plateau rests in between these two ranges, where the major cities and industrial areas of the country are located.
- **Population, Cities, and American Residents:** The population of Switzerland totals 6.8 million people (1992 est.). Germans account for 65 percent of the population; French account for 18 percent, Italian for 10 percent, and Romansh for 1 percent. Five percent are comprised of other groups.

    Most American residents are employed in Switzerland's three largest cities: Bern with 305,000 people, Zurich with 700,000, and Geneva with 375,000 (1988 est.).
- **Language and Currency:** There are three official languages in Switzerland: German, French, and Italian. A fourth "national" language is Romansh, spoken by only 1 percent of the people. Most Swiss are multilingual and English is a fifth language, spoken throughout business and tourist areas. The monetary unit is the Swiss franc (SFr), which is divided into 100 centimes. It remains one of the most dominant currencies in the world. The exchange rate is 1 Swiss franc = U.S.$.66 (July 30, 1993).
- **Climate:** Switzerland has a moderate continental climate. Summers are generally warm and winters cold, but conditions vary depending on the altitude, and precipitation is most frequent in spring and summer. The north wind, or "bise," brings cold, brisk weather during the winter and cool breezes in the summer. Another wind, the Fohn, brings warm, humid air from the south during the warmer months.
- **Economy and Resources:** Switzerland is a world leader in banking. Swiss banking institutions are known for their secret accounts and have attracted large amounts of foreign funds. Until recently, banking laws were very relaxed. Zurich and Geneva are the main financial centers. Switzerland's economy is very dependent on commerce, with exports accounting for 25 percent of the gross domestic product (GDP) and imports for 30 percent. The industrial sector must rely on importing raw materials, due to the lack

of natural resources. Major exports include machinery and equipment, precision instruments, metal products, and foodstuffs. Over half of the exports go to the European Community. Unemployment remains low, at less than 1 percent. Of the labor force, 42 percent work in services, 39 percent in industry and crafts, and 11 percent in government. Throughout the years, the Swiss have worked long and hard to achieve a thriving economy, of which tourism and services are a large part. The mountainous country has a small amount (10 percent) of arable land, and very limited natural resources, yet its people have created one of the most efficient industrial economies in the world.

- **Cost of Living:** At 168, the cost of living is much higher than in the United States.
- **Work Permits, Visas, etc.:** A valid passport is required to travel in Switzerland, and you'll need a visa if your stay is more than three months. If you plan on working in Switzerland, a work or residence permit must be obtained prior to your trip. When entering Switzerland from the United States, no vaccinations are required. For official or other information, direct inquiries to the embassy or consulate at the addresses below.
- **Taxation:** Residents of Switzerland are subject to taxes at the federal, cantonal, and communal levels. You are considered a resident if you live in Switzerland for three to six months of a calendar year. Foreign residents are responsible for taxes earned on a worldwide basis, but a treaty is in effect between Switzerland and the United States to avoid double taxation.
- **Principal International Schools:** Private schools are one of the major service industries of Switzerland, with institutions located throughout the country. Tuition for an American school is about $10,000 per year.
- **Health Care:** Medical facilities throughout most of Switzerland are modern and well-equipped. Specialists are available and prescription drugs may be easily obtained at local establishments. Medical fees are very high compared to the United States; a check-up with a general practitioner will cost about $250. Sanitary conditions are very good, and you'll find most public facilities exceptionally clean. The Swiss are very conscientious about controlling pollution, and laws are strictly enforced. There are no prevalent diseases or health hazards that pose a threat to travelers.
- **Crime:** Switzerland is considered one of the safest countries in the world, in most areas. There is a drug problem, however, as there is in many wealthy countries, but drug-associated violence is still rare.
- **Pros and Cons of Living and Working in Switzerland:** Switzerland is proverbial for its political stability and majestic scenery. It has long been a major tourist attraction, with abundant lakes and snow-capped mountains, and museums and medieval towns. Switzerland is an exceptionally clean and inviting country, and telecommunications and transportation are very good. Wearing seat belts is

EMBASSY AND CONSULATE CONTACT INFORMATION:

EMBASSY OF SWITZERLAND
2900 CATHEDRAL AVE. NW
WASHINGTON, DC 20008
TEL: 202-745-7900

CONSULATE GENERAL OF SWITZERLAND
665 FIFTH AVE.
NEW YORK, NY 10022
TEL: 212-758-2560

mandatory. Health and sanitary standards are very high. Housing is available, but may cost more than comparable U.S. accommodations, as do many everyday items.

OTHER SOURCES OF INFORMATION:

SWISS NATIONAL TOURIST OFFICE
608 FIFTH AVE.
NEW YORK, NY 10020
TEL: 212-757-5944

COMPANIES/ORGANIZATIONS WITH OPERATIONS IN SWITZERLAND:

ALLIS MINERAL SYSTEMS/SVEDALA
   INDUSTRIES, INC., 118
AM INTERNATIONAL, INC., 119
AMERICAN HOME PRODUCTS
   CORPORATION, 126
AMGEN, INC., 131
ANDREW CORPORATION, 134
AUGAT, INC., 146
BANKAMERICA CORPORATION, 155
THE BARDEN CORPORATION, 157
BATTELLE MEMORIAL INSTITUTE, 159
BAUSCH & LOMB, INC., 159
BEAR STEARNS COMPANIES, INC., 161
BECKMAN INSTRUMENTS, INC., 162
BIO-RAD LABORATORIES, 166
BOSE CORPORATION, 172
BROWN & SHARPE MANUFACTURING
   COMPANY, 176
BURSON-MARSTELLER, 180
CARRIER CORPORATION, 186
CHARTER MEDICAL CORPORATION, 190
CHASE MANHATTAN CORPORATION, 190
CHEMICAL BANKING CORPORATION, 191
CHEVRON CHEMICAL COMPANY, 192
CHRISTIAN BLIND MISSION
   INTERNATIONAL, 543
CIGNA CORPORATION, 197
CITICORP, 198
COMMODORE INTERNATIONAL LTD., 206
CS FIRST BOSTON, INC., 219
DATA GENERAL CORPORATION, 225
DDB NEEDHAM WORLDWIDE, INC., 227
DEAN WITTER, DISCOVER & COMPANY,
   228
DELTA AIR LINES, INC., 232
DETROIT DIESEL CORPORATION, 232
THE DEXTER CORPORATION, 233
DONALDSON LUFKIN & JENRETTE, INC.,
   238
ELI LILLY AND COMPANY, 250
EMERY WORLDWIDE, 252

ENCYCLOPEDIA BRITANNICA, INC., 253
ENSERCH INTERNATIONAL DEVELOPMENT,
   INC., 254
FEDERAL EXPRESS CORPORATION, 260
FIRST CHICAGO CORPORATION, 262
GALEN HEALTH CARE, 271
GANNETT COMPANY, INC., 272
GENERAL SIGNAL CORPORATION, 278
GERHARD'S BICYCLE ODYSSEYS, 280
THE GILLETTE COMPANY, 283
W. R. GRACE & COMPANY, 285
HANSON INDUSTRIES, 295
HASBRO, INC., 297
HERTZ CORPORATION, 300
HEWLETT-PACKARD COMPANY, 300
HOLIDAY INNS WORLDWIDE, 302
HONEYWELL, INC., 303
HUGHES AIRCRAFT COMPANY, 307
HYATT INTERNATIONAL CORPORATION,
   308
IMO INDUSTRIES, 310
INFORMATION BUILDERS, INC., 312
INTERNATIONAL MONETARY FUND, 552
ITW FINISHING SYSTEMS & PRODUCTS,
   322
JONES, DAY, REAVIS & POGUE, INC., 326
KIDDER PEABODY GROUP & COMPANY,
   INC., 335
KLYNVELD PEAT MARWICK GOERDELER
   (KPMG), 337
KRAFT GENERAL FOODS INTERNATIONAL,
   341
LEVI STRAUSS ASSOCIATES, INC., 344
LINTAS: WORLDWIDE, 346
MAGNETEK, INC., 358
MCGRAW-HILL, INC., 357
MEASUREX CORPORATION, 366
MERCK & COMPANY, INC., 368
MERISEL, INC., 369
MERRILL LYNCH & COMPANY, INC., 369
METALLURG CORPORATION, 370

MILLIPORE CORPORATION, 374
MONSANTO COMPANY, 377
MOTOROLA, INC., 381
NEWSWEEK INTERNATIONAL, 387
NORDSON CORPORATION, 389
NYNEX CORPORATION, 392
OCCIDENTAL PETROLEUM CORPORATION, 393
OFFICE OF INTERNATIONAL HEALTH, 557
OWENS-ILLINOIS, INC., 401
PAINE WEBBER GROUP, INC., 403
PFIZER, INC., 412
PHILIP MORRIS COMPANIES, INC., 413
PHILIPP BROTHERS CHEMICALS, INC., 414
PITNEY BOWES, INC., 417
PRICE WATERHOUSE, 424
PROJECT HOPE, 563
PUROLATOR PRODUCTS COMPANY, 427
R. J. REYNOLDS TOBACCO COMPANY, 429
RALSTON PURINA COMPANY, 430
READER'S DIGEST ASSOCIATION, INC., 432
RELIANCE ELECTRIC COMPANY, 435
REVLON, INC., 437
REYNOLDS METALS COMPANY, 438
RUBBERMAID, INC., 445
RUDER FINN, INC., 445
SB POWER TOOLS, INC. (SKIL CORP.), 450
A. SCHULMAN, INC., 451
SEA-LAND SERVICE, INC., 454

SENSORMATIC ELECTRONICS CORPORATION, 457
SGS CONTROL SERVICES, 458
SHEARSON LEHMAN BROTHERS, 460
SHIPLEY COMPANY, INC., 461
SMITH BARNEY, HARRIS UPHAM & COMPANY, INC., 466
SRI INTERNATIONAL, 475
STANDARD COMMERCIAL CORPORATION, 476
STORAGE TECHNOLOGY CORPORATION, 481
SUNDSTRAND CORPORATION, 485
TEXACO OIL COMPANY, 493
TLC BEATRICE INTERNATIONAL HOLDINGS, INC., 498
TRACOR, INC., 500
TRANE COMPANY, 501
TRW, INC., 503
UNITED NATIONS INDUSTRIAL DEVELOPMENT ORGANIZATION (UNIDO), 568
UNITED TECHNOLOGIES CORPORATION, 512
WARNER ELECTRIC BRAKE & CLUTCH COMPANY, 521
WEYERHAEUSER COMPANY, 526
WORLD COURIER MANAGEMENT, INC., 529
WORLD INTELLECTUAL PROPERTY ORGANIZATION, 586
YOUNG & RUBICAM, INC., 533

COUNTRY PROFILES

TAIWAN

- **Official Name:** Republic of China

- **Capital:** Taipei

- **Location:** Taiwan consists of one main island with 75 smaller ones. The main island is located approximately 100 miles off the southeastern coast of mainland China. It separates the Pacific Ocean from the South China Sea, approximately one-third of the way from Hong Kong to Japan. The 75 smaller islands make up the Penghu Archipelago (Pescodores). The island is divided through the middle from north to south, by a range of mountains descending to a broad, fertile, western plain. Over half the land is densely forested.

- **Population, Cities, and American Residents:** Taiwan has 21 million people (1992 est.), with the Taiwanese accounting for 84 percent of the population. Fourteen percent are descended from mainland Chinese, and 2 percent are aborigine.

  Most American residents are employed in Taiwan's three largest cities: Taipei with 2.7 million people, Kaohsiung with 1.4 million, and Taichung with 762,000 (1990 est.).

- **Language and Currency:** The official language of Taiwan is Mandarin Chinese, and Taiwanese and Hakka dialects are also used. However, English is the language of international business, as is Japanese. The monetary unit is the New Taiwan Dollar. Hsin Taibi has 100 fen (cents). Americans tend to quote prices in 'NT' as in "the total comes to 125 NT." Bills are in denominations of 1,000, 500, 100, 10, 5, and 1 dollar(s). Coins are 1 and 5 dollars, and 50, 20, and 10 fen. The exchange rate is 1 Taiwan dollar = U.S.$.037; 27 Taiwan dollars equal U.S.$1 (July 30, 1993).

- **Climate:** Surrounded by water, Taiwan is humid most of the time. Spring and fall are the best seasons, as summers can be very hot and extremely humid, and winters are cool and damp. The rainy season precedes summer in the months of May and June. Temperatures average 40°F in winter and 95°F in the summer. Taiwan is subject to typhoons, which arrive during summer and fall.

- **Economy and Resources:** Once a tiny, poor, and backward island, Taiwan has been transformed into one of Asia's major trading nations. Taiwan's foreign currency reserves remain high, second only to Japan's in Asia. The two leading industries are textiles and electronics, and major exports are electrical machinery, textiles, general machinery, and communications equipment. The United States is Taiwan's biggest export customer. Nearly 41 percent of the people work in industry or commerce-related areas. Natural resources include natural gas, marble, and asbestos. Environmental regulations have been costly, and structural reforms are currently in progress. These include opening the banking sector to private firms, privatizing telecommunications, and liberalizing the insurance industry. Changes will occur on a wide scale if the government will allow foreigners to participate in the economy without hindrance.

- **Cost of Living:** At 133, the cost of living is much higher than in the United States.

- **Work Permits, Visas, etc.:** A valid passport and visa are required for any visit in Taiwan, and resident visas, free to U.S. citizens, are required if the length of stay is longer than two months. Applications must be made at the Department of Consular Affairs, in the office of the Ministry of Foreign Affairs in Taipei, upon arrival. Along with the application, you must present a document stating the purpose of the visit and the name and address of your sponsor or company in Taiwan. If you are entering Taiwan from the United States, no vaccinations are required. For official or other information, direct inquiries to the embassy or consulate at the addresses below.

- **Taxation:** There are 19 different taxes levied in Taiwan. If you are a resident of Taiwan, or a foreigner living in the country for more than 91 days, income tax is collected at various progressive rates. For more information, contact the Foreign Affairs Office, National Tax Administration of Taipei, Ministry of Finance, 547 Chunghsiao East Road, Section 4, Taipei.

- **Principal International Schools:** There are two American schools in Taiwan for children of American residents. One is in Taipei; and the other one is the Morison Academy in T'ai-chung. Tuition for American schools averages $9,500 per year.

- **Health Care:** Taiwan has very good health care, as many of its professional medical staff were trained in the United States or Canada. Taipei's Mackay Memorial Hospital, a missionary facility with Western doctors on staff, is used frequently by Americans. Compared to U.S. prices, prescriptions and various drugs can be expensive in Taiwan, and hospital and emergency clinics insist on payment in advance in the local currency (NT$). Tap water is unsafe, so you must boil it for all usage, or buy bottled water. Appropriate precautions should be taken with all fruits and vegetables, and avoid many of the sidewalk restaurants if they do not appear clean. Hepatitis is a serious problem in Taiwan, and travelers should consider a Hepatitis B vaccination before arriving as there is a slight risk the disease can be spread through food preparation.

- **Crime:** With the increasing prosperity of Taipei, common crime is on the rise. Though foreign residents are not special targets, be as careful as you would in any tourist area. The media sometimes overdramatize kidnappings and other crimes. The local police say that streets are safe, day or night.

- **Pros and Cons of Living and Working in Taiwan:** Taiwan is a very busy economic center and has museums, temples, and the various coastal islands to attract tourists. Public transportation is good and reasonably priced, but usually crowded, and telecommunications are very good. Doctors are qualified in the major cities, but sanitary conditions could use improvement. It is ill-advised to drive on your own in Taiwan. Roads are crowded, and no one seems to obey the rules of the road, especially in the cities. Licenses and insurance can be costly. Housing is available, but in most cases a two years' rent in advance is required. Don't bring antiques or expensive furniture, as the air is humid, and mildew may ruin any fine items.

EMBASSY AND CONSULATE CONTACT INFORMATION:

AMERICAN INSTITUTES IN TAIWAN
WASHINGTON HDQTRS.
1700 N. MONROE ST., 17TH FL.
ARLINGTON, VA 22209
TEL: 703-525-8474
FAX: 703-841-1385

OTHER SOURCES OF INFORMATION:

TOURISM BUREAU OF THE REPUBLIC OF
CHINA
1 WORLD TRADE CENTER, RM. #9753
NEW YORK, NY 10048
TEL: 212-466-0692
FAX: 212-432-6436

COMPANIES/ORGANIZATIONS WITH OPERATIONS IN TAIWAN:

AIRBORNE EXPRESS, 112
AMERICAN CYANAMID COMPANY, 124
AMERICAN PRESIDENT COMPANIES, LTD.,
  128
AMERICAN TOOL COMPANIES, INC., 129
AMPEX CORPORATION, 133
AST RESEARCH, INC., 144
AT&T INTERNATIONAL, 145
ATARI CORPORATION, 146

AVNET, INC., 148
BANDAG, INC., 153
THE BANK OF NEW YORK COMPANY,
  INC., 154
BAUSCH & LOMB, INC., 159
BECHTEL GROUP, INC., 162
BLOCK DRUG COMPANY, INC., 169
BROWN GROUP, INC., 176
BURLINGTON AIR EXPRESS, 179

A
M
E
R
I
C
A
N

J
O
B
S

A
B
R
O
A
D

CH2M HILL INTERNATIONAL, LTD., 195
COOPER POWER SYSTEMS, 213
CTS CORPORATION, 220
LEO A. DALY COMPANY, 223
DDB NEEDHAM WORLDWIDE, INC., 227
DH TECHNOLOGY, INC., 233
DIGITAL EQUIPMENT CORPORATION, 236
DOW CORNING CORPORATION, 240
E-SYSTEMS, INC., 245
EBASCO OVERSEAS CORPORATION, 248
EG & G, INC., 249
FERRO CORPORATION, 261
FLOW INTERNATIONAL CORPORATION, 265
FORD MOTOR COMPANY, 267
GENERAL DYNAMICS SERVICES
 COMPANY, 275
GENERAL INSTRUMENT CORPORATION,
 276
GOLDMAN SACHS & COMPANY, 283
GRACO, INC., 286
HERCULES, INC., 299
HONEYWELL, INC., 303
ICF KAISER ENGINEERS, 308
IDB COMMUNICATIONS, INC., 309
ILLINOIS TOOL WORKS, INC., 309
INDUCTOTHERM CORPORATION, 311
INTERNATIONAL PAPER COMPANY, 318
ITT CORPORATION, 321
ITT HARTFORD INSURANCE GROUP, 321
JOHNSON & HIGGINS, 324
JOHNSON & JOHNSON, 325
L. A. GEAR, INC., 342
LIZ CLAIBORNE, INC., 348
MATTEL, INC., 363
METROPOLITAN LIFE INSURANCE
 COMPANY, 371
MORTON INTERNATIONAL, 380

MOTOROLA, INC., 381
NIKE, INC., 388
NORWEST CORPORATION, 391
OLIN CORPORATION, 396
OTIS ELEVATOR COMPANY: WORLD
 HEADQUARTERS, 399
PARSONS BRINKERHOFF, 406
J. C. PENNEY COMPANY, INC., 407
PENTAIR, INC., 409
PFIZER, INC., 412
PPG INDUSTRIES, 421
PROCTER & GAMBLE COMPANY, 425
PRUDENTIAL INSURANCE COMPANY OF
 AMERICA, 427
QUAKER OATS COMPANY, 428
QUME CORPORATION, 429
ROCKWELL INTERNATIONAL
 CORPORATION, 441
SCOTT PAPER COMPANY, 453
SEALED AIR CORPORATION, 455
SHAKLEE CORPORATION, 459
SHEARMAN & STERLING, 460
SILICONIX, 462
SONOCO PRODUCTS COMPANY, 470
TANDY CORPORATION, 487
TEKTRONIX, INC., 488
TEXAS INTRUMENTS, INC., 494
TORRINGTON COMPANY, 499
TOYS ''R'' US, INC., 500
TRW, INC., 503
UNION CARBIDE CORPORATION, 507
U.S. WHEAT ASSOCIATES, 511
THE UPJOHN COMPANY, 515
WARNER BROTHERS INTERNATIONAL, 521
JERVIS B. WEBB COMPANY, 523
WILLIAM WRIGLEY JR. COMPANY, 529
YORK INTERNATIONAL, INC., 532

TANZANIA

- **Official Name:** United Republic of Tanzania

- **Capital:** Dar es Salaam

- **Location:** Tanzania is located on the eastern coast of Africa, and includes the islands of Zanzibar and Pemba. It lies approximately 25 miles off the Tanganyika coast in the Indian Ocean. It is bounded by Burundi and Rwanda to the northwest, Uganda and

Kenya to the north, the Indian Ocean to
the east, Mozambique and Malawi to the
south, Zambia to the southwest, and Zaire
to the west. Its total land area is 342,102
square miles, making it approximately
three times the size of Arizona. Forests,
meadows, and pastures dominate Tanzania, with plains along the coast and
highlands in the north and the south.

- **Language and Currency:** English and
Swahili are the official languages of Tanzania. The monetary unit is the Tanzanian
shilling. The current exchange rate is
unavailable.

COMPANIES/ORGANIZATIONS WITH OPERATIONS IN TANZANIA:

LOUIS BERGER INTERNATIONAL INC., 165

THAILAND

- **Official Name:** Kingdom of Thailand
- **Capital:** Bangkok
- **Location:** Thailand is located in Southeast Asia and occupies the western half of the
Indochinese peninsula. It shares this area with Myanmar (formerly called Burma), Laos,
Kampuchea (formerly called Cambodia), Vietnam, and Malaysia. Thailand's coast is
extensive along the Gulf of Thailand and the Andaman Sea. Its land area totals 198,475
square miles, comparable to the size to France. The main sector of Thailand is the
heavily populated central plain around Bangkok. Extensively irrigated by the Chao
Phraya and smaller rivers, it is a fertile area. The western section towards Myanmar and
the area to the north of the mountains are less populated. The northeast and eastern
sections are occupied by the Korat plateau, a hilly region used for raising livestock. The
Malay peninsula to the south is mountainous and filled with dense jungles.
- **Population, Cities, and American Residents:** The population of Thailand totals
57.2 million people (1991 est.). Nearly 90 percent of the population is composed of
ethnic Thais, 8 percent Chinese, and the remaining 2 percent of Malay, Khmer,
Burmese, and Indian strains.

    Most American residents are employed in Thailand's three largest cities: Bangkok
with 5.9 million people, Songkhla with 173,000 and Chon Buri with 115,000 (1990
est.).
- **Language and Currency:** The official language of the country is Thai, with its own

written script based on Pali and Sanskrit. English, however, is widely used in offices, stores, and tourist areas, but it is rarely spoken in rural areas of the country. The unit of currency is the baht (shortened to B). There are 100 satang in 1 baht, with coins and bills color-coded for identification. Coins are in 50 and 25 satang (copper); B5, B2, and B1 (silver); and bills are in B500 (purple), 100 (red), 50 (blue), 20 (green), and 10 (brown). The exchange rate is 1 Thai baht = U.S.$.40 (July 30, 1993).

- **Climate:** Except at high elevations, Thailand's climate is tropical and can be extremely hot and humid most of the year. Temperatures above 90°F are common. Most of the rain occurs from June to October, and the coolest months are from November through February where daytime highs drop to 80°F in northern areas. Monsoons are most frequent in the southern region of Thailand.

- **Economy and Resources:** Thailand has a thriving and almost unbridled capitalist economy, in part due to a strict limit on government spending during the last 30 years. Agriculture is the strongest economic sector enabling Thailand to be a major food exporter, and nearly 73 percent of the labor force work in agriculture. It is the world's second largest exporter of rice (8.5 percent of exports in 1988), and the third largest exporter of rubber and tin. It is also a major exporter of textiles and tungsten. Teak was once a major export, but teak cutting was halted in 1989 in an effort to conserve the rain forests. Thailand's economic growth is credited to exports, but animal husbandry has been targeted as a growth industry by the government. As the country tries to improve its herds, experts forecast increasing opportunities in Thailand for Western specialists in livestock genetics.

- **Cost of Living:** At 101, the cost of living is practically equal to that of the United States.

- **Work Permits, Visas, etc.:** A valid passport and a return ticket are required for visits up to 15 days. For longer stays, a visa must be obtained in advance from the Embassy of Thailand. Business visas require a company letter stating the reason for the visit and the length of stay. If you are entering Thailand from the United States, no vaccinations are required, but malaria tablets and polio and typhoid shots are recommended. For official or other information, direct inquiries to the embassy or consulate at the addresses below.

- **Taxation:** Personal income tax is collected on residents who spend more than 180 days of any tax year in Thailand. Rates are established on a case-by-case basis.

- **Principal International Schools:** There is a selection of international schools in Bangkok with classes in English, French, German, and Japanese. The U.S. international school has a curriculum similar to the California program and charges about $4,500 per year for tuition.

- **Health Care:** Medical facilities in Bangkok are equipped with well-trained doctors, including specialists and dentists, who speak fluent English. Hospitals have modern equipment and charges are reasonable. Two used most often by American residents in Bangkok are Ramathibodi Hospital on Rama IV Road, and the Bangkok Christian Hospital at 1245 Silom Road. Health standards in Thailand are not comparable to those in the United States. Tap water is not chlorinated so you must boil all water or use bottled fluids. Dairy products carry many infectious diseases (use only canned milk), and all meat must be thoroughly cooked. Rabies is prevalent in all fur-bearing animals in the country, so keep children away from all stray animals. The AIDS epidemic is rampant in Thailand, particularly among the large population of prostitutes.

- **Crime:** Crime is not a major problem in Thailand, but muggings occur. Watch out for pickpockets, and don't carry valuables or large amounts of cash in crowded areas. Burglary is a problem, so lock doors upon leaving your home, and keep valuables in a safe, concealed place.

- **Pros and Cons of Living and Working in Thailand:** Thailand is an exotic, friendly country offering cultural events, relaxing beaches, and sightseeing adventures. Most costs are reasonable. Bangkok has a wild night life with lively cabarets and discos, that stay open well into the morning hours. Transportation and telecommunications services are good, and housing is available and affordable. Parking poses problems, as there is next to none for private vehicles. Sanitation is also a drawback, as many areas are unhealthy compared to U.S. standards. Bangkok's high heat and humidity during summer months can be oppressive, and the humidity and insects may ruin books, fine fabrics, or expensive clothing.

EMBASSY AND CONSULATE CONTACT INFORMATION:

ROYAL THAI EMBASSY
2300 KALORAMA RD. NW
WASHINGTON, DC 20008
TEL: 202-483-7200

THAILAND CONSULATE GENERAL
53 PARK PLACE, RMS. 505-507
NEW YORK, NY 10017
TEL: 212-732-8166

OTHER SOURCES OF INFORMATION:

U.S. STATE DEPARTMENT
DESK OFFICER FOR THAILAND
WASHINGTON, DC 20025
TEL: 202-647-0978

COMPANIES/ORGANIZATIONS WITH OPERATIONS IN THAILAND:

ADVANCED MICRO DEVICES, INC., 112
AMERICAN APPRAISAL ASSOCIATES, INC., 121
AMERICAN CYANAMID COMPANY, 124
AMERICAN PRESIDENT COMPANIES, LTD., 128
AMERICAN STANDARD, INC., 128
AT&T INTERNATIONAL, 145
BANDAG, INC., 153
THE BANK OF NEW YORK COMPANY, INC., 154
BLACK & VEATCH, 168
THE CHUBB & SON CORPORATION, 196
CONTINENTAL AIRLINES HOLDINGS, INC., 210
D'ARCY MASIUS BENTON & BOWLES INC., 225
DATA GENERAL CORPORATION, 225
DDB NEEDHAM WORLDWIDE, INC., 227

DE KALB GENETICS CORPORATION, 227
DOW CHEMICAL COMPANY, 240
ELI LILLY AND COMPANY, 250
EXXON COMPANY, INTERNATIONAL, 258
FERRO CORPORATION, 261
GTE CORPORATION, 288
H. J. HEINZ COMPANY, 290
HUGHES AIRCRAFT COMPANY, 307
HUGHES CHRISTENSEN COMPANY, 307
INTERNATIONAL DATA GROUP, INC., 316
INTERNATIONAL VOLUNTARY SERVICES, INC., 555
KENDALL INTERNATIONAL, 332
KENNAMETAL, INC., 333
KIMBERLY-CLARK CORPORATION, 336
KOLMAR LABORATORIES, INC., 340
LOCTITE CORPORATION, 349
NATIONAL SEMICONDUCTOR CORPORATION, 383

NORTHWEST AIRLINES, INC., 390
PACIFIC TELESIS INTERNATIONAL, 403
PARSONS BRINKERHOFF, 406
PARSONS CORPORATION, 406
J. C. PENNEY COMPANY, INC., 407
PEPSICO FOODS INTERNATIONAL, 409
PEPSICO, INC., 410
PIONEER HI-BRED INTERNATIONAL, INC.,
    417
POPULATION COUNCIL, 562
PPG INDUSTRIES, 421

PREMARK INTERNATIONAL, INC., 423
SCOTT PAPER COMPANY, 453
SEAGATE TECHNOLOGY, INC., 454
STANDARD COMMERCIAL CORPORATION,
    476
3M COMPANY, 496
TLC BEATRICE INTERNATIONAL HOLDINGS,
    INC., 498
TRITON ENERGY CORPORATION, 502
UNOCAL CORPORATION, 513
WARNER BROTHERS INTERNATIONAL, 521

A
M
E
R
I
C
A
N

J
O
B
S

A
B
R
O
A
D

TRINIDAD AND TOBAGO

- **Official Name:** Republic of Trinidad and Tobago
- **Capital:** Port-of-Spain
- **Location:** Trinidad and Tobago is a country comprised of two main islands in the southeastern Caribbean Sea. Trinidad, the largest of the two, is located seven miles east of Venezuela. Tobago lies 20 miles northeast of Trinidad. With a total land area of 1,980 square miles, the island country is comparable in size to Delaware. Nearly half of the territory is covered by forests. Tropical wilderness and rich flatlands cover most of Trinidad; a mountain range exists in the north; and low hills can be found toward the central and southern regions. In Tobago, a mountain range lies in the center of the island, and wide sandy beaches prevail along the coast.
- **Language and Currency:** The official language of Trinidad and Tobago is English, which is used throughout business and government. The monetary unit is the Trinidad and Tobago dollar. The exchange rate is 5.7 Trinidad and Tobago dollars = U.S.$1 (November 1993).
- **Print Sources of Information:** U.S. Department of Commerce's *Foreign Economic Trends—Trinidad and Tobago* (Dec. 1987) is available from the Superintendent of Documents, U.S. Government Printing Office, Washington, D.C., 20402

EMBASSY AND CONSULATE CONTACT INFORMATION:

EMBASSY OF TRINIDAD AND TOBAGO
1708 MASSACHUSETTS AVE. NW
WASHINGTON, DC 20036
TEL: 202-467-6490

COMPANIES/ORGANIZATIONS WITH OPERATIONS IN TRINIDAD AND TOBAGO:

CUNA MUTUAL INSURANCE GROUP, 222
DOW CHEMICAL COMPANY, 240
NL INDUSTRIES, INC., 388

TUNISIA

- **Official Name:** Republic of Tunisia
- **Capital:** Tunis
- **Location:** Tunisia is located on the Mediterranean coast of Africa. It is bounded by Libya to the southeast, Algeria to the west, and the Mediterranean Sea to the north and east. Its land area covers 63,379 square miles and it is slightly larger than the state of Georgia. Tunisia has four regions: the mountainous north comprises one-third of the land area; the central area is a large plateau; south of the plateau there is a region of shallow salt lakes; and lastly, the southern sector of Tunisia is comprised of Saharan sand and rock. Along the eastern coastline are many beaches and harbors where several resorts are located. Tunisia has a comparatively smooth landscape, each area blending into the other with no sharp geographic features to divide its territory.
- **Language and Currency:** Arabic is the official language of Tunisia, with French, German, and English spoken in the major cities. French is the accepted language of commerce, and a working knowledge of that language is important if you are on a long-term assignment in Tunisia. The monetary unit is the Tunisian dinar (DT). The exchange rate is 1 Tunisian dinar = U.S.$1 (November 1993).

EMBASSY AND CONSULATE CONTACT INFORMATION:

EMBASSY OF TUNISIA/CONSULAR SECTION
2408 MASSACHUSETTS AVE. NW
WASHINGTON, DC 20008
TEL: 202-862-1850

OTHER SOURCES OF INFORMATION:

OVERSEAS PRIVATE INVESTMENT
CORPORATION
1615 M ST.
WASHINGTON, DC 20527
TEL: 202-457-7139

MINISTRY OF THE INTERIOR
AVE. DU 7 NOVEMBRE
TUNIS, TUNISIA
TEL-243-000

COMPANIES/ORGANIZATIONS WITH OPERATIONS IN TUNISIA:

FREEPORT-MCMORAN, INC., 268
MARATHON PETROLEUM COMPANY, 359
USX CORPORATION, 516

TURKEY

- **Official Name:** Republic of Turkey
- **Capital:** Ankara
- **Location:** Turkey creates a land bridge between Europe and the Middle East. With an area of 296,000 square miles, it is slightly bigger than Texas. The Bosphorous Bridge in Istanbul (the only city in the world to connect two continents) is the fourth longest bridge

in the world, connecting Europe with Asia Minor. The two main parts of Turkey are European Turkey (Thrane), and Asia Minor (called Anatolia by the Turks). Asia Minor has 97 percent of the territory and 85 percent of the population. Asia Minor is separated from European Turkey by three bodies of water connecting the Mediterranean and Black Seas, known as the Turkish Straits. Anatolia is bordered to the north and east by the Black Sea, to the east and south by Iran, and to the southeast by Iraq and Syria. Cypress lies offshore to the south and is currently divided between Greek and Turkish sectors. European Turkey contains Istanbul. Its widest end, toward the west, borders on Greece and Bulgaria.

- **Language and Currency:** The official language of the country is Turkish, but many Turks in the business sector speak European and Middle Eastern languages. Many better-educated people speak fluent English and use it in business and government circles. The monetary unit is the lira. Bills are in: TL10,000, 5,000, 1,000, 500, 100, 50, 20, 10, and 5. Coins are in: TL20, 10, 5, 2.5, and 1. The exchange rate is 11,248 lira = U.S.$1 (July 30, 1993). Do not become involved in the exchange of currency in the streets. Violators are punished severely, and illegal exchanges sometimes result in receiving counterfeit currency. The black market exists not because there is a lack of money, but because Turks wish to acquire American money to travel abroad.

- **Climate:** The climate of Turkey has three separate zones. The Black Sea area, which includes Istanbul and European Turkey, has warm summers and mild winters with an average temperature of 41°F in January and 75°F in July. Rainfall is greatest in this area. The central region, including Ankara, has warm and dry summers with an average temperature of 72°F. Winter temperatures average about 37°F. The coastal region has a Mediterranean climate with average temperatures in January of 45°F, and 79°F in July. Turkey's climate is comparable to that of the mid-Atlantic seaboard of the United States.

- **Economy and Resources:** Turkey experienced some major changes in the 1980s. Free market principles made Turkey one of the fastest growing economies in the OECD. Private industry has become more important, too, but the State Economic Enterprise (SEE) is still responsible for 40 percent of the total industrial output of the country. Industry accounts for 24 percent of the gross domestic product (GDP), producing mainly textiles, metals, and motor vehicles. Agriculture, however, is the backbone of Turkey's economy, generating 19 percent of the GDP and 25 percent of major exports. Over half of the people work in agriculture-related areas. Major exports include wheat, cotton, fruits and nuts, tobacco, and sugar beets. Mining reserves are sufficient, but Turkey is still dependent on imported oil. It is currently searching for other energy alternatives, including hydroelectric and nuclear sources.

- **Cost of Living:** At 101, the cost of living is practically equal to that of the United States.

- **Work Permits, Visas, etc.:** A valid passport is needed for a visit of up to three months, and longer stays require a multiple-entry visa. For a business visa, an employee must apply through his/her company, which in turn, contacts the Minister of the Interior in Turkey. The Turkish consulate approves the visa. Resident visas can only be obtained after arrival in Turkey. When entering Turkey from the United States, no vaccinations are required. For official or other information, contact the embassy or consulate at the addresses below.

- **Taxation:** All income earned while living in Turkey is subject to Turkish income tax, especially for foreign residents. Currently, no treaty exists between the United States and Turkey for the avoidance of double taxation, but individuals may qualify for deductions and personal allowances.

- **Principal International Schools:** Principal international schools are available in Istanbul. Tuition rates range from $825 to $4,675 per year. One American-sponsored school is the Istanbul International Community School, PK. 29 Bebek 80801, Istanbul, Turkey.

- **Health Care:** Medical care in Turkey is considered adequate. Their equivalent to our Red Cross is the Red Crescent, and it provides government-paid health stations throughout Turkey. Large cities have well-equipped medical facilities,but the outlying rural areas do not. Turkish doctors are well-trained and most of the medical personnel in Istanbul hospitals speak English. Americans often use the American Hospital in Istanbul. Tap water is safe in Istanbul, but use bottled water elsewhere. Appropriate precautions should be taken with all fruits and vegetables. Air pollution creates some problems, so be prepared for some eye or nose irritation.

- **Crime:** It is generally a safe country except for isolated incidents, but the State Department has issued a travel alert for U.S. citizens traveling to Turkey, as there have been a number of urban terrorist attacks in the past. Check with the U.S. Embassy in Ankara or a U.S. Consulate in Istanbul or Izmir on travel and safety conditions before going to Turkey. Take precautions, do not leave valuables unattended, and park vehicles in guarded lots. Women should be especially careful and not visit unknown parts of the country on their own.

- **Pros and Cons of Living and Working in Turkey:** Turkey offers cultural and sightseeing opportunities, and Istanbul has interesting cobblestone streets, medieval architecture, and peddlers offering wares. As the only city in the world to be built on two continents, Istanbul, originally called Constantinople, has been an important crossroads in world history. Costs for most items are reasonable throughout Turkey, and transportation and communications are good. Though housing is adequate and reasonably priced, it may be difficult to find, and in some cases you might have to provide one year's rent in advance when signing a lease. Traffic in the cities is very congested, and the streets are noisy with people and music at all hours, including late into the night. Air pollution presents some problems, and Turkey is in an earthquake-prone area. Turkey is an Is-

EMBASSY AND CONSULATE CONTACT INFORMATION:

EMBASSY OF THE REPUBLIC OF TURKEY
1606 23RD ST. NW
WASHINGTON, DC 20008
TEL: 202-387-3200

CONSULATE GENERAL OF TURKEY
50 ROCKEFELLER PLAZA
NEW YORK, NY 10020
TEL: 212-949-0160

lamic culture, with customs strictly adhered to; showing open signs of affection in public is forbidden, and shoes must be removed when visiting mosques. Study the culture before taking a trip to Turkey, and you'll know what to expect.

OTHER SOURCES OF INFORMATION:

TURKISH GOVERNMENT TOURISM AND
INFORMATION OFFICE
821 UNITED NATIONS PLAZA
NEW YORK, NY 10017
TEL: 212-687-2194

COMPANIES/ORGANIZATIONS WITH OPERATIONS IN TURKEY:

THE BANK OF NEW YORK COMPANY,
   INC., 154
BLACK & VEATCH, 168
BROWN & WILLIAMSON TOBACCO
   CORPORATION, 177
DE LEUW, CATHER INTERNATIONAL, 228
GENERAL DYNAMICS CORPORATION, 274
INTERNATIONAL DATA GROUP, INC., 316

INTERNATIONAL FLAVORS &
   FRAGRANCES, INC., 317
ITT CORPORATION, 321
JAMES RIVER CORPORATION, 323
MOBIL OIL CORPORATION, 375
PARSONS BRINKERHOFF, 406
PHILIP MORRIS COMPANIES, INC., 413
STANDARD COMMERCIAL CORPORATION,
   476

UKRAINE

- **Official Name:** Ukraine
- **Capital:** Kiev
- **Location:** Located in east-central Europe, Ukraine has a total land area of 233,090 square miles, making it twice the size of Arizona. It is bounded by Belarus to the north; Russian Federation to the northeast and east; Sea of Azov and the Black Sea to the south; Moldova and Romania to the southwest; and Hungary, Slovakia, and Poland to the west. It is a country rich in farmlands, and it also has significant industrial and mining regions.
- **Language and Currency:** The official language of Ukraine is Ukrainian. Russian and other ethnic languages are also spoken. If you are going to live or work in this country, you should have a basic knowledge of Ukrainian. The monetary unit is the ruble. The current exchange rate is .000603 Rubles = U.S.$1 (March 1994).

**EMBASSY AND CONSULATE CONTACT
INFORMATION:**

EMBASSY OF UKRAINE
3350 M ST. NW
WASHINGTON, DC 20007
TEL: 202-333-0606

OTHER SOURCES OF INFORMATION:

U.S. COMMERCE DEPARTMENT
OFFICE OF EAST EUROPEAN AND SOVIET
AFFAIRS
WASHINGTON, DC 20230
TEL: 202-377-4655

COMPANIES/ORGANIZATIONS WITH OPERATIONS IN UKRAINE:

NATIONAL DEMOCRATIC INSTITUTE, 557

TAMBRANDS, INC., 486

UNITED ARAB EMIRATES

- **Official Name:** United Arab Emirates
- **Capital:** Abu Dhabi
- **Location:** Seven countries are joined together to form the United Arab Emirates (UAE), located on the eastern side of the Arabian peninsula. They are Abu Dhabi, Dubai, Sharjah, Ras al-Khaimah, Ajman, Umm al Quaiwain, and Fujairah. The land area totals 77,700 square miles, making it comparable in size to South Dakota. The UAE is bounded by the Persian Gulf to the north, the Gulf of Oman to the northeast, Oman to the southeast, Saudi Arabia to the south and west, and Qatar to the northwest. Most of the country is hot and dry with the exception of the extreme northeast section where some rain does fall, allowing for a little cultivation. The most populous areas are along the coastal sections of the United Arab Emirates.
- **Population, Cities, and American Residents:** The population of the United Arab Emirates totals 2.4 million (1992 est.). Less than 25 percent of the people were born in the UAE. Nearly 50 percent are South Asian, 23 percent are Arab, 19 percent are Emirian, and 8 percent are other groups, including expatriates, Westerners, and East Asian people.

  Most American residents are employed in The UAE's three largest cities: Abu Dhabi with 670,000 people, Dubai with 419,000, and Sharjah with 269,000 (1987 est.).
- **Language and Currency:** The official language of the United Arab Emirates is Arabic, but English is widely spoken in business circles. Other languages spoken are Farsi and Urdu. The monetary unit is the UAE dirham. It is hard currency and has had a fixed rate to the dollar since 1980. The exchange rate is: UD3.67= U.S.$1 (July 30, 1993).
- **Climate:** Summers in the United Arab Emirates are extremely hot and humid, especially along the coast. Temperatures range from 90°F to 120°F from July through September. During the winter season, temperatures range from 65°F to 80°F, with cool nights. January is the coldest month, with daytime temperatures in Abu Dhabi averaging at 60°F. Rain is infrequent except for an occasional torrential downfall at the end of winter. Sandstorms are frequent and can be very annoying.
- **Economy and Resources:** The United Arab Emirates is the sixth largest exporter of oil in the Middle East. Exploration is performed on a continuing basis, and oil production is expected to continue for at least the next 75 years. Abu Dhabi accounts for 60 percent of UAE's gross domestic product (GDP), and Dubai accounts for 25 percent. Oil and gas are the country's only natural resources, so officials are searching for other channels of economic development for the future. The seven UAE countries are coordinating economic policies to manage mutual investment funds, to increase labor mobility, and to stimulate capital flow. Nearly 80 percent of the work force is foreign-born and 85 percent is engaged in industry and commerce. Major trading partners are the United States and the European Community.
- **Cost of Living:** At 104, the cost of living is slightly higher than in the United States.

- **Work Permits, Visas, etc.:** A valid passport and visa are required to travel in the UAE, but entry to the country will be denied if there is any evidence of travel to Israel or South Africa. A residence permit and identification card are required to work in the UAE. When entering the UAE from the United States, no vaccinations are required, but precautions against hepatitis, typhoid, polio, malaria, and tetanus are advisable. For official or other information, direct inquiries to the embassy or consulate at the addresses below.

- **Taxation:** There are no federal, personal income, sales, or property taxes in the United Arab Emirates. There are various other taxes, however, including municipal taxes on rental, commercial, or residential properties.

- **Principal International Schools:** International schools available are in Abu Dhabi and Dubai. The annual tuition for an American school is about $6,000 in Abu Dhabi, and $12,000 in Dubai.

- **Health Care:** Medical care is adequate in the major cities of the United Arab Emirates, as most medical personnel are recruited in Europe and the Western Hemisphere. Fees for services are reasonable, and most simple medical problems can be handled locally. For serious health ailments, however, seek another facility in Europe. Sanitary standards are below those in the United States. Water is supposed to be safe in large cities, but unless you're in a major hotel, boil or filter tap water before drinking. The dry winds can also cause problems, especially for people who already have respiratory problems.

- **Crime:** Serious crime is not a major problem in the United Arab Emirates. Legal codes can be a bit confusing, however, as each emirate is different. Two legal codes exist in the country: the civil-criminal system and the customary Sharia code of Islam. In Abu Dhabi, alcohol is allowed, but in Sharjah it is strictly forbidden. There are stiff fines for violating the laws of the country, so learning the legal codes can save a great deal of trouble in the long run.

- **Pros and Cons of Living and Working in the United Arab Emirates:** The United Arab Emirates offer museums, forts, and archaeological sites. Housing is available, although largely in the form of cement-block bungalows or apartment complexes. For rentals, advance payment in full is usually required. Be careful when driving, as pedestrians have the absolute right of way and animals wander freely in the streets. Should an accident happen, fines may be severe and court cases drag on for a very long time. It's wise to know the basic laws of each emirate and to remember that the country is conservative and religious. As in all Islamic countries, everything shuts down on Friday for religious observances.

EMBASSY AND CONSULATE CONTACT INFORMATION:

EMBASSY OF THE UNITED ARAB EMIRATES
600 NEW HAMPSHIRE AVE. NW
WASHINGTON, DC 20037
TEL: 202-338-6500
VISA INFO.: 202-337-1121

U.S. CONSULATE GENERAL
DUBAI INTERNATIONAL TRADE CENTER
PO BOX #9343, DUBAI

OTHER SOURCES OF INFORMATION:

ARAB INFORMATION CENTER
747 THIRD AVE.
NEW YORK, NY 10017
TEL: 212-838-8700

COMPANIES/ORGANIZATIONS WITH OPERATIONS IN UNITED ARAB EMIRATES:

ABB VETCO GRAY, INC., 108
BECHTEL GROUP, INC., 162
BLACK & DECKER CORPORATION, 167
CHADBOURNE & PARKE, 189
CORE LABORATORIES, 214
D'ARCY MASIUS BENTON & BOWLES INC., 225
DE LEUW, CATHER INTERNATIONAL, 228
EASTMAN KODAK COMPANY, 246
FMC CORPORATION, 266
FUGRO-MCCLELLAND USA, INC., 269
HALLIBURTON COMPANY, 292
HOLIDAY INNS WORLDWIDE, 302
HUGHES CHRISTENSEN COMPANY, 307
HYATT INTERNATIONAL CORPORATION, 308
IMS AMERICA, LTD., 311
KEYSTONE INTERNATIONAL, 334
MCDERMOTT INTERNATIONAL, INC., 356
MERRILL LYNCH & COMPANY, INC., 369

NL INDUSTRIES, INC., 388
OCEANEERING INTERNATIONAL, INC., 393
OFFSHORE LOGISTICS, 394
PARSONS CORPORATION, 406
PENROD DRILLING CORPORATION, 408
PEPSICO FOODS INTERNATIONAL, 409
READING & BATES, 433
SEA-LAND SERVICE, INC., 454
SHEARMAN & STERLING, 460
SMITH INTERNATIONAL, INC., 467
SONAT, INC., 469
SONAT OFFSHORE, 470
SOUTHWIRE COMPANY, 472
SPERRY-SUN, INC., 473
STONE & WEBSTER ENGINEERING CORPORATION, 480
TRANE COMPANY, 501
TURNER STEINER INTERNATIONAL, INC., 504

COUNTRY PROFILES

UNITED KINGDOM

- **Official Name:** The United Kingdom of Great Britain and Northern Ireland
- **Capital:** Great Britain
- **Location:** Great Britain is located on the British islands off the coast of northwestern Europe. It is bounded to the west by the Republic of Ireland and the Atlantic Ocean, to the northwest by the Atlantic, to the east by the North Sea, and separated from France by the English Channel to the south. Its total land area is 94,249 square miles, making it comparable in size to Oregon. The United Kingdom has four basic parts: England, the most dominant, shares the island of Great Britain with Scotland and Wales. The fourth part (on the northeast corner of the island of Ireland) is Northern Ireland. The United Kingdom also includes the Channel Islands off the coast of France, and the Isle of Man located in the Irish Sea.
- **Population, Cities, and American Residents:** The population of Great Britain totals 57.6 million (1992 est.). The two main population groups are the English, with 81.5 percent, and the Scottish, with 9.6 percent. Irish, Welsh, Ulster, Indian, West Indian, and Pakistani account for the balance. Descendants from the current population are from various groups who settled in the country prior to the start of the 11th century. Today, approximately 46 million people are English, 5 million are Scottish, 3 million are Welsh, and 1.5 million are Northern Irish. The remainder is composed of other mixed groups.

Most American residents are employed in Great Britain's three major cities: London with 6.8 million people, Birmingham with 2.4 million, and Glasgow with 900,000 (1989 est.).

- **Language and Currency:** The official language of the United Kingdom is English. The monetary unit is the British pound, divided into 100 pence. Money is written with the mark of the pound, £, or "p" for pence. Only one identifying letter is used on currency. The exchange rate is 1 British pound = U.S.$1.48 (July 30, 1993).

- **Climate:** The United Kingdom has a very damp climate, and the winds off the ocean, the stone construction of most buildings, and the lack of central heating make it feel much colder than it really is. England's daytime temperature ranges from 20°F to 81°F. The warmest month is July (about 73°F), and the coldest month is January (average 30°F). The substantial amount of rain and fog allow for the foliage to be lush and green, evident in the abundant flowering gardens. Scotland has a temperate climate, with a good deal of rain, and winters tend to be on the cold side (about 20°F). Wales, in the western region of the United Kingdom, will see snow for four to five months in the winter. Northern Ireland has warm summers and cold winters accompanied by strong winds. Rain gear is recommended throughout the year.

- **Economy and Resources:** The United Kingdom is a main manufacturing and trading nation. One-third of the gross domestic product (GDP) is derived from industry, concentrating on durable goods. These include aerospace products, electrical equipment, machinery, chemicals, and oil. Nearly one-quarter of the GDP is generated by overseas trade, with the United States as its biggest trading partner. The United Kingdom is almost self-sufficient in food products, but is a net importer of manufactured goods. Natural resources include coal, crude oil, and tin. Chief exports are manufactured goods and machinery, fuels, and transport equipment. Of the labor force, 52.1 percent of the people work in goods and services, and 23.4 are engaged in manufacturing and construction. The labor market has been disrupted by economic restructuring, and the country has been troubled by unemployment and inflation. The south of England has maintained its prosperity better than Scotland and other regions in the northern section of the country.

- **Cost of Living:** The cost of living in the United Kingdom varies with each area. England at 151, is much higher than the United States. Belfast is at 118 and Oxfordshire is at 126.

- **Work Permits, Visas, etc.:** To travel in Great Britain, a valid passport is required. To work in the country, a foreign national needs a work permit issued by the British Department of Employment in England, Scotland, and Wales, and the Department of Economic Development in Northern Ireland. It must be presented upon arrival in Britain, and those holding work permits must be registered with the police after arrival in the country. Contact the British Information Service for more information. If you are entering the United Kingdom from the United States, no vaccinations are required. For official or other information, direct inquiries to the embassy or consulate at the addresses below.

- **Taxation:** Residents are taxed on income from all sources while living in the United

Kingdom. Nonresidents are taxed on U.K. income only. An individual is considered a resident if he or she is actually present in the U.K. for a period of six months of the income tax year, running from April 6 to April 5. You are also deemed a resident if you are present in the U.K. for two-to-three months for four successive years or own property there.

- **Principal International Schools:** Many international schools are scattered throughout the United Kingdom. Tuition for an American school is about $6,000.

- **Health Care:** Medical facilities in the United Kingdom are comparable to those in the United States. The National Health Service is free and usually made available to foreign residents who work in the country for more than six months. It is important to get your name on the "list" of a local practitioner as soon as possible once you are in the United Kingdom. These lists are available at local pharmacies or post offices, and are sometimes full, so take care of this before you need medical attention. Sanitary conditions throughout the country are good, and water is safe to drink.

- **Crime:** Britain has a high incidence of common crime, one of the highest in Europe. Be on guard for pickpockets and purse snatchers and be especially careful at night. Avoid poorly lit streets, and try to stay in a group of people, particularly when riding subways or public transportation systems.

- **Pros and Cons of Living and Working in The United Kingdom:** The United Kingdom has a great deal to offer. The countryside is quite beautiful, and London is regarded by many as the theater capital of the world. It also offers parks, museums, and an array of other tourist attractions. Transportation and telecommunications services are very good, although installation can be quite slow. Living in the United Kingdom, particularly London, can be more expensive than in the United States. Housing is becoming difficult to find, and is very costly. Be extremely cautious when signing lease agreements; having a lawyer present is recommended. Pack your umbrella and warm clothing, as Britain has a damp, chilly climate a good deal of the time.

EMBASSY AND CONSULATE CONTACT INFORMATION:

BRITISH EMBASSY
3100 MASSACHUSETTS AVE. NW
WASHINGTON, DC 20008
TEL: 202-462-1340

OTHER SOURCES OF INFORMATION:

BRITISH-AMERICAN CHAMBER OF COMMERCE
275 MADISON AVE.
NEW YORK, NY 10016
TEL: 212-889-0680

COMPANIES/ORGANIZATIONS WITH OPERATIONS IN UNITED KINGDOM:

ABB VETCO GRAY, INC., 108
ABBOTT LABORATORIES, 109
ACCO WORLD CORPORATION, 110
ACUSHNET COMPANY, 111
ADVANCE MACHINE COMPANY, 111
ADVANCED MICRO DEVICES, INC., 112
AIRBORNE EXPRESS, 112
AKZO AMERICA, INC., 113

ALARM DEVICE MANUFACTURING COMPANY, 114
ALBANY INTERNATIONAL CORPORATION, 114
ALBERTO-CULVER COMPANY, 115
ALDUS CORPORATION, 115
ALEXANDER & ALEXANDER SERVICES, INC., 116
ALLEN-BRADLEY COMPANY, INC., 116

A
M
E
R
I
C
A
N

J
O
B
S

A
B
R
O
A
D

ALLIS MINERAL SYSTEMS/SVEDALA
INDUSTRIES, INC., 118
AM INTERNATIONAL, INC., 119
AMDAHL CORPORATION, 120
AMERADA HESS CORPORATION, 121
AMERICAN APPRAISAL ASSOCIATES, INC.,
121
AMERICAN BANKERS INSURANCE GROUP,
INC., 122
AMERICAN CYANAMID COMPANY, 124
AMERICAN EXPRESS BANK, LTD., 124
AMERICAN EXPRESS COMPANY—TRAVEL
RELATED SERVICES, 125
AMERICAN GREETINGS CORPORATION,
126
AMERICAN HOME PRODUCTS
CORPORATION, 126
AMERICAN MANAGEMENT SYSTEMS, INC.,
127
AMERICAN UNIFORM COMPANY, 129
AMETEK, INC., 130
AMGEN, INC., 131
AMR/AMERICAN AIRLINES, 133
ANDREW CORPORATION, 134
ANSELL INTERNATIONAL, 135
ANTHONY INDUSTRIES, 135
AON CORPORATION, 136
APPLE COMPUTER, INC., 136
APPLIED BIOSCIENCE INTERNATIONAL,
INC., 137
APPLIED MATERIALS, INC., 137
ARCHER-DANIELS-MIDLAND COMPANY,
138
ARCO COAL COMPANY, 139
ARCO INTERNATIONAL OIL AND GAS
COMPANY, 139
ARETHUSA OFFSHORE, 140
ARMCO, INC., 140
ARMOUR SWIFT ECKRICH, INC., 141
ARMSTRONG WORLD INDUSTRIES, INC.,
141
ASEA BROWN BOVERI, 142
ASHLAND OIL, INC., 143
ASSOCIATED PRESS, 144
ATARI CORPORATION, 146
AUGAT, INC., 146
AUTOMATIC SWITCH COMPANY, 147
AVERY DENNISON CORPORATION, 147
AVNET, INC., 148
AVX CORPORATION, 150

BADGER COMPANY, INC., 151
BAILEY CONTROLS COMPANY, 151
BAKER HUGHES, INC., 152
BANCTEC, INC., 152
BANDAG, INC., 153
THE BANK OF NEW YORK COMPANY,
INC., 154
BANKAMERICA CORPORATION, 155
BANYAN SYSTEMS, INC., 156
C. R. BARD, INC., 157
THE BARDEN CORPORATION, 157
BAXTER HEALTHCARE CORPORATION, 160
JIM BEAM BRANDS COMPANY, 161
BEAR STEARNS COMPANIES, INC., 161
BELL HELICOPTER TEXTRON, INC., 163
BELL & HOWELL COMPANY, 164
LOUIS BERGER INTERNATIONAL INC., 165
BETZ LABORATORIES, 166
BIO-RAD LABORATORIES, 166
BISSELL, INC., 167
BLACK & DECKER CORPORATION, 167
BLACK & VEATCH, 168
BLOCK DRUG COMPANY, INC., 169
BLOUNT, INC. (BLOUNT CONSTRUCTION
DIVISION), 169
BORDEN, INC., 170
BORG-WARNER CORPORATION, 171
BORLAND INTERNATIONAL, INC, 172
BOSE CORPORATION, 172
BP AMERICA, INC., 173
W. H. BRADY COMPANY, 173
BROWN & SHARPE MANUFACTURING
COMPANY, 176
BROWNING-FERRIS INDUSTRIES, 177
BRUSH WELLMAN, INC., 178
BUCK CONSULTANTS, INC., 178
BURLINGTON AIR EXPRESS, 179
BURNS INTERNATIONAL SECURITY
SERVICES, 179
BURSON-MARSTELLER, 180
CALGON CORPORATION, 182
CALIFORNIA PELLET MILL COMPANY, 182
CAMPBELL SOUP COMPANY, 183
CARGILL INCORPORATED, 184
CARLSON TRAVEL NETWORK, 185
CARRIER CORPORATION, 186
CARTER-WALLACE, INC., 187
J. I. CASE COMPANY, 187
CHARTER MEDICAL CORPORATION, 190
CHASE MANHATTAN CORPORATION, 190

CHEMICAL BANKING CORPORATION, 191
CHEMICAL FABRICS CORPORATION, 192
CHEVRON OVERSEAS PETROLEUM, INC., 194
CH2M HILL INTERNATIONAL, LTD., 195
CIGNA CORPORATION, 197
CINCOM SYSTEMS, INC., 197
CLARCOR, INC., 198
CLOROX COMPANY, 199
CLUB CORPORATION INTERNATIONAL, 200
THE COASTAL GROUP, 201
COHERENT, INC., 202
COLTEC INDUSTRIES, INC., 204
COMMERCE CLEARING HOUSE, 205
COMMERCIAL INTERTECH CORPORATION, 205
COMMODORE INTERNATIONAL LTD., 206
COMPAQ COMPUTERS CORPORATION, 207
COMPUTERVISION CORPORATION, 208
CONTINENTAL AIRLINES HOLDINGS, INC., 210
CONTINENTAL BANK CORPORATION, 210
CONTINENTAL GRAIN COMPANY, 211
CONTINUUM COMPANY, INC., 211
CONVERSE, INC., 212
COOPER ENERGY SERVICES, LTD., 212
COOPER INDUSTRIES, INC., 213
COOPERS & LYBRAND, 214
CORE LABORATORIES, 214
CORE STATES FINANCIAL CORPORATION, 215
WILLIS CORROON, 216
CPC INTERNATIONAL, INC., 217
JOHN CRANE, INC., 218
CRS SIRRINE, INC., 219
CTS CORPORATION, 220
CUBIC CORPORATION, 220
CUC INTERNATIONAL, INC., 221
CUMMINS ENGINE COMPANY, INC., 221
D-M-E COMPANY, 222
D'ARCY MASIUS BENTON & BOWLES INC., 225
DAY & ZIMMERMAN, 226
DAYCO PRODUCTS, INC., 226
DDB NEEDHAM WORLDWIDE, INC., 227
DEAN WITTER, DISCOVER & COMPANY, 228
DEBEVOISE & PLIMPTON, 229
DEERE & COMPANY, 229
DELL COMPUTER CORPORATION, 231

DELOITTE & TOUCHE, 231
DELTA AIR LINES, INC., 232
THE DEXTER CORPORATION, 233
DH TECHNOLOGY, INC., 233
DIAMOND M-ODECO DRILLING, INC., 234
DIEBOLD INCORPORATED, 235
DIGICON, INC., 235
DIGITAL EQUIPMENT CORPORATION, 236
DIXON TICONDEROGA COMPANY, 236
DOMINO'S PIZZA, INC., 237
DONALDSON COMPANY, INC., 237
DONALDSON LUFKIN & JENRETTE, INC., 238
R. R. DONNELLEY & SONS COMPANY, 238
REUBEN H. DONNELLY, 239
DOVER CORPORATION, 239
DOW CHEMICAL COMPANY, 240
DOW CORNING CORPORATION, 240
DRUMMOND COMPANY, INC., 242
DUN & BRADSTREET CORPORATION, 243
DURACELL, INC., 244
DURIRON COMPANY, INC., 244
EAGLE-PICHER INDUSTRIES, INC., 246
EASTMAN KODAK COMPANY, 246
EATON CORPORATION/CUTLER HAMMER, 247
EBASCO OVERSEAS CORPORATION, 248
EG & G, INC., 249
ELECTRONIC DATA SYSTEMS CORPORATION, 249
ELI LILLY AND COMPANY, 250
ELIZABETH ARDEN COMPANY, 251
EMERY WORLDWIDE, 252
ENCYCLOPEDIA BRITANNICA, INC., 253
ENGELHARD CORPORATION, 253
ENRON CORPORATION, 254
ENSERCH INTERNATIONAL DEVELOPMENT, INC., 254
EXPEDITORS INTERNATIONAL OF WASHINGTON, INC., 257
EXXON CORPORATION, 258
FAIRCHILD PUBLICATIONS, INC., 259
FEDERAL EXPRESS CORPORATION, 260
FIBRONICS INTERNATIONAL, INC., 261
FIGGIE INTERNATIONAL, INC., 262
FIRST CHICAGO CORPORATION, 262
FISCHER & PORTER COMPANY, 263
FISHER CONTROLS INTERNATIONAL, INC., 263

COUNTRY PROFILES

A
M
E
R
I
C
A
N

J
O
B
S

A
B
R
O
A
D

FLUOR CORPORATION, 266
FMC CORPORATION, 266
FORD MOTOR COMPANY, 267
FRITZ COMPANIES, 269
FULLER COMPANY, 269
GAF CORPORATION, 270
GAFNEY, CLINE & ASSOCIATES, INC., 271
GALEN HEALTH CARE, 271
GANNETT COMPANY, INC., 272
THE GATES RUBBER COMPANY, 273
GATX CORPORATION, 273
GENERAL ELECTRIC COMPANY (GE), 275
GENERAL FOODS USA, 276
GENERAL INSTRUMENT CORPORATION, 276
GENERAL MOTORS CORPORATION (GM), 277
GETZ BROTHERS COMPANY, INC., 281
GIDDINGS & LEWIS, INC., 282
GILBERT/COMMONWEALTH INTERNATIONAL, INC., 282
THE GILLETTE COMPANY, 283
GOODYEAR TIRE & RUBBER COMPANY, 284
W. R. GRACE & COMPANY, 285
GRACO, INC., 286
GRANT THORNTON INTERNATIONAL, 286
GREAT LAKES CARBON INTERNATIONAL CORPORATION, 287
GREAT LAKES CHEMICAL CORPORATION, 287
A. P. GREEN INDUSTRIES, INC., 287
GREY ADVERTISING, INC., 288
H. J. HEINZ COMPANY, 290
HALLIBURTON COMPANY, 292
HALLIBURTON COMPANY/HALLIBURTON SERVICES DIVISION, 293
HALLMARK CARDS, INC., 294
HAMLIN, INC., 294
HANSON INDUSTRIES, 295
HARRIS CORPORATION, 296
HAZLETON WASHINGTON CORPORATION, 297
HELLMUTH, OBATA & KASSABAUM, INC., 298
HERCULES, INC., 299
HERTZ CORPORATION, 300
HEWLETT-PACKARD COMPANY, 300
HOECHST CELANESE, INC., 302
HONEYWELL, INC., 303

HORMEL FOODS CORPORATION, 304
HOUSEHOLD INTERNATIONAL, INC., 305
HUBBELL, INC., 306
HUGHES AIRCRAFT COMPANY, 307
HUGHES CHRISTENSEN COMPANY, 307
ICF KAISER ENGINEERS, 308
IDB COMMUNICATIONS, INC., 309
ILLINOIS TOOL WORKS, INC., 309
IMCERA GROUP, INC., 310
IMO INDUSTRIES, 310
INDUCTOTHERM CORPORATION, 311
INFORMATION BUILDERS, INC., 312
INGERSOLL ENGINEERS, 312
INGERSOLL INTERNATIONAL, INC., 313
INGERSOLL-RAND COMPANY, 313
INTEL CORPORATION, 314
INTERNATIONAL DAIRY QUEEN, INC., 316
INTERNATIONAL FLAVORS & FRAGRANCES, INC., 317
INTERNATIONAL PAPER COMPANY, 318
INTERNATIONAL RECTIFIER CORPORATION, 319
INTERNATIONAL TOTALIZATOR SYSTEMS, INC., 319
IOMEGA CORPORATION, 320
ITT CORPORATION, 321
ITT HARTFORD INSURANCE GROUP, 321
ITT SHERATON CORPORATION, 322
ITW FINISHING SYSTEMS & PRODUCTS, 322
JAMES RIVER CORPORATION, 323
JMK INTERNATIONAL/JAMACK FABRICATIONS, INC., 323
JOHNSON CONTROLS, INC., 324
JOHNSON & JOHNSON, 325
JONES, DAY, REAVIS & POGUE, INC., 326
JOURNAL OF COMMERCE, 326
JOY TECHNOLOGIES, INC., 327
JWP, INC., 328
KAMAN CORPORATION, 328
A. T. KEARNEY, INC., 329
KELLOGG COMPANY, 330
M. W. KELLOGG COMPANY, 331
KELLWOOD COMPANY, 331
KENDALL INTERNATIONAL, 332
KENNAMETAL, INC., 333
KENNECOTT CORPORATION, 333
KETCHUM INTERNATIONAL, 334
KEYSTONE INTERNATIONAL, 334
KFC CORPORATION, 335

KIDDER PEABODY GROUP & COMPANY, INC., 335
KIMBALL INTERNATIONAL, INC., 336
KIMBERLY-CLARK CORPORATION, 336
KNIGHT-RIDDER, INC., 338
KNOLL INTERNATIONAL, 338
KOHLER COMPANY, 339
LAMBDA ELECTRONICS, INC., 343
LAW COMPANIES GROUP, INC., 343
LAWTER INTERNATIONAL, INC., 344
LIANT SOFTWARE CORPORATION, 345
THE LIMITED, INC., 345
THE LINCOLN ELECTRIC COMPANY, 346
LINTAS: WORLDWIDE, 346
ARTHUR D. LITTLE, INC., 347
LIZ CLAIBORNE, INC., 348
LOCTITE CORPORATION, 349
LORAL CORPORATION, 350
LORD CORPORATION, 350
LOUISIANA LAND & EXPLORATION COMPANY, 352
LUBRIZOL CORPORATION, 353
LYKES LINES, 354
MACDERMID, INC., 355
MALLINCKRODT, INC., 359
MARATHON PETROLEUM COMPANY, 359
MARION MERRELL DOW, INC., 360
MARRIOTT CORPORATION, 360
MASCO CORPORATION, 361
MASONEILAN INDUSTRIES, INC., 361
MASTER LOCK COMPANY, 362
MAYTAG CORPORATION, 364
MCCANN-ERICKSON WORLDWIDE, 354
MCCORMICK & COMPANY, INC., 355
MCDONALD'S CORPORATION, 356
MCGRAW-HILL, INC., 357
MEAD CORPORATION, 365
MEASUREX CORPORATION, 366
MEMOREX TELEX CORPORATION, 367
MERCK & COMPANY, INC., 368
MERISEL, INC., 369
MERRILL LYNCH & COMPANY, INC., 369
METALLURG CORPORATION, 370
METROPOLITAN LIFE INSURANCE COMPANY, 371
MGM INCORPORATED, 372
MILLER BREWING COMPANY, 372
HERMAN MILLER, INC., 373
MILLIKEN & COMPANY, 373
MMS INTERNATIONAL, 374

MONSANTO COMPANY, 377
MOORE PRODUCTS COMPANY, 378
J. P. MORGAN & COMPANY, INC., 378
MORGAN STANLEY GROUP, INC., 379
MORRISON KNUDSEN CORPORATION, 379
MORTON INTERNATIONAL, 380
MOTION PICTURE EXPORT ASSOCIATION OF AMERICA, 380
MOTOROLA, INC., 381
NABORS INDUSTRIES, INC., 381
NATIONAL DATA CORPORATION, 382
NELLCOR, INC., 385
NEW YORK TIMES COMPANY, 386
NEWSWEEK INTERNATIONAL, 387
NICOLET INSTRUMENT CORPORATION, 387
NORDSON CORPORATION, 389
NORTHWEST AIRLINES, INC., 390
NORTON COMPANY, 390
NOVELL, INC., 392
NYNEX CORPORATION, 392
OCCIDENTAL PETROLEUM CORPORATION, 393
OCEANEERING INTERNATIONAL, INC., 393
OGDEN CORPORATION, 395
OGILVY & MATHER, 395
OLIN CORPORATION, 396
OMNICOM GROUP, INC., 397
ONAN CORPORATION, 397
OPPENHEIMER GROUP, 398
ORACLE SYSTEMS, INC., 398
ORYX ENERGY, 398
OTIS ELEVATOR COMPANY: WORLD HEADQUARTERS, 399
OVERSEAS SHIPHOLDING GROUP, INC., 400
OWENS-CORNING FIBERGLAS CORPORATION, 400
PACCAR, INC., 401
PACIFIC TELESIS INTERNATIONAL, 403
PAINE WEBBER GROUP, INC., 403
PALL CORPORATION, 404
PARKER HANNIFIN CORPORATION, 405
PARSONS BRINKERHOFF, 406
PARSONS CORPORATION, 406
PENTAIR, INC., 409
PEPSICO FOODS INTERNATIONAL, 409
PEPSICO, INC., 410
PERKIN-ELMER CORPORATION, 410
PETROLITE CORPORATION, 411
PFAUDLER COMPANIES, INC., 411

C
O
U
N
T
R
Y

P
R
O
F
I
L
E
S

A
M
E
R
I
C
A
N

J
O
B
S

A
B
R
O
A
D

PHELPS DODGE CORPORATION, 412
PHIBRO ENERGY, INC., 413
PHILIPP BROTHERS CHEMICALS, INC., 414
PHILLIPS PETROLEUM COMPANY, 415
PILLSBURY COMPANY, 416
PINKERTON'S, INC., 416
PITNEY BOWES, INC., 417
PITTSBURGH-DES MOINES CORPORATION, 418
PITTWAY CORPORATION, 418
PIZZA HUT, INC., 419
PLAYTEX APPAREL, INC., 419
PMI FOOD EQUIPMENT GROUP, 420
POLAROID CORPORATION, 420
R. L. POLK & COMPANY, 421
PPG INDUSTRIES, 421
PRC, INC., 422
PRECISION VALVE CORPORATION, 422
PREFORMED LINE PRODUCTS COMPANY, 423
PREMARK INTERNATIONAL, INC., 423
PRICE WATERHOUSE, 424
PRIMERICA CORPORATION, 424
PRINTRONIX, INC., 425
PROCTER & GAMBLE COMPANY, 425
PROCTER & GAMBLE COSMETICS AND FRAGRANCE PRODUCTS, 426
QUAKER CHEMICAL CORPORATION, 428
QUAKER OATS COMPANY, 428
QUME CORPORATION, 429
RANCO, INC., 431
RAYTHEON COMPANY, 432
READER'S DIGEST ASSOCIATION, INC., 432
READING & BATES, 433
RECOGNITION EQUIPMENT, INC., 433
REDKEN LABORATORIES, INC., 434
REED TOOL COMPANY, 434
REEVES BROTHERS, INC., 435
RELIANCE ELECTRIC COMPANY, 435
RELIANCE INTERNATIONAL, 436
REMINGTON PRODUCTS, INC., 436
REVLON, INC., 437
REYNOLDS METALS COMPANY, 438
RHONE-POULENC RORER, 438
RJR NABISCO, 439
ROBERT HALF INTERNATIONAL, INC., 440
ROBERTSON CECO, 440
ROCKWELL GRAPHIC SYSTEMS, 441

ROCKWELL INTERNATIONAL CORPORATION, 441
ROGERS CORPORATION, 442
ROWAN COMPANIES, INC., 444
RUDER FINN, INC., 445
RUSSELL CORPORATION, 446
RUSSELL REYNOLDS ASSOCIATES, INC., 446
RYDER SYSTEMS, INC., 447
SAINT JUDE MEDICAL, INC., 448
SALOMON, INC., 449
A. SCHULMAN, INC., 451
SCI SYSTEMS, 452
SCIENTIFIC ATLANTA, INC., 452
SCM CHEMICALS, 453
SCOTT PAPER COMPANY, 453
SEA-LAND SERVICE, INC., 454
SEAGATE TECHNOLOGY, INC., 454
SEALED AIR CORPORATION, 455
SEARLE COMPANY, 455
SENCO PRODUCTS, 456
SENSORMATIC ELECTRONICS CORPORATION, 457
SEQUA CORPORATION, 457
SGS CONTROL SERVICES, 458
SGS-THOMSON MICROELECTRONICS, 458
SHAKLEE CORPORATION, 459
SHEAFFER PEN, INC., 459
SHEARMAN & STERLING, 460
SHEARSON LEHMAN BROTHERS, 460
SHERWIN-WILLIAMS COMPANY, 461
SHIPLEY COMPANY, INC., 461
SIGNODE PACKAGING SYSTEMS, 462
SILICONIX, 462
SIMON & SCHUSTER, INC., 463
SIMPLEX TIME RECORDER COMPANY, 463
SIMPLICITY PATTERN COMPANY INC., 464
SKADDEN, ARPS, SLATE, MEAGHER & FLOM, 465
SMITH CORONA CORPORATION, 466
A. O. SMITH CORPORATION, 467
J. M. SMUCKER COMPANY, 468
SNAP-ON TOOLS CORPORATION, 468
SONAT, INC., 469
SONAT OFFSHORE, 470
SONOCO PRODUCTS COMPANY, 470
SONY PICTURES ENTERTAINMENT, 471
SOTHEBY'S HOLDINGS, INC., 471
SOUTHLAND CORPORATION, 472
SPRINGS INDUSTRIES, INC., 473

SPS TECHNOLOGIES, INC., 474

SQUARE D COMPANY, 475

SRI INTERNATIONAL, 475

STANDEX INTERNATIONAL, 477

STANHOME, INC., 477

STATE STREET BOSTON CORPORATION, 478

STEBBINS ENGINEERING & MANUFACTURING CORPORATION, 479

STONE CONTAINER CORPORATION, 480

STONE & WEBSTER ENGINEERING CORPORATION, 480

STORAGE TECHNOLOGY CORPORATION, 481

STRUCTURAL DYNAMICS RESEARCH CORPORATION, 481

SULLIVAN & CROMWELL, 483

SUN COMPANY, INC., 483

SUN ELECTRIC CORPORATION, 484

SUN MICROSYSTEMS, INC., 484

SYMBOL TECHNOLOGIES, INC., 485

SYNTEX CORPORATION, 486

TAMBRANDS, INC., 486

TANDY CORPORATION, 487

TEKTRONIX, INC., 488

TELLABS OPERATIONS, INC., 489

TENNECO, INC., 492

TENNESSEE ASSOCIATES INTERNATIONAL, INC., 492

TERADYNE, INC., 493

TEXACO OIL COMPANY, 493

TEXAS INTRUMENTS, INC., 494

TEXTRON, INC., 494

THERMCO SYSTEMS, INC., 495

THOMAS & BETTS, 495

3M PHARMACEUTICALS, 497

TIME-WARNER, INC., 498

TORRINGTON COMPANY, 499

TOWERS PERRIN, INC., 499

TOYS ''R'' US, INC., 500

TRANE COMPANY, 501

TRANSAMERICA, CORPORATION, 501

TRINOVA CORPORATION, 502

TRITON ENERGY CORPORATION, 502

TRW, INC., 503

TURNER BROADCASTING SYSTEM, INC., 503

UAL CORPORATION, 506

UNILEVER UNITED STATES, INC., 506

UNION CAMP CORPORATION, 507

UNION CARBIDE CORPORATION, 507

UNISYS CORPORATION, 508

UNITED ENGINEERS & CONSTRUCTORS INTERNATIONAL, 508

UNITED PRESS INTERNATIONAL, 509

U.S. ELECTRICAL MOTORS (EMERSON ELECTRIC), 510

U.S. FEDERAL AVIATION ADMINISTRATION, 577

UNITED STATES SHOE CORPORATION, 510

UNITED STATES SURGICAL CORPORATION, 511

UNITED TECHNOLOGIES CORPORATION, 512

UNOCAL CORPORATION, 513

UNUM CORPORATION, 514

UOP, INC., 514

THE UPJOHN COMPANY, 515

US WEST, INC., 515

USAIR GROUP, INC., 516

USX CORPORATION, 516

VF CORPORATION, 517

VISA INTERNATIONAL, 517

VISHAY INTERTECHNOLOGY, 518

WALKER MANUFACTURING COMPANY, 519

WANG LABORATORIES, INC., 519

WARNACO, INC., 520

WARNER-LAMBERT COMPANY, 522

WATERS CHROMATOGRAPHY (MILLIPORE), 523

WEIGHT WATCHERS INTERNATIONAL, INC., 524

WENDY'S INTERNATIONAL, INC., 524

WEST COMPANY, INC., 525

WESTINGHOUSE ELECTRIC CORPORATION, 525

WHITMAN CORPORATION, 527

WMX TECHNOLOGIES/WASTE MANAGEMENT, INC., 527

WOODWARD GOVERNOR COMPANY, 528

WORLD COURIER MANAGEMENT, INC., 529

WILLIAM WRIGLEY JR. COMPANY, 529

WYETH-AYERST LABORATORIES, 530

WYNN'S INTERNATIONAL, INC., 530   YORK INTERNATIONAL, INC., 532
XEROX CORPORATION, 531   YOUNG & RUBICAM, INC., 533

A
M
E
R
I
C
A
N

J
O
B
S

A
B
R
O
A
D

U.S. VIRGIN ISLANDS

- **Official Name:** Virgin Islands of the United States
- **Capital:** Charlotte Amalie
- **Location:** The U.S. Virgin Islands comprise three inhabited islands, St. Croix, St. Thomas, and St. John. It also includes 50 smaller ones, mostly uninhabited and all the islands are located in the northeastern Caribbean Sea. The British Virgin Islands lie to the north, the Netherlands Antilles to the east, the Caribbean Sea to the south, and Puerto Rico (about 40 miles) to the west. The total land area is 136 square miles, making the U.S. Virgin Islands nearly twice the size of Washington, D.C. The southern part of the island is predominantly flat, with hills forming in the northern areas. Numerous sandy beaches and a pleasant year-round climate attract tourists from around the world.
- **Language and Currency:** The official language is English and the monetary unit is the U.S. dollar.
- **Print Source of Information:** Zeller, Margaret, editor. *Fielding's Caribbean.* New York: Fielding Travel Books, William Morrow & Co., 1992.

COMPANIES/ORGANIZATIONS WITH OPERATIONS IN U.S. VIRGIN ISLANDS:

AMERICAN CANADIAN CARIBBEAN LINE, 123

URUGUAY

- **Official Name:** Oriental Republic of Uruguay
- **Capital:** Montevideo
- **Location:** Located on the southeastern coast of South America, Uruguay lies on the mouth of the Rio de la Plata. It is the second-smallest independent country in South America. Uruguay has a total land area of 68,500 square miles, making it comparable in size to Washington. It is bounded by Brazil to the north, the Atlantic Ocean to the east and south, and Argentina to the west. A very scenic country, Uruguay has no distinct land features. Uruguay is primarily composed of coastal plains, the vast interior lowlands, and an abundance of sandy beaches.
- **Population, Cities, and American Residents:** The total population of Uruguay is 3 million people (1992 est.). Nearly 90 percent of the population is white, with mestizo and black accounting for the remainder.

Most Americans are employed in Uruguay's two major cities: Montevideo with 1.3 million and Salto with 88,000 people (1989 est.).

- **Language and Currency:** The official language of Uruguay is Spanish. If you plan to live or work in Uruguay, you should have a basic knowledge of Spanish. The monetary unit is the new Uruguayan peso (written as N$Ur). The current exchange rate is 4.6 N$Ur = U.S.$1 (March 1994).

- **Economy and Resources:** Uruguay, once a rich country, is still recovering from a recession that began during the 1950s. Complicating a troubled economy was the internal political unrest of the 1960s and 1970s. Military officers took control of the government in 1973. The people bitterly protested and when democratic elections were held in 1984, civilian government finally returned.

   Agriculture dominates the economy, accounting for 20 percent of GDP. Chief exports including wheat, rice, corn, and sorghum are traded mainly to the United States, Brazil, Argentina, and Germany. Of the labor force, 25 percent work in government, another 19 percent in manufacturing, 12 percent in agriculture, 12 percent in commerce, and 12 percent in utilities, construction, transport, and communications areas.

   Escalating foreign debt and rising unemployment are two major concerns facing Uruguay today. Domestic growth has been slow due to adverse weather conditions, workers' strikes, and a need to modernize the economic structure. New government reforms include the sale of some state-owned firms, a cut in government spending, and improved financial relationships with other countries. It is hoped that these measures will strengthen the struggling economy.

- **Cost of Living:** At 119, the cost of living is slightly higher than in the United States.

- **Work Permits, Visas, etc.:** A passport is required to travel in Uruguay. A visa is not required for stays up to three months. Official or diplomatic passports and visas must be obtained in advance of the trip. If you are entering Uruguay from the United States, no vaccinations are required. For official or other information, direct inquiries to the embassy or the consulate at the addresses below.

- **Taxation:** Contact the Embassy of Uruguay for current tax information.

- **Principal International Schools:** American schools are available.

- **Health Care:** Sanitation standards and medical facilities are good in Uruguay. There are a number of private hospitals with well-trained personnel. Food and water are safe for consumption, and there are no particular health risks with food.

- **Crime:** Violent crime is not a serious problem in Uruguay. However, street crime is increasing, and travelers should be careful in major tourist areas. Pickpockets and muggers may be present in crowded shopping areas. Take the normal precautions you would in any large city.

- **Pros and Cons of Living and Working in Uruguay:** Uruguay is a fairly modern nation and it offers various tourist sites for travelers. Sandy beaches, the colorful sidewalk cafes of Montevideo, and sporting events are among the attractions. Soccer is the most popular sport in this country, bringing huge crowds to city stadiums. Health and sanitation standards are good in most areas. Telecommunications are good and it's important to remember that Uruguay is two time zones ahead of Eastern Standard Time. Transportation services are adequate, with most roads paved, and taxi service reliable and fairly inexpensive. For best housing selection, arrange in advance for accommodations. United States and Uruguay relations remain friendly, especially since Uruguay's return to democracy. The small nation is still in the process of developing its economy, so there may be a shortage of some goods and services.

EMBASSY AND CONSULATE CONTACT INFORMATION:

EMBASSY OF URUGUAY
1918 F ST. NW
WASHINGTON, DC 20006
TEL: 202-331-1313

OTHER SOURCES OF INFORMATION:

FOR CURRENT UPDATES ON FOREIGN TRAVEL IN URUGUAY, CONTACT: U.S. STATE DEPT.
FOREIGN TRAVEL ADVISORIES
WASHINGTON, DC 20520
TEL: 202-647-5225

COMPANIES/ORGANIZATIONS WITH OPERATIONS IN URUGUAY:

CAMP DRESSER & MCKEE INTERNATIONAL, INC., 183

RESOURCES MANAGEMENT INTERNATIONAL, 437

VENEZUELA

- **Official Name:** Republic of Venezuela
- **Capital:** Caracas
- **Location:** Venezuela is located on the northern coast of South America. It is bounded by the Caribbean Sea to the north, Guiana to the east, Brazil to the south, and Colombia to the west. Venezuela has 1,800 miles of coastline on the Caribbean Sea and 347,031 square miles of total land area, making it about one-and-a-half times the size of Texas. The country has four distinct geographic regions: in the north are the Andean Highlands; to the northwest is the basin of Lake Maracaibo; in the center are the llanos (great plains) and forests; and to the southeast the Guiana Highlands. The Orinoco River, which has over seventy mouths and a delta of almost 9,000 square miles flows into the Atlantic Ocean in the northeastern corner of the country.
- **Population, Cities, and American Residents:** The population of Venezuela totals 20.7 million people (1992 est.). Nearly 67 percent of Venezuelans are mestizos (of mixed ethnic background), 21 percent are white, 10 percent black, and 2 percent Indian.

  Most American residents are employed in Venezuela's three largest cities: Caracas with 3.3 million people, Maracaibo with 1.3 million, and Valencia with 1.2 million (1989 est.).
- **Language and Currency:** The official language of Venezuela is Spanish. Many

executives throughout the country speak English, but that should not be expected. A working knowledge of Spanish is recommended if you are planning on an extended stay in Venezuela. The unit of currency is the bolivar, abbreviated as Bs. There are 100 centimos in each bolivar. The floating exchange rate is 1 Venezuelan bolivar = U.S.$.011; 91 bolivars equal U.S.$1 (July 30, 1993).

- **Climate:** Generally, Venezuela has a tropical climate. However, there are considerable variations depending upon the altitude. Up to 2,500 feet in elevation, the climate is tropical with a temperature range of 75°F to 95°F; between 2,500 and 6,000 feet, the climate is subtropical, with a daily mean temperature range of 50°F to 77°F; between 6,000 and 9,000 feet the climate is temperate; and above 9,000 feet the climate is cold. The rainy season occurs from May to October.

- **Economy and Resources:** Until the early 1900s, the economy was dominated by agriculture and livestock production. Petroleum is now the mainstay of the economy accounting for 17 percent of the gross domestic product (GDP), 52 percent of central government revenues, and 87 percent of export earnings. State-owned Petroleos de Venezuela is the fourth largest oil company in the world. Recently, the country has concentrated on the sale of refined products, in addition to exporting crude oil, through joint ventures with consuming countries. Being so dependent on oil has not had entirely positive effects. The fall of oil prices in the 1980s highlighted the country's over-dependence on oil. Venezuela, fortunately, had sufficient foreign reserves to survive the crisis. Of the labor force, 56 percent work in services, 28 percent in industry, and 16 percent are engaged in agriculture. Major industries include petroleum, iron ore mining, and construction materials. In addition to petroleum, exports include bauxite, aluminum, iron ore, and agricultural products. Over half of all exports go to the United States. Venezuela still has an enormous ($32 billion) foreign debt, and faces many economic challenges. It must continue to diversify its economy. Industries targeted for development include aluminum production, chemical/petrochemical, pulp and paper, industrial glass, and cement projects.

- **Cost of Living:** At 74, the cost of living is much lower than in the United States.

- **Work Permits, Visas, etc.:** You'll need a valid passport to travel in Venezuela, and for stays of longer than two months, a visa is required. These cannot be processed by mail; they must be obtained through an embassy or consulate in the United States. If you want to work in Venezuela, enter the country on a tourist visa, or you will have to get a tax clearance before departing for home. Business visas may also be obtained through an embassy or consulate. When entering Venezuela from the United States, no vaccinations are required, but tetanus and yellow fever shots and antimalarial drugs are recommended. For official or other information, direct inquiries to the embassy or consulate at the addresses below.

- **Taxation:** Any income earned by an individual living in Venezuela is taxable whether or not it comes from Venezuelan sources. Tax rates are different for individuals, partnerships, and corporations.

- **Principal International Schools:** International schools are available in Venezuela,

A
M
E
R
I
C
A
N

J
O
B
S

A
B
R
O
A
D

but they are crowded, so try to make arrangements in advance. Tuition for an American school is about $4,500 per year.

- **Health Care:** Medical facilities in Venezuela are adequate. Caracas has qualified doctors and dentists, but nursing is below U.S. standards. Laboratory work can be costly, and replacing lenses or eyeglasses can be very expensive; it's best to bring along an extra pair. Sanitation conditions in the major cities of Venezuela are acceptable. In rural areas, water may be potable, but it is so heavily chlorinated that most local people, as well as foreigners, use bottled water. Avoid swimming in lakes or streams while traveling in Venezuela, as water may contain bacteria or disease.

- **Crime:** Crime is not a main problem in Venezuela, although common crimes occur, particularly in the cities. Do not leave valuables unattended or carry large sums of money with you on a casual basis. If you go out in the evening, avoid poorly lit streets or remote areas outside the main cities.

- **Pros and Cons of Living and Working in Venezuela:** Venezuela is one of the most developed nations in South America. It has magnificent scenery, with waterfalls, snow-capped mountains, and an abundance of wildlife. Eagles (more than 30 species) make their homes throughout the forests and along riverbanks. The highest waterfall in the world (3,212 feet), Angel Falls, is found in Venezuela. Sporting events are plentiful, including "winter ball," for which Venezuela hosts many U.S. major league baseball players from October through February. Telecommunications are good, but new phones are scarce, and nearly impossible to get installed. Roads in Venezuela are good, but driving laws are strictly enforced. Learn the rules of the road before you set out. Gas is extremely cheap in the country (less than 30 cents a gallon), but there is a traffic reduction system, which means you aren't allowed to drive for part of one day a week. Housing is available and very reasonably priced, but bring along your own furniture as the selection in Venezuela is limited and may not be suitable to your taste. Many expatriates work in the country, so it should be fairly easy to get to know others if you are on short or long-term assignment in Venezuela. A working knowledge of Spanish is needed to make daily life easier.

EMBASSY AND CONSULATE CONTACT INFORMATION:

EMBASSY OF VENEZUELA
2445 MASSACHUSETTS AVE. NW
WASHINGTON, DC 20008
TEL: 202-797-3800

CONSULATE GENERAL OF VENEZUELA
7 EAST 51 ST.
NEW YORK, NY 10020
TEL: 212-826-1660

OTHER SOURCES OF INFORMATION:

VENEZUELA INFORMATION
40 WEST 57 ST.
NEW YORK, NY 10020
TEL: 212-956-8504

COMPANIES/ORGANIZATIONS WITH OPERATIONS IN VENEZUELA:

ABB LUMMUS CREST, 108
ABB VETCO GRAY, INC., 108
ACCO WORLD CORPORATION, 110
ALBERTO-CULVER COMPANY, 115

AMERICAN EXPRESS COMPANY—TRAVEL
RELATED SERVICES, 125
AMERICAN HOME PRODUCTS
CORPORATION, 126
ASEA BROWN BOVERI, 142

BAXTER HEALTHCARE CORPORATION, 160

BECHTEL GROUP, INC., 162

BROWNING-FERRIS INDUSTRIES, 177

CALGON CORPORATION, 182

CAPITOL CITIES/ABC, INC., 184

CHASE MANHATTAN CORPORATION, 190

CHEMICAL BANKING CORPORATION, 191

CHURCH & DWIGHT COMPANY, INC., 196

CIGNA CORPORATION, 197

CONTINENTAL BANK CORPORATION, 210

CORE LABORATORIES, 214

THE DEXTER CORPORATION, 233

DIAMOND SHAMROCK R & M, INC., 234

DIGICON, INC., 235

DOMINO'S PIZZA, INC., 237

ELI LILLY AND COMPANY, 250

EXXON CORPORATION, 258

FEDERAL-MOGUL CORPORATION, 260

FORD MOTOR COMPANY, 267

FOSTER WHEELER CORPORATION, 268

FRITZ COMPANIES, 269

THE GILLETTE COMPANY, 283

GOODYEAR TIRE & RUBBER COMPANY, 284

GTE DIRECTORIES CORPORATION, 289

J. M. HUBER CORPORATION, 306

IDB COMMUNICATIONS, INC., 309

ILLINOIS TOOL WORKS, INC., 309

INGERSOLL-RAND COMPANY, 313

INTERNATIONAL PAPER COMPANY, 318

ITT SHERATON CORPORATION, 322

JOHNSON & HIGGINS, 324

KELLOGG COMPANY, 330

KELSEY-HAYES COMPANY, 332

KENDALL INTERNATIONAL, 332

KRAFT GENERAL FOODS INTERNATIONAL, 341

L. A. GEAR, INC., 342

LINTAS: WORLDWIDE, 346

LIQUID CARBONIC CORPORATION, 347

LOCTITE CORPORATION, 349

LYKES LINES, 354

MCCORMICK & COMPANY, INC., 355

MCDERMOTT INTERNATIONAL, INC., 356

MEASUREX CORPORATION, 366

NORTON COMPANY, 390

OCCIDENTAL PETROLEUM CORPORATION, 393

OLIN CORPORATION, 396

OTIS ELEVATOR COMPANY: WORLD HEADQUARTERS, 399

OWENS-ILLINOIS, INC., 401

PEPSICO FOODS INTERNATIONAL, 409

PEPSICO, INC., 410

PHELPS DODGE CORPORATION, 412

PHILIP MORRIS COMPANIES, INC., 413

PHILLIPS PETROLEUM COMPANY, 415

PILLSBURY COMPANY, 416

PPG INDUSTRIES, 421

PRECISION VALVE CORPORATION, 422

PREMARK INTERNATIONAL, INC., 423

PROCTER & GAMBLE PHARMACEUTICALS, INC., 426

PUROLATOR PRODUCTS COMPANY, 427

REVLON, INC., 437

ROWAN COMPANIES, INC., 444

SEARLE COMPANY, 455

SGS CONTROL SERVICES, 458

SONY PICTURES ENTERTAINMENT, 471

TOWERS PERRIN, INC., 499

TRANE COMPANY, 501

UNISYS CORPORATION, 508

UNITED TECHNOLOGIES CORPORATION, 512

UNOCAL CORPORATION, 513

WARNER-LAMBERT COMPANY, 522

JERVIS B. WEBB COMPANY, 523

WORLD COURIER MANAGEMENT, INC., 529

COUNTRY PROFILES

YUGOSLAVIA

- **Official Name:** Federal Republic of Yugoslavia

- **Capital:** Belgrade

- **Location:** Yugoslavia is located on the northwestern region of the Balkan Peninsula in southeastern Europe. Consisting of two republics, Serbia and Montenegro, its land area is 39,449 square miles, making Yugoslavia slightly smaller than Ohio. Most of the terrain is mountainous with some lowland hills and plains scattered throughout the republics.

- **Language and Currency:** The official language of Yugoslavia is Serbian. Albanian and Hungarian are also spoken in some regions. Having a working knowledge of Serbian is useful if you are on a long-term assignment in Yugoslavia. The monetary unit is the dinar. The exchange rate fluctuates greatly. In November 1993, one U.S. dollar was worth approximately 2 million dinars.

- **Important Note:** Dramatic changes have taken place in Yugoslavia over the past three years. Once a federation of six republics, the "new" Yugoslavia now has two—Serbia and Montenegro. The others, Bosnia and Herzegovina, Croatia, Macedonia, and Slovenia desired independence and in 1992 separated from the federation.

The conflict between Yugoslavia and its former republics should be taken seriously. A travel warning has been issued by the U.S. State Department (February 11, 1994) for all U.S. citizens going to Yugoslavia. For safety reasons, the United States has brought home all non-essential personnel from its embassy in Yugoslavia.

The United Nations has imposed strict economic sanctions against the country and all international and commercial air links have been severely cut. Internal travel is unreliable and unsafe. Contact the Citizen's Emergency Center in Washington, D.C., for a current update on travel in Yugoslavia.

EMBASSY AND CONSULATE CONTACT INFORMATION:

EMBASSY OF THE FEDERAL REPUBLIC OF YUGOSLAVIA
2410 CALIFORNIA ST. NW
WASHINGTON, DC 20008
TEL: 202-462-6566

EMBASSY OF THE REPUBLIC OF CROATIA
236 MASSACHUSETTS AVE. NE
WASHINGTON, DC 20002
TEL: 202-543-5580

EMBASSY OF THE REPUBLIC OF MACEDONIA
1015 15TH ST. NW
WASHINGTON, DC 20005
TEL: 202-682-0519

EMBASSY OF THE REPUBLIC OF SLOVENIA
1300 19TH ST. NW
WASHINGTON, DC 20036
TEL: 202-828-1650

EMBASSY OF THE REPUBLIC OF BOSNIA AND HERZEGOVINA
** THERE IS NO EMBASSY OR CONSULAR OFFICE CURRENTLY LOCATED IN THE UNITED STATES

OTHER SOURCES OF INFORMATION:

YUGOSLAV NATIONAL TOURIST OFFICE
630 FIFTH AVE., STE. 280
NEW YORK, NY 10111
TEL: 212-757-2801

COMPANIES/ORGANIZATIONS WITH OPERATIONS IN YUGOSLAVIA:

GENERAL MOTORS CORPORATION (GM),
277
JOHNSON & JOHNSON, 325

ZAIRE

- **Official Name:** Republic of Zaire
- **Capital:** Kinshasa
- **Location:** Lying deep within central Africa, Zaire has only a small, narrow neck of land reaching the Atlantic Ocean to keep it from being landlocked. It is bounded by the Central African Republic and Sudan to the north; Uganda, Rwanda, Burundi, and Tanzania to the east; Zambia to the south; Angola to the southwest; the Atlantic Ocean, the Cabinda district of Angola, and Congo to the west. Its land area totals 905,365 square miles, approximately 1.5 times the size of Alaska. Nearly 80 percent is covered by forests. One of the world's densest rain forests covers most of the northern sector. Thick grasslands cover most of southern Zaire where the Congo River flows through the country.
- **Language and Currency:** Zaire's official language is French, used throughout business and government and taught in most schools. You should have a working knowledge of French if you are on a long-term assignment in Zaire. The monetary unit is the (new) zaire. The exchange rate is 4.01 zaires = U.S.$1 (November 1993).
- **Print Sources of Information:** The U.S. Department of Labor's *Foreign Labor Trends* is available from the Superintendent of Documents, U.S. Government Printing Office, Washington, D.C., 20402.

EMBASSY AND CONSULATE CONTACT INFORMATION:

EMBASSY OF THE REPUBLIC OF ZAIRE
1800 NEW HAMPSHIRE AVE. NW
WASHINGTON, DC 20008
TEL: 202-234-7690

COMPANIES/ORGANIZATIONS WITH OPERATIONS IN ZAIRE:

LOUIS BERGER INTERNATIONAL INC., 165

ZAMBIA

- **Official Name:** Republic of Zambia

- **Capital:** Lusaka

- **Location:** Zambia is a landlocked country in south central Africa and borders Zaire to the north, Tanzania to the northeast, Malawi to the east, Mozambique to the southeast, Zimbabwe to the south, Namibia to the southwest, and Angola to the west. Its total land area is 284,994 square miles, making it slightly bigger than Texas. Almost half of the territory is covered by meadows and pastures, and one fourth by forests. Most of Zambia is a high plateau 3,000-5,000 feet above sea level. The northern region comprises the "Copperbelt," an area rich in mineral resources and the backbone of the Zambian economy. The broad Zambezi River forms most of the country's southern border and is the origin of Zambia's name. Victoria Falls, on the Zambezi, is a major tourist attraction.

- **Language and Currency:** The official language of Zambia is English, which is used throughout the country. The monetary unit is the kwacha, divided into 100 wee. The exchange rate is 355 kwachas = U.S.$1 (November 1993).

EMBASSY AND CONSULATE CONTACT INFORMATION:

EMBASSY OF THE REPUBLIC OF ZAMBIA
2419 MASSACHUSETTS AVE. NW
WASHINGTON, DC 20008
TEL: 202-265-9717

OTHER SOURCES OF INFORMATION:

ZAMBIA NATIONAL TOURIST BOARD
ZAMBIA HOUSE
237 EAST 52ND ST.
NEW YORK, NY 10022
TEL: 212-308-2155

COMPANIES/ORGANIZATIONS WITH OPERATIONS IN ZAMBIA:

ITT CORPORATION, 321

ZIMBABWE

- **Official Name:** Republic of Zimbabwe
- **Capital:** Harare
- **Location:** Zimbabwe is a landlocked country resting on a high plateau in southern Africa. It is bounded by Zambia to the northwest, Mozambique to the east, South Africa to the south, and Botswana to the southwest. With a total land area of 149,293 square miles, Zimbabwe is slightly larger than Montana. Most of the territory is a high plateau, with mountains forming in the eastern region. Nearly two-thirds of the land is covered by forests.
- **Population, Cities, and American Residents:** The population of Zimbabwe is 10.3 million (1992 est.), with black Africans accounting for 98 percent. Whites, Asians, and other mixed groups account for the remainder.

  Most American residents are employed in Zimbabwe's two largest cities: Harare with 730,000 people and Bulawayo with 415,000 (1987 est.).
- **Language and Currency:** The official language of Zimbabwe is English, used throughout the country. ChiShona and Si Ndebele are also spoken. The monetary unit is the Zimbabwe dollar. The exchange rate is 6.9 Zimbabwe dollars = U.S.$1 (December 1993).
- **Climate:** Most of Zimbabwe is 3,000 to 5,000 feet above sea level, which creates a pleasant climate, primarily subtropical and moderated by the altitude. Summers are usually hot and wet, with average temperatures of 54°F-85°F. Winters (May to August) are cool and dry with a minimum temperature range of 37°F-47°F. Most of the rain falls from October to April, with the annual amount averaging about 30 inches.
- **Economy and Resources:** Agriculture plays a key role in the Zimbabwean economy,

employing three-fourths of the people and accounting for 40 percent of major exports. Mineral resources are Zimbabwe's main source of foreign earnings. The country also has a strong industrial base. Chief exports include such products as gold, nickel, asbestos, tobacco, and coffee. Major trading partners are members of the European Community.

An uneven growth rate, due to sporadic agricultural production, was a main concern in the early 1990s. Lack of rain in 1992 led to heavy crop failures, and Zimbabwe had to import food for its starving people. The drought was the worst one in Africa in 20 years. Economic assistance and aid from various organizations and private donors nations helped to alleviate the famine.

- **Cost of Living:** At 73, the cost of living is less than in the United States.
- **Work Permits, Visas, etc.:** A passport is required to travel in Zimbabwe. Visitors must declare currency upon arrival. If you are entering Zimbabwe from the United States no vaccinations are required. For official or other information direct inquiries to the embassy or consulate at the addresses below.
- **Taxation:** Contact the embassy or consulate of the Republic of Zimbabwe for current tax information.
- **Principal International Schools:** American schools are available.
- **Health Care:** Medical facilities are good in major cities, but certain drugs and pharmaceuticals may not be available. It is recommended that anyone on a long-term assignment in Zimbabwe have supplemental health insurance for overseas coverage; U.S. coverage does not always apply. AIDS is a major problem in this country. Take precautions. Water is potable in major urban areas, but not in rural sections.
- **Crime:** Since Britain recognized the independence of Zimbabwe in 1980, political tensions have eased. There are still sporadic outbreaks, and fighting occurs among black ethnic groups. Travelers should note current conditions. Take precautions against street crime. Muggings and break-ins are on the rise, especially in popular tourist areas.
- **Pros and Cons of Working and Living in Zimbabwe:** Zimbabwe offers some unique natural surroundings and a fairly pleasant climate. Victoria Falls on the Zambezi River is a major attraction, as are the "Great Zimbabwe" ruins near Masvingo. There are several parks and game preserves. There are strict rules against some photography, with many places off-limits (embassies and government buildings). Transportation and telecommunications services are adequate, but the buses tend to be crowded, unreliable, and sometimes unsafe (negligent drivers or poorly maintained vehicles). Housing is available but selection is limited, so accommodations should be made well in advance. Nationwide electrical blackouts occasionally occur and may last for several hours. Zimbabwean officials treat drug offenders very seriously, handing out stiff fines and mandatory jail sentences.

EMBASSY AND CONSULATE CONTACT INFORMATION:
EMBASSY OF THE REPUBLIC OF ZIMBABWE
1608 NEW HAMPSHIRE AVE. NW
WASHINGTON, DC 20009
TEL: 202-332-7100

COMPANIES/ORGANIZATIONS WITH OPERATIONS IN ZIMBABWE:

CROWN CORK & SEAL COMPANY, INC., 218
CUMMINS ENGINE COMPANY, INC., 221

INTERNATIONAL VOLUNTARY SERVICES, INC., 555
POPULATION COUNCIL, 562

J O B   C A T E G O R Y   I N D E X

ACADEMIC DIRECTORS

World Learning Center, 586

ACCOUNTANTS

ABB Lummus Crest, 108
American International Group, 127
American Tool Companies, Inc., 129
Bank of Boston Corporation, 153
The Bank of New York Company,
    Inc., 154
Borg-Warner Corporation, 171
Borland International, Inc, 172
Bridgestone-Firestone, Inc., 174
The Coca-Cola Company, 202
Conoco, Inc., 209
Coopers & Lybrand, 214
CUNA Mutual Insurance Group, 222
Dames & Moore, 223
Daniel, Mann, Johnson & Mendenhall,
    224
Data General Corporation, 225
DDB Needham Worldwide, Inc., 227
Dean Witter, Discover & Company,
    228
Debevoise & Plimpton, 229

Deloitte & Touche, 231
Delta Air Lines, Inc., 232
Diamond Shamrock R & M, Inc.,
    234
Dow Chemical Company, 240
Dow Corning Corporation, 240
Drummond Company, Inc., 242
Dun & Bradstreet Corporation, 243
Eagle-Picher Industries, Inc., 246
Eastman Kodak Company, 246
Eaton Corporation/Cutler Hammer,
    247
EG & G, Inc., 249
Electronic Data Systems Corporation,
    249
Elizabeth Arden Company, 251
Ernst & Young, 255
Federal Express Corporation, 260
Figgie International, Inc., 262
First Chicago Corporation, 262
Fischer & Porter Company, 263
Fisher Controls International, Inc.,
    263
Flow International Corporation, 265
FMC Corporation, 266
Ford Motor Company, 267
Freeport-McMoran, Inc., 268

Gannett Company, Inc., 272
GATX Corporation, 273
General Electric Company (GE), 275
General Instrument Corporation, 276
General Tire, Inc., 279
Giddings & Lewis, Inc., 282
The Gillette Company, 283
Grant Thornton International, 286
Great Lakes Carbon International
    Corporation, 287
GTECH Corporation, 289
Halliburton Company, 292
Halliburton Company/Halliburton
    Services Division, 293
Halliburton-NUS Corporation, 293
Hallmark Cards, Inc., 294
Harris Corporation, 296
Hasbro, Inc., 297
Hazleton Washington Corporation, 297
Helene Curtis Industries, Inc., 298
Hellmuth, Obata & Kassabaum, Inc.,
    298
Holiday Inns Worldwide, 302
Hormel Foods Corporation, 304
Hughes Aircraft Company, 307
Hyatt International Corporation, 308
IMS America, Ltd., 311
Intel Corporation, 314
International Dairy Queen, Inc., 316
International Data Group, Inc., 316
International Flavors & Fragrances,
    Inc., 317
International Rescue Committee, 554
Intertrans Corporation, 320
ITT Hartford Insurance Group, 321
Johnson Controls, Inc., 324
Klynveld Peat Marwick Goerdeler
    (KPMG), 337
Lubrizol Corporation, 353
Mallinckrodt, Inc., 359
MCI Communications Corporation,
    365
J. P. Morgan & Company, Inc., 378
Morton International, 380
NCR Corporation, 384
Price Waterhouse, 424
Rayovac Corporation, 431

ADMINISTRATION

A. L. Laboratories Inc., 107

Agency for International Development,
    536
Alarm Device Manufacturing Company,
    114
Alberto-Culver Company, 115
Allen-Bradley Company, Inc., 116
American Building Maintenance
    Industries, Inc., 123
American Institute for Free Labor
    Development, 537
Anacomp, Inc., 134
Andrew Corporation, 134
Anthony Industries, 135
Arby's, Inc., 138
Archer-Daniels-Midland Company, 138
ARCO Coal Company, 139
ASA Foundation, 539
Asarco, Inc., 142
Avery Dennison Corporation, 147
Badger Company, Inc., 151
BankAmerica Corporation, 155
Baroid Corporation, 158
Block Drug Company, Inc., 169
Blount, Inc. (Blount Construction
    Division), 169
Borland International, Inc, 172
BP America, Inc., 173
Brown & Williamson Tobacco
    Corporation, 177
California Pellet Mill Company, 182
Camp Dresser & McKee International,
    Inc., 183
Capitol Cities/ABC, Inc., 184
CARE, 541
Catholic Relief Services, 542
Champion International Corporation,
    189
Chase Manhattan Corporation, 190
Bernard Chaus, Inc., 191
Chevron Chemical Company, 192
Child Reach International, 542
Christian Blind Mission International,
    543
Christian Children's Fund, Inc., 543
The Coastal Group, 201
Colgate-Palmolive Company, 203
ConAgra, Inc., 208
Continental Airlines Holdings, Inc.,
    210
Continental Bank Corporation, 210

Continental Grain Company, 211
Continuum Company, Inc., 211
Willis Corroon, 216
Crown Cork & Seal Company, Inc., 218
CRS Sirrine, Inc., 219
CUNA Mutual Insurance Group, 222
Inter-American Development Bank, 547
Inter-American Foundation, 547
International Fund for Agricultural Development (IFAD), 549
International Management Development Institute, 551
International Monetary Fund, 552
International Organization for Migration, 553
International Planned Parenthood Federation, 553
International Rescue Committee, 554
International Wildlife Coalition, 556
JWP, Inc., 328
Kellogg Company, 330
Ketchum International, 334
Kraft General Foods International, 341
Levi Strauss Associates, Inc., 344
Loral Corporation, 350
McCann-Erickson Worldwide, 354
McCormick & Company, Inc., 355
McDermott International, Inc., 356
McGraw-Hill, Inc., 357
McKinsey & Company, Inc., 357
Macro Systems, Inc., 358
Marathon Petroleum Company, 359
Masco Corporation, 361
Maxus Energy Corporation, 363
MCI Communications Corporation, 365
Mead Corporation, 365
Medtronic, Inc., 366
MGM Incorporated, 372
Monsanto Company, 377
Motorola, Inc., 381
Nabors Industries, Inc., 381
National Aeronautics and Space Administartion (NASA), 556
National Democratic Institute, 557
National Semiconductor Corporation, 383

New York Life Insurance Company, 385
Newmont Mining Corporation, 386
Norton Company, 390
NYNEX Corporation, 392
Occidental Petroleum Corporation, 393
Oceaneering International, Inc., 393
Offshore Logistics, 394
Offshore Pipelines, Inc., 394
OMI International, 396
Organization of American States, 558
Owens-Illinois, Inc., 401
Pacific Telesis International, 403
Pan American Health Organization, 560
Parsons Corporation, 406
Pathfinders International, 561
J. C. Penney Company, Inc., 407
Pfizer, Inc., 412
Population Council, 562
Price Waterhouse, 424
Primerica Corporation, 424
Procter & Gamble Cosmetics and Fragrance Products, 426
Qume Corporation, 429
R. J. Reynolds Tobacco Company, 429
Ralston Purina Company, 430
Reading & Bates, 433
RJR Nabisco, 439
Rockwell International Corporation, 441
Rogers Corporation, 442
Rowan Companies, Inc., 444
Ruder Finn, Inc., 445
Save the Children Federation, Inc., 564
Scientific Atlanta, Inc., 452
Scott Paper Company, 453
Searle Company, 455
Skadden, Arps, Slate, Meagher & Flom, 465
Snap-On Tools Corporation, 468
South Pacific Commission, 564
Springs Industries, Inc., 473
Technoserve, Inc., 565
Textron, Inc., 494
United Engineers & Constructors International, 508
United Nations Childrens' Fund, 565

A
M
E
R
I
C
A
N

J
O
B
S

A
B
R
O
A
D

United Nations Environment Program, 567
United Nations High Commissioner for Refugees, 567
United Nations Industrial Development Organization (UNIDO), 568
United Service Organizations, Inc., 569
U.S. Central Intelligence Agency, 570
U.S. Department of the Air Force, 572
U.S. Department of Defense, 572
U.S. Department of Justice, 574
U.S. Department of the Navy, 574
U.S. Department of State, 575
U.S. Department of Transportation, 576
U.S. Department of Treasury, 576
U.S. Environmental Protection Agency, 577
U.S. Federal Aviation Administration, 577
U.S. Federal Bureau of Investigation, 578
U.S. General Services Administration, 580
United States Information Agency, 580
U.S. Marine Corps, 581
U.S. Peace Corps, 582
United States Surgical Corporation, 511
U.S. Total Army Personnel Command, 582
Wendy's International, Inc., 524
World Bank Group, 584
World Relief, 587
World Vision Relief and Development, Inc., 588

ADMINISTRATIVE ASSISTANTS

Metco Perkin-Elmer, 371

AGENTS—INSURANCE

Alexander & Alexander Services, Inc., 116
American Bankers Insurance Group, Inc., 122

Aon Corporation, 136
Willis Corroon, 216
Donaldson Lufkin & Jenrette, Inc., 238
Johnson & Higgins, 324
New York Life Insurance Company, 385
Reliance International, 436
Rollins Hudig Hall International, 443
Transamerica, Corporation, 501
UNUM Corporation, 514

AGENTS—INVESTIGATIVE

U.S. Department of Justice, 574
U.S. Federal Bureau of Investigation, 578

AGRICULTURAL SPECIALISTS

Agency for International Development, 536
Food & Agriculture Organization of the United Nations, 546
International Fertilizer Development Center, 549
International Voluntary Services, Inc., 555
United Nations Employment Information & Assistance Division, 566
Volunteers in Technical Assistance, Inc, 584
World Concern, 585

AIRCRAFT MAINTENANCE

Northwest Airlines, Inc., 390

AIRLINE WORKERS

AMR/American Airlines, 133
UAL Corporation, 506
USAir Group, Inc., 516

AIRPORT MANAGEMENT

AMR/American Airlines, 133
Delta Air Lines, Inc., 232
UAL Corporation, 506

ANALYSTS

Oppenheimer Group, 398

ANTHROPOLOGISTS

Conservation International, 545

APPRAISERS

American Appraisal Associates, Inc.,
    121

ARCHITECTS

Black & Veatch, 168
Burns & Roe, Inc., 180
Leo A. Daly Company, 223
Daniel, Mann, Johnson & Mendenhall,
    224
Day & Zimmerman, 226
De Leuw, Cather International, 228
HDR Incorporated, 298
Hellmuth, Obata & Kassabaum, Inc.,
    298
ICF Kaiser Engineers, 308
The Kuljian Company, 341
Law Companies Group, Inc., 343
Parsons Brinkerhoff, 406
Rust International, Inc., 447
Skidmore, Owings & Merrill, 465
VTN Corporation, 518

ATTORNEYS

Chadbourne & Parke, 189
Coudert Brothers Law Firm, 217
Debevoise & Plimpton, 229
Hellmuth, Obata & Kassabaum, Inc.,
    298
International Labor Office, 550
Jones, Day, Reavis & Pogue, Inc.,
    326
Organization of American States, 558
Shearman & Sterling, 460
Skadden, Arps, Slate, Meagher &
    Flom, 465
Sullivan & Cromwell, 483
United Nations Employment
    Information & Assistance
    Division, 566
U.S. Department of Justice, 574

World Intellectual Property
    Organization, 586

AUDITORS

U.S. General Accounting Office, 579

BARTENDERS

International Maritime Resources, 317

BIOLOGISTS

Conservation International, 545

BROKERS—INSURANCE

Alexander & Alexander Services, Inc.,
    116
American International Group, 127
Willis Corroon, 216

BROKERS—SECURITIES &
FINANCIAL

Aon Corporation, 136
The Bank of New York Company,
    Inc., 154
Bankers Trust New York Corporation,
    155
Dean Witter, Discover & Company,
    228
Donaldson Lufkin & Jenrette, Inc.,
    238
Figgie International, Inc., 262
Goldman Sachs & Company, 283
Johnson & Higgins, 324
Merrill Lynch & Company, Inc., 369
Paine Webber Group, Inc., 403
Shearson Lehman Brothers, 460
Smith Barney, Harris Upham &
    Company, Inc., 466
Standard & Poor's Corporation, 476
UNUM Corporation, 514

BUSINESS DEVELOPMENT

Navistar International Transportation
    Corporation, 383
Teledyne, Inc., 489

CAPTAINS

American Canadian Caribbean Line, 123
Commodore Cruise Lines, 206

CARPENTERS

Pacific Architects & Engineers, Inc., 402

CHEFS

American Canadian Caribbean Line, 123
Clipper Cruise Lines, 199
Commodore Cruise Lines, 206
International Maritime Resources, 317

CHEMICAL ENGINEERS

American Home Products Corporation, 126
Cabot Corporation, 181
W. R. Grace & Company, 285
International Fertilizer Development Center, 549
Mobil Oil Corporation, 375
Morton International, 380
United Nations Industrial Development Organization (UNIDO), 568
Unocal Corporation, 513

CHEMISTS

Applied Bioscience International, Inc., 137
Betz Laboratories, 166
Chevron Chemical Company, 192
Chiron Corporation, 194
Core Laboratories, 214
Diamond Shamrock R & M, Inc., 234
Exxon Chemical Company, 257
GAF Corporation, 270
Hazleton Washington Corporation, 297
Hercules, Inc., 299
Johnson & Johnson, 325
Kolmar Laboratories, Inc., 340
Mallinckrodt, Inc., 359
Procter & Gamble Pharmaceuticals, Inc., 426

United Nations Industrial Development Organization (UNIDO), 568
Warner-Lambert Company, 522
Wyeth-Ayerst Laboratories, 530

CLERICAL ASSISTANTS

Champion International Corporation, 189
DDB Needham Worldwide, Inc., 227
Gannett Company, Inc., 272
General Electric Company (GE), 275
H & R Block, 291
Hoechst Celanese, Inc., 302
Intertrans Corporation, 320
Mead Corporation, 365
Pacific Architects & Engineers, Inc., 402
PepsiCo, Inc., 410
Sizzler International, 464
U.S. Central Intelligence Agency, 570
U.S. Defense Intelligence Agency, 571
U.S. Department of State, 575

COMMUNICATIONS

Academy for Educational Development, 535
Electronic Data Systems Corporation, 249
Volunteers in Technical Assistance, Inc, 584

COMPTROLLERS

Data General Corporation, 225

COMPUTER PROGRAMMERS

AMR/American Airlines, 133
Astronautics Corporation of America, 145
Hellmuth, Obata & Kassabaum, Inc., 298
Inter-American Foundation, 547
UAL Corporation, 506

CONSERVATION SPECIALISTS

Conservation International, 545
U.S. Environmental Protection Agency, 577

CONSTRUCTION WORKERS

Bechtel Group, Inc., 162
Blount, Inc. (Blount Construction
    Division), 169
Ebasco Overseas Corporation, 248
Foster Wheeler Corporation, 268
Gannett Fleming, Inc., 272
The Kuljian Company, 341
Morrison Knudsen Corporation, 379
Offshore Pipelines, Inc., 394
United Engineers & Constructors
    International, 508
World Concern, 585

CONSULTANTS— ENGINEERING

CH2M Hill International, Ltd., 195
Parsons Main, Inc., 407

CONSULTANTS—FINANCIAL

Buck Consultants, Inc., 178
Burson-Marsteller, 180
Cargill Incorporated, 184

CONSULTANTS— MANAGEMENT

Ingersoll Engineers, 312
International Management Development
    Institute, 551
A. T. Kearney, Inc., 329
Klynveld Peat Marwick Goerdeler
    (KPMG), 337
McKinsey & Company, Inc., 357
PRC, Inc., 422
SRI International, 475
Stone & Webster Engineering
    Corporation, 480
Tennessee Associates International,
    Inc., 492

CONTRACT ADMINISTRATION

Ebasco Overseas Corporation, 248

CONTRACTORS

Dyncorp, 245
M. W. Kellogg Company, 331

Pittsburgh-Des Moines Corporation,
    418
Rowan Companies, Inc., 444
Stebbins Engineering & Manufacturing
    Corporation, 479

COOPERATIVE DEVELOPMENT

International Voluntary Services, Inc.,
    555

COUNSELORS

AMIDEAST, 538
ORT International Cooperation, 559

CUSTOM ENGINEERS

Wang Laboratories, Inc., 519

CUSTOMER SERVICES

Banyan Systems, Inc., 156
Bell Helicopter Textron, Inc., 163
Burlington Air Express, 179
Flow International Corporation, 265
Northwest Airlines, Inc., 390

DATA PROCESSORS

Organization for Economic Cooperation
    & Development, 559
Robert Half International, Inc., 440

DECK HANDS

American Canadian Caribbean Line,
    123
Clipper Cruise Lines, 199
Commodore Cruise Lines, 206

DEMOGRAPHERS

United Nations Employment
    Information & Assistance
    Division, 566

DENTISTS

Project Concern International, 562

A
M
E
R
I
C
A
N

J
O
B
S

A
B
R
O
A
D

DESIGN

ABB Lummus Crest, 108
Aldus Corporation, 115
Bernard Chaus, Inc., 191
Leo A. Daly Company, 223
Daniel, Mann, Johnson & Mendenhall, 224
De Leuw, Cather International, 228
Giddings & Lewis, Inc., 282
Gilbert/Commonwealth International, Inc., 282
Gould Pumps, Inc., 285
Guardian Industries Corporation, 290
Holmes & Narver, Inc., 303
Illinois Tool Works, Inc., 309
Intergraph Corporation, 314
The Kuljian Company, 341
Liz Claiborne, Inc., 348
Mead Corporation, 365
Scientific Atlanta, Inc., 452

DESIGN ENGINEERS

Bechtel Group, Inc., 162
Bendix Field Engineering Corporation, 165
Boeing Company, 170
Commodore International Ltd., 206
General Motors Corporation (GM), 277

DESIGN PLANNERS

Skidmore, Owings & Merrill, 465

DEVELOPMENT SPECIALISTS

Church World Service & Witness, 544
United Nations Employment Information & Assistance Division, 566

DIVERS

Oceaneering International, Inc., 393
Offshore Pipelines, Inc., 394

DRAFTSMEN

Hellmuth, Obata & Kassabaum, Inc., 298

DRILLING OPERATORS

Parker Drilling Company, 405

DRIVERS

Pacific Architects & Engineers, Inc., 402
Yellow Freight System, Inc., 532

ECONOMISTS

Agency for International Development, 536
Asian Development Bank, 540
Gannett Fleming, Inc., 272
International Labor Office, 550
Organization of American States, 558
Organization for Economic Cooperation & Development, 559
United Nations Employment Information & Assistance Division, 566
United Nations Industrial Development Organization (UNIDO), 568
United Nations Secretariat, 568
U.S. Department of State, 575
U.S. Foreign Agriculture Service, 579
World Bank Group, 584
World Concern, 585

EDITORS

Dow Jones & Company, Inc., 241
McGraw-Hill, Inc., 357
New York Times Company, 386
Newsweek International, 387
Reader's Digest Association, Inc., 432
Simon & Schuster, Inc., 463
United Press International, 509

ELECTRICAL ENGINEERS

E-Systems, Inc., 245
Emerson Electric Company, 251
General Railway Signal Company, 278

ELECTRICIANS

Pacific Architects & Engineers, Inc., 402

ENGINE ROOM STAFF

International Maritime Resources, 317

ENGINEERS

ABB Lummus Crest, 108
Abex Inc./Fisher Scientific International, Inc., 110
Advanced Micro Devices, Inc., 112
Aldus Corporation, 115
Amdahl Corporation, 120
AMP, Inc., 132
Applied Bioscience International, Inc., 137
ARCO International Oil and Gas Company, 139
Arethusa Offshore, 140
Armco, Inc., 140
Asarco, Inc., 142
Ashland Oil, Inc., 143
Asian Development Bank, 540
AST Research, Inc., 144
Astronautics Corporation of America, 145
Badger Company, Inc., 151
Banyan Systems, Inc., 156
The Barden Corporation, 157
Baroid Corporation, 158
Bechtel Group, Inc., 162
Louis Berger International Inc., 165
Betz Laboratories, 166
Black & Veatch, 168
Boeing Company, 170
Borg-Warner Corporation, 171
Borland International, Inc, 172
BP America, Inc., 173
Bristol Babcock, Inc., 174
Burns & Roe, Inc., 180
Camp Dresser & McKee International, Inc., 183
Chevron Corporation, 193
Chevron Overseas Petroleum, Inc., 194
CLARCOR, Inc., 198
Coin Acceptors, Inc., 203
Conoco, Inc., 209
Cooper Industries, Inc., 213
Corning Incorporated, 215
John Crane, Inc., 218
CRS Sirrine, Inc., 219

Cubic Corporation, 220
Cummins Engine Company, Inc., 221
Dames & Moore, 223
Daniel, Mann, Johnson & Mendenhall, 224
Day & Zimmerman, 226
De Leuw, Cather International, 228
DH Technology, Inc., 233
Diamond M-ODECO Drilling, Inc., 234
Diamond Shamrock R & M, Inc., 234
Digicon, Inc., 235
Duriron Company, Inc., 244
Ebasco Overseas Corporation, 248
EG & G, Inc., 249
Encore Computer Corporation, 252
Fibronics International, Inc., 261
Flow International Corporation, 265
Fluor Corporation, 266
FMC Corporation, 266
Foster Wheeler Corporation, 268
Freeport-McMoran, Inc., 268
Fugro-McClelland USA, Inc., 269
Fuller Company, 269
Gafney, Cline & Associates, Inc., 271
General Dynamics Corporation, 274
General Dynamics Services Company, 275
Geraghty & Miller, Inc., 279
Gilbert/Commonwealth International, Inc., 282
Guardian Industries Corporation, 290
Halliburton Company, 292
Halliburton Company/Halliburton Services Division, 293
Hartford Steam Boiler Inspection/ Insurance Company, 296
HDR Incorporated, 298
Holmes & Narver, Inc., 303
Hughes Aircraft Company, 307
ICF Kaiser Engineers, 308
Illinois Tool Works, Inc., 309
Ingersoll-Rand Company, 313
Intergraph Corporation, 314
International Rectifier Corporation, 319
International Rescue Committee, 554
Johnson Controls, Inc., 324
M. W. Kellogg Company, 331

JOB CATEGORY INDEX

A M E R I C A N   J O B S   A B R O A D

Kennecott Corporation, 333
Kohler Company, 339
The Kuljian Company, 341
Law Companies Group, Inc., 343
Litton Industries, Inc., 348
Loral Corporation, 350
Lord Corporation, 350
Louisiana Land & Exploration Company, 352
McDermott International, Inc., 356
Marathon Petroleum Company, 359
Maxus Energy Corporation, 363
Mead Corporation, 365
Metcalf & Eddy International, Inc., 370
Morrison Knudsen Corporation, 379
Nellcor, Inc., 385
Occidental Petroleum Corporation, 393
Olin Corporation, 396
ONAN Corporation, 397
Overseas Shipholding Group, Inc., 400
Owens-Illinois, Inc., 401
Parker Hannifin Corporation, 405
Parsons Brinkerhoff, 406
Phelps Dodge Corporation, 412
Phillips Petroleum Company, 415
PPG Industries, 421
Printronix, Inc., 425
Quaker Chemical Corporation, 428
Qume Corporation, 429
Raytheon Company, 432
Reading & Bates, 433
Recognition Equipment, Inc., 433
Resources Management International, 437
Rust International, Inc., 447
SCI Systems, 452
Scientific Atlanta, Inc., 452
Seagate Technology, Inc., 454
Sealed Air Corporation, 455
Siliconix, 462
Skidmore, Owings & Merrill, 465
Smith International, Inc., 467
Sonat, Inc., 469
SPS Technologies, Inc., 474
Stebbins Engineering & Manufacturing Corporation, 479
Stone & Webster Engineering Corporation, 480

Structural Dynamics Research Corporation, 481
STV Group, 482
Sun Company, Inc., 483
Sun Microsystems, Inc., 484
Sundstrand Corporation, 485
Symbol Technologies, Inc., 485
Tandem Computers, Inc., 487
Technoserve, Inc., 565
Tellabs Operations, Inc., 489
Telxon Corp., 490
Tenneco Automotive, 491
Teradyne, Inc., 493
Texaco Oil Company, 493
Tracor, Inc., 500
Trinova Corporation, 502
TRW, Inc., 503
Turner Steiner International, Inc., 504
United Nations Industrial Development Organization (UNIDO), 568
U.S. Army Corps of Engineers, 570
U.S. Department of Energy, 573
U.S. Department of State, 575
United Technologies Corporation, 512
USX Corporation, 516
VTN Corporation, 518
Jervis B. Webb Company, 523
WMX Technologies/Waste Management, Inc., 527

ENTERTAINERS

Carnival Cruise Lines, 185

ENVIRONMENTAL SPECIALISTS

Conoco, Inc., 209
Ecology and Environment, Inc., 248
International Voluntary Services, Inc., 555
International Wildlife Coalition, 556
Organization for Economic Cooperation & Development, 559
United Nations Employment Information & Assistance Division, 566
United Nations Environment Program, 567
Volunteers in Technical Assistance, Inc, 584

World Wildlife Fund, 588

EPIDEMIOLOGISTS

Office of International Health, 557

ESTIMATORS

United Engineers & Constructors
　International, 508

EVALUATORS

U.S. General Accounting Office, 579

EXECUTIVE MANAGEMENT

Abbott Laboratories, 109
Albany International Corporation, 114
Aldus Corporation, 115
Amerada Hess Corporation, 121
American Express Bank, Ltd., 124
American Express Company—Travel
　Related Services, 125
American Standard, Inc., 128
Backer Spielvogel & Bates Worldwide,
　Inc., 150
Baker Hughes, Inc., 152
BankAmerica Corporation, 155
Bankers Trust New York Corporation,
　155
Battelle Memorial Institute, 159
Bear Stearns Companies, Inc., 161
Bristol-Meyers Squibb Company, 175
Chemical Banking Corporation, 191
Chiron Corporation, 194
Citicorp, 198
Commerce Clearing House, 205
Cooper Industries, Inc., 213
Coopers & Lybrand, 214
CS First Boston, Inc., 219
Digicon, Inc., 235
Duriron Company, Inc., 244
Eastman Kodak Company, 246
Encyclopedia Britannica, Inc., 253
Enron Corporation, 254
Exxon Chemical Company, 257
Exxon Corporation, 258
Fairchild Publications, Inc., 259
Federal Express Corporation, 260
Federal-Mogul Corporation, 260

First Chicago Corporation, 262
Ford Foundation, 546
Ford Motor Company, 267
General Dynamics Corporation, 274
General Electric Company (GE), 275
General Mills, Inc., 277
General Motors Corporation (GM),
　277
Getz Brothers Company, Inc., 281
Goodyear Tire & Rubber Company,
　284
A. P. Green Industries, Inc., 287
GTE Corporation, 288
H. J. Heinz Company, 290
Hanson Industries, 295
Honeywell, Inc., 303
International Business Machines (IBM),
　315
International Paper Company, 318
ITT Corporation, 321
S. C. Johnson Wax, 325
M. W. Kellogg Company, 331
Kidder Peabody Group & Company,
　Inc., 335
Arthur D. Little, Inc., 347
Metropolitan Life Insurance Company,
　371
Mobil Oil Corporation, 375
ONAN Corporation, 397
Oppenheimer Group, 398
Owens-Corning Fiberglas Corporation,
　400
Paccar, Inc., 401
Pentair, Inc., 409
Philip Morris Companies, Inc., 413
Pillsbury Company, 416
Pitney Bowes, Inc., 417
Prudential Insurance Company of
　America, 427
Reynolds Metals Company, 438
Russell Reynolds Associates, Inc.,
　446
Shearson Lehman Brothers, 460
Sprint Corporation, 474
State Street Boston Corporation, 478
Stone Container Corporation, 480
Time-Warner, Inc., 498
Turner Broadcasting System, Inc.,
　503
Unisys Corporation, 508

Universal Foods Corporation, 513
William Wrigley Jr. Company, 529

EXECUTIVE RECRUITERS

Korn/Ferry International, 340

FABRICATORS

Jervis B. Webb Company, 523

FACTORY MANAGEMENT

Bridgestone-Firestone, Inc., 174

FAMILY PLANNING SPECIALISTS

Christian Children's Fund, Inc., 543
International Planned Parenthood
    Federation, 553
Pathfinders International, 561

FIELD ENGINEERS

Bendix Field Engineering Corporation,
    165
Exxon Corporation, 258
Halliburton Company, 292
Oryx Energy, 398
Parsons Corporation, 406
United Engineers & Constructors
    International, 508

FIELD SERVICE POSITIONS

Save the Children Federation, Inc.,
    564
United Nations Childrens' Fund, 565
United Nations High Commissioner for
    Refugees, 567
United Nations Industrial Development
    Organization (UNIDO), 568
United Nations Secretariat, 568
United States Information Agency,
    580
U.S. Total Army Personnel Command,
    582
World Vision Relief and Development,
    Inc., 588
World Wildlife Fund, 588

FIELD TECHNICIANS

Enserch International Development,
    Inc., 254
Nabors Industries, Inc., 381
Penrod Drilling Corporation, 408
Texaco Oil Company, 493

FINANCE

Agency for International Development,
    536
Amdahl Corporation, 120
American Express Bank, Ltd., 124
American Express Company—Travel
    Related Services, 125
American Standard, Inc., 128
Ampex Corporation, 133
AT&T International, 145
Atari Corporation, 146
Avery Dennison Corporation, 147
Avon Products, Inc., 149
Backer Spielvogel & Bates Worldwide,
    Inc., 150
Badger Company, Inc., 151
BancTec, Inc., 152
Bank of Boston Corporation, 153
Bankers Trust New York Corporation,
    155
Battelle Memorial Institute, 159
Bausch & Lomb, Inc., 159
Baxter Healthcare Corporation, 160
Bear Stearns Companies, Inc., 161
Bell & Howell Company, 164
Louis Berger International Inc., 165
Bio-Rad Laboratories, 166
Borden, Inc., 170
Bridgestone-Firestone, Inc., 174
Bristol-Meyers Squibb Company, 175
Brown Group, Inc., 176
Brush Wellman, Inc., 178
Buck Consultants, Inc., 178
Campbell Soup Company, 183
Capitol Cities/ABC, Inc., 184
Chemical Banking Corporation, 191
Chevron Overseas Petroleum, Inc.,
    194
Child Reach International, 542
The Chubb & Son Corporation, 196
Club Corporation International, 200
Club Med, Inc., 201

Compaq Computers Corporation, 207
Continental Airlines Holdings, Inc., 210
Continental Bank Corporation, 210
Continental Grain Company, 211
Continuum Company, Inc., 211
Cooper Industries, Inc., 213
Core States Financial Corporation, 215
John Crane, Inc., 218
Crown Cork & Seal Company, Inc., 218
Dana Corporation, 224
DDB Needham Worldwide, Inc., 227
Delta Air Lines, Inc., 232
The Dexter Corporation, 233
Donaldson Company, Inc., 237
Donaldson Lufkin & Jenrette, Inc., 238
Dow Chemical Company, 240
Duriron Company, Inc., 244
Eastman Kodak Company, 246
Eaton Corporation/Cutler Hammer, 247
EG & G, Inc., 249
Electronic Data Systems Corporation, 249
Eli Lilly and Company, 250
Emerson Electric Company, 251
Enron Corporation, 254
Exxon Corporation, 258
Fairchild Publications, Inc., 259
Fibronics International, Inc., 261
Figgie International, Inc., 262
Fisher Controls International, Inc., 263
Fluor Corporation, 266
FMC Corporation, 266
Ford Foundation, 546
Ford Motor Company, 267
GATX Corporation, 273
General Foods USA, 276
General Railway Signal Company, 278
Goldman Sachs & Company, 283
Great Lakes Carbon International Corporation, 287
Halliburton Company, 292
Hanson Industries, 295
Helene Curtis Industries, Inc., 298
Hertz Corporation, 300

Hewlett-Packard Company, 300
Hoechst Celanese, Inc., 302
Holiday Inns Worldwide, 302
Household International, Inc., 305
Hyatt International Corporation, 308
ICF Kaiser Engineers, 308
Ingersoll Engineers, 312
Ingersoll-Rand Company, 313
Inter-American Development Bank, 547
Inter-American Foundation, 547
International Fund for Agricultural Development (IFAD), 549
International Monetary Fund, 552
Intertrans Corporation, 320
ITT Corporation, 321
ITT Sheraton Corporation, 322
JWP, Inc., 328
A. T. Kearney, Inc., 329
Keithley Instruments, Inc., 329
Kellogg Company, 330
KFC Corporation, 335
Knight-Ridder, Inc., 338
Korn/Ferry International, 340
L. A. Gear, Inc., 342
Levi Strauss Associates, Inc., 344
Liz Claiborne, Inc., 348
McCormick & Company, Inc., 355
McDonald's Corporation, 356
McGraw-Hill, Inc., 357
Marriott Corporation, 360
Montgomery Ward Holding Company, 377
Newsweek International, 387
Northwest Airlines, Inc., 390
NYNEX Corporation, 392
Oppenheimer Group, 398
Organization for Economic Cooperation & Development, 559
Paccar, Inc., 401
Parsons Corporation, 406
J. C. Penney Company, Inc., 407
PepsiCo Foods International, 409
Pfizer, Inc., 412
Philip Morris Companies, Inc., 413
Pillsbury Company, 416
PPG Industries, 421
Primerica Corporation, 424
Prudential Insurance Company of America, 427

A
M
E
R
I
C
A
N

J
O
B
S

A
B
R
O
A
D

R. J. Reynolds Tobacco Company, 429
Ralston Purina Company, 430
Rayovac Corporation, 431
Robert Half International, Inc., 440
Rockwell International Corporation, 441
Rubbermaid, Inc., 445
Saatchi & Saatchi, 448
Saint Jude Medical, Inc., 448
Salomon, Inc., 449
Scott Paper Company, 453
Sequa Corporation, 457
Smith Barney, Harris Upham & Company, Inc., 466
Sotheby's Holdings, Inc., 471
Southland Corporation, 472
State Street Boston Corporation, 478
Symbol Technologies, Inc., 485
Tambrands, Inc., 486
Technoserve, Inc., 565
Tenneco Automotive, 491
Textron, Inc., 494
United Nations Employment Information & Assistance Division, 566
United Parcel Service of America, Inc., 509
U.S. Department of Treasury, 576
United States Information Agency, 580
Visa International, 517
Volunteers in Technical Assistance, Inc, 584
Weight Watchers International, Inc., 524
World Bank Group, 584
Wyeth-Ayerst Laboratories, 530

FINANCIAL ADVISORS

Asian Development Bank, 540
Chase Manhattan Corporation, 190
CS First Boston, Inc., 219
Dean Witter, Discover & Company, 228
Ernst & Young, 255
Klynveld Peat Marwick Goerdeler (KPMG), 337
Arthur D. Little, Inc., 347

Merrill Lynch & Company, Inc., 369
Paine Webber Group, Inc., 403
Reliance International, 436

FINANCIAL CONSULTANTS

J. P. Morgan & Company, Inc., 378
Morgan Stanley Group, Inc., 379

FISHERIES

Food & Agriculture Organization of the United Nations, 546

FORESTRY

Food & Agriculture Organization of the United Nations, 546
U.S. Foreign Agriculture Service, 579

GARDENERS

Pacific Architects & Engineers, Inc., 402

GEOCHEMISTS

Core Laboratories, 214

GEOLOGISTS

Chevron Corporation, 193
Conoco, Inc., 209
Core Laboratories, 214
Maxus Energy Corporation, 363

GEOPHYSICISTS

Conoco, Inc., 209

GUARDS

Pinkerton's, Inc., 416

HEALTH PROFESSIONALS

Amnesty International, USA, 539
CARE, 541
Galen Health Care, 271
Project Concern International, 562
Project HOPE, 563
United Nations Childrens' Fund, 565

United Nations High Commissioner for
   Refugees, 567
World Relief, 587
World Vision Relief and Development,
   Inc., 588

HOSPITAL ADMINISTRATION

Charter Medical Corporation, 190

HOTEL MANAGEMENT

Carnival Cruise Lines, 185
Marriott Corporation, 360

HUMAN RESOURCES

Academy for Educational
   Development, 535
Agency for International Development,
   536
Bristol-Meyers Squibb Company, 175
Omnicom Group, Inc., 397
PepsiCo Foods International, 409
Robert Half International, Inc., 440
Tambrands, Inc., 486
United Nations Employment
   Information & Assistance
   Division, 566

INSURANCE

American International Group, 127

INVESTMENT COUNSELORS

MMS International, 374
Morgan Stanley Group, Inc., 379
Paine Webber Group, Inc., 403
Shearson Lehman Brothers, 460

JOURNALISTS

International Data Group, Inc., 316

LAB TECHNICIANS

Hospital Corporation International,
   Ltd., 304

LEGAL PERSONNEL

Amnesty International, USA, 539

Chadbourne & Parke, 189
Debevoise & Plimpton, 229
Jones, Day, Reavis & Pogue, Inc.,
   326

MAIL CLERKS

Gannett Company, Inc., 272

MAINTENANCE

American Building Maintenance
   Industries, Inc., 123
Cooper Energy Services, Ltd., 212
Dyncorp, 245
The Kuljian Company, 341
Pacific Architects & Engineers, Inc.,
   402
United Engineers & Constructors
   International, 508

MAINTENANCE ENGINEERS

Gannett Fleming, Inc., 272

MANAGEMENT

ABB Vetco Gray, Inc., 108
ACCO World Corporation, 110
Acushnet Company, 111
Airborne Express, 112
AKZO America, Inc., 113
Alexander & Alexander Services, Inc.,
   116
Allied-Signal, Inc., 117
Allis Mineral Systems/Svedala
   Industries, Inc., 118
Aluminum Company of America, 118
AMAX, Inc., 119
Amerace Corporation (Elastimold), 121
American Bankers Insurance Group,
   Inc., 122
American Cyanamid Company, 124
American Greetings Corporation, 126
American International Group, 127
American Management Systems, Inc.,
   127
American President Companies, Ltd.,
   128
American Red Cross, 538
American Tool Companies, Inc., 129

A
M
E
R
I
C
A
N

J
O
B
S

A
B
R
O
A
D

American Uniform Company, 129
Ameriwood, Inc., 130
Ametek, Inc., 130
Amoco Corporation, 131
Ansell International, 135
Apple Computer, Inc., 136
Applied Bioscience International, Inc., 137
Arby's, Inc., 138
ARCO Coal Company, 139
ARCO International Oil and Gas Company, 139
Arethusa Offshore, 140
Armco, Inc., 140
Armour Swift Eckrich, Inc., 141
Armstrong World Industries, Inc., 141
Asea Brown Boveri, 142
Ashland Oil, Inc., 143
AST Research, Inc., 144
Astronautics Corporation of America, 145
Augat, Inc., 146
Avery Dennison Corporation, 147
Avis, Inc., 148
Avnet, Inc., 148
BancTec, Inc., 152
Bank of Boston Corporation, 153
C. R. Bard, Inc., 157
The Barden Corporation, 157
BASF Corporation, 158
Bausch & Lomb, Inc., 159
Baxter Healthcare Corporation, 160
Jim Beam Brands Company, 161
Bechtel Group, Inc., 162
Beckman Instruments, Inc., 162
Bemis Company, Inc., 164
Bendix Field Engineering Corporation, 165
Louis Berger International Inc., 165
Betz Laboratories, 166
Bio-Rad Laboratories, 166
Bissell, Inc., 167
Black & Decker Corporation, 167
Black & Veatch, 168
Blount, Inc. (Blount Construction Division), 169
Boeing Company, 170
Borden, Inc., 170
Borland International, Inc, 172
Boy Scouts of America, 541

W. H. Brady Company, 173
Bridgestone-Firestone, Inc., 174
Bristol Babcock, Inc., 174
Brown Group, Inc., 176
Brown & Sharpe Manufacturing Company, 176
Browning-Ferris Industries, 177
Brush Wellman, Inc., 178
Burlington Air Express, 179
Calgon Corporation, 182
Campbell Soup Company, 183
Cargill Incorporated, 184
Carlson Travel Network, 185
Carrier Corporation, 186
J. I. Case Company, 187
Centocor, Inc., 188
Champion International Corporation, 189
Chase Manhattan Corporation, 190
Chevron Corporation, 193
Chevron Overseas Petroleum, Inc., 194
Child Reach International, 542
Chrysler Corporation, 195
The Chubb & Son Corporation, 196
Church & Dwight Company, Inc., 196
CLARCOR, Inc., 198
Club Corporation International, 200
Club Med, Inc., 201
The Coastal Group, 201
The Coca-Cola Company, 202
Coherent, Inc., 202
Coltec Industries, Inc., 204
Commodore International Ltd., 206
Compaq Computers Corporation, 207
Computer Associates International, Inc., 207
Computervision Corporation, 208
ConAgra, Inc., 208
Conoco, Inc., 209
Continental Bank Corporation, 210
Continuum Company, Inc., 211
Cooper Power Systems, 213
Core States Financial Corporation, 215
CPC International, Inc., 217
CTS Corporation, 220
CUC International, Inc., 221
Cummins Engine Company, Inc., 221
D-M-E Company, 222

DAKA International, 222
Dana Corporation, 224
D'Arcy Masius Benton & Bowles Inc., 225
Dayco Products, Inc., 226
De Kalb Genetics Corporation, 227
De Leuw, Cather International, 228
Del Monte Corporation, 230
Dell Computer Corporation, 231
Deloitte & Touche, 231
Detroit Diesel Corporation, 232
Diebold Incorporated, 235
Digicon, Inc., 235
Digital Equipment Corporation, 236
Dixon Ticonderoga Company, 236
Domino's Pizza, Inc., 237
Donaldson Company, Inc., 237
Reuben H. Donnelly, 239
Dover Corporation, 239
Dresser Industries, Inc., 241
Dun & Bradstreet Corporation, 243
DuPont Merck Pharmaceutical Company, 243
Duracell, Inc., 244
Dyncorp, 245
Ebasco Overseas Corporation, 248
Emerson Electric Company, 251
Emery Worldwide, 252
Encore Computer Corporation, 252
Engelhard Corporation, 253
Enserch International Development, Inc., 254
Esco Corporation, 255
Ethicon, Inc., 256
Ethyl Corporation, 256
Expeditors International of Washington, Inc., 257
Exxon Company, International, 258
Exxon Corporation, 258
Federal-Mogul Corporation, 260
Fischer & Porter Company, 263
Fleming Companies, Inc., 264
Fluor Corporation, 266
Foster Wheeler Corporation, 268
Freeport-McMoran, Inc., 268
Fritz Companies, 269
Fugro-McClelland USA, Inc., 269
Fuller Company, 269
GAF Corporation, 270
The Gates Rubber Company, 273

GATX Corporation, 273
General Dynamics Services Company, 275
General Foods USA, 276
General Railway Signal Company, 278
General Signal Corporation, 278
General Tire, Inc., 279
Getz Brothers Company, Inc., 281
Goldman Sachs & Company, 283
Gould Pumps, Inc., 285
W. R. Grace & Company, 285
Grant Thornton International, 286
Great Lakes Chemical Corporation, 287
Grey Advertising, Inc., 288
GTE Directories Corporation, 289
Guardian Industries Corporation, 290
H & R Block, 291
Hamlin, Inc., 294
M. A. Hanna Company, 295
Hellmuth, Obata & Kassabaum, Inc., 298
Hercules, Inc., 299
Hill & Knowlton, Inc., 301
Holmes & Narver, Inc., 303
Household International, Inc., 305
Hubbell, Inc., 306
J. M. Huber Corporation, 306
Hughes Aircraft Company, 307
Hughes Christensen Company, 307
IDB Communications, Inc., 309
Illinois Tool Works, Inc., 309
IMCERA Group, Inc., 310
IMO Industries, 310
Inductotherm Corporation, 311
Information Builders, Inc., 312
Intergraph Corporation, 314
International Business Machines (IBM), 315
International Dairy Queen, Inc., 316
International Data Group, Inc., 316
International Flavors & Fragrances, Inc., 317
International Labor Office, 550
International Rectifier Corporation, 319
International Voluntary Services, Inc., 555
Iomega Corporation, 320
ITT Sheraton Corporation, 322

A
M
E
R
I
C
A
N

J
O
B
S

A
B
R
O
A
D

ITW Finishing Systems & Products, 322
James River Corporation, 323
JMK International/Jamack Fabrications, Inc., 323
Johnson & Higgins, 324
Johnson & Johnson, 325
JWP, Inc., 328
Kaman Corporation, 328
Kayser-Roth Corporation, 329
Kellogg Company, 330
Kellwood Company, 331
Kelsey-Hayes Company, 332
Kendall International, 332
Kennametal, Inc., 333
Keystone International, 334
KFC Corporation, 335
Kimball International, Inc., 336
Kimberly-Clark Corporation, 336
Knight-Ridder, Inc., 338
Knoll International, 338
Koch Industries, Inc., 339
Korn/Ferry International, 340
Lawter International, Inc., 344
Liant Software Corporation, 345
The Lincoln Electric Company, 346
Lintas: Worldwide, 346
Lockheed Corporation, 349
Louisiana Land & Exploration Company, 352
LTV Steel Co., 352
LTX Corporation, 353
Lykes Lines, 354
MacDermid, Inc., 355
McDonald's Corporation, 356
MagneTek, Inc., 358
Marion Merrell Dow, Inc., 360
Masoneilan Industries, Inc., 361
George S. May International, Inc., 364
Maytag Corporation, 364
Memorex Telex Corporation, 367
Merisel, Inc., 369
Merrill Lynch & Company, Inc., 369
Miller Brewing Company, 372
Herman Miller, Inc., 373
Milliken & Company, 373
Millipore Corporation, 374
MMS International, 374
Modine Manufacturing Company, 375

Molex, Inc., 376
Monroe Auto Equipment Company, 376
Morrison Knudsen Corporation, 379
Motion Picture Export Association of America, 380
Nabors Industries, Inc., 381
National Data Corporation, 382
Nicolet Instrument Corporation, 387
NIKE, Inc., 388
NL Industries, Inc., 388
Nordson Corporation, 389
North American Philips Corporation, 389
Northwest Airlines, Inc., 390
Norwest Corporation, 391
Ogden Corporation, 395
Ogilvy & Mather, 395
Olin Corporation, 396
Omnicom Group, Inc., 397
Oracle Systems, Inc., 398
Oryx Energy, 398
Otis Elevator Company: World Headquarters, 399
Outboard Marine Corporation, 399
Owens-Illinois, Inc., 401
Paine Webber Group, Inc., 403
Pall Corporation, 404
Paramount Communications, Inc., 404
Parker Hannifin Corporation, 405
Parsons Brinkerhoff, 406
Pennzoil Company, 408
Penrod Drilling Corporation, 408
PepsiCo, Inc., 410
Perkin-Elmer Corporation, 410
Petrolite Corporation, 411
Pfaudler Companies, Inc., 411
Phelps Dodge Corporation, 412
Phibro Energy, Inc., 413
Philipp Brothers Chemicals, Inc., 414
Philips Technologies, 414
Phillips-Van Heusen Corporation, 415
Pinkerton's, Inc., 416
Pioneer Hi-Bred International, Inc., 417
Pittsburgh-Des Moines Corporation, 418
Pittway Corporation, 418
Pizza Hut, Inc., 419
Playtex Apparel, Inc., 419

Polaroid Corporation, 420
R. L. Polk & Company, 421
PPG Industries, 421
PRC, Inc., 422
Precision Valve Corporation, 422
Preformed Line Products Company, 423
Premark International, Inc., 423
Printronix, Inc., 425
Procter & Gamble Company, 425
Purolator Products Company, 427
Quaker Chemical Corporation, 428
Quaker Oats Company, 428
Rain Bird Sprinkler Manufacturing Corporation, 430
Ranco, Inc., 431
Reader's Digest Association, Inc., 432
Reading & Bates, 433
Reed Tool Company, 434
Reliance Electric Company, 435
Reliance International, 436
Remington Products, Inc., 436
Resources Management International, 437
Revlon, Inc., 437
Rhone-Poulenc Rorer, 438
Riverwood International, Inc., 439
Robertson Ceco, 440
Rohm & Haas Company, 442
Rosemount, Inc., 443
RPM, Inc., 444
Rubbermaid, Inc., 445
Russell Corporation, 446
Rust International, Inc., 447
Ryder Systems, Inc., 447
Saint Jude Medical, Inc., 448
Salomon, Inc., 449
Sara Lee Corporation, 449
SB Power Tools, Inc. (Skil Corp.), 450
Schering-Plough Corporation, 450
Schlegel Corporation, 451
A. Schulman, Inc., 451
SCM Chemicals, 453
Seagate Technology, Inc., 454
Sealed Air Corporation, 455
Sears Roebuck and Company, 456
Senco Products, 456
Sequa Corporation, 457
SGS Control Services, 458

SGS-Thomson Microelectronics, 458
Shaklee Corporation, 459
Sheaffer Pen, Inc., 459
Sherwin-Williams Company, 461
Shipley Company, Inc., 461
Signode Packaging Systems, 462
Simplex Time Recorder Company, 463
Simplicity Pattern Company Inc., 464
Sizzler International, 464
Smith Corona Corporation, 466
A. O. Smith Corporation, 467
Smith International, Inc., 467
J. M. Smucker Company, 468
Sonat Offshore, 470
Sonesta International Hotels Corporation, 470
Sonoco Products Company, 470
Sony Pictures Entertainment, 471
Sotheby's Holdings, Inc., 471
Southland Corporation, 472
Southwire Company, 472
Sperry-Sun, Inc., 473
Square D Company, 475
SRI International, 475
Standard Commercial Corporation, 476
Standard & Poor's Corporation, 476
Standex International, 477
Stanhome, Inc., 477
Stanley Works, 478
Sterling Winthrop, Inc., 479
Stone & Webster Engineering Corporation, 480
Storage Technology Corporation, 481
Structural Dynamics Research Corporation, 481
Sun Electric Corporation, 484
Syntex Corporation, 486
Tandy Corporation, 487
Tektronix, Inc., 488
Teledyne, Inc., 489
Tennant Company, 490
Tenneco, Inc., 492
Tennessee Associates International, Inc., 492
Teradyne, Inc., 493
Texas Intruments, Inc., 494
Thermco Systems, Inc., 495
Thomas & Betts, 495

3M Company, 496
3M Pharmaceuticals, 497
Time, Inc., 497
TLC Beatrice International Holdings,
    Inc., 498
Torrington Company, 499
Towers Perrin, Inc., 499
Toys "R" Us, Inc., 500
Tracor, Inc., 500
Trane Company, 501
Transamerica, Corporation, 501
Trinova Corporation, 502
Triton Energy Corporation, 502
TRW, Inc., 503
TW Holdings, Inc., 504
Tyson Foods, Inc., 505
Unilever United States, Inc., 506
Union Camp Corporation, 507
Union Carbide Corporation, 507
United Engineers & Constructors
    International, 508
United Nations Industrial Development
    Organization (UNIDO), 568
United Parcel Service of America,
    Inc., 509
U.S. Department of Defense, 572
U.S. Department of Energy, 573
U.S. Electrical Motors (Emerson
    Electric), 510
United States Shoe Corporation, 510
U.S. Wheat Associates, 511
United Technologies Corporation, 512
Unocal Corporation, 513
UOP, Inc., 514
The Upjohn Company, 515
US West, Inc., 515
USAir Group, Inc., 516
VF Corporation, 517
Visa International, 517
Vishay Intertechnology, 518
VTN Corporation, 518
Walker Manufacturing Company, 519
Wang Laboratories, Inc., 519
Ward Howell International, Inc., 520
Warnaco, Inc., 520
Warner Brothers International, 521
Warner Electric Brake & Clutch
    Company, 521
Warner-Lambert Company, 522
Washington Post Company, 522

Jervis B. Webb Company, 523
Weight Watchers International, Inc.,
    524
West Company, Inc., 525
Westinghouse Electric Corporation,
    525
Weyerhaeuser Company, 526
Whirlpool Corporation, 526
Whitman Corporation, 527
WMX Technologies/Waste
    Management, Inc., 527
Woodward Governor Company, 528
Woolworth Corporation, 528
World Concern, 585
World Courier Management, Inc., 529
Wyeth-Ayerst Laboratories, 530
Wynn's International, Inc., 530
Yellow Freight System, Inc., 532
York International, Inc., 532
Young & Rubicam, Inc., 533

MANAGEMENT TRAINING

Arby's, Inc., 138
Avis, Inc., 148
Diamond Shamrock R & M, Inc.,
    234
Duro-Test International Corporation,
    245
Hertz Corporation, 300
International City Management
    Association, 548
International Management Development
    Institute, 551
KFC Corporation, 335
McDonald's Corporation, 356
Wendy's International, Inc., 524

MANUFACTURING

Advance Machine Company, 111
Advanced Micro Devices, Inc., 112
Alberto-Culver Company, 115
Allis Mineral Systems/Svedala
    Industries, Inc., 118
Ameracc Corporation (Elastimold), 121
Ametek, Inc., 130
AMP, Inc., 132
Ampex Corporation, 133
Anthony Industries, 135
Apple Computer, Inc., 136

Applied Materials, Inc., 137
Archer-Daniels-Midland Company, 138
Astronautics Corporation of America, 145
AVX Corporation, 150
Bell & Howell Company, 164
Borg-Warner Corporation, 171
Bose Corporation, 172
Calgon Corporation, 182
Catholic Relief Services, 542
Chrysler Corporation, 195
Clorox Company, 199
Coin Acceptors, Inc., 203
Conoco, Inc., 209
Corning Incorporated, 215
Del Monte Corporation, 230
Flow International Corporation, 265
The Gates Rubber Company, 273
Graco, Inc., 286
H. J. Heinz Company, 290
Hamlin, Inc., 294
Hubbell, Inc., 306
Ingersoll Engineers, 312
Ingersoll International, Inc., 313
Kelsey-Hayes Company, 332
Kendall International, 332
Keystone International, 334
Masoneilan Industries, Inc., 361
Measurex Corporation, 366
Nellcor, Inc., 385
Otis Elevator Company: World
    Headquarters, 399
Owens-Illinois, Inc., 401
PMI Food Equipment Group, 420
Tambrands, Inc., 486
Tennant Company, 490
3M Company, 496
3M Pharmaceuticals, 497
Torrington Company, 499
Waters Chromatography (Millipore), 523
Whitman Corporation, 527

MARKETING

Academy for Educational
    Development, 535
ACCO World Corporation, 110
Airborne Express, 112
AMAX, Inc., 119

American President Companies, Ltd., 128
American Standard, Inc., 128
Ameriwood, Inc., 130
Anacomp, Inc., 134
Ansell International, 135
Armco, Inc., 140
Armstrong World Industries, Inc., 141
Asarco, Inc., 142
Asea Brown Boveri, 142
Astronautics Corporation of America, 145
AVX Corporation, 150
Backer Spielvogel & Bates Worldwide, Inc., 150
Bandag, Inc., 153
Bell Helicopter Textron, Inc., 163
Bemis Company, Inc., 164
Boeing Company, 170
Browning-Ferris Industries, 177
Brush Wellman, Inc., 178
Buck Consultants, Inc., 178
Burlington Air Express, 179
Capitol Cities/ABC, Inc., 184
Carrier Corporation, 186
Champion International Corporation, 189
The Chubb & Son Corporation, 196
CLARCOR, Inc., 198
Club Corporation International, 200
Coin Acceptors, Inc., 203
Columbian Rope Company, 204
Commerce Clearing House, 205
Coopers & Lybrand, 214
Corning Incorporated, 215
CRS Sirrine, Inc., 219
CUC International, Inc., 221
Cummins Engine Company, Inc., 221
Leo A. Daly Company, 223
D'Arcy Masius Benton & Bowles Inc., 225
Day & Zimmerman, 226
Deloitte & Touche, 231
R. R. Donnelley & Sons Company, 238
Drummond Company, Inc., 242
Dun & Bradstreet Corporation, 243
Duracell, Inc., 244
Dyncorp, 245
Eastman Kodak Company, 246

A
M
E
R
I
C
A
N

J
O
B
S

A
B
R
O
A
D

Eaton Corporation/Cutler Hammer, 247

Electronic Data Systems Corporation, 249

Emery Worldwide, 252

Ernst & Young, 255

Esco Corporation, 255

Expeditors International of Washington, Inc., 257

Federal Express Corporation, 260

Figgie International, Inc., 262

Fluor Corporation, 266

FMC Corporation, 266

Freeport-McMoran, Inc., 268

Fugro-McClelland USA, Inc., 269

GAF Corporation, 270

Gafney, Cline & Associates, Inc., 271

The Gates Rubber Company, 273

GATX Corporation, 273

General Dynamics Corporation, 274

General Dynamics Services Company, 275

General Electric Company (GE), 275

Geraghty & Miller, Inc., 279

Getz Brothers Company, Inc., 281

Gould Pumps, Inc., 285

W. R. Grace & Company, 285

Grant Thornton International, 286

Great Lakes Carbon International Corporation, 287

A. P. Green Industries, Inc., 287

Grey Advertising, Inc., 288

Guardian Industries Corporation, 290

Hach Company, 292

Halliburton Company, 292

Halliburton Company/Halliburton Services Division, 293

Hartford Steam Boiler Inspection/ Insurance Company, 296

HDR Incorporated, 298

Hercules, Inc., 299

Hill & Knowlton, Inc., 301

Holmes & Narver, Inc., 303

IMS America, Ltd., 311

International Fertilizer Development Center, 549

International Flavors & Fragrances, Inc., 317

International Paper Company, 318

Intertrans Corporation, 320

ITW Finishing Systems & Products, 322

James River Corporation, 323

JMK International/Jamack Fabrications, Inc., 323

Kaman Corporation, 328

A. T. Kearney, Inc., 329

Kennecott Corporation, 333

Ketchum International, 334

Kimball International, Inc., 336

Kimberly-Clark Corporation, 336

Knoll International, 338

Kohler Company, 339

Kolmar Laboratories, Inc., 340

Law Companies Group, Inc., 343

Lintas: Worldwide, 346

LTV Steel Co., 352

Lykes Lines, 354

McCann-Erickson Worldwide, 354

Macro Systems, Inc., 358

Masco Corporation, 361

Masonite Corporation, 362

George S. May International, Inc., 364

Mead Corporation, 365

Metcalf & Eddy International, Inc., 370

MGM Incorporated, 372

Herman Miller, Inc., 373

Milliken & Company, 373

Modine Manufacturing Company, 375

Morrison Knudsen Corporation, 379

Morton International, 380

Motion Picture Export Association of America, 380

National Data Corporation, 382

Newmont Mining Corporation, 386

Ogilvy & Mather, 395

Omnicom Group, Inc., 397

ONAN Corporation, 397

Otis Elevator Company: World Headquarters, 399

Outboard Marine Corporation, 399

Overseas Shipholding Group, Inc., 400

Paccar, Inc., 401

Paramount Communications, Inc., 404

Parsons Brinkerhoff, 406

Parsons Corporation, 406

PRC, Inc., 422

Preformed Line Products Company, 423
Price Waterhouse, 424
Reeves Brothers, Inc., 435
Riverwood International, Inc., 439
Robert Half International, Inc., 440
Robertson Ceco, 440
Rogers Corporation, 442
Ruder Finn, Inc., 445
Russell Reynolds Associates, Inc., 446
Rust International, Inc., 447
Ryder Systems, Inc., 447
Saatchi & Saatchi, 448
Sea-Land Service, Inc., 454
Sealed Air Corporation, 455
SGS Control Services, 458
Signode Packaging Systems, 462
Skadden, Arps, Slate, Meagher & Flom, 465
Sonoco Products Company, 470
Sony Pictures Entertainment, 471
Sotheby's Holdings, Inc., 471
SRI International, 475
Standex International, 477
Stebbins Engineering & Manufacturing Corporation, 479
Stone Container Corporation, 480
Stone & Webster Engineering Corporation, 480
STV Group, 482
Tennessee Associates International, Inc., 492
Textron, Inc., 494
Time-Warner, Inc., 498
Torrington Company, 499
Towers Perrin, Inc., 499
Trane Company, 501
TRW, Inc., 503
Turner Broadcasting System, Inc., 503
Turner Steiner International, Inc., 504
Union Camp Corporation, 507
United Parcel Service of America, Inc., 509
U.S. Foreign Agriculture Service, 579
United Technologies Corporation, 512
Universal Foods Corporation, 513
USX Corporation, 516
Vishay Intertechnology, 518

Ward Howell International, Inc., 520
Warner Brothers International, 521
West Company, Inc., 525
Weyerhaeuser Company, 526
WMX Technologies/Waste Management, Inc., 527
World Courier Management, Inc., 529
Yellow Freight System, Inc., 532
York International, Inc., 532
Young & Rubicam, Inc., 533

MARKETING—AGRICULTURAL

Archer-Daniels-Midland Company, 138
Cargill Incorporated, 184
Central Soya Company, 188
Continental Grain Company, 211
De Kalb Genetics Corporation, 227
Exxon Chemical Company, 257
Monsanto Company, 377
Philipp Brothers Chemicals, Inc., 414
Pioneer Hi-Bred International, Inc., 417
Rain Bird Sprinkler Manufacturing Corporation, 430
U.S. Wheat Associates, 511
Universal Foods Corporation, 513

MARKETING—AUTOMOTIVE

Allied-Signal, Inc., 117
Chrysler Corporation, 195
Coltec Industries, Inc., 204
Cooper Industries, Inc., 213
Dana Corporation, 224
Dayco Products, Inc., 226
Eaton Corporation/Cutler Hammer, 247
Ford Motor Company, 267
General Motors Corporation (GM), 277
General Tire, Inc., 279
Goodyear Tire & Rubber Company, 284
Hertz Corporation, 300
Kelsey-Hayes Company, 332
Monroe Auto Equipment Company, 376
Navistar International Transportation Corporation, 383
Purolator Products Company, 427

Rockwell International Corporation, 441

A. O. Smith Corporation, 467

Sun Electric Corporation, 484

Tenneco Automotive, 491

Walker Manufacturing Company, 519

Warner Electric Brake & Clutch Company, 521

Wynn's International, Inc., 530

MARKETING—CHEMICALS

AKZO America, Inc., 113

Aluminum Company of America, 118

Amerace Corporation (Elastimold), 121

Amoco Corporation, 131

Asarco, Inc., 142

BASF Corporation, 158

Betz Laboratories, 166

BP America, Inc., 173

Cabot Corporation, 181

Calgon Corporation, 182

Chevron Chemical Company, 192

Church & Dwight Company, Inc., 196

Diamond Shamrock R & M, Inc., 234

Dow Chemical Company, 240

Dow Corning Corporation, 240

Eastman Kodak Company, 246

Engelhard Corporation, 253

Ethyl Corporation, 256

Exxon Chemical Company, 257

Exxon Corporation, 258

GAF Corporation, 270

W. R. Grace & Company, 285

Great Lakes Chemical Corporation, 287

M. A. Hanna Company, 295

Hercules, Inc., 299

Hoechst Celanese, Inc., 302

J. M. Huber Corporation, 306

IMCERA Group, Inc., 310

Koch Industries, Inc., 339

Lawter International, Inc., 344

Loctite Corporation, 349

Lord Corporation, 350

Lubrizol Corporation, 353

MacDermid, Inc., 355

Mallinckrodt, Inc., 359

Merck & Company, Inc., 368

Metco Perkin-Elmer, 371

Mobil Oil Corporation, 375

Monsanto Company, 377

Morton International, 380

Nalco Chemical Company, 382

Olin Corporation, 396

OMI International, 396

Pennzoil Company, 408

Petrolite Corporation, 411

Philipp Brothers Chemicals, Inc., 414

Phillips Petroleum Company, 415

PPG Industries, 421

Quaker Chemical Corporation, 428

Rohm & Haas Company, 442

RPM, Inc., 444

Rubbermaid, Inc., 445

A. Schulman, Inc., 451

SCM Chemicals, 453

Sherwin-Williams Company, 461

Shipley Company, Inc., 461

3M Pharmaceuticals, 497

Union Camp Corporation, 507

Union Carbide Corporation, 507

UOP, Inc., 514

The Upjohn Company, 515

Wynn's International, Inc., 530

MARKETING—CONSUMER GOODS

Acushnet Company, 111

Alberto-Culver Company, 115

American Greetings Corporation, 126

American Tool Companies, Inc., 129

Avery Dennison Corporation, 147

Bissell, Inc., 167

Brown & Williamson Tobacco Corporation, 177

Calgon Corporation, 182

Carter-Wallace, Inc., 187

Bernard Chaus, Inc., 191

Church & Dwight Company, Inc., 196

Clorox Company, 199

Colgate-Palmolive Company, 203

Converse, Inc., 212

Corning Incorporated, 215

CPC International, Inc., 217

Dixon Ticonderoga Company, 236

Dow Chemical Company, 240

Elizabeth Arden Company, 251

Florsheim Shoe Company, 264
The Gillette Company, 283
Hallmark Cards, Inc., 294
Hasbro, Inc., 297
Helene Curtis Industries, Inc., 298
James River Corporation, 323
S. C. Johnson Wax, 325
Kayser-Roth Corporation, 329
Kellwood Company, 331
Kimberly-Clark Corporation, 336
Kinney Shoe Corporation, 337
L. A. Gear, Inc., 342
Levi Strauss Associates, Inc., 344
The Limited, Inc., 345
Liz Claiborne, Inc., 348
Master Lock Company, 362
Mattel, Inc., 363
Maytag Corporation, 364
Montgomery Ward Holding Company,
    377
NIKE, Inc., 388
J. C. Penney Company, Inc., 407
Philip Morris Companies, Inc., 413
Phillips-Van Heusen Corporation, 415
Pitney Bowes, Inc., 417
Playtex Apparel, Inc., 419
Premark International, Inc., 423
Procter & Gamble Company, 425
Procter & Gamble Cosmetics and
    Fragrance Products, 426
R. J. Reynolds Tobacco Company,
    429
Ralston Purina Company, 430
Redken Laboratories, Inc., 434
Remington Products, Inc., 436
Revlon, Inc., 437
RJR Nabisco, 439
Rubbermaid, Inc., 445
Russell Corporation, 446
SB Power Tools, Inc. (Skil Corp.),
    450
Scott Paper Company, 453
Sears Roebuck and Company, 456
Senco Products, 456
Shaklee Corporation, 459
Sheaffer Pen, Inc., 459
Simplicity Pattern Company Inc., 464
Snap-On Tools Corporation, 468
Southland Corporation, 472
Springs Industries, Inc., 473

Standard Commercial Corporation,
    476
Stanhome, Inc., 477
Stanley Works, 478
Tambrands, Inc., 486
3M Company, 496
Toys "R" Us, Inc., 500
Unilever United States, Inc., 506
United States Shoe Corporation, 510
VF Corporation, 517
Warnaco, Inc., 520
Warner-Lambert Company, 522
Weight Watchers International, Inc.,
    524
Whirlpool Corporation, 526
Whitman Corporation, 527
Woolworth Corporation, 528
Wynn's International, Inc., 530

MARKETING—ELECTRONICS

Advanced Micro Devices, Inc., 112
Alarm Device Manufacturing Company,
    114
Aldus Corporation, 115
Allen-Bradley Company, Inc., 116
Aluminum Company of America, 118
AM International, Inc., 119
Amdahl Corporation, 120
American Management Systems, Inc.,
    127
AMP, Inc., 132
Ampex Corporation, 133
Andrew Corporation, 134
Apple Computer, Inc., 136
AST Research, Inc., 144
Atari Corporation, 146
Augat, Inc., 146
Avnet, Inc., 148
Bailey Controls Company, 151
BancTec, Inc., 152
Banyan Systems, Inc., 156
Beckman Instruments, Inc., 162
Bell & Howell Company, 164
Bose Corporation, 172
Cincom Systems, Inc., 197
Commodore International Ltd., 206
Compaq Computers Corporation, 207
Computer Associates International,
    Inc., 207

A
M
E
R
I
C
A
N

J
O
B
S

A
B
R
O
A
D

Computervision Corporation, 208
Cooper Industries, Inc., 213
CTS Corporation, 220
Data General Corporation, 225
Dell Computer Corporation, 231
Diebold Incorporated, 235
Digital Equipment Corporation, 236
Duro-Test International Corporation, 245
E-Systems, Inc., 245
Emerson Electric Company, 251
Encore Computer Corporation, 252
John Fluke Manufacturing Company, 265
General Electric Company (GE), 275
General Instrument Corporation, 276
General Signal Corporation, 278
GTECH Corporation, 289
Harris Corporation, 296
Hewlett-Packard Company, 300
Honeywell, Inc., 303
Hubbell, Inc., 306
IDB Communications, Inc., 309
IMO Industries, 310
Information Builders, Inc., 312
Intel Corporation, 314
Intergraph Corporation, 314
International Totalizator Systems, Inc., 319
Iomega Corporation, 320
Johnson Controls, Inc., 324
JWP, Inc., 328
Keithley Instruments, Inc., 329
Lambda Electronics, Inc., 343
Liant Software Corporation, 345
Loral Corporation, 350
Lotus Development Corporation, 351
LTX Corporation, 353
MagneTek, Inc., 358
Measurex Corporation, 366
Memorex Telex Corporation, 367
Merisel, Inc., 369
Methode Electronics, Inc., 371
Molex, Inc., 376
Motorola, Inc., 381
National Semiconductor Corporation, 383
NCR Corporation, 384
Nicolet Instrument Corporation, 387

North American Philips Corporation, 389
Novell, Inc., 392
Oracle Systems, Inc., 398
Perkin-Elmer Corporation, 410
Pittway Corporation, 418
Polaroid Corporation, 420
Printronix, Inc., 425
Qume Corporation, 429
Ranco, Inc., 431
Raytheon Company, 432
Rockwell International Corporation, 441
SCI Systems, 452
Seagate Technology, Inc., 454
Sensormatic Electronics Corporation, 457
SGS-Thomson Microelectronics, 458
Siliconix, 462
Simplex Time Recorder Company, 463
Smith Corona Corporation, 466
Solectron Corporation, 469
Southwire Company, 472
Square D Company, 475
Storage Technology Corporation, 481
Structural Dynamics Research Corporation, 481
Sun Microsystems, Inc., 484
Symbol Technologies, Inc., 485
Tandem Computers, Inc., 487
Tandy Corporation, 487
Tektronix, Inc., 488
Telxon Corp., 490
Texas Intruments, Inc., 494
Thomas & Betts, 495
Unisys Corporation, 508
U.S. Electrical Motors (Emerson Electric), 510
Vishay Intertechnology, 518
Westinghouse Electric Corporation, 525
Xerox Corporation, 531

MARKETING—FINANCIAL SERVICES

Alexander & Alexander Services, Inc., 116

American Bankers Insurance Group, Inc., 122

American Express Bank, Ltd., 124

American Express Company—Travel Related Services, 125

Aon Corporation, 136

AT&T International, 145

Bank of Boston Corporation, 153

Bear Stearns Companies, Inc., 161

Chase Manhattan Corporation, 190

Chemical Banking Corporation, 191

Continental Bank Corporation, 210

Core States Financial Corporation, 215

CS First Boston, Inc., 219

CUNA Mutual Insurance Group, 222

Ford Motor Company, 267

Fritz Companies, 269

General Electric Company (GE), 275

General Motors Corporation (GM), 277

Goldman Sachs & Company, 283

Household International, Inc., 305

ITT Hartford Insurance Group, 321

Johnson & Higgins, 324

Merrill Lynch & Company, Inc., 369

Metropolitan Life Insurance Company, 371

MMS International, 374

New York Life Insurance Company, 385

Paine Webber Group, Inc., 403

Primerica Corporation, 424

Prudential Insurance Company of America, 427

Reliance International, 436

Rollins Hudig Hall International, 443

Salomon, Inc., 449

Sears Roebuck and Company, 456

Shearson Lehman Brothers, 460

Smith Barney, Harris Upham & Company, Inc., 466

State Street Boston Corporation, 478

Textron, Inc., 494

Transamerica, Corporation, 501

UNUM Corporation, 514

Visa International, 517

MARKETING—FOOD/FOOD SERVICES

Alberto-Culver Company, 115

American Home Products Corporation, 126

Arby's, Inc., 138

Armour Swift Eckrich, Inc., 141

Jim Beam Brands Company, 161

Cargill Incorporated, 184

The Coca-Cola Company, 202

ConAgra, Inc., 208

CPC International, Inc., 217

DAKA International, 222

Del Monte Corporation, 230

Domino's Pizza, Inc., 237

Fleming Companies, Inc., 264

General Foods USA, 276

General Mills, Inc., 277

Gerber Products Company, 280

H. J. Heinz Company, 290

Hershey Foods Corporation, 299

Holiday Inns Worldwide, 302

Hormel Foods Corporation, 304

International Dairy Queen, Inc., 316

KFC Corporation, 335

Kraft General Foods International, 341

McCormick & Company, Inc., 355

McDonald's Corporation, 356

Marriott Corporation, 360

Miller Brewing Company, 372

PepsiCo Foods International, 409

PepsiCo, Inc., 410

Philip Morris Companies, Inc., 413

Pillsbury Company, 416

Pizza Hut, Inc., 419

Procter & Gamble Company, 425

Quaker Oats Company, 428

Ralston Purina Company, 430

RJR Nabisco, 439

Sara Lee Corporation, 449

Sizzler International, 464

J. M. Smucker Company, 468

Southland Corporation, 472

TLC Beatrice International Holdings, Inc., 498

TW Holdings, Inc., 504

Tyson Foods, Inc., 505

Wendy's International, Inc., 524

William Wrigley Jr. Company, 529

MARKETING—HEALTH & MEDICAL SUPPLIES

Abex Inc./Fisher Scientific
    International, Inc., 110
AKZO America, Inc., 113
American Cyanamid Company, 124
American Home Products Corporation,
    126
C. R. Bard, Inc., 157
Bausch & Lomb, Inc., 159
Baxter Healthcare Corporation, 160
Bio-Rad Laboratories, 166
Chiron Corporation, 194
Eli Lilly and Company, 250
Ethicon, Inc., 256
Johnson & Johnson, 325
Kendall International, 332
Mallinckrodt, Inc., 359
Medtronic, Inc., 366
Nellcor, Inc., 385
Pall Corporation, 404
Pfizer, Inc., 412
Saint Jude Medical, Inc., 448
Schering-Plough Corporation, 450
United States Surgical Corporation,
    511
Warner-Lambert Company, 522

MARKETING—INDUSTRIAL

Advance Machine Company, 111
Allis Mineral Systems/Svedala
    Industries, Inc., 118
Aluminum Company of America, 118
Ametek, Inc., 130
Automatic Switch Company, 147
W. H. Brady Company, 173
Bristol Babcock, Inc., 174
J. I. Case Company, 187
Chemical Fabrics Corporation, 192
Coltec Industries, Inc., 204
Commercial Intertech Corporation,
    205
Cooper Energy Services, Ltd., 212
Cooper Industries, Inc., 213
Cooper Power Systems, 213
John Crane, Inc., 218

Crown Cork & Seal Company, Inc.,
    218
D-M-E Company, 222
Detroit Diesel Corporation, 232
The Dexter Corporation, 233
DH Technology, Inc., 233
Dover Corporation, 239
Duriron Company, Inc., 244
Falk Corporation, 259
Federal-Mogul Corporation, 260
Fisher Controls International, Inc.,
    263
Flow International Corporation, 265
Giddings & Lewis, Inc., 282
Graco, Inc., 286
Hamlin, Inc., 294
Hanson Industries, 295
Illinois Tool Works, Inc., 309
Inductotherm Corporation, 311
Ingersoll International, Inc., 313
Ingersoll-Rand Company, 313
Joy Technologies, Inc., 327
Kennametal, Inc., 333
Keystone International, 334
Kysor Industrial Corporation, 342
The Lincoln Electric Company, 346
Liquid Carbonic Corporation, 347
Melroe Company, 367
Metallurg Corporation, 370
Moore Products Company, 378
Nordson Corporation, 389
Norton Company, 390
Parker Hannifin Corporation, 405
Pentair, Inc., 409
Petrolite Corporation, 411
PMI Food Equipment Group, 420
Precision Valve Corporation, 422
Ranco, Inc., 431
Reliance Electric Company, 435
Reynolds Metals Company, 438
Rockwell Graphic Systems, 441
Rosemount, Inc., 443
Schlegel Corporation, 451
Sequa Corporation, 457
SPS Technologies, Inc., 474
Tennant Company, 490
Trinova Corporation, 502
Woodward Governor Company, 528

MARKETING—PETROLEUM/ NATURAL GAS

Amoco Corporation, 131
ARCO International Oil and Gas Company, 139
Arethusa Offshore, 140
Ashland Oil, Inc., 143
Baroid Corporation, 158
BP America, Inc., 173
Cabot Corporation, 181
Chevron Overseas Petroleum, Inc., 194
The Coastal Group, 201
Diamond M-ODECO Drilling, Inc., 234
Engelhard Corporation, 253
Enron Corporation, 254
Enserch International Development, Inc., 254
Exxon Company, International, 258
Exxon Corporation, 258
Freeport-McMoran, Inc., 268
Koch Industries, Inc., 339
Marathon Petroleum Company, 359
Mobil Oil Corporation, 375
Occidental Petroleum Corporation, 393
Oceaneering International, Inc., 393
Oryx Energy, 398
Parker Drilling Company, 405
Pennzoil Company, 408
Penrod Drilling Corporation, 408
Phibro Energy, Inc., 413
Phillips Petroleum Company, 415
Reading & Bates, 433
Reed Tool Company, 434
Rowan Companies, Inc., 444
Smith International, Inc., 467
Sonat, Inc., 469
Sonat Offshore, 470
Sperry-Sun, Inc., 473
Sun Company, Inc., 483
Tenneco, Inc., 492
Texaco Oil Company, 493
Triton Energy Corporation, 502
Unocal Corporation, 513
USX Corporation, 516

MARKETING— PHARMACEUTICALS

A. L. Laboratories Inc., 107
Allergan, Inc., 117
American Cyanamid Company, 124
American Home Products Corporation, 126
Bausch & Lomb, Inc., 159
Block Drug Company, Inc., 169
Carter-Wallace, Inc., 187
Centocor, Inc., 188
Chiron Corporation, 194
DuPont Merck Pharmaceutical Company, 243
Eli Lilly and Company, 250
Johnson & Johnson, 325
Mallinckrodt, Inc., 359
Marion Merrell Dow, Inc., 360
Merck & Company, Inc., 368
Monsanto Company, 377
Pfizer, Inc., 412
Procter & Gamble Pharmaceuticals, Inc., 426
Revlon, Inc., 437
Rhone-Poulenc Rorer, 438
Schering-Plough Corporation, 450
Searle Company, 455
Sterling Winthrop, Inc., 479
Syntex Corporation, 486
3M Pharmaceuticals, 497
The Upjohn Company, 515
Warner-Lambert Company, 522
Wyeth-Ayerst Laboratories, 530

MARKETING—PUBLISHING

Bell & Howell Company, 164
Capitol Cities/ABC, Inc., 184
Reuben H. Donnelly, 239
Dun & Bradstreet Corporation, 243
Encyclopedia Britannica, Inc., 253
Fairchild Publications, Inc., 259
GTE Directories Corporation, 289
International Data Group, Inc., 316
Knight-Ridder, Inc., 338
McGraw-Hill, Inc., 357
New York Times Company, 386
Paramount Communications, Inc., 404
Pittway Corporation, 418
R. L. Polk & Company, 421

JOB CATEGORY INDEX

A
M
E
R
I
C
A
N

J
O
B
S

A
B
R
O
A
D

Reader's Digest Association, Inc., 432
Simon & Schuster, Inc., 463
Time, Inc., 497
Time-Warner, Inc., 498
Washington Post Company, 522

MARKETING—SCIENTIFIC

ABB Vetco Gray, Inc., 108
Abex Inc./Fisher Scientific
    International, Inc., 110
Allied-Signal, Inc., 117
Aluminum Company of America, 118
Amgen, Inc., 131
Applied Bioscience International, Inc.,
    137
Applied Materials, Inc., 137
BASF Corporation, 158
Beckman Instruments, Inc., 162
Bio-Rad Laboratories, 166
Brown & Sharpe Manufacturing
    Company, 176
Coherent, Inc., 202
Coltec Industries, Inc., 204
Computervision Corporation, 208
Dresser Industries, Inc., 241
Eagle-Picher Industries, Inc., 246
EG & G, Inc., 249
Fischer & Porter Company, 263
Hazleton Washington Corporation, 297
Honeywell, Inc., 303
Hughes Aircraft Company, 307
IMCERA Group, Inc., 310
International Rectifier Corporation,
    319
JWP, Inc., 328
Lockheed Corporation, 349
Millipore Corporation, 374
Olin Corporation, 396
Raytheon Company, 432
Rockwell International Corporation,
    441
Rosemount, Inc., 443
Sundstrand Corporation, 485
Thermco Systems, Inc., 495
Tracor, Inc., 500
TRW, Inc., 503
Waters Chromatography (Millipore),
    523

MARKETING—TELECOMMUNICATIONS

AT&T International, 145
ITT Corporation, 321
MCI Communications Corporation,
    365
NYNEX Corporation, 392
Pacific Telesis International, 403
Scientific Atlanta, Inc., 452
Sprint Corporation, 474
US West, Inc., 515

MARKETING—TRAVEL

American Express Company—Travel
    Related Services, 125
Carlson Travel Network, 185
Club Med, Inc., 201
Continental Airlines Holdings, Inc.,
    210
Delta Air Lines, Inc., 232
Holiday Inns Worldwide, 302
Hyatt International Corporation, 308
ITT Sheraton Corporation, 322
Marriott Corporation, 360
Northwest Airlines, Inc., 390
UAL Corporation, 506

MATES

American Canadian Caribbean Line,
    123
Clipper Cruise Lines, 199
Commodore Cruise Lines, 206

MEDICAL PERSONNEL

American Friends Service Committee,
    537
American Red Cross, 538
CARE, 541
Christian Blind Mission International,
    543
International Medical Corps, 551
International Rescue Committee, 554
International Voluntary Services, Inc.,
    555
Office of International Health, 557
Pan American Health Organization,
    560
Pathfinders International, 561

U.S. Department of State, 575
World Concern, 585
World Vision Relief and Development,
Inc., 588

MEDICAL TECHNICIANS

Charter Medical Corporation, 190

NURSES

Charter Medical Corporation, 190
Christian Blind Mission International,
543
Hospital Corporation International,
Ltd., 304
International Medical Corps, 551
International Rescue Committee, 554

NUTRITIONISTS

International Medical Corps, 551

OFFICE MANAGEMENT

Aon Corporation, 136
Archer-Daniels-Midland Company, 138
Atari Corporation, 146
The Bank of New York Company,
Inc., 154
Dames & Moore, 223
The Dexter Corporation, 233
R. R. Donnelley & Sons Company,
238
Fibronics International, Inc., 261
H & R Block, 291
Kysor Industrial Corporation, 342
Liquid Carbonic Corporation, 347
Loctite Corporation, 349
Lotus Development Corporation, 351
Marathon Petroleum Company, 359
Robert Half International, Inc., 440

OPHTHALMOLOGISTS

Christian Blind Mission International,
543

PAINTERS

Pacific Architects & Engineers, Inc.,
402

PEDIATRICIANS

International Medical Corps, 551

PETROLEUM ENGINEERS

Core Laboratories, 214

PHOTOGRAPHERS

United Press International, 509

PHYSICIANS

Charter Medical Corporation, 190
Christian Blind Mission International,
543
Hospital Corporation International,
Ltd., 304
International Rescue Committee, 554
Population Council, 562
Project Concern International, 562

PILOTS

Offshore Logistics, 394
Rowan Companies, Inc., 444

PLANT ENGINEERS

Bridgestone-Firestone, Inc., 174
Hughes Christensen Company, 307

PLANT MANAGERS

Archer-Daniels-Midland Company, 138
Bridgestone-Firestone, Inc., 174
Cabot Corporation, 181
Central Soya Company, 188
Columbian Rope Company, 204
Falk Corporation, 259
Fisher Controls International, Inc.,
263
John Fluke Manufacturing Company,
265
FMC Corporation, 266
Masonite Corporation, 362
Mattel, Inc., 363
Norton Company, 390
Reeves Brothers, Inc., 435

PLUMBERS

Pacific Architects & Engineers, Inc.,
402

POLITICAL SCIENTISTS

International Republican Institute, 554
National Democratic Institute, 557
U.S. Department of State, 575

PRESS OFFICERS

United Nations Employment
Information & Assistance
Division, 566

PRODUCT DEVELOPMENT

AKZO America, Inc., 113
Allergan, Inc., 117
Aluminum Company of America, 118
Amgen, Inc., 131
C. R. Bard, Inc., 157
Betz Laboratories, 166
Campbell Soup Company, 183
Chemical Fabrics Corporation, 192
Colgate-Palmolive Company, 203
Coltec Industries, Inc., 204
Computer Associates International,
Inc., 207
Converse, Inc., 212
Cooper Industries, Inc., 213
Cooper Power Systems, 213
CTS Corporation, 220
Dell Computer Corporation, 231
DH Technology, Inc., 233
Donaldson Company, Inc., 237
Dow Corning Corporation, 240
E-Systems, Inc., 245
Eastman Kodak Company, 246
EG & G, Inc., 249
Elizabeth Arden Company, 251
Exxon Chemical Company, 257
Florsheim Shoe Company, 264
GAF Corporation, 270
General Motors Corporation (GM),
277
Gerber Products Company, 280
Giddings & Lewis, Inc., 282
The Gillette Company, 283
W. R. Grace & Company, 285

Great Lakes Chemical Corporation,
287
H. J. Heinz Company, 290
Hach Company, 292
Hallmark Cards, Inc., 294
Harris Corporation, 296
Hasbro, Inc., 297
Hercules, Inc., 299
Hewlett-Packard Company, 300
IMCERA Group, Inc., 310
IMO Industries, 310
Information Builders, Inc., 312
Intel Corporation, 314
International Flavors & Fragrances,
Inc., 317
Johnson Controls, Inc., 324
Johnson & Johnson, 325
S. C. Johnson Wax, 325
Kaman Corporation, 328
Kellogg Company, 330
Kimberly-Clark Corporation, 336
Kraft General Foods International,
341
L. A. Gear, Inc., 342
Levi Strauss Associates, Inc., 344
Liz Claiborne, Inc., 348
Lotus Development Corporation, 351
LTV Steel Co., 352
LTX Corporation, 353
MagneTek, Inc., 358
Mallinckrodt, Inc., 359
Marion Merrell Dow, Inc., 360
Mattel, Inc., 363
Maytag Corporation, 364
Measurex Corporation, 366
Memorex Telex Corporation, 367
Herman Miller, Inc., 373
Modine Manufacturing Company, 375
Monsanto Company, 377
Motorola, Inc., 381
Nalco Chemical Company, 382
NCR Corporation, 384
Nicolet Instrument Corporation, 387
NIKE, Inc., 388
NL Industries, Inc., 388
Oracle Systems, Inc., 398
Outboard Marine Corporation, 399
PepsiCo, Inc., 410
Pfaudler Companies, Inc., 411
Pfizer, Inc., 412

Polaroid Corporation, 420
Premark International, Inc., 423
Procter & Gamble Company, 425
Quaker Oats Company, 428
Qume Corporation, 429
Recognition Equipment, Inc., 433
Redken Laboratories, Inc., 434
Reliance Electric Company, 435
Rhone-Poulenc Rorer, 438
Rockwell International Corporation, 441
Saint Jude Medical, Inc., 448
Sara Lee Corporation, 449
SCI Systems, 452
Sensormatic Electronics Corporation, 457
SGS-Thomson Microelectronics, 458
Siliconix, 462
Solectron Corporation, 469
Sony Pictures Entertainment, 471
Springs Industries, Inc., 473
SPS Technologies, Inc., 474
Sterling Winthrop, Inc., 479
Storage Technology Corporation, 481
Sun Electric Corporation, 484
Syntex Corporation, 486
Tandy Corporation, 487
Texas Intruments, Inc., 494
Unisys Corporation, 508
Warner-Lambert Company, 522
Westinghouse Electric Corporation, 525

PROJECT MANAGERS

General Railway Signal Company, 278
International Republican Institute, 554
Partners in Economic Reform, Inc., 560

PSYCHIATRISTS

Charter Medical Corporation, 190

PUBLIC ADMINISTRATORS

United Nations Employment Information & Assistance Division, 566

PUBLIC HEALTH ADMINISTRATORS

American Home Products Corporation, 126
Project Concern International, 562

PUBLIC RELATIONS

Borland International, Inc, 172
Burson-Marsteller, 180
Capitol Cities/ABC, Inc., 184
Clipper Cruise Lines, 199
Ruder Finn, Inc., 445

PURSERS

Carnival Cruise Lines, 185
Commodore Cruise Lines, 206
International Maritime Resources, 317

QUALITY ASSURANCE

Brown Group, Inc., 176
Converse, Inc., 212

RADIO ENGINEERS

Voice of America: Bureau of Broadcasting, 583

RELIEF WORKERS

World Vision Relief and Development, Inc., 588

REPORTERS

Associated Press, 144
Dow Jones & Company, Inc., 241
Journal of Commerce, 326
New York Times Company, 386
Newsweek International, 387
United Press International, 509

RESEARCH & DEVELOPMENT

A. L. Laboratories Inc., 107
Abex Inc./Fisher Scientific International, Inc., 110
Applied Materials, Inc., 137
Asea Brown Boveri, 142
Battelle Memorial Institute, 159

JOB CATEGORY INDEX

A
M
E
R
I
C
A
N

J
O
B
S

A
B
R
O
A
D

Block Drug Company, Inc., 169
Carter-Wallace, Inc., 187
Centocor, Inc., 188
Coherent, Inc., 202
Compaq Computers Corporation, 207
Digital Equipment Corporation, 236
Dow Chemical Company, 240
DuPont Merck Pharmaceutical
 Company, 243
Helene Curtis Industries, Inc., 298
Kolmar Laboratories, Inc., 340
Parker Drilling Company, 405
Pioneer Hi-Bred International, Inc.,
 417
Procter & Gamble Cosmetics and
 Fragrance Products, 426
Rosemount, Inc., 443
Schering-Plough Corporation, 450
Searle Company, 455
3M Company, 496
The Upjohn Company, 515

RESEARCH TECHNICIANS

Merck & Company, Inc., 368
U.S. Defense Intelligence Agency, 571

RESEARCHERS

Flow International Corporation, 265
Gannett Company, Inc., 272
IMS America, Ltd., 311
McKinsey & Company, Inc., 357
Mobil Oil Corporation, 375
Office of International Health, 557
Syntex Corporation, 486

RIGGING SERVICES

Nabors Industries, Inc., 381

RURAL DEVELOPMENT

American Friends Service Committee,
 537
International Labor Office, 550

SAFETY INSPECTORS

International Labor Office, 550
U.S. Federal Aviation Administration,
 577

SALES

ACCO World Corporation, 110
American President Companies, Ltd.,
 128
American Standard, Inc., 128
Ameriwood, Inc., 130
Anacomp, Inc., 134
Ansell International, 135
Armco, Inc., 140
Armstrong World Industries, Inc., 141
Asarco, Inc., 142
Asea Brown Boveri, 142
Bandag, Inc., 153
The Barden Corporation, 157
Bell Helicopter Textron, Inc., 163
Bemis Company, Inc., 164
Boeing Company, 170
Browning-Ferris Industries, 177
Brush Wellman, Inc., 178
Burlington Air Express, 179
Capitol Cities/ABC, Inc., 184
Carrier Corporation, 186
Champion International Corporation,
 189
Coin Acceptors, Inc., 203
Columbian Rope Company, 204
Corning Incorporated, 215
CRS Sirrine, Inc., 219
R. R. Donnelley & Sons Company,
 238
Drummond Company, Inc., 242
Dun & Bradstreet Corporation, 243
Duracell, Inc., 244
Eagle-Picher Industries, Inc., 246
Eastman Kodak Company, 246
Eaton Corporation/Cutler Hammer,
 247
Esco Corporation, 255
Federal Express Corporation, 260
Figgie International, Inc., 262
Fluor Corporation, 266
FMC Corporation, 266
GAF Corporation, 270
The Gates Rubber Company, 273
General Electric Company (GE), 275
Gould Pumps, Inc., 285
W. R. Grace & Company, 285
Great Lakes Carbon International
 Corporation, 287

A. P. Green Industries, Inc., 287
Guardian Industries Corporation, 290
Hach Company, 292
Hercules, Inc., 299
International Flavors & Fragrances, Inc., 317
International Paper Company, 318
ITW Finishing Systems & Products, 322
James River Corporation, 323
JMK International/Jamack Fabrications, Inc., 323
Kennecott Corporation, 333
Kimball International, Inc., 336
Kimberly-Clark Corporation, 336
Knoll International, 338
LTV Steel Co., 352
Lykes Lines, 354
Masco Corporation, 361
Masonite Corporation, 362
Mead Corporation, 365
Herman Miller, Inc., 373
Milliken & Company, 373
Modine Manufacturing Company, 375
Morton International, 380
National Data Corporation, 382
Ogden Corporation, 395
Otis Elevator Company: World Headquarters, 399
Outboard Marine Corporation, 399
Preformed Line Products Company, 423
Reeves Brothers, Inc., 435
Riverwood International, Inc., 439
Robertson Ceco, 440
Rogers Corporation, 442
Ryder Systems, Inc., 447
Sea-Land Service, Inc., 454
Sealed Air Corporation, 455
SGS Control Services, 458
Signode Packaging Systems, 462
Sonoco Products Company, 470
Sony Pictures Entertainment, 471
Sotheby's Holdings, Inc., 471
Standex International, 477
Stone Container Corporation, 480
Textron, Inc., 494
Time-Warner, Inc., 498
Torrington Company, 499
Trane Company, 501

Turner Broadcasting System, Inc., 503
Union Camp Corporation, 507
United Parcel Service of America, Inc., 509
United Technologies Corporation, 512
Universal Foods Corporation, 513
USX Corporation, 516
Vishay Intertechnology, 518
Warner Brothers International, 521
West Company, Inc., 525
Weyerhaeuser Company, 526
WMX Technologies/Waste Management, Inc., 527
York International, Inc., 532

SALES—ADVERTISING

Backer Spielvogel & Bates Worldwide, Inc., 150
D'Arcy Masius Benton & Bowles Inc., 225
Grey Advertising, Inc., 288
Ketchum International, 334
Lintas: Worldwide, 346
McCann-Erickson Worldwide, 354
Saatchi & Saatchi, 448
Young & Rubicam, Inc., 533

SALES—AGRICULTURAL

Cargill Incorporated, 184
Central Soya Company, 188
Continental Grain Company, 211
De Kalb Genetics Corporation, 227
Deere & Company, 229
Exxon Chemical Company, 257
Monsanto Company, 377
Philipp Brothers Chemicals, Inc., 414
Pioneer Hi-Bred International, Inc., 417
Rain Bird Sprinkler Manufacturing Corporation, 430
Universal Foods Corporation, 513

SALES—AUTOMOTIVE

Allied-Signal, Inc., 117
Bridgestone-Firestone, Inc., 174
Chrysler Corporation, 195
Coltec Industries, Inc., 204

A
M
E
R
I
C
A
N

J
O
B
S

A
B
R
O
A
D

Cooper Industries, Inc., 213
Dana Corporation, 224
Eaton Corporation/Cutler Hammer, 247
Ford Motor Company, 267
General Motors Corporation (GM), 277
Hertz Corporation, 300
Kelsey-Hayes Company, 332
Monroe Auto Equipment Company, 376
Navistar International Transportation Corporation, 383
Purolator Products Company, 427
Rockwell International Corporation, 441
A. O. Smith Corporation, 467
Sun Electric Corporation, 484
Tenneco Automotive, 491
Walker Manufacturing Company, 519
Warner Electric Brake & Clutch Company, 521
Wynn's International, Inc., 530

SALES—CHEMICALS

AKZO America, Inc., 113
Aluminum Company of America, 118
Amerace Corporation (Elastimold), 121
Amoco Corporation, 131
Asarco, Inc., 142
BASF Corporation, 158
BP America, Inc., 173
Calgon Corporation, 182
Chevron Chemical Company, 192
Church & Dwight Company, Inc., 196
Dow Chemical Company, 240
Dow Corning Corporation, 240
Eastman Kodak Company, 246
Engelhard Corporation, 253
Ethyl Corporation, 256
Exxon Chemical Company, 257
Exxon Corporation, 258
GAF Corporation, 270
W. R. Grace & Company, 285
Great Lakes Chemical Corporation, 287
M. A. Hanna Company, 295
Hercules, Inc., 299
Hoechst Celanese, Inc., 302

J. M. Huber Corporation, 306
IMCERA Group, Inc., 310
Koch Industries, Inc., 339
Lawter International, Inc., 344
Loctite Corporation, 349
Lord Corporation, 350
Lubrizol Corporation, 353
MacDermid, Inc., 355
Merck & Company, Inc., 368
Metco Perkin-Elmer, 371
Monsanto Company, 377
Morton International, 380
Nalco Chemical Company, 382
NL Industries, Inc., 388
OMI International, 396
Pennzoil Company, 408
Petrolite Corporation, 411
Philipp Brothers Chemicals, Inc., 414
Phillips Petroleum Company, 415
PPG Industries, 421
Quaker Chemical Corporation, 428
Rohm & Haas Company, 442
RPM, Inc., 444
Rubbermaid, Inc., 445
A. Schulman, Inc., 451
SCM Chemicals, 453
Sherwin-Williams Company, 461
Shipley Company, Inc., 461
3M Pharmaceuticals, 497
Union Camp Corporation, 507
Union Carbide Corporation, 507
UOP, Inc., 514
The Upjohn Company, 515
Wynn's International, Inc., 530

SALES—CONSUMER GOODS

Acushnet Company, 111
American Greetings Corporation, 126
Avery Dennison Corporation, 147
Avon Products, Inc., 149
Brown & Williamson Tobacco Corporation, 177
Calgon Corporation, 182
Carter-Wallace, Inc., 187
Bernard Chaus, Inc., 191
Church & Dwight Company, Inc., 196
Clorox Company, 199
Colgate-Palmolive Company, 203
Converse, Inc., 212

Corning Incorporated, 215
CPC International, Inc., 217
Dixon Ticonderoga Company, 236
Dow Chemical Company, 240
Elizabeth Arden Company, 251
Florsheim Shoe Company, 264
The Gillette Company, 283
Hallmark Cards, Inc., 294
Hasbro, Inc., 297
Helene Curtis Industries, Inc., 298
James River Corporation, 323
S. C. Johnson Wax, 325
Kayser-Roth Corporation, 329
Kellwood Company, 331
Kimberly-Clark Corporation, 336
Kinney Shoe Corporation, 337
L. A. Gear, Inc., 342
Levi Strauss Associates, Inc., 344
The Limited, Inc., 345
Liz Claiborne, Inc., 348
Master Lock Company, 362
Mattel, Inc., 363
Maytag Corporation, 364
Montgomery Ward Holding Company, 377
NIKE, Inc., 388
J. C. Penney Company, Inc., 407
Pfaudler Companies, Inc., 411
Philip Morris Companies, Inc., 413
Phillips-Van Heusen Corporation, 415
Pitney Bowes, Inc., 417
Playtex Apparel, Inc., 419
Premark International, Inc., 423
Procter & Gamble Company, 425
Procter & Gamble Cosmetics and Fragrance Products, 426
Ralston Purina Company, 430
Redken Laboratories, Inc., 434
Remington Products, Inc., 436
Revlon, Inc., 437
RJR Nabisco, 439
Rubbermaid, Inc., 445
Russell Corporation, 446
SB Power Tools, Inc. (Skil Corp.), 450
Scott Paper Company, 453
Sears Roebuck and Company, 456
Senco Products, 456
Shaklee Corporation, 459
Sheaffer Pen, Inc., 459

Simplicity Pattern Company Inc., 464
Snap-On Tools Corporation, 468
Springs Industries, Inc., 473
Standard Commercial Corporation, 476
Stanhome, Inc., 477
Stanley Works, 478
Tambrands, Inc., 486
3M Company, 496
Toys "R" Us, Inc., 500
United States Shoe Corporation, 510
VF Corporation, 517
Warnaco, Inc., 520
Warner-Lambert Company, 522
Whirlpool Corporation, 526
Whitman Corporation, 527
Woolworth Corporation, 528
Wynn's International, Inc., 530

SALES—DEFENSE INDUSTRY

Boeing Company, 170
E-Systems, Inc., 245
General Dynamics Corporation, 274
Loral Corporation, 350
Teledyne, Inc., 489
TRW, Inc., 503
Westinghouse Electric Corporation, 525

SALES—ELECTRONICS

Advanced Micro Devices, Inc., 112
Alarm Device Manufacturing Company, 114
Aldus Corporation, 115
Allen-Bradley Company, Inc., 116
Aluminum Company of America, 118
AM International, Inc., 119
Amdahl Corporation, 120
American Management Systems, Inc., 127
Ampex Corporation, 133
Andrew Corporation, 134
Apple Computer, Inc., 136
AST Research, Inc., 144
Atari Corporation, 146
Augat, Inc., 146
Avnet, Inc., 148
Bailey Controls Company, 151
BancTec, Inc., 152

AMERICAN JOBS ABROAD

Banyan Systems, Inc., 156
Beckman Instruments, Inc., 162
Bell & Howell Company, 164
Bose Corporation, 172
Cincom Systems, Inc., 197
Compaq Computers Corporation, 207
Computer Associates International, Inc., 207
Computervision Corporation, 208
Cooper Industries, Inc., 213
CTS Corporation, 220
Dell Computer Corporation, 231
Diebold Incorporated, 235
Digital Equipment Corporation, 236
Duro-Test International Corporation, 245
E-Systems, Inc., 245
Emerson Electric Company, 251
Encore Computer Corporation, 252
John Fluke Manufacturing Company, 265
General Electric Company (GE), 275
General Instrument Corporation, 276
General Signal Corporation, 278
GTECH Corporation, 289
Harris Corporation, 296
Hewlett-Packard Company, 300
Honeywell, Inc., 303
Hubbell, Inc., 306
IDB Communications, Inc., 309
IMO Industries, 310
Information Builders, Inc., 312
Intel Corporation, 314
Intergraph Corporation, 314
International Totalizator Systems, Inc., 319
Iomega Corporation, 320
Johnson Controls, Inc., 324
JWP, Inc., 328
Keithley Instruments, Inc., 329
Lambda Electronics, Inc., 343
Liant Software Corporation, 345
Loral Corporation, 350
Lotus Development Corporation, 351
LTX Corporation, 353
MagneTek, Inc., 358
Measurex Corporation, 366
Memorex Telex Corporation, 367
Merisel, Inc., 369
Methode Electronics, Inc., 371

Molex, Inc., 376
Motorola, Inc., 381
National Semiconductor Corporation, 383
NCR Corporation, 384
Nicolet Instrument Corporation, 387
North American Philips Corporation, 389
Perkin-Elmer Corporation, 410
Pittway Corporation, 418
Polaroid Corporation, 420
Printronix, Inc., 425
Qume Corporation, 429
Ranco, Inc., 431
Raytheon Company, 432
Recognition Equipment, Inc., 433
Rockwell International Corporation, 441
SCI Systems, 452
Seagate Technology, Inc., 454
Sensormatic Electronics Corporation, 457
Siliconix, 462
Simplex Time Recorder Company, 463
Smith Corona Corporation, 466
Solectron Corporation, 469
Southwire Company, 472
Square D Company, 475
Storage Technology Corporation, 481
Structural Dynamics Research Corporation, 481
Sun Microsystems, Inc., 484
Symbol Technologies, Inc., 485
Tandem Computers, Inc., 487
Tandy Corporation, 487
Tektronix, Inc., 488
Telxon Corp., 490
Texas Intruments, Inc., 494
Thomas & Betts, 495
Unisys Corporation, 508
U.S. Electrical Motors (Emerson Electric), 510
Vishay Intertechnology, 518
Westinghouse Electric Corporation, 525
Xerox Corporation, 531

SALES—FINANCIAL SERVICES

American Bankers Insurance Group, Inc., 122
American Express Bank, Ltd., 124
American Express Company—Travel Related Services, 125
AT&T International, 145
Continental Bank Corporation, 210
Willis Corroon, 216
CUNA Mutual Insurance Group, 222
Ford Motor Company, 267
Fritz Companies, 269
General Electric Company (GE), 275
General Motors Corporation (GM), 277
New York Life Insurance Company, 385
Paine Webber Group, Inc., 403
Primerica Corporation, 424
Rollins Hudig Hall International, 443
Salomon, Inc., 449
Sears Roebuck and Company, 456
Textron, Inc., 494

SALES—FOOD/FOOD SERVICES

American Home Products Corporation, 126
Arby's, Inc., 138
Armour Swift Eckrich, Inc., 141
Jim Beam Brands Company, 161
Campbell Soup Company, 183
Cargill Incorporated, 184
The Coca-Cola Company, 202
ConAgra, Inc., 208
CPC International, Inc., 217
DAKA International, 222
Del Monte Corporation, 230
Domino's Pizza, Inc., 237
Fleming Companies, Inc., 264
General Foods USA, 276
General Mills, Inc., 277
Gerber Products Company, 280
H. J. Heinz Company, 290
Hershey Foods Corporation, 299
Holiday Inns Worldwide, 302
Hormel Foods Corporation, 304
Kellogg Company, 330
KFC Corporation, 335

Kraft General Foods International, 341
McCormick & Company, Inc., 355
Marriott Corporation, 360
Miller Brewing Company, 372
PepsiCo, Inc., 410
Philip Morris Companies, Inc., 413
Pillsbury Company, 416
Pizza Hut, Inc., 419
Procter & Gamble Company, 425
Quaker Oats Company, 428
Ralston Purina Company, 430
RJR Nabisco, 439
Sara Lee Corporation, 449
Sizzler International, 464
J. M. Smucker Company, 468
TLC Beatrice International Holdings, Inc., 498
TW Holdings, Inc., 504
Tyson Foods, Inc., 505
William Wrigley Jr. Company, 529

SALES—HEALTH & MEDICAL SUPPLIES

Abex Inc./Fisher Scientific International, Inc., 110
AKZO America, Inc., 113
American Cyanamid Company, 124
American Home Products Corporation, 126
C. R. Bard, Inc., 157
Bausch & Lomb, Inc., 159
Johnson & Johnson, 325
Kendall International, 332
Medtronic, Inc., 366
Nellcor, Inc., 385
Pall Corporation, 404
Pfizer, Inc., 412
Saint Jude Medical, Inc., 448
Schering-Plough Corporation, 450
United States Surgical Corporation, 511
Warner-Lambert Company, 522

SALES—INDUSTRIAL

Advance Machine Company, 111
Allis Mineral Systems/Svedala Industries, Inc., 118
Aluminum Company of America, 118

A
M
E
R
I
C
A
N

J
O
B
S

A
B
R
O
A
D

Ametek, Inc., 130
Automatic Switch Company, 147
W. H. Brady Company, 173
Bristol Babcock, Inc., 174
California Pellet Mill Company, 182
J. I. Case Company, 187
Chemical Fabrics Corporation, 192
Coltec Industries, Inc., 204
Commercial Intertech Corporation, 205
Cooper Energy Services, Ltd., 212
Cooper Industries, Inc., 213
Cooper Power Systems, 213
John Crane, Inc., 218
Crown Cork & Seal Company, Inc., 218
D-M-E Company, 222
Detroit Diesel Corporation, 232
The Dexter Corporation, 233
DH Technology, Inc., 233
Donaldson Company, Inc., 237
Dover Corporation, 239
Falk Corporation, 259
Federal-Mogul Corporation, 260
Fisher Controls International, Inc., 263
Flow International Corporation, 265
Giddings & Lewis, Inc., 282
Graco, Inc., 286
Hanson Industries, 295
Illinois Tool Works, Inc., 309
Ingersoll International, Inc., 313
Ingersoll-Rand Company, 313
Joy Technologies, Inc., 327
Kennametal, Inc., 333
Keystone International, 334
Kysor Industrial Corporation, 342
The Lincoln Electric Company, 346
Liquid Carbonic Corporation, 347
Masoneilan Industries, Inc., 361
Melroe Company, 367
Metallurg Corporation, 370
Moore Products Company, 378
Norton Company, 390
Parker Hannifin Corporation, 405
Pentair, Inc., 409
Petrolite Corporation, 411
Phelps Dodge Corporation, 412
PMI Food Equipment Group, 420
Precision Valve Corporation, 422

Ranco, Inc., 431
Reliance Electric Company, 435
Reynolds Metals Company, 438
Rockwell Graphic Systems, 441
Rosemount, Inc., 443
Schlegel Corporation, 451
Sequa Corporation, 457
SPS Technologies, Inc., 474
Sullair Corporation, 482
Teledyne, Inc., 489
Trinova Corporation, 502
Jervis B. Webb Company, 523
Woodward Governor Company, 528

SALES—PETROLEUM/ NATURAL GAS

Amoco Corporation, 131
Ashland Oil, Inc., 143
Baroid Corporation, 158
BP America, Inc., 173
Chevron Overseas Petroleum, Inc., 194
Diamond M-ODECO Drilling, Inc., 234
Engelhard Corporation, 253
Enserch International Development, Inc., 254
Exxon Company, International, 258
Exxon Corporation, 258
Hughes Christensen Company, 307
Koch Industries, Inc., 339
Marathon Petroleum Company, 359
NL Industries, Inc., 388
Occidental Petroleum Corporation, 393
Pennzoil Company, 408
Phibro Energy, Inc., 413
Phillips Petroleum Company, 415
Sonat, Inc., 469
Sperry-Sun, Inc., 473
Sun Company, Inc., 483
Tenneco, Inc., 492
Texaco Oil Company, 493
USX Corporation, 516

SALES—PHARMACEUTICALS

A. L. Laboratories Inc., 107
Abbott Laboratories, 109
Allergan, Inc., 117
American Cyanamid Company, 124

J
O
B

C
A
T
E
G
O
R
Y

I
N
D
E
X

American Home Products Corporation, 126
Bausch & Lomb, Inc., 159
Block Drug Company, Inc., 169
Carter-Wallace, Inc., 187
Centocor, Inc., 188
DuPont Merck Pharmaceutical Company, 243
Johnson & Johnson, 325
Marion Merrell Dow, Inc., 360
Merck & Company, Inc., 368
Monsanto Company, 377
Pfizer, Inc., 412
Procter & Gamble Pharmaceuticals, Inc., 426
Revlon, Inc., 437
Rhone-Poulenc Rorer, 438
Schering-Plough Corporation, 450
Searle Company, 455
Sterling Winthrop, Inc., 479
Syntex Corporation, 486
3M Pharmaceuticals, 497
The Upjohn Company, 515
Warner-Lambert Company, 522
Wyeth-Ayerst Laboratories, 530

SALES—PUBLISHING

Bell & Howell Company, 164
Capitol Cities/ABC, Inc., 184
Reuben H. Donnelly, 239
Dow Jones & Company, Inc., 241
Dun & Bradstreet Corporation, 243
Encyclopedia Britannica, Inc., 253
GTE Directories Corporation, 289
International Data Group, Inc., 316
New York Times Company, 386
Pittway Corporation, 418
R. L. Polk & Company, 421
Reader's Digest Association, Inc., 432
Simon & Schuster, Inc., 463
Time, Inc., 497
Time-Warner, Inc., 498

SALES—SCIENTIFIC

ABB Vetco Gray, Inc., 108
Abex Inc./Fisher Scientific International, Inc., 110
Allied-Signal, Inc., 117
Aluminum Company of America, 118
Amgen, Inc., 131
Applied Materials, Inc., 137
BASF Corporation, 158
Battelle Memorial Institute, 159
Beckman Instruments, Inc., 162
Bio-Rad Laboratories, 166
Brown & Sharpe Manufacturing Company, 176
Coherent, Inc., 202
Coltec Industries, Inc., 204
Computervision Corporation, 208
Dresser Industries, Inc., 241
Eagle-Picher Industries, Inc., 246
Fibronics International, Inc., 261
Fischer & Porter Company, 263
Hazleton Washington Corporation, 297
Honeywell, Inc., 303
Hughes Aircraft Company, 307
IMCERA Group, Inc., 310
International Rectifier Corporation, 319
JWP, Inc., 328
Lockheed Corporation, 349
Millipore Corporation, 374
Raytheon Company, 432
Rockwell International Corporation, 441
Rosemount, Inc., 443
Sundstrand Corporation, 485
Teradyne, Inc., 493
Tracor, Inc., 500
TRW, Inc., 503
Waters Chromatography (Millipore), 523

SALES—TELECOMMUNICATIONS

AT&T International, 145
ITT Corporation, 321
MCI Communications Corporation, 365
NYNEX Corporation, 392
Pacific Telesis International, 403
Sprint Corporation, 474
Tellabs Operations, Inc., 489
US West, Inc., 515

SALES—TRAVEL

American Express Company—Travel
Related Services, 125
Carlson Travel Network, 185
Continental Airlines Holdings, Inc.,
210
Delta Air Lines, Inc., 232
Holiday Inns Worldwide, 302
Marriott Corporation, 360
Northwest Airlines, Inc., 390
USAir Group, Inc., 516

SCIENTISTS

Hartford Steam Boiler Inspection/
Insurance Company, 296
Hospital Corporation International,
Ltd., 304
Organization of American States, 558
U.S. Department of Energy, 573

SEAMEN

International Maritime Resources, 317

SECURITY OFFICERS

Burns International Security Services,
179
U.S. Federal Aviation Administration,
577

SERVICE ENGINEERS

Fuller Company, 269

STATISTICIANS

International Labor Office, 550
United Nations Employment
Information & Assistance
Division, 566

STEWARDS

American Canadian Caribbean Line,
123
Clipper Cruise Lines, 199
Commodore Cruise Lines, 206
International Maritime Resources, 317

TAX PREPARERS

H & R Block, 291

TEACHERS

Academy for Educational
Development, 535
Agency for International Development,
536
AMIDEAST, 538
Amnesty International, USA, 539
ASA Foundation, 539
Boy Scouts of America, 541
Catholic Relief Services, 542
Church World Service & Witness,
544
Department of Defense Dependents
Schools, 545
Food & Agriculture Organization of
the United Nations, 546
International Fund for Agricultural
Development (IFAD), 549
International Organization for
Migration, 553
International Planned Parenthood
Federation, 553
International Rescue Committee, 554
Organization of American States, 558
ORT International Cooperation, 559
Project HOPE, 563
South Pacific Commission, 564
U.S. Department of Defense, 572
United States Information Agency,
580
World Concern, 585
World Relief, 587

TECHNICAL ASSISTANTS

Smith International, Inc., 467

TECHNICAL DESIGN

Hughes Aircraft Company, 307

TECHNICAL FIELD SUPPORT

American Institute for Free Labor
Development, 537
ASA Foundation, 539

Astronautics Corporation of America, 145

Burns & Roe, Inc., 180

CARE, 541

Christian Blind Mission International, 543

Church World Service & Witness, 544

Data General Corporation, 225

Day & Zimmerman, 226

Deere & Company, 229

Donaldson Company, Inc., 237

Emery Worldwide, 252

Exxon Company, International, 258

Ferro Corporation, 261

Ford Foundation, 546

Gafney, Cline & Associates, Inc., 271

Gannett Fleming, Inc., 272

Geraghty & Miller, Inc., 279

GTE Corporation, 288

Halliburton-NUS Corporation, 293

Hospital Corporation International, Ltd., 304

Inductotherm Corporation, 311

Inter-American Foundation, 547

International Fund for Agricultural Development (IFAD), 549

Kolmar Laboratories, Inc., 340

Louisiana Land & Exploration Company, 352

Milliken & Company, 373

Mobil Oil Corporation, 375

National Aeronautics and Space Administartion (NASA), 556

Newmont Mining Corporation, 386

Novell, Inc., 392

Ogden Corporation, 395

Oracle Systems, Inc., 398

Organization of American States, 558

ORT International Cooperation, 559

Paramount Communications, Inc., 404

Pennzoil Company, 408

PepsiCo, Inc., 410

Phibro Energy, Inc., 413

Phillips Petroleum Company, 415

Reed Tool Company, 434

Rockwell Graphic Systems, 441

Sea-Land Service, Inc., 454

Sonat, Inc., 469

Sonat Offshore, 470

Sun Company, Inc., 483

Tenneco, Inc., 492

Triton Energy Corporation, 502

Turner Steiner International, Inc., 504

United Engineers & Constructors International, 508

U.S. Department of the Air Force, 572

U.S. Department of the Navy, 574

U.S. Department of Transportation, 576

U.S. Environmental Protection Agency, 577

U.S. General Services Administration, 580

U.S. Marine Corps, 581

USX Corporation, 516

World Concern, 585

TECHNICAL SERVICE MANAGERS

Navistar International Transportation Corporation, 383

TECHNICAL WRITERS

Borland International, Inc, 172

TECHNICIANS

Airborne Express, 112

Astronautics Corporation of America, 145

Baroid Corporation, 158

Beckman Instruments, Inc., 162

Bridgestone-Firestone, Inc., 174

Carrier Corporation, 186

Commodore International Ltd., 206

Dames & Moore, 223

Digital Equipment Corporation, 236

Hartford Steam Boiler Inspection/ Insurance Company, 296

Hubbell, Inc., 306

International Business Machines (IBM), 315

Litton Industries, Inc., 348

MGM Incorporated, 372

National Semiconductor Corporation, 383

PRC, Inc., 422

A
M
E
R
I
C
A
N

J
O
B
S

A
B
R
O
A
D

UAL Corporation, 506

**TELECOMMUNICATIONS
OFFICERS**

U.S. Central Intelligence Agency, 570

TOUR LEADERS

Gerhard's Bicycle Odysseys, 280

TRAINING SPECIALISTS

Bankers Trust New York Corporation,
155
International Labor Office, 550
International Republican Institute, 554
International Voluntary Services, Inc.,
555
National Democratic Institute, 557
Partners in Economic Reform, Inc.,
560

TRANSLATORS

Organization for Economic Cooperation
& Development, 559
Pacific Architects & Engineers, Inc.,
402

TRUCK DRIVERS

Diamond Shamrock R & M, Inc.,
234

UNDERWRITERS

CIGNA Corporation, 197
Metropolitan Life Insurance Company,
371
J. P. Morgan & Company, Inc., 378
Prudential Insurance Company of
America, 427
Salomon, Inc., 449

URBAN DEVELOPMENT

Agency for International Development,
536

VESSEL OPERATORS

Offshore Logistics, 394

VETERINARIANS

World Concern, 585